ICD-10-PCS
Coding System

Education, Planning, and Implementation

Carline A. Dalgleish
BS, MA, RHIA

DELMAR
CENGAGE Learning®

ICD-10-PCS Coding System: Education, Planning, and Implementation
Dalgleish, Carline A.

Vice President, Editorial: Dave Garza

Director of Learning Solutions: Matthew Kane

Executive Editor: Rhonda Dearborn

Managing Editor: Marah Bellegarde

Senior Product Manager: Jadin Babin-Kavanaugh

Editorial Assistant: Lauren Whalen

Vice President, Marketing: Jennifer Baker

Marketing Director: Wendy Mapstone

Senior Marketing Manager: Nancy Bradshaw

Marketing Coordinator: Piper Huntington

Production Director: Wendy Troeger

Production Manager: Andrew Crouth

Senior Content Project Manager: Kenneth McGrath

Senior Art Director: Jack Pendleton

Technology Product Manager: Mary Colleen Liburdi

Technology Project Managers: Patricia Allen Chris Catalina

For product information and technology assistance, contact us at
Cengage Learning Customer & Sales Support, 1-800-354-9706
For permission to use material from this text or product,
submit all requests online at **www.cengage.com/permissions**
Further permissions questions can be e-mailed to
permissionrequest@cengage.com

Library of Congress Control Number: 2011926483

ISBN-13: 978-1-4390-5730-8

ISBN-10: 1439057303

Delmar
5 Maxwell Drive
Clifton Park, NY 12065-2919
USA

Cengage Learning is a leading provider of customized learning solutions with office locations around the globe, including Singapore, the United Kingdom, Australia, Mexico, Brazil, and Japan. Locate your local office at:
international.cengage.com/region

Cengage Learning products are represented in Canada by Nelson Education, Ltd.

To learn more about Delmar, visit **www.cengage.com/delmar**

Purchase any of our products at your local college store or at our preferred online store **www.cengagebrain.com**

Notice to the Reader
Publisher does not warrant or guarantee any of the products described herein or perform any independent analysis in connection with any of the product information contained herein. Publisher does not assume, and expressly disclaims, any obligation to obtain and include information other than that provided to it by the manufacturer. The reader is expressly warned to consider and adopt all safety precautions that might be indicated by the activities described herein and to avoid all potential hazards. By following the instructions contained herein, the reader willingly assumes all risks in connection with such instructions. The publisher makes no representations or warranties of any kind, including but not limited to, the warranties of fitness for particular purpose or merchantability, nor are any such representations implied with respect to the material set forth herein, and the publisher takes no responsibility with respect to such material. The publisher shall not be liable for any special, consequential, or exemplary damages resulting, in whole or part, from the readers' use of, or reliance upon, this material.

Printed in the United States of America
1 2 3 4 5 6 7 14 13 12

Table of Contents

Preface   vii

About the Author   xii

Reviewers   xiii

Technical Reviewer   xiv

Acknowledgements   xv

How to Use StudyWare™   xvi

How to Use *EncoderPro* .com—Expert Online Encoder Software   xix

UNIT I: ICD-9 TO ICD-10

Chapter 1: ICD-10 History, Preview, and Impacts   1

Introduction 2
ICD-10: Now is the Time! 2
History of The International Classification of Diseases (ICD) 3
Why the Classification System is Changing 4
ICD-10-CM 7
ICD-10-CM Implementation 7
Layout and Structure of the ICD-10-CM Diagnostic Classification System . . . 8
The ICD-10-CM Coding Manual 9
ICD-10-PCS (Procedural Coding System) 13
ICD-10-PCS Code Structure. 14
The ICD-10-PCS Coding Manual. 15

Chapter 2: HIPAA, ARRA, HITECH, Transactions, and Code Sets   23

Introduction 24
Health Insurance Portability and Accountability Act (HIPAA). 25
HIPAA Title II: Administrative Simplification 27
The Electronic Health Record (EHR) and Health Information Exchanges (HIE) 33
Transaction Standards 37
ANSI, ASC x12 and version 5010, D.0, and 3.0 40
Version 5010 43
HIPAA Code Sets 51

Chapter 3: General Equivalency Mappings   60

Introduction 61
General Equivalency Mappings 61
Diagnosis Codes and Levels of Specificity. 62
Diagnosis Codes in Combination. . . . 65

General Equivalency Mappings for Diagnostic Coding 67
Migration Choices for Systems and Applications 69
General Equivalency Mapping: ICD-9-CM to ICD-10-CM 69
v26 MS-DRG General Equivalency Mappings 78

UNIT 2: ICD-10-PCS

Chapter 4: ICD-10-PCS (Procedural Coding System)   91

Introduction 93
History of the ICD-10-PCS 93
ICD-10-PCS Legislation. 93
The ICD-10-PCS Code Structure . . . 93
ICD-10-PCS Codebook Layout 95
Medical Documentation 96
Character Assignment and Definitions 107
ICD-10-PCS Coding Guidelines 118
Steps in ICD-10-PCS Coding 119
Appendices in the ICD-10-PCS 122
Other Character Assignments in Certain Sections 123

Chapter 5: Root Operations in the Medical and Surgical Section   130

Introduction 131
Root Operations in the ICD-10-PCS 132
ICD-10-PCS Root Operation Guidelines 132
Root Operations That Take Out Some or All of a Body Part 136
Using the Index for Root Objectives That Take Out Some or All of a Body Part. 139
Root Operations That Take Out a Solid, Fluid, or Gas From a Body Part 148
Root Operations That Involve Cutting or Separation. 154
Root Operations that Put In, Put Back, or Move Some or All of a Body Part. 157
Root Operations That Alter the Diameter or Route of a Tubular Body Part 162
Root Operations That Include Other Repairs 168
Root Operations Involving Examination Only. 171

Root Operations That Always Involve a Device 172
Root Operations That Involve Other Objectives 177

Chapter 6: Medical and Surgical Section Coding   182

Introduction .183
The Medical and Surgical Section (0) 184
Body System (Character 2) Values in the Medical and Surgical Section. 186
Body Part (Character 4) Values in the Medical and Surgical Section 187
Approach (Character 5) Values in the Medical and Surgical Section. 192
Device (Character 6) Values in Medical and Surgical Section 194
Qualifier (Character 7) Values in the Medical and Surgical Section 199
Putting it All Together 207
Assigning Code Character Values to Match Procedural Statements . . . 207
Coding a detachment root operation 208
Coding device procedures. 209
Coding multiple procedures 212
Coding from an Operative Report . . . 219

Chapter 7: Section 1: Obstetrics   228

Introduction .229
Section 1, Obstetrics (I02–I0Y) . . .229
Character 3: Root Operations 232
Character 4: Body Parts 234
Approach (Character 5) Values in the Obstetrics Section 236
Device (Character 6) Values in the Obstetrics Section. 242
Qualifier (Character 7) Values in the Obstetrics Section. 243
Using the ICD-10-PCS Coding Manual for the Obstetric Section. . . 249

Chapter 8: Placement, Administration, Monitoring & Measuring Sections   255

Introduction .258
Placement Section (2W0–2W6 and 2Y0–2Y5) 258
Placement Section, Anatomical Regions (2W0–2W6) 258
Placement Section, Anatomical Orifices (2Y0–2Y5) 267

Administration Section
(302–3E1) 269
Root Operations in the
Administration Section. 270
Measurement and Monitoring
(4A0–4B0) Section 281
Measurement and Monitoring Root
Operations 282
Root Operation Measurement
and Physiological Devices 289
Root Operation Monitoring and
Physiological Systems 290

**Chapter 9: Extracorporeal
Sections   300**
Introduction 302
Extracorporeal Assistance and
Performance 5A0–5A2 302
Root Operations 303
Extracorporeal Therapies
6A0–6A9 314
Root Operations 314
Body System, Duration, and Qualifier
Values for Extracorporeal
Therapies 316
Coding Extracorporeal Therapies in
Root Operations in ICD-10-PCS . . . 316

**Chapter 10: Osteopathic,
Other Procedures,
Chiropractic, and Imaging   321**
Introduction 322
Osteopathic Section 322
Chiropractic (9WB) 324
Other Procedures (8E0) 326
Body System: Physiological
Systems and Anatomical
Regions 326
Imaging .333
Body System (Character 2) Values
in Imaging Section. 333
Root Type (Character 3) Values
in the Imaging Section. 334

Body Part (Character 4) Values
in the Imaging Section 335
Contrast (Character 5) Values
in the Imaging Section 335
Qualifier (Characters 6 and 7)
Values Used in Imaging
Section. 342
Coding Imaging Section
Procedures using the
ICD-10-PCS 344

**Chapter 11: Nuclear
Medicine and Radiation
Oncology   353**
Introduction 354
Nuclear Medicine (C01–CW7) 355
Body System (Character 2) Values
in the Nuclear Medicine
Section. 355
Root Type (Character 3) Values in the
Nuclear Medicine Section 355
Body Part (Character 4) Values in the
Nuclear Medicine Section 357
Radionuclides (Character 5) Values
in the Nuclear Medicine
Section. 361
Coding Nuclear Medicine
Procedures 361
Radiation Oncology 367
Body System (Character 2) Values
in Radiation Oncology Section . . . 367
Root Types (Character 3) Values
in the Radiation Oncology
Section. 368
Treatment Site (Character 4) in the
Radiation Oncology Section 368
Modality Qualifier (Character 5) in the
Radiation Oncology
Section. 372
Isotope (Character 6) Values in the
Radiation Oncology Section 373
Qualifier (Character 7) Values in the
Radiation Oncology Section 375
Coding Radiation Oncology
Procedures 375

**Chapter 12: Rehabilitation
Mental Health and Substance
Abuse   381**
Introduction 383
Physical Rehabilitation and
Diagnostic Audiology (F00–F15) . 384
Character 3, Root Types 385
Character 4, Body System
and Region 387
Character 5, Type Qualifier 389
Character 6, Equipment 394
Coding Physical Rehabilitation
and Diagnostic Audiology in
ICD-10-PCS. 398
Mental Health (GZ1–GZJ) 402
Character 3, Root Type 403
Character 4, Type Qualifiers
in Mental Health 403
Coding Mental Health in ICD-10-PCS. . 405
Substance Abuse (HZ2–HZ9) 407
Characters 3 and 4, Root
Types and Type Qualifiers 407
Coding Substance Abuse
Procedures in ICD-10-PCS 409

**Appendix A: ICD-10-PCS
2012 Guidelines   414**

**Appendix B: ICD-10 Quick
Reference   429**

**Appendix C: Institutional
Claim 4010A to 5010   432**

**Appendix D: Professional
Claim 4010A to 5010   526**

**Appendix E: GEM Fact
Sheet   620**

**Appendix F: GEM
Guidelines   625**

**Appendix G: GEM 2012
Updates   651**

Index   662

List of Tables

Table 1-1   ICD-9-CM to ICD-10-CM Comparison

Table 1-2   Example of ICD-10-CM Codes with Specificity

Table 1-3   Definitions of Character Assignments

Table 2-1   Types of Health Care Systems

Table 2-2   HIPAA Titles

Table 2-3   PHI Identifiers

Table 2-4   HIPAA Transactions

Table 3-1   Terminology Differences between ICD-9-CM and ICD-10-CM

Table 3-2   Other Differences that Impact Data Comparison between ICD-9-CM and ICD-10-CM

Table 3-3   Reading the GEMs

Table 3-4   Terminology Differences between ICD-9-CM and ICD-10-PCS

Table 4-1   Character Values for Code 0JH63M7

Table 4-2   ICD-10-PCS Code Character Assignment Values

Table 4-3   Abstracting Procedural Statements

Table 4-4   Table for Code Characters

Table 4-5   Character Values for Table Sections of the ICD-10-PCS

Table 4-6   Character Values for Character 2: Body System, Used in the Medical and Surgical Section (0)

Table 4-7   Root Operations (Character 3) Value, Term, and Definition

Table 4-8   Character 5, Approach, Terms, Character Values, and Definitions

Table 4-9   Device Types (Character 6)

Table 4-10   Examples of Devices and Device Values from ICD-10-PCS

Table 4-11   Excerpt from Appendix D, Components of Approach Definitions

Table 5-1   Root Operation by Group Objective

Table 5-2   List of Root Operation Guidelines and Topics

Table 5-3   Root Operation Guideline B3.3a through B3.3d

Table 5-4   Guidelines B3.4 Discontinued Procedures

Table 5-5   Guidelines B3.8 Excision versus Resection

Table 5-6   Root Operations that Take Out a Solid, Fluid, or Gas from a Body Part

Table 5-7   Root Operations that Put In, Put Back, or Move Some or All of a Body Part

Table 5-8   Root Operations that Alter the Diameter or Route of a Tubular Body Part

Table 5-9   Guidelines for Root Operation Inspection

Table 5-10   Root Operations that Always Involve a Device

Table 5-11   Guidelines for Root Operation Fusion

Table 6-1   Body System (Character 2) Values in Medical and Surgical Table

Table 6-2   Body System Specific Coding Guidelines

Table 6-3   Approach (Character 5) Values and Definitions

Table 6-4   Device Types

Table 6-5   Device (Character 6) Values and Associated Root Operation

Table 6-6   Qualifier (Character 7) Values with Applicable Root Operations and Body System Values

Table 6-7   Character Assignment for Extraction Procedure

Table 6-8   Character Assignment for Detachment Procedure

Table 6-9   Character Assignment for Occlusion Procedure

Table 6-10   Character Assignment for Replacement Procedure

Table 6-11   Character Assignment for Free Skin Graft from Back, Open

Table 6-12   Character Assignment for Percutaneous Laser Ablation of Sigmoid Colon Lesion

Table 6-13   Character Assignment for Bypass, Sigmoid Colon Procedure

Table 7-1   Character Value Assignments Used in Obstetrics

Table 7-2   Body Part Values Used in Obstetrics Section

Table 7-3   Body Part Values in Comparison to Root Operation in Obstetrics Section

Table 7-4   Approaches Applicable to Obstetric Section Root Operations and Body Parts

Table 7-5   Approach Values and Definitions Used in Obstetrics Section of ICD-10-PCS

Table 7-6   Device Character Values in Obstetrics Section of ICD-10-PCS

Table 7-7   Qualifiers Used in Obstetrics Section of ICD-10-PCS

Table 7-8   Root Operation, Body Part, Approach, and Qualifier Values in Obstetrics Section of ICD-10-PCS

Table 8-1   Body System/Region Values and Descriptions in Placement Section

Table 8-2   Devices for Root Operation and/or Body Part in Placement Section

Table 8-3   Approach Values and Definitions and Approaches Available with the Root Operations and Body System/Regions

Table 8-4   Substance Values and Related Qualifiers for Root Operation Introduction

Table 8-5   Character Values and Definitions for Irrigation Table 3E1

Table 8-6   Body System/Region, Approach, and Substance Values for Root Operation Transfusion

Table 8-7   Approach Values used with Character 4 Body Systems

Table 8-8   Measurement Functions by Body System

Table 8-9   Relationships between Physiological System and Approaches in Monitoring Tables

Table 8-10   Root Operation Monitoring Approach and Function Values

Table 9-1   Duration Values in Root Operation Assistance

Table 9-2   Function Values in Root Operation Assistance

Table 9-3   Qualifiers Used by Body System and Function

Table 9-4   Duration Values used with Assistance Root Operation

Table 9-5   Functions Used with Root Operation Performance

Table 9-6   Root Operations, Values, and Definitions

Table 9-7   Body System, Duration, and Qualifier Values for Root Operations

Table 10-1   Approaches Used in Osteopathic Treatment

Table 10-2   Body Regions Used with Other Procedures (8E0)

Table 10-3a Body Regions Applicable to Approach Values

Table 10-3b Method Values by Body Region in Other Procedures Root Operation

Table 10-4   Body Systems Values in the Imaging Section

Table 10-5   Body Part Values within each Body System

Table 10-6   Root Types Associated with Contrast Values

Table 11-1   Body Systems in the Nuclear Medicine Section

Table 11-2   Root Types in Nuclear Medicine

Table 11-3   Body Parts Associated with Body Systems and Root Types

Table 11-4   Radionuclides used in Nuclear Medicine

Table 11-5   Body System Values in Radiation Oncology

Table 11-6   Treatment Sites and Values by Body System and Root Types

Table 11-7   Modality Values by Root Type

Table 11-8   Isotopes used in Radiation Oncology

Table 12-1   Root Types by Procedure Category

Table 12-2   Body System and Region Values Associated with Each Root Type

Table 12-3   Character 5 Type Qualifier Values by Category and Root Type

Table 12-4   Character 6 Equipment by Category and Root Type

Table 12-5   Root Types, Values, and Definitions used in Mental Health

Table 12-6   Type Qualifiers, Values, and Definitions by Root Type

Table 12-7   Type Qualifiers and Root Types in the Substance Abuse Section

Preface

INTRODUCTION

On January 15, 2009, the final rule was issued for the mandatory replacement of ICD-9-CM with the ICD-10-CM (diagnostic) and ICD-10-PCS (procedural) code sets by October 1, 2013. The structure of the new code sets is radically different from the current codes in use today. ICD-10 implementation will impact virtually all processes, technology and people, within a health care enterprise.

The changes in the diagnostic and procedural coding format and structure that comes with adoption of ICD-10-CM and ICD-10-PCS are so significant that retraining of existing coders will be required, and all allied health care providers, hospitals, and related entities will be required to retool their accounting and clinical documentation procedures and software applications to accommodate the changes.

In addition, and perhaps most importantly, coders currently using ICD-9-CM, and those students enrolled in educational courses that include diagnostic and procedural coding, will need extensive training in the new, complex, and expanded ICD-10-CM and ICD-10-PCS diagnostic and procedural codes.

The Time Is Now!

It seems like a long way away, October 13, 2013, but because of the massive changes that will need to take place in technology, people and processes—not the least of which is coding education—preparation should begin now.

Canada implemented ICD-10-CM only between 2002 and 2005. They reported several major unexpected outcomes, including:

- Underestimation of amount of work involved in preparing technology for the change
- Timelines and budgets grossly underestimated due to delays and unknown variables
- Magnitude of change was underestimated

Even their expected outcome, training of certified coders, proved insufficient in scope!

This coding instruction and implementation textbook will serve as a training manual for current and prospective coders, hospitals, physicians, and other medical professionals as well as any health care provider, payer, vendor, or related entity that uses the diagnostic and procedural code sets.

It will also serve to introduce students to the General Equivalency Maps (GEMs) that act as translation guides between ICD-9 and ICD-10 code sets. The new version 5010 electronic transaction standards are introduced, with comparisons of the paper provider and institutional claims to the 837P and 837I HIPAA transactions. Last, but not least, an entire chapter is devoted to strategy and planning for implementation of the ICD-10 code sets.

Audience

The audience for this textbook is anyone in the health care industry, professionals and instructors alike, who need to know what changes are coming in order to prepare for the impact that this transition will have on providers of care and health care facilities. This may include:

* Existing coders (inpatient and outpatient)

* New Coders and educators of new coders (career colleges, community colleges)

* Medical facilities (hospitals, physician practices, physical therapy, etc.)

* Medical professional associations

* Insurance carriers, third party payers

ICD-10-PCS Impacts and Training

* Compare structural changes to coding guidelines, terminology and functionality between ICD-10-PCS and CPT

* Compare structural changes to coding guidelines, terminology and functionality between ICD-10-PCS and Volume III of the ICD-9

* Identify the layout, terminology, and punctuation of the Tabular List.

* Understand the Guidelines and Conventions as they apply to the ICD-10-PCS

* Apply the steps for accurate and appropriate procedural coding by as defined by the 17 Sections and seven characters of the ICD-10-PCS

Facilities Impact & Implementation

* Provide comprehensive overview of the objectives, edits and changes

* Deliver crosswalk and guides for ICD-9-CM (Volumes 1 & 2) to ICD-10-CM, and ICD-9-CM (Volume 3) to ICD-10-PCS

* Prepare and develop policy & procedure manual changes, staff training needs and requirements

* Deliver phased checklists and templates for HIM and non-HIM staff, physician, allied health personnel education

* Learn impacts to and requirements for upgrading existing software applications, including claims editors, billing and claims, and electronic data interchange clearinghouses

* In-depth training for use of ICD-10 Official Coding Guidelines and coding manuals, for both ICD-10-CM and ICD-10-PCS

ORGANIZATION OF THE TEXTBOOK

Chapter is a basic overview of ICD-10 including the history of the code sets and a high-level overview of the significant changes brought about by ICD-10-CM and ICD-10-PCS. Chapters 2 and 3 discuss the General Equivalency Maps (GEMs), HIPAA Transactions and the new ASC x12 version 5010 transaction standards. Chapters 4 through 12 cover the same type of information for ICD-10-PCS procedural coding.

FEATURES OF THE TEXTBOOK

Each textbook chapter contains the following elements:

- Learning Objectives at the beginning to help organize the material.

- Key Terms and Definitions assist students in learning the technical vocabulary associated with coding systems.

- Practice Exercises reinforce the presented content.

- Chapter Summary encapsulates the chapter content so that students can review to make sure they understand all covered concepts.

- Chapter Review features multiple choice, matching, short answer, and coding practice questions to allow for mastery of covered concepts in a given chapter.

- CAAHEP and CAHIIM Competencies.

- Supplementary Material is provided as Appendices and includes coding guidelines, GEM instructions and maps, ASC x12 version 5010 examples of the 837I and 837P HIPAA transactions.

SUPPLEMENTS

The following supplements are available for this textbook:

- Student Workbook
- Instructor's Manual
- Instructor Resources
- Companion Website with StudyWARE™
- WebTutor™ Course Cartridges for Blackboard and Angel®

Student Workbook (978-1-4390-5728-5)

The *Workbook to Accompany ICD-10-PCS Coding System* follows the chapter organization of the textbook, and contains application-based assignments. Each chapter of the workbook contains a list of objectives and instructions for completing the assignment.

Instructor's Manual (978-1-4390-5727-8)

The Instructor's Manual contains learning objectives, lecture outlines, answers to chapter exercises and reviews, answers to workbook questions and activities. The Instructor's Manual also contains implementation guides for coding programs, including accreditation guidelines, calendars, syllabi, and course outlines.

Instructor Resources CD-ROM (978-1-1111-2748-0)

Spend less time planning and more time teaching with Delmar Cengage Learning's *Instructor Resources to Accompany ICD-10-PCS Coding System*. As an instructor, you will find this CD-ROM offers invaluable assistance by giving you access to all of your resources, anywhere, at any time*. Features of the Instructor CD-ROM include:

- Instructor's Manual in electronic format, containing class preparation information, sample syllabi, and complete answer keys for the textbook and workbook.

- Computerized test bank in ExamView® makes generating tests and quizzes a snap. With approximately 250 questions, you can create customized assessments for your students with the click of a button.

- Customizable instructor support slide presentations in PowerPoint™ format focus on key points in each chapter.

*All of these same great resources are also available online at www.CengageBrain.com

WebTutor™ Course Cartridges

(Blackboard: 978-1-4390-5722-3; Angel: 978-1-4390-5721-6)

WebTutor™ is an internet-based course management and delivery system designed to accompany the textbook. WebTutor content is available for use in Blackboard®, Angel®, and other platforms upon request. Available to supplement on-campus course delivery, or as the course management system for an online course, WebTutor contains the following:

- Video clips

- Online quizzes by chapter

- Discussion topics and learning links

- Online glossary

- Answer keys to textbook exercises and reviews

- Instructor presentations in PowerPoint™

- Test bank

- Communication tools, including a course calendar, chat, e-mail, and threaded discussions

To learn more, visit http://webtutor.cengage.com.

Companion Websites

Additional resources for students and instructors can be found at the online companion site for the textbook as follows:

Student Resources at the Student Companion Site

Some resources located at the Student Companion site are free to access, while others (such as StudyWARE) will require passcode entry. To access passcode-protected content, follow the instructions on the printed access card that is bound into this textbook.

Instructor Resources at the Instructor Companion Site

All instructor resources can be accessed by going to www.cengagebrain.com to create a unique user login. Contact your sales representative for more information. Online instructor resources at the Instructor Companion site are password-protected and include the following:

- All resources found on the Instructor Resources CD-ROM, including test bank, presentations in PowerPoint™, and electronic Instructor's Manual

- If there are any revisions to the textbook, workbook, or answer keys due to code changes, they will be posted here

- Access to all student supplements, including StudyWARE™

About the Author

Carline Dalgleish, BS, MA, RHIA

AHIMA Approved ICD-10-CM/PCS Trainer, AHIMA ICD-10 Ambassador

Carline has been working in health care since 1970, starting in the Medical Records department of the Army/Air Force Hospital in Nuremberg, Germany. Over the years, she has worked in almost every administrative and managerial position for physicians, clinics, and hospitals, and even Medicare.

Carline has real-world experience in administrative and financial departments, as well as management experience in business office administration, regulatory compliance, information technology, and is a subject matter expert in medical billing and coding and administrative medical assisting. In addition, she has created the curriculum for and instructed multiple administrative medical courses, with an emphasis in physician and hospital coding, insurance billing and administrative medical assisting.

Carline holds a Bachelor's degree in Business Information Systems, and a Master's degree in Leadership, a post-baccalaureate in Health Information Management, and is an AHIMA-Approved ICD-10-CM/PCS Trainer and ICD-10 Ambassador. She is a member of the American Health Information Management Association (AHIMA) and the American Association of Health care Administrative Management (AAHAM), and owns her own educational consulting firm, AnnGrant Education Services, LLC.

Reviewers

The publisher and author would like to acknowledge the following instructors for their invaluable insights and suggestions on this edition.

Cheryl H. Bordwine, BHA, MBA, RMA (AMT)
Director/Professor Medical Assisting Program
College of the Mainland
Texas City, TX

Mary M. Cantwell, RHIT, CPC, CPC-I, CPC-H, CPC-P, RMC
Professor, Health Information
Metro Community College
Omaha, NE

Marie T. Conde, MPA, RHIA, CCS
HIT Program Director and Instructor
City College of San Francisco
San Francisco, CA

Rhoda Cooper, CPC, RMC, NCICS
Director of HIM
PVCC
Charlottesville, VA

Linda H. Donahue, RHIT, CCS, CCS-P, CPC
Assistant Professor, Health Information Technology
Delgado Community College
New Orleans, LA

Carrie Heinz, RHIT
Health Information Management
Presentation Medical Center and Rolette Community Care Center
Rolla and Rolette, ND

Judy Hurtt, Med
Instructor
East Central Community College
Decatur, MS

Anne C. Karl, RHIA, CCS-P, CPC, CCC
Associate Instructor
Rasmussen College
Eden Prairie, MN

Joshua Maywalt, NCICS, NCMOA
MBC Instructor
City College
Casselberry, FL

Tracey McKethan, MBA, CCA
Department Chair/Assistant Professor
Springfield Technical Community College
Springfield, MA

Della Moon, RHIT, CCS, CTR
HIM Instructor
San Jacinto College
Houston, TX

Donna Otis, LPN
Medical Program Director
Metro Business College
Rolla, MO

June M. Petillo, MBA, RMC, NCP
Director of EMR & Adjunct Instructor
Women's Health USA & Capital Community College
Avon, CT & Hartford, CT

Technical Reviewer

A special thank you to Patricia Griffin, who reviewed this book and provided content corrections and insight. The timeliness of your work was greatly appreciated.

Patricia J. Griffin, AAS, RHIT, HIC
United Methodist Homes
Elizabeth Church Campus
Binghamton, New York

Acknowledgements

To my beloved Grant, who I miss more with each passing day;

To my wonderful family, both here in the United States as well as Canada, especially Mom, Aunt Ruby, Gail, Kelly, Greg, and my sweeties, Evan and Cole, and a host of aunts, cousins and family too numerous to mention;

To Frank Hern, Jr. my best friend, whose encouragement (and threats) kept me laughing and on-track during this long process;

To Greg, my favorite nephew, whose late night pep talks revived me when I wanted to give up;

To Sharon L. Ansley, whose unwavering faith planted the seeds 17 years ago that launched my journey in Christ;

To Jadin Kavanaugh for keeping me motivated, the reviewers (especially Patricia Griffin) who pushed me to make this text the best it could be, and of course, to Rhonda Dearborn, who gave me the chance to write this book, and to everyone at Cengage Learning who helped me accomplish this goal;

And, finally to all my friends, who have touched and blessed my life in incredible ways.

How to Use StudyWARE™

Delmar Cengage Learning's StudyWARE software helps you learn terms and concepts presented in the *ICD-10-PCS Coding System* textbook. As you study each chapter of the text, be sure to complete the activities for the corresponding content areas in StudyWARE. Use StudyWARE as your own private tutor to help you learn and review the material in your textbook.

MENUS

You can access any of the menus from wherever you are in the program.

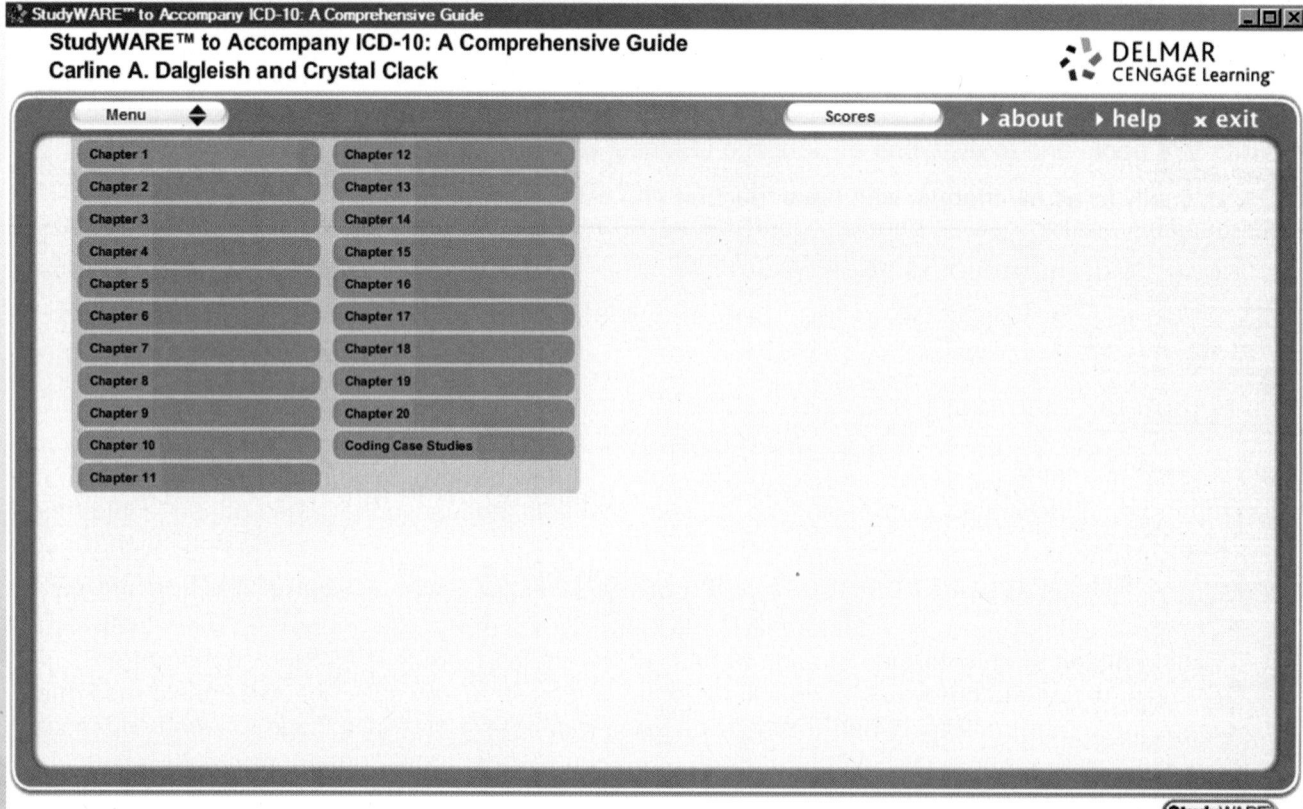

QUIZZES

Quizzes include multiple-choice, true-false, and fill-in-the-blank questions. You can take the quizzes in both Practice Mode and Quiz Mode.

- Use Practice Mode to improve your mastery of the material. You have multiple tries to get the answers correct. Instant feedback tells you whether you're right or wrong, and helps you learn quickly by explaining why an answer was correct or incorrect.

- Use Quiz Mode when you are ready to test yourself and keep a record of your scores. In Quiz Mode, you have one try to get the answers right, but you can take each Quiz as many times as you want.

- You can view your last scores for each quiz and print out your results to submit to your instructor.

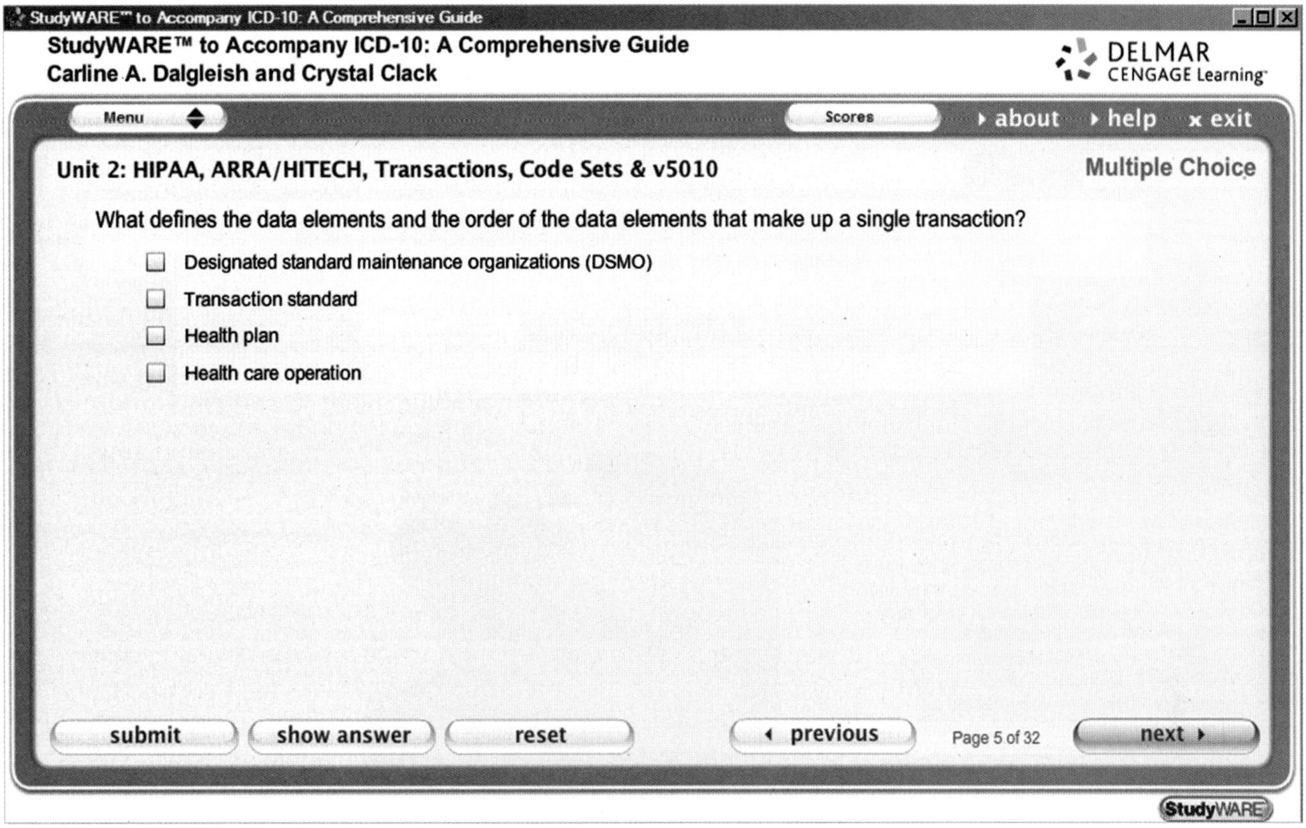

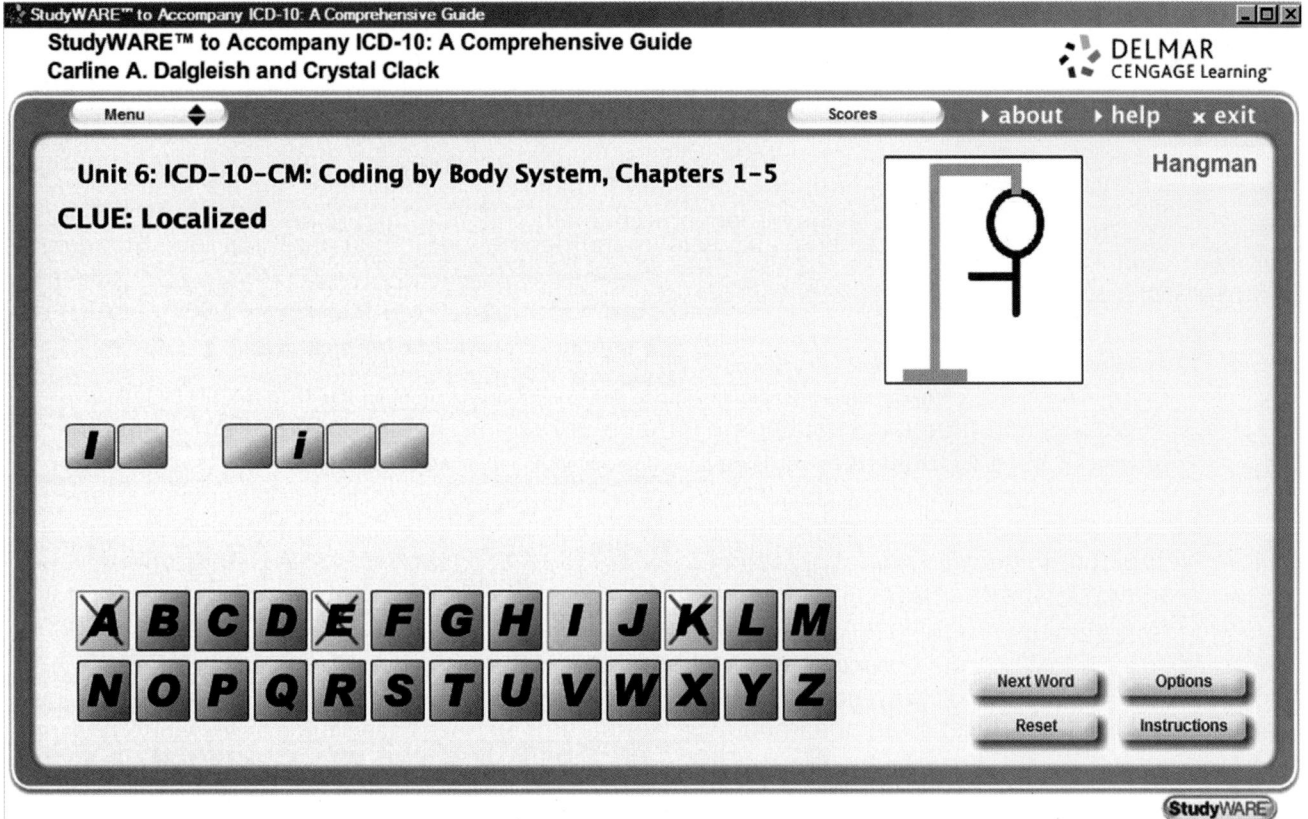

ACTIVITIES

Activities include hangman and concentration. Have fun while increasing your knowledge!

CODING CASES

Coding cases are patient scenarios that include images and videos. Read each case, view the animation or video, and code each case correctly to challenge your coding knowledge!

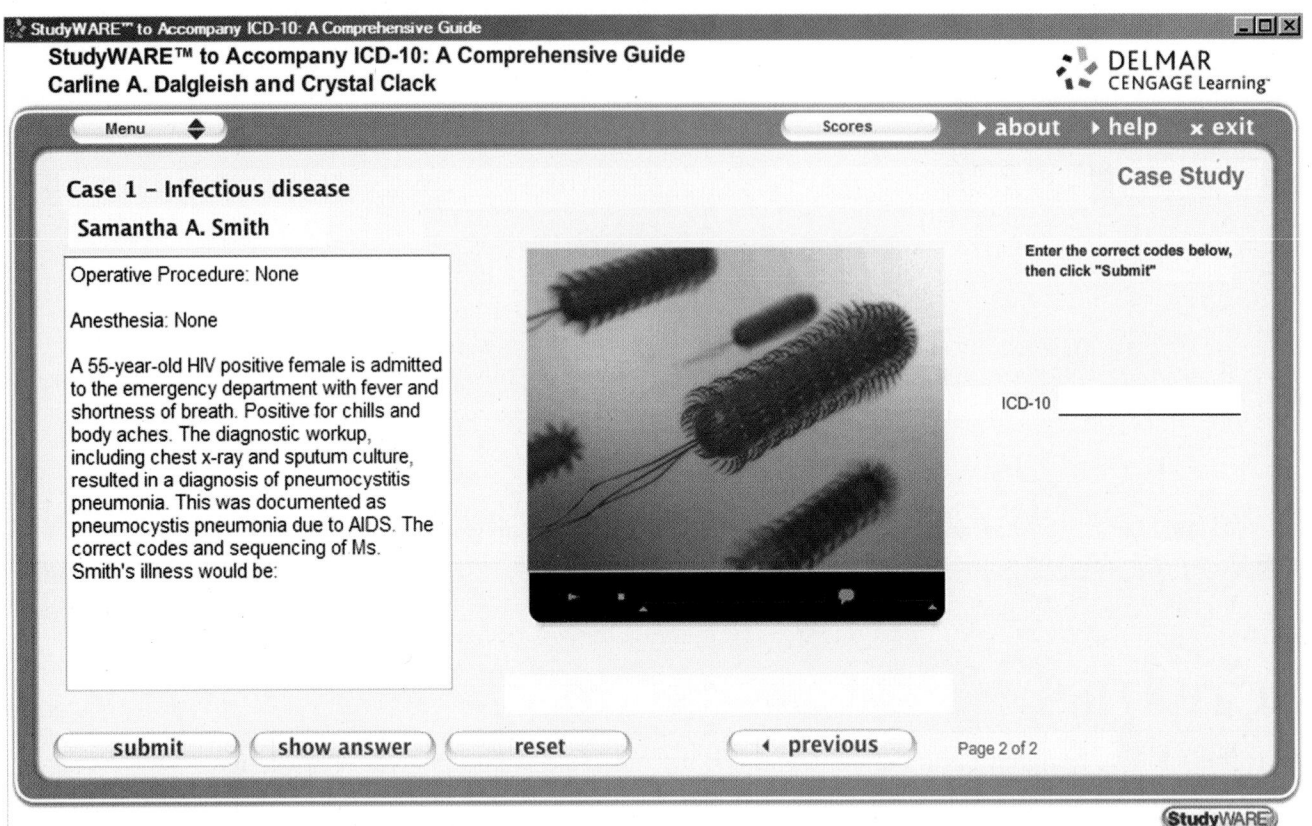

StudyWARE™ to Accompany ICD-10: A Comprehensive Guide

StudyWARE™ to Accompany ICD-10: A Comprehensive Guide
Carline A. Dalgleish and Crystal Clack

DELMAR
CENGAGE Learning

Menu   Scores   ▸ about   ▸ help   ✕ exit

Case 1 – Infectious disease   Case Study

Samantha A. Smith

Operative Procedure: None   Enter the correct codes below, then click "Submit"

Anesthesia: None

A 55-year-old HIV positive female is admitted to the emergency department with fever and shortness of breath. Positive for chills and body aches. The diagnostic workup, including chest x-ray and sputum culture, resulted in a diagnosis of pneumocystitis pneumonia. This was documented as pneumocystis pneumonia due to AIDS. The correct codes and sequencing of Ms. Smith's illness would be:

ICD-10 _____

submit   show answer   reset   ◂ previous   Page 2 of 2

StudyWARE

HOW TO USE THE ENCODERPRO.COM—EXPERT 59-DAY TRIAL

With the purchase of this textbook you receive free 59-day access to *EncoderPro.com—Expert*, the powerful online medical coding solution from Ingenix® . With *EncoderPro.com*, you can simultaneously search across all three code sets.

How to Access the Free Trial

Information on how to access your 59-day trial of *EncoderPro.com* is included on the printed tear-out card bound into this textbook. Your unique user access code is also printed on the card. **NOTE:** be sure to check with your instructor before beginning your free trial bxecause it will expire 59 days after your initial login.

Features and Benefits of EncoderPro.com

EncoderPro.com is the essential code lookup software for CPT® , ICD-9-CM, and HCPCS code sets from Ingenix® . It gives users fast searching capabilities across all code sets. EncoderPro can greatly reduce the time it takes to build or review a claim, and helps improve overall coding accuracy.

EncoderPro.com | **INGENIX**

Login

EncoderPro.com Product Suite
Access Current, Code-specific Information Now!

Learn which HCPCS codes can be used to report equipment and services and which are covered for reimbursement.

Ligation or banding?
Know the difference by referencing our Coders' Desk Reference lay descriptions for procedures.

Extra Digits
Our ICD-9-CM color codes tell you instantly whether a diagnosis is valid, specific, and covered (or not).

Take our most comprehensive code lookup, billing, and compliance tool, **EncoderPro.com/Expert**, for a free trial now!

Username: / Password: / Login / Forgot your username or password?

Click here to purchase your **Subscription** to EncoderPro.com ►► Get it now!

Click here for a **30-day FREEtrial** ►► try it now!

MEDICODE

View our support message board

Contact Us | AMA Copyright | Terms of Use | Support
© Ingenix, Inc. 2010. All Rights Reserved.
CPT Only © 2009 American Medical Association. All Rights Reserved.
CPT® is a registered trademark of the American Medical Association.

During your free trial period to *EncoderPro.com—Expert*, the following tools will be available to you:

- **Powerful Ingenix CodeLogic™ search engine**. Search all three code sets simultaneously using lay terms, acronyms, abbreviations, and even misspelled words.
- **Lay descriptions for thousands of CPT® codes.** Enhance your understanding of procedures with easy-to-understand descriptions.
- **Color-coded edits.** Understand whether a code carries an age or sex edit, is covered by Medicare, or contains bundled procedures.
- **ICD-10 Mapping Tool**. Crosswalk from ICD-9-CM codes to the appropriate ICD-10 code quickly and easily.
- **Great value.** Get the content from over 20 code and reference books in one powerful solution.

EncoderPro.com Video-based Autodemo

View Ingenix's online EncoderPro.com video-based Autodemo at http://www.shopingenix.com by scrolling your mouse over Products and eSolutions, and clicking on the eSolution Online Demos link. Then, click on the EncoderPro.com link to start the Autodemo, which is approximately 5 minutes in length. The EncoderPro.com features are described and using the encoder to locate a code is demonstrated.

For more information about *EncoderPro.com*, or to become a subscriber beyond the free trial, e-mail us at **esales@cengage.com**.

ICD-10 History, Preview, and Impacts

Learning Objectives

At the conclusion of this chapter, the learner should be able to:

* Understand what the International Classification of Diseases (ICD) coding system is and its use.
* Understand the development history of the International Classification of Diseases (ICD).
* Describe the four major objectives that guided the development of ICD-10-CM and PCS.
* Identify when the new ICD-10 coding systems must be implemented.
* Understand who will be impacted by the change from ICD-9 to ICD-10.
* Describe the advantages of implementation of ICD-10.
* Distinguish between ICD-10-CM (Clinical Modification) and ICD-10-PCS (Procedural Coding System).
* Identify the main changes in structure from ICD-9-CM to ICD-10-CM.
* Identify the main changes in structure from procedural coding to ICD-10-PCS.

Key Terms and Definitions

Alphabetic Index	An alphabetical reference used to locate approximate codes or code ranges, which are then used to find the most accurate code in the Tabular List of the ICD-10-CM or Tables of the ICD-10-PCS.
Approach	The fifth character of an ICD-10-PCS that identifies the method used to reach the site of the procedure.
Body Part	The fourth character of an ICD-10-PCS code that describes the exact body part upon which the procedure is being performed.
Body System	The second character of an ICD-10-PCS code that describes the general body system on which a procedure is performed.
Code Sets	The diagnostic and procedure codes mandated by law. As of October 1, 2013, they are the ICD-10-CM, ICD-10-PCS. The existing CPT and HCPCS codes are the existing procedure codes for physicians, outpatient and ambulatory care providers.
Cooperating parties	Four agencies responsible for the maintenance and upgrade of the ICD-10-CM. The American Hospital Association (AHA), The Centers for Medicare and Medicaid Services (CMS), the National Center for Health Statistics (NCHS) and the American Health Information Management Association (AHIMA).

Device	The sixth character of an ICD-10-PCS code is used to identify any devices left in the patient at the end of a procedure.
HIPAA	Health Insurance Portability and Accountability Act. A US law that sets privacy standards protecting patients' medical records and other health information provided to health plans, physicians, hospitals, and other health care providers. It also sets standards for electronic transmission of data and coding classification system requirements.
ICD-9-CM (International Classification of Diseases, 9th Edition, Clinical Modification).	A 3-volume coding manual containing diagnostic and procedural codes. It is being replaced by ICD-10-CM and ICD-10-PCS.
ICD-10-CM	A diagnostic code classification system.
ICD-10-PCS	A procedure code classification system.
Provider	Any individual or organization that renders care, treatment, or performs a procedure on a patient.
Qualifier	The seventh character of an ICD-10-PCS code provides additional information regarding the procedure being performed.
Root Operation	The third character of an ICD-10-PCS code that describes the type of procedure performed.
Section	The first character of an ICD-10-PCS code containing groupings of similar types of procedures. The largest section is the Medical/Surgical section.
Tabular List	In the ICD-10-CM it is a numerical list of diagnosis codes and their descriptions, divided by chapter.
Transactions	The HIPAA-mandated data elements required for electronic submission of healthcare data.
Transaction and Code Sets (TCS)	Electronic data transmission standards and diagnostic and procedural codes.

Introduction

Use of the new ICD-10 coding classification system, by law, must replace ICD-9 no later than October 1, 2013. This chapter will explain why the new codes are important, how they were developed, what they look like, and who they affect. In addition, it will explain the development of disease classification systems like the ICD-9 and ICD-10, describe the differences between the current edition (9th) of the ICD and the newly mandated 10th edition, and outline the benefits and advantages of the new system. The differences between ICD-10-CM and ICD-10-PCS codes will be explained, and finally, this chapter will provide an overview comparison of ICD-9-CM to ICD-10-CM and ICD-10-PCS, including the new features and structure.

Later chapters will present instruction in coding diseases, injuries, and conditions using the ICD-10-CM, and procedures and services using the ICD-10-PCS. The guidelines for diagnostic and procedural coding, the format of coding manuals, and the steps for coding will also be presented in future chapters. Complete planning and implementation guidelines will also be presented for health care entities, to assist them in preparing the organization for implementation of ICD-10-CM and ICD-10-PCS.

ICD-10: Now is the Time!

For students who already know how to use the ICD-9 codes, the basic guidelines for diagnostic coding are generally the same. However, the ICD-10 diagnostic and procedural codes are radically different in structure, layout, and form, which means there is plenty to learn. This book will teach diagnostic and procedural coding "from the ground up" using ICD-10.

ICD-10, like its predecessor ICD-9, is a system of codes used for many purposes. These codes translate intricate diagnoses and complicated procedures into a standardized "language" that everyone in health care can understand–from physicians to hospitals to insurance carriers. For the medical coder, this language is primarily used for insurance billing, but these codes are used for many other purposes, including reporting, morbidity, and mortality and other statistical analyses.

History of The International Classification of Diseases (ICD)

Classification systems like ICD-9 and ICD-10 are used by health care organizations to organize health care data and make retrieval meaningful. The early Greeks were the first to group data by disease processes. Captain John Graunt of London was the first to publish mortality and morbidity statistics in his publication, *London Bills of Mortality*.

This was the first real attempt at studying disease processes from a statistical viewpoint. Later, in the 1830s, William Farr introduced uniformity in the use of statistics. His work helped classify diseases by anatomical site. His *International List of Causes of Death* provided the foundation for current vital statistics.

In 1893, Dr. Jacques Bertillon developed the *Bertillon Classification of Causes of Death*. The American Public Health Association (APHA) recommended adoption of this classification system by Canada, Mexico, and the United States, and further recommended that it be revised every ten years.

Subsequent revisions were called the *International Classification System of Causes of Death*.; multiple revisions were made until 1938. The World Health Organization (WHO) took over in 1948 by publishing the first International Classification of Diseases (ICD). This coding system was developed to provide international consistency for reporting mortality (death) statistics only. Numbers were added with subsequent revisions to identify the new "version." ICD-9 and ICD-10, the most current versions, are copyrighted by WHO. ICD-10 is the latest version.

Effective from January 15, 1999, ICD-10 implementation officially began in the United States when ICD-10-CM codes were used for reporting the cause of death on death certificates.

In the 1950s, the U.S. Public Health Service adopted the International Classification of Diseases (ICD-A), which was used for indexing hospital records by diseases and operations. Subsequent modifications, in 1962, provided greater detail and introduced a classification for *surgical operations*. In 1968, due to a need for even greater detail and specificity, the eighth revision of ICD-A (ICDA-8), adapted for use in the United States, was published. The ninth revision of ICD was published in 1975, retitled *International Classification of Diseases, Ninth Revision (ICD-9)*. In 1979, the World Health Organization adopted it as the global statistical classification system and, that same year, the National Center for Health Statistics (NCHS) developed a modification of ICD-9 for use in the United States. The modification, *International Classification of Diseases, Ninth Revision, Clinical Modification* (ICD-9-CM) has been in use in the United States since that time.

Four organizations in the United States are responsible for maintaining the ICD-9-CM classification. They are responsible for developing official guidelines and for proper application of ICD-9-CM, and now the ICD-10-CM. They are known as the **cooperating parties**, and include:

- The American Hospital Association (AHA)

- The American Health Information Management Association (AHIMA)

- The Centers for Medicare and Medicaid Services (CMS)

- The National Center for Health Statistics (NCHS)

The Final Rule mandating the use of ICD-10-CM and ICD-10-PCS went into effect on January 15, 2009.

All health care providers and insurance companies must begin using ICD-10-CM for diagnostic coding no later than October 1, 2013. The ICD-10-PCS, on the other hand, need only be implemented by hospitals, acute care facilities, and insurance payors on this date. Physicians and other outpatient providers, such as ambulatory surgery centers, emergency departments, or outpatient facilities, may continue to perform procedural coding using the Current Procedural Terminology (CPT) developed by the American Medical Association (AMA) and the Healthcare Common Procedural Coding System (HCPCS), developed by the Centers for Medicare and Medicaid Services (CMS). The guidelines for ICD-10 implementation include:

- Implementation by October 1, 2013, in hospitals, and all health care organizations that interact with hospital insurance billing and data gathering. Clearinghouses are also affected.

- Physicians and other ambulatory care providers may continue to use CPT and HCPCS to code procedures and services rendered to the patient.

Because the structure of ICD-10-CM is radically different from that of the ninth edition, there is, and will be, a large learning curve, both in the impact of ICD-10 on the entire health care industry and in the medical coder's skill sets and knowledge. It is time to prepare and plan now!

Why the Classification System is Changing

Federal legislation regarding the privacy and portability of health insurance, called the Health Insurance Portability and Accountability Act (HIPAA), created the need to replace the outdated, obsolete ninth edition of the ICD because it does not meet HIPAA standards in the area of electronic transactions and code sets. HIPAA includes laws that govern the privacy and security of health information. Included in HIPAA are rules for the transmission of data electronically over the internet. The Transactions & Code Sets (TCS) provision of HIPAA defines how the data is structured and transmitted. **Transactions** are data transmitted electronically, which must be arranged in a specific format. **Code sets** are diagnosis and procedure codes. Until the new ICD-10 law goes into effect, the code sets being used are ICD-9-CM, CPT and HCPCS. Electronic transactions and code sets, also called electronic data interchange (EDI), enable employers, physicians, and hospitals to submit insurance claims and other information to insurance companies for reimbursement using the internet.

With Medicare, particularly, there are payment systems in place that require more emphasis on (1) documentation in the health record, (2) coding and reimbursement education, and (3) data quality. To this end, ICD-10's design addresses deficiencies in ICD-9-CM. In addition, ICD-10 enhances the efficiency of clinical data collection and quality of administrative data. These payments systems, especially Medicare Severity-Diagnosis Related Groups (MS-DRG) and Prospective Payment Systems (PPS) will be discussed in Chapter 3 of this textbook.

Coded data currently have many uses. The first and most important is to have a standardized "language" understood by hospitals, providers, insurance carriers, and others. ICD-10-CM codes are used throughout the health care industry, throughout the world. Researchers, scientists, physicians, and other health care workers in Japan, Russia, Germany, and everywhere in between can view a diagnosis or procedure code and know exactly what is wrong with a patient, and what treatment was provided. As of October 1, 2013, ICD-10-CM codes will be used in the United States.

Medical billers and coders use the codes to identify the diagnosis and treatment for a patient, and submit an insurance claim for reimbursement. Researchers and hospitals use the codes to gather statistical data on disease and death, and success or failure rates of treatment and surgical procedures. This data is evaluated to determine the safety and quality of medical care, as well as its effectiveness. Uses for diagnostic and procedure codes include:

1. Assist in processing of insurance claims both on paper and electronically
2. Measuring safety, quality, and efficacy of medical care
3. Designing health care delivery systems
4. Setting health care policy
5. Monitoring resource utilization
6. Improving financial, clinical, and administrative performance

7. Providing health care consumers with data on cost and outcome(s) of treatment options

8. Identifying, tracking, and managing public health risks and disease processes

9. Recognizing and identifying abusive or fraudulent reimbursement trends

10. Conducting health care research and clinical trials

11. Participating in epidemiological studies.

For medical billers and coders, the most important uses, and the ones that affect them the most, are the design of payment systems and the identification of abuse and fraud. In order for a coder or biller to submit an insurance claim, the patient's diagnoses, procedures, services, and treatments, must be translated into a standardized code recognizable by a specific payor, and submitted using the required guidelines and rules. Some of the reasons ICD-9-CM is being replaced include:

- Inadequate description of many procedures

- Lack of specificity

ICD-9-CM diagnosis codes	ICD-10-CM diagnosis codes
• 3-5 characters in length	• 3-7 characters in length
• Approximately 13,000 codes	• Approximately 68,000 available codes
• First digit may be alpha (E or V) or numeric; Digits 2-5 are numeric	• Digit 1 is alpha; Digits 2 and 3 are numeric; Digits 4-7 are alpha or numeric
• Limited space for adding new codes	• Flexible for adding new codes
• Lacks detail	• Very specific
• Lacks laterality	• Has laterality
• Difficult to analyze data due to non-specific codes	• Specificity improves coding accuracy and richness of data for analysis
• Codes are non-specific and do not adequately define diagnoses needed for medical research	• Detail improves the accuracy of data used for medical research
• Does not support interoperability because it is not used by other countries	• Supports interoperability and the exchange of health data between other countries and the U.S.
ICD-9-CM procedure codes	ICD-10-PCS procedure codes
• 3-4 numbers in length	• 7 alpha-numeric characters in length
• Approximately 3,000 codes	• Approximately 87,000 available codes
• Based upon outdated technology	• Reflects current usage of medical terminology and devices
• Limited space for adding new codes	• Flexible for adding new codes
• Lacks detail	• Very specific
• Lacks laterality	• Has laterality
• Generic terms for body parts	• Detailed descriptions for body parts
• Lacks description of methodology and approach for procedures	• Provides detailed descriptions of methodology and approach for procedures
• Limits DRG assignment	• Allows DRG definitions for better recognize new technologies and devices
• Lacks precision to adequately define procedures	• Precisely defines procedures with detail regarding body part, approach, any device used and qualifying information

Department of Health and Human Services, Federal Register, Vol. 73, No. 164, Friday, August 22, 2008.

© Cengage Learning 2013

Figure 1-1 Comparison of ICD-9 and ICD-10 Diagnostic and Procedure Codes

- No consistent identification of devices or procedural approaches

- Difficult to update and expand

- Virtually no room for expansion

- Limits accuracy of MS-DRG definitions.

Figure 1-1 is a comparison of ICD-9 and ICD-10 diagnostic and procedure codes, and illustrates the radical differences between the two classification systems. For example, the ICD-9-CM diagnosis codes are 3–5 numeric characters in length, with approximately 13,000 codes. ICD-10-CM codes can be 3–7 characters in length, and the number of codes available are now approximately 68,000—more than five times the number of codes in the ICD-9-CM! There are approximately 3,000 ICD-9-CM procedure codes, compared to 87,000 ICD-10-PCS procedure codes, with the ICD-9-CM codes comprised of 3–4 numbers, and the ICD-10-PCS codes comprised of 7 alphanumeric characters.

Let's Review 1–1:

1. The implementation date for ICD-10-CM/PCS is:
   a. January 15, 2009
   b. January 15, 2013
   c. October 1, 2011
   d. October 1, 2013

2. Which of the following is/are correct:
   a. ICD-10-CM must be implemented by all health care organizations
   b. ICD-10-PCS is only required to be implemented for hospital inpatient coding
   c. ICD-10-PCS must be implemented by physicians and ambulatory care providers
   d. A and B

3. The new diagnostic classification system is:
   a. ICD-10-CM
   b. ICD-10-PCS
   c. Both the ICD-10-CM and the ICD-10-PCS
   d. None of the above

4. The ICD-10 classification systems are updated annually by:
   a. The Cooperating Parties
   b. The American Hospital Association
   c. The World Health Organization
   d. The Centers for Medicare and Medicaid Services

5. Transactions and code sets (TCS) are defined as:
   a. Standards for electronic data interchange
   b. Electronic transmission standards and diagnosis and procedure codes
   c. Privacy and portability standards for HIPAA
   d. Standards for diagnosis and procedure codes

6. One difference between ICD-10-CM and ICD-9-CM is:
   a. ICD-9-CM uses 3–5 numbers; ICD-10-CM uses 3–7 characters
   b. ICD-9-CM uses 3–5 characters; ICD-10-CM requires 6 characters
   c. ICD-10-CM has an eighth character that identifies an initial or secondary encounter, or sequela; ICD-9-CM does not
   d. ICD-10-CM uses only letters and no numbers; ICD-9-CM uses only numbers

ICD-10-CM

Diagnoses, conditions, illnesses, and injuries are translated into ICD-10-CM codes. ICD-10-CM is the abbreviation for International Classification of Diseases, 10ᵗʰ Edition, Clinical Modification. In the past, coders used Volumes I and II of the ICD-9-CM to select these codes. Previous editions of the ICD-9-CM were comprised of three volumes. Volumes I and II were the alphabetical and tabular indexes for diseases, symptoms, signs, and health issues. Volume III included tabular and alphabetical hospital procedure codes. Volumes I and II are being replaced by ICD-10-CM, and volume III is being replaced, in hospital inpatient settings, by ICD-10-PCS.

Generally, upon purchase of an ICD-9-CM coding manual, especially in a hospital billing and coding environment, all three volumes were included. A physician or ambulatory care provider typically used only volumes I and II for their diagnostic coding. When coding procedures and office visits, physicians and other providers use the CPT (Current Procedural Terminology) and HCPCS (Healthcare Common Procedural Coding System).

Please be aware that this textbook does not include physician CPT and HCPCS procedure coding guidelines and instructions. The focus here is on the new ICD-10 classification systems: ICD-10-CM for diagnosis coding in all health care settings, and ICD-10-PCS for procedure coding in inpatient settings.

ICD-10-CM Implementation

The tenth revision of the ICD system was published in 1992 in order to:

- Expand the content, purpose, and scope of system
- Include ambulatory care services
- Increase clinical detail
- Capture risk factors in primary care
- Include emergent diseases
- Group diagnoses for epidemiological purposes

The projected benefits of transitioning to ICD-10-CM and ICD-10-PCS include:

- More accurate payment
- Fewer rejected or improper claims
- Better understanding of procedural coding
- Improved disease management
- Better understanding of health conditions and health care outcomes
- Harmonization of disease monitoring and reporting worldwide

The advantages and benefits of ICD-10-CM are significant in both quality and usefulness of data for various health care settings.

Changes to the United States versions of the ICD-10 are made annually through a review process to further clarify some codes and to create new codes needed as a result of medical discoveries and advancements, or for other administrative reasons. This review process is under the direction of the Centers for Medicare & Medicaid Services (CMS), the American Hospital Association (AHA), and the National Center for Health Statistics (NCHS), and the American Health Information Management Association (AHIMA).

Layout and Structure of the ICD-10-CM Diagnostic Classification System

The layout of the ICD-10-CM coding manual is comparable to the ICD-9-CM. There is still a Tabular List and an Alphabetical Index, which were included in volumes I and II of the ICD-9-CM. However, where ICD-9-CM codes were numeric (with the exception of V and E codes), ICD-10-CM codes are a combination of alphabetic and numeric characters. An ICD-9-CM code for gastroesophageal reflux disease (GERD), for example, is 530.81. In the ICD-10-CM, the code is K21.9. ICD-10-CM codes can be up to seven (7) alphanumeric characters, compared to the maximum five (5) for ICD-9-CM. This allows for even greater accuracy and specificity in code selection. In ICD-9-CM a diagnosis of *astigmatism, irregular, of the left eye*, did not include identification of the eye involved. The closest specific code available, 367.22, described only the *irregular astigmatism*. In the ICD-10-CM, not only is the *irregular astigmatism* identified with the code H52.21, but the addition of a sixth character (2) for a code of H52.212 identifies the left eye.

ICD-10-CM also incorporates additional information related to ambulatory care and managed-care encounters that is not available in ICD-9-CM. When coding injuries, the ICD-10-CM groups them first by site (arm, shoulder, ankle), and then by type (fracture, sprain), rather than only by type, as in the ICD-9-CM. Other new or expanded features of the ICD-10-CM include:

- Combination codes are used for both symptom and diagnosis; and etiology and manifestations.
- Codes are expanded to include laterality (identification of a specific side of the body) which was missing from ICD-9-CM.
- Classifications that indicate a patient's trimester are included in the obstetrics chapter.
- In the section on diabetes, codes are included for types of diabetes that require insulin therapy and types that do not.
- Codes for postoperative complications have been expanded.
- Expanded codes allow for distinctions between intraoperative complications and postprocedural disorders.
- Code groupings are more logical, and have been expanded to add four new chapters not found in the ICD-9-CM.
- Category *and* subcategory codes now contain full descriptions.
- Characters are added to provide more precise coding and are incorporated into the code listing.
- Laterality, or identification of body side, is now possible.
- Expanded code detail with addition of the sixth and seventh digits.

Table 1-1 ICD-9-CM to ICD-10-CM Comparison

Characteristic	ICD-9-CM	ICD-10-CM
Character type	Numeric, except letters V and E	All codes are alphanumeric, beginning with letters A through Z except I and O.
Code length	Maximum of five digits	Maximum of seven characters
Supplementary codes	V codes and E codes	None (added to main code book)
Laterality (left vs. right)	No	Yes
Trimester	No	Yes
Structure of injuries	Wound type	Body part

- A seventh character allows the coder to provide additional information with the code.

- Coding of etiology (origin) and manifestation (the disease or condition), which required two codes with the ICD-9-CM, have been replaced by a single "combination" code.

- Category and subcategory code titles have been changed to reflect new technology and terminology.

- Codes have been added to describe post-operative conditions.

- Codes in the pregnancy, delivery, and puerperium (period of time beginning immediately after birth) chapter includes designation of the trimester in which the condition occurs.

- Many new codes are incorporated into the ICD-10-CM, including blood typing and alcohol level.

ICD-10-CM Structure

There are 21 chapters within the ICD-10-CM tabular list. A sixth character has been added for more specificity, and in obstetrics, injuries, and external causes of injury, a seventh character is added to identify an initial or subsequent encounter, or whether sequelae (late effects) exist. In all cases the structure of the ICD-10-CM code is as shown below. Alpha characters are not case sensitive.

Character 1 is an alpha character

- Character 2 is numeric

- Characters 3–7 are alphabetic or numeric

  - Examples:

    - A66 Yaws

    - A6.20 Lyme disease, unspecified

    - 09.311 Physical abuse complicating pregnancy, first trimester

    - S42.001A Closed fracture of unspecified part of right clavicle, initial encounter

The ICD-10-CM Coding Manual

The ICD-10-CM coding manual is divided into a Tabular List and an **Alphabetic Index**. The Alphabetic Index is used to help search for diagnoses, conditions, illnesses, and injuries by name. Each named disease, condition, illness, or injury references the primary category code in the Tabular List. The **Tabular List** contains all the codes in alphanumeric order, as well as code descriptions, and is subdivided by chapters.

Appendix A in this text contains the 2011 ICD-10-CM Official Coding Guidelines (Guidelines). The Guidelines are instructions for using the codes in the ICD-10-CM to classify diseases and conditions documented in the medical record. Take a moment to review Appendix A. The Guidelines begin with

Table 1-2 Example of ICD-10-CM Codes with Specificity

Appendicitis	
K35.0	Acute appendicitis with generalized peritonitis
K35.1	Acute appendicitis with peritoneal abscess
K35.9	Acute appendicitis, unspecified
Stress Fracture, left tibia	
M84.362A	Stress fracture, left tibia, initial encounter for fracture
M84.362D	Stress fracture, left tibia, subsequent encounter for fracture with routine healing
M84.362G	Stress fracture, left tibia, subsequent encounter for fracture with delayed healing

Section I: Conventions, general coding guidelines, and chapter-specific guidelines, which details all of the Guidelines for classifying diagnoses, regardless of the Chapter in use, followed by the Guidelines for specific chapters of the ICD-10-CM coding manual. Next is Section II, which outlines the rules for selection of the principal diagnosis, and Section III, Reporting Additional Diagnoses. Section IV of the Official Coding Guidelines presents the diagnostic coding and reporting guidelines for outpatient services. There is also an Appendix (I) that includes the Present on Admission (POA) reporting guidelines. All of the sections, and the Appendix, will be discussed in detail in later chapters of this textbook.

The ICD-10-CM Coding Manual

Depending upon the publisher, the layout of the ICD-10-CM may vary slightly, but typically, the ICD-10-CM coding manual will contain a preface and introduction, a guide to using the ICD-10-CM, and all of the Guidelines, including the conventions, general and chapter-specific guidelines. Then, there are two main sections in the ICD-10-CM coding manual. First, is the Alphabetic Index (Figure 1-2), which lists all diseases, illnesses, conditions, and injuries. The search for the proper diagnostic code begins here, in the Alphabetic Index of the coding manual. The second section is the Tabular List (Figure 1-3), which begins with Chapter I–Certain Infectious and Parasitic Diseases (A00-B99). In addition there are two tables, and a second index specifically for external cause codes. These will be covered in depth in a later chapter. Right now, take a look at the ICD-10-CM coding manual and review the following items:

- Look at the header of the Tabular Index pages. The chapter title, "Certain Infectious and Parasitic Diseases," as well as the code range (A00-B99) for the chapter, is shown in the header.

- Look at the codes in the Tabular List. Note that all codes begin with an alpha character. The remaining characters are usually, but not always, numeric. The Chapter 1 code range begins with the letter A,

---

ICD-10-CM INDEX TO DISEASES and INJURIES

A

Aarskog's syndrome Q87.1

Abandonment - see Maltreatment, abandonment

Abasia (-astasia) (hysterical) F44.4

Abderhalden-Kaufmann-Lignac syndrome (cystinosis) E72.04

Abdomen, abdominal - see also condition

- acute R10.0

- angina K55.1

- muscle deficiency syndrome Q79.4

Abdominalgia - see Pain, abdominal

Abduction contracture, hip or other joint - see Contraction, joint

Aberrant (congenital) - see also Malposition, congenital

- adrenal gland Q89.1

- artery (peripheral) Q27.8

- - basilar NEC Q28.1

- - cerebral Q28.3

- - coronary Q24.5

- - digestive system Q27.8

- - eye Q15.8

© Cengage Learning 2013

Figure 1-2 Excerpt from the ICD-10-CM Alphabetic Index

> # CHAPTER 1
> ## Certain infectious and parasitic diseases (A00-B99)
> Includes: diseases generally recognized as communicable or transmissible
>
> Use additional code for any associated drug resistance (Z16)
>
> Excludes 1: carrier or suspected carrier of infectious disease (Z22.-)
>
> >certain localized infections - see body system-related chapters
> >
> >infectious and parasitic diseases complicating pregnancy, childbirth and the puerperium (O98.-)
> >
> >influenza and other acute respiratory infections (J00-J22)
>
> Excludes2: infectious and parasitic diseases specific to the perinatal period (P35-P39)
>
> This chapter contains the following blocks:
>
> | | |
> |---|---|
> | A00-A09 | Intestinal infectious diseases |
> | A15-A19 | Tuberculosis |
> | A20-A28 | Certain zoonotic bacterial diseases |
> | A30-A49 | Other bacterial diseases |
> | A50-A64 | Infections with a predominantly sexual mode of transmission |
> | A65-A69 | Other spirochetal diseases |
> | A70-A74 | Other diseases caused by chlamydiae |
> | A75-A79 | Rickettsioses |
> | A80-A89 | Viral infections of the central nervous system |
> | A90-A99 | Arthropod-borne viral fevers and viral hemorrhagic fevers |
> | B00-B09 | Viral infections characterized by skin and mucous membrane lesions |
> | B10 | Other human herpesviruses |
> | B15-B19 | Viral hepatitis |
> | B20 | Human immunodeficiency virus [HIV] disease |
> | ICD-10-CM Tablular | Page2   2010 |

Figure 1-3 Excerpt from ICD-10-CM 2011 Tabular List

followed by two zeros (A00), and ends with the letter B and the number 99 (B99). All the codes for "Chapter 1, Certain Infectious and Parasitic Diseases" fall in the code range A00 through B99.

The following is an example from the ICD-10-CM from the Alphabetic Index and Tabular List for the diagnosis *orthopnea*.

In the Alphabetic Index excerpt (Figure 1-4), search for *orthopnea*. The code shown is in the general category: R06.0. Now, go to the Tabular List section (Figure 1-5) and locate R06.0. Since

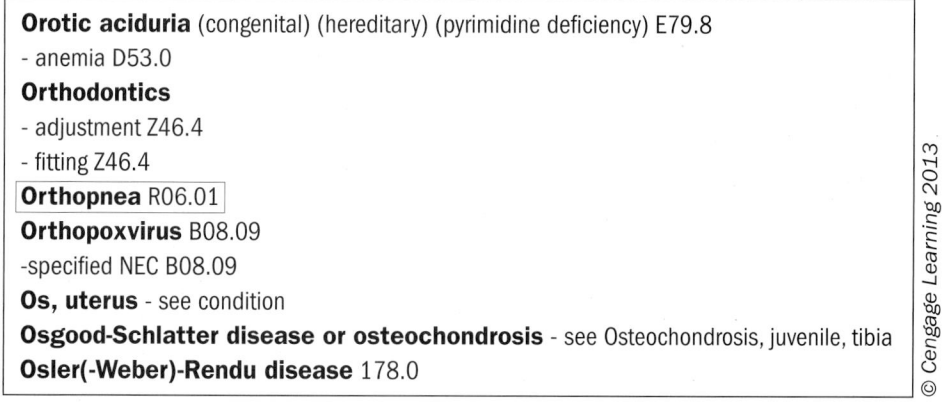

> **Orotic aciduria** (congenital) (hereditary) (pyrimidine deficiency) E79.8
> - anemia D53.0
> **Orthodontics**
> - adjustment Z46.4
> - fitting Z46.4
> **Orthopnea** R06.01
> **Orthopoxvirus** B08.09
> -specified NEC B08.09
> **Os, uterus** - see condition
> **Osgood-Schlatter disease or osteochondrosis** - see Osteochondrosis, juvenile, tibia
> **Osler(-Weber)-Rendu disease** 178.0

Figure 1-4 Excerpt from the ICD-10-CM Alphabetic Index for Orthopnea

R06 Abnormalities of breathing

    Excludes1: acute respiratory distress syndrome (J80)

              respiratory arrest (R09.2)

              respiratory arrest of newborn (P28.81)

              respiratory distress syndrome of newborn (P22.-)

              respiratory failure (J96.-)

              respiratory failure of newborn (P28.5)

R06.0 Dyspnea

    Excludes1: tachypnea NOS (R06.82)

              transient tachypnea of newborn (P22.1)

    R06.00 Dyspnea NOS

    R06.01 Orthopnea

    R06.02 Shortness of breath

    R06.09 Other forms of dyspnea

R06.1 Stridor

    Excludes1: congenital laryngeal stridor (P28.89)

              laryngismus (stridulus) (J38.5)

R06.2 Wheezing

    Excludes1: Asthma (J42.-)

© Cengage Learning 2013

Figure 1-5 Excerpt from ICD-0-CM 2011 Tabular Index for category R06

The Tabular List starts with an alpha character representing the category, making it relatively easy to quickly find the "R" category. Now, look above code R06.0 for a moment. Note that subcategory "06" is labeled "Abnormalities of Breathing." Next, at R06.0, find *dyspnea* (difficult breathing). Remember, the diagnosis being sought is *orthopnea*—so R06.0 is not the best choice. Look below R06.0, to find the even more specific code for *orthopnea*, which is R06.01. It is important to find a code that best matches the diagnosis. R06.0 did not match the diagnosis of *orthopnea*, but R06.01 did. This is a very basic example of how diagnostic coding is performed. In later chapters, more detail will be provided, including how to use the Official Guidelines, the layout and format of the ICD-10-CM coding manual, and the precise steps for diagnostic coding.

Let's Review 1–2:

1. ICD-10-CM replaces:
    a. ICD-9-CM, Volume I only
    b. ICD-9-CM, Volumes I and II only
    c. ICD-9-CM, Volumes I, II and III
    d. ICD-9-PCS

2. The seventh character of an ICD-10-CM code, when used, specifies:
    a. Laterality
    b. Initial and subsequent encounter or sequela
    c. In which chapters (such as obstetrics and injuries) it should be used
    d. A and C

3. One new feature of the ICD-10-CM classification system of codes is:
   a. Post- and intraoperative complication codes
   b. Combination codes that identify both etiology and manifestation
   c. Obstetrics codes that identify the trimester of care
   d. All of the above

4. The Tabular List:
   a. Contains procedural Tables for each section, body part, and root operation
   b. Contains 21 Chapters, and lists all the diagnosis codes and code descriptions
   c. Is used to look up alphabetically a disease or condition to find an approximate code or code range
   d. Contains the diagnostic coding Guidelines, Preface and Introduction

5. ICD-10-CM is required for:
   a. Only hospital inpatient billing
   b. Only outpatient and ambulatory care providers
   c. All health care organizations, providers, clearinghouses, and payors
   d. None of the above

6. Which of the following is not a projected benefit of transitioning to ICD-10-CM?
   a. Fewer rejected claims and more accurate payment
   b. Harmonization of disease monitoring and reporting
   c. Improved disease management
   d. Increase in development of new medical techniques and procedures

ICD-10-PCS (Procedural Coding System)

In 1991, the Centers for Medicare and Medicaid Services (CMS) awarded a contract to 3M Health Information Systems to develop a new procedure coding system. While this system includes "International Classification of Diseases" in its title, these codes are not diagnosis codes, nor do they have any relation to the World Health Organization's design of ICD-10-CM, or the National Centers for Health Care Statistics' (NCHS) adaptation of the ICD-10-CM for use in the United States. The final draft version was completed in 1998, and the ICD-10-PCS has been updated annually since.

The new ICD-10-PCS system utilizes a seven-digit alphanumeric coding system, which allows for completeness, expandability, multiple procedure coding, and standardized terminology. One major enhancement is the inclusion of qualifier characters, which allow for better documentation of underlying issues affecting the procedure performed or the treatment given.

Like ICD-10-CM, implementation of ICD-10-PCS falls under the same rules and regulations of HIPAA, with the only exception being physicians, outpatient health care facilities, and ambulatory care providers, who are exempt from implementing the ICD-10-PCS.

Four major objectives have guided the development of ICD-10 PCS:

1. **Completeness:** There should be a unique code for all substantially different procedures. Currently, procedures on different body parts, with different approaches, or of different types are sometimes assigned to the same code.

2. **Expandability:** As new procedures and medical technologies are developed, the increased length and values built into the structure of the ICD-10-PCS code should allow them to be easily incorporated as unique codes.

3. **Multiaxial:** ICD-10-PCS should have a multiaxial structure, with each code character having the same meaning within the specific procedure section and across all procedure sections, to the extent

possible. For example, all the medical and surgical codes will begin with the number 0. The root operation Extirpation will always be assigned the code value C, regardless which body system or body part is involved in the treatment or procedure.

4. **Standardized terminology:** ICD-10-PCS includes definitions of the terminology used. While the meaning of specific words can vary in common usage, ICD-10-PCS does not include multiple meanings for the same term. Using the example of the root operation Extirpation, it will always have the same meaning regardless which body part or system is involved.

Procedures, services, treatments, surgeries, and diagnostic tests translate into ICD-10-PCS codes. ICD-10-PCS is the abbreviation for International Classification of Diseases, 10ᵗʰ Edition, Procedural Coding System. In the past, coders selected codes from Volume III of the ICD-9-CM in a hospital setting. Physicians and other ambulatory care providers used two other coding classification systems for procedures and services: (1) the CPT (Current Procedural Terminology) and (2) a CMS-developed coding system called the Health Care Common Procedural Coding System (HCPCS). ICD-10-PCS must be implemented in hospital inpatient coding environments by October 1, 2013, but physicians may continue to use the CPT and HCPCS classification systems for procedural coding.

ICD-10-PCS Code Structure

The structure of an ICD-10-PCS code is significantly different than the code structure used in Volume III of the ICD-9-CM. While ICD-9-CM uses up to four numeric characters, ICD-10-PCS has 7 characters that must all be used when coding a procedure or service. The characters use the Numbers 0 through 9, and all letters of the alphabet except I and O, which are not used in order not to be confused with the numbers one (1) and zero (0). The alphabetic characters are not case sensitive, meaning a capital or lowercase letter is allowed.

Every procedure code assigned must include all seven (7) characters.

In Figure 1-6, each character represents specific information related to the procedure performed. The first character of an ICD-10-PCS code describes the **section** of the ICD-10-PCS coding system where the code is located. There are 16 Sections, including, but not limited to, Medical-Surgical, Osteopathic and Chiropractic, Nuclear Medicine, Diagnostic Imaging, Obstetrics, and Measuring & Monitoring.

Character 2 represents the general body system involved in the procedure. The third character is the **root operation**, which identifies the objective of the procedure. Examples of root operations include Alteration, Bypass, Excision, Drainage, Fusion, and Reattachment. Characters 4, 5, 6, and 7 increase the specificity of the code. Character 4 is the specific body part affected and character 5 is the approach. The **approach** is the technique used to reach the site of the procedure, e.g. endoscopic, percutaneous (through the skin), external, and open approach. Character 6 specifies any **devices** that remain after the procedure is completed. Devices do not include stitches or staples, which are a normal part of a surgical procedure. Instead, they describe biological, synthetic, therapeutic, mechanical, or electronic appliances, such as skin grafts, an IUD (intrauterine device), a radioactive implant (used in cancer treatment), a pacemaker, or a joint replacement or pin. Last, Character 7 is a qualifier. The **qualifier** contains unique

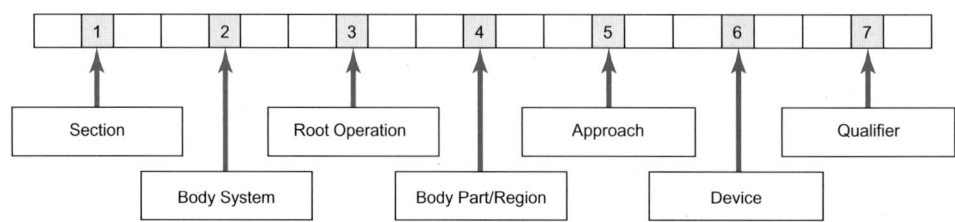

Figure 1-6 ICD-10-PCS Character Assignment
© Cengage Learning 2013

values for individual procedures. For example, the qualifier can be used to identify the destination site for a bypass procedure. Table 1-3 provides definitions for each of the seven character assignments. All seven characters must be used for a code to be correct. In characters 6 and 7, device and qualifier, a Z is used when there is no other value to choose.

To illustrate how this works, look at Figure 1-7. At the top of the graphic are the character assignments—Section, Body System, Root, etc. The options for an excision involving the gastrointestinal system for the purpose of obtaining a biopsy are listed below the characters and character assignments.

Characters 1, 2, and 3 describe the Section: Medical/Surgical (0); the Body System: Gastrointestinal (D); and the Root Operation: Excision (B). The specific body part, character 4, in Figure 1-7 is the stomach (6). The Approach for character 5 is "via natural or artificial opening endoscopic" (8). In this table, there is no option for a device, making character 6 the letter Z. Last but not least, the procedure was diagnostic; therefore, the qualifier, or seventh character, is X.

The ICD-10-PCS Coding Manual

As mentioned with the ICD-10-CM coding manual, the layout may vary between publishers, but generally, there will be a preface and introduction, the current year's ICD-10-PCS Official Coding Guidelines, an alphabetic index, the code Tables (also referred to as the Tabular List), and several appendices that are primarily definitions for root operations, approaches and code character meanings. Appendix B in this textbook contains the ICD-10-PCS Draft Coding Guidelines. It contains three sections, the Conventions, Medical and Surgical Section Guidelines, and Obstetrics Guidelines. These guidelines will be covered in depth in later chapters, but for now, take a quick look at the main sections of an ICD-10-PCS coding manual, the Alphabetic Index and the Tables.

Table 1-3 Definitions of Character Assignments

Name	Character	Description/Definition
Section	1	Type of procedure
Body System	2	General body system
Root Operation	3	Objective of procedure
Body Part/Region	4	Specific body system part upon which procedure is being performed
Approach	5	Technique used to reach site of procedure
Device	6	Any devices that remain after procedure is completed
Qualifier	7	Provides additional information about procedure

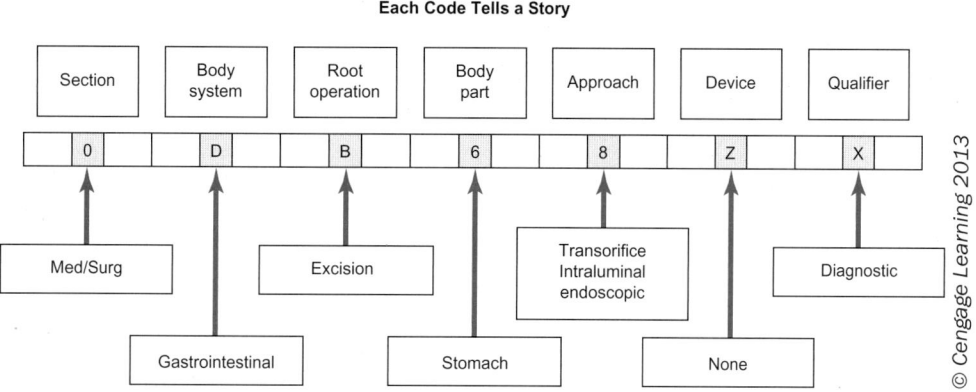

Figure 1-7 ICD-10-PCS Character Assignment Example

ICD-10-PCS Alphabetic Index and Tables (Tabular List)

Section   o Medical and Surgical

Body System S Lower Joints

Operation   G Fusion: Joining together portions of an articular body part rendering the articular body part immobile

Body Part	Approach	Device	Qualifier
0 Lumber Vertebral Joint **1** Lumber Vertebral Joints, 2 or more **3** Lumbosacral Joint	**0** Open **3** Percutaneous **4** Percutaneous Endoscopic	**3** Interbody Internal Fixation Device **4** Internal Fixation Device **7** Autologous Tissue Substitute **H** Interbody Synthetic Substitute **J** Synthetic Substitute **K** Nonautologous Tissue Substitute **N** Interbody Nonautologous Tissue Substitute **Z** No Device	**0** Anterior Approach, Anterior Column **1** Posterior Approach, Posterior Column **J** Posterior Approach, Anterior Column **K** Lateral Transverse Process Approach, Posterior Column
5 Sacrococcygeal Joint **6** Coccygeal Joint **7** Sacroiliac Joint, Right **8** Sacroiliac Joint, Left	**0** Open **3** Percutaneous **4** Percutaneous Endoscopic	**4** Internal Fixation Device **7** Autologous Tissue Substitute **J** Synthetic Substitute **K** Nonautologous Tissue Substitute **Z** No Device	**Z** No Qualifier
9 Hip Joint, Right **B** Hip Joint, Left **C** Knee Joint, Right **D** Knee Joint, Left **F** Ankle Joint, Right **G** Ankle Joint, Left **H** Tarsal Joint, Right **J** Tarsal Joint, Left **K** Metatarsal-Tarsal Joint, Right **L** Metatarsal-Tarsal Joint, Left **M** Metatarsal-Phalangeal Joint, Right **N** Metatarsal-Phalangeal Joint, Left **P** Toe Phalangeal Joint, Right **Q** Toe Phalangeal Joint, Left	**0** Open **3** Percutaneous **4** Percutaneous Endoscopic	**4** Internal Fixation Device **5** External Fixation Device **7** Autologous Substitute **J** Synthetic Substitue **K** Nonautologous Tissue Substitute **Z** No Device	**Z** No Qualifier

Figure 1-8 Example from Medical/Surgical (0) Table

Figure 1-8 is an excerpt from a Table in the ICD-10-PCS coding manual. Note that the Section, Body System, and Root Operation are at the top of the table in the first three rows, called the header. This table represents the Medical and Surgical Section, Lower Joints Body System, and the Root Operation Fusion. Characters 1, 2, and 3 of the code will be 0SG. The definition of the Root Operation of Fusion is also provided.

The fourth character is Body Part, located in the first column of the 0SG table. In Figure 1-8, first column, first row, there are three specific body part choices:

0   Lumbar vertebral joint

1   Lumbar Vertebral joint (2–4)

3   Lumbosacral joint

The next or second column is the Approach. In the first row of the second column, there are three choices here, as well:

0   Open
3   Percutaneous
4   Percutaneous Endoscopic

In the third column are the options for character 6, Device. There are many choices, including internal and external fixation devices and tissue substitutes, as well as the Z placeholder character, which is used to indicate that no device was left in the patient. The last column, which is the seventh character Qualifier in Figure 1-8, relates to the character 5 Approach–in this case, two of the choices include an anterior (0) or posterior (1) approach—in other words, whether the surgeon went in from the patient's abdomen or back.

Now, let's put this together to illustrate how the Table works. Any code selected from this table will automatically begin with 0SG. The remaining four characters will change as the body part, approach, device, and qualifier change. A percutaneous *endoscopic fusion of three lumbar vertebral joints with a posterior approach and column, leaving an internal fixation device* in the patient would produce the code 0SG1441, from the first row of this Table, while a *percutaneous endoscopic fusion of the right sacroiliac joint leaving no device* in the patient would result in a code of 0SG74ZZ from the second row of this table. If the needed body part, approach, device, or qualifier is not found within this table, the next option would be to find another Table that matched all seven characters to the medical documentation.

This was just a quick illustration of how the Tables are used–more will be revealed in later chapters. Before moving on to the next chapter, take a few moments to review Appendix C in this textbook. This appendix contains fact sheets developed by the Centers for Medicare and Medicaid Services (CMS) for ICD-10-CM and ICD-10-PCS.

Let's Review 1–3:

1. ICD-10-PCS was developed by:
   a. The World Health Organization
   b. The American Hospital Association
   c. 3M Health Information Systems
   d. The Department of Health and Human Services

2. ICD-10-PCS is required for use by:
   a. All health care organizations
   b. Hospital inpatient coding only
   c. Physicians and ambulatory care providers only
   d. Hospital outpatient coding only

3. The seven characters in an ICD-10-PCS code represent (in correct order):
   a. Section, Body System, Approach, Root Operation, Device, Body Part, and Qualifier
   b. Section, Root Operation, Approach, Body System, Body Part, Device, and Qualifier
   c. Section, Body System, Root Operation, Body Part, Approach, Device, and Qualifier
   d. Section, Qualifier, Body System, Body Part, Device, Approach, and Root Operation

4. The Root Operation is:
   a. The method by which the procedure site is accessed
   b. The type of procedure performed
   c. Any additional information required to match the code to the procedure's description
   d. The section or table in which the code is located

(Continues)

5. The sections of an ICD-10-PCS coding manual (book) contain:
  a. Tables and Alphabetic Index
  b. Diagnostic coding guidelines
  c. Tabular List and Alphabetic Index
  d. A and B

6. Types of devices include:
  a. Stitches or staples
  b. Internal fixation devices
  c. Endoscopic instruments
  d. A and B

Chapter Summary

The Final Rule mandating the use of ICD-10-CM and ICD-10-PCS went into effect from January 15, 2009. ICD-10-CM (diagnostic coding) must be implemented no later than October 1, 2013, in physician facilities, hospitals, insurance companies, and all other affected groups, such as clearinghouses.
ICD-10 diagnostic and procedural codes are radically different in structure, layout, and form. ICD-10, like its predecessor ICD-9, is a system of codes used for many purposes. These codes translate intricate diagnoses and complicated procedures into a standardized "language" that everyone in the health care industry can understand. For the medical coder, it is primarily used in insurance billing, but, these codes are used for many other purposes, including reporting, morbidity and mortality, and other statistical analysis.

Four organizations in the United States are responsible for maintaining the ICD-10-CM classification. They are responsible for developing official guidelines and for proper application of ICD-9-CM, and now the ICD-10-CM. They are known as the cooperating parties, and include the American Hospital Association (AHA), the American Health Information Management Association (AHIMA), the Centers for Medicare and Medicaid Services (CMS), and the National Center for Health Statistics (NCHS). The Centers for Medicare and Medicaid Services (CMS) are responsible for the annual updates of the ICD-10-CM.

All health care providers and insurance companies must begin using ICD-10-CM for diagnostic coding no later than October 1, 2013. The ICD-10-PCS, on the other hand, need only be implemented by hospitals and insurance payers on this date. Physicians and other providers, such as ambulance or medical equipment supply companies will continue to perform procedural coding using the Current Procedural Terminology (CPT) and Health Care Common Procedural Coding System (HCPCS). The Transactions & Code Sets (TCS) provision of HIPAA defines how the data is structured and transmitted. Transactions are the data transmitted electronically, which must be arranged in a specific format. Code sets are the diagnosis and procedure codes.

ICD-9-CM diagnosis codes are 3–5 numeric characters in length, with approximately 13,000 codes. ICD-10-CM codes can be 3–7 characters in length, with approximately 68,000 codes. There are approximately 3000 ICD-9-CM procedure codes, as compared to 87,000 ICD-10-PCS procedure codes, with the ICD-9-CM codes being 3–4 numbers in length, and the ICD-10-PCS codes being 7 alphanumeric characters.

Diagnoses, conditions, illnesses, and injuries are translated into ICD-10-CM codes. ICD-10-CM is the abbreviation for International Classification of Diseases, 10th Edition, Clinical Modification.

The layout of the ICD-10-CM coding manual is comparable to the ICD-9-CM. There is still a Tabular List and an Alphabetic Index, which were in Volumes I and II of the ICD-9-CM. However, where ICD-9-CM codes were numeric (with the exception of V and E codes), ICD-10-CM codes are a combination of alphabetic and numeric characters. There are 21 chapters within the ICD-10-CM Tabular List.

The ICD-10-CM coding manual is divided into a Tabular List, and Alphabetic Index. The Alphabetic Index is used to help search for diagnoses, conditions, illnesses and injuries by name. Each named disease, condition, illness, or injury references the primary category code in the Tabular List. The Tabular List contains all the codes, in alphanumeric order, and code descriptions, subdivided by chapters.

In 1991, the Centers for Medicare and Medicaid Services (CMS) awarded a contract to 3M Health Information Systems to develop a new procedure coding system, which became the ICD-10-PCS, or procedural coding system. The ICD-10-PCS replaces Volume III of the ICD-9-CM, which was used by hospitals to code inpatient procedures.

The new ICD-10-PCS system utilizes a seven character alphanumeric coding system, which is significantly different than Volume III of the ICD-9-CM. While ICD-9-CM (Volume III) used up to four numeric characters, ICD-10-PCS has 7 characters that must all be used when coding a procedure or service. The characters use the numbers 0 through 9; and all letters of the alphabet except I and O.

The first character of an ICD-10-PCS code describes the location of a code in one of the 16 sections of the ICD-10-PCS. Character 2 represents the general body system involved in the procedure. The third character is the root operation, which identifies the objective of the procedure. Character 4 is the specific body part affected, and character 5 is the approach, or technique used to reach the site of the procedure. Character 6 specifies any devices that remain after the procedure is completed. Finally, Character 7 is a qualifier. The qualifier contains unique values for individual procedures.

Review

Matching

Instructions: Match the key term to the appropriate definition.

_____ **1.** Health Insurance Portability and Accountability Act (HIPAA)

_____ **2.** ICD-10-CM

_____ **3.** ICD-10-PCS

_____ **4.** Provider

_____ **5.** Transaction and Code Sets (TCS)

_____ **6.** Tabular List

_____ **7.** Root Operation

_____ **8.** Body Part

_____ **9.** Approach

_____ **10.** Device

a. Sets the standards for electronic transmission of data, and coding classification system requirements

b. The third character of an ICD-10-PCS code that describes the type of procedure performed

c. The fourth character of an ICD-10-PCS code that describes the exact body part upon which the procedure is being performed

d. Diagnostic code classification system

e. The sixth character of an ICD-10-PCS code is used to identify any devices left in the patient at the end of a procedure

f. Electronic data transmission standards and diagnostic and procedural codes

g. The fifth character of an ICD-10-PCS that identifies the method used to reach the site of the procedure

h. Procedure code classification system

i. In the ICD-10-CM it is a numerical list of diagnosis codes and their descriptions, divided by chapter

j. Any individual or organization that renders care, treatment, or performs a procedure on a patient

Short Answer

Instructions: Write responses for the following.

1. The cooperating parties who maintain the ICD-10 are
   a. _____
   b. _____
   c. _____
   d. _____

2. The seven characters in an ICD-10-PCS code describe:
   a. _____
   b. _____
   c. _____
   d. _____
   e. _____
   f. _____
   g. _____

3. When used, the seventh character in an ICD-10-CM code describes:
   a. _____
   b. _____
   c. _____

4. Give three potential benefits of ICD-10 implementation:
   a. _____
   b. _____
   c. _____

5. Describe the layout of the Tabular List of the ICD-10-CM:
   a. _____

6. Explain the parts of a Table in the ICD-10-PCS
   a. _____
   b. _____
   c. _____

7. By what date does the ICD-10-CM/PCS need to be implemented in health care organizations?
   a. _____

8. How often is the ICD-10-CM and ICD-10-PCS updated:
   a. _____

9. Define a root operation and give one example:
   a. _____
   b. _____

10. Explain who must use ICD-10-CM and ICD-10-PCS:

    a. ICD-10-CM: _____

    b. ICD-10-PCS: _____

Multiple Choice

Instructions: Circle the most appropriate response.

1. ICD-10-PCS codes are used for:

    a. Diagnosis and procedure coding

    b. Diagnosis coding

    c. Procedure coding

    d. None of the above

2. ICD-10-CM codes are used for:

    a. Diagnosis and procedure coding

    b. Diagnosis coding

    c. Procedure coding

    d. None of the above

3. The mandatory implementation date for ICD-10-CM and PCS is _____.

    a. January 15, 2013

    b. October 1, 2013

    c. January 15, 2015

    d. October 1, 2015

4. Physicians and other ambulatory care providers are exempt from the mandatory implementation of:

    a. CPT and HCPCS codes

    b. ICD-10-CM

    c. ICD-10-PCS

    d. All of the above

5. The designation CM (clinical modification) represents _____ code sets for statistical and reimbursement uses.

    a. Procedural

    b. Diagnostic

    c. Procedural and Diagnostic

    d. None of the above

6. The most *significant* change (having the most impact) in the ICD-10 is:

    a. ICD-10 uses alphanumeric characters

    b. ICD-10 no longer includes procedure codes

    c. ICD-10's layout (chapters, categories) have changed

    d. ICD-10 is more specific

7. ICD-10-CM code set adoption became a more urgent issue in the United States as a direct result of federal mandates included in:

    a. The Centers for Medicare and Medicaid Services (CMS)

    b. The American Health Information Management Assn. (AHIMA)

    c. The Administrative Simplification Act (aka HIPAA)

    d. The Department of Health and Human Services (DHHS)

8. The following best describes the new ICD-10-CM coding system

    a. ICD-10 codes are alphanumeric, a maximum of 12 digits, and codes are for diagnostic coding only

     b. ICD-10 codes are numeric, a maximum of 6 digits, and are used for diagnostic coding only

     c. ICD-10 codes are alphanumeric, a maximum of 6 digits and are used for procedural coding only

     d. ICD-10-CM codes are alphanumeric, a maximum of 6 or 7 digits and codes are used for diagnostic coding only

9. The Federal Agency responsible for use and adoption of the ICD-10-CM system in the United States is:

     a. The National Centers for Disease Control (NCDC)
     b. The Department of Health and Human Services (DHHS)
     c. The National Centers for Health Statistics (NCHS)
     d. The Health Care Financing Administration (HCFA)

10. ICD-10-PCS codes:

     a. Are seven (7) alphabetic and numeric characters
     b. Require all seven (7) characters are used when coding a procedure
     c. Were developed by 3M Health Information Systems at the request of CMS
     d. All of the above

11. The (free) draft version of the ICD-10-CM can be found on the _____ website:

     a. National Centers for Disease Control (NCDC)
     b. American Health Information Management Association (AHIMA)
     c. World Health Organization (WHO)
     d. National Center for Health Statistics (NCHS)

12. The (free) draft version of the ICD-10-PCS can be found on the _____ website:

     a. Centers for Medicare and Medicaid Services (CMS)
     b. American Health Information Management Association (AHIMA)
     c. World Health Organization (WHO)
     d. National Center for Health Statistics (NCHS)

Coding Practice

Let's try a few coding practices. Using the ICD-10-CM and ICD-10-PCS coding manuals, try to find the code. (Hint: You can look up the diagnosis or procedure in the Alphabetic Index of the two coding manuals to find the approximate location in the Tabular List).

Using ICD-10-CM, code the following:

1. Tachycardia (unspecified) _____

2. Pain, right upper quadrant _____

3. Diarrhea (unspecified) _____

Using the ICD-10-PCS, code the following:

4. Change bladder catheter. (Approach is external, Device is drainage device, and there is no qualifier)

    _____

5. Insertion of radioactive element into right upper arm percutaneously _____

    _____

6. Cholelithotripsy (Hint: Root Operation is fragmentation, Body part is gallbladder, approach is percutaneous endoscopic, and there is no device and no qualifier) _____

    _____

HIPAA, ARRA, HITECH, Transactions, and Code Sets

Learning Objectives

At the conclusion of this chapter, the learner should be able to:

- Acquire a basic understanding of the Health Insurance Portability and Accountability Act (HIPAA), especially as it relates to transactions and code sets.
- Describe the impacts of the American Recovery and Reinvestment Act (ARRA) and Health Information Technology for Economic and Clinical Health (HITECH), especially as it relates to transactions and code sets.
- Understand basic terminology associated with HIPAA and ARRA.
- Describe the purpose and origin of the ASC x12 version 5010 (v5010) standards, and when implementation is required.
- Identify and list the HIPAA-mandated transactions and their uses.
- Compare the provider CMS1500 paper claim form to the ASC x12 version 5010 (v5010) 837 Professional (837-P) transaction.
- Compare the institutional CMS1450 paper claim form to the ASC x12 version 5010 (v5010) 837 Institutional (837-I) transaction.
- Describe the use of the ASC x12 version D.0 and 3.0.

Key Terms and Definitions

Business associate	A person or an organization that performs services on behalf of a covered entity.
Covered entities	Organizations or individuals required by law to comply with HIPAA.
Designated Standard Maintenance Organizations (DSMO)	Responsible for developing, maintaining, and modifying electronic data interchange (EDI) standards.
Electronic Data Interchange (EDI)	The exchange of health data electronically across the internet
Electronic Protected Health Information (EPHI)	PHI in electronic form.
Enterprise Integration	The electronic linkage of health care providers, health plans, the government, and other interested parties, to enable electronic exchange and use of health information among all the components in the health care infrastructure in accordance with applicable law.

Health care	Care, services, or supplies related to the health of an individual.
Health care clearinghouses	Entities that process nonstandard information they receive from another entity into a standard format or data content.
Health care operations	Administrative, financial, legal, and quality-improvement activities of a covered entity that are necessary to run its business.
Health care provider	A person or organization that furnishes, bills for, or is paid for health care.
Health Information Exchange (HIE)	The electronic movement of health-related information among organizations according to nationally recognized standards.
Health Insurance Portability and Accountability Act (HIPAA)	Laws that allow individuals to maintain insurance coverage even if they change jobs or move, and that establish standards for the privacy, security, and electronic transmission of health data across the internet.
Health plan	Pays the cost of medical care.
Identifiers	Any data that could reveal the identity of a patient.
Protected Health Information	Any health information maintained by a covered entity where the individual could, in any possible way, be identified.
Payment	Various activities of health care providers to get paid or be reimbursed for their services.
Regional Health Information Organization (RHIO)	A health information organization that brings together stakeholders within a defined geographic area and governs health information exchange among them for the purpose of improving health and care in that community.
Transaction	Exchange of information between two parties to carry out financial or administrative activities related to health care.
Transaction standard	Defines the data elements and the order of the data elements that make up a single transaction.
Treatment	Provision, coordination, or management of health care and related services among health care providers or by a health care provider with a third party.

Introduction

While the focus of this textbook is on the ICD-10 coding classification systems, it is important to understand the laws and intent behind their use, and identify other rules that go hand-in-hand with the use of ICD-10-CM and ICD-10-PCS. This chapter will include a high-level overview of the Health Insurance Portability and Accountability Act (HIPAA), as well as the American Reinvestment and Recovery Act (ARRA)/Health Information Technology for Economic and Clinical Health (HITECH) Act, and how they work together to ensure the privacy and security of protected health information, drive the use of the ICD-10 transaction and code sets, and create the standards used when transmitting health data electronically.

The HIPAA, and now the new ARRA/HITECH, rules not only require use of the ICD-10 code sets, but establish standards for how these codes must be sent electronically. These standards include specific formatting instructions for various transactions, such as an electronically submitted health insurance claim form, and requirements for transmitting the transactions electronically. HIPAA requires the use of specific formats for transactions such as insurance claims, health insurance eligibility and verification of benefits, health plan enrollment and disenrollment, insurance claim status inquiries, explanation of payment (remittance advice), and others. HIPAA also requires the use of standards for transmitting these transactions electronically. ARRA/HITECH laws established new transactions and code sets, electronic transaction standards, and compliance dates for the new standards. Effective as of January 1, 2012, all health care organizations transmitting information electronically must use the ASC x 12 version 5010 (abbreviated as v5010 or 5010) standards and transactions and, effective from October 1, 2013, the ICD-10 code sets must be implemented. This chapter will provide a high-level overview of HIPAA, ARRA and HITECH, the ASC x12 standards, the HIPAA transactions, and how these rules pertain to the ICD-10 code sets.

Health Insurance Portability and Accountability Act (HIPAA)

HIPAA is the acronym for **Health Insurance Portability and Accountability Act**, a group of federal laws that took effect on August 21, 1996. HIPAA was created for several reasons, but those most important to this textbook, and to ICD-10, establish standards for (1) the privacy and security of health care information, and (2) the identification of the transactions and code sets required for electronic transmission of health data over the internet, more commonly known as **Electronic Data Interchange (EDI)**. HIPAA is also known as Public Law 104-191 [H.R. 3103] or the Kennedy-Kassebaum bill. HIPAA is one of the first laws to address privacy, security, and standardization of EDI in the health care industry. The law in turn has influenced many state and federal laws. HIPAA has also had an indirect impact on many other industries that do business with the health care industry.

HIPAA consists of five different Titles, or parts, that address portability of insurance, fraud and abuse, tax issues, group health plans, and revenue offsets within the health care industry. Title II of HIPAA, known as Administrative Simplification, will be the main focus of this chapter, because it directly impacts the ICD-10 code sets and establishes the standards for EDI and health care data transactions. Figure 2-1 is a high-level overview of the five HIPAA Titles and what major provisions are covered in each.

There are six main reasons Congress passed the HIPAA legislation:

- To make it easier to transfer health insurance coverage for both group and individual health care plans
- To fight waste, fraud, and abuse in health insurance and health care delivery.
- To promote the use of medical savings accounts
- To improve access to long-term care services and coverage

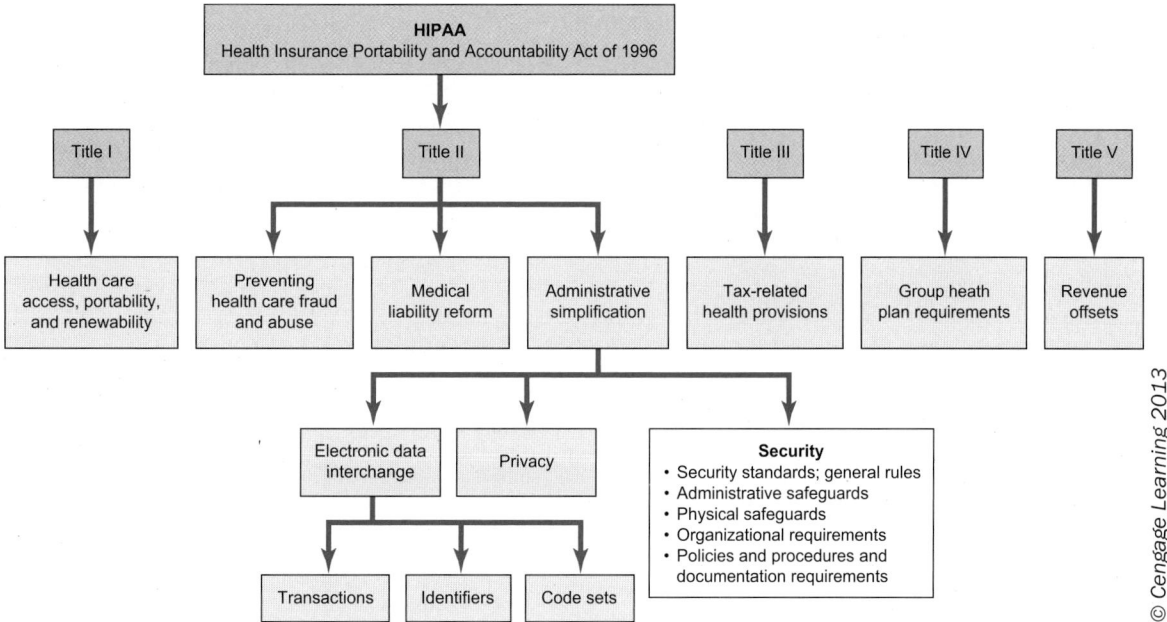

Figure 2-1 Overview of HIPAA

- To simplify the administration of health insurance

- To promote the safe exchange of health data electronically (over the Web).

In this chapter the focus is on the sixth reason: *to promote the safe exchange of health data electronically*. HIPAA Title II, also known as Administrative Simplification, is the section of the HIPAA rules pertinent to the code sets currently in use (ICD-9-CM). Later, we'll focus on the American Recovery and Reinvestment Act (ARRA) Title XIII, the Health Information Technology for Economic and Clinical Health (HITECH) Act, and how they have impacted the code sets, and the HIPAA transaction standards.

It should not be surprising to learn that the health care industry is a trillion-dollar industry. In addition, it is undergoing a rapid transformation. More than 10 million people work in the health care industry, and the U.S. Department of Labor recognizes 400 different job titles in this field. There is little doubt that the health care industry is highly fragmented and very complex. In addition, the new millennium brought with it great advances in technology. Unlike 20th-century businesses, most companies today use the Internet and e-mail to conduct business and electronic data interchange. The health care industry in particular has had a hard time keeping up with these advances in technology. Many health care organizations face huge roadblocks, including

- Limited budgets for technology

- Multiple homegrown, or proprietary, systems that often cannot easily communicate with other mainstream systems

- Multiple older, or legacy, systems that must be integrated with modern networking technology and operating systems

- Reliance on paper-based procedures.

In health care, many obstacles disrupt the information flow. For one, the software programs used by health care systems are often out of date, and have trouble communicating with modern systems. For another, the programs are diverse. They can be difficult to manage in a centralized, efficient way. Table 2-1 is just a sampling of the many health care systems in use today.

Think about this for a minute. When these software systems cannot easily communicate with one another, it becomes costly and burdensome to trade information. This contributes to the rising cost of health care in our country. And it is not only communication that has become a problem. Picture an old-fashioned file storeroom with rows of filing cabinets stuffed with thousands of file folders. All those records occupy a huge amount of space, and retrieving or filing information can be time-consuming. In addition, errors in filing, and lost or missing files or documents, can add to the misery. These days, most information is stored electronically, and, since electronic files take up practically no physical space, it is easier for companies to store and distribute large amounts of data. For health care organizations, the quick exchange of critical data electronically can be life-saving. But there is a downside, including cases of fraud, loss of privacy, and unethical disclosures of sensitive patient information. Even worse, electronic information is open to attack from computer viruses. It is easy to imagine the damage that a virus can cause. It can destroy or corrupt data.

Table 2-1 Types of Health Care Systems

Call/contact center	Materials management
Claims clearing houses	Nurse triage
Claims processing	Operating room
Customer relations management	Patient accounting/billing
Document imaging management	Practice management
Emergency departments	Quality review
Enterprise resource planning	Research databases
General financial systems	Technology-enabled marketing

All of this was a concern for Senators Edward Kennedy and Nancy Kassebaum, who introduced the HIPAA bill into Congress. Another of their concerns was health care portability. In the past, many individuals were discouraged from accepting new job opportunities if they had a pre-existing medical condition. Portability allows workers to continue health care coverage if they change jobs even when a pre-existing condition exists. Workers can now move their coverage from one job to the next.

HIPAA is composed of five parts, known as Titles. While the focus of this chapter is mostly on Title II, Administrative Simplification, and the American Recovery and Reinvestment Act (ARRA)/Health Information Technology for Economic and Clinical Health (HITECH) Act, it is important to be familiar with the terminology and applicable laws, since they do impact health care. Table 2-2 lists the five HIPAA Titles, ARRA Title XIII/HITECH, and the main topics covered in each.

HIPAA Title II: Administrative Simplification

Administrative Simplification includes three main bodies of standards. These standards or rules (1) promote efficiency and lower overhead costs for the exchange of information electronically, (2) outline requirements to prevent health care fraud and abuse, and (3) require safeguards to protect the privacy and confidentiality of patient records. Most of our discussion of Administrative Simplification will focus on the first rule: promoting efficiency and lowering overhead costs associated with the electronic exchange of information. It is important to note that even though the focus of this chapter is only on those parts of HIPAA, ARRA, and HITECH that affect ICD-10 directly, a health care worker should have an in-depth understanding of the rules for the privacy and security of health care information. Take a course specifically designed to delve into the HIPAA privacy and security rules, or contact the Privacy/Compliance Officer within the health care organization to obtain training in this very important legislation.

Often, news events influence the law-making process. Think back to the early days of Internet use. It is not rare to see stories on the news about breaches of personal information or patient medical record data. These electronic breaches, along with some accidental or inadvertent leaks of health care information, helped fuel the need for a federal law to protect health information. Another motivation for HIPAA was the need for standards in the sharing of health information, especially electronically. Technological advances have created an explosion of electronic information. This in turn has led to a need for standards to allow all entities involved in the diagnosis, treatment, and payment of patient can communicate seamlessly. Administrative Simplification intends to accomplish several goals:

- To create standards for electronic transactions and code sets
- To create patient health information privacy rules.
- To secure the confidentiality, integrity, and availability of electronic health data.

Table 2-2 HIPAA Titles

Title	Description
Title I	Health Care Insurance Access, Portability, Renewability
Title II	Preventing Health Care Fraud and Abuse Administrative Simplification Medical Liability Reform
Title III	Tax-related Health Provisions
Title IV	Application/Enforcement of Group Health Insurance
Title V	Revenue Offsets
ARRA Title XIII/HITECH	ICD-10 Code Sets ASC x12 v 5010 Transaction Standards Revision of Privacy Breach Notification rules Requirement for Electronic Health Record and Health Information Exchange(s)

The Administrative Simplification portion of HIPAA is made up of three main bodies of standards, also called rules:

- Standards for Electronic Transmissions, also called Transactions, Code Sets, and Identifiers.
- Standards for the Privacy of Individually Identifiable Health Information, also called the Privacy Rule.
- Security Standards, also called the Security Rule.

The intent is to save billions of dollars each year for health care businesses. Having national standards will lower the costs of developing and maintaining software. It will also reduce the time and expense needed to handle health care transactions. The U.S. Department of Health and Human Services (HHS) estimates that HIPAA's transaction standards could save approximately $29 billion over 10 years.

Compliance Deadlines

To get a sense of HIPAA's progress so far, let's look at some of the deadlines set when HIPAA was enacted in 1996:

- October 16, 2002: Transactions and Code Sets (extended to October 16, 2003).
- April 14, 2003: Privacy.
- April 21, 2005: Security.

In 2009, President Obama signed into law the ARRA/HITECH Act. Included as part of that legislation were new transactions and code sets, with additional compliance dates:

- January 1, 2012: Version 5010 Transaction format.
- October 1, 2013: ICD-10 Code Sets.

Organizations involved in HIPAA

The organizations affected by or involved with HIPAA consist of covered entities, health care providers, health plans, health care clearinghouses, business associates, government organizations, standards organizations, and others.

The most important players in the HIPAA arena are the **covered entities**. These are the organizations or individuals that are required by law to comply with HIPAA. Sometimes a covered entity is referred to as a CE. The three types of CEs that must comply with HIPAA are health care providers, health plans, and health care clearinghouses. One way of deciding if an organization is a covered entity is to ask: Does the person, business, or agency furnish, bill for, or receive payment for health care in the normal course of business? If the answer is no, the organization is not a covered entity. If the answer is yes, ask a second question: Is information sent electronically? If the answer to that question is no, it is not a covered entity. If the answer is yes, it is.

A **health care provider** is an institutional provider, such as a hospital. This category also includes physicians, dentists, and chiropractors. In short, any person or organization that furnishes, bills for, or is paid for health care is a health care provider.

A **health plan** is the CE that pays the cost of medical care. Health plans include health, dental, vision, and prescription drug insurers. Other examples of health plans are health maintenance organizations (HMOs), Medicare, Medicaid, Medicare + Choice, and Medicare supplement insurers. Even a long-term care insurer can be considered a health plan. Health plans also include employer-sponsored group health plans, government and church-sponsored health plans, and multiemployer health plans.

Health care clearinghouses are entities that process nonstandardized information they receive from aa health care provider into a standard format or data content. They are known by other names such as billing services, repricing companies, or value-added networks (or switches). A switch is like a central bus station. People arrive from all over and are shipped off to different locations. If a clearinghouse functions as a switch, it means that nonstandard transaction files from all over come into one central station. They are then reformatted into a common "language" or data transmission file, and shipped off to all sorts of different locations as standard transaction files. If a switch is a value-added network, it is like a bus station with a snack bar and a hair salon. That means that the switch provides extra services over and above translating files and routing information.

Business Associates

A **business associate** (BA) is a person or an organization that performs services on behalf of a covered entity. BAs also need to be concerned about HIPAA. Business associates can be those organizations that perform functions or tasks such as:

- Claims processing
- Transcription
- Management
- Data analysis
- Billing
- Accounting
- Accreditation

To make things a little more complicated, consider this. A covered entity can be a business associate of another covered entity. For example, a health plan might provide claims processing services for another health plan. Figure 2-2 describes ways to determine if an organization is a business associate.

Government Organizations involved in HIPAA

Government agencies play a huge role in administering HIPAA, including the Department of Health and Human Services (HHS), the Centers for Medicare and Medicaid Services (CMS), the Office of Civil Rights (OCR), the Workgroup for Electronic Data Interchange (WEDI), Health Level Seven (HL7), the American National Standards Institute (ANSI), Washington Publishing Company (WPC), the National Council for Prescription Drug Programs (NCPDP), and the National Committee on Vital and Health Statistics (NCVHS), to name just a few. All of these agencies work together to establish the standards for electronic data interchange, transactions, and code sets.

U.S. Department of Health and Human Services (HHS) The Department of Health and Human Services (HHS or DHHS) is one of the largest federal agencies, and its main mission is to protect the

An organization is a business associate if:

- It performs services on behalf of a health plan, a health provider, or a health care clearinghouse.
- It is not a member of the covered entity's workforce.
- The services provided involve the use of individually identifiable health information.
- It is not a bank (HIPAA excludes normal banking operations in its definition of a business associate).
- It is not a conduit, such as a post office, UPS, or an Internet Service Provider (Conduits are also excluded from HIPAA regulations)

© Cengage Learning 2013

Figure 2-2 Identifying a Business Associate

health of all Americans. It is the federal agency responsible for creating the rules and standards of HIPAA, as well as enforcing HIPAA. It is also responsible for the ARRA and HITECH Acts. All the other HIPAA government entities mentioned here operate under the HHS umbrella, even though they are separate entities. This agency is made up of 12 operating divisions and is responsible for dozens of programs, including public health, biomedical research, Medicare and Medicaid, welfare, and social services.

Centers for Medicare and Medicaid Services (CMS) The Center for Medicare and Medicaid Services (CMS) is one of the divisions under HHS. It has a huge responsibility. First, this agency is responsible for enforcing all parts of Administrative Simplification except the Privacy Rule and the Security Rule, which are enforced by the Office of Civil Rights (OCR). It also provides health insurance for over 74 million Americans through Medicare, Medicaid, and the State Children's Health Insurance Program (SCHIP). In addition to providing health insurance, CMS also performs a number of quality-focused activities. It regulates laboratory testing, develops coverage policies, works to improve quality of care, and works along with the individual states to oversee the survey and certification of nursing homes and continuing care providers. This includes home health agencies, intermediate care facilities for the developmentally disabled, and hospitals. CMS makes all the information it gathers available to beneficiaries, providers, researchers, and state surveyors.

Office of Civil Rights (OCR) Think of the Office of Civil Rights (OCR) as a kind of watchdog for HHS. OCR investigates and enforces the rights of individuals who are eligible for services provided by HHS. OCR enforces patient privacy, health plan member privacy, and the rights of Medicare and Medicaid beneficiaries. In addition, OCR is responsible for providing a variety of resources to providers, advocates, patients, foster parents, and long-term care recipients. Finally, OCR is responsible for enforcing the HIPAA Privacy Rules, and on July 27, 2009, Secretary of the Department of Health and Human Services (HHS) Kathleen Sebelius delegated authority for the administration and enforcement of the Security Standards for the Protection of Electronic Protected Health Information (Security Rule) to the OCR.

Standards Organizations

In addition to covered entities and government agencies, HHS named six organizations to maintain the Administrative Simplification standards. These organizations are referred to as **Designated Standard Maintenance Organizations** (DSMO). They are responsible for developing, maintaining, and modifying EDI standards. The six DSMOs are

- Accredited Standards Committee (ASC) X12

  The Accredited Standards Committee (ASC) X12, chartered by the American National Standards Institute in 1979, develops EDI standards and related documents for national and global markets.

- Dental Content Committee of the American Dental Association (DeCC).

  Maintain the data content and some of the code set elements for dental claims.

- Health Level Seven (HL7).

  Health care institutions often have independent systems. This makes it difficult for them to share clinical information. Health Level Seven (HL7) tries to address the differences between independent health care systems and helps coordinate their integration with electronic transactions particularly in the area of claims attachments and other related data standards. There are several HL7 documents, including those that cover ambulances, clinical reports, emergency departments, laboratory results, medications, and rehabilitation services.

- National Council for Prescription Drug Programs (NCPDP).

  A not-for-profit ANSI-Accredited Standards Development Organization representing virtually every sector of the pharmacy services industry.

- National Uniform Billing Committee (NUBC).

- Formed to develop a single billing form and standard data set that could be used nationwide by institutional providers and payers for handling health care claims

- National Uniform Claim Committee (NUCC).

  Created to develop a standardized data set for use by the noninstitutional health care community to transmit claim and encounter information to and from all third-party payers.

There are other affilitated organizations that should be mentioned as well, such as the Workgroup for WEDI, the Washington Publishing Company (WPC), and the National Committee on Vital and Health Statistics (NCVHS).

Workgroup for Electronic Data Interchange (WEDI) WEDI has been around since 1991. It is officially designated as an advisory group to HHS. Its original mission was to address administrative costs in the nation's health care system. WEDI is a voluntary task force, with a combination of public and private organizations and individuals as members. Today, WEDI works to streamline health care administration by standardizing electronic communication through the use of EDI. WEDI members work together to help solve some of the issues that can prevent organizations from easily exchanging information.

In addition, it publishes educational papers that help organizations understand how to comply with HIPAA.

Washington Publishing Company (WPC) The Washington Publishing Company (WPC) specializes in managing and distributing EDI information. WPC produces documentation for organizations that develop, maintain, and implement EDI standards. Picture a standard HIPAA transaction, like an insurance claim or health insurance claim status request. Each one has its own implementation guide that explains in detail how to map the data elements to the HIPAA standard format. WPC is responsible for all of these implementation guides. These can be downloaded from the WPC Web site or ordered as a paper, or hard copy.

National Committee on Vital and Health Statistics (NCVHS) The last standards organization is the National Committee on Vital and Health Statistics (NCVHS). NCVHS is an advisory committee to the Secretary of Health and Human Services.

Other Terminology Associated with HIPAA, HITECH

Probably the most important definition to learn is that of **Protected Health Information**, or PHI. The definition that HIPAA uses is shown in Figure 2-3. HIPAA is not concerned with all health information, but only with individually identifiable health information, which is called PHI. PHI is health information created or maintained by a covered entity or a business associate and includes data elements that identify an individual (or there is a reasonable basis to believe that someone could use it to identify an individual). HIPAA created an official set of data elements called identifiers. **Identifiers** turn ordinary health information into individually identifiable health information. If this information is under the control of a covered entity, it becomes protected under HIPAA. Some of the more common identifiers are found in Table 2-3.

> Health information means any information, whether oral or recorded in any form or medium, that is created or received by a health care provider, health plan, public health authority, employer, life insurer, school or university, or health care clearinghouse; and relates to the past, present, or future physical or mental health or condition of an individual; the provision of health care to an individual; or the past, present, or future payment for the provision of health care to an individual.

Figure 2-3 HIPAA Definition of PHI
© Cengage Learning 2013

Table 2-3 PHI Identifiers

Identifiers	
Name of an individual	City or county of residence
ZIP code	Social Security number
Fingerprint	Telephone number
Medical record number	Fax number
Photograph of an individual	Driver's license number

There are many other identifiers, but what is important to remember is that any health information maintained by a covered entity where the individual could, in any possible way, be identified, needs to be treated as protected health information. **Electronic Protected Health Information (EPHI)** is basically PHI in electronic form. EPHI includes PHI that is created, received, maintained, or transmitted electronically. For example, EPHI may be transmitted over the Internet, or stored on a computer, CD, disk, magnetic tape, or by other means. The Privacy Rule covers all PHI, no matter what form it takes. The Security Rule only focuses on EPHI.

Other HIPAA terminology to understand includes **health care, treatment, payment and health care operations (TPO)**, and **designated record set. Health care** is care, services, or supplies related to the health of an individual. Health care includes the diagnosis, cure, mitigation, treatment, and prevention of physical or mental disease. The next three terms are used often when discussing HIPAA privacy. The abbreviation **TPO** represents all three: Treatment, Payment, and Health Care Operations. Often people refer to all of the activities described below as the TPO Umbrella.

- **Treatment:** The definition of treatment covers a lot of territory. It includes the provision, coordination, or management of health care and related services among health care providers or by a health care provider with a third party. It also includes consultation between health care providers regarding a patient. Finally, it includes the referral of a patient from one health care provider to another.

- **Payment:** This encompasses the various activities of health care providers to get paid or be reimbursed for their services. One example is a health plan obtaining premium payments. Also included is a health plan fulfilling its responsibilities to provide benefits under the plan, and to obtain or provide reimbursement for the provision of health care. In addition, the Privacy Rule gives other examples of common payment activities. Some of the most common ones are:

  - Determining eligibility or coverage under a plan

  - Adjudicating claims

  - Risk adjustments

  - Billing and collection

  - Reviewing health care services for medical necessity, coverage, and justification of charges

  - Utilization review activities

  - Disclosures to consumer reporting agencies.

- **Health care operations:** This is defined as certain administrative, financial, legal, and quality-improvement activities of a covered entity that are necessary to run its business. It also includes activities to support the core functions of treatment and payment. These activities include:

  - Conducting quality assessment and improvement activities for the purpose of improving health or reducing health care costs.

  - Performing case management and care coordination.

  - Reviewing the competence or qualifications of health care professionals.

- Evaluating provider and health plan performance; training health care and nonhealth care professionals; accreditation, certification, licensing, or credentialing activities.

- Underwriting and other activities relating to the creation, renewal, or replacement of a contract of health insurance or health benefits, and ceding, securing, or placing a contract for reinsurance of risk relating to health care claims.

- Conducting or arranging for medical review, legal, and auditing services, including fraud and abuse detection and compliance programs.

- Conducting business planning and development, such as performing cost-management and planning analyses related to managing and operating the entity.

The Designated Record Set (DRS) is a group of records maintained by or for a covered entity. Such records are used to make decisions about individuals. They can also be a provider's medical and billing records about individuals. Or they can be a health plan's enrollment, payment, claims adjudication, and case or medical management systems.

The Electronic Health Record (EHR) and Health Information Exchanges (HIE)

For a long time there has been talk in the health care industry about making all patient health records completely electronic. There has even been talk of having a national database of electronic health records. In fact, the original act of 1996 that made HIPAA a law also included a section that charged the National Committee for Vital and Health Statistics (NCVHS) with "study(ing) the issues related to the adoption of uniform data standards for patient medical record information and the electronic exchange of such information." Since then, NCVHS has been working to establish standards for the information and terminologies that would make up a universal electronic patient health record that would standardize the data so that it is understood by any and all health care providers and organizations.

Electronic Health Record

There are new laws (ARRA and HITECH, covered later in this chapter) that require implementation of an Electronic Health Record (EHR) and the development of Health Information Exchanges (HIEs) locally, regionally, and nationally. Many companies are already investing in EHR projects and initiatives, although the final deadline for implementing the EHR in all health care facilities (including physicians' offices) is not until January 1, 2014. The benefits of EHR are pretty obvious:

- Easy and efficient access to patient records—no lost charts.

- Easy to transfer patient information to other physicians.

- Reduces cost of paper.

- Integrates with patient medicine or prescription software and helps alert to drug interactions and patient allergies.

The standards that HIPAA established will support the ARRA/HITECH EHR initiatives. This means that organizations that are already compliant with HIPAA and already exchanging electronic health information will be in a good position to implement an electronic health record.

ARRA Title XIII/ HITECH

This legislation, which went into effect in January of 2010, requires health care data sent electronically (called transactions) to use a specific standard and mandates the use of ICD-10 diagnostic and procedure code sets.

The American Recovery and Reinvestment Act (ARRA) is officially Public Law 111-5 and was signed on February 17, 2009, by President Barack Obama. ARRA provides many different stimulus opportunities, one of which is $19.2 billion for health information technology (HIT). Title XIII of ARRA was given a subtitle: Health Information Technology for Economic and Clinical Health Act (HITECH). It is this section that deals with many of the health information communication and technology provisions, including Subpart D—Privacy.

The HITECH provisions of the 2009 federal stimulus bill are complex and can be divided into seven broad categories as shown below. The two areas specific to ICD-10 include Health Information Exchanges (HIE) and privacy and security.

- HITECH-ARRA Overview

- Meaningful Use

- Privacy and Security

- Health Information Exchange

- State-level Activity

- HITECH Workforce

- Other Resources

On January 16, 2009, HHS announced the final rules for v5010 electronic transactions and ICD-10-CM and ICD-10-PCS code sets, intended to improve patient care quality, enhance claim processing, improve reporting, and promote interoperability. On March 5, 2009, the Obama Administration released their decision to proceed with both final rules on ICD-10 and the Electronic Transaction Standards without changes to the effective dates. Compliance dates include January 1, 2012 for the Transaction Code Sets of Version 5010, Version D.0 and Version 3.0, with small health plans having until January 2013 for Version 3.0 compliance. (These transactions are discussed in detail later in this chapter.) This provides lead time for industry compliance with the October 1, 2013 requirement for ICD-10 code sets used to report health care diagnoses and procedures.

The new ARRA Title XIII/HITECH laws will require health care providers to implement an EHR, essentially forcing them to transmit claims and other health care data electronically starting in 2012. In the meantime, some providers are choosing to avoid HIPAA compliance. This might be a valid choice for some small providers. However, a provider considering this option should think about it carefully. In a high-tech age, it is very hard for a provider to conduct business efficiently without using electronic transactions. Also, Medicare and Medicaid claims must now be sent electronically, and most other health care plans are following Medicare and Medicaid's policy. A provider who avoids HIPAA compliance also has to choose not to have any Medicare or Medicaid patients. In the foreseeable future, this will extend to most other health care insurance plans.

In short, sticking with paper records is not a good solution for most providers. For smaller ones with an exclusive clientele, this might be an option. For most providers, it is not. Unlike providers, health plans do not have any choice about using standard transactions. If a provider submits a standard transaction, a health plan must be able to receive it. And that health plan cannot in any way delay processing of a standard transaction. Also, the health plan cannot charge providers for sending standard electronic transactions. If a health plan does not comply, it could be subject to penalties under HIPAA.

Let's take a minute to review the new ARRA/HITECH laws regarding EHRs. The term EHR, or electronic health record, means an electronic record of health-related information on an individual that is created, gathered, managed, and consulted by authorized health care clinicians and staff. Physicians and hospitals can receive thousands of dollars in funding and incentives if they can demonstrate "meaningful use" of EHR. The meaningful use criteria include

- Use of a certified EHR system.

- Use of a system that has e-prescribing capability.

- Participation in a HIE that works to enhance the coordination of patient care among providers.

- Implementation of quality measures. Providers must demonstrate that they use EHR to track key clinical conditions such as hypertension and diabetes, and to provide data on these conditions for care coordination purposes.

In addition to the EHR initiatives, ARRA/HITECH pushes for the development of HIEs. The goal of HIEs are to exchange health care data between health care providers and hospitals at a local, regional, and even national level. **Health Information Exchanges** are defined as the electronic movement of health-related information among organizations according to nationally recognized standards. This is also known as **Enterprise Integration**, which is the electronic linkage of health care providers, health plans, the government, and other interested parties, to enable electronic exchange and use of health information among all the components in the health care infrastructure, in accordance with applicable law. It includes related application protocols and other related standards. One form of HIE is the **Regional Health Information Organization (RHIO)**, defined as a health information organization that brings together stakeholders within a defined geographic area and governs health information exchange among them for the purpose of improving health and care in that community.

The ability to exchange health information electronically is a basic and critical capability that is the foundation of efforts to improve health care in the United States. The increased availability of relevant health information through HIE:

- Provides a key building block for improved patient care, quality, and safety

- Makes relevant health care information available where and when it is needed

- Provides the connecting point for an organized, standardized process for data exchange across local, regional, and statewide HIT initiatives

- Provides the means to reduce duplication of services with a resultant reduction of health care costs

- Facilitates reduced operational costs by enabling automation of many (currently manual) administrative tasks

- Provides governance and management over the data exchange process.

- Enables the integration of sick (illness)-care with well-care

- Links first-responder teams with trauma care teams

- Stimulates consumer education and involvement in their health care process

- Promotes transparency of service and cost

- Creates a potential for feedback loop between research and actual practice

- Enables public health to meet its commitment to the community

- Facilitates the efficient deployment of emerging technology and health care services, such as e-prescribing

- Provides a basic level of interoperability between physician-maintained EHRs and patient-maintained Patient Health Records (PHR).

ARRA/HITECH impacts the HIE in several key ways. There is specific funding for HIE development, and additional funding to accelerate physician and hospital adoption of EHR. The transactions and code sets, including the ICD-10, established by HIPAA and ARRA/HITECH will help in the creation of standards for the content and format of the EHR and the HIE.

Before moving on from the topic of ARRA/HITECH, here are a few more provisions of these laws. While they do not impact ICD-10 or transactions directly, it is important to be aware of them since they impact health care services and delivery. The main impact of ARRA/HITECH is the required implementation of an EHR, and transmission of claims and data. electronically. All providers (physicians and hospitals) are required to comply. The second biggest impact of ARRA/HITECH on HIPAA and privacy is the new requirement to advise patients when there has been a breach in security/privacy of records. The relationship between HIPAA and ARRA/HITECH also includes (a) the extension of consumers' rights to request restrictions on disclosures under certain conditions (i.e, payment of a bill out of pocket by the patient to avoid disclosing health care provided to the insurance company); and (b) requiring the CEs that maintain EHRs to provide individuals with copies of their PHI in electronic format upon request, or transmit it as directed. Also:

1. Health care covered entities must notify consumers when their individually identifiable information is breached. (Applies to HIPAA-covered entities and their business associates).

2. A breach, under the new HITECH rules, is the unauthorized acquisition, access, use, or disclosure of PHI that compromises the security and privacy of the information (i.e., information is not encrypted in any way). HITECH covers breaches from any media (paper or electronic).

3. If a business associate becomes aware of a breach by the CE (and vice versa), they have an obligation to report it if the responsible party does not do so within a reasonable period of time.

4. If unintentional access by an employee or other person acting on behalf of the covered entity or business associate occurs, it is forgivable—provided the PHI was reviewed in good faith and was not further accessed (cases like these must, however, be documented by the covered entity).

Let's Review 2–1:

1. One of HIPAA's objectives is to:
   a. Expand budgets for technology throughout health care
   b. Promote a safe exchange of health information electronically
   c. Create a health care clearinghouse for the exchange of health care data
   d. Create a new diagnostic and procedural coding system

2. The acronym HIPAA stands for:
   a. Health Insurance Privacy and Accessibility Act
   b. Health Care Industry Privacy and Accountability Act
   c. Health Insurance Portability and Accountability Act
   d. Heath Insurance Portability and Accessibility Act

3. Another name for HIPAA is:
   a. Public Law 104-191 (H.R. 3103)
   b. ARRA/HITECH
   c. Kennedy-Kassebaum Bill (Act)
   d. A and B only
   e. A and C only

4. ARRA/HITECH's rule/rules pertinent to ICD-10 is/are:
   a. Use of ICD-10-CM required
   b. Use of ICD-10-PCS required
   c. Use of version 5010 standards and transaction sets required
   d. Compliance deadlines for ICD-10 and version 5010
   e. All of the above

5. Title II of HIPAA includes:
  a. ICD-10 code sets and version 5010 standards
  b. Health care insurance access, portability, and renewability
  c. Group health insurance application and enforcement
  d. Administrative Simplification
  e. Revenue Offsets

6. An HIE is:
  a. A system for the transfer of information between hospitals in a specific region
  b. A system for the transfer of information between hospitals that are part of a group
  c. A system for the transfer of health information between organizations, regionally, and/or nationally
  d. None of the above

Transaction Standards

Most people are familiar with Microsoft Word and can e-mail Word documents with ease. When a Word document is sent, the recipient is usually able to easily open, read, and even edit the document. But just for a minute, imagine being the only person in the world with Microsoft Word. It is possible to send a document, but no one else has software that can read it. In order to send documents, or exchange information, a common format that is compatible with both computer operating systems and software must be established. In the health care industry, there were more than 150 standards for transmitting health claim information, which made electronic exchange of health care data, such as insurance claims, very difficult and, ultimately, very costly. The U.S. Government Accounting Office (GAO) estimated in 2009 that more than 20 cents of every health care dollar was spent on administrative overhead in our health care system, and a significant portion were costs in time, materials, and resources, associated with mailing health data (rather than using EDI), as well as the cost of translating data into a "language" that could be understood by all the organizations handling an electronic transaction.

For this reason, HIPAA, especially Title II's Administrative Simplification rules, created standards for EDI between health care organizations, including providers, hospitals, insurance carriers, federal and state agencies and clearinghouses; and made electronic transactions mandatory for any provider submitting federal or state insurance claims, such as Medicare and Medicaid. Not only that, but HIPAA's Administrative Simplification rules created specific standards for each type of health care transaction. A **transaction** is the exchange of information between two parties to carry out financial or administrative activities related to health care. A **transaction standard** clearly defines the data elements and the order of the data elements that make up a single transaction. This means that any organization that exchanges the transaction electronically does it the exact same way. Imagine that each transaction is a menu item in a restaurant. A transaction standard provides the detailed recipe for that menu item, so any chef in the kitchen can cook the identical item. In other words, there are standards for electronic submission of health insurance claims, checking on the status of submitted insurance claims, verification of insurance benefits, and several others, and, all health care entities must use the same transaction standards. In the Transactions portion of the Administrative Simplification rule, HIPAA mandated that eight key tasks, or business transactions, must be standardized when information is exchanged electronically:

- Verification of insurance eligibility
- Enrollment in insurance plans
- Inquiries into the status of insurance claims
- Submission of insurance claims (institutional, professional, dental)
- Billing and claims receipt acknowledgment

- Electronic remittance advice
- Insurance premium payment
- Referrals and authorizations.

More Terminology Associated with Transactions

Under HIPAA, if a covered entity conducts one of the adopted transactions electronically, they must use the adopted standard. This means that they must adhere to the content and format requirements of each standard. HIPAA also adopted specific code sets for diagnosis and procedures to be used in all transactions, which will be covered in more detail later in this chapter.

When HHS began the task of setting standards for HIPAA, the planners thought hard about how they could use existing standards from the American National Standards Institute (ANSI) for common healthcare EDI transactions. ANSI is the organization that developed the transaction standards for banking, credit and debit cards, and all financial and administrative transactions used in the United States and the world today. The standard they decided on is called the ANSI Accredited Standards Committee (ASC) X12 standard. HHS adopted this ASC X12 standard and modified it to meet the needs of specific information exchanges in the health care industry. It used the existing X12 standard to create 12 HIPAA standards for electronic transactions of health care information, which are described in Table 2-4.

Now, take a look at the various transactions in a little more detail. Most, but not all, of these transactions will use the ICD-10 code sets as part of the transaction standard.

Transaction 270, Health Plan Eligibility Inquiry, is sent from the provider to the health plan. The information includes questions such as whether the patient is covered in the health plan and the type of coverage availability. General eligibility requests ask for one or more of the following:

- Eligibility status (in other words, active or not active in the plan)
- Maximum benefits (policy limits)
- Exclusions

Table 2-4 HIPAA Transactions

HIPAA Standard Transactions		Definition
270	Health Plan Eligibility Inquiry	Providers verify insurance eligibility and benefits electronically
271	Health Plan Eligibility Response	Providers receive an electronic response to an insurance eligibility inquiry
276	Health Care Claim Status Request	Providers check the status of an insurance claim electronically.
277	Health Care Claim Status Response	Providers receive an electronic response to an insurance claim status inquiry.
278	Certification and Authorization of Referrals—Request for Review	Providers obtain authorization for referrals electronically.
278	Certification and Authorization of Referrals—Response	Providers obtain a response to a request for a referral authorization.
820	Health Plan Premium Payments	An insured party makes an electronic payment of health plan premiums.
834	Enrollment or Disenrollment in a Health Plan	An insured party electronically enrolls into or out of a health plan.
835	Health Care Claim Payment/Remittance Advice	An insurance claim payer responds with payment and an itemized remittance statement.
837-P	Health Care Claim—Professional	A physician's office files an insurance claim electronically using this format. The hard copy (paper) version is called the CMS1500.
837-D	Health Care Claim—Dental	A dentist's office files an insurance claim electronically using this format. The hard copy (paper) version is the ADA form.
837-I	Health Care Claim—Institutional	A hospital files an insurance claim electronically using this format. The hard copy (paper) version is called the UB-04 (CMS1450).

- In-plan and out-of-plan benefits
- Coordination of benefits information
- Deductible
- Co-pays.

Specific eligibility requests on the 270 transaction may ask for one or more of the following:

- Procedure coverage dates
- Procedure coverage maximum amount allowed
- Deductible amount
- Remaining deductible amount
- Coinsurance amount
- Co-pay amount
- Coverage limitation percentage
- Patient responsibility amount
- Noncovered amount.

The 271 transaction, Health Plan Eligibility Response, is sent from the health plan to the Provider as a reply to a 270 request. A 276 transaction, Health Care Claim Status Request, is sent from the provider or provider's billing service to the health plan to determine the status of the claim or whether the claim has been processed. The 277 transaction, Health Care Claim Status Response, is the reply from the health plan to the provider or billing service indicating the status of the claim. The reply may be in the form of a request for additional information from the provider. The health plan may also send an unsolicited notification of a health care claim status.

The 278 is a combined transaction for Certification and Authorization of Referrals. It is typically initiated or sent from the provider to the health plan, asking for preauthorization to perform a specific procedure or service, or to authorize a referral. The procedure or service and the related diagnoses are required on a 278 transaction in the form of ICD-10-CM and ICD-10-PCS codes. The same transaction is used by the health plan to approve or reject the request. The types of information on a 278 transaction include:

- Precertifying a patient to be admitted to a hospital.
- Precertifying a patient to receive surgery.
- Patient arrival notice.
- Patient discharge notice.
- Certification or service change notice.
- Authorizing referrals or other services.
- Requests for a UMO to review a claim.
- Notification of certification or authorization to the primary provider, other providers, and UMOs.

The 820, Health Plan Premium Payments, is sent from an employer or employer's bank to the health plan or health plan's bank for routine payment of a health plan premium. This transaction usually involves moving money from one account to another. The 820 transaction

- Can be sent to a bank to move money only.
- Can be sent to a bank to move money as well as detailed or summary remittance (payment) information.
- Can be sent directly to a payee to move detailed or summary remittance information.

An employer typically sends the 834 transaction, Enrollment or Disenrollment in a Health Plan, to the health plan to enroll, update, or disenroll employees and dependents in a health plan policy.

Next is the 835 transaction, the Health Care Claim Payment or Remittance Advice. This is sent from the health plan or the health plan's bank to the provider or provider's bank. After a health plan processes a claim, it sends the money to the provider or to the provider's bank. Like the 820, this transaction usually involves moving money from one account to another. An 835 is also used to send explanation of benefits (EOB) information to the patient explaining how the claim was processed and paid. As a side note, the Remittance Advice (RA) is sent to the provider of service. The Explanation of Benefits (EOB) is sent to the patient. The remittance advice will use the ICD-10-PCS codes submitted on an insurance claim. The EOB typically only provides the description of the service to make it easier for patients to understand.

The last transaction is the 837, and there are actually three forms of this transaction. This is the electronic insurance claim submitted by the provider of service to the health plan. It contains three general sections. The first section includes all of the patient demographic and insurance information needed for the health care plan to identify the insured person. The next section includes the services, diagnoses, and other pertinent information about the patient's care, including dates of service, whether the patient was hospitalized or off work, and most importantly, the diagnoses and procedures and services rendered to the patient. The diagnoses and procedures are transmitted using the ICD-10-CM and ICD-10-PCS codes:

- The 837-P or 837 Professional is sent from the provider or provider's billing service to the health plan. It is the electronic form of the paper, or hard copy, insurance claim form called the CMS1500. This is the bill that a provider sends to a health plan after a patient visit, service, or stay. An 837 Professional transaction means that the bill is coming from a single provider, for example, a physician, surgeon, radiologist, or mental health professional.

- An 837 Institutional (837-I) transaction comes from a provider facility, such as a hospital. The information in an 837 Institutional is the electronic equivalent of the UB-04/CMS1450 paper insurance claim form.

- Finally, the 837 Dental (837-D) transaction comes from a dentist's office. The information in the 837 Dental is the electronic equivalent of the ADA paper insurance claim form.

There is one additional transaction, the 275, Health Care Claims Attachment. This transaction is not yet a HIPAA standard, but it should be soon—especially with the requirement to use the ASC X12 version 5010 standards that must be in place by January 1, 2012 and the ICD-10 code sets, mandated for use by October 1, 2013. Unlike the other transactions, which use the ANSI X12 standard as a foundation, Health Level 7 (HL7) sets the standards for claims attachments. The other big difference between this standard and the others is that it is capable of capturing all sorts of data in electronic form, including photographs, x-rays, and other types of multimedia information. ANSI x12 standards, by comparison, are strictly text files, and thus are not capable of transmitting photographs or x-rays.

The 275, Health Care Claims Attachment, can help providers send health plans and extra information about claims. It also can be used outside of this standard context to send multimedia information to all sorts of different organizations. Currently, CMS has a proposed standard for claims attachments. The proposed standard should one day become a final standard and be brought in as part of the Transactions and Code Sets rules.

ANSI, ASC x12 and version 5010, D.0, and 3.0

There is more to know about the HIPAA-mandated transactions for electronic data interchange. Not only must these transactions be standardized as has been outlined, but there are specific rules for the transmission of these transactions electronically. The American National Standards Institute (ANSI) developed standards for electronic transactions for businesses years ago, with particular emphasis on banking transactions. Nowadays, it is possible to bank online, and even pay for fast food using a debit or credit card. When the process began to integrate health care transactions into the electronic "world," those same standards, known as Accredited Standards Committee x12, or ASC x12, were used as the foundation for the transaction. HIPAA's Title II rules required that the ASC x12 standards be used with each health care transaction, i.e. the transactions mandated by HIPAA, and also required that a specific version of the ASC x12 standards be used. Currently, the following transaction standard versions are in use:

- Providers (including hospitals): ASC x12 version 4010A1

- Pharmacy: ASC x12 version 5.1 or 1.0

ARRA/HITECH rules updated the ASC x12 standards to a newer version which must replace the old versions no later than January 1, 2012. The new versions are:

- Providers (including hospitals): ANSI ASC X12 version 5010 (v5010)

- Pharmacy: ANSI ASC X12 version D.0 or 3.0 (vD.0 or v3.0)

These versions are required by the modifications made to the Health Insurance Portability and Accountability Act (HIPAA) of 1996 in January 2009 by Congress as part of ARRA Title XIII, and HITECH, which was signed into law by President Obama.

As with other HIPAA standards, CMS has a dual role related to the Version 5010, D.0, and 3.0 standards. The CMS Office of E-Health Standards & Services (OESS) is responsible for the policies and enforcement of the Administrative Simplification provisions for transactions and code sets covered under HIPAA.

ASC x12

The following is a timeline that led to the newest regulations concerning the use of transactions and code sets.

- HIPAA mandated the use of standard formats for electronic claims and claims-related transactions, such as the 837-P, 837-I, 270/271, and 278 transactions.

- The transactions and code sets' final rule was published on August 17, 2000. This adopted the use of the standard transactions and the ICD-9-CM code sets.

- The Administrative Simplification Compliance Act (ASCA) of 2001 required the use of electronic claims from providers to receive Medicare reimbursement—effective from October 16, 2003.

- The HIPAA Administrative Simplification: Modifications to Medical Data Code Set Standards to Adopt ICD-10-CM and ICD-10-PCS Final Rule replaced the current versions of the standards with version 5010 and D.0, respectively, and established a new standard called NCPDP 3.0, which allows Medicaid to recoup payments made to pharmacies when a third party payer had primary financial responsibility instead of Medicaid.

The covered entities affected by the transition from v4010A1 to v5010 are providers, such as physicians, rehabilitation clinics and hospitals, health plans, and health care clearinghouses. Business associates that use the affected transactions, such as billing services and agents, and vendors, are also affected. For the purposes of this textbook, the emphasis will be to provide a high-level overview of the ASC x12 version 5010 (v5010) standards, which affect providers and hospitals sending and exchanging health care data. The goal is to generate understanding of the transactions and new version requirements as they relate to ICD-10, not to provide in-depth instruction in the process or details of v5010 implementation. ASC x12 version D.0 is exclusively for Medicare Part D prescription drug claims, and version 3.0 is only for Medicaid pharmacy claims subrogation. Thus, as they do not impact ICD-10-CM or PCS, they will not be covered in this chapter or textbook. All transactions, including the following, will now require use of v5010 electronic transaction standards no later than January 1, 2012:

- Claims (837-P, 837-I, and 837-D)

- Remittance Advice (835)

- Claims Status Inquiry and Response (276/277)
- Eligibility Inquiry and Response (270/271)

Systems that submit claims, receive remittances, and exchange claims status or eligibility inquiries and responses must be analyzed to identify software and business process changes. According to CMS, version 5010 is essential the adoption of the ICD-10 code sets, and requires upgrades to existing computer systems because of the following changes:

- ICD-10 increases the field size for code lengths from 5 bytes to 7 bytes
- Addition of a one-digit version indicator to the ICD code version to indicate version 10 is the code used, versus a code from ICD-9.
- Increases the number of diagnoses allowed on a claim
- Adds additional data modifications to the standards.

Version 5010 will accommodate those changes, and also makes the following improvements to the old ASC x12 version 4010A1:

- Standardizes the business information related to the transaction
- Uses reporting guidelines that represent data consistently and which are less confusing
- Accommodates the reporting of clinical data such as diagnosis and procedure codes
- Distinguishes between principal diagnosis, admitting diagnosis, external cause of injury and patient reason for visit codes
- Supports monitoring of certain illness mortality rates, outcomes for specific treatment options, some hospital length of stays, and clinical reasons for care
- Adds indicator on institutional claims to accommodate "present on admission" rules.

The timeline for implementation of version 5010 and D.0 is shown in Figure 2-4. By January 1, 2010, Level I, internal testing, should have been completed. Level II testing, which includes testing with trading partners and accepting new v5010/D.0 transactions, while still accepting the older v4010 transactions, should begin no later than January 1, 2011. By January 1, 2012, no older versions should be accepted, only v5010 and D.0 transactions are accepted, and facilities should be in full compliance.

Date	Compliance Step
January 1, 2010	Payers and providers should begin internal testing of Version 5010 standards for electronic claims
December 31, 2010	Internal testing of Version 5010 must be complete to achieve Level I Version 5010 compliance
January 1, 2011	• Payers and providers should begin external testing of Version 5010 for electronic claims • CMS begins accepting Version 5010 claims • Version 4010 claims continue to be accepted
December 31, 2011	• External testing of Version 5010 for electronic claims must be complete to achieve Level II Version 5010 compliance
January 1, 2012	• All electronic claims must use Version 5010 • Version 4010 claims are no longer accepted
October 1, 2013	• Claims for services provided on or after this date must use ICD-10 codes for medical diagnosis and inpatient procedures • CPT codes will continue to be used for outpatient services

© Cengage Learning 2013

Figure 2-4 Transaction and Code Sets Compliance Dates

Version 5010

With the move to electronic exchange of health information, it became necessary to convert the information on the paper insurance claim form (CMS-1500) to the electronic file format (837 Professional) using the ASC x12 version 5010 standards. Figure 2-5 is an example of the paper CMS-1500 claim form. Note that every block on the claim form requires specific information. Block 1a requires the insured's identification number, Block 21 includes the diagnosis codes, and Blocks 24a through j are required charge-specific fields.

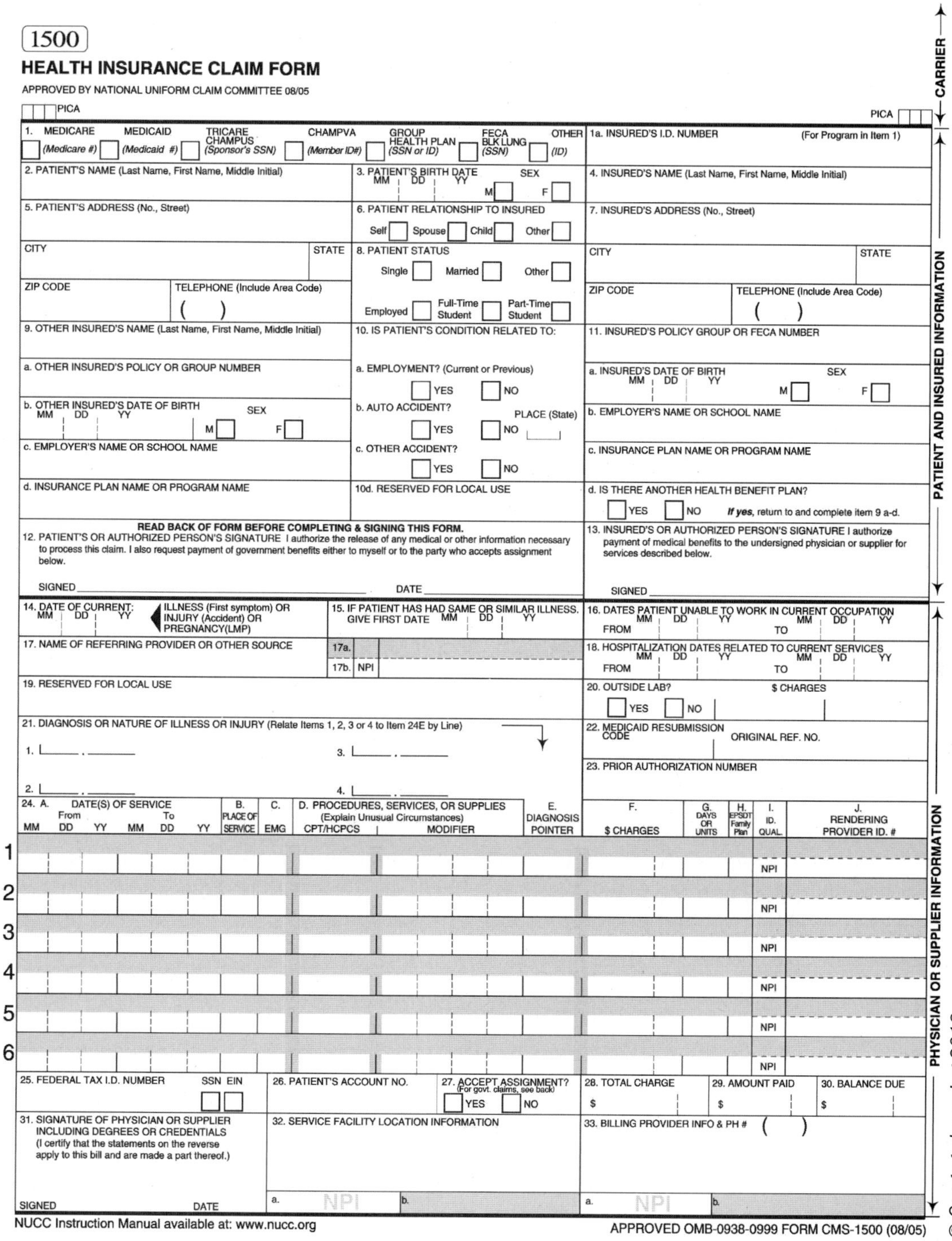
1500
HEALTH INSURANCE CLAIM FORM
APPROVED BY NATIONAL UNIFORM CLAIM COMMITTEE 08/05

PICA | PICA

1. MEDICARE (Medicare #) | MEDICAID (Medicaid #) | TRICARE CHAMPUS (Sponsor's SSN) | CHAMPVA (Member ID#) | GROUP HEALTH PLAN (SSN or ID) | FECA BLK LUNG (SSN) | OTHER (ID)
1a. INSURED'S I.D. NUMBER (For Program in Item 1)
2. PATIENT'S NAME (Last Name, First Name, Middle Initial)
3. PATIENT'S BIRTH DATE MM DD YY SEX M F
4. INSURED'S NAME (Last Name, First Name, Middle Initial)
5. PATIENT'S ADDRESS (No., Street)
6. PATIENT RELATIONSHIP TO INSURED Self Spouse Child Other
7. INSURED'S ADDRESS (No., Street)
CITY STATE
8. PATIENT STATUS Single Married Other
CITY STATE
ZIP CODE TELEPHONE (Include Area Code) ( )
Employed Full-Time Student Part-Time Student
ZIP CODE TELEPHONE (Include Area Code) ( )
9. OTHER INSURED'S NAME (Last Name, First Name, Middle Initial)
10. IS PATIENT'S CONDITION RELATED TO:
11. INSURED'S POLICY GROUP OR FECA NUMBER
a. OTHER INSURED'S POLICY OR GROUP NUMBER
a. EMPLOYMENT? (Current or Previous) YES NO
a. INSURED'S DATE OF BIRTH MM DD YY SEX M F
b. OTHER INSURED'S DATE OF BIRTH MM DD YY SEX M F
b. AUTO ACCIDENT? YES NO PLACE (State)
b. EMPLOYER'S NAME OR SCHOOL NAME
c. EMPLOYER'S NAME OR SCHOOL NAME
c. OTHER ACCIDENT? YES NO
c. INSURANCE PLAN NAME OR PROGRAM NAME
d. INSURANCE PLAN NAME OR PROGRAM NAME
10d. RESERVED FOR LOCAL USE
d. IS THERE ANOTHER HEALTH BENEFIT PLAN? YES NO *If yes,* return to and complete item 9 a-d.
READ BACK OF FORM BEFORE COMPLETING & SIGNING THIS FORM.
12. PATIENT'S OR AUTHORIZED PERSON'S SIGNATURE I authorize the release of any medical or other information necessary to process this claim. I also request payment of government benefits either to myself or to the party who accepts assignment below.
SIGNED DATE
13. INSURED'S OR AUTHORIZED PERSON'S SIGNATURE I authorize payment of medical benefits to the undersigned physician or supplier for services described below.
SIGNED
14. DATE OF CURRENT: MM DD YY ILLNESS (First symptom) OR INJURY (Accident) OR PREGNANCY(LMP)
15. IF PATIENT HAS HAD SAME OR SIMILAR ILLNESS. GIVE FIRST DATE MM DD YY
16. DATES PATIENT UNABLE TO WORK IN CURRENT OCCUPATION FROM MM DD YY TO MM DD YY
17. NAME OF REFERRING PROVIDER OR OTHER SOURCE
17a.
17b. NPI
18. HOSPITALIZATION DATES RELATED TO CURRENT SERVICES FROM MM DD YY TO MM DD YY
19. RESERVED FOR LOCAL USE
20. OUTSIDE LAB? YES NO $ CHARGES
21. DIAGNOSIS OR NATURE OF ILLNESS OR INJURY (Relate Items 1, 2, 3 or 4 to Item 24E by Line)
1. 2. 3. 4.
22. MEDICAID RESUBMISSION CODE ORIGINAL REF. NO.
23. PRIOR AUTHORIZATION NUMBER
24. A. DATE(S) OF SERVICE From MM DD YY To MM DD YY
B. PLACE OF SERVICE
C. EMG
D. PROCEDURES, SERVICES, OR SUPPLIES (Explain Unusual Circumstances) CPT/HCPCS MODIFIER
E. DIAGNOSIS POINTER
F. $ CHARGES
G. DAYS OR UNITS
H. EPSDT Family Plan
I. ID. QUAL.
J. RENDERING PROVIDER ID. #
1 NPI
2 NPI
3 NPI
4 NPI
5 NPI
6 NPI
25. FEDERAL TAX I.D. NUMBER SSN EIN
26. PATIENT'S ACCOUNT NO.
27. ACCEPT ASSIGNMENT? (For govt. claims, see back) YES NO
28. TOTAL CHARGE $
29. AMOUNT PAID $
30. BALANCE DUE $
31. SIGNATURE OF PHYSICIAN OR SUPPLIER INCLUDING DEGREES OR CREDENTIALS (I certify that the statements on the reverse apply to this bill and are made a part thereof.)
SIGNED DATE
32. SERVICE FACILITY LOCATION INFORMATION
a. NPI b.
33. BILLING PROVIDER INFO & PH # ( )
a. NPI b.
NUCC Instruction Manual available at: www.nucc.org
APPROVED OMB-0938-0999 FORM CMS-1500 (08/05)

Figure 2-5 CMS-1500 Provider Paper Insurance Claim Form (Permission to reuse in accordance with http://www.coms.hhs.gov Content Reuse and Linking Policy.)

Each of these blocks on the CMS1500 was converted to a field in the 837 Professional transaction format. Then, that 837 professional transaction was embedded in the electronic transaction standard file, version 5010. To put this another way, ASC x12 version 5010 is the format any transaction must be in to be sent electronically.

Each transaction, i.e. the 837s, 277/278, etc. must be in its own specific format within the ASC x12 v5010 transaction standards. An insurance claim sent by a physician must be in an 837 Professional transaction format. An insurance claim sent by a hospital or acute care facility must be in an 837 Institutional transaction format. And, a health claims status inquiry must be in a 276 Health Care Claim Status Request format, and the response from the insurer must be in a 277 Health Care Claim Status Response format, etc.

Compare Figure 2-5 to Figure 2-6, which is an excerpt from the 837 Professional transaction, in ASC x12 version 5010 standard. While the focus of this textbook is on ICD-10 coding, it is important to have a familiarity with the format of the transactions and electronic data transmission requirements, and what they look like.

Each row in Figure 2-5 represents one item required either for the 837 Professional transaction or for the v5010 standards. For example, in rows that have an element identifier that starts with PA, note that the patient relationship code, employment status code, student status code from blocks 6 and 8 on the CMS1500 matches the 5010 transaction standards (Figure 2-5). In rows with element identifiers that start with NM1, the patient's last and first name are found on both the CMS1500 form in block 2, and the 837-P transaction (NMI103 through NMI105 (Figure 2-6).

Take just a minute to look at the columns in Figure 2-6, the 837-P, 5010 transaction. Each required element has an element identifier, which is found in the first column; the description of that element is in the second column. Any element, for example, that begins with PAT will be some type of specific patient information. PAT01 is the relationship code, PAT02 the location code, PAT03 the employment status code, and so on. The third column contains an internal identification code established and used by the provider. The fourth column defines how many characters can be used; for example, on NUM103, Patient Last Name, between 1 and 60 characters may be entered for the patient's last name. A last name of Jones would use five of these characters, while Mastroantonio would use thirteen. Column five identifies whether the field is required (R), never used (NU), or suggested (S).

The next two fields are internal fields identifying whether an element is repeated, and how many times; and the final column represents the allowable values that can be entered in a particular field. For example, for PAT01, Individual relationship code, the field length must be 2 characters, the code is required and the allowable values are 01, 19, 20, 21, 39, 40, 53, and G8. To find the complete definitions for the values in columns 3 through 8 requires a data dictionary. The data dictionary explains what each column is used for, what the codes and values are, and what they mean. The implementation guides for each transaction, the data dictionary, and the v5010 standards can be obtained from the Centers for Medicare and Medicaid Services (CMS), as well as the various standards associations, such as WEDI, ANSI and ASC, which were discussed earlier in the chapter. Again, this is only an overview to explain the relationship between the transaction standards and the ICD-10 codes and provide insight into how the ICD-10 codes are used in electronic data interchange. It is not intended to use as a guide to setting up the ASC x12 v5010 transactions.

Now that a bit has been explained regarding the transactions and electronic data transmission standards, it should be mentioned that there are conversion guides provided to help those organizations and facilities who already use the ASC x12 version 4010A1 to submit transactions electronically and identify what changes have occurred to which data elements. An excerpt from a 4010A1 to 5010 837-P Professional conversion guide is shown in Figure 2-7. In Figure 2-7 there is only one difference between v4010A1 and v5010—in the last row, for element identifier GS08, version identifier code. In v5010 an allowable value code change has been made (see the Values column).

Before leaving this topic, look for just a moment at a sample UB-04/CMS1450 paper (hard copy) insurance claim used by hospitals (Figure 2-8), and the version 5010, 837 Institutional (837-I) claim electronic transaction (Figure 2-9). Essentially, the look of the v5010, 837-I is similar to the 837-P;

Element Identifier	Description	ID	Min Max.	Usuage Reg.	Loop	Loop Repeat	Values	
			5010					
			837-P 5010					
HL	PATIENT HIERARCHICAL LEVEL		1	S	2000C	>1		
HL01	Hierarchical ID Number	AN	1-12	R				
HL02	Hierarchical Parent ID Number	AN	1-12	R				
HL03	Hierarchical Level Code	ID	1-2	R			23	
HL04	Hierarchical Child Code	ID	1-1	R	2000C		0	
PAT	PATIENT INFORMATION		1	R				
PAT01	Individual Relationship Code	ID	2-2	R			01, 19, 20, 21, 39, 40, 53, G8	Code Deleted
PAT02	Patient Location Code	ID	1-1	N/U				
PAT03	Employment Status Code	ID	2-2	N/U				
PAT04	Student Status Code	ID	1-1	N/U				
PAT05	Date Time Period Format Qualifier	ID	2-3	S			D8	
PAT06	Patient Death Date	AN	1-35	S			CCYYMMDD	
PAT07	Unit or Basis for Measurement Code	ID	2-2	S			01	
PAT08	Patient Weight 9(6)V99	R	1-10	S				
PAT09	Pregnancy Indicator	ID	1-1	S			Y	
NM1	PATIENT NAME		1	R	2010CA	1		
NM101	Entity Identifier Code	ID	2-3	R			QC	
NM102	Entity Type Qualifier	ID	1-1	R			1	
NM103	Patient Last Name	AN	1-60	R				Increase from 35-60
NM104	Patient First Name	AN	1-35	S				Increase from 25-35
NM105	Patient Middle Name	AN	1-25	S				Usage changed to Situational
NM106	Name Prefix	AN	1-10	N/U				
NM107	Patient Name Suffix	AN	1-10	S				
NM108	Identification Code Qualifier	ID	1-2	N/U				Code Deleted
NM109	Patient Primary Identifier	AN	2-80	N/U				Usage changed to Not used
NM110	Entity Relationship Code	ID	2-2	N/U				Usage changed to Not Used

Figure 2-6 v5010 837 Professional Record Example

4010A1							
Element Identifier	Description	ID	Min.Max	Usuage Reg.		Loop	Loop Repeat
837-P-4010A1							
ISA	INTERCHANGE CONTROL HEADER		1	R	__	1	
ISA01	Authorization Information Qualifier	ID	2-2	R			00,03
ISA02	Authorization Information	AN	10-10	R			
ISA03	Security Information Qualifier	ID	2-2	R			00,01
ISA04	Security Information	AN	10-10	R			
ISA05	Interchange ID Qualifier	ID	2-2	R			,14, 20, 27, 28, 29,30, 33, ZZ
ISA06	Interchange Sender ID	AN	15-16	R			
ISA07	Interchange ID Qualifier	ID	2-2	R			01, 14, 20, 27, 28, 29, 30, 33, ZZ
ISA08	Interchange Receiver ID	AN	15-15	R			
ISA09	Interchange Date	DT	6-6	R			YYMMDD
ISA10	Interchange Time	TM	4-4	R			HHMM
ISA11	Interchange Control Standards ID	ID	1-1	R			U
ISA12	Interchange Control Version Number	ID	5-5	R			00401
ISA13	Interchange Control Number	NO	9-9	R			
ISA14	Acknowledgement Requested	ID	1-1	R			0,1
ISA15	Usage Indicator	ID	1-1	R			P,T
ISA16	Component Element Separator	AN	1-1	R			
	FUNCTIONAL GROUP HEADER		1	R	–	>1	
GS							
GS01	Functional Identifier Code	ID	2-2	R			HC
GS02	Application Sender Code	AN	2-15	R			
GS03	Application Receiver Code	AN	2-15	R			CCYYMMDD
GS04	Date	DT	8-8	R			
GS05	Time	TM	4-8	R			HHMMSSDD
GS06	Group Control Number	NO	1-9	R			
GS07	Responsible Agency Code	ID	1-2	R			X
GS08	Version Identifier Code	AN	1-12	R			004010X098A1

5010							
Element Identifier	Description	ID	Min. Max.	Usage Reg.	Loop	Loop Repeat	Values
837-P 5010							
ISA	INTERCHANGE CONTROL HEADER		1	R	–	1	
ISA01	Authorization Information Qualifier	ID	2-Feb	R			00, 03
ISA02	Authorization Information	AN	10-Oct	R			
ISA03	Security Information Qualifier	ID	2-Feb	R			00, 01
ISA04	Security Information	AN	10-Oct	R			
ISA05	Interchange ID Qualifier	ID	2-Feb	R			01, 14, 20, 27, 28, 29, 30, 33, ZZ
ISA06	Interchange Sender ID	AN	15-15	R			
ISA07	Interchange ID Qualifier	ID	2-Feb	R			01, 14, 20, 27, 28, 29, 30, 33, ZZ

Figure 2-7 v4010A1 to v5010 837 Professional Conversion Example

ISA08	Interchange Receiver ID	AN	15-15	R				
ISA09	Interchange Date	DT	6-Jun	R				YYMMDD
ISA10	Interchange Time	TM	4-Apr	R				HHMM
ISA11	Interchange Control Standards ID		1-Jan	R				
ISA12	Interchange Control Version Number	ID	5-May	R				501
ISA13	Interchange Control Number	NO	9-Sep	R				
ISA14	Acknowledgement Requested	ID	1-Jan	R				0, 1
ISA15	Usage Indicator	ID	1-Jan	R				P, T
ISA16	Component Element Separator	AN	1-Jan	R				
GS	FUNCTIONAL GROUP HEADER		1	R	–	1		
GS01	Functional Identifier Code	ID	2-Feb	R				
GS02	Application Sender Code	AN	15-Feb	R				
GS03	Application Receiver Code	AN	15-Feb	R				
GS04	Date	DT	8-Aug	R				CCYYMMDD
GS05	Time	TM	8-Apr	R				HHMM
GS06	Group Control Number	NO	9-Jan	R				
GS07	Responsible Agency Code	ID	2-Jan	R				X Code Change
GS08	Version Identifier Code	AN	12-Jan	R				005010X222

© Cengage Learning 2013

Figure 2-7 (*Continued*)

however, much more information is required from the hospital when billing an insurance claim. Therefore, the v5010, 837-I is much more complex, with many more data elements. Hospitals and other acute care facilities must use the v5010 transaction standards, and the 837-I transaction, when submitting health insurance claims for payment. They cannot use the 837-P or 837-D. Figure 2-9 also illustrates the v4010A1 version. The changes made in v5010 are on the far right side of the table.

The Health Care Clearinghouse

The covered entity that helps everyone with the exchange of financial and administrative information is the health care clearinghouse. Remember, the job of a clearinghouse is to take data that is in a proprietary, or nonstandard, format and translate it into the HIPAA standards in this case the v5010 standards, the HIPAA transactions, and the ICD-10-CM and ICD-10-PCS code sets. While not required, both health care providers and health plans may use a clearinghouse to do this. Figure 2-10 is an illustration of the relationship of the clearinghouse to providers. Let's say a provider sends its non-standard CMS1500 insurance claim form to the clearinghouse. The clearinghouse translates it into the 837-P claim form transaction, and the ASC x12 v5010 electronic transaction standards. The clearinghouse then takes the translated data and sends it to the health plan for processing. When the health plan processes the electronic claim for payment, it transmits the remittance advice (RA) and payment back through the clearinghouse. The clearinghouse translates the data into a format the provider's financial software system will understand, and transmits the RA and payment to the provider and/or the provider's bank. The clearinghouse acts as the ultimate mediator for information.

Not all providers and health plans use a clearinghouse. The provider and the health plan may exchange information directly with each other. There are all sorts of different arrangements. For example, some providers and health plans may use a clearinghouse to exchange some transactions but not others. Or a health plan may use a clearinghouse to exchange information with only one particular provider.

Another entity that can be involved in exchanging health information is an employer. An employer needs to send information to its health plan. Employees are hired, get fired, have babies, and get married. The employer needs to let the health plan know so it can keep track of who is and is not

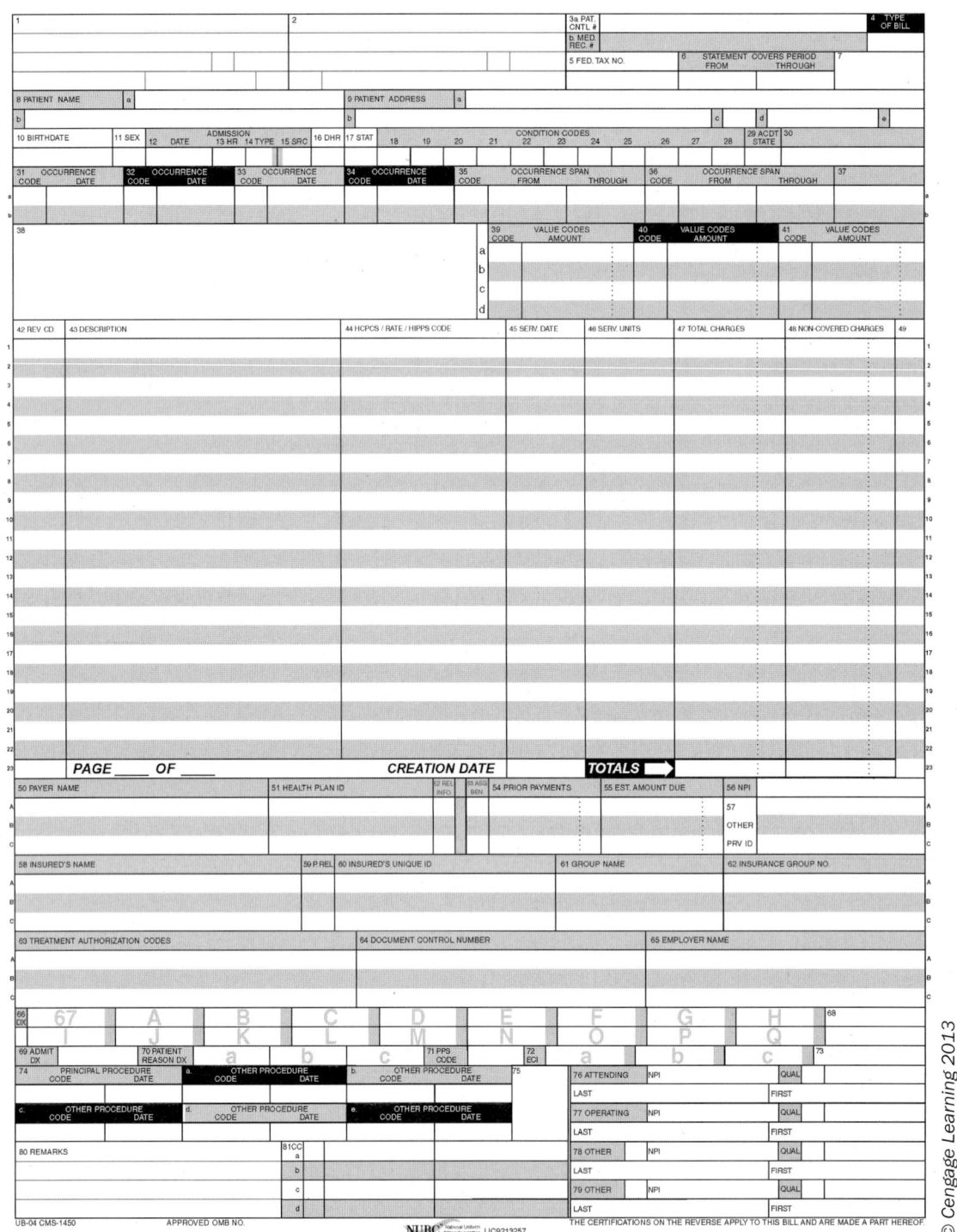

Figure 2-8 UB-04 Institutional Paper Insurance Claim Form (Permission to reuse in accordance with http://www .cms.hhs.gov Content Reuse and Linking policy.)

covered. Because an employer is not a covered entity under HIPAA (unless the employer has a self-insured, self-administered health plan), an employer does not have to use the HIPAA standard transactions when it exchanges information; however, most employers will choose to use the standard, since it makes it easier to exchange information with a health plan. When the employer does not use the standard, the clearinghouse can perform the same translation on the transaction to make it understandable by all organizations involved in the transaction.

INSTITUTIONAL CLAIM

Element Identifier	Description	ID	Min. Max.	Usage Reg.	Loop	Loop Repeat	Values
							4010A1
ST	TRANSACTION SET HEADER		1	R	—	>1	
					837-I 4010A1		
ST01	Transaction Set Identifier Code	ID	3-3	R			837
ST02	Transaction Set Control Number	AN	4-9	R			
BHT	BEGINNING OF HIERARCHICAL TRANSACTION		1	R	—	1	
BHT01	Hierarchical Structure Code	ID	4-4	R			0019
BHT02	Transaction Set Purpose Code	ID	2-2	R			00,18
BHT03	Originator Application Transaction ID	AN	1-30	R			
BHT04	Transaction Set Creation Date	DT	8-8	R			CCYMMDD
BHT05	Transaction Set Creation Time	TM	4-8	R			HHMM, HHMMSS, HHMMSSDD
BHT06	Claim or Encounter ID	ID	2-2	R			CH, RP
REF	TRANSMISSION TYPE IDENTIFICATION		1	S			
REF01	Reference Identification Qualifier	ID	2-3	R			87
REF02	Reference Identification	AN	1-30	R			
REF03	Description	AN	1-80	N/U			
REF04	Reference Identifier			N/U			
NM1	SUBMITTER NAME		1	R	1000A	1	
NM101	Entity Identifier Code	ID	2-3	R			41
NM102	Entity Type Qualifier	ID	1-1	R			1, 2
NM103	Submitter Last or Organization Name	AN	1-35	R			
NM104	Submitter First Name	ASN	1-25	S			
NM105	Submitter Middle Name	AN	1-25	S			
NM106	Name Prefix	AN	1-10	N/U			
NM107	Name Suffix	AN	1-10	N/U			
NM108	Identification Code Qualifier	ID	1-2	R			46
NM109	Submitter Identifier	AN	2-80	R			
NM110	Entity Relationship Code	ID	2-2	N/U			
NM111	Entity Identifier Code	ID	2-3	N/U			

Figure 2-9 v5010 837 Institutional Record Example

5010

Element Identifier	Description	Usage Reg.	ID	Loop	Min. Max.	Loop Repeat	Values	Notes
837-I 5010								
ST	TRANSACTION SET HEADER					>1	—	
STO1	Transaction Set Identifier Code	R	ID		3-3		837	
STO2	Transaction Set Control Number	R	AN		4-9			
STO3	Implementation Convention Reference	R	AN		1-35			New Element
BHT	BEGINNING OF HIERARCHICAL TRANSACTION					1	—	
BHT01	Hierarchical Structure Code	R	ID		4-4		0019	
BHT02	Transaction Set Purpose Code	R	ID		2-2		00, 18	
BHT03	Originator Application Transaction ID	R	AN		1-50			Increase from 30 - 50
BHT04	Transaction Set Creation Date	R	DT		8-8		CCYYMMDD	
BHT05	Transaction Set Creation Time	R	TM		4-8		HHMM, HHMMSS, HHMMSSD, HHMMSSDD	
BHT06	Claim or Encounter ID	R	ID		2-2		31, CH, RP	Code Added
NM1	SUBMITTER NAME	R		1000A		1		Segment Deleted
NM101	Entity Identifier Code	R	ID		2-3		41	
NM102	Entity Type Qualifier	R	ID		1-1		1, 2	
NM103	Submitter Last or Organization Name	R	AN		1-60			Increase from 35-60
NM104	Submitter First Name	S	AN		1-35			Increase from 25-35
NM105	Submitter Middle Name	S	AN		1-25			
NM106	Name Prefix	N/U	AN		1-10			
NM107	Name Suffix	N/U	AN		1-10			
NM108	Identification Code Qualifier	R	ID		1-2		46	
NM109	Submitter Identifier	R	AN		2-80			
NM110	Entity Relationship Code	N/U	ID		2-2			
NM111	Entity Identifier Code	N/U	ID		2-3			
NM112	Name Last or Organization Name	N/U	AN		1-60			New Element

Figure 2-9 (Continued)

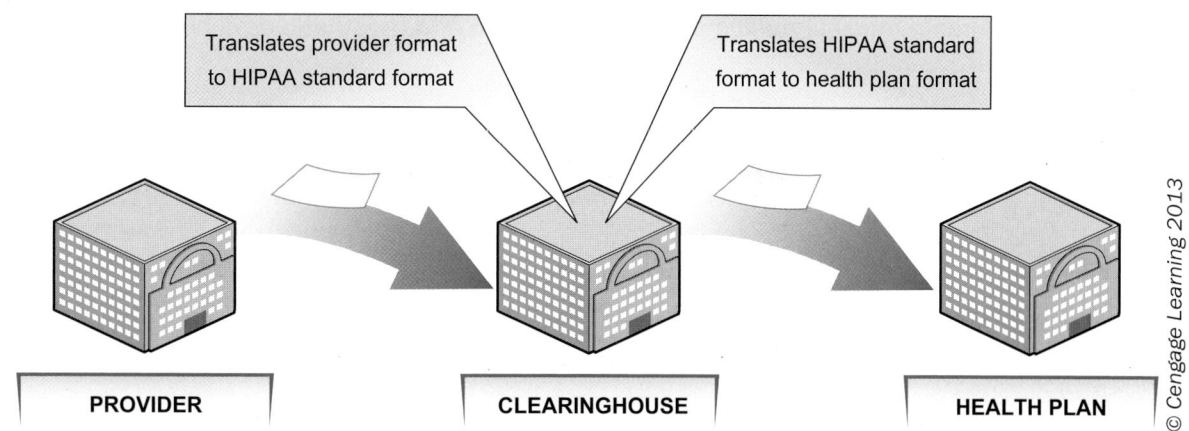

Figure 2-10 Clearinghouse Transaction Process

When discussing the exchange of all of this information, keep in mind that many Covered Entities (CE) use outside organizations to help them perform some of their functions. Many times a provider, a health plan, or even a clearinghouse will hire another company to conduct electronic transactions on its behalf. Here are a few common examples of how a Business Associate (BA) may assist a CE in conducting electronic transactions:

- A provider may hire a billing service to send claims to health plans and receive payments from health plans and patients.

- A health plan may hire a Third Party Administrator (TPA) to process, pay, and settle (or adjudicate) claims.

- A clearinghouse may hire a software vendor to assist in the process of translating nonstandard files to standard files.

HIPAA Code Sets

Code set: A **code set** is any group of codes used for encoding data elements. Data elements include tables of terms, medical concepts, medical diagnostic codes, and medical procedure codes. Code sets also include codes that are a part of the ANSI X12 v5010 transaction set, as well as CPT codes, CDT codes, ICD 9-CM, ICD-10-CM, and ICD-10-PCS codes, and others. The following are brief examples of the code sets including those currently in use, as well as the newly mandated ICD-10.

- CPT: (Current Procedural Terminology) Procedure codes used by physicians. After October 1, 2013 physicians and outpatient providers will still be allowed to use CPT codes to report procedures and services rendered.

- CDT: (Current Dental Terminology): Procedure codes used by dentists. Dentists will be allowed to continue using CDT codes to report dental procedures and services.

- ICD-9 (International Classification of Diseases, 9th Edition, volumes 1, 2, and 3: Procedure and diagnosis codes used by hospitals and other acute care facilities. Hospitals and other acute care facilities must begin using the new ICD-10-CM and ICD-10-PCS codes no later than October 1, 2013.

- ICD-10-CM, 10th Edition: Diagnosis codes that must be in use by all health care providers, including physicians and hospitals, effective October 1, 2013.

- ICD-10-PCS, 10th Edition: Procedure codes must be in use by hospitals and other acute care facilities, effective from October 1, 2013. Physicians and other outpatient providers are exempt from using ICD-10-PCS.

- Health Care Common Procedural Coding System (HCPCS), Level II: HCPCS Level II is the required code set to identify or describe health-related services that are not physician services, dentist services, or hospital surgical procedures. The codes include medical and surgical supplies, certain drugs, certain durable medical equipment (DME), orthotic and prosthetic devices, and procedures and services performed by nonphysicians.

Interrelationship between v5010, Transactions, and Code Sets

Figure 2-11 is an illustration of the relationship between the ASC x12, version 5010 standards; the HIPAA transactions, like the 837, 270/271, and 277/278 transactions; and the ICD-10-CM and ICD-10-

5010/D.0 & ICD-10 Interrelationships
Understand the Connections between the 5010 and ICD-10 Regulations

5010/D.0	ICD-10-CM/PCS
Introduction	
Compliance date:	• Compliance date:
• January 1, 2012	• October 1, 2013
• Covered entities	• All covered entities
• January 1, 2013	
• Small health plans	
Who Is Affected?	
• All HIPAA covered entities	• All HIPAA covered entities
• Providers	• Providers
• Health plans	• Health plans
• Clearinghouses	• Clearinghouses
• Business associates of covered entities that use the affected transactions	• Business associates of covered entities that use ICD-9 codes/data
• Billing/service agents	• Billing/service agents
Format Changes	
• Increases the field size for ICD codes from 5 bytes to 7 bytes	
• Adds a one-digit version indicator to the ICD code to indicate version 9 vs 10	• ICD-9-CM→ ICD-10-PCS
• Increases the number of diagnosis codes allowed on a claim	• Increases the field size for ICD codes from 3-5 bytes to 3-7 bytes
• Includes some of the other data modifications in the standards adopted by Medicare FFS	• Increased clinical specificity with over 100,000 additional codes
• Enhanced data elements	• Increased clinical categories by over 1,200
	• Increased procedural specificity with over 190,000 additional codes
	• Allows for alphanumeric codes
	• New procedures for In-patient coding
Requirements	
• Required for submission of ICD-9 and ICD-10 codes	• Required for claim reimbursement on patient discharges starting on October 1, 2013
• New ASC X12 standard acknowledgment and rejection transactions	• Patient discharges prior to October 1, 2013 will be submitted with ICD-9 codes
• Enhanced Electronic Transmission of claims	• Additional specificity will require expanded knowledge of Anatomy and Physiology
• Transaction (TR3) Data Content	• Clinical documentation will be cornerstone to coding accurately
• Present on Admission indicator	
• NPI unique identifier	
• Physical address for billing provider	
• Unique Patient ID 5 Subscriber, not patient	
Contact Holly Gaebel, Coordinator, at (312) 915-9227; hgaebel@himss.org or Pam Matthews CPHIMS, HIMSS, Senior Director of Healthcare Information Systems at (706) 838-0583; pmatthews@himss.org	

© Cengage Learning 2013

Figure 2-11 Interrelationship between v5010 and ICD-10

PCS code sets. Remember that the compliance date for v5010 and the HIPAA transactions is January 1, 2012, for everyone except small health plans. The compliance date for implementation of the ICD-10 code sets is October 1, 2013. The covered entities for both v5010 and ICD-10 are the same, making everyone responsible for ensuring compliance. Read through the format changes. In later chapters, these format changes will be discussed at length, but the main thing to remember at this point is that the ICD-10 code sets will require changes to any software programs used by an organization and that ASC x12 version 5010 will help accommodate those changes. The new ASC x12 v5010 standards will include

- New standard (claim) acknowledgement and rejection transactions
- Enhanced electronic claims transmission
- New transaction data content
  - Present on Admission indicator for acute care facilities
  - National Provider Identifier (NPI)
  - Physical address for the billing provider, and
  - Unique Patient Identifier (PI)

Requirements for ICD-10-CM/PCS include

- Codes must be in use no later than October 1, 2013
- Additional specificity in ICD-10-CM/PCS codes will require expanded knowledge of anatomy and physiology
- The cornerstone to accurate coding will be in the clinical documentation

Let's Review 2–2:

1. The transaction standards that must be in place by January 1, 2012 are:
   a. ICD-10-CM and ICD-10-PCS
   b. ASC x12 v5010
   c. 837 Professional (claim) transaction
   d. ASC x12 version 4010A1
   e. ASC x12 version 276-277

2. Which federal rules/laws require use of the 837-P and 837-I transactions?
   a. HIPAA
   b. ARRA
   c. HITECH
   d. ASC x 12 Standards Committee
   e. NCPDP

3. The 837-P transaction replaces the:
   a. ASC x12 v4010A1
   b. UB-04/CMS1450 institutional paper claim
   c. CMS150 provider paper insurance claim
   d. The 837-I
   e. None of the above

(Continues)

4. CMS recommends that Level I version 5010 internal testing should be complete by:
   a. January 1, 2010
   b. December 31, 2010
   c. January 1, 2011
   d. January 1, 2012
   e. December 31, 2011

5. A code set is/are:
   a. Procedure codes used by physicians
   b. Procedure codes used by hospitals and acute care facilities
   c. Diagnosis codes used by all providers
   d. Any group of codes used to encode data elements
   e. All of the above

6. The ICD-10-PCS are:
   a. Diagnostic codes
   b. Procedure codes used only by physicians
   c. Procedure codes used only by dentists
   d. Procedure codes used by hospitals and acute care facilities
   e. A and D only

Chapter Summary

HIPAA is the acronym for Health Insurance Portability and Accountability Act, a group of federal laws that took effect on August 21, 1996. HIPAA was created, in part, to establish standards for (1) the privacy and security of health care information; and (2) identification of the transactions and code sets required for electronic transmission of health data over the Internet, known as EDI. Administrative Simplification, or Title II, requires use of the ICD-10 code sets and establishes the standards for EDI. The six reasons Congress passed the HIPAA legislation include ease in transfer of health insurance coverage; fighting waste, fraud, and abuse in health insurance and health care delivery; promoting the use of medical savings accounts; improving access to long-term care services and coverage; simplifying the administration of health insurance; and promoting the safe exchange of health data electronically.

HIPAA Title II, Administrative Simplification, includes standards, which promote efficiency and lower overhead costs for the exchange of information electronically, outline requirements to prevent health care fraud and abuse, and require safeguards to protect the privacy and confidentiality of patient records. The Administrative Simplification portion of HIPAA is made up of three main bodies of rules: (1) standards for electronic transmissions, also called transactions, code sets, and identifiers, (2) standards for the privacy of individually identifiable health information, also called the privacy rule, and (3) security standards, also called the security rule.

The Department of Health and Human Services (HHS or DHHS) is responsible for creating the rules and standards of HIPAA, as well as for enforcing HIPAA. It is also responsible for the ARRA and HITECH Acts. The Center for Medicare and Medicaid Services (CMS) is responsible for enforcing all parts of Administrative Simplification except the Privacy Rule. The Office of Civil Rights (OCR) investigates and enforces the rights of individuals who are eligible for services provided by HHS. OCR enforces patient privacy, health plan member privacy, the rights of Medicare and Medicaid beneficiaries, and the HIPAA Privacy and Security Rules. Protected Health Information (PHI) is health information created or maintained by a covered entity or a business associate and includes data elements that identify an individual. HIPAA created an official set of data elements called identifiers. Identifiers include the patient's name, date of birth, social security number, driver's license number, and other data that turns ordinary health information into individually identifiable health information. Electronic Protected Health Information (EPHI) includes PHI that is created, received, maintained, or transmitted electronically.

ARRA/HITECH includes new laws that require implementation of an EHR and the development of HIEs locally, regionally, and nationally. This legislation, which went into effect in January 2010, requires health care data sent electronically (called transactions) to use a specific standard, and mandates the use of ICD-10 diagnostic and procedure code sets.

Title XIII of ARRA is called the Health Information Technology for Economic and Clinical Health (HITECH) Act , and deals with many of the health information communication and technology provisions of HIPAA and ARRA. On January 16, 2009, HHS announced the final rules for 5010 and ICD-10, intended to improve patient care quality, enhance claim processing, improve reporting, and promote interoperability Compliance dates are (1) January 1, 2012 for the ASC x12 Version 5010, Version D.0 and Version 3.0 with small health plans having until January 2013 for Version 3.0 compliance, and (2) October 1, 2013, for implementation of ICD-10-CM and ICD-10-PCS to replace ICD-9-CD.

HIPAA, especially Title II's Administrative Simplification rules, created standards for EDI between health care organizations—including providers, hospitals, insurance carriers, federal and state agencies—and made electronic transactions mandatory for any provider submitting federal or state insurance claims, such as Medicare and Medicaid. They created specific standards for each type of health care transaction. A transaction is the exchange of information between two parties to carry out financial or administrative activities related to health care. A transaction standard clearly defines the data elements and the order of the data elements that make up a single transaction. There is a standard for electronic submission of health insurance claims, checking on the status of submitted insurance claims, and verification of insurance benefits, and several others. In the Transactions portion of the Administrative Simplification rule, HIPAA mandated that eight key tasks, or business transactions, must be standardized when that information is exchanged electronically:

- Verification of insurance eligibility.
- Enrollment in insurance plans.
- Inquiries into the status of insurance claims.
- Submission of insurance claims (institutional, professional, dental).
- Billing and claims receipt acknowledgment.
- Electronic remittance advice.
- Insurance premium payment.
- Referrals and authorizations.

The standard is called ANSI ASC X12 standard. HHS adopted this X12 standard and modified it to meet the needs of specific information exchanges in the health care industry. HHS used the existing X12 standard to create 12 HIPAA standards for electronic transactions. The 271, Health Plan Eligibility Response, is sent from the health plan to the Provider, and is a reply to a 270 request. A 276, Health Care Claim Status Request, is sent from the provider or provider's billing service to the health plan to determine the status of the claim or whether the claim has been processed, and the 277, Health Care Claim, is the response from the health plan. The 278 is a combined transaction for Certification and Authorization of Referrals. The 820, Health Plan Premium Payments, is sent from an employer or employer's bank to the health plan or health plan's bank for routine payment of a health plan premium. The 835 transaction, Health Care Claim Payment or Remittance Advice, is sent from the health plan or health plan's bank to the provider or provider's bank. There are three forms of the 837 transaction. The 837-P or 837 Professional, is sent from a provider or provider's billing service to the health plan. It is the electronic form of the paper, or hard copy, insurance claim form called the CMS1500. An 837 Institutional (837-I) transaction comes from a provider facility, such as a hospital. The information in an

837 Institutional is the electronic equivalent of the UB-04/CMS1450 paper form. The third form is the 837 Dental (837-D) transaction, which comes from a dentist's office. The information in the 837 Dental is the electronic equivalent of the ADA paper form. The 275, Health Care Claims Attachment, transaction is not yet a HIPAA standard, but will allow for the transmission of data other than text, which the ASC x12 transactions are. Unlike the other transactions, Health Level 7 (HL7) sets the standards for claims attachments since it is capable of capturing of data in electronic form, including photographs, x-rays, and other types of multimedia information.

ARRA/HITECH rules updated the ASC x12 standards that were to be used to a newer version which must replace the old versions no later than January 1, 2012. The new versions are:

- Providers (including hospitals): ANSI ASC X12 version 5010 (v5010)

- Pharmacy: ANSI ASC X12 version D.0 or 3.0 (vD.0 or v3.0)

The covered entities affected by the transition from v40101A to v5010 and vD.0 are providers, such as physicians, rehabilitation clinics and hospitals, health plans, and health care clearinghouses.

A code set is any group of codes used for encoding data elements. Data elements include tables of terms, medical concepts, medical diagnostic codes, and medical procedure codes. Code sets also include codes that are a part of the ANSI X12 v 5010 transaction set, as well as CPT codes, CDT codes, ICD 9-CM, ICD-10-CM, and ICD-10-PCS codes, and others.

Review

Matching

Instructions: Match the key term to the appropriate definition.

_____ 1. electronic data interchange (EDI)

_____ 2. Electronic Protected Health Information (EPHI)

_____ 3. Health Insurance Portability and Accountability Act (HIPAA)

_____ 4. Identifiers

_____ 5. Treatment

_____ 6. Payment

_____ 7. Health care operations

_____ 8. Transaction

_____ 9. Transaction standard

_____ 10. Health Information Exchange (HIE)

a. Laws that allow individuals to maintain insurance coverage, and establish standards for the privacy, security and electronic transmission of health data across the internet.

b. The electronic movement of health-related information among organizations according to nationally recognized standards

c. Administrative, financial, legal, and quality-improvement activities of a covered entity that are necessary to run its business

d. The exchange of health data electronically across the internet

e. Exchange of information between two parties to carry out financial or administrative activities related to health care

f. Defines the data elements and the order of the data elements that make up a single transaction

g. Provision, coordination, or management of health care and related services among health care providers or by a health care provider with a third party

h. PHI in electronic form

i. Various activities of health care providers to get paid or be reimbursed for their services

j. Any data that could reveal the identity of a patient

Short Answer

Instructions: Write brief responses to the following.

1. Briefly describe the transaction and code sets part of HIPAA
   a. Transactions: _____
   b. Code Sets: _____

2. What is EDI?
   a. _____

3. Name three reasons why Congress passed the Health Insurance Portability and Privacy Act.
   a. _____
   b. _____
   c. _____

4. List five types of health care systems.
   a. _____
   b. _____
   c. _____
   d. _____
   e. _____

5. List two provisions of the HIPAA Title II laws.
   a. _____
   b. _____

6. List two provisions of the ARRA Title XIII/HITECH Act.
   a. _____
   b. _____

7. Name three federal agencies involved in HIPAA and briefly describe their purpose.
   a. _____
   b. _____
   c. _____

8. List five of the eight transactions standardized by the HIPAA rules.
   a. _____
   b. _____
   c. _____
   d. _____
   e. _____

9. Name the new transaction standards that must be in place for providers by January 1, 2012.
   a. _____

10. Describe the 837-P transaction and what paper form it replaces.
    a. _____

Multiple Choice

Instructions: Circle the most appropriate response.

1. Another name for the HIPAA laws is:
   a. Kennedy-Kasselbaum Act
   b. Public Law 104-191 (H.R. 3103)
   c. The American Hospital Association Act
   d. A and B

2. One of the reasons HIPAA was enacted was to:
   a. Promote the safe exchange of health data electronically
   b. Prevent medical malpractice
   c. Create rules for establishing an Electronic Health Record
   d. Create Health Information Exchanges

3. Title II of HIPAA includes:
   a. ICD-10 Code Sets and ASC x12 v5010 transactions
   b. Health care insurance access, portability, renewability
   c. Administrative simplification, medical liability reform, preventing health care fraud and abuse
   d. Tax related health provisions, revenue offsets

4. The deadline for implementing Version 5010 transactions in all health care organizations is:
   a. October 1, 2013
   b. January 1, 2012
   c. October 1, 2012
   d. January 1, 2013

5. One important difference between ANSI ASC x12 version 5010 (v5010) transactions and Health Level 7 (HL7) transactions is that:
   a. V5010 is only capable of electronic transmission of text files; HL7 can transmit digital images
   b. HL7 is only capable of electronic transmission of text files; v5010 can transmit digital images
   c. V5010 is for electronic transmission of health insurance claims; HL7 is for electronic transmission of pharmacy claims
   d. HL7 is for electronic transmission of health insurance claims; v5010 is for electronic transmission of pharmacy claims.

6. An 837-P transaction is used for:
   a. Electronic transmission of professional (physician) insurance claims
   b. Electronic transmission of hospital inpatient claims
   c. Electronic transmission of health insurance claim status requests
   d. Electronic transmission of dental insurance claims

7. The benefits of an electronic health record (EHR) include all of the following except:
   a. Easy and efficient access to patient records—no lost charts.
   b. Easy to transfer patient information to other physicians (this benefit could be compromised if there is no standardization).
   c. Allows for insurance claim attachments
   d. Integrates with patient medicine or prescription software and helps alert to drug interactions and patient allergies.

8. The provisions of ARRA/HITECH specific to ICD-10 implementation include:
    a. Meaningful Use
    b. Health Information Exchange
    c. Privacy and Security
    d. All of the above

9. Look at Figure 2-6, on the line labeled NM103, Patient Last Name. What is the allowable length of the field on the ASC x12 v5010 transaction?
    a. 1-60
    b. 1-25
    c. AN
    d. R

10. Look at Figure 2-7. What are the values for the ISA12, Interchange Control Number, in the old v4010a and the new v5010:
    a. V4010a: 00601; v5010: 00401
    b. V4010a: 00401, v5010: 00601
    c. V4010a: CCYYMMDD; v5010: CCYYMMDD
    d. Both versions are 00601

11. Column five of the ASC x12 v5010 transaction guide indicates:
    a. Whether the field is required (R), never used (NU), or suggested (S)
    b. The allowable values for the field
    c. How many characters may be used in the field
    d. The description of the code/identifier

12. A code set is/are:
    f. Procedure codes used by physicians
    g. Procedure codes used by hospitals and acute care facilities
    h. Diagnosis codes used by all providers
    i. Any group of codes used to encode data elements
    j. All of the above

General Equivalency Mappings

Learning Objectives

At the conclusion of this chapter, the learner should be able to:

- Describe what General Equivalency Mappings (GEMs) are, and their uses
- Know what types of GEMs are available, and where to find them
- Describe the benefits and disadvantages of GEMs
- Identify the structure of General Equivalency Maps
- Understand the concepts of one-to-one, one-to-many, and combination code mappings
- Describe what General Equivalency Maps can and cannot be used for
- Identify the 10 steps for using GEMs
- Understand the purpose and definition of Medicare Severity-Diagnosis Related Groups (MS-DRGs), and how they relate to diagnostic and procedural coding
- Identify the relationship between billing, reimbursement, and diagnostic and procedural coding
- Know the difference between GEMs for coding, reimbursement, and MS-DRGs
- Identify how to find the GEMs for Reimbursement
- Describe the uses and contraindications for Reimbursement GEMs
- Describe what v26 MS-DRG conversion GEMs are and their uses

Key Terms and Definitions

Applied mapping	Technique used when goal is to translate ICD-10-CM/PCS codes back to ICD-9-CM codes so that an application can continue to be used.
Attributes	Designate if the GEM match can be a combination or cluster (4th character), and which type the match is, i.e. combination is represented by the number 1 and cluster codes are represented by the number 2 in the 5th character position.
Backward (reverse) mapping	Going from new to old, i.e. ICD-10-CM or ICD-10-PCS to ICD-9-CM.
Coding Clinic	Quarterly coding advice guidelines created by the American Hospital Association (AHA).

Combination (codes)	When one ICD-9-CM or ICD-10-CM code contains more than one.
Cluster (codes)	When more than one ICD-10-CM or ICD-10-PCS code is required to make a complete translation of one ICD-9-CM code.
Conversion	Approach to take when migrating coding data systems and applications in such a way that the same general action is taken whether the encounter is coded in ICD-9-CM or ICD-10-CM/PCS, or when the goal is to improve data accuracy by taking advantage of the increased detail in ICD-10-CM/PCS.
Forward mapping	Going from old to new, i.e. ICD-9-CM to ICD-10-CM/PCS.
Flags	On GEMs indicate whether a match exists, and whether it is a one-to-one match, or a one-to-many match.
General Equivalency Mappings (GEMs)	Translation "maps" or guides to find equivalent, or near-equivalent translations from ICD-9-CM to ICD-10-CM/PCS, and vice versa.
One-to-one	The one "best" matching code.
One-to-many	Searching for all the possible code matches.
Source codes	Originating codes.
Target code	Code being sought.

Introduction

General Equivalency Mappings (GEMs) were created by the Centers for Medicare and Medicaid Services (CMS) to provide translation "crosswalks" between ICD-9-CM codes and ICD-10-CM/PCS codes. There are four types of GEMs available. Two are for diagnostic and procedural coding; the other two are for reimbursement, and conversion of Medicare Severity-Diagnosis Related Groups (MS-DRGs). This chapter will provide an introduction to each GEM, explain how these maps can and cannot be used, and provide instruction in the use of the GEMs. One misconception is that a GEM is a literal, one-to-one mapping between ICD-9-CM and ICD-10-CM/PCS; however, there are very few instances where a direct correlation exists. There are one-to-one mappings, one-to-many, combination, and cluster code relationships, which will be explained in this chapter.

Chapter 3 is written under the assumption that the student already has experience in ICD-9-CM coding. It is designed as a guide to help understand how to transition existing code sets to the new ICD-10-CM and ICD-10-PCS code sets using the GEMs. However, *all* students learning ICD-10-CM and ICD-10-PCS coding–with or without a background in ICD-9-CM–need to understand the concepts of reimbursement, billing, and principal (first-listed) diagnosis; and the purpose and definition of MS-DRGs and their relationship to diagnostic and procedural coding.

General Equivalency Mappings

The new ICD-10-CM and ICD-10-PCS code sets include more specific data and codes which accommodate the ever-changing needs of the health care industry, incorporating changes in medical science, clinical terminology, and technology. For this reason, ICD-10-CM and ICD-10-PCS are replacing ICD-9-CM codes effective from October 1, 2013. The National Center for Health Statistics (NCHS) is the U.S. government agency that, jointly with the CMS, is responsible for the modification of ICD-10-CM. The ICD-9-CM Coordination and Maintenance Committee maintains and updates translation "maps" or guides to find equivalent, or near-equivalent translations from ICD-9-CM to ICD-10-CM/PCS, and vice versa. These maps are called **General Equivalency Mappings**, or GEMs. GEMS were developed to serve a specific, limited, short-term need—to allow the health care industry to migrate their systems, applications, and data from ICD9-CM to ICD-10-CM/PCS. They help make the complex process of translation from one code set to another more meaningful.

Hospitals and coders versed in ICD-9-CM codes and guidelines can use these GEMs as crosswalks to find matching or near-matching ICD-10-CM or ICD-10-PCS codes. There are also GEMs which can be used to translate reimbursement equivalents, as well as map to MS-DRG classifications.

Mapping is not a straightforward correlation between codes of the two classification systems, so caution must be exercised when using them. Never use these maps to classify diagnoses or procedures directly. There are few one-to-one direct matches. Coding from the medical record should only be done using the correct version–and current year–of the coding manual. Optimally, the selection of the best code alternatives should be based upon the available documentation, and the ultimate use of the data. In most instances, the best practice is to code from the medical record directly to the ICD-10-CM or ICD-10-PCS, and ignore the GEMs. The GEMs are guides meant only to assist in the translation and migration of codes in software systems and applications from the old code set (ICD-9-CM) to the new code sets (ICD-10-CM/PCS), and will help point the coder to equivalent codes. In most instances there is not a straightforward alternative in the ICD-10-CM/ PCS for an ICD-9-CM code. General Equivalency Mappings were created to be used as a general translation tool for use by all providers, payers, and data users. They are free of charge, and in public domain for all to use. There are four reasons GEMs are needed: to (1) organize, (2) navigate, (3) identify, and (4) manage.

Organize: The GEMS give all reasonable translation alternatives for the complete meaning of the code being looked up, or the source system code. They include Tabular instructions, index entries, guidelines, and appropriate Coding Clinic advice. **Coding Clinics** are quarterly coding advice guidelines published by the American Hospital Association (AHA) and are the official publication endorsed by the CMS for ICD-9-CM coding guidelines and advice. Their purpose is to promote accuracy and consistency in the use of the ICD-9-CM, and, going forward, the ICD-10-CM. All guidelines and supporting information published in Coding Clinics are approved by the NCHS, CMS, the American Health Information Management Association (AHIMA) and AHA.

Navigate: There may be multiple translation alternatives for a source system code, or just one best alternative. The decision of which code to use is based on which is the closest match, depending upon the need.

Identify: GEMs help identify untranslatable types of information, which is common because ICD-10-CM/ PCS contains so much more specificity and detail. In addition, they identify ICD-10-CM/PCS **clusters**. When more than one ICD-10-CM or ICD-10-PCS code is required to make a complete translation of one ICD-9-CM code, this is called a **cluster**. The importance of identifying clusters will be revealed later in this chapter.

Manage: Some concepts expressed by one ICD-10-CM or ICD-10-PCS code need more than one ICD-9-CM code for a complete translation, and vice versa.

Diagnosis Codes and Levels of Specificity

Instead of a simple crosswalk, the GEM files attempt to organize differences in a meaningful way, by linking a code to all valid alternatives in the other code set from which choices can be made, depending on how the code is to be used. It is important to understand the kinds of differences that need to be reconciled in linking coded data. The method used to reconcile these differences may vary, depending on whether the data is used for research, claims adjudication, or analyzing coding patterns between the two code sets. When the desired outcome is to look at all the possible code matches, it is called **one-to-many** mapping. If it is to find the one "best" compromise, this is known as **one-to-one** mapping. The scope of the differences varies, is complex, and cannot be overlooked if quality mapping and useful coded data are the desired outcomes.

Figure 3-1 illustrates that ICD-10-CM codes may be have more characters than an ICD-9-CM code. In addition, there are about five times as many of them. ICD-10 is much more specific than ICD-9-CM, and, just as important for purposes of mapping, the level of precision in an ICD-10 code is more consistent

I-9 and I-10 Code Sets Compared:

Code Length and Set Size

Comparison	ICD-9-CM	ICD-10-CM
# of Characters	3-5 Numeric (+V and E codes)	3-7 Alphanumeric
# of codes	~13,500	~68,000

© Cengage Learning 2013

Figure 3-1 Comparison of ICD-9-CM and ICD-10-CM Code Lengths and Code Set Size

within clinically pertinent ranges of codes. For example, ICD-9-CM category 733, *other disorders of bone and cartilage*, contains the codes:

- 733.93 *Stress fracture of tibia or fibula*
- 733.94 *Stress fracture of the metatarsals*
- 733.95 *Stress fracture of other bone*
- 733.96 *Stress fracture of femoral neck*
- 733.97 *Stress fracture of shaft of femur*
- 733.98 *Stress fracture of pelvis*

Five of the six codes specify the exact site of the fracture. One code, 733.95, is an "umbrella" code for all other bones in this anatomical location. In practical terms this means that code 733.95 represents more than one possible fracture site. Diagnoses that are identified by umbrella codes lose their uniqueness as coded data. When only the coded ICD-9-CM data is available, it is impossible to tell which bone was fractured. On the other hand, in many instances ICD-10-CM provides specific codes for all likely sites of a stress fracture, including more specificity for the bones of the extremities, the pelvis, and the vertebra. Stress fracture data coded in ICD-10 possesses a consistent level of specificity. Note in Figure 3-2 the increased specificity for a stress fracture in

M84.35	**Stress fracture, pelvis and femur**	
	Stress fracture, hip	
	M84.350	Stress fracture, pelvis
	M84.351	Stress fracture, right femur
	M84.352	Stress fracture, left femur
	M84.353	Stress fracture, unspecified femur
	M84.359	Stress fracture, hip, unspecified
M84.36	**Stress fracture, tibia and fibula**	
	M84.361	Stress fracture, right tibia
	M84.362	Stress fracture, left tibia
	M84.363	Stress fracture, right fibula
	M84.364	Stress fracture, left fibula
	M84.369	Stress fracture, unspecified tibia and fibula
M84.37	**Stress fracture, ankle, foot and toes**	
	M84.371	Stress fracture, right ankle
	M84.372	Stress fracture, left ankle
	M84.373	Stress fracture, unspecified ankle
	M84.374	Stress fracture, right foot
	M84.375	Stress fracture, left foot
	M84.376	Stress fracture, unspecified foot
	M84.377	Stress fracture, right toe(s)
	M84.378	Stress fracture, left toe(s)
	M84.379	Stress fracture, unspecified toe(s)

© Cengage Learning 2013

Figure 3-2 Stress Fracture Codes in ICD-10-CM

anatomical location and laterality in the ICD-10-CM. For example, the fracture can be of the ankle only, the entire foot, or the toes, of either the left or right side.

Other Differences between ICD-9-CM and ICD-10-CM

There are significant terminology differences between ICD-9-CM and ICD-10-CM. In addition, there are differences in meaning and definitions, as well as other differences impacting the comparison of data between the two code sets. Table 3-1 illustrates differences in terminology between ICD-9-CM and ICD-10-CM.

Table 3-1 Terminology Differences between ICD-9-CM and ICD-10-CM

ICD-9-CM	ICD-10-CM
Fracture: • Open, closed	• Open, closed • Salter-Harris Types I, II, III and IV • Lefort I, II, and III • Avulsion • Wedge compression • Stable and unstable burst Zone I, II, and III • Barton's, Smith's • Greenstick, transverse, oblique, spiral, comminuted, segmental, torus • Maisonneuve's open fracture types I, II, IIIA, IIIB, IIIC with delayed healing
Asthma: • Extrinsic, intrinsic • Chronic obstructive asthma w/status asthmaticus • Chronic obstructive asthma w/(acute) exacerbation • Exercise-induced bronchospasm • Cough variant asthma	• Mild intermittent • Mild persistent • Moderate persistent • Severe persistent w/status asthmaticus • Severe persistent w/(acute) exacerbation • Exercise-induced bronchospasm • Cough variant asthma (Chronic obstructive asthma is classified to COPD)
• Open wound, laceration • Penetrating wound or penetration • Traumatic amputation complicated w/tendon involvement	• Avulsion, laceration • Penetrating wound • Puncture wound • Open bite • Traumatic amputation (Complicated aspects specifically identified in either the same code or separately)
• Aftercare • Late effect • Complications, surgical procedure	• Subsequent encounter • Sequela • Intraoperative complication • Postprocedural complication

Note for example *complications, surgical procedure* in the ICD-9-CM. ICD-10-CM adds additional terminology to identify whether the complication was intraoperative (during the procedure) or a complication that arose after the procedure was completed. Asthma illustrates another interesting difference between ICD-9-CM and ICD-10-CM. First, *chronic asthma* is no longer classified with other asthma conditions in the ICD-10-CM, instead, it is classified to *chronic obstructive pulmonary disease (COPD)*. In addition, the severity has several levels in the ICD-10, ranking from *mild intermittent* to *mild persistent* to *moderate* and *severe persistent*, with or without *status asthmaticus*. A big difference in terminology is in the fractures category. In ICD-9-CM the two main types of fractures are open and closed, while in ICD-10-CM, there are over a dozen types listed, describing types of fractures as well as levels of severity and location. This is one area especially where a firm foundation both in medical terminology and anatomy and physiology is essential.

There are other differences between terms in ICD-9-CM and in ICD-10-CM that impact data comparisons. For example, myocardial infarction (MI) code descriptions in ICD-9-CM include episodes of care, and define post–myocardial infarction treatment as still being acute if follow-up care is within eight weeks of the initial MI. In ICD-10-CM, the MI is coded as acute if the follow-up care occurs within four weeks, rather than eight, of the initial MI. Additionally, there is no episode of care requirement. Another example is in the cutoff date between abortion and fetal death. In ICD-9-CM it is considered a fetal death, not an abortion, after 22 weeks gestation, but in the ICD-10-CM it is considered fetal death after the 20th week. The ICD-9-CM also requires an episode of care for obstetrics coding. The ICD-10-CM does not require an episode of care, but does require identification of the trimester. Table 3-2 outlines other differences that impact data comparisons. Note especially that *Septicemia NOS* and *Sepsis* are coded to different chapters and categories of the two code sets.

Diagnosis Codes in Combination

One ICD-9-CM or ICD-10-CM code can contain more than one diagnosis. For purposes of mapping, these are called **combination codes**. A combination code consists of more than one diagnosis. For example, a combination code can consist of a chronic condition with a current acute manifestation, as in ICD-9-CM code 250.21, *Diabetes with hyperosmolarity, type I (juvenile type), not stated as uncontrolled*. Or a combination code can consist of two acute conditions found together, as in ICD-10-CM code R65.21 *Severe sepsis with septic shock*. Or a combination code can consist of an acute condition and its external cause, as in ICD-10-CM code T58.01 *Toxic effect of carbon monoxide from motor vehicle exhaust, accidental (unintentional)*. If a combination code in one code set has a corresponding combination code

Table 3-2 Other Differences that Impact Data Comparison between ICD-9-CM and ICD-10-CM

ICD-9-CM	ICD-10-CM
Tuberculosis	Tuberculosis
Codes are differentiated by confirmation method	There is no distinction between methods of confirmation when coding
Septicemia NOS	Septicemia NOS
Classified to Infection Diseases chapter and Septicemia category	Classified to Bacteremia code in Symptoms chapter
Sepsis	Sepsis
Classified to type of infection + SIRS subcategory code (SIRS: Systemic Inflammatory Response Syndrome)	Classified to type of infection in Infectious Diseases chapter

in the other code set, then the two entries are linked in the usual way. It is only when a combination code in one set is broken into discrete diagnosis codes in the other set that another method of mapping is needed.

Mapping in cases where a combination code in one set corresponds to two or more discrete diagnosis codes in the other set requires the combination code to be linked as a unit to two or more codes in the other code set. Each discrete diagnosis code is a partial expression of the information contained in the combination code and must be linked together as one GEM entry to fully describe the same conditions specified in the combination code. Entries of this type are linked using a special mapping flag that indicates the allowable choices.

For example, in Figure 3-3, a mapping of combination codes from ICD-9-CM to ICD-10-CM, notice that code 115.11, *histoplasmosis duboisii meningitis*, requires two codes in the ICD-10-CM, B39.5 to identify the *Histoplasmosis duboisii* (etiology) and G02 to describe the *meningitis* (manifestation). Similarly, in Figure 3-4, illustrating ICD-10-CM to ICD-9-CM combination code mapping, only one code, I25.710 for *atherosclerosis of autologous vein coronary artery bypass grafts, with unstable angina pectoris*, requires two codes to map back to ICD-9-CM, 414.02 for the *coronary atherosclerotic autologous vein bypass graft*, and 411.1 for the *intermediate coronary syndrome* (describing the angina).

I-9 to I-10 mapping, combination entry:

Histoplasma duboisii meningitis

ICD-9-CM Source	to	ICD-10-CM Target
115.11 Histoplasma duboisii meningitis	≈	B39.5 Histoplasmosis duboisii **AND** G02 Meningitis in other infectious and parasitic diseases classified elsewhere

© Cengage Learning 2013

Figure 3-3 ICD-9-CM to ICD-10-CM Combination Code Mapping

I-10 to I-9 mapping, combination entry:

Atherosclerosis of autologous vein coronary artery bypass graft(s) with unstable angina pectoris

ICD-10-CM Source	to	ICD-9-CM Target
125.710 Atherosclerosis of autologous vein coronary artery bypass graft(s) with unstable angina pectoris	≈	414.02 Coronary atherosclerosis of autologous vein bypass graft **AND** 411.1 Intermediate coronary syndrome

© Cengage Learning 2013

Figure 3-4 ICD-10-CM to ICD-9-CM Combination Code Mapping

Let's Review 3–1:

1. General Equivalency Mappings (GEMs) are:
   a. Translation maps that assist in finding equivalent codes between ICD-9 and ICD-10
   b. Designed to help the health care industry migrate from ICD-9 to ICD-10
   c. Seldom exact matches
   d. All of the above

2. Coding Clinics are:
   a. Classes/seminars held by the American Health Information Association to teach ICD-10 coding
   b. Quarterly coding advice guidelines published by the American Hospital Association
   c. Coding classes taught by the Medicare Learning Network (part of The Centers for Medicare and Medicaid Services)
   d. None of the above

3. In the GEMs, a cluster is defined as:
   a. When more than one ICD-10-CM or ICD-10-PCS code is required to make a complete translation of one ICD-9-CM code
   b. When more than one ICD-9-CM code is required to make a complete translation of one ICD-10-CM or ICD-10-PCS code
   c. When several codes have a same or similar meaning
   d. When one code can have more than one meaning

4. In the GEMs, a combination is defined as:
   a. When an ICD-9 or ICD-10 code description contains more than one diagnosis
   b. When only an ICD-10 code contains more than one diagnosis
   c. When only an ICD-9 code contains more than one diagnosis
   d. When an ICD-9 or ICD-10 code description contains only one diagnosis

5. A one-to-one match means:
   a. There is an approximate match between one code in the ICD-9 and one in the ICD-10
   b. Either a cluster or combination code match exists
   c. There is an exact match between one code in the ICD-9 and one code in the ICD-10
   d. None of the above

6. A conversion is:
   a. A type of approach to take when migrating old coding data/applications to the new ICD-10 code sets
   b. A type of approach to take when mapping the new ICD-10-CM code set back to a legacy system
   c. Moving from the new code set (ICD-10) to the old code set (ICD-9) when using the GEMs
   d. All of the above

General Equivalency Mappings for Diagnostic Coding

Mappings between ICD-9-CM and ICD-10-CM attempt to find a corresponding diagnosis code or codes between the two code sets. In some areas of classification the correlation between codes is fairly close, and since the two code sets share the conventions of organization and formatting common to both revisions of the International Classification of Diseases, translating between them is straightforward. Many infectious disease, neoplasm, eye, and ear codes are examples of fairly straightforward correlation between the two code sets. In other areas—obstetrics, for example—whole chapters are organized along a different axis of classification. In such cases, translating between them can, the majority of the time, offer only a series of possible compromises, rather than the mirror image of one code in the other code set. Figure 3-5 is an example of a straightforward match between ICD-9-CM and ICD-10-CM. The equal sign between the first two columns indicates the match is exact.

I-10 Description	Correlation	I-9 Description	Unequal Axis of classification
A02.21 Salmonella meningitis	=	003.21 Salmonella meningitis	None
C92.01 Acute myeloid leukemia, in remission	=	205.01 Myeloid leukemia, acute, in remission	None

Figure 3-5 Example of Exact Match between ICD-9-CM and ICD-10-CM

Unfortunately, most codes do not map directly from ICD-9-CM to ICD-10-CM and vice versa. For example, in Figure 3-6, the equal sign between the first two columns has a slash through it, indicating there is no direct match. In this case, more information about the trimester of the pregnancy would need to be abstracted from the medical record, in order to choose the appropriate ICD-10-CM code. Note too, that ICD-9-CM codes reference an episode of care. Episodes of care are not used in the ICD-10-CM. At this point, if the medical documentation stated *spotting, complicating pregnancy, second trimester*, it is now possible to select O26.852 as the probable ICD-10-CM code. The next step would be to review the code description for O26.852 in the Tabular List in the ICD-10-CM code manual to confirm it matches the medical documentation exactly.

I-10 Description	Correlation	I-9 Description	Unequal Axis of classification
O26.851 Spotting complicating pregnancy, first trimester O26.852 Spotting complicating pregnancy, second trimester O26.853 Spotting complicating pregnancy, third trimester O26.859 Spotting complicating pregnancy, unspecified trimester	≠	649.50 Spotting complicating pregnancy, unspecified episode of care 649.51 Spotting complicating pregnancy, delivered 649.53 Spotting complicating pregnancy, antepartum	Stage of pregnancy (I-10) vs. Episode of care (I-9)

Figure 3-6 Example of No Match between ICD-9-CM and ICD-10-CM

Migration Choices for Systems and Applications

There are two choices when migrating from ICD-9-CM to ICD-10-CM/PCS, **conversion** or **applied mapping**. If the goal of the health care organization is to migrate coding data systems and applications in such a way that the same general action is taken whether the encounter is coded in ICD-9-CM or ICD-10-CM/PCS, or, more importantly, if the goal is to improve data accuracy by taking advantage of the increased detail in ICD-10-CM/PCS, then the choice should be to convert the applications to ICD-10-CM/PCS. With this choice, the goal would be to convert, or upgrade, existing systems and applications—or lease or purchase new systems—to ICD-10-CM/PCS, which would require field length changes and other programming adjustments to accommodate the new codes. Remember, too, that these systems would also need to be upgraded to the ASC X12 version 5010 transactions as well. This choice, unlike applied mapping, is a massive project and very costly, since all applications will either be completely updated, or new systems that already accommodate the new transactions and code sets purchased or leased. If the goal of the health care organization is to translate incoming ICD-10-CM/PCS codes back to ICD-9-CM codes so that ICD-9-CM applications can continue to be used, then applied mapping might be an appropriate choice. Two examples where this might be useful are reimbursement applications, and those using MS-DRG data. The same upgrades would need to be made to existing applications and software as with the conversion option, but depending upon the application and use, it might be less costly since it is a phased approach rather than the "all-at-once" approach of the conversion option. Another example where applied mapping could be useful is as an interim measure while applications are being converted to an ICD-10-CM/PCS-based application.

General Equivalency Mapping: ICD-9-CM to ICD-10-CM

AHIMA gives the following guidelines for using the General Equivalency Maps after a search of all applications in the health care organization that look at or use ICD-9-CM codes.

- For converting applications to ICD-10-CM/PCS, perform a reverse lookup using an ICD-10-CM/PCS to ICD-9-CM GEM

- To translate historical data, use an ICD-9-CM to ICD-10-CM/PCS GEM

- Use bidirectional GEMs when working with small conversion projects, with access to original records or additional clinical information, or for forecasting, planning, and general education

These maps are bidirectional—in other words, maps from ICD-9-CM to ICD-10-CM/PCS are available, as well as maps from ICD-10-CM/PCS to ICD-9-CM. GEMs are structured by source and target. The originating codes are the **source** codes, and the code being sought is the **target** code. For example, if the original code is ICD-9-CM and an ICD-10-CM code is needed, the ICD-9-CM code is the source, and the ICD-10-CM code is the target. Going from ICD-9-CM to ICD-10-CM/PCS is called **forward mapping** (going from old to new). Searching for an ICD-9-CM code, when the source code is ICD-10-CM or PCS is called **backward** or **reverse mapping** (going from new to old).

Figure 3-7 is an example of a forward mapping GEM for diagnosis codes. As GEMs are all text files, it is recommended that they be uploaded into Microsoft Excel or another spreadsheet software application to make them easier to use. Remember, these GEMs only point toward possible matches between the two code sets. It will always be necessary to confirm the code or codes found in the Tabular List of the code manual to ensure that the code selected is appropriate and accurate for its intended use. If the intended use is to translate an assigned diagnosis or procedure code from a medical record, the code chosen must also be compared against the original medical record documentation to ensure accuracy.

In Figure 3-7, in the first column are the **source** codes which are all ICD-10-CM diagnosis codes. For those familiar with the ICD-9-CM code, note that the decimal normally found after the third character is not used. The second column contains the **target** codes, in this case ICD-10-CM diagnosis codes. Before looking at the third column, it is necessary to know what each of the numbers in the third column represent. Because the ICD-10-CM/PCS codes contain much more specificity and complexity, it is seldom possible

```
File   Edit   Format   View   Help
0010          A000            00000
0011          A001            00000
0019          A009            00000
0020          A0100           10000
0021          A011            00000
0022          A012            00000
0023          A013            00000
0029          A014            00000
0030          A020            00000
0031          A021            00000
00320         A0220           00000
00321         A0221           00000
00322         A0222           00000
00323         A0223           00000
00324         A0224           00000
00329         A0229           10000
0038          A028            00000
0039          A029            00000
```

© Cengage Learning 2013

Figure 3-7 Excerpt from ICD-9-CM to ICD-10-CM General Equivalency Map

to map an ICD-9-CM code directly to an ICD-10-CM or PCS code. What the third column numbers indicate are essentially how closely matched the codes are to one another (approximate), and whether cluster or combination codes exist. The first three characters in the third column are **flags** that indicate whether a match exists, and whether it is a one-to-one match or a one-to-many match. The last two characters in the third column are attributes. **Attributes** designate whether the match can be a combination or cluster (4th character), and which type of match it is, i.e. a combination is represented by the number 1 and cluster codes are represented by the number 2 in the 5th character position. Each number in the third column signifies the following flags or attributes. The flags are read as 1 = On, and 0 = Off.

- Flag (Approximate): First Character in the Third Column
  - The translation is an approximate match = 1
  - An exact match exists = 0
- Flag: Second Character in Third Column
  - No plausible translation for source system code = 1
  - There is at least one plausible translation for source system code = 0
- Flag: Third Character in Third Column
  - Code maps to more than one code = 1
  - Code maps to a single code = 0
- Attribute: Fourth Character in Third Column
  - If the third character was 1, indicating a one-to-many match exists, the fourth character indicates that a combination or cluster code does (or does not) exist. In most instances, if there is a 1 in the 3rd character field, the 4th character will be also be a 1 to indicate yes. A 0 will indicate there is not a combination or cluster code match.
- Attribute: Fifth Character in Third Column
  - 1 = Combination codes exist
  - 2 = Cluster codes exist

Here are some examples of how the flags work. These are reverse mapping examples from an ICD-10-PCS (procedure) code to an ICD-9-CM (procedure) code.

- Examples for First Character
  - Example of approximate but not identical match (1)
    - T1500xA   9300   **1**0111
    - T1500xA   E914   **1**0112
      - Each of these codes is an Approximate match
  - Example of diagnosis Identical match (0)
    - 41411   I2542   **0**0000
      - ICD-9-CM code 414.11 is an Identical match to ICD-10-CM code I2542
- Examples for Second Character

ICD-10-PCS	ICD-9-CM	Flag
- T500x6A	NODX	1**1**000
- T500x6D	NODX	1**1**000
- T500x6S	NODX	1**1**000

- **T500x6A** Underdosing of mineralocorticoids and their antagonists, initial encounter
  - *Maps to* NODX No description found (Notice the NODX "No Description Found" entry instead of a code number in middle column)
- **T500x6D** Underdosing of mineralocorticoids and their antagonists, subsequent encounter
  - *Maps to* NODX No description found
- **T500x6S** Underdosing of mineralocorticoids and their antagonists, sequela
  - *Maps to* NODX No description found
- Examples for Third Character

ICD-10-PCS	ICD-9-CM	Flags
- T1500xA	9300	10**1**12
- T1500xA	E914	10**1**12
- T1500xD	9300	10**1**12
- T1500xD	E914	10**1**12
- T1500xS	9085	10**0**00

- **T1500xA** Foreign body in cornea, unspecified eye, initial encounter
  - *Maps to ICD-9 cluster* (Flag 3 is 1)
    - 9300 Corneal foreign body (ICD-9-Code)
    - E914 Foreign body accidentally entering eye and adnexa (ICD-9 Code)
- **T1500xD** Foreign body in cornea, unspecified eye, subsequent encounter
  - *Maps to ICD-9 cluster* (Flag 3 is 1)
    - 9300 Corneal foreign body
    - E914 Foreign body accidentally entering eye and adnexa
- **T1500xS** Foreign body in cornea, unspecified eye, sequela (Flag 3 is 0)
  - *Maps to* 9085 Late effect of foreign body in orifice

Looking again at Figure 3-7, the source code (ICD-9-CM) is 0010, and the target (ICD-10-CM) is A000. The five zeros (00000) in the fifth column indicate there is a direct (exact) match. In other words, 0010 is an exact match to A000. The next two source codes, 0011 and 0019, are also exact matches to the target codes, A001 and A009, respectively. If the need is to code a diagnosis from a medical record, the medical record drives the code selection. If the need is to map to reimbursement or an MS-DRG, the reimbursement or MS-DRG application drives the code selection. In this illustration, some of the codes have exact matches, and a few do not have an exact match, such as source code 0020 and target code A0100, or source code 00329 and target code A0229. If there is an approximate match, but no indication that there is a combination or cluster code attribute, then a comparison of the source and target codes must be done using the appropriate coding manuals.

Figure 3-8 contains forward mapping (ICD-9-CM to ICD-10-CM) examples of both cluster and combination diagnostic code equivalent mapping. Look at Table 3-3, which illustrates how to read GEMs using several of the ICD-9-CM diagnostic source codes in Figure 3-8, starting with code 04112.

04100	B955	00000
04101	B950	00000
04102	B951	00000
04103	B954	10000
04104	B952	00000
04105	B954	10000
04109	B954	10000
04110	B958	00000
04111	B956	00000
04112	B956	10111
04112	Z16	10112
04119	B957	00000

© Cengage Learning 2013

Figure 3-8 GEM Illustrating Cluster and Combination Code Mappings

Using source code 04112, *Methacillin-resistant Staphylococcus aureus (MRSA)* in the ICD-9-CM in the first row of Table 3-3, the general ICD-10 tabular reference is B956, *Staphylococcus aureus as the cause of disease classified elsewhere*, which is an approximate—but not exact—match, thus the 1 in the first character space of the third column. Based on the 2nd character flag, there is no exact match, and the 3rd character flag of 1 indicates there is a one-to-many match available of either a cluster or combination code. The fifth character of 1 indicates that the code match will be a combination of codes.

Table 3-3 Reading the GEMs

Source	Target	Third Column				
ICD-9	ICD-10	Flags			Attributes	
		1st Character	2nd Character	3rd Character	4th Character	5th Character
		Type of Match?	Plausible Translation?	# of Codes Mapped?	Cluster/Combo?	Type
04112	B956	1–Approximate	0 = Yes	1–More than 1	1–Yes	1–Combo
04112	Z16	1–Approximate	0 = Yes	1–More than 1	1–Yes	2–Cluster
04119	B957	0–Exact	0 = Yes	0–Single Code	0–No (see 3rd character)	0–Neither

Look at Figure 3-9, an excerpt from code 041.12 in the ICD-9-CM. The code description is *Methacillin-resistant Staphylococcus aureus (MRSA)*. Now, compare the code description with Figure 3-10, an excerpt from code B95.6 in the ICD-10-CM, *Staphylococcus aureus as the cause of disease classified elsewhere*. It is probably difficult to understand how the same code can map to more than one code. Using the first line of Table 3-3, the description of diagnosis code 041.12 in the Tabular List of the ICD-9-CM is *methicillin-resistant Staphylococcus aureus*. The difference becomes even clearer when looking at code B95.6 in the ICD-10-CM. There, the description only describes *Staphylococcus aureus as the cause of diseases classified elsewhere*, with no mention of the methicillin-resistance. Going back to the first row of Table 3-3, B95.6 maps to one part of the diagnostic statement and ICD-9-CM code—the *Staphylococcus aureus*. Another code is needed to match 041.12 directly to B95.6. In this example, it is the Z16 ICD-10-CM code on the second row of Table 3-3. The code description for Z16 is infection with drug-resistant microorganism, which matches the rest of ICD-9-code 041.12. Therefore, in order to forward map 041.12 from the ICD-9-CM to the ICD-10-CM, two codes are needed, B95.6 and Z16. The only step left is to determine the manifestation (infection) source from the medical record, find the ICD-9-CM code for that part of the diagnosis, and map it to ICD-10-CM using the forward mapping ICD-9-CM to ICD-10-CM GEM.

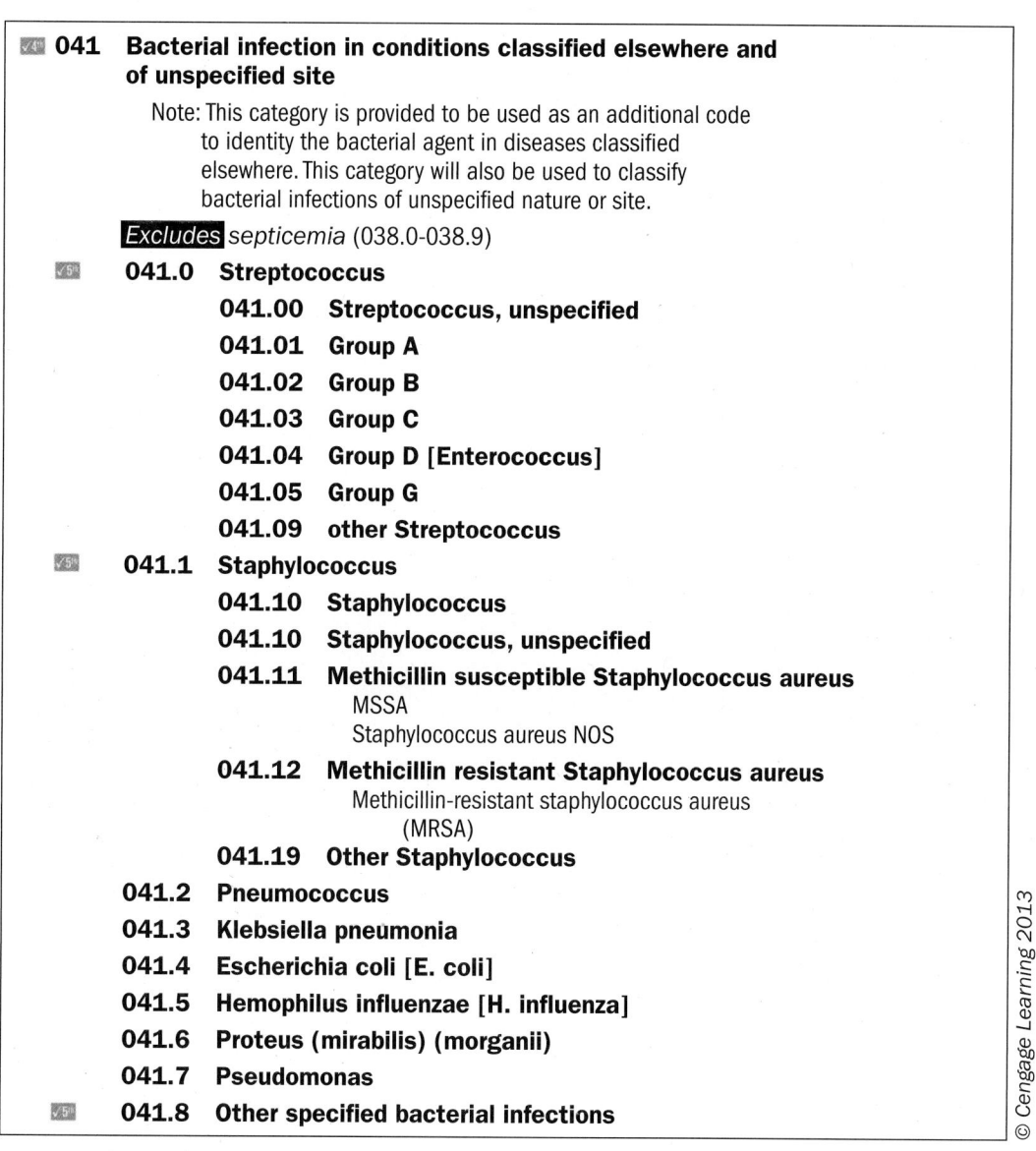

Figure 3-9 Excerpt from Code 041.12 in the ICD-9-CM

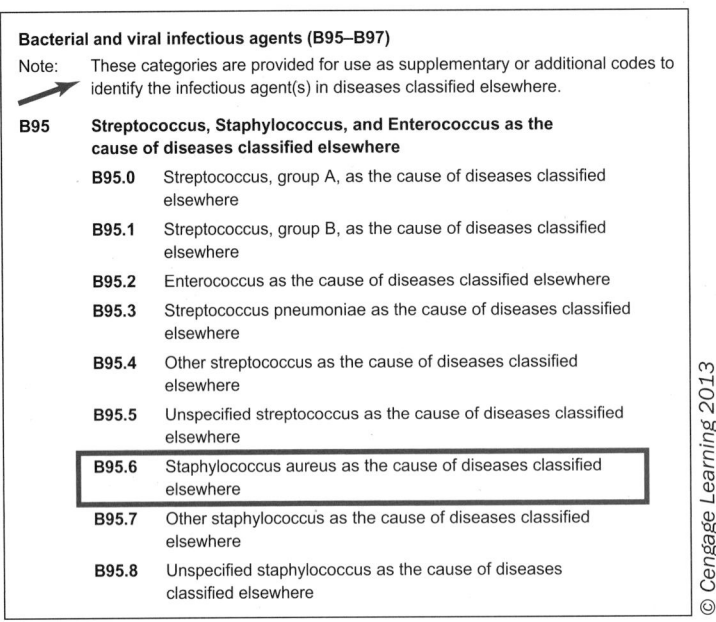

Bacterial and viral infectious agents (B95–B97)

Note: These categories are provided for use as supplementary or additional codes to identify the infectious agent(s) in diseases classified elsewhere.

B95   **Streptococcus, Staphylococcus, and Enterococcus as the cause of diseases classified elsewhere**

B95.0   Streptococcus, group A, as the cause of diseases classified elsewhere

B95.1   Streptococcus, group B, as the cause of diseases classified elsewhere

B95.2   Enterococcus as the cause of diseases classified elsewhere

B95.3   Streptococcus pneumoniae as the cause of diseases classified elsewhere

B95.4   Other streptococcus as the cause of diseases classified elsewhere

B95.5   Unspecified streptococcus as the cause of diseases classified elsewhere

B95.6   Staphylococcus aureus as the cause of diseases classified elsewhere

B95.7   Other staphylococcus as the cause of diseases classified elsewhere

B95.8   Unspecified staphylococcus as the cause of diseases classified elsewhere

© Cengage Learning 2013

Figure 3-10 Excerpt from Code B95.6 in the ICD-10-CM

As a reminder, here are the definitions once again of combination and cluster codes.

- Combination codes: when one ICD-9-CM or ICD-10-CM code contains more than one diagnosis
- Cluster codes: when more than one ICD-10-CM or ICD-10-PCS code is required to make a complete translation of one ICD-9-CM code

The 5th character of 1 in Table 3-3 means that a *combination* code exists in the ICD-10-CM that includes the entire diagnosis description, rather than a *cluster* (more than one code) using B95.6 and another code. One clue that it is a combination code, rather than a cluster, is the instructional note at the top of the category. *Note: These categories are provided for use as supplementary or additional codes to identify the infectious agent(s) in diseases classified elsewhere.* To prove that a combination code exists, start with a search of the Alphabetic Index of the ICD-10-CM for MRSA (Figure 3-11), which leads to code Z16. In the Tabular Index, the code description for Z16 (Figure 3-12) does not specifically state MRSA exists, but does indicate it should be used for an infection with resistance to drug treatment. It is important to note here that (1) there is an instructional note stating the infection should be coded first; (2) all parts of the original 041.12 have been identified; and most importantly, (3) a determination must now be made on how this combination code is to be used. If it is solely to match the ICD-9-CM MRSA diagnosis to the ICD-10-CM MRSA code in a software application, for example, that has been accomplished—041.12 matches Z16. However, if it is to match a diagnosis from a medical record, more codes will need to be added.

Movements, dystonic R25.8
Moyamoya disease I67.5
MRSA (Methacillin Resistant Staphylococcus Aureus) **Z16**
Mucha-Habermann disease L41.0
Mucinosis (cutaneous) (focal) (papular) (skin) L98.5
-oral K13.79

Figure 3-11 Alphabetic Index of ICD-10-CM for MRSA
© Cengage Learning 2013

Z16   Infection with drug resistant microorganisms
This category is intended for use as an additional code for infectious conditions classified elsewhere to indicate the presence of drug-resistance of the infectious organism
Code first the infection

Figure 3-12 Tabular Index of ICD-10-CM for MRSA
© Cengage Learning 2013

This is illustrated more clearly in the second entry in Table 3-3. Note that the source code is again 041.12, but this time the target is Z16. The fifth character in the third column now indicates a *cluster* of codes is required, or, to put it another way, more than one code will be needed to make an exact match to a diagnosis, most likely a combination code that includes the manifestation (infection) and the etiology (cause), but possibly two codes, one for the infection (manifestation) and code B95.6, *Staphylococcus aureus in diseases classified elsewhere*, to identify the etiology. To prove this, it would be necessary to have the complete diagnosis from the medical record, and map to that diagnosis using the coding manual, not the GEM. In that case, all the GEM has done is provided a starting point to begin the search in the coding manual.

To summarize, if the purpose of the mapping is to find an equivalent match between the two coding manuals to be used in a software application, such as revenue or code set conversion, the original cluster code in the ICD-10, Z19, maps directly to the drug resistance, Z19 in the ICD-9. If the purpose is to map to a diagnosis in a medical record, a combination of cluster code or codes would most likely be required.

Finally, the last entry in Table 3-3 has 04119 as the source code, and B95.7 as the target code, but the third column indicates there is no equivalent code. In this case, direct research of the Tabular List in the ICD-10-CM, starting with the B95.7, is required to find a map to 041.19 in the ICD-9-CM.

Before proceeding to the steps for using the GEMs, it is important to reiterate that these conversion maps are only a tool to assist in finding approximate or direct matches between ICD-9-CM, and ICD-10-CM or ICD-10-PCS. AHIMA provides a specific list of when GEMs should not be used:

- When only a small number of codes are being converted

- When access to the medical record is available

- When direct access to text descriptions or clinical terms describing the diagnosis or procedure is available

Above all else, GEMs should not be used for coding medical records. Mapping is not the same as coding. Mapping only links concepts in two code sets, but does not consider context or patient medical record information. Coding involves the assignment of the most appropriate code based on medical record documentation and applicable coding rules and guidelines—which is the primary reason why GEMs should never be used for coding medical records.

10 Steps for Using GEMs

As stated earlier, an applied mapping can be used to create a one-to-one mapping when incoming ICD-10-CM/PCS codes are going to be converted to ICD-9-CM codes in legacy systems instead of converting, upgrading, or purchasing new systems. The existing ICD-9-CM codes in a software application will simply be replaced by the appropriate ICD-10-CM/PCS code. In the example of source code 04112 from Table 3-3, where cluster code Z19 in the ICD-10-CM was a direct match, the software application ICD-9-CM code 04112 would be replaced with code Z19.

For a conversion of software systems, where an entire upgrade or replacement of a system is planned with the ICD-10 code sets built in, the goal would be to link the historical ICD-9-CM data to the appropriate ICD-10-CM/PCS data. Regardless of whether an application mapping or conversion approach is used, the GEMs will help translate, or map, the older codes to the newer codes, and vice versa.

There are 10 basic steps for using GEMs in conversion or application mapping projects. Figure 3-13 is an illustration of the steps. For an application mapping, stop at step 8. For a conversion mapping, perform steps 9 and 10. The first step is to find any lists, or files, that contain ICD-9-CM codes. Next, use the reverse lookup, where the source is ICD-10 and the target is ICD-9, and find translations, or maps, for each code in the list. If the application has already been upgraded to ICD-10 codes, steps 1 and 2 would be to find the ICD-10 code lists in the application, then do a forward mapping from ICD-9 (source) to ICD-10 (target) and find the translation codes. Step 3 is to replace ICD-9 lists with all the ICD-10 codes that have been identified. If the application is already upgraded, and the intent is to map the ICD-9 lists in any legacy (nonupgraded) system, then do not replace the codes. In this instance, the codes would simply

Let's Review 3–2:

1. Which of the following is true?
   a. Both ICD-9-CM and ICD-10-CM code sets have similar guidelines and conventions
   b. There are virtually no differences in each chapter's code descriptions between ICD-9-CM and ICD-10-CM
   c. The structure of an ICD-9-CM code and an ICD-10-CM/PCS code is mostly the same
   d. Episodes of care in obstetrics coding are used in both the ICD-9 and ICD-10

2. Using the ICD-10 to ICD-9 GEM is called:
   a. Reverse mapping
   b. Forward mapping
   c. Bidirectional mapping
   d. There is no ICD-10 to ICD-9 GEM

3. If the goal in using the GEMs is to translate historical data, AHIMA recommends:
   a. Using a forward mapping
   b. Using a reverse mapping
   c. Using a bidirectional mapping
   d. Using a cluster mapping

4. Source codes are:
   a. The originating code
   b. The target code
   c. The destination code
   d. A and B only

5. In any GEM, there are:
   a. A source code
   b. A target code
   c. Flags and attributes
   d. All of the above

6. If the flags and attributes from the third column of a GEM are 00000, which answer is true?
   a. An exact match exists
   b. An approximate match exists
   c. A combination match exists
   d. A cluster match exists

be interfaced so that the new system would be able to pull in legacy system data when needed. The next two steps are to identify and resolve any conflicts between the two code lists, and identify and capture cluster and combination codes where needed. Then, perform one final quality assurance evaluation. For application mappings, replace ICD-9-CM code lists with the new ICD-10-CM/PCS code lists. For conversions, replace any ICD-9 code lists in the upgraded system with the mapped ICD-10 code lists.

AHIMA makes it clear in all their resources and documentation on implementation of ICD-10 that GEMs are "tools to facilitate the transition, not 'magic bullets,' and that linked codes in the GEMs do not necessarily have equivalent meanings." As always, any potential match found on any of the general equivalency maps must be confirmed by analysis of both the ICD-9-CM and ICD-10-CM or ICD-10-PCS coding manuals.

General Equivalency Mappings for ICD-10-PCS Coding

One of the largest issues when using the ICD-10-PCS to map procedures to Volume 3 of the ICD-9-CM is the difference in terminology. For example, in the ICD-9-CM, the term *replacement* can have several different meanings, and change the code significantly in the ICD-10-PCS. The ICD-10 uses root

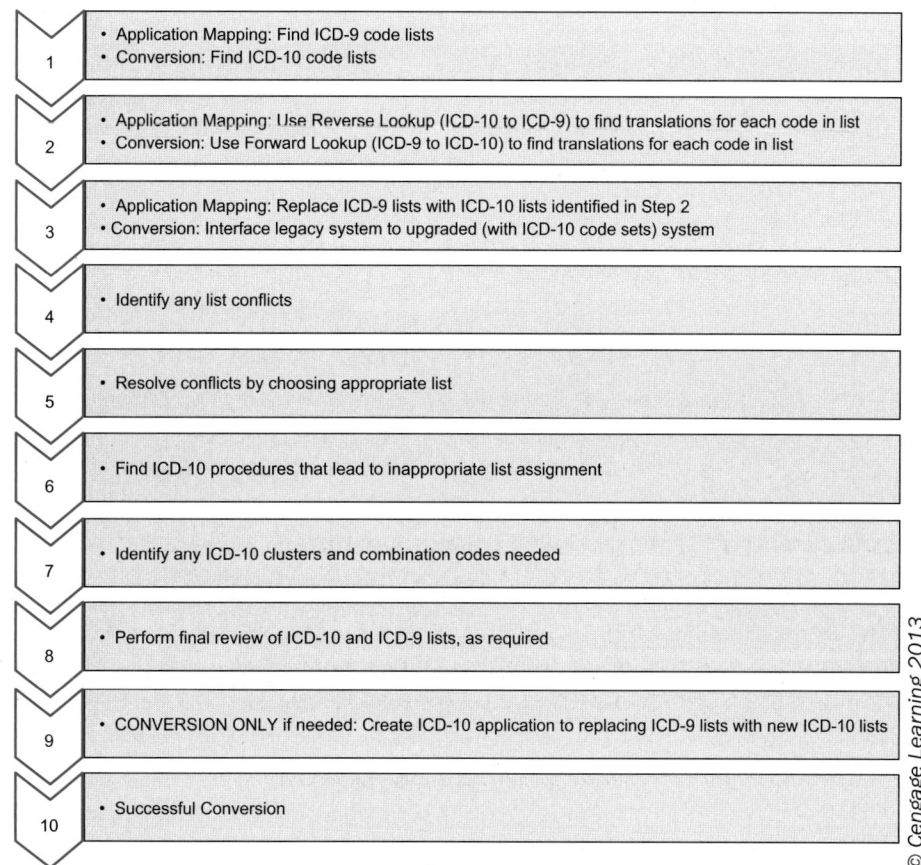

1
- Application Mapping: Find ICD-9 code lists
- Conversion: Find ICD-10 code lists

2
- Application Mapping: Use Reverse Lookup (ICD-10 to ICD-9) to find translations for each code in list
- Conversion: Use Forward Lookup (ICD-9 to ICD-10) to find translations for each code in list

3
- Application Mapping: Replace ICD-9 lists with ICD-10 lists identified in Step 2
- Conversion: Interface legacy system to upgraded (with ICD-10 code sets) system

4
- Identify any list conflicts

5
- Resolve conflicts by choosing appropriate list

6
- Find ICD-10 procedures that lead to inappropriate list assignment

7
- Identify any ICD-10 clusters and combination codes needed

8
- Perform final review of ICD-10 and ICD-9 lists, as required

9
- CONVERSION ONLY if needed: Create ICD-10 application to replacing ICD-9 lists with new ICD-10 lists

10
- Successful Conversion

© Cengage Learning 2013

Figure 3-13 Steps to Using the GEMs

operations to identify the goal of the procedure, and the term *replacement* from the ICD-9-CM can translate to several root operations in the ICD-10-PCS, including replacement, insertion, removal, and revision. Table 3-4 gives additional examples of how one term in the ICD-9-CM can have several meanings in the ICD-10-CM, depending on the objective of the procedure. These root operations and their definitions and uses are discussed in detail in a later chapter.

Table 3-4 Terminology Differences between ICD-9-CM and ICD-10-PCS

ICD-9-CM	ICD-10-PCS
Replacement	Insertion Removal Replacement Revision
Excision	Excision Destruction Revision
Resection	Drainage Extirpation Insertion Inspection Removal Revision

Table 3-4 Terminology Differences between ICD-9-CM and ICD-10-PCS (continued)

Repair	Dilation
	Fragmentation
	Reattachment
	Release
	Repair
	Replacement
	Reposition
	Restriction
	Revision
	Supplement

v26 MS-DRG General Equivalency Mappings

When Medicare was established in 1965, payment was based primarily on the cost of services provided. In the late 1960s, Congress authorized Yale University to develop a system for monitoring quality and utilization of services, and Diagnosis-Related Groups (DRGs) were established. DRGs established predetermined reimbursement rates for hospital inpatient stays. Under the DRG system, patients were classified based on diagnosis, and each diagnosis was assigned to a Major Diagnostic Category (MDC) which was largely based on body systems. Patients within each DRG require approximately equal use of hospital resources (costs), typically resulting in a similar length of stay, and are reimbursed at the same rate. Reimbursement for each DRG could be adjusted higher if certain comorbidities and complicating

Let's Review 3–3:

Using the following third column flags from a GEM, determine whether an exact match, combination, or cluster code exists.

1. 10111
   a. Exact match
   b. Cluster match
   c. Combination match
   d. No match

2. 00000
   a. Exact match
   b. Cluster match
   c. Combination match
   d. No match

3. 10112
   a. Exact match
   b. Cluster match
   c. Combination match
   d. No match

4. 10000
   a. Approximate match (single code)
   b. Cluster match
   c. Combination match
   d. No match

5. 10112
   a. Exact match
   b. Cluster match
   c. Combination match
   d. No match

6. 11000
   a. Exact match
   b. Cluster match
   c. Combination match
   d. No match

conditions (CC) increased the severity, and thus the costs and lengths of stay. Comorbidities are defined as other illnesses or diseases that exist in addition to the primary diagnostic DRG.

In 2008, the methodology for DRGs changed in order to recognize the severity of an illness based on its complexity, DRGs were renamed MS-DRGs. The principal diagnosis determines the MDCs, and within each MDC there are surgical and medical DRGs. There are three subcategories within MS-DRGs:

- DRG with Major Comorbidity or Complication (MCC)

- DRG with Comorbidity or Complication (CC)

- Non-MCC or CC DRGs

Reimbursement for MS-DRGs is based on a relative weight assigned to the MS-DRG times the hospital-specific payment rate established by the CMS. As of the first quarter of 2011, the MS-DRG General Equivalency Maps version in use is version 26 (v.26), which is used for this text. Be sure to check the CMS website to ensure that the v26 MS-DRG GEM is still in use before proceeding with an MS-DRG applied mapping or conversion in any health care organization.

Using GEMs for MS-DRG and Reimbursement Conversion

Before discussing how the GEMs are used for MS-DRG conversions, take a quick look at Figures 3-14 and 3-15, which are examples of the MS-DRG categories for ICD-9-CM and ICD-10-CM. Note that the MS-DRG categories have little variation between ICD-9-CM and ICD-10-CM. The difference lies in the principal diagnoses included in each MS-DRG category.

Whenever possible, assign an ICD-10-CM/PCS MS-DRG to the same ICD-9-CM MS-DRG category as illustrated in Figure 3-16. Here, note that in the top box, all similar diagnoses from both the ICD-9-CM and the ICD-10-CM that fall within an MS-DRG—in this case, benign neoplasms of the colon—are included. Below that, in the lower box, the three applicable MS-DRGs are listed. MS-DRG 393 is for *other digestive system diagnoses with a major comorbidity and/or complication* (MCC), 394 is for *other digestive system diagnoses with a comorbidity and/or complication (CC)* that is not major, and 395 is for *other digestive system diagnoses without an MCC or CC*. Below that, the principal diagnoses that fall into one of the three MS-DRG categories are listed. If the diagnosis is D120, *benign neoplasm of the cecum*, the next step would be to review the medical documentation to determine whether an MCC or CC is present as well, in order to assign the correct MS-DRG.

The trick with the MS-DRG assignments is not in the MS-DRG category, since those for the most part match directly. MS-DRG 393 in the ICD-9-CM, for example, is the same in the ICD-10-CM. The real mastery lies in converting ICD-9-CM diagnoses into appropriate ICD-10-CM diagnoses. Figure 3-17 is an example from CMS. Note that the MS-DRGs are the same in both boxes. The principal diagnoses, however, are different. In ICD-9-CM, there are only four principal diagnoses that fall within any of the

MS-DRG	FY2010 Final Rule Post-Acute DRG	FY 2010 Final Rule Special Pay DRG	MDC	TYPE	MS-DRG Title
001	No	No	PRE	SURG	HEART TRANSPLANT OR IMPLANT OF HEART ASSIST SYSTEM W MCC
002	No	No	PRE	SURG	HEART TRANSPLANT OR IMPLANT OF HEART ASSIST SYSTEM W/O MCC
003	Yes	No	PRE	SURG	ECMO OR TRACH W MV 96+HRS OR PDX EXC FACE, MOUTH & NECK W MAJ O.R.
004	Yes	No	PRE	SURG	TRACH W MV 96+HRS OR PDX EXC FACE, MOUTH & NECK W/O MAJ O.R.
005	No	No	PRE	SURG	LIVER TRANSPLANT W MCC OR INTESTINAL TRANSPLANT
006	No	No	PRE	SURG	LIVER TRANSPLANT W/O MCC
007	No	No	PRE	SURG	LUNG TRANSPLANT
008	No	No	PRE	SURG	SIMULTANEOUS PANCREAS/KIDNEY TRANSPLANT
009	No	No	PRE	SURG	BONE MARROW TRANSPLANT
010	No	No	PRE	SURG	PANCREAS TRANSPLANT
011	No	No	PRE	SURG	TRACHEOSTOMY FOR FACE, MOUTH & NECK DIAGNOSES W MCC
012	No	No	PRE	SURG	TRACHEOSTOMY FOR FACE, MOUTH & NECK DIAGNOSES W CC
013	No	No	PRE	SURG	TRACHEOSTOMY FOR FACE, MOUTH & NECK DIAGNOSES W/O CC/MCC
020	No	No	01	SURG	INTRACRANIAL VASCULAR PROCEDURES W PDX HEMORRHAGE W MCC
021	No	No	01	SURG	INTRACRANIAL VASCULAR PROCEDURES W PDX HEMORRHAGE W CC
022	No	No	01	SURG	INTRACRANIAL VASCULAR PROCEDURES W PDX HEMORRHAGE W/O CC/MCC
023	No	No	01	SURG	CRANIO W MAJOR DEV IMPL/ACUTE COMPLEX CNS PDX W MCC OR CHEMO IMPLANT
024	No	No	01	SURG	CRANIO W MAJOR DEV IMPL/ACUTE COMPLED CNS PDX W/O MCC
025	Yes	No	01	SURG	CRANIOTOMY & ENDOVASCULAR INTRACRANIAL PROCEDURES W MCC
026	Yes	No	01	SURG	CRANIOTOMY & ENDOVASCULAR INTRACRANIAL PROCEDURES W CC
027	Yes	No	01	SURG	CRANIOTOMY & ENDOVASCULAR INTRACRANIAL PROCEDURES W/O CC/MCC
028	Yes	Yes	01	SURG	SPINAL PROCEDURES W MCC
029	Yes	Yes	01	SURG	SPINAL PROCEDURES W CC OR SPINAL NEUROSTIMULATORS
030	Yes	Yes	01	SURG	SPINAL PROCEDURES W/O CC/MCC
031	Yes	No	01	SURG	VENTRICULAR SHUNT PROCEDURES W MCC
032	Yes	No	01	SURG	VENTRICULAR SHUNT PROCEDURES W CC
033	Yes	No	01	SURG	VENTRICULAR SHUNT PROCEDURES W/O CC/MCC
034	No	No	01	SURG	CAROTID ARTERY STENT PROCEDURE W MCC

Figure 3-14 Excerpt of MS-DRG Categories for ICD-9-CM

Draft ICD-10-CM/PCS MS-DRGv26 Definitions Manual

MS-DRG INDEX

DRG 001   Heart transplant or implant of heart assist system w MCC

DRG 002   Heart transplant or implant of heart assist system w/o MCC

DRG 003   ECMO or trach w MV 96+ hrs or PDX exc face, mouth & neck w maj O.R.

DRG 004   Trach w MV 96+ hrs or PDX exc face, mouth & neck w/o w maj O.R.

DRG 005   Liver transplant w MCC or intestinal transplant

DRG 006   Liver transplant w/o MCC

DRG 007   Lung transplant

DRG 008   Simultaneous pancreas/kidney transplant

DRG 009   Bone marrow transplant

DRG 010   Pancreas transplant

DRG 011   Tracheostomy for face, mouth & neck diagnoses w MCC

DRG 012   Tracheostomy for face, mouth & neck diagnoses w CC

DRG 013   Tracheostomy for face, mouth & neck diagnoses w/o CC/MCC

DRG 020 (MDC 01)   Intracranial vascular procedures w PDX hemorrhage w MCC

DRG 021 (MDC 01)   Intracranial vascular procedures w PDX hemorrhage w CC

DRG 022 (MDC 01)   Intracranial vascular procedures w PDX hemorrhage w/o CC/MCC

DRG 023 (MDC 01)   Cranio w major dev impl/acute complex CNS PDX w MCC or chemo implant

DRG 024 (MDC 01)   Cranio w major dev impl/acute complex CNS PDX w/o MCC

DRG 025 (MDC 01)   Craniotomy & endovascular intracranial procedures w MCC

DRG 026 (MDC 01)   Craniotomy & endovascular intracranial procedures w CC

DRG 027 (MDC 01)   Craniotomy & endovascular intracranial procedures w/o CC/MCC

DRG 028 (MDC 01)   Spinal procedures w MCC

DRG 029 (MDC 01)   Spinal procedures w CC or spinal neurostimulators

DRG 030 (MDC 01)   Spinal procedures w/o CC/MCC

DRG 031 (MDC 01)   Ventricular shunt procedures w MCC

DRG 032 (MDC 01)   Ventricular shunt procedures w CC

DRG 033 (MDC 01)   Ventricular shunt procedures w/o CC/MCC

DRG 034 (MDC 01)   Carotid artery stent procedure w MCC

DRG 035 (MDC 01)   Carotid artery stent procedure w CC

DRG 036 (MDC 01)   Carotid artery stent procedure w/o CC/MCC

Figure 3-15 Excerpt of MS-DRG Categories for ICD-10-CM

MS-DRG assignments in the box on the left. In ICD-10-CM, there are twenty-eight principal diagnoses that fall within MS-DRG 385, 386 and/or 387. For this reason, in order to perform MS-DRG mappings, it is necessary to analyze the diagnoses to determine (1) whether there is a match, and (2) whether that match still falls within that MS-DRG.

In ICD-9-CM, Volume 3, mapping to ICD-10-PCS, the difference is even more dramatic, as shown in Figure 3-18. Note again, that the MS-DRGs are the same in both boxes, however, there are only two ICD-9-CM operating room procedures, while there are 112 operating room procedures included in the same three MS-DRG categories in the ICD-10-PCS. It becomes imperative, once again, to abstract the procedures found in the medical documentation and map those procedures from the ICD-9-CM to the ICD-10-PCS to ensure that there is a match, and that it falls into the same MS-DRG. If it does, the same ICD-10-PCS MS-DRG category may be used. If it does not, use a forward mapping ICD-9-CM to ICD-10-PCS GEM to map the procedures to the correct code. Then, return to the MS-DRG GEM to locate those codes and the new and correct MS-DRG category.

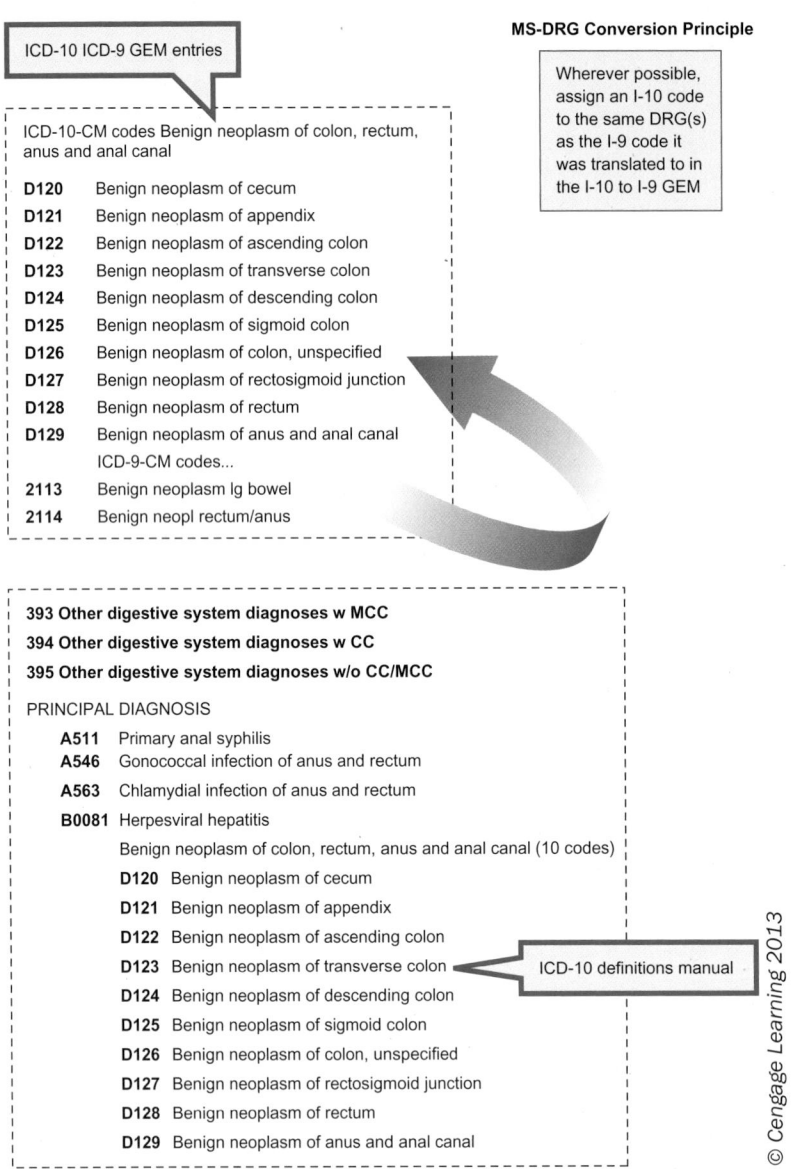

Figure 3-16 CMS Example of the MS-DRG Conversion Principle

According to CMS, the "find and replace" conversion of MS-DRGs includes four guidelines: it must be *fundamental, repeatable, adaptable*, and *flexible*.

- Fundamental. The task of ICD-10 conversion consists of a straightforward replacement of individual ICD-9 codes and lists of codes within the ICD-10.

- Repeatable. The process can be used as many times as needed to replicate the hierarchy of relationships in MS-DRGs.

- Adaptable. The MS-DRG conversion maps can be used to convert any ICD-9-based application or system so that it can process comparable ICD-10 codes.

- Flexible. The process can be used to convert code "list to list" or "code to code" applications. For example, it works for any size of application of MS-DRGs from a multi-specialty, multi-facility organization to a facility's one-page document outlining the treatment protocol for MRSA.

Important to remember is that MS-DRG categories are essentially the same in both ICD-9 and ICD-10; only the individual codes or code lists within an application or use may need to be converted.

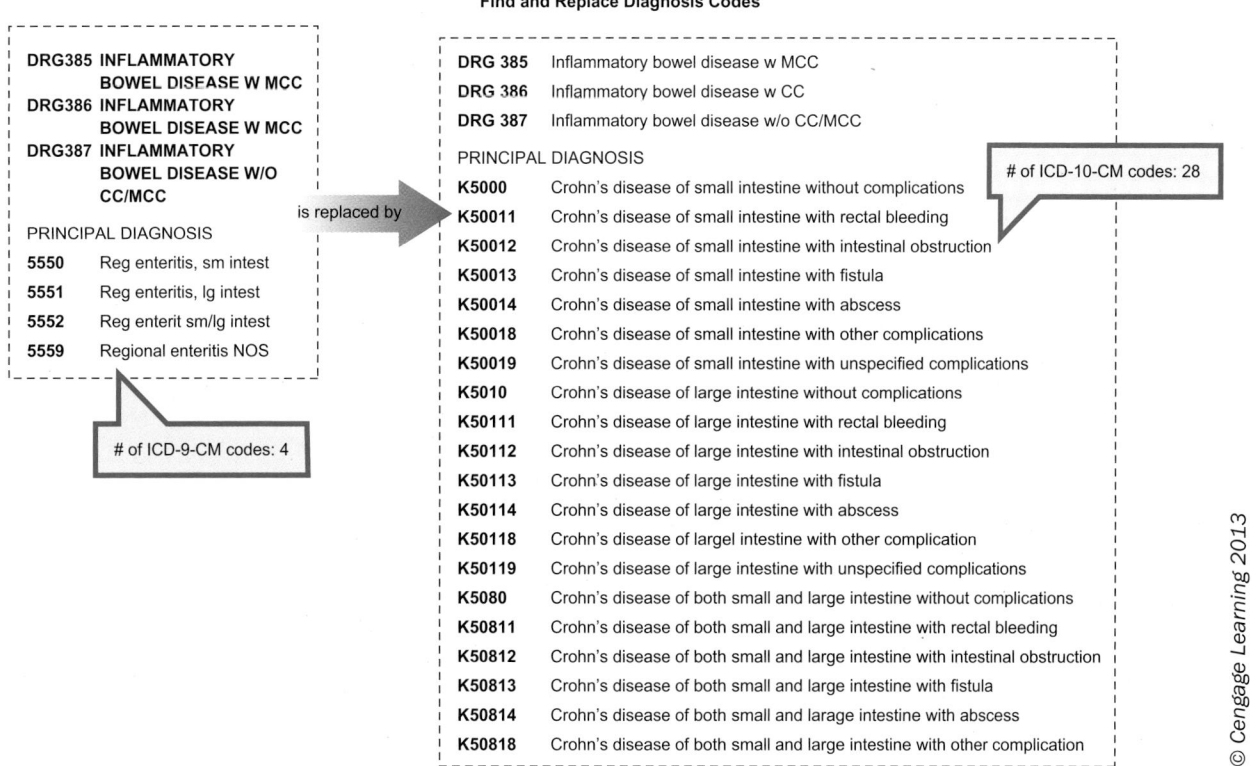

Figure 3-17 ICD-9-CM to ICD-10-CM Diagnosis Conversion

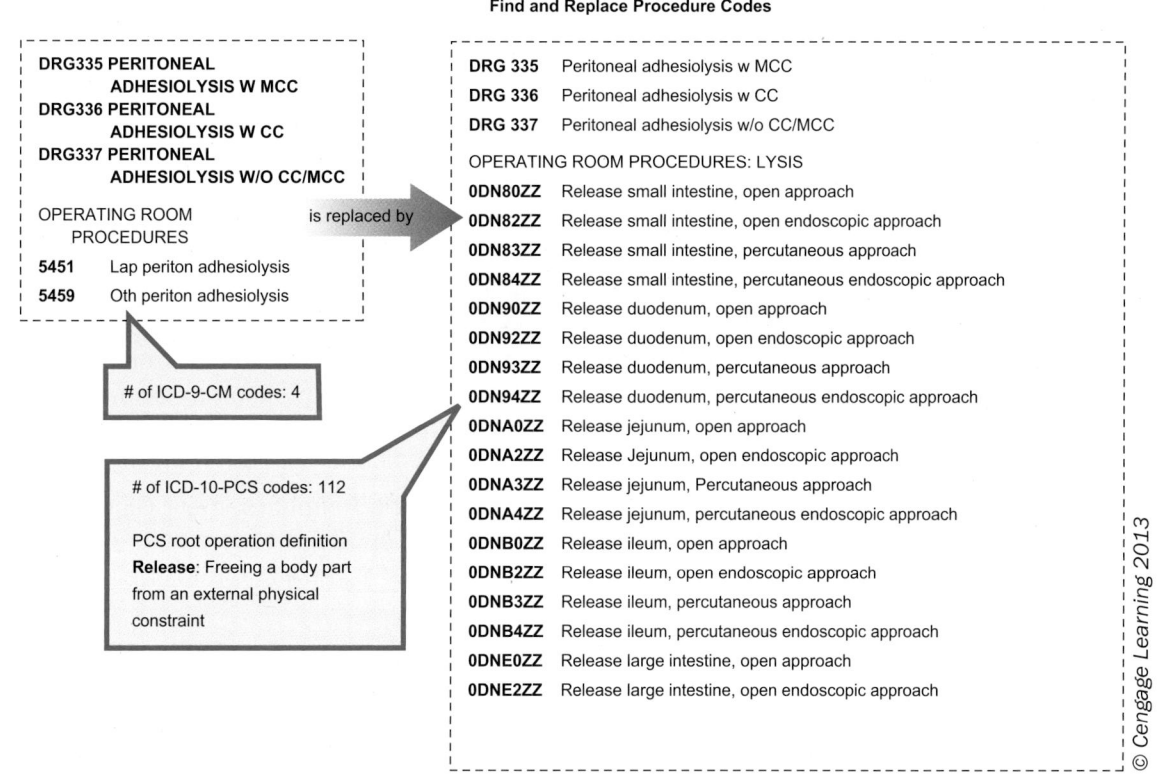

Figure 3-18 MS-DRG Mapping for Procedures

The logic and category of the MS-DRG remains unchanged, and the steps needed for conversion are to "find and replace" the ICD-9 codes with the appropriate ICD-10 codes.

- Find: For the ICD-9 code in an MS-DRG, find the corresponding ICD-10 codes in the GEMs
- Replace: Convert (replace) each ICD-9 code or code list with the appropriate ICD-10 codes assigned by the ICD-10 to ICD-9 GEM.

Once the "find and replace" process is complete, review and evaluate the results of the replacements to ensure accuracy.

GEMs and Reimbursement Mapping

The GEMS are a general purpose translation aid for finding and replacing codes or lists of codes, and are designed to aid in converting applications and systems from ICD-9 to ICD-10. Reimbursement mapping GEMs are designed to be interposed between data submitting using ICD-10 codes and legacy systems using ICD-9 codes, so that "older" data can continue to be used without converting the legacy system to ICD-10. It is considered an interim measure by CMS, to be used only while systems are being upgraded or converted to ICD-10. The purpose of the reimbursement mappings is to find the closest code match between ICD-9 and ICD-10, based on the code lists used for reimbursement. The goal here is to match similarly reimbursed codes for financial applications, especially those specific to Medicare and other health care payer reimbursement amounts. If, for example, the charges submitted for reimbursement of services for a principal diagnosis of *benign neoplasm of the cecum, with no comorbidities and/or complications* (MS-DRG 395) are $1000, the next step is to find that same principal diagnosis in the ICD-10-CM, verify that the MS-DRG is the same, and then link it to the ICD-9-CM reimbursement code or codes.

The Reimbursement Mappings were developed by CMS in response to non-Medicare industry requests for a "standard one-to-one reimbursement crosswalk," which is a temporary mechanism for mapping ICD-10-CM/PCS codes submitted on or after October 1, 2013, back to "reimbursement equivalent" ICD-9-CM codes. In order to develop the Reimbursement Mappings, CMS used the GEMs as a starting point by selecting the best ICD-9-CM code that maps to each ICD-10 code based on Medicare data. The Reimbursement Mappings identify the best matching ICD-9-CM code that can be used for reimbursement purposes for each ICD-10 code.

In the GEMs, a single ICD-9 code is often translated into more than one ICD-10 code. For example, 109.89, *Other specified rheumatic heart diseases*, in the ICD-9-CM is often associated with other diagnostic codes, such as 397.1, *rheumatic diseases of the pulmonary valve*, or 398.99, *other rheumatic heart diseases*. The reimbursement mappings clarify which alternative ICD-9 code is an appropriate choice for reimbursement. As with the ICD-10 to ICD-9, ICD-9 to ICD-10, and MS-DRG general equivalency mapping, it will be necessary to review the complete code description to find the appropriate match.

To develop reimbursement mappings, start with the ICD-10 to ICD-9 GEM. Where an ICD-10 code translates to one ICD-9 code, no additional review is necessary. Where an ICD-10 code translates to more than one ICD-9 code, historical ICD-9 code frequency data is needed to determine the ICD-9 code most commonly used by the facility. In the vast majority of cases, there is almost always a dominant code in terms of frequency, which makes it fairly easy to determine which ICD-10 code is appropriate for reimbursement purposes. In rare cases, a clinical review of medical documentation will be necessary.

All ICD-10 codes with an entry in the GEMs are included in the Reimbursement GEMs, and each ICD-10 code is assigned back to a single or cluster ICD-9 code. An ICD-9 code cluster contains two or more ICD-9 codes that must be used in combination to attain the complete meaning of one ICD-10 code, as shown in Figure 3-19.

The example given for a direct or single code match in Figure 3-19 is S72032G, *displaced midcervical fracture of the left femur, subsequent encounter for closed fracture with delayed healing*. The direct map for reimbursement back to the ICD-9-CM is 820.02, *fracture of midcervical section of femur, closed*. For a cluster ICD-9 match, the ICD-10-PCS code 02733D6 describes a *dilation of four or more coronary artery sites, bifurcated, with implantation of an intraluminal device (such as a stent) using a percutaneous approach*. In order to map this procedure back to ICD-9, it is necessary to use

Reimbursement Mappings

- All I-10 codes with an
  entry in the GEMs are
  included
- Each I-10 code is
  assigned to a single I-9
  code or I-9 code
  cluster
  - I-9 code sluster contains
    two or more I-9 codes
    that must be used in
    combination to attain the
    complete meaning of
    one I-10 code

Assigned for reimbursement:
*S72.032G displaced midcervical fracture of
left femur, subsequent encounter for closed
fracture with delayed healing*
is assigned to this I-9 single code:
*820.02 Fracture of midcervical section of
femur, closed*

Assigned for reimbursement:
*02733D6 Dilation of coronary artery, four or
more sites, bifurcation, with intraluminal
device, percutaneous approach*
is assigned to this I-9 code cluster:
00.66 [PTCA] or coronary atherectomy
00.43 Procedure on four or more vessels
00.48 Insertion of four or more vascular stents
*36.06 Insertion of non-drug eluting coronary
stent(s)*
00.44 Procedure on vessel bifurcation

© Cengage Learning 2013

Figure 3-19 Reimbursement Mapping Code Assignments

several ICD-9 codes, specifically 00.66, 00.43, 00.48, 36.06, and 00.44, to match all parts of the ICD-10 procedural statement. The coronary atherectomy is covered with code 00.66, the four vessels are covered by 00.43, the intraluminal device (stents) insertion, and the type of stent (drug-eluting) is covered by 00.48 and 36.06, and the bifurcation is covered by 00.44.

The Reimbursement Maps are different from the other General Equivalency Maps. First, there are only two files, one for diagnosis codes, and a second for procedure codes. Figure 3-20 is an excerpt from the reimbursement map with an example for ICD-10-CM and ICD-10-PCS. In the left column, is the ICD-10 code. The middle column indicates how many codes the ICD-10 code maps to, and in the right column is the matching ICD-9 code or cluster. The first five codes in Figure 3-20 map to a single code. The next seven codes map to ICD-9 clusters of four, five, and six. ICD-10-PCS code 2700T6, for example, maps to six ICD-9-CM codes, 36.03, 00.40, 00.45, 36.06, 00.44, and 92.27.

25V3ZZ	1	3865				
25V4ZZ	1	3865				
25W0ZZ	1	3865				
25W3ZZ	1	3865				
25W4ZZ	1	3865				
270046	5	3603	0040	0045	3607	0044
27004Z	4	3603	0040	0045	3607	
2700D6	5	3603	0040	0045	3606	0044
2700DZ	4	3603	0040	0045	3606	
2700T6	6	3603	0040	0045	3606	0044	9227
2700TZ	5	3603	0040	0045	3606	9227
2700Z6	3	3603	0040	0044		
2700ZZ	2	3603	0040			
270346	5	0066	0040	0045	3607	0044
27034Z	4	0066	0040	0045	3607	
2703D6	5	0066	0040	0045	3606	0044
2703DZ	4	0066	0040	0045	3606	
2703T6	6	0066	0040	0045	3606	0044	9227
2703TZ	5	0066	0040	0045	3606	9227

© Cengage Learning 2013

Figure 3-20 Excerpt from Reimbursement Map

Let's Review 3–4:

1. MS-DRGs:
   a. Are groups of diagnoses that are related
   b. Are predetermined reimbursement rates
   c. Designate Medicare severity
   d. All of the above

2. In most instances, what determines the major diagnostic category (MDC)?
   a. Comorbidities and complications
   b. Reimbursement rates
   c. Principal diagnosis
   d. A and B only

3. When reviewing an MS-DRG General Equivalency Map, which of the following are true?
   a. There is little variation in the MS-DRG category between ICD-9 and ICD-10
   b. There are major differences in the MS-DRG categories between ICD-9 and ICD-10
   c. There is little variation in the diagnoses included in an MS-DRG between ICD-9 and ICD-10
   d. None of these statements are true

4. What are the three classifications with each MS-DRG?
   a. MCC, CC, and without MCC or CC
   b. MDC, principal diagnosis, and CC
   c. MCC, MDC, and CC
   d. Principal diagnosis, MCC, and CC

5. The major difference in ICD-10-PCS maps for MS-DRG is:
   a. There is no major difference
   b. There are many more ICD-10 surgical procedures within a specific MS-DRG map than there are ICD-9 surgical procedures
   c. There are many more ICD-10-PCS principal diagnoses within a specific MS-DRG map than there are ICD-9-CM, Volume 3, principal diagnoses
   d. B and C

6. A Reimbursement Map has a 6 in the middle column of the Table which is the correct interpretation of that information?
   a. There are six different matches between the source code and the target code
   b. Six is the page number where an exact match is found between the source code and the target code
   c. It will take six target codes to map back to the one original source code
   d. It is impossible to determine the correct interpretation

Chapter Summary

GEMs were created by the CMS to provide translation "crosswalks" between ICD-9-CM codes and ICD-10-CM/PCS codes. The four types of GEMs available are diagnostic and procedural coding, and reimbursement and MS-DRGs. GEMs are not a literal, one-to-one mapping between ICD-9-CM and ICD-10-CM/PCS. There are very few instances where a direct correlation exists. There are one-to-one mappings, one-to-many, combination, and cluster code relationships. A one-to-one map is where an exact match or approximate single code match exists. A one-to-many map can be an exact or approximate match between the two code sets. Two codes used to define one diagnosis are called cluster codes, and when one code contains more than one diagnosis, this is called a combination code.

A General Equivalency Map (GEM) contains three columns. The first column is the source code, or originating code. The second column is the target code, or code equivalent being sought. For example, if the search is for an equivalent ICD-9 code in the ICD-10, then the GEM that will be used is an ICD-9 to ICD-10. The ICD-9 code will be in the first column of the GEM and is the source code. The ICD-9 code equivalent will be in the second column and is the target code. The third column contains flags and attributes that help direct the user to an exact or approximate match. There are five numbers in the third column. The first three determine whether an exact or approximate match exists, and whether it is a single code or a combination or cluster code match. The last two numbers in the third column determine whether a combination code or cluster of codes are required to find an equivalent match.

The first three numbers in the third column are called flags, which help determine whether an equivalent code does or does not exist. If the first number in the third column is 0, there is an exact match available between the source and target codes. If it is a 1, then an approximate match exists. If the second number in the third column is a 0, then there is at least one approximate translation available. If it is a 1, there is no approximate translation, making it necessary to go directly to the coding manuals to find an equivalent match. If the third number in the GEM is a 0, then the source code maps to a single target code. If it is a 1, then it maps to more than one code.

The last two numbers in the third column are called attributes and help determine what type of equivalent code exists. If the third character is 1, which indicates more than one code is needed to map the source to the target code, then a 1 in the fourth position of the third column means yes, there is a cluster or combination code available. If the third position of the third column is 0, then a 0 in the fourth position means there is no cluster or combination because it mapped to a single code. In the fifth number of the third column, a 0 means there is no cluster or combination, a 1 indicates that the code being sought is a combination code, and a 2 indicates that the code being sought is a cluster of codes.

DRGs were created by CMS as a method of standardizing reimbursement for certain groups of diagnoses. Reimbursement for MS-DRGs is based on a relative weight assigned to the MS-DRG, multiplied by the hospital-specific payment rate established by the CMS. As of the first quarter of 2011, the MS-DRG general equivalency maps version in use is version 26 (v26). The trick with the MS-DRG assignments is not in the MS-DRG category, since those for the most part match directly.

The real mastery lies in converting ICD-9-CM diagnoses into appropriate ICD-10-CM diagnoses. In order to perform MS-DRG mappings, it is necessary to analyze the diagnoses to determine 1) whether there is a match; and 2) whether that match still falls within that MS-DRG. The steps needed for conversion are to "find and replace" the ICD-9 codes with the appropriate ICD-10 codes. For the ICD-9 code in an MS-DRG, find the corresponding ICD-10 codes in the GEMs. Then, replace each ICD-9 code or code list to the appropriate ICD-10 codes assigned by the ICD-10 to ICD-9 GEM.

The purpose of Reimbursement Maps is to find the closest code match between ICD-9 and ICD-10, based on the code lists used for reimbursement. The goal here is to match similarly reimbursed codes for financial applications, especially those specific to Medicare and other health care payer reimbursement amounts.

The reimbursement maps are different from the other General Equivalency Maps. First, there are only two files—one for diagnosis codes and a second for procedure codes. In the left column is the ICD-10 code. The middle column indicates how many codes the ICD-10 code maps to, and the right column contains the matching ICD-9 code or cluster.

Review

Matching

Instructions: Match the key term to the appropriate definition.

_____ **1.** General Equivalency Mapping (GEM)

_____ **2.** Coding Clinic

_____ **3.** Source codes

_____ **4.** Target code

_____ **5.** Forward mapping

_____ **6.** Backward (reverse) mapping

_____ **7.** One-to-one

_____ **8.** One-to-many

_____ **9.** Combination (codes)

_____ **10.** Cluster (codes)

_____ **11.** Flags

_____ **12.** Attributes

A. Code being sought

B. Crosswalks that help translate ICD-9-CM codes to ICD-10-CM and ICD-10-PCS codes

C. When one ICD-9-CM or ICD-10-CM code contains more than one diagnosis

D. On GEMs, indicates whether a match exists, whether it is a one-to-one match, or a one-to-many match.

E. Quarterly coding advice guidelines

F. Originating codes

G. Going from old to new, i.e. ICD-9-CM to ICD-10-CM/PCS

H. Going from new to old, i.e. ICD-10-CM or ICD-10-PCS to ICD-9-CM

I. When more than one ICD-10-CM or ICD-10-PCS code is required to make a complete translation of one ICD-9-CM code

J. The one "best" matching code, or exact match

K. Code matches that are approximate, and map to more than one code

L. Designates if the GEM match can be a combination or cluster (4th character), and which type the match is

Short Answer

Instructions: Look at the ICD-9 to ICD-10 GEM map (Figure 3-21) and determine what type of match, if any exists. Acceptable answers are Exact, No match, Single Code, Combination, and Cluster.

Example: A3981 is an <u>exact</u> match to 0361.

1. A3982 is a(n) _____ match to 03681

2. A3983 is a(n) _____ match to 03681

A3981	0361	00000
A3982	03681	10000
A3983	03682	00000
A3984	03682	10000
A3989	03689	00000
A399	0369	00000
A400	99591	10111
A400	0380	10112
A401	99591	10111

© Cengage Learning 2013

Figure 3-21 ICD-10 to ICD-9 GEM for Let's Code It! Activity 3-6

3. A399 is a(n) _____ match to 0369

4. A400 is a(n) _____ match to 99591

5. A400 is a(n) _____ match to 0380

Multiple Choice

Instructions: Circle the most appropriate response.

1. What agency maintains the General Equivalency Maps?
   a. National Center for Health Care Statistics (NCHS)
   b. ICD-9 Coordination and Maintenance Committee
   c. Centers for Medicare and Medicaid Services (CMS)
   d. American Health Information Management Association (AHIMA)

2. The types of GEMs available are:
   a. ICD-9 to ICD-10 and ICD-10-to ICD-9 code maps
   b. Reimbursement maps
   c. MS-DRG maps
   d. All of the above

3. Quarterly coding advice data comes from:
   a. American Hospital Association (AHA)
   b. Centers for Medicare and Medicaid Services (CMS)
   c. American Health Information Management Association (AHIMA)
   d. National Centers for Health Care Statistics (NCHS)

4. Differences in ICD-9 and ICD-10 include:
   a. Terminology is more specific in ICD-10 than ICD-9
   b. Length and format of codes
   c. There are treatment and procedure codes in the ICD-10-CM
   d. A and B only

5. A code that consists of more than one diagnosis is:
   a. A cluster code   c. A one-to-many code
   b. A combination code   d. A forward mapping code

6. A diagnosis that requires more than one code to map completely is:
   a. A cluster code
   b. A combination code
   c. A one-to-many code
   d. A forward mapping code

7. One reason to use applied mapping, rather than a conversion, would be:
   a. To map back to a legacy system
   b. As an interim measure until legacy systems can be converted
   c. For MS-DRG or reimbursement mappings
   d. All of the above

8. The originating codes are called:
   a. Source codes
   b. Target codes
   c. One-to-one codes
   d. One-to-many codes

9. Using a GEM that goes from ICD-10 to ICD9 is called:
   a. Forward mapping
   b. Applied mapping
   c. Reverse (backward) mapping
   d. Conversion mapping

10. The third column in the GEM contains:
    a. Flags
    b. Attributes
    c. A and B
    d. None of the above

11. In the third column of a GEM, a flag of 0 in the first position means:
    a. An exact match exists
    b. An approximate match exists
    c. A combination match exists
    d. A cluster match exists

12. In the third column of a GEM, an attribute of 2 in the fifth position means:
    a. An exact match exists
    b. An approximate match exists
    c. A combination match exists
    d. A cluster match exists

13. In the third column of the GEM it lists 00000. Which of the following is true?
    a. There is an exact match
    b. There is an approximate match to a combination code
    c. There is an approximate match for a cluster code
    d. There is no match

14. In the third column of the GEM it lists 10112. Which of the following is true?
    a. There is an exact match
    b. There is a match to a combination code
    c. There is an approximate match for a cluster code
    d. There is no match

15. In the third column of the GEM it lists, 10000. Which of the following is true?
    a. There is an exact match
    b. There is a single code approximate match
    c. There is a combination code match
    d. There is a cluster code match

ICD-10-PCS (Procedural Coding System)

Learning Objectives

At the conclusion of this chapter, the learner should be able to:

- Understand the history and development of the ICD-10-PCS
- Learn the layout and guidelines of the ICD-10-PCS
- Identify the characters that make up an ICD-10-PCS code and identify each character's purpose
- Understand the terminology used in the layout and structure of the ICD-10-PCS codebook
- Know what a table is, and how it is used when creating an ICD-10-PCS code
- Know the Sections of the ICD-10-PCS and what each Section is used for

Key Terms and Definitions

Approach	In most of the 17 sections of the ICD-10-PCS codebook, the fifth character of the code is the approach or technique used to reach the site of the procedure.
Body Part	In ICD-10-PCS, the Body Part refers to the specific body part affected by the procedure. It is always the fourth character of the ICD-10-PCS code. In some sections it is labeled body region.
Body Region	See Body Part.
Body System	In ICD-10-PCS, Body System is always the second character of the ICD-10-PCS code and refers to the body system affected by the procedure.
Character	In ICD-10-PCS, there are seven characters. Each character is a letter or number that represents a specific value of the ICD-10-PCS code.
Code value	Each character of the ICD-10-PCS code has a specific purpose and identifies each of the characters within a code. There are 34 code values, 10 digits (0 through 9) and 24 letters (A through H, J through N, and P through Z).
Completeness	One of the four attributes of the new ICD-10-PCS codes, assigning a unique code for all substantially different procedures.

Device	Character 6 in the ICD-10-PCS almost always designates a device. A device is any object left in or on the body during a procedure, such as a pacemaker, or screws and pins.
Expandability	One of the four attributes of the new ICD-10-PCS codes, which allows for easy incorporation of newly developed procedures.
Function	In the Measurement and Monitoring section, the sixth character is represented by the physiological function assisted or performed during the procedure, such as oxygenation or ventilation.
ICD-10-PCS	International Classification of Diseases, 10th Revision, Procedure Classification System. A procedure coding system mandated by Centers for Medicare and Medicaid Services (CMS) for implementation and use by October 1, 2013 in all acute care settings. It replaces ICD-9-CM, Volume III.
Index	An alphabetic list containing main and modifying terms, which is used to point to the most appropriate table in the ICD-10-PCS.
Isotope	In the Radiation Oncology section, the sixth character identifies the isotope introduced into the body.
Method	In three Sections of the ICD-10-PCS, the sixth character is method, rather than approach. Method refers to the method by which the procedure is accomplished in osteopathic, chiropractic, and certain other procedures.
Modality qualifier	In Radiation Oncology section, the fifth character is the modality qualifier, which specifies the instrument used to introduce the radiation isotope into the body.
Multiaxial	One of the four attributes of the new ICD-10-PCS codes, assigning independent characters within a code that retains its meaning across broad ranges of codes.
Qualifier	In ICD-10-PCS the seventh character is always a qualifier. A qualifier contains unique values specific to the procedure performed.
Radionuclide	In the Nuclear Medicine section, the fifth character identifies the source of the radiation, or radionuclide.
Root operation	In ICD-10-PCS, the Root Operation identifies the objective of the procedure. It is always the third character of the ICD-10-PCS code.
Root type	In the Radiation Oncology section, the third character of the ICD-10-CM code is the general modality used. In the Mental Health section, the root type specifies the procedure type, such as crisis intervention or counseling.
Section	In ICD-10-PCS, a Section identifies the general type of procedure, i.e. medical/surgical (med-surg), obstetrics, etc. It is always the first character of the ICD-10-PCS code. There are 17 Sections in the ICD-10-PCS codebook.
Standardized	One of the four attributes of the new ICD-10-PCS codes. Standardized terminology definitions are included in ICD-10-PCS to prevent multiple meanings for the same term.
Substance	In the Administration section of the ICD-10-PCS, the sixth character identifies the substance being introduced to the body during the procedure.
Table	Each section of the ICD-10-PCS codebook is arranged in rows that specify valid combinations of codes that can be used within that Section. The rows collectively are called a Table.
Tabular List	All of the Tables within the ICD-10-PCS codebook are collectively known as the Tabular List. It is from the Tabular list that the final code determination should be made.
Type qualifier	In the Substance Abuse Treatment section, the fourth character specifies the procedure type, such as cognitive-behavioral, 12-step, or interpersonal counseling.

Introduction

The Centers for Medicare and Medicaid Services contracted with 3M to develop a procedural code set to replace the ICD-9-CM, Volume III, used in acute care settings. All acute care facilities must begin using ICD-10-PCS no later than October 1, 2013. This chapter introduces the layout and general guidelines for use of the ICD-10-PCS codebook in selecting procedure codes. The ICD-10-PCS code contains seven characters, and each character has a specific value and purpose. The objective is to introduce the character assignments and basic guidelines for ICD-10-PCS, and lay the foundation for an in-depth understanding of the terminology used and the coding steps required for procedural coding, which will be presented in the chapters that follow.

History of the ICD-10-PCS

The **International Classification of Diseases, 10th Revision, Procedure Classification System (ICD-10-PCS)**, is a procedure coding system mandated by Centers for Medicare and Medicaid Services (CMS) for implementation and use by October 1, 2013 in all acute care settings. It replaces ICD-9-CM, Volume III. Volume III of the ICD-9-CM has been used in the United States for classifying acute care (inpatient) procedures since 1979. Despite rapidly changing and new technologies over the years, these new technologies could not be incorporated into Volume III due to the restrictive and finite nature of the code structure. For this reason, in 1995, the CMS contracted with 3M to create a new procedural coding system. They designed the new ICD-10-PCS procedural coding system that was unveiled in 1998. Since that time, the coding system has been updated and revised annually. The timeline for 3M's ICD-10-PCS development is:

- 1991: Contract for preliminary design
- 1995: Contract for entire system
- 1998: First draft completed
- 1998-2000: Multiple field tests of system
- November 2000: Updated version released incorporating results of field tests
- 2001 to present: Annual updates, revisions, and refinements

ICD-10-PCS Legislation

Prior to January 16, 2009, the code sets in use in the United States were ICD-9-CM, Volumes I and II, for diagnostic coding, ICD-9-CM, Volume III for procedural coding in acute care settings, and in ambulatory care settings, the Current Procedural Terminology (CPT) and Health care Common Procedural Coding System (HCPCS). The law was changed on January 16, 2009, requiring that by October 1, 2013, the following code sets were to be used:

- All health care providers, payers, and facilities must use ICD-10-CM for diagnostic coding
- All acute care facilities must use ICD-10-PCS for procedure coding
- Ambulatory care providers (physicians) may continue to use CPT and HCPCS for procedural coding

The ICD-10-PCS Code Structure

The structure of ICD-9-CM, Volume III, procedure codes was two digits, followed by up to two additional digits used as modifiers. Using an abstracted procedural statement of *initial percutaneous insertion of dual array rechargeable pacemaker under subcutaneous tissue and fascia of the chest*, the ICD-9-CM procedure code would be 37.83, *initial insertion of dual chamber-device*. With this example, it is easy to see the lack of specificity and detail. The CPT code provides a little more specificity, with 33213,

Table 4-1 Character Values for Code OJH63M7

Character Value	Character Title	Description
0	Section	Medical and surgical
J	Body System	Subcutaneous tissue and fascia
H	Root Operation	Insertion
6	Body Part	(Subcutaneous tissue and fascia) chest
3	Approach	Percutaneous
M	Device	Stimulator generator (pacemaker)
7	Qualifier	Dual-array, rechargeable

insertion or replacement of pacemaker or pulse generator . . . dual chamber. Again, the CPT code lacks specificity regarding the approach taken or the body system and part affected.

The ICD-10-PCS code is seven characters in length with each character representing a specific value, such as the approach, the body system and part involved, the device implanted (if any) and the objective of the procedure, to name a few. Using the same abstracted procedure above, the ICD-10-PCS code would be OJH63M7. Table 4-1 illustrates the value of each character in the ICD-10-PCS code. Note how every part of the procedural statement is accounted for by a character within the code. Now, it is time to find out what all these values and terms mean.

Benefits of ICD-10-PCS

This revolutionary new system (ICD-10-PCS) utilizes a seven-digit alphanumeric coding system, which allows for completeness, expandability, multiaxial coding, and standardized terminology. One major enhancement is the inclusion of qualifier digit(s). These qualifier(s) allows for better documentation of the underlying issues affecting the procedure performed. This is something that medical providers have wanted for many years. The four major objectives guiding the development of ICD-10 PCS are:

- **Completeness:** There should be a unique code for all substantially different procedures. Currently, procedures on different body parts, with different approaches, or of different types are sometimes assigned to the same code.

- **Expandability:** As new procedures are developed, the structure of ICD-10-PCS should allow them to be easily incorporated as unique codes.

- **Multiaxial:** ICD-10-PCS should have a multiaxial structure, with each code character having the same meaning within the specific procedure Section and across procedure Sections, to the extent possible.

- **Standardized terminology:** ICD-10-PCS should include definitions of the terminology used. While the meaning of specific words can vary in common usage, ICD-10-PCS should not include multiple meanings for the same term.

Code Structure

- ICD-10-PCS has a seven-character alphanumeric code structure.

- All seven characters must be used. A placeholder (the letter Z) is used to fill any character position for which there is no assigned value.

- Each character has up to 34 different values (see next bullet).

- Up to 10 digits (0-9), and 24 letters, A-H, J-N, and P-Z, may be assigned to each character. The letters O and I are not used in order to avoid confusion with the numbers 0 and 1.

Character Assignment

Figure 4-1 lists the title or assignment of each character. Do not confuse this with the value of the character. Remember, there can be up to 34 different values for each of one these characters. The following are the seven character titles are: (1) Section, (2) Body System, (3) Root Operation, (4) Body Part or Region, (5) Approach, (6) Device, and (7) Qualifier, as shown in Table 4-2.

ICD-10-PCS Codebook Layout

The ICD-10-PCS codebook includes five Sections. In the front of the codebook is an introduction that details the history of ICD-10-PCS development, and describes the terminology and layout of the codebook. The next section is an **Index** arranged in alphabetical order, generally by the Root Operation (objective of the procedure) and then the body part affected. The Index is used much like an index from any book, but rather than pointing to a specific page number, it points toward the correct Table in the **Tabular List**, which is the third section – and the section used to determine the best and most accurate code. The Tabular List contains all procedure codes used in an acute care setting and is arranged in a series of tables. Each row in the table lists characters available to use in combination to create a code. The fourth section is actually found between the Introduction and the Index. It contains the Guidelines, or rules, for using the codes. Last, in most published versions of the ICD-10-PCS codes, is a section containing various appendices, such as Appendix A, which lists the definitions of all Root Operations, or Appendix C, which includes all the medical and surgical approach definitions. These appendices will prove immensely valuable, especially to the novice coder.

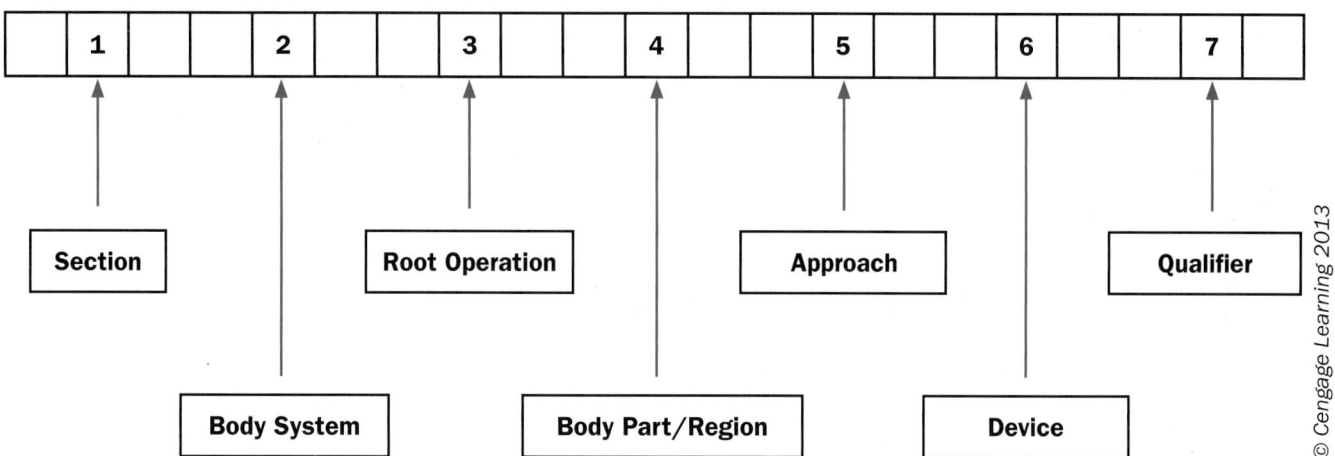

© Cengage Learning 2013

Figure 4-1 ICD-10-PCS Code Character Numbers and Names

Table 4-2 ICD-10-PCS Code Character Assignment Values

Character Title	Character Value	Definition
1	Section	Division of the coding system, i.e. medical and surgical, obstetrics, imaging, etc.
2	Body System	The body system affected by the procedure, female reproductive, urinary, gastrointestinal, etc.
3	Root Operation	The objective of the procedure, i.e. insertion, resection, excision
4	Body Part	The specific body part affected, e.g. uterus, vein, bladder
5	Approach	The method used to perform the procedure, open, percutaneous, via natural or artificial opening etc.
6	Device	Certain objects remaining in the body after the procedure, e.g. pacemakers, pins, and screws
7	Qualifier	Provides unique detail to a character assignment within a code

Abstracting and Main or Modifying Term Selection

There are several steps to selecting a procedure code. The first is to abstract procedural statements from the patient record. Next is the selection of main and modifying terms from the procedural statement. Once that's done, a search for the main and modifying terms is performed using the Alphabetic Index, and finally, the last step is selecting, from the ICD-10-PCS Tabular List, a code or codes whose description matches the procedural statement as closely as possible.

The goal in procedural coding is to learn how to use the ICD-10-PCS coding manual properly—not to memorize the codes. As there are over 72,000 codes in the ICD-10-PCS, it would obviously be impossible to memorize them. However, a thorough understanding of the layout, structure, guidelines, and terminology will definitely make it easier to find the best possible procedure code. Understanding the terminology used in the ICD-10-PCS coding manual is the first and most important step. Next, interpreting the guidelines and the Tabular List tables and understanding how to build a procedure code is the second step in the process. This text is devoted to develop the skills and knowledge necessary to use the coding manual and find the most specific and accurate procedural code available to match the procedural statement.

A procedural statement is the patient's documented procedure or treatment provided during an encounter with a health care provider. It can be as simple as *destruction of a mole* written on a progress note, or as complex as *bifurcation dilation of two coronary arteries using a percutaneous endoscopic approach with insertion of a drug-eluting intraluminal device* listed on an operative report.

Medical Documentation

The steps for using the ICD-10-PCS manual begin by abstracting the procedural and therapeutic statements from the medical documentation. Information pertinent to code selection comes from a variety of medical documents. Sources of procedural statements include the Encounter form, History and Physical (H&P, HPE), Progress/Treatment notes, Discharge Summary, and Operative Report. There are many other sources, but these are the primary medical record (chart) documents used.

Encounter Form

The Encounter form is also called a superbill, fee slip, or charge ticket. An encounter is defined as the meeting of a patient and health care provider for a specific medical reason. An office visit with a physician is an encounter, as is the patient's arrival at a hospital for admission, a lab or x-ray facility for procedural testing, or a consultant's office for a second opinion. An encounter occurs whenever a patient sees a health care provider in the doctor's office, a hospital, or any other health care facility.

Encounter forms are used by physicians, in ambulatory care settings, and have CPT or HCPCS codes preprinted on them. Acute care settings, such as hospitals, use a type of encounter form, but will use ICD-10-PCS codes instead of the CPT and HCPCS codes. Figure 4-2 is an example of an acute care setting encounter form with ICD-10-CM and ICD-10-PCS codes preprinted on the form. The physician either writes down the procedure or circles the appropriate procedure.

The components of an encounter form are:

- The practice name, address, and phone number
- The attending physician's name
- The practice's and physician's tax and insurance identification numbers
- Basic patient demographic and insurance information
- A list of procedures and services commonly used by the practice, and the corresponding CPT, HCPCS, and ICD-10-PCS codes (remember, physicians can use CPT and HCPCS—use of ICD-10-PCS is optional.)

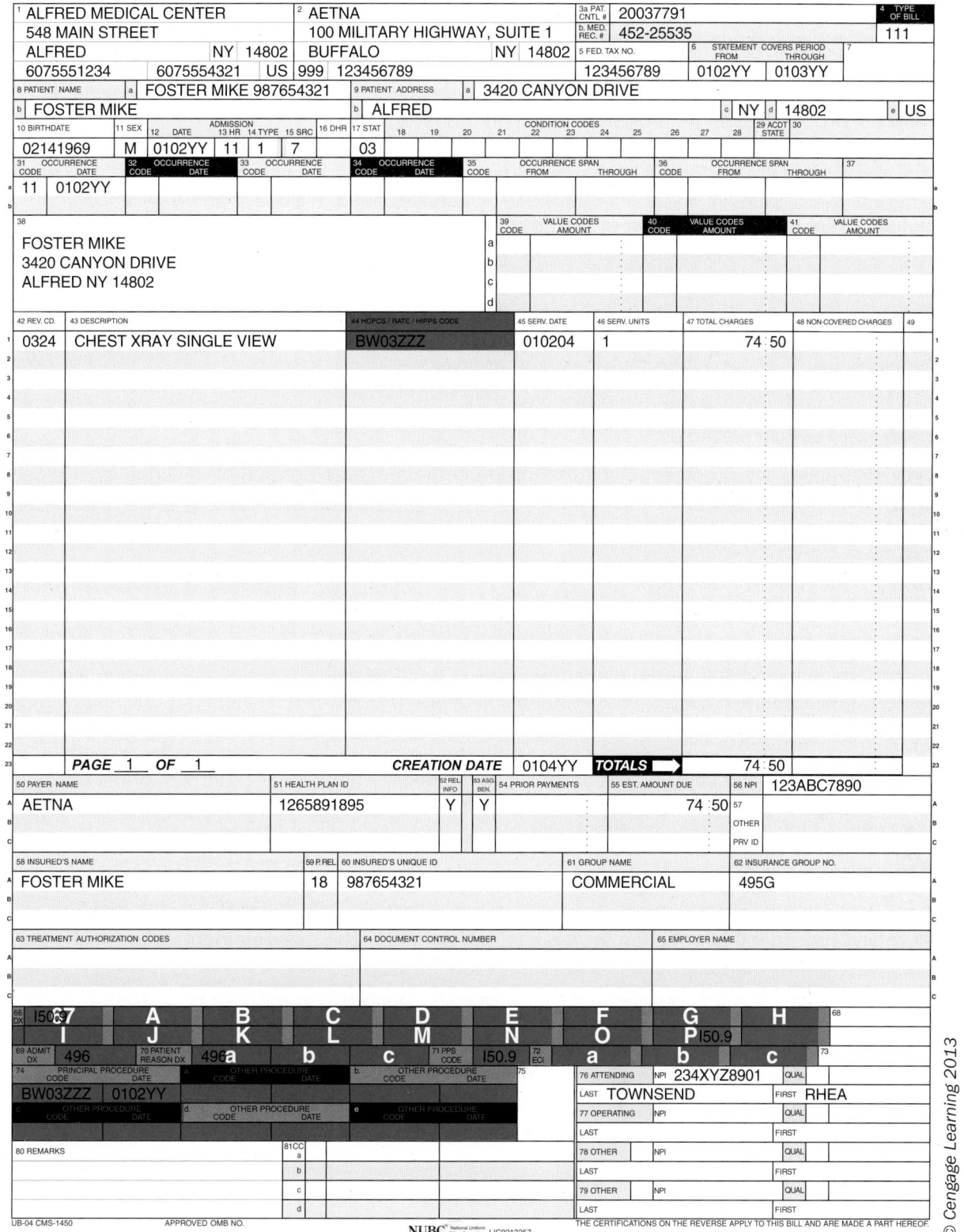

Figure 4-2 Encounter form with ICD-10-CM and ICD-10-PCS Codes

- A list of common procedures encountered in that practice, and the associated ICD-10-PCS code; *or* blank lines where the physician can write in the patient procedure or diagnosis.

Treatment or Progress Notes

Treatment notes, also known as progress notes, are another medical document from which procedural information can be obtained. Progress notes are exactly what they sound like – a record of the patient's progress and current status. Typically, the progress notes are used for established patients to document their progress through an illness or injury while the patient is hospitalized, or on return encounters with the provider. In Table 4-3, the section of the progress note highlighted is for the treatment, procedure, or service performed during the encounter. They are also used to list any new problems the patient may have. Progress notes include:

- Patient current status: how they feel on the date of the encounter, or their **chief complaint** (CC), if a new problem exists. The chief complaint is the main reason the patient sought the encounter with the physician, such as a sore throat, cough, or fever.
- Procedures performed during the encounter
- Preliminary or final diagnosis

    When abstracting the procedure, look for entries in the progress notes that describe what procedure was performed, or what treatment was given.

History & Physical Exam (H&P)

The History and Physical Exam (H&P, HPE) is the starting point of the new patient's "story" as to why they sought medical attention or are now receiving medical attention.

    The layout of the HPE includes the Chief Complaint, and all other subjective information related by the patient concerning the reason for the encounter. Next is the physician's physical examination, and review of systems. These are the objective or measurable findings. The last two sections are the assessment or diagnosis, and the plan, which includes any procedures or treatments the patient will receive during the encounter, or which will be planned for soon after the encounter. When searching for procedures and therapeutic treatments, the plan is most pertinent to the coder. The plan for treatment of the condition (or procedure), and can include x-rays, lab work, surgery, or administration of medications. Figure 4-3 is an example of the H&P with the Plan section of the history and physical highlighted.

Discharge Summary

The discharge summary is one of the two medical documents most commonly used to abstract procedure and procedural information for hospitalized patients. The main elements of a Discharge Summary (Figure 4-4) include:

1. Patient demographic information,
2. Admission date and date of discharge,
3. HPE findings,
4. Procedures and therapies rendered while hospitalized
5. Aftercare plan and instructions

    The procedural statements are obtained from the fourth section, procedures and therapies rendered.

Operative Report

The operative report is used for extracting procedure and procedural information for patients who underwent surgery as an outpatient or inpatient. An Operative Report (Figure 4-5) includes the preliminary and final procedure and procedure information, and a detailed description of the operation from start to finish. The coder uses the final procedure to search for, and select, an appropriate procedure code.

CODING REGIONAL HOSPITAL
123 MAIN STREET, ANYWHERE, USA

HISTORY AND PHYSICAL EXAMINATION

PATIENT NAME: GREENE, ROBERT   **Elizabeth Diamond, MD**

ADMITTED: 09/16/20YY

This office note serves as the History and Physical for the above patient. Patient was seen in my office on 09/14/20YY for preoperative H & P.

CHIEF COMPLAINT: Patient complains of swelling, soreness, pain of right foot

BUNION PAIN: Condition is chronic with a recent increase in severity of pain and discomfort. The severity of the condition is moderate. Duration is constant. Pain is made worse with daily activity, wearing shoes and weight bearing. Bunion is located along the medial aspect of the right foot.

CONTRACTED TOE PAIN: The contracture deformity is present in the 2-5 digits of the right foot. Pain is worse with wearing shoes and weight bearing. Previous treatment of the condition has been shoe modification and this has failed to eliminate symptoms.

PAST MEDICAL HISTORY, SOCIAL HISTORY: COPD. HTN, Rheumatoid Arthritis

MEDS: Benicar HCT, Celebrex, Hydrocodone

No known allergies

ROS:
ENT: Chronic sinusitis
Respiratory: SOB and bronchitis
C/V: Hypertension
GI: No history GI problems and denies any present problems

EXAM:
VS: 67 inches, weight 160 pounds, healthy appearing male.
Skin: Skin turgor and texture WNL
MS: Hallux abducto valgus deformity of right foot. Pain on end range of motion on the right 1st metatarsal joint. There is also equinus deformity of the left ankle. There is significant forefoot abduction on the right. Muscle strength and tone is WNL. There is collapse of the medial arch on the right with pain on palpation over the medial arch.
Neuro: Sensory testing to modalities of pain (pin prick) shows no evidence of loss bilaterally.
Vascular: Palpable DP and PT pulses bilaterally. Capillary refill 5 seconds.

(Continued)

PATIENT NAME: GREENE, ROBERT   **Elizabeth Diamond, MD**

ADMITTED: 09/16/20YY

IMPRESSION:
1. Foot/Toe Pain
2. Arthritis, Degenerative
3. Hallux Abducto Valgus with Bunion on Right
4. Hammertoe Deformity 2-5 Right
5. Achilles tendon Equinus

TREATMENT PLAN: CT scan showed arthritic changes. Discussed treatment options with patient. He would need reconstructive surgery on the right to correct.

Surgery has been scheduled for 09/16/20YY.

Elizabeth Diamond, MD

Page 2 of 2

© Cengage Learning 2013

Figure 4-3 Example of History and Physical with Plan Highlighted

CODING REGIONAL HOSPITAL
123 MAIN STREET, ANYWHERE, USA

DISCHARGE SUMMARY

PATIENT NAME: GREENE, ROBERT

DATE OF BIRTH: 03/01/1956
ADMITTED: 09/16/20YY
DISCHARGED: 09/18/20YY

DIAGNOSES:
1. Painful flatfoot deformity, right
2. Rheumatoid arthritis
3. Degenerative joint disease, right
4. Hallux abducto valgus
5. Equinus deformity
6. Hypertension
7. Chronic obstructive pulmonary disease

PROCEDURES:
1. **Gastroenemius resection**
2. **Navicular cuneiform arthrodesis**
3. **Cuneiform osteotomy**
4. **Double calcaneal ostotomy (all right foot)**

REASON FOR ADMISSION: Patient had flatfoot reconstruction done on his right foot and was admitted for postoperative pain problems and edema control.

HOSPITAL COURSE: Once the patient was stable from the PACU, he was transferred to the floor. He was placed on Lortab and Dilaudid and Toradol for pain control. He was non-weight bearing on his right foot. He was seen the next day. He was doing well, however, experiencing some significant pain as well as edema. On the 2nd postoperative day, the dressing was taken down, the incision sites were not red and there was no drainage. A new dressing was placed and a below-the-knee cast placed on the right lower extremity. Patient was discharged at this point.

Elizabeth Diamond, MD

Figure 4-4 Sample Discharge Summary with Procedures Highlighted

CODING REGIONAL HOSPITAL
123 MAIN STREET, ANYWHERE, USA

OPERATIVE REPORT

PATIENT NAME: GREENE, ROBERT

DATE OF BIRTH: 03/01/1956
DATE OF ADMISSION: 09/16/20YY
DATE OF SURGERY: 09/16/20YY

PREOPERATIVE DIAGNOSIS:
1. Painful flatfoot deformity with arthritic changes along the medial column on the right foot.
2. Equinus deformity
3. Rheumatoid arthritis

POSTOPERATIVE DIAGNOSIS:
1. Painful flatfoot deformity with arthritic changes along the medial column on the right foot.
2. Equinus deformity
3. Rheumatoid arthritis

PROCEDURES:
1. **Double calcaneal osteotomy which was an Evans and Posterior displacement calcaneal osteotomy on right side**
2. **Gastroenemius recession**
3. **Navicular cuneiform arthrodesis**
4. **Cuneiform osteotomy of bone grafting**

Patient is a male who presents with painful flatfoot deformity on his right foot and he also has rheumatoid arthritis. Patient has continued pain upon ambulation with foot gear. Patient foregoes further conservation measures, requests surgical intervention.

Patient consented to procedure and was brought to OR and placed in the supine position. After general anesthesia, right lower extremity prepped and draped in aseptic manner. Attention directed to the posterior aspect of the right gastroenemius head where a 5 cm linear incision was made where it was carried through the subcutaneous layer. The fascial layer was excised then a transverse incision was made through the junction of the gastroenemius and soleus. This released both medial and lateral as well as the median raphe bands.

Attention was then directed to the lateral aspect of the right foot. The peroneal tendons were retracted, the fascial layer excised. The calcaneocuboid joint was identified and a Evans type osteotomy was performed. An iliac crest bone wedge was fashioned and placed in the area.

© Cengage Learning 2013

Figure 4-5 Sample Operative Report with Procedures Highlighted

Main and Modifying Terms

Table 4-3 provides notes and instructions for abstracting the procedural statements highlighted in Figures 4-3 through 4-5. In ICD-10-PCS, the main term is almost always the main objective of the procedure, or the Root Operation. A modifying term is almost always a body system or part. This will be a little confusing at first, because there are 30 different Root Operations, so a simple tonsillectomy would not just be a matter of looking up tonsillectomy in the Alphabetic Index (although that is sometimes possible). A tonsillectomy could be considered an extraction or a resection procedure or Root Operation. The main term would therefore be either *extraction* or *resection* (depending upon the medical documentation's description of the procedure), and the

Table 4-3 Abstracting Procedural Statements

Progress Note (follow up visit for burn)	Excerpt from a progress note using SOAP formatting* O: sloughing blister noted with serosanguineous drainage inner aspect right thigh, 2 × 2 inches, with a 3/4 × 3/4-inch eschar area. Cleaned w/ normal saline, then dressed with Silvadene, a dry 4 × 4, and secured with tape. Dressing changes b.i.d. A: Second-degree burn to right inner thigh with eschar. P: Debridement and dressing changes approximately two times per week. _____	The procedural statement comes from the Plan (P) area on a progress note, but it is also important to look at the objective/exam findings. **Procedural Statement:** First, the progress note itself indicates there was an encounter, which should be coded. The dressing change with Silvadene application is a second procedural statement *SOAP formatting: Subjective Findings (statements made by patient about condition and medical history) Objective Findings (measurable results of examination) Assessment (diagnosis(es)) Plan (plan for further testing and/or treatment)
Progress Note	This is an excerpt from a progress note for patient Robert Greene Plan: **1.** Physical therapy for gait training **2.** Discontinue Foley **3.** Continue pain meds **4.** Casting, right foot **5.** Discharge If coding for hospital, code #2, 3, 4, and 5 as hospital services performed If physical therapy was done while patient was inpatient, and coding is being performed for the hospital, code the physical therapy If physical therapy was done as outpatient, and coding is being performed for the physical therapist or the hospital, code the physical therapy If coding for the attending physician/surgeon, code the cast application, and any encounters for follow-up (see note in next column), and the encounter to perform the discharge.	The progress note in this case is for a subsequent (follow-up) hospital encounter. Code the encounter, if applicable. (Note: If the patient is being seen for a follow-up visit immediately after surgery, the encounter may be bundled into the surgery code. Check the ICD-10-PCS guidelines on surgical procedures and follow-up encounters). Look for additional documentation, such as an H&P or operative report, to gather more information for the procedural statement abstract
History & Physical (H&P)	See Figure 4-3 for patient Robert Greene Surgery scheduled for 9/16/20xx	The procedural statement is taken from the Plan section of the History & Physical. There is no true procedural statement here, only a note that surgery is scheduled. In this case, the Operative Report and/or Discharge Summary will be the source of procedural statements

Table 4-3 Abstracting Procedural Statements (continued)

Discharge Summary	See Figure 4-4 for patient Robert Greene Procedures: 1. Gastrocnemius resection 2. Navicular cuneiform arthrodesis 3. Cuneiform osteotomy 4. Double calcaneal osteotomy (right foot)	Note that the Discharge Summary captured more detail than the progress note or H&P
Operative Report	See Figure 4-5 for patient Robert Greene Post-Operative Diagnosis 1. Double calcaneal osteotomy (Evans and Posterior displacement) calcalneal osteotomy on right side 2. Gastrocnemius resection 3. Navicular cuneiform arthrodesis 4. Cuneiform osteotomy of bone grafting Note in the body of the operative report that an "iliac crest bone wedge" was harvested and used as a bone graft. The harvesting of the bone wedge would also be included as part of the procedural statement.	The surgical procedures listed on the Operative Report provide even more detail than those found on the Discharge Summary. The operative report should be the primary source for coding the surgical procedure.

modifying term would be *tonsil*. Figure 4-6 is an excerpt from the Index showing the root operation *resection* and *excision* for tonsil.

Using this same example, if the term *tonsillectomy* is used for the search, the Index will provide a See instructional note, which will direct the coder to look for the root operation, then the body system or part. Under tonsillectomy, for example, three are two See notes (Figure 4-7). The first is *See excision, mouth and throat (0CB)*, and the second is *See resection, mouth and throat (0CT)*. At this point, the coder would move to either *excision* or *resection* in the Index, then choose the body part (tonsil). Knowing the definitions of each Root Operation will lead to the correct root operation and to the correct table in the Tabular List.

Later in this and subsequent chapters of this text, Root Operations and their definitions will be covered in depth with multiple examples to help understand how to select a main and modifying term. For the time being, know that this is an important part of the steps for selecting an ICD-10-PCS procedure code.

Index

The Alphabetic Index structure includes main terms, modifying terms, and subterms.

- Main terms: appear in **bold** type and are the Root Operation (procedure)
- Modifying terms: are indented two spaces to the right under the main term, and are generally divided by either the Body System or Body Part
- Subterms: indented two additional spaces from the level the modifying term, and describes the specific body system or part

The Alphabetic Index is organized by main terms, usually the Root Operation or procedure objective. For example, in *reattachment* of the *right thumb*, (Figure 4-8) the main term is reattachment. Note that the main term is in bolded font. In this instance, the modifying term (indented two spaces under the main term) is by Body Part, and the subterm (indented two spaces under the modifying term) is thumb. The Index will normally provide the first three characters of the code. In this example, the first character, Section, is Medical and Surgical, represented by the character 0 (zero). The second character is Body System, represented by the character X, the assignment for *upper extremities*, and the third character, Root

4-6 (a)
Resection continued

Tendon **continued**

Hip
Left **OLTK**
Right **OLTJ**
Knee
Left **OLTR**
Right **OLTQ**
Lower Arm and wri
Left **OLT6**
Right **OLT5**
Lower Leg
Left **OLTP**
Right **OLTN**
Perineum **OLTH**
Shoulder
Left **OLT2**
Right **OLT1**
Thorax
Left **OLTD**
Right **OLTC**

Trunk
Left **OLTB**
Right **OLT9**
Upper Arm
Left **OLT4**
Right **OLT3**
Upper Leg
Left **OLTM**
Right **OLTL**
Testis
Bilateral **OVTC**
Left **OVTB**
Right **OVT9**
Thymus **07TM**
Thyroid Gland
Left Lobe **OGTG**
Right Lobe **OGTH**
Tibia
Left **OQTH0ZZ**
Right **OQTG0ZZ**
Tongue **OCT7**
Tonsils **OCTP**

4-6 (b)
Excision continued

Tarsal
Left **OQBM**
Right **OQBL**
Tendon
Abdomen
Left **OLBG**
Right **OLBF**
Ankle
Left **OLBT**
Right **OLBS**
Foot
Left **OLBW**
Right **OLBV**
Hand
Left **OLB8**
Right **OLB7**
Head and
Neck **OLB0**
Hip
Left **OLBK**
Right **OLBJ**

Knee
Left **OLBR**
Right **OLBQ**
Lower Arm and Wrist
Left **OLB6**
Right **OLB5**
Lower Leg
Left **OLBP**
Right **OLBN**
Perineum **OLBH**
Shoulder
Left **OLB2**
Right **OLB1**
Thorax
Left **OLBD**
Right **OLBC**
Trunk
Left **OLBB**
Right **OLB9**
Upper Arm
Left **OLB4**
Right **OLB3**

Upper Leg
Left **OLBM**
Right **OLBL**
Testis
Bilateral **OVBC**
Left **OVBB**
Right **OVB9**
Thalamus **00B9**
Thymus **07BM**
Thyroid Gland
Left Lobe **OGBG**
Right Lobe **OGBH**
Tibia
Left **OQBH**
Right **OQBG**
Tongue **OCB7**
Tonsils **OCBP**

© Cengage Learning 2013

Figure 4-6a-b Alphabetic Index Listing for Resection and Excision of Tonsils 4-6a Resection; 4-6b Excision

Tonsillectomy
see Excision, Mouth and Throat **OCB**
see Resection, Mouth and Throat **OCT**

Figure 4-7 Alphabetic Index Listing for Tonsillectomy
© Cengage Learning 2013

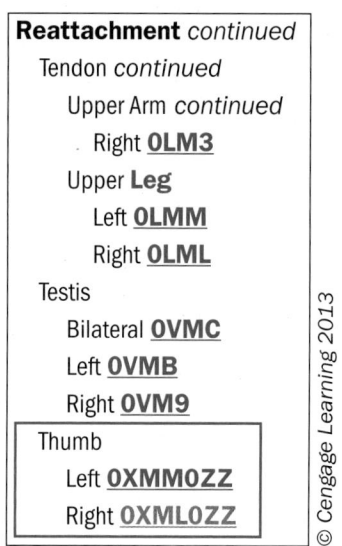

Reattachment *continued*
Tendon *continued*
Upper Arm *continued*
Right **OLM3**
Upper **Leg**
Left **OLMM**
Right **OLML**
Testis
Bilateral **OVMC**
Left **OVMB**
Right **OVM9**
Thumb
Left **OXMM0ZZ**
Right **OXML0ZZ**

© Cengage Learning 2013

Figure 4-8 Alphabetic Index Listing for Reattachment of Thumb

Operation, *reattachment,* is represented by the character M, which results in a table reference of 0XM. The next step would be to go to the Tabular List and find the Table 0XM. It is important to note that Figure 4-8, the Index entry in this instance lists the entire code for reattachment of the right thumb, 0XML0ZZ. In most instances, the Index gives only the first three or four characters, therefore, this is a good time to mention that a code should never be selected only from the Index. The proper procedure is always to verify the code in the Tabular List, even when, as in this example, the entire code is provided.

Tabular List (Tables)

Table 4-4 is an example of a Table in the Tabular List for the example used in Figure 4-8, reattachment of right thumb. Each Section of the ICD-10-PCS codebook is arranged in rows that specify valid

Table 4-4 Table for Code Characters

Section	**0**	Medical and Surgical		
Body System	**X**	Anatomical Regions, Upper Extremities		
Operation	**M**	Reattachment: Putting back in or on all or a portion of a separated body part to its normal location or other suitable location		

Body Part	Approach	Device	Qualifier
0 Forequater, right			
1 Forequater, left			
2 Shoulder region, right			
3 Shoulder region, left			
4 Axilla, right			
5 Axilla, left			
6 Upper extremity, right			
7 Upper extremity, left			
8 Upper arm, right			
9 Upper arm, left			
B Elbow region, right			
C Elbow region, left			
D Lower arm, right			
F Lower arm, left			
G Wrist region, right	**0** open	**Z** No device	**Z** No qualifier
H Wrist region, left			
J Hand, right			
K Hand, left			
L Thumb, right			
M Thumb, left			
N Index finger, right			
P Index finger, left			
Q Middle finger, right			
R Middle finger, left			
S Ring finger, right			
T Ring finger, left			
V Little finger, right			
W Little finger, left			

combinations of codes that can be used within that Section, and columns that identify the body part, approach, device, and qualifier. The rows and columns collectively are called a **Table**.

In Table 4-4, the first row lists the Section (0, medical and surgical), the Body System (X, anatomical region, upper extremities), and the Root Operation (M, reattachment). The next row contains columns for each of the four remaining code characters. Character 4 is the Body Part (note that right thumb is given the character L). Character 5 is the Approach. In this table, the only option for the Approach is 0, open. Character 6 is the Device, and character 7 is the Qualifier. There is no Device or Qualifier for this procedure, therefore, a Z is used as a placeholder for both. Thus, the code for reattachment of the right thumb is 0XML0ZZ. When selecting a code it is important to stay within the same row within the Table being used.

Character Assignment and Definitions

It is time to explain some of the terminology associated with character assignments, and to learn what values are allowed. This chapter will contain only high-level definitions for these terms. In subsequent chapters, more detailed explanations and examples will be given.

Section, Character 1

In ICD-10-PCS, a **Section** identifies the part of the codebook within which the code is located, i.e. Medical and Surgical, Obstetrics, Imaging, or Radiation Oncology. It is always the first character of the ICD-10-PCS code. There are 17 Sections in the ICD-10-PCS codebook (Table 4-5). Each section is represented by a different character value. The character for a specific section never changes, and it is always the first character of a code.

- Medical and Surgical (0) Section is by far the largest and includes almost all of the Root Operations (objective of the procedure, character 3).

- Obstetrics (1) includes procedures performed on the products of conception only. Procedures on the pregnant female are coded in the medical and surgical Section (0).

Table 4-5 Character Values for Table Sections of the ICD-10-PCS

Section Value	Term/Label
0	Medical & Surgical
1	Obstetric
2	Placement
3	Administration
4	Measurement and monitoring
5	Extracorporeal assistance and performance
6	Extracorporeal therapies
7	Osteopathic
8	Other procedures
9	Chiropractic
B	Imaging
C	Nuclear medicine
D	Radiation oncology
F	Physical rehabilitation and diagnostic audiology
G	Mental health
H	Substance abuse treatment

- Placement (2) codes represent procedures for putting a device in or on a body region for the purpose of protection, immobilization, stretching, compression, or packing, such as traction, splints, casts, braces, and pressure dressings.

- Administration (3) codes represent procedures for putting on, or in the body, a therapeutic, prophylactic, protective, diagnostic, nutritional, or physiological substance, including transfusions, infusions, and injections.

- Measurement and Monitoring (4) includes any procedures performing for determining the level of a physiological or physical function, including vital signs, basal metabolic rate, and pulmonary function.

- Extracorporeal Assistance and Performance (5) includes any equipment used outside the body to assist or perform a physiological function, such as mechanical ventilation or hemodialysis.

- Extracorporeal Therapies (6) include equipment used outside the body that does not involve the assistance or performance of a physiological function. These therapies include raising or lowering of body temperature, elimination of undissolved gas from body fluids, and treatment with electromagnetic waves.

- Osteopathic (7) includes all procedures performed by a doctor of osteopathy. These procedures are manual treatments to eliminate or alleviate somatic dysfunction and related disorders.

- Other Procedures (8) include acupuncture, suture removal, and in vitro fertilization.

- Chiropractic (9) codes include procedures performed by a doctor of chiropractic. Like the osteopathic Section, these procedures involve the manual manipulation of a body part, and are designed to eliminate or alleviate a somatic dysfunction.

- Imaging (B) procedures include x-rays, fluoroscopy, computer tomography (CT) scans, magnetic resonance imaging (MRI), and ultrasound

- Nuclear Medicine (C) procedures include uptakes and scans. The procedures include the introduction of radioactive material into the body to create an image, to diagnose and treat pathological conditions, or to assess metabolic functions.

- Radiation Oncology (D) code procedures include the introduction of encapsulated radioactive material for the treatment of cancers.

- Physical Rehabilitation and Diagnostic Audiology (F) includes procedures such as physical and occupational therapy, as well as speech-language pathology therapies.

- Mental Health (G) codes are used for therapies that include individual psychotherapy, counseling, electroconvulsive therapy, and biofeedback

- Substance Abuse Therapies (H) include detoxification, individual and group counseling, and 12-step program therapies

Let's Review 4–1:

Match each of the following procedures or therapies to the Section in which it would be found:

1. Spontaneously aborted fetus _____
2. Delivery of spontaneously aborted fetus _____
3. Application of a splint and traction _____
4. Osteopathic manipulation therapy _____
5. Radiation therapy for cancer _____
6. Hearing test _____

Body System, Character 2

In ICD-10-PCS, Body System is always the second character of the ICD-10-PCS code and refers to the body system affected by the procedure. In the Medical and Surgical Section, there are 31 body systems represented. In future chapters, discussion of Body Systems included in specific Sections will be discussed at length. For now, the focus will be on the medical and surgical Section, and only on a few unique descriptions. Most of the body systems listed are clearly recognizable as a body system, such as the central (0) and peripheral (1) nervous system, and the respiratory (B), gastrointestinal (D), and endocrine (G) systems. Table 4-6 is a complete listing of Body Systems represented by character 2.

There are 13 anatomical regions assignments in the Body Systems character (2) that are unique. These will be discussed in-depth in their respective chapters, however, for now, let's review some

Table 4-6 Character Values for Character 2: Body System, Used in the Medical and Surgical Section (0)

Body System Character Value	Term
0	Central nervous system
1	Peripheral nervous system
2	Heart and great vessels
3	Upper arteries
4	Lower arteries
5	Upper veins
6	Lower veins
7	Lymphatic and hemic system
8	Eye
9	Ear, nose, sinus
B	Respiratory system
C	Mouth and throat
D	Gastrointestinal system
F	Hepatobiliary system and pancreas
G	Endocrine system
H	Skin and breast
J	Subcutaneous tissue and fascia
K	Muscles
L	Tendon
M	Bursa and ligaments
N	Head and facial bones
P	Upper bones
Q	Lower bones
R	Upper joints
S	Lower joints
T	Urinary system
U	Female reproductive system
V	Male reproductive system
W	Anatomic regions, general
X	Anatomic regions, upper extremities
Y	Anatomic regions, lower extremities

Body System guidelines for the Medical and Surgical Section. There are three Body System specific guidelines in ICD-10-PCS.

- **Guideline B2.1.a.** The procedure codes in the general anatomical regions body systems should only be used when the procedure is performed on an anatomical region rather than a specific body part, or on the rate occasion when no information is available to support assignment of a code to a specific body part. **Guideline B2.1.b.** Body systems designated as *upper* or *lower* contain body parts located above or below the diaphragm, respectively. For example, veins that are found above the diaphragm are found in *the upper veins body system*.

Not Elsewhere Classified (NEC)

ICD-10-PCS has limited "not elsewhere classified" (NEC) code options. In ICD-9, NEC was a common used term throughout the diagnostic and procedural code sets. ICD-10-PCS has only two NEC options, the first is for the Root Operation *repair* in the Medical and Surgical section, and the second is for Other Devices in the character 6 position of the procedure code, which has a value of Y. The sixth position value of Y will be used only when the specific device being coded is not listed in the table within which the rest of the code character values are located. These will be discussed more thoroughly in the next two chapters.

Let's Review 4–2:

Match the Body System with the appropriate code character value.

1. Upper arteries _____
2. Lower arteries _____
3. Lymphatic and hemic system _____
4. Eye _____
5. Central nervous system _____
6. Respiratory system _____

Using the procedural statements below, determine the Section and Body System characters (Hint: you'll need to use your ICD-10-PCS code manual to find some of the body systems specific to sections other than Medical and Surgical):

1. Reattachment of right thumb _____
2. Imaging of the lymphatic system _____ .
3. Repositioning of the uterus _____
4. Nuclear medicine procedure on the central nervous system _____
5. Radiation oncology on the endocrine system _____
6. Hearing test _____
7. Measurement of a physiological system _____
8. Administration (of a substance) into the circulatory system (3 administration, 0 circulatory) _____
9. Placement of immobilization on an anatomical region, general _____
10. Thoracentesis _____

Root Operation

In ICD-10-PCS, the **Root Operation** identifies the objective of the procedure, and is always the third character of the ICD-10-PCS code. There are 31 Root Operations that each have precise definitions. Regardless of which section the Root Operation is located in, its definition remains the same. Chapter 5 in this textbook will delvelop into Root Operations thoroughly. For now, Table 4-7 lists the 31 Root Operations terms, their values, and definitions.

Table 4-7 Root Operations (Character 3) Value, Term, and Definition

Root Operations Value	Term	Definition
0	Alteration	Modifying the natural anatomic structure of a Body Part without affecting the function of the body part
1	Bypass	Altering the route of passage of the contents of a tubular body part
2	Change	Taking out or off a device from a body part and putting back an identical or similar device in or on the same body part without cutting or puncturing the skin or a mucus membrane
3	Control	Stopping, or attempting to stop, postprocedural bleeding
4	Creation	Making a new structure that does not take over the place of a body part
5	Destruction	Physical eradication of all or a portion of a body part by direct use of energy, force, or a destructive agent
6	Detachment	Cutting off all or a portion of the upper or lower extremities
7	Dilation	Expanding an orifice or the lumen of a tubular body part
8	Division	Cutting into a body part without draining fluids or gasses from the body part in order to separate or transect a body part
9	Drainage	Taking or letting out fluids and gases from a body part
B	Excision	Cutting out or off, without replacement, a portion of a body part
C	Extirpation	Taking or cutting out solid matter from a body part
D	Extraction	Pulling or stripping out or off all or a portion of a body part by the use of force
F	Fragmentation	Breaking solid matter in a body part into pieces
G	Fusion	Joining together portions of an articular body part, rendering the body part immobile
H	Insertion	Putting in a nonbiological appliance that monitors, assists, performs or prevents a physiological function but that does not physically take the place of a body part
J	Inspection	Visually and manually exploring a body part
K	Map	Locating the route of passage of electrical impulses and locating functional areas in a body part
L	Occlusion	Completely closing an orifice or lumen of a tubular body part
M	Reattachment	Putting back in or on all or a portion of a separated body part into its normal location or other suitable location
N	Release	Freeing a body part from an abnormal physical constraint
P	Removal	Taking out or off a device from a body part
Q	Repair	Restoring, to the extent possible, a body part to its normal anatomical structure and function
R	Replacement	Putting in or on biological or synthetic material that physically takes the place and function of all or a portion of a body part
S	Reposition	Moving to its normal location or other suitable location all or a portion of a body part
T	Resection	Cutting out or off, without replacement, all of a body part
U	Supplement	Putting in or on biological or synthetic material that physically reinforces and augments the function of a portion of a body part
V	Restriction	Partially closing an orifice or lumen of a tubular body part
W	Revision	Correcting, to the extent possible, a malfunctioning or displaced device
X	Transfer	Moving, without taking out, all or a portion of a body part to another location to take over the function of all or a portion of a body part
Y	Transplantation	Putting in or on all or a portion of a living body part taken from another individual or animal to physically take the place and function of all or a portion of a similar body part

Let's Review 4–3:

Match the following root operations to their definition:

1. Alteration
2. Change
3. Dilation
4. Extirpation
5. Inspection
6. Map
7. Release
8. Replacement
9. Reattachment
10. Fusion

   a. Modifying the natural anatomic structure of a body part without affecting the function of the body part
   b. Taking out or off a device from a body part and putting back an identical or similar device in or on the same body part without cutting or puncturing the skin or a mucus membrane
   c. Expanding an orifice or the lumen of a tubular body part
   d. Taking or cutting out solid matter from a body part
   e. Visually or manually exploring a body part
   f. Locating the route of passage of electrical impulses or locating functional areas in a body part
   g. Freeing a body part from an abnormal physical constraint
   h. Putting in or on biological or synthetic material that physically takes the place and function of all or a portion of a body part
   i. Putting back in or on all or a portion of a separated body part into its normal location or other suitable location
   j. Joining together portions of an articular body part, rendering the body part immobile

Body Part

In ICD-10-PCS, the Body Part refers to the specific or general body part affected by the procedure. It is always the fourth character of the ICD-10-PCS code. In some sections, it is labeled Body Region or given a different value. These will be covered in later chapters of this textbook. The character that represents each body part will change depending on the Table Section (Character 1) and Body System (Character 2) within which the code is being identified. Figure 4-9 is an example of body part character assignments for the Medical Surgical Section (0), and Hepatobiliary System and Pancreas (F) Body System, with the Root Operation *drainage* (9). In this example, the character assignment for the body parts associated with the hepatobiliary system and pancreas are:

- Liver   0
- Liver, right lobe   1
- Liver, left lobe   2
- Gallbladder   4
- Hepatic duct, right   5
- Hepatic duct, left   6

Section	0	Medical and Surgical
Body System	F	Hepatobiliary System and pancreas
Operation	9	Drainage: Taking or letting out fluids and/or gases from a body part

Body Part	Approach	Device	Qualifer
0 Liver **1** Liver, Right Lobe **2** Liver, Left Lobe **4** Gallbladder **G** Pancreas	**0** Open **3** Percutaneous **4** Percutaneous Endoscopic	**0** Drainage Device	**Z** No Qualifier
0 Liver **1** Liver, Right Lobe **2** Liver, Left Lobe **4** Gallbladder **G** Pancreas	**0** Open **3** Percutaneous **4** Percutaneous Endoscopic	**Z** No Device	**X** Diagnostic **Z** No Qualifier
5 Hepatic Duct, Right **6** Hepatic Duct, Left **8** Cystic Duct **9** Common Bile Duct **C** Ampulla of Vater **D** Pancreatic Duct **F** Pancreatic Duct, Accessory	**0** Open **3** Percutaneous **4** Percutaneous Endoscopic **7** Via Natural or Artifical Opening **8** Via Natural or Artifical Opening Endoscopic	**0** Drainage Device	**Z** No Qualifier
5 Hepatic Duct, Right **6** Hepatic Duct, Left **8** Cystic Duct **9** Common Bile Duct **C** Ampulla of Vater **D** Pancreatic Duct **F** Pancreatic Duct, Accessory	**0** Open **3** Percutaneous **4** Percutaneous Endoscopic **7** Via Natural or Artifical Opening **8** Via Natural or Artifical Opening Endoscopic	**Z** No Device	**X** Diagnostic **Z** No Qualifier

© Cengage Learning 2013

Figure 4-9 Example of Body Part Assignments for Category 0F9

- Cystic duct   B
- Ampulla of Vater   C
- Pancreatic duct   D
- Pancreatic duct, accessory   F
- Pancreas   G

Note that in Figure 4-9, there are four distinct rows, and that some of the values are repeated in more than one row, *hepatic duct*, for example. This is done when the Approach, Device, or Qualifier is distinctly different. Using Body Part value 5, *hepatic duct, right,* for example, note the following differences:

- Approaches are the same in both the third and fourth row
- Different Device characters are used in rows three and four. In row three, is the character 0 to indicate there was a drainage device left in the body. In row four, however, there is no device, and the placeholder Z is the only option. The first six characters for an open drainage of the right hepatic duct *with* drainage device left in the body would be coded 0F9500. In the same procedure where no drainage device is left, the first six characters would be 0F950Z.

- Different Qualifiers are used in the third and fourth row. Z is used as a placeholder in both rows—indicating there is no qualifier. In the fourth row, the qualifier X would be used to indicate this was a diagnostic open drainage of the right hepatic duct with no device left behind. Using the diagnosis from the previous bullet, the code for open drainage of the right hepatic duct *with* drainage device is 0F9500Z. If no device was left behind, and it was a diagnostic open drainage of the right hepatic duct, the code would be 0F950ZX.

Within Sections, and individual Body Systems, the Body Parts character assignments will remain the same. For example, in the same section and body system shown in Figure 4-9, when the Root Operation changes to *excision*, the body part, *liver,* is still 0, the *liver, right lobe*, is still 1, and the *ampulla of Vater* is still C, etc. Be warned however, there are some sections where the body system character assignment is different than that used in the Medical and Surgical Section. In future chapters, these will be identified and discussed.

Approach

In most of the 17 sections of the ICD-10-PCS codebook, the fifth character of the code is the **approach** or technique used to reach the site of the procedure. In some sections, the fifth character represents a different value – which will be discussed in later chapters of this textbook. An example of a different term used for Character 5 is in Section 5, Extracorporeal Assistance and Performance. The fifth character in Section 5 is *duration*, and is used to indicate the length of time for the assistance or performance.

There are seven approaches listed in the Medical and Surgical (0) Section. Table 4-8 illustrates the Approach term, the value, and the definition.

The Approach includes three components: (1) the access location, (2) the method, and (3) the type of instrumentation.

- The **access location** specifies the external site through which the site of the procedure is reached, if the procedure is performed on an internal body part. The two general types of access location are the skin or mucous membranes and external orifices.

  - Every approach value except External includes one of these two access locations.

Table 4-8 Character 5, Approach, Terms, Character Values, and Definitions

Approach Value	Term	Definition
0	Open	Cutting through the skin or mucous membrane and any other body layers necessary to expose the site of the procedure
2	Open with percutaneous endoscopic assistance	Cutting through the skin or mucous membrane and any other body layers necessary to expose the site of the procedure; and entry, by puncture or minor incision, of instrumentation through the skin or mucous membrane and any other body layers necessary to aid in the performance of the procedure
3	Percutaneous	Entry, by puncture or minor incision, of instrumentation through the skin or mucous membrane and any other body layers necessary to **reach** the site of the procedure
4	Percutaneous endoscopic	Entry, by puncture or minor incision, of instrumentation through the skin or mucous membrane and any other body layers necessary to **reach and visualize the** site of the procedure
7	Via natural or artificial opening	Entry of instrumentation through a natural or artificial external opening to **reach** the site of the procedures
8	Via natural or artificial opening endoscopic	Entry of instrumentation through a natural or artificial external opening to **reach and visualize** the site of the procedures
X	External	Procedures performed directly on the skin or mucous membrane, and procedures performed indirectly by the application of external force through the skin or mucous membrane

- The skin or mucous membrane can be cut or punctured to reach the procedure site.
- All open and percutaneous Approach values use this access location.
- The site of the procedure can also be reached through an external opening. External openings can be natural or artificial.
- For procedures performed on an internal body part, the **method** specifies how the external access location is entered.
  - Open: Cutting through the skin or mucous membrane and any other body layers necessary to expose the site of the procedure.
  - An instrumental method specifies entry of the instrument though the access location to the procedure site.
  - Instrumentation can by introduced by puncture or minor incision, or through an external opening. The puncture or minor incision does not constitute an open approach because it does not expose the site of the procedure.
  - An Approach can define multiple methods, i.e. *open with percutaneous endoscopic assistance,* which describes both the open approach that exposes the body part and the placement of instrumentation in the body part to aid in the performance of the procedure.
- **Type of Instrumentation** means that specialized equipment is used to perform the procedure. Instrumentation is used in all internal approaches other than the basic open approach.
  - Instrumentation may or may not include the capacity to visualize the site, for example a colonoscopy's instrumentation allows visualization of the internal colon; while the instrument used to perform a needle biopsy does not.
  - If the term *endoscopic* is used in the procedural statement, this always includes instrumentation that allows the site to be visualized.

Let's Review 4–4:

In the following procedures, determine which Approach character is appropriate (Hint: Appendix C in the ICD-10-PCS coding manual will be very helpful in this activity):

1. Instrumental approach through the skin and membrane with the purpose of visualizing the site of the procedure _____
2. Instrumental approach without visualization entering through the mouth _____
3. Closed fracture reduction _____
4. Needle biopsy of the lung _____
5. Colostomy tube insertion _____
6. Abdominal splenectomy _____

Device

Character 6 in the ICD-10-PCS in most Sections designates a **Device**, or any object purposely left in the body during a procedure, such as a pacemaker or screws and pins. It does not include staples or sutures. There are four different types of devices. The Device values, terms, and definitions are shown in Table 4-9.

Table 4-9 Device Types (Character 6)

Biological or synthetic material that takes the place of all or a portion of a body part, e.g. skin grafts and joint prostheses
Biological or synthetic material that assists or prevents a physiological function, e.g. IUD
Therapeutic material that is not absorbed or eliminated by, or incorporated into a body part, e.g. radioactive implant
Mechanical or electronic appliances used to assist, monitor, take the place of, or prevent a physiological function, e.g. pacemaker or orthopedic screws and pins

Table 4-10 Examples of Devices and Device Values from ICD-10-PCS

Section	Body System	Root Operation	Body Part	Approach	Device	Description
0 Med/Surg	H Skin/Breast	9 Drainage	T Breast/right	0 Open	0	Drainage device
0 Med/Surg	J SubQ tissue/fascia	H Insertion	0 Scalp	3 Percutaneous	M	Stimulator generator
"	"	"	H Chest	0 Open	P	Pacemaker/defibrillator
"	"	"	"	"	H	Contraceptive device
"	"	"	"	"	N	Tissue expander
"	"	"	"	"	V	Infusion pump
"	"	"	"	"	W	Reservoir
"	"	"	"	"	X	Vascular access device
"	"	"	S Head/Neck	0 Open	1	Radioactive element
"	"	"	"	"	3	Infusion device

Depending upon the previous characters (Section, Body System, Root Operation, Body Part, and Approach), the specific device will be included in the Table with a corresponding character assignment. Table 4-10 is a short list of Devices with their value and description from different Sections of the ICD-10-PCS code manual.

Specific Device characters are always used with the Root Operations Change, Insertion, Removal, Replacement and Revision. In addition, Device characters are also generally found with the Root Operations of Alteration, Bypass, Creation, Dilation, Drainage, Fusion, Occlusion, Exposition, and Restriction, but their use with these Root Operations is optional.

- If the objective of the procedure is to put in a device, then the Root Operation is Insertion.

- If the device is put in to meet an objective other than Insertion, then the Root Operation defining the underlying objective of the procedure is used, e.g. a total left hip replacement would use the Root Operation Replacement, and the Device character would be the device that replaced the hip joint.

Figure 4-10 contains the Table that illustrates the Device and Qualifier character options for a total hip replacement. First, look at the Device character. The section is Medical and Surgical (0), the Body System is lower joints (S), the Root Operation is replacement (R), the Body Part is hip joint, left (B), the Approach is open (0) and there is one Device character listed, J, Synthetic substitute. The code, so far is 0SRB0J. The final character will be the Qualifier, which, in this instance, will describe the synthetic substitute.

Section	**0**	Medical and Surgical
Body System	**S**	Lower Joints
Operation	**R**	Replacement: Putting in or on biological or synthetic material that physically takes the place and/or function of all or a portion of a body part

Body Part	Approach	Device	Qualifier
0 Lumbar Vertebral Joint **3** Lumbosacral Joint	**0** Open	**7** Autologous Tissue Substitute **K** Nonautologous Tissue Substitute	**Z** No Qualifier
0 Lumbar Vertebral Joint **3** Lumbosacral Joint	**0** Open	**J** Synthetic Substitute	**4** Facet **Z** No Qualifier
2 Lumbar Vertebral Disc **4** Lumbosacral Disc **5** Sacrococcygeal Joint **6** Coccygeal Joint **7** Sacroiliac Joint, Right **8** Sacroiliac Joint, Left **C** Knee Joint, Right **D** Knee Joint, Left **F** Ankle Joint, Right **G** Ankle Joint, Left **H** Tarsal Joint, Right **J** Tarsal Joint, Left **K** Metatarsal-Tarsal Joint, Right **L** Metatarsal-Tarsal Joint, Left **M** Metatarsal-Phalangeal Joint, Right **N** Metatarsal-Phalangeal Joint, Left **P** Toe Phalangeal Joint, Right **Q** Toe Phalangeal Joint, Left **T** Knee Joint, Femoral Surface, Right **U** Knee Joint, Femoral Surface, Left **V** Knee Joint, Tibial Surface, Right **W** Knee Joint, Tibial Surface, Left	**0** Open	**7** Autologous Tissue Substitute **J** Synthetic Substitute **K** Nonautologous Tissue Substitute	**Z** No Qualifier
9 Hip Joint, Right **B** HiD Joint, Left	**0** Open	**7** Autologous Tissue Substitute **K** Nonautoloaous Tissue Substitute	**Z** No Qualifier
9 Hip Joint, Right **B** Hip Joint, Left	**0** Open	**J** Synthetic Substitute	**5** Metal on Polyethylene **6** Metal on Metal **7** Ceramic on Ceramic **8** Ceramic on Polyethylene **Z** No Qualifier
A Hip Joint, Acetabular Surface, Right **E** Hip Joint, Acetabular Surface, Left	**0** Open	**7** Autologous Tissue Substitute **K** Nonautologous Tissue Substitute	**Z** No Qualifier

© Cengage Learning 2013

Figure 4-10 Device and Qualifier Characters for Total Hip Replacement

Qualifier

In ICD-10-PCS, the seventh character is always a qualifier. A **qualifier** contains unique values specific to the procedure performed. Using Figure 4-10, and the example of a total left hip replacement, the Qualifier column contains five different options for the type of Device J, synthetic substitute:

- 5 Metal on Polyethylene
- 6 Metal on Metal
- 7 Ceramic on Ceramic
- 8 Ceramic on Polyethylene

- Z No qualifier (In reality, this should seldom, if ever, be used. If the medical documentation did not specify which synthetic substitute was used for the hip replacement, the provider or surgeon who performed the replacement would be queried and asked to update the medical record to specify it.)

ICD-10-PCS Coding Guidelines

- As of January 2011, the Coding Guidelines are considered in draft form and subject to change before the final version is released. The date final version of the ICD-10-PCS Coding Guidelines will be released has not yet been established – remember, therefore, that the information being presented with these or any other Guidelines is subject to change. There are three distinct types of Guidelines in the ICD-10-PCS, labeled A, B, and C. Guidelines in the A section are general guidelines for use regardless the Section. Those will be presented in this Chapter B guidelines are for the Medical and Surgical Section (0) exclusively and will be presented in Chapter 6. Last, the sole C Guideline, C.1, applies only to the Obstetrics Section (1) and will be covered in Chapter 7. Earlier, guidelines associated with the Body Systems in the Medical and Surgical Section (0) were introduced (B2.1a and B2.1b).

   The A guidelines will be presented in this chapter. The guidelines give general and specific rules for using certain characters when coding.

ICD-10-PCS Draft Coding Guidelines: Conventions

- **Guideline A1.** ICD-10-PCS codes are seven characters. Exact character specifies certain information about the procedure performed. A code character will have the same definition within a defined code range for that section. For example, in the Medical and Surgical Section, the first character will always be a 0, to identify that section, and the second character will always define the body system, etc.

- **Guideline A2.** One of 34 possible values can be assigned to each character (also called axis of classification) in an ICD-10-PCS code: the numbers 0 through 9 and the alphabet (except I and O so that they aren't confused with 1 and 0).

- **Guideline A3.** The valid values for any code character can be added to as needed. For example, if a significantly new type of device is developed, a new device value can be added to the device values during the annual upgrade to the ICD-10-PCS.

- **Guideline A4.** The meaning of any single value in a code character is a combination of its character placement in a code and any preceding values on which it might be dependent. For example, the meaning of a body part value (character 4) in the Medical and Surgical section is always dependent on the body system value (character 2). Therefore, the body part value 0 in the central nervous body system is body part *brain*, while the value 0 in the peripheral nervous body system is body part *cervical plexus*.

- **Guideline A5:** As the system is expanded to become increasingly detailed, over time, more values will depend on preceding values for their meaning. For example, in the lower joints body system, the device value 3 in the root operation 3 is *infusion device*, while the device value 3, in the root operation Fusion, is *interbody fusion device*. (This convention seems to mean the same thing as A4, however, it's referring more to the fact that there are more new technologies and devices than the 34 possible device values available, so the same character value will represent many different devices depending on the section, body system, root operation, body part or approach.)

- **Guideline A6.** The purpose of the Alphabetic Index is to locate the appropriate table that contains all the information necessary to construct a procedure code. The appropriate Table should always be used to find the most valid code.

- **Guideline A7.** It is not required to consult the alphabetic index first before proceeding to the tables to complete the code.

- **Guideline A8.** All seven characters must be used in order for a code to be valid. If the documentation is incomplete, the physician should be queried to supply the information needed that will enable all seven characters to be identified.

- **Guideline A9.** Use the same row in a table that contains the code values that match the procedural statement. 0JHT3VZ is a valid code because all the characters come from the same row, while code values 0JHW3VZ, for example, do not.

- **Guideline A10.** "And", when used in a code description means "and" or "or".

- **Guideline A11.** Many of the terms used to construct PCS codes are defined, the conder is not required to query the physician when the correlation between the documentation and the defined PCS terms is clear. In addition, the physician is not expected to use terms used in the PCS code descriptions. For example, if the coder documents a partial resection, the coder can independently correlate the documentation to the root operation Excision without need to query the physician.

Steps in ICD-10-PCS Coding

There are eight basic steps required for accurate ICD-10-PCS procedural coding as follows:

1. Review the medical documentation to abstract the procedure or treatment performed during the encounter.

2. Determine the main terms (typically the root operation) and the modifying term (usually the Body System or Body Part) within the procedural statement.

3. Locate the main term in the Alphabetic Index, then the modifying term. Write down the table reference characters associated with the main and modifying term.

   a. Review any See notes, if necessary.

4. Confirm the code(s) found in the Index by going next to the Tabular List

5. Find the table in the Tabular List that contains the Section, Body System (or part), and Root Operation characters found in the Index.

6. Work through the row or rows to find the correct Body Part, Approach, Device, and Qualifier characters.

7. Review the Official Coding Guidelines for guidance, to ensure there is nothing to contraindicate use of the code selected.

8. Write the code(s) found next to the procedural statement.

Using the following abstracted procedural statement, here is how the character assignments and steps work.

EXAMPLE: Open bypass of the lower jejunum to transverse colon using an autologous tissue substitute.

Before working the steps on this example, let's take a quick look at a bypass procedure guideline. **Guideline B3.6.a** states that bypass procedures are coded according to the direction of flow of a tubular body part. Therefore, the body part value identifies the origin or start of the bypass, and the Qualifier identifies the destination of the bypass. In this example, the origination of the bypass is the jejunum (body part value, character 4), and the destination is the transverse colon (qualifier value, character 7).

- First, break down the statement to find the main and modifying term. The main term is the root operation, or the objective of the procedure. In looking at the example, the objective would be to bypass the lower jejunum. The root operation for this procedure, and thus the main term, is bypass. This makes the modifying term the jejunum (which is part of the gastrointestinal system).

- Next, look for bypass in the Index of the ICD-10-PCS coding manual. Scroll down the list of modifying terms indented under bypass until finding the subterm gastrointestinal system under the modifying term *by Body System*, or in this case, since the body part is known (jejunum), find the modifying term *by Body Part* and then search for jejunum. The Index gives a code of 0D1A for *bypass*, by Body Part, *jejunum.*

Section	0	Medical and Surgical
Body System	D	Gastrointestinal System
Operation	1	Bypass: Altering the route of passage of the contents of a tubular body part

Body Pan	Approach	Device	Qualifier
1 Esophagus, Upper **2** Esophagus, Middle **3** Esophagus, Lower **5** Esophagus	**0** Open **4** Percutaneous Endoscopic **8** Via Natural or Artificial Opening Endoscopic	**7** Autologous Tissue Substitute **J** Synthetic Substitute **K** Nonautologous Tissue Substitute **Z** No Device	**4** Cutaneous **6** Stomach **9** Duodenum **A** Jejunum **B** Ileum
1 Esophagus, Upper **2** Esophagus, Middle **3** Esophagus, Lower **5** Esophagus	**3** Percutaneous	**J** Synthetic Substitute	**4** Cutaneous
6 Stomach **9** Duodenum	**0** Open **4** Percutaneous Endoscopic **8** Via Natural or Artificial Opening Endoscopic	**7** Autologous Tissue Substitute **J** Synthetic Substitute **K** Nonautologous Tissue Substitute **Z** No Device	**4** Cutaneous **9** Duodenum **A** Jejunum **B** Ileum **L** Transverse Colon
6 Stomach **9** Duodenum	**3** Percutaneous	**J** Synthetic Substitute	**4** Cutaneous
A Jejunum	**0** Open **4** Percutaneous Endoscopic **8** Via Natural or Artificial Opening Endoscopic	**7** Autologous Tissue Substitute **J** Synthetic Substitute **K** Nonautologous Tissue Substitute **Z** No Device	**4** Cutaneous **A** Jejunum **B** Ileum **H** Cecum **K** Ascending Colon **L** Transverse Colon **M** Descending Colon **N** Sigmoid Colon **P** Rectum **Q** Anus
A Jejunum	**3** Percutaneous	**J** Synthetic Substitute	**4** Cutaneous
B Ileum	**0** Open **4** Percutaneous Endoscopic **8** Via Natural or Artificial Opening Endoscopic	**7** Autologous Tissue Substitute **J** Synthetic Substitute **K** Nonautologous Tissue Substitute **Z** No Device	**4** Cutaneous **A** Jejunum **B** Ileum **H** Cecum **K** Ascending Colon **L** Transverse Colon **M** Descending Colon **N** Sigmoid Colon **P** Rectum **Q** Anus
B Ileum	**3** Percutaneous	**J** Synthetic Substitute	**4** Cutaneous

Figure 4-11 Table for Code OD1A: Bypass of the Jejunum

- Go to the Tabular List and find the Table for OD1 (Section 0, Medical and Surgical, Body System D, gastrointestinal system, Root Operation 1, Bypass).

- Find the row or rows that contain Body Part A, *jejunum* in Table OD1 (See the excerpt in Figure 4-11.) Note there are two rows containing the body part *jejunum*. It is time to break down the procedural statement even further to find the Approach, Device, and Qualifier.

- Look at the procedural statement again: *Open bypass of the lower jejunum to transverse colon using an autologous tissue substitute. Bypass* and *jejunum* can be deleted from the statement since they can be identified as the Body Part and Root Operation respectively, so next is the Approach. There is no instrumentation listed, so any endoscopic approach can be ruled out. Looking back at the Approaches listed in Table 4-8, this leaves open (0), external (X), and via natural or artificial opening (7) as the available choices. The diagnostic statement states *open bypass*, So the approach will be 0, open.

- Now, look at the second row in the table that contains the body part, jejunum. Open is not one of the Approach choices available, but it is in the row right above that. This will be the row from which the entire code will now be constructed. So far, identification of the first five characters of the code have been identified as 0D1A0.

- Device is the sixth character. Looking back at the procedural statement, there are two parts remaining, *autologous tissue substitute* and *to the transverse colon*. This helps determine the sixth character, Device, since to the transverse colon is the destination, and thus the qualifier. In the same row that the first five characters were chosen from, 7 is the Device assignment for *autologous tissue substitute*. Now the code is built to the sixth character: 0D1A07.

- The seventh character, Qualifier, in this table designates the destination of the bypass. The procedural statement again provides this clue, the *transverse colon*. The qualifier for transverse colon is L. The seven-character code for *Open bypass of the lower jejunum to transverse colon using an autologous tissue substitute* is 0D1A07L.

The character assignments are always built in the same order:

- Character 1: Section
- Character 2: Body System
- Character 3: Root Operation
- Character 4: Body Part
- Character 5: Approach
- Character 6: Device
- Character 7: Qualifier

In later chapters, the ICD-10-PCS guidelines will be addressed in more detail, as well as Root Operations, and other differences in character assignments in sections other than Medical and Surgical. However, all the fundamentals needed to begin understanding and coding procedures have been covered in this chapter. To that end, here are some actual coding activities. Some of them may be a little tricky, but most likely, enough information has been provided so far to make you feel like you're already becoming a procedure coding star!

Let's Review 4–5:

Part 1: Using the ICD-10-PCS coding manual Index, find the main term (Root Operation) for the following procedures. Part 2: Using the procedures in Part I: find the appropriate Table for the following procedures. Then, go to that Table in the Tabular List, and construct the code. (Hint: All of these procedures will come from Section 0 – Medical and Surgical).

1. Percutaneous endoscopic bypass of the duodenum to the skin (cutaneous) using an autologous tissue substitute _____

2. Diagnostic percutaneous drainage of peritoneum _____

3. Percutaneous endoscopic inspection of the left lower lobe of lung _____

4. Reattachment of right thumb _____

5. Lacrimal duct dilation, right duct, via natural opening to duct leaving an intraluminal device in the duct to maintain the dilation _____

6. Lacrimal duct dilation, right duct, via natural opening, no device _____

Appendices in the ICD-10-PCS

In the January 2011 version of the ICD-10-PCS Official Draft Code Set, there are five Appendices. Like the draft Guidelines, these are subject to change, and sometimes also vary by publisher. At present, there are six appendices, but bear in mind, they might not be in the same order in the ICD-10-PCS manual. They are:

- Appendix A: Root Operations by Definitions. This is a complete list of all Root Operations, their values, and definitions. In addition, an explanation and examples accompany each Root Operation definition.

Figure 4-12 is an excerpt from Appendix A. Note that the definition for Alteration (0) is given. The explanation states "the principal purpose (of this Root Operation) is to improve appearance". Examples include face lift and breast augmentation.

- Appendix B: Comparison of Medical and Surgical Root Operations. This is a very helpful Appendix. It divides up Root Operations into groups of similar operations, and describes the action and target. In addition, it provides additional clarification of the definition and gives examples.

Figure 4-13 is an excerpt from Appendix B. This groups all similar Root Operations that fall under the description "procedures that take out some or all of a body part". The five Root Operations that fit this description are Excision, Resection, Extraction, Destruction, and Detachment. The action for Excision and Resection is the same, "cutting out or off"; it is at the target where they first differ. Excision is for a portion of a body part, while Resection is cutting out or off all of a body part. The clarification is the same for both. The example for Excision is a sigmoid polypectomy, illustrating that only a portion of a body part was removed. The Resection example is total nephrectomy, which indicates the removal of the entire kidney, not just a portion.

Appendix A: Root Operations Definitions

0 Medical and Surgical			
0	Alteration	Definition:	Modifying the natural anatomic structure of a body part without affecting the function of the body part
		Explanation:	Principal purpose is to improve appearance
		Examples:	Face lift, breast augmentation
1	Bypass	Definition:	Altering the route of passage of the contents of a tubular body part
		Explanation:	Rerouting contents around an area of a body part to another distal (downstream) area in the normal route; rerouting the contents to another different but similar route and body part; or to an abnormal route and another dissimilar body part. It includes one or more concurrent anastomoses with or without the use of a device such as autografts, tissue substitutes, and synthetic substitutes.
		Examples:	Coronary artery bypass, colostomy formation

© Cengage Learning 2013

Figure 4-12 Excerpt from Appendix A of ICD-10-PCS Coding Manual for Definition of Alteration

Appendix B: Comparison of Medical and Surgical Root Operations

Procedures That Take Out Some or All of a Body Part

Operation	Action	Target	Clarification	Example
Excision	Cutting out or off	Portion of a body part	Without replacing body part	Sigmoid polypectomy
Resection	Cutting out or off	All of a body part	Without replacing body part	Total nephrectomy
Extraction	Pulling out or off	All or a portion of a body part	Without replacing body part	Suction D&C
Destruction	Eradicating	All or a portion of a body part	Without taking out or replacing body part	Rectal polyp fulguration
Detachment	Cutting off	All or a portion of an extremity	Without replacing extremity	Below knee amputation

© Cengage Learning 2013

Figure 4-13 Excerpt from Appendix B of ICD-10-PCS Coding Manual Comparing Similarities in Root Operations

- Appendix C: Body Part Key; This handy appendix lists anatomical terms and the corresponding PCS description. For example, if the documentation states acetabulofemoral joint, the corresponding ICD-10-PCS description is hip joint (left or right). Another example is the anatomical term anterior cerebral artery. The PCS description is the intracranial artery.

- Appendix D: Components of the Medical and Surgical Approach Definitions. This is another helpful Index that describes the Access location (first column), method (second column), type of instrumentation (third column), and approach (fourth column) for Character 5, Approach, used in the Medical and Surgical Section. The fifth column provides an example for each. The following (Table 4-11) is an excerpt from the first few lines of the chart in Appendix D.

- Appendix E: Character Meanings. Every character meaning for every section of the ICD-10-PCS coding manual is contained in this Appendix. Each section is further subdivided by the Body System, and individual columns list each applicable character available. For example, Figure 4-14 is an excerpt from Appendix E for the Medical Surgical Section (0), and upper joints Body System (R). Note there is a column for every Root Operation, Body Part, Approach, Device, and Qualifier that is used in this Section and Body System. This is by far the largest appendix in the coding manual. In future chapters, this Appendix will be used extensively.

- Appendix F: Device Table. Gives link to brand name devices to appropriate device value.

- Appendix G: Device Aggregation Table. Links a specific device for a specific root operation to the general device character value.

Other Character Assignments in Certain Sections

In certain sections of the ICD-10-PCS codebook other terms may be used in lieu of Body Part (Character 4), Approach (Character 5), and Device (Character 6). The Section, Body System, Root Operation and Qualifier will almost always be the terms used for characters 1, 2, 3 and 6, respectively. This chapter will provide a brief look at these terms and their definitions. In later chapters, they will be discussed at length. These terms include Method, Radionuclide, Root Type (the one exception to the third character, Root Operation), Modality qualifier, Isotope, Substance, Function, Body region, and Type qualifier.

- Method: In three Sections of the ICD-10-PCS, the sixth character is method, rather than approach. **Method** refers to the method or manner by which the procedure is accomplished in osteopathic, chiropractic, and certain other procedures.

- Radionuclide: In the nuclear medicine Section, the fifth character identifies the source of the radiation, or **radionuclide**.

Table 4-11 Excerpt from Appendix D, Components of Approach Definitions

Access Location	Method	Type of Instrumentation	Approach	Example
Skin and mucus membrane	Open	None	Open	Abdominal hysterectomy
Same	Instrumental	Without visualization	Percutaneous	Needle biopsy of liver
Same	Instrumental	With visualization	Percutaneous endoscopic	Arthroscopy
Orifice	Instrumental	Without visualization	Via natural or artificial opening	Endotracheal tube insertion
Orifice	Instrumental	With visualization	Via natural or artificial opening endoscopic	Laparoscopic-assisted vaginal hysterectomy

0: Medical and Surgical

R: Upper Joints

Operation-Character 3	Body Part-Character 4	Approach-Character 5	Device-Character 6	Qualifier-Character 7
2 Change	0 Occipital-cervical Joint	0 Open	0 Drainage Device	0 Anterior
5 Destruction	1 Cervical Vertebral Joint	3 Percutaneous	3 Infusion Device	1 Posterior
9 Drainage	2 Cervical Vertebral Joint, 2 or more	4 Percutaneous Endoscopic	4 Internal Fixation Device	2 Interspinous Process
B Excision	3 Cervical Vertebral Disc	X External	5 External Fixation Device	3 Pedicle-based Dynamic Stabilization
C Extirpation	4 Cervicothoracic Vertebral Joint		7 Autologous Tissue Substitute	4 Facet
G Fusion	5 Cervicothoracic Vertebral Disc		8 Spacer	X Diagnostic
H Insertion	6 Thoracic Vertebral Joint		J Synthetic Substitute	Z No Qualifier
J Inspection	7 Thoracic Vertebral Joint, 2 to 7		K Nonautologous Tissue Substitute	
N Release	8 Thoracic Vertebral Joint, 8 or more		Y Other Device	
P Removal	9 Thoracic Vertebral Disc		Z No Device	
Q Repair	A Thoracolumbar Vertebral Joint			
R Replacement	B Thoracolumbar Vertebral Disc			
S Reposition	C Temporomandibular Joint, Right			
T Resection	D Temporomandibular Joint, Left			
U Supplement	E Sternoclavicular Joint, Right			
W Revision	F Sternoclavicular Joint, Left			
	G Acromioclavicular Joint, Right			
	H Acromioclavicular Joint, Left			
	J Shoulder Joint, Right			
	K Shoulder Joint, Left			
	L Elbow Joint, Right			
	M Elbow Joint, Left			
	N Wrist Joint, Right			
	P Wrist Joint, Left			
	Q Carpal Joint, Right			
	R Carpal Joint, Left			
	S Metacarpocarpal Joint, Right			
	T Metacarpocarpal Joint, Left			
	U Metacarpophalangeal Joint, Right			
	V Metacarpophalangeal Joint, Left			
	W Finger Phalangeal Joint, Right			
	X Finger Phalangeal Joint, Left			
	Y Upper Joint			

*Includes synovial membrane.

Figure 4-14 Excerpt from Appendix E of ICD-10-PCS Coding Manual Describing Character Meanings

- **Root type:** In the radiation oncology Section, the third character of the ICD-10-CM code is the general modality used. In the mental health Section, the root type specifies the procedure type, such as crisis intervention or counseling

- **Modality qualifier:** In Radiation oncology Section, the fifth character is the modality qualifier, which specifies the instrument used to introduce the radiation isotope into the body

- **Isotope:** In the radiation oncology Section, the sixth character identifies the isotope (substance) introduced into the body

- **Substance:** In the Administration Section of the ICD-10-PCS, the sixth character identifies the substance being introduced to the body during the procedure

- **Function:** In the Measurement and Monitoring Section, the sixth character is represented by physiological function assisted or performed during the procedure, such as oxygenation or ventilation

- **Body region:** See Body Part

- **Type qualifier:** In the substance abuse treatment Section, the fourth character specifies the procedure type, such as cognitive-behavioral, 12-step, or interpersonal counseling procedure

Chapter Summary

The Centers for Medicare and Medicaid Services contracted with 3M to develop a procedural code set to replace the ICD-9-CM, Volume III, used in acute care settings. All acute care facilities must begin using ICD-10-PCS no later than October 1, 2013. In 1995, the Centers for Medicare and Medicaid Services (CMS) contracted with 3M to create a new procedural coding system, which became the ICD-10-PCS. The ICD-10-PCS code is seven characters in length, with each character representing a specific value, such as the approach, the body system and part involved, the device implanted (if any), and the objective of the procedure.

- ICD-10-PCS has a seven-character alphanumeric code structure.

- All seven characters must be used. A placeholder (the letter Z) is used to fill any character position for which there is no assigned value.

- Each character has up to 34 different values

- Up to 10 digits (0-9), and 24 letters, A-H, J-N, and P-Z, may be assigned to each character. The letters O and I are not used in order to avoid confusion with the digits O and 1.

The ICD-10-PCS codebook includes five Sections. At the beginning of the codebook is an introduction that details the history of ICD-10-PCS development, and describes the terminology and layout of the codebook. The next section is an Index arranged in alphabetical order, generally by the Root Operation (objective of the procedure) and then by the body part affected. The Tabular List contains all procedure codes used in an acute care setting and is arranged in a series of Tables. Each row in the table lists characters that are available to use in combination to create a code. The fourth section is actually found between the Introduction and the Index and contains the coding guidelines.

There are several steps to selecting a procedure code. The first is to abstract procedural statements from the patient record. Next is the selection of main and modifying terms from the procedural statement. Once that's done, a search for the main and modifying terms is performed using the Alphabetic Index, and finally, the last step is selecting, from the ICD-10-PCS Tabular List, a code or codes whose description matches the procedural statement as closely as possible.

Sources of procedural statements include the Encounter form, History and Physical (H&P, HPE), Progress/Treatment notes, Discharge Summary, and Operative Report.

In ICD-10-PCS, the main term is almost always the main objective of the procedure, or the Root Operation, and a modifying term is almost always a body system or part.

The Alphabetic Index is organized by main terms that usually describe the Root Operation or procedure objective.

In ICD-10-PCS, a section identifies the part of the codebook within which the code is located, i.e. Medical and Surgical, Obstetrics, Imaging, Radiation Oncology, and so on. This is always the first character of the ICD-10-PCS code. There are 17 Sections in the ICD-10-PCS codebook. Each section is represented by a different character value. The character for a specific section never changes, and it is always the first character of a code.

In ICD-10-PCS, Body System is always the second character of the ICD-10-PCS code and refers to the body system affected by the procedure. In the Medical and Surgical Section, there are 31 body systems represented. There are thirteen anatomical regions assignments in the Body Systems character (2) that are unique

In ICD-10-PCS. The Root Operation identifies the objective of the procedure, and is always the third character of the ICD-10-PCS code. There are 31 Root Operations that each have precise definitions. Regardless of which section the Root Operation is located in, its definition remains the same.

The Body Part character refers to the specific or general body part affected by the procedure. It is always the fourth character of the ICD-10-PCS code. In some sections, it is labeled either Body Region or Body Part. The character that represents each Body Part will change depending on the Table Section (Character 1) and Body System (Character 2) within which the code is being identified. Within sections, and individual Body Systems, the Body Parts character assignments will remain the same. In most of the seventeen sections of the ICD-10-PCS codebook, the fifth character of the code is the approach or technique used to reach the site of the procedure. There are seven approaches listed in the Medical and Surgical (0) Section. The Approach includes three components: 1) the access location, 2) the method, and 3) the type of instrumentation.

Character 6 in in most sections of the ICD-10-PCS designates a Device, or any object purposely left in the body during a procedure, such as a pacemaker, or screws and pins. It does not include staples or sutures. There are four different types of devices.

Specific Device characters are always used with the Root Operations Change, Insertion, Removal, Replacement and Revision. In addition, Device characters are also generally found with the Root Operations of Alteration, Bypass, Creation, Dilation, Drainage, Fusion, Occlusion, Exposition, and Restriction, but their use with these Root Operations is optional. In ICD-10-PCS, the seventh character is always a Qualifier. A qualifier contains unique values specific to the procedure performed.

There are three distinct types of guidelines in the ICD-10-PCS, labeled A, B and C. The guidelines give general and specific rules for using certain characters when coding, some of which include:

- Do not construct a procedure code from the alphabetic Index.

- Choose a valid code only from the tables, which contain exclusive coding instructions unavailable elsewhere in the ICD-10-PCS coding manual.

- All seven characters of a code must be used, and must contain valid values, to be considered a valid procedure code.

- The columns in the tables contain the values for characters four through seven. The rows delineate the valid combinations of values. Any combination of values not contained in a single row of the tables is invalid.

- "And", when used in a code description means "and/or",

There are eight basic steps required for accurate ICD-10-PCS procedural coding.

1. Review the medical documentation to abstract the procedure or treatment performed during the encounter.

2. Determine the main terms (typically the Root Operation) and the modifying term (usually the Body System or Body Part) within the procedural statement.

3. Locate the main term in the Alphabetic Index, and then the modifying term. Write down the characters associated with the main and modifying terms.

   a. Review any See notes, if necessary

4. Confirm the code(s) found in the Index by going next to the Tabular List.

5. Find the Table in the Tabular list that contains the Section, Body System (or part), and Root Operation characters found in the Index.

6. Work through the row or rows to find the correct Body Part, Approach, Device and Qualifier character.

7. Review the Official Coding Guidelines for guidance, to ensure there is nothing to contraindicate use of the code selected.

8. Write the code(s) found next to the procedural statement.

Review

Matching

Instructions:

_____ 1. Index

_____ 2. Table

_____ 3. Tabular list

_____ 4. Qualifier

_____ 5. Device

_____ 6. Approach

_____ 7. Root Operation

_____ 8. Body System

_____ 9. Section

_____ 10. Character value

a. In ICD-10-PCS, the Root Operation identifies the objective of the procedure. It is always the third character of the ICD-10-PCS code.

b. In ICD-10-PCS, a Ssection identifies the general type of procedure, i.e. Medical/Surgical (med-surg), Obstetrics, etc. It is always the first character of the ICD-10-PCS code. There are 17 Sections in the ICD-10-PCS codebook.

c. In ICD-10-PCS, Body System is always the second character of the ICD-10-PCS code and refers to the body system affected by the procedure.

d. Each character of the ICD-10-PCS code has a specific purpose and identifies each of the characters within a code. There are 34 character values, 10 digits (0 through 9) and 24 letters (A through H, J through N, and P through Z).

e. An alphabetic list containing main and modifying terms, which is used to point to the most appropriate table in the ICD-10-PCS.

f. In ICD-10-PCS the seventh character is always a Qualifier. A qualifier contains unique values specific to the Table in which it is found.

g. In most of the seventeen sections of the ICD-10-PCS codebook, the fifth character of the code is the Approach, or technique used to reach the site of the procedure.

h. Each section of the ICD-10-PCS codebook is arranged in rows that specify valid combinations of codes that can be used within that section. The rows collectively are called a Table.

i. All of the tables within the ICD-10-PCS codebook are collectively known as the Tabular List. It is from the Tabular list that the final code determination should be made.

j. Any object left in or on the body during a procedure, such as a pacemaker, or screws and pins.

Short Answer

Instructions: Provide the main term shown in the Index, and at least three characters of the Index listing for the following statements (Hint, Appendix A should be very helpful with this activity):

1. Drainage of the cervical plexus nerve _____

2. Esophagogastroduodenoscopy _____

3. Excision of abdominal tendon _____

4. Electroneurogram _____

5. Inspection, general autonomic region _____

6. Visualization of the inner ear _____

7. Humeral head replacement _____

8. Repair subcutaneous tissue of right foot _____

9. Exchange device in eye for new one _____

10. Plastic surgery on drooping left eyelid _____

Let's Code: Procedures

Instructions: Code the following procedures from the Medical and Surgical Section (0)

1. Change drainage device in brain using an external approach _____

2. Insertion of monitoring device in coronary vein using percutaneous endoscopic approach

   _____

3. Percutaneous destruction of right ulnar artery _____

4. Open repair of azygos vein _____

5. Percutaneous endoscopic dilation of left brachial vein with placement of intraluminal device

   _____

6. Excision of right eye via external approach (non-diagnostic) _____

7. Drainage of right lung, endoscopic, via mouth (orifice) with placement of a drainage device

   _____

8. Open revision of gallbladder with placement of an infusion device _____

9. External excision of right breast, diagnostic _____

10. Extraction of subcutaneous tissue of anterior neck via open approach
   _____

11. Open adrenalorrhaphy of left adrenal gland _____

12. Open division of anal sphincter _____

13. Digital rectal exam _____

14. Percutaneous ligation of right renal vein _____

15. Release of scar contracture, skin of right ear _____

Root Operations in the Medical and Surgical Section

Learning Objectives

At the conclusion of this chapter, the learner should be able to:
- Describe the root operations used in the Medical and Surgical section and give examples
- Understand the differences and similarities between related root operations
- Apply the general and root operation-specific guidelines for the ICD-10-PCS appropriately
- Perform a search in the Index for the appropriate root operation and determine the best Table reference from that search

Key Terms and Definitions

Ablation	A minimally invasive alternative therapy to traditional (open) surgery. It is used to remove abnormal tissue that occurs with some types of cancer, and heart, vascular and reproductive conditions.
Alteration	Modifying the anatomic structure of a body part without affecting the function of the body part.
Bypass	Altering the route of passage of the contents of a tubular body part.
Change	Taking out or off a device from a body part and putting back an identical or similar device in or on the same body part without cutting or puncturing the skin or a mucous membrane.
Control	Stopping or attempting to stop postprocedural bleeding.
Creation	Making a new genital structure that does not take over the function of a body part.
Destruction	Physical eradication of all or a portion of a body part by the direct use of energy, force, or a destructive agent.
Detachment	Cutting off all or a portion of the upper or lower extremities.
Dilation	Expanding an orifice or the lumen of a tubular body part.
Division	Cutting into a body part, without draining fluids and/or gases from the body part, in order to separate or transect a body part.
Drainage	Taking or letting out fluids and/or gases from a body part.
Excision	Cutting out or off, without replacement, a portion of a body part.
Extirpation	Taking or cutting out solid matter from a body part.

Extraction	Pulling or stripping out or off all or a portion of a body part by the use of force.
Fragmentation	Breaking solid matter in a body part into pieces.
Fusion	Joining together portions of an articular body part, rendering the articular body part immobile.
Insertion	Putting a nonbiological appliance that monitors, assists, performs, or prevents a physiological function but does not physically take the place of a body part.
Inspection	Visually and/or manually exploring a body part.
Mapping	Locating the route of passage of electrical impulses and/or locating functional areas in a body part.
Occlusion	Completely closing an orifice or the lumen of a tubular body part.
Reattachment	Putting back in or on all or a portion of a separated body part to its normal location or other suitable location.
Release	Freeing a body part from an abnormal physical constraint.
Removal	Taking out or off a device from a body part.
Repair	Restoring, to the extent possible, a body part to its normal anatomic structure and function.
Replacement	Putting in or on biological or synthetic material that physically takes the place and/or function of all or a portion of a body part.
Reposition	Moving to its normal location, or other suitable location, all or a portion of a body part.
Resection	Cutting out or off, without replacement, all of a body part.
Restriction	Partially closing an orifice or the lumen of a tubular body part.
Revision	Correcting, to the extent possible, a portion of a malfunctioning device or the position of a displaced device.
Supplement	Putting in or on a biological or synthetic material that physically reinforces and/or augments the function of a portion of a body part.
Transfer	Moving, without taking out, all or a portion of a body part to another location to take over the function of all or a portion of a body part.
Transplantation	Putting in or on all of a portion of a living body part taking from another individual or animal to physically take the place and/or function of all or a portion of a similar body part.

Introduction

The Medical and Surgical Section of the ICD-10-PCS is by far the largest. Each of the seven code character values for the Medical and Surgical section is important, but the root operation is the key to searching for and selecting the correct Table, and the best procedure code. There are 31 root operations with very precise definitions and objectives. Because the root operation is used to perform an Index search, this entire chapter will be devoted exclusively to root operations in this section. Definitions and examples of root operations will be covered, and instructions for use of root operations in abstracting and searching the Index will be introduced. Guidelines from the ICD-10-PCS that assist in selecting the appropriate root operation, and guidelines specific to coding in general, will also be presented. In the next chapter, the remaining six code characters will be analyzed, followed by in-depth instruction in using the Index and Tables to code Medical and Surgical procedures.

Root Operations in the ICD-10-PCS

Coding procedures from the ICD-10-PCS begins with a search for the root operation of the procedure. The root operation is the third character in a procedure code. The first and largest section of the ICD-10-PCS coding manual is the Medical and Surgical section; as discussed in the last chapter, there are 31 root operations. Each root operation has a specific definition and describes a specific objective and purpose. The root operations, their definitions, and their objectives will be covered in depth in this chapter because of their importance in proper coding of medical and surgical procedures. The 31 root operations will be divided into nine groups, each of which will contain root operations with similar objectives. The nine groups are root operations that:

1. Take out some or all of a body part

2. Take out solids, fluids, or gases from a body part

3. Involve cutting or separation only

4. Put in/put back, or move some or all of a body part

5. Alter the diameter or route of a body part

6. Include other repairs

7. Involve examination only

8. Always involve a device

9. Include other objectives

Table 5-1 lists the root operations found in each of these nine groups. Understanding the objective of the root operation, and its proper use when coding, is the key to successful coding. The root operation guides the coder from the abstract to selection of the main term and a successful Index search. From there, the root operation is the foundation for selection of the remaining six code character values in the Medical and Surgical section Tables in the Tabular List.

The ICD-10-PCS coding manual contains a Section 0 Appendix that lists all the root operations, provides definitions, and in some cases provides further explanation and examples. Figure 5-1 is an excerpt from that appendix.

ICD-10-PCS Root Operation Guidelines

There are several groups of guidelines in the ICD-10-PCS. In the previous chapter, several general guidelines were presented from the guidelines in group A. A few of these will be repeated here, with more explanation, as well as guidelines for specific root operations. Those guidelines will be covered as the related root operations are introduced.

There are two general root operation guidelines B3.1a and B3.1b, and several others, such as multiple procedures (B3.2), discontinued procedures (B3.3), biopsies followed by a more definitive treatment (B3.4), and overlapping body parts (B3.5) that are not specific to any particular root operation. These will be covered first, followed by specific root operation guidelines that will be introduced. Table 5-2 lists the remainder of the guidelines to be covered in this chapter.

Guideline B3.1a: *In order to determine the appropriate root operation, the full definition of that root operation, as it is found in the Tables, must be applied.* Many of the root operations have similar definitions. For example, the definitions for Excision and Resection both begin with *cutting out or off, without replacement*. Excision, however, only cuts out or off *part* of a body part; while resection cuts out or off *all* of a body part. Using the full definition as a guide will prevent errors in root operation, and thus code, selection.

Table 5-1 Root Operation by Group Objective

Group	Value	Root Operation
Take out some or all of a body part	B	Excision
	T	Resection
	6	Detachment
	5	Destruction
	D	Extraction
Take out solids/fluids/gases from a body part	9	Drainage
	C	Extirpation
	F	Fragmentation
Involving cutting or separation only	8	Division
	N	Release
Put in/put back or move some/all of a body part	Y	Transplantation
	M	Reattachment
	X	Transfer
	S	Reposition
Alter the diameter or route of a tubular body part	V	Restriction
	L	Occlusion
	7	Dilation
	1	Bypass
Include other repairs	3	Control
	Q	Repair
Involving examination only	J	Inspection
	K	Map
Always involve a device	H	Insertion
	R	Replacement
	U	Supplement
	2	Change
	P	Removal
	W	Revision
Include other objectives	G	Fusion
	0	Alteration
	4	Creation

Guideline is B3.1b: *Components of a procedure necessary to complete the objective of a procedure is considered integral to the procedure and are not coded separately.* An example of B3.2 would be a joint replacement procedure. Resection of the joint in order to replace it is considered an integral part of the procedure, and as such is not coded separately.

Guideline for Multiple Procedures (B3.2a Through B3.2d)

In ICD-10-PCS, it is certainly possible and advisable to code multiple procedures. This guideline on multiple procedures, B3.2, has four subparts, A through D, which identify when it is appropriate to code multiple procedures from the same operative episode. The guideline in its entirety is shown in Table 5-3.

Section 0 – Medical and Surgical
Character 3 – Operation *(continued)*

Creation	**Definition:** Making a new genital structure that does not take over the function of a body part
	Explanation: Used only for sex change operations
	Includes/Examples: Creation of vagina in a male, creation of penis in a female
Destruction	**Definition:** Physical eradication of all or a portion of a body part by the direct use of energy, force, or a destructive agent
	Explanation: None of the body part is physically taken out
	Includes/Examples: Fulguration of rectal polyp, cautery of skin lesion
Detachment	**Definition:** Cutting off all or a portion of the upper or lower extremities
	Explanation: The body part value is the site of the detachment, with a qualifier if applicable to further specify the level where the extremity was detached
	Includes/Examples: Below knee amputation, disarticulation of shoulder
Dilation	**Definition:** Expanding an orifice or the lumen of a tubular body part
	Explanation: The orifice can be a natural orifice or an artificially created orifice. Accomplished by stretching a tubular body part using intraluminal pressure or by cutting part of the orifice or wall of the tubular body part
	Includes/Examples: Percutaneous transluminal angioplasty, pyloromyotomy

© Cengage Learning 2013

Figure 5-1 Excerpt from Medical and Surgical Section (0) Appendix

Table 5-2 List of Root Operation Guidelines and Topics

Guideline	Topic and/or Root Operation
B3.2	Multiple Procedures
B3.3	Discontinued Procedures
B3.4	Biopsy followed by more definitive treatment
B3.5	Overlapping Body Layers
B3.6a–B3.6c	Bypass Procedures
B3.7	Control versus more definitive root operations
B3.8	Excision versus Resection
B3.9	Excision for Graft
B3.10a–B3.10c	Fusion Procedures of the Spine
B3.11a–B3.11c	Inspection Procedures
B3.12	Occlusion versus Restriction for Vessel Embolization Procedures
B3.13	Release Procedures
B3.14	Release versus Division
B3.15	Reposition for Fracture Treatment

An example of B3.2a is *diagnostic excision of the liver and pancreas.* The liver and pancreas each have a separate body part value; therefore, a separate code for the diagnostic excision of each would be required.

An example for B3.2b would be *excision of gastrocnemius muscle and soleus muscles.* Both muscles are included in the lower legs muscle body part value; therefore, multiple procedures would be coded to

Table 5-3　Root Operation Guideline B3.3a through B3.3d

B3.2. During the Same Operative Episode, Multiple Procedures are Coded If:	
a	The same root operation is performed on different body parts as definite by distinct values of the body part character
b	The same root operation is repeated at different body sites that are included in the same body part value
c	Multiple root operations with distinct objectives are performed on the same body part
d	The intended root operation is attempted using one approach, but is converted to a different approach

indicate two separate excisions of two different muscles. Another example would be the destruction of two separate skin sites on the face. The body part value is defined as Skin, Face; therefore, each of the two facial destruction sites would have their own code.

Guideline B3.2c states that it is appropriate to code multiple procedures if *multiple root operations with distinct objectives are performed on the same body part*. For example, destruction of a sigmoid colon lesion and a bypass of the sigmoid colon, performed at the same time, have individual, distinct objectives—specifically, the destruction and the bypass, which are two different root operations. Each procedure, the destruction and the bypass, would be coded separately.

Guideline B3.2d, indicates that multiple procedures should be coded if the intended root operation is attempted using one approach, but is converted to a different approach. If a procedure starts out, for example, as a laparoscopic procedure and ends up being converted to an open procedure, this would qualify for multiple procedure coding. If a laparoscopic cholecystectomy is converted to an open cholecystectomy during the same operative episode, both procedures would be coded. In this example, the laparoscopic procedure would be coded as an endoscopic inspection root operation, and the open cholecystectomy coded as an open resection root operation.

Guideline is B3.3, referring to discontinued procedures (Table 5-4).

An example of B3.3 would be a *ureteroscopy with an unsuccessful excision of a ureteral stone*. This would be coded as an inspection of the urethra because the attempt to extract the stone was unsuccessful. If a portion of the stone was excised, but the procedure was discontinued for any reason before completion, code to the root operation Excision.

Let's look at the remaining two guidelines B3.4 and B3.5 before proceeding on to the root operation-specific guidelines.

Guideline B3.4 describes the rules for procedures that start with a biopsy but are then followed by more definitive procedures. If a diagnostic (i.e., with biopsy) excision, extraction, or drainage procedure is performed, followed (during the same procedure) by a more definitive objective, such as a destruction, excision, or resection, both procedures should be assigned an ICD-10-PCS code. An example is a biopsy of the breast, followed by a resection of the breast based on the results of the biopsy. The original biopsy, and the breast resection would both be coded.

Last is **guideline B3.5,** concerning overlapping body layers. If the root operations excision, repair, or inspection are performed on overlapping layers of the musculoskeletal system, the body part

Table 5-4　Guidelines B3.4 Discontinued Procedures

B3.3. Discontinued Procedures
If the intended procedure is discontinued or incomplete, code the procedure to the specific root operation actually performed
If a procedure is discontinued before any other root operation is performed, code the root operation *Inspection* of the body part or anatomical region

(character 4) should specify the deepest layer. If the skin, subcutaneous tissue, and muscle are debrided to remove dead tissue, for example, the body part value would be the muscle, since it is the deepest layer involved in the debridement.

Root Operations and Documentation

It is important to apply the correct root operation regardless of the documentation in the medical record. When reading operative reports or procedural notes, many times words like *removal, excision,* and *resection* are used somewhat interchangeably. In ICD-10-PCS, however, there are very specific rules and definitions for each root operation.

The most important thing to remember when coding any procedure is to determine the objective of the procedure, and select the root operation definition that best matches that objective. If the medical documentation states that an entire body part is excised, the tendency would be to select excision as the root operation. However, the definition of Excision is *cutting out some or a portion of a body part*. The documentation states that the entire body part was removed, which means the root operation that best describes it is Resection, *cutting out all of a body part*.

Be careful to read the documentation thoroughly to determine the objective of the procedure, and then match the root operation to that objective. The importance of this fundamental principle cannot be stressed enough.

Root Operations That Take Out Some or All of a Body Part

There are five root operations that qualify as those that take out some or all of a body part group. They are Excision, Resection, Detachment, Destruction, and Extraction. There are two guidelines specific to the use of the root operations Excision and Resection, B3.8 and B3.9. Table 5-5 describes guideline B3.8, and the differences between excision and resection. Guideline B3.9 is specific to grafts and will be covered later in this chapter.

Another perfect example of when to use excision or resection is with lymph nodes. If an entire lymph node chain is cut out, the procedure is coded to the root operation resection. When a lymph node or a few nodes are cut out of a lymph chain, the procedure is coded to the root operation excision.

Excision (B) and Resection (T) Root Operations

The root operation **excision** has the character value B, and will always be in the third position of the code. The definition of Excision is *cutting out or off, without replacement, a portion of a body part*. The two keys to this root operation are (1) it is without replacement, in other words, the procedure cuts a part of a body part out or off and it is not replaced, and (2) only a portion of a body part is cut off or out. Examples of an excision root operation include a *partial nephrectomy, liver biopsy,* and *breast lumpectomy*. In a partial nephrectomy, only a section of the kidney is removed, and nothing replaces the removed section. The key here is to first identify the body part, then determine whether or not all of the body part is removed. The body part value for kidney is 0 for the right kidney and 1 for the left kidney. In the Urinary System Table, with the root operation Excision, there is also a body part

Table 5-5 Guidelines B3.8 Excision versus Resection

B3.8 Excision versus Resection
Resection is coded whenever "all of a body part" is cut out or off without replacement. "All of a body part" includes any anatomical subdivision that has its own body part value. Therefore, resection of a specific anatomical subdivision body part is coded, whenever possible, rather than Excision of the less specific body part
EXAMPLE: Breast has its own body part value (T, right breast, U, left breast). A total mastectomy would be coded to Resection because the entire breast is cut off. A partial mastectomy would be coded to Excision, since it is not the entire body part being cut out or off.

value for the kidney pelvis, but as it is not part of the procedural statement, it is not an appropriate code character value. Since the procedure description includes the word *partial*, and there is no indication that replacement of that partial body part occurred, then the correct root operation would be Excision.

In liver biopsy and breast lumpectomy, only part of the body part is removed, with no replacement of that body part, so in both instances the root operation is Excision. There is another consideration when the term *biopsy* occurs in the procedural statement. Whenever this term is in the procedural statement, the seventh character of the code will use the diagnostic qualifier, X. One further important note is that bone marrow and endometrial biopsies are not coded to excision. They are coded to the root operation extraction, which will be discussed later in this chapter.

Guideline B3.9 states that if an autograft is obtained from a different body part in order to complete the objective of the procedure, the autograft is coded separately. For example, if a bypass procedure is done to replace the femoral artery with the saphenous vein and the saphenous vein is harvested during the bypass procedure, both the bypass and the saphenous vein harvesting are coded.

It is important to remember that all root operations employing cutting to accomplish the objective allow the use of any sharp instrument including but not limited to scalpel, wire, scissors, bone saws, and electrocautery tips. The key, again, for use of the root operation excision is that a portion of a body part is cut out or off.

The definition of root operation **resection**, character value T, is very similar to excision. Like Excision, Resection is cutting out or off, without replacement, but here *it is all of a body part rather than some or part of a body part. Some examples include total nephrectomy,* where the entire kidney is cut off or out, *total lobectomy of the lung,* and *total mastectomy.* Here the word *total* with nephrectomy, and the knowledge that the kidney has its own body part value (0 or 1), indicates that Resection, rather than Excision, is the correct root operation. The same is true for each lobe of the lung and the breast. They all have their own body part value, and the procedure description includes the total or whole body part that is cut off or out. Figure 5-2 provides additional guidelines for root operation Resection, taken from a handout from an ICD-10-PCS Root Operation audio seminar sponsored by AHIMA in 2010.

The key in choosing the root operation Resection or Excision is that the part being cut out or off is a portion of a body part or an entire body part. A prostatectomy is the cutting out of the entire prostate, while a transurethral resection of the prostate (TURP) is the removal only of the section of the prostate that is causing symptoms. The prostatectomy is coded to root operation Resection, the TURP is

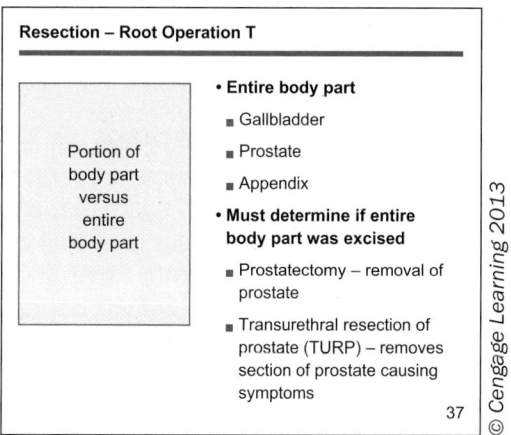

Figure 5-2 Guidelines for Using Root Operation Resection

coded to Excision. It is important to remember that a body part is not necessarily the entire organ. For example, the liver and lung lobes each have their own body part value. Therefore, if a lung or liver lobe is cut out completely, Resection would be the correct root operation; if only a portion of the lung or liver lobe is cut out, the root operation would be Excision.

Root Operation Detachment (6)

The character value for root operation **detachment** is 6. The definition is *cutting off all or part of the upper or lower extremities.* This root operation is very specific, in that it affects the extremities only. Examples of root operation detachment would be below the knee amputation, a disarticulation of the shoulder, or amputation above the elbow. A Detachment represents a narrow range of procedures, specifically amputation. There are specific qualifiers used for a detachment, depending on the body part values in the upper and lower extremities. Examples are complete, partial, high, mid, or low, among others. In the next chapter, these qualifiers will be covered at length, however, here it is important only to know the root operations and their appropriate uses.

Root Operation Destruction (5)

The character value for the root operation **destruction** is 5. The definition is *physical eradication of all or a portion of a body part by the direct use of energy, force, or a destructive agent.* With this root operation, no body part is cut off or out. Examples include *fulguration of rectal polyp or of endometrium, or cautery of a skin lesion.*

While none of the body part is cut out or off, destruction takes out a body part in the sense that it obliterates it. Terms like *ablation, destruction, fulguration, cryotherapy, cautery,* and *coagulation* all conform to the definition of destruction as the root operation. This root operation defines a broad range of common procedures since it can be used anywhere on the body to treat a variety of conditions, such as skin and genital warts, nasal and colon polyps, esophageal varices, endometrial implants, or nerve lesions.

From the Mayo Clinic, here is an interesting overview of the term ablation:

Ablation therapy is a minimally invasive alternative to traditional (open) surgery. It is used to remove abnormal tissue that occurs with some types of cancer, and heart, vascular and reproductive conditions. Ablation therapy helps spare healthy tissue and decreases the risks and discomforts of open surgery.

Ablation injures or destroys abnormal tissue. The ablation technique used depends on the condition being treated. Usually images such as a CT scan or ultrasound guide ablation. During ablation, the doctor inserts a probe through the skin or a narrow tube (catheter) through an artery, or uses energy beams to reach the area being treated. Heat in the form of high-energy radio waves (radiofrequency ablation), gas that creates extreme cold (cryoablation) or a chemical substance is then released to destroy the abnormal tissue.

Root Operation Extraction (D)

The definition for root operation **extraction**, which has a character value of D, is *pulling or stripping out or off all or a portion of a body part by the use of force.* Extraction is coded when the method employed to take out the body part is pulling or stripping. Minor cutting, such as that used in vein stripping procedures, is included in extraction, since the objective of the procedure is to pull or strip the veins. Other examples include *dilatation and curettage (D&C),* and extraction of teeth. As always, read the documentation carefully. It is important to convert common terminology to the appropriate root operation according to the real intent of the procedure. For example, a procedure documented as a removal might, in actuality, be coded to extraction, for example removal of a tooth or thumbnail. Both procedures involve pulling or stripping; therefore, the root operation is extraction, not removal. The root operation **removal** is defined as *taking out or off a device from a body part*—which is not the objective when removing teeth or a thumbnail.

Here are a few more examples with some descriptions that may help in determining whether Extraction is the correct root operation. Bone and endometrial biopsies, unlike most other biopsies which are coded to excision with a diagnostic qualifier of X, are coded to extraction, because the tissue obtained is pulled or stripped from the bone or endometrium. Let's take the procedure *phacoemulsification without implant*. **Phacoemulsification** is a procedure in which the lens clouded by a cataract is broken up by ultrasound, irrigated, and suctioned out. Extraction is the pulling or stripping out of a body part, and by this definition, it is the correct root operation. One important note, if there is an implant of a new lens performed during the same procedure as the phacoemulsification, that would be coded to the root operation replacement rather than extraction because the objective of the procedure would be to implant the lens. The phacoemulsification becomes part of the process, and is no longer the objective. This means that in any procedure where a replacement of a body part is part of the definition, the objective not simply the extraction, and another root operation, like replacement, would be used. Here's another example. If a non-excisional debridement is done, it is coded to Extraction; however, if an excisional debridement done, it is coded to Excision. The final example is liposuction. If the liposuction is done for medical reasons, it is coded to Extraction; however, if it was done for cosmetic reasons, the root operation is Alteration.

Using the Index for Root Objectives That Take Out Some or All of a Body Part

Before beginning this section, remember that with all of these root operations, it is permissible, based on Guideline A7, to go straight to the appropriate Table for the root operation to confirm the values and complete the code character value selection. A search of the Index is not a requirement, although especially when first learning how to code procedures using ICD-10-PCS, the Index will be the best starting place.

As mentioned earlier, the key to abstracting and searching the Index for an appropriate Table reference is in determining the objective of the procedure performed. Let's take some procedure examples from the root operations excision, resection, detachment, destruction, and extraction, identifying the objective, the correct root operation, and the steps for finding the root operation in the Index. In this chapter, the goal is to determine the objective, and search the Index. In the following chapter, the real fun will begin as the next step is determining values for all seven code characters, and coding the entire procedure using the Tables in the Medical and Surgical Section of the ICD-10-PCS.

Using the Index to Find the Root Operation Excision or Resection

Before even turning to the Index, the first step is to determine the procedure objective. If the objective is to cut out some or part of a body part the root operation is Excision. If the objective is to cut out all of a body part, the root operation is Resection. A search for Excision in the Index leads to several pages. An excerpt is shown in Figure 5-3.

Let's take a closer look at this excerpt. First, note that Excision is in bold font. This makes it a main term. Indented below Excision are the modifying terms, which in this case are generally body systems. The first body system listed is Bursa and Ligament. Indented below the modifying term are subterms, which in most instances will be the specific body part. The entire excerpt in Figure 5-3 identifies the body system Bursa and Ligaments, and the associated anatomical body parts for that body system. All of the subterms, from hand, to hip, to buttocks, colon, cornea, discs and ducts, are all body parts found in this body system. Using the procedure *excision of the bursa of the left wrist*, the search would begin with *excision* as the main term, *bursa and ligaments* as the modifying term, and *wrist, left* as the subterms.

In Figure 5-3, the Table reference for this procedure is 0MB6. The first character 0 represents the Medical and Surgical Section, and M represents the Bursa and Ligament body system. The third character B is the root operation, excision, and the fourth character 6 is the body part, left wrist.

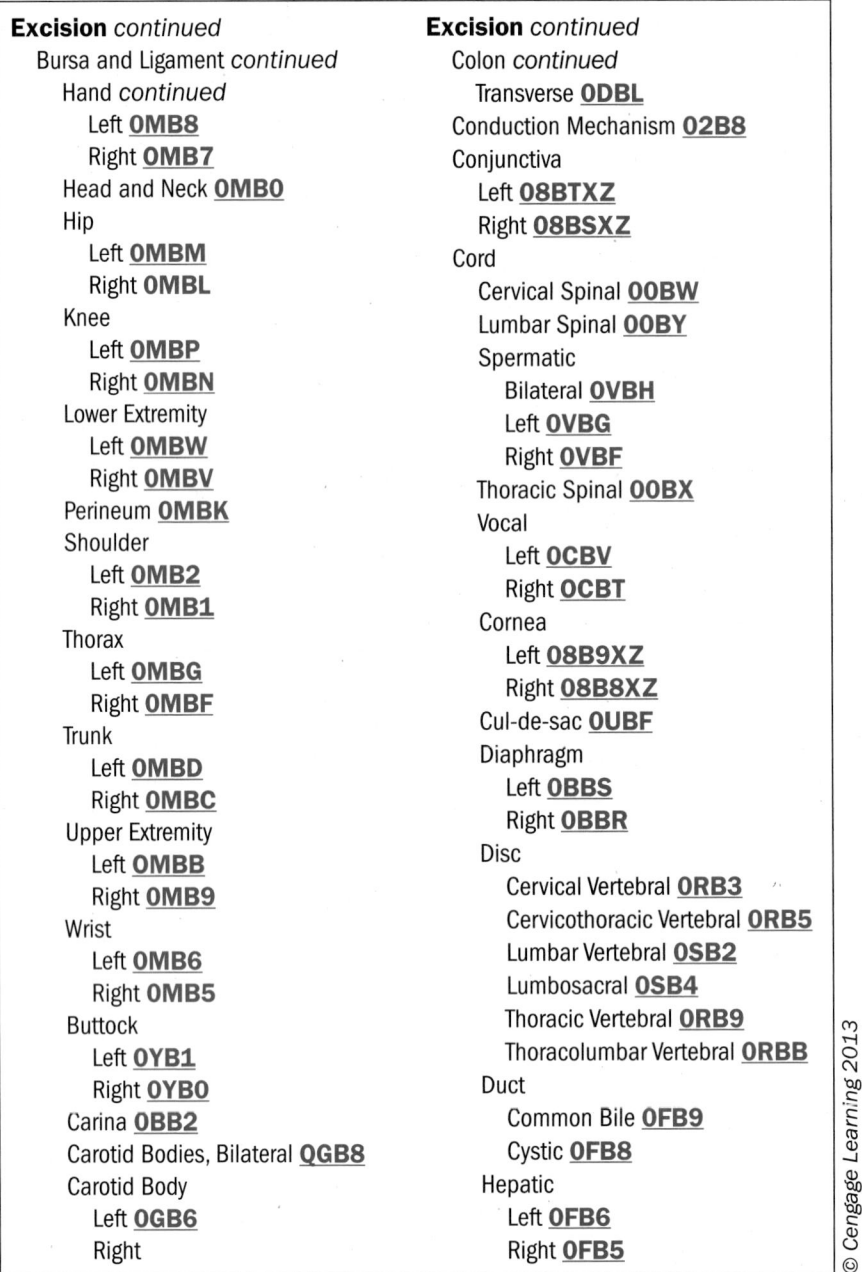

Excision *continued*	Excision *continued*
Bursa and Ligament *continued*	Colon *continued*
Hand *continued*	Transverse **0DBL**
Left **0MB8**	Conduction Mechanism **02B8**
Right **0MB7**	Conjunctiva
Head and Neck **0MB0**	Left **08BTXZ**
Hip	Right **08BSXZ**
Left **0MBM**	Cord
Right **0MBL**	Cervical Spinal **00BW**
Knee	Lumbar Spinal **00BY**
Left **0MBP**	Spermatic
Right **0MBN**	Bilateral **0VBH**
Lower Extremity	Left **0VBG**
Left **0MBW**	Right **0VBF**
Right **0MBV**	Thoracic Spinal **00BX**
Perineum **0MBK**	Vocal
Shoulder	Left **0CBV**
Left **0MB2**	Right **0CBT**
Right **0MB1**	Cornea
Thorax	Left **08B9XZ**
Left **0MBG**	Right **08B8XZ**
Right **0MBF**	Cul-de-sac **0UBF**
Trunk	Diaphragm
Left **0MBD**	Left **0BBS**
Right **0MBC**	Right **0BBR**
Upper Extremity	Disc
Left **0MBB**	Cervical Vertebral **0RB3**
Right **0MB9**	Cervicothoracic Vertebral **0RB5**
Wrist	Lumbar Vertebral **0SB2**
Left **0MB6**	Lumbosacral **0SB4**
Right **0MB5**	Thoracic Vertebral **0RB9**
Buttock	Thoracolumbar Vertebral **0RBB**
Left **0YB1**	Duct
Right **0YB0**	Common Bile **0FB9**
Carina **0BB2**	Cystic **0FB8**
Carotid Bodies, Bilateral **0GB8**	Hepatic
Carotid Body	Left **0FB6**
Left **0GB6**	Right **0FB5**
Right	

Figure 5-3 Excerpt from Alphabetic Index Search for Root Operation Excision

Take a quick peek at Figure 5-4, which is the 0MB Table in the Tabular List. Note the heading of the Table. The Table heading always includes the section, body system, and operation. The columns in the Tables for the Medical and Surgical section represent the fourth through seventh characters of the code. The body part—wrist, bursa and ligament, left hand—is in the first column, which represents the body part. The remaining columns give the allowable values for the procedure approach, device, and qualifier. (The Tables, including the definitions and use of headings and columns, will be discussed at length in the next chapter.)

Going back to the procedure, *excision of the bursa of the left wrist,* the Index search leads to the Table reference 0MB6.

Section **0** Medical and Surgical			
Body System **M** Bursae and Ligaments			
Operation **B** Excision: Cutting out or off, without replacement, a portion of a body part			
Body Part	Approach	Device	Qualifier
0 Head and Neck Bursa and Ligament	**0** Open	**Z** No Device	**X** Diagnostic
1 Shoulder Bursa and Ligament, Right	**3** Percutaneous	**Z** No Qualifier	
2 Shoulder Bursa and Ligament, Left	**4** Percutaneous Endoscopic		
3 Elbow Bursa and Ligament, Right			
4 Elbow Bursa and Ligament, Left			
5 Wrist Bursa and Ligament, Right			
6 Wrist Bursa and Ligament, Left			
7 Hand Bursa and Ligament, Right			
8 Hand Bursa and Ligament, Left			
9 Upper Extremity Bursa and Ligament, Right			
B Upper Extremity Bursa and Ligament, Left			
C Trunk Bursa and Ligament, Right			
D Trunk Bursa and Ligament, Left			
F Thorax Bursa and Ligament, Right			
G Thorax Bursa and Ligament, Left			
H Abdomen Bursa and Ligament, Right			
J Abdomen Bursa and Ligament, Left			
K Perineum Bursa and Ligament			
L Hip Bursa and Ligament, Right			
M Hip Bursa and Ligament, Left			
N Knee Bursa and Ligament, Right			
P Knee Bursa and Ligament, Left			
Q Ankle Bursa and Ligament, Right			
R Ankle Bursa and Ligament, Left			
S Foot Bursa and Ligament, Right			
T Foot Bursa and Ligament, Left			
V Lower Extremity Bursa and Ligament, Right			
W Lower Extremity Bursa and Ligament, Left			

© Cengage Learning 2013

Figure 5-4 Table 0MB in the Tabular List

Here is another example, this time using the root operation resection. The procedure is *total hysterectomy*. This is the removal of the entire uterus, i.e., the entire body part (uterus) is cut out. The definition for resection is cutting out an entire body part. The search in the Index, therefore, will begin with the main term (root operation) resection. As with the root operation excision, the Index has several pages of resection procedures. An excerpt from resection, which includes the body part uterus, is shown in Figure 5-5. In this excerpt, the Table reference for the main term resection, and the modifying term, uterus, is 0UT9. The 0 is for the Medical and Surgical section, the U represents the female reproductive body system, and the T identifies the root operation resection. The fourth character body part value, 9, is the value for the body part uterus. From this reference, the next step in the coding process would be to go to the 0UT Table in the Tabular List and find the row in which the body part value 9 is listed.

Now, what happens if the medical documentation lists only a specific procedure, but does not give enough information to determine the objective? Let's use the example of an *abdominohysterectomy*.

Resection *continued*

Tendon *continued*

Hip

Left **OLTK**

Right **OLTJ**

Knee

Left **OLTR**

Right **OLTO**

Lower Arm and Wrist

Left **OLT6**

Right **OLT5**

Lower Leg

Left **OLTP**

Right **OLTN**

Perineum **OLTH**

Shoulder

Left **OLT2**

Right **OLT1**

Thorax

Left **OLID**

Right **OLTC**

Trunk

Left **OLTB**

Right **OLT9**

Upper Arm

Left **OLT4**

Right **OLT3**

Upper Leg

Left **OLTM**

Right **OLTL**

Testis

Bilateral **OVTC**

Left **OVTB**

Right **OVT9**

Thymus **07JH**

Thyroid Gland

Left Lobe **OGTG**

Right Lobe **OGTH**

Tibia

Left **OOTHOZZ**

Right **OOTGOZZ**

Tongue **OCT7**

Tonsils **OCTP**

Tooth

Lower **OCTXOZ**

Upper **OCTWOZ**

Trachea **OBT1**

Tunica Vaginalis

Left **OVT7**

Right **OVT6**

Turbinate, Nasal **09TL**

Ulna

Left **OPTLOZZ**

Right **OPTKOZZ**

Ureter

Left **OTT7**

Right **OTT6**

Urethra **OTTD**

Uterine Supporting Structure **OUT4**

Uterus **OUT9**

© Cengage Learning 2013

Figure 5-5 Alphabetic Index Excerpt for Root Operation Resection

Going to the Index, we find this procedure listed (Figure 5-6). Note that there is an instructional note to *see* both Excision and Resection, along with a Table reference for each one. The first step is to follow the instructional note and look in the Index under excision and resection, and then look for the appropriate body part. Starting with excision, and the body part uterus again, look at Figure 5-7. Then look back at Figure 5-5 for the root operation Resection, and body part uterus. Note that the only code value that changes is the third character. With Excision, the values are 0UB9, and with resection, the values are 0UT9—the same as the Table reference given in Figure 5-6 for abdominohysterectomy.

At this point, it is still impossible to tell which root operation is correct, which leads us to the real point: The medical documentation must contain enough information to determine what the objective of the procedure is. This is the only way to identify the correct root operation. Taking the same procedure again, abdominohysterectomy, the documentation does reveal the objective, which is to totally remove the uterus (hyster = uterus, ectomy = surgical removal), allowing selection of the resection Table reference from the Index. Here's one final procedure example, *total cholecystectomy*. In this example, a search in the Index can start with Resection, since the word *total* indicates removal of the entire gallbladder, or the index search can begin with the procedure *cholecystectomy*. A search for

Abdominohysterectomy

see Excision, Uterus **0UB9**

see Resection, Uterus **0UT9**

Figure 5-6 Alphabetic Index Excerpt for Abdominohysterectomy
© Cengage Learning 2013

Excision *continued*

Tooth

Lower **0CBX**

Upper **0CBW**

Trachea **0BB1**

Trunk, Pulmonary **02BP**

Tunica Vaginalis

Left **0VB7**

Right **0VB6**

Turbinate, Nasal **09BL**
Ulna

Left **0PBL**

Right **0PBK**

Ureter

Left **0TB7**

Right **0TB6**

Urethra **0TBD**

Uterine Supporting Structure **0UB4**

Uterus **0UB9**

© Cengage Learning 2013

Figure 5-7 Alphabetic Index Excerpt for Root Operation Excision and Body Part Uterus

Cholecystectomy

see Excision, Gallbladder **0FB4**

see Resection, Gallbladder **0FT4**

Figure 5-8 Alphabetic Index Excerpt for Cholecystectomy
© Cengage Learning 2013

cholecystectomy in the Index (Figure 5-8), leads to cholecystectomy as the main term, which has an instructional note to *see* excision, gallbladder, or *see* resection, gallbladder. The Table reference for *resection, gallbladder* is 0FT4. The third character is T, which is the value for the root operation resection. The 0 and F values represent the Medical and Surgical section, and the Hepatobiliary System and Pancreas body system, respectively. The fourth character, 4, is for the body part gallbladder. A search for the main term resection, and body part gallbladder, will lead to the same Table reference (Figure 5-9). The next step is to turn to the Table referenced, and select the remaining values.

Using the Index to Find the Root Operation Detachment

The objective of the root operation **detachment** is to cut off all or part of an upper or lower extremity. The main term, when doing a search in the Index, can be either *amputation* or *detachment*. A search for amputation leads to the instructional note to *see* Detachment. Indented under Detachment in the Index (Figure 5-10), are all the modifying and subterms, all of which are an upper or lower extremity body part. For example, in Figure 5-10, a *detachment of the left little finger* reveals the Table reference 0X6W0Z,

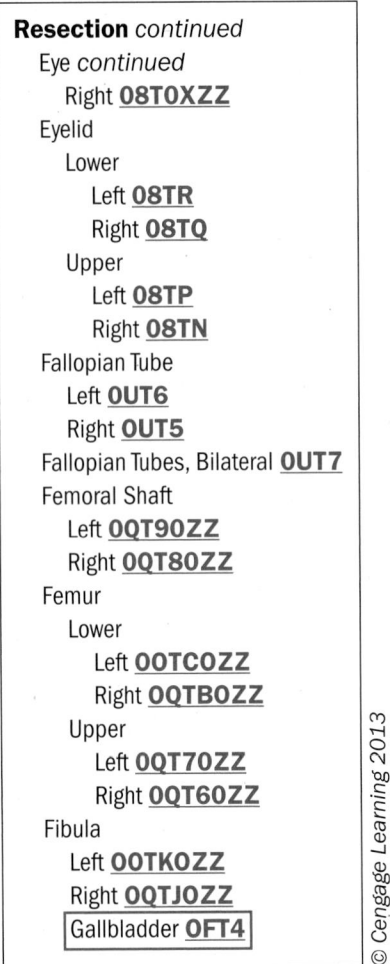

Resection *continued*
  Eye *continued*
    Right **08T0XZZ**
  Eyelid
    Lower
      Left **08TR**
      Right **08TQ**
    Upper
      Left **08TP**
      Right **08TN**
  Fallopian Tube
    Left **0UT6**
    Right **0UT5**
  Fallopian Tubes, Bilateral **0UT7**
  Femoral Shaft
    Left **0QT90ZZ**
    Right **0QT80ZZ**
  Femur
    Lower
      Left **0OTC0ZZ**
      Right **0QTB0ZZ**
    Upper
      Left **0QT70ZZ**
      Right **0QT60ZZ**
  Fibula
    Left **0OTK0ZZ**
    Right **0QTJ0ZZ**
  Gallbladder **0FT4**

© Cengage Learning 2013

Figure 5-9 Alphabetic Index Excerpt for Resection, Gallbladder

or the first six code character values. The next step would be to go to Table 0X6, then verify the six character values are correct and match the procedural statement, and finally, determine the seventh and final code character.

Using the Index to Find the Root Operation Destruction

Surgical techniques such as fulguration, cautery, coagulation, ablation, and cryotherapy fulfill the objective of the root operation **destruction.** The objective is *physical eradication of all or a portion of a body part by the direct use of energy, force or a destructive agent.* A search in the Index for these common terminologies—*fulguration, cryotherapy, ablation,* and *coagulation*—all lead to an instructional note to *see* destruction. A search for Destruction in the Index reveals several pages of destruction root operations. Figure 5-11 is a small excerpt from the Index for the main term Destruction. Note that indented below the root operation are once again, body parts as modifying terms, and in many instances, subterms indented below that to identify laterality, etc. For example, under *destruction, artery,* the subterm lists the specific arteries, such as anterior tibial. Indented below that is another subterm indicating the left or right anterior tibial artery. Just above that, in Figure 5-11, is the modifying term aorta, with the subterms abdominal and thoracic.

Here is an example. If the procedure was *ablation of abdominal aortic cyst,* the first search in the Index could be for ablation. There, an instructional note to *see* Destruction would lead to that root operation (main term) in the Index. From there, the modifying term would be *aorta,* the subterm would be *abdominal,* and the Index Table reference would be 0450. As illustrated in Figure 5-12, the first character 0 would be the Medical and Surgical Section, second character 4 the body system lower arteries, and

Detachment
  Arm
    Lower
      Left **0X6F0Z**
      Right **0X6D0Z**
    Upper
      Left **0X690Z**
      Right **0X680Z**
    Elbow Region
      Left **0X6C0ZZ**
      Right **0X6B0ZZ**
    Femoral Region
      Left **0Y680ZZ**
      Right **0Y670ZZ**
    Finger
      Index
        Left **0X6P0Z**
        Right **0X6N0Z**
      Little
        Left **0X6W0Z**
        Right **0X6V0Z**
      Middle
        Left **0X6R0Z**
        Right **0X6Q0Z**
      Ring
        Left **0X6T0Z**
        Right **0X6S0Z**
    Foot
      Left **0Y6N0Z**
      Right **0Y6M0Z**
    Fore quarter
      Left **0X610ZZ**
      Right **0X600ZZ**
    Hand
      Left **0X6K0Z**
      Right **0X630Z**
    Hind quarter
      Bilateral **0Y640ZZ**
      Left **0Y630ZZ**
      Right **0Y620ZZ**
    Knee Region
      Left **0Y6G0ZZ**

© Cengage Learning 2013

Figure 5-10 Alphabetic Index Excerpt for Detachment, Finger, Little, Left

Destruction *continued*
  Adenoids **0C5Q**
  Ampulla of Vater **0F5C**
  Anterior Chamber
    Left **08533ZZ**
    Right **08523ZZ**
  Anus **0D5Q**
  Aorta
    Abdominal **0450**
    Thoracic **025W**
  Aortic Body **0G5D**
  Appendix **0D5J**
  Artery
  Anterior Tibial
    Left **0450**
    Right **045P**
  Axillary
    Left **0356**
    Right **0355**
  Brachial
    Left **0358**
    Right **0352**
  Celiac **0451**
  Colic
    Left **0457**
    Middle **0458**
    Right **0456**
  Common Carotid
    Left **035J**
    Right **035H**

Destruction *continued*
  Artery *continued*
    Internal Mammary *continued*
    Left **0351**
    Right **0350**
  Intracranial **035G**
  Lower **045Y**
  Peroneal
    Left **045U**
    Right **0451**
  Popliteal
    Left **045N**
    Right **045M**
  Posterior Tibial
    Left **045S**
    Right **045R**
  Pulmonary
    Left **025R**
    Right **025Q**
  Radial
    Left **035C**
    Right **035B**
  Renal
    Left **045A**
    Right **0459**
  Splenic **0454**
  Subclavian
    Left **0354**
    Right **0353**
  Superior Mesenteric **0455**

© Cengage Learning 2013

Figure 5-11 Alphabetic Index Excerpt for Root Operation Destruction

Section	**0** Medical and Surgical
Body System	**4** Lower Arteries
Operation	**5** Destruction: Physical eradication of all or a portion of a body part by the direct use of energy, force, or a destructive agent

Body Part	Approach	Device	Qualifier
0 Abdominal Aorta **1** Celiac Artery **2** Gastric Artery **3** Hepatic Artery **4** Splenic Artery **5** Superior Mesenteric Artery **6** Colic Artery, Right **7** Colic Artery, Left **8** Colic Artery, Middle **9** Renal Artery, Right **A** Renal Artery, Left **B** Inferior Mesenteric Artery **C** Common Iliac Artery, Right **D** Common Iliac Artery, Left **E** Internal Iliac Artery, Right **F** Internal Iliac Artery, Left **H** External Iliac Artery, Right **J** External Iliac Artery; Left **K** Femoral Artery, Right **L** Femoral Artery, Left **M** Popliteal Artery, Right **N** Popliteal Artery, Left **P** Anterior Tibial Artery, Right **Q** Anterior Tibial Artery, Left **R** Posterior Tibial Artery, Right **S** Posterior Tibial Artery, Left **T** Peroneal Artery, Right **U** Peroneal Artery, Left **V** Foot Artery, Right **W** Foot Artery, Left **Y** Lower Artery	**0** Open **3** Percutaneous **4** Percutaneous Endoscopic	**Z** No Device	**Z** No Qualifier

Figure 5-12 Medical and Surgical Table 045 for Root Operation Destruction

© Cengage Learning 2013

third character 5 the root operation destruction. In the first column of the Table, the fourth character body part is 0, abdominal aorta. All that is left to do is identify the correct approach, device, and qualifier values in Table 045.

Using the Index to Find the Root Operation Extraction

The objective of this root operation is *pulling or stripping out or off all or a portion of a body part by the use of force*. Examples used earlier were vein stripping, tooth extraction, and thumbnail removal. A search for stripping in the Index leads to the instructional note *see Extraction*. A search for removal, leads to a completely different root operation, which will be covered later in this chapter. The key here again, is that it is the pulling or stripping out by the use of force. Whenever the procedure includes that type of wording, even if the word removal is included, the root operation will be extraction. Figure 5-13 is an excerpt from the Index of the ICD-10-PCS for the root operation Extraction.

Extraction *continued*
  Bursa and Ligament *continued*
    Knee *continued*
      Left **OMPP**
      Right **OMDN**
    Lower Extremity
      Left **OMDW**
      Right **OMDV**
    Perineum **OMDK**
    Shoulder
      Left **OMD2**
      Right **OMD1**
    Thorax
      Left **OMDG**
      Right **OMDF**
    Trunk
      Left **OMDD**
      Right **OMDC**
    Upper Extremity
      Left **OMDB**
      Right **OMD9**
    Wrist
      Left **OMD6**
      Right **OMD5**
  Cord
    Left **OCDV**
    Right **OCDT**
  Cornea
    Left **08D9XZ**
    Right **08D8XZ**
  Dura Mater **OOD2**
  Endometrium **OUDB**
  Hair **OHDSXZZ**
  Kidney
    Left **OTD1**
    Right **OTDO**
  Lens
    Left **08DK3ZZ**
    Right **08DJ3ZZ**
  Marrow
    Iliac **07DR**
    Sternum **07DQ.**

Extraction *continued*
Nerve *continued*
  Glossopharyngeal **OODP**
    Head and Neck Sympathetic **01PK**
    Hypoglossal **OODS**
    Lumbar **01DB**
    Lumbar Sympathetic **01DN**
    Median **D1D5**
    Oculomotor **OODH**
    Olfactory **OODF**
    Optic **OODG**
    Peroneal **01DH**
    Phrenic **01D2**
    Pudendal **OIDC**
    Radial **01D6**
    Sacral **01DR**
    Sacral Sympathetic **01DP**
    Sciatic **01DF**
    Thoracic **01D8**
    Thoracic Sympathetic **01DL**
    Tibial **01DG**
    Trigeminal **OODK**
    Trochlear **OODJ**
    Ulnar **01D4**
    Vagus **ODPQ**
  Ossicle
    Left **09DAOZZ**
    Right **09D90ZZ**
  Ova **OUDN**
  Pleura
    Left **OBDP**
    Right **OBDN**
  Plexus
    Brachial **Q1D3**
    Cervical **01DO**
    Lumbar **01D9**
    Lumbosacral **01DA**
    Sacral **01DQ**
  Products of Conception
    Classical **10D00Z0**
    Ectopic **10D2**

© Cengage Learning 2013

Figure 5-13 Alphabetic Index Excerpt for Root Operation Extraction

The modifying terms are typically all body systems or body parts, with subterms that add further specificity to the modifying terms. The first modifying term indented under Extraction is the body system bursa and ligaments. Indented below that is the body part subterm, i.e., knee, lower extremity, perineum, shoulder and thorax. Indented below most of these are subterms that identify laterality. For example, under Extraction, bursa and ligament, shoulder, is the Table reference for the left shoulder (OMD2) and right shoulder (OMD1). The first three characters in both Table references represent the Medical and Surgical Section (0), the Bursa and Ligament body system (M), and the root operation Extraction (D). The fourth character represents the body part. The left shoulder body part value is 2, and the right shoulder is 1.

Let's Review 5–1:

Identify the correct root operation for the following procedures, and give at least three characters from the Index Table Reference.

1. Glossopharyngeal nerve removal by force _____
2. Trans-metatarsal amputation of foot at left big toe _____
3. Total prostatectomy _____
4. Cutting out two left inguinal lymph nodes _____
5. Bone marrow biopsy, sternum _____
6. Suction curettage (D&C), non-obstetric _____

Table 5-6 Root Operations that Take Out a Solid, Fluid, or Gas from a Body Part

Root Operation	Value	Definition
Drainage	9	Taking or letting out fluids and/or gases from a body part
Extirpation	C	Taking or cutting out solid matter from a body part
Fragmentation	F	Breaking solid body matter into pieces

Root Operations That Take Out a Solid, Fluid, or Gas From a Body Part

The common trait of this root operation is that a solid, gas, or fluid is taken out of the body part. There are three root operations that share this common attribute: Drainage, Extirpation, and Fragmentation. Table 5-6 gives the definitions and values for these root operations.

Root Operation Drainage (9)

The third character, root operation **drainage**, has a value of 9. Its definition is *taking or letting out fluids and/or gases from a body part*. Examples of procedures that use the root operation drainage include thoracentesis (pleural tap), paracentesis, incision and drainage (I&D), and amniocentesis. **Paracentesis** is simply the removal of fluid from any body cavity using a needle, trocar, cannula, or other hollow instrument. During a thoracentesis procedure, the surgeon or the physician inserts a needle through the skin of the chest wall into the space around the lung to remove or drain the fluids from that space. In amniocentesis, the fluid or gas is removed from the amniotic sac. Incision and drainage, and clinical lancing, are minor surgical procedures to release fluids, pus or pressure (gas) built up under the skin, such as from an abscess, boil, or infected paranasal sinus.

Uses of the root operation Drainage include both diagnostic and therapeutic procedures. When drainage is accomplished by putting in a catheter to remove the fluid or gas, it is considered therapeutic. If the fluid or gas drained is to be examined, it is a diagnostic drainage. In the next chapter, devices and qualifiers will be covered in depth, but for now just know that if a catheter is used for the drainage procedure, the sixth character will have a device value for the catheter used. If the fluid or gas taken or let out is to be examined for diagnostic purposes, i.e., for a biopsy, a seventh character, Qualifier, diagnostic (character value X), is used.

Root Operation Extirpation

Extirpation (pronounced ex-tur–*pay*-shun) has a character value of C. An **extirpation** procedure is when solid matter or material is taken or cut out from a body part. In the ICD-10-PCS coding manual Medical and Surgical section root operation appendix, an explanation of extirpation states it can be either an abnormal byproduct of a biological function such as a calculus (stone) or a foreign body. The matter can be embedded in a natural body part, e.g., the gallbladder, or in the lumen of a tubular body part such as an artery or a vein. Whether or not the solid matter or material was previously broken into pieces does not affect use of the root operation Extirpation. The key to this root operation is the definition *taking or cutting out solid matter*. Examples where Extirpation is the root operation include *thrombotomy, choledocholithotomy*, and the taking or cutting out of some type of foreign body.

In an Extirpation procedure the body part itself is really not the focus of what is occurring in that particular procedure. Instead, the objective of the procedure is to remove solid material from the body part. Examples include foreign body removal, or removal of a thrombus or calculus.

Root Operation Fragmentation (F)

Fragmentation has a character value of F and is defined as *breaking solid matter in a body part into pieces*. A good example of Fragmentation is lithotripsy, where a calculus (stone) is broken into multiple pieces. During the fragmentation procedure, physical force is applied, either directly or indirectly. The root operation does not change, whether it is direct or indirect fragmentation. The objective, and the key to using this root operation, is that the solid matter is broken into pieces. As with the root operation Extirpation, the solid matter may either be an abnormal byproduct of a biological function, such as a calculus, or a foreign body. An extracorporeal shock wave lithotripsy (ESWL) would be an example of when the root operation Fragmentation would be used. If the solid material being broken into pieces is then subsequently removed, the objective, and thus the root operation, changes to Extraction.

Using the Index to Search for Root Operation Drainage

Most procedures with the suffix -*centesis* are drainage procedures, including thoracentesis, amniocentesis, and paracentesis. A search in the Index for any procedure with the suffix -centesis leads to an instructional note to *see* Drainage. For example, a search for arthrocentesis (Figure 5-14) results in a *see* Drainage instruction for the upper and lower joints. The procedure incision and drainage, commonly known by its abbreviation, I&D, has the objective of incising and draining fluid or gases from a body part as well. A search for I&D, or incision and drainage, returns no results in the Index, although incision of abscess does lead to an instructional note to *see* drainage. It is therefore good to remember to simply go to the main term Drainage when searching for an I&D procedure. For all -centesis and I&D procedures, the appropriate action is to go to Drainage in the Index, find the appropriate body system or body part, and confirm the Table reference.

Searching for Drainage in the Index (Figure 5-15) reveals several pages of drainage procedures. The modifying terms indented under this main term are generally either the body system or the body part. The excerpt in Figure 5-15 starts with the body part, *bone*. The first subterm indented below that is *temporal*, and additional subterms indented below *temporal* specify the left or right side. In the procedure *drainage of the left temporal bone*, the Table reference is 0N96. The Medical and Surgical section is 0, the body system is head and facial bones (N), and the root operation is drainage (9). The first column of the 0N9 Table represents the body part *temporal bone, left*, with a fourth character value of 6, as shown in Figure 5-16.

Arthrocentesis
  see Drainage, Upper Joints **0R9**
  see Drainage, Lower Joints **0S9**

Figure 5-14 Alphabetic Index Excerpt for Arthrocentesis
  © Cengage Learning 2013

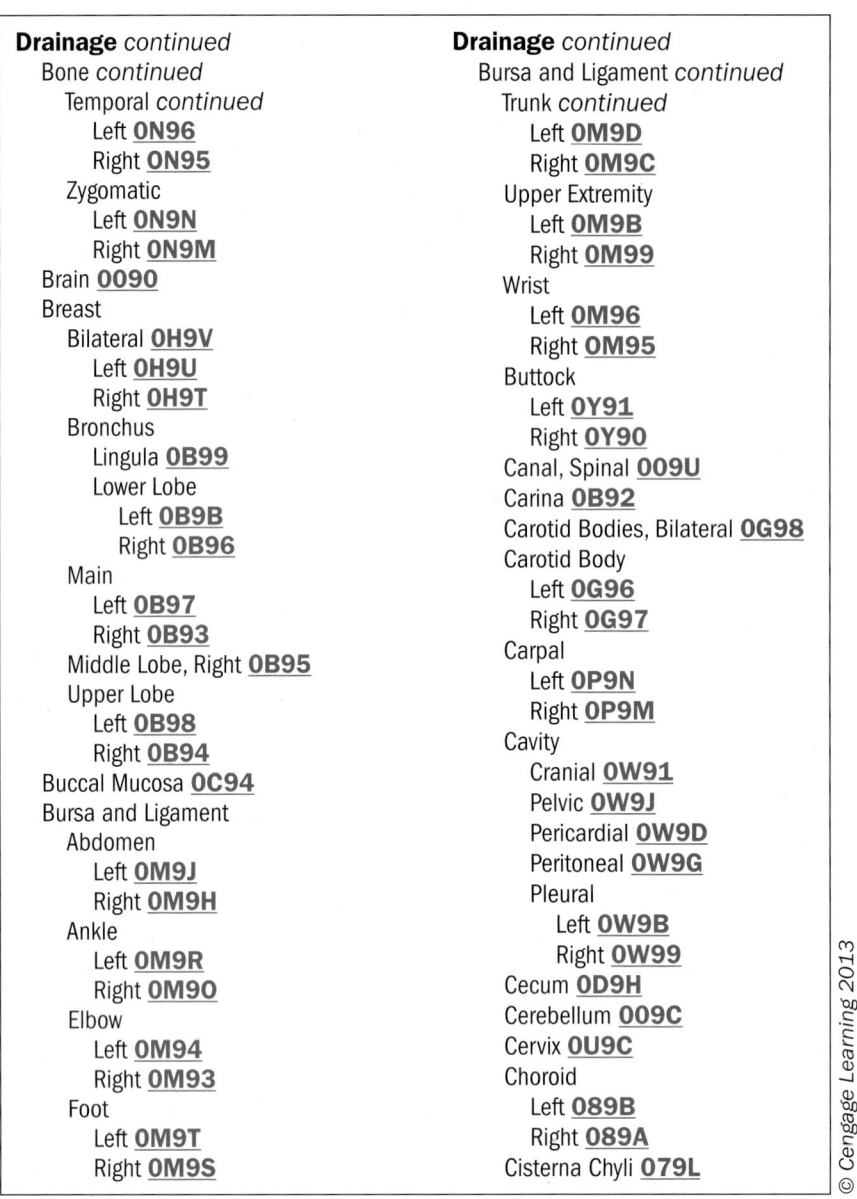

Drainage *continued*
   Bone *continued*
      Temporal *continued*
         Left <u>ON96</u>
         Right <u>ON95</u>
      Zygomatic
         Left <u>ON9N</u>
         Right <u>ON9M</u>
   Brain <u>0090</u>
   Breast
      Bilateral <u>OH9V</u>
      Left <u>OH9U</u>
      Right <u>OH9T</u>
   Bronchus
      Lingula <u>OB99</u>
      Lower Lobe
         Left <u>OB9B</u>
         Right <u>OB96</u>
      Main
         Left <u>OB97</u>
         Right <u>OB93</u>
      Middle Lobe, Right <u>OB95</u>
      Upper Lobe
         Left <u>OB98</u>
         Right <u>OB94</u>
   Buccal Mucosa <u>OC94</u>
   Bursa and Ligament
      Abdomen
         Left <u>OM9J</u>
         Right <u>OM9H</u>
      Ankle
         Left <u>OM9R</u>
         Right <u>OM9O</u>
      Elbow
         Left <u>OM94</u>
         Right <u>OM93</u>
      Foot
         Left <u>OM9T</u>
         Right <u>OM9S</u>

Drainage *continued*
   Bursa and Ligament *continued*
      Trunk *continued*
         Left <u>OM9D</u>
         Right <u>OM9C</u>
      Upper Extremity
         Left <u>OM9B</u>
         Right <u>OM99</u>
      Wrist
         Left <u>OM96</u>
         Right <u>OM95</u>
      Buttock
         Left <u>OY91</u>
         Right <u>OY90</u>
   Canal, Spinal <u>009U</u>
   Carina <u>OB92</u>
   Carotid Bodies, Bilateral <u>OG98</u>
   Carotid Body
      Left <u>OG96</u>
      Right <u>OG97</u>
   Carpal
      Left <u>OP9N</u>
      Right <u>OP9M</u>
   Cavity
      Cranial <u>OW91</u>
      Pelvic <u>OW9J</u>
      Pericardial <u>OW9D</u>
      Peritoneal <u>OW9G</u>
      Pleural
         Left <u>OW9B</u>
         Right <u>OW99</u>
   Cecum <u>OD9H</u>
   Cerebellum <u>009C</u>
   Cervix <u>OU9C</u>
   Choroid
      Left <u>089B</u>
      Right <u>089A</u>
   Cisterna Chyli <u>079L</u>

© Cengage Learning 2013

Figure 5-15 Alphabetic Index Excerpt for Root Operation Drainage

Using the Index to Search for Root Operation Extirpation

The clue for root operation Extirpation is use of the suffix -*otomy,* as in thrombotomy or choledocholithotomy, or medical documentation of the removal of a foreign body. A search of the Index for *foreign body* leads to a few listings. For example, under *magnet extraction, ocular foreign body* in the Index, is an instructional note to *see* extirpation and a Table reference of 08C. As always, the first character 0 is for the Medical and Surgical section, the body system is represented by 8, eye, and the third character C represents the root operation extirpation. A search of the Index for any term ending in the suffix -otomy is more successful, but will sometimes lead to a different root operation; thus, it is important to remember that the root operation Extirpation has as its objective the cutting or taking out of solid matter or material from a body part.

For example, a search for cholescystotomy has an instructional note to *see* Drainage, gallbladder; while a search for choledocolithotomy has an instructional note to *see* Extirpation, duct, common bile. Consider that cholecystotomy means *creating an opening in the gallbladder* (cyst- is the root word for bladder), thus, the most logical root operation would be Drainage, since there is normally no solid matter

Section	**0** Medical and Surgical			
Body System	**N** Head and Facial Bones			
Operation	**9** Drainage: Taking or letting out fluids and/or gases from a body part			

Body Part	Approach	Device	Qualifier
0 Skull **1** Frontal Bone, Right **2** Frontal Bone, Left **3** Parietal Bone, Right **4** Parietal Bone, Left **5** Temporal Bone, Right **6** Temporal Bone, Left **7** Occipital Bone, Right **8** Occipital Bone, Left **B** Nasal Bone **C** Sphenoid Bone, Right **D** Sphenoid Bone, Left **F** Ethmoid Bone, Right **G** Ethmoid Bone, Left **H** Lacrimal Bone, Right **J** Lacrimal Bone, Left **K** Palatine Bone, Right **L** Palatine Bone, Left **M** Zygomatic Bone, Right **N** Zygomatic Bone, Left **P** Orbit, Right **Q** Orbit, Left **R** Maxilla, Right **S** Maxilla, Left **T** Mandible, Right **V** Mandible, Left **X** Hyoid Bone	**0** Open **3** Percutaneous **4** Percutaneous Endoscopic	**0** Drainage Device	**Z** No Qualifier

Figure 5-16 Medical and Surgical Section Table for 0N9

© Cengage Learning 2013

in the gallbladder. The definition of choledocholithotomy, on the other hand, is surgical incision of the common bile duct for removal of a gallstone. Removal of a gallstone from the bile duct would meet the objective of extirpation, as would a surgical opening (-otomy) made to remove other solid matter, like an embolus, foreign body, or calculus.

Going directly to Extirpation in the Index (Figure 5-17), the structure is the same as with other root operations in the Medical and Surgical section. The first indented term under the main term Extirpation is the body system or body part, and the subterms indented below the modifying term are the specific body parts, and where appropriate, additional specificity and/or laterality. For example, in Figure 5-16, searching for a *thrombotomy of the left popliteal artery* leads to Extirpation, artery, popliteal and left, with a Table reference of 04CN.

Using the Index to Search for Root Operation Fragmentation

The definition of root operation **fragmentation** is *breaking solid matter in a body part into pieces*, such as in ESWL or urethral lithotripsy. The suffix *-lithotripsy* is the key in reading the medical documentation. When this suffix is used, it points directly to the root operation fragmentation. Do not forget, however, that if the solid material being broken into pieces is subsequently removed during the same procedure, the objective and, thus the root operation, changes to extraction.

A search for ESWL or any lithotripsy will find an instructional note to see Fragmentation. A search for the root operation Fragmentation leads to a list of body systems and parts indented below the main

Extirpation *continued*	**Extirpation** *continued*
Artery *continued*	Bone *continued*
Internal Iliac *continued*	Lacrimal
Left **04CF**	Left **0NCJ**
Right **04CE**	Right **0NCH**
Internal Mammary	Nasal **0NCB**
Left **03C1**	Occipital
Right **03C0**	Left **0NC8**
Intracranial **03CG**	Right **0NC7**
Lower **04CY**	Palatine
Peroneal	Left **0NCL**
Left **04CU**	Right **0NCK**
Right **04CT**	Parietal
Popliteal	Left **0NC4**
Left **04CN**	Right **0NC3**
Right **04CM**	Pelvic
Posterior Tibial	Left **0QC3**
Left **04CS**	Right **0QC2**
Right **04CR**	Sphenoid
Pulmonary	Left **0NCD**
Left **02CR**	Right **0NCC**
Right **02CQ**	Temporal
Radial	Left **0NC6**
Left **03CC**	Right **0NC5**
Right **03CB**	Zygomatic
Renal	Left **0NCN**
Left **04CA**	Right **0NCM**
Right **04C9**	Brain **00C0**
Splenic **04C4**	Breast
Subclavian	Bilateral **0HCV**
Left **03C4**	Left **0HCU**
Right **03C3**	Right **0HCT**
Superior Mesenteric **04C5**	Bronchus
Temporal	Lingula **0BC9**
Left **03CT**	Lower **Lobe**
Right **03CS**	Left **0BCB**
Thyroid	Right **0BC6**

© Cengage Learning 2013

Figure 5-17 Alphabetic Index Excerpt for Root Operation Extirpation

term. Figure 5-18 is an excerpt from the Index for the root operation Fragmentation. For the procedure *urethral lithotripsy*, first determine the objective of the procedure, then the affected body part. In this case, it is fragmentation (-tripsy) of stones (lith-) in the urethra. In the Index, the search can begin with urethral lithotripsy, but the associated instructional note states to *see* Fragmentation. Indented below the root operation Fragmentation, find the body part urethra (Figure 5-18). The Table reference is 0TFD, broken down as:

- First character   Section   0   Medical and Surgical
- Second character   Body System   T   Urinary System
- Third character   Root Operation   F   Fragmentation
- Fourth character   Body Part   D   Urethra

Fragmentation *continued*
  Fallopian Tube *continued*
    Right **OUF5**
  Fallopian Tubes, Bilateral **OUF7**
  Gallbladder **0FF4**
  Gastrointestinal Tract **OWFP**
  Genitourinary Tract **OWFR**
  Ileum **ODFB**
  Intestine
    Large **ODFE**
      Left **ODFG**
      Right **ODFF**
    Small **ODF8**
  Jejunum **ODFA**
  Kidney Pelvis
      Left **OTF4**
      Right **OTF3**
  Mediastinum **OWFC**
  Oral Cavity and Throat **OWF3**
  Pericardium **02FN**
  Rectum **ODFP**
  Respiratory Tract **OWFQ**
  Stomach **ODF6**
  Subarachnoid Space **OOF5**
  Subdural Space **OOF4**
  Trachea **OBF1**
  Ureter
      Left **OTF7**
      Right **OTF6**
  Urethra **OTFD**
  Uterus **OUF9**
  Ventricle, Cerebral **OOF6**
  Vitreous
      Left **08F5**
      Right **08F4**

© Cengage Learning 2013

Figure 5-18 Alphabetic Index Excerpt for Root Operation Fragmentation

Let's Review 5–2:

Identify the root operation and a minimum of three characters of the Table reference value for the following:

1. Thoracentesis _____
2. Choledocholithotomy _____
3. Thrombotomy, right brachial artery _____
4. Incision and drainage, perineal cyst, female _____
5. Diagnostic ovariocentesis _____
6. Foreign body removal, left eye _____

Root Operations That Involve Cutting or Separation

The common trait in this grouping are that each of these two root operations involves cutting or separation of a body part. The two root operations are division and release.

During a **division** procedure, a body part is cut into without draining fluids or gases from that body part. If gases or fluids were drained, the root operation would of course be drainage. The objective of the root operation Division is to cut into a body part to separate or transect it. In a division procedure, which has a character value of 8, either all or a portion of a body part is separated into two or more portions. One example of a division procedure is a *spinal cord cordotomy*. During this procedure, a surgical division of the tracts of the spinal cord is performed. Two other examples that would qualify for the root operation Division are osteotomy and neurotomy. A coder would use the root operation Division when the objective of the procedure is to cut into, transect, or otherwise separate, either all or a portion of the body part. Division should not be used if the objective of the procedure is either to cut or to separate the area around the body part, the attachments to a body part, or cutting and separating between subdivisions of a body part. In that case, the root operation Release should be used. There is one guideline in the ICD-10-PCS for use of the root operations release and division.

Guideline B3.14 states: If the sole objective of the procedure is to separate or transect a body part, the root operation is Division. If the sole objective of the procedure is to free a body part, without cutting that body part, the root operation is Release.

Release is the second root operation in this group, and has a character value of N. During a release procedure, *the body part is freed from an abnormal physical constraint by either cutting that body part or using force*. During the release procedure, some of the restraining tissue may be removed, but to use the root operation release, none of the body part that's being freed may be removed or taken out—only restraining tissue, as described in Guideline B3.13, which states that the body part value coded is the body part being feed, and not the tissue being manipulated or cut to free the body part.

A common example of a release procedure would be a *carpal tunnel release*. When a carpal tunnel release procedure is performed, the transverse carpal ligament is cut, which releases the pressure placed on the median nerve of the wrist. Another common example of a release procedure would be adhesiolysis procedures. Adhesiolysis means cutting through or lysing adhesions. Lysis procedures would almost always be coded to the root operation Release. A release procedure can be performed on an area around the body part, on attachments to a body part, or between subdivisions of a body part that are causing the abnormal constraint.

In the root operation Release, the body part value is the body part being freed, and not the tissue being manipulated or cut to free the body part. In the carpal tunnel release example, the body part released is the median nerve. Even if the documentation states the cut was made to the transverse carpal ligament, it was the median nerve that was released, and therefore, the fourth code character body part value is the median nerve.

Using the Index to Search for Root Operations Division and Release

Division is to cut into a body part to separate or transect the body part, e.g., a *spinal cord cordotomy, osteotomy,* or *neurotomy.* A Release procedure has as its objective the freeing of a body part from an abnormal physical constraint; for example, a *carpal tunnel release* or *lysis of adhesions.* Searching the Index for terms with the suffix *-otomy,* will lead to a division procedure, but can just as often lead to other root operations. For both Division and Release root operations, the key is matching the procedure objective to the correct definition of the root operation, and then searching for that root operation in the Index.

Searching for root operation division Let's start with a root operation Division example, *sphincterotomy, anal.* In the Index, there are two instructional notes to *see* either Drainage or Division (Figure 5-19). Without knowing the objective, it would be difficult to select the correct root operation, which is why it is so important to know the root operation definitions. Now, look at Figure 5-20, an excerpt from the Index for the root operation Division. As always, indented below the main term Division

Sphincterotomy, anal
see Drainage, Sphincter, Anal **0D9R**
see Division, Sphincter, Anal **0D8R**

Figure 5-19 Alphabetic Index Excerpt for Sphincterotomy
© Cengage Learning 2013

Division *continued*
  Bursa and Ligament *continued*
    Upper Extremity *continued*
      Left **0M8B**
      Right **0M89**
    Wrist
      Left **0M86**
      Right **0M85**
    Carpal
      Left **0P8N**
      Right **0P8M**
    Chordae Tendineae **0289**
    Clavicle
      Left **0P8B**
      Right **0P89**
    Coccyx **0Q8S**
    Conduction Mechanism **0288**
    Cord
      Cervical Spinal **008W**
      Lumbar Spinal **008Y**
      Thoracic Spinal **008X**
    Esophagogastric Junction **0D84**
    Femoral Shaft
      Left **0Q89**
      Right **0Q88**
  Femur
    Lower
      Left **0Q8C**
      Right **0Q8B**
    Upper
      Left **0Q87**
      Right **0Q86**
    Fibula
      Left **0Q8K**
      Right **0Q8J**
    Gland, Pituitary **0G80**
    Glenoid Cavity
      Left **0P88**
      Right **0P87**
    Hemisphere, Cerebral **0087**
    Humeral Head
      Left **0P8D**
      Right **0P8C**
    Humeral Shaft
      Left **0P8G**
      Right **0P8F**
    Hymen **0U8K**
    Kidneys, Bilateral **0T82**

Division *continued*
  Muscle
    Abdomen
      Left **0K8L**
      Right **0K8K**
    Facial **0K81**
    Foot
      Left **0K8W**
      Right **0K8V**
    Hand
      Left **0K8D**
      Right **0K8C**
    Head **0K80**
    Hip
      Left **0K8P**
      Right **0K8N**
    Lower Arm and Wrist
      Left **0K8B**
      Right **0K89**
    Lower Leg
      Left **0K8T**
      Right **0K8S**
    Neck
      Left **0K83**
      Right **0K82**
    Papillary **028D**
    Perineum **0K8M**
    Shoulder
      Left **0K86**
      Right **0K85**
    Thorax
      Left **0K8J**
      Right **0K8H**
    Tongue, Palate, Pharynx **0K84**
    Trunk
      Left **0K8G**
      Right **0K8F**
    Upper Arm
      Left **0K88**
      Right **0K87**
    Upper Leg
      Left **0K8R**
      Right **0K8Q**
  Nerve Abdominal Sympathetic **018M**
    Abducens **008L**
    Accessory **008R**
    Acoustic **008N**

© Cengage Learning 2013

Figure 5-20 Alphabetic Index Excerpt for Root Operation Division

is the body system or body part modifying term, and below the modifying terms are subterms that add more specificity to it. A *division of the bursa of the lower left femur* has a Table reference of 0Q8C. The first four code character values are assigned as follows:

- First character   Section   0   Medical and Surgical
- Second character   Body System   Q   Bursa and Ligament
- Third character   Root Operation   8   Division
- Fourth character   Body Part   C   Femur, Lower, Left

Searching for root operation release in the index The key in searching the Index for procedures with the root operation release are (1) that the procedure indicates freeing a body part from an abnormal physical constraint, and (2) to code to the body part being released, not to the tissue or body part being cut to create the release.

Terminology that includes the suffix *-lysis* will generally be found to be release procedures. A search In the Index for terms ending with the suffix -lysis leads to an instructional note to *see* Release. Figure 5-21 is an excerpt from the Index for the root operation release. Using the example, *phrenic nerve*

Release *continued*
  Muscle *continued*
    Foot *continued*
      Right **0KNV**
    Hand
      Left **0KND**
      Right **0KNC**
    Head **0KN0**
    Hip
      Left **0KNP**
      Right **0KNN**
    Lower Arm and Wrist
      Left **0KNB**
      Right **0KN9**
    Lower Leg
      Left **0KNT**
      Right **0KNS**
    Neck
      Left **0KN3**
      Right **0KN2**
    Papillary **02ND**
    Perineum **0KNM**
    Shoulder
      Left **0KN6**
      Right **0KN5**
    Thorax
      Left **0KNJ**
      Right **0KNH**
    Tongue, Palate, Pharynx **0KN4**
    Trunk
      Left **0KNG**
      Right **0KNF**
    Upper Arm
      Left **0KN8**
      Right **0KN7**
    Upper Leg
      Left **0KNR**
      Right **0KNQ**

Release *continued*
  Nerve *continued*
    Phrenic **01N2**
    Pudendal **01NC**
    Radial **01N6**
    Sacral **01NR**
    Sacral Sympathetic **01NP**
    Sciatic **01NF**
    Thoracic **01N8**
    Thoracic Sympathetic **01NL**
    Tibial **01NG**
    Trigeminal **00NK**
    Trochlear **00NJ**
    Ulnar **01N4**
    Vagus **00NQ**
  Nipple
    Left **0HNX**
    Right **0HNW**
  Nose **09NK**
  Omentum
    Greater **0DNS**
    Lesser **0DNT**
  Orbit
    Left **0NNQ**
    Right **0NNP**
  Ossicle
    Left **09NA0ZZ**
    Right **09N90ZZ**
  Ovary
    Bilateral **0UN2**
    Left **0UN1**
    Right **0UN0**
  Palate
    Hard **0CN2**
    Soft **0CN3**
  Pancreas **0FNG**
  Para-aortic Body **0GN9**

© Cengage Learning 2013

Figure 5-21 Alphabetic Index Excerpt for Root Operation Release

release, the root operation would be Release, the modifying term would be nerve, and the subterm would be phrenic. The Table reference for this procedure is 01N2, broken down as follows:

- First character   Section   0   Medical and Surgical
- Second character   Body System   1   Peripheral Nervous System
- Third character   Root Operation   N   Release
- Fourth character   Body Part   2   Phrenic Nerve

The next step would be to go to that Table (01N) in the Tabular List, confirm the first four characters, and then find the correct values for the remaining three code characters.

Let's Review 5–3:

Identify the root operation, and list a minimum of three characters of the Table reference for the following:

1. Open posterior tarsal tunnel release _____
2. Anal sphincterotomy _____
3. Lysis of intestinal adhesions _____
4. Open osteotomy of right capitates _____
5. Retrogasserian rhizotomy _____

Root Operations that Put In, Put Back, or Move Some or All of a Body Part

There are four root operations included in this group: transplantation, reattachment, transfer, and reposition. The common trait between each is that the objective is to put in, put back, or move, some or all of a body part. Table 5-7 identifies the root operation character values, and the definitions of the four operations in this group.

Root Operation Transplantation (Y)

Transplantation, with a third character root operation value of Y, is defined as *putting in or putting on all or a portion of a living body part that has been taken either from another individual or from an animal.* The living body part that's being transplanted physically takes the place or the function of either all or a portion of that

Table 5-7 Root Operations that Put In, Put Back, or Move Some or All of a Body Part

Root Operation	Value	Definition
Transplantation	Y	Putting in or on all or a portion of a living body part taken from an individual or animal to physically take the place and/or function of all or a portion of a similar body part
Reattachment	M	Putting back in or on all or a portion of a separated body part to its normal location or other suitable location
Transfer	X	Moving, without taking out, all or a portion of a body part in order to take over the function of all or a portion of a body part
Reposition	S	Moving to its normal location, or other suitable location, all or a portion of a body part

similar body part. During a transplantation procedure, the native body part being replaced may or may not actually be taken out. Only a small number of procedures are coded to the root operation Transplantation, such as a donor-matched liver transplant, or a heart valve transplant using a porcine valve. There is also a guideline to further help identify when the Transplantation root operation should be used.

Guideline B3.16 states: *Putting in a mature and functioning living body part taken from another individual or animal is coded to the root operation Transplantation. Putting in autologous or nonautologous cells is coded to the Administration section.*

This guideline means that only a body part, such as the heart, kidney, or part of the liver, taken from another individual or animal is coded to transplantation. Cells, bone marrow, stem cells, or pancreatic islet cells, for example, that are taken from another individual, animal, or even the patient, are coded to the Administration section of the ICD-10-PCS, which will be covered in a later chapter.

To perform a search in the Index, read the medical documentation carefully to find the objective, and to identify the body part. If the objective is to put in a living body part, rather than cells, and the body part is from another individual or an animal, then the root operation is transplantation. Figure 5-22 is the Index listing for Transplantation. Note that there are only a few body parts listed, including the esophagus, heart, intestine, kidney, liver, ovary, pancreas, spleen, stomach, and thymus. Using the procedure *transplant of right lower lobe of the lung*, the search would begin with the main term *transplantation*, the modifying term *lung*, and the subterms *lower lobe* and *right*, which leads to the Table reference OBYFOZ. For now, concentrate only on the first four characters in the Table reference;

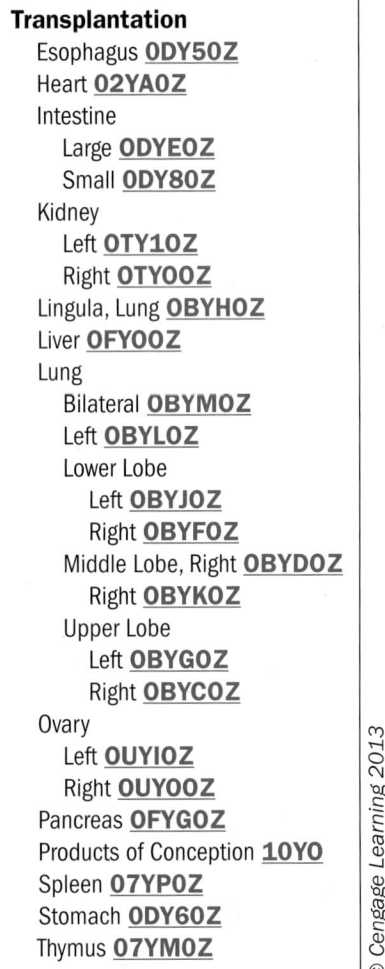

Transplantation
  Esophagus **ODY50Z**
  Heart **02YA0Z**
  Intestine
      Large **ODYE0Z**
      Small **ODY80Z**
  Kidney
      Left **OTY1OZ**
      Right **OTYOOZ**
  Lingula, Lung **OBYHOZ**
  Liver **OFYOOZ**
  Lung
      Bilateral **OBYMOZ**
      Left **OBYLOZ**
      Lower Lobe
          Left **OBYJOZ**
          Right **OBYFOZ**
      Middle Lobe, Right **OBYDOZ**
          Right **OBYKOZ**
      Upper Lobe
          Left **OBYGOZ**
          Right **OBYCOZ**
  Ovary
      Left **OUYIOZ**
      Right **OUYOOZ**
  Pancreas **OFYGOZ**
  Products of Conception **10YO**
  Spleen **07YPOZ**
  Stomach **ODY60Z**
  Thymus **07YMOZ**

© Cengage Learning 2013

Figure 5-22 Alphabetic Index Excerpt for Root Operation Transplantation

the fifth through seventh character code values will be covered in the next chapter. The first character 0 is the Medical and Surgical section, the second character is the body system, *respiratory*, and the third character is the root operation *transplantation*, represented by the value Y. The fourth character, F, is the *left lower lobe* body part.

Root Operation Reattachment (M)

The second root operation in this group is **Reattachment**, which has a character value of M. During a reattachment procedure, a body part that's either been separated or avulsed from the body is put back in or on its normal location or in some other suitable location. The vascular circulation and the nervous pathways may or may not be reestablished when the procedure is being performed. Some examples of a reattachment procedure include a body part that may have been detached or avulsed, such as a thumb, finger, toe, or tooth. Reattachment will be the main term, and thus the root operation, found in medical documentation for any procedures where the objective is to put back in or on a body part that has been separated from the body. To perform a search in the Index, find the main term Reattachment (Figure 5-23), then the body part affected. For example, for the procedure *reattachment of the left index finger*, the Table reference is OXMPOZZ. Again, in this chapter, the search is only for the first three or four code character values. The Medical and Surgical section is the first character, 0, the body system is *Anatomical Regions, Upper Extremities* (X), and the root operation is M, *reattachment*. The fourth character body part is *index finger, left*, which is represented by the character value M.

Root Operation Transfer (X)

The third root operation in this group is **Transfer**, which has a character value of X. Transfer is defined as *moving all or a portion of a body part to another location so that it can take over the function of all or a*

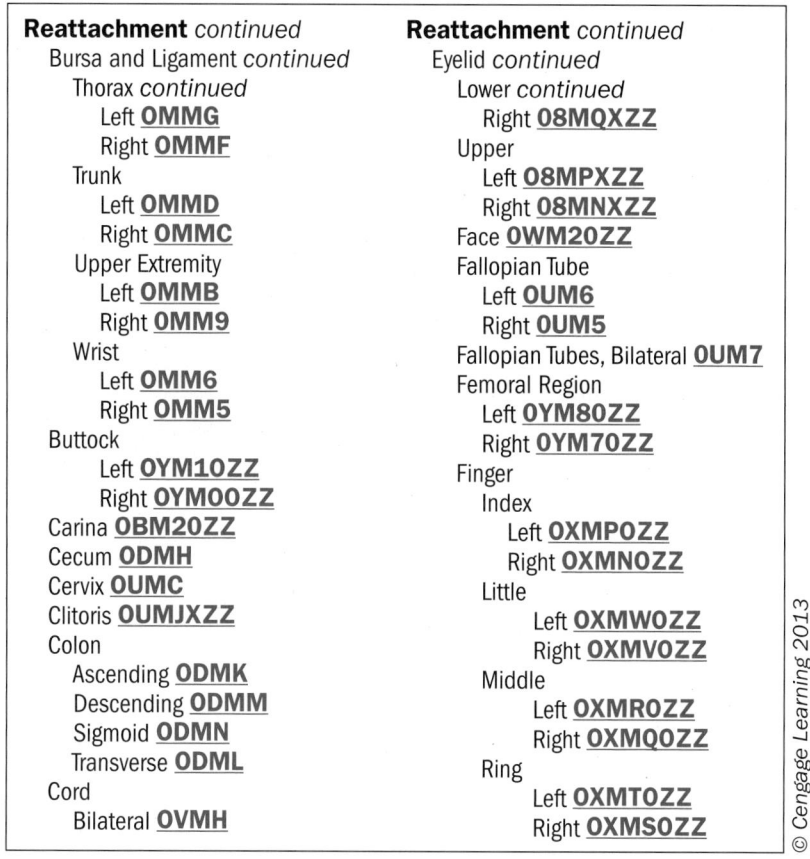

Figure 5-23 Alphabetic Index Excerpt for Root Operation Reattachment

portion of a body part or another body part. A key note when using the root operation transfer is that, during the procedure, the body part being transferred must remain connected to its vascular and nerve supply; for example, an adjacent skin transfer. In the surgical procedure *adjacent skin transfer*, the transferred skin remains attached to its nerve and vascular supply. A tendon transfer would be another example of a procedure that would use the root operation transfer. In other words, transfer is used only to represent or code those procedures in which the body part is moved to another location without disrupting either the vascular or the nerve supply. A free skin graft, on the other hand, would not use this root operation because in a free skin graft the skin is removed from the donor site, and thus from its vascular and nerve supply. With a free skin graft, Replacement is the correct root operation and not Transfer.

A search in the Index for *Graft* to find the root operation Transfer will be unsuccessful, since it leads to instructional notes to *see* Replacement and *see* Supplement, or it will lead to a bypass graft, which is a completely different root operation. Searches using common terminology will sometimes lead to Transfer as a root operation. For example, searching for *opponensplasty* or *pollicization* will lead to an instructional note to *see* Transfer, tendon, or *see* Transfer, Anatomical Regions, Upper Extremities. The best way, however, is to know the objective of the root operation, match its definition to the procedure, and search for the root operation as the main term. Figure 5-24 is an Index excerpt for Transfer. For the procedure *skin flap pedicle transfer, anterior neck*, the root operation is transfer, the body system is *subcutaneous tissue and fascia*, and *anterior neck* is the body part subterm. The Table reference is 0JX4, which is the Medical and Surgical section (0), the *subcutaneous tissue and fascia* body system (J), the root operation *transfer* (J), and the body part *anterior neck* (4).

Root Operation Reposition (S)

The character value of the root operation **Reposition** is S. It is defined as *moving, to its normal location, or other suitable location, all or a portion of a body part.* In the Medical and Surgical Section 0 Root Operations Appendix, the following additional information is provided: *The body part is moved to a new location from an abnormal location, or from a normal location where it is not functioning correctly. The body part may or may not be cut out or off to be moved to the new location.* Examples include fracture reduction, and repositioning an undescended testicle.

There is a guideline for this root operation, **Guideline B3.15**, which states: *A reduction of a displaced fracture is coded to the root operation Reposition. The application of a cast or splint in conjunction with the reposition procedure is not coded separately.*

Reposition (and any subsequent application of a cast or splint) is used only for displaced fractures, that are out of their normal position.

Non-displaced fractures that do not require repositioning, are coded to other root operations. For example, placing a pin in a nondisplaced fracture is coded to the root operation Insertion, since a device is being inserted. Another example is the casting or splinting of a nondisplaced fracture, which would be coded to the root operation Immobilization, in the Placement section of ICD-10-PCS. The objective of the root operation Reposition is to move a body part to a normal position, not to immobilize or insert a device into that body part. Therefore, in the case of a fractured bone, if the objective is to put the bone back in its normal position, then the correct root operation is Reposition. Some common terminology associated with reposition includes, but is not limited to, those listed below. When searching in the Index, in all cases, these terms reveal an instructional note to *see* Reposition:

- Fitting. A search in the Index for fitting leads to the modifying term *arch bars for fracture reduction*, and an instructional note to *see* Reposition.

- Fixation. A search for this main terms, leads to several root operations. With the modifying terms external with fracture reduction, and internal with fracture reduction, the instructional note is to *see* Reposition. (In this case Fixation would be used to mean fracture reduction, not fixating the bone by inserting pins or screws.)

Figure 5-24 Alphabetic Index Excerpt for Root Operation Transfer

- Reduction. Under this main term in the Index, are several modifying terms that lead to the instructional note *see Reposition*, including dislocation, fracture, prolapsed, torsion, and volvulus.

- Suffix—*pexy* (arthropexy, cecopexy, cystopexy, etc.). Two root operations are found under these procedures Repair and Reposition. It is important, therefore, to know the objective of the procedure in order to select the correct root operation.

- Autotransplant. Adrenal gland and kidney repositioning searches in the Alphabetic Index lead to an instructional note to *see Reposition*. There are other root operations here as well including transfer and reattachment.

Figure 5-25 is an excerpt from the Index for root operation Reposition. For a *fracture reduction of the left zygomatic bone*, the first action is to determine the objective of the procedure and match it with the definition of the correct root operation. A fracture reduction, without insertion of a device, or immobilization of the fracture as the objective, leads to the root operation Reposition. The search would begin with the main term *Reposition*, followed by the modifying term *bone*, and the subterms *left* and *zygomatic*. The Table reference for this procedure is 0NSN.

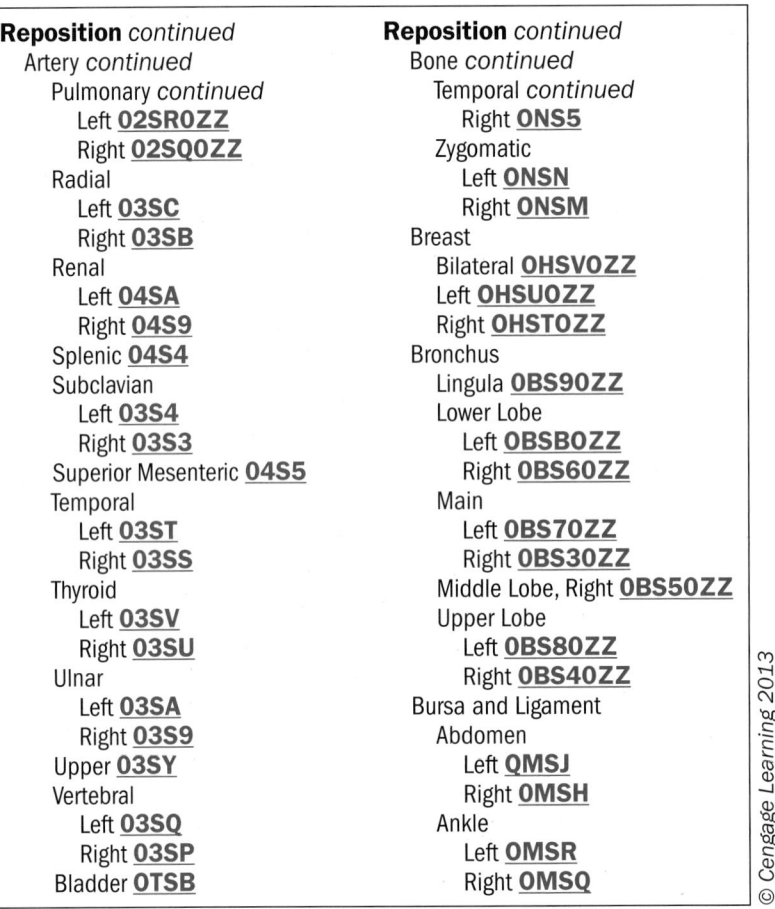

Figure 5-25 Alphabetic Index Excerpt for Root Operation Reposition

Let's Review 5–4:

Determine the root operation, and find a minimum of three characters of a Table reference for the following:

1. Closed reduction fracture, right humerus (*hint:* upper arm) _____
2. Relocation of bilateral undescended testicle _____
3. Endoscopic radial to median nerve transfer _____
4. Kidney transplant, left _____
5. Attachment of traumatic amputation left thumb _____

Root Operations That Alter the Diameter or Route of a Tubular Body Part

There are four root operations that belong to this group: restriction, occlusion, dilation, and bypass. Table 5-8 lists the character values and definitions for these four root operations.

Table 5-8 Root Operations that Alter the Diameter or Route of a Tubular Body Part

Root Operation	Value	Definition
Restriction	V	Partially closing an orifice or lumen of a tubular body part
Occlusion	L	Completely closing an orifice or lumen of a tubular body part
Dilation	7	Expanding an orifice or the lumen of a tubular body part
Bypass	1	Altering the route of passage of the contents of a tubular body part

Root Operation Restriction (V)

The first root operation in this group is **Restriction**, which has a third character value of V. It is defined as *partially closing an orifice or lumen of a tubular body part.* In the Medical and Surgical section Appendix for root operations, it is noted that the orifice can either be a natural orifice or an artificially created orifice. In addition, the objective can be accomplished from within the lumen (intraluminal) or from outside (extraluminal). An example of an intraluminal restriction would be insertion of a stent into the thoracic duct. Extraluminal restriction procedures include banding of an artery, or clipping an aneurysm.

Other procedures that use the root operation restriction include *esophagogastric fundoplication* and *cervical cerclage*. In the fundoplication, used to treat gastric reflux disease, the fundus of the stomach is wrapped (plicated) around the lower end of the esophagus, which reinforces the closing function of the esophageal sphincter. This wrapping or plication restricts the esophagogastric junction. A cervical cerclage procedure is done to treat an incompetent cervix. In cerclage, a strong thread is stitched around the cervix to help keep the cervical opening (lumen) closed. The objective of these procedures, fundoplication and cerclage, is restriction.

Terminology associated with Restriction that might be found in medical documentation includes *banding*. A search in the Index under banding leads to an instructional note to *see* Restriction. Another term is *bioactive intraluminal device*, but searching for that term in the Index will lead not just to the root operation restriction, but also to occlusion. Again, care must be taken to ensure that the proper objective and definition is determined for the root operation before performing an Index search.

In addition, almost every term ending with the suffix *-plication* will lead, if not directly to a Table reference, then at least to an instructional note to *see* Restriction. For example, under *cecoplication*, the instructional note is to *see* Restriction, cecum. Searches for cerclage, clipping, plication, and fundoplication will all lead to a *see* Restriction instructional note as well.

Figure 5-26 is an Index excerpt for the root operation Restriction. The modifying terms are generally body systems, organs, or parts, and include bones, arteries, veins, and other structures. Indented below the modifying terms are subterms that include more specific body parts, and laterality. A restriction procedure on the *right common iliac vein*, for example, would lead to the Table reference 06VC. Restriction is the main term, *vein* is the modifying term, and *right, common iliac* the subterm.

Root Operation Occlusion (L)

The root operation **Occlusion**, with a character value L, has the objective *to completely close an orifice or lumen of a tubular body part.* The orifice can be natural or artificially created. The best known example of an occlusion procedure is a *tubal ligation of the fallopian tubes*, which involves severing and sealing the fallopian tube openings to prevent pregnancy. If the ligation is done using sutures, clips, or rings, the appropriate root operation is Restriction. However, if it is done with electrocoagulation or cauterization, for example, then the root operation would be Destruction and not Occlusion. Another example is ligation of the inferior vena cava, which is done to prevent recurrent pulmonary emboli due to venous thrombosis or trauma in the lower extremities or pelvis. Occlusion, like Restriction, includes both intraluminal and extraluminal methods.

Restriction *continued*	Restriction *continued*
Duodenum **ODV9**	Vein *continued*
Esophagogastric Junction **ODV4**	Brachial
Esophagus **ODV5**	Left **05VA**
Lower **ODV3**	Right **05V9**
Middle **ODV2**	Cephalic
Upper **ODV1**	Left **05VF**
Heart **02VA**	Right **05VD**
Ileum **ODVB**	Colic **06V7**
Intestine	Common Iliac
Large **ODVE**	Left **06VD**
Left **ODVG**	Right **06VC**
Right **ODVF**	Esophageal **06V3**
Small **ODV8**	External Iliac
Jejunum **ODVA**	Left **06VG**
Kidney Pelvis	Right **06VF**
Left **OTV4**	External Jugular
Right **OTV3**	Left **05VQ**
	Right **05VP**

© Cengage Learning 2013

Figure 5-26 Alphabetic Index Excerpt for Root Operation Restriction

Guideline, B3.12, discusses occlusion versus restriction for vessel embolization procedures. If the objective of an embolization procedure is to complete close a vessel, the root operation occlusion is coded. If the objective is to narrow the lumen of a vessel, the root operation Restriction is coded. For example, in aneurysm procedures, if the objective of the procedure is not to close off the blood vessel complete, but to narrow the lumen of the vessel where the vessel has been widened by the aneurysm, restriction is the correct root operation.

When searching the Index, some common medical documentation terminology includes clamping, collapse, embolization, interruption, and ligation. A search for any of these terms results in an instructional note to *see* Occlusion. Figure 5-27 is an Index excerpt for Occlusion. Using the procedure *clamping of left vertebral artery,* the search would be by the main term Occlusion, the body system artery as a modifying term, and left vertebral as the subterm, with a Table reference of 03LQ. The Medical and Surgical section value 0 is the first character, 3 represents the second character value for the *Upper Arteries* body system, and L is the third character value for the root operation *Occlusion.* The body part value, L is the *left vertebral artery.*

Root Operation Dilation (7)

The character value for the root operation **Dilation** is 7, and the objective is *to expand the orifice or lumen of a natural or artificially created body part.* The procedure is accomplished by stretching a tubular body part using intraluminal pressure or by cutting parts of the orifice or wall of the tubular body part. Some examples are *percutaneous transluminal angioplasty* (PTA) and *percutaneous transluminal coronary angioplasty* (PTCA). During a PTA or PTCA, the narrowed or obstructed blood vessel is mechanically widened, typically using a balloon catheter, which is passed into the narrowed lumen. The balloon is then inflated, which crushes the fatty deposits within the blood vessel. If a device is placed to maintain the new diameter of the orifice or lumen, this is an integral part of the Dilation procedure, and would not be coded separately.

Common terminology associated with this root operation includes terms ending in the suffix -plasty, such as angioplasty, however, other root operations are also found with the same suffix. Once again, knowing the objective of the procedure, and matching it correctly to the root operation definition is key when preparing to search for those types of procedures. Cannulation, catheterization, and enlargement are other terms where the root operation dilation might be found in the Index, but bypass, drainage, and irrigation, and other root operations can be found within those terms as well. Those terms, and others, such as *percutaneous transluminal coronary artery angioplasty,* all have a *see* Dilation instructional note.

Root Operation Revision (W)

Revision has a third character value of W and is defined as *correcting, to the extent possible, a malfunctioning or displaced device.* Revision is coded when the objective of the procedure is to correct the position or function of a previously placed device, without taking the entire device out and putting a whole new device in its place.

Here's an example of a Revision procedure: A previous fracture repair was performed, and a plate was installed during the repair. Subsequently, a screw holding the plate in place comes loose. The loose screw is removed and replaced with a new, larger, screw. The applicable root operation for removal of the screw and replacement with a larger screw to correct the placement and function of the screw meets the definition and objective of Revision. Another example of a revision procedure is the recementing of a prosthesis that's come loose after a total hip replacement surgery.

Root Operations That Involve Other Objectives

The last group of root operations are those that include other objectives from root operations in any other group. This group, which includes Fusion, Alteration and Creation, have no real similarities, and thus, do not fit into any of the other groups covered in this chapter. Fusion, Alteration, and Creation are root operations that describe procedures performed for three very distinct and different reasons.

A fusion procedure, which has the character value G, puts a dysfunctional joint out of service rather than restoring the function for that joint. Alteration encompasses a whole range of procedures that are done to improve a person's physical appearance. Creation represents only two very specific sex change operations.

Root Operation Fusion (G)

During a **Fusion** procedure, portions of an articular body part, or joint, are joined together, which renders that joint immobile. In a Fusion procedure, the body part can be joined together by fixation devices, bone grafts, or by some other means. Two examples include a *spinal fusion* and an *ankle arthrodesis*. There are three guidelines for the root operation Fusion, which are shown in Table 5-11, along with an example.

Root Operation Alteration (0)

Alteration has a character value of 0 , and is used for coding cosmetic procedures. The definition for alteration is *modifying the natural structure of a body part without affecting the function of that body part.* Alteration is coded for all procedures performed where the sole objective is to improve a person's appearance. This root operation is used only for cosmetic procedures. If there is a medical purpose for performing the procedure, then a different root operation would be used, depending upon the objective of the procedure.

Root Operation Creation (4)

Creation, which has a third character value 4, is defined as *making a new genital structure that does not physically take the place of a body part.* The root operation Creation is used only to code sex change operations. The two examples of creation procedures would be creation of a vagina in a male or creation of a penis in female.

Table 5-11 Guidelines for Root Operation Fusion

B3.10a: The body part coded for a spinal vertebral joint(s) rendered immobile by a spinal fusion procedure is classified by the level of the spine affected, i.e., cervical or thoracic. There are distinct body part values for a single vertebral joint and for multiple vertebral joints at each spinal level. For example, in the lumbar vertebra body part column, there are distinct values for two or more lumbar vertebral joints, as well as for a single lumbar vertebral joint.
B3.10b: Joints between two areas of the spine have their own body part values and are coded separately. Example: Fusion of the C5/6 joint and C7-T1 joint are coded separately.
B3.10c: If multiple vertebral joints included in the same body part value are fused, a separate procedure is coded **for each joint that uses a different device and/or qualifier.** Example: Fusion of C4/5 with fixation device and C5/6 with bone graft are coded separately

Chapter Summary

Coding procedures from the ICD-10-PCS begins with a search for the root operation of the procedure. The root operation is the third character in a procedure code.

The 31 root operations will be divided into nine groups. Each group will contain root operations with similar objectives. The nine groups are root operations that:

1. Take out some or all of a body part

2. Take out solids, fluids, or gases from a body part

3. Involve cutting or separation only

4. Put in/put back, or move some or all of a body part

5. Alter the diameter or route of a body part

6. Include other repairs

7. Involve examination only

8. Always involve a device

9. Include other objectives

It is important to apply the correct root operation regardless of the documentation in the medical record. When reading operative reports or procedural notes, many times words like *removal, excision, or resection,* are used somewhat interchangeably in the medical documentation. In ICD-10-PCS, however, there are very specific rules and definitions for each of the root operations.

There are five root operations that qualify as those that take out some or all of a body part group: Excision, Resection, Detachment, Destruction, and Extraction. There are two guidelines specific to the use of the root operations Excision and Resection, B3.8 and B3.9. Table 5-5 describes both guidelines.

The root operation Excision has the character value B, and this will always be in the third position of the code. The definition of excision is *cutting out or off, without replacement, a portion of a body part.* The two keys to this root operation are (1) it is without replacement, in other words, the procedure cuts a body part out or off and it is not replaced, and (2) only a portion of a body part is cut off or out.

The definition of root operation Resection, character value T, is very similar to Excision. Like excision, resection is cutting out or off, without replacement, but here it is *all* of a body part rather than s*ome* or *part* of a body part. The character value for root operation Detachment is 6. The definition is cutting off all or part of the upper or lower extremities. The character value for the root operation destruction is 5. The definition *is physical eradication of all or a portion of a body part by the direct use of energy, force or a destructive agent.* The definition for root operation extraction, which has a character value of D, is *pulling or stripping out or off all or a portion of a body part by the use of force.* Extraction is coded when the method employed to take out the body part is pulling or stripping. The objective of the root operation detachment is to cut off all or part of an upper or lower extremity. The main term, when doing a search in the Index can be either *amputation* or *detachment.*

Surgical techniques such as *fulguration, cautery, coagulation, ablation,* and *cryotherapy* fulfill the objective of the root operation destruction. The objective is *physical eradication of all or a portion of a body part by the direct use of energy, force, or a destructive agent.*

Root operations that take out a solid, fluid, or gas from a body part include Drainage, Extirpation, and Fragmentation. Table 5-6 gives the definitions and values for these three root operations.

Root operations that involve cutting or separation have two root operations, Division and Release.

Root operations that put in, put back, or move some or all of a body part include four root operations: Transplantation, Reattachment, Transfer, and Reposition. The common trait between each is that the objective is to put in, put back, or move some or all of a body part. Table 5-7 identifies the root operation character values, and the definitions of the four operations in this group.

Root operations that alter the diameter or route of a tubular body part include the root operations Restriction, Occlusion, Dilation, and Bypass. Table 5-8 lists the character values and definitions for these four root operations.

Root operations that include other repairs include only two root operations: Control and Repair. Control has the character value 3, and has a very specific definition: *stopping, or attempting to stop, postprocedural bleeding*. The root operation repair has the character value Q. Its definition is *restoring, to the extent possible, a body part to its normal anatomic structure and function*.

Root operations involving examination only include Inspection and Map. The character value for Inspection is J. The definition of root operation inspection is *visually and/or manually exploring a body part*, with or without optical instrumentation. A manual exploration may be performed directly or through intervening body layers.

There are three guidelines that are appropriate for Inspection (Table 5-9).

Review

Matching

Instructions:

_____ 1. Bypass

_____ 2. Change

_____ 3. Destruction

_____ 4. Excision

_____ 5. Extirpation

_____ 6. Insertion

_____ 7. Reposition

_____ 8. Revision

_____ 9. Removal

_____ 10. Resection

a. Cutting out or off, without replacement, a portion of a body part
b. Correcting, to the extent possible, a portion of a malfunctioning device or the position of a displaced device
c. Taking out or off a device from a body part and putting back an identical or similar device in or on the same body part without cutting or puncturing the skin or a mucous membrane
d. Taking or cutting out solid matter from a body part
e. Moving to its normal location, or other suitable location, all or a portion of a body part
f. Altering the route of passage of the contents of a tubular body part
g. Cutting out or off, without replacement, all of a body part
h. Taking out or off a device from a body part
i. Putting a nonbiological appliance that monitors, assists, performs, or prevents a physiological function but does not physically take the place of a body part
j. Physical eradication of all or a portion of a body part by the direct use of energy, force, or a destructive agent

Short Answer

Instructions: Determine the correct root operation and the Table reference for the following procedures:

1. Endometrial biopsy
   a. Root Operation _____
   b. Table Reference _____

2. Left fourth toe amputation, mid proximal phalanx
   a. Root Operation _____
   b. Table Reference _____

3. Total mastectomy
   a. Root Operation _____
   b. Table Reference _____

4. Open reduction with internal fixation, right humerus
   a. Root Operation _____
   b. Table Reference _____

5. Adhesions rupture, manual, shoulder joint, right
   a. Root Operation _____
   b. Table Reference _____

6. ERCP with lithotripsy of common bile duct calculus
   a. Root Operation _____
   b. Table Reference _____

7. Transurethral cystoscopy with removal of ureteral calculus
   a. Root Operation _____
   b. Table Reference _____

8. Cryotherapy esophageal varices
   a. Root Operation _____
   b. Table Reference _____

9. Percutaneous paracentesis for ascites
   a. Root Operation _____
   b. Table Reference _____

10. Anal sphincterotomy
    a. Root Operation _____
    b. Table Reference _____

Coding Practice

Instructions: Give at least the first three characters for the following root operations. As in Chapter 10, try to code the complete procedure based on what has been learned so far. It is permissible to use an x as a placeholder for the remaining, unidentified, character values for this activity.

1. Kidney transplant, right, synegenic _____

2. External replantation of three avulsed teeth, lower jaw _____

3. Endoscopic radial to median nerve transfer _____

4. Endoscopic restriction of thoracic duct with intraluminal stent _____

5. Inferior mesenteric artery embolization, percutaneous endoscopic, extraluminal device _____

6. Dilation of upper esophageal stricture via mouth/esophagus _____

7. Femoral-popliteal artery bypass, open, autologous vein (femoral artery is being bypassed by the popliteal artery) _____

8. Post-op prostatectomy hemorrhage control, percutaneous (*Hint:* perineum) _____
   _____

9. Pyelography, open, right kidney pelvis _____

10. Diagnostic endoscopic arthroscopy, left knee _____

11. Percutaneous mapping, basal ganglia _____

12. Insertion of central venous infusion catheter, right subclavian, open _____
    _____

13. Removal of drainage device, external, gallbladder _____

14. Open reposition of right metacarpal bone, no device _____

15. Diagnostic biopsy of left ankle bursa/ligament, endoscopic (*Hint:* Excision) _____
    _____

Medical and Surgical Section Coding

Learning Objectives

At the conclusion of this chapter, the learner should be able to:

- Understand how each of the seven code characters are combined to form a complete and accurate procedure code
- Apply the Medical and Surgical section and general guidelines appropriately when assigning an ICD-10-PCS code
- Identify the body systems, body parts, and anatomical regions as used in the Medical and Surgical section of the ICD-10-PCS
- Understand the Approaches used in the Medical and Surgical section, and how to apply them properly
- Identify the types of Devices used, and with which root operations and body systems and parts they are appropriate for use
- Determine how Qualifiers are used, and when to use them when coding procedures
- Apply the procedural coding steps and guidelines to translate procedural statements into ICD-10-PCS codes

Key Terms and Definitions

Access location	One of the three determining factors for the Approach value. It specifies the external site through which the site of the procedure is reached.
Allogenic	A transplanted body part or tissue taken from a different individual of the same species.
Approach	The method used to perform the procedure based on access location, method and type of instrumentation.
Deep Inferior Epigastric Artery Perforator (DIEP) Flap	A breast reconstruction procedure similar to the TRAM flap, except that it uses only skin and fat from the abdominal wall, and leaves the muscle intact.
Cardiac resynchronization therapy (CRT)	Used to treat the delay in heart ventricle contractions that occur in some people with advanced heart failure.
Ductus arteriosus	A normal fetal structure that allows blood to bypass circulation to the lungs, which closes in most cases within 24 hours. When it does not close, it is termed a Patent Ductus Arteriosus, and may require intervention with infusion of chemicals, placement of plugs, or surgical closure.

External approach	Procedures performed directly on the skin or mucous membrane, and procedures performed indirectly by the application of external force through the skin or mucous membrane.
Free TRAM Flap	Procedure in which fat, muscle, and blood vessels are removed from the lower abdominal wall and moved to the chest wall to reconstruct the breast.
Latissimus Dorsi (LD) Flap	Breast reconstruction procedure that takes muscle and skin from the upper back, which is then used to replace missing breast tissue.
Method	One of the three determining factors for the Approach value. It specifies how the external access location is entered during the approach.
Open approach	Cutting through the skin or mucous membrane and any other body layers necessary to expose the site of the procedure.
Open endoscopic approach	Cutting through the skin or mucous membrane and any other body layers necessary to expose the site of the procedure; and entry, by puncture or minor incision, of instrumentation through the skin or mucous membrane and any other body layers necessary to aid in the performance of the procedure.
Pacemaker	A surgically implanted electronic device that regulates a slow or erratic heartbeat.
Percutaneous approach	Entry, by puncture or minor incision, of instrumentation through the skin or mucous membrane and any other body layers necessary to reach the site of the procedure.
Percutaneous endoscopic approach	Entry, by puncture or minor incision, of instrumentation through the skin or mucous membrane and any other body layers necessary to reach and visualize the site of the procedure.
Ray	Refers to the metacarpal and metatarsal bones of the hand and foot, respectively, when using the root operation Detachment.
Syngeneic	Tissue or a body part taken from someone with identical genes like an identical twin.
Type of Instrumentation	One of the three determining factors for the Approach value. It identifies whether specialized equipment is used to perform the procedure.
Via natural or artificial opening approach	Entry of instrumentation through a natural or artificial external opening to reach the site of the procedures.
Via natural or artificial opening approach endoscopic	Entry of instrumentation through a natural or artificial external opening to reach and visualize the site of the procedures Tissue or a body part.
Zooplastic	taken from an animal.

Introduction

In the previous chapter, the definitions and objectives of the 31 root operations in the Medical and Surgical section were covered, in addition to information on how to use the Index to begin the search for an appropriate Table in the Tabular List. In this chapter, the remaining code characters, their values, and their definitions will be introduced, along with a detailed discussion of the Tables in the Medical and Surgical section, and how they are used to select the best and most accurate procedure code.

More information about the body system and body part characters and their values will be included in this chapter, in addition to Approach, Device, and Qualifier values. All codes in the Medical and Surgical section will begin with the first character value 0. And all of the codes will, of course, be seven characters in length. There are also more guidelines for use of the Body System, Body Parts, Approaches, Devices, and Qualifiers in the Medical and Surgical section. Many of the root operations,

Index Table references, and procedures from the previous chapter will be brought forward into this chapter, where the remaining code values will be combined to build a complete procedure code based on the guidelines and Tables from the Medical and Surgical section.

This is by far the largest section of the ICD-10-PCS procedural coding manual. It represents the code sets mandated for use in all procedures performed in an inpatient or acute care setting. For physicians, ambulatory care providers, and most other outpatient settings, the Current Procedural Terminology (CPT) and Health Care Common Procedural Coding System (HCPCS) code will continue to be the procedural code sets for transactions, billing, and reporting purposes.

The Medical and Surgical Section (0)

As mentioned earlier, the first character of a code from the Medical and Surgical section will always be 0. (This is a zero, the alphabetic character O is not used in ICD-10-PCS.) The remaining six characters, in order, are:

Character 2	Body System
Character 3	Root Operation
Character 4	Body Part (or Anatomical Region)
Character 5	Approach
Character 6	Device
Character 7	Qualifier

Character 2 represents general body system values, while character 4 is a more specific body part within the general body system. Character 3 is the root operation, which is the specific objective of the procedure. The fifth character is the approach used to reach the procedure site, such as *open, percutaneous endoscopic,* or *via natural or artificial opening.* Character 6 is any device left in or on the body as part of the objective of the procedure. Examples of devices includes pacemakers, tissue substitutes, and fracture fixation devices. Character 7, Qualifiers, are generally specific to a root operation. For example, in a Bypass root operation, the Qualifier is used to identify the destination site of the bypass. The first through fifth characters of a Medical and Surgical section code will have unique, specific, values, but there are instances where no unique value is assigned to the sixth and seventh characters. If there is no applicable Device or Qualifier for a root operation or procedure, the default character value is Z, which means No Device and/or No Qualifier.

The Tables in the Medical and Surgical section Tabular List are identical in layout regardless of which body system or root operation is involved. Figure 6-1 is an example of a Table from the Medical and Surgical section.

At the top of each Table is the heading. It will always contain the section, body system, and root operation values and titles. In addition, the definition of the root operation is included. Figure 6-1's header is from the Medical and Surgical section, value 0; the body system (and character 2 of the code) is 0, the value for the Central Nervous System, and the root operation is P, Removal (taking out or off a device from a body part). The first three characters of a code will always be the section, body system, and root operation, so for this example, the code would start with 00P. Next are four columns. The first column represents the body part, the second represents the approach values possible for each body part, next is the device, and the last column is the qualifier.

Note that in Figure 6-1, there are six rows below the header, and that in some the same body part value is repeated. For example, the body parts Brain (0) and Spinal Cord (V) appear in rows 1 and 2. The difference between the rows in this example are the allowable approach values. In the first row, three approach values are available, while in the second, only an external approach is shown. If the procedure was an *open removal of a drainage device from the brain,* row 1 would be the only appropriate row to use since the open approach is only found in row 1. If the same procedure was documented as external,

Section	0	Medical and Surgical
Body System	0	Central Nervous System
Operation	P	Removal: Taking out or off a device from a body part

Body Part	Approach	Device	Qualifier
0 Brain **V** Spinal Cord	**0** Open **3** Percutaneous **4** Percutaneous Endoscopic	**0** Drainage Device **2** Monitoring Device **3** Infusion Device **7** Autologous Tissue Substitute **J** Synthetic Substitute **K** Nonautologous Tissue Substitute **M** Neurostimulator Lead	**Z** No Qualifier
0 Brain **V** Spinal Cord	**X** External	**0** Drainage Device **2** Monitoring Device **3** Infusion Device **M** Neurostimulator Lead	**Z** No Qualifier
6 Cerebral Ventricle **U** Spinal Canal	**0** Open **3** Percutaneous **4** Percutaneous Endoscopic	**0** Drainage Device **2** Monitoring Device **3** Infusion Device **J** Synthetic Substitute **M** Neurostimulator Lead	**Z** No Qualifier
6 Cerebral Ventricle **U** Spinal Canal	**X** External	**0** Drainage Device **2** Monitoring Device **3** Infusion Device **M** Neurostimulator Lead	**Z** No Qualifier
E Cranial Nerve	**0** Open **3** Percutaneous **4** Percutaneous Endoscopic	**0** Drainage Device **2** Monitoring Device **3** Infusion Device **7** Autologous Tissue Substitute **M** Neurostimulator Lead	**Z** No Qualifier
E Cranial Nerve	**X** External	**0** Drainage Device **2** Monitoring Device **3** Infusion Device **M** Neurostimulator Lead	**Z** No Qualifier

© Cengage Learning 2013

Figure 6-1 Example of a Medical and Surgical Section Table

the only appropriate row would be row 2, which contains the External approach value. Once a row has been chosen, the remainder of the code values must come from that row. Using the same procedure example, *open removal of a drainage device from the brain,* the first row contains all the matching values for the procedure, which arrives at the code 00P000Z, broken down as follows:

1st Character	Section	Medical and Surgical	Value 0
2nd Character	Body System	Central Nervous System	Value 0
3rd Character	Root Operation	Removal	Value P
4th Character	Body Part	Brain	Value 0
5th Character	Approach	Open	Value 0
6th Character	Device	Drainage Device	Value 0
7th Character	Qualifier	None	Value Z

If, after a row is selected, one of the character values does not match the procedural statement, another row must be selected. This will be explained more fully later in this chapter.

Body System (Character 2) Values in the Medical and Surgical Section

Body system characters and guidelines were discussed in an earlier chapter, but here is a brief recap of character 2, Body System. In ICD-10-PCS, the body system is always the second character of the ICD-10-PCS code and refers to the body system affected by the procedure. There are 31 body systems represented in the Medical and Surgical section. Most are clearly recognizable as body systems, such as the central (0) and peripheral (1) nervous system, and the respiratory (B), gastrointestinal (D), and endocrine (G) systems. Table 6-1 lists the body systems and their values found in the Medical and Surgical section.

Table 6-1 Body System (Character 2) Values in Medical and Surgical Table

Body System Character Value	Term
0	Central nervous system
1	Peripheral nervous system
2	Heart and great vessels
3	Upper arteries
4	Lower arteries
5	Upper veins
6	Lower veins
7	Lymphatic and hemic system
8	Eye
9	Ear, nose, sinus
B	Respiratory system
C	Mouth and throat
D	Gastrointestinal system
F	Hepatobiliary system and pancreas
G	Endocrine system
H	Skin and breast
J	Subcutaneous tissue and fascia
K	Muscles
L	Tendon
M	Bursa and ligaments
N	Head and facial bones
P	Upper bones
Q	Lower bones
R	Upper joints
S	Lower joints
T	Urinary system
U	Female reproductive system
V	Male reproductive system
W	Anatomic regions, general
X	Anatomic regions, upper extremities
Y	Anatomic regions, lower extremities

Body system values are called general values, in that they generally represent an entire body system, and not a specific body part within that system. In most instances, they are relevant primarily to the preliminary Index search, and used only to confirm that the correct Table has been selected. The body system can be repeated in several Tables, depending upon the root operation. In other words, the same body systems and values can be found in a Table for root operation Removal, as illustrated in Table 6-1, and for any of the remaining 30 root operations in the Medical and Surgical section.

In ICD-9-CM, Volume III, the body systems used common terminology like endocrine system, female respiratory system, and so forth. In ICD-10-PCS, most of these same body systems have a character value, but there are many new divisions which use different terminology. For example, in ICD-9-CM, all of the veins and arteries were part of the circulatory system. In ICD-10-PCS they are separated into their own categories, and further subdivided by location, such as upper and lower arteries, upper and lower veins, etc. When using the more general body systems like anatomical regions, lower extremities, or heart and great vessels, or upper and lower arteries and veins, the Body Part Key in Appendix C in the ICD-10-PCS will prove extremely valuable. Remember, depending on the publisher, the Appendix ID may be different. Where most medical documentation lists specific anatomical sites, Appendix C will guide the coder to the most appropriate body system. For example, if the medical documentation states the arcuate artery, Appendix C lists the ICD-10-PCS definition as foot artery. This guides the coder to the lower arteries body system, character value 4, and the more specific fourth character body part value for foot artery.

Body System Guidelines

There are two guidelines applicable to the body systems characters B2.1a and B2.1b. These guidelines determine body system character usage regardless of which Table or section of the ICD-10-PCS coding manual is used. Table 6-2 lists each of the Guidelines, and provides examples of each.

Later in this chapter, more examples of body system guidelines will be introduced, and the proper selection of body system, root operation, and code character values will be discussed in far more detail. For now, let's look at the rest of the characters that make up the ICD-10-PCS code.

Body Part (Character 4) Values in the Medical and Surgical Section

The fourth character of an ICD-10-PCS code is the body part. The body part represents the specific part of the body upon which the procedure is performed. It is always the first column in a table from the Medical and Surgical section.

The character that represents each body part will change depending on the Table section (Character 1), body system (Character 2), and occasionally the root operation (Character 3) within which the code is identified.

Table 6-2 Body System Specific Coding Guidelines

Body System Guideline B2.1a
When a procedure is performed that spans more than one body system, a value from one of the three anatomic region character assignments should be used: • Anatomic region, general • Anatomic region, upper extremities • Anatomic region, lower extremities EXAMPLE: *Control of post-operative hemorrhage is coded to the general anatomic region body system.*
Body System Guideline B2.1b
B2.3 Body systems designated as upper or lower contain body parts located above or below the diaphragm, respectively EXAMPLE: *Upper vein* Body Parts are above the diaphragm, *lower vein* Body System structures are below the diaphragm

In the ICD-10-PCS coding manual, there is an appendix titled **Section 0—Medical and Surgical, Character 4—Body Part**. This is a very handy appendix, because it states explicitly what is included in each body part. For example, the body part *abdominal aorta* includes six different arteries, the inferior phrenic, lumbar, medial sacral, middle suprarenal, ovarian, and testicular. Some of these arteries have individual body part values. Figure 6-2 is an excerpt from the Section 0, Character 4 body part appendix.

Section 0 - Medical and Surgical
Character 4 - Body Part *(continued)*

Bone, Ethmoid, Left Bone, Ethmoid, Right	**Includes:** Cribriform plate
Bone, Frontal, Left Bone, Frontal, Right	**Includes:** Zygomatic process of frontal bone
Bone, Nasal	**Includes:** Vomer
Bone, Occipital, Left Bone, Occipital, Right	**Includes:** Foramen magnum
Bone, Pelvic, Left Bone, Pelvic, Right	**Includes:** Iliac crest Ilium Ischium Pubis
Bone, Sphenoid, Left Bone, Sphenoid, Right	**Includes:** Greater wing Lesser wing Optic foramen Pterygoid process Sella turcica
Bone, Temporal, Left Bone, Temporal, Right	**Includes:** Mastoid process Petrous part of temporal bone Tympanic part of temporal bone Zygomatic process of temporal bone
Brain	**Includes:** Corpus callosum Encephalon
Breast, Bilateral Breast, Left Breast, Right	**Includes:** Mammary duct Mammary gland
Buccal Mucosa	**Includes:** Buccal gland Labial gland Molar gland Palatine gland

Figure 6-2 Excerpt from Body Part Appendix in ICD-10-PCS Coding Manual

When the body part is *brain*, to give another example, the structures *corpus callosum* and *encephalon* are included within that body part value. Included in the *breast* body part are the *mammary ducts* and *glands*. If, during the abstracting procedure, the documentation states *drainage of three mammary ducts of the left breast,* the body part value will default to *breast* since there is no body part value for *mammary ducts.*

Though there are far too many body parts to list here, an important note to remember is that the same values—0 through 9, and A-D, F-H, J-N, and P-Z—will be designated to different body part values, depending upon the body system. Figure 6-3 shows a table from the body system *Lower Veins*. Note that that 0 represents the inferior vena cava, 1 the splenic vein, 2 the gastric vein and so on, through Y, lower vein. Now look at Figure 6-4, which is a Table from the body system *Lymphatic and Hemic Systems*. Almost all of the same letter and number values are in this Table; however, 0 is now lymphatic, head; 1 is right neck lymphatic; and 2 is lymphatic, left neck, etc. For this reason, trying to memorize the body part values would be a fruitless endeavor, since unlike the root operations, they will change as the body system changes.

Body Part Guidelines

There are eight guidelines specific to the use of body part values B4.1a through B4.7, Of these, B4.1a and B4.1b are general guidelines which apply to all body parts. The rest are body part-specific guidelines. Before reviewing the body part guidelines, let's cover some general information about body parts. Body parts can sometimes include general values, like the esophagus, and in the same Table, have even more specific values, such as *upper esophagus. Esophagus* is a general body part value, while

Section	**0**	Medical and Surgical		
Body System	**6**	Lower Veins		
Operation	**S**	Reposition: Moving to its normal location, or other suitable location, all or a portion of a body part		

Body Part	Approach	Device	Qualifier
0 Inferior Vena Cava **1** Splenic Vein **2** Gastric Vein **3** Esophageal Vein **4** Hepatic Vein **5** Superior Mesenteric Vein **6** Inferior Mesenteric Vein **7** Colic Vein **8** Portal Vein **9** Renal Vein, Right **B** Renal Vein, Left **C** Common Iliac Vein, Right **D** Common Iliac Vein, Left **F** External Iliac Vein, Right **G** External Iliac Vein, Left **H** Hypogastric Vein, Right **J** Hypogastric Vein, Left **M** Femoral Vein, Right **N** Femoral Vein, Left **P** Greater Saphenous Vein, Right **Q** Greater Saphenous Vein, Left **R** Lesser Saphenous Vein, Right **S** Lesser Saphenous Vein, Left **T** Foot Vein, Right **V** Foot Vein, Left **Y** Lower Vein	**0** Open **3** Percutaneous **4** Percutaneous Endoscopic	**Z** No Device	**Z** No Qualifier

Figure 6-3 Medical and Surgical Table Example for Lower Vein Body Part

Section	**0**	Medical and Surgical
Body System	**7**	Lymphatic and Hemic Systems
Operation	**B**	Excision: Cutting out or off, without replacement, a portion of a body part

Body Part	Approach	Device	Qualifier
0 Lymphatic, Head **1** Lymphatic, Right Neck **2** Lymphatic, Left Neck **3** Lymphatic, Right Upper Extremity **4** Lymphatic, Left Upper Extremity **5** Lymphatic, Right Axillary **6** Lymphatic, Left Axillary **7** Lymphatic, Thorax **8** Lymphatic, Internal Mammary, Right **9** Lymphatic, Internal Mammary, Left **B** Lymphatic, Mesenteric **C** Lymphatic, Pelvis **D** Lymphatic, Aortic **F** Lymphatic, Right Lower Extremity **G** Lymphatic, Left Lower Extremity **H** Lymphatic, Right Inguinal **J** Lymphatic, Left Inguinal **K** Thoracic Duct **L** Cisterna Chyli **M** Thymus **P** Spleen	**0** Open **3** Percutaneous **4** Percutaneous Endoscopic	**Z** No Device	**X** Diagnostic **Z** No Qualifier

© Cengage Learning 2013

Figure 6-4 Body Part Values for Lymphatic and Hemic System

esophagus, upper is a specific body part value. Use the specific body part value whenever possible, but when a specific value is not available, use a general body part value in the following instances:

- When a procedure is performed on a general body part as a whole

- When the specific body part cannot be determined

- In the root operations *Change, Removal, and Revision,* when the specific body part is not in the Tabular List Table

   EXAMPLES:

   1. If, in any of the above conditions, the procedure documentation states only *esophagus* (the general body part) it is acceptable to use just that general body part when selecting the code.

   2. Another example might be *treatment of esophageal varices.* If the medical documentation does not specify a specific section of the esophagus, it can be assumed that the varices treatment was applied to the entire esophagus. In this case, the general body part value for *esophagus* is appropriate.

   3. For the root operation Removal, in a procedure that removes a device from the esophagus, even if a specific body part such as upper esophagus is mentioned in the medical documentation, the body part value for a Removal procedure will still be *esophagus,* because there is no *upper esophagus* value in the Removal root operation Tables.

General body part guidelines B4.1a and B4.1b These two guidelines are specific to all body part values within the Medical and Surgical section:

- **Guideline B4.1a:** If a procedure is performed on a portion of a body part that does not have a separate value, code the value corresponding to the whole body part. For example, a procedure performed on the alveolar process of the mandible is coded to the Mandible body part. Remember, the ICD-10-PCS coding manual has Appendix C, titled Body Part Key, which lists all the body parts and the structures included in that body part. Refer back to Figure 6-2 for an excerpt from this appendix.

- **Guideline B4.1b:** If the prefix *peri-* is used with a body part to identify the site of the procedure, the body part value is defined as the body part named. For example, perihepatic is coded to the *liver* body part. Note also, if the procedure documentation uses a body part to further specify the site of the procedure, the body part value is defined as the body part on which the procedure is performed. An example is a body part identified in the medical documentation as *prostatic urethra.* Prostatic is an adjective (think of it as a modifying or sub-term) for the body part urethra, therefore, the procedure is actually performed on the body part *urethra*.

Guideline B4.2, Branches of Body Parts, states that when a specific branch of a body part, for example the *mandibular branch of the trigeminal nerve*, does not have its own body part value, code to the closest proximal branch that does. In this example, the value selected would be for the *trigeminal nerve* body part.

Guideline B4.3, Bilateral Body Part Values, the bilateral body part values are available for a limited number of body parts. They are included in a system on the basis of frequency and common practice. If the identical procedure is performed on bilateral body parts, i.e., both knees, eyes, or hips, etc., and a bilateral body part value exists for that body part, a single procedure is coded using the bilateral body part value.

If no bilateral body part value exists, code each procedure separately using the appropriate body part value. For example, there is a bilateral body part value for *fallopian tubes* in the female reproductive system, so if a procedure is performed on both fallopian tubes, code it as one procedure using the bilateral body part value. The knee joint, on the other hand, does not have a bilateral body part value, therefore, if a bilateral arthroplasty of the knee is performed, two separate procedures would be coded using the body part value for the appropriate knee (right or left).

Guideline B4.4: coronary arteries Guideline B4.4 is specific to the coronary arteries in the heart and great vessels body system. The guideline states that coronary arteries are classified as a single body part. There is no differentiation between, for example, a left or right coronary artery, but they are differentiated by the number of sites treated. Separate body part values exist to indicate the number of sites treated when the same procedure is performed on multiple sites in the coronary arteries. Refer back to the Bypass root operation guideline B3.6 for additional information about coding coronary artery body parts.

For example, if two sites in the coronary arteries were dilated using stents, the body part description and value would be 1, *coronary artery, two sites.* Now, if two dilations were performed using two different devices, then two separate codes would be needed, and the body part value for each coronary artery dilation procedure would be 0, for one site, with a different device character value for the sixth code character. These two principles are shown in Figure 6-5.

Guideline B4.5: Procedures performed on tendons, ligaments, bursae, and fascia supporting a joint are coded to the body part that is the focus of the procedure in the respective body system. Procedures performed on joint structures are coded to the body part in the joint body systems. For example, *repair of the anterior cruciate ligament (ACL) of the knee* is coded to the Knee body part in the Bursae and Ligaments body system, because the focus is on the repair of the ACL. In a *shoulder arthroscopy, with shaving of the articular cartilage*, the focus of the arthroscopy is the shoulder, and is, therefore, coded to the Shoulder Joint body part.

Guideline B4.6: In body systems containing skin, subcutaneous tissue, muscle, and tendon body part values, where a specific body part value does not exist for the area surrounding a joint, the corresponding body part value is coded as follows:

- Shoulder is coded to Upper Arm

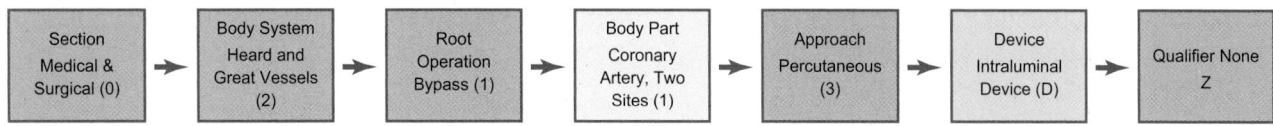

Example 1 above: percutaneous dilation two sites using intraluminal devices (02113DZ)

Example 2 below: percutaneous dilation two sites, 1st site intraluminal device, 2nd site drug-eluting intraluminal device (02103DZ and 021034Z)

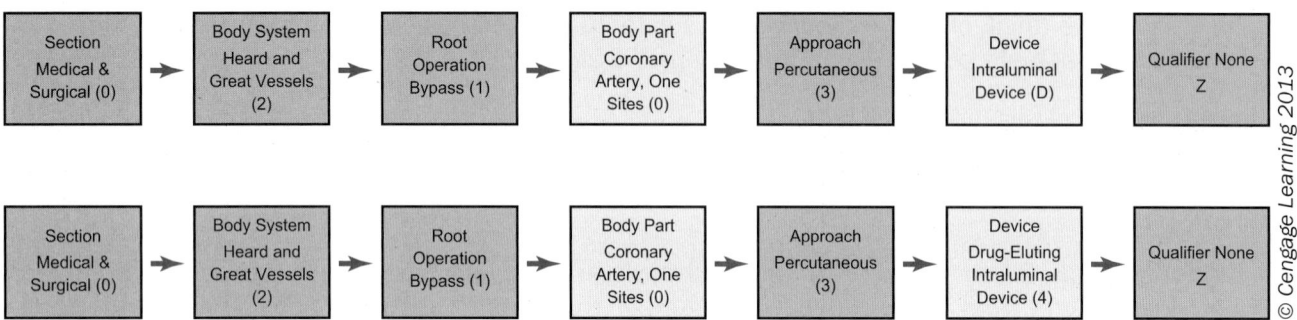

© Cengage Learning 2013

Figure 6-5 Medical and Surgical Table for Coronary Artery Bypass Procedure

- Elbow is coded to Lower Arm
- Wrist is coded to Lower Arm
- Hip is coded to Upper Leg
- Knee is coded to Lower Leg
- Ankle is coded to Foot

Guideline B4.7 Guideline B4.7 discusses coding for fingers and toes. If a body system does not contain a separate body part value for fingers or toes, procedures performed on the fingers or toes are coded to the body part value for hand or foot, respectively. For example, *excision of a finger muscle* is coded to the Hand Muscle body part value.

Approach (Character 5) Values in the Medical and Surgical Section

There are seven approaches listed in the Medical and Surgical (0) section. These were mentioned in an earlier chapter, but because of their importance, let's look at them in depth this time. Table 6-3 illustrates the approach terms, values, and definitions in the Medical and Surgical section.

The approach includes three components: (1) the access location; (2) the method; and (3) the type of instrumentation.

The **access location** specifies the external site through which the site of the procedure is reached, if the procedure is performed on an internal body part. The two general types of access location are the skin or mucous membranes and external orifices. Every approach value except External includes one of these two access locations. The skin or mucous membrane can be cut or punctured to reach the procedure site. All open and percutaneous approach values use this access location. The site of the procedure can also be reached through an external opening. External openings can be natural or artificial.

For procedures performed on an internal body part, the **method** specifies how the external access location is entered.

- Open: Cutting through the skin or mucous membrane and any other body layers necessary to expose the site of the procedure.

Table 6-3 Approach (Character 5) Values and Definitions

Approach Value	Term	Definition
0	Open	Cutting through the skin or mucous membrane and any other body layers necessary to **expose the site of the procedure**
2	Open with percutaneous endoscopic assistance	Cutting through the skin or mucous membrane and any other body layers necessary to **expose the site of the procedure**; and **entry, by puncture or minor incision, of instrumentation through the skin or mucous membrane** and any other body layers necessary to aid in the performance of the procedure
3	Percutaneous	Entry, by puncture or minor incision, of instrumentation through the skin or mucous membrane and any other body layers necessary to **reach** the site of the procedure
4	Percutaneous endoscopic	Entry, by puncture or minor incision, of instrumentation through the skin or mucous membrane and any other body layers necessary to **reach and visualize** the site of the procedure
7	Via natural or artificial opening	Entry of instrumentation through a natural or artificial external opening to **reach** the site of the procedures
8	Via natural or artificial opening endoscopic	Entry of instrumentation through a natural or artificial external opening to **reach and visualize** the site of the procedures
X	External	Procedures **performed directly on the skin or mucous membrane**, and procedures **performed indirectly by the application of external force** through the skin or mucous membrane

- An instrumental method specifies entry of the instrument through the access location to the procedure site.

- Instrumentation can by introduced by puncture or minor incision, or through an external opening. The puncture or minor incision does not constitute an open approach because it does not expose the site of the procedure.

- An Approach can define multiple methods, such as open with percutaneous endoscopic assistance includes both the open approach that exposes the body part and the placement of instrumentation in the body part to aid in the performance of the procedure.

Type of Instrumentation means that specialized equipment is used to perform the procedure. Instrumentation is used in all internal approaches other than the basic open approach.

- Instrumentation may or may not include the capacity to visualize the site, for example a colonoscopy's instrumentation allows visualization of the internal colon; while the instrument used to perform a needle biopsy does not.

- If the term *endoscopic* is used in the procedural statement, this always includes instrumentation that allows the site to be visualized.

Guidelines for Character 5 Approach

There are four guidelines specific to the fifth character approach. Guideline B5.2 discusses the open approach with percutaneous assistance. B5.3a and B5.3b discusses external approaches, and the final approach guideline, B5.4 covers percutaneous procedures using a device. There is no B5.1 guideline as of the 2011 upgrade to ICD-10-PCS.

Guideline B5.2: Procedures performed using the open approach with percutaneous endoscopic assistance are coded to the approach value Open, 0. For example, a *laparoscopic-assisted sigmoidectomy*, where the sigmoid colon is surgically removed is coded to Open Approach. The use of the laparoscope is only to assist in the surgical removal.

Procedures performed via natural or artificial opening with percutaneous endoscopic assistance are coded to approach value F, via natural or artificial opening with percutaneous endoscopic assistance. A laparoscopic-assisted vaginal hysterectomy (LAVH) is the surgical removal of the uterus via the vagina—a natural opening. The surgical removal of the uterus through the vagina makes the Approach via natural opening, which would normally be value 7, but with the laparoscopic assistance, it changes to value F, which combines via natural opening and percutaneous endoscopic assistance into one approach value.

Guideline B5.3a: Procedures performed within an orifice on structures that are visible without the aid of any instrumentation are coded to X, External, i.e., a resection of the tonsils.

Guideline B5.3b: Procedures performed indirectly by the application of external force through the intervening body layers are coded to approach value X, External, such as a closed reduction of a fracture.

Guideline B5.4: Procedures performed via indwelling devices are coded to approach value 3, Percutaneous, for example, the fragmentation of a kidney stone performed via percutaneous nephrostomy.

Procedures performed on a device, as defined in the root operations Change, Irrigation, Removal, and Revision, are coded to the procedure performed. For example, an irrigation of a percutaneous nephrostomy tube is coded to the root operation Irrigation of Indwelling Device—which is in the Administration section, not the Medical and Surgical section, of the ICD-10-PCS.

Let's Review 6–1:

In the following procedures, determine which Approach character is appropriate:

1. Open abdominal appendectomy _____

2. Instrumental approach entering through the anus Closed fracture reduction _____

3. Diagnostic arthroscopy _____

4. Biopsy of left lower lobe of lung _____

Device (Character 6) Values in Medical and Surgical Section

Character 6 in the ICD-10-PCS in most sections designates a Device, or any object purposely left in the body during a procedure, such as a pacemaker, or screws and pins. It does not include staples or sutures that are incidental to the procedure performed. There are several different types of devices, biological or synthetic materials, therapeutic materials, and mechanical or electronic appliances. The descriptions of each type of device are in Table 6-4, and the devices, values, and applicable root operations are in Table 6-5.

Table 6-4 Device Types

Device Types (Character 6)
Biological or synthetic material that takes the place of all or a portion of a body part, e.g., skin grafts and joint prostheses
Biological or synthetic material that assists or prevents a physiological function, e.g., IUD
Therapeutic material that is not absorbed or eliminated by, or incorporated into a body part, e.g., radioactive implant
Mechanical or electronic appliances used to assist, monitor, take the place of, or prevent a physiological function, e.g., pacemaker or orthopedic screws and pins

The first thing to notice is that the alphabetic or numeric value is duplicated in different body systems, and can either have a similar or completely different meaning. For example, the device value M, in most root operations, represents a cardiac or neurostimulator lead, but in the skin and skeletal body systems, M is the value for bone growth stimulator and tissue expander, respectively. The duplication occurs in the existing (as of 2011) draft version of ICD-10-PCS with the values 3, 4, 8, 9, and B, G, M and N; however, be aware that this version has not been finalized, so more value duplications, and even more devices, will most likely be added.

Next, take a few minutes to review Tables 6-4 and 6-5, and note there are several root operations for certain devices.

Table 6-5 Device (Character 6) Values and Associated Root Operation

Value	Device	Root Operation
0	Drainage Device	Change Drainage Insertion Removal Revision
1	Radioactive Element	Insertion Removal
2	Monitoring Device	Insertion Removal Revision
3*	Infusion Device	Fusion Insertion Removal Revision
3*	Interbody Internal Fixation Device	**Body System: Upper Joints*** **Fusion**
4*	Drug-eluting Intraluminal Device	Bypass Dilation Fusion Insertion Removal Reposition Revision
4*	Internal Fixation Device	**Body System Upper Bones*** Insertion Removal Replacement Reposition
5	External Fixation Device	Insertion Removal Revision Replacement Reposition
6	Intramedullary Fixation Device	Insertion Removal Revision

7	Autologous Tissue Substitute	Alteration Bypass Fusion Removal Supplement Revision Replacement
8*	Zooplastic Tissue	Removal Replacement Supplement
8*	Spacer	**Body System: Upper Joints*** Insertion Removal Revision
9*	Autologous Venous Tissue	Bypass Removal Revision
9*	Liner	**Body System: Lower Joints*** Insertion Removal Supplement
A	Autologous Arterial Tissue	Bypass Removal Revision
B*	Bioactive Intraluminal Device	Occlusion Removal Restriction Revision
B*	Airway	**Ear, Nose, Throat Body System** **Gastrointestinal System** Insertion Removal Revision
B*	Resurfacing Device	**Body System: Lower Joints*** Insertion Removal Supplement
C	Extraluminal Device	Occlusion Removal Restriction Revision
D	Intraluminal Device	Bypass Dilation Insertion Occlusion Removal Restriction Revision
E	Endotracheal Airway	Change Insertion Removal Revision

Table 6-5 Device (Character 6) Values and Associated Root Operation (continued)

Value	Device	Root Operation
F	Tracheostomy Device	Insertion Bypass Removal Revision
G	Endobronchial Valve	Insertion Revision Removal
G*	Pessary	**Body System: Female Reproductive*** Insertion Removal
H	Contraceptive Device	Fusion Change Insertion Removal
J	Synthetic Substitute	Alteration Bypass Fusion Removal Supplement Revision Replacement
K	Nonautologous tissue substitute	Alteration Bypass Fusion Removal Replacement Revision Supplement
L	Artificial Sphincter	Insertion Removal Revision
M*	Neurostimulator/Cardiac Lead	Insertion Removal Revision
M*	Diaphragmatic Pacemaker Lead	**Respiratory System Only*** Insertion Removal Revision
M*	Stimulator Generator	**Subcutaneous Tissue and Fascia Only*** Insertion Removal Revision
M*	Bone Growth Stimulator	**Body System: Skeletal*** Insertion Removal
N*	Tissue Expander	Insertion Removal Revision
N	Interbody Nonautologous Tissue	**Body System: Upper Joints*** Fusion

Q	Implantable Heart Assist System	Insertion Removal Revision
R	External Heart Assist System	Insertion Removal Revision
S	Hearing Device	Insertion Removal
T	Radioactive Intraluminal Device	Dilation Removal Revision
U	Feeding Device	Change Insertion Removal Revision
V	Infusion Pump	Insertion Removal Revision
W	Reservoir	Insertion Removal Revision
X	Vascular Access Device	Insertion Removal Revision
Y	Other Device	Change Insertion Removal Revision
Z	No Device	Any Root Operations

Device Guidelines

Before talking about the Device-specific Guidelines, there is a new feature with the 2012 upgrades: ICD-10-PCS added a PCS to PCS Device Aggregation Table between root operations that use both general and specific devices and root operations like Removal and Revision that only use general devices. This table will help identify which category of device matches the medical documentation. This table will be found in most published versions of the ICD-10-PCS. In addition, there are two new device table listings, one listed by device brand name, and one with the PCS device value. There are four guidelines for any use of code character six device. They are B6.1a through B6.1c, and B6.2. Most of these have already been discussed here, but the entire guideline text, along with an example, is shown below:

- **Guideline B6.1a:** A device is coded only if a device remains after the procedure is completed. If no device remains (device value Z) no device is coded in the sixth code character position.

- **Guideline B6.1b:** Materials such as sutures, ligatures, radiological markers, and temporary post-operative wound drains are considered integral to the performance of the procedure, and are not coded as devices.

- **Guideline B6.1c:** Procedures performed only on a device and not on an actual body part are specified in the root operations Change, Irrigation, Removal, and Revision, depending upon the objective of the procedure.

- **Guideline B6.2:** A separate procedure to put in a drainage device is coded to the root operation Drainage, value 9, with the device value 0 for drainage device. Remember it is the objective of the procedure that must be considered. While it might seem that putting in a drainage device should be coded to the root operation Insertion, the objective of drainage is taking or letting out fluids and/or gases from a body part—which is the objective of putting in a drainage device.

Let's Review 6–2:

Determine the correct root operation and device for each of the procedures, and give the Device and Root Operation values.

1. Coronary artery bypass, one site, with autologous arterial tissue cut from the right greater saphenous vein _____

2. Insertion of drainage device into right lacrimal gland (Hint: Guideline B6.3) _____

3. Putting in a hearing device, right ear _____

4. Adding (augmenting) autologous tissue to left external ear _____

5. Joining together two or more lumbar vertebral joints using an interbody nonautologous tissue substitute _____

Qualifiers (Character 7) Values in the Medical and Surgical Section

In ICD-10-PCS, the seventh character is always a qualifier. A qualifier contains unique values specific to the procedure performed, and thus, the root operation. The body system can also affect qualifier usage. In root operations that use no qualifier, the value is Z. Most root operations, however, do use qualifiers, and each qualifier is unique or specific to the root operation and/or body system. For example, qualifiers used with the Bypass procedures identify the bypass destination body part, or, in the case of bypassed coronary arteries, the qualifier is the name of the vessel bypassed. An **open bypass** of **the right axillary artery** to an **upper arm artery right** using autologous arterial tissue would be coded 03150A0 as follows from the Upper Arteries, Bypass Table 031 (Figure 6-6).

Section (Character 1):	Medical and Surgical	0
Body System (Character 2):	Upper Arteries	3
Root Operation (Character 3):	**Bypass**	1
Body Part (Character 4):	**Axillary Artery, right**	5 (Bypass origin)
Approach (Character 5):	**Open**	0
Device (Character 6):	Autologous Arterial Tissue	A
Qualifier (Character 7):	**Upper arm artery, right**	0 (Bypass destination)

The qualifier in Transfer and Replacement root operations represents the body part used for the Transfer operation. For example, a replacement of tissue of the thumb, with autologous tissue from the toe, results in the fourth character assignment of thumb (left or right), and a seventh character qualifier value for the autologous tissue used as replacement for the left or right toe. Remember that the replacement root operation objective is to *put in or on biological or synthetic material that physically takes the place and/or function of all or a portion of a body part.*

The transfer of any body part to a new location has a qualifier for the body part transferred, therefore, the fourth character body part value would be the new location, and the seventh character body part would be the one transferred. Again, it is important to know the definition of a transfer operation in order to properly determine whether a qualifier is used. It is *moving one body part to another location to take over the function of all or a part of another body part.* So with Replacement, the qualifier value will, in most instances be tissue or material, while in Transfer, an entire body part will be moved from one location to another.

Section	0	Medical and Surgical
Body System	3	Upper Arteries
Operation	1	Bypass: Altering the route of passage of the contents of a tubular body part

Body Part	Approach	Device	Qualifier
2 Innominate Artery **5** Axillary Artery, Right **6** Axillary Artery, Left	**0** Open	**9** Autologous Venous Tissue **A** Autologous Arterial Tissue **7** Upper Leg Artery, Left **J** Synthetic Substitute **K** Nonautologous Tissue Substitute **Z** No Device	**0** Upper Arm Artery, Right **1** Upper Arm Artery, Left **2** Upper Arm Artery, Bilateral **3** Lower Arm Artery, Right **4** Lower Arm Artery, Left **5** Lower Arm Artery, Bilateral **6** Upper Leg Artery, Right **8** Upper Leg Artery, Bilateral **9** Lower Leg Artery, Right **B** Lower Leg Artery, Left **C** Lower Leg Artery, Bilateral **D** Upper Arm Vein **F** Lower Arm Vein **J** Extracranial Artery, Right **K** Extracranial Artery, Left
3 Subclavian Artery, Right **4** Subclavian Artery, Left	**0** Open	**9** Autologous Venous Tissue **A** Autologous Arterial Tissue **J** Synthetic Substitute **K** Nonautologous Tissue Substitute **Z** No Device	**0** Upper Arm Artery, Right **1** Upper Arm Artery, Left **2** Upper Arm Artery, Bilateral **3** Lower Arm Artery, Right **4** Lower Arm Artery, Left **5** Lower Arm Artery, Bilateral **6** Upper Leg Artery, Right **7** Upper Leg Artery, Left **8** Upper Leg Artery, Bilateral **9** Lower Leg Artery, Right **B** Lower Leg Artery, Left **C** Lower Leg Artery, Bilateral **D** Upper Arm Vein **F** Lower Arm Vein **J** Extracranial Artery, Right **K** Extracranial Artery, Left **M** Pulmonary Artery, Right **N** Pulmonary Artery, Left

Figure 6-6 Medical and Surgical Table for Bypass Root Operation, Lower Arteries

Table 6-6 lists the qualifier values found in the Medical and Surgical section that are associated with a root operation. The Table lists the qualifier, its root operation, and applicable body system(s).

Let's look at some of the other terminology used in the qualifier column in Table 6-5.

Qualifier Ductus Arteriosus (T)

The root operations Dilation, Occlusion, and Restriction, along with the body system heart and great vessels include a unique qualifier identify a fetal heart defect, called the ductus arteriosus. The **ductus arteriosus** is a normal fetal structure that allows blood to bypass circulation to the lungs during gestation. At birth, high levels of oxygen causes this structure to close, typically within 24 hours. Failure of the ductus arteriosus to close results in a defect known as patent ductus arteriosus (PDA). This defect may correct itself within several months of birth, but in some cases intervention is required by the infusion of chemicals, the placement of plugs via catheters, or surgical closure. The three root operations performed for a correction of a PDA are dilation, occlusion, and restriction. The heart and great vessels are the only body system in which the qualifier *ductus arteriosus* is found, and is used to indicate that the dilation, occlusion, or restriction root operation was performed to correct that defect.

Table 6-6 Qualifier (Character 7) Values with Applicable Root Operations and Body System Values

Qualifier	Root Operation	Body System
Destination Body Part	Bypass	All Body Systems/Origin Body Part
X–Diagnostic	Drainage Excision	All Body Systems
Destination Body Part	Transfer	All Body Systems/Origin Body Part
6–Bifurcation	Dilation	Heart and Great Vessels
T–Ductus Arteriosus	Dilation Occlusion Restriction	Heart and Great Vessels
G–Pressure Sensor S–Biventricular A–Pacemaker Lead E–Defibrillator Lead	Insertion	Heart and Great Vessels
0–Allogeneic 1–Syngeneic 2–Zooplastic	Transplantation	Any Body Systems/Body Parts
T–via Umbilical Vein	Insertion	Lower Veins
C–Hemorrhoidal Plexus	Occlusion	Lower Veins
5–Intraocular Telescope	Replacement	Eye
1–Bone Conduction 2–Cochlear Prosthesis, Single Channel 3–Cochlear Prosthesis, Multiple Channel Y–Other Hearing Device	Insertion	Ear, Nose Sinus
0–Single 1–Multiple 2–All	Destruction Drainage Excision Extraction Reattachment Release Repair Replacement Reposition Resection	Mouth and Throat
D–Multiple	Destruction	Skin and Breast
3–Full Thickness 4–Partial Thickness 5–Latissimus Dorsi (LD) Myocutaneous Flap 6–Transverse Rectus Abdominus Myocutaneous (TRAM) Flap 7–Deep Inferior Epigastric Artery Perforator (DIEP) Flap 8–Superficial Inferior Epigastric Artery Flap 9–Gluteal Artery Perforator Flap	Replacement	Skin and Breast
0–Pacemaker, Single Chamber 1–Pacemaker, Single Chamber, Rate Responsive 2–Pacemaker, Dual Chamber 3–Cardiac Resynchronization Pacemaker Pulse Generator 4–Defibrillator Generator 5–Cardiac Rescynchronization Defibrillator Pulse Generator 6–Single Array 7–Dual Array 8–Single Array Rechargeable	Insertion	Subcutaneous Tissue and Fascia

9—Dual Array Rechargeable A—Contractility Modulation Device D—Hemodynamic Y—Other Cardiac Rhythm-Related Device		
3—Monoplanar 4—Ring 5—Hybrid	Insertion Reposition	Lower Bones Upper Bones
3—Monoplanar 4—Ring 5—Hybrid 9—Limb Lengthening Device	Insertion Upper Bones	Lower Bones
0—Anterior Approach, Anterior Column 1—Posterior Approach, Posterior Column J—Posterior Approach, Anterior Column	Fusion	Upper Joints
0—Anterior Approach, Anterior Column 1—Posterior Approach, Posterior Column J—Posterior Approach, Anterior Column K—Lateral Transverse Process Approach	Fusion	Lower Joints
2—Interspinous Process 3—Pedicle-based Dynamic Stabilization	Insertion	Lower Joints Upper Joints
4—Facet	Replacement Supplement	Lower Joints Upper Joints
5—Metal on Polyethylene 6—Metal on Metal 7—Ceramic on Ceramic 8—Ceramic on Polyethylene F—Metal G—Ceramic H—Polyethylene	Replacement	Lower Joints
C—Patellar Surface	Supplement	Lower Joints
0—Vagina 1—Penis	Creation	Anatomic Regions, General
2—Stoma	Repair	Anatomic Regions, General
0—Complete 1—High 2—Mid 3—Low 4—Complete first Ray 5—Complete second Ray 6—Complete third Ray 7—Complete fourth Ray 8—Complete fifth Ray 9—Partial first Ray B—Partial second Ray C—Partial third Ray D—Partial fourth Ray F—Partial fifth Ray	Detachment	**Anatomical Regions:** Lower Extremities Upper Extremities
N—Toe, Right P—Toe, Left	Replacement	Anatomical Regions: Upper Extremities

Qualifiers with Root Operation Detachment

The root operation Detachment is defined as the cutting off all or part of a body part. If a leg is detached, the detachment may be high, mid, or lower leg. When this root operation is used for the long bones of the hand or foot, the detachment is classified by the term **ray**. A **ray** refers to the metacarpal and metatarsal bones of the hand and foot, respectively, when using the root operation Detachment. Metacarpal bones are the long bones of the hand, often called the knuckle bones. Metatarsal bones are the long bones of the foot between the ankle and the toes. Rays are numbered 1, 2, 3, 4, and 5.

The first ray is on the medial side of the hand or foot, which is on the thumb-side or the large toe side of the foot. The next ray moving laterally is the long bone leading to the index finger or second toe, and has the value 2, and so on until 5, which is the long bone leading to the little finger or toe. Look at Figure 6-7 for an illustration showing the ray designations for the hand and foot. When a metacarpal or metatarsal bone is detached, it can be either complete or partial, i.e., if the metatarsal at the big toe is

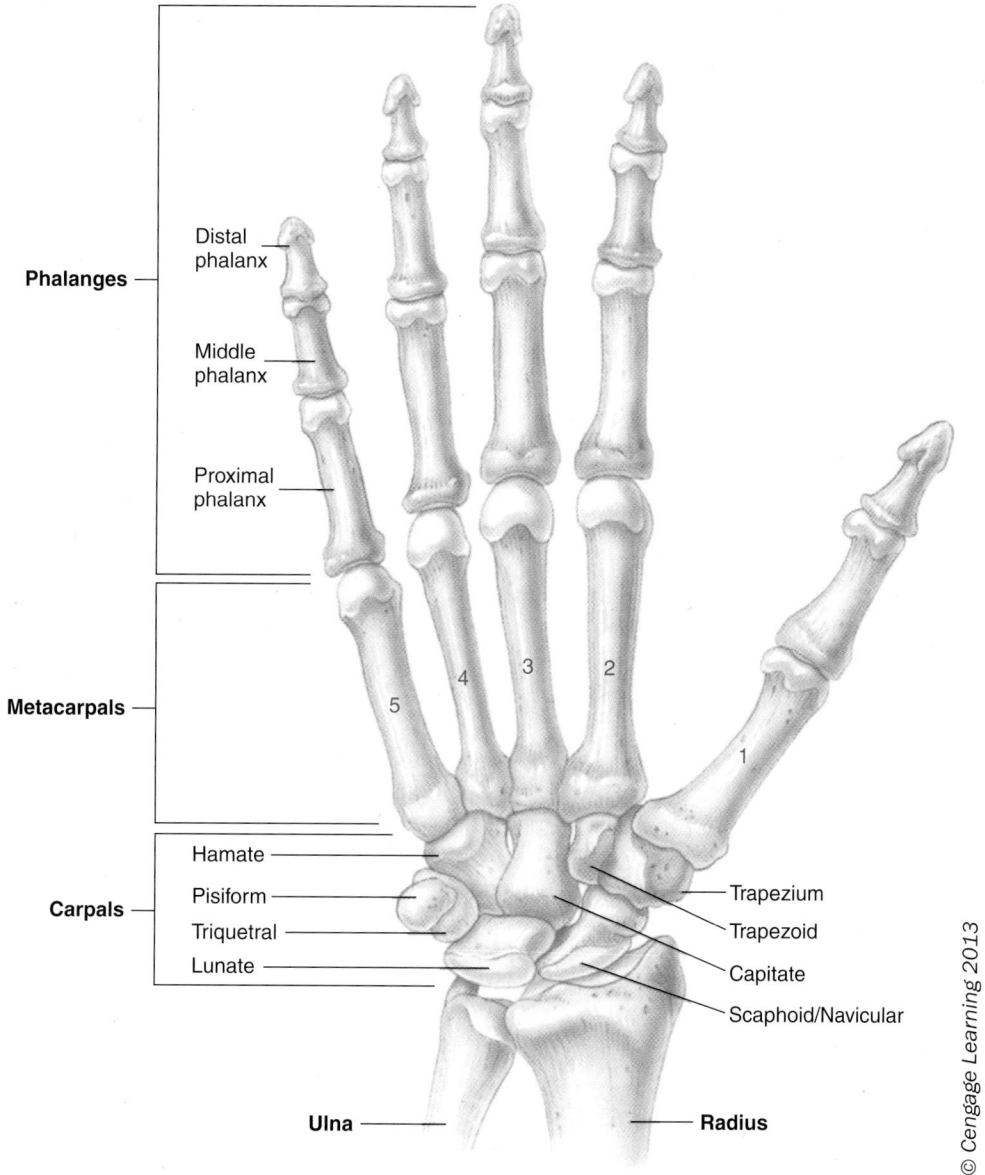

© Cengage Learning 2013

Figure 6-7 Illustration of RAY Designation in Metacarpal and Metatarsal Bones

removed, that is a complete detachment of the first ray, which has a Qualifier value of 4, if only part of the metatarsal bone is removed, that is a partial detachment of the first ray.

Do not confuse the qualifier 0, complete, with a complete ray. The complete qualifier with the value 0 is meant to indicate an entire extremity, such as a complete detachment of the left leg. A complete ray, on the other hand, means the removal of an entire metacarpal or metatarsal section of the hand or foot was detached.

Qualifiers in Transplantation

There are three qualifier values used with the root operation Transplantation: allogenic, syngeneic, and zooplastic. A transplanted body part or tissue taken from a different individual of the same species is **allogenic**. **Syngeneic** is when tissue or a body part has been taken from someone who has identical genes, such as an identical twin. **Zooplastic** tissue comes from an animal.

Qualifiers with Insertion for Body System Ear, Nose, and Sinus

There are four qualifiers for the root operation Insertion and body system ear, nose, and sinus. Each of these qualifiers refers to a type of hearing device inserted into the ear. These include a single or multiple channel cochlear implant, a bone conduction hearing device, and other hearing device. The values for each of these qualifiers are:

1—Bone Conduction

2—Cochlear Prosthesis, Single Channel

3—Cochlear Prosthesis, Multiple Channel

Y—Other Hearing Device

A qualifier from this list is only used with the root operation Insertion, and the body system ear, nose, and sinus. They are not associated with any other root operations or body systems.

Qualifiers with Replacement for Body System Lower Joints

Total hip replacements of the lower joints body system use a variety of materials that replace the bone, including metal, ceramic, and polyethylene. These materials, as of 2012, are found under the Device value. When the root operation is Replacement, the body system is lower joints, and the body part is hip, the devices and qualifiers used for the replacement are identified by the following values:

DEVICES	QUALIFIERS
E—Synthetic Substitute, Metal on Polyethylene	5—Cemented
F—Synthetic Substitute - Metal on Mental	6—Uncemented
G—Synthetic Substitute, Ceramic on Ceramic	Z—None
H—Synthetic substitute, Ceramic on Polyethylene	
J—Synthetic Substitute	

These materials are not used for coding for other lower joints, like the knee or ankle, nor are they used in coding upper joints.

Qualifiers with Insertion for Body System Subcutaneous Tissue and Fascia

A **pacemaker** is a surgically implanted electronic device that regulates a slow or erratic heartbeat. An insulated wire called a lead is inserted into an incision above the collarbone and guided through a large vein into the chambers of the heart. Depending on the configuration of the pacemaker and the clinical needs of the patient, as many as three leads may be used in a pacing system. Current pacemakers have a double or bipolar electrode attached to the end of each lead. The electrodes deliver an electrical charge to the heart to regulate heartbeat. They are positioned on the areas of the heart that require stimulation. The leads are then attached to the pacemaker device, which is implanted under the skin of the patient's chest.

Cardiac resynchronization therapy (CRT) is used to treat the delay in heart ventricle contractions that occur in some people with advanced heart failure. The CRT pacing device (also called a biventricular pacemaker) is an electronic, battery-powered device that is surgically implanted under the skin. The device has two or three leads (wires) that are positioned in the heart to help the heart beat in a more balanced way. The leads are implanted through a vein in the right atrium and right ventricle and into the coronary sinus vein to pace the left ventricle.

Some patients with heart failure may benefit from a combination of CRT and an implantable cardiac defibrillator (ICD). These devices combine biventricular pacing with anti-tachycardia pacing and internal defibrillators to deliver treatment as needed. The CRT/ICD combination devices:

- Resynchronize the heartbeat
- Slow down an abnormal fast heart rhythm
- Prevent abnormally slow heart rhythms
- Record a history of the patient's heart rate and rhythm

The qualifier options for the root operation Insertion, and body system subcutaneous tissue and fascia are shown below. These are used only for the insertion of the device under the skin. The placement of the leads is another separate procedure, and would be coded separately, using the Insertion root operation, and the body system heart and great vessels.

0—Pacemaker, Single Chamber

1—Pacemaker, Single Chamber, Rate Responsive

2—Pacemaker, Dual Chamber

3—Cardiac Resynchronization Pacemaker Pulse Generator

4—Defibrillator Generator

5—Cardiac Rescynchronization Defibrillator Pulse Generator

6—Single Array

7—Dual Array

8—Single Array Rechargeable

9—Dual Array Rechargeable

A—Contractility Modulation Device

D—Hemodynamic

Y—Other Cardiac Rhythm-Related Device

Qualifiers with Replacement: Skin and Breast Body System

There are many techniques for the replacement or reconstruction of the breast after a mastectomy. In the previous chapter, the TRAM Flap procedure was discussed for the root operation Replacement. Remember that a replacement procedure not only puts in or on a material that physically takes the place or function of all or a portion of a body part, but also differs from the root operation Transfer in that r tissue does not remain connected to its blood and nerve supply in root operation Replacement. In flap procedures, skin and muscle tissue from various locations on the body, i.e., autologous tissue, are completely detached from their origin, and moved to the missing body part.

In a **Free TRAM Flap**, fat, muscle, and blood vessels are removed from the lower abdominal wall and moved to the chest wall to reconstruct the breast. The blood and nerve supply from that tissue is connected to the blood and nerve supply of the chest wall. A **Deep Inferior Epigastric Artery Perforator (DIEP) Flap** is similar to the TRAM flap, except it uses only skin and fat from the abdominal wall, but leaves the muscle intact. A **Latissimus Dorsi (LD) Flap** breast reconstruction procedure that takes muscle and skin from the upper back, which is then used to replace missing breast tissue and muscle. From these descriptions it should be easy to determine the origin of the replacement tissue used for breast reconstruction procedures in the replacement root operation for the skin and breast body system. All of the qualifiers for this root operation and body system are shown below:

3—Full Thickness

4—Partial Thickness

5—LD Myocutaneous Flap

6—TRAM Flap

7—DIEP Flap

8—Superficial Inferior Epigastric Artery Flap

9—Gluteal Artery Perforator Flap

Let's Review 6–3:

List the body system, root operation, body part, approach, and device character values for the following procedures, based on the qualifier.

1. Percutaneous endoscopic fusion, anterior approach and column, lumbosacral vertebral joint, using internal fixation device.
   a. Body System: _____
   b. Root Operation: _____
   c. Approach: _____
   d. Device: _____
   e. Qualifier: _____

2. Biopsy, percutaneous, right kidney pelvis
   a. Body System: _____
   b. Root Operation: _____
   c. Body Part: _____
   d. Approach: _____
   e. Device: _____
   f. Qualifier: _____

3. Change feeding device, upper intestinal tract
   a. Body System: _____
   b. Root Operation: _____
   c. Body Part: _____
   d. Approach: _____
   e. Device: _____
   f. Qualifier: _____

4. Transplant syngeneic tissue to stomach
   a. Body System: _____
   b. Root Operation: _____
   c. Body Part: _____
   d. Approach: _____
   e. Device: _____
   f. Qualifier: _____

5. Open bypass right hepatic duct to common bile duct using intraluminal device
   a. Body System: _____
   b. Root Operation: _____
   c. Body Part (origin): _____
   d. Approach: _____
   e. Device: _____
   f. Qualifier (destination): _____

Putting it All Together

In this chapter, and the previous two chapters, all the steps, character values, definitions, and guidelines were presented. Now, it is time to apply everything to the coding process, starting with main and modifying term determination, and then selecting the seven code characters that most accurately match the procedural statement. Throughout these introductory chapters on ICD-10-PCS coding, especially in the root operations chapter, many procedural statements were presented to demonstrate one or several of the ICD-10-PCS coding steps.

For example, in the root operations chapter, the steps for abstracting, determining the main and modifying terms, and performing an index search began the coding process. Now, those root operation examples will be used to assign the Approach, Device, and Qualifier values to make a complete and accurate code. The first step is a review of the ICD-10-PCS coding steps, after which the steps will be applied to each of the examples brought forward.

Coding Steps Review

The seven steps required for accurate ICD-10-PCS procedural coding start with 1. a review of the medical documentation to abstract the procedure or treatment performed during the encounter, followed by a 2. determination of the main term, generally the root operation, and modifying terms, which, typically are the body system or body part values. 3. With the main and modifying terms in hand, find the main term in the Index of the ICD-10-PCS coding manual, followed by the modifying term, and select the Table reference or references for those terms. The remaining steps are performed within the Tables of the Medical and Surgical section in the Tabular List, as shown here:

4. Confirm the code(s) found in the Index by going next to the Tabular List and find the Table in the Tabular list that contains the first three code characters that represent the Section, Body System, and Root Operation, characters found in the Index Table reference.

5. Work through the row or rows to find the correct Body Part, Approach, Device, and Qualifier character

6. Review the Guidelines for guidance, to ensure there is nothing to contraindicate use of the code selected.

7. Write the code(s) found next to the procedural statement.

Assigning Code Character Values to Match Procedural Statements

Now it is time to begin applying everything learned in this and the previous two chapters, and start coding! The remainder of this chapter will walk through all the steps in coding procedures using several different root operations, which should help provide a thorough understanding of the coding steps, and how to properly assign all seven code characters to the procedural statement.

Remember, the most important rule in assigning the proper code is correct identification of the root operation. Regardless of what terminology is used in the medical documentation, the objective of the procedure is the determining factor when selecting the root operation. The documentation, for example, may say *excision of varicose veins*—but varicose veins are removed by stripping or pulling out the vein, so the correct root operation is actually Extraction, not Excision. Another example is a phacoemulsification of the lens in the eye is performed. If the phacoemulsification is the sole objective and no intraocular lens (IOL) is implanted, then the objective is extraction. However, if the procedure is to put in an IOL, the extraction of the lens becomes an integral part of the procedure, and is no longer the objective. Under that circumstance, the root operation changes to replacement.

Coding an Extraction Root Operation

Using the procedure *percutaneous endoscopic glossopharyngeal nerve removal by force*, the first step is to determine the main and modifying terms from this procedural statement. For this procedure, the term *percutaneous endoscopic* identifies the approach, the *glossopharyngeal nerve* is the body part, and

Section	**0**	Medical and Surgical		
Body System	**0**	Central Nervous System		
Operation	**D**	Extraction: Pulling or stripping out or off all or a portion of a body part by the use of force		

Body Part	Approach	Device	Qualifier
1 Cerebral Meninges **2** Dura Mater **F** Olfactory Nerve **G** Optic Nerve **H** Oculomotor Nerve **J** Trochlear Nerve **K** Trigeminal Nerve **L** Abducens Nerve **M** Facial Nerve **N** Acoustic Nerve **P** Glossopharyngeal Nerve **Q** Vagus Nerve **R** Accessory Nerve **S** Hypoglossal Nerve **T** Spinal Meninges	**0** Open **3** Percutaneous **4** Percutaneous Endoscopic	**Z** No Device	**Z** No Qualifier

© Cengage Learning 2013

Figure 6-8 Medical and Surgical Table 00D

removal by force of that body part establishes the procedure objective. A comparison of the root operation definitions, based on the objective, will lead to a match for the root operation Extraction. This, therefore, becomes the main term, and the body part is the modifying term. In reality, when doing a search in the Index, it is not always necessary to know the section or body system. That is actually identified from the Table reference in the Index, and the Table itself. Once the Table reference is found in the Alphabetic Index, which in this case is 00DP, the next step is to go to the appropriate Table in the Tabular List.

Table 00D is shown in Figure 6-8. Now, the section and body system can be verified. The section description for the first character in Table 00D is the Medical and Surgical section. Looking at the heading again for Table 00D, the second character (body system) is 0, Central Nervous System. The third character, D, is the root operation Extraction, and the fourth character is the body part, P, glossopharyngeal nerve, found in the first column, and only row, in this Table. At this point, the first four character values from Table 00D match the procedural statement, indicating this is the correct Table.

The fifth character of the code identifies the approach, which is found in Column 2 of the Table. In Table 00D, there are three approach values: Open (0), Percutaneous (3), and Percutaneous endoscopic (4). A review of the procedural statement reveals *percutaneous endoscopic* as the appropriate Approach value, so the fifth character value is 4. No device or qualifier was mentioned in the procedural statement or in the 00D Table, making it appropriate to use Z as the sixth and seventh code character value. As a result, the code description for all seven characters (00DP4ZZ) matches the procedural statement exactly. Table 6-7 breaks the procedure down by the character and title, procedure description, and value.

Coding a detachment root operation

Here is a procedure to code using the root operation Detachment: *Amputation, complete, first metatarsal, right foot.* First, identify the character assignments for the root operation and body part. The root operation is determined from the procedure objective, amputation, when compared against the definition of the root operation, which in this case is Detachment. Detachment becomes the main term. The body part is the metatarsal bone of the foot. Go to the Index and find the main term Detachment, then search

Table 6-7 Character Assignment for Extraction Procedure

Character	Title	Procedure Description	Value
1	Section	Medical and Surgical	0
2	Body System	Central Nervous System	0
3	Root Operation	Extraction	D
4	Body Part	Glossopharyngeal nerve	P
5	Approach	Percutaneous endoscopic	4
6	Device	No device	Z
7	Qualifier	No qualifier	Z

for the modifying term *metatarsal*. The metatarsal bone is not found under Detachment. The next search option for a modifying term is to look for the more general body part *foot*. This search leads to the Table reference 0Y6.

Now, turn to Table 0Y6 in the Tabular List, shown in Figure 6-9, and look at the heading. The section should be Medical and Surgical (0), the Body System should be Anatomical Regions, Lower Extremities (Y), and the root operation is Detachment, which means that, so far, this is the correct Table. In the first column, for the fourth character body part, the right and left foot values are shown in the third row. Also note that there is no body part value for metatarsal, which means choosing foot instead of metatarsal as the body part was accurate. At this point, the first four characters of the code, 0Y6 and M (right foot), have been confirmed The only approach value available is 0, which will be the fifth code character. There is no device listed in the third column of Table 0Y6, nor is there one in the procedural statement, so the sixth character will be Z.

The only remaining character value to select is the seventh character, which is the qualifier. Here is where the metatarsal bone amputation can be identified. Had this been a complete amputation of the foot, the qualifier 0, *complete*, would be the seventh character of the code. However, the procedural statement documents a *complete first metatarsal bone*, which, as discussed earlier in the chapter, is identified by the **ray** assignment. The qualifier identifies the ray in Detachment procedures involving the long bones (metacarpals and metatarsals) of the hand and foot. The qualifier value is 4 for a complete first ray. The breakdown of the code character assignments for this procedure is shown in Table 6-8. The final code is 0Y6M0Z4 for *Amputation, complete, first metatarsal, right foot*.

Coding device procedures

A procedure example here would be *percutaneous endoscopic intraluminal stent closure of left pulmonary artery to repair a patent ductus arteriosus (PDA)*. As a quick review, there are three root operations that use a *ductus arteriosus* qualifier: Dilation, Restriction, and Occlusion. There are only three approach values for these three root operations: Open (0), Percutaneous (3), and Percutaneous endoscopic (4).

The device character values for root operation Dilation are drug-eluting intraluminal device (4), intraluminal device (D), and radioactive intraluminal device (T). Occlusion and Restriction root operations both use only two devices, extraluminal (C) and intraluminal (D). All three root operations also have a character value Z if no device is used. The seventh character qualifier values for all three root objectives are either Z, for no qualifier, or T, for *ductus arteriosus*.

The first decision is determination of the objective, in order to select the root operation. If, when reading the medical documentation, the objective is to expand the lumen of the tubular body part causing the PDA, the root operation is Dilation. If it is to completely close off the lumen, the root operation is Occlusion. If the objective is to partially close the lumen, the root operation is Restriction.

Section	0	Medical and Surgical
Body System	Y	Anatomical Regions, Lower Extremities
Operation	6	Detachment: Cutting off all or a portion of the upper or lower extremities

Body Part	Approach	Device	Qualifier
2 Hindquarter, Right **3** Hindquarter, Left **4** Hindquarter, Bilateral **7** Femoral Region, Right **8** Femoral Region, Left **F** Knee Region, Right **G** Knee Region, Left	**0** Open	**Z** No Device	**Z** No Qualifier
C Upper Leg, Right **D** Upper Leg, Left **H** Lower Leg, Right **J** Lower Leg, Left	**0** Open	**Z** No Device	**1** High **2** Mid **3** Low
M Foot, Right **N** Foot, Left	**0** Open	**Z** No Device	**0** Complete **4** Complete 1st Ray **5** Complete 2nd Ray **6** Complete 3rd Ray **7** Complete 4th Ray **8** Complete 5th Ray **9** Partial 1st Ray **B** Partial 2nd Ray **C** Partial 3rd Ray **D** Partial 4th Ray **F** Partial 5th Ray
P 1st Toe, Right **Q** 1st Toe, Left **R** 2nd Toe, Right **S** 2nd Toe, Left **T** 3rd Toe, Right **U** 3rd Toe, Left **V** 4th Toe, Right **W** 4th Toe, Left **X** 5th Toe, Right **Y** 5th Toe, Left	**0** Open	**Z** No Device	**0** Complete **1** High **2** Mid **3** Low

© Cengage Learning 2013

Figure 6-9 Medical and Surgical Table 0Y6

Table 6-8 Character Assignment for Detachment Procedure

Character	Title	Procedure Description	Value
1	Section	Medical and Surgical	0
2	Body System	Anatomical Regions, Lower Extremities	Y
3	Root Operation	Detachment (amputation)	6
4	Body Part	Foot, right	M
5	Approach	Open	0
6	Device	No device	Z
7	Qualifier	Complete 1 Ray	4

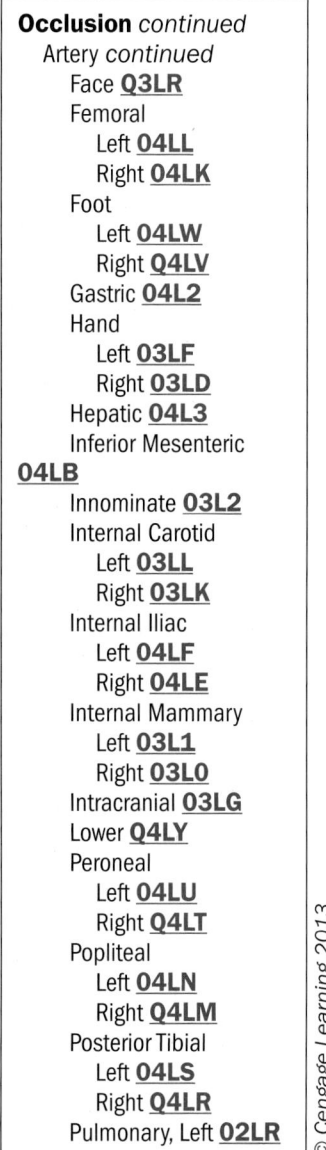

Occlusion *continued*
Artery *continued*
Face **Q3LR**
Femoral
Left **04LL**
Right **04LK**
Foot
Left **04LW**
Right **Q4LV**
Gastric **04L2**
Hand
Left **03LF**
Right **03LD**
Hepatic **04L3**
Inferior Mesenteric
04LB
Innominate **03L2**
Internal Carotid
Left **03LL**
Right **03LK**
Internal Iliac
Left **04LF**
Right **04LE**
Internal Mammary
Left **03L1**
Right **03L0**
Intracranial **03LG**
Lower **Q4LY**
Peroneal
Left **04LU**
Right **Q4LT**
Popliteal
Left **04LN**
Right **Q4LM**
Posterior Tibial
Left **04LS**
Right **Q4LR**
Pulmonary, Left **02LR**

© Cengage Learning 2013

Figure 6-10 Alphabetic Index Excerpt for Root Operation Occlusion

Using the procedure *percutaneous endoscopic intraluminal stent closure of left pulmonary artery to repair a PDA*, first separate out the procedure objective to determine which root operation is appropriate. In this procedural statement, the objective is the vein *closure* making the root operation Occlusion. The next step is determining the body part, which is the *left pulmonary artery*. A search in the Index for Occlusion as the main term, *artery* as the modifying term, and *pulmonary* and *left* as the subterms, reveals the Table reference 02LR (Figure 6-10).

The next step is to go to the 02L Table in the Tabular List (Figure 6-11). First, confirm that the root operation and body part are in this Table, then break down the remainder of the procedural statement to assign all the character values, as shown in Table 6-9.

In this procedure, *percutaneous endoscopic* is the approach (value 0), *intraluminal stent* is the device (value D), *closure* is the root operation Occlusion (value L), *left pulmonary artery* is the body part (value R), and *ductus arteriosus* is the qualifier (value T). The *left pulmonary artery* is in the Heart and Great Vessels Body System (value 2), and of course, this is a Medical and Surgical procedure, which identifies the section (value 0). The code for this procedure is 02LR0DT.

Section	**0**	Medical and Surgical		
Body System	**2**	Heart and Great Vessels		
Operation	**L**	Occlusion: Completely closing an orifice or the lumen of a tubular body part		

Body Part	Approach	Device	Qualifier
R Pulmonary Artery, Left	**0** Open **3** Percutaneous **4** Percutaneous Endoscopic	**C** Extraluminal Device **D** Intraluminal Device **Z** No Device	**T** Ductus Arteriosus
S Pulmonary Vein, Right **T** Pulmonary Vein, Left **V** Superior Vena Cava	**0** Open **3** Percutaneous **4** Percutaneous Endoscopic	**C** Extraluminal Device **D** Intraluminal Device **Z** No Device	**Z** No Qualifier

© Cengage Learning 2013

Figure 6-11 Medical and Surgical Table 02L for Root Operation Occlusion

Table 6-9 Character Assignment for Occlusion Procedure

Character	Title	Procedure Description	Value
1	Section	Medical and Surgical	0
2	Body System	Heart and Great Vessels	2
3	Root Operation	Occlusion	L
4	Body Part	Pulmonary Artery, left	R
5	Approach	Open	0
6	Device	Intraluminal Device (Stent)	D
7	Qualifier	Ductus Arteriosus (repair)	T

Coding multiple procedures

Guideline B3.2 states that if a procedure is performed with two or more distinct objectives, separate codes are required for each objective. Here are two examples of how to determine whether multiple procedures are required, as well as the steps for coding each procedure.

The first procedure is *closure of complex open wound, subcutaneous tissue and fascia of left chest, open approach, using free skin graft from percutaneous harvest of subcutaneous tissue and fascia, (performed during the same procedure).* In breaking down the procedure into the root operation and body part, it becomes obvious that two separate procedures were performed. One procedure is the wound closure using a skin graft, and the other is the harvesting of the skin graft.

Looking at the closure using a skin graft, there are two potential root operations, Transfer and Replacement. The root operation Transfer is defined as moving, without taking out, all or a portion of a body part to another location to take over the function of all or a portion of a body part. Remember, in a Transfer procedure, the tissue moved must maintain it is original blood and nerve supply, it cannot be taken or cut out, otherwise it no longer fits the definition of Transfer.

In the procedure example, a free skin graft was used which eliminates Transfer as the correct root operation. If the skin graft or flap is cut free from its vascular and nerve supply, it is coded as a free skin graft, and the root operation changes to Replacement. The root operation Replacement is defined as *putting in or on a biological or synthetic material on all or a portion of a body part that physically takes the place and/or function of a body part.* Skin cut free of its nerve and blood supply fits the definition of a biological material, which in this procedure would be put on the open chest wound to perform the function of the skin that is missing.

To finish coding the first part of the procedure, the root operation Replacement has been identified, as well as the body part, the *subcutaneous tissue and fascia of the chest.* In the Index, Replacement is the main term, with the modifying term *subcutaneous tissue and fascia*, and subterm of *chest* (Figure 6-12). The Table reference is 0JR6.

Replacement *continued*
  Omentum *continued*
    Greater **ODRS**
    Lesser **ODRT**
  Orbit
    Left **ONRO**
    Right **ONRP**
  Ossicle
    Left **09RA0**
    Right **09R90**
  Palate
    Hard **OCR2**
    Soft **OCR3**
  Patella
    Left **OORF**
    Right **OORD**
  Pericardium **02RN**
  Peritoneum **ODRW**
  Phalanx
    Finger
      Left **OPRV**
      Right **OPRT**
    Thumb
      Left **OPRS**
      Right **OPRR**
    Toe
      Left **OORR**
      Right **OORO**
  Pharynx **OCRM**
  Radius
    Left **OPR3**
    Right **OPRH**
  Rib
    Left **OPR2**
    Right **OPR1**
  Sacrum **OOR1**
  Scapula
    Left **OPR6**
    Right **OPR5**
  Sclera
    Left **08R7X**
    Right **08R6X**
  Septum
    Atrial **02R5**
    Nasal **09RM**
    Ventricular **02RM**
  Skin
    Abdomen **OHR7**
    Back **OHR6**
    Buttock **OHR8**
    Chest **OHR5**

Replacement *continued*
  Skin *continued*
    Hand *continued*
      Left **OHRG**
      Right **OHRF**
    Lower Arm
      Left **OHRE**
      Right **OHRD**
    Lower Leg
      Left **OHRL**
      Right **OHRK**
    Neck **OHR4**
    Perineum **OHR9**
    Scalp **OHRO**
    Upper Arm
      Left **OHRC**
      Right **OHRB**
    Upper Leg
      Left **OHRJ**
      Right **OHRH**
  Skull **ONRO**
  Sphincter, Anal **OPRR**
  Sternum **OPRO**
  Subcutaneous Tissue and Fascia
    Abdomen **OJR8**
    Back **OJR7**
    Bttock **OJR9**
    Chest **OJR6**
    Face **OJR1**
    Foot
      Left **OJRR**
      Right **OJRO**
    Hand
      Left **OJRK**
      Right **OJRJ**
    Lower Arm
      Left **OJRH**
      Right **OJRG**
    Lower Leg
      Left **OJRP**
      Right **OJRN**
    Neck
      Anterior **OJR4**
      Posterior **OJR5**
    Pelvic Region **OJRC**
    Perineum **OJRB**
    Scalp **OJRO**
    Upper Arm
      Left **OJRF**
      Right **OJRD**

© Cengage Learning 2013

Figure 6-12 Alphabetic Index Excerpt for Root Operation Replacement

Under Replacement, with the modifying term skin, there is also a Table reference to OHR5. It is easy to interchange the term skin for subcutaneous tissue and fascia, especially in the medical documentation. But, it is important to make a distinction, since it will lead to two different Tables. In Figures 6-13 and 6-14, take a look at the Tables and see what happens. Had the body part *skin* been chosen, a value for skin of the chest is found in the Body Part column of Table OHR, however, looking across the row, the only Approach is external. The procedure in this example clearly states an Open Approach was used.

Section	**0**	Medical and Surgical
Body System	**J**	Subcutaneous Tissue and Fascia
Operation	**R**	Replacement: Putting in or on biological or synthetic material that physically takes the place and/or function of all or a portion of a body part

Body Part	Approach	Device	Qualifier
0 Subcutaneous Tissue and Fascia, Scalp **1** Subcutaneous Tissue and Fascia, Face **4** Subcutaneous Tissue and Fascia, Anterior Neck **5** Subcutaneous Tissue and Fascia, Posterior Neck **6** Subcutaneous Tissue and Fascia, Chest **7** Subcutaneous Tissue and Fascia, Back **8** Subcutaneous Tissue and Fascia, Abdomen **9** Subcutaneous Tissue and Fascia, Buttock **B** Subcutaneous Tissue and Fascia, Perineum **C** Subcutaneous Tissue and Fascia, Pelvic Region **D** Subcutaneous Tissue and Fascia, Right Upper Arm **F** Subcutaneous Tissue and Fascia, Left Upper Arm **G** Subcutaneous Tissue and Fascia, Right Lower Arm **H** Subcutaneous Tissue and Fascia, Left Lower Arm **J** Subcutaneous Tissue and Fascia, Right Hand **K** Subcutaneous Tissue and Fascia, Left Hand **L** Subcutaneous Tissue and Fascia, Right Upper Leg **M** Subcutaneous Tissue and Fascia, Left Upper Leg **N** Subcutaneous Tissue and Fascia, Right Lower Leg **P** Subcutaneous Tissue and Fascia, Left Lower Leg **Q** Subcutaneous Tissue and Fascia, Right Foot **R** Subcutaneous Tissue and Fascia, Left Foot	**0** Open **3** Percutaneous	**7** Autologous Tissue Substitute **J** Synthetic Substitute **K** Nonautologous Tissue Substitute	**Z** No Qualifier

© Cengage Learning 2013

Figure 6-13 Medical and Surgical Table 0JR, Body System Skin and Breast

Section	**0**	Medical and Surgical
Body System	**H**	Skin and Breast
Operation	**R**	Replacement: Putting in or on biological or synthetic material that physically takes the place and/or function of all or a portion of a body part

Body Part	Approach	Device	Qualifier
0 Skin, Scalp **1** Skin, Face **2** Skin, Right Ear **3** Skin, Left Ear **4** Skin, Neck **5** Skin, Chest **6** Skin, Back **7** Skin, Abdomen **8** Skin, Buttock **9** Skin, Perineum **A** Skin, Genitalia **B** Skin, Right Upper Arm **C** Skin, Left Upper Arm **D** Skin, Right Lower Arm **E** Skin, Left Lower Arm **F** Skin, Right Hand **G** Skin, Left Hand **H** Skin, Right Upper Leg **J** Skin, Left Upper Leg **K** Skin, Right Lower Leg **L** Skin, Left Lower Leg **M** Skin, Right Foot **N** Skin, Left Foot	**X** External	**7** Autologous Tissue Substitute **K** Nonautologous Tissue Substitute	**3** Full Thickness **4** Partial Thickness

© Cengage Learning 2013

Figure 6-14 Medical and Surgical Table 0HR, Body System Subcutaneous Tissue and Fascia

Table 6-10 Character Assignment for Replacement Procedure

Character	Title	Procedure Description	Value
1	Section	Medical and Surgical	0
2	Body System	Subcutaneous tissue and fascia	J
3	Root Operation	Replacement	R
4	Body Part	Subcutaneous tissue and fascia, chest	6
5	Approach	Open	0
6	Device	Autologous tissue substitute	7
7	Qualifier	None	Z

In addition, there are two Qualifier values in the last column of the Table that reference full or partial thickness skin replacement. There is no mention of skin thickness in the procedural statement.

In addition, the procedural statement includes *subcutaneous tissue and fascia*, which is not identified in Table 0HR, and the Approach and Qualifier values do not fit the procedural statement, therefore, the correct Table to have chosen is 0JR. In that Table, the body system is *subcutaneous tissue and fascia*, and the body part is *subcutaneous tissue and fascia, chest*, which is a better match to the procedural statement. In addition, the character five Approach value Open is found, as is the Device value for *autologous tissue substitute*.

To finish coding this procedure, note there is no Qualifier value, which makes Z the seventh character. The code for the first half of the procedure *closure of complex open wound, subcutaneous tissue and fascia of left chest, open approach* is 0JR607Z. Table 6-10 is a character-by-character breakdown of the procedure.

Now, it is time to code the second half of the procedure *using free skin graft from percutaneous harvest of subcutaneous tissue and fascia (same procedure)*. The first step, as always, is to determine the procedure objective. In this case, it is to cut out (harvest) a portion of a body part (subcutaneous tissue and fascia, back). Looking at the definitions for root operations, the best fit is Excision, which is defined as *cutting out or off, without replacement, a portion of a body part*. The subcutaneous tissue and fascia cut out of the back will not be replaced by any other material. The excised subcutaneous tissue and fascia will become an autologous free skin graft in the Replacement procedure of the chest wall wound.

The root operation is Excision, and the body part is subcutaneous tissue and fascia, back. Figure 6-15 is an excerpt from the Index for the main term Excision and modifying term Subcutaneous Tissue and Fascia. (Once again, be precise in use of terminology; a choice of the body part *skin* here will lead to the same issues found when coding the Replacement procedure.) The Table reference is 0JB7. The next step is to turn to Table 0JB in the Medical and Surgical section of the Tabular List (Figure 6-16).

The heading of Table 0JB includes the body system subcutaneous tissue and fascia, and the root operation Excision determined from the procedural statement. There is only one row in this Table, and subcutaneous tissue and fascia, chest is found in that row. The procedure Approach is percutaneous, which will have a value of 3, and there is no device left behind, nor is there a Qualifier for this procedure, since the procedure was not diagnostic. The breakdown of characters for this part of the procedure is 0JB73ZZ, as shown in Table 6-11.

Let's look at another multiple procedure coding example. In this example, the procedure is *percutaneous endoscopic laser ablation of sigmoid colon lesion, and open bypass of sigmoid colon to the rectum*. In this procedure, there are two objectives: *Eradication of a lesion*, and a *sigmoid colon bypass*. Starting with the lesion eradication objective, the root operation definition that best matches is Destruction, defined as *the physical eradication of all or a portion of a body part by the direct use of energy, force, or destructive agent*. Ablation is a term defined in the previous chapter that helps identify the procedure as a Destruction root operation. The body part is the sigmoid colon.

```
Excision continued
   Skin continued
      Foot
         Left OHBNXZ
         Right OHBMXZ
      Genitalia OHBAXZ
      Hand
         Left OHBGXZ
         Right OHBFXZ
      Lower Arm
         Left OHBEXZ
         Right OHBDXZ
      Lower Leg
         Left OHBLXZ
         Right OHBKXZ
      Neck OHB4XZ
      Perineum OHB9XZ
      Scalp OHBOXZ
      Upper Arm
         Left OHBCXZ
         Right OHBBXZ
      Upper Leg
         Left OHB3XZ
         Right OHBHXZ
   Skull ONBO
   Sphincter, Anal ODBR
   Spleen 07BP
   Sternum OPBO
   Stomach ODB6
      Pylorus ODB7
   Subcutaneous Tissue and Fascia
      Abdomen QJB8
      Back QJB7
```

© Cengage Learning 2013

Figure 6-15 Alphabetic Index Excerpt for Excision, Subcutaneous Tissue and Fascia

Section	0	Medical and Surgical
Body System	J	Subcutaneous Tissue and Fascia
Operation	B	Excision: Cutting out or off, without replacement, a portion of a body part

Body Part	Approach	Device	Qualifier
0 Subcutaneous Tissue and Fascia, Scalp **1** Subcutaneous Tissue and Fascia, Face **4** Subcutaneous Tissue and Fascia, Anterior Neck **5** Subcutaneous Tissue and Fascia, Posterior Neck **6** Subcutaneous Tissue and Fascia, Chest **7** Subcutaneous Tissue and Fascia, Back **8** Subcutaneous Tissue and Fascia, Abdomen **9** Subcutaneous Tissue and Fascia, Buttock **B** Subcutaneous Tissue and Fascia, Perineum **C** Subcutaneous Tissue and Fascia, Pelvic Region **D** Subcutaneous Tissue and Fascia, Right Upper Arm **F** Subcutaneous Tissue and Fascia, Left Upper Arm **G** Subcutaneous Tissue and Fascia, Right Lower Arm **H** Subcutaneous Tissue and Fascia, Left Lower Arm **J** Subcutaneous Tissue and Fascia, Right Hand **K** Subcutaneous Tissue and Fascia, Left Hand **L** Subcutaneous Tissue and Fascia, Right Upper Leg **M** Subcutaneous Tissue and Fascia, Left Upper Leg **N** Subcutaneous Tissue and Fascia, Right Lower Leg **P** Subcutaneous Tissue and Fascia, Left Lower Leg **Q** Subcutaneous Tissue and Fascia, Right Foot **R** Subcutaneous Tissue and Fascia, Left Foot	**0** Open **3** Percutaneous	**Z** No Device	**X** Diagnostic **Z** No Qualifier

© Cengage Learning 2013

Figure 6-16 Medical and Surgical Table, 0HR, Body System Subcutaneous Tissue and Fascia

Table 6-11 Character Assignment for Free Skin Graft from Back, Open

Character	Title	Procedure Description	Value
1	Section	Medical and Surgical	0
2	Body System	Subcutaneous tissue and fascia	J
3	Root Operation	Excision	B
4	Body Part	Subcutaneous tissue and fascia, back	7
5	Approach	Percutaneous	3
6	Device	None	Z
7	Qualifier	None	Z

Turning to the Index, under the main term Destruction is the modifying term *colon,* and subterm *sigmoid,* and the Table reference 0D5N (Figure 6-17). The next steps are to go to the Medical and Surgical section Table 0D5, confirm the root operation and body part, then find the appropriate row and assign the remaining code character values. Figure 6-18 is the Medical and Surgical section Table 0D5. Assign the remaining characters, based on the procedural statement as shown in Table 6-12, resulting in a code of 0D5N4ZZ for percutaneous endoscopic ablation.

The second procedure objective for this statement is *bypass of sigmoid colon to the rectum.* The Approach will remain the same as with the first procedure, as will the body system and part. The root operation will change to Bypass, since the objective of this procedure is to alter the route of passage of the contents of a tubular body part (sigmoid colon). The alteration will move reroute the passage of the

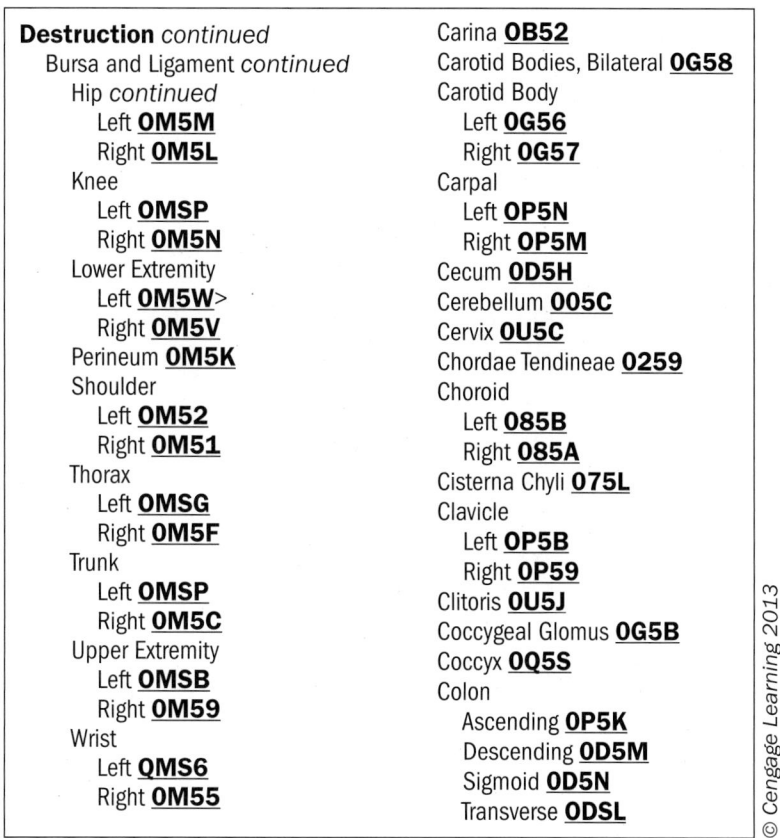

Destruction *continued*
  Bursa and Ligament *continued*
    Hip *continued*
      Left **OM5M**
      Right **OM5L**
    Knee
      Left **OMSP**
      Right **OM5N**
    Lower Extremity
      Left **OM5W**>
      Right **OM5V**
    Perineum **OM5K**
    Shoulder
      Left **OM52**
      Right **OM51**
    Thorax
      Left **OMSG**
      Right **OM5F**
    Trunk
      Left **OMSP**
      Right **OM5C**
    Upper Extremity
      Left **OMSB**
      Right **OM59**
    Wrist
      Left **QMS6**
      Right **OM55**

Carina **OB52**
Carotid Bodies, Bilateral **OG58**
Carotid Body
  Left **OG56**
  Right **OG57**
Carpal
  Left **OP5N**
  Right **OP5M**
Cecum **OD5H**
Cerebellum **005C**
Cervix **OU5C**
Chordae Tendineae **0259**
Choroid
  Left **085B**
  Right **085A**
Cisterna Chyli **075L**
Clavicle
  Left **OP5B**
  Right **OP59**
Clitoris **OU5J**
Coccygeal Glomus **OG5B**
Coccyx **OQ5S**
Colon
  Ascending **OP5K**
  Descending **OD5M**
  Sigmoid **OD5N**
  Transverse **ODSL**

© Cengage Learning 2013

Figure 6-17 Alphabetic Index Excerpt for Destruction, Sigmoid Colon

Section	**0**	Medical and Surgical	
Body System	**D**	Gastrointestinal System	
Operation	**5**	Destruction: Physical eradication of all or a portion of a body part by the direct use of energy, force, or a destructive agent	

Body Part	Approach	Device	Qualifier
1 Esophagus, Upper **2** Esophagus, Middle **3** Esophagus, Lower **4** Esophagogastric Junction **5** Esophagus **6** Stomach **7** Stomach, Pylorus **8** Small Intestine **9** Duodenum **A** Jejunum **B** Ileum **C** Ileocecal Valve **E** Large Intestine **F** Large Intestine, Right **G** Large Intestine, Left **H** Cecum **J** Appendix **K** Ascending Colon **L** Transverse Colon **M** Descending Colon **N** Sigmoid Colon **P** Rectum	**0** Open **3** Percutaneous **4** Percutaneous Endoscopic **7** Via Natural or Artificial Opening **8** Via Natural or Artificial Opening Endoscopic	**Z** No Device	**Z** No Qualifier
Q Anus	**0** Open **3** Percutaneous **4** Percutaneous Endoscopic **7** Via Natural or Artificial Opening **8** Via Natural or Artificial Opening Endoscopic **X** External	**Z** No Device	**Z** No Qualifier
R Anal Sphincter **S** Greater Omentum **T** Lesser Omentum **V** Mesentery **W** Peritoneum	**0** Open **3** Percutaneous **4** Percutaneous Endoscopic	**Z** No Device	**Z** No Qualifier

Figure 6-18 Medical and Surgical Table 0D5, Root Operation Destruction, Gastrointestinal System

Table 6-12 Character Assignment for Percutaneous Laser Ablation of Sigmoid Colon Lesion

Character	Title	Procedure Description	Value
1	Section	Medical and Surgical	0
2	Body System	Gastrointestinal System	D
3	Root Operation	Destruction	5
4	Body Part	Sigmoid Colon	N
5	Approach	Percutaneous endoscopic	4
6	Device	None	Z
7	Qualifier	None	Z

Section	**0**	Medical and Surgical
Body System	**D**	Gastrointestinal System
Operation	**1**	Bypass: Altering the route of passage of the contents of a tubular body part

Body Part	Approach	Device	Qualifier
H Cecum	**0** Open **4** Percutaneous Endoscopic **8** Via Natural or Artificial Opening Endoscopic	**7** Autologous Tissue Substitute **J** Synthetic Substitute **K** Nonautologous Tissue Substitute **Z** No Device	**4** Cutaneous **H** Cecum **K** Ascending Colon **L** Transverse Colon **M** Descending Colon **N** Sigmoid Colon **P** Rectum
H Cecum	**3** Percutaneous	**J** Synthetic Substitute	**4** Cutaneous
K Ascending Colon	**0** Open **4** Percutaneous Endoscopic **8** Via Natural or Artificial Opening Endoscopic	**7** Autologous Tissue Substitute **J** Synthetic Substitute **K** Nonautologous Tissue Substitute **Z** No Device	**4** Cutaneous **K** Ascending Colon **L** Transverse Colon **M** Descending Colon **N** Sigmoid Colon **P** Rectum
K Ascending Colon	**3** Percutaneous	**J** Synthetic Substitute	**4** Cutaneous
L Transverse Colon	**0** Open **4** Percutaneous Endoscopic **8** Via Natural or Artificial Opening Endoscopic	**7** Autologous Tissue Substitute **J** Synthetic Substitute **K** Nonautologous Tissue Substitute **Z** No Device	**4** Cutaneous **L** Transverse Colon **M** Descending Colon **N** Sigmoid Colon **P** Rectum
L Transverse Colon	**3** Percutaneous	**J** Synthetic Substitute	**4** Cutaneous
M Descending Colon	**0** Open **4** Percutaneous Endoscopic **8** Via Natural or Artificial Opening Endoscopic	**7** Autologous Tissue Substitute **J** Synthetic Substitute **K** Nonautologous Tissue Substitute **Z** No Device	**4** Cutaneous **M** Descending Colon **N** Sigmoid Colon **P** Rectum
M Descending Colon	**3** Percutaneous	**J** Synthetic Substitute	**4** Cutaneous
N Sigmoid Colon	**0** Open **4** Percutaneous Endoscopic **8** Via Natural or Artificial Opening Endoscopic	**7** Autologous Tissue Substitute **J** Synthetic Substitute **K** Nonautologous Tissue Substitute **Z** No Device	**4** Cutaneous **N** Sigmoid Colon **P** Rectum
N Sigmoid Colon	**3** Percutaneous	**J** Synthetic Substitute	**4** Cutaneous

Figure 6-19 Medical and Surgical Table 0D1, Bypass Procedure, Gastrointestinal System

contents of the sigmoid colon to the rectum. Remember, the origin of the bypass is the Body Part; in this example, it is the sigmoid colon. The destination is the Qualifier, which will be the rectum. A search of the Index for the main term Bypass, and Body Part *colon, sigmoid* will reveal a Table reference of 0D1N. The Medical and Surgical section Table 0D1 header lists the body system as Gastrointestinal, and the root operation as Bypass (Figure 6-19). The approach is percutaneous endoscopic (4), the device is Z (none), and the qualifier, which in this case identifies the destination, rectum, is P.

The seven character code for this procedure is 0D1N4ZP, as shown in Table 6-13. The two codes for this procedural statement *percutaneous endoscopic laser ablation of sigmoid colon lesion, and bypass of sigmoid colon to the rectum* are 0D5N4ZZ and 0D1N4ZP, respectively.

Coding from an Operative Report

In Figure 6-20, an operative report is shown for a total left hip replacement with metal on metal prosthesis insertion. The name of the procedure is *hip arthroplasty total, with titanium prosthesis, left*. In addition, other abstracted items are highlighted to add information that helps identify the entire procedural statement.

Table 6-13 Character Assignment for Bypass, Sigmoid Colon Procedure

Character	Title	Procedure Description	Value
1	Section	Medical and Surgical	0
2	Body System	Gastrointestinal System	D
3	Root Operation	Bypass	1
4	Body Part	Sigmoid Colon	N
5	Approach	Percutaneous endoscopic	4
6	Device	None	Z
7	Qualifier	Rectum	P

Pre-Operative Diagnosis: Osteoarthritis, left hip

Post-Operative Diagnosis: Severe degenerative osteoarthritis, left hip

Procedure Performed: Hip arthroplasty, total, w/ titanium prosthesis, left

Date: March 10, 20YY

Surgeon: Frank Hern, M.D.

Procedure Description:

Under general anesthesia, the patient was placed in the lateral decubitus position with left side exposed. Left hip was prepped and draped in usual fashion. An 8-inch modified anterio-lateral approach (Hardinge) incision was made at the greater trochanter of left hip. As incision was deepened, small bleeders were cauterized. The short external rotator was divided close to the bone, together with the posterior capsule. The hip was posteriorly dislocated, where severe degenerative osteoarthritis was clearly visualized.

The femoral neck was cut at the appropriate level and angle, at which time the acetabulum was exposed. The floor was cleared of soft tissue and osteophytes were excised. The acetabulum was reamed progressively to 50 mm in diameter, and then under-reamed by 2 mm. A trial with a 52 mm trial acetabular component was performed, revealing excellent fit and alignment. The trial component was removed, and a 52-mm titanium porous-coated acetabular component was press-fit into place. Excellent alignment and fixation were noted. Liner was inserted with an overhang posteriorly and inferiorly.

Femoral canal was prepared by ream and broach to 13.5-mm size. Trial of neutral neck 32-mm head component was attempted and hip was reduced. Good range of movement was noted, and an AP view x-ray showed good position and length. Hip was re-dislocated and trial femoral component was removed. Femoral canal was brushed and washed to prepare for cementing. Canal plugged with the Universal© cement restrictor plug, after which canal was lavaged with pulsatile lavage and dried thoroughly. Two bags of cement were missed in the vacuum mixer and a 13.5 mm nonporous stem with a 14-mm centralizer was cemented into place using the cement syringe. On setting of the cement, excellent alignment and fixation were noted. The 4-mm neck and 32-mm head component was tapped onto the femoral stem and the hip was reduced. A stable range of movement was noted. Hemostasis was checked and one Hemovac drain was placed for drainage.

Closure was performed using #1 Vicryl to reattach the short external rotators and posterior capsule, and fascial layer. Subcutaneous layer was closed with 2-0 and 3-0 Vicryl, and skin was closed with staples. Incision was dressed with Xeriform gauze, 4 X 4 gauze, and a Cover-Roll dressing.
Patient tolerated the procedure well and left for recovery room in stable condition.

Figure 6-20 Operative Report for a Total Left Hip Replacement

The next step is to identify the main and modifying terms. It is permissible to use *arthroplasty* as the main term; however, a search for it in the Index leads to an instructional note to *see* three different root operations: Repair, Replacement, and Supplement. It will be necessary to determine the procedure objective and match it to the root operation definition that best fits in order to determine the main term and know where to begin the search in the Index.

The objective of the procedure is to *insert a titanium (metal) prosthesis to take the place and/or function of the hip joint*. The titanium prosthesis is a synthetic substitute. With that objective in mind, the best root operation definition is Replacement, which is defined as *putting in or on biological or synthetic material that takes the place and/or function of all or a portion of a body part*. The main term is, therefore, Replacement, and the body part is the left hip.

Looking in the Index, indented under Replacement is the body part *hip* with subterms for the right and left hip, and other specific body parts including the *acetabular* and *femoral surfaces* (Figure 6-21). Here's where it might get a little confusing. When reading the operative report, both the acetabular and femoral surfaces are clearly mentioned, which might lead to selection of the Table references for both surfaces, rather than the left hip. However, that's the key. If only one surface were mentioned in the operative report, then just that one would be selected, and the procedure becomes a partial hip replacement. Since both the acetabulum and femur were included in the same procedure, this is a total

Figure 6-21 Alphabetic Index Excerpt for Replacement, Hip

Section	**0**	Medical and Surgical
Body System	**S**	Lower Joints
Operation	**R**	Replacement: Putting in or on biological or synthetic material that physically takes the place and/or function of all or a portion of a body part

Body Part	Approach	Device	Qualifier
0 Lumbar Vertebral Joint **2** Lumbar Vertebral Disc **3** Lumbosacral Joint **4** Lumbosacral Disc **5** Sacrococcygeal Joint **6** Coccygeal Joint **7** Sacroiliac Joint, Right **8** Sacroiliac Joint, Left **H** Tarsal Joint, Right **J** Tarsal Joint, Left **K** Metatarsal-Tarsal Joint, Right **L** Metatarsal-Tarsal Joint, Left **M** Metatarsal-Phalangeal Joint, Right **N** Metatarsal-Phalangeal Joint, Left **P** Toe Phalangeal Joint, Right **Q** Toe Phalangeal Joint, Left	**0** Open	**7** Autologous Tissue Substitute **J** Synthetic Substitute **K** Nonautologous Tissue Substitute	**Z** No Qualifier
9 Hip Joint, Right **B** Hip Joint, Left	**0** Open	**1** Synthetic Substitute, Metal **2** Synthetic Substitute, Metal on Polyethylene **3** Synthetic Substitute, Ceramic **4** Synthetic Substitute, Ceramic on Polyethylene **J** Synthetic Substitute	**9** Cemented **A** Uncemented **Z** No Qualifier
9 Hip Joint, Right **B** Hip Joint, Left	**0** Open	**7** Autologous Tissue Substitute **K** Nonautologous Tissue Substitute	**Z** No Qualifier
A Hip Joint, Acetabular Surface, Right **E** Hip Joint, Acetabular Surface, Left	**0** Open	**0** Synthetic Substitute, Polyethylene **1** Synthetic Substitute, Metal **3** Synthetic Substitute, Ceramic **J** Synthetic Substitute	**9** Cemented **A** Uncemented **Z** No Qualifier
A Hip Joint, Acetabular Surface, Right **E** Hip Joint, Acetabular Surface, Left	**0** Open	**7** Autologous Tissue Substitute **K** Nonautologous Tissue Substitute	**Z** No Qualifier

Figure 6-22 Medical and Surgical Table 0SR, for Root Operation Replacement, Body System Hip

hip replacement. The only appropriate choice from the Index, therefore, is the *left hip* Table reference, 0SRB.

Next, turn to Table 0SR, for the Medical and Surgical section, lower joints body system, and root operation Replacement (Figure 6-22). The *left hip joint* value is found in the second and third rows of the first column titled Body Part. The character value is B. Now, it will be important to see which row's approach, device, and qualifier best matches the procedural statement. Determining the approach value for this procedure is easy, since the only option in either row is Open, which makes the fifth code character 0.

It is in the Device column that the proper row will be revealed. In the third row, the only two choices are *autologous* and *nonautologous tissue substitutes* values. There is no mention in the operative report of a *tissue* substitute. The last two rows have separate joint surfaces, but this is a total hip replacement, so the entire joint is needed. The devices column in the second row includes a metal (titanium) synthetic substitute with a value of 1, which is now the sixth character of the code. The only character left to determine is the seventh, the Qualifier, which must come from the same row (second) row of the Table. The seventh character will be 9, cemented, since that is mentioned in the operative report description. The code for the total left hip replacement is 0SRB019.

Chapter Summary

The Medical and Surgical section is by far the largest in the ICD-10-PCS procedural coding manual. It represents the code sets mandated for use in all procedures performed in an inpatient setting. The first character of a code from the Medical and Surgical section will always be 0 (the alphabetic character O is not used in ICD-10-PCS). The remaining six characters, in order, are, Character 2, Body System; Character 3, Root Operation; Character 4, Body Part (or Anatomical Region); Character 5, Approach; Character 6, Device; and Character 7, Qualifier.

Character 2 represents general body system values, while character 4 is a more specific body part within the general body system. Character 3 is the root operation, which is the specific objective of the procedure. Character 5 is the approach used to reach the procedure site. Character 6 is any device left in or on the body as part of the objective of the procedure.

The Tables in the Medical and Surgical section Tabular List are identical in layout regardless of which body system or root operation is involved. At the top of each Table is the heading. It will always contain the section, body system, and root operation values and titles. In addition, the definition of the root operation is included. The first three characters of a code will always be the section, body system, and root operation.

Next are four columns. The first column represents the body part, the second represents the approach values possible for each body part, next is the device, and the last column is the qualifier.

In ICD-10-PCS, body system is always the second character of the ICD-10-PCS code and refers to the body system affected by the procedure. There are 31 body systems represented in the Medical and Surgical section. These are called general values, in that they generally represent an entire body system, and not a specific body part.

The fourth character of an ICD-10-PCS code is the body part. The body part represents the specific part of the body upon which the procedure is performed. It is always the first column in a Table from the Medical and Surgical section. In the ICD-10-PCS coding manual, there is an appendix titled Section 0—Medical and Surgical, Character 4—Body Part. This is a very handy appendix, because it states explicitly what comprises each body part.

There are seven approaches listed in the Medical and Surgical (0) section. These were discussed at length in an earlier chapter, but because of their importance, let's look at them again. Table 6-3 illustrated the approach terms, values, and definitions in the Medical and Surgical section.

The approach includes three components: (1) the access location, (2) the method, and (3) the type of instrumentation. The access location specifies the external site through which the site of the procedure is reached, if the procedure is performed on an internal body part. For procedures performed on an internal body part, the method specifies how the external access location is entered. Type of Instrumentation means that specialized equipment is used to perform the procedure. Instrumentation is used in all internal approaches other than the basic open approach. Character 6 in the ICD-10-PCS in most sections designates a device, or any object purposely left in the body during a procedure, such as a pacemaker, or screws and pins. It does not include staples or sutures that are incidental to the procedure performed. There are several different types of devices—biological or synthetic materials, therapeutic materials, and mechanical or electronic appliances. The descriptions of each type of device were in Table 6-4, and the devices, values, and applicable root operations were in Table 6-5. There are four general guidelines for any use of code character six, device. They are B6.1 through B6.4.

In ICD-10-PCS, the seventh character is always a qualifier. A qualifier contains unique values specific to the procedure performed, and thus, the root operation. The body system will also affect qualifier usage. Most root operations use no qualifier. The value for no qualifier is Z.

In this chapter, the coding process and steps were reintroduced, starting with main and modifying term determination, and moving through selection of the seven code characters that most accurately matched the procedural statement. The eight steps required for accurate ICD-10-PCS procedural coding start with a review of the medical documentation to abstract the procedure or treatment performed during the encounter, followed by a determination of the main term, generally the root operation, and modifying terms, which, typically are the body part values. With the main and modifying term in hand, the third step is to find the main term in the Index of the ICD-10-PCS coding manual, followed by the modifying term, and then select the Table reference or references for those terms. Steps four through eight are performed within the Tables of the Medical and Surgical section in the Tabular List, and are listed here again as well:

1. Confirm the code(s) found in the Index by going next to the Tabular List.

2. Find the Table in the Tabular list that contains the first three code characters that represent the Section, Body System, and Root Operation, found in the Index Table reference.

3. Work through the row or rows to find the correct Body Part, Approach, Device, and Qualifier characters.

4. Review the guidelines to ensure there is nothing to contraindicate use of the code selected.

5. Write the code(s) found next to the procedural statement.

The most important rule in assigning the proper code is correct identification of the root operation. Regardless what terminology is used in the medical documentation, the objective of the procedure is the determining factor when selecting the root operation.

Chapter Review

Matching

Instructions: Match the term with its definition.

_____ 1. Allogenic

_____ 2. Cardiac resynchronization therapy (CRT)

_____ 3. External approach

_____ 4. Method

_____ 5. Open approach

_____ 6. Open endoscopic approach

_____ 7. Percutaneous approach

_____ 8. Percutaneous endoscopic approach

_____ 9. Ray

_____ 10. Via natural or artificial opening approach endoscopic

_____ 11. Via natural or artificial opening approach

_____a. One of the three determining factors for the Approach value. It specifies how the external access location is entered during the approach.

_____b. Refers to the metacarpal and metatarsal bones of the hand and foot, respectively, when using the root operation Detachment.

_____c. A transplanted body part or tissue taken from a different individual of the same species.

_____d. Entry of instrumentation through a natural or artificial external opening to reach and visualize the site of the procedures.

_____e. Procedures performed directly on the skin or mucous membrane, and procedures performed indirectly by the application of external force through the skin or mucous membrane.

_____ f. Used to treat the delay in heart ventricle contractions that occur in some people with advanced heart failure.

_____g. Entry, by puncture or minor incision, of instrumentation through the skin or mucous membrane and any other body layers necessary to reach and visualize the site of the procedure.

_____h. Entry of instrumentation through a natural or artificial external opening to reach the site of the procedures.

_____ i. Entry, by puncture or minor incision, of instrumentation through the skin or mucous membrane and any other body layers necessary to reach the site of the procedure.

_____ j. Cutting through the skin or mucous membrane and any other body layers necessary to expose the site of the procedure.

_____k. Cutting through the skin or mucous membrane and any other body layers necessary to expose the site of the procedure; and entry, by puncture or minor incision, of instrumentation through the skin or mucous membrane and any other body layers necessary to aid in the performance of the procedure.

Short Answer

Instructions: List the code characters and their values for the following procedures.

1. Endometrial biopsy, endoscopic vaginal approach
    a. Section _____
    b. Body System _____
    c. Root Operation _____
    d. Body Part _____
    e. Approach _____
    f. Device _____
    g. Qualifier _____

2. Breast, left, lumpectomy, open
    a. Section _____
    b. Body System _____

    c. Root Operation _____

    d. Body Part _____

    e. Approach _____

    f. Device _____

    g. Qualifier _____

3. Left fourth toe amputation, mid proximal phalanx

    a. Section _____

    b. Body System _____

    c. Root Operation _____

    d. Body Part _____

    e. Approach _____

    f. Device _____

    g. Qualifier _____

4. Open reduction with internal fixation, right humerus shaft

    a. Section _____

    b. Body System _____

    c. Approach _____

    d. Body Part _____

    e. Approach _____

    f. Device _____

    g. Qualifier _____

5. TRAM flap skin and subcutaneous tissue closure of complex open wound, subcutaneous tissue and fascia, left chest

    a. Section _____

    b. Body System _____

    c. Root Operation _____

    d. Body Part _____

    e. Approach _____

    f. Device _____

    g. Qualifier _____

6. Orthotopic heart transplant using porcine heart

    a. Section _____

    b. Body System _____

    c. Root Operation _____

    d. Body Part _____

    e. Approach _____

    f. Device _____

    g. Qualifier _____

7. ERCP with lithotripsy of common bile duct calculus

    a. Section _____

    b. Body System _____

    c. Root Operation _____

    d. Body Part _____

    e. Approach _____

    f. Device _____

    g. Qualifier _____

8. Transurethral endoscopic cystoscopy with removal of ureteral calculus

    a. Section _____

    b. Body System _____

    c. Root Operation _____

      d. Body Part _____

      e. Approach _____

      f. Device _____

      g. Qualifier _____

9. Fulgeration nasal polyps, external

      a. Section _____

      b. Body System _____

      c. Root Operation _____

      d. Body Part _____

      e. Approach _____

      f. Device _____

      g. Qualifier _____

10. Anal sphincterotomy, open (division)

      a. Section _____

      b. Body System _____

      c. Root Operation _____

      d. Body Part _____

      e. Approach _____

      f. Device _____

      g. Qualifier _____

Coding Practice

1. Open thoracotomy with extraluminal device banding, left pulmonary artery for ductus arteriosis

   _____

2. Percutaneous incision with removal of K-wire internal fixation, left metacarpal

   _____

3. Diagnostic endometrium extraction, vaginal _____

4. Drainage, with drainage device, left middle ear, open _____

5. Cholelithotripsy, external (*Hint:* Fragmentation) _____

6. Endoscopic removal impacted fecal mass, ascending colon, via colon (*Hint:* Extirpation)

   _____

7. Incision and removal of right lacrimal duct stone _____

8. Open dilation of previous (old) anastamosis, splenic artery _____

9. Percutaneous division of right foot tendon _____

10. Destruction of left retina, percutaneous _____

11. Percutaneous biopsy of left gastrocnemius muscle _____

12. Removal impaction submaxillary gland, right, percutaneous (*Hint:* Extirpation)

   _____

13. Open resection pulmonary valve _____

14. Reattachment of left thumb _____

15. Bilateral breast enlargement with saline implants, percutaneous (*Hint:* Alteration)

   _____

Section 1: Obstetrics

Learning Objectives

At the conclusion of this chapter, the learner should be able to:

- Understand terms used in the Obstetrics section and identify the two new root operations
- Identify the Body System, Root Operation, Body Parts, Approach, Device, and Qualifiers used in the Obstetrics section
- Understand the Guidelines that impact code selection in the Obstetrics section
- Differentiate how the Root Operations are used in the Obstetrics section, how to apply the correct Body Part, Approach, Device, and Qualifier for each Root Operation
- Know how to use the Index and Tables to select the correct code from the Obstetrics section

Key Terms and Definitions

Abortifacient	Any substance that causes pregnancy to end prematurely and causes an abortion.
Abortion	Root operation A in the Obstetrics section. Artificially eliminating a pregnancy.
Breech	Baby is inverted; where the buttocks are presenting for delivery instead of the head.
Complete breech	The baby's legs are crossed under and in front of the body.
Delivery	Root operation E in the Obstetrics section. It is defined as assisting the passage of the products of conception from the genital canal.
Ectopic	Outside the uterus, as in an ectopic pregnancy where the development of the fetus occurs in the fallopian tubes, ovaries, or even the cervix, rather than in the uterus.
Footling breech	One leg or both legs are positioned to enter the birth canal.
Frank breech	The baby's legs are folded up against its body.
Incomplete abortion	A miscarriage, in which part, but not all of the uterine contents are expelled.
Induced abortion	The deliberate (elective) termination of a pregnancy.
Laminaria	A small rod-shaped piece of dried seaweed. When placed within the cervix, a laminaria causes it to gradually dilate (widen). The species of seaweed serving this purpose is *Laminaria digitata*.
Mechanical means	In the obstetrics section, these are instruments such as forceps, cervical dilators, vacuum aspiration, or curettes used to perform a dilatation and curettage (D&C) during delivery or abortion.

Medication abortion	Abortion methods that include introduction of a substance (such as a laminaria) or medication (abortifacient) that induces the abortion.
Missed abortion	A miscarriage in which the fetus and other products of conception remain in the uterus for four or more weeks.
Products of conception	The human fetus, placenta, amniotic sac, and other structures associated with pregnancy and childbirth.
Spontaneous abortion	Another term for missed or incomplete abortion, also known as miscarriage.
Version	Technique used by an obstetrician; may attempt to turn a breech presentation baby to a (normal) vertex or head down position.
Vertex presentation	Baby descends head first into the vaginal canal.

Introduction

The Obstetrics section of the ICD-10-PCS is presented in this chapter. Specific terminology associated with Obstetrics will be covered here, as well as discussion of the body systems, root operations, body parts, approaches, devices, and qualifiers used in the Obstetrics section. Guidelines specific to Obstetrics coding are presented, along with a discussion of the differences in root operations, devices, and qualifiers found in the Obstetrics section.

The first character of an Obstetrics section code is always 1. In addition, the body system value will always be a 2 for Obstetrics. As would be expected, there is a smaller list of body parts and root operations applicable to this section, as well as approaches, devices, and qualifiers. Each of these will be discussed in this chapter. There are eleven root operations, nine of which were also found in the Medical and Surgical section. The two new root operations are delivery and abortion.

Section 1, Obstetrics (I02–I0Y)

Figure 7-1 is an illustration of the male and female reproductive systems. In the male, the reproductive organs are the testes. In the female, they are the ovaries. All other structures support the activity of reproduction; for example, in the male, the scrotum and vas deferens are ancillary structures, and in the female the fallopian tubes and uterus are.

In ICD-10-PCS, Obstetrics is given the section character assignment of 1 and includes delivery and abortion codes. The codes in Section 1 are only for delivery, abortion, or procedures performed on the fetus during delivery. Rather than use the term *fetus* or *baby*, this section uses the term **products of conception**, which refers not only to the fetus, but to the placenta, amniotic sac, and other structures associated with pregnancy. Codes for any treatment or procedures performed on the pregnant female, even during delivery, such as an episiotomy, are actually found in Section 0, Medical and Surgical. Obstetrics section codes are used only for the products of conception (including, but not limited to, the fetus). For the purposes of this chapter, the term *fetus* or *baby* will be used, in lieu of *products of conception,* where appropriate.

Within the Obstetrics Section, there is no differentiation in coding based on gestational age. In addition, the terms *zygote, embryo,* and *fetus* are not used nor is there any reference to trimester in the procedure codes for this section. Use of those terms is required in ICD-10-CM diagnosis coding, but not in the Obstetrics section of the ICD-10-PCS, where coding is done only for procedures (root operations) performed on the fetus or other products of conception. When coding from the Medical and Surgical section for the pregnant female, any procedures or treatments performed on the products of conception at the same encounter, including delivery of the baby, would be coded from the Obstetrics section if they are part of the medical documentation.

There is only one body system character assignment for Obstetrics: 0, which is pregnancy. Every code within this Section will start with 10. The rest of the value assignments, for characters three through seven, are in Table 7-1.

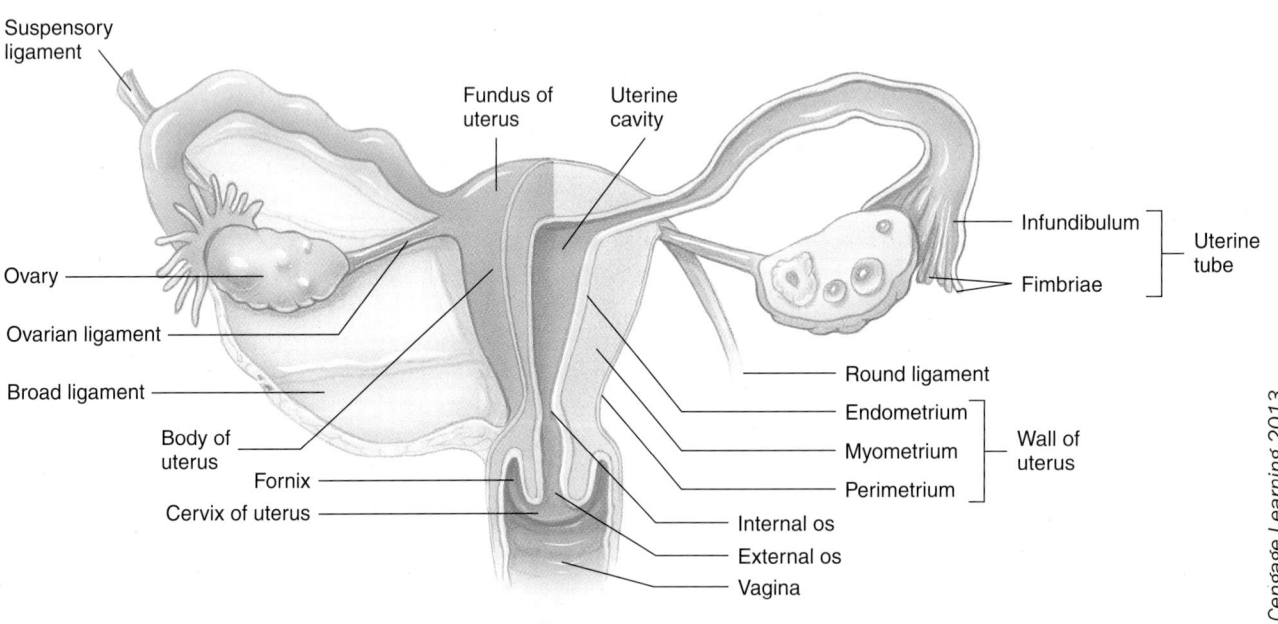

Figure 7-1 Illustration of Male (A) and Female (B) Reproductive System

Table 7-1 Character Value Assignments Used in Obstetrics

Root Operations	Body Parts	Approaches	Devices	Qualifiers
2–Change	0–Products of conception	0–Open	3–Monitoring electrode	Z–No device
9–Drainage	1–Products of conception, retained	3–Percutaneous	Y–Other device	9–Fetal blood
A–Abortion	2–Products of conception, ectopic	4–Percutaneous endoscopic	Z–No device	A–Fetal cerebrospinal fluid
D–Extraction		7–via natural or artificial opening		B–Fetal fluid, other
E–Delivery		8–Via natural or artificial opening, endoscopic		C–Amniotic fluid, therapeutic
F–Insertion		X–External		D–Fluid, other
J–Inspection				U–Amniotic fluid, diagnostic
P–Removal				W–Laminaria
5–Reposition				X–Abortifacient
T–Resection				0–Classical
Y–Transplantation				1–Low cervical
				2–Extraperitoneal
				3–Low forceps
				4–Mid forceps
				5–High forceps
				6–Vacuum
				7–Internal version
				8–Other
				E–Nervous system
				F–Cardiovascular system
				G–Lymphatics and hemic
				H–Eye
				J–Ear, nose, sinus
				K–Respiratory system
				L–Mouth and throat
				M–Gastrointestinal system
				N–Hepatobiliary and pancreas
				P–Endocrine system
				Q–Skin
				R–Musculoskeletal system
				S–Urinary system
				T–Female reproductive system
				V–Male reproductive system
				Y–Other body system

Guidelines Specific to the Obstetrics Section

There are two obstetric-specific guidelines, C1, which defines the products of conception, and C2, concerning procedures following a delivery or an abortion.

- **Guideline C1,** Products of Conception: Procedures performed on the products of conception (the fetus, placenta, amniotic sac, etc.) are coded to the Obstetrics section. Procedures performed on the pregnant female are coded to the appropriate root operation in the Medical and Surgical section of the ICD-10-PCS. For example, amniocentesis is a procedure performed on the products of conception which includes the amniotic sac, and is coded to the Obstetrics section. The *repair of an obstetrical laceration of the urethra* in a pregnant female, on the other hand, is coded to the *urethra* body part in the medical and surgical section.

- **Guideline C2,** Procedures following delivery or abortion: Procedures performed following a delivery or abortion for curettage of the endometrium or evacuation of retained products of conception are all coded to the obstetrics section using the root operation extraction, and the body part products of conception, retained. Diagnostic or therapeutic dilation and curettage (D&C) performed during times other than the postpartum or post abortion period are all coded in the Medical and Surgical section, using the root operation Extraction and the body part Endometrium.

Character 3: Root Operations

There are eleven root operations used in the Obstetrics section. The root operations and their values are:

- Change (2)
- Drainage (9)
- **Abortion (A)**
- Extraction (D)
- **Delivery (E)**
- Insertion (F)
- Inspection (J)
- Removal (P)
- Reposition (5)
- Resection (T)
- Transplantation (Y)

In the root operations list above, there are two new Root Operations (in bold font) that have not yet been discussed, Abortion (A) and Delivery (E). The rest of the root operation definitions have exactly the same definitions as those found in the Medical and Surgical section (0), and are used in the same way. Let's look at the root operations Abortion and Delivery more thoroughly.

Root Operation Abortion (A)

Root Operation A, **Abortion,** is defined as artificially eliminating a pregnancy. This root operation is subdivided according to whether an additional device such as a laminaria or abortifacient is used; or whether the abortion was performed by mechanical means. **Laminaria** is a small rod-shaped piece of dried seaweed that, when placed within the cervix, causes it to gradually dilate (widen). The species of seaweed serving this purpose is *Laminaria digitata.*

An **abortifacient** is any substance that causes pregnancy to end prematurely and causes an abortion. Other terms for a medication abortion are medical abortion, elective abortion, and induced abortion. Abortion methods that use introduction of a substance (such as a laminaria or abortifacient) or medication to induce the abortion are called medical or medication abortions. **Mechanical means** of abortions include instruments such as forceps, cervical dilators, vacuum aspirators, or curettes (Figure 7-2) used in dilatation and curettage (D&C) procedures. Figure 7-2 is an illustration of different types of curettes used in delivery and abortion procedures. Figure 7-3 is an illustration of different types of delivery forceps. The instruments shown in Figure 7-2 are used for many different types of female reproductive system procedures, and the instruments in both Figures 7-2 and 7-3 are used to assist in delivery and abortion procedures.

An **incomplete abortion** is a miscarriage in which part, but not all, of the uterine contents are expelled. A **missed abortion** is also a miscarriage; however, in a missed abortion the fetus and other products of conception can remain in the uterus for four or more weeks. Two alternative terms for a missed abortion are **miscarriage** and **spontaneous abortion**, in that it occurs without provocation. The last type is an **induced abortion**, which is the deliberate termination of a pregnancy.

Root Operation Delivery (E)

The definition of root operation **Delivery** (E) is assisting the passage of the products of conception from the genital canal. This root operation is used only for manually assisted, vaginal delivery of the products of conception. For the Delivery root operation, there is neither differentiation in the procedure coding between live-born or stillborn, nor does the trimester or gestational age matter when using this root operation. Assisting in a vaginal birth, where no instrumentation is used, is coded to the root operation Delivery. If instruments such as forceps or vacuum aspirators are used, or if a cesarean delivery is performed, then the procedure is not coded to Delivery but to Extraction, which is defined as pulling out all or a portion of a body part. In a manually assisted spontaneous abortion, since the pregnancy is not artificially (electively) terminated, the root operation is Delivery, since this captures the procedure objective.

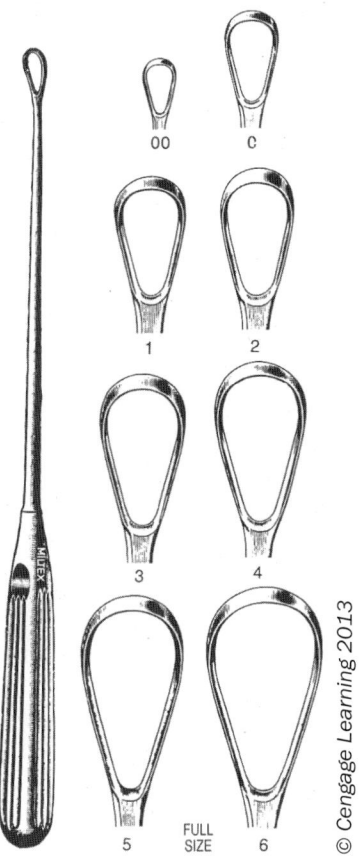

Figure 7-2 Illustration of Types of Uterine Curettes

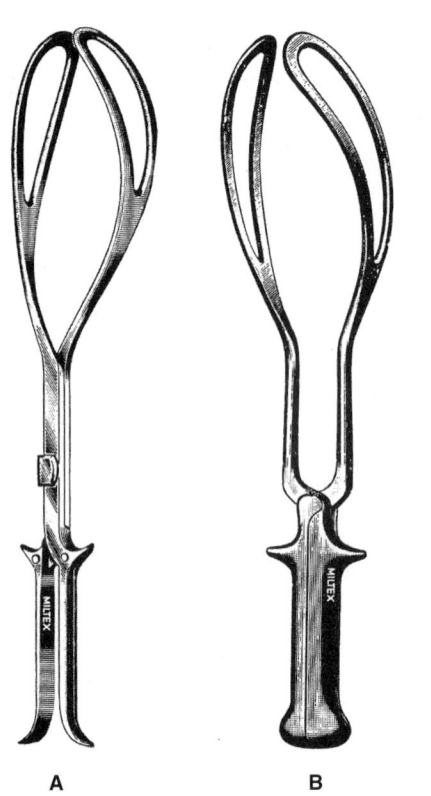
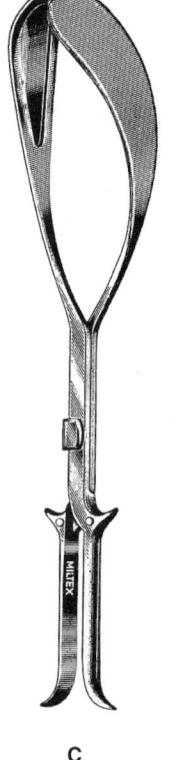
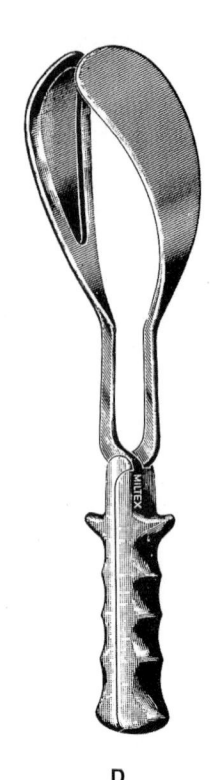

A   B   C   D

© Cengage Learning 2013

Figure 7-3 (A–D) Illustration of Types of Delivery Forceps

Character 4: Body Parts

There are only three body part values for character 4 in the Obstetrics section. They are *products of conception* (0), *products of conception, retained* (1), and *products of conception, ectopic* (2). Table 7-1 lists the three body part character values available in the Obstetrics section. Value 0, identifies any fully removed fetus or other product of conception. Table 7-2 identifies which of the three body part values can be used with a specific root operation in this Section.

As indicated in Table 7-2, body part value 0 is used with every root operation except Resection. Value 1 (products of conception, retained), is used only with Extraction and Inspection root operations. Additionally, body part value 2 (products of conception, ectopic) is used only with the root operations Extraction, Inspection, Reposition, and Resection. Let's look more closely at why only certain body part values can be used with these twelve root operations. Table 7-3 compares the body part value and the root operation definition.

Table 7-2 Body Part Values Used in Obstetrics Section

Value	Body Part	Change	Drainage	Abortion	Extraction	Delivery	Insertion	Inspection	Removal	Repair	Reposition	Resection	Transplantation
0	Product of conception	X	X	X	X	X	X	X	X	X	X		X
1	Product of conception, retained				X		X						
2	Product of conception, ectopic				X		X				X	X	

Table 7-3 Body Part Values in Comparison to Root Operation in Obstetrics Section

Body Part	Root Operation	Definition
0	2-Change	Taking out all of a device from a body part and putting back an identical or similar device in or on the same body part without cutting or puncturing the skin or a mucous membrane Objective: To exchange an existing device for another similar device If approach is external, use root operation Change, if internal approach, use Removal. **EXAMPLE:** Fetal heart monitor electrode
0	9-Drainage	Taking or letting out fluids and gases from a body part **EXAMPLE:** Amniocentesis, fetal spinal tap, percutaneous
0	A-Abortion	Artificially terminating a pregnancy Objective: Abortion of products of conception
0 1 2	D-Extraction	Pulling or stripping out all or a portion of a body part by use of force **EXAMPLE:** Dilatation and curettage, vacuum-suction products of conception
0	E-Delivery	Assisting the passage of products of conception from the genital cavity
0	H-Insertion	Putting in a nonbiological appliance that monitors, assists, performs, or prevents a physiological function, but does not physically take the place of a body part **EXAMPLE:** insertion of central venous catheter
0 1 2	J-Inspection	Visually and manually exploring a body part **EXAMPLE:** Fetogram
0	P-Removal	Taking out or off a device from a body part, region, or orifice If approach is external, use root operation Change, if internal approach, use Removal. **EXAMPLE:** Drainage tube removal
0	Q-Repair	Restoring, to the extent possible, a body part to its normal anatomic structure and function **EXAMPLE:** Suture of laceration, herniorrhaphy
0 2	5-Reposition	Moving to its normal location or other suitable location all or a portion of a body part Explanation: Body part is moved from an aberrant location to a normal location **EXAMPLE:** Reposition viable ectopic pregnancy to uterus
2	T-Resection	Cutting out or off, without replacement, all of a body part If part of a body part use Root Operation Excision, if all of a body part, use Resection **EXAMPLE:** Resection of ectopic products of conception from fallopian tube
0	Y-Transplantation	Putting in or on all of a portion of a living body part taken from another individual or animal to physically take the place and/or function of all or a portion of a similar body part **EXAMPLE:** Kidney transplant

Given the definition of the root operations Change, Drainage, and Extraction, these procedures would not normally be performed on retained (1) or ectopic (2) products of conception. For example, consider the objective of the root operation Change (Figure 7-4).

It can be assumed that retained and ectopic products of conception are not living, while the products of conception (value 0) can be considered an unborn, but living, fetus. In the example given for the root operation Change, a heart monitor lead might be placed and subsequently changed, on a living fetus in preparation for delivery, but not on a non viable one. On the other hand, in the root operation Extraction (Figure 7-5), all three body part values are applicable—since the body part, whether complete, retained, or ectopic, can be pulled or stripped out of the body by force. This includes all methods used to pull or strip out the products of conception (i.e., fetus, ectopic pregnancy contents, or retained substances or structures such as the placenta). This is not the same as Delivery. In Extraction, instruments or manual force pulls or strips out the contents. Delivery is an assist in passage of the products "naturally" from the uterus and through the vagina, without the use of instrumentation.

Section	1	Obstetrics		
Body System	0	Pregnancy		
Operation	2	Change: Taking out or off a device from a body part and putting back an identical or similar device in or on the same body part without cutting or puncturing the skin or a mucous membrane		

Body Part	Approach	Device	Qualifier
0 Products of Conception	7 Via Natural or Artificial Opening	3 Monitoring Electrode Y Other Device	Z No Qualifier

Figure 7-4 Root Operation Change in Obstetrics Section of ICD-10-PCS
© Cengage Learning 2013

Section	1	Obstetrics		
Body System	0	Pregnancy		
Operation	D	Extraction: Pulling or stripping out or off all or a portion of a body part		

Body Part	Approach	Device	Qualifier
0 Products of Conception	0 Open	Z No Device	0 Classical 1 Low Cervical 2 Extraperitoneal
0 Products of Conception	7 Via Natural or Artificial Opening	Z No Device	3 Low Forceps 4 Mid Forceps 5 High Forceps 6 Vacuum 7 Internal Version 8 Other
1 Products of Conception, Retained 2 Products of Conception, Ectopic	7 Via Natural or Artificial Opening 8 Via Natural or Artificial Opening Endoscopic	Z No Device	Z No Qualifier

© Cengage Learning 2013

Figure 7-5 Root Operation Extraction in Obstetrics Section of ICD-10-PCS

Approach (Character 5) Values in the Obstetrics Section

Essentially, the same seven approaches used in the Medical and Surgical section are used in the Obstetrics section. Table 7-4 illustrates which approaches are applicable with specific root operations and body parts.

Let's look at the applicable approach values from Table 7-4 more closely. As a reminder, Table 7-5 lists the approach value, title, and definition.

Approach X, External, is used only with root operations Delivery and Inspection. The definition of an External approach is a procedure performed directly on the skin or mucous membrane, or performed indirectly by application of external force through the skin or mucous membrane. In an Abortion root operation, if a laminaria or abortifacient is used, the approach is *via natural or artificial opening*.

With the root operation Delivery (Figure 7-6) for example, using the External approach means the delivery is accomplished by applying external manual force while assisting in passage of the fetus through the vaginal canal. An External approach in Inspection (Figure 7-7) would be to physically palpate the skin of the fetus to inspect it. An additional note about the root operation Inspection is that it is the only root operation applicable to all body part and approach values. In other words, an Inspection can be done on the products of conception; products of conception, retained; and products of conception, ectopic; and all approach values can be used for any of the body parts in the Obstetrics section.

Table 7-4 Approaches Applicable to Obstetric Section Root Operations and Body Parts

Root Operation	Body Part	Approach
2–Change 9–Drainage	0–Products of conception 0–Products of conception	0–Open 0–Open 3–Percutaneous 4–Percutaneous endoscopic 7–Via natural or artificial opening 8–Via natural or artificial opening endoscopic
A–Abortion	0–Products of conception	0–Open 2–Open endoscopic 3–Percutaneous 4–Percutaneous endoscopic 7–Via natural or artificial opening 8–Via natural or artificial opening endoscopic
D–Extraction	0–Products of conception	0–Open 7–Via natural or artificial opening
	1–Products of conception, retained 2–Products of conception, ectopic	7–Via natural or artificial opening 8–Via natural or artificial opening endoscopic
E–Delivery	0–Products of conception	X–external
H–Insertion	0–Products of conception	0–Open 7–Via natural or artificial opening
J–Inspection	0–Products of conception	0–Open
	1–Products of conception, retained 2–Products of conception, ectopic	2–Open endoscopic 3–Percutaneous 4–Percutaneous endoscopic 7–Via natural or artificial opening 8–Via natural or artificial opening endoscopic X–External
P–Removal	0–Products of conception	0–Open 7–Via natural or artificial opening
Q–Repair	0–Products of conception	0–Open 2–Open endoscopic 3–Percutaneous 4–Percutaneous endoscopic 7–Via natural or artificial opening 8–Via natural or artificial opening endoscopic
S–Reposition	0–Products of conception	7–Via natural or artificial opening 8–Via natural or artificial opening endoscopic
	2–Products of conception, ectopic	0–Open 2–Open endoscopic 3–Percutaneous 4–Percutaneous endoscopic 7–Via natural or artificial opening 8–Via natural or artificial opening endoscopic
T–Resection	2–Products of conception, ectopic	0–Open 2–Open endoscopic 3–Percutaneous 4–Percutaneous endoscopic 7–Via natural or artificial opening 8–Via natural or artificial opening endoscopic
Y–Transplantation	0–Products of conception	3–Percutaneous 4–Percutaneous endoscopic 7–Via natural or artificial opening

Table 7-5 Approach Values and Definitions Used in Obstetrics Section of ICD-10-PCS

Approach	Approach Definition
0–Open	Cutting through the skin or mucous membrane and any other body layers necessary to expose the site of the procedure
2–Open endoscopic	Cutting through the skin or mucous membrane and any other body layers necessary to expose the site of the procedure; **and** entry, by puncture or minor incision, of instrumentation through the skin or mucous membrane and any other body layers necessary to aid in the performance of the procedure
3–Percutaneous	Entry, by puncture or minor incision, of instrumentation through the skin or mucous membrane and any other body layers necessary to **reach** the site of the procedure
4–Percutaneous endoscopic	Entry, by puncture or minor incision, of instrumentation through the skin or mucous membrane and any other body layers necessary to **reach and visualize** the site of the procedure
7–Via natural or artificial opening	Entry of instrumentation through a natural or artificial external opening to **reach** the site of the procedures
8–Via natural or artificial opening endoscopic	Entry of instrumentation through a natural or artificial external opening to **reach and visualize** the site of the procedures
External	Procedures performed directly on the skin or mucous membrane, and procedures performed indirectly by the application of external force through the skin or mucous membrane

Section	**1**	Obstetrics
Body System	**0**	Pregnancy
Operation	**E**	Delivery: Assisting the passage of the products of conception from the genital canal

Body Part	Approach	Device	Qualifier
0 Products of Conception	**X** External	**Z** No Device	**Z** No Qualifier

Figure 7-6 Root Operation Delivery in Obstetrics Section of ICD-10-PCS
© Cengage Learning 2013

Section	**1**	Obstetrics
Body System	**0**	Pregnancy
Operation	**J**	Inspection: Visually and manually exploring a body part

Body	Part Approach	Device	Qualifier
0 Products of Conception **1** Products of Conception, Retained **2** Products of Conception, Ectopic	**0** Open **2** Open Endoscopic **3** Percutaneous **4** Percutaneous Endoscopic **7** Via Natural or Artificial Opening **8** Via Natural or Artificial Opening Endoscopic **X** External	**Z** No Device	**Z** No Qualifier

Figure 7-7 Root Operation Inspection in Obstetrics Section of ICD-10-PCS

© Cengage Learning 2013

With root operations Abortion (A), and Repair (Q), and body part 0, products of conception, all approach values except External are acceptable. No other body part values except 0 are used in Abortion (Figure 7-8) or Repair (Figure 7-9).

Another example is the use of approach values 7 and 8 only with the root operations Extraction (D) and Reposition (4). With root operation Extraction (Figure 7-5), these two approach values are only used with body part values 1 and 2, products of conception retained and *products of conception,*

Section	**1**	Obstetrics
Body System	**0**	Pregnancy
Operation	**A**	Abortion: Artificially terminating a pregnancy

Body Part	Approach	Device	Qualifier
0 Products of Conception	**0** Open **2** Open Endoscopic **3** Percutaneous **4** Percutaneous Endoscopic **8** Via Natural or Artificial Opening Endoscopic	**Z** No Device	**Z** No Qualifier
0 Products of Conception	**7** Via Natural or Artificial Opening	**Z** No Device	**6** Vacuum **W** Laminaria **X** Abortifacient **Z** No Qualifier

© Cengage Learning 2013

Figure 7-8 Root Operation Abortion in Obstetrics Section of ICD-10-PCS

Section	**1**	Obstetrics
Body System	**0**	Pregnancy
Operation	**Q**	Repair: Restoring, to the extent possible, a body part to its normal anatomic structure and function

Body Part	Approach	Device	Qualifier
0 Products of Conception	**0** Open **2** Open Endoscopic **3** Percutaneous **4** Percutaneous Endoscopic **7** Via Natural or Artificial Opening **8** Via Natural or Artificial Opening Endoscopic	**Y** Other Device **Z** No Device	**E** Nervous System **F** Cardiovascular System **G** Lymphatics and Hemic **H** Eye **J** Ear, Nose, and Sinus **K** Respiratory System **L** Mouth and Throat **M** Gastrointestinal System **N** Hepatobiliary and Pancreas **P** Endocrine System **Q** Skin **R** Musculoskeletal System **S** Urinary System **T** Female Reproductive System **V** Male Reproductive System **Y** Other Body System

© Cengage Learning 2013

Figure 7-9 Root Operation Repair in Obstetrics Section of ICD-10-PCS

ectopic, respectively. A procedural example would be *extraction of retained products of conception after missed abortion*. The first four character values would be 10D1—Section 1, *Obstetrics*; Body System 0, *Pregnancy*; Root Operation D, *Extraction*; and Body Part 1, *products of conception*, retained. The fifth character, the approach, can be either 7 or 8, depending on whether the Extraction was performed via a natural opening (vaginal canal) and whether it was performed with (character value 7) or without (character value 8) endoscopic assistance. The device and qualifier values for this example will be discussed later in the chapter.

With the Reposition root operation (Figure 7-10), only body part value 1, *products of conception*, is acceptable. Approach value 7 is via natural or artificial opening, and value 8 is via natural or artificial opening, endoscopic, which means that an Extraction (Figure 7-5) of an ectopic pregnancy (body part value 2), can only be performed using one of these two approaches. If the root operation is Reposition, then repositioning the fetus from breech (buttocks first) to vertex (head first), for example, can only be done via approach 7 or 8 as well.

Section	1	Obstetrics			
Body System	0	Pregnancy			
Operation	S	Reposition: Moving to its normal location or other suitable location all or a portion of a body part			

Body Part	Approach	Device	Qualifier
0 Products of Conception	**7** Via Natural or Artificial Opening **X** External	**Z** No Device	**Z** No Qualifier
2 Products of Conception, Ectopic	**0** Open **2** Open Endoscopic **3** Percutaneous **4** Percutaneous Endoscopic **7** Via Natural or Artificial Opening **8** Via Natural or Artificial Opening Endoscopic	**Z** No Device	**Z** No Qualifier

Figure 7-10 Root Operation Reposition in Obstetrics Section of ICD-10-PCS

Section	1	Obstetrics			
Body System	0	Pregnancy			
Operation	T	Resection: Cutting out or off, without replacement, all of a body part			

Body Part	Approach	Device	Qualifier
2 Products of Conception, Ectopic	**0** Open **2** Open Endoscopic **3** Percutaneous **4** Percutaneous Endoscopic **7** Via Natural or Artificial Opening **8** Via Natural or Artificial Opening Endoscopic	**Z** No Device	**Z** No Qualifier

Figure 7-11 Root Operation Resection in Obstetrics Section of ICD-10-PCS

Section	1	Obstetrics			
Body System	0	Pregnancy			
Operation	9	Drainage: Taking or letting out fluids and gases from a body part			

Body Part	Approach	Device	Qualifier
0 Products of Conception	**0** Open **3** Percutaneous **4** Percutaneous Endoscopic **7** Via Natural or Artificial Opening **8** Via Natural or Artificial Opening Endoscopic	**Z** No Device	**9** Fetal Blood **A** Fetal Cerebrospinal Fluid **B** Fetal Fluid, Other **C** Amniotic Fluid, Therapeutic **D** Fluid, Other **U** Amniotic Fluid, Diagnostic

Figure 7-12 Root Operation Drainage in Obstetrics Section of ICD-10-PCS

Another rule with root operation Reposition (S) involves body part value 2, *products of conception, ectopic*. All approach values for root operation Reposition (S) and body part value 2 are applicable except External. In addition, all approach values except External may be used with root operation Resection (T), shown in Figure 7-11, and body part value 2, *products of conception, ectopic*.

This leaves root operations Drainage (9), Insertion (H), Removal (P), and Transplantation (Y). With root operation Drainage (Figure 7-12), the appropriate body part value is 0 (products of conception) and approach values are 0 (open) 3 (percutaneous), 4 (percutaneous endoscopic), 7 (via natural or artificial opening), and 8 (via natural or artificial opening, endoscopic). The only applicable body part value for

Section	**1**	Obstetrics
Body System	**0**	Pregnancy
Operation	**H**	Insertion: Putting in a nonbiological appliance that monitors, assists, performs, or prevents a physiological function but does not physically take the place of a body part

Body Part	Approach	Device	Qualifier
0 Products of Conception	**0** Open **7** Via Natural or Artificial Opening	**3** Monitoring Electrode **Y** Other Device	**Z** No Qualifier

Figure 7-13 Root Operation Insertion in Obstetrics Section of ICD-10-PCS
© Cengage Learning 2013

Section	**1**	Obstetrics
Body System	**0**	Pregnancy
Operation	**P**	Removal: Taking out or off a device from a body part, region, or orifice

Body Part	Approach	Device	Qualifier
0 Products of Conception	**0** Open **7** Via Natural or Artificial Opening	**3** Monitoring Electrode **Y** Other Device	**Z** No Qualifier

Figure 7-14 Root Operation Removal in Obstetrics Section of ICD-10-PCS
© Cengage Learning 2013

Section	**1**	Obstetrics
Body System	**0**	Pregnancy
Operation	**Y**	Transplantation: Putting in or on all or a portion of a living body part taken from another individual or animal to physically take the place and/or function of all or a portion of a similar body part

Body Part	Approach	Device	Qualifier
0 Products of Conception	**3** Percutaneous **4** Percutaneous Endoscopic **7** Via Natural or Artificial Opening	**Z** No Device	**E** Nervous System **F** Cardiovascular System **G** Lymphatics and Hemic **H** Eye **J** Ear, Nose, and Sinus **K** Respiratory System **L** Mouth and Throat **M** Gastrointestinal System **N** Hepatobiliary and Pancreas **P** Endocrine System **Q** Skin **R** Musculoskeletal System **S** Urinary System **T** Female Reproductive System **V** Male Reproductive System **Y** Other Body System

© Cengage Learning 2013

Figure 7-15 Root Operation Transplantation in Obstetrics Section of ICD-10-PCS

root operations Insertion (Figure 7-13) and Removal (Figure 7-14) is 0 (products of conception); and the only applicable approach values for these two root operations are 0 (open) and 7 (via natural or artificial opening).

Last is root operation Transplantation (Y), shown in (Figure 7-15) defined as *putting in or on all of a portion of a living body part taken from another individual or animal to physically take the place and/or function of all or a portion of a similar body part*. With this root operation, the only applicable body part value is 0, and the only acceptable approaches are 3, percutaneous, 4, percutaneous endoscopic, or 7, via natural or artificial opening.

Table 7-6 Device Character Values in Obstetrics Section of ICD-10-PCS

Root Operation	Body Part	Devices
2—Change	0—Products of conception	3—Monitoring electrode Y—Other device
H—Insertion	0—Products of conception	3—Monitoring electrode Y—Other device
P—Removal	0—Products of conception	3—Monitoring electrode Y—Other device
Q—Repair	0—Products of conception	Y—Other device
All Other Root Operations	0, 1, or 2	Z—No device

Device (Character 6) Values in the Obstetrics Section

In most root operations, the only device character value is Z, no device. The only two other devices listed in the Obstetrics section are monitoring electrode (3), and other device (Y), shown in Table 7-6. These two devices are listed only with the root operations Change (2), Insertion (H), and Removal (P). The device value Y, other device, is found by itself in the root operation Repair (Q). The only body part value applicable with any device from this section is 0, products of conception.

Let's Review 7–1:

1. The body part codes in Obstetrics (Section 1) are _____
2. List and define five root operations found in the Obstetrics section.? _____
3. Differentiate between medication abortions and mechanical abortions _____
4. Describe the difference between incomplete, missed, spontaneous, and induced abortion. _____
5. The root operation Delivery is used only for: _____
6. What is the difference between root operation extraction and delivery? _____

Electronic Fetal Monitoring

Electronic Fetal Monitoring (EFM) is frequently used during labor to assess fetal well-being. EFM involves the use of an electronic fetal heart rate (FHR) monitor to record the baby's heart rate. There are two methods of applying the electrodes. The first is an open surgical procedure (approach 0), and the second is via a natural or artificial opening (approach 7). The electrodes (device character value 3) are placed on the fetus and connected to the monitor. The EFM detects the baby's heart rate as well as the uterine contractions. The monitor then records the FHR and contractions as a pattern on a strip of paper called a tracing. EFM can be used either externally or internally.

Internal monitoring does not use ultrasound, is more accurate than electronic monitoring, and provides continuous monitoring for the high-risk mother and fetus. An internal monitor requires that the amniotic sac be ruptured (approach character value 7, via natural or artificial opening) and that the pregnant woman is at least two to three centimeters dilated. It is used in high-risk situations, or when it is difficult to obtain an accurate FHR tracing.

Other Devices

Telemetry is still used occasionally in some hospitals, but was more popular in the 1990s. Telemetry uses radio waves transmitted from an instrument on the mother's thigh, which allows the mother to remain mobile. It provides continuous fetal monitoring and uterine contraction times. Besides EFM and telemetry, which is usually continuous, there is intermittent monitoring using a hand-held Doppler to assess the FHR. If these devices are specified in the medical documentation as part of the procedure, the device character value assigned is Y, other device. More rarely, a special stethoscope is used, called a *fetoscope*. Since the fetoscope is not a device left in place as part of the procedure, the appropriate device character value when a fetoscope is mentioned as part of the procedural statement is Z, no device.

Earlier in the chapter, an example of the procedure *extraction of retained products of conception after missed abortion* was used. The first four character values were shown as 10D1—Section 1, Obstetrics, Body System 0, Pregnancy, Root Operation D, Extraction, and Body Part 1, products of conception, retained. The fifth character, Approach, would be either 7 or 8, depending on whether the Extraction was performed via a natural opening (vaginal canal) with or without endoscopic assistance, respectively. In this example, the fifth character would be Z, no device, since (1) the root operation Extraction doesn't list any device as applicable and (2) no device is used with any body part except 0, *products of conception*. There is no qualifier, which makes the seventh character Z. The correct code for this procedure example would now be either 10D17ZZ (if the approach was via natural or artificial opening) or 10D18ZZ (if the approach was via natural or artificial opening, endoscopic).

Example 2: If a fetal heart monitor is used during labor and delivery, the electrode(s) from the monitor, placed on the fetus, would use device character 3, monitoring electrode. In the previous example, the root operation Extraction was used, but this time, it will be Insertion (Figure 7-13). The first three characters of the code will be 10H, Section Obstetrics (1), Body System Pregnancy (0), Root Operation Insertion (H). Body Part 0, products of conception, will be the fourth character, making the code 10H0. In this example, the approach will be through the vaginal canal and cervix to the fetus. The Approach therefore will be 7, via natural or artificial opening. The code is now 10H07. The device is 3, monitoring electrode, resulting in the first six characters 10H073. There is no qualifier for this procedure, thus, the full code would be 10H073Z.

Qualifier (Character 7) Values in the Obstetrics Section

The list in Table 7-7 looks daunting, but in reality, only a few of these qualifiers are used with any specific root operation. As usual, the placeholder Z is used in the seventh character position when no qualifier is applicable. In the Obstetrics section, Z, no qualifier, is used with the following root operations:

- Change (2)
- Abortion (A) when the approach is any method except 7, via natural or artificial opening
- Extraction (D) when the body part values are 1 and 2, products of conception, retained and ectopic, respectively
- Delivery (E)
- Insertion (H)
- Inspection (J)
- Removal (P)
- Reposition (5)
- Resection (T)

This leaves four root operations (Table 7-8): Abortion (A), when the approach is 7; Extraction when the body part value is 0; Repair (Q); and Transplantation (Y).

Table 7-7 Qualifiers Used in Obstetrics Section of ICD-10-PCS

Qualifiers
Z–No qualifier
9–Fetal blood
A–Fetal cerebrospinal fluid
B–Fetal fluid, other
C–Amniotic fluid, therapeutic
D–Fluid, other
U–Amniotic fluid, diagnostic
W–Laminaria
X–Abortifacient
0–Classical
1–Low cervical
2–Extraperitoneal
3–Low forceps
4–Mid forceps
5–High forceps
6–Vacuum
7–Internal version
8–Other
E–Nervous system
F–Cardiovascular system
G–Lymphatics and hemic
H–Eye
J–Ear, nose, sinus
K–Respiratory system
L–Mouth and throat
M–Gastrointestinal system
N–Hepatobiliary and pancreas
P–Endocrine system
Q–Skin
R–Musculoskeletal system
S–Urinary system
T–Female reproductive system
V–Male reproductive system
Y–Other body system

Go back and look at other devices in, Example 2. The first six code characters for *vaginal canal approach to fetus for insertion of a fetal heart monitor electrode* are 10H073. The first three characters are Section Obstetrics (1), Body System Pregnancy (0), and Root Operation Insertion (H). Body Part 0, products of conception, is next, and the approach chosen for this example is 7, via natural or artificial opening. The

Table 7-8 Root Operation, Body Part, Approach, and Qualifier Values in Obstetrics Section of ICD-10-PCS

Root Operation	Body Part	Approach	Qualifier
A–Abortion	0–Products of conception	7–Via natural or artificial opening	W–Laminaria X–Abortifacient Z–No qualifier
D–Extraction	0–Products of conception	0–Open	0–Classical 1–Low cervical 2–Extraperitoneal
		7–Via natural or artificial opening	3–Low forceps 4–Mid forceps 5–High forceps 6–Vacuum 7–Internal version 8–Other
Q–Repair	0–Products of conception	0–Open 2–Open endoscopic 3–Percutaneous 4–Percutaneous endoscopic 7–Via natural or artificial opening 8–Via natural or artificial opening, endoscopic	E–Nervous system F–Cardiovascular system G–Lymphatics and hemic H–Eye J–Ear, nose, and sinus K–Respiratory system L–Mouth and throat M–Gastrointestinal system N–Hepatobiliary and pancreas P–Endocrine system Q–Skin R–Musculoskeletal system S–Urinary system T–Female reproductive system V–Male reproductive system Y–Other body system
Y–Transplantation	0–Products of conception	3–Percutaneous 4–Percutaneous endoscopic 7–Via natural or artificial opening	E–Nervous system F–Cardiovascular system G–Lymphatics and hemic H–Eye J–Ear, nose, and sinus K–Respiratory system L–Mouth and throat M–Gastrointestinal system N–Hepatobiliary and pancreas P–Endocrine system Q–Skin R–Musculoskeletal system S–Urinary system T–Female reproductive system V–Male reproductive system Y–Other body system

device remaining after the procedure is 3, monitoring electrode. Now it is time to select the qualifier. For root operation Insertion, the only qualifier available is Z, no qualifier. This example now has a complete code for the procedure, 10H073Z.

Qualifiers Used with Extraction Root Operation

Before applying any qualifiers, let's look at some terms that will help in understanding a few of the qualifiers. The first two are vertex and breech presentation.

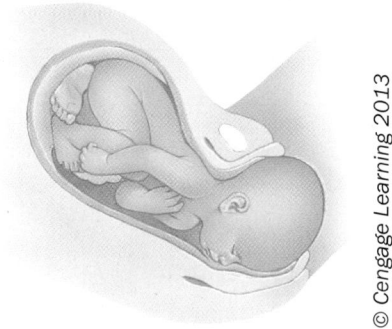

© Cengage Learning 2013

Figure 7-16 Illustration of a Vertex Presentation at Delivery

A **vertex** presentation is when the fetus descends into the vaginal canal head first and face down (Figure 7-16). If no instruments are used to deliver the baby, the root operation for a vertex presentation is Delivery (E). A breech presentation, on the other hand, is when the baby's buttocks present first instead of the head. Using a technique called a **version**, an obstetrician may attempt to turn the baby to a head down position. The only time the qualifier Version (7) is used in the Obstetrics section is with the root operation Extraction. The risks with breech presentation are much higher than with a head-first (vertex) presentation. For this reason, review the medical documentation carefully to determine whether there was a successful version. If the version was not successful, look for an extraction by c-section. In that case, use the root operation Extraction but change the qualifier to forceps or vacuum aspiration.

There are three types of breech presentation. In a **frank breech**, the baby's legs are folded up against its body. In a **complete breech**, the baby's legs are crossed under and in front of the body, and in a **footling breech**, one or both legs are positioned to enter the birth canal.

Forceps delivery Although not used as much as in earlier times, forceps can be used if the baby's head is very low in the birth canal. Also, if there is some sudden change in the maternal-fetal status, the doctor may opt for a forceps delivery if it would be faster than a cesarean section. Forceps are spoon-shaped devices that can be placed around the baby's head while the doctor gently pulls the baby out of the vagina.

Half of the forceps are slid into the vagina and around the side of the baby's head to gently grasp it. When both forceps are in place, the doctor pulls on them to help the baby through the birth canal during a uterine contraction. In the root operation Extraction (D), the Qualifiers 3, 4, and 5 all describe types of forceps deliveries. The American College of Obstetricians and Gynecologists (ACOG) provides specific criteria for these types of forceps deliveries:

- Low forceps (Qualifier 3): The leading point of the fetal skull is at a station greater than or equal to 2 cm and is not on the pelvic floor; any degree of rotation may be present.

- Mid forceps (Qualifier 4): The station is above 2 cm, but the head is engaged.

High forceps (Qualifier 5): This is not included in the classification. Previous systems classified high-forceps deliveries as procedures performed when the head is not engaged.

If the medical documentation states that forceps were used to assist in the delivery, the only appropriate root operation is Extraction, and only the qualifiers 3, 4, or 5 may be used to code the delivery.

Vacuum-assisted birth A vacuum-assisted birth is a newer method of delivering a baby, and is considered a gentler alternative to forceps. Similar to forceps deliveries, vacuum-assisted births can only be used with a fully dilated cervix and a well-descended head. In this procedure, a device called a vacuum extractor is used by placing a large rubber or plastic cup against the baby's head. A pump then creates suction that gently pulls on the cup to ease the baby out of the birth canal. The qualifier 7, vacuum, is found only with the root operation Extraction (D) in the Obstetrics section. If the medical documentation states vacuum aspiration or a vacuum aspirator is used, the only root operation appropriate is Extraction.

Cesarean sections A cesarean section, also called a c-section, is a surgical procedure in which an incision is made through a woman's abdomen and uterus to deliver her baby. This procedure is performed whenever abnormal conditions complicate labor and vaginal delivery such that the life or health of the mother or baby is threatened. The procedure is performed in the United States on nearly one in every four women, resulting in more than 900,000 babies each year being delivered by c-section. The procedure is often used in women who have had a previous c-section, but if the incision on the uterus is not vertical, the woman can try a vaginal birth after cesarean (VBAC).

One factor for cesarean section delivery is fetal distress, a condition where the fetus is not getting enough oxygen. Fetal brain damage can result from oxygen deprivation. Fetal distress is often related to abnormalities in the position of the fetus or abnormalities in the birth canal, causing reduced blood flow through the placenta. The c-section is performed surgically by making one or more incisions through a mother's abdomen (laparotomy) and uterus (hysterotomy) to deliver one or more babies, or to remove a dead fetus. Figure 7-17 is an illustration of a surgical c-section in which the laparotomy is complete, and the uterus is exposed. The hysterotomy would be done next. A c-section is performed only by an Open Approach (Character value 0). There are three types of c-sections, indicated by the qualifier values 0, 1, and 2:

- Character 0: Classical

  ◦ The *classical cesarean section* involves a midline longitudinal incision, which allows a larger space to deliver the baby. However, it is rarely performed today as it is more prone to complications. a method for surgically delivering a baby through a vertical midline incision of the upper segment of the uterus. For many practitioners this is the fastest method of cesarean delivery. However, it produces a weaker scar, and, because the upper segment is thicker and more vascular, more bleeding occurs during surgery. The lower uterine segment section is the procedure most commonly used today; it involves a transverse cut just above the edge of the bladder and results in less blood loss and is easier to repair. Figure 7-17 is an illustration of a classical (7-17A), low cervical, vertical (7.17B) and low cervical, horizontal (7.17C) c-section incision.

- Character 1: Low cervical

  ◦ A surgical procedure to deliver a baby through a transverse incision in the thin supracervical part of the lower uterine segment, behind the bladder and the bladder flap. This incision bleeds

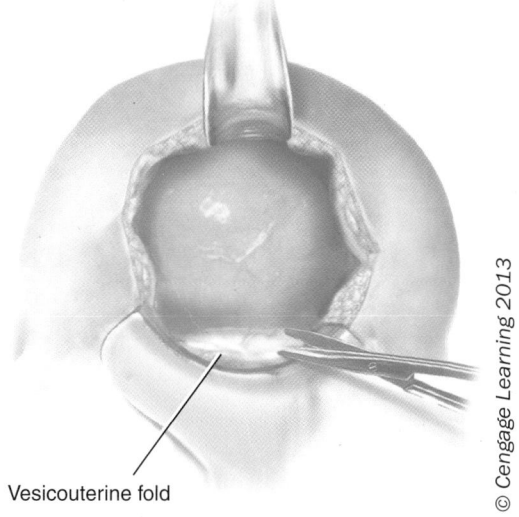

Vesicouterine fold

© Cengage Learning 2013

Figure 7-17 Illustration of a C-Section Procedure with Uterus Exposed

less during surgery and heals with a stronger scar than the higher vertical scar of the classic cesarean section.

- Character 2: Extraperitoneal

  - An extraperitoneal cesarean section is a method for surgically delivering a baby through an incision in the lower uterine segment without entering the peritoneal cavity. The uterus is approached through the paravesical space. Paravesical means around the bladder. The paravesical space (also known as perivesical space) is the space under and around the bladder. Rather than make the surgical incision through the peritoneum, the incision is made below the peritoneum, through the paravesical space, to the uterus, where the hysterotomy is then performed. This procedure is performed most often to prevent spread of infection from the uterus into the peritoneal cavity.

Ectopic Pregnancy

A *salpingostomy* is a surgical incision into a fallopian tube. This procedure may be done to repair a damaged tube or to remove an ectopic pregnancy (one that occurs outside of the uterus). During a normal pregnancy, the fertilized egg passes from the fallopian tubes into the uterus and then implants into the lining of the uterus. If the fertilized egg implants anywhere outside of the uterus, it is called an ectopic (or tubal) pregnancy. The majority of ectopic pregnancies occur in the fallopian tubes, but may also occur in the uterine muscle, the abdomen, the ovaries, and rarely, the cervix.

In ICD-10-PCS, the root operation is Extraction (D), since the objective of the salpingostomy is to extract an ectopic pregnancy (body part 2, products of conception, ectopic). As an ectopic pregnancy progresses, the fallopian tubes are unable to contain the growing embryo and may rupture. A ruptured ectopic pregnancy is considered a medical emergency as it can cause significant hemorrhaging (excessive bleeding). If an ectopic pregnancy is diagnosed early (i.e., before rupture has occurred), it may be possible to manage medically. The drug *methotrexate* targets rapidly dividing fetal cells, preventing the fetus from developing further. If medical management is not possible or has failed, surgical intervention may be necessary. A salpingostomy may then be performed to remove the pregnancy.

Qualifiers Used with Repair and Transplantation Root Operation

The objective of the root operations Repair and Transplantation are to fix or transplant a body part. In Repair, the objective is restoring, to the extent possible, a body part to its normal anatomic structure and function. The qualifiers all represent a body part or system being restored. In Transplantation, the objective is to put in or on all of a portion of a living body part taken from another individual or animal to physically take the place and/or function of all or a portion of a similar body part. As with Repair, the qualifiers for Transplantation are the same, and represent an anatomical structure or body system. The qualifiers used with both Repair and Transplantation are:

- E–Nervous system
- F–Cardiovascular system
- G–Lymphatics and hemic
- H–Eye
- J–Ear, nose, and sinus
- K–Respiratory system
- L–Mouth and throat
- M–Gastrointestinal system
- N–Hepatobiliary and pancreas

- P–Endocrine system
- Q–Skin
- R–Musculoskeletal system
- S–Urinary system
- T–Female reproductive system
- V–Male reproductive system
- Y–Other body system

Let's look at an example of a repair of a fetal heart valve. The allowed body part value to use with Repair is 0, products of conception. The approach may be open (0), open endoscopic (2), percutaneous (3), percutaneous endoscopic (4), via natural or artificial opening (7), or via natural or artificial endoscopic (8). Expanding the procedural statement to *percutaneous endoscopic repair of fetal mitral heart valve* results in a code of 10Q04ZF, broken down as follows:

- 1–Section, Obstetrics
- 0–Body System, Pregnancy
- Q–Root Operation, Repair
- 0–Body Part, products of conception
- Z–Device, none (the statement did not indicate a device)
- F–Cardiovascular system (the mitral valve is located in the heart)

The qualifier with root operation Repair designates the body system upon which the repair was done. In Transplantation, the qualifier represents the body system from which the transplant came. For example, let's take the same procedure but change the root Operation to Transplantation. This results in the code 10Y04ZF. The third character changes from Repair (Q) to Transplantation (Y). The section, body system, body part, device, and qualifier are the same as those used in the repair of the heart valve. There is no device, because the qualifier in this instance represents the source of the transplanted objective, i.e., the valve, which came from the cardiovascular system.

Using the ICD-10-PCS Coding Manual for the Obstetric Section

Before using the ICD-10-PCS coding manual, the medical documentation is reviewed and the procedural statements abstracted. Next, the main and modifying terms are determined. Here's a simple example of a procedural statement: *delivery of live-born male*. The main term (root operation) is Delivery. Going to the Index, under Delivery is the modifying term bo*dy part,* and under that one subterm, *products of conception* (Figure 7-18). The code characters shown are 10E0. Turning to the Tabular List, look for Table 10E0 (also shown in Figure 7-6). Composing the remainder of the code is easy with this procedure, since there is only one character value assigned to the approach, device, and qualifier. Thus, the code is 10E0XZZ.

Let's try another one. The procedural statement is mid-forceps delivery of live-born female. It would seem appropriate to select as the main term the root operation Delivery, since that is in the procedural statement. The trick is remembering the root operation definitions, and the objective of each root operation. With Delivery, the objective is to manually assist in the passage of the products of

> **Delivery**
> *by* Body Part
>   Products of Conception 10E0

Figure 7-18 Alphabetic Index Excerpt for Root Operation Delivery
© Cengage Learning 2013

```
┌─────────────────────────────────────────┐
│ Extraction continued                      │
│   Nerve continued                         │
│     Thoracic Sympathetic 01DL             │
│     Tibial 01DG                           │
│     Trigeminal 00DK                       │
│     Trochlear 00DJ                        │
│     Ulnar 01D4                            │
│     Vagus 00DQ                            │
│   Ova 0UDN                                │
│   Pleura                                  │
│     Left 0BDP                             │
│     Right 0BDN                            │
│   Products of Conception                  │
│     Classical 10P00Z0                     │
│     Ectopic 10D2                          │
│     Extraperitoneal 10D00Z2               │
│     High Forceps 10D07Z5                  │
│     Internal Version 10D07Z7              │
│     Low Cervical 10D00Z1                  │
│     Low Forceps 10D07Z3                   │
│     Mid Forceps 10D07Z4                   │
│     Other 10D07Z8                         │
│     Retained 10D1                         │
│     Vacuum 10D07Z6                        │
└─────────────────────────────────────────┘
```
© Cengage Learning 2013

Figure 7-19 Alphabetic Index Excerpt for Root Operation Extraction

conception from the genital cavity. Using forceps does not qualify as a manual assist. After a review of root operation definitions and objectives, the best choice would be Extraction. The objective of Extraction is to pull or strip out all or a portion of a body part by the use of force. Forceps, in this instance, pull the fetus out of the genital canal by force. The main term, therefore, is Extraction, and the modifying term will be *by body part, products of conception*. In the Index (Figure 7-19), find the root operation Extraction, then find the modifying (*by body part*) and subterms (*products of conception*). The code characters given are 10D0. Next, go to the Tabular List and find Table 10D0 (Obstetrics (1), Pregnancy (0), Extraction (D), Products of Conception (0)) (this was shown earlier in Figure 7-5).

There are two rows in this Table for 10D0, with a different approach in each row. The procedural statement does not indicate this was an open procedure, which means the Approach must be 7, via natural or artificial opening, which is the second row. Staying in that row, the next character will be the device. There's only one value in the device column in this row: Z, no device. At this point, the code is 10D07Z. The seventh character will complete the procedural statement coding, by choosing the appropriate qualifier. The procedural statement indicates a mid-forceps delivery, which would be qualifier value 4. The complete code for *mid-forceps delivery of live-born female is* 10D07Z4.

Here's one more example. The procedural statement is *manual rupture, vaginally, of amniotic sac for drainage of amniotic fluid*. The objective of the procedure is drainage of the amniotic sac, which makes the main term Drainage. In the Index, under Drainage, look for the modifying term *by body part,* and the subterm *products of conception.* (Remember, products of conception includes the amniotic sac.) This search produces the code value 1090.

Moving to that Table in the Tabular List (Figure 7-12) indicates there are five approaches (Open, Percutaneous, Percutaneous endoscopic, via natural or artificial opening, via natural or artificial opening endoscopic). The procedural statement indicates the approach is vaginal, thus, the correct approach value is 7, via natural or artificial opening. There is one value for device, which is Z, no device. Next, select the qualifier. This was to drain amniotic fluid. There are two choices, amniotic fluid, therapeutic (C) and amniotic fluid, diagnostic (U). Since there is no indication that the fluid was drained for diagnostic purposes, i.e., a laboratory analysis, the correct qualifier is C, amniotic fluid, therapeutic. The final code is 10907ZC.

Chapter Summary

In ICD-10-PCS, Obstetrics is given the section character assignment of 1 and includes delivery and abortion codes. The codes in section 1 are only for delivery, abortion, or procedures performed on the fetus during delivery. Rather than use the term *fetus* or *baby*, this section uses the term products of conception, which refers not only to the fetus, but to the placenta, amniotic sac, and other structures that are associated with pregnancy. Codes for any treatment or procedures performed on the pregnant female, even during delivery, such as an episiotomy, are actually found in Section 0, Medical and Surgical. Obstetrics section codes are only for the products of conception (including, but not limited to, the fetus). For the purposes of this chapter, the term *fetus* or *baby* will be used, in lieu of *products of conception*, where appropriate.

When coding for the Obstetrics section, coding is done only for procedures (root operations) performed on the fetus, or other products of conception. There is only one body system character assignment for Obstetrics, 0, which is pregnancy, therefore, every code within this section will start with 10. The rest of the character value assignments for characters three through seven are in Table 7-1.

There are 11 root operations used in the Obstetrics section. The root operations and their values are: Change (2), Drainage (9), Abortion (A), Extraction (D), Delivery (E), Insertion (F), Inspection (J), Removal (P), Reposition (5), Resection (T), and Transplantation (Y).

Root Operation A, Abortion, is defined as artificially eliminating a pregnancy. This root operation is subdivided according to whether an additional device such as a laminaria or abortifacient is used; or whether the abortion was performed by mechanical means. There are several types of abortion, including spontaneous and induced. An incomplete abortion is a miscarriage in which part, but not all, of the uterine contents are expelled. A missed abortion is also a miscarriage, however, in a missed abortion the fetus and other products of conception can remain in the uterus for four or more weeks. Two alternative terms for missed abortion are miscarriage or spontaneous abortion, in that it occurs without provocation. The last type is an induced abortion, which is the deliberate termination of a pregnancy.

The definition of root operation Delivery (E) is assisting the passage of the products of conception from the genital canal. This root operation is used only for manually assisted, vaginal delivery of the products of conception. With the Delivery root operation, there is no differentiation in the procedure coding between live-born or stillborn, nor does the trimester or gestational age matter when using it. If instruments such as forceps or vacuum aspirators are used, or if a cesarean delivery is performed, then the procedure is not coded to Delivery, but rather to root operation Extraction, defined as pulling out all or a portion of a body part.

There are only three body part values for character 4 in the Obstetrics Section. They are products of conception (0), products of conception, retained (1), and products of conception, ectopic (2).

A vertex presentation is when the fetus descends into the vaginal canal head first and face down. If no instruments are used to deliver the baby, the root operation for a vertex presentation is Delivery (E). A breech presentation, on the other hand, is when the baby's buttocks present first instead of the head. Using a technique called a version, an obstetrician may attempt to turn the baby to a head-down position. There are three types of breech presentation. In a frank breech, the baby's legs are folded up against its body. In a complete breech, the baby's legs are crossed under and in front of the body, and in a footling breech, one or both legs are positioned to enter the birth canal.

In the root operation Extraction (D), the qualifiers 3–5 all describe types of forceps deliveries. The ACOG provides specific criteria for these types of forceps deliveries:

- Low forceps (Qualifier 3): The leading point of the fetal skull is at a station greater than or equal to 2 cm and is not on the pelvic floor; any degree of rotation may be present.

- Mid forceps (Qualifier 4): The station is above 2 cm, but the head is engaged.

- High forceps (Qualifier 5): The head is not engaged.

A vacuum-assisted birth is a newer method of delivering a baby, and is considered a gentler alternative to forceps. Similar to forceps deliveries, vacuum-assisted births can only be used with a fully dilated cervix and a well-descended head. A cesarean section, also called a c-section, is a surgical procedure in which an incision is made through a woman's abdomen and uterus to deliver her baby. There are three types of c-sections, indicated by the qualifier values 0–2:

- Character 0: Classical

  - The classical cesarean section involves a midline longitudinal incision, which allows a larger space to deliver the baby.

- Character 1: Low cervical

  - A surgical procedure to deliver a baby through a transverse incision in the thin supracervical part of the lower uterine segment, behind the bladder and the bladder flap.

- Character 2: Extraperitoneal

  - An extraperitoneal cesarean section is a method for surgically delivering a baby through an incision in the lower uterine segment without entering the peritoneal cavity. The uterus is approached through the paravesical space. Paravesical means around the bladder. The paravesical space (also known as perivesical space) is the space under and around the bladder.

A salpingostomy is a surgical incision into a fallopian tube. This procedure may be done to repair a damaged tube or to remove an ectopic pregnancy (one that occurs outside of the uterus). During a normal pregnancy, the fertilized egg passes from the fallopian tubes into the uterus and then implants into the lining of the uterus. If the fertilized egg implants anywhere outside of the uterus, it is called an ectopic (or tubal) pregnancy. The majority of ectopic pregnancies occur in the fallopian tubes, but they may also occur in the uterine muscle, the abdomen, the ovaries, and rarely, the cervix. In ICD-10-PCS, the root operation is Extraction (D), since the objective of the salpingostomy is to extract an ectopic pregnancy (body part 2, products of conception, ectopic).

Chapter Review

Matching

Instructions: Match the term to its definition.

_____ **1.** Abortion

_____ **2.** Delivery

_____ 3. Laminaria

_____ 4. frank breech

_____ 5. footling breech

_____ 6. Abortifacient

_____ 7. Ectopic

_____ 8. Incomplete abortion

_____ 9. Products of conception

_____ 10. Mechanical means

_____ 11. Version

a. One or both legs are positioned to enter the birth canal.

b. Root operation A in the Obstetrics section. Artificially eliminating a pregnancy.

c. Technique used by an obstetrician may attempt to turn a breech presentation baby to a (normal) vertex or head down position.

d. In the Obstetrics section, these are instruments such as forceps, cervical dilators, vacuum aspiration, or curettes used to perform a dilatation and curettage (D&C) during delivery or abortion.

e. Outside the uterus, as in an ectopic pregnancy where the development of the fetus occurs in the fallopian tubes, ovaries, or even the cervix, rather than in the uterus.

f. Root operation E in the Obstetrics section. It is defined as assisting the passage of the products of conception from the genital canal.

g. A miscarriage, in which part, but not all of the uterine contents are expelled.

h. A small rod-shaped piece of dried seaweed. When placed within the cervix, a laminaria causes it to gradually dilate (widen). The species of seaweed serving this purpose is _Laminaria digitata_.

i. The baby's legs are folded up against its body

j. The human fetus, placenta, amniotic sac, and other structures associated with pregnancy and childbirth

k. Any substance that causes pregnancy to end prematurely and causes an abortion

Short Answer

Instructions: List the root operation for the following procedures

1. Rupture of amniotic sac membrane for therapeutic drainage of amniotic fluid

_____

2. Low cervical cesarean section _____

3. Exchange of malfunctioning monitoring electrode _____

4. Fetal spinal tap _____

5. Assisting in the passage of fetus from the vaginal cavity _____

6. Percutaneous endoscopic repair of septal rupture _____

7. Excision of all products of conception in ectopic pregnancy_____

8. Repair of episiotomy tear (Repair) _____

9. Hysterectomy (Resection) _____

10. Manual change of breech presentation to vertex presentation (Reposition) _____
_____

Coding Practice

Instructions: Code the following procedures

1. Transvaginal abortion using vacuum aspiration technique _____

2. Manually-assisted delivery _____

3. Fetal spinal tap, open _____

4. Amniocentesis, diagnostic, percutaneous _____

5. Percutaneous therapeutic drainage of amniotic fluid from amniotic sac _____
_____

6. Vaginal extraction of retained fetus and placenta after spontaneous abortion _____
_____

7. Medication induced abortion after insertion of laminaria in cervix _____
_____

8. Endoscopic assisted extraction of ectopic pregnancy _____

9. Cutting out entire ectopic pregnancy from fallopian tube, open, endoscopic-assisted _____
_____

10. Percutaneous endoscopic repair of mitral valve, in vitro fetus _____

11. Transvaginal abortion using vacuum aspiration technique_____

12. External visualization of fetus _____

13. Diagnostic amniocentesis, percutaneous, amniotic fluid _____

14. C-section, low cervical, opening _____

15. Removal ectopic pregnancy, open (*Hint:* Resection) _____

Placement, Administration, Monitoring & Measuring Sections

Learning Objectives

At the conclusion of this chapter, the learner should be able to:

- Understand terms used in the Placement section and identify new character values
- Identify the Body System, Root Operation, Body Parts, Approach, Device, and Qualifiers used in the Placement section
- Understand the guidelines that impact code selection in the Placement section
- Differentiate how the root operations are used in the Placement section, and how to apply the correct Body Part, Approach, Device, and Qualifier for each root operation
- Know how to use the Index and Tables to select the correct code from the Placement section
- Understand terms used in the Administration section and identify new character values
- Identify the Body System, Root Operation, Body Parts, Approach, Device, and Qualifiers used in the Administration section
- Understand the guidelines that impact code selection in the Administration section
- Differentiate how the root operations are used in the Administration section, and how to apply the correct Body Part, Approach, Device, and Qualifier for each root operation
- Know how to use the Index and Tables to select the correct code from the Administration section
- Understand terms used in the Measurement and Monitoring section and identify new character values
- Identify the Body Systems, Root Operations, Body Parts, Approaches, Functions or Devices, and Qualifiers used in the Measurement and Monitoring section
- Differentiate between physiological systems and physiological devices as used in the Measurement and Monitoring section
- Understand the guidelines that impact code selection in the Measurement and Monitoring section

- Differentiate how the root operations are used in the Measurement and Monitoring section, and how to apply the correct Body Part, Approach, Device, and Qualifier for each root operation
- Know how to use the Index and Tables to select the correct code from the Measurement and Monitoring section

Key Terms and Definitions

Acuity	Keenness or acuteness, especially in the senses (vision, smell) or thought.
Antiarrhythmic	A drug used to treat an abnormal heart rhythm.
Antineoplastic	Inhibiting or preventing the growth or development of malignant cells.
Autologous	Coming from one's own body (self).
Brachytherapy	Radiation treatment given by placing radioactive material directly in or near the target, which is often a tumor. Brachytherapy for prostate cancer, for example, is also called interstitial radiation therapy or seed implantation. In brachytherapy for prostate cancer, radioactive seeds are implanted in the prostate. The seeds might be titanium-encased pellets containing the radioisotope iodine-125.
Compression	Root operation 1 in Placement section. Defined as putting pressure on a body region.
Conductivity	The ability of a physiological system to conduct electricity, heat, fluid, or sound.
Contractility	The capability or quality of shrinking or contracting, especially by muscle fibers.
Contrast	A radiopaque substance injected into a part of the body, as the stomach or duodenum, to provide a contrasting background for the tissues in an x-ray or fluoroscopic examination.
Dialysate	A chemical bath used in dialysis to draw fluids and toxins out of the bloodstream and supply electrolytes and other chemicals to the bloodstream.
Dressing	Root operation 2 in the Placement section. Putting material on a body region for protection.
Holter® monitor	Device worn on a strap or belt around the waist. Its electrodes from the monitor are placed on specific areas of the chest. During the prescribed time period, the monitor records the heart and pulse rates, and electrical activity.
Immobilization	Root operation 3 in Placement section. Limiting or preventing motion of a body region.
Injection	The forcing or administering of a liquid into a part, as into the subcutaneous tissues, the vascular tree, or an organ.
Interleukin-2	A chemical messenger or substance that can improve the body's response to disease. It stimulates the growth of certain disease-fighting blood cells in the immune system. Also called IL-2.
Intermittent pressure device	An instrument which increases and decreases pressure intermittently, such as those used to obtain lower extremity segmented blood pressures.
Intradermal	Injection made into the dermis or substance of the skin.
Intramuscular	Injection made into a muscle.

Intravenous	Injection one made into a vein.
Introduction	Root Operation 0 in the Administration section. Putting in or on a therapeutic, diagnostic, nutritional, physiological, or prophylactic substance except blood or blood products.
Irrigation	Root Operation 1 in the Administration section. Putting in or on a cleansing substance.
Measurement	Determining the level of function of a physiological or physical system at a set point in time.
Metabolism	Complete set of chemical reactions that happen in human beings to maintain life.
Monitoring	Determining the level of function of a physiological or physical system over a specific period of time.
Monoclonal antibody	An antibody produced by a single clone cells, and used as a pure homogeneous type of antibody. Monoclonal antibodies can be made in large amounts in the laboratory and are a cornerstone of immunology.
Motility	Spontaneous movement, i.e., the automatic stomach contractions that move the food content along from the stomach into the intestines.
Natriuretic	An agent causing natriuresis, the excretion of an excessively large amount of sodium in the urine.
Nonautologous	Coming from a source other than one's own body.
Oxazolidinones	A type of antibacterial, effective by both the intravenous and oral route of administration.
Packing	Root operation 4 in Placement section. Putting material in a body region or orifice.
Radioisotope	A version of a chemical element that has an unstable nucleus and emits radiation. Radioisotopes have important uses in medical diagnosis, treatment, and research, some types include radioactive iodine, Iodine-131, and MIBG (iodine-131-meta-iodobenzylguanidine).
Recombinant bone morphogenetic protein	A protein created by recombinant DNA technology that induces bone formation.
Recombinant human-activated protein C	A vitamin K–dependent plasma protein that, when activated by thrombin, inhibits clotting.
Saturation	The level at which a chemical compound, gas, vapor, or solution, unites with any other substance. For example, the level (amount) of gases (oxygen, nitrogen, hydrogen) found within human arterial blood.
Stereotactic apparatus	An external, three-dimensional frame, for example a halo frame for immobilizing the head.
Subcutaneous	Injection made into the subcutaneous tissues.
Substance	Character 6 value in Administration section. The material, medication, or other substance being introduced to the body.
Traction	Root operation 6 in Placement section. Exerting a pulling force on a body region in a distal direction.
Transfusion	Root Operation 2 in the Administration section. Putting in blood or blood products.
Vasopressor	Stimulating contraction of the muscular tissue of the capillaries and arteries.

Introduction

Three sections of the ICD-10-PCS are covered in this chapter:

- Placement

- Administration

- Measurement and Monitoring

The Placement section describes procedures during which a device is put on or into a body region. Placement section contains seven root operations: Change, Compression, Dressing, Immobilization, Packing, Removal, and Traction, and placement codes always begin with the number 2. The approach is always external for Placement section codes, and any devices, such as splints, casts, braces, or traction devices, are identified in the sixth character, in the device column of a Placement table.

The Administration section is used to report procedures where therapeutic, prophylactic, protective, diagnostic, nutritive, or physiological substances are put into or on the body. These include transfusions, electrolytes and water infusions, heat or cold therapy, and many others.

The Measurement and Monitoring (4A0-4B0) section presents procedures that determine the level of a physiological or physical function, such as measuring or monitoring cardiac output. The body system, approach, function and devices, and qualifiers for each of the root operations in these three sections will be covered in detail.

Placement Section (2W0–2W6 and 2Y0–2Y5)

Placement section codes represent procedures for putting a device in or on a body region for the purpose of protection, immobilization, stretching, compression, or packing. It includes only those procedures that can be performed without making an incision or puncture. The Placement section character value is 2, which will always be the first character of a Placement code. There are two body systems character values for this section. Body system character W represents anatomical regions, and body system character value Y represents anatomical orifices. The letter W or Y will always be the second character of a Placement code. In the ICD-10-PCS, there are two Placement sections. The first is *Placement Section, anatomical regions*, represented by code range 2W0 through 2W6. The second is *Placement Section, anatomical orifices*. The codes for that section range from 2Y0 through 2Y5. The primary difference between the two are the body parts included within each. In the first section, the body part values identify a body region, i.e., upper leg or wrist. In the anatomical orifices portion of the Placement section, they identify natural body openings, i.e., the ear or vagina.

Placement Section, Anatomical Regions (2W0–2W6)

Body System character W represents the Placement section (2) anatomical regions (W). A code from *Placement section, anatomical regions,* will always begin with 2W as the first two character values.

Root Operations

The root operations in the Placement section include only those procedures that are performed without making an incision or a puncture. The root operations Change and Removal are in this section, as well as several new root operations—Compression, Dressing, Immobilization, Packing, and Traction. The definitions and objectives of the Change and Removal root operations are the same as they were for all sections within the ICD-10-PCS coding manual but the character values are different. Change is now character value 0, and Removal is character value 5. The definitions of all the root operations and the character values for each one are provided below. The new root operations are in bold font for easy recognition.

- Change (0): Taking out or off a device from a body part and putting back in an identical or similar device in or on the same body part without cutting or puncturing the skin or mucous membrane (Figure 8-1)
- Removal (5): Taking out or off a device from a body part (Figure 8-2)
- **Compression** (1): Putting pressure on a body region (Figure 8-3)
- **Dressing** (2): Putting material on a body region for protection (Figure 8-4)
- **Immobilization** (3): Limiting or preventing motion of a body region (Figure 8-5)
- **Packing** (4): Putting material in a body region or orifice (Figure 8-6)
- **Traction** (6): Exerting a pulling force on a body region in a distal direction (Figure 8-7)

Body System/Regions

In Placement, the character 4 title (name) is changed from Body Parts to Body System/Region. Table 8-1 describes the anatomical regions used for all root operations in the Placement section (2), Body System, anatomical regions (W).

Section	2	Placement
Body System	W	Anatomical Regions
Operation	0	Change: Taking out or off a device from a body part and putting back an identical or similar device in or on the same body part without cutting or puncturing the skin or a mucous membrane

Body Region	Approach	Device	Qualifier
0 Head	X External	0 Traction Apparatus 1 Splint 2 Cast 3 Brace 4 Bandage 5 Packing Material 6 Pressure Dressing 7 Intermittent Pressure Device 8 Stereotactic Apparatus Y Other Device	Z No Qualifier
1 Face	X External	0 Traction Apparatus 1 Splint 2 Cast 3 Brace 4 Bandage 5 Packing Material 6 Pressure Dressing 7 Intermittent Pressure Device 9 Wire Y Other Device	Z No Qualifier

Figure 8-1 Excerpt from Root Operation Change in Placement Section

Section	2	Placement
Body System	W	Anatomical Regions
Operation	5	Removal: Taking out or off a device from a body part

Body Region	Approach	Device	Qualifier
0 Head	**X** External	**0** Traction Apparatus **1** Splint **2** Cast **3** Brace **4** Bandage **5** Packing Material **6** Pressure Dressing **7** Intermittent Pressure Device **8** Stereotactic Apparatus **Y** Other Device	**Z** No Qualifier
1 Face	**X** External	**0** Traction Apparatus **1** Splint **2** Cast **3** Brace **4** Bandage **5** Packing Material **6** Pressure Dressing **7** Intermittent Pressure Device **9** Wire **Y** Other Device	**Z** No Qualifier

© Cengage Learning 2013

Figure 8-2 Root Operation Removal in Placement Section

Section	2	Placement
Body System	W	Anatomical Regions
Operation	1	Compression: Putting pressure on a body region

Body Region	Approach	Device	Qualifier
0 Head **1** Face **2** Neck **3** Abdominal Wall **4** Chest Wall **5** Back **6** Inguinal Region, Right **7** Inguinal Region, Left **8** Upper Extremity, Right **9** Upper Extremity, Left **A** Upper Arm, Right **B** Upper Arm, Left **C** Lower Arm, Right **D** Lower Arm, Left **E** Hand, Right **F** Hand, Left **G** Thumb, Right **H** Thumb, Left **J** Finger, Right **K** Finger, Left **L** Lower Extremity, Right **M** Lower Extremity, Left **N** Upper Leg, Right **P** Upper Leg, Left **Q** Lower Leg, Right **R** Lower Leg, Left **S** Foot, Right **T** Foot, Left **U** Toe, Right **V** Toe, Left	**X** External	**6** Pressure Dressing **7** Intermittent Pressure Device	**Z** No Qualifier

© Cengage Learning 2013

Figure 8-3 Root Operation Compression in Placement Section

Section	2	Placement
Body System	W	Anatomical Regions
Operation	4	Packing: Putting material in a body region or orifice

Body Region	Approach	Device	Qualifier
0 Head **1** Face **2** Neck **3** Abdominal Wall **4** Chest Wall **5** Back **6** Inguinal Region, Right **7** Inguinal Region, Left **8** Upper Extremity, Right **9** Upper Extremity, Left **A** Upper Arm, Right **B** Upper Arm, Left **C** Lower Arm, Right **D** Lower Arm, Left **E** Hand, Right **F** Hand, Left **G** Thumb, Right **H** Thumb, Left **J** Finger, Right **K** Finger, Left **L** Lower Extremity, Right **M** Lower Extremity, Left **N** Upper Leg, Right **P** Upper Leg, Left **Q** Lower Leg, Right **R** Lower Leg, Left **S** Foot, Right **T** Foot, Left **U** Toe, Right **V** Toe, Left	**X** External	**5** Packing Material	**Z** No Qualifier

Figure 8-6 Root Operation Packing in Placement Section

Except for casts for fractures and dislocations, the devices in the Placement section are considered "off the shelf" materials. In other words, there is no extensive design, fabrication, or fittings required for these devices. If design, fabrication, or fitting device descriptions are part of the medical documentation, then codes would be selected from the Rehabilitation section, not the Placement section. Table 8-2 lists the devices available for each root operation and/or body part.

A **stereotactic apparatus** (Figure 8-8) is an external, three-dimensional frame—for example, a halo frame for immobilizing the head. To code the application of a halo frame, the objective is immobilization. The root operation would be 3. While both the head and neck are immobilized by the halo frame, the body system/region would be determined from the medical documentation. If for example, the halo frame is applied to immobilize a fracture of the neck, the body part character value would be 2, neck. If the halo frame was used to immobilize the head due to a skull fracture, the body part character value would be 0, *head*. In most but not all instances, the body part used for application of a stereotactic apparatus would be for cervical vertebra fractures or injuries, which would indicate 2, *neck*, as the body part character value to use.

An **Intermittent pressure device** is an instrument that increases and decreases pressure intermittently, such as the sphygmomanometer instrument used to obtain segmented blood pressures to increase poor cardiac output. In patients with poor cardiac output or reduced peripheral blood

Section	**2**	Placement
Body System	**W**	Anatomical Regions
Operation	**6**	Traction: Exerting a pulling force on a body region in a distal direction

Body Region	Approach	Device	Qualifier
0 Head **1** Face **2** Neck **3** Abdominal Wall **4** Chest Wall **5** Back **6** Inguinal Region, Right **7** Inguinal Region, Left **8** Upper Extremity, Right **9** Upper Extremity, Left **A** Upper Arm, Right **B** Upper Arm, Left **C** Lower Arm, Right **D** Lower Arm, Left **E** Hand, Right **F** Hand, Left **G** Thumb, Right **H** Thumb, Left **J** Finger, Right **K** Finger, Left **L** Lower Extremity, Right **M** Lower Extremity, Left **N** Upper Leg, Right **P** Upper Leg, Left **Q** Lower Leg, Right **R** Lower Leg, Left **S** Foot, Right **T** Foot, Left **U** Toe, Right **V** Toe, Left	**X** External	**0** Traction Apparatus **Z** No Device	**Z** No Qualifier

Figure 8-7 Excerpt from Root Operation Traction in Placement Section

flow, sphygomomanometers are wrapped around the top of each leg, as close as possible to the inguinal area. The sphygmomanometers are inflated, and at specific intervals, deflated, to simulate and stimulate circulation to the lower extremities. Let's use the example *application of intermittent pressure sphygmomanometer to left upper leg*. The objective is (intermittent) compression, which is root operation 1. The body system/region is P, upper leg, left. Looking at Figure 8-3, the device character for intermittent pressure device in root operation Compression is character value 7. The code is 2W1PX7Z, broken down as follows:

2–Section: Placement

W–Body System: Anatomical Regions

1–Root Operation: Compression

P–Body Part: Left Upper Leg

X–Approach: External

7–Device: Intermittent Pressure Device

Z–Qualifier: No qualifier

In root operation Traction (6), there are two device character values. If manual traction was applied to a body part, but no traction apparatus was applied, use character value Z to indicate there was no device used.

Table 8-1 Body System/Region Values and Descriptions in Placement Section

Root Operations	Body System/Region Value	Body System/Regions
All Root Operations	0	Head
0–Change	1	Face
1–Compression	2	Neck
2–Dressing	3	Abdominal wall
3–Immobilization	4	Chest wall
4–Packing	5	Back
5–Removal	6	Inguinal region, right
6–Traction	7	Inguinal region, left
	8	Upper extremity, right
	9	Upper extremity, left
	A	Upper arm, right
	B	Upper arm, left
	C	Lower arm, right
	D	Lower arm, left
	E	Hand, right
	F	Hand, left
	G	Thumb, right
	H	Thumb, left
	J	Finger, right
	K	Finger, left
	L	Lower extremity, right
	M	Lower extremity, left
	N	Upper leg, right
	P	Upper leg, left
	Q	Lower leg, right
	R	Lower leg, left
	S	Foot, right
	T	Foot, left
	U	Toe, right
	V	Toe, left

This character would be used, for example, to designate manual traction exerted on a closed wrist dislocation to realign the bones. In all other instances, the traction apparatus character value 0 would be used, as long as the device is applied without cutting or puncturing the skin or mucous membranes.

Qualifiers

There are no qualifier characters specified in the Placement section; therefore, the qualifier character value is always Z, no qualifier. Review Figure 8-1 through Figure 8-7 and note that the qualifier value for all root operations is Z, which indicates there are no qualifiers used in the Placement section, Anatomical Regions body system.

Table 8-2 Devices for Root Operation and/or Body Part in Placement Section

Root Operation	Body Part	Device
0–Change 5–Removal	0–Head	0–Traction Apparatus 1–Splint 2–Cast 3–Brace 4–Bandage 5–Packing Material 6–Pressure Dressing 7–Intermittent Pressure Device 8–Stereotactic device Y–Other device
	1–Face	0–Traction Apparatus 1–Splint 2–Cast 3–Brace 4–Bandage 5–Packing Material 6–Pressure Dressing 7–Intermittent Pressure Device 9–Wire Y–Other Device
	All Remaining Body System/Regions 2–9, A–H, J–N, and P–V	0–Traction Apparatus 1–Splint 2–Cast 3–Brace 4–Bandage 5–Packing Material 6–Pressure Dressing 7–Intermittent Pressure Device Y–Other device
1–Compression	All Body System/Regions 0–9, A–H, J–N, and P–V	6–Pressure dressing 7–Intermittent pressure device
2–Dressing	All Body System/Regions 0–9, A–H, J–N, and P–V	4–Bandage
	0–Head	1–Splint 2–Cast 3–Brace 8–Stereotactic apparatus Y–Other Device
	1–Face	1–Splint 2–Cast 3–Brace 9–Wire Y–Other Device
	All Remaining Body System/Regions	1–Splint 2–Cast
	2–9, A–H, J–N, and P–V	3–Brace Y–Other device
4–Packing	All Body System/Regions 0–9, A–H, J–N, and P–V	5–Packing Material
5–Traction	All Body System/Regions 0–9, A–H, J–N, and P–V	0–Traction apparatus Z–No Device

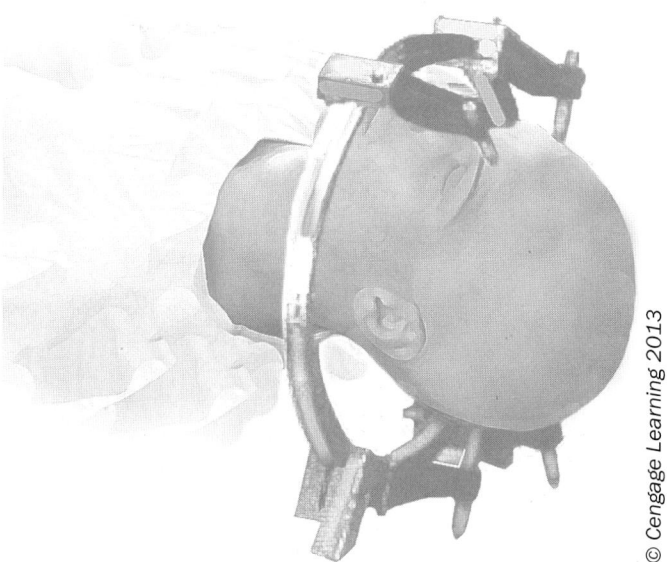

© Cengage Learning 2013

Figure 8-8 Illustration of a Stereotactic Apparatus/Frame

Using ICD-10-PCS Code Book

As always, the first step in coding is to abstract the procedural statement from the medical record. The next step is to determine the main and modifying terms. The main term will be one of the following root operations: Change, Removal, Compression, Dressing, Immobilization, Packing, or Traction. The modifying term will be either *by Body System* or *by Body Part/Region*, with a subterm that will be the general region or specific body part value.

For example, look at Figure 8-9, an excerpt from the Index for the root operation (main term) Dressing. The main term is Dressing, and indented below are the specific body parts, beginning with *foot* and ending with *right toe*. Using the procedure *application of bandage to left hand*, and after determining the objective was to apply a dressing, the root operation will be Dressing. In Figure 8-9, under the main term Dressing, and the modifying term *by Body Part*, the subterm *hand* is found. Here, the Index indicates 2W2 as the appropriate Table. Moving to the Table for the root operation Dressing (Figure 8-4), the code would be 2W2FX4Z, which fully defines the procedural statement, as follows:

2–Section: Placement

W–Body System: Anatomical Region

2–Root Operation: Dressing

F–Body Part: Hand, left

X–Approach: External

4–Device: Bandage

Z–Qualifier: No qualifier

Placement Section, Anatomical Orifices (2Y0–2Y5)

Body system character Y represents the Placement section anatomical orifices. A code from Placement section, anatomical orifices, will always begin with 2Y as the first two characters.

Look at Figure 8-10. In this section, note there are no changes to the approach or qualifier values from the Anatomical Regions section. The approach will always be External and use the character value X. There are also no qualifiers unique to this section, which means the character value will always be Z. Packing material, character value 5, is the only device character for each of the three root

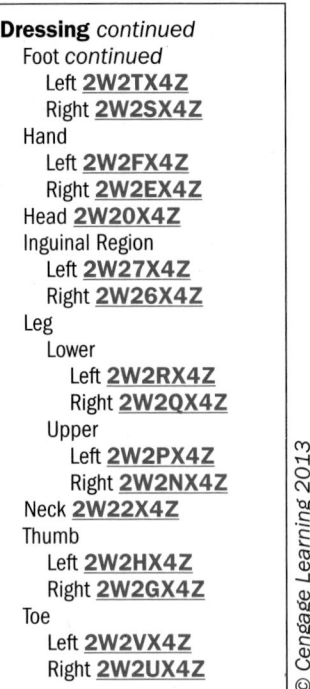

```
Dressing continued
    Foot continued
        Left 2W2TX4Z
        Right 2W2SX4Z
    Hand
        Left 2W2FX4Z
        Right 2W2EX4Z
    Head 2W20X4Z
    Inguinal Region
        Left 2W27X4Z
        Right 2W26X4Z
    Leg
        Lower
            Left 2W2RX4Z
            Right 2W2QX4Z
        Upper
            Left 2W2PX4Z
            Right 2W2NX4Z
    Neck 2W22X4Z
    Thumb
        Left 2W2HX4Z
        Right 2W2GX4Z
    Toe
        Left 2W2VX4Z
        Right 2W2UX4Z
```

© Cengage Learning 2013

Figure 8-9 Alphabetic Index Excerpt for Root Operation Dressing in Placement Section

Section	2	Placement
Body System	Y	Anatomical Orifices
Operation	0	Change: Taking out or off a device from a body part and putting back an identical or similar device in or on the same body part without cutting or puncturing the skin or a mucous membrane

Body Region	Approach	Device	Qualifier
0 Mouth and Pharynx **1** Nasal **2** Ear **3** Anorectal **4** Female Genital Tract **5** Urethra	**X** External	**5** Packing Material	**Z** No Qualifier

Section	2	Placement
Body System	Y	Anatomical Orifices
Operation	4	Packing: Putting material in a body region or orifice

Body Region	Approach	Device	Qualifier
0 Mouth and Pharynx **1** Nasal **2** Ear **3** Anorectal **4** Female Genital Tract **5** Urethra	**X** External	**5** Packing Material	**Z** No Qualifier

Section	2	Placement
Body System	Y	Anatomical Orifices
Operation	5	Removal: Taking out or off a device from a body part

Body Region	Approach	Device	Qualifier
0 Mouth and Pharynx **1** Nasal **2** Ear **3** Anorectal **4** Female Genital Tract **5** Urethra	**X** External	**5** Packing Material	**Z** No Qualifier

© Cengage Learning 2013

Figure 8-10a-c Examples from Placement Section of ICD-10-PCS Coding Manual Illustrating Root Operations(8-10a) Root Operation Change; (8-10b) Root Operation Packing; and (8-10c) Root Operation Removal

operations in this section. There are three root operations, Change (0), Packing (4), and Removal (5). The body system/regions are the same in all three root operation Tables and include:

0–Mouth and Pharynx

1–Nasal

2–Ear

3–Anorectal

4–Female Genital Tract

5–Urethra

As would be expected in this section, the body regions all relate to an opening or orifice in the body. Coding from this Section of the ICD-10-PCS is relatively straightforward. For example, *changing the packing material in the vaginal canal*, would be coded 2Y04X5Z, broken down as follows:

2–Section: Placement

Y–Body System: Anatomical Orifices

0–Root Operation: Change

4–Body Part: Female Genital Tract

X–Approach: External

5–Device: Packing Material

Z–Qualifier: No qualifier

When searching in the Index, look under the root operation for the main term Change, Packing or Removal. Then, find the specific orifice under the modifying term *by Body Region*. In the example *packing applied to nasal cavity*, the Index listing for Packing, by body region *nasal* is 2Y41. In the root operation Table for 2Y41, the remaining code character values would be X (External approach), device value 5 (Packing Material), and Z, no qualifier. The code for *packing applied to nasal cavity* is 2Y41X5Z.

Let's Review 8–1:

Determine the root operation, and code the following procedures:

1. Cast applied to left lower arm _____

2. Application of packing material to chest wall _____

3. Removal of cast from entire right leg _____

4. Replacing broken cast on left lower arm _____

5. Manual traction for displaced rotator cuff of right shoulder _____

Administration Section (302-3E1)

The administration section is used to code procedures that *put in or on the body a therapeutic, prophylactic, protective, diagnostic, nutritional, or physiological substance*. The section includes administration of transfusions, infusions, and injections, as well as irrigation and tattooing procedures used in Radiation Oncology. Administration section codes always begin with a first character value of 3. There are three body system (character 2) values: indwelling catheter (C), physiological systems and anatomical regions (E), and circulatory (0). Body system value C, indwelling catheter, is used in only one Table with the root operation Irrigation. The Circulatory body system (character value 0) is used only for transfusion procedures and uses only one root operation: Transfusion (character value 2). The first two characters for Administration section codes will always be either 3C, 3E, or 30:

- 3E represents the Administration section, and Body System physiological systems and anatomical regions, found in all the Introduction root operations Tables, and in one of two Irrigation root operation Tables.
- 3C represents Body System Indwelling Catheter, found only in one Administration Table, with only one Root Operation, which is Irrigation
- 30 represents the Body System Circulatory, found only in the Table with Root Operation Transfusion.

There are some new root operations in the Administration section, and new terminology for the approach and qualifier values. The sixth character changes as well, from Device to Substance, to identify what substance is being administered.

Root Operations in the Administration Section

There are three root operations in the Administration section: Introduction, Irrigation, and Transfusion. The root operation character values and definitions are:

0–**Introduction:** Putting in or on a therapeutic, diagnostic, nutritional, physiological, or prophylactic substance except blood or blood products (Figure 8-11). This is the largest portion of the Administration section.

1–**Irrigation:** Putting in or on a cleansing substance. There are two tables in which Root Operation Irrigation appears. (1) Body System Indwelling Catheter (value C) shown in Figure 8-12, and (2) Body System Physiological Systems and Anatomical Regions (Figure 8-13).

2–**Transfusion:** Putting in blood or blood products (Figure 8-14). There is only one Table in which Root Operation Transfusion appears, which is Circulatory (value 2).

Root operation introduction

The root operation Introduction is a large portion of the Administration section, and includes virtually all Body System/Regions and Approaches found in other Sections of the ICD-10-PCS coding manual. There are approximately 20 different substance character values and almost as many qualifier values. The definition of the Introduction root operation *is putting in or on a therapeutic, diagnostic, nutritional, physiological, or prophylactic substance except blood or blood products*. Blood and blood products administered use the root operation Transfusion, found in Table 302 (Administration (3), Circulatory System (0), Transfusion (2)).

Body System/Region in Introduction Root Operation The fourth character of an ICD-10-PCS code, as always, identifies the body system or body region. It identifies the site where the substance is administered, not the site where the substance takes effect. Sites include skin and mucous membrane, subcutaneous tissue, and muscle and usually involve an injection procedure. An **injection** is the forcing or administering of a liquid into a part, as into the subcutaneous tissues, the vascular tree, or an organ. There are four types of percutaneous injections, depending upon where the injection is administered:

Intradermal: into the dermis or skin

Subcutaneous: into the subcutaneous tissues

Intramuscular: into a muscle

Intravenous: into a vein

Arteries and Veins Body Systems/Regions The body system regions for arteries and veins are (1) peripheral artery, (2) central artery, (3) peripheral vein, and (4) central vein. The peripheral artery or

Section	**3**	Administration	
Body System	**E**	Physiological Systems and Anatomical Regions	
Operation	**0**	Introduction: Putting in or on a therapeutic, diagnostic, nutritional, physiological, or prophylactic substance except blood or blood products	

Body System/Region	Approach	Substance	Qualifier
0 Skin and Mucous Membranes	**X** External	**0** Antineoplastic	**5** Other Antineoplastic **M** Monoclonal Antibody
0 Skin and Mucous Membranes	**X** External	**2** Anti-infective	**8** Oxazolidinones **9** Other Anti-infective
0 Skin and Mucous Membranes	**X** External	**3** Anti-inflammatory **4** Serum, Toxoid and Vaccine **B** Local Anesthetic **K** Other Diagnostic Substance **M** Pigment **N** Analgesics, Hypnotics, Sedatives **T** Destructive Agent	**Z** No Qualifier
0 Skin and Mucous Membranes	**X** External	**G** Other Therapeutic Substance	**C** Other Substance
1 Subcutaneous Tissue	**3** Percutaneous	**0** Antineoplastic	**5** Other Antineoplastic **M** Monoclonal Antibody
1 Subcutaneous Tissue	**3** Percutaneous	**2** Anti-infective	**8** Oxazolidinones **9** Other Anti-infective
1 Subcutaneous Tissue	**3** Percutaneous	**3** Anti-inflammatory **4** Serum, Toxoid, and Vaccine **6** Nutritional Substance **7** Electrolytic and Water Balance Substance **B** Local Anesthetic **H** Radioactive Substance **J** Contrast Agent **K** Other Diagnostic Substance **N** Analgesics, Hypnotics, Sedatives **T** Destructive Agent	**Z** No Qualifier
1 Subcutaneous Tissue	**3** Percutaneous	**G** Other Therapeutic Substance	**C** Other Substance
1 Subcutaneous Tissue	**3** Percutaneous	**V** Hormone	**G** Insulin **J** Other Hormone
2 Muscle	**3** Percutaneous	**0** Antineoplastic	**5** Other Antineoplastic **M** Monoclonal Antibody
2 Muscle	**3** Percutaneous	**2** Anti-infective	**8** Oxazolidinones **9** Other Anti-infective

© Cengage Learning 2013

Figure 8-11 Excerpt from Root Operation Introduction in Administration Section

Section	**3**	Administration	
Body System	**C**	Indwelling Device	
Operation	**1**	Irrigation: Putting in or on a cleansing substance	

Body System / Region	Approach	Substance	Qualifier
Z None	**X** External	**8** Irrigating substance	**Z** No Qualifier

Figure 8-12 Excerpt from Root Operation Irrigation in Administration Section
© Cengage Learning 2013

Section	3	Administration
Body System	E	Physiological Systems and Anatomical Regions
Operation	1	Irrigation: Putting in or on a cleansing substance

Body System/Region	Approach	Substance	Qualifier
0 Skin and Mucous Membranes **C** Eye	**3** Percutaneous **X** External	**8** Irrigating Substance	**X** Diagnostic **Z** No Qualifier
9 Nose **B** Ear **F** Respiratory Tract **G** Upper GI **H** Lower GI **J** Biliary and Pancreatic Tract **K** Genitourinary Tract **N** Male Reproductive **P** Female Reproductive	**3** Percutaneous **7** Via Natural or Artificial Opening **8** Via Natural or Artificial Opening Endoscopic	**8** Irrigating Substance	**X** Diagnostic **Z** No Qualifier
L Pleural Cavity **Q** Cranial Cavity and Brain **R** Spinal Canal **S** Epidural Space **U** Joints **Y** Pericardial Cavity	**3** Percutaneous	**8** Irrigating Substance	**X** Diagnostic **Z** No Qualifier
M Peritoneal Cavity	**3** Percutaneous	**8** Irrigating Substance	**X** Diagnostic **Z** No Qualifier
M Peritoneal Cavity	**3** Percutaneous	**9** Dialysate	**Z** No Qualifier

© Cengage Learning 2013

Figure 8-13 Excerpt 2 from Root Operation Irrigation in Administration Section

vein is generally used when a substance is introduced locally, usually by injection, into an artery or vein. In general, any substance introduced into a peripheral artery or vein has a systemic effect. An example would be when an antineoplastic substance for chemotherapy is introduced into a peripheral artery or vein by a percutaneous approach.

Central arteries or veins are used when the site where the substance is introduced is distant from the point of entry. For example, the introduction of a substance directly at the site of a clot within an arter or vein using a catheter, is coded as an introduction of a thrombolytic substance into a central artery or vein by a percutaneous approach.

Approaches Used in the Administrative Section for All Three Root Operations

The approach (character 5) includes the same approach values as found in the Medical and Surgical section. The approach for intradermal, subcutaneous, and intramuscular injections is given the character value 7, percutaneous. Table 8-3 illustrates which approach values and definitions are used in the Administration section and indicates which root operations and body system/regions are used with each approach.

Many of the body system/regions overlap into several approach group categories because some of the sixth and seventh character values for substances and qualifiers require different approaches, depending upon the body system. For example, the approach to the cranial cavity and brain can be open, percutaneous, or via natural or artificial opening—but, it is not appropriate to use an External approach, even though it seems that an approach through the nasal cavities would be an external approach. However, that would actually use the via natural or artificial opening approach character value. Read the medical documentation carefully to determine the appropriate approach based on the root operation and body system/region documented.

Section	**3**	Administration
Body System	**0**	Circulatory
Operation	**2**	Transfusion: Putting in blood or blood products

Body System/Region	Approach	Substance	Qualifier
3 Peripheral Vein **4** Central Vein	**0** Open **3** Percutaneous	**A** Stem Cells, Embryonic	**Z** No Qualifier
3 Peripheral Vein **4** Central vein	**0** Open **3** Percutaneous	**G** Bone Marrow **H** Whole Blood **J** Serum Albumin **K** Frozen Plasma **L** Fresh Plasma **M** Plasma Cryoprecipitate **N** Red Blood Cells **P** Frozen Red Cells **Q** white Cells **R** Platelets **S** Globulin **T** Fibrinogen **V** Antihemophilic Factors **W** Factor IX **X** Stem Cells, Cord Blood **Y** Stem Cells, Hematopoietic	**0** Autologous **1** Nonautologous
5 Peripheral Artery **6** Central Artery	**0** Open **3** Percutaneous	**G** Bone Marrow **H** Whole Blood **J** Serum Albumin **K** Frozen Plasma **L** Fresh Plasma **M** Plasma Cryoprecipitate **N** Red Blood Cells **P** Frozen Red Cells **Q** White Cells **R** Platelets **S** Globulin **T** Fibrinogen **V** Antihemophilic Factors **W** Factor IX **X** Stem cells, Cord Blood **Y** Stem Cells, Hematopoietic	**0** Autologous **1** Nonautologous

© Cengage Learning 2013

Figure 8-14 Excerpt from Root Operation Transfusion in Administration Section

Substances Used in the Administration Section In the Administration section, the sixth character is defined as a **substance** rather than a device, as in previous sections. A substance is the material, medication, or other substance being introduced to the body. The sixth character specifies the substance being introduced. Anesthetic, contrast, dialysate, and blood products such as platelets, are a few of the substance materials included here.

Definitions of terms used in the substance column of the administration section The following are a few definitions of the substances listed in the Administration section Table substance column. When it is not possible to determine a specific substance, consult a pharmacology reference book or ask the documenting physician to clarify which substance character value is most appropriate to use:

- **Antineoplastic**: Inhibiting or preventing the growth or development of malignant cells.

- **Contrast:** A radiopaque substance injected into a part of the body, as the stomach or duodenum, to provide a contrasting background for the tissues in an x-ray or fluoroscopic examination.

Table 8-3 Approach Values and Definitions and Approaches Available with the Root Operations and Body System/Regions

Root Operation	Body System/Region	Approach
2-Transfusion	3-Peripheral vein 4-Central vein	0-Open 3-Percutaneous
	7-Products of conception, circulatory	0-Open 3-Percutaneous
1-Irrigation	Z-Whole body	X-External
0-Introduction	0-Skin and mucous membranes	X-External
	1-Subcutaneous tissue 2-Muscle A-Bone marrow L-Pleural cavity M-Peritoneal cavity Q-Cranial cavity and brain R-Spinal canal S-Epidural space T-Peripheral nerves and plexi U-Joints V-Bones W-Lymphatics X-Cranial nerves Y-Pericardial cavity	3-Percutaneous
	3-Peripheral vein 4-Central vein 5-Peripheral artery 6-Central artery Q-Cranial cavity and brain R-Spinal canal	0-Open 3-Percutaneous
	9-Nose B-Ear C-Eye D-Mouth and pharynx E-Products of conception F-Respiratory Tract G-Upper GI H-Lower GI J-Biliary and pancreatic tract K-Genitourinary tract N-Male reproductive P-Female reproductive	3-Percutaneous 7-Via natural or artificial opening X-External
	L-Pleural cavity M-Peritoneal cavity P-Female reproductive Q-Cranial cavity and brain R-Spinal canal	0-Open
	P-Female reproductive Q-Cranial cavity and brain R-Spinal canal S-Epidural space U-Joints Y-Pericardial cavity	3-Percutaneous 7-Via natural or artificial opening
	J-Biliary and pancreatic tract	3-Percutaneous 7-Via natural or artificial opening 8-Via natural or artificial opening, endoscopic

- **Antiarrhythmic:** A drug used to treat an abnormal heart rhythm.
- **Dialysate:** A chemical bath used in dialysis to draw fluids and toxins out of the bloodstream and supply electrolytes and other chemicals to the bloodstream.
- **Vasopressor:** Stimulating contraction of the muscular tissue of the capillaries and arteries.

Qualifiers used with root operation introduction There are quite a few qualifiers used with the root operation Introduction. Each qualifier is dependent upon the substance administered. Table 8-4 lists the substance values and the related qualifier(s).

Table 8-4 Substance Values and Related Qualifiers for Root Operation Introduction

Substance	Qualifier Description
0–Antineoplastic	2–High-dose interleukin-2 3–Low-dose interleukin-2 4–Liquid brachytherapy radioisotope 5–Other antineoplastic M–Monoclonal antibiody
2–Anti-infective	8–Oxazolidinones 9–Other anti-infective
3–Anti-inflammatory 4–Serum, toxoid, and vaccine 5–Adhesion barrier 6–Nutritional substance 7–Electrolytic and water balance substance A–Stem cells, embryonic B–Local anesthetic C–Regional anesthetic H–Radioactive substance J–Contrast agent K–Other diagnostic substance M–Pigment N–Analgesics, hypnotics, sedatives P–Platelet inhibitor R–Antirhythmic T–Destructive agents X–Vasopressor	Z–No qualifier
C–Other therapeutic substance	B–Recombinant bone morphogenetic protein C–Other substance N–Blood-brain barrier disruption
V–Hormone	G–Insulin H–Human B-type natriuretic J–Other hormone
E–Stem cells, somatic Q–Fertilized ovum U–Pancreatic islet cells	0–Autologous 1–Nonautologous
W–Immunotherapeutic	K–Immunostimulator L–Immunosuppressor
1–Thrombolytic	6–Recombinant human-activated protein C 7–Other thrombohemolytic
S–Gas	D–Nitric oxide F–Other gas

Qualifier terms and definitions

- **Interleukin-2:** A chemical messenger or substance that can improve the body's response to disease. It stimulates the growth of certain disease-fighting blood cells in the immune system. Also called IL-2.

- **Brachytherapy:** Radiation treatment given by placing radioactive material directly in or near the target, which is often a tumor. Brachytherapy for prostate cancer, for example, is also called interstitial radiation therapy or seed implantation. In brachytherapy for prostate cancer, radioactive seeds are implanted in the prostate. The seeds might be titanium-encased pellets containing the radioisotope iodine-125.

- **Radioisotope:** A version of a chemical element that has an unstable nucleus and emits radiation. Radioisotopes have important uses in medical diagnosis, treatment, and research, some types include radioactive iodine, Iodine-131, and MIBG (iodine-131-meta-iodobenzylguanidine).

- **Monoclonal antibiody** An antibody produced by a single clone cells, and used as a pure homogeneous type of antibody. Monoclonal antibodies can be made in large amounts in the laboratory and are a cornerstone of immunology.

- **Oxazolidinones**: A type of antibacterial, effective by both the intravenous and oral route of administration.

- **Recombinant bone morphogenetic protein**: A protein created by recombinant DNA technology that induces bone formation. Bone morphogenetic proteins (BMPs) are a group of growth factors originally used for their ability to induce the formation of bone and cartilage, but now considered to promote tissue growth throughout throughout the body.

- **Natriuretic:** An agent causing natriuresis, the excretion of an excessively large amount of sodium in the urine.

- **Recombinant human-activated protein C**: A vitamin K–dependent plasma protein that, when activated by thrombin, inhibits clotting.

Using ICD-10-PCS Code Book for Root Operation Introduction

Determining that a code might come from the Administration section is fairly straightforward, based on the section definition. Establishing the root operation Introduction is also relatively simple, based on the root operation definition. Where it gets tricky is in deciphering the appropriate approach, substance and qualifier, once the correct Table is found. First, remember that the Administration section is always 3, and that the root operation Introduction (value 0) is only found in Tables with the body system value E, Physiological Systems and Anatomical Regions. Therefore, the first three characters of the code will always be 3E0. In the Index, under the root operation Introduction, the first three characters of every body system listed are 3E0. The fourth character shown in the Index identifies the body part, system or region, i.e., ear (B), genitourinary tract (K), heart (8), and skin and mucous membranes (0).

Let's focus on the Index which leads to the 3E0 Table containing the root operation Introduction, and use the procedure *anti-inflammatory intramuscular injection*. After some practice, it will be automatic to remember that the objective of an injection is the introduction of a substance into the body, which makes the root operation Introduction. In Introduction, the modifying term is, as always, by body system, and in this example, the subterm will be *muscle* (it is an intramuscular injection). In the Index, the character value is 3E02.

Moving to the Index, and Table 3E0, the first column, Body System/Region muscle is found in four rows. The approach in all four rows is percutaneous, so we need to identify the substance and maybe even the qualifier before finding the correct row. The first two rows are shown in Figure 8-11. The first row lists the substance as antineoplastic—so this row can be ignored. The second row does include the substance anti-infective, but under the qualifier value, it lists oxazolidinones (8) and other anti-infective (9). The procedural statement does not include either qualifier. We can ignore the second row in Figure 8-11. Now look at Figure 8-15, which shows the two remaining rows containing the body system/region *muscle* in the 3E0 Table. In the first row, the Substance anti-infective is listed, and the qualifier

Section	3 Administration		
Body System	E Physiological Systems and Anatomical Regions		
Operation	0 Introduction: Putting in or on a therapeutic, diagnostic, nutritional, physiological, or prophylactic substance except blood or blood products		

Body System / Region	Approach	Substance	Qualifier
2 Muscle	3 Percutaneous	3 Anti-inflammatory 4 Serum, Toxoid and Vaccine 6 Nutritional Substance 7 Electrolytic and Water Balance Substance B Local Anesthetic H Radioactive Substance J Contrast Agent K Other Diagnostic Substance N Analgesics, Hypnotics, Sedatives T Destructive Agent	Z No Qualifier
2 Muscle	3 Percutaneous	G Other Therapeutic Substance	C Other Substance

© Cengage Learning 2013

Figure 8-15 Administration Table 3E0 Illustrating Body System/Region Muscle

value for the first row is Z, no qualifier. In the second row, the substance is C, other substance. Since the procedural statement *anti-inflammatory intramuscular injection* does not specify a qualifier, the most appropriate row is the first one in Figure 8-15. The code is 3E0233Z, as follows:

3–Section: Administrative

E–Body System: Physiological Systems and Anatomical Regions

0–Root Operation: Introduction

2–Body System/Region: Muscle

3–Approach: Percutaneous (injections are always either open or percutaneous, and the only option given in this row is percutaneous)

3–Substance: Anti-infective

Z–Qualifier: No qualifier

Changing the procedure *anti-inflammatory intramuscular injection* by adding the word *oxazolidinones* changes the row to the second row in Figure 8-11, because of the qualifier. The code would change to 3E02328, with the sixth character being anti-infective (2) and the seventh character qualifier 8 representing the *oxazolidinones*.

Root Operation Irrigation

There are two Irrigation Tables in the Tabular List based on Body System. Figure 8-12 is the Irrigation Table for the Body System titled Indwelling Catheter, which has a character value of C. There is only one Body System/Region, Approach, Substance, and Qualifier value in this Table:

- Body System/Region: Z, Whole Body
- Approach: X, External
- Substance, 8, Irrigating Substance
- Qualifier: Z, No qualifier

Do not be confused by the approach value here. The codes from this Table are used only for the irrigating substance, not the placement or insertion of the indwelling catheter. The procedure for inserting the catheter would be coded from the Medical and Surgical section. The irrigation procedure is coded from the Administration section.

Now, look at Figure 8-13. This is the second Irrigation root operation Table found in the Administration section. In this Irrigation root operation, the body system is not indwelling catheter (2), but rather physiological systems and anatomical regions (character value E). It is quite different from the first Irrigation root operation Table. There are more Body System/Region, Approach, Substance, and Qualifier character values, as shown in Table 8-5.

As shown in Figure 8-12, for root operation Irrigation (1) there is no qualifier when the body system value is C, Indwelling Device. In this Table, the seventh character will always be Z, indicating no qualifier is applicable. However, in Figure 8-13, where the body system value is E, *physiological systems and anatomic regions*, note that there is one additional qualifier, diagnostic, with a character value of X. If the substance irrigated from the anatomical site is subsequently analyzed as part of the procedure, then the qualifier X, diagnostic, is used.

Root Operation Transfusion

There is one Table in the Administration section in which root operation Transfusion appears: Table 302 (Administration section (3), Body System Circulatory (0), and root operation Transfusion (2)). The body system/region, approaches, and substances for this Table are shown in Table 8-6.

All of the substances listed with the Circulatory body system and root operation Transfusion are blood or blood products. Any other substances are coded to the Introduction root operation. With the exception of the body System/region *products of conception, circulatory*, the approach is either open or percutaneous. With *products of conception, circulatory* the approach is either percutaneous or via natural or artificial opening. All of the substances are the same for each body system/region, except bone marrow and stem cells, which cannot be administered via a peripheral or central artery, nor through the fetal circulatory system. Delivery of those substances can only be administered through a peripheral or central vein.

Table 8-5 Character Values and Definitions for Irrigation Table 3E1

Section: 3–Administration Body System: E–Physiological Systems and Anatomical Regions Root Operation: 1–Irrigation			
Body System/Region	Approach	Substance	Qualifier
0–Skin and mucous membrane C–Eye	3–Percutaneous X–External	8–Irrigating Substance	X–Diagnostic Z–No qualifier
9–Nose B–Ear F–Respiratory tract G–Upper GI H–Lower GI J–Biliary and pancreatic tract K–Genitourinary tract N–Male reproductive P–Female reproductive	3–Percutaneous 7–Via natural or artificial opening 8–Via natural or artificial opening endoscopic	8–Irrigating Substance	X–Diagnostic Z–No qualifier
L–Pleural cavity M–Peritoneal cavity Q–Cranial cavity and brain R–Spinal canal S–Epidural space U–Joints Y–Pericardial cavity	3–Percutaneous	8–Irrigating Substance	X–Diagnostic Z–No qualifier
M–Peritoneal cavity	3–Percutaneous	9–Dialysate	Z–No qualifier

Table 8-6 Body System/Region, Approach, and Substance Values for Root Operation Transfusion

Section: 3–Administration
Body System: 0–Circulatory
Root Operation: 2–Transfusion

Body System/Region	Approach	Substance
3-Peripheral Vein 4-Central Vein 3-Peripheral Vein 4-Central Vein	0-Open 3-Percutaneous 0-Open 3-Percutaneous	A-Stem Cells, Embryonic G-Bone Marrow H-Whole Blood J-Serum Albumin K-Frozen Plasma L-Fresh Plasma M-Plasma Cryoprecipitate N-Red Blood Cells P-Frozen Red Cells Q-White Cells R-Platelets S-Globulin T-Fibrinogen V-Antihemophilic Factors W-Factor IX X-Stem Cells, Cord Blood Y-Stem Cells, Hematopoietic
5-Peripheral Artery 6-Central Artery	0-Open 3-Percutaneous	H-Whole Blood J-Serum Albumin K-Frozen Plasma L-Fresh Plasma M-Plasma Cryoprecipitate
		N-Red Blood Cells P-Frozen Red Cells Q-White Cells R-Platelets S-Globulin T-Fibrinogen V-Antihemophilic Factors W-Factor IX
7-Products of conception, circulatory	3-Percutaneous 7-via natural or artificial opening	H-Whole Blood J-Serum Albumin K-Frozen Plasma L-Fresh Plasma M-Plasma Cryoprecipitate N-Red Blood Cells P-Frozen Red Cells Q-White Cells R-Platelets S-Globulin T-Fibrinogen V-Antihemophilic Factors W-Factor IX

Qualifiers used with transfusion root operation There are two qualifier values used with the root operation Transfusion, autologous and nonautologous. **Autologous** means the substance administered comes from one's own body (self). **Nonautologous** means the source is coming from someone or something other than the patient to whom the substance was administered. For example, in *administration of bone marrow percutaneously through a central vein*, the qualifier can be 0, *autologous*, meaning the bone marrow came from the patient; or 1, *nonautologous*, meaning it came from a donor other than the patient. In this procedure example, if the bone marrow came from a donor, the code would be 30243G1, broken down as follows:

3–Section: Administration

0–Body System: Circulatory

2–Root Operation: Transfusion (remember, bone marrow is a blood product)

4–Body System/Region: Central Vein

3–Approach: Percutaneous

G–Substance: Bone Marrow

1–Nonautologous

Using ICD-10-PCS Code Book for Root Operation Transfusion

After abstracting the procedural statements from the medical record, the next step is to determine the root operation, or main term. For the procedural statement *percutaneous donor blood (whole) infusion via peripheral vein*, the objective is to put blood into the system. This makes the root operation Transfusion. In the Index, a search of modifying terms under Transfusion (Figure 8-16), yields two, *by Body System* and *by Body Part.* Under the modifying term *by Body System*, the peripheral vein is found, with the character values 3023. Note that under *by Body Part* whole blood is found, with a character value of 3023. Either one will lead to the correct Table.

In the Tabular List, Table 302 is found in the Administration section (3), Circulatory body system (0), and Transfusion root operation (2). In the body system/region column, *peripheral vein* is found in the

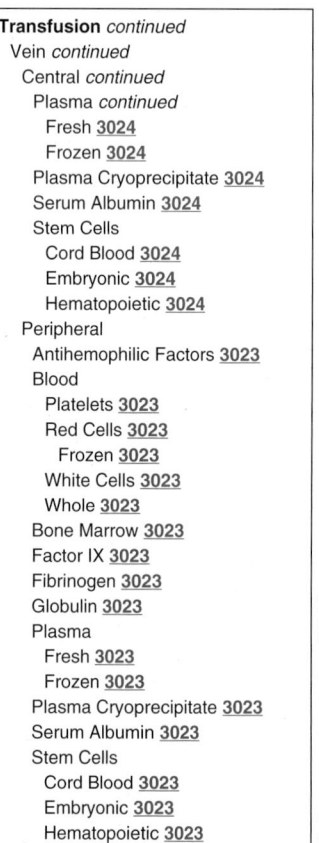

Transfusion *continued*
  Vein *continued*
    Central *continued*
      Plasma *continued*
        Fresh **3024**
        Frozen **3024**
        Plasma Cryoprecipitate **3024**
        Serum Albumin **3024**
      Stem Cells
        Cord Blood **3024**
        Embryonic **3024**
        Hematopoietic **3024**
    Peripheral
      Antihemophilic Factors **3023**
      Blood
        Platelets **3023**
        Red Cells **3023**
          Frozen **3023**
        White Cells **3023**
        Whole **3023**
      Bone Marrow **3023**
      Factor IX **3023**
      Fibrinogen **3023**
      Globulin **3023**
      Plasma
        Fresh **3023**
        Frozen **3023**
        Plasma Cryoprecipitate **3023**
        Serum Albumin **3023**
      Stem Cells
        Cord Blood **3023**
        Embryonic **3023**
        Hematopoietic **3023**

© Cengage Learning 2013

Figure 8-16 Alphabetic Index Excerpt for Root Operation Transfusion

first two rows. The approach is the same in both rows, but in the first, the only substance listed in the Substance column is A, *stem cells, embryonic*, making that row inappropriate. In row two, whole blood is included in the Substance column, with the character value of H. Next, look for the correct qualifier. In this case, the procedure states that donor blood was infused, which means the correct qualifier would be 1, nonautologous. The final code for the procedural statement is 30233H1, broken down as follows:

3–Section: Administration

0–Body System: Circulatory

2–Root Operation: Transfusion

3–Body System/Region: Peripheral vein

3–Approach: Percutaneous

H–Device: Whole Blood

1–Qualifier: Nonautologous

Coding for root operation Transfusion is relatively easy once an understanding of the definition and objective of the root operation is achieved. Seeing the administration of any blood or blood product in the procedural statement should lead right to the root operation Transfusion.

Measurement and Monitoring (4A0–4B0) Section

The codes within the Measurement and Monitoring section include procedures for determining the level of physiological or physical functions. Measurement is described as determining the level of function at a set point in time. Monitoring, on the other hand, is the determination of function levels over a specific period of time. Examples from this Section include electrocardiogram (EKG), cardiac catheterization, intracranial pressure measurement, cardiac rate and rhythm monitoring, and pulmonary function measurements and monitoring. Figures 8-17 and 8-18 are excerpts from the measurement and monitoring subsections of the Measurement and Monitoring section of the ICD-10-PCS.

The Measurement and Monitoring section character value is 4, and there are two body systems represented: Physiological systems (A) and physiological devices (B). The first two characters of a Measurement and Monitoring Section code will always be either 4A (physiological systems) or 4B (physiological devices). There are two root operations in this section: Measurement, character value 0, and Monitoring, character value 1. Body System B, physiological devices, is found with both the Measurement and Monitoring root operations. The first three characters of a Measurement root operation code will be either 4A0 (Measurement and Monitoring Section (4), Physiological Systems (A), Measurement (0)), or 4B0 (Measurement and Monitoring section (4), Physiological Devices (A), Measurement (0)). In the Monitoring subsection the first three characters will be either 4B1, Monitoring section (4), Physiological Devices (B), root operation Monitoring (1) or 4A2, Measurement and Monitoring section (4), Physiological Systems (A), root operation Monitoring (1).

In the Medical and Surgical section, the fourth character title was Body Part, indicating a specific body part from the general body system represented by character 2 of the code. Somewhat confusingly, in the Measurement and Monitoring section, the second and fourth characters are both titled Body System. In Character 2, the body system value is the general physiological system; the fourth character, the body system value, specifies the specific physiological system measured or monitored. The fifth character, approach, uses the same character values as the Medical and Surgical section. The sixth character, function/device, identifies the physiological or physical function measured or monitored. Examples of physiological or physical function include rate, conductivity, metabolism, pulse, temperature, volume, pressure, and electrical activity. The measurement and monitoring section codes are only for the measurement or monitoring procedure, and the devices used are always extracorporeal (outside the body). If a device is used to perform the measurement or monitoring is inserted and left in, then insertion of the device is coded as a separate procedure, and the function is coded from the

Section	4	Measurement and Monitoring
Body System	A	Physiological Systems
Operation	0	Measurement: Determining the level of a physiological or physical function at a point in time

Body System	Approach	Function/Device	Qualifier
0 Central Nervous	**0** Open	**2** Conductivity **4** Electrical Activity **B** Pressure	**Z** No Qualifier
0 Central Nervous	**3** Percutaneous **7** Via Natural or Artificial Opening	**B** Pressure **K** Temperature **R** Saturation	**D** Intracranial
0 Central Nervous	**X** External	**2** Conductivity **4** Electrical Activity	**Z** No Qualifier
1 Peripheral Nervous	**0** Open **3** Percutaneous **X** External	**2** Conductivity	**9** Sensory **B** Motor
2 Cardiac	**0** Open **3** Percutaneous	**4** Electrical Activity **9** Output **C** Rate **F** Rhythm **H** Sound **P** Action Currents	**Z** No Qualifier
2 Cardiac	**0** Open **3** Percutaneous	**N** Sampling and Pressure	**6** Right Heart **7** Left Heart **8** Bilateral
2 Cardiac	**X** External	**4** Electrical Activity **9** Output **C** Rate **F** Rhythm **H** Sound **P** Action Currents	**Z** No Qualifier
2 Cardiac	**X** External	**M** Total Activity	**4** Stress
3 Arterial	**0** Open **3** Percutaneous	**5** Flow **J** Pulse	**1** Peripheral **3** Pulmonary **C** Coronary
3 Arterial	**0** Open **3** Percutaneous	**B** Pressure	**1** Peripheral **3** Pulmonary **C** Coronary **F** Other Thoracic
3 Arterial	**0** Open **3** Percutaneous	**H** Sound **R** Saturation	**1** Peripheral

© Cengage Learning 2013

Figure 8-17 Excerpt from the Measurement Table in the ICD-10-PCS Coding Manual

Measurement and Monitoring section. In most instances, the seventh character qualifier will contain specific values as needed to further specify the body part, i.e., *pulmonary, intracranial, right heart,* or a value unique to the function, e.g., *sensory* or *motor.*

Measurement and Monitoring Root Operations

There are two subsections in the Measurement and Monitoring section, one for measurement and one for monitoring. Each one will be covered separately; the fourth character body system, approaches, functions or devices, and qualifiers for each will be discussed as well. There are two body system character values used with root operation Measurement: Physiological systems, with a value of A, and physiological devices, with the character value B.

Section	4	Measurement and Monitoring		
Body System	A	Physiological Systems		
Operation	1	Monitoring: Determining the level of a physiological or physical function repetitively over a period of time		

Body System	Approach	Function/Device	Qualifier
0 Central Nervous	**0** Open	**2** Conductivity **B** Pressure	**Z** No Qualifier
0 Central Nervous	**0** Open	**4** Electrical Activity	**G** Intraoperative **Z** No Qualifier
0 Central Nervous	**3** Percutaneous **7** Via Natural or Artificial Opening	**B** Pressure **K** Temperature **R** Saturation	**D** Intracranial
0 Central Nervous	**X** External	**2** Conductivity	**Z** No Qualifier
0 Central Nervous	**X** External	**4** Electrical Activity	**G** Intraoperative **Z** No Qualifier
1 Peripheral Nervous	**0** Open **3** Percutaneous **X** External	**2** Conductivity	**9** Sensory **B** Motor
2 Cardiac	**0** Open **3** Percutaneous	**4** Electrical Activity **9** Output **C** Rate **F** Rhythm **H** Sound	**Z** No Qualifier
2 Cardiac	**X** External	**4** Electrical Activity	**5** Ambulatory **Z** No Qualifier
2 Cardiac	**X** External	**9** Output **C** Rate **F** Rhythm **H** Sound	**Z** No Qualifier
2 Cardiac	**X** External	**M** Total Activity	**4** Stress
3 Arterial	**0** Open **3** Percutaneous	**5** Flow **B** Pressure **J** Pulse	**1** Peripheral **3** Pulmonary **C** Coronary
3 Arterial	**0** Open **3** Percutaneous	**H** Sound **R** Saturation	**1** Peripheral
3 Arterial	**X** External	**5** Flow **B** Pressure **H** Sound **J** Pulse **R** Saturation	**1** Peripheral

© Cengage Learning 2013

Figure 8-18 Excerpt from Monitoring Table in the ICD-10-PCS Coding Manual

Root Operation Measurement with Physiological System Body System Values

The objective of root operation **Measurement** is determining the level of function of a physiological or physical system at a set point in time. Examples of Measurement functions include conductivity (intracranial), electrical activity (cardiac), pressure (arterial), temperature (body), and flow (biliary). For example, an electrocardiogram (EKG) procedure would determine the level of cardiac electrical activity at the time of the procedure. Taking vital signs would determine the body temperature as well as the pulse, respiration, and heart rate at the time the vital signs were taken. The first three characters of any code from the Measurement and Monitoring section, Physiological System body system (character 2), and root operation Measurement, will always be 4A0.

Measurement approaches The approaches in the Measurement subsection are of the same value and type as those found in the Medical and Surgical Section. Table 8-7 lists the type and values used in Measurement and associated with the various body system (character 4) values found in this subsection.

In Table 8-7, there are six approach values: open, percutaneous, percutaneous endoscopic, via natural or artificial opening with or without endoscopic assistance, and external. With most fourth character body systems, there is more than one approach, and with others, like visual and olfactory, there is only one—X, for External. As always, the definitions are the same for the approach values.

Using the procedure *percutaneous peripheral venous flow test*, the section, body system, root operation, body system, and approach can now be determined. The objective is to determine arterial flow, which means this is a measurement. If there had been a time period mentioned in the procedural statement, then it would be a monitoring root operation, for example, a 24-hour Holter to test the cardiac function. So, the root operation, or main term, will be Measurement, the general body system will be physiological systems (A), and the approach will be percutaneous. Therefore, the first five characters of the code will be 4A043, broken down as follows:

4–Section: Measurement and Monitoring

A–Body System: Physiological Systems

Table 8-7 Approach Values used with Character 4 Body Systems

Section: Measurement and Monitoring (4) Body System: Physiological Systems (A) Root Operation: Measurement (0)	
Body System (Character 4)	Approach
0–Central nervous system	0–Open 3–Percutaneous 7–Via natural or artificial opening X–External
1–Peripheral nervous system 2–Cardiac 3–Arterial 4–Venous	0–Open 3–Percutaneous X–External
5–Circulatory	X–External
6–Lymphatic	0–Open 3–Percutaneous
7–Visual 8–Olfactory G–Whole body	X–External
9–Respiratory	7–Via natural or artificial opening 8–Via natural or artificial opening, endoscopic X–external
B–Gastrointestinal H–Products of conception, cardiac J–Products of conception, nervous	7–Via natural or artificial opening 8–Via natural or artificial opening, endoscopic
C–Biliary	3–Percutaneous 4–Percutaneous Endoscopic 7–Via natural or artificial opening 8–Via natural or artificial opening, endoscopic
D–Urinary G–Whole body	7–Via natural or artificial opening
F–Musculoskeletal	3–Percutaneous X–External

0–Root Operation: Measurement

4–Body System: Venous

3–Approach: Percutaneous

In searching the Index, first find the root operation Measurement (Figure 8-19). Note that the Index lists the modifying terms *by Body System* or *by Body Part,* such as peripheral nervous, respiratory, and urinary. Instead, the modifying term is *by Function*. Indented below this term is a list of functions. Look at the procedural statement again. The function being measured is flow. In Figure 8-19, the modifying term Venous and subterm *Flow* is listed. Indented below that are four additional subterms, central, peripheral, portal, and pulmonary. The Table reference for Measurement, venous, flow, and peripheral (four of the five words in the diagnostic statement) is 4A04. Turning to that Table in the Tabular list, it can be confirmed that 4A04 is the correct section (Measurement and Monitoring), Body System (Physiological Systems), Root Operation (Measurement), and Body System (venous). All that is left is to determine the approach, which in the procedural statement is percutaneous (3). Now, let's find the function or device, and qualifier for this procedure.

Measurement function/devices The measurement functions from this subsection include conductivity, electrical activity, pressure, temperature, saturation, sampling and pressure, output, rate, rhythm, sound, action currents, total activity, flow, pulse, volume, acuity, mobility, capacity, resistance, secretion, metabolism, and temperature. Some of these functions can be performed on a number of body systems, while a few are unique to a specific body system. Table 8-8 identifies which of the measurement functions apply to each body system.

The approach values will differ depending on the function being tested. Using the procedural statement from above, *percutaneous peripheral venous flow test,* and the first five code characters 4A043, the sixth character function value can be established as 5, *flow.* Look at Figure 8-20.

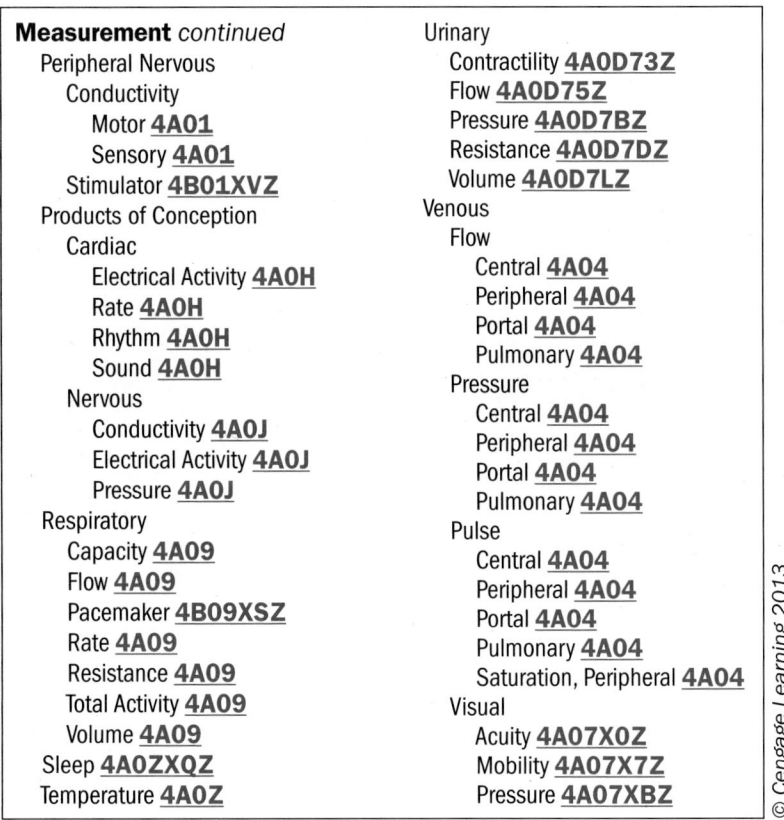

Measurement *continued*
 Peripheral Nervous
  Conductivity
   Motor **4A01**
   Sensory **4A01**
   Stimulator **4B01XVZ**
 Products of Conception
  Cardiac
   Electrical Activity **4A0H**
   Rate **4A0H**
   Rhythm **4A0H**
   Sound **4A0H**
  Nervous
   Conductivity **4A0J**
   Electrical Activity **4A0J**
   Pressure **4A0J**
 Respiratory
  Capacity **4A09**
  Flow **4A09**
  Pacemaker **4B09XSZ**
  Rate **4A09**
  Resistance **4A09**
  Total Activity **4A09**
  Volume **4A09**
 Sleep **4A0ZXQZ**
 Temperature **4A0Z**

Urinary
 Contractility **4A0D73Z**
 Flow **4A0D75Z**
 Pressure **4A0D7BZ**
 Resistance **4A0D7DZ**
 Volume **4A0D7LZ**
Venous
 Flow
  Central **4A04**
  Peripheral **4A04**
  Portal **4A04**
  Pulmonary **4A04**
 Pressure
  Central **4A04**
  Peripheral **4A04**
  Portal **4A04**
  Pulmonary **4A04**
 Pulse
  Central **4A04**
  Peripheral **4A04**
  Portal **4A04**
  Pulmonary **4A04**
  Saturation, Peripheral **4A04**
Visual
 Acuity **4A07X0Z**
 Mobility **4A07X7Z**
 Pressure **4A07XBZ**

© Cengage Learning 2013

Figure 8-19 Alphabetic Index Excerpt for Root Operation Measurement

Table 8-8 Measurement Functions by Body System

Section: Measurement and Monitoring (4) Body System: Physiological Systems (A) Root Operation: Measurement (0)		
Body System (Character 4)	Function/Device	Example
0–Central nervous system	2–Conductivity 4–Electrical activity B–Pressure K–Temperature R–Saturation	Electroencephalogram
1–Peripheral Nervous System	2–Conductivity	Nerve conduction study
2–Cardiac	N–Sampling and pressure 4–Electrical activity 9–Output C–Rate F–Rhythm H–Sound P–Action currents M–Total activity	Electrocardiogram Blood Pressure Cardiac Stress Test
3–Arterial	B–Pressure H–Sound R–Saturation 5–Flow B–Pressure H–Sound J–Pulse R–Saturation	Arterial Blood Gases
Body System (Character 4)	Function/Device	Example
4–Venous	5–Flow B–Pressure H–Sound J–Pulse R–Saturation	Venous Blood Gases
5–Circulatory	L–Volume	
6–Lymphatic	5–Flow B–Pressure	
7–Visual	0–Acuity 7–Mobility B–Pressure	Snellen eye chart/eye exam
8–Olfactory	0–Acuity	
9–Respiratory	1–Capacity 5–Flow C–Rate D–Resistance L–Volume M–Total Activity	Spirometry Lung volume tests
B–Gastrointestinal	8–Motility B–Pressure G–Secretion	
C–Biliary	5–Flow B–Pressure	

Table 8-8 Measurement Functions by Body System (continued)

D–Urinary	3–Contractibility 5–Flow B–Pressure D–Resistance L–Volume	
F–Musculoskeletal	3–Contractibility	
G–Whole body	6–Metabolism K–Temperature Q–Sleep	Vital signs Sleep studies
H–Products of conception, cardiac	4–Electrical Activity C–Rate F–Rhythm H–Sound	Electrocardiogram (EKG)
J–Products of conception, nervous	2–Conductivity 4–Electrical Activity B–Pressure	Electroencephalogram (EEG)

There are three rows in the 4A0 Table for Measurement and Monitoring, which include the body system Venous. The first two rows contain the right approach (3—percutaneous), but only the first row includes the function *flow* in the sixth character position. Since the procedure specifically states it is a venous flow test, the only function column option is the first row, where *flow* appears. The code is now 4A0435, with only the qualifier to determine. Take just a moment to compare the procedural statement to the code. Note that all the pertinent words in *percutaneous peripheral venous flow test* now have a character assignment except the word *peripheral*, which will be found in the Qualifier column.

The following are definitions of some of the functions listed in the Measurement and Monitoring section:

- **Conductivity** is the ability of a physiological system to conduct electricity, heat, fluid, or sound
- **Contractility** is the capability or quality of shrinking or contracting, especially by muscle fibers
- **Saturation** defines the level at which a chemical compound, gas, vapor, or solution, unites with any other substance. For example, the level (amount) of gases (oxygen, nitrogen, hydrogen) found within human arterial blood
- **Motility** is defined as spontaneous movement, i.e., the automatic stomach contractions (peristalsis) that move the food content along from the stomach into the intestines
- **Acuity** is keenness or acuteness, especially in the senses (vision, smell), i.e., keen vision, or an acute sense of smell
- **Metabolism** complete set of chemical reactions that happen in human beings to maintain life

Measurement qualifiers There are two types of qualifier values in the Measurement subsection. The seventh character qualifier will either contain specific values as needed to further specify the body part, i.e., pulmonary, intracranial, or right heart, **or** values unique to the function, for example, in functions of the peripheral nervous system measuring *sensory* or *motor* conductivity. Sensory or motor are the qualifiers added to the conductivity function. Look back at Figure 8-20, the procedural statement is *percutaneous peripheral venous flow test,* and the first six characters of the code (4A0435). In the first row, with the body system Venous (which was established as the appropriate row based on the approach and Function), there are four qualifiers: 0, Central; 1. Peripheral; 2, Portal; and 3, Pulmonary. The procedural statement includes the term *peripheral,* making 1 the final code value. 4A04351 is the correct code for *percutaneous peripheral venous flow test.*

Section	4	Measurement and Monitoring
Body System	A	Physiological Systems
Operation	0	Measurement: Determining the level of a physiological or physical function at a point in time

Body System	Approach	Function / Device	Qualifier
3 Arterial	X External	5 Flow B Pressure H Sound J Pulse R Saturation	1 Peripheral
4 Venous	0 Open 3 Percutaneous	5 Flow B Pressure J Pulse	0 Central 1 Peripheral 2 Portal 3 Pulmonary
4 Venous	0 Open 3 Percutaneous	R Saturation	1 Peripheral
4 Venous	X External	5 Flow B Pressure J Pulse R Saturation	1 Peripheral
5 Circulatory	X External	L Volume	Z No Qualifier
6 Lymphatic	0 Open 3 Percutaneous	5 Flow B Pressure	Z No Qualifier
7 Visual	X External	0 Acuity 7 Mobility B Pressure	Z No Qualifier
8 Olfactory	X External	0 Acuity	Z No Qualifier
9 Respiratory	7 Via Natural or Artificial Opening 8 Via Natural or Artificial Opening Endoscopic X External	1 Capacity 5 Flow C Rate D Resistance L Volume M Total Activity	Z No Qualifier
B Gastrointestinal	7 Via Natural or Artificial Opening 8 Via Natural or Artificial Opening Endoscopic	8 Motility B Pressure G Secretion	Z No Qualifier
C Biliary	3 Percutaneous 4 Percutaneous Endoscopic 7 Via Natural or Artificial Opening 8 Via Natural or Artificial Opening Endoscopic	5 Flow B Pressure	Z No Qualifier

© Cengage Learning 2013

Figure 8-20 Measurement Table 4A0

Here are two examples which do not include the term *measurement*, or the root operation Measurement. Here's how to find the appropriate Index entry, and the correct code:

1. Electrocardiogram: In the Index, look under electrocardiogram or EKG. Both tests are listed by that term, with the Table reference 4A02. From that Table the rest of the code can be built. It takes knowledge of anatomy, physiology, and function, but with a good medical terminology foundation, it can be done even now. Breaking down the medical term *electrocardiogram*, the root word refers to the heart, gram is a recording or tracing, and the prefix *electro-* refers to electrical activity. The EKG electrodes are placed on the skin, making the approach external. In Table 4A0, the fourth character will be body system 2 (Cardiac), the approach X, external, the function 4, electrical activity, and in this case, there is no associated qualifier. The code is 4A02X4Z.

2. Electroencephalogram: In the Index, there is a listing for Electroencephalogram (EEG), leading to Table 4A00 (Measurement and Monitoring, Physiological Systems, Measurement, Central Nervous

System). Breaking down the term yields the procedure recording (-gram) of electrical activity (electro-) of the brain (encephalo-). The electrodes for the recording are placed on the scalp, making the approach external. The brain is part of the central nervous system. In Table 4A00, the approach will be X, external, the function will be electrical activity (4), and there is no qualifier value for this row. The code for electroencephalogram is 4A00X4Z.

Bear in mind, most measurement and monitoring tests are listed by the test name. The same will be true for other tests that do not come from this section. For example, echocardiography might seem like a measurement test, but when searching for it in the Index, the reference value will lead to the Imaging Table (B24) rather than the Measurement and Monitoring Table. The best aid to understanding the test performed will be a good foundation in medical terminology, anatomy and physiology, and a medical reference guide. Whenever there is a doubt, ask the documenting physician or another clinician for clarification on the type and purpose of any procedures performed that are difficult to decipher.

Root Operation Measurement and Physiological Devices

The second body system (character 2) values in the Measurement subsection is physiological devices (B). The first three characters of a code from a Measurement root operation using the body system physiological devices (B) are 4B0. There are five character 4 body system values, one approach (external), three devices, and no qualifiers in this Table (Figure 8-21). The three device values in the 4B0 Table are V, stimulator; S, pacemaker; and T, defibrillator.

The first thing to consider is what is being measured in the Measurement root operation. Think of the *physiological device* measurements as tests of the *device* function, while *physiological systems* measurements are tests of the *body system* function. Review the medical documentation thoroughly to determine the objective of the procedure. If it is to measure physiological or physical levels of function, it is a Measurement root operation, and physiological systems body system. If the objective is to measure the device level of function, it is a Measurement root operation, and a physiological devices, character 2, body system value.

The body system (character 4) values are shown in Figure 8-21, with the corresponding device values. A stimulator device (Y) measurement uses only body systems central or peripheral nervous system (0 or 1, respectively), and musculoskeletal system (F). The respiratory system (9) uses only S, pacemaker device, and the cardiac system (2) allows two device values—S, pacemaker, and T, defibrillator.

Looking up devices by name in the Index can lead to an incorrect Table. For example, looking under *pacemaker* in the Index, will lead to the Insertion procedure, not to Measurement or Monitoring. The key is remembering the objective of the procedure. If the objective is measurement, monitoring, recording, tracing, reading, or *determining the level of function* of a *device*, it will be a root operation Measurement (0) or Monitoring (1), code character value 2, physiological device (B). For the procedure *evaluation of*

Section	4	Measurement and Monitoring		
Body System	B	Physiological Devices		
Operation	0	Measurement: Determining the level of a physiological or physical function at a point in time		

Body System	Approach	Function/Device	Qualifier
0 Central Nervous **1** Peripheral Nervous **F** Musculoskeletal	**X** External	**V** Stimulator	**Z** No Qualifier
2 Cardiac	**X** External	**S** Pacemaker **T** Defibrillator	**Z** No Qualifier
9 Respiratory	**X** External	**S** Pacemaker	**Z** No Qualifier

© Cengage Learning 2013

Figure 8-21 Measurement and Physiological Devices Table 4B0

defibrillator function, the first place to look in the Index is for the root operation Measurement. Look back at Figure 8-19. Indented under Measurement is the modifying term *by Function*, and indented below that is the subterm *defibrillator, cardiac* with the Table reference value 4B02.

Turning to Table 4B02 in the Tabular List, the approach value is external (X), the function/device is defibrillator (T), and there is no qualifier (Z). The code for the procedure is 4B02XTZ. Using this same procedure, if the root operation Monitoring is searched for in the Index, there would be no subterm leading to the defibrillator device, since all Monitoring subterms refer only to a function or body system. There are no devices listed under Monitoring. This should automatically move the search in the Index to Measurement, based on the definition and objective of the root operation.

Let's Review 8–2:

1. Oral pulmonary function test, volume _____
2. External cardiac pacemaker measurement _____
3. Body temperature, oral _____
4. Transvaginal electrocardiograph, fetal _____
5. Measurement from external muscle stimulator _____

Root Operation Monitoring and Physiological Systems

The objective of the root operation Monitoring is to determine the level of a physiological or physical body system or device function repetitively over a period of time. There is one body system (character 2) value, physiological systems (value A). There are no physiological device character values in the Monitoring subsection, which means no device functioning monitoring procedures are coded from here—only body systems monitoring. A device may be listed in the procedural statement, but the key is in the objective and purpose of the procedure, and thus, the root operation. For example, in the procedure *cardiac electrical activity via 24-hour Holter onitor*. Even though a device is part of the procedure, the objective is to monitor electrical activity of the heart.

The first three characters of a Monitoring root operation code will always be 4A1—Measurement and Monitoring Section (4), Physiological Systems body system (A), and root operation Monitoring (1). Figure 8-22 is an excerpt from the 4A1 Table in the Tabular List.

In this excerpt, notice that there are five rows that contain the character four (first column) body system value central nervous system. In each row, either the approach, function or device alters the procedure objective. For example, look at the first two rows. The approach is the same for both, but the function or device values are different in both, and each row is affected by different qualifier values. An *open central nervous system monitoring procedure to determine the level of conductivity* would be coded 4A1002Z as follows:

4–Section: Measurement and Monitoring

A–Body System: Physiological Systems

1–Root Operation: Monitoring

0–Central Nervous

0–Approach: Open

2–Function/Device: Conductivity

Z–Qualifier: No Qualifier

Section	4	Measurement and Monitoring
Body System	A	Physiological Systems
Operation	1	Monitoring: Determining the level of a physiological or physical function repetitively over a period of time

Body System	Approach	Function / Device	Qualifier
0 Central Nervous	**0** Open	**2** Conductivity **B** Pressure	**Z** No Qualifier
0 Central Nervous	**0** Open	**4** Electrical Activity	**G** Intraoperative **Z** No Qualifier
0 Central Nervous	**3** Percutaneous **7** Via Natural or Artificial Opening	**B** Pressure **K** Temperature **R** Saturation	**D** Intracranial
0 Central Nervous	**X** External	**2** Conductivity	**Z** No Qualifier
0 Central Nervous	**X** External	**4** Electrical Activity	**G** Intraoperative **Z** No Qualifier
1 Peripheral Nervous	**0** Open **3** Percutaneous **X** External	**2** Conductivity	**9** Sensory **B** Motor
2 Cardiac	**0** Open **3** Percutaneous	**4** Electrical Activity **9** Output **C** Rate **F** Rhythm **H** Sound	**Z** No Qualifier
2 Cardiac	**X** External	**4** Electrical Activity	**5** Ambulatory **Z** No Qualifier
2 Cardiac	**X** External	**9** Output **C** Rate **F** Rhythm **H** Sound	**Z** No Qualifier
2 Cardiac	**X** External	**M** Total Activity	**4** Stress
3 Arterial	**0** Open **3** Percutaneous	**5** Flow **B** Pressure **J** Pulse	**1** Peripheral **3** Pulmonary **C** Coronary
3 Arterial	**0** Open **3** Percutaneous	**H** Sound **R** Saturation	**1** Peripheral
3 Arterial	**X** External	**5** Flow **B** Pressure **H** Sound **J** Pulse **R** Saturation	**1** Peripheral

© Cengage Learning 2013

Figure 8-22 Table 4A1 from Monitoring Section of the ICD-10-PCS

Changing the term *conductivity* in this procedural statement to *electrical activity* requires a move to the second row, since *electrical activity* is not a function/device in the first row. The code changes to 4A1004Z, as shown here:

4–Section: Measurement and Monitoring

A–Body System: Physiological Systems

1–Root Operation: Monitoring

0–Central Nervous

0–Approach: Open

4–Function/Device: Electrical Activity

Z–Qualifier: No Qualifier

For the seventh character, qualifier, the procedure example does not specify a qualifier, therefore, the qualifier value Z is used. Had the procedural statement example stated that monitoring was performed intraoperatively (i.e., during a surgical procedure), the seventh character value would change to G, *intraoperative*.

Monitoring Approaches

The approach values for Monitoring are essentially identical and use the same character 2 body system values as those in the Measurement subsection. Table 8-9 illustrates the relationships between the physiological systems and approaches in the Monitoring subsection. Comparing Table 8-7 with Table 8-9 indicates one or two variances in approach for specific physiological systems. For example, approach value 7, *via natural or artificial opening, endoscopic*, has been added to *products of conception, cardiac* and *nervous* in the Monitoring subsection.

Review the medical documentation carefully to ensure the correct approach is chosen, since it impacts the code selection significantly. For example, *monitoring a percutaneous central venous pressure level of function* would be coded 4A143B0, broken down as follows:

4–Section: Measurement and Monitoring

A–Body System: Physiological Systems

1–Root Operation: Monitoring

4 Venous 3–Approach: Percutaneous

Table 8-9 Relationships between Physiological System and Approaches in Monitoring Tables

Section: Measurement and Monitoring (4) Body System: Physiological Systems (A) Root Operation: Monitoring (1)	
Body System (Character 4)	Approach
0–Central nervous system	0–Open 3–Percutaneous 7–Via natural or artificial opening X–External
1–Peripheral nervous system 2–Cardiac 3–Arterial 4–Venous	0–Open 3–Percutaneous X–External
5–Circulatory	X–External
6–Lymphatic	0–Open 3–Percutaneous
7–Visual 8–Olfactory	X–External
9–Respiratory G–Whole body	7–Via natural or artificial opening X–external
H–Products of conception, cardiac J–Products of conception, nervous	7–Via natural or artificial opening 8–Via natural or artificial opening, endoscopic X–External
B–Gastrointestinal	7–Via natural or artificial opening 8–Via natural or artificial opening, endoscopic
D–Urinary	7–Via natural or artificial opening
F–Musculoskeletal	3–Percutaneous X–External

B–Function/Device: Pressure

0–Device: Central

Changing the function of this example from *pressure* to *saturation* changes the code from 4A143**B**0 to 4A143**R**0, which is found in a different row since the function, *saturation,* is not in the same row as the first code found, even though the section, body system, root Operation, and approach are the same.

The same is true if the approach changes, even if the body System and function remain the same. For example, an *external venous flow monitoring* procedure is coded to a different row in the table if the approach changes to a *percutaneous venous flow monitoring* procedure. Look back at the first and third rows of Figure 8-22. The first four characters of the procedure are 4A1. Look in the Function/Device column. The same three functions are in both rows. The approach and qualifier values are the only values that are different, depending on the row. If the procedural statement states that the approach is percutaneous, the first six characters of the code would be built from row one, 4A1435. If the same statement describes an external approach, then a code would be built from row three, with the first six characters 4A14X5. The only value that changed in the first six characters is the fifth character approach value.

Monitoring function/devices There are fewer body systems and function monitored, than were found with the Measurement body systems and functions, for example, in Measurement, visual acuity measurement was a function value. There is no Monitoring root operation for visual acuity where the level of function is monitored over a period of time. Table 8-10 describes the body system, approach

Table 8-10 Root Operation Monitoring Approach and Function Values

Section: Measurement and Monitoring (4) Body System: Physiological Systems (A) Root Operation: Monitoring (1)		
Body System (Character 4)	Approach	Function/Device
0–Central nervous	0–Open	2–Conductivity 4–Electrical activity B–Pressure
0–Central nervous	3–Percutaneous 7–via natural or artificial opening	B–Pressure K–Temperature R–Saturation
0–Central nervous	X–External	2–Conductivity 4–Electrical activity
1–Peripheral nervous	0–Open 3–Percutaneous X–External	2–Conductivity
2–Cardiac	0–Open 3–Percutaneous	4–Electrical activity 9–Output C–Rate F–Rhythm H–Sound
2–Cardiac	X–External	4–Electrical activity 9–Output C–Rate F–Rhythm H–Sound M–Total activity
3–Arterial	0–Open 3–Percutaneous X–External	5–Flow B–Pressure J–Pulse H–Sound R–Saturation

4–Venous	0–Open 3–Percutaneous X–External	5–Flow B–Pressure J–Pulse
4–Venous	0–Open 3–Percutaneous	R–Saturation
6–Lymphatic	0–Open 3–Percutaneous	5–Flow B–Pressure
9–Respiratory	7–Via natural or artificial opening X–external	1–Capacity 5–Flow C–Rate D–Resistance L–Volume
B–Gastrointestinal	7–Via natural or artificial opening 8–Via natural or artificial opening, endoscopic	8–Motility B–Pressure G–Secretion
D–Urinary	7–Via natural or artificial opening	3–Contractibility 5–Flow B–Pressure D–Resistance L–Volume
G–Whole body	7–Via natural or artificial opening X–External	K–Temperature
G–Whole body	X–External	Q–Sleep
H–Products of conception, cardiac	7–Via natural or artificial opening 8–Via natural or artificial opening, endoscopic	4–Electrical activity C–Rate F–Rhythm H–Sound
J–Products of conception, nervous	7–Via natural or artificial opening 8–Via natural or artificial opening, endoscopic	2–Conductivity 4–Electrical activity B–Pressure

and functions found with root operation Monitoring. Conversely, in the respiratory system, capacity, flow, rate, resistance, and volume can be both measured (one time) and monitored (over a period of time); thus, the respiratory system is found in both Table 4A0 and 4A1 for root operations Measurement (0) and Monitoring (1), in the Measurement and Monitoring section (4), and in the physiological systems (A) body system.

Remember, the qualifier may change the approach or function, and thus, the row in which all the correct code characters are located. For example, a *central nervous system pressure monitoring* procedure uses the approaches *open, percutaneous,* or *via natural opening*. If the procedure includes the qualifier *intercranial,* the code characters will appear in a row separate from one that does not contain a qualifier—even though the body system and function are the same. In addition, the approach will be different. For an *intracranial pressure monitoring* procedure, the approach can only be percutaneous or via natural opening, resulting in code 4A103BD, where percutaneous is the approach; or 4A107BD, where the approach is via natural or artificial opening. Drop the word *intracranial* from the procedural statement, and the only row option is the one containing the qualifier Z, and open approach. The code would then be 4A100BZ with open approach (0) and no qualifier (Z).

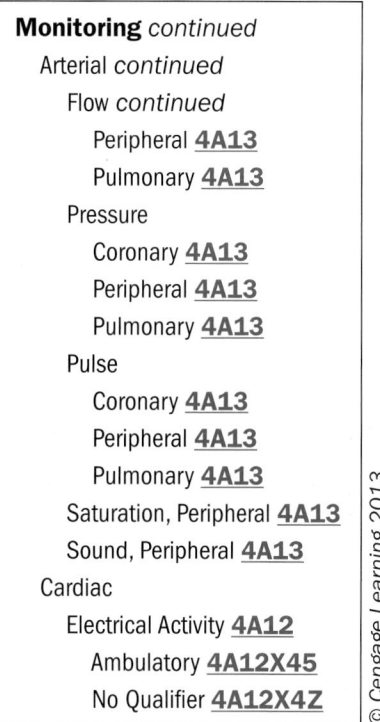

Figure 8-23 Alphabetic Index Excerpt for Root Operation Monitoring

Coding Monitoring Root Operations in ICD-10-PCS

Using the procedure *24-hour Holter monitor of cardiac electrical activity*, the root operation is Monitoring, determining the level of function of a physiological system repeatedly over a period of time. In the Index, under the main term Monitoring, (Figure 8-23), the modifying term is *cardiac,* and indented below that, within subterms based on the function, is the subterm *electrical activity.* The procedural statement indicates this is *cardiac,* so the Table reference value refers to Table 4A12. Moving to Table 4A1 in the Tabular List (Figure 8-24), 4A12 identifies the Measurement and Monitoring section (4), physiological systems value A, root operation Monitoring, and body system cardiac, 2. To determine the fifth character, approach, an understanding of how a Holter® Monitor works is needed. A **Holter® monitor** is worn on a strap or belt around the waist, and electrodes from the monitor are placed on specific areas of the chest. During the prescribed time period, the monitor records the heart and pulse rates, and electrical activity as the patient continues his normal daily activity. Based on this description, the approach can be identified as external and the qualifier as *ambulatory*. There are three rows with code character values 4A12X, but only one that identifies the function electrical activity, value 4, and the qualifier, ambulatory (5). The code for this procedure is 4A12X45, broken down as follows:

4–Section: Measurement and Monitoring

A–Body System: Physiological Systems

1–Root Operation: Monitoring

2–Body System: Cardiac

X–Approach: External

4–Function: Electrical Activity

5–Qualifier: Ambulatory

If the patient was hospitalized and confined to a bed during the cardiac monitoring, the qualifier ambulatory (5) would be omitted, and the seventh character of the code would be Z, no qualifier.

Section	4	Measurement and Monitoring	
Body System	A	Physiological Systems	
Operation	1	Monitoring: Determining the level of a physiological or physical function repetitively over a period of time	

Body System	Approach	Function/Device	Qualifier
0 Central Nervous	**0** Open	**2** Conductivity **B** Pressure	**Z** No Qualifier
0 Central Nervous	**0** Open	**4** Electrical Activity	**G** Intraoperative **Z** No Qualifier
0 Central Nervous	**3** Percutaneous **7** Via Natural or Artificial Opening	**B** Pressure **K** Temperature **R** Saturation	**D** Intracranial
0 Central Nervous	**X** External	**2** Conductivity	**Z** No Qualifier
0 Central Nervous	**X** External	**4** Electrical Activity	**G** Intraoperative **Z** No Qualifier
1 Peripheral Nervous	**0** Open **3** Percutaneous **X** External	**2** Conductivity	**9** Sensory **B** Motor
2 Cardiac	**0** Open **3** Percutaneous	**4** Electrical Activity **9** Output **C** Rate **F** Rhythm **H** Sound	**Z** No Qualifier
2 Cardiac	**X** External	**4** Electrical Activity	**5** Ambulatory **Z** No Qualifier
2 Cardiac	**X** External	**9** Output **C** Rate **F** Rhythm **H** Sound	**Z** No Qualifier
2 Cardiac	**X** External	**M** Total Activity	**4** Stress
3 Arterial	**0** Open **3** Percutaneous	**5** Flow **B** Pressure **J** Pulse	**1** Peripheral **3** Pulmonary **C** Coronary
3 Arterial	**0** Open **3** Percutaneous	**H** Sound **R** Saturation	**1** Peripheral
3 Arterial	**X** External	**5** Flow **B** Pressure **H** Sound **J** Pulse **R** Saturation	**1** Peripheral

Figure 8-24 Monitoring Table 4A1

Let's Review 8–3

Code the following procedures:

1. Cardiac stress test _____

2. Intracranial pressure monitoring, percutaneous approach _____

3. Open peripheral arterial flow monitoring _____

4. Percutaneous pulmonary artery flow monitoring _____

5. Sensory conductivity monitoring, peripheral nervous system, external _____

Chapter Summary

Placement section codes represent procedures for *putting a device in or on a body region for the purpose of protection, immobilization, stretching, compression, or packing.* The Placement section character value is 2, There are two Body Systems character values for this section. Body system character W represents anatomical regions, and body system character value Y represents anatomical orifices. The root operations in the Placement section include only those procedures that are performed without making an incision or a puncture. The root operations Change and Removal are in this section, as well as several new root operations: Compression, Dressing, Immobilization, Packing, and Traction.

The ICD-10-PCS Guidelines provide specific instructions for using the anatomical regions. In a procedure performed on body layers that span more than one body system or region, a general anatomical region character value should be used. Since all Placement procedures are performed directly on the skin or mucous membrane, or performed indirectly by applying external force through the skin or mucous membrane, the approach value is always X, external. The device character is always specified, except in the case of manual traction. If the procedure includes manual traction, the sixth character should be Z, no device. Devices include splints, casts, bandages, etc.

In root operation Traction (6), there are two device character values. If manual traction was applied to a body part, but no traction apparatus was applied, use character value Z to indicate no device used.

The Administration section is used to code procedures that *put in or on the body a therapeutic, prophylactic, protective, diagnostic, nutritional, or physiological substance.* The section includes administration of transfusions, infusions, and injections, as well as irrigation and tattooing procedures. Administration section codes always begin with a first character value of 3. There are three body system (character 2) values: indwelling catheter (C), physiological systems and anatomical regions (E) and circulatory (O).

There are three root operations in the Administration section: Introduction, Irrigation, and Transfusion. The root operation Introduction is a large portion of the Administration section, and includes virtually all body system/regions and approaches found in other sections of the ICD-10-PCS coding manual. There are approximately 20 different substance character values and almost as many qualifier values. The definition of the Introduction root operation is *putting in or on a therapeutic, diagnostic, nutritional, physiological, or prophylactic substance except blood or blood products.*

Determining that a code might come from the Administration section is fairly straightforward, based on the section definition. There are two qualifier values used with the root operation Transfusion, autologous and nonautologous. Autologous means the substance administered comes from one's own body (self). Nonautologous means the source is coming from someone or something other than the patient to whom the substance was administered.

The Measurement and Monitoring section character value is 4, and there are two body systems represented: Physiological systems (A) and physiological devices (B).

In the Measurement and Monitoring section, the second and fourth character are both titled Body System. In Character 2, the body system value is the general physiological system and the fourth character, body system, specifies the specific physiological system measured or monitored. The fifth character, approach, uses the same character values as the Medical and Surgical section. The sixth character, function/device, identifies the physiological or physical function measured or monitored. The objective of root operation Measurement is determining the level of function of a physiological or physical system at a set point in time. Examples of Measurement functions include conductivity (intracranial), electrical activity (cardiac), pressure (arterial), temperature (body), and flow (biliary).

The objective of the root operation Monitoring is to determine the level of a physiological or physical body system or device function repetitively over a period of time. There is one body system (character 2) value, physiological systems (value A). There are no physiological device character values in the Monitoring subsection, which means no device functioning monitoring procedures are coded from here—only body systems monitoring.

Chapter Review

Matching

Instructions: Match the key term to the appropriate definition.

_____ 1. Intradermal

_____ 2. Injection

_____ 3. Transfusion

_____ 4. Stereotactic apparatus

_____ 5. Antiarrhythmic

_____ 6. Brachytherapy

_____ 7. Radioisotope

_____ 8. Intramuscular

_____ 9. Antineoplastic

_____ 10. Vasopressor

a. An external, three-dimensional frame, for example a halo frame for immobilizing the head.

b. Injection made into a muscle.

c. Root operation 2 in the Administration section. Putting in blood or blood products.

d. Injection made into the dermis or substance of the skin.

e. A drug used to treat an abnormal heart rhythm.

f. The forcing or administering of a liquid into a part, as into the subcutaneous tissues, the vascular tree, or an organ.

g. Radiation treatment given by placing radioactive material directly in or near the target, which is often a tumor.

h. Inhibiting or preventing the growth or development of malignant cells.

i. A version of a chemical element that has an unstable nucleus and emits radiation.

j. Stimulating contraction of the muscular tissue of the capillaries and arteries.

Short Answer

Instructions: Define the following terms:

1. Conductivity _____

2. Measurement _____

3. Monitoring _____

4. Contractility _____

5. Saturation _____

6. Motility _____

7. Acuity _____

8. Metabolism _____

9. Intradermal _____

10. Injection _____

Coding Practice

Instructions: Code the following procedures

1. Placement of packing material, left ear _____

2. Change vaginal packing _____

3. Splint removal, right shoulder _____

4. Neck brace placement _____

5. Traction, mechanical, left leg _____

6. Sterile dressing to left groin _____

7. Intermittent pneumatic compression device, right arm _____

8. Pressure dressing exchange, left thigh _____

9. Apply intermittent pressure device to both legs to improve circulation in lower extremities
   (hint: Do not forget about Guideline B4.5) _____

10. Measurement of cardiac output, external _____

11. Arterial blood gasses (ABG), peripheral, percutaneous (*hint:* Saturation of gas (02, nitrogen, etc.)
    in arterial blood) _____

12. Respiratory pacemaker measurement (*hint:* This is a device) _____

13. Portal vein pulse monitoring _____

14. Respiratory resistance monitoring, external _____

15. Heart rate monitoring using Holter® monitor _____

Extracorporeal Sections

Learning Objectives

At the conclusion of this chapter, the learner should be able to:

- Understand terms used in the Extracorporeal Assistance and Performance section and identify new character values
- Identify the Body System, Root Operation, Body Parts, Approach, Device, and Qualifiers used in the Extracorporeal Assistance and Performance section
- Understand the guidelines that impact code selection in the Extracorporeal Assistance and Performance section
- Differentiate how the root operations are used in the Extracorporeal Assistance and Performance section, and how to apply the correct Body Part, Approach, Device, and Qualifier for each root operation
- Know how to use the Index and Tables to select the correct code from the Extracorporeal Assistance and Performance section
- Understand terms used in the Extracorporeal Therapies section and identify new character values
- Identify the Body System, Root Operation, Body Parts, Approach, Device, and Qualifiers used in the Extracorporeal Therapies section
- Understand the guidelines that impact code selection in the Extracorporeal Therapies section
- Differentiate how the root operations are used in the Extracorporeal Therapies section, and how to apply the correct Body Part, Approach, Device, and Qualifier for each root operation
- Know how to use the Index and Tables to select the correct code from the Extracorporeal Therapies section

Key Terms and Definitions

Assistance	Root operation 0 in Extracorporeal Assistance and Performance. Taking over a portion of a physiological function by extracorporeal means.
Atmospheric control	Root operation 0 in Extracorporeal Therapies. Extracorporeal control of atmospheric pressure and composition.
Balloon pump	Device inserted into a heart vessel. In Extracorporeal Assistance, the balloon is inflated and deflated with gas (usually helium), which assists in cardiac output by pumping blood through the heart.
Cardioversion	Converting one cardiac rhythm or electrical pattern to another.
Decompression	Root operation 1 in Extracorporeal Therapies section. Extracorporeal elimination of undissolved gas from body fluids.
Duration	The length of time extracorporeal assistance, performance, or restoration is performed, or the type of delivery.
Electromagnetic therapy	Root operation 2 in Extracorporeal Therapies section. Extracorporeal treatment by electromagnetic rays.
Extracorporeal	Outside of the body.
Filtration	Process where fluids pass through a filter or filtering medium, e.g., dialysis.
Hyperbaric	Pertaining to gas pressures greater than 1 atm* of pressure. Also pertaining to solutions that are more dense than the medium to which they are added. The term "hyperbaric" is derived from Greek roots: "hyper-" meaning high, beyond, excessive, above normal, and "baros" meaning weight.
Hyperthermia	Root operation 3 in Extracorporeal Therapies section. Extracorporeal raising of body temperature.
Hypothermia	Root operation 4 in Extracorporeal Therapies section. Extracorporeal lowering of body temperature.
IPAP	Inspiratory Positive Airway Pressure.
Output	The amount of blood pumped by the heart per unit time, measured in liters per minute (L/min).
Oxygenation	The addition of oxygen to any system, or the process of treating a patient with oxygen.
Pacing	Controlling the rate and rhythm of the heart.
Performance	Root operation 1 in Extracorporeal Assistance and Performance. Completely taking over a physiological function by extracorporeal means.
Pheresis	Root operation 5 in Extracorporeal Therapies section. Extracorporeal separation of blood products.
Phototherapy	Root operation 6 in Extracorporeal Therapies section. Extracorporeal treatment by light rays.
Pulsatile compression	Intermittent compression to a body member, used in Extracorporeal Assistance Table 5A0 to assist in cardiac output.
Restoration	Root operation 2 in Extracorporeal Assistance and Performance. Returning or attempting to return, a physiological function to its original state by extracorporeal means.

Shockwave therapy	Root operation 9 in Extracorporeal Therapies section. Extracorporeal treatment by shock waves.
Ultrasound therapy	Root operation 7 in Extracorporeal Therapies section. Extracorporeal treatment by ultrasound.
Ultraviolet light therapy	Root operation 8 in Extracorporeal Therapies section. Extracorporeal treatment by ultraviolet light.
Ventilation	The exchange of air between the lungs and the environment.

Introduction

These two sections cover therapies, assistance, and performance treatments undertaken outside the body (extracorporeal). They are Extracorporeal Assistance and Performance (5A0–5A2) and Extracorporeal Therapies (6A0–6A9). The Extracorporeal Assistance and Performance section (5A0–5A2) represents procedures that assist or perform the function of a body system or part, e.g., respiratory ventilation or oxygenation procedures. The second section, Extracorporeal Therapies (6A0–6A9), includes codes for environmental control therapies, such as decompression, atmospheric control, and hyperthermic and hypothermic procedures.

Extracorporeal Assistance and Performance 5A0–5A2

The codes in this section range from 5A0 through 5A2, and include three root operations that assist, perform, or restore physiological functions by extracorporeal means. **Extracorporeal** means *outside the body*, in the anatomic sense. In extracorporeal assistance and performance procedures, external equipment is used to assist or perform a physiological function. This section includes procedures performed in a critical care setting such as mechanical ventilation and cardioversion, as well as other services like hyperbaric oxygen treatment and dialysis. Other examples include using a balloon pump or pulsatile compression to assist the heart function, applying nonmechanical ventilation to perform respiratory functions, or using CPR to restore cardiac rhythm.

The first character in this Section is 5, Extracorporeal Assistance and Performance. The second character, representing the general body system is A, physiological systems. The three root operations and values for the third code character are Assistance (0), Performance (1), and Restoration (2). There are only five Body System (character 4) values in this Section, cardiac (2), circulatory (5), respiratory (9), biliary (C), and urinary (D).

In this section, the fifth character value is Duration, rather than Approach. **Duration** indicates the length of time assistance, performance, or restoration is performed—less than 24 hours, 24–96 hours, or more than 96 hours. It can also describe the form or type of delivery, e.g., single, intermittent, or continuous. The sixth character Function values are output, oxygenation, ventilation, pacing, filtration, and rhythm. Qualifiers in this section describe the extracorporeal device used in the root operation, and include breathing devices (continuous or intermittent positive airway pressure or continuous or intermittent negative airway pressure) and cardiac function devices (balloon pump, pulsatile compression, or hyperbaric chamber (device).

It is important to note that all of the root operations in this section are designed to assist, perform, or restore vital physiological functions of the heart and lungs especially, but also the biliary and urinary systems that are so important to body function and life.

Root Operations

The three root operations and values for the third code character are Assistance (0), Performance (1), and Restoration (2). The first three characters from any code in this Section will be 5A0, 5A1, or 5A2. The first character is the section, Extracorporeal Assistance and Performance (5), the second character is the body system, Physiological Systems (A), and the third character represents the root operation:

- 5A0 is root operation Assistance
- 5A1 is root operation Performance
- 5A2 is root operation Restoration

Table 5A with Root Operation Assistance (0)

The objective of root operation **Assistance** is to take over a portion of a physiological function by extracorporeal means. These are procedures that support a physiological function, but do not take complete control. Some examples are intra-aortic balloon pumps to support cardiac output, and hyperbaric oxygen treatment. Assistance differs from the root operation Performance in that it only assists in cardiac, respiratory, or circulatory function, whereas Performance takes over the entire physiological function. In a sense, all of the codes with this root operation, or the other two in this section, can be life-saving or life-prolonging functions.

In the root operation Assistance, procedures are applied to the heart, lungs, or circulatory system to assist in their functioning. Figure 9-1 is an excerpt from the Extracorporeal Assistance and Performance Table (5A) for root operation Assistance (0). In this Table are three fourth character body system values: Cardiac (2), circulatory (5), and respiratory (9).

Approaches used in root operation assistance In this section, the fifth character value is Duration, rather than Approach. Duration indicates the length of time assistance is performed, or the type of delivery. The values are shown in Table 9-1.

Duration values that describe length of time are applicable to the respiratory system only. Intermittent or continuous duration values are appropriate for either the cardiac or circulatory systems. For example, respiratory ventilation assistance performed continuously for over 96 hours would have a duration value of 5. Intermittent cardiac output assistance would have a duration value of 1, intermittent.

Section	**5**	Extracorporeal Assistance and Performance		
Body System	**A**	Physiological Systems		
Operation	**0**	Assistance: Taking over a portion of a physiological function by extracorporeal means		

Body System	Duration	Function	Qualifier
2 Cardiac	**1** Intermittent **2** Continuous	**1** Output	**0** Balloon Pump **5** Pulsatile Compression **6** Other Pump **D** Impeller Pump
5 Circulatory	**1** Intermittent **2** Continuous	**2** Oxygenation	**1** Hyperbaric **3** Membrane **C** Supersaturated
9 Respiratory	**3** Less than 24 Consecutive Hours **4** 24–96 Consecutive Hours **5** Greater than 96 Consecutive Hours	**5** Ventilation	**7** Continuous Positive Airway Pressure **8** Intermittent Positive Airway Pressure **9** Continuous Negative Airway Pressure **B** Intermittent Negative Airway Pressure **Z** No Qualifier

© Cengage Learning 2013

Figure 9-1 Extracorporeal Assistance and Performance Table 5A0

Table 9-1 Duration Values in Root Operation Assistance

Duration Type	Value	Name	Description	Body System
Length of Time	3	Less than 24 hours	Assistance provided for less than 24 hours	Respiratory
	4	24–96 hours	Assistance provided between 24 and 96 hours	Respiratory
	5	Greater than 96 hours	Assistance provided continuously for more than 96 hours	Respiratory
Form of Assist	1	Intermittent	Assistance provided intermittently, as needed	Cardiac or Circulatory
	2	Continuous	Assistance provided continuously, as needed	Cardiac or Circulatory

Table 9-2 Function Values in Root Operation Assistance

Function	Value	Description	Body System
Output	1	The amount of blood that is pumped by the heart	Cardiac
Oxygenation	2	The addition of oxygen to any system	Circulatory
Ventilation	3	The exchange of air between the lungs and the environment	Respiratory

Functions used in root operation assistance There are three functions used with root operation Assistance: Output (1), oxygenation (2), and ventilation (3). Table 9-2 illustrates the function and value, as well as the body system to which the function is applicable.

Output is the amount of blood that is pumped by the heart per unit time, measured in liters per minute (L/min). **Oxygenation** is the addition of oxygen to any system, including the human body. Oxygenation may also refer to the process of treating a patient with oxygen. **Ventilation** is essentially breathing, which is the exchange of air between the lungs and the environment. Ventilation assistance in respiratory function helps the patient to breathe using a device like the Continuous Positive Airway Pressure (CPAP) or cardiopulmonary bypass (Figure 9-2).

The Output function in root operation Assistance is used only with cardiac function. For example, *continuous cardiac output function assistance* using a balloon pump (5A02210) is an appropriate code; but there are no function or duration values available for *continuous pulmonary output function assistance*. Note in Figure 9-1 that there is neither a function value *output* in the row for the respiratory system, nor a duration value of *continuous*.

The Oxygenation function is applicable only to the circulatory system. Again, in Figure 9-1, note that there is no function value *oxygenation* in the row for the respiratory or the cardiac system. And last, the Ventilation function is applicable only to the respiratory system. In Figure 9-1, there is no function value *ventilation* in either the cardiac or circulatory system rows.

Qualifiers used with root operation assistance There are several qualifiers used with the Assistance root operation. Table 9-3 indicates the qualifiers used by body system and function in the root operation Assistance Table.

The balloon pump (0), pump (6), and pulsatile compression (5) qualifiers are used only with the cardiac system, and the cardiac output function. A **balloon pump** or simply, pump, is a device inserted into a heart vessel. Extracorporeally, the balloon is inflated and deflated with gas (usually helium) helping assist in cardiac output by manually pumping blood through the heart. A **pulsatile compression** device (Figure 9-3), which is sometimes called a pneumatic tourniquet system, applies intermittent compression to one or more extremities to assist in cardiac output.

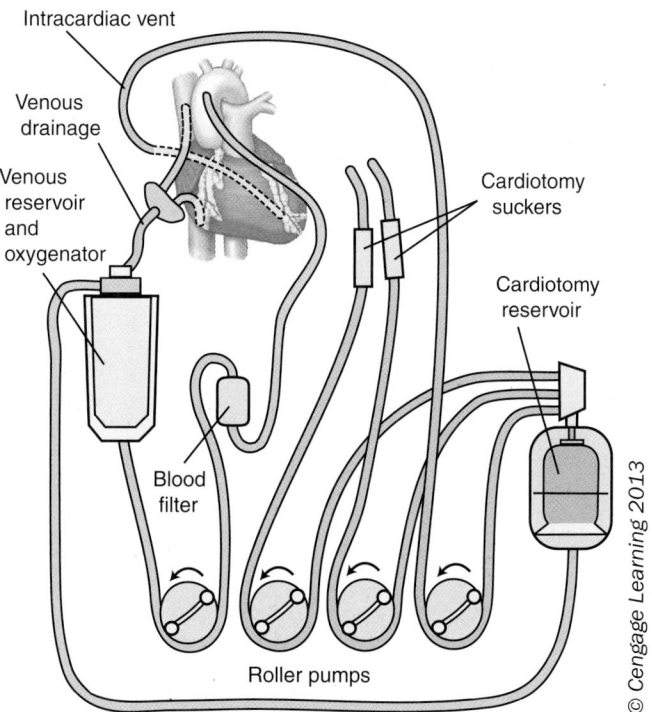

Figure 9-2 Illustration of Cardiopulmonary Bypass

Table 9-3 Qualifiers Used by Body System and Function

Body System	Value	Qualifier
Cardiac	0	Balloon Pump
	5	Pulsatile Compression
	6	Pump
Circulatory	1	Hyperbaric
	3	Membrane
	C	Supersaturated
Respiratory	7	Continuous Positive Airway Pressure (CPAP)
	8	Intermittent Positive Airway Pressure (IPAP)
	9	Continuous Negative Airway Pressure
	B	Intermittent Negative Airway Pressure
	Z	No Qualifier

The qualifiers hyperbaric (1), membrane (3), and supersaturated (C) are used only with the circulatory system, and the oxygenation function. **Hyperbaric** oxygenation is an increased amount of oxygen in organs and tissues resulting from the administration of oxygen in a compression chamber. The term "hyperbaric" is derived from Greek roots: "hyper-" meaning high, beyond, excessive, above normal; and "baros" meaning weight. Hyperbaric oxygen is used to treat gangrene, some soft tissue wounds and infections, and other conditions in which high concentrations of oxygen are beneficial.

Supersaturated (qualifier value C) oxygenation is, like hyperbaric, an increase in available oxygen. This qualifier is used only with the circulatory system, and oxygenation function in root operation Assistance in the Extracorporeal Assistance and Performance section.

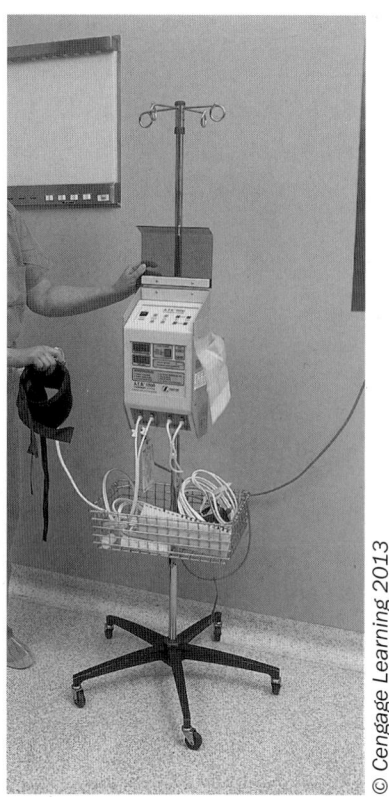

© Cengage Learning 2013

Figure 9-3 Pneumatic Tourniquet System (Pulsatile Compression Device)

CPAP represented by qualifier value 7, is a device that delivers a continuous stream of air through a mask or nasal cannula. It is an effective treatment for obstructive sleep apnea. CPAP patients wear a face mask connected to a pump that forces air into the nasal passages at pressures high enough to overcome obstructions in the airway and stimulate normal breathing. The airway pressure delivered into the upper airway is continuous during both inspiration and expiration. Figure 9-4 illustrates the respiratory system processes and functions. Intermittent positive airway pressure devices (Qualifier value 8) deliver an intermittent flow of air. Continuous or intermittent negative airway pressure devices work in a similar fashion, however, instead of forcing air in, it draws air from the lungs to force expiration of breath. The qualifier values 9 and B represent continuous negative airway pressure, and intermittent negative airway pressure, respectively.

Qualifier value 3, extracorporeal membrane oxygenation (ECMO) is a special procedure that uses an artificial heart-lung machine (Figure 9-5) to take over the work of the lungs (and sometimes also the heart). ECMO is used most often in newborns and young children, but it can also be used as a last resort for adults whose heart or lungs are failing. This qualifier is used only with the circulatory system, and oxygenation function.

Coding Assistance Root Operations in ICD-10-PCS

To find a Table reference in the Alphabetic Index from this section of the ICD-10-PCS, it is important to determine the objective of the procedure. For example, if the procedure states *intermittent balloon pump to increase cardiac output*, the objective would be to take over the cardiac output physiological function. Because it is intermittent, it can be assumed that it is not completely taking over that function, so it stands to reason that it is taking over only a portion of the cardiac output function. That objective fits the root operation definition for Assistance. A search using the terms *cardiac, output,* or even *function* reveals no Index entry or Table reference characters. As is almost always the case, the root operation would be required to begin the search. In the objective definition above, Assistance is the root operation (main term) used to begin the search in the Index.

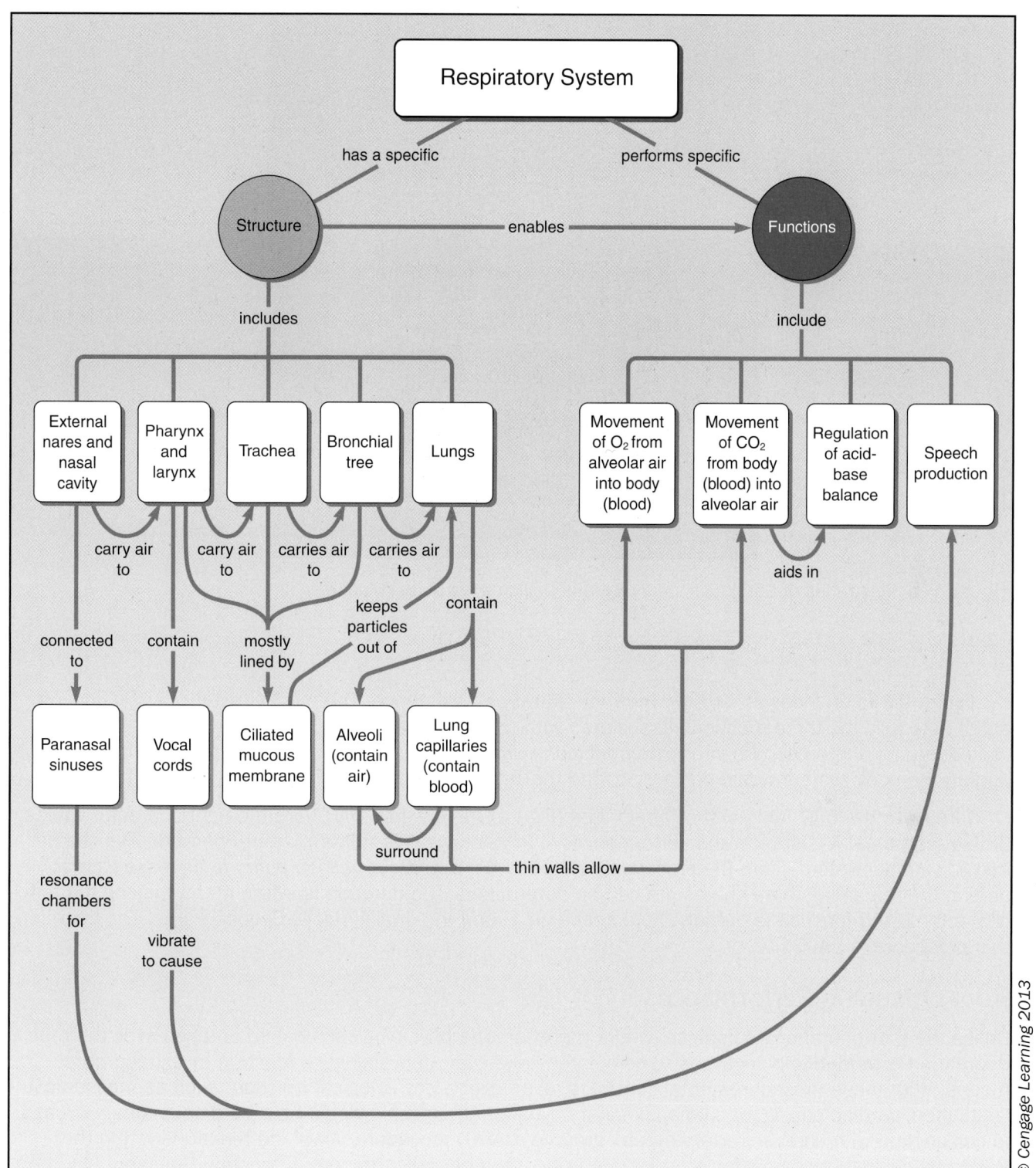

Figure 9-4 Illustration of the Respiratory System Structure, Process, and Function

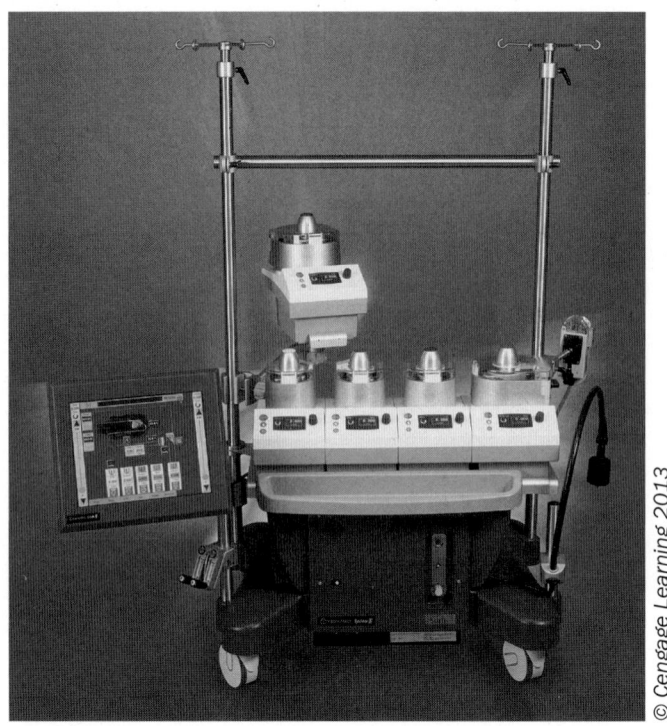

Figure 9-5 Illustration of Cardiopulmonary Bypass Device (Heart-Lung Machine)

© Cengage Learning 2013

Figure 9-6 is an Index excerpt for the root operation Assistance. The modifying term is *by Function* and it lists only the three functions associated with this root operation: Output, oxygenation, and ventilation. For the procedure *intermittent balloon pump to increase cardiac output,* the function would be output, the body system would be cardiac, and the Table reference value is 5A02.

Turning to the 5A0 Table in the Tabular List (Figure 9-1), confirm 5A02 are the right character values. 5: Extracorporeal Assistance and Performance, A: Physiological Systems, 0: root operation Assistance, and 2: cardiac system. From the procedural statement, *intermittent balloon pump to increase cardiac output,* the remaining three characters can be determined. The duration is intermittent, making the fifth character 1, the function is output, character value 1, and the qualifier is 0, Balloon Pump. The code for this procedure is 5A02110.

Root Operation Performance

Unlike the root operation Assistance, where a portion of a physiological function is taken over, the root operation **Performance** objective is to completely take over a physiological function by extracorporeal means. With these procedures, total control is taken over a physiological function, such as mechanical ventilation, cardiac pacing, or cardiopulmonary bypass. An example would be a cardiopulmonary bypass in conjunction with coronary artery bypass grafting (CABG) procedure. All of the functions within the Performance root operation Table are meant to take the place of the normal function to essentially keep the body alive.

Figure 9-7 illustrates the Table containing the root operation Performance in the Extracorporeal Assistance and Performance section. The character value for this root operation is 1, so a code from this section, body system, and root operation will always begin with the characters 5A1. There are five body system values for character 4, cardiac (2), circulatory (5), respiratory (9), biliary (C), and urinary (D). By definition, root operation Performance means that the function of the heart, circulatory, and respiratory system are completely taken over, as well as the functions of the biliary and urinary systems.

```
Assistance
    Cardiac
        Continuous
            Balloon Pump 5A02210
            Impeller Pump 5A0221D
            Other Pump 5A02216
            Pulsatile Compression 5A02215
        Intermittent
            Balloon Pump 5A02110
            Impeller Pump 5A0211D
            Other Pump 5A02116
            Pulsatile Compression 5A02115
    Circulatory
        Continuous
            Hyperbaric 5A05221
            Supersaturated 5A0522C
        Intermittent
            Hyperbaric 5A05121
            Supersaturated 5A0512C
    Respiratory
        24-96 Consecutive Hours
            Continuous Negative Airway Pressure 5A09459
            Continuous Positive Airway Pressure 5A09457
```

© Cengage Learning 2013

Figure 9-6 Alphabetic Index Excerpt for Root Operation Assistance

Section | **5** | Extracorporeal Assistance and Performance
Body System | **A** | Physiological Systems
Operation | **1** | Performance: Completely taking over a physiological function by extracorporeal means

Body System	Duration	Function	Qualifier
2 Cardiac	**0** Single	**1** Output	**2** Manual
2 Cardiac	**1** Intermittent	**3** Pacing	**Z** No Qualifier
2 Cardiac	**2** Continuous	**1** Output **3** Pacing	**Z** No Qualifier
5 Circulatory	**2** Continuous	**2** Oxygenation	**3** Membrane
9 Respiratory	**0** Single	**5** Ventilation	**4** Nonmechanical
9 Respiratory	**3** Less than 24 Consecutive Hours **4** 24-96 Consecutive Hours **5** Greater than 96 Consecutive Hours	**5** Ventilation	**Z** No Qualifier
C Biliary **D** Urinary	**0** Single **6** Multiple	**0** Filtration	**Z** No Qualifier

© Cengage Learning 2013

Figure 9-7 Root Operation Performance Table

The duration (fifth character) values are single (0), intermittent (1), continuous (2), less than 24 hours (3), 24–96 hours (4), greater than 96 consecutive hours (5), and multiple (6). There are five function values (sixth character): Filtration (0), output (1), oxygenation (2), pacing (3), and ventilation (5). Let us take a closer look at the duration, function, and qualifier values for the root operation Performance.

Duration values used with performance root operations The fifth character duration values and their definitions are the same as those for Assistance, with two new values added, *single* and *multiple* (Table 9-4).

Values intermittent (1), continuous (2), less than 24 hours (3), 24–96 hours (4), and greater than 96 consecutive hours (5) have the same value and definition as those with root operation Assistance. The new duration values are single (0) and multiple (6), and are used to indicate the function has been

Table 9-4 Duration Values used with Assistance Root Operation

Duration Type	Value	Name	Description	Body System
Length of Time	3	Less than 24 hours	Performed for less than 24 hours	Respiratory
	4	24–96 hours	Performed between 24 and 96 hours	Respiratory
	5	Greater than 96 hours	Performed more than 96 hours continuously	Respiratory
Form of Assist	1	Intermittent	Performed intermittently, as needed	Cardiac or Circulatory
	2	Continuous	Performed continuously, as needed	Cardiac or Circulatory
	0	Single	Performed once	Biliary or Urinary
	6	Multiple	Performed multiple times	Biliary or Urinary

Table 9-5 Functions Used with Root Operation Performance

Function	Value	Description	Body System
Output	1	The amount of blood that is pumped by the heart	Cardiac
Pacing	3	The rate and rhythm of the heart	Cardiac
Oxygenation	2	Addition of oxygen to any system	Circulatory
Ventilation	5	Exchange of air between the lungs and the environment	Respiratory
Filtration	0	Process where fluids pass through a filter or a filtering medium	Biliary and Urinary

performed one or multiple times. Duration values that specify a length of time are applicable only to the respiratory system. Intermittent or continuous functions are used with the cardiac or circulatory system. The duration values single and multiple are applicable only to the biliary and urinary systems.

Performance function/devices Table 9-5 describes the Functions used with root operation Performance.

The two new functions used with the root operation Performance are pacing and filtration. Performance of the **pacing** function means to control the rate and rhythm of the heart. It is used only with the cardiac system. **Filtration** is a process where fluids pass through a filter or filtering medium. The best-known example of a filtration device is dialysis (Figure 9-8), used to filter out toxins from the urinary system.

These functions are not interchangeable by body system. Filtration, for example, will be a root operation Performance function only for the biliary and urinary systems. Output and pacing are functions performed only on the cardiac system, e.g., there will not be a respiratory, circulatory, biliary, or urinary system function output found with this root operation and section.

Qualifiers used with root operation performance There are only four qualifier values for the root operation Performance:

- Z–No qualifier
- 2–Manual
- 3–Membrane
- 4–Nonmechanical

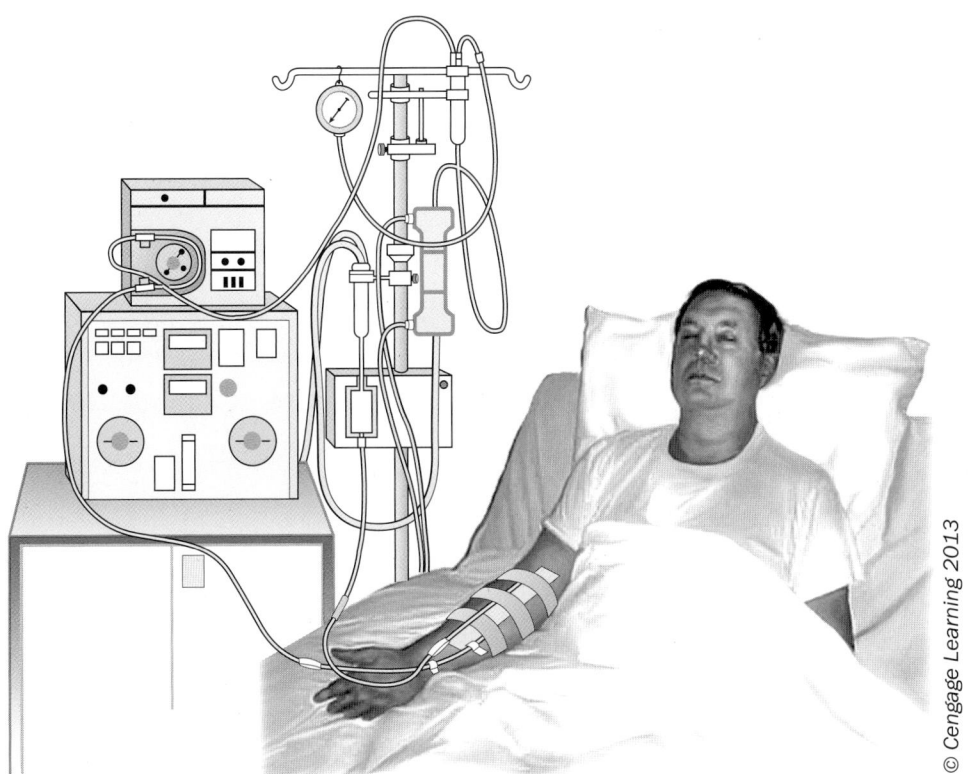

© Cengage Learning 2013

Figure 9-8 Dialysis Filtration System

The qualifier value 2, manual, is used only with a single cardiac output performance performed manually. The best example would be the chest compressions in cardiopulmonary resuscitation (CPR). The code for chest compressions in CPR would be as follows:

5–Section: Extracorporeal Assistance and Performance

A–Body System: Physiological Systems

1–Root Operation: Performance

2–Body System: Cardiac

0–Duration: Single

1–Function: Output

2–Qualifier: Manual

The qualifier membrane (3) is used only with continuous oxygenation of the circulatory system. The code for this procedure is 5A13223. Performance of continuous respiratory ventilation is the only time the qualifier nonmechanical (4) is used in this section and root operation. It would not be used when a heart-lung machine is performing the function, but only when ventilation is performed manually, as in mouth-to-mouth resuscitation (part of CPR). The code for this procedure would be 5A19054, broken down as:

5–Section: Extracorporeal Assistance and Performance

A–Body System: Physiological Systems

1–Root Operation: Performance

9–Body System: Respiratory

0–Duration: Single

5–Function: Ventilation

4–Qualifier: Nonmechanical

```
┌─────────────────────────────────────────────┐
│ Performance                                   │
│   Biliary                                     │
│     Multiple, Filtration 5A1C60Z              │
│     Single, Filtration 5A1C00Z                │
│   Cardiac                                     │
│     Continuous                                │
│        Output 5A1221Z                         │
│        Pacing 5A1223Z                         │
│     Intermittent, Pacing 5A1213Z              │
│     Single, Output, Manual 5A12012            │
│   Circulatory, Continuous, Oxygenation, Membrane 5A15223 │
│   Respiratory                                 │
│     24-96 Consecutive Hours, Ventilation 5A1945Z │
│     Greater than 96 Consecutive Hours, Ventilation 5A1955Z │
│     Less than 24 Consecutive Hours, Ventilation 5A1935Z │
│     Single, Ventilation, Nonmechanical 5A19054 │
│   Urinary                                     │
│     Multiple, Filtration 5A1D60Z              │
│     Single, Filtration 5A1D00Z                │
└─────────────────────────────────────────────┘
```
© Cengage Learning 2013

Figure 9-9 Alphabetic Index Excerpt for Root Operation Performance

Coding Performance Root Operations in ICD-10-PCS

As always, after abstracting the procedural statement from the medical documentation, the next step is to determine the main term, which is typically the root operation. Take the procedural statement continuous membrane oxygenation, circulatory system and consider what the purpose of this procedure is. The word oxygenation gives a clue that part or all of a physiological function has been taken over. Continuous adds a further clue that it might be all of a physiological function. Taking over all of a physiological function by extracorporeal means is the definition of root operation Performance.

Figure 9-9 is an excerpt from the Index for the root operation Performance. The modifying terms are by body system, with the functions listed as subterms below each body system. The function in this exam is continuous membranous circulatory system oxygenation, with the Table reference code 5A15.

Turning to that Table (Figure 9-7) in the Tabular list, the next steps are to confirm 5A15 is the correct table and row, then to determine the duration, function, and qualifier values. The reference value 5A15 represents the Extracorporeal Assistance and Performance section, the physiological systems body system, and the root operation Performance. The body system circulatory is found in only one row (the fourth), therefore, this is the row from which the function and will now be chosen. The function is oxygenation, value 2, and the qualifier is membrane (value 3). The code for continuous membrane oxygenation, circulatory system is 5A15223, broken down as follows:

5–Section: Extracorporeal Assistance and Performance

A–Body System: Physiological Systems

1–Root Operation: Performance

5–Body System: Circulatory

2–Duration: Continuous

2–Function: Oxygenation

3–Qualifier: Membrane

Here is another example, manual chest compressions. Looking again for clues from the procedure, the chest compressions are taking the place of a physiological function—in this case, cardiac output. These clues form the definition of root operation Performance. In Table 5A12 (Figure 9-7), there are three rows containing body system cardiac. The next step is to look for the duration, function, and qualifier that match the procedure, and are all contained in one row. The statement does not include a duration, but the function, *output*, limits the choice to row 1 or 3. Row 1 contains the qualifier manual, but row 3 does not—thus, the correct row from this Table is row 1. There is only one duration value (0, single), which makes building the code easier. (If there were multiple duration values listed, the medical documentation would need to be reviewed to determine the duration, or the provider of the chest compressions would need to be queried.) The code for *manual chest compressions* is 5A12012, broken down as follows:

5–Section: Extracorporeal Assistance and Performance
A–Body System: Physiological Systems
1–Root Operation: Performance
2–Body System: Cardiac
0–Duration: Single
1–Function: Output
2–Qualifier: Manual

It is time to review the final root operation for this section, Restoration.

Root Operation Restoration

There is only one body system, duration, function and qualifier for root operation Restoration. **Restoration** is returning, or attempting to return, a physiological function to its original state by extracorporeal means, and the character value is 2. The best example of a procedure from this root operation is using a defibrillator to shock the heart back into normal rhythm. The only other procedure using this root operation from this section is **cardioversion.** Cardioversion is conversion of one cardiac rhythm or electrical pattern to another, almost always from an abnormal to a normal one. This conversion can be accomplished by pharmacologic means, using medications; or by electrical cardioversion, using a defibrillator. The only code possible from this Table is 5A2204Z, which includes the procedures defibrillation and cardioversion. The code values are:

5–Section: Extracorporeal Assistance and Performance
A–Body System: Physiological Systems
2–Root Operation: Restoration
2–Body System: Cardiac
0–Duration: Single
4–Function: Rhythm
Z–Qualifier: None

Let's Review 9–1:

List the root operation and code for the following:
   1. Chest compressions as part of CPR _____
   2. Defibrillation to heart to restore rhythm _____
   3. Continuous pulsatile compression stocking to assist in cardiac output _____
   4. Hyperbaric chamber, continuous, for circulatory oxygenation assistance _____
   5. CPAP for sleep apnea, 10p.m. to 7a.m. _____

Extracorporeal Therapies 6A0–6A9

In this section, equipment outside the body is used for a therapeutic purpose that does not involve assistance, performance, or restoration of a physiological function. Examples of extracorporeal therapies include extracorporeal dialysis and extracorporeal shock wave lithotripsy. Extracorporeal therapies have a character value of 6. There is only one character 2 value for body systems: Physiological Systems, which has a character value of A. All codes from this section will begin with the characters 6A. There are 10 root operations in the extracorporeal therapy section. Table 9-6 lists the root operations, values, and definitions.

The fourth character specifies the body system on which the therapy is performed, e.g., skin, circulatory, musculoskeletal, and other body systems. Duration is the fifth character value, and is similar to the duration values in the Extracorporeal Assistance and Performance section. In this section, the sixth and seventh characters are qualifiers (In previous sections, character 6 has described the device or function). In this section, there are no valid sixth character values, so the sixth character in any code from this section will be Z, no device. There are only two root operations that use a seventh character qualifier. In the root operation Pheresis, the qualifier specifies the blood component on which pheresis is performed, e.g., erythrocytes, platelets, or plasma. In root operation Ultrasound Therapy, the qualifier is used to specify the treatment site, i.e., the head and neck vessels, heart, or other vessels.

Root Operations

Let us examine the root operations more closely, along with valid body system, duration, and qualifier values. Table 9-7 contains each of the 10 root operations, and the values for character four, body system, character five, duration, and characters six and seven, qualifiers.

Root Operation Definitions and Examples

- **Atmospheric Control** is root operation 0 in Extracorporeal Therapies. It is defined as extracorporeal control of atmospheric pressure and composition; for example, in allergy treatments, controlling the atmosphere with antigen-free air conditioning.

- **Decompression**, root operation 1, is the extracorporeal elimination of undissolved gas from body fluids. This consists of a single type of procedure, treatment for decompression sickness (known as the bends) using a hyperbaric chamber.

Table 9-6 Root Operations, Values, and Definitions

Root Operation	Value	Description
Atmospheric Control	0	Extracorporeal control of atmospheric pressure and composition
Decompression	1	Extracorporeal elimination of undissolved gas from body fluids
Electromagnetic Therapy	2	Extracorporeal treatment by electromagnetic rays
Hyperthermia	3	Extracorporeal raising of body temperature
Hypothermia	4	Extracorporeal lowering of body temperature
Pheresis	5	Extracorporeal separation of blood products
Phototherapy	6	Extracorporeal treatment by light rays
Shock wave therapy	7	Extracorporeal treatment by shock waves
Ultrasound therapy	8	Extracorporeal therapy by ultrasound
Ultraviolet light therapy	9	Extracorporeal therapy by ultraviolet light

Table 9-7 Body System, Duration, and Qualifier Values for Root Operations

Root Operation Character 3	Body System Character 4	Duration Character 5	Qualifier Character 6	Qualifier Character 7
0–Atmospheric Control	G–Whole body	0–Single 6–Multiple	Z–No qualifier	Z–No qualifier
1–Decompression	5–Circulatory	0–Single 6–Multiple	Z–No qualifier	Z–No qualifier
2–Electromagnetic Therapy	1–Urinary 2–Central nervous	0–Single 6–Multiple	Z–No qualifier	Z–No qualifier
3–Hyperthermia	G–Whole body	0–Single 6–Multiple	Z–No qualifier	Z–No qualifier
4–Hypothermia	G–Whole body	0–Single 6–Multiple	Z–No qualifier	Z–No qualifier
5–Pheresis	5–Circulatory	0–Single 6–Multiple	Z–No qualifier	0–Erythrocytes 1–Leukocytes 2–Platelets 3–Plasma T–Stem Cells, cord V–Stem cells, hematopoietic
6 –Phototherapy	0–Skin 5–Circulatory	0–Single 6–Multiple	Z–No qualifier	Z–No qualifier
7–Ultrasound Therapy	5–Circulatory	0–Single 6–Multiple	Z–No qualifier	4–Head and neck vessels 5–Heart 6–Peripheral vessels 7–Other vessels Z–No qualifier
8–Ultraviolet Light Therapy	0–Skin	0–Single 6–Multiple	Z–No qualifier	Z–No qualifier
9–Shock Wave Therapy	3–Musculoskeletal	0–Single 6–Multiple	Z–No qualifier	Z–No qualifier

- **Electromagnetic Therapy** is extracorporeal treatment by electromagnetic rays, represented by character value 2. An example of Electromagnetic Therapy is transcranial magnetic stimulation (TMS).

- **Hyperthermia**, Root Operation 3, is the extracorporeal raising of body temperature. It is used to treat temperature imbalances, or as an adjunct radiation treatment for cancer. If the procedure is to treat a temperature imbalance, the code should be selected from Extracorporeal Therapies section, root operation Hyperthermia. If Hyperthermia is used as a cancer treatment, this is classified as a modality (device) in the Radiation Oncology section.

- **Hypothermia** is the extracorporeal lowering of body temperature, e.g., whole body hypothermia treatments. The character value for Hypothermia is 4.

- **Pheresis** is the extracorporeal separation of blood products. It is used in medical practice for two purposes: (1) to treat diseases where too much of a blood component is produced (leukemia); or (2) to remove a blood product from a donor to use in transfusion into a patient who needs the blood product.

- **Phototherapy**, root operation 6, is defined as extracorporeal treatment by light rays. In the circulatory system phototherapy is used to expose the blood to light rays using a machine that recirculates the blood and returns it to the body after the phototherapy is complete.

- Root operation 7 is **Ultrasound Therapy,** extracorporeal treatment by ultrasound. A good example of Ultrasound Therapy is Ultrasound-assisted thrombolysis. Ultrasound-assisted thrombolysis uses ultrasound waves to target and break down blood clots. Benefits include a more targeted, immediate solution than pharmaceutical blood-thinning treatment, and reduced complications and healing time than is usually associated with invasive surgical procedures.

- **Ultraviolet light therapy**, Root Operation 8 in the Extracorporeal Therapies section, is extracorporeal treatment by ultraviolet light, e.g., ultraviolet light phototherapy, used in some acne treatments.

- **Shock wave therapy** is root operation 9. Defined as extracorporeal treatment by shock waves. It is used in this section to treat the musculoskeletal system, such as *shoc kwave therapy of the plantar fascia of the foot.*

Body System, Duration, and Qualifier Values for Extracorporeal Therapies

The only character five body system values used in this section are the whole body, and the urinary, central nervous, circulatory, and integumentary (skin) systems. The whole body value G is used only with root operations Atmospheric Control, Hyperthermia, and Hypothermia. The circulatory system, value 5, is used with root operations Decompression, Pheresis, Phototherapy, and Ultrasound therapy. The urinary and central nervous system values (1 and 2, respectively) are used in root operation 2, Electromagnetic Therapy only. And root operation Shock Wave Therapy uses the musculoskeletal system (value 3) only. There are only two duration values, 0, to indicate a single treatment, and 6, to indicate multiple treatments for the specific root operation. The sixth character qualifier for all ten root operations is Z, no qualifier, and in all but two operations the seventh character qualifier is also Z. In root operation Pheresis, there are six qualifiers in the seventh position:

0–Erythrocytes

1–Leukocytes

2–Platelets

3–Plasma

T–Stem Cells, Cord Blood (from umbilical cord)

V–Stem Cells, Hematopoietic (blood cells produced by the body)

Pheresis is the extracorporeal separation of blood products, and the seventh character qualifier indicates which blood products were separated. Pheresis is an automated blood collection technology that allows a donor to give specific blood components, such as platelets. During the procedure, all but the needed blood components are returned to the donor. Shock wave Therapy is extracorporeal treatment using shock waves. This therapy uses high-intensity magnets (magnetotherapy) and affects nerves, vessels, muscles, and bones. The therapy produces a powerful impulse that is stated to restore nerve conduction, and stimulate muscle fiber, and also assists in reabsorption and "breaking" of salt deposits in the tissues.

Coding Extracorporeal Therapies in Root Operations in ICD-10-PCS

In the Index, each of the root operations is listed individually. If the procedure is Shock wave Therapy, that root operation is, like all root operations, found in the Index. The same is true regardless of which of the ten root operations is being searched for. For example, use the procedure *electromagnetic therapy, central nervous system (CNS), six treatments.* In the Index, *electromagnetic therapy* is the main term, and indented below that are two subterms, *central nervous* and *urinary systems.* Beside the central nervous system is the Table reference 6A22. In the Tabular List for Table 6A22, all that remains is to determine the duration, and qualifiers. In this procedure, the duration is listed as multiple treatments, making the fifth character 6, with Z representing the sixth and seventh characters. The code is 6A226ZZ.

Another example would be *separation of blood plasma from donor blood*. The objective of this procedure is to separate the blood, which is the definition of the root operation Pheresis. In the Index, indented under Pheresis is the subterm *circulatory system*, and a reference to Table 6A55. This references the Extracorporeal Therapies section (6), the body system Physiology (A), the root operation Pheresis (5), and the body system Circulatory. The duration is 1, single (a single donor), the sixth character qualifier is Z, and the seventh character qualifier is 3, plasma. The code is 6A551Z3. As with all Indexing, the key is in determining the objective of the procedure, which leads to the root operation. When in doubt, review either Appendix A in the ICD-10-PCS codebook to find examples, explanations, and definitions of the root operations, or Appendix B, which groups similar root operations together to help identify the specific, and most appropriate root operation.

Let's Review 9–2:

Identify the root operation and code the following procedures:

1. Antigen-free air conditioning, series treatment (Atmospheric Control) _____
2. Hyperbaric decompression treatment, single (Decompression) _____
3. Therapeutic leukapheresis, single treatment (Pheresis) _____
4. Peripheral vessel therapeutic ultrasound, series treatment (Ultrasound Therapy) _____
5. Plantar fascia shock wave therapy, single treatment (Shock wave Therapy) _____

Chapter Summary

The codes the Extracorporeal Assistance and Performance section range from 5A0 through 5A2, and include three root operations that assist, perform, or restore, physiological functions by extracorporeal means. Extracorporeal means *outside the body*. In extracorporeal assistance and performance procedures, equipment outside the body is used to assist or perform a physiological function. The second character, representing the general body system is A, Physiological Systems. The three root operations and values for the third code character are Assistance (0), Performance (1), and Restoration (2). There are only five body system (character 4) values in this section: Cardiac (2), circulatory (5), respiratory (9), biliary (C), and urinary (D). In this section, the fifth character value is duration, rather than approach. Duration indicates the length of time assistance, performance, or restoration was performed, for example less than 24 hours, 24–96 hours, or greater than 96 hours. It can also describe the form or type of delivery, e.g., single, intermittent, or continuous.

The first three characters from any code in this Section will be 5A0, 5A1, or 5A2:

- 5A0 is root operation Assistance
- 5A1 is root operation Performance
- 5A2 is root operation Restoration

The objective of root operation Assistance is to take over a portion of a physiological function by extracorporeal means. These are procedures that support a physiological function, but do not take complete control. In the root operation Assistance, procedures are applied to the heart, lungs, or circulatory system to assist in their functioning (Figure 9-1). In this Table are three fourth character body system values: Cardiac (2), circulatory (5), and respiratory (9). The fifth character value is duration, rather than approach. Duration indicates the length of time assistance was performed, or the type of delivery. The values are shown in Table 9-1. Duration values that describe length of time are applicable to the respiratory system only. Intermittent or continuous duration values are appropriate for either the cardiac or circulatory system.

There are three functions used with root operation Assistance: Output (1), oxygenation (2), and ventilation (Table 9-2). The output function in root operation Assistance is used only with cardiac function and the oxygenation function is applicable only to the circulatory system. There are several qualifiers used with the Assistance root operation (Table 9-3). The qualifiers hyperbaric (1), membrane (3), and supersaturated (C) are used only with the circulatory system, and the oxygenization function.

To find a Table reference in the index from this section of the ICD-10-PCS, it is important to determine the objective of the procedure. Unlike the root operation Assistance, where a portion of a physiological function is taken over, the objective of the root operation Performance is to completely take over a physiological function by extracorporeal means. With these procedures, total control is taken over a physiological function, such as mechanical ventilation, cardiac pacing, or cardiopulmonary bypass.

The root operation Performance means that the function of the heart, circulatory, and respiratory system are completely taken over, as well as the functions of the biliary and urinary systems. The duration (fifth character) values are single (0), intermittent (1), continuous (2), less than 24 hours (3), 24–96 hours (4), greater than 96 consecutive hours (5), and multiple (6). There are five function values (sixth character): filtration (0), output (1), oxygenation (2), pacing (3), and ventilation (5).

The two new functions used with the root operation Performance are pacing and filtration. Performance of the pacing function means to control the rate and rhythm of the heart. It is used only with the cardiac system in this root operation. Filtration is a process where fluids pass through a filter or filtering medium. Restoration is returning, or attempting to return, a physiological function to its original state by extracorporeal means, and the character value is 2.

In the Extracorporeal Therapies section, equipment outside the body is used for a therapeutic purpose that does not involve assistance, performance, or restoration of a physiological function. Extracorporeal therapies have a character value of 6. There is only one character 2 value for body systems: Physiological systems, with a character value of A. All codes from this section will begin with the characters 6A. There are 10 root operations in the Extracorporeal Therapies section (Table 9-6). The fourth character specifies the body system on which the therapy is performed, e.g., skin, circulatory, musculoskeletal, and other body systems. Duration is the fifth character value, and is similar to the duration values in the Extracorporeal Assistance and Performance section. In this section, the sixth and seventh characters are qualifiers. There are no valid sixth character values, so the sixth character in any code from this section will be Z, no device, and there are only two root operations that use a seventh character qualifier. In the root operation Pheresis, the qualifier specifies the blood component on which Pheresis is performed, e.g., erythrocytes, platelets, or plasma. In root operation Ultrasound Therapy, the qualifier is used to specify the treatment site, i.e., the head and neck vessels, heart, or other vessels.

Chapter Review

Matching

Instructions: Match the term to its definition.

_____ 1. Extracorporeal

_____ 2. Restoration

_____ 3. CPAP

_____ 4. Assistance

_____ 5. Performance

_____ 6. Atmospheric control

_____ 7. Decompression

_____ 8. Hypothermia

_____ 9. Pheresis

_____ 10. Duration

a. Outside of the body.

b. Root operation 2 in Extracorporeal Assistance and Performance. Returning, or attempting to return, a physiological function to its original state by extracorporeal means.

c. Continuous positive airway pressure device that delivers a continuous stream of air through a mask or nasal cannula.

d. Root operation 0 in Extracorporeal Assistance and Performance. Taking over a portion of a physiological function by extracorporeal means.

e. Root operation 1 in Extracorporeal Assistance and Performance. Completely taking over a physiological function by extracorporeal means.

f. Root operation 0 in Extracorporeal Therapies. Extracorporeal control of atmospheric pressure and composition.

g. Root operation 1 in the Extracorporeal Therapies section. Extracorporeal elimination of undissolved gas from body fluids.

h. Root operation 4 in the Extracorporeal Therapies section. Extracorporeal lowering of body temperature.

i. Root operation 5 in the Extracorporeal Therapies section. Extracorporeal separation of blood products.

j. Length of time extracorporeal assistance, performance, or restoration was performed, or the type of delivery.

Short Answer

Instructions: Determine the root operation for the following procedures.

1. Ultraviolet light phototherapy, series treatment _____

2. Hyperbaric oxygenation of wound

3. Cardiopulmonary bypass in conjunction with CABG (code the Extracorporeal Assistance and Performance only) _____

4. Attempted cardiac defibrillation, unsuccessful _____

5. Whole body hypothermia treatment, series _____

6. Temperature elevation, whole body, single treatment _____

7. Therapeutic plasmapheresis, multiple treatments _____

8. Therapeutic ultrasound of head and neck vessels, single treatment _____

9. Transcranial magnetic stimulation (TMS), series treatment _____

10. Cardioversion, successful _____

Coding Practice

Instructions: Now that the root operation has been identified, code the following procedures.

1. Ultraviolet light phototherapy, series treatment _____

2. Hyperbaric oxygenation of wound _____

3. Cardiopulmonary bypass in conjunction with CABG (code the Extracorporeal Assistance and Performance only) _____

4. Attempted cardiac defibrillation, unsuccessful _____

5. Whole body hypothermia treatment, series _____

6. Temperature elevation, whole body, single treatment _____

7. Therapeutic plasmapheresis, multiple treatments _____

8. Therapeutic ultrasound of head and neck vessels, single treatment

   _____

9. Transcranial magnetic stimulation (TMS), series treatment _____

10. Cardioversion, successful _____

Osteopathic, Other Procedures, Chiropractic, and Imaging

Learning Objectives

At the conclusion of this chapter, the learner should be able to:

- Define and understand the key terms and definitions associated with the Osteopathic, Chiropractic, Other Procedures, and Imaging sections of the ICD-10-PCS coding manual
- Identify the character values, definitions, and uses for the Osteopathic, Chiropractic, Other Procedures, and Imaging sections of the ICD-10-PCS coding manual
- Know the guidelines specific to the Osteopathic, Chiropractic, Other Procedures, and Imaging sections of the ICD-10-PCS coding manual
- Understand how to search in the Alphabetic Index for procedures from the Osteopathic, Chiropractic, Other Procedures, and Imaging sections of the ICD-10-PCS coding manual
- Perform coding steps for procedures, services, and treatments related to the Osteopathic, Chiropractic, Other Procedures, and Imaging sections of the ICD-10-PCS coding manual

Key Terms and Definitions

Computer assisted procedures	Navigation systems that provide additional information during a procedure, to increase surgical accuracy and reduce the chance of malposition of implants.
Contrast	Substance used in imaging procedures to enhance visualization of internal organs and structures.
Contrast Agents (radiocontrast agents)	A type of medical substance used to improve the visibility of internal bodily structures in imaging root types.
Densitometry	A test measuring bone density.
Fluoroscopy	Single or bi-plane real time display of an image developed from the capture of radiation on a fluorescent screen.
Magnetic Resonance Imaging (MRI)	Computerized digital display of multiplanar images developed from the capture of radiofrequency signals emitted within a magnetic field.

Manipulation	Manual procedure that involves a directed thrust to move a joint past the physiological range of motion, without exceeding the anatomical limit. It is also known as an adjustment and is found only in the Chiropractic section.
Multiplanar	A technique used to generate sagittal, coronal, and oblique views (multiple planes).
Near-infrared spectroscopy	Monitoring method in detecting oxygen saturation in the field of neurosurgery and cardiovascular surgery and neonatal ICU.
Osmole	Amount of a substance that dissociates (separates) in a solution.
Osmolarity	The concentration of osmotically active particles in a solution.
Other procedures	Methodologies that attempt to alleviate somatic dysfunction and related disorders.
Plain Radiography	The capture of external radiation developed as an image on photographic or photoconductive plate. Also known simply as an X-ray or radiological image.
Root type	Third character title for Imaging section code, replacing Root Operation.
Robotic-assisted procedures	A computerized system with a motorized construction (usually an arm) capable of interacting with the environment.
Treatment	The manual treatment to alleviate somatic dysfunction and related disorders. In the Osteopathic section, root operation value 0.
Ultrasonography	Real time display of anatomical structure or flow images developed from the capture of high-frequency sound waves.

Introduction

Four chapters of the ICD-10-PCS coding manual are presented here. They are:

- Osteopathic (7W0)
- Chiropractic (9WB)
- Other Procedures (8E0)
- Imaging (B00-BY4)

   The body systems, body parts, root operations, and other character values are discussed at length, as well as any applicable guidelines. The character value names and definitions for most of these chapters are different than those presented in other chapters of the ICD-10-PCS. Their definitions and uses are included here. Directions will be given on how to search the Alphabetic Index for procedures included in these chapters, and how to read the associated Tables. Last, but not least, multiple procedure coding examples are presented for Osteopathic, Chiropractic, Other Procedures and Imaging procedures, treatments, and services.

Osteopathic Section

Osteopathic procedure codes have a first character value of 7. The body system (character 2) value is Anatomical Regions (W), and there is only one root operation for the Osteopathic section, which is Treatment, character value 0. The first three characters for any Osteopathic section code is 7W0. The root operation **Treatment** is manual treatment to alleviate somatic dysfunction and related disorders. An example is *fascia release of abdomen, osteopathic manipulation treatment* (OMT). The Osteopathic Table is illustrated in Figure 10-1. Note that the character meanings differ slightly from other sections. The second

Section	**7**	Osteopathic		
Body System	**W**	Anatomical Regions		
Operation	**0**	Treatment: Manual treatment to eliminate or alleviate somatic dysfunction and related disorders		

Body Region	Approach	Method	Qualifier
0 Head **1** Cervical **2** Thoracic **3** Lumbar **4** Sacrum **5** Pelvis **6** Lower Extremities **7** Upper Extremities **8** Rib Cage **9** Abdomen	**0** Articulatory-Raising **1** Fascial Release **2** General Mobilization **3** High Velocity-Low Amplitude **4** Indirect **X** External **6** Lymphatic Pump **7** Muscle Energy-Isometric **8** Muscle Energy-Isotonic **9** Other Method	**5** Low Velocity-High Amplitude	**Z** None

Figure 10-1 Osteopathic Table in the ICD-10-PCS

© Cengage Learning 2013

and third characters still represent the general body system, and the root operation. Character 4 is the Body Region, and character 6, rather than the device or function, represents the Method by which the root operation treatment is delivered. Character 5, is still the approach, and has only one value, X, external. Character 7, the qualifier, is always none in the Osteopathic section, with the character value Z.

Body Regions in the Osteopathic Section

There are 10 body regions (character 4) in the first column of the Osteopathic Table:

0—Head

1—Cervical

2—Thoracic

3—Lumbar

4—Sacrum

5—Pelvis

6—Lower extremities

7—Upper extremities

8—Rib cage

9—Abdomen

The root operation Treatment is aimed at one of these specific body regions. For example, if Treatment is aimed at the fourth and fifth lumbar, the specific body region is 3, lumbar. If it is aimed at the lumbar, sacrum, and pelvis, there would be three individual codes, in accordance with Guideline B3.2 on multiple procedures. Each code would have the same character values except for character 4, Body Region, unless the method (character 6) differs with each or all of the Treatment procedures. Let us take a look at the methods in Osteopathic Treatment.

Approaches in Osteopathic Treatment

Character 5 identifies the Treatment approaches performed during the procedure. There are 10 approach values. Table 10-1 identifies the approaches, their values, and basic definitions for each.

In earlier procedure coding versions, especially in the ambulatory care facilities, the Osteopathic Treatment was coded simply as an Osteopathic Manipulation Technique (OMT) without a specific indication of the method used. This is one of many areas that require more detailed medical record documentation by the provider to add the precise method of Treatment given. There are no qualifiers in the Osteopathic Section, therefore, the seventh character will always be Z, no qualifier. The final two

Table 10-1 Approaches Used in Osteopathic Treatment

Value	Name	Description
0	Articulatory-Raising	Passive joint and muscle stretching techniques used by the body via palpation and movement
1	Fascial and Myofascial Relase	Fascial release is a very old osteopathic technique, which can use direct or indirect forces to treat fascial restrictions
2	General Mobilization	Massage designed to enhance fluid movement through the tissues
3	High Velocity Low Amplitude (HVLA)	Uses forces quickly applied to a discrete area. This is familiar to many people as a thrusting or "popping" technique. This is most commonly performed as a direct technique
4	Indirect	Can be any one of the techniques shown here as including an indirect approach
5	Lymphatic Pump	The rib cage and thoracic spine are manipulated with the intent of improving the lymphatic circulation of the chest. Also known as lymphatic drainage massage
6	Muscle Energy, Isometric	A form of resistance exercise in which one's muscles are used in opposition with other muscle groups
7	Muscle Energy, Isotonic	A form of resistance exercise in which one's muscles are used in harmony with other muscle groups
8	Other Methods	Balanced Tension: This technique balances the tension of or across a given level to set up a condition where the body is less affected by the pathology and can treat itself. Percussion: The use of percussion using a Foredom percussor over precise areas of the body at a specific speed and length of time

characters of an Osteopathic section code are the Method (character 6) and Qualifier (character 7). There is only one method value, low velocity, high-amplitude (value 5), This method uses forces applied slowly to the treatment area, similar to stretching rather than popping or thrusting. The qualifier (character 7) value in the Osteopathic section is always Z, none.

Coding Osteopathic Root Operation Treatment in ICD-10-PCS

There is only one Root Operation in this Section, Treatment; therefore, whenever an Osteopathic procedure is performed, the Root Operation will be Treatment in the Index. A search under Osteopathic gives the instruction *See Treatment*. Under Treatment, the modifying term is *Osteopathic*, and the subterms include all 10 body regions, starting with Abdomen and ending with Upper Extremities. For the procedure *Osteopathic manipulation of pelvis using isometric muscle energy technique*, the Index reference for Pelvis is Table 7W02. In Table 7W0, (Osteopathic section, Anatomical Regions, root operation Treatment), the approach will always be X for External. The method used in this procedure is *isometric muscle energy* (character value 7) and there is no qualifier, so the seventh character value will be Z. The code is 7W0X7Z.

Chiropractic (9WB)

The first three characters of a chiropractic section code are 9WB. The section (9) is Chiropractic; the body system is W, Anatomical Regions, and the only root operation is Manipulation, character B. The fourth character represents the body region upon which the chiropractic manipulation is performed. There are 10 body region values, as follows:

0—Head

1—Cervical (vertebra)

2—Thoracic (vertebra)

3—Lumbar (vertebra)

4—Sacrum

5—Pelvis

6—Lower Extremities

7—Upper Extremities

8—Rib Cage

9—Abdomen

The fourth character approach with a chiropractic manipulation is always external, represented by character value X. In the Chiropractic Table, the only root operation is manipulation, defined as a manual procedure that involves a directed thrust to move a joint past the physiological range of motion, without exceeding the anatomical limit. An example is manipulation of the cervical spine. A manipulation is also called an adjustment in Chiropractic. There are nine character 6 method values in this section. All procedures consist of the following components:

1. High or low velocity thrust applied singly or of multiple repetitions. This thrust has a variable amplitude, specific direction and is applied through a long and/or short lever system

2. Contact and different hand positioning

3. Patient and doctor positioning

4. Indications and contraindications

At times, a mechanical device is used to assist in the manipulation; the method them becomes value K, mechanically assisted. A non-manual manipulation is performed using specific patient positions and gravity, rather than a hands-on manipulation of the body part. Extraarticular methods (value D) are manipulations away from joints in the spine or body. Indirect and direct visceral (values C and F) manipulations typically are applied to the body region abdomen (9). A short-lever thrust is usually applied to the smaller, shorter, bones, i.e., to individual vertebra, while long-lever thrusts are applied to longer bones, such as the leg, upper body, or head.

Coding Chiropractic Root Operation Manipulation in ICD-10-PCS

In the Index, searching for the root operation Manipulation results in an instructional note (Figure 10-2) to *See Chiropractic Manipulation*. For this reason, consider the root operation a Chiropractic Manipulation, not just a manipulation. Figure 10-3 is an excerpt from the Alphabetic Index for root operation Manipulation. Note that it contains the instruction to SEE chiropractic manipulation. Figure 10-4 is the Index listing for Chiropractic Manipulation. The modifying terms with this root operation identify the body region, starting with Abdomen and ending with Thoracic.

Using the procedure *short-lever thoracic vertebral adjustment*, a search of the Index reveals the body region *thoracic* as a modifying term indented under Chiropractic Manipulation. The Table reference is

Section	9	Chiropractic		
Body System	W	Anatomical Regions		
Operation	B	Manipulation: Manual procedure that involves a directed thrust to move joint past the physiological range of motion, without exceeding the anatomical limit		

Body Region	Approach	Method	Qualifier
0 Head **1** Cervical **2** Thoracic **3** Lumbar **4** Sacrum **5** Pelvis **6** Lower Extremities **7** Upper Extremities **8** Rib Cage **9** Abdomen	**X** External	**B** Non-Manual **C** Indirect Visceral **D** Extra-Articular **F** Direct Visceral **G** Long Lever Specific Contact **H** Short Lever Specific Contact **J** Long and Short Lever Specific Contact **K** Mechanically Assisted **L** Other Method	**Z** None

© Cengage Learning 2013

Figure 10-2 Chiropractic Table for Root Operation Manipulation

> **Manipulation**
> Adhesions see Release
> Chiropractic see Chiropractic Manipulation

Figure 10-3 Alphabetic Index for Root Operation Manipulation   © Cengage Learning 2013

> **Chiropractic Manipulation**
> Abdomen **9WB9X**
> Cervical **9WB1X**
> Extremities
>   Lower **9WB6X**
>   Upper **9WB7X**
> Head **9WB0X**
> Lumbar **9WB3X**
> Pelvis **9WB5X**
> Rib Cage **9WB8X**
> Sacrum **9WB4X**
> Thoracic **9WB2X**
>
> © Cengage Learning 2013

Figure 10-4 Alphabetic Index Excerpt for Chiropractic Manipulation

9WB2X. Turning to that Table (Figure 10-2), first confirm that 9WB2X are the correct character values for the section, body system, root operation, body region, and approach. The method is short lever, value H, for the sixth character, and as always, there is no qualifier in the Chiropractic table, so the seventh character value will be Z. The code for a *short-lever thoracic vertebral adjustment*, is 9WB2XHZ.

Other Procedures (8E0)

The root operation for the Other Procedures Table is also named Other Procedures, and is defined as *methodologies that attempt to alleviate somatic dysfunction and related disorders.* The procedures included in the Other Procedures section are for non-traditional, whole-body therapies, including acupuncture and meditation. The Other Procedures section is represented by the value 8. There are two body system character values: C, indwelling Catheter, and E, anatomical systems and anatomical regions. The root operation will always be 0, Other Procedures.

In addition to acupuncture and meditation, other procedures include collection of body fluids from an indwelling catheter, near infrared spectroscopy, therapeutic massage, suture removal, piercing, sperm collection, in vitro fertilization, and yoga therapy. The fourth through seventh character assignments are:

- Character 4: Body Region
- Character 5: Approach
- Character 6: Method
- Character 7: Qualifier

Body System: Physiological Systems and Anatomical Regions

For Body System C, indwelling catheter (Figure 10-5) the first three characters of the code will be 9C0. There are two body regions—the nervous system (value 1), and the circulatory system (value 2). The approach for both body systems is X, external, and the method is Collection (value 6) for both body systems. The qualifier identifies the substance collected. For the nervous system, the substance will be either cerebrospinal fluid (3) or other fluid (L). For the circulatory system, the substance will be blood (K) or other fluid (L). This Table is not for coding insertion of an indwelling catheter, or any other procedure except for collection of a substance from that catheter.

Body System: Indwelling Catheter

Section	**8**	Other Procedures
Body System	**C**	Indwelling Device
Operation	**0**	Other Procedures: Methodologies which attempt to remediate or cure a disorder or disease

Body Region	Approach	Method	Qualifier
1 Nervous System	**X** External	**6** Collection	**J** Cerebrospinal Fluid **L** Other Fluid
2 Circulatory System	**X** External	**6** Collection	**K** Blood **L** Other Fluid

Figure 10-5 Body System C, Indwelling Catheter in other Procedures Table

Table 10-2 Body Regions Used with Other Procedures (8E0)

Value	Body Region
1	Nervous System
2	Circulatory System
9	Head and Neck Region
H	Integumentary System and Breast
K	Musculoskeletal System
U	Female Reproductive System
V	Male Reproductive System
W	Trunk Region
X	Upper Extremity
Y	Lower Extremity
Z	None

The body regions, approaches, methods and qualifiers are different in the physiological systems and anatomical regions body system. Codes from this Table will begin with 8E0. There are multiple body regions, approaches, methods, and qualifiers in the Other Procedures section. Table 10-2 identifies the Body Regions used with the procedures in this section.

Body Regions (Character 4) Used in Other Procedures

The same body region will be found in several rows of the Table, depending on the approach, method, and qualifier, as shown in Figure 10-6. Note for example, the body region Head and Neck (9). This body region appears in four rows in the Other Procedures Table. In one row, there are multiple approaches; in the other three the approach is external. In those three rows the method and qualifier determine the correct row for the procedure. For example, a robotic-assisted procedure of the head and neck region has an external approach and no qualifier. A computer-assisted procedure has an external approach also, but in this row, there are four qualifiers that could apply.

Body region character Z (Figure 10-7) is used in this section to denote procedures that are not applicable specifically to any of the other body regions. These include other methods of treatment identified by the qualifier. There are four qualifiers for body region Z, with an external approach, and a Y for other method: In vitro fertilization (1), yoga therapy (4), meditation (5), and isolation therapy (6).

Approach (Character 5) Values Used with Other Procedures

All six approaches found in other sections are used here in the Other Procedures section, including open, percutaneous, percutaneous endoscopic, via natural or artificial opening with or without endoscopic assistance, and external. Table 10-3a lists each approach, and the appropriate body regions for each.

Section	8	Other Procedures
Body System	E	Physiological Systems and Anatomical Regions
Operation	0	Other Procedures: Methodologies which attempt to remediate or cure a disorder or disease

Body Region	Approach	Method	Qualifier
1 Nervous System **U** Female Reproductive System	**X** External	**Y** Other Method	**7** Examination
2 Circulatory System	**3** Percutaneous	**D** Near Infrared Spectroscopy	**Z** No Qualifier
9 Head and Neck Region	**0** Open **3** Percutaneous **4** Percutaneous Endoscopic **7** Via Natural or Artificial Opening **8** Via Natural or Artificial Opening Endoscopic	**C** Robotic Assisted Procedure	**Z** No Qualifier
9 Head and Neck Region **W** Trunk Region	**X** External	**B** Computer Assisted Procedure	**F** With Fluoroscopy **G** With Computerized Tomography **H** With Magnetic Resonance Imaging **Z** No Qualifier
9 Head and Neck Region **W** Trunk Region	**X** External	**C** Robotic Assisted Procedure	**Z** No Qualifier
9 Head and Neck Region **W** Trunk Region	**X** External	**Y** Other Method	**8** Suture Removal
H Integumentary System and Breast	**3** Percutaneous	**0** Acupuncure	**0** Anesthesia **Z** No Qualifier
H Integumentary System and Breast	**X** External	**6** Collection	**2** Breast Milk
H Integumentary System and Breast	**X** External	**Y** Other Method	**9** Piercing
K Musculoskeletal System	**X** External	**1** Therapeutic Massage	**Z** No Qualifier
K Musculoskeletal System	**X** External	**Y** Other Method	**7** Examination
V Male Reproductive System	**X** External	**1** Therapeutic Massage	**C** Prostate **D** Rectum
V Male Reproductive System	**X** External	**6** Collection	**3** Sperm
X Upper Extremity **Y** Lower Extremity	**0** Open **3** Percutaneous **4** Percutaneous Endoscopic	**C** Robotic Assisted Procedure	**Z** No Qualifier
X Upper Extremity **Y** Lower Extremity	**X** External	**B** Computer Assisted Procedure	**F** With Fluoroscopy **G** With Computerized Tomography **H** With Magnetic Resonance Imaging **Z** No Qualifier
X Upper Extremity **Y** Lower Extremity	**X** External	**C** Robotic Assisted Procedure	**Z** No Qualifier

Figure 10-6 Other Procedures Table with Root Operation E, Other Procedures

Section	**8**	Other Procedures		
Body System	**E**	Physiological Systems and Anatomical Regions		
Operation	**0**	Other Procedures: Methodologies which attempt to remediate or cure a disorder or disease		

Body Region	Approach	Method	Qualifier
Z None	**X** External	**Y** Other Method	**1** In Vitro Fertilization **4** Yoga Therapy **5** Meditation **6** Isolation

© Cengage Learning 2013

Figure 10-7 Body Region Z

Table 10-3a Body Regions Applicable to Approach Values

Value	Approach	Body Region
0	Open	9—Head and Neck Region W—Trunk Region X—Upper Extremity Y—Lower Extremity
3	Percutaneous	2—Circulatory System 9—Head and Neck Region W—Trunk Region X—Upper Extremity Y—Lower Extremity H—Integumentary System and Breast
4	Percutaneous endoscopic	9—Head and Neck Region W—Trunk Region X—Upper Extremity Y—Lower Extremity
7	Via natural or artificial opening	9—Head and Neck Region W—Trunk Region
8	Via natural or artificial opening, endoscopic	9—Head and Neck Region W—Trunk Region
X	External	1—Nervous System 9—Head and Neck Region H—Integumentary System and Breast K—Musculoskeletal System U—Female Reproductive System V—Male Reproductive System W—Trunk Region X—Upper Extremity Y—Lower Extremity Z—None

All body regions are included in approach X, external, including body region Z. The head and neck region (8) and trunk region (W) are the only two body regions that use approaches 7 and 8, via natural or artificial opening, with or without endoscopic assistance. Most body regions have options for percutaneous (3) or percutaneous endoscopic (4) approaches. The open (0) approach is applicable only to the head and neck region (9), trunk region (W), and the upper and lower extremities (values X and Y, respectively).

Table 10-3b Method Values by Body Region in Other Procedures Root Operation

Value	Method	Body Region
B	Computer-Assisted Procedure	9—Head and Neck Region W—Trunk Region X—Upper Extremity Y—Lower Extremity
C	Robotic-Assisted Procedure	9—Head and Neck Region W—Trunk Region X—Upper Extremity Y—Lower Extremity
D	Near Infrared Spectroscopy	2—Circulatory System
Y	Other Method	1—Nervous System K—Musculoskeletal System H—Integumentary System and Breast Z—None
0	Acupuncture	H—Integumentary System and Breast
1	Therapeutic Massage	K—Musculoskeletal System V—Male Reproductive System
6	Collection	H—Integumentary System and Breast V—Male Reproductive System

Method (Character 6) Values Used with Other Procedures

There are seven values for the method column (code character 6). Table 10-3b lists the method values and the applicable body regions.

The first thing to consider about Other Procedures is they are not the actual surgeries. In most instances, codes from this section are used when a procedure from the Medical and Surgical section describes a computer-assisted or robotic-assisted component of the surgery. In other words, the surgery itself would be coded from the Medical and Surgical section, and the computer or robotic assistance would be coded from the Other Procedures section. Let us take a look at descriptions of a few of the methods.

Computer assisted procedures describe navigation systems that provide additional information during a procedure. The goal of computer-assisted navigation (CAN) is to increase surgical accuracy and reduce the chance of malposition of implants. Proper implant alignment is believed to be an important factor for minimizing long-term wear, risk of osteolysis, and loosening of the prosthesis found with other, more aggressive, approaches. The character value for this method is B, computer assisted procedure. In the Other Procedures section, the only body regions associated with this method are the head and neck (9), trunk (W), and upper (X) and lower (Y) extremities.

Robotic-assisted procedures use a computerized system with a motorized construction (usually an arm) capable of interacting with the environment. In its most basic form, it contains sensors, which provide feedback data on the robot's current situation, and a system to process this information so that the next action can be determined. The value for this method is C, and is used only with the following body regions: head and neck (9), trunk (W), and upper (X) and lower (Y) extremities.

Near-infrared spectroscopy is a monitoring method used to detect oxygen saturation. It is used in the field of neurosurgery and cardiovascular surgery and neonatal ICU. With near-infrared spectroscopy, for example, circulatory system oxygenation is promptly and continuously monitored during resuscitation or surgical procedures. The value for this method is D, and is used only with the circulatory system body region as an adjunct to monitor circulation.

The collection method is for the collection of either sperm from the male reproductive system (V), or breast milk from the integumentary system and breast body region. Where value Y, other methods, is found, the qualifier specifies the other method. For example, in the body regions head and neck, trunk, and upper and lower extremities, the method value is Y, and the qualifier value is 8, suture removal.

Qualifiers (Character 7) Values Used with Other Procedures

There are 15 qualifier values in the character 7 position, as well as value Z, to indicate there is no qualifier. Figure 10-6 is an excerpt from the Other Procedures Table for root operation E. As always, each Table rows identify which qualifiers are used with specific body regions, approaches, and methods.

The qualifiers include:

- Value 2, Breast Milk, is used only when milk is extracted from the breast manually or mechanically, e.g., with a breast pump. The body region is the integumentary system and breast, the approach is external, and the method is collection (6).

- Value 3, Sperm, is used for collection of sperm from the male reproductive system. Approach is external, and the method is collection (6).

- Value 7, Examination, which is used with body regions nervous system (1), musculoskeletal system (K), and female reproductive system (U). The approach is external (X), and the method is Y, *other method*. An example of this qualifier in use would be the pelvic exam that occurs when a pap smear is taken. The pap smear procedure would be coded from the Medical and Surgical section, and the exam from Other Procedures.

- Value 8, Suture Removal. This is an external approach, and the method value is other method *(Y)*. It is used only with the body regions head and neck, trunk, and upper and lower extremites, for the removal of external sutures.

- Value 9, Piercing, is used only when the skin or breast are pierced for remediation or attempts to cure a disorder or disease. The approach is external, the body region is H, integumentary system and breast, and the method value is Y, other method.

- Values C, Prostate and D, Rectum. These two values are used with therapeutic massage (method value 1) of the musculoskeletal system and the male reproductive system. In the male reproductive system it is used typically to massage the prostate gland. The approach for both body regions is external.

- Values F, G, and H are adjuncts used with a computer assisted procedure of the head and neck, trunk, and upper and lower extremity body regions. The approach can be any one of the six values: open, external, percutaneous with and without endoscopic assistance, and via natural or artificial opening with or without endoscopic assistance. The values are:
  - F: with Fluoroscopy
  - G: with Computerized Tomography (CT)
  - H: with Magnetic Resonance Imaging (MRI)

- Values 1, 4, 5, and 6 are used only with body region Z, external approach (X), and Y, other method. These values are:
  - 1: In vitro fertilization
  - 4: Yoga therapy
  - 5: Meditation
  - 6: Isolation

Coding Other Procedures in ICD-10-PCS

For most of these procedures, a search in the Index by method usually results in a Table reference value listing. Searching for *acupuncture* in the index yields the characters 8E0H, which leads to the Other Procedures Table. Searching for *collection* in the Index (Figure 10-8) leads to several modifying terms, including *indwelling catheter, breast milk,* and *sperm.* The Table reference for each modifying term leads to the correct Table in the Tabular list. In the Table, select the row with the values that correspond to the correct body region, approach, method, and qualifier.

Before moving on to the next section, here is an example using the procedure *computer-assistance with MRI imaging, external (for total knee replacement).* (Note, coding will be done only for the computer-assisted procedure. The knee replacement would, in all other instances, be coded as well from the Medical and Surgical section). In the Index, search by the method, which in this instance is *computer-assisted procedure* (Figure 10-9). Then, search the modifying terms indented below, for the body region Knee. Note that knee is not found, but lower extremity is listed as a body region value. Indented below this is the value for MRI. The Table reference appears to be an entire code 8E0YXBH, and it most likely is the correct code, however, remember that all codes must be verified in the appropriate Table in the Tabular List.

Moving to Table 8E0, Other Procedures, find the row with the appropriate body region, approach, method, and qualifier. Look back at Figure 10-6, again. In the body region column, lower extremity (value Y) is listed in several rows, but the approach external, from the procedural statement, is shown only in the second row that includes the body region Y, lower extremity. The method is computer-assisted procedure (B), and in the same row, the qualifier is MRI, value H. The final, correct code is 8E0YXBH. All parts of the procedure description are represented by the appropriate character value.

```
Collection from
    Breast, Breast Milk 8E0HX62
    Indwelling Device
        Circulatory System
            Blood 8C02X6K
            Other Fluid 8C02X6L
        Nervous System
            Cerebrospinal Fluid 8C01X6J
            Other Fluid 8C01X6L
    Integumentary System, Breast Milk 8E0HX62
    Reproductive System, Male, Sperm 8E0VX63
```

© Cengage Learning 2013

Figure 10-8 Index Listing for Method Collection

```
Computer Assisted Procedure
    Extremity
        Lower
            No Qualifier 8E0YXBZ
            With Computerized Tomography 8E0YXBG
            With Fluoroscopy 8E0YXBF
            With Magnetic Resonance Imaging 8E0YXBH
        Upper
            No Qualifier 8E0XXBZ
            With Computerized Tomography 8E0XXBG
```

© Cengage Learning 2013

Figure 10-9 Index Listing for Computer-Assisted Procedure

Let's Review 10–1:

List the Method and code the following procedures:

1. External robotic assisted procedure of the trunk region _____
2. Collection of cerebrospinal fluid from indwelling catheter _____
3. Therapeutic massage of prostate _____
4. Acupuncture, skin, with anesthesia _____
5. Breast milk collection via breast pump _____
6. Suture removal, thigh _____
7. Extraarticular manipulation of the cervical spine _____
8. Mechanically assisted manipulation of the rib cage _____
9. Direct visceral adjustment of the abdomen _____

Imaging

The Imaging section (character value B) is the first one that does not include a root operation. In fact, sections ranging from Imaging through Substance Abuse Treatment (character value H) do not include the term root operation. In the imaging section, this term is replaced by *root type,* and includes types of imaging procedures, like a CT scan or MRI. This is also a huge section, since each Table includes a separate body system (character 2) and separate root operation (character 3). The Table ranges include B00 through BY4. Figure 10-10 is an excerpt from the first Imaging table, B00. The section is B, Imaging.

In addition, the fifth character is now named Contrast, rather than approach, and the sixth and seventh characters of an Imaging code are now both titled qualfiers. The body system is the central nervous system (value 0), and the root type is Plain Radiography (0). This Table includes only one character 4 body part, the spinal cord (character value B). The fourth character value is Contrast (rather than the usual approach value). Additionally, both the sixth and seventh characters are qualifiers. The imaging section is only for diagnostic imaging procedures. Therapeutic radiation procedure codes are in the Radiation Oncology section. In addition, other types of scans, uptakes, or nuclear medicine procedures are found in the Nuclear Medicine section, rather than here in Imaging.

Body System (Character 2) Values in Imaging Section

In the Imaging section, there is a separate Table for each body system, divided by the five root types (Plain Radiography, Fluoroscopy, CT, MRI, and Ultrasonography). For example, body system 4, lower

Section	**B**	Imaging
Body System	**0**	Central Nervous System
Type	**0**	Plain Radiography: Planar display of an image developed from the capture of external ionizing radiation on photographic or photoconductive plate

Body Part	Contrast	Qualifier	Qualifier
B Spinal Cord	**0** High Osmolar **1** Low Osmolar **Y** Other Contrast **Z** None	**Z** None	**Z** None

© Cengage Learning 2013

Figure 10-10 Imaging Table B00

arteries, is found in Table B40, Plain Radiography, B41, Fluoroscopy, B42, Computerized Tomography (CT scan), B43, MRI, and B44, Ultrasonography. Table 10-4 lists all the character 2 body system values found in the Imaging section.

Body system value 7, lymphatic system, is found only with root type Plain Radiography, and not with the other four Imaging root types. Body system D, gastrointestinal system, is associated with only three Imaging root types: Fluoroscopy, CT, and Ultrasonography. Body system G, endocrine system, contains three root types: CT, MRI, and Ultrasonography. Body systems H, skin, subcutaneous tissue, and breast, N, skull and facial bones, and Y, fetal and obstetrical, use root types Plain Radiography, MRI, and Ultrasonography only. Connective tissue, body system L, appears only in an MRI and Ultrasonography Table. The female reproductive body system (U) is included with all root types except CT. Muscles, which in the Medical and Surgical section has its own value, is included with the skeletal system values, e.g., non-axial or axial skeletal bones.

Root Type (Character 3) Values in the Imaging Section

Rather than the traditional root operation found in the third character position of an ICD-10-PCS code, the name of the Imaging procedure becomes character three of an ICD-10-PCS Imaging code. For

Table 10-4 Body Systems Values in the Imaging Section

Value	Body System (Character 2)
0	Central Nervous System
2	Heart
3	Upper Arteries
4	Lower Arteries
5	Veins
7	Lymphatic System
8	Eye
9	Ear, Nose, Mouth and Throat
B	Respiratory System
D	Gastrointestinal System
F	Hepatobiliary System and Pancreas
G	Endocrine System
H	Skin, Subcutaneous Tissue and Breast
L	Connective Tissue
N	Skull and Facial Bones
P	Non-axial (Skeleton) Upper Bones
Q	Non-axial Lower Bones
R	Axial Skeleton, except Skull and Facial Bones
T	Urinary System
U	Female Reproductive System
V	Male Reproductive
W	Anatomical Regions
X	Fetus and Obstetrical

example, for CT scan procedures, the third character value is 2, for MRI the value is 3, etc. There are four root type values for character 3:

- 0—**Plain Radiography.** The capture of external radiation developed as an image on photographic or photoconductive plate. Also known simply as an X-ray or radiological image.

- 1—**Fluoroscopy.** Single or bi-plane real time display of an image developed from the capture of radiation on a fluorescent screen.

- 3—**Magnetic Resonance Imaging (MRI).** Computerized digital display of multiplanar images developed from the capture of radiofrequency signals emitted within a magnetic field. Multiplanar is defined as a technique used to generate views of more than one anatomical plane, such as sagittal, coronal, and oblique.

- 4—**Ultrasonography.** Real time display of anatomical structure or flow images developed from the capture of high-frequency sound waves.

Body Part (Character 4) Values in the Imaging Section

It is character 4 that separates each of the body systems into individual body parts, and has the most detail. Table 10-5 is a listing of the body parts for each body system, and the character value of each. The first thing to notice is that character values of each body part change as the body system changes. In the *upper arteries* body system, for example, the value 0 is thoracic aorta, and 2 is subclavian artery, left, but, in the *lower arteries* body system, 0 is abdominal artery and 2 is hepatic artery. In the body system *veins*, value 0 is epidural veins, and 2 is intracranial sinuses, and in the body system *axial skeleton, except skull and facial bones*, 0 is cervical spine, and 2 is thoracic (vertebra) discs.

Also, depending on the root type, not every body part will be included in every Table from the corresponding body system. For example, in the body system *heart,* body parts B, *heart with aorta*, and D, *pediatric heart,* appear only within a root type Ultrasonography Table, while values 4 (heart, right), 5 (heart, left) and 6 (heart, right and left) are used with all five imaging root types. Another example is the body system upper arteries. Here, the ophthalmic arteries (value V) appear only with an Ultrasonography root type Table, as shown in Figure 10-11. Body system Y, *fetus and obstetrical*, is found only with MRI and ultrasound imaging tables. It is not necessary to memorize the changes in character values, or which body parts appear with specific root types; just be aware that they exist, and will impact code character selection.

Figure 10-12 is an illustration of some of the major blood vessels of the circulatory system. Much like coding from the Medical and Surgical section, it is easy to see that a thorough understanding of the anatomy of the human body and a comprehensive review of the medical documentation is essential in order to code from the Imaging section, as well.

Contrast (Character 5) Values in the Imaging Section

There are five contrast values in the fifth character position: high osmolar (0), low osmolar (1), other contrast (Y), and no contrast (Z). Contrast is the new fifth character value in the Imaging section, replacing Approach. **Contrast** is defined as the substance used to improve visability of body structures during certain imaging procedures. **Contrast agents,** also known as radiocontrast agents, are a type of medical substance used to improve the visibility of internal bodily structures in Imaging root types, e.g. CT or Plain Radiography (commonly known as X-ray imaging). These agents are typically iodine or barium compounds. The contrast agent can be delivered as high or low osmolarity. To understand what that means, a brief description of an osmole would be helpful. In biochemistry, an **osmole** is the amount of a substance that dissociates in solution. The amounts form active particles groups, and each group is an osmole. **Osmolarity,** therefore, is the concentration of osmotically active particles in solution. A large number of osmoles per contrast solution, has a high

Table 10-5 Body Part Values within each Body System

Body System Value	Body System (Character 2)	Body Parts (Character 4)
0	Central Nervous System	0—Brain 7—Cisterna 9—Cerebral Ventricles 9—Sella Turcica/Pituitary Gland B—Spinal Cord C—Acoustic Nerves
2	Heart	0—Coronary Artery, Single 1—Coronary Arteries, Multiple 2—Coronary Artery Bypass Graft, Single 3—Coronary Artery Bypass Grafts, Multiple 4—Heart, Right 5—Heart, Left 6—Heart, Right And Left 7—Internal Mammary Bypass Graft, Right 8—Internal Mammary Bypass Graft, Left B—Heart With Aorta D—Pediatric Heart F—Bypass Graft, Other
3	Upper Arteries	0—Thoracic Aorta 1—Brachiocephalic-Subclavian Artery, Right 2—Subclavian Artery, Left 3—Common Carotid Artery, Right 4—Common Carotid Artery, Left 5—Common Carotid Arteries, Bilateral 6—Internal Carotid Artery, Right 7—Internal Carotid Artery, Left 8—Internal Carotid Arteries, Bilateral 9—External Carotid Artery, Right B—External Carotid Artery, Left C—External Carotid Arteries, Bilateral D—Vertebral Artery, Right F—Vertebral Artery, Left G—Vertebral Arteries, Bilateral H—Upper Extremity Arteries, Right J—Upper Extremity Arteries, Left K—Upper Extremity Arteries, Bilateral L—Intercostals And Bronchial Arteries M—Spinal Arteries N—Upper Arteries, Other P—Thoraco-Abdominal Aorta Q—Cervico-Cerebral Arch R—Intercranial Arteries S—Pulmonary Artery, Right T—Pulmonary Artery Left V—Ophthalmic Arteries
4	Lower Arteries	0—Abdominal Aorta 1—Celiac Artery 2—Hepatic Artery 3—Splenic Artery 4—Superior Mesenteric Artery 5—Inferior Mesenteric Artery 6—Renal Artery, Right 7—Renal Artery, Left 8—Renal Arteries, Bilateral 9—Lumbar Arteries B—Intra-Abdominal Arteries, Other

Table 10-5 Body Part Values within each Body System (continued)

		C—Pelvic Arteries D—Aorta And Bilateral Lower Extremity Arteries F—Lower Extremity Arteries, Right G—Lower Extremity Arteries, Left H—Lower Extremity Arteries, Bilateral J—Lower Arteries, Other K—Celiac And Mesenteric Arteries L—Femoral Artery M—Renal Artery Transplant N—Penile Arteries
5	Veins	0—Epidural Veins 1—Cerebral And Cerebellar Veins 2—Intracranial Sinuses 3—Jugular Veins, Right 5—Jugular Veins, Bilateral 6—Subclavian Vein, Right 7—Subclavian Vein, Left 8—Superior Vena Cava 9—Inferior Vena Cava B—Lower Extremity Veins, Right C—Lower Extremity Veins, Left D—Lower Extremity Veins, Bilateral F—Pelvic (Iliac) Veins, Right G—Pelvic (Iliac) Veins, Left H—Pelvic (Iliac) Veins, Bilateral J—Renal Vein, Right K—Renal Vein, Left L—Renal Veins, Bilateral J—Renal Vein, Right K—Renal Vein, Left L—Renal Veins, Bilateral M—Upper Extremity Veins, Right N—Upper Extremity Veins, Left P—Upper Extremity Veins, Bilateral Q—Pulmonary Vein, Right R—Pulmonary Vein, Left S—Pulmonary Veins, Bilateral T—Portal And Splanchnic Veins V—Veins, Other W—Dialysis Shunt/Fistula
7	Lymphatic System	0—Abdominal/Retroperitoneal Lymphatics, Unilateral 1—Abdominal/Retroperitoneal Lymphatics, Bilateral 4—Lymphatics, Head And Neck 5—Upper Extremity Lymphatics, Right 6—Upper Extremity Lymphatics, Left 7—Upper Extremity Lymphatics, Bilateral 8—Lower Extremity Lymphatics, Right 9—Lower Extremity Lymphatics, Left B—Lower Extremity Lymphatics, Bilateral C—Lymphatics, Pelvic
8	Eye	0—Lacrimal Duct, Right 1—Lacrimal Duct, Left 2—Lacrimal Ducts, Bilateral 3—Optic Foramina, Right 4—Optic Foramina, Left 5—Eye, Right 6—Eye, Left 7—Eyes, Bilateral

Body System Value	Body System (Character 2)	Body Parts (Character 4)
9	Ear, Nose, Mouth and Throat	0—Ear 2—Paranasal Sinuses 6—Parotid Glands, Bilateral 9—Submandibular Glands, Bilateral B—Salivary Gland, Right C—Salivary Gland, Left D—Salivary Glands, Bilateral F—Nasopharynx/Oropharynx H—Mastoids J—Larynx
B	Respiratory System	2—Lung, Right 3—Lung, Left 4—Lungs, Bilateral 6—Diaphragm 7—Tracheobronchial Tree, Right 8—Tracheobronchial Tree, Left 9—Tracheobronchial Trees, Bilateral B—Pleural C—Mediastinum D—Upper Airways F—Trachea/Airways G—Lung Apices
D	Gastrointestinal System	1—Esophagus 2—Stomach 3—Small Bowel 4—Colon 5—Upper GI 5—Upper GI And Small Bowel 7—Gastrointestinal Tract 8—Appendix 9—Duodenum B—Mouth/Otopharynx C—Rectum
F	Hepatobiliary System and Pancreas	0—Bile Ducts 1—Biliary And Pancreatic Ducts 2—Gallbladder 3—Gallbladder And Bile Ducts 4—Gallbladder, Bile Ducts And Pancreatic Ducts 5—Liver 6—Liver And Spleen 7—Pancreas 8—Pancreatic Ducts C—Hepatobiliary System, All
G	Endocrine System	0—Adrenal Gland, Right 1—Adrenal Gland, Left 2—Adrenal Glands, Bilateral 3—Parathyroid Glands 4—Thyroid Gland
H	Skin, Subcutaneous Tissue, and Breast	0—Breast, Right 1—Breast, Left 2—Breasts, Bilateral 3—Single Mammary Duct, Right 4—Single Mammary Duct, Left 5—Multiple Mammary Ducts, Right 6—Multiple Mammary Ducts, Left

Table 10-5 Body Part Values within each Body System (continued)

		7—Extremity, Upper 8—Extremity, Lower 9—Abdominal Wall B—Chest Wall C—Head And Neck D—Subcutaneous Tissue, Head/Neck F—Subcutaneous Tissue, Upper Extremity G—Subcutaneous Tissue, Thorax H—Subcutaneous Tissue, Abdomen And Pelvis J—Subcutaneous Tissue, Lower Extremity
L	Connective Tissue	0—Connective Tissue, Upper Extremity 1—Connective Tissue, Lower Extremity 2—Tendons, Upper Extremity 3—Tendons, Lower Extremity
N	Skull and Facial Bones	0—Skull 1—Orbit, Right 2—Orbit, Left 3—Orbits, Bilateral 4—Nasal Bones 5—Facial Bones 6—Mandible 7—Temporomandibular Joint, Right 8—Temporomandibular Joint, Left 9—Temporomandibular Joints, Bilateral B—Zygomatic Arch, Right C—Zygomatic Arch, Left D—Zygomatic Arches, Bilateral F—Temporal Bones G—Tooth, Single H—Teeth, Multiple J—Teeth, All
P	Non-axial (Skeleton) Upper Bones	0—Sternoclavicular Joint, Right 1—Sternoclavicular Joint, Left 2—Sternoclavicular Joints, Bilateral 3—Acromioclavicular Joints, Bilateral 4—Clavicle, Right 5—Clavicle, Left 6—Scapula, Right 7—Scapula, Left 8—Shoulder, Right 9—Shoulder, Left A—Humerus, Right B—Humerus, Left D—Hand/Finger Joint, Left E—Upper Arm, Right F—Upper Arm, Left G—Elbow, Right H—Elbow, Left J—Forearm, Right K—Forearm, Left Wrist, Right M—Wrist, Left N—Hand, Right P—Hand, Left Q—Hands And Wrists, Bilateral R—Finger(S), Right S—Finger(S), Left T—Upper Extremity, Right

Body System Value	Body System (Character 2)	Body Parts (Character 4)
		U—Upper Extremity, Left V—Upper Extremities, Bilateral X—Ribs, Right Y—Ribs, Left
Q	Non-axial (Skeleton) Lower Bones	0—Hip, Right 1—Hip, Left 2—Hips, Bilateral 3—Femur, Right 4—Femur, Left 7—Knee, Right 8—Knee, Left 9—Knees, Bilateral D—Lower Leg, Right F—Lower Leg, Left G—Ankle, Right H—Ankle, Left J—Calcaneus, Right K—Calcaneus, Left L—Foot, Right M—Foot, Left P—Toe(S), Right Q—Toe(S), Left R—Lower Extremity, Right S—Lower Extremity, Left V—Patella, Right W—Patella, Left X—Foot/Toe Joint, Right Y—Foot/Toe Joint, Left
R	Axial Skeleton, Except Skull and Facial Bones	0—Cervical Spine 1—Cervical Disc(S) 2—Thoracic Disc(S) 3—Lumbar Disc(S) 4—Cervical Facet Joints 5—Thoracic Facet Joints 6—Lumbar Facet Joints 7—Thoracic Spine 8—Thoracolumbar Joint 9—Lumbar Spine B—Lumbosacral Joint C—Pelvis D—Sacroiliac Joints F—Sacrum And Coccyx G—Whole Spine H—Sternum
T	Urinary System	0—Bladder 1—Kidney, Right 2—Kidney, Left 3—Kidneys, Bilateral 4—Kidneys, Ureters, And Bladder 5—Urethra 6—Ureter, Right 7—Ureter, Left 9—Kidney Transplant B—Bladder And Urethra C—Ileal Diversion Loop

Table 10-5 Body Part Values within each Body System (continued)

		D—Kidney, Ureter And Bladder, Right F—Kidney, Ureter And Bladder, Left G—Ileal Loop, Ureters And Kidneys J—Kidneys And Bladder
U	Female Reproductive System	0—Fallopian Tube, Right 1—Fallopian Tube, Left 2—Fallopian Tubes, Bilateral 3—Ovary, Right 4—Ovary, Left 5—Ovaries, Bilateral 6—Uterus 8—Uterus And Fallopian Tubes 9—Vagina B—Pregnant Uterus C—Uterus And Ovaries
V	Male Reproductive	0—Corpora Cavernosa 1—Epididymis, Right 2—Epididymis, Left 3—Prostate 4—Scrotum 5—Testicle, Right 6—Testicle, Left 7—Testicles, Bilateral 8—Vaso Vasorum 9—Prostate And Seminal Vesicles B—Penis
W	Anatomical Regions	0—Abdomen 1—Abdomen And Pelvis 3—Chest 4—Chest And Abdomen 5—Chest, Abdomen And Pelvis 8—Head 9—Head And Neck B—Long Bones, All C—Lower Extremity F—Neck G—Pelvic Region H—Retroperitoneum J—Upper Extremity K—Whole Body L—Whole Skeleton M—Whole Body, Infant P—Brachial Plexus
X	Fetus and Obstetrical	0—fetal head 1—fetal heart 2—fetal thorax 3—fetal abdomen 4—fetal spine 5—fetal extremities 6—whole fetus 7—fetal umbilical cord 8—placenta 9—first trimester, single fetus B—first trimester, multiple gestation C—second trimester, single fetus D—second trimester, multiple gestation F—third trimester, single fetus G—third trimester, multiple gestation

Section	**B**	Imaging			
Body System	**3**	Upper Arteries			
Type	**4**	Ultrasonography: Real time display of images of anatomy or flow information developed from the capture of reflected and attenuated high frequency sound waves			

Body Part	Contrast	Qualifier	Qualifier
0 Thoracic Aorta **1** Brachiocephalic-Subclavian Artery, Right **2** Subclavian Artery, Left **3** Common Carotid Artery, Right **4** Common Carotid Artery, Left **5** Common Carotid Arteries, Bilateral **6** Internal Carotid Artery, Right **7** Internal Carotid Artery, Left **8** Internal Carotid Arteries, Bilateral **H** Upper Extremity Arteries, Right **J** Upper Extremity Arteries, Left **K** Upper Extremity Arteries, Bilateral **R** Intracranial Arteries **S** Pulmonary Artery, Right **T** Pulmonary Artery, Left **V** Ophthalmic Arteries	**Z** None	**Z** None **Z** None	**3** Intravascular

© Cengage Learning 2013

Figure 10-11 Table B34 Inclusion of Body Part Ophthalmic Artery

osmolarity; a smaller number has a low osmolarity. The character value for high osmolarity is 0, and for low osmolarity, 1. The two other character values for the Imaging section are Y, other contrast, and Z, none. Table 10-6 identifies which of the root types are associated with each contrast value.

MRI and Ultrasonography root types use only Y or Z contrast values. The only Ultrasonography Table in which Y, other contrast, is used, is the Table associated with imaging of the heart (Figure 10-13). Contrast value Y is used with virtually every MRI Table in Imaging. The rest of the root types can use any one of the four contrast values as a fifth character in the code.

Qualifier (Characters 6 and 7) Values Used in Imaging Section

In the Imaging section, character valued 6 and 7 are qualifiers. There are only two qualifier values in the sixth character position: 0, unenhanced and enhanced, or Z, none. When qualifier value 0, unenhanced and enhanced, is used, it means that the imaging procedure was done without (unenhanced) and with (enhanced) contrast. For example, in a CT of the brain, with and without contrast, the sixth character value would be 0. In a CT scan using no contrast, the fifth and sixth characters would be Z, indicating that no contrast was used, and no sixth character qualifier applied. If the CT scan was done with high or low osmolar contrast, or other contrast, but the medical documentation did not state images were taken with and without contrast, the sixth character value would be Z, no qualifier.

Qualifier values for character 7 are Z in almost every Imaging Table except for the following:

- B21, Imaging, Heart, Fluoroscopy (Figure 10-14). In this Table, the qualifier for character seven is 0, intraoperative, meaning the Fluoroscopy imaging was performed during surgery on these body regions.

- B21, Imaging, Heart, Fluoroscopy. In this Table, note that the sixth character qualifier value is 1, to identify a laser surgery.

- B24, Imaging, Heart, Ultrasonography (Figure 10-15). The seventh character qualifier is 3, intravascular.

- B34, Imaging, Heart, Ultrasonography. The seventh character qualifier is 3, intravascular.

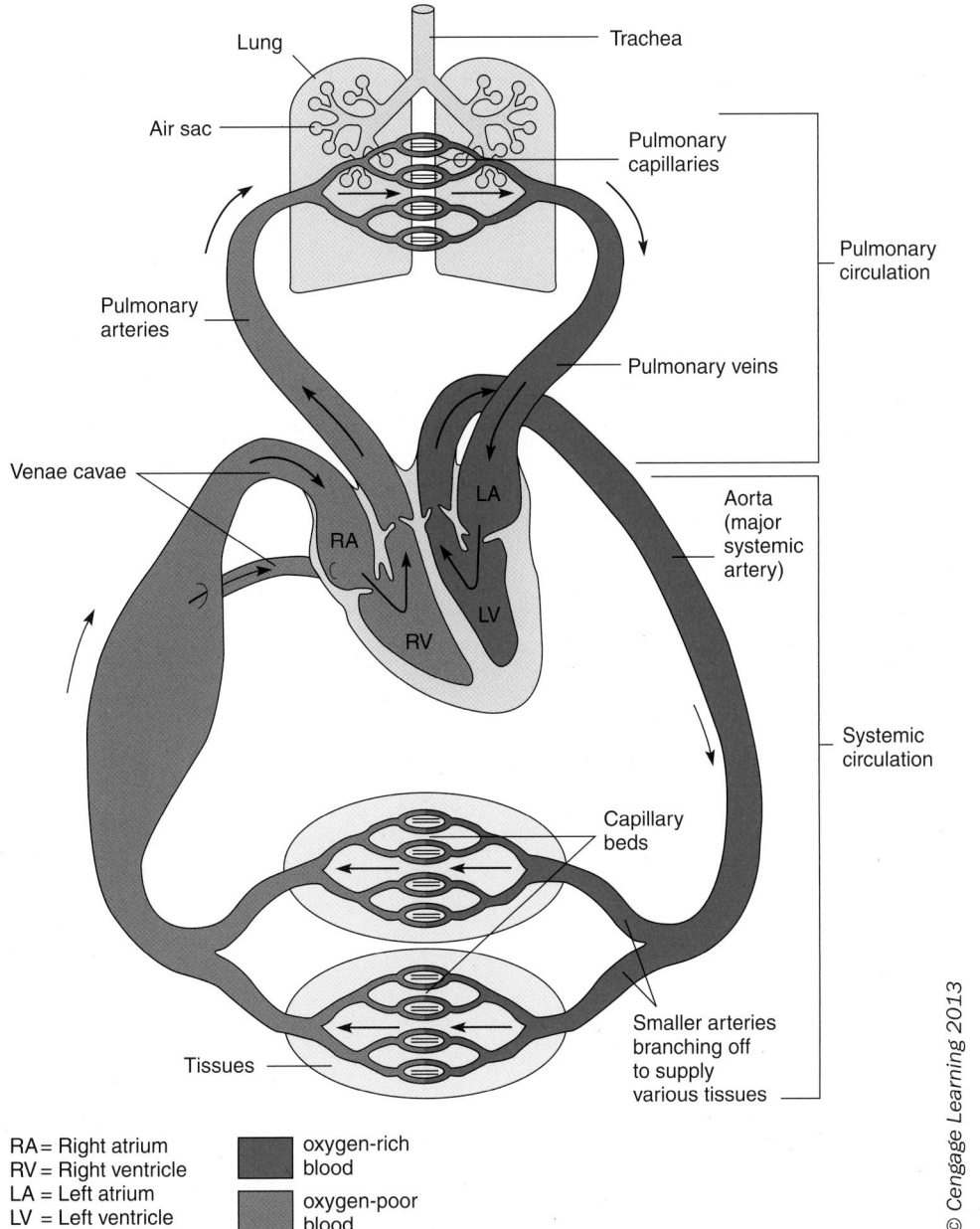

Figure 10-12 Illustration of the Main Arteries and Veins of the Human Body

- B44, Imaging, Lower Arteries, Ultrasonography. The seventh character qualifier is 3, intravascular.

- B54, Imaging, Veins, Ultrasonography. The seventh character qualifier is 3, intravascular.

- BP4, Imaging, Non-axial Upper Bones, Plain Radiography. The qualifier for the seventh character is 1, **densitometry** (Figure 10-16), which tests bone density.

- BQ0, Imaging, Non-axial Lower Bones, Plain Radiography. The qualifier for the seventh character is 1, densitometry.

- BE0, Imaging, Axial Skeleton, Except Skull and Facial Bones, Plain Radiography. The qualifier for the seventh character is 1, densitometry.

With these Imaging section qualifier values, intraoperative (0), intravascular (3), and densitometry (1), review the medical documentation carefully to ensure assignment tof the seventh code character is appropriate.

Table 10-6 Root Types Associated with Contrast Values

Contrast Value (Character 5)	Root Types
0—High Osmolar	0—Plain Radiography 1—Fluoroscopy 2—Computerized Tomography (CT)
1—Low Osmolar	0—Plain Radiography 1—Fluoroscopy 2—Computerized Tomography (CT)
Y—Other Contrast	3—Magnetic Resonance Imaging (MRI)
Z—None	0—Plain Radiography 1—Fluoroscopy 2—Computerized Tomography (CT) 3—Magnetic Resonance Imaging (MRI) 4—Ultrasound

Section	B	Imaging		
Body System	2	Heart		
Type	4	Ultrasonography: Real time display of images of anatomy or flow information developed from the capture of reflected and attenuated high frequency sound waves		

Body Part	Contrast	Qualifier	Qualifier
0 Coronary Artery, Single **1** Coronary Arteries, Multiple **4** Heart, Right **5** Heart, Left **6** Heart, Right and Left **B** Heart with Aorta **C** Pericardium **D** Pediatric Heart	**Y** Other Contrast	**Z** None	**Z** None
0 Coronary Artery, Single **1** Coronary Arteries, Multiple **4** Heart, Right **5** Heart, Left **6** Heart, Right and Left **B** Heart with Aorta **C** Pericardium **D** Pediatric Heart	**Z** None	**Z** None	**3** Intravascular **Z** None

Figure 10-13 Use of Y, Other Contrast in Body System Heart in Imaging Section

Coding Imaging Section Procedures using the ICD-10-PCS

When searching the Index, look for the root types as the main term. For example, Figure 10-17 is an excerpt from the Index for root type Plain Radiography. The modifying terms are all body parts and are indented below the main term. For example, a Plain Radiography of the abdomen has a Table reference for BW0ZZZ. As always, even though all seven characters might be referenced in the Index, the code must always be confirmed in the appropriate Table. The next step, therefore, would be to go to the BW0 Table, and confirm that the code characters match the procedural statement.

It is also possible to look for a specific imaging test in the Index. For example, in Figure 10-18, the Imaging procedures Angiocardiography and Angiography are listed. Note that there is an instructional note to *See Plain Radiography or Fluoroscopy*, along with a Table reference. Under Angiocardiography,

Section	B	Imaging
Body System	2	Heart
Type	1	Fluoroscopy: Single plane or bi-plane real time display of an image developed from the capture of external ionizing radiation on a fluorescent screen. The image may also be stored by either digital or analog means

Body Part	Contrast	Qualifier	Qualifier
0 Coronary Artery, Single **1** Coronary Arteries, Multiple **2** Coronary Artery Bypass Graft, Single **3** Coronary Artery Bypass Grafts, Multiple	**0** High Osmolar **1** Low Osmolar **Y** Other Contrast	**1** Laser	**0** Intraoperative
0 Coronary Artery, Single **1** Coronary Arteries, Multiple **2** Coronary Artery Bypass Graft, Single **3** Coronary Artery Bypass Grafts, Multiple	**0** High Osmolar **1** Low Osmolar **Y** Other Contrast	**Z** None	**Z** None
4 Heart, Right **5** Heart, Left **6** Heart, Right and Left **7** Internal Mammary Bypass Graft, Right **8** Internal Mammary Bypass Graft, Left **F** Bypass Graft, Other	**0** High Osmolar **1** Low Osmolar **Y** Other Contrast	**Z** None	**Z** None

© Cengage Learning 2013

Figure 10-14 Qualifier 7 Value in Imaging Table B21

Section	B	Imaging
Body System	2	Heart
Type	4	Ultrasonography: Real time display of images of anatomy or flow information developed from the capture of reflected and attenuated high frequency sound waves

Body Part	Contrast	Qualifier	Qualifier
0 Coronary Artery, Single **1** Coronary Arteries, Multiple **4** Heart, Right **5** Heart, Left **6** Heart, Right and Left **B** Heart with Aorta **C** Pericardium **D** Pediatric Heart	**Y** Other Contrast	**Z** None	**Z** None
0 Coronary Artery, Single **1** Coronary Arteries, Multiple **4** Heart, Right **5** Heart, Left **6** Heart, Right and Left **B** Heart with Aorta **C** Pericardium **D** Pediatric Heart	**Z** None	**Z** None	**3** Intravascular **Z** None

© Cengage Learning 2013

Figure 10-15 Qualifier 7 Value in Imaging Table B24

four different body parts are listed, along with the instructional note, and a Table reference. Two body regions are indented below the Angiography main term, with the *See* instructional note, and individual Table reference. It is permissible to go straight to the Table referenced from the Imaging procedure listing in the Index, or to go to the root type listed in the instructional note.

It is time to code a procedure. The procedural statement is *angiocardiography, left heart, with high osmolar contrast.* First, determine the main term (or root type), then look in the Index for that main term or root type. Using *angiocardiography* as the main term in the Index, look next for the body region or part. In Figure 10-18, the second indented modifying term *Left Heart* has a note to *See* Plain Radiography, Heart, Left, and a Table reference of B205.

Section	**B**	Imaging		
Body System	**P**	Non-Axial Upper Bones		
Type	**4**	Ultrasonography: Real time display of images of anatomy or flow information developed from the capture of reflected and attenuated high frequency sound waves		

Body Part	Contrast	Qualifier	Qualifier
8 Shoulder, Right **9** Shoulder, Left **G** Elbow, Right **H** Elbow, Left **L** Wrist, Right **M** Wrist, Left **N** Hand, Right **P** Hand, Left	**Z** None	**Z** None	**1** Densitometry **Z** None

© Cengage Learning 2013

Figure 10-16 Qualifier 7 Value in Imaging Table BP4

Plain Radiography
Abdomen **BW00ZZZ**
Abdomen and Pelvis **BW01ZZZ**
Abdominal Lymphatic
   Bilateral **B701**
   Unilateral **B700**
Airway, Upper **BB0DZZZ**
Ankle
   Left **BQ0H**
   Right **BQ0G**
Aorta
   Abdominal **B400**
   Thoracic **B300**
   Thoraco-Abdominal **B30P**
Aorta and Bilateral Lower Extremity Arteries **B40D**
Arch
   Bilateral **BN0DZZZ**
   Left **BN0CZZZ**
   Right **BN0BZZZ**
Arm
   Left **BP0FZZZ**
   Right **BP0EZZZ**
Artery
   Brachiocephalic-Subclavian, Right **B301**

Bronchial **B30L**
Bypass Graft, Other **B20F**
Cervico-Cerebral Arch **B30Q**
Common Carotid
   Bilateral **B305**
   Left **B304**
   Right **B303**
Coronary
   Bypass Graft
      Multiple **B203**
      Single **B202**
   Multiple **B201**
   Single **B200**
External Carotid
   Bilateral **B30C**
   Left **B30B**
   Right **B309**
Hepatic **B402**
Inferior Mesenteric **B405**
Intercostal **B30L**
Internal Carotid
   Bilateral **B308**
   Left **B307**
   Right **B306**

© Cengage Learning 2013

Figure 10-17 Alphabetic Index Excerpt for Root Type Plain Radiography

---

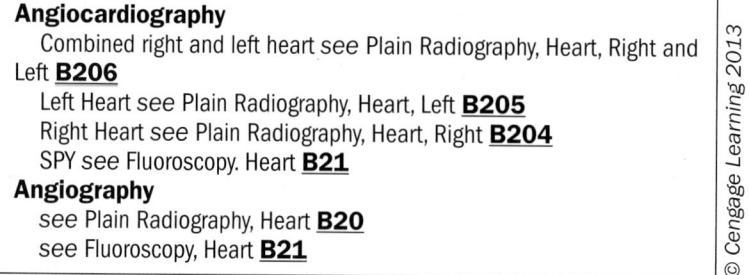

Angiocardiography
   Combined right and left heart *see* Plain Radiography, Heart, Right and Left **B206**
      Left Heart *see* Plain Radiography, Heart, Left **B205**
      Right Heart *see* Plain Radiography, Heart, Right **B204**
      SPY *see* Fluoroscopy. Heart **B21**
Angiography
   see Plain Radiography, Heart **B20**
   see Fluoroscopy, Heart **B21**

© Cengage Learning 2013

Figure 10-18 Alphabetic Index Excerpt for Imaging Procedure Angiography

Section	B	Imaging
Body System	2	Heart
Type	0	Plain Radiography: Planar display of an image developed from the capture of external ionizing radiation on photographic or photoconductive plate

Body Part	Contrast	Qualifier	Qualifier
0 Coronary Artery, Single 1 Coronary Arteries, Multiple 2 Coronary Artery Bypass Graft, Single 3 Coronary Artery Bypass Grafts, Multiple 4 Heart, Right 5 Heart, Left 6 Heart, Right and Left 7 Internal Mammary Bypass Graft, Right 8 Internal Mammary Bypass Graft, Left F Bypass Graft, Other	0 High Osmolar 1 Low Osmolar Y Other Contrast	Z None	Z None

© Cengage Learning 2013

Figure 10-19 Table B20: Plain Radiography Imaging of Heart

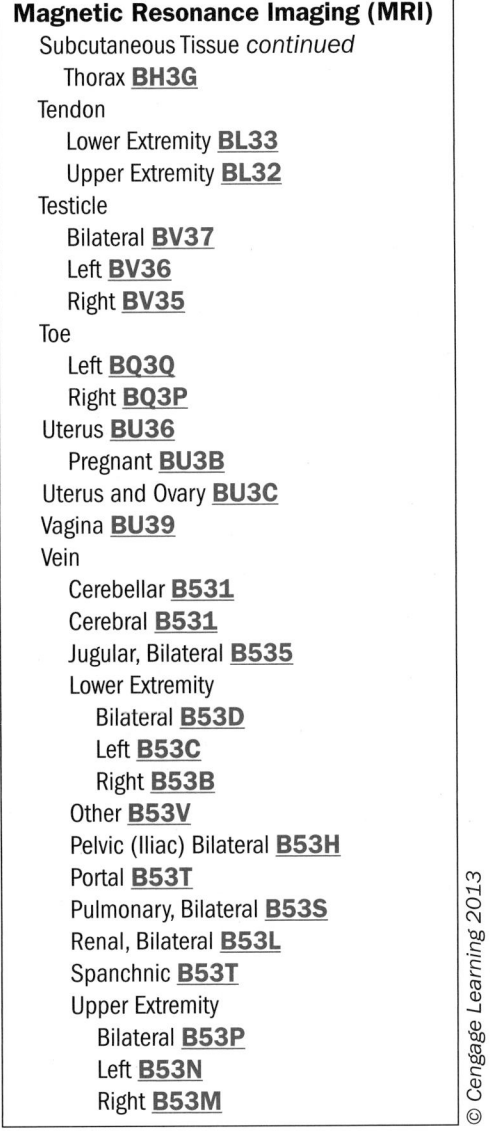

Magnetic Resonance Imaging (MRI)

Subcutaneous Tissue *continued*
   Thorax **BH3G**
Tendon
   Lower Extremity **BL33**
   Upper Extremity **BL32**
Testicle
   Bilateral **BV37**
   Left **BV36**
   Right **BV35**
Toe
   Left **BQ3Q**
   Right **BQ3P**
Uterus **BU36**
   Pregnant **BU3B**
Uterus and Ovary **BU3C**
Vagina **BU39**
Vein
   Cerebellar **B531**
   Cerebral **B531**
   Jugular, Bilateral **B535**
   Lower Extremity
      Bilateral **B53D**
      Left **B53C**
      Right **B53B**
   Other **B53V**
   Pelvic (Iliac) Bilateral **B53H**
   Portal **B53T**
   Pulmonary, Bilateral **B53S**
   Renal, Bilateral **B53L**
   Spanchnic **B53T**
   Upper Extremity
      Bilateral **B53P**
      Left **B53N**
      Right **B53M**

© Cengage Learning 2013

Figure 10-20 Alphabetic Index Excerpt for Magnetic Resonance Imaging

Section	**B**	Imaging		
Body System	**5**	Veins		
Type	**3**	Magnetic Resonance Imaging (MRI): Computer reformatted digital display of multiplanar Images developed from the capture of radio frequency signals emitted by nuclei in a body site excited within a magnetic field		
Body Part		Contrast	Qualifier	Qualifier
1 Cerebral and Cerebellar Veins **2** Intracranial Sinuses **5** Jugular Veins, Bilateral **8** Superior Vena Cava **9** Inferior Vena Cava **B** Lower Extremity Veins, Right **C** Lower Extremity Veins, Left **D** Lower Extremity Veins, Bilateral **H** Pelvic (Iliac) Veins, Bilateral **L** Renal Veins, Bilateral **M** Upper Extremity Veins, Right **N** Upper Extremity Veins, Left **P** Upper Extremity Veins, Bilateral **S** Pulmonary Veins, Bilateral **T** Portal and Splanchnic Veins **V** Veins, Other		**Y** Other Contrast	**0** Unenhanced and Enhanced **Z** None	**Z** None
1 Cerebral and Cerebellar Veins **2** Intracranial Sinuses **5** Jugular Veins, Bilateral **8** Superior Vena Cava **9** Inferior Vena Cava **B** Lower Extremity Veins, Right **C** Lower Extremity Veins, Left **D** Lower Extremity Veins, Bilateral **H** Pelvic (Iliac) Veins, Bilateral **L** Renal Veins, Bilateral **M** Upper Extremity Veins, Right **N** Upper Extremity Veins, Left **P** Upper Extremity Veins, Bilateral **S** Pulmonary Veins, Bilateral **T** Portal and Splanchnic Veins **V** Veins, Other		**Z** None	**Z** None	**Z** None

Figure 10-21 Table B53 Magnetic Resonance Imaging of Veins

Turn to the B20 Table. The B20 Table is found in Figure 10-19. Now, it is time to confirm the first four characters of the code referenced in the Index. The section is Imaging (B), the body system is heart (2) and the root type is Plain Radiography (0). The body part 5 is heart, left. So far, these four characters match the procedure. The fifth character will identify whether contrast was used, and if so, which type. The procedural statement indicates a high osmolar contrast was used, making the fifth character of the code 0. In this Table the only qualifier value in the sixth and seventh position is Z, none. The code for *angiocardiography, left heart, with high osmolar contrast* is B2050ZZ.

Here is another procedure: *MRI of lower extremity veins, unenhanced, and enhanced using contrast.* The main term, or root type, will be MRI. The acronym MRI is not found in the Index, making it necessary to search for MRI in the Index. Figure 10-20 is an excerpt from the root type MRI, which includes the body part *vein.* Indented under *vein* are several subterms, including *cerebellar, jugular, lower extremity, pelvic,* and *renal,* among others. The body part described in this procedure is lower extremity. Below that are references for the right, left, or bilateral.

For the procedure example, a clue is in the use of the word *veins.* Given the three body part subterms, the most logical choice will be bilateral. This leads to the Table reference B53D. In the Table (Figure 10-21), confirm that the first four characters match the procedure. The section is B,

Imaging, the body system is 5, veins, and the root type is 3, MRI. In the first column, D is the body part value for lower extremity veins, bilateral. So far, so good.

In the Contrast column, there are two values, one in each row. The procedural statement indicates contrast was used, so the first row must be chosen with the value Y. The second row cannot be used since it includes only the value Z, for no contrast. In the character 6 column of the first row, Qualifier, there are two values, Z for no qualifier, and 0 for unenhanced and enhanced. The procedural statement indicates the MRI was performed
with and without contrast enhancement, therefore the sixth character is 0. The seventh character Qualifier is Z, none. The code is B53DY0Z for *MRI of lower extremity veins, unenhanced, and enhanced using contrast.*

It is easy to get lost when searching for the right Imaging Table, because the body regions are repeated in several Tables and root types. It is important to stay focused on the root type and body region when searching in the Index, and reviewing the Tables in the Imaging section.

Let's Review 10–2:

Identify the root type(s) for the following imaging procedures:

1. Angiography (Plain Radiography) _____
2. Aortagraphy (Plain Radiography, Fluoroscopy) _____
3. Arthrography (Plain Radiography) _____
4. MR Angiography (Magnetic Resonance Imaging) _____
5. Bronchography (Plain Radiography, Floroscopy) _____
6. Densitometry (Plain Radiography, Ultrasonography) _____

Chapter Summary

Osteopathic procedure codes have a first character value of 7. The body system character 2 value is Anatomical Regions (W), and there is only one root operation for the Osteopathic section, which is Treatment, character value 0. The first three characters for any Osteopathic section code is 7W0. Whenever an Osteopathic procedure is performed the root operation will be Treatment in the Alphabetic Index. The root operation for the Other Procedures Table is also named Other Procedures, defined as *methodologies that attempt to alleviate somatic dysfunction and related disorders.* The procedures included in the Other Procedures section are for non-traditional, whole-body therapies, including Acupuncture and Meditation. The section Other Procedures is represented by the value 8. There are two body system character values: C, indwelling catheter, and E, anatomical systems and anatomical regions. The root operation will always be 0, Other Procedures.

The fourth through seventh character assignments are:

Character 4: Body Region

Character 5: Approach

Character 6: Method (this is the technique used during the procedure)

Character 7: Qualifier (the Qualifier identifies the procedure performed)

Body region character Z (Figure 10-4) is used in this section to denote procedures that are not applicable specifically to any of the other body regions. These include other methods of treatment identified by the qualifier value. There are four qualifiers for body region Z, with an external approach, and Y for other method: In vitro fertilization (1), yoga therapy (4), meditation (5), and isolation therapy (6). There are 15 Qualifier values in the character 7 position, as well as value Z, to indicate there is no qualifier.

The first three characters of a Chiropractic section code are 9WB. The section (9) is Chiropractic; the body system is W, Anatomical Regions, and the only root operation is Manipulation, character B. The fourth character represents the body region upon which the chiropractic manipulation is performed. Manipulation is defined as *a manual procedure that involves a directed thrust to move a joint past the physiological range of motion, without exceeding the anatomical limit.* If a mechanical device is used to assist in the manipulation, the method then would be value K, mechanically assisted. A non-manual manipulation is performed using specific patient positions and gravity, rather than a hands-on manipulation of the body part.

The Imaging section (character value B) is the first one that does not include a root operation. This term is replaced by root type, and includes types of Imaging procedures, like CT scan or MRI. Each Table includes a separate body system (character 2) and separate root operation (character 3). The Table ranges include B00 through BY4. Rather than the traditional root operation found in the third character position of an ICD-10-PCS code, the name of the Imaging procedure becomes character three of an ICD-10-PCS Imaging code. There are four root type values for character three: Plain Radiography, Fluoroscopy, Magnetic Resonance Imaging (MRI), and Ultrasonography. It is character 4 that separates each of the body systems into individual body parts, and has the most detail (Table 10-5).

The character values of body parts change as the body system changes. In the upper arteries body system, for example, the value 0 is thoracic aorta, and 2 is subclavian artery, left, but, in the lower arteries body system, 0 is abdominal artery and 2 is hepatic artery. There are five contrast values in the fifth character position: high osmolar (0), low osmolar (1), other contrast (Y), and no contrast (Z). In the Imaging section, character value 6 is a qualifier. With these Imaging section qualifier values, intraoperative (0), intravascular (3), and densitometry (1), review the medical documentation carefully to ensure assignment of the seventh code character is appropriate.

When searching the Index, look for the root types as the main term. The modifying terms are all body parts and are indented below the main term. It is easy to get lost when searching for the right Imaging Table, because the body regions are repeated in several Tables and Root Types. It is important to stay focused on the Root type and body region when searching in the Index, and reviewing the Tables in the Imaging section.

Review

Matching

Instructions:

_____ 1. Treatment

_____ 2. Manipulation

_____ 3. Computer assisted procedures

_____ 4. Near-infrared spectroscopy

_____ 5. Fluoroscopy.

_____ 6. Magnetic Resonance Imaging (MRI)

_____ 7. Multiplanar

_____ 8. Ultrasonography

_____ 9. Contrast agents

_____ 10. densitometry

a. A test measuring bone density.

b. Manual movement or adjustment used to alleviate somatic dysfunction and related disorders. In the Osteopathic section, the root operation value is 0.

c. Manual procedure that involves a directed thrust to move a joint past the physiological range of motion, without exceeding the anatomical limit. It is also known as an adjustment.

d. A type of medical substance used to improve the visibility of internal bodily structures in imaging root types.

e. Real time display of anatomical structure or flow images developed from the capture of high-frequency sound waves monitoring method in detecting oxygen saturation in the field of neurosurgery and cardiovascular surgery and neonatal ICU.

f. Single or bi-plane real time display of an image developed from the capture of radiation on a fluorescent screen.

g. Computerized digital display of multiplanar images developed from the capture of radiofrequency signals emitted within a magnetic field.

h. A technique used to generate sagittal, coronal, and oblique views (multiple planes).

i. Monitoring method used to detect oxygen saturation in the field of neurosurgery and cardiovascular surgery and neonatal ICU.

j. Describe navigation systems that provide additional information during a procedure, to increase surgical accuracy and reduce the chance of malposition of implants.

Short Answer

Instructions: Provide a brief answer to the following questions.

1. List the operation(s) and approach(es) for Section 7, Osteopathic
   a. Operation: treatment
   b. Approach: external

2. List the operation(s) and approach(es) for Section 8, Other Procedures
   a. Operation: Other Procedures
   b. Approach: External, percutaneous, percutaneous endoscopic, via natural or artificial opening, and via natural or artificial opening, endoscopic

3. List the operation(s) and approach(es) for Section 9, Chiropractic
   a. Operation: Manipulation
   b. Approach: External

4. Briefly describe a *computerized tomography* for Section B, Imaging
   a. Obtain from definitions in ICD-10-PCS code book

5. Briefly describe *magnetic resonance imaging (MRI)* for Section B, Imaging

6. Briefly describe *ultrasonography* for Section B, Imaging

7. Briefly describe *positron emission tomographic (PET) imaging* for Section C, Imaging

8. List the qualifiers used in Table 8C0 (Other Procedures, Indwelling Devices)

9. List four methods found in Table 8E0 (Other Procedures, Physiological Systems and Anatomic Regions)

10. List at least three contrasts used in Section B, Imaging

Coding Practice

Instructions:

1. Myelogram of brain via CT scan _____

2. Intravascular Doppler study common carotid arteries, bilateral _____

3. Fluoroscopic bronchography, bilateral lungs _____

4. Densitometry study, left hip (requires determination of correct root type) _____
_____

5. MR angiography, heart, unenhanced and enhanced with other contrast _____
_____

6. Aortagraphy, fluoroscopic, right upper extremity arteries _____

7. Arthrography, skull _____

8. Computer-assisted surgery of trunk region, with magnetic resonance imaging _____
_____

9. Osteopathic treatment of rib cage using fascial release _____

10. Collection of blood from circulatory system _____

11. Yoga therapy _____

12. Short level manipulation of pelvis _____

13. Ultrasound of single coronary artery, using other contrast _____

14. X-ray imaging of optic foramina, right _____

15. Enhanced and unenhanced CT of colon, other contrast _____

Nuclear Medicine and Radiation Oncology

Learning Objectives

At the conclusion of this chapter, the learner should be able to:

- Understand key terms used in the Nuclear Medicine and Radiation Oncology sections and identify new character names and values
- Identify the Body System, Root Type, Body Regions, Radionuclides, and Qualifiers used in the Nuclear Medicine section
- Identify the Body System, Root Type, Treatment Site, Modality Qualifier, Isotope, and Qualifier used in the Radiation Oncology section
- Understand the guidelines that impact code selection in the Nuclear Medicine and Radiation Oncology sections
- Differentiate how the root types are used in the Nuclear Medicine section, and how to apply the correct character values
- Differentiate how the root types are used in the Radiation Oncology section, and how to apply the correct character values
- Know how to use the Index and Tables to select the correct code from the Nuclear Medicine section
- Know how to use the Index and Tables to select the correct code from the Radiation Oncology section
- Understand the guidelines and instructional notes that impact code selection in the Nuclear Medicine and Radiation Oncology sections

Key Terms and Definitions

Beam Radiation	Radiation therapy that uses a machine located outside of the body to aim radiation at cancer cells.
Brachytherapy	Internal radiation treatment done by implanting radioactive material directly into the tumor or close to it. Also called internal radiation therapy.
Electron beam	A stream of high-energy atomic particles used to treat cancer.

Intensity Modulated Radiation Therapy (IMRT)	A method of radiation therapy in which the beams are aimed from many directions. Also called conformal radiation therapy.
Isotope	Character 6 of a radiation oncology code that identifies the type of radioactive substance used in the procedure.
Modality qualifier	Character 5 of a radiation oncology code that gives further specificity to the type of radiation used.
Nonimaging Nuclear Medicine Assay	Introduction of radioactive material into the body for the study of body fluids and blood elements, by the detection of radioactive emissions. Root type value 6 in the Nuclear Medicine section.
Planar nuclear medicine imaging	Root type value 1 in the Nuclear Medicine section. Introduction of radioactive materials into the body for single-plane display of images developed from capture of radioactive emissions.
Plaque therapy	Radioactive material is placed (seeded) into an implantable container called a plaque.
Port	The area of the body through which external beam radiation is directed to reach a tumor. Also called treatment site.
Positron Emission Tomographic (PET) Scan	Imaging root type value 3 in the Nuclear Medicine section. Introduction of radioactive materials into the body for three-dimensional display of images developed from the simultaneous capture, 180 degrees apart, of radioactive emissions.
Radionuclide	Radiation source. A chemical substance that exhibits radioactivity. Used in the Nuclear Medicine section. They are sometimes referred to as tracers.
Stereotactic radiosurgery	Radiation treatment that gives a large dose of radiation to a small tumor area. Also called fractionated radiosurgery or Stereotactic radiotherapy.
Systemic radiation	Uses radioactive materials taken by mouth or injected into the body to kill cancer cells.
Systemic therapy	Introduction of unsealed radioactive materials into the body for treatment. Root type value 7 in the Nuclear Medicine section.
Tattoo	A pinpoint or freckle-sized dot made using India ink that creates a permanent mark outlining the treatment site.
Tomographic (Tomo) Nuclear Medicine Imaging	Root type value 2 in the Nuclear Medicine section. Introduction of radioactive materials into the body for three-dimensional display of images developed from capture of radioactive emissions.
Treatment site	Character 4 of a radiation oncology code that identifies the site of the body being treated.

Introduction

The Nuclear Medicine and Radiation Oncology sections of the ICD-10-PCS coding manual are introduced in this chapter. There are many new key terms, especially those related to oncology procedures, as well as new character names and values in all of the Tables in these two sections. In this chapter, the goal is to identify terminology, including root types, radionuclides, isotopes, PET scans, and others. Also covered are the guidelines relevant to nuclear medicine and radiation oncology coding, and discussion on how to perform the coding steps properly.

Nuclear Medicine (C01–CW7)

Nuclear medicine is a branch of medicine that uses radiation to provide information about the functioning of a person's body systems or organs or to treat disease. The thyroid, bones, heart, liver, blood, and many other organs and systems can be visualized, revealing disorders in their functioning. In some cases, radiation can be used to treat diseased organs or tumors. Nuclear medicine procedures introduce radioactive material into the body. The image created by the radioactive material helps to diagnose and treat pathological conditions, or to assess metabolic functions.

The first character value for Nuclear Medicine procedures is C. The second character identifies the body system on which a procedure is performed. There are seven root types in the Nuclear Medicine section, including nonimaging uptakes, probes, and assays, single plane and tomographic imaging, and positron emission tomography, also called PET scans. Character 4 of the Nuclear Medicine code identifies the body part or region being studied or assessed, and the fifth character is the radionuclide, or radiation source used in the procedure. Characters 6 and 7 are qualifier categories, and in the entire Nuclear Medicine section, the values are always Z, no qualifiers.

Figure 11-1 is an excerpt from a Table in the Nuclear Medicine section illustrating some of the values within each column. The section value is C, Nuclear Medicine, and in this example, the body system is B, the respiratory system. The root type is planar (single-plane) nuclear medicine imaging, and has a value of 1. There are two rows in this Table: The body parts in row 1 are the lungs and bronchi, with a character value of 2. The second row body part is the respiratory system (Y). In the second column, under Radionuclide, the radiation sources are listed, and in both qualifier columns in both rows the character value is Z, meaning there are no qualifiers for these procedures.

Body System (Character 2) Values in the Nuclear Medicine Section

As always, the second character in an ICD-10-PCS code identifies the body system. In Nuclear Medicine, the body systems and their values are represented in Table 11-1.

Body systems not given a specific character value, such as the female reproductive system, are found within the character 2 body system, Anatomical Regions (value W). The female reproductive system is included in the *pelvic region* body part column (value J).

Root Type (Character 3) Values in the Nuclear Medicine Section

There are seven nuclear medicine root types. The values and definitions of each are shown in Table 11-2.

Section	**C**	Nuclear Medicine		
Body System	**B**	Respiratory System		
Type	**1**	Planar Nuclear Medicine Imaging: Introduction of radioactive materials into the body for single plane display of images developed from the capture of radioactive emissions		
Body Part	Radionuclide	Qualifier	Qualifier
---	---	---	---
2 Lungs and Bronchi	**1** Technetium 99m (Tc-99m) **9** Krypton (Kr-81m) **T** Xenon 127 (Xe-127) **V** Xenon 133 (Xe-133) **Y** Other Radionuclide	**Z** None	**Z** None
Y Respiratory System	**Y** Other Radionuclide	**Z** None	**Z** None

Figure 11-1 Nuclear Medicine Table CB1

Table 11-1 Body Systems in the Nuclear Medicine Section

Value	Body System
0	Central Nervous System
2	Heart
5	Veins
7	Lymphatic and Hematologic Systems
8	Eye
9	Ear, Nose, Mouth, and Throat
B	Respiratory System
D	Gastrointestinal System
F	Hepatobiliary System and Pancreas
G	Endocrine System
H	Skin, Subcutaneous Tissue, and Breast
P	Musculoskeletal System
T	Urinary System
V	Male Reproductive
W	Anatomical Regions

Table 11-2 Root Types in Nuclear Medicine

Value	Root Type	Definition
1	**Planar imaging**	Introduction of radioactive materials into the body for **single-plane display** of images developed from capture of radioactive emissions
2	**Tomographic (tomo) imaging**	Introduction of radioactive materials into the body for **three-dimensional display** of images developed from capture of radioactive emissions
3	**Positron Emission Tomography (PET) Scan**	Introduction of radioactive materials into the body for three-dimensional display of images developed from the **simultaneous capture, 180 degrees apart**, of radioactive emissions
4	**Nonimaging Uptake**	Introduction of radioactive materials into the body for **measurements of organ function**, from the detection of radioactive emissions
5	**Nonimaging probe**	Introduction of radioactive materials into the body for the **study of distribution and fate of certain substances**, by the detection of radioactive emissions from an **external source.** Or alternatively, **measurement of absorption of radioactive emissions** from an external source
6	**Nonimaging assay**	Introduction of radioactive material into the body for the **study of body fluids and blood elements**, by the detection of radioactive emissions
7	**Systemic therapy**	Introduction of unsealed radioactive materials into the body for treatment

Almost all of the root types in the Nuclear Medicine section include the introduction of a radioactive material into the body. This material then emits radioactivity, and the emissions are captured and displayed as images. Each root type has a specific objective. Planar imaging (value 1) is a single body plane display, i.e., sagittal, coronal, or frontal. Tomographic imaging (2) creates a three-dimensional display for diagnostic evaluation. The PET scan (3) simultaneously captures images 180 degrees apart; for example, frontal and posterior images, which can both be viewed at the same time. Nonimaging uptakes (4) are performed to measure organ function, and nonimaging probes (5) are used to study how the radioactive emissions distribute throughout the body part, and what happens to them. For example, a nonimaging probe procedure on the brain can monitor how the radioactive particles flow through the brain, and determine in which part of the brain they collect, and whether they are absorbed by cells or enter the blood stream.

A nonimaging probe can also measure the rate of absorption of radioactive materials. Root type 6, nonimaging assay, is used only in the Table containing the Blood and Lymphatic systems. The assay studies body fluids (like lymph) or blood elements. The systemic therapy root type (7) is found only with Tables that include the body system *anatomical regions*. For some medical conditions, it is useful to destroy or weaken malfunctioning cells using radiation. In most cases, beta radiation causes the destruction of the damaged cells. This systemic therapy is not to be confused with radiation oncology. Radiation Oncology deals only with procedures that are used to treat cancer.

The systemic therapy root type is a non-cancer treatment. Iodine-131 and phosphorus-32 are examples of two radioisotopes used for systemic nuclear medicine therapy. Iodine-131 is used to treat the thyroid for abnormal conditions such as hyperthyroidism. It is also used to treat thyroid cancers, which will be discussed later in the Radiation Oncology section of this textbook. Phosphorus-32 is used to control an excess of red blood cells in the disease *polycythemia vera*. There are several other techniques of diagnostic nuclear medicine.

- Scintigraphy ("scint") is the use of internal radioisotopes to create two-dimensional images. Scintigraphy is coded to nuclear medicine, typically tomographic (tomo) nuclear medicine imaging, value 2 (even though scintigraphy is only two-dimensional). The most common term for scintigraphy is bone scan.

- Single photon emission computed tomography (SPECT, or less commonly, SPET) is a nuclear medicine tomographic imaging technique using gamma rays. It is very similar to conventional nuclear medicine planar imaging, except it provides true three-dimensional information. This information is typically presented as cross-sectional slices through the patient, but can be freely reformatted or manipulated as required. The root type value for SPECT is 2, tomographic (tomo) nuclear medicine imaging.

Body Part (Character 4) Values in the Nuclear Medicine Section

As in the Imaging section, not every body part will be associated with each root type. It is also not unusual to see the same body parts repeated in several rows in a Table, or in several Tables. In Body System W, anatomical region, there are many regional and combination values. An example of a regional body part value would be lower extremity, or abdomen, where one region is targeted by the root type. Abdomen and pelvis, and head and neck, are two examples of combination values, where two or more body areas are included in the nuclear medicine procedure. In Table 11-3, the body parts identified in the Nuclear Medicine section are shown with the applicable body systems and root types.

In Tables C01, C02, and C03, for the body system Central Nervous System, the three root types target the same three body parts listed in Table 11-3. The same is true for the body parts and root types in Tables CH1 and CH2, and CT2 and CT6. In some of the same body systems, the body parts will change depending upon the root type. In CW1, for example, there are 12 different body parts under the root type planar imaging, but when the root type changes to Tomographic Imaging, body part Z, *anatomical regions, other* is not an option. In CW3, with the root type PET Imaging, only body part N, *whole body* is an appropriate value. Table CG4 is the only instance where the root type Nonimaging Uptake is used, for measurement of thyroid and endocrine system functioning.

Note too, that the body part character values change as the body system changes. The value 1, for example, identifies the body parts left breast, skull, and abdomen and pelvis within which the body system the body part is found, i.e., skull is in the musculoskeletal system, while the abdomen and pelvis are in the Anatomical Regions body system. It is also important to remember that some body part values will be in different rows of one Table, depending upon the Radionuclide (fifth character) used in the procedure. For example, look at Figure 11-2. This is the Table for Nuclear Medicine, Anatomical Regions, Planar Imaging (CW1). In Table 11-3, all of the body parts for Table CW1 are listed, however, in the Table, they are divided into four rows. The body parts abdomen through whole body are in one row, with several radionuclides in the second column. In the second, third, and fourth rows, only one body

Table 11-3 Body Parts Associated with Body Systems and Root Types

Tables	Body System	Root Type(s)	Body Part(s) (Fourth Character)
C01 C02 C03	0—Central Nervous System	1—Planar Imaging 2—Tomographic Imaging 3—Pet Imaging	0—Brain S—Cerebrospinal Fluid Y—Central Nervous System
C05	0—Central Nervous System	5—Nonimaging Probe	0—Brain Y—Central Nervous System
C21 C22	2—Heart	1—Planar Imaging 2—Tomograpic Imaging	6—Heart, Right And Left G—Myocardium Y—Heart
C23	2—Heart	3—PET Imaging	G—Myocardium Y—Heart
C25	2—Heart	5—Nonimaging Probe	6—Heart, Right And Left Y—Heart
C51	5—Veins	1—Planar Imaging	B—Lower Extremity Veins, Right C—Lower Extremity Veins, Left D—Lower Extremity Veins, Bilateral N—Upper Extremity Veins, Right P—Upper Extremity Veins, Left Q—Upper Extremity Veins, Bilateral R—Central Veins Y—Veins
C71	7—Lymphatic And Hematologic	1—Planar Imaging	0—Bone Marrow 2—Spleen 3—Blood 5—Lymphatics, Head And Neck D—Lymphatics, Pelvic J—Lymphatics, Head K—Lymphatics, Neck L—Lymphatics, Upper Chest M—Lymphatics, Trunk N—Lymphatics, Upper Extremity P—Lymphatics, Lower Extremity Y—Lymphatics And Hematologic System
C72	7—Lymphatic And Hematologic	2—Tomographic Imaging	2—Spleen Y—Lymphatics And Hematologic System
C75	7—Lymphatic And Hematologic	5—Nonimaging Probe	5—Lymphatics, Head And Neck D—Lymphatics, Pelvic J—Lymphatics, Head K—Lymphatics, Neck L—Lymphatics, Upper Chest M—Lymphatics, Trunk N—Lymphatics, Upper Extremity P—Lymphatics, Lower Extremity Y—Lymphatics And Hematologic System
C76	7—Lymphatic And Hematologic	6—Nonimaging Assay	3—Blood Y—Lymphatic And Hematologic System
C81	8—Eye	1—Planar Imaging	9—Lacrimal Ducts, Bilateral Y—Eye
C91	9—Ear, Nose, Mouth, And Throat	1—Planar Imaging	B—Salivary Glands, Bilateral Y—Ear, Nose, Mouth, And Throat
CB1 CB2 CB3	B—Respiratory System	1—Planar Imaging 2—Tomographic Imaging 3—Pet Imaging	2—Lungs and Bronchi Y—Respiratory System

CD1	D—Gastrointestinal System	1—Planar Imaging	5—Upper Gastrointestinal Tract 7—Gastrointestinal Tract Y—Digestive System
CD2	D—Gastrointestinal System	2—Tomographic Imaging	7—Gastrointestinal Tract Y—Digestive System
CF1	F—Hepatobiliary And Pancreas	1—Planar Imaging	4—Gallbladder 5—Liver 6—Liver And Spleen C—Hepatobiliary System, All Y—Hepatobiliary System And Pancreas
CF2	F—Hepatobiliary And Pancreas	2—Tomographic Imaging	4—Gallbladder 5—Liver 6—Liver And Spleen Y—Hepatobiliary System And Pancreas
CG1	G—Endocrine System	1—Planar Imaging	1—Parathyroid Glands 2—Thyroid Gland 4—Adrenal Glands, Bilateral Y—Endocrine System
CG2	G—Endocrine System	2—Tomographic Imaging	1—Parathyroid Glands Y—Endocrine System
CG4	G—Endocrine System	4—Nonimaging Uptake	2—Thyroid Gland Y—Endocrine System
CH1 CH2	H—Skin, Subcutaneous Tissue, and Breast	1—Planar Imaging 2—Tomographic Imaging	0—Breast, Right 1—Breast, Left 2—Breasts, Bilateral Y—Skin, Subcutaneous Tissue, and Breast
CP1	P—Musculoskeletal System	1—Planar Imaging	1—Skull 4—Thorax 5—Spine 6—Pelvis 7—Spine And Pelvis 8—Upper Extremity, Right 9—Upper Extremity, Left B—Upper Extremities, Bilateral C—Lower Extremity, Right D—Lower Extremity, Left F—Lower Extremities, Bilateral Y—Musculoskeletal System, Other Z—Musculoskeletal System, All
CP2	P—Musculoskeletal System	2—Tomographic Imaging	1—Skull 2—Cervical Spine 3—Skull And Cervical Spine 4—Thorax 6—Pelvis 7—Spine And Pelvis 8—Upper Extremity, Right 9—Upper Extremity, Left B—Upper Extremities, Bilateral C—Lower Extremity, Right D—Lower Extremity, Left F—Lower Extremities, Bilateral G—Thoracic Spine H—Lumbar Spine J—Thoracolumbar Spine Y—Musculoskeletal System, Other

Table 11-3 Body Parts Associated with Body Systems and Root Types (continued)

Tables	Body System	Root Type(s)	Body Part(s) (Fourth Character)
CP3	P—Musculoskeletal System	5—Nonimaging Probe	5—Spine N—Upper Extremities P—Lower Extremities Y—Musculoskeletal System, Other
CT1	T—Urinary System	1—Planar Imaging	3—Kidneys, Ureters, and Bladder H—Bladder and Ureters Y—Urinary System
CT2 CT6	T—Urinary System	6—Nonimaging Assay	3—Kidneys, Ureters, and Bladder Y—Urinary System
CV1	V—Male Reproductive	1—Planar Imaging	9—Testicles, Bilateral Y—Male Reproductive System
CW1	W—Anatomical Regions	1—Planar Imaging	0—Abdomen 1—Abdomen And Pelvis 3—Chest 4—Chest And Abdomen 6—Chest And Neck B—Head And Neck D—Lower Extremity J—Pelvic Region M—Upper Extremity N—Whole Body Y—Anatomical Regions, Multiple Z—Anatomical Regions, Other
CW2	W—Anatomical Regions	2—Tomographic Imaging	0—Abdomen 1—Abdomen And Pelvis 3—Chest 4—Chest And Abdomen 6—Chest And Neck B—Head And Neck D—Lower Extremity J—Pelvic Region M—Upper Extremity Y—Anatomical Regions, Multiple
CW3	W—Anatomical Regions	3—PET Imaging	N—Whole Body
CW5	W—Anatomical Regions	5—Nonimaging Probe	0—Abdomen 1—Abdomen And Pelvis 3—Chest 4—Chest And Abdomen 6—Chest And Neck B—Head And Neck D—Lower Extremity J—Pelvic Region M—Upper Extremity
CW7	W—Anatomical Regions	7—Systemic Therapy	0—Abdomen 3—Chest G—Thyroid N—Whole Body Y—Anatomical Regions, Multiple

Section	**C**	Nuclear Medicine		
Body System	**W**	Anatomical Regions		
Type	**1**	Planar Nuclear Medicine Imaging: Introduction of radioactive materials into the body for single plane display of images developed from the capture of radioactive emissions		

Body Part	Radionuclide	Qualifier	Qualifier
0 Abdomen **1** Abdomen and Pelvis **4** Chest and Abdomen **6** Chest and Neck **B** Head and Neck **D** Lower Extremity **J** Pelvic Region **M** Upper Extremity **N** Whole Body	**1** Technetium 99m (Tc-99m) **D** Indium 111 (In-111) **F** Iodine 123 (I-123) **G** Iodine 131 (I-131) **L** Gallium 67 (Ga-67) **S** Thallium 201 (Tl-201) **Y** Other Radionuclide	**Z** None	**Z** None
3 Chest	**1** Technetium 99m (Tc-99m) **D** Indium 111 (In-111) **F** Iodine 123 (I-123) **G** Iodine 131 (I-131) **K** Fluorine 18 (F-18) **L** Gallium 67 (Ga-67) **S** Thallium 201 (Tl-201) **Y** Other Radionuclide	**Z** None	**Z** None
Y Anatomical Regions, Multiple	**Y** Other Radionuclide	**Z** None	**Z** None
Z Anatomical Region, Other	**Z** None	**Z** None	**Z** None

© Cengage Learning 2013

Figure 11-2 Body Part Row Distribution for Table CW1

part value is listed, chest, anatomical regions, multiple, and anatomical region, other, respectively. Each of those three rows have different or additional radionuclides shown.

Radionuclides (Character 5) Values in the Nuclear Medicine Section

A **radionuclide** is the radiation source used in nuclear medicine. It is a chemical substance that exhibits radioactivity. Used in the Nuclear Medicine section. Radionuclides are sometimes referred to as tracers. Diagnostic radiopharmaceuticals are used to examine blood flow to the brain, or functioning of the thyroid, lungs, liver, or gastrointestinal systems. Another important use is to predict the effects of surgery and assess changes since treatment.

Table 11-4 contains the Radionuclides, or radiation sources, used in the Nuclear Medicine section.

The radioinuclide used in most nuclear medicine procedures is technetium-99m. Myocardial Perfusion Imaging (MPI) procedures that detect coronary artery disease use thallium-201 chloride or technetium-99m. One last note about the Nuclear Medicine section. Characters 6 and 7 are both qualifier values, however, there are no qualifiers used in the nuclear medicine section. The value for both qualifier characters is always Z.

Coding Nuclear Medicine Procedures

In most instances, the root type is the main search word in the Index. However, it is also possible to find at least some information using terms like scan, or diagnostic imaging. In both of those examples, the Index includes the instructional note to See Imaging, or See whichever root type is appropriate. For example, looking up scan (Figure 11-3) leads to references to See either an Imaging section CT scan or Planar Nuclear Medicine Imaging. A search for a PET scan leads to the instructional note See PET Imaging. It is also possible to look in the Index under Nuclear Medicine, and find all of the root types listed, as shown in Figure 11-4.

Table 11-4 Radionuclides used in Nuclear Medicine

Value	Radionuclide
1	Technetium 99m (Tc-99m)
7	Cobalt 58 (Co-58)
8	Samarium 153 (Sm-153)
9	Krypton (Kr-81m)
B	Carbon 11 (C-11)
C	Cobalt 57 (Co-57)
D	Indium 111 (In-111)
F	Iodine 123 (I-123)
G	Iodine 131 (I-131)
H	Iodine 125 (I-125)
K	Fluorine 18 (F-18)
L	Gallium 67 (Ga-67)
M	Oxygen 15 (O-15)
N	Phosphorus 32 (P-32)
P	Strontium 89 (Sr-89)
Q	Rubidium 82 (Rb-82)
R	Nitrogen 13 (N-13)
S	Thallium 201 (Tl-201)
T	Xexon 127 (Xe-127)
V	Xenon 133 (Xe-133)
Y	Other Radionuclide
Z	None

> **Scan**
> Computerized Tomography (CT) *see* Computerized Tomography (CT Scan)
> Radioisotope *see* Planar Nuclear Medicine Imaging

Figure 11-3 Alphabetic Index Listing for Scan © *Cengage Learning 2013*

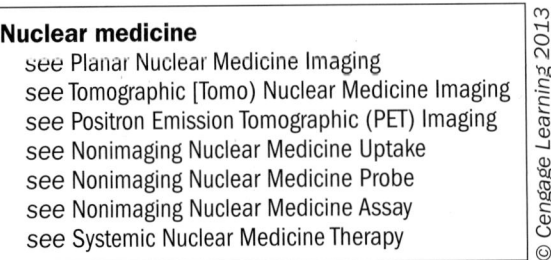

> **Nuclear medicine**
> see Planar Nuclear Medicine Imaging
> see Tomographic [Tomo] Nuclear Medicine Imaging
> see Positron Emission Tomographic (PET) Imaging
> see Nonimaging Nuclear Medicine Uptake
> see Nonimaging Nuclear Medicine Probe
> see Nonimaging Nuclear Medicine Assay
> see Systemic Nuclear Medicine Therapy

© *Cengage Learning 2013*

Figure 11-4 Alphabetic Index Listing for Nuclear Medicine

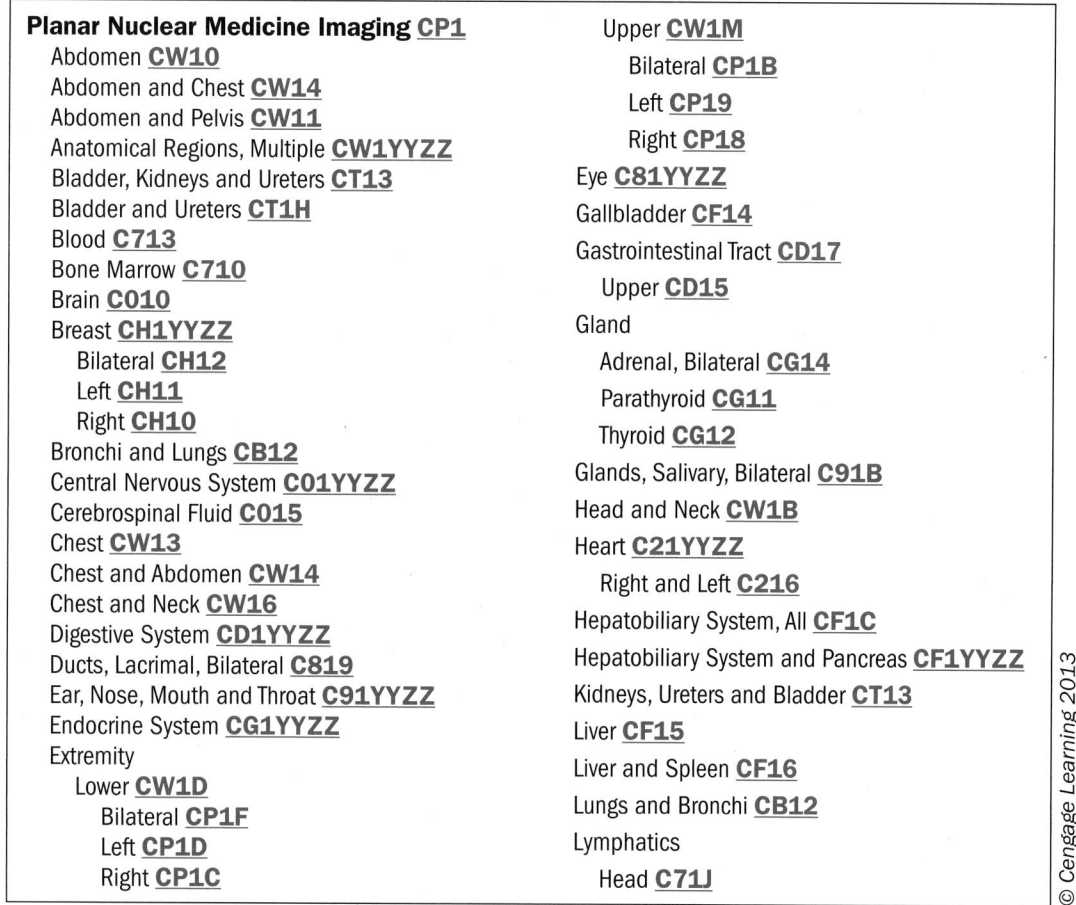

Figure 11-5 Alphabetic Index Listing for Planar Nuclear Medicine Imaging

Figures 11-6 through 11-12 are excerpts in the Index for each one of the root types in the Nuclear Medicine section. These are not complete lists, but are meant to illustrate how they appear in the Index. Use these as an aid to understanding how to conduct the Index search for nuclear medicine procedures. There are some examples given here that will use a few of these Figures. Indented as a modifying term under each of the bolded root types is the body system or body part along with the Table reference. Search for the root type as the main term, then the body part, region, or system identified in the procedure. Use Figure 11-5, for example.

Now, it is time to code a few nuclear medicine procedures. The first procedure example is *diagnostic myocardial imaging, 3D, contrast Tc-99m*. Finding the main term rests in knowing the definitions of the root types. A three-dimensional (3D) diagnostic imaging would lead to tomographic (tomo) nuclear medicine imaging. A search can be started using Nuclear Medicine (Figure 11-4) which lists each nuclear medicine procedure, or by going directly to Tomographic (tomo) nuclear medicine imaging in the Index (Figure 11-6). Indented below the root type is the body part, myocardium, and the Table reference C22G, for the nuclear medicine section (C), body system heart (2), and root type tomographic (tomo) nuclear medicine imaging. In Table C22, the first column body part value G, myocardium is in the second row (Figure 11-12). The fifth character (column 2) identifies the radionuclide. The correct radioisotope is 1, Technetium 99m (Tc-99m). Both qualifier values are Z. The code C22G1ZZ matches the procedure *diagnostic myocardial imaging, 3D, contrast Tc-99m*.

Here is another one, *systemic thyroid therapy, I-131*. The key words are *systemic* and *therapy,* which should lead to systemic nuclear medicine therapy in the Index (Figure 11-11). The Table reference for thyroid is CW7G. Going to Table CW7, shown in Figure 11-13, the section, body system, and root type

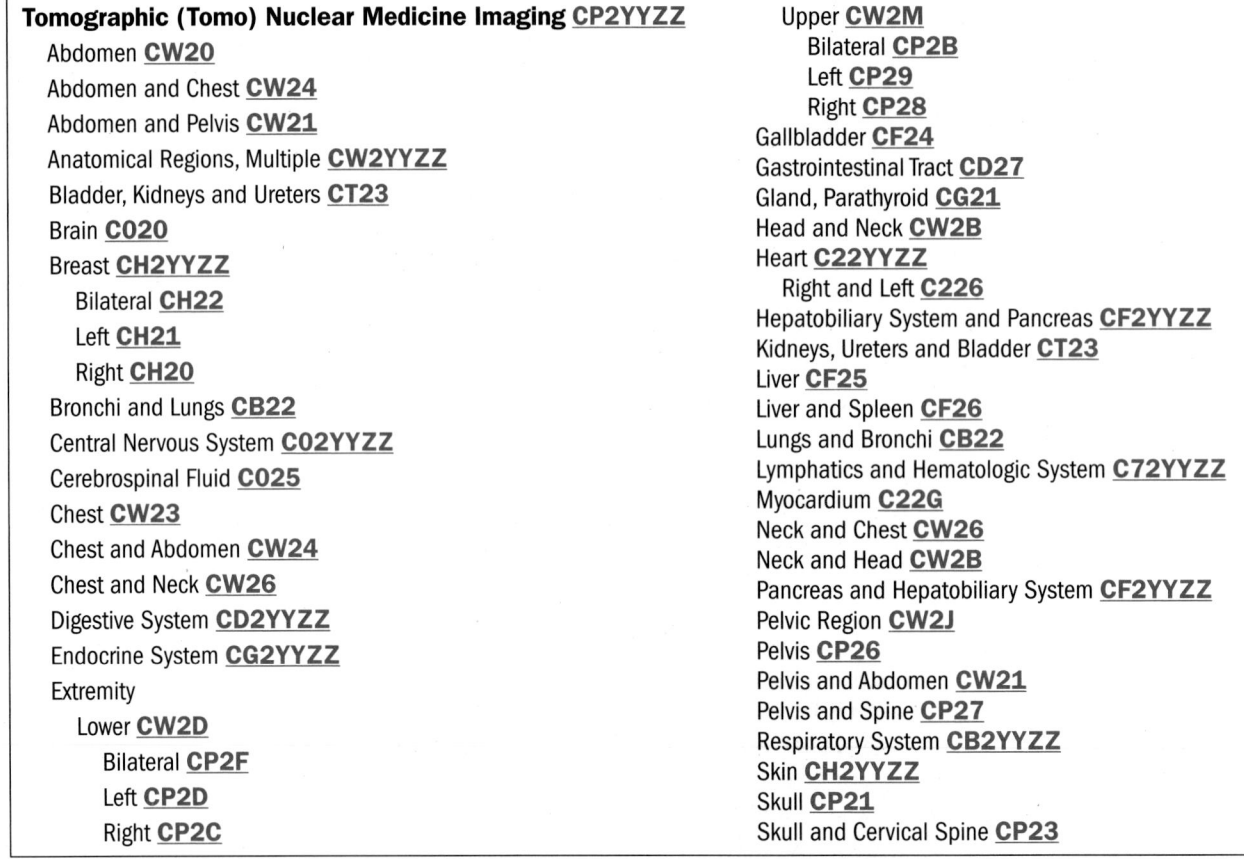

Tomographic (Tomo) Nuclear Medicine Imaging CP2YYZZ
- Abdomen **CW20**
- Abdomen and Chest **CW24**
- Abdomen and Pelvis **CW21**
- Anatomical Regions, Multiple **CW2YYZZ**
- Bladder, Kidneys and Ureters **CT23**
- Brain **C020**
- Breast **CH2YYZZ**
  - Bilateral **CH22**
  - Left **CH21**
  - Right **CH20**
- Bronchi and Lungs **CB22**
- Central Nervous System **C02YYZZ**
- Cerebrospinal Fluid **C025**
- Chest **CW23**
- Chest and Abdomen **CW24**
- Chest and Neck **CW26**
- Digestive System **CD2YYZZ**
- Endocrine System **CG2YYZZ**
- Extremity
  - Lower **CW2D**
    - Bilateral **CP2F**
    - Left **CP2D**
    - Right **CP2C**
- Upper **CW2M**
  - Bilateral **CP2B**
  - Left **CP29**
  - Right **CP28**
- Gallbladder **CF24**
- Gastrointestinal Tract **CD27**
- Gland, Parathyroid **CG21**
- Head and Neck **CW2B**
- Heart **C22YYZZ**
  - Right and Left **C226**
- Hepatobiliary System and Pancreas **CF2YYZZ**
- Kidneys, Ureters and Bladder **CT23**
- Liver **CF25**
- Liver and Spleen **CF26**
- Lungs and Bronchi **CB22**
- Lymphatics and Hematologic System **C72YYZZ**
- Myocardium **C22G**
- Neck and Chest **CW26**
- Neck and Head **CW2B**
- Pancreas and Hepatobiliary System **CF2YYZZ**
- Pelvic Region **CW2J**
- Pelvis **CP26**
- Pelvis and Abdomen **CW21**
- Pelvis and Spine **CP27**
- Respiratory System **CB2YYZZ**
- Skin **CH2YYZZ**
- Skull **CP21**
- Skull and Cervical Spine **CP23**

© Cengage Learning 2013

Figure 11-6 Alphabetic Index Listing for Tomography Nuclear Medicine Imaging

Positron Emission Tomographic (PET) Imaging
- Brain **C030**
- Bronchi and Lungs **CB32**
- Central Nervous System **C03YYZZ**
- Heart **C23YYZZ**
- Lungs and Bronchi **CB32**
- Myocardium **C23G**
- Respiratory System **CB3YYZZ**
- Whole Body **CW3NYZZ**

© Cengage Learning 2013

Figure 11-7 Alphabetic Index Listing for Positron Emission Tomographic Imaging

Nonimaging Nuclear Medicine Uptake
- Endocrine System **CG4YYZZ**
- Gland, Thyroid **CG42**

Figure 11-8 Alphabetic Index Listing for Nonimaging Nuclear Medicine Uptake
© Cengage Learning 2013

are shown as Nuclear Medicine (C), anatomical regions (W), and systemic nuclear medicine therapy (7). The body part thyroid is in the first column, second row, and has the value G. In the second column, and second row, there are two radionuclide values. With this procedure the value G, Iodine 131 (I-131) will be used, and as always in the nuclear medicine section, there are no character 6 or 7 Qualifiers, so those values are both Z. For the procedure *systemic thyroid therapy, I-13,* the code is CW7GGZZ.

Nonimaging Nuclear Medicine Probe CP5YYZZ
Abdomen **CW50**
Abdomen and Chest **CW54**
Abdomen and Pelvis **CW51**
Brain **C050**
Central Nervous System **C05YYZZ**
Chest **CW53**
Chest and Abdomen **CW54**
Chest and Neck **CW56**
Extremity
    Lower **CP5**
    Upper **CP5**
Head and Neck **CW5B**
Heart **C25YYZZ**
   Right and Left **C256**
Lymphatics
    Head **C75J**
    Head and Neck **C755**
    Lower Extremity **C75P**
    Neck **C75K**
    Pelvic **C75D**
    Trunk **C75M**
    Upper Chest **C75L**
    Upper Extremity **C75N**
Lymphatics and Hematologic System **C75YYZZ**
Neck and Chest **CW56**
Neck and Head **CW5B**
Pelvic Region **CW5J**
Pelvis and Abdomen **CW51**
Spine **CP55ZZZ**

© Cengage Learning 2013

Figure 11-9 Alphabetic Index Listing for Nonimaging Nuclear Medicine Probe

Nonimaging Nuclear Medicine Assay
   Bladder, Kidneys and Ureters **CT63**
   Blood **C763**
   Kidneys, Ureters and Bladder **CT63**
   Lymphatics and Hematologic System **C76YYZZ**
   Ureters, Kidneys and Bladder **CT63**
   Urinary System **CT6YYZZ**

© Cengage Learning 2013

Figure 11-10 Alphabetic Index Listing for Nonimaging Nuclear Medicine Assay

Systemic Nuclear Medicine Therapy
   Abdomen **CW70**
   Anatomical Regions, Multiple **CW7YYZZ**
   Chest **CW73a**
   Thyroid **CW7G**
   Whole Body **CW7N**

Figure 11-11 Alphabetic Index Listing for Systemic Nuclear Medicine Therapy   © Cengage Learning 2013

Section	**C** Nuclear Medicine			
Body System	**2** Heart			
Type	**2** Tomographic (Tomo) Nuclear Medicine Imaging: Introduction of radioactive materials into the body for three dimensional display of images developed from the capture of radioactive emissions			
Body Part	Radionuclide	Qualifier	Qualifier	
6 Heart, Right and Left	**1** Technetium 99m (Tc-99m) **Y** Other Radionuclide	**Z** None	**Z** None	
G Myocardium	**1** Technetium 99m (Tc-99m) **D** Indium 111 (In-111) **K** Fluorine 18 (F-18) **S** Thallium 201 (Tl-201) **Y** Other Radionuclide **Z** None	**Z** None	**Z** None	
Y Heart	**Y** Other Radionuclide	**Z** None	**Z** None	

© Cengage Learning 2013

Figure 11-12 Nuclear Medicine Table C22

Section	**C** Nuclear Medicine		
Body System	**W** Anatomical Regions		
Type	**7** Systemic Nuclear Medicine Therapy: Introduction of unsealed radioactive materials into the body for treatment		
Body Part	Radionuclide	Qualifier	Qualifier
0 Abdomen **3** Chest	**N** Phosphorus 32 (P-32) **Y** Other Radionuclide	**Z** None	**Z** None
G Thyroid	**G** Iodine 131 (I-131) **Y** Other Radionuclide	**Z** None	**Z** None
N Whole Body	**8** Samarium 153 (Sm-153) **G** Iodine 131 (I-131) **N** Phosphorus 32 (P-32) **P** Strontium 89 (Sr-89) **Y** Other Radionuclide	**Z** None	**Z** None
Y Anatomical Regions, Multiple	**Y** Other Radionuclide	**Z** None	**Z** None

© Cengage Learning 2013

Figure 11-13 Radiation Oncology Table CW7

Let's Review 11–1:

1. SPECT analysis, spleen, Tc-99 (Remember the root type for SPECT is tomographic nuclear medicine imaging) _____

2. Nonimaging assay, blood, Cobalt 58 _____

3. Nonimaging probe, CNS, other radioisotope _____

4. Sagittal plane imaging of lymphatics, head, Tc-99m (Hint: sagittal is a single anatomical plane) _____

5. PET scan, lungs and bronchi, F-18 _____

Section	**D**	Radiation Oncology
Body System	**0**	Central and Peripheral Nervous System
Modality	**0**	Beam Radiation

Treatment Site	Modality Qualifier	Isotope	Qualifier
0 Brain **1** Brain Stem **6** Spinal Cord **7** Peripheral Nerve	**0** Photons < 1 MeV **1** Photons 1 – 10 MeV **2** Photons >10 MeV **4** Heavy Particles (Protons,Ions) **5** Neutrons **6** Neutron Capture	**Z** None	**Z** None
0 Brain **1** Brain Stem **6** Spinal Cord **7** Peripheral Nerve	**3** Electrons	**Z** None **Z** None	**0** Intraoperative

© Cengage Learning 2013

Figure 11-14 Table D00 from Radiation Oncology Section

Radiation Oncology

Radiation oncology therapy is a local therapy, meaning it treats a specific localized area of the body. This is in contrast to systemic therapies, such as chemotherapy, which travel throughout the body. There are two main types of radiation therapy: external radiation therapy, where a beam of radiation is directed from outside the body (root type 0, Beam Therapy), and internal radiation therapy, which is also called **Brachytherapy** or implant therapy (root type 1), where a source of radioactivity is surgically placed inside the body near the tumor. In addition to Beam Radiation and Brachytherapy, there are two additional root types, Stereotactic Radiosurgery (2) and Other Radiation. **Stereotactic Radiosurgery** is a type of radiation treatment that gives a large dose of radiation to a small tumor area, usually in a single session. It is mostly used for brain tumors and other tumors inside the head. Root type Y, Other Radiation, includes any radiological modalities used for cancer treatment other than Beam Radiation, Brachytherapy, and Stereotactic radiation.

Figure 11-14 is Table D00 from the Radiation Oncology section illustrating the character assignments in this section. The first character in the radiation oncology section is always D. The second character is the body system, and the third character is one of four root types: Beam Radiation (0), Brachytherapy (1), Stereotactic Radiation (2), and Other Radiation (Y). The fourth character is called the **treatment site** rather than body part or body region, and it identifies the area of the body being treated. The names of the fifth and sixth characters are also different from those found in most other sections of the ICD-10-PCS. Character 5 gives further specificity to the type of radiation used, and is labeled **modality qualifier**. The sixth character in a radiation oncology code is the **isotope**, which is the type of radioactive substance introduced into the body. The seventh character is the qualifier, which has only two values, Z, no qualifier, and 0, intraoperative, which describes radiation therapy given during the course of a surgery.

Body Systems (Character 2) Values in Radiation Oncology Section

The body system characters in the radiation therapy section are similar to those used in the Imaging and Nuclear Medicine sections. The exceptions are heart, and veins, which are not part of the Radiation Oncology section, and therefore, no value is assigned. In Radiation Oncology, the breast has a separate body system value, M. In most other sections, the breast is included in the Skin and Subcutaneous Tissue body system. Table 11-5 lists the body systems and their corresponding values. Body system values can be repeated in different tables depending upon the root type. For example, the Central and Peripheral Nervous System (0) is found in Tables for all four root types.

Table 11-5 Body System Values in Radiation Oncology

Value	Body System
0	Central Nervous System
7	Lymphatic and Hematologic Systems
8	Eye
9	Ear, Nose, Mouth, and Throat
B	Respiratory System
D	Gastrointestinal System
F	Hepatobiliary System and Pancreas
G	Endocrine System
H	Skin
M	Breast
P	Musculoskeletal System
T	Urinary System
U	Female Reproductive
V	Male Reproductive
W	Anatomical Regions

Root Types (Character 3) Values in the Radiation Oncology Section

There are four root types in the Radiation Oncology section: Beam Radiation, Brachytherapy, Stereotactic Radiation, and Other Radiation. **Beam Radiation** (value 0) is also called external radiation. External radiation uses a machine located outside of the body to aim high-energy rays at cancer cells. **Brachytherapy** (value 1) is a type of internal radiation treatment performed by implanting radioactive material directly into the tumor or close to it. Brachytherapy is also called internal radiation therapy, or IRT.

Stereotactic Radiosurgery is a type of radiation treatment that gives a large dose of radiation to a small tumor area, usually in a single session. It is mostly used for tumors inside the brain or head. Sometimes doctors give the radiation in many smaller treatments to deliver the same or slightly higher dose, which is then called fractionated radiation therapy.

Other terms used in radiation therapy, especially in root type Y, Other Radiation, include **Intensity Modulated Radiation Therapy (IMRT)**, a method of radiation therapy in which the beams are aimed from many directions and the strength of the beams is controlled by computers. IMRT allows more radiation to reach the treatment site, while reducing the radiation to healthy tissues. A **port** is another word for treatment site. It is the area of the body through which external Beam Radiation is directed in order to reach a tumor. **Tattoos** in radiation oncology are dots the size of pinpoints or freckles, made using India ink, that create a permanent mark outlining the treatment site. The tattoos are used as treatment site guides each time radiation therapy is administered. Tattoos are coded from the Other Procedures section of the ICD-10-PCS. There are many more terms unique to the Radiation Oncology section, which will be discussed later in this chapter.

Treatment Site (Character 4) in the Radiation Oncology Section

Treatment site is the first column title, known in other sections as body part or body region. The treatment site is the site upon which the radiation therapy is being performed. The treatment sites and values are listed in Table 11-6 along with the related body system and root types. Note that the body parts, like the body systems, can be repeated in each of the root type Tables.

Table 11-6 Treatment Sites and Values by Body System and Root Types

Tables	Body System	Root Type(s)	Treatment Sites(s) (Fourth Character)
D00 D01 D02 D0Y	Central and Peripheral Nervous	Beam Radiation Brachytherapy Stereotactic Radiosurgery Other Radiation	0—Brain 1—Brain Stem 6—Spinal Cord Z—Peripheral Nerve
D70 D71 D72 D7Y	Lymphatic and Hematologic	Beam Radiation Brachytherapy Stereotactic Radiosurgery Other Radiation	0—Bone Marrow 1—Thymus 2—Spleen 3—Lymphatics, Neck 4—Lymphatics, Axillary 5—Lymphatics, Thorax 6—Lymphatics, Abdomen 7—Lymphatics, Pelvis 8—Lymphatics, Inguinal
D80 D81 D82 D8Y	Eye	Beam Radiation Brachytherapy Stereotactic Radiosurgery Other Radiation	0—Eye
D90 D91	Ear, Nose, Mouth, Throat	Beam Radiation Brachytherapy	0—Ear 1—Nose 3—Hypopharynx 4—Mouth 5—Tongue 6—Salivary Glands 7—Sinuses 8—Hard Palate 9—Soft Palate B—Larynx D—Nasopharynx F—Oropharynx
D92	Ear, Nose, Mouth, Throat	Stereotactic Radiosurgery	0—Ear 1—Nose 3—Hypopharynx 4—Mouth 5—Tongue 6—Salivary Glands 7—Sinuses 8—Hard Palate 9—Soft Palate B—Larynx C—Pharynx F—Oropharynx
D9Y	Ear, Nose, Mouth, Throat	Other Radiation	0—Ear 1—Nose 3—Hypopharynx 4—Mouth 5—Tongue 6—Salivary Glands 7—Sinuses 8—Hard Palate 9—Soft Palate B—Larynx C—Pharynx D—Nasopharynx F—Oropharynx

Table 11-6 Treatment Sites and Values by Body System and Root Types (continued)

Tables	Body System	Root Type(s)	Treatment Sites(s) (Fourth Character)
DB0 DB1 DB2 DBY	Respiratory	Beam Radiation Brachytherapy Stereotactic Radiosurgery Other Radiation	0—Trachea 1—Bronchus 2—Lung 5—Pleura 6—Mediastinum 7—Chest Wall 8—Diaphragm
DD0 DD1 DD2	Gastrointestinal	Beam Radiation Brachytherapy Stereotactic Radiosurgery	0—Esophagus 1—Stomach 2—Duodenum 3—Jejunum 4—Ileum 5—Colon 7—Rectum
DDY	Gastrointestinal	Other Radiation	0—Esophagus 1—Stomach 2—Duodenum 3—Jejunum 4—Ileum 5—Colon 7—Rectum 8—Anus
DF0 DF1 DF2 DFY	Hepatobiliary and Pancreas	Beam Radiation Brachytherapy Stereotactic Radiosurgery Other Radiation	0—Liver 1—Gallbladder 2—Bile Ducts 3—Pancreas
DG0 DG1	Endocrine	Beam Radiation Brachytherapy	0—Pituitary Gland 1—Pineal Body
DG2 DGY		Stereotactic Radiosurgery Other Radiation	2—Adrenal Glands 4—Parathyroid Glands 5—Thyroid
DH0	Skin	Beam Radiation	2—Skin, Face 3—Skin, Neck 4—Skin, Arm 7—Skin, Back 8—Skin, Abdomen 9—Skin, Buttock B—Skin, Leg
DHY		Other Radiation	2—Skin, Face 3—Skin, Neck 4—Skin, Arm 5—Skin, Hand 7—Skin, Back 8—Skin, Abdomen 9—Skin, Buttock B—Skin, Leg C—Skin, Foot
DM0 DM1 DM2 DMY	Breast	Beam Radiation Brachytherapy Stereotactic Radiosurgery Other Radiation	0—Breast, left 1—Breast, right

DP0 DP1 DP2 DPY	Musculoskeletal	Beam Radiation Brachytherapy Stereotactic Radiosurgery Other Radiation	0—Skull 2—Maxilla 3—Mandible 4—Sternum 5—Rib(S) 6—Humerus 7—Radius/Ulna 8—Pelvic Bones 9—Femur B—Tibia/Fibula C—Other Bone
DT0 DT1 DT2 DTY	Urinary	Beam Radiation Brachytherapy Stereotactic Radiosurgery Other Radiation	0—Kidney 1—Ureter 2—Bladder 3—Urethra
DU0 DU1 DU2 DUY	Female Reproductive	Beam Radiation Brachytherapy Stereotactic Radiosurgery Other Radiation	0—Ovary 1—Cervix 2—Uterus
DV0 DV1 DV2 DVY	Male Reproductive	Beam Radiation Brachytherapy Stereotactic Radiosurgery Other Radiation	0—Prostate 1—Testis
DW0 DWY	Anatomical Regions	Beam Radiation Other Radiation	1—Head and Neck 2—Chest 3—Abdomen 4—Hemibody 5—Whole Body 6—Pelvic Region
DW1 DW2	Anatomical Regions	Brachytherapy Stereotactic Radiosurgery	1—Head and Neck 2—Chest 3—Abdomen 6—Pelvic Region

Note that in a few instances, a treatment site is added to or omitted from some Tables. For example, in the Ear, Nose, Mouth, and Throat treatment site, the pharynx is not included with Beam Radiation or Brachytherapy, but it is a part of the Stereotactic Radiosurgery and Other Radiation root types. In addition, the treatment site nasopharynx (D) is part of all root types except Stereotactic Radiosurgery. In the Gastrointestinal system, the treatment site anus (8) is only included with the root type Other Radiation. In the Integumentary system (Skin), the skin of the hand (5) and foot (C) is included in the Other Radiation Tables, but neither treatment site appears with the other three root types. Additionally, only Beam Radiation and Other Radiation root types are used with the treatment site skin. Brachytherapy and Stereotactic Radiosurgery are not root types for these treatment sites.

For all treatment sites in the Musculoskeletal System, the Treatment Site is identified by the bones of the skeleton. If the radiation therapy is administered to a muscle or group of muscles, it is preferable to use Anatomical Regions Tables. For example, if the treatment site is the pectoralis muscle(s) use the Anatomical Region (W) and the treatment site chest (2). And last, in the Anatomical Regions body system, hemibody (4) and whole body (5) are used only with Beam Radiation and Other Radiation root types. They are not included in the treatment site list for Brachytherapy or Stereotactic radiation.

Modality Qualifier (Character 5) in the Radiation Oncology Section

The **modality qualifier** is character 5, which in earlier sections contained the approach value. The modality qualifier describes the type of radiation therapy administered. Generally, the values in the sixth character column, Isotope, are used only when the procedure inserts radioactive material into the body (internal), which is called Brachytherapy (1). For radioactive material beamed or directed from an external source, the root type is generally Beam Radiation (0). There are several types of modalities, including photons, electrons, and neutrons, as well as several other types that fall in the Other Radiation (Y) root type. The energy (source of radiation) used in external radiation therapy may come from the following:

- X-rays or gamma rays, which are both forms of electromagnetic radiation. Although they are produced in different ways, both use photons (packets of energy).

  - **X-rays** can be used to destroy cancer cells on the surface of the body (lower energy) or deeper into tissues and organs (higher energy).

  - **Gamma rays** are produced when isotopes of certain elements (such as iridium and cobalt 60) release radiation energy as they break down.

- **Three-dimensional (3-D) conformal radiation therapy (3DCRT).** Typically, radiation treatment planning is done in two dimensions (width and height). Three-dimensional (3-D) conformal radiation therapy targets a tumor using width, height, and depth. Computed tomography (CT), magnetic resonance imaging (MRI), PET, or SPECT can all be used to obtain a 3-D imagine of a tumor. Using information from the image, special computer programs design radiation beams that "conform" to the shape of the tumor.

- **Electron beam.** A stream of high-energy particles called electrons used with Beam Radiation root types to treat cancer.

In Table 11-7, each of the modality qualifiers found in radiation oncology is listed by their root type.

Brachytherapy has two types of modalities depending upon the treatment site. Radioactive substances such as Cesium, Iridium, and Iodine are used with all treatment sites, except certain body systems, and the anatomical regions treatment site. Note also that the treatment site skin is omitted from both Brachytherapy and Stereotactic Radiosurgery, since the skin is too broad a treatment site for either Brachytherapy, an internal radiation oncology procedure, or Stereotactic Radiosurgery, which treats small, localized internal tumors.

Stereotactic Radiosurgery (Root Type 2) Modalities

There are three modality qualifiers for Stereotactic Radiosurgery: Photon, particulate, and gamma beam. These differ from external Beam Radiation only by the objective of the root type. Photon, particulate, and gamma beams are used as external sources of radiation for the Beam Radiation root type, which typically targets tumors in larger body areas. In Stereotactic Radiosurgery, the radiation source is still external, but it targets smaller, more localized, tumors, like those in the brain.

Other Radiation (Root Type Y) Modalities

Other Radiation uses modalities such as contact radiation, hyperthermia, plaque radiation, and any radiation oncology procedures that are not beamed, internal (Brachytherapy), or Stereotactic in their root operation objective. Radioactive **plaque therapy** is a form of treatment where radioactive material is seeded into an implant (plaque). The plaque is then inserted into the treatment site. Plaque therapy is used often in treatment of tumors of the eye, especially when the objective is to avoid removal of the eye.

Particle beams use fast-moving subatomic particles instead of photons. This type of radiation may be called Particle Beam Radiation therapy or Particulate Radiation. Particle beam therapy uses electrons, neutrons, or heavy ions (such as protons); which are small, negatively charged atomic particles. Because they are so small, they are often used to treat cancers located on the surface of or just below the skin. **Proton beam therapy** is a type of particle Beam Radiation therapy. Protons deposit

Table 11-7 Modality Values by Root Type

Root Type	Modality Qualifier and Value
0–Beam Radiation	0–Photons [1 MeV 1–Photons 1-10 MeV 2–Photons] 10 MeV 3–Electrons 4–Heavy Particles (Protons, Ions) 5–Neutrons 6–Neutron Capture
1–Brachytherapy • all Treatment sites except those listed on next row (Treatment Site Skin Excluded)	7–Cesium 137 (Cs-137) 8–Iridium 192 (Ir-192) 9–Iodine 125 (I-125) B–Pallidium 103 (Pd 103) C–Californium 252 (Cf 252) Y–Other Isotope
1–Brachytherapy • Lymphatic and Hematologic System • Eye • Ear, Nose, Mouth, and Throat • Respiratory System • Gastrointestinal System • Hepatobiliary System and Pancreas • Endocrine System • Breast • Urinary System • Male Reproductive System • Anatomical Regions	B–Low Dose Rate (LDR) 9–High Dose Rate (HDR)
2–Stereotactic Radiosurgery (Treatment Site Skin Excluded)	D–Stereotactic Other Photon Radiosurgery H–Stereotactic Particulate Radiosurgery J–Stereotactic Gamma Beam Radiosurgery
Y–Other Radiation	7–Contact Radiation 8–Hyperthermia C–Intraoperative Radiation Therapy (IORT) F–Plaque Radiation G–Isotope Administration K–Laser Interstitial Thermal Therapy

their energy over a very small area. Proton beam therapy emits high doses of proton beam therapy to a tumor while doing less damage to normal tissues. **Intraoperative radiation therapy (IORT)** is a form of external radiation given during surgery. IORT treats cancers that cannot be completely removed or that have a high risk of recurring in nearby tissues. After all or most of the cancer is removed during the surgical procedure, one large, high-energy dose of radiation is aimed directly at the tumor site.

Isotope (Character 6) Values in the Radiation Oncology Section

Character 6 in the Radiation Oncology section is **Isotope**, which is the radiation source. Isotopes are also called radioisotopes. An isotope is a species of atoms of a chemical element with the same atomic number and position in the periodic table, which have nearly identical chemical behavior. There are two broad categories of isotopes, stable and unstable. Stable isotopes do not undergo radioactive decay, and remain unchanged in structure indefinitely. Unstable, or radioactive, isotopes undergo spontaneous disintegration. When a combination of neutrons and protons, which does not already exist in nature, is produced artificially, the atom will be unstable and is called a radioactive isotope or radioisotope.

The radioactive substances used include iridium, cesium, iodine, and phosphorus. Radiation therapy is delivered in volts, specifically in millions of electron volts, abbreviated MeV. In the Modality Qualifier column of Beam Radiation root type Tables, the three values that include MeV are all photons, as follows:

0—photons [1 MeV: The character [means less than, so for this value, less than 1 million electron volts of photons were administered.

1—photons 1–10 MeV. This means between 1 and 10 million electron volts.

2—photons>10 MeV. This means greater than 10 million electron volts.

Character 6 isotope values are found only in the Brachytherapy Tables. In Beam Radiation, Stereotactic Radiosurgery, and Other Radiation, the sixth character value is Z, no qualifier. For example, for the procedure *Beam Radiation, brain, [1MeV photons*, the code would be D0000ZZ, with the code characters represented as follows:

Section D: Radiation Oncology

Body System 0: Central and Peripheral Nervous System

Root Type 0: Beam Radiation

Body Part 0: Brain

Modality 0: Photon 1MeV

Isotope Z: none

Qualifier Z: none

Another example is *Brachytherapy, spinal cord, high dose rate, Cesium 137*. The code would be D01697Z, broken down as follows:

Section D: Radiation Oncology

Body System 0: Central and Peripheral Nervous System

Root Type 1: Brachytherapy

Body Part 6: Spinal cord

Modality 9: High Dose Rate (HDR)

Isotope 7: Cesium 137 (Cs-137)

Qualifier Z: none

Table 11-8 lists the isotopes used in the Radiation Oncology section.

Table 11-8 Isotopes used in Radiation Oncology

Value	Isotope
These values are found only with Brachytherapy root type	
7	Cesium 137 (Cs-137)
8	Iridium 192 (Ir-192)
9	Iodine 125 (I-125)
B	Pallidium 103 (Pd-103)
C	Californium 252 (Cf-252)
The following are used only with root type Y, Other Radiation and Modality Qualifier G, Isotope Administration	
D	Iodine 131 (I-131)
F	Phosphorus 32 (P-32)
G	Strontium 90 (Sr-90)
Y	Other Isotope

Qualifier (Character 7) Values in the Radiation Oncology Section

There are only two seventh character qualifier values in Radiation Oncology. The first is Z, no qualifier, and the second is 0, intraoperative. When radiation therapy is administered during the course of a surgery, use value 0 for the seventh character qualifier.

Coding Radiation Oncology Procedures

The quickest method for finding a Radiation Oncology procedure in the Index is by looking for the root type, i.e., Beam Radiation, Brachytherapy, or Stereotactic Radiosurgery. For radiation procedures in the Other Radiation root type Tables, search for the terms in the modality column, such as plaque radiation (Figure 11-15), contact radiation, or isotope administration. There is no main term listing in the Index for Other Radiation.

There are other options; for example, looking under Hyperthermia in the index (Figure 11-16) leads to the modifying term *radiation oncology*, with all the treatment sites indented below that. In Figure 11-16, note that the third character in all Table references is Y, indicating the root type is Other Radiation. The term *isotope administration* in the Index lists all the treatment sites as modifying terms (Figure 11-17).

Note here too, that the third character in the Table reference is Y, Other Radiation.

Starting with the procedure *Isotope Administration I-131*, look in the Index under Isotope Administration (Figure 11-17). There is one modifying term, *whole body*, and one Table reference to DWY5GDZ. The next step is to confirm the reference in the DWY Table in the Tabular List. Each code character description matches the procedure. It is appropriate to assume that the treatment site is

Figure 11-15 Alphabetic Index Excerpt for Plaque Radiation

Hyperthermia	Esophagus **DDY08ZZ**
Radiation Oncology	Eye **D8Y08ZZ**
Abdomen **DWY38ZZ**	Femur **DPY98ZZ**
Adrenal Gland **DGY28ZZ**	Fibula **DPYB8ZZ**
Bile Ducts **DFY28ZZ**	Gallbladder **DFY18ZZ**
Bladder **DTY28ZZ**	Gland
Bone, Other **DPYC8ZZ**	Adrenal **DGY28ZZ**
Bone Marrow **D7Y08ZZ**	Parathyroid **DGY48ZZ**
Brain **D0Y08ZZ**	Pituitary **DGY08ZZ**
Brain Stem **D0Y18ZZ**	Thyroid **DGY58ZZ**
Breast	Glands, Salivary **D9Y68ZZ**
Left **DMY08ZZ**	Head and Neck **DWY18ZZ**
Right **DMY18ZZ**	Hemi body **DWY48ZZ**
Bronchus **DBY18ZZ**	Humerus **DPY68ZZ**
Cervix **DUY18ZZ**	Hypopharynx **D9Y38ZZ**
Chest **DWY28ZZ**	Ileum **DDY48ZZ**
Chest Wall **DBY78ZZ**	Jejunum **DDY38ZZ**
Colon **DDY58ZZ**	Kidney **DTY08ZZ**
Diaphragm **DBY88ZZ**	Larynx **D9YB8ZZ**
Duodenum **DDY28ZZ**	Liver **DFY08ZZ**
Ear **D9Y08ZZ**	Lung **DBY28ZZ**

© Cengage Learning 2013

Figure 11-16 Alphabetic Index Excerpt for Hyperthermia

Isotope Administration, Whole Body DWY5G

Figure 11-17 Alphabetic Index Excerpt for Isotope Administration   © Cengage Learning 2013

whole body (5) since that is the only row in Table DWY that includes the Isotope Administration modality, and Isotope values in the procedural statement.

Look at the next procedure, *intraoperative electron beam radiation to abdomen*. This procedure lists the root type Beam Radiation, so the main term is easily identifiable. In the Index, under *beam radiation* (Figure 11-18), search for the treatment site abdomen.

Abdomen is listed as a modifying term, and it has its own reference (DW03). It is possible to go to that Table and find the appropriate row; but, indented just below abdomen, is the subterm intraoperative, and the Table reference DW033Z0, which, while it still has to be verified in the Table, is still a more specific reference than DW03.

Going to Table DW0, each character of the code DW033Z0 matches the procedure, as follows:

D: Section, Radiation Oncology

W: Body System, Anatomical Regions

0: Root Type, Beam Radiation

3: Treatment site, Abdomen

3: Modality Qualifier, Electrons

Z: Isotope, none

0: Qualifier, Intraoperative

Let us look at one more, *IORT, prostate*. First, break down the abbreviation to find the main term, IORT, which in this case is a modality qualifier in the Other Radiation Tables. A search of the Index finds IORT with all the treatment sites indented below it as modifying terms (Figure 11-19). The Table reference for the modifying term prostate is DVY0CZZ. Turn to the Table DVY in the Tabular List. Confirm that the

Beam Radiation
  Abdomen **DW03**
    Intraoperative **DW033Z0**
  Adrenal Gland **DG02**
    Intraoperative **DG023Z0**
  Bile Ducts **DF02**
    Intraoperative **DF023Z0**
  Bladder **DT02.**
    Intraoperative **DT023Z0**
  Bone
    Other **DP0C**
      Intraoperative **DP0C3Z0**
  Bone Marrow **D700**
    Intraoperative **D7003Z0**
  Brain **D000**
    Intraoperative **D0003Z0**
  Brain Stem **D001**
    Intraoperative **D0013Z0**
  Breast
    Left **DM00**
      Intraoperative **DM003Z0**
    Right **DM01**
      Intraoperative **DM013Z0**
  Bronchus **DB01**
    Intraoperative **DB013Z0**
  Cervix **DU01**
    Intraoperative **DU013Z0**
  Chest **DW02**
    Intraoperative **DW023Z0**
  Chest Wall **DB07**
    Intraoperative **DB073Z0**
  Colon **DD05**
    Intraoperative **DD053Z0**
  Diaphragm **DB08**
    Intraoperative **DB083Z0**
  Duodenum **DD02**
    Intraoperative **DD023Z0**

© *Cengage Learning 2013*

Figure 11-18 Alphabetic Index Excerpt for Beam Radiation

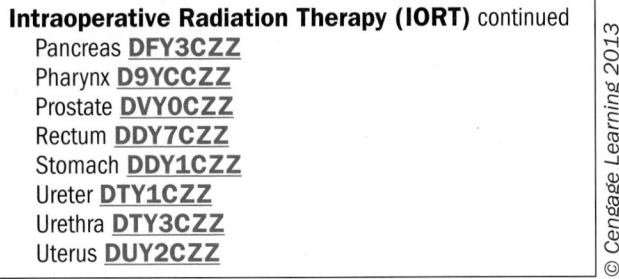

Intraoperative Radiation Therapy (IORT) continued
  Pancreas **DFY3CZZ**
  Pharynx **D9YCCZZ**
  Prostate **DVY0CZZ**
  Rectum **DDY7CZZ**
  Stomach **DDY1CZZ**
  Ureter **DTY1CZZ**
  Urethra **DTY3CZZ**
  Uterus **DUY2CZZ**

© *Cengage Learning 2013*

Figure 11-19 Alphabetic Index Excerpt for IORT

code character descriptions match the procedure *IORT, prostate.* DVY is the correct section, body system, and root type. The fourth character 0, is the treatment site prostate, and the fifth character modality qualifier value for IORT is C. There is no Isotope, nor is there a qualifier, therefore the sixth and seventh characters are both Z. DVY0CZZ is confirmed as the correct code for procedure *IORT, prostate.*

Chapter Summary

Nuclear Medicine is branch of medicine that uses radiation to provide information about the functioning of a person's specific organs or to treat disease. In some cases radiation is also used to treat diseased organs, or tumors. Nuclear medicine procedures introduce radioactive material into the body. The image created by the radioactive material helps to diagnose and treat pathologic conditions, or to assess metabolic functions.

The first character value for nuclear medicine procedures is C. The second character of a nuclear medicine code identifies the body system on which a nuclear medicine procedure is performed. There are seven root types in the Nuclear Medicine section, including nonimaging uptakes, probes, and assays, single plane and tomographic imaging, and positron emission tomography, also called PET scans. Character 4 of the Nuclear Medicine code identifies the body part or region being studied or assessed, and the fifth character is the radionuclide, or radiation source. Characters 6 and 7 are qualifier categories,

There are seven nuclear medicine root types (Table 11-2). Each root type has a specific objective. Planar Imaging (value 1) is a single body plane display. Tomographic Imaging (2) creates a three-dimensional display for diagnostic evaluation. The PET Scan (3) simultaneously captures images 180 degrees apart, which can both be viewed at the same time. Nonimaging Uptakes (4) are performed to measure organ function, and Nonimaging Probes (5) are used to study how the radioactive emissions distribute throughout the body part, and what happens to them.

An isotope is a species of atoms of a chemical element with the same atomic number and position in the periodic table, which have nearly identical chemical behavior. There radiation therapy is a local therapy, meaning it treats a specific localized area of the body. This is in contrast to systemic therapies, such as chemotherapy, which travel throughout the body. There are two main types of radiation therapy: external radiation therapy, where a beam of radiation is directed from outside the body (root type 0, Beam Therapy), and internal radiation therapy, which is also called Brachytherapy or implant therapy (root type 1), where a source of radioactivity is surgically placed inside the body near the tumor. There are two additional root types, Stereotactic Radiosurgery (2) and Other Radiation. Stereotactic Radiosurgery is a type of radiation treatment that gives a large dose of radiation to a small tumor area, usually in a single session. Root type Y, Other Radiation, includes any modalities other than Beam Radiation, Brachytherapy, and Stereotactic Radiation.

The first character in the radiation oncology section is always D. The second character is the body system, and the third character is one of four root types: Beam Radiation (0), Brachytherapy (1), Stereotactic Radiation (2), and Other Radiation (Y). The fourth character is called the Treatment Site rather than body part or body region, and it identifies the area of the body being treated. Character 5 gives further specificity to the type of radiation used, and is labeled Modality. The sixth character in a radiation oncology code is the Isotope, which is the type of radioactive substance introduced into the body. The seventh character is the qualifier, which has only two values, Z, no qualifier, and 0, intraoperative, which describes radiation therapy given during the course of a surgery.

For all treatment sites in the Musculoskeletal System, the treatment site is identified by the bones of the skeleton. If the radiation therapy is administered to a muscle or group of muscles, it is preferable to use Anatomical Regions Tables. Character 6 in the Radiation Oncology section is Isotope, which is the radiation source. Isotopes are also called radioisotopes. The radioactive substances used include iridium, cesium, iodine, and phosphorus. Radiation therapy is delivered in volts. The quickest method for finding a Radiation Oncology procedure in the Index is by looking for the root type, i.e., Beam Radiation, Brachytherapy, and Stereotactic Radiosurgery.

For radiation procedures in the Other Radiation root type Tables, search for the terms in the modality column, such as plaque radiation (Fig 11-15), contact radiation, or Isotope Administration. Other options exist, for example, looking under *hyperthermia* in the index (Figure 11-16) leads to the modifying term *radiation oncology*, with all the treatment sites indented below that.

Review

Matching

Instructions: Match the following terms to their definition:

_____ 1. Beam Radiation

_____ 2. Brachytherapy

_____ 3. Intensity Modulated Radiation Therapy

_____ 4. Port

_____ 5. Stereotactic Radiosurgery

_____ 6. Systemic radiation

_____ 7. Unsealed radiation

_____ 8. Modality Qualifier

_____ 9. Isotope

_____ 10. Plaque therapy

a. Character 6 of a radiation oncology code that identifies the type of radioactive substance used in the procedure.

b. Uses radioactive materials taken by mouth or injected into the body to kill cancer cells.

c. The area of the body through which external Beam Radiation is directed to reach a tumor. Also called treatment site.

d. Radiation therapy that uses a machine located outside of the body to aim radiation at cancer cells.

e. Character 5 of a radiation oncology code that gives further specificity to the type of radiation used.

f. Internal radiation treatment done by implanting radioactive material directly into the tumor or close to it. Also called internal radiation therapy.

g. Radioactive material is placed (seeded) into an implantable container called a plaque.

h. Radiation treatment that gives a large dose of radiation to a small tumor area. Also called fractionated radiosurgery or Stereotactic Radiotherapy.

i. Radiation substances that swallowed or given by injecting a radioactive substance into the bloodstream or a body cavity. Also called radiopharmaceutical.

j. A method of radiation therapy in which the beams are aimed from many directions. Also called conformal radiation therapy.

Short Answer

Instructions: Provide a brief answer to the following questions.

1. List at least four *radionuclides* used in Section 6, Nuclear Medicine _____

2. What character 5 qualifiers appear in Section D, Radiation Oncology? _____

3. In Section D, Radiation Oncology, what is the difference between *modality* and *isotope*? _____
_____

4. Define *stereotactic therapy*, from Section D, Radiation Oncology and list at least one type _____
_____

5. In Section D, Radiation Oncology, describe *brachytherapy* and list at least two treatment sites where it is used. _____

6. List two types of Section D, Radiation Oncology, modalities used on the Lymphatic System _____
_____

7. Define *hyperthermia* and list at least three treatment sites it might be used on in Section D, Radiation Oncology _____

8. What is the primary difference between Section C, Nuclear Medicine, and Section D, Radiation Oncology? _____

9. What is the difference between a PET scan in Section B, Imaging and Section D, Nuclear Medicine?
_____

10. Name the seven character values for Radiation Oncology.

Coding Practice

Instructions:

1. Neutron beam radiation, colon _____

2. Contact radiation, larynx _____

3. >10 meV photons, radiation therapy, spleen _____

4. Intraoperative electron beam therapy, bone marrow _____

5. IORT, cervix _____

6. Intraoperative beam radiation, left breast _____

7. Proton beam radiation gallbladder (Hint: proton is a heavy particle) _____

8. Plaque radiation, esophagus _____

9. Neutron capture external radiation therapy, chest wall _____

10. Nonimaging nuclear medicine probe, spine _____

Rehabilitation Mental Health and Substance Abuse

Learning Objectives

At the conclusion of this chapter, the learner should be able to:

- Understand terms used in the Physical Rehabilitation and Diagnostic Audiology section and identify new character names and values
- Identify the Body System, Root type, Body System and Regions, Type Qualifier, Equipment, and Qualifier values for the Physical Rehabilitation and Diagnostic Audiology section
- Understand the Guidelines and instructional notes that impact code selection in the Physical Rehabilitation and Diagnostic Audiology section
- Differentiate how the root types are used in the Physical Rehabilitation and Diagnostic Audiology Section, and how to apply the correct character values
- Know how to use the Index and Tables to select the correct code from the Physical Rehabilitation and Diagnostic Audiology section
- Understand terms used in the Mental Health section identify new character names and values
- Identify the Body System, Root Type, and Qualifier values for the Mental Health section
- Understand the guidelines and instructional notes that impact code selection in the Mental Health section
- Differentiate how the root types are used in the Mental Health Section, and how to apply the correct character values
- Know how to use the Index and Tables to select the correct code from the Mental Health section
- Understand terms used in the Substance Abuse section and identify new character names and values
- Identify the Body System, Root Type, and Qualifier values for the Substance Abuse section
- Understand the guidelines and instructional notes that impact code selection in the Substance Abuse section

- Differentiate how the root types are used in the Substance Abuse section, and how to apply the correct character values
- Know how to use the Index and Tables to select the correct code from the Substance Abuse section

Key Terms and Definitions

Antabuse	A drug used to support the treatment of chronic alcoholism by producing an acute sensitivity to alcohol.
Aphasia	One in a group of speech disorders in which there is a defect or loss of the power of expression by speech, writing, or signs, or a defect or loss of the power of comprehension of spoken or written language.
Assessments	In Physical Rehabilitation section, measures functionality or level of impairment.
Audiometry	Measurement of the acuity of hearing for the various frequencies of sound waves.
Augmentative communications	Sometimes referred to as alternative communication (AAC). A method of communication used by individuals with severe speech and language disabilities.
Binaural	Pertaining to both ears.
Bupropion	An antidepressant also used as a smoking cessation aid.
Caregiver Training	Teaches family members and caregivers how to support and help the patient achieve an optimal level of functioning.
Clonidine	A medication used to treat hypertension, opioid detoxification, sleep sweats (hyperhydrosis), and to counter the side effects of stimulant medications such as amphetamine.
Cochlear implant	A small complex electronic device that is surgically placed (implanted) within the inner ear to help persons with certain types of deafness to hear.
Cognitive integration skills	Basic mental abilities used to think, study, and learn.
Dichotic	Simultaneous, occurring at the same time. In audiology assessment, it means different words or sounds spoken simultaneously in each ear, to determine the ability to differentiate between them.
Dix-Hallpike dynamic	(Also called Nylen-Barany test) determines whether vertigo is triggered by certain head movements, and helps determine the cause of vertigo as either the inner ear or the brain.
Dynamic orthosis	Allows motion through transfer of movement from other body parts or by use of outside forces.
Electroconvulsive therapy (ECT)	A medical treatment for severe mental illness in which a small, carefully controlled amount of electricity is introduced into the brain.
Electrophysiologic somatosensory	The electric activity associated with a bodily part or function. Of or relating to the perception of sensory stimuli from the skin and internal organs.
Fittings	Facilitate or support higher levels of functioning.
Filtered speech	A form of speech analysis to evaluate a hearing-impaired person's ability to hear certain words or word parts.
Halo orthosis	A cervical device consisting of a stiff halo attached to the upper skull and to a rigid jacket on the chest to provide maximal rigidity.

Levo-alpha-acetyl-methadol (LAAM)	Synthetic opioid similar in structure to methadone, used as a second-line treatment for the treatment and management of opioid dependence if patients fail to respond to drugs like methadone or bupropion.
Methadone	A synthetic opioid, used medically as an analgesic, antitussive and more commonly, as an anti-addictive for use in patients addicted to opioids.
Monoaural	Pertaining to one ear.
Naltrexone	Medication used in the management of alcohol and opioid dependence.
Narcosynthesis	Psychotherapy under partial anesthesia, induced by barbiturates, first used to treat acute mental disorders in a combat setting.
Neurophysiologic intraoperative	Measures neurological systems function during surgery.
Oral peripheral mechanism	In speech production, measurement of the parts of the body, other than the larynx that help form sounds and words, including the lips, tongue, and teeth.
Orthosis	An orthopedic appliance or apparatus used to support, align, prevent, or correct deformities or to improve function of movable parts of the body.
Otoacoustic emission (OAE)	Echoes emitted by the outer hair cells of the inner ear.
Phonetically balanced speech discrimination	An audiological word test evaluation measuring the ability to hear and understand spoken words.
Prosthesis	An artificial substitute for a missing body part, such as an arm, leg, eye, or tooth; used for functional or cosmetic reasons or both.
Range of motion integrity	The range through which a joint can be moved, usually its range of flexion and extension.
Root type	Third character title for several sections, replacing Root Operation. In the Physical Rehabilitation section, there are four categories of root type, assessment, treatment, caregiver training, and fittings.
Section qualifier	The second character of a Section F, Physical Rehabilitation and Diagnostic Audiology code.
Spondee (words)	Two-syllable words that have equal stress on each syllable.
Staggered spondaic words	Measurement of central auditory pathway integrity in which two different two-syllable words with the same emphasis on each word are presented simultaneously, one in each ear, to test selective listening in the auditory system.
Static orthosis	Does not allow movement, and body parts are kept in the desired position.
Treatments	Apply techniques to improve, augment, or compensate for impairments.
Tympanometry	Indirect measurement of the compliance (mobility) and impedance of the tympanic membrane and ossicles of the middle ear.
Type qualifier	The type qualifier adds detail to the type of procedures coded from this section.

Introduction

The final three chapters of the ICD-10-PCS coding manual are discussed here: Physical Rehabilitation, Mental Health, and Substance Abuse. New terms, new character values and definitions, and a few guidelines and instructional notes are presented for these three chapters of the ICD-10-PCS. Root types, especially those used in the Physical Rehabilitation section, are introduced, as well as other concepts impacting Mental Health and Substance Abuse coding. The goal is to understand these new terms, learn how to properly search for Rehabilitation, Mental Health and Substance Abuse codes, and to properly apply the coding steps and guidelines to arrive at the most accurate code possible.

Physical Rehabilitation and Diagnostic Audiology (F00-F15)

Physical rehabilitation provides treatment and assistance in removing or reducing disabilities. Diagnostic Audiology may at first not seem to fit in this section, but the objective in diagnostic audiology is also to assess and treat disabilities, such as hearing loss and equilibrium disturbances. Physical Rehabilitation procedures include physical and occupational therapy, and speech-language pathology codes. The character value for this section is F, thus, all codes within Physical Rehabilitation and Diagnostic Audiology will begin with the letter F. A Table from Physical Rehabilitation and Diagnostic Audiology is shown in Figure 12-1. The range of codes for this section is F00-F15.

Section	F	Physical Rehabilitation and Diagnostic Audiology
Section Qualifier	0	Rehabilitation
Type	0	Speech Assessment: Measurement of speech and related functions

Body System/Region	Type Qualifier	Equipment	Qualifier
3 Neurological System - Whole Body	**G** Communicative/Cognitive Integration Skills	**K** Audiovisual **M** Augmentative/Alternative Communication **P** Computer **Y** Other Equipment **Z** None	**Z** None
Z None	**0** Filtered Speech **3** Staggered Spondaic Word **1** Audiometer **Q** Performance Intensity Phonetically Balanced Speech Discrimination **R** Brief Tone Stimuli **S** Distorted Speech **T** Dichotic Stimuli **V** Temporal Ordering of Stimuli **W** Masking Patterns	**2** Sound Field/Booth **K** Audiovisual **Z** None	**Z** None
Z None	**1** Speech Threshold **2** Speech/Word Recognition	**1** Audiometer **2** Sound Field/Booth **9** Cochlear Implant **K** Audiovisual **Z** None	**Z** None
Z None	**4** Sensorineural Acuity Level	**1** Audiometer **2** Sound Field/Booth **Z** None	**Z** None
Z None	**5** Synthetic Sentence Identification	**1** Audiometer **2** Sound Field/Booth **9** Cochlear Implant **K** Audiovisual	**Z** None
7 Nonspoken Language **Z** None	**6** Speech and Language Screening **C** Aphasia **8** Receptive/Expressive Language **G** Communicative/Cognitive Integration Skills **L** Augmentative/Alternative Communication System	**K** Audiovisual **M** Augmentative/Alternative Communication **P** Computer **Y** Other Equipment **Z** None	**Z** None
Z None	**9** Articulation/Phonology	**K** Audiovisual **P** Computer **Q** Speech Analysis **Y** Other Equipment **Z** None	**Z** None

© Cengage Learning 2013

Figure 12-1 Table from Physical Rehabilitation and Diagnostic Audiology (F00)

Section F - Physical Rehabilitation and Diagnostic Audiology
Character 3 - Type

Activities of Daily Living (ADL) Assessment	**Definition:** Measurement of functional level for ADL
ADL Treatment	**Definition:** Exercise or activities to facilitate functional competence for ADL
ADL Caregiver Training	**Definition:** Training in activities to support patient's optimal level of function
Cochlear Implant Treatment	**Definition:** Application of techniques to improve the communication abilities of individuals with cochlear implant
Device Fitting	**Definition:** Fitting of a device designed to facilitate or support achievement of a higher level of function
Hearing Aid Assessment	**Definition:** Measurement of the appropriateness and effectiveness of a hearing device
Hearing Assessment	**Definition:** Measurement of hearing and related functions
Hearing Treatment	**Definition:** Application of techniques to improve, augment, or compensate for hearing and related functional impairment
Motor Function Assessment Nerve Function Assessment	**Definition:** Measurement of motor, nerve, and related functions
Motor Treatment	**Definition:** Exercise or activities to increase or facilitate motor function
Speech Assessment	**Definition:** Measurement of speech and related functions
Speech Treatment	**Definition:** Application of techniques to improve, augment, or compensate for speech and related functional impairment

© Cengage Learning 2013

Figure 12-2 Excerpt from Section F with Root type Definitions

The second character in this section is titled **Section Qualifier** rather than body system or region. There are only two character two section qualifier values in this section. The first is Rehabilitation, represented by value 0. The second is Diagnostic Audiology, which has a value of 1. There are eleven root types associated with value 0, Rehabilitation, and three with Diagnostic Audiology. The body region or part upon which the procedure is performed is represented by the fourth character, Body System or Region. The fifth character is called the type qualifier, and adds more specificity to the type of rehabilitation or diagnostic audiology procedure performed. Most ICD-10-PCS coding manual versions provide definitions for assessment, caregiver training, fitting, and treatment type qualifiers. Look for an Appendix in the ICD-10-PCS that lists the section Type and Type Qualifier definitions.

An Appendix excerpt for character 3 Type Qualifier definitions for Section F, Physical Rehabilitation and Diagnostic Audiology, is shown in Figure 12-2, and many of those definitions are included in this chapter, as well. Character 6 in the Physical Rehabilitation and Diagnostic Audiology section identifies the general categories of equipment used, such as adaptive or supportive types of equipment, or equipment used in aerobic endurance and conditioning rehabilitation procedures.

Character 3, Root Types

There are 14 root type values, which can be classified into four basic types of procedures: Assessment, caregiver training, and fittings, i.e., for prosthetics or hearing aids, and treatment. Table 12-1 groups each of the 14 root type values and their definitions by procedure type and second character value.

Assessments measure functionality or level of impairment. **Treatments** apply techniques to improve, augment, or compensate for impairments. **Fittings** facilitate or support higher levels of functioning, and **Caregiver Training** teaches family members and caregivers how to support and help the patient achieve an optimal level of functioning. The character 2 value Rehabilitation is used for all categories in Table 12-1, while Diagnostic Audiology (value 1) is used only in the Assessments category, specifically, hearing, hearing aid, and vestibular assessment. The six types of Assessments are (1) speech, (2) motor and nerve function, (3) activities of daily living (ADL), (4) hearing, (5) hearing aid, and

Table 12-1 Root Types by Procedure Category

Category	Character 2 Value	Root Type (Value)	Root Type Definition
Assessments	Rehabilitation (0)	**Speech Assessment (0)**	Measurement of speech and related functions
		Motor and Nerve Function Assessment (1)	Measurement of motor, nerve, and related functions
		Activities of Daily Living (ADL) Assessment (2)	Measurement of functional level for ADL
	Diagnostic Audiology (1)	**Hearing Assessment (3)**	Measurement of hearing and related functions
		Hearing Aid Assessment (4)	Measurement of the appropriateness and effectiveness of a hearing device
		Vestibular Assessment (5)	Measurement of the vestibular system and related functions
Treatments	Rehabilitation (0)	**Speech Treatment (6)**	Application of techniques to improve, augment, or compensate for speech and related functional impairment
		Motor Treatment (7)	Exercise or activities to increase or facilitate motor function
		ADL Treatment (8)	Exercise or activities to facilitate functional competence for ADL
		Hearing Treatment (9)	Application of techniques to improve, augment, or compensate for hearing and related functional impairment
		Cochlear Implant Treatment (B)	Application of techniques to improve the communication abilities of individuals with cochlear implant
		Vestibular Treatment (C)	Application of techniques to improve, augment, or compensate for vestibular and related functional impairment
Fittings	Rehabilitation (0)	**Device Fittings (D)**	Fitting of a device designed to facilitate or support achievement of a higher level of function
Caregiver Training	Rehabilitation (0)	**Caregiver Training (F)**	Training in activities to support patient's optimal level of function

(6) vestibular. Treatment values are given for all of the root types found in the Assessment category, with the following differences: (1) cochlear implant treatment is added to the Treatment values and (2) there is no hearing aid treatment. In a cochlear implant, electrodes are implanted in the cochlea (the surgery is coded to Chapter 9, Ear, Nose, and Sinus, in the Medical and Surgical Section of the ICD-10-PCS). The implant transmits signals to the electrodes, which provides limited hearing for a patient who qualifies for the implant. Figure 12-3 is an illustration of a cochlear implant. Hearing aids, as well as prostheses, and orthotics, are included in the Fittings category. Balance and equilibrium are measured, and disorders are treated, in the vestibular assessment and vestibular treatment categories. The vestibule is the cavity that extends from the outer to the inner ear, and contains the structures for hearing and equilibrium within the middle and inner ear.

The following are the fourteen root types and their character values.

- Assessments
  - Speech Assessment (0)
  - Motor and/or Nerve Function Assessment (1)

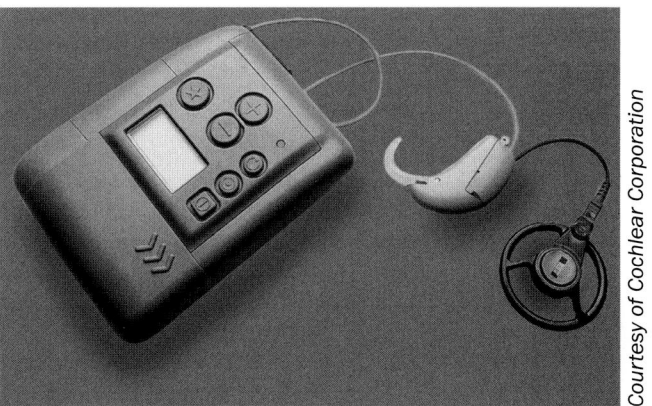

Courtesy of Cochlear Corporation

Figure 12-3 Illustration of a Cochlear Implant Prosthesis
AST, Inc, *Surgical Technology for the Surgical Technologist*

- ◦ ADL Assessment (2)
- ◦ Hearing Assessment (3)
- ◦ Hearing Aid Assessment (4)
- ◦ Vestibular Assessment (5)
- Treatments
  - ◦ Speech Treatment (6)
  - ◦ Motor Treatment (7)
  - ◦ ADL Treatment (8)
  - ◦ Hearing Treatment (9)
  - ◦ Vestibular Treatment (C)
- Caregiver Training (F)
- Device Fitting (D)

Character 4, Body System and Region

The fourth character body system and region values associated with each root type are shown in Table 12-2.

The body system or region character 4 value identifies the target of the Assessment, Treatment, Fitting, or Caregiver Training. For example, the target of a vestibular treatment can be the neurological, integumentary, or musculoskeletal system involving the whole body. For device fittings, caregiver training, hearing and cochlear implant treatment, no specific body system or region is involved, therefore, the body system value is Z, none.

In the Assessment category, hearing, hearing aid, and vestibular assessments are not associated with any specific body system or region. Z, none, therefore represents the character 4 body system or region. Motor or nerve function assessments and treatments are performed on several systems, and several regions within that system. For example, the musculoskeletal system values are broken down into four general regions: Head and neck, upper back/upper extremity, lower back/lower extremity, and whole body. Depending upon the region of the system on which the assessment or treatment is performed, the value will change. A motor and nerve function assessment of the legs would have a fourth character value of L; if the same assessment was performed on the head and neck, the fourth character value would be J. A whole body circulatory system motor and nerve function assessment would be 7 for the fourth character value.

Table 12-2 Body System and Region Values Associated with Each Root Type

Root type (Value)	Value–Associated Body System and Region
Speech Assessment (0)	3-Neurological System, Whole Body Z-None
Motor and Nerve Function Assessment (1)	0-Neurological System-Head and Neck 1-Neurological System-Upper Back/Upper Extremity 2-Neurological System-Lower Back/Lower Extremity 3-Neurological System-Whole Body D-Integumentary System-Head and Neck F-Integumentary System-Upper Back/Upper Extremity G-Integumentary System-Lower Back/Lower Extremity J-Musculoskeletal System-Head and Neck K-Musculoskeletal System-Upper Back/Upper Extremity L-Musculoskeletal System-Lower Back/Lower Extremity M-Musculoskeletal System-Whole Body N-Genitourinary System Z-None
Activities of Daily Living (ADL) Assessment (2)	0-Neurological System-Head and Neck 1-Neurological System-Upper Back/Upper Extremity 2-Neurological System-Lower Back/Lower Extremity 3-Neurological System-Whole Body 4-Circulatory System-Head and Neck 5-Circulatory System-Upper Back/Upper Extremity 6-Circulatory System-Lower Back/Lower Extremity 7-Circulatory System-Whole Body 8-Respiratory System-Head and Neck 9-Respiratory System-Upper Back/Upper Extremity B-Respiratory System-Lower Back/Lower Extremity C-Respiratory System-Whole Body Z-None
Hearing Assessment (3)	Z-None
Hearing Aid Assessment (4)	Z-None
Vestibular Assessment (5)	Z-None
Speech Treatment (6)	3-Neurological Systems-Whole Body Z-None
Motor Treatment (7)	0-Neurological System-Head and Neck 1-Neurological System-Upper Back/Upper Extremity 2-Neurological System-Lower Back/Lower Extremity 3-Neurological System-Whole Body 4-Circulatory System-Head and Neck 5-Circulatory System-Upper Back/Upper Extremity 6-Circulatory System-Lower Back/Lower Extremity 7-Circulatory System-Whole Body 8-Respiratory System-Head and Neck 9-Respiratory System-Upper Back/Upper Extremity B-Respiratory System-Lower Back/Lower Extremity C-Respiratory System-Whole Body D-Integumentary System-Head and Neck F-Integumentary System-Upper Back/Upper Extremity G-Integumentary System-Lower Back/Lower Extremity J-Musculoskeletal System-Head and Neck K-Musculoskeletal System-Upper Back/Upper Extremity L-Musculoskeletal System-Lower Back/Lower Extremity M-Musculoskeletal System-Whole Body N-Genitourinary System Z-None

Table 12-2 Body System and Region Values Associated with Each Root Type (continued)

Activities of Daily Living (ADL) Treatment (8)	D-Integumentary System-Head and Neck F-Integumentary System-Upper Back/Upper Extremity G-Integumentary System-Lower Back/Lower Extremity J-Musculoskeletal System-Head and Neck K-Musculoskeletal System-Upper Back/Upper Extremity L-Musculoskeletal System-Lower Back/Lower Extremity M-Musculoskeletal System-Whole Body Z-None
Hearing Treatment (9)	Z-None
Cochlear Implant Treatment (B)	Z-None
Vestibular Treatment (C)	3-Neurological System-Whole Body H-Integumentary System-Whole Body M-Musculoskeletal System-Whole Body
Device Fittings (D)	Z-None
Caregiver Training (F)	Z-None

Character 5, Type Qualifier

The **type qualifier** adds more specificity to the type of rehabilitation or diagnostic audiology procedure performed. There are several dozen types of rehabilitation and diagnostic audiology procedures performed, and again, they are divided into the same four basic categories, assessment, treatment, fitting, and caregiver training. Figure 12-4 is an appendix excerpt from the Section F, Physical Rehabilitation and Diagnostic Audiology, which provides definitions of the character 5 Type Qualifiers used in this section. The type qualifiers, separated by category and root type, are shown in Table 12-3.

In the Assessment category, there are over 100 different type qualifiers. Some of these are repeated in different root types; however, most are unique to the individual root type. For example, there is no overlap in type qualifiers between speech, motor and nerve function, hearing, and hearing aid assessments. The same is true of root type Treatments, hardly any of the type qualifiers are listed in more than one root type value. There is a correlation between some treatments and caregiver training categories, such as bathing and dressing, bed mobility, grooming, and feeding, for example. When the patient is taught how do perform these functions, the type qualifier is chosen from ADL or another Treatment category. When the patient's caregiver is taught how to perform these activities, the type qualifier is chosen from the Caregiver Training root type.

Type Qualifier Definitions

Many of the type qualifiers are easily understood. For example, in Caregiver Training, bathing, showering, dressing, grooming, and bed or wheelchair mobility are all procedures that should need no explanation or further definition. However, for many of the type qualifiers found in the Assessment and Treatment categories, an explanation or definition is needed. To this end, some of the definitions are provided below:

- **Aphasia.** One in a group of speech disorders in which there is a defect or loss of the power of expression in speech, writing, or signs, or a defect or loss of the power of comprehension of spoken or written language. An aphasia assessment measures expressive and receptive speech and language function, including reading and writing. Aphasia treatment is applying techniques to improve, augment, or compensate for receptive/expressive language impairments.

Section F - Physical Rehabilitation and Diagnostic Audiology Character 5 - Type Qualifier	
Acoustic Reflex Decay	**Definition:** Measures reduction in size/strength of acoustic reflex over time
	Includes/Examples: Includes site of lesion test
Acoustic Reflex Patterns	**Definition:** Defines site of lesion based upon presence/absence of acoustic reflexes with ipsilateral vs. contralateral stimulation
Acoustic Reflex Threshold	**Definition:** Determines minimal intensity that acoustic reflex occurs with ipsilateral or contralateral stimulation
Aerobic Capacity and Endurance | Endurance and Aerobic Capacity	**Definition:** Measures autonomic responses to positional changes; perceived exertion, dyspnea or angina during activity; performance during exercise protocols; standard vital signs; and blood gas analysis or oxygen consumption
Alternate Binaural or Monaural Loudness Balance	**Definition:** Determines auditory stimulus parameter that yields the same objective sensation
	Includes/Examples: Sound intensities that yield same loudness perception
Anthropometric Characteristics	**Definition:** Measures edema, body fat composition, height, weight, length, and girth
Aphasia (Assessment)	**Definition:** Measures expressive and receptive speech and language function including reading and writing

© Cengage Learning 2013

Figure 12-4 Section F Appendix Type Qualifier Definitions

Table 12-3 Character 5 Type Qualifier Values by Category and Root Type

Category	Root Type (Value)	Type Qualifiers (Character 5 Value)
Assessments	**Speech Assessment (0)**	0–Filtered Speech 1–Speech Threshold 2–Speech/Word Recognition 3–Staggered Spondiac Word 4–Sensorineural Acuity Level 5–Synthetic Sentence Identification 6–Speech and Language Screening 7–Nonspoken Language 8–Receptive/Expressive Language B–Motor Speech C–Aphasia D–Fluency F–Voice G–Communicative/Cognitive Integration Skills H–Bedside Swallowing and Oral Function K–Orofacial Myofunctional L–Augmentive/Alternative Communication System M–Voice Prosthetic N–Non-invasive Instrumental Status P–Oral Peripheral Mechanism Q–Performance Intensity Phonetically Balanced Speech R–Brief Tone Stimuli S–Distorted Speech T–Dichotic Stimuli V–Temporal Ordering of Stimuli W–Masking Patterns X–Other Specified Central Auditory Process

Table 12-3 Character 5 Type Qualifier Values by Category and Root Type (continued)

Category	Root Type (Value)	Type Qualifiers (Character 5 Value)
	Motor and Nerve Function Assessment (1)	0–Muscle Performance 1–Integumentary Integrity 2–Visual Motor Integration 3–Coordination/Dexterity 4–Motor Function 5–Range of Motion and Joint Integrity 6–Sensory Awareness/Processing/Integrity 7–Facial Nerve Function 8–Neurophysiologic Intraoperative 9–Somatosensory Evoked Potentials B–Bed Mobility C–Transfer F–Wheelchair Mobility D–Gait and Balance
	Activities of Daily Living (ADL) Assessment (2)	0–Bathing/Showering 1–Dressing 2–Feeding/Eating 3–Grooming/Personal Hygiene 4–Home Management 7–Aerobic Capacity and Endurance 8–Anthropometric Characteristics 9–Cranial Nerve Integrity B–Environmental, Home, and Work Barriers C–Ergonomics and Body Mechanics D–Neuromotor Development F–Pain G–Ventilation, Respiration, and Circulation H–Vocational Activities and Functional Community or Work Reintegration Skills
	Hearing Assessment (3)	0–Hearing Screening 1–Pure Tone Audiometry, Air 2–Pure Tone Audiometry, Air, and Bone 3–Bekesy Audiometry 4–Conditioned Play Audiometry 5–Select Picture Audiometry 6–Visual Reinforcement Audiometry 7–Alternate Binaural or Monaural Loudness Balance 8–Tone Decay 9–Short Increment Sensitivity Index B–Stenger C–Pure Tone Stenger D–Tympanometry F–Eustachian Tube Function G–Acoustic Reflex Patterns H–Acoustic Reflex Threshold J–Acoustic Reflex Decay K–Electrocochleography L–Auditory Evoked Potentials M–Evoked Otoacoustic Emissions, Screening N–Evoked Otoacoustic Emissions, Diagnostic P–Aural Rehabilitation Status Q–Auditory Processing

	Hearing Aid Assessment (4)	0–Cochlear Implant 1–Ear Canal Probe Microphone 2–Monaural Hearing Aid 3–Binaural Hearing Aid 4–Assistive Listening System/Device Selection 5–Sensory Aids 6–Binaural Electroacoustic Hearing Aid Check 7–Ear Protector Attenuation 8–Monaural Electroacoustic Hearing Aid Check
	Vestibular Assessment (5)	0–Bithermal, Binaura Caloric Irrigation 1–Bithermal, Monaural Caloric Irrigation 2–Unithermal Binaural Screen 3–Oscillating Tracking 4–Sinusoidal Vertical Axis Rotational 5–Dix-Hallpike Dynamic 6–Computerized Dynamic Posturography 7–Tinnitus Masker
Treatments	Speech Treatment (6)	0–Nonspoken Language 1–Speech-Language Pathology and Related Disorders Counseling 2–Speech-Language Pathology and Related Disorders Prevention 3–Aphasia 4–Articulation/Phonology 5–Aural Rehabilitation 6–Communicative/Cognitive Integration Skills 7–Fluency 8–Motor Speech 9–Orofacial Myofunctional B–Receptive/Expressive Language C–Voice D–Swallowing Dysfunction
	Motor Treatment (7)	0–Range of Motion and Joint Mobility 1–Muscle Performance 2–Coordination/Dexterity 3–Motor Function 4–Wheelchair Mobility 5–Bed Mobility 6–Therapeutic Exercise 8–Transfer Training 9–Gait Training/Functional Ambulation
	ADL Treatment (8)	0–Bathing/Showering Techniques 1–Dressing Techniques 2–Grooming/Personal Hygiene 3–Feeding/Eating 4–Home Management 5–Wound Management 6–Psychosocial Skills
	Hearing Treatment (9)	0–Hearing and Related Disorders Counseling 1–Hearing and Related Disorders Prevention 2–Auditory Processing 3–Cerumen Management
	Cochlear Implant Treatment (B)	0–Cochlear Implant Rehabilitation
	Vestibular Treatment (C)	0–Vestibular 1–Perceptual Processing 2–Visual Motor Integration 3–Postural Control

Table 12-3 Character 5 Type Qualifier Values by Category and Root Type (continued)

Category	Root Type (Value)	Type Qualifiers (Character 5 Value)
Fittings	**Device Fittings (D)**	0–Tinnitus Masker 1–Monaural Hearing Aid 2–Binaural Hearing Aid 3–Augmentive/Alternative Communication System 4–Voice Prosthetic 5–Assistive Listening Device 6–Dynamic Orthosis 7–Static Orthosis 8–Prosthesis 9–Assistive, Adaptive, Supportive, or Protective Devices
Caregiver Training	**Caregiver Training (F)**	0–Bathing/Showering Technique 1–Dressing 2–Feeding and Eating 3–Grooming/Personal Hygiene 4–Bed Mobility 5–Transfer 6–Wheelchair Mobility 7–Therapeutic Exercise 8–Airway Clearance Techniques 9–Wound Management B–Vocational Activities and Functional Community or Work Reintegration Skills C–Gait Training/Functional Ambulation D–Application, Proper Use, and Care of Assistive, Adaptive, Supportive, or Protective Devices F–Application, Proper Use, and Care of Orthosis G–Application, Proper Use, and Care of Prosthesis H–Home Management J–Communication Skills

- **Audiometry.** Measurement of the acuity of hearing for the various frequencies of sound waves.

- **Augmentative communications.** Augmentative or alternative communication (AAC) is a method of communication used by individuals with severe speech and language disabilities caused by, for example, cerebral palsy, ALS, or stroke. AAC is for those individuals who are cognitively able to speak, but are unable, or when speaking, are difficult to understand. These individuals will use gestures, communications boards, pictures, symbols, or drawings as adaptive methods of communication. In assessing the patient, determination is made of the appropriateness of aids, techniques, symbols, and strategies that help augment or replace speech and enhance communication. Training the patient in the use of these techniques and strategies is coded to root type category Treatment, specifically speech treatment.

- **Bekesy audiometer.** An instrument that tests hearing by emitting discrete or continuously varying pure tones, or a choice of pulsed or continuous signals. The patient presses a signal button when the tone is heard, and the audiometer records and maps the hearing levels by decibels.

- **Binaural.** Pertaining to both ears

- **Cognitive integration skills.** The basic mental abilities we use to think, study, and learn. They include a wide variety of mental processes used to analyze sounds and images, recall information from memory, make associations between different pieces of information, and maintain concentration on particular tasks. They can be individually identified and measured. Examples of these skills include orientation, attention span, initiation and termination of activities, memory, judgment, and proving solving skill assessments. In the Treatment category, these include activities which facilitate the use of cognitive and communication functions.

- **Dichotic.** The term dichotic means simultaneous. In audiology assessment, it means different words or sounds spoken simultaneously in each ear, to determine the ability to differentiate between them.

- **Dix-Hallpike Dynamic.** The Dix-Hallpike test (also called Nylen-Barany test) determines whether vertigo is triggered by certain head movements. The test locates the cause of vertigo as either the inner ear or the brain. If the problem is in the ear, this test can determine which ear is affected. The maneuver involves turning the head to the left or right 30° to 45° and having the patient lie quickly back with the head hanging over the edge of the exam table. The Dix-Hallpike Dynamic measures the nystagmus (involuntary eye movements) after the maneuver is performed.

- **Electrophysiologic somatosensory.** The electric activity associated with a bodily part or function, or relating to the perception of sensory stimuli from the skin and internal organs. In Assessment, it is the testing or assessment of sensory response.

- **Filtered speech.** A form of speech analysis to evaluate a hearing-impaired person's ability to hear certain words or word parts, for example, determining that words with *sh*, *ch*, or other vowels or consonants are understood and understood correctly.

- **Monoaural.** Pertaining to one ear

- **Neurophysiologic Intraoperative.** Measures neurological systems function during surgery.

- **Oral peripheral mechanism.** In speech production, measurement of the parts of the body, other than the larynx, that help form sounds and words, including the lips, tongue, and teeth.

- **Phonetically balanced speech discrimination.** This audiological evaluation consists of two word tests—the Speech Reception Threshold (SRT) and the Speech Discrimination (SD) test. It measures the ability to hear and understand spoken words.

- **Range of motion integrity.** The range through which a joint can be moved, usually its range of flexion and extension. Due to an injury, the knee may for example lack 10° of full extension.

- **Speech Reception Threshold.** Measurement of speech capabilities where patient is asked to repeat a list of easy-to-distinguish, familiar spondee (see spondee) words.

- **Speech Discrimination.** The purpose of SD testing (sometimes called word recognition testing) is to determine how well a patient hears and understands speech when the volume is set at their Most Comfortable Level (MCL).

- **Spondee (words).** Two-syllable words that have equal stress on each syllable. When a spondee is spoken out loud, each syllable has the same volume and takes the same length of time to say.

- **Staggered spondaic words.** Measurement of central auditory pathway integrity in which two different two-syllable words with the same emphasis on each word are presented simultaneously, one in each ear. The purpose is to test selective listening in the auditory system.

Character 6, Equipment

In the Physical Rehabilitation and Diagnostic Audiology section, the sixth character represents the equipment used by root type and type qualifier. A specific piece of equipment is not typically used for the equipment column, instead broad categories of equipment are listed, such as assistive or adaptive equipment, etc. Table 12-4 lists the Equipment categories by type qualifier and root type.

Table 12-4 Character 6 Equipment by Category and Root Type

Category	Type Qualifier	Equipment
Assessments	0-Speech	1-Audiometer 2-Sound Field/Booth 9-Cochlear Implant K-Audiovisual M-Augmentative/Alternative Communication N-Biosensory Feedback P-Computer Q-Speech Analysis S-Voice Analysis T-Aerodynamic Function V-Speech Prosthesis W-Swallowing Y-Other Equipment Z-None
	1-Motor and Nerve Function	3-Somatosensory 7-Electrophysiologic E-Orthosis F-Assistive, Adaptive, Supportive, or Protective K-Audiovisual M-Augmentative/Alternative Communication N-Biosensory Feedback P-Computer Q-Speech Analysis S-Voice Analysis U-Prosthesis Y-Other Equipment Z-None
	2-Activities of Daily Living (ADL)	C-Mechanical E-Orthosis F-Assistive, Adaptive, Supportive, or Protective G-Aerobic Endurance and Conditioning K-Audiovisual M-Augmentative/Alternative Communication N-Biosensory Feedback P-Computer Q-Speech Analysis S-Voice Analysis U-Prosthesis Y-Other Equipment Z-None
	3-Hearing	0-Occupational Hearing 1-Audiometer 2-Sound Field/Booth 3-Tympanometer 4-Electroacoustic Immittance/Acoustic Reflex 7-Electrophysiologic 8-Vestibular/Balance 9-Cochlear Implant K-Audiovisual L-Assistive Listening P-Computer Y-Other Equipment Z-None

	4–Hearing Aid	0–Occupational Hearing 1–Audiometer 2–Sound Field/Booth 3–Tympanometer 4–Electroacoustic Immittance/Acoustic Reflex 5–Hearing Aid Selection/Fitting/Test 7–Electrophysiologic K–Audiovisual L–Assistive Listening P–Computer Y–Other Equipment Z–None
	5–Vestibular	8–Vestibular/Balance 5–Hearing Aid Selection/Fitting/Test Z–None
Treatment	6–Speech	4–Electroacoustic Immittance/Acoustic Reflex K–Audiovisual L–Assistive Listening M–Augmentative/Alternative Communication N–Biosensory Feedback P–Computer Q–Speech Analysis S–Voice Analysis T–Aerodynamic Function V–Speech Prosthesis W–Swallowing Y–Other Equipment Z–None
	7–Motor	B–Physical Agents C–Mechanical D–Electrotherapeutic E–Orthosis F–Assistive, Adaptive, Supportive, and Protective G–Aerobic Endurance and Conditioning H–Mechanical or Electromechanical U–Prosthesis Y–Other Equipment Z–None
	8–ADL	B–Physical Agents C–Mechanical D–Electrotherapeutic E–Orthosis F–Assistive, Adaptive, Supportive, and Protective G–Aerobic Endurance and Conditioning H–Mechanical or Electromechanical U–Prosthesis Y–Other Equipment Z–None
	9–Hearing	K–Audiovisual L–Assistive Listening P–Computer X–Cerumen Management Y–Other Equipment Z–None

Table 12-4 Character 6 Equipment by Category and Root Type (continued)

Category	Type Qualifier	Equipment
	B–Cochlear Implant	1–Audiometer 2–Sound Field/Booth 9–Cochlear Implant K–Audiovisual P–Computer Y–Other Equipment
	C–Vestibular	E–Orthosis F–Assistive, Adaptive, Supportive, or Protective K–Assistive Listening N–Biosensory Feedback P–Computer Q–Speech Analysis S–Voice Analysis T–Aerodynamic Function U–Prosthesis Y–Other Equipment Z–None
Fitting	D–Device	1–Audiometer 2–Sound Field/Booth 5–Hearing Aid Selection/Fitting K–Audiovisual L–Assistive Listening M–Augmentative/Alternative Communication S–Voice Analysis U–Prosthesis V–Speech Prosthesis Z–None
Caregiver	F–Caregiver Training	E–Orthosis F–Assistive, Adaptive, Supportive, Protective K–Audiovisual L–Assistive Listening M–Augmentative/Alternative Communication P–Computer U–Prosthesis Z–None

As in the type qualifiers, much of the vocabulary used in the Equipment category is fairly straightforward. The section F appendix found in most ICD-10-PCS coding manuals provides definitions for all the equipment listed in the Equipment columns of the Physical Rehabilitation and Diagnostic Audiology Tables, but here are a few of them:

- **Audiometer.** An electrical instrument for measuring the threshold of hearing for pure tones of normally audible frequencies generally varying from 200 to 8000 Hz and recorded in decibels.

- **Tympanometry.** Indirect measurement of the compliance (mobility) and impedance of the tympanic membrane and ossicles of the middle ear.

- **Prosthesis.** An artificial substitute for a missing body part, such as an arm, leg, eye, or tooth, used for functional or cosmetic reasons or both.

- **Orthosis.** An orthopedic appliance or apparatus used to support, align, prevent, or correct deformities or to improve function of movable parts of the body. Examples of orthosis include customized and prefabricated splints, inhibitory casts, spinal and other braces, and protective devices.

- ○ **Dynamic Orthosis.** Allows motion through transfer of movement from other body parts or by use of outside forces.

- ○ **Static Orthosis.** Do not allow movement, and body parts are kept in the desired position.

- **Otoacoustic Emission (OAE).** Echoes emitted by the outer hair cells of the inner ear. These echoes are used to evaluate the integrity of the inner ear and to screen hearing in newborns.

- **Halo orthosis.** A cervical orthosis consisting of a stiff halo attached to the upper skull and to a rigid jacket on the chest, providing maximal rigidity.

- **Cochlear implant.** A small complex electronic device that is surgically placed (implanted) within the inner ear to help persons with certain types of deafness to hear. In Assessment, the cochlear implant type qualifier measures candidacy for a cochlear implant. In cochlear implant rehabilitation (treatment category) the definition is applying techniques to improve the communication abilities of individuals with cochlear implant; includes programming the device, providing patients/families with information.

The seventh character value for the qualifier column in both root types of Physical Rehabilitation (0) and Diagnostic Audiology (1) is Z, none.

Coding Physical Rehabilitation and Diagnostic Audiology in ICD-10-PCS

It is once again time to put all this information together and identify how to use the Index and Tables when coding rehabilitation and diagnostic audiology procedures. Starting with the Index, the best option is to search by one of the four Root types, assessment, treatment, caregiver training, and fittings. Figure 12-5 is the Index listing for Root type Assessment.

Note that all eight of the assessment types are indented below the main term *assessment,* including speech, motor and nerve function, hearing, hearing aid, and ADL, followed by the Table reference. From the Index, select the appropriate assessment type, and turn to that Table in the Tabular List.

A search for the root type for Treatment is a little trickier. Rather being a separate listing in the Index, with each of the Treatment type qualifiers indented below, the main terms for the Treatment root type are found throughout the Index, according to the actual treatment name. For example, *gait training, exercise, cochlear implant treatment, hearing treatment, motor treatment, motor function treatment, hydrotherapy, occupational or physical therapy, physiatry,* and *cardiac and vocational rehabilitation* are listed separately and alphabetically, as main terms, with the associated root type and Table reference. Figure 12-6, for example, shows the Index listing for *cardiac and vocational retraining (treatment).* Figure 12-7 is an excerpt from the Index for *physical therapy, physiatry, and physical medicine.*

Assessment
   Activities of daily living *see* Activities of Daily Living Assessment, Rehabilitation **F02**
      Hearing *see* Heating Assessment, Diagnostic Audiology **F13**
      Hearing aid *see* Hearing Aid Assessment, Diagnostic Audiology **F14**
      Motor function *see* Motor Function Assessment, Rehabilitation **F01**
      Nerve function *see* Motor Function Assessment, Rehabilitation **F01**
      Speech *see* Speech Assessment, Rehabilitation **F00**
      Vestibular *see* Vestibular Assessment, Diagnostic Audiology **F15**
      Vocational *see* Activities of Daily Living Treatment, Rehabilitation **F08**
Assistance

© Cengage Learning 2013

Figure 12-5 Alphabetic Index Listing for Root Type Assessment

> **Retraining**
> Cardiac *see* Motor Treatment, Rehabilitation **F07**
> Vocational *see* Activities of Daily Living Treatment, Rehabilitation **F08**

Figure 12-6 Alphabetic Index Listing for Cardiac and Vocational Retraining
© Cengage Learning 2013

> **Physiatry** *see* Motor Treatment. Rehabilitation **F07**
> **Physical medicine** *see* Motor Treatment, Rehabilitation **F07**
> **Physical therapy** *see* Motor Treatment, Rehabilitation **F07**

Figure 12-7 Alphabetic Index Listing for Physiatry and Physical Medicine and Therapy
© Cengage Learning 2013

> **Fitting**
> Arch bars, for Fracture reduction *see* Reposition, Mouth, and Throat **0CS**
> Arch bars, for immobilization *see* Immobilization, Face **2W31**
> Artificial limb *see* Device Fitting, Rehabilitation **F0D**
> Hearing aid *see* Device Fitting, Rehabilitation **F0D**
> Ocular prosthesis **F0DZ8UZ**
> Prosthesis, limb *see* Device Fitting, Rehabilitation **F0D**
> Prosthesis, ocular **F0DZ8UZ**

Figure 12-8 Alphabetic Index Listing for Fittings
© Cengage Learning 2013

> **Activities of Daily Living Assessment F02**
> **Activities of Daily Living Treatment F08**

Figure 12-9 Alphabetic Index Listing for Activities of Daily Living (ADL)
© Cengage Learning 2013

Caregiver Training is found in the Index with the Table reference F0FZ, and Fittings is found under both Device Fittings, with Table reference F0DZ, and under Fitting (Figure 12-8). Note that in Figure 12-6, there are some Index references for Fitting from different sections of the ICD-10-PCS. Be sure, when beginning a search for a procedure in the Index, that the correct Table reference is selected based on the root type and the correct section of the coding manual.

Now, let's look at a few procedures, and walk through the steps for coding them properly. The first procedure will be *ADL assessment for ventilation, respiration, and circulation of the whole respiratory system using aerobic endurance and conditioning equipment.* The root type Assessment will be the main term (Figure 12-5). Indented below that are the various root types, including ADL, with an instructional note to *See* ADL Assessment, Rehabilitation, and a Table reference of F02. From here, the options are to follow the instructional note, or to go straight to the Table referenced. Looking under ADL Assessment in the Index leads to the same Table reference (Figure 12-9). Note, too, in Figure 12-9 that ADL Treatment is found in the Index right below the ADL Assessment listing. Since the procedure example is an assessment, the next step is to go to the Table referenced for the assessment, F02 (Figure 12-10).

The section is F, Physical Rehabilitation and Diagnostic Audiology, the root type is Rehabilitation (0), and the root type is ADL Assessment (2). The next step is determining the fourth character body system/region. From the procedure description, choose respiratory system, whole body (value C).

Section	F	Physical Rehabilitation and Diagnostic Audiology		
Section Qualifier	0	Rehabilitation		
Type	2	Activities of Daily Living (ADL) Assessment: Measurement of functional level for ADL		

ADL Body System/Region	Type Qualifier	Equipment	Qualifier
0 Neurological System - Head and Neck	**9** Cranial Nerve Integrity **D** Neuromotor Development	**Y** Other Equipment **Z** None	**Z** None
1 Neurological System - Upper Back/Upper Extremity **2** Neurological System - Lower Back/Lower Extremity **3** Neurological System - Whole Body	**D** Neuromotor Development **Z** None	**Y** Other Equipment	**Z** None
4 Circulatory System - Head and Neck **5** Circulatory System - Upper Back/Upper Extremity **6** Circulatory System - Lower Back/Lower Extremity **8** Respiratory System - Head and Neck **9** Respiratory System - Upper Back/Upper Extremity **B** Respiratory System - Lower Back/Lower Extremity	**C** Mechanical **G** Ventilation, Respiration, and Circulation **Y** Other Equipment **Z** None	**G** Aerobic Endurance and Conditioning **Z** None	**Z** None
7 Circulatory System - Whole Body **C** Respiratory System - Whole Body	**7** Aerobic Capacity and Endurance	**E** Orthosis **G** Aerobic Endurance and Conditioning **U** Prosthesis **Y** Other Equipment **Z** None	**Z** None
7 Circulatory System - Whole Body **C** Respiratory System - Whole Body	**G** Ventilation, Respiration, and Circulation	**C** Mechanical **G** Aerobic Endurance and Conditioning **Y** Other Equipment **Z** None	**Z** None
Z None	**0** Bathing/Showering **1** Dressing **3** Grooming/Personal Hygiene **4** Home Management	**E** Orthosis **F** Assistive, Adaptive, Supportive, or Protective **U** Prosthesis **Z** None	**Z** None
Z None	**2** Feeding/Eating **8** Anthropometric Characteristics **F** Pain	**Y** Other Equipment	

Figure 12-10 Table F02, Activities of Daily Living (ADL) Assessment

Value C appears in two rows of this Table, so it is now necessary to determine the type qualifier and equipment to identify the correct row. In the procedural statement, the type qualifier will be G, ventilation, respiration, and circulation, found only in the one row. Staying in that same row, it is now possible to find aerobic endurance and conditioning equipment, which has the value G. There is no seventh character qualifier, so the final code character will be Z. The code for the procedure *ADL assessment for ventilation, respiration, and circulation of the whole respiratory system using aerobic endurance and conditioning equipment* is F02CGGZ.

Here is another procedure to code: *audiovisual hearing disorders counseling*. This one is a little trickier. Looking for *counseling in* the Index leads to substance abuse and mental health counseling root types (Figure 12-11), which makes it necessary to figure out a different main term. A search for the

Counseling
Family, for substance abuse, Other Family Counseling **HZ63ZZZ**
Group
    12-Step **HZ43ZZZ**
    Behavioral **HZ41ZZZ**
    Cognitive **HZ40ZZZ**
    Cognitive-Behavioral **HZ42ZZZ**
    Confrontational **HZ48ZZZ**
    Continuing Care **HZ49ZZZ**
    Infectious Disease
        Post-Test **HZ4CZZZ**
        Pre-Test **HZ4CZZZ**
Interpersonal **HZ44ZZZ**
Motivational Enhancement **HZ47ZZZ**
Psychoeducation **HZ46ZZZ**

© Cengage Learning 2013

Figure 12-11 Alphabetic Index Listing for Counseling

Hearing Aid Assessment F14Z
Hearing Assessment F13Z
Hearing Device
Insertion of device in
    Bone
        Left **0NH6**
        Right **0NH5**
    Ear
        Left **09HE**
            Other Hearing Device **09HE0SY**
        Right **09HD**
            Other Hearing Device **09HD0SY**
Removal of device from
    Ear
        Left **09PE**
        Right **09PD**
    Skull **0NP0**
Revision of device in
    Ear
        Left **09WE**
        Right **09WD**
    Skull **0NW0**
Hearing Treatment F09Z

© Cengage Learning 2013

Figure 12-12 Alphabetic Index Listing for the Term Hearing

word hearing in the Index reveals several root types and type qualifier modifiers, most of which are types of Assessments, but it does also include Hearing Treatment (Figure 12-12) with Table reference F09Z. Using *acoustic* leads to several listings in the Index, mostly as a modifying term to the body system nerve, but none that point toward hearing disorder counseling of any type. As discussed earlier, a search for Treatment will not lead to that as a main term heading in the Index.

This leaves the Index listing for *hearing treatment* with a Table reference of F09Z, for now, as the only option. It will soon become apparent whether that reference will lead to the correct code. Turn to Table F09 in the Tabular list, shown in Figure 12-13. The definition of the root type for hearing treatment is application of techniques to improve, augment, or compensate for hearing and related functional impairments. Counseling for hearing disorders does fall under the hearing treatment root type. The

Section	F	Physical Rehabilitation and Diagnostic Audiology		
Section Qualifier	0	Rehabilitation		
Type	9	Hearing Treatment: Application of techniques to improve, augment, or compensate for hearing and related functional impairment		

Body System/Region	Type Qualifier	Equipment	Qualifier
Z None	**0** Hearing and Related Disorders Counseling **1** Hearing and Related Disorders Prevention	**K** Audiovisual **Z** None	**Z** None
Z None	**2** Auditory Processing	**K** Audiovisual **L** Assistive Listening **P** Computer **Y** Other Equipment **Z** None	**Z** None
Z None	**3** Cerumen Management	**X** Cerumen Management **Z** None	**Z** None

Figure 12-13 Table F09 Hearing Treatment

© Cengage Learning 2013

section qualifier is rehabilitation, which is also a clue that this is the correct Table. In the first row of the Table, in the type qualifier column, the first value, 0, matches the procedural statement closely (except for acoustic)–*hearing and related disorders counseling*. The equipment category includes acoustic (value K). The code therefore is F09Z0KZ for the procedure *acoustic hearing disorder counseling*.

Let's Review 12–1:

Code the following Physical Rehabilitation and Diagnostic Audiology procedures:
   1. Motor speech assessment, computer _____
   2. Neurologic muscle performance, prosthetic, left lower leg _____
   3. Gait training, electrotherapeutic _____
   4. Wound management, muscle, upper back, ADL, physical agents _____
   5. Binaural hearing aids selection, fitting, and testing _____

Mental Health (GZ1-GZJ)

The first character value for the mental health section is G. The second character value representing the body system is always Z, none, in this section. Therefore, a Mental Health procedure code will always begin with GZ. This section contains Mental Health root types (character 3) including psychological testing, counseling, individual, family, and group psychotherapy, crisis intervention, and medication management. The fourth character in the Mental Health section is the type qualifier, which describes the type of mental health service provided. For example, in root type 1, psychological tests, the type qualifier describes the type of testing, i.e., personality and behavioral, neuropsychological, or developmental. The fifth through seventh characters in a mental health section code are all qualifiers, and all three qualifiers have the character value, Z, none. A Mental Health section code, therefore, will always begin with GZ, and the last three characters will always be Z. Only the third character, root type, and fourth character type qualifier values will change.

Character 3, Root Type

There are twelve root types in the Mental Health section. The values and descriptions of these are shown in Table 12-5.

Most ICD-10-PCS coding manuals will contain an appendix which includes definitions for some examples of these root types in the Mental Health section. For example, the monitoring of, and techniques used in, biofeedback include electroencephalogram (EEG), blood pressure, regulation of bowel or bladder activity, and regulation of gastric motility, among others. For patients suffering from seasonal affective depression disorder (SADD), one mental health procedure that has proven effective is light therapy, root type value J. **Electroconvulsive therapy (ECT)** is medical treatment for severe mental illness in which a small, carefully controlled amount of electricity is introduced into the brain. This electrical stimulation, used in conjunction with anesthesia and muscle relaxant medications, produces a mild generalized seizure or convulsion. While used to treat a variety of psychiatric disorders, it is most effective in the treatment of severe depression. **Narcosynthesis** is essentially psychotherapy under partial anesthesia, induced by barbiturates, first used to treat acute mental disorders in a combat setting.

Character 4, Type Qualifiers in Mental Health

The character four type qualifier values and definitions are listed in Table 12-7. The definitions, and some examples, can usually also be found in the type qualifiers appendix in the ICD-10-PCS coding manual.

Table 12-5 Root Types, Values, and Definitions used in Mental Health

Root Type	Value	Description
Psychological Tests	1	The administration and interpretation of standardized psychological tests and measurement instruments for the assessment of psychological function
Crisis Intervention	2	Treatment of a traumatized, acutely disturbed, or distressed individual for the purpose of short-term stabilization
Medication Management	3	Monitoring and adjusting the use of medications for a mental health disorder
Individual Psychotherapy	5	Treatment of an individual with a mental health disorder by behavioral, cognitive, psychoanalytic, psychodynamic, or psychophysiological means to improve function or well being
Counseling	6	The application of psychological methods to treat an individual with normal developmental issues and psychological problems in order to increase function, improve well-being, alleviate distress, maladjustment, or resolve crises
Family Psychotherapy	7	Treatment that includes one or more family members of an individual with a mental health disorder by behavioral, cognitive, psychoanalytic, psychodynamic, or psychophysiological means to improve functioning or well-being
Electroconvulsive Therapy (ECT)	B	The application of controlled electrical voltages to treat mental health disorders
Biofeedback	C	Provision of information from the monitoring and regulating of physiological processes in conjunction with cognitive-behavioral techniques to improve patient functioning or well-being
Hypnosis	F	Introduction of a state of heightened suggestibility by auditory, visual, and tactile techniques to elicit an emotional or behavioral response
Narcosynthesis	G	Introduction of intravenous barbiturates in order to release suppressed or repressed thoughts
Group Psychotherapy	H	Treatment of two or more individuals with a mental health disorder by behavioral, cognitive, psychoanalytic, psychodynamic, or psychophysiological means to improve functioning or well-being
Light Therapy	J	Application of specialized light treatments to improve functioning or well being

Table 12-6 Type Qualifiers, Values, and Definitions by Root Type

Type Qualifier (Value)	Definition	Root Type(s)
0–Developmental	Evaluating age-normed developmental status of cognitive, social, and adaptive behaviors	Psychological Tests
1–Personality and Behavior	Mood, emotion, behavior, social functioning, psychopathological conditions, personality traits, and characteristics testing	
2–Intellectual and Psychoeducational	Intellectual abilities, academic achievements, learning capabilities, including behaviors, and emotional factors affecting learning	
3–Neuropsychological	Thinking, reasoning and judgment, acquired knowledge, attention, memory, visual spatial abilities, language functions, and planning testing	
4–Neurobehavioral and cognitive status	Includes neurobehavioral status exam(s), interview(s), and observation for the clinical assessment of thinking, reasoning and judgment, acquired knowledge, attention, memory, visual spatial abilities, language functions, and planning.	
Z–None		Crisis Intervention
Z–None		Medication Management
0–Interactive	Uses primarily physical aids and other non-oral interaction with a patient who is psychologically or developmentally unable to use ordinary language for communication	Individual Psychotherapy
1–Behavioral	Primarily to modify behavior, including role playing, positive reinforcement, self-managing skills training.	
2–Cognitive	To correct cognitive distortions and errors.	
3–Interpersonal	Helps an individual make changes in interpersonal behaviors to reduce psychological dysfunction	
4–Psychoanalysis	Methods of obtaining a detailed account of past and present mental and emotional experiences to determine the source and eliminate or diminish the undesirable effects of unconscious conflicts	
5–Psychodynamic	Exploration of past and present emotional experiences to understand motives and drives using insight-oriented techniques to reduce the undesirable effects of internal conflicts on emotions and behavior.	
6–Supportive	Formation of therapeutic relationship primarily for providing emotional support to prevent further deterioration in functioning and during periods of particular stress.	
8–Cognitive-Behavioral	Combining cognitive and behavioral treatment strategies to improve functioning.	
9–Psychophysiological	Monitoring and alteration of physiological processes to help the individual associate physiological reactions combined with cognitive and behavioral strategies to gain improved control of these processes and help the individual cope more effectively.	
0–Educational 1–Vocational 3–Other Counseling	Application of psychological methods to treat an individual with normal developmental issues and psychological problems, in order to increase function, improve well-being, alleviate stress, or resolve crises in school, work, or other pursuits.	Counseling
2–Other Family Psychotherapy		Family Psychotherapy

Table 12-6 Type Qualifiers, Values, and Definitions by Root Type (continued)

Type Qualifier (Value)	Definition	Root Type(s)
0–Unilateral-Single Seizure 1–Unilateral–Multiple Seizure 2–Bilateral–Single Seizure 3–Bilateral Multiple Seizure 4–Other Electroconvulsive Therapy (ECT)	Applying single or multiple electrical shocks unilaterally or bilaterally to the brain to treat a mental health disorder.	ECT
9–Other Biofeedback	Using devices, i.e., EEG, electrocardiogram (ECG/EKG), electrogastrogram to monitor and regulate physiological processes, e.g., blood pressure, respirations, gastric motility, in conjunction with cognitive-behavioral techniques, i.e., learning principles, information processing models, to improve patient functioning or well-being.	Biofeedback
Z–None		Hypnosis
Z–None		Narcosynthesis
Z–None		Group Psychotherapy
Z–None		Light Therapy

Coding Mental Health in ICD-10-PCS

The most effective search method for Mental Health procedures is by root type. For example, a search of the prefix *psycho-* in the Index reveals listings for psychoanalysis and psychological testing (Figure 12-14). A search for *psychotherapy* as the main term lists *individual*, *family*, and *group* as modifiers, and the type qualifiers as subterms indented below the modifiers (Figure 12-15). Searching for *Biofeedback* or *ECT* arrives at Table references for each one. In *biofeedback*, the Table reference is GZC9ZZZ. In *ECT* (Figure 12-16), each type qualifier is indented below as a modifier, with its own Table reference.

In a search for *Counseling*, the modifying term is *Mental Health Services*, with the types of counseling indented as subterms below the modifying term (Figure 12-17).

Remember, all Mental Health codes begin with GZ, and end with ZZZ. The only values that change are the fourth character root type, and the fifth character type qualifier. Therefore, a search for the root type will always lead to a full code in the Index, or to modifying and subterms describing the type qualifier. The next, and final, step is to confirm the Table reference from the Index in the appropriate Table.

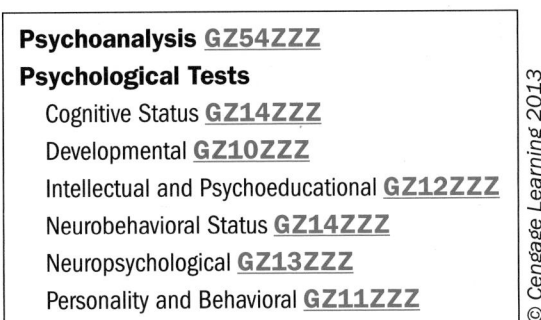

Psychoanalysis GZ54ZZZ
Psychological Tests
   Cognitive Status GZ14ZZZ
   Developmental GZ10ZZZ
   Intellectual and Psychoeducational GZ12ZZZ
   Neurobehavioral Status GZ14ZZZ
   Neuropsychological GZ13ZZZ
   Personality and Behavioral GZ11ZZZ

© Cengage Learning 2013

Figure 12-14 Alphabetic Index Search Results for Prefix Psycho

Psychotherapy
 Family, Mental Health Services <u>GZ72ZZZ</u>
 Group
  <u>GZHZZZZ</u>
  Mental Health Services <u>GZHZZZZ</u>
Individual
 see Psychotherapy, Individual, Mental Health Services for substance abuse
  12-Step <u>HZ53ZZZ</u>
  Behavioral <u>HZ51ZZZ</u>
  Cognitive <u>HZ50ZZZ</u>
  Cognitive-Behavioral <u>HZ52ZZZ</u>
  Confrontational <u>HZ58ZZZ</u>
  Interactive <u>HZ55ZZZ</u>
  Interpersonal <u>HZ54ZZZ</u>
  Motivational Enhancement <u>HZ57ZZZ</u>
  Psychoanalysis <u>HZ5BZZZ</u>
  Psychodynamic <u>HZ5CZZZ</u>
  Psychoeducation <u>HZ56ZZZ</u>
  Psychophysiological <u>HZ5DZZZ</u>
  Supportive <u>HZ59ZZZ</u>
 Mental Health Services
  Behavioral <u>GZ51ZZZ</u>
  Cognitive <u>GZ52ZZZ</u>
  Cognitive-Behavioral <u>GZ58ZZZ</u>
  Interactive <u>GZ50ZZZ</u>
  Interpersonal <u>GZ53ZZZ</u>
  Psychoanalysis <u>GZ54ZZZ</u>
  Psychodynamic <u>GZ55ZZZ</u>
  Psychophysiological <u>GZ59ZZZ</u>
  Supportive <u>GZ56ZZZ</u>

© Cengage Learning 2013

Figure 12-15 Alphabetic Index Search Results for Psychotherapy

Electroconvulsive Therapy
 Bilateral-Multiple Seizure <u>GZB3ZZZ</u>
 Bilateral-Single Seizure <u>GZB2ZZZ</u>
 Electroconvulsive Therapy, Other <u>GZB4ZZZ</u>
 Unilateral-Multiple Seizure <u>GZB1ZZZ</u>
 Unilateral-Single Seizure <u>GZB0ZZZ</u>

Figure 12-16 Alphabetic Index Search Results for Electroconvulsive Therapy
© Cengage Learning 2013

Counseling
 Family, for substance abuse, Other Family Counseling **HZ63ZZZ**
 Group
  12-Step **HZ43ZZZ**
  Behavioral **HZ41ZZZ**
  Cognitive **HZ40ZZZ**
  Cognitive-Behavioral **HZ42ZZZ**
  Confrontational **HZ48ZZZ**
  Continuing Care **HZ49ZZZ**
  Infectious Disease
   Post-Test **HZ4CZZZ**
   Pre-Test **HZ4CZZZ**
  Interpersonal **HZ44ZZZ**
  Motivational Enhancement **HZ47ZZZ**
  Psychoeducation **HZ46ZZZ**

© Cengage Learning 2013

Figure 12-17 Index Search Results for Counseling

Let's Review 12–2:

1. Developmental testing, psychological _____

2. Medication management, mental health _____

3. Bilateral, multiple seizure ECT _____

4. Cognitive-behavioral psychotherapy, individual _____

5. Educational counseling, mental health _____

Substance Abuse (HZ2–HZ9)

Procedures from the Substance Abuse section of the ICD-10-PCS will always begin with HZ. The H identifies the section, substance abuse; and the second character value is always Z, none to identify the body system. There are seven root type values for the third character, and 24 fourth character values. The last three characters in a Substance Abuse code are qualifiers and the value for each is Z, none.

Characters 3 and 4, Root Types and Type Qualifiers

There is some overlap in the procedures in the Substance Abuse section and the Mental Health section. For example, there are values for psychotherapy and counseling in both sections. The significant difference between the two is that in the Substance Abuse section the psychotherapy and counseling and other therapies are directed at individuals with addictions, while in the Mental Health section the therapies and treatments are directed at individuals with psychological and mental health problems generally unrelated to addiction. That is not to say the two are mutually exclusive, since an individual could receive treatment for both a psychological or mental health issue and an addiction. In that case, of course, the appropriate codes would be chosen from each section, which would result in multiple codes for one encounter.

The seven root type values for the Substance Abuse section are:

- Detoxification Services (2)
- Individual Counseling (3)
- Group Counseling (4)
- Individual Psychotherapy (5)
- Family Counseling (6)
- Medication Management (7)
- Pharmacotherapy (9)

Table 12-7 lists the Type Qualifiers and values for each of the seven root types.

The definitions for most psychotherapy and counseling root types have already been defined in the Mental Health section of this chapter. There are a few items to point out about the type qualifiers for the substance abuse section. First, notice that in the root types for counseling and psychotherapy, the type qualifiers have the same character values, except values 9, B, and C. In individual counseling and group counseling, the values for the type of counseling are 9, continuing care, B, spiritual, and C, pre/post-test infectious disease. In individual psychotherapy, however, the values are replaced by types of psychotherapy procedures. Value 9 is now supportive, B is psychoanalysis, and C is psychodynamic. Family counseling does not differentiate between types of counseling, but instead uses only the value 3, for other family counseling.

Table 12-7 Type Qualifiers and Root Types in the Substance Abuse Section

Type Qualifier (Value)	Root Type	Root Type Definition
Z-None	2-Detoxification	Detoxification from alcohol and drugs
0-Cognitive 1-Behavioral 2-Cognitive-Behavioral 3-Twelve-Step 4-Interpersonal 5-Vocational 6-Psychoeducational 7-Motivational Enhancement 8-Confrontational 9-Continuing Care B-Spiritual	3-Individual counseling	Application of psychological methods to treat an individual with addictive behavior
C-Pre/Post-Test Infectious Disease		
	4-Group Counseling	Application of psychological methods to treat groups of individuals with addictive behaviors
0-Cognitive 1-Behavioral 2-Cognitive-Behavioral 3-Twelve-Step 4-Interpersonal 5-Vocational 6-Psychoeducational 7-Motivational Enhancement 8-Confrontational 9-Supportive B-Psychoanalysis C-Psychodynamic D-Psychophysiological	5-Individual Psychotherapy	Treatment of an individual with addictive behavior by behavioral, cognitive, psychoanalytic, psychodynamic, or psychophysiological techniques
3-Other Family Counseling	6-Family counseling	The application of psychological methods that includes one or more family members to treat an individual with addictive behaviors
0-Nicotine Replacement 1-Methadone Maintenance 2-Levo-alpha-acetyl-methadol (LAAM) 3-Antabuse 4-Naltrexone 5-Naloxone 6-Clonidine 7-Bupropion 8-Psychiatric Medication 9-Other Replacement Medication	8-Medication Management 9-Pharmacotherapy	Monitoring and adjusting the use of medications for the treatment of addiction The use of replacement medications for the treatment of addiction

The only other important differentiation to be aware of is with the root types medication management (8) and pharmacotherapy (9). The same medications in the type qualifier column are found in both Tables. The difference lies in the objective of the root type. Medication management is simply monitoring and adjusting the replacement medications used for the treatment of addiction. In pharmacotherapy, the medication is used specifically as a replacement for the substance the individual is addicted to. The best example of this would be **methodone**, which is a synthetic heroin. A code from pharmacotherapy would be used if methodone was prescribed as a replacement for a heroin-addicted individual. As the medication is monitored and adjusted throughout the length of its use, a code from medication management will be used.

Here are a few definitions of some of the drugs shown in this section:

- **Antabuse** is a drug used to support the treatment of chronic alcoholism by producing an acute sensitivity to alcohol.

- **Bupropion** is an antidepressant, and is also used as a smoking cessation aid. The most recognizable brand name for bupropion is Wellbutrin.

- **Clonidine** is a direct-acting medication prescribed historically as an antihypertensive agent. It has found new uses, including treatment of some types of neuropathic pain, opioid detoxification, sleep sweats (hyperhydrosis), anesthetic use, and to counter the side effects of stimulant medications such as amphetamine. It is also used to treat insomnia, and for relief of menopausal symptoms. Clonidine is also used treat attention deficit hyperactivity disorder (ADHD) and Tourette's syndrome.

- **Levo-alpha-acetyl-methadol (LAAM)** is a synthetic opioid similar in structure to methadone. LAAM is indicated as a second-line treatment for the treatment and management of opioid dependence if patients fail to respond to drugs like methadone or bupropion.

- **Methadone** is a synthetic opioid, used medically as an analgesic, antitussive, and more commonly, as an anti-addictive for use in patients on opioids.

- **Naltrexone** is used in the management of alcohol and opioid dependence.

Coding Substance Abuse Procedures in ICD-10-PCS

In the Index, the most effective way to begin the search for a Table reference is by the root type. For example, a search for *counseling* or *psychotherapy* will lead to references both to the Mental Health Tables and the Substance Abuse Tables. It will be necessary to know whether the patient is being treated for an addiction or for mental health issues, in order to determine which code to reference. The modifying term is typically the type qualifier, but occasionally it will have an ICD-10-PCS section reference. For example, under *counseling,* each type of counseling is listed below the main term as

---

Counseling *continued*
Group *continued*
Spiritual **HZ4BZZZ**
Vocational **HZ45ZZZ**
Individual
12-Step **HZ33ZZZ**
Behavioral **HZ31ZZZ**
Cognitive **HZ30ZZZ**
Cognitive-Behavioral **HZ32ZZZ**
Confrontational **HZ38ZZZ**
Continuing Care **HZ39ZZZ**
Infectious Disease
Post-Test **HZ3CZZZ**
Pre-Test **HZ3CZZZ**
Interpersonal **HZ34ZZZ**
Motivational Enhancement **HZ37ZZZ**
Psychoeducation **HZ36ZZZ**
Spiritual **HZ3BZZZ**
Vocational **HZ35ZZZ**
Mental Health Services
Educational **GZ60ZZZ**
Other Counseling **GZ63ZZZ**
Vocational **GZ61ZZZ**

© Cengage Learning 2013

Figure 12-18 Index Listing for Group Counseling

illustrated in Figure 12-18. All of the Substance Abuse section type qualifiers modifying and subterms are listed, such as *group counseling* with the type qualifier Twelve-Step (Table reference HZ43ZZZ), and *post-test infectious disease counseling*, with the Table reference HZ4CZZZ.

Since a mental health section code will always begin with HZ, and end with the last three characters of ZZZ, the only selection will be of the correct root type and type qualifier.

Let's Review 12–3:

1. Methadone maintenance replacement for heroin addiction _____
2. Follow-up methadone monitoring and adjustment _____
3. Family member counseling for addicted individual _____
4. Confrontational psychotherapy, individual _____
5. Spiritual group counseling _____

Chapter Summary

Physical Rehabilitation and Diagnostic Audiology (F00–F15)

Physical Rehabilitation provides treatment and assistance in removing or reducing disabilities. Physical rehabilitation procedures include physical and occupational therapy, and speech-language pathology codes. The character value for this section is F, and all codes within Physical Rehabilitation and Diagnostic Audiology will begin with the letter F. The range of codes for this section is F00–F15. There are only two character two values in this section. The first is Rehabilitation, represented by value 0. The second is Diagnostic Audiology, which has a value of 1. There are 11 root types associated with value 0, rehabilitation, and three with Diagnostic Audiology.

These 14 root type values can be classified into four basic types of procedures, Assessment, Caregiver Training, Fittings, i.e., prosthetics or hearing aids, and Treatment. The body region or part upon which the procedure is performed is represented by the fourth character, body system or region. The fifth character is called the type qualifier, and adds more specificity to the type of rehabilitation or diagnostic audiology procedure performed. Assessments measure functionality or the level of impairment. Treatments apply techniques used to improve, augment, or compensate for impairments. Fittings facilitate or support higher levels of functioning, and Caregiver Training teaches family members and caregivers how to support and help the patient achieve an optimal level of functioning. The six types of assessments are speech, motor and nerve function, ADL, hearing, hearing aid, and vestibular.

Treatment values are given for all of the root types found in the Assessment category, with the following differences: (1) cochlear implant treatment is added to the Treatment values (there is no cochlear implant assessment) and (2) there is no hearing aid treatment. Hearing aids, as well as prostheses and orthotics, are included in the Fittings category. Balance and equilibrium are measured, and disorders are treated, in the vestibular assessment and vestibular treatment categories. The fourth character body system and region values associated with each root type are shown in Table 12-2. The body system or region character 2 value identifies the target of the assessment, treatment, fitting, or caregiver training. The type qualifier adds more specificity to the type of rehabilitation or diagnostic audiology procedure performed. In the Assessment category, there are over 100 different type qualifiers. Some of these values are repeated in different root types; however, most are unique to the individual root type. A specific piece of equipment is not typically used for the equipment column; instead, broad categories of equipment are listed, such as assistive or adaptive equipment. The seventh character value for the qualifier column in both root types of Physical Rehabilitation (0) and Diagnostic Audiology (1) is Z, none. When coding Rehabilitation and Diagnostic Audiology procedures, start with the Index and search by one of the four root types: Assessment, Treatment, Caregiver training, or Fittings.

In the Mental Health (GZ1-GZJ) section the first character value is G. The second character value representing the body system is always Z, none. This section contains mental health root types (character 3) that include psychological testing, counseling, individual, family, and group psychotherapy, crisis intervention, and medication management. The fourth character in the mental health section is the type qualifier, which describes the type of mental health service provided. The fifth through seventh characters in a mental health section code are all qualifiers, and all three Qualifiers have the character value, Z, none. The most effective search method for mental health procedures is by root type. A search for psychotherapy as the main term lists individual, family, and group as modifiers, and the type qualifiers as subterms indented below the modifiers.

Substance Abuse (HZ2-HZ9). Procedures from the Substance Abuse section of the ICD-10-PCS will always begin with HZ. H identifies the section, Substance Abuse; and the second character value is always Z, none, to identify the body system. There are seven root type values for the third character, and 24 fourth character values. The last three characters in a Substance Abuse code are qualifiers, and the value for each is Z, none. The seven root type values for the Substance Abuse section are: Detoxification services (2), Individual counseling (3), Group Counseling (4), Individual Psychotherapy (5), Family Counseling (6), Medication Management (7), and Pharmacotherapy (9).

In the Index, the most effective way to begin the search for a Table reference is by the root type. It will be necessary to know whether the patient is being treated for an addiction or for mental health issues, in order to determine which code to reference. The modifying term is typically the type qualifier, but occasionally it will have an ICD-10-PCS section reference. Since a Mental Health section code will always begin with HZ, and end with the last three characters of ZZZ, the only selection will be of the correct root type and type qualifier.

Review

Matching

Instructions: Match the term to its definition.

_____ 1. Antabuse

_____ 2. Audiometry

_____ 3. Binaural

_____ 4. Bupropion

_____ 5. Dynamic Orthosis

_____ 6. Narcosynthesis

_____ 7. Tympanometry

_____ 8. Static Orthosis

_____ 9. Spondee (words)

_____ 10. Otoacoustic Emission (OAE)

a. Pertaining to both ears.

b. Echoes emitted by the outer hair cells of the inner ear.

c. A drug used to support the treatment of chronic alcoholism by producing an acute sensitivity to alcohol.

d. Indirect measurement of the compliance (mobility) and impedance of the tympanic membrane and ossicles of the middle ear.

e. Two-syllable words that have equal stress on each syllable.

f. Does not allow movement, and body parts are kept in the desired position.

g. Psychotherapy under partial anesthesia, induced by barbiturates, first used to treat acute mental disorders in a combat setting.

h. Measurement of the acuity of hearing for the various frequencies of sound waves.

i. An antidepressant, but is also used as a smoking cessation aid. The most recognizable brand name is Wellbutrin.

j. Allows motion through transfer of movement from other body parts or by use of outside forces.

Short Answer

Instructions: Provide a brief answer for the following questions.

1. Define ADL and give at least two examples _____

2. Give three examples of *type qualifiers* for Section, F, Physical Rehabilitation and Diagnostic Audiology _____

3. Give four examples of *section qualifiers* for Physical Rehabilitation _____
_____

4. What is the difference between *motor treatment* and *motor assessment* in Section F, Physical Rehabilitation and Diagnostic Audiology? _____

5. Define *acoustic reflex decay* and give an example _____

6. Define *assistive, adaptive, supportive,* or *protective devices* in Section F, Physical Rehabilitation and Diagnostic Audiology _____

7. Describe the difference between crisis intervention and counseling in Section G, Mental Health
_____

8. Give examples of character 3, Type, in Section H, Substance Abuse Treatment _____
_____

9. What does the character 4 qualifier in Section G, Mental Health describe? _____
_____

10. Explain the primary difference between codes in Section G, Mental Health, and Section H, Substance Abuse _____

Coding Practice

Instructions: Code the following procedures.

1. Bedside swallowing and oral function assessment _____

2. Non-invasive instrumental status assessment, aerodynamic function equipment _____
_____

3. Range of motion and joint integrity neurological assessment, whole body, other equipment _____
_____

4. ADL training, using assistive and adaptive equipment, for bathing, showering techniques _____
_____

5. Cerumen management, using cerumen management equipment _____

6. Dynamic orthosis device fitting, using orthosis _____

7. Personality and behavioral psychological testing _____

8. Suicide prevention (Hint: Think crisis intervention) _____

9. Medication management, mental health disorder _____

10. Individual addiction counseling, 12-Step _____

11. Hearing aid acoustic reflex assessment _____

12. Analysis (voice) of voice prosthetic _____

13. Assistive vestibular treatment for musculoskeletal system, posture control _____
_____

14. Chlonidine management for substance abuse _____

15. Neurobehavioral and cognitive testing _____

Appendix A: ICD-10-PCS 2012 Guidelines

ICD-10-PCS Coding Guidelines

Table of Contents

A. Conventions 1
B. Medical and Surgical Section Guidelines 4
     2. Body System 4
     3. Root Operation...5
     4. Body Part 9
     5. Approach 12
     6. Device 13
C. Obstetrics Section Guidelines..14

Conventions

A1

ICD-10-PCS codes are composed of seven characters. Each character is an axis of classification that specifies information about the procedure performed. Within a defined code range, a character specifies the same type of information in that axis of classification.
Example: The fifth axis of classification specifies the approach in sections 0 through 4 and 7 through 9 of the system.

A2

One of 34 possible values can be assigned to each axis of classification in the seven-character code: they are the numbers 0 through 9 and the alphabet (except I and O because they are easily confused with the numbers 1 and 0). The number of unique values used in an axis of classification differs as needed.
Example: Where the fifth axis of classification specifies the approach, seven different approach values are currently used to specify the approach.

A3

The valid values for an axis of classification can be added to as needed.
Example: If a significantly distinct type of device is used in a new procedure, a new device value can be added to the system.

A4

As with words in their context, the meaning of any single value is a combination of its axis of classification and any preceding values on which it may be dependent.
Example: The meaning of a body part value in the Medical and Surgical section is always dependent on the body system value. The body part value 0 in the Central Nervous body system specifies Brain and the body part value 0 in the Peripheral Nervous body system specifies Cervical Plexus.

1

A5

As the system is expanded to become increasingly detailed, over time more values will depend on preceding values for their meaning.
Example: In the Lower Joints body system, the device value 3 in the root operation Insertion specifies Infusion Device and the device value 3 in the root operation Fusion specifies Interbody Fusion Device.

A6

The purpose of the alphabetic index is to locate the appropriate table that contains all information necessary to construct a procedure code. The PCS Tables should always be consulted to find the most appropriate valid code.

A7

It is not required to consult the index first before proceeding to the tables to complete the code. A valid code may be chosen directly from the tables.

A8

All seven characters must be specified to be a valid code. If the documentation is incomplete for coding purposes, the physician should be queried for the necessary information.

A9

Within a PCS table, valid codes include all combinations of choices in characters 4 through 7 contained in the same row of the table. In the example below, 0JHT3VZ is a valid code, and 0JHW3VZ is *not* a valid code.

Section: 0 Medical and Surgical
Body System: J Subcutaneous Tissue and Fascia
Operation: H Insertion: Putting in a nonbiological appliance that monitors, assists, performs, or prevents a physiological function but does not physically take the place of a body part

Body Part	Approach	Device	Qualifier
S Subcutaneous Tissue and Fascia, Head and Neck V Subcutaneous Tissue and Fascia, Upper Extremity W Subcutaneous Tissue and Fascia, Lower Extremity	0 Open 3 Percutaneous	1 Radioactive Element 3 Infusion Device	Z No Qualifier
T Subcutaneous Tissue and Fascia, Trunk	0 Open 3 Percutaneous	1 Radioactive Element 3 Infusion Device V Infusion Pump	Z No Qualifier

A10

"And," when used in a code description, means "and/or."
Example: Lower Arm and Wrist Muscle means lower arm and/or wrist muscle.

A11

Many of the terms used to construct PCS codes are defined within the system. It is the coder's responsibility to determine what the documentation in the medical record equates to in the PCS definitions. The physician is not expected to use the terms used in PCS

2

code descriptions, nor is the coder required to query the physician when the correlation between the documentation and the defined PCS terms is clear.

Example: When the physician documents "partial resection" the coder can independently correlate "partial resection" to the root operation Excision without querying the physician for clarification.

Medical and Surgical Section Guidelines (section 0)

B2. Body System

General guidelines
B2.1a
The procedure codes in the general anatomical regions body systems should only be used when the procedure is performed on an anatomical region rather than a specific body part (e.g., root operations Control and Detachment, drainage of a body cavity) or on the rare occasion when no information is available to support assignment of a code to a specific body part.
Example: Control of postoperative hemorrhage is coded to the root operation Control found in the general anatomical regions body systems.

B2.1b
Body systems designated as upper or lower contain body parts located above or below the diaphragm respectively.
Example: Vein body parts above the diaphragm are found in the Upper Veins body system; vein body parts below the diaphragm are found in the Lower Veins body system.

B3. Root Operation

General guidelines
B3.1a
In order to determine the appropriate root operation, the full definition of the root operation as contained in the PCS Tables must be applied.

B3.1b
Components of a procedure specified in the root operation definition and explanation are not coded separately. Procedural steps necessary to reach the operative site and close the operative site are also not coded separately.
Example: Resection of a joint as part of a joint replacement procedure is included in the root operation definition of Replacement and is not coded separately. Laparotomy performed to reach the site of an open liver biopsy is not coded separately.

Multiple procedures
B3.2
During the same operative episode, multiple procedures are coded if:
a.   The same root operation is performed on different body parts as defined by distinct values of the body part character.
        Example: Diagnostic excision of liver and pancreas are coded separately.
b.   The same root operation is repeated at different body sites that are included in the same body part value.
        Example: Excision of the sartorius muscle and excision of the gracilis muscle are both included in the upper leg muscle body part value, and multiple procedures are coded.
c.   Multiple root operations with distinct objectives are performed on the same body part.
        Example: Destruction of sigmoid lesion and bypass of sigmoid colon are coded separately.
d.   The intended root operation is attempted using one approach, but is converted to a different approach.
        Example: Laparoscopic cholecystectomy converted to an open cholecystectomy is coded as percutaneous endoscopic Inspection and open Resection.

Discontinued procedures
B3.3
If the intended procedure is discontinued, code the procedure to the root operation performed. If a procedure is discontinued before any other root operation is performed, code the root operation Inspection of the body part or anatomical region inspected.
Example: A planned aortic valve replacement procedure is discontinued after the initial thoracotomy and before any incision is made in the heart muscle, when the patient becomes hemodynamically unstable. This procedure is coded as an open Inspection of the mediastinum.

5

Biopsy followed by more definitive treatment
B3.4

If a diagnostic Excision, Extraction, or Drainage procedure (biopsy) is followed by a more definitive procedure, such as Destruction, Excision or Resection at the same procedure site, both the biopsy and the more definitive treatment are coded.
Example: Biopsy of breast followed by partial mastectomy at the same procedure site, both the biopsy and the partial mastectomy procedure are coded.

Overlapping body layers
B3.5

If the root operations Excision, Repair or Inspection are performed on overlapping layers of the musculoskeletal system, the body part specifying the deepest layer is coded.
Example: Excisional debridement that includes skin and subcutaneous tissue and muscle is coded to the muscle body part.

Bypass procedures
B3.6a

Bypass procedures are coded by identifying the body part bypassed "from" and the body part bypassed "to." The fourth character body part specifies the body part bypassed from, and the qualifier specifies the body part bypassed to.
Example: Bypass from stomach to jejunum, stomach is the body part and jejunum is the qualifier.

B3.6b

Coronary arteries are classified by number of distinct sites treated, rather than number of coronary arteries or anatomic name of a coronary artery (e.g., left anterior descending). Coronary artery bypass procedures are coded differently than other bypass procedures as described in the previous guideline. Rather than identifying the body part bypassed from, the body part identifies the number of coronary artery sites bypassed to, and the qualifier specifies the vessel bypassed from.
Example: Aortocoronary artery bypass of one site on the left anterior descending coronary artery and one site on the obtuse marginal coronary artery is classified in the body part axis of classification as two coronary artery sites and the qualifier specifies the aorta as the body part bypassed from.

B3.6c

If multiple coronary artery sites are bypassed, a separate procedure is coded for each coronary artery site that uses a different device and/or qualifier.
Example: Aortocoronary artery bypass and internal mammary coronary artery bypass are coded separately.

Control vs. more definitive root operations
B3.7

The root operation Control is defined as, "Stopping, or attempting to stop, postprocedural bleeding." If an attempt to stop postprocedural bleeding is initially unsuccessful, and to stop the bleeding requires performing any of the definitive root operations Bypass,

6

Detachment, Excision, Extraction, Reposition, Replacement, or Resection, then that root operation is coded instead of Control.

Example: Resection of spleen to stop postprocedural bleeding is coded to Resection instead of Control.

Excision vs. Resection
B3.8

PCS contains specific body parts for anatomical subdivisions of a body part, such as lobes of the lungs or liver and regions of the intestine. Resection of the specific body part is coded whenever all of the body part is cut out or off, rather than coding Excision of a less specific body part.

Example: Left upper lung lobectomy is coded to Resection of Upper Lung Lobe, Left rather than Excision of Lung, Left.

Excision for graft
B3.9

If an autograft is obtained from a different body part in order to complete the objective of the procedure, a separate procedure is coded.

Example: Coronary bypass with excision of saphenous vein graft, excision of saphenous vein is coded separately.

Fusion procedures of the spine
B3.10a

The body part coded for a spinal vertebral joint(s) rendered immobile by a spinal fusion procedure is classified by the level of the spine (e.g. thoracic). There are distinct body part values for a single vertebral joint and for multiple vertebral joints at each spinal level.

Example: Body part values specify Lumbar Vertebral Joint, Lumbar Vertebral Joints, 2 or More and Lumbosacral Vertebral Joint.

B3.10b

If multiple vertebral joints are fused, a separate procedure is coded for each vertebral joint that uses a different device and/or qualifier.

Example: Fusion of lumbar vertebral joint, posterior approach, anterior column and fusion of lumbar vertebral joint, posterior approach, posterior column are coded separately.

B3.10c

Combinations of devices and materials are often used on a vertebral joint to render the joint immobile. When combinations of devices are used on the same vertebral joint, the device value coded for the procedure is as follows:

- If an interbody fusion device is used to render the joint immobile (alone or containing other material like bone graft), the procedure is coded with the device value Interbody Fusion Device

7

- If internal fixation is used to render the joint immobile and an interbody fusion device is *not* used, the procedure is coded with the device value Internal Fixation Device
- If bone graft is the *only* device used to render the joint immobile, the procedure is coded with the device value Nonautologous Tissue Substitute or Autologous Tissue Substitute
- If a mixture of autologous and nonautologous bone graft (with or without biological or synthetic extenders or binders) is used to render the joint immobile, code the procedure with the device value Autologous Tissue Substitute

Examples: Fusion of a vertebral joint using a cage style interbody fusion device containing morsellized bone graft is coded to the device Interbody Fusion Device.
Fusion of a vertebral joint using a bone dowel interbody fusion device made of cadaver bone and packed with a mixture of local morsellized bone and demineralized bone matrix is coded to the device Interbody Fusion Device.
Fusion of a vertebral joint using rigid plates affixed with screws and reinforced with bone cement is coded to the device Internal Fixation Device.
Fusion of a vertebral joint using both autologous bone graft and bone bank bone graft is coded to the device Autologous Tissue Substitute.

Inspection procedures
B3.11a
Inspection of a body part(s) performed in order to achieve the objective of a procedure is not coded separately.
Example: Fiberoptic bronchoscopy performed for irrigation of bronchus, only the irrigation procedure is coded.

B3.11b
If multiple tubular body parts are inspected, the most distal body part inspected is coded. If multiple non-tubular body parts in a region are inspected, the body part that specifies the entire area inspected is coded.
Examples: Cystoureteroscopy with inspection of bladder and ureters is coded to the ureter body part value.
Exploratory laparotomy with general inspection of abdominal contents is coded to the peritoneal cavity body part value.

B3.11c
When both an Inspection procedure and another procedure are performed on the same body part during the same episode, if the Inspection procedure is performed using a different approach than the other procedure, the Inspection procedure is coded separately.
Example: Endoscopic Inspection of the duodenum is coded separately when open Excision of the duodenum is performed during the same procedural episode.

Occlusion vs. Restriction for vessel embolization procedures
B3.12

8

If the objective of an embolization procedure is to completely close a vessel, the root operation Occlusion is coded. If the objective of an embolization procedure is to narrow the lumen of a vessel, the root operation Restriction is coded.

Examples: Tumor embolization is coded to the root operation Occlusion, because the objective of the procedure is to cut off the blood supply to the vessel.

Embolization of a cerebral aneurysm is coded to the root operation Restriction, because the objective of the procedure is not to close off the vessel entirely, but to narrow the lumen of the vessel at the site of the aneurysm where it is abnormally wide.

Release procedures

B3.13

In the root operation Release, the body part value coded is the body part being freed and not the tissue being manipulated or cut to free the body part.

Example: Lysis of intestinal adhesions is coded to the specific intestine body part value.

Release vs. Division

B3.14

If the sole objective of the procedure is freeing a body part without cutting the body part, the root operation is Release. If the sole objective of the procedure is separating or transecting a body part, the root operation is Division.

Examples: Freeing a nerve root from surrounding scar tissue to relieve pain is coded to the root operation Release. Severing a nerve root to relieve pain is coded to the root operation Division.

Reposition for fracture treatment

B3.15

Reduction of a displaced fracture is coded to the root operation Reposition and the application of a cast or splint in conjunction with the Reposition procedure is not coded separately. Treatment of a nondisplaced fracture is coded to the procedure performed.

Examples: Putting a pin in a nondisplaced fracture is coded to the root operation Insertion.

Casting of a nondisplaced fracture is coded to the root operation Immobilization in the Placement section.

Transplantation vs. Administration

B3.16

Putting in a mature and functioning living body part taken from another individual or animal is coded to the root operation Transplantation. Putting in autologous or nonautologous cells is coded to the Administration section.

Example: Putting in autologous or nonautologous bone marrow, pancreatic islet cells or stem cells is coded to the Administration section.

9

B4. Body Part

General guidelines
B4.1a
If a procedure is performed on a portion of a body part that does not have a separate body part value, code the body part value corresponding to the whole body part.
Example: A procedure performed on the alveolar process of the mandible is coded to the mandible body part.

B4.1b
If the prefix "peri" is combined with a body part to identify the site of the procedure, the procedure is coded to the body part named.
Example: A procedure site identified as perirenal is coded to the kidney body part.

Branches of body parts
B4.2
Where a specific branch of a body part does not have its own body part value in PCS, the body part is coded to the closest proximal branch that has a specific body part value.
Example: A procedure performed on the mandibular branch of the trigeminal nerve is coded to the trigeminal nerve body part value

Bilateral body part values
B4.3
Bilateral body part values are available for a limited number of body parts. If the identical procedure is performed on contralateral body parts, and a bilateral body part value exists for that body part, a single procedure is coded using the bilateral body part value. If no bilateral body part value exists, each procedure is coded separately using the appropriate body part value.
Example: The identical procedure performed on both fallopian tubes is coded once using the body part value Fallopian Tube, Bilateral. The identical procedure performed on both knee joints is coded twice using the body part values Knee Joint, Right and Knee Joint, Left.

Coronary arteries
B4.4
The coronary arteries are classified as a single body part that is further specified by number of sites treated and not by name or number of arteries. Separate body part values are used to specify the number of sites treated when the same procedure is performed on multiple sites in the coronary arteries.
Examples: Angioplasty of two distinct sites in the left anterior descending coronary artery with placement of two stents is coded as Dilation of Coronary Arteries, Two Sites, with Intraluminal Device.
Angioplasty of two distinct sites in the left anterior descending coronary artery, one with stent placed and one without, is coded separately as Dilation of Coronary Artery, One Site with Intraluminal Device, and Dilation of Coronary Artery, One Site with no device.

10

Tendons, ligaments, bursae and fascia near a joint
B4.5
Procedures performed on tendons, ligaments, bursae and fascia supporting a joint are coded to the body part in the respective body system that is the focus of the procedure. Procedures performed on joint structures themselves are coded to the body part in the joint body systems.
Example: Repair of the anterior cruciate ligament of the knee is coded to the knee bursa and ligament body part in the bursae and ligaments body system. Knee arthroscopy with shaving of articular cartilage is coded to the knee joint body part in the Lower Joints body system.

Skin, subcutaneous tissue and fascia overlying a joint
B4.6
If a procedure is performed on the skin, subcutaneous tissue or fascia overlying a joint, the procedure is coded to the following body part:
- Shoulder is coded to Upper Arm
- Elbow is coded to Lower Arm
- Wrist is coded to Lower Arm
- Hip is coded to Upper Leg
- Knee is coded to Lower Leg
- Ankle is coded to Foot

Fingers and toes
B4.7
If a body system does not contain a separate body part value for fingers, procedures performed on the fingers are coded to the body part value for the hand. If a body system does not contain a separate body part value for toes, procedures performed on the toes are coded to the body part value for the foot.
Example: Excision of finger muscle is coded to one of the hand muscle body part values in the Muscles body system.

B5. Approach

Open approach with percutaneous endoscopic assistance
B5.2
Procedures performed using the open approach with percutaneous endoscopic assistance are coded to the approach Open.
Example: Laparoscopic-assisted sigmoidectomy is coded to the approach Open.

External approach
B5.3a
Procedures performed within an orifice on structures that are visible without the aid of any instrumentation are coded to the approach External.
Example: Resection of tonsils is coded to the approach External.

B5.3b
Procedures performed indirectly by the application of external force through the intervening body layers are coded to the approach External.
Example: Closed reduction of fracture is coded to the approach External.

Percutaneous procedure via device
B5.4
Procedures performed percutaneously via a device placed for the procedure are coded to the approach Percutaneous.
Example: Fragmentation of kidney stone performed via percutaneous nephrostomy is coded to the approach Percutaneous.

B6. Device

General guidelines
B6.1a
A device is coded only if a device remains after the procedure is completed. If no device remains, the device value No Device is coded.

B6.1b
Materials such as sutures, ligatures, radiological markers and temporary post-operative wound drains are considered integral to the performance of a procedure and are not coded as devices.

B6.1c
Procedures performed on a device only and not on a body part are specified in the root operations Change, Irrigation, Removal and Revision, and are coded to the procedure performed.
Example: Irrigation of percutaneous nephrostomy tube is coded to the root operation Irrigation of indwelling device in the Administration section.

Drainage device
B6.2
A separate procedure to put in a drainage device is coded to the root operation Drainage with the device value Drainage Device.

Obstetric Section Guidelines (section 1)

C. Obstetrics Section

Products of conception
C1
Procedures performed on the products of conception are coded to the Obstetrics section. Procedures performed on the pregnant female other than the products of conception are coded to the appropriate root operation in the Medical and Surgical section.
Example: Amniocentesis is coded to the products of conception body part in the Obstetrics section. Repair of obstetric urethral laceration is coded to the urethra body part in the Medical and Surgical section.

Procedures following delivery or abortion
C2
Procedures performed following a delivery or abortion for curettage of the endometrium or evacuation of retained products of conception are all coded in the Obstetrics section, to the root operation Extraction and the body part Products of Conception, Retained. Diagnostic or therapeutic dilation and curettage performed during times other than the postpartum or post-abortion period are all coded in the Medical and Surgical section, to the root operation Extraction and the body part Endometrium.

14

Appendix B: ICD-10 Quick Reference

Quick Reference Information

➤➤➤➤➤➤➤➤➤➤➤➤➤➤➤➤➤➤➤➤➤➤➤➤➤➤➤➤

ICD-10-CM Classification Enhancements

The compliance date for implementation of the International Classification of Diseases, 10th Edition, Procedure Coding System/Clinical Modification (ICD-10-PCS/CM) is October 1, 2013 for all covered entities. ICD-10-CM, including the *ICD-10-CM Official Guidelines for Coding and Reporting*, will replace the International Classification of Diseases, 9th Edition, Clinical Modification (ICD-9-CM) diagnosis code set in all health care settings for diagnosis reporting with dates of service, or dates of discharge for inpatients, that occur on or after October 1, 2013. This publication discusses the benefits of ICD-10-CM, similarities and differences between the two coding systems, and new features and additional changes that can be found in ICD-10-CM.

BENEFITS OF ICD-10-CM

ICD-10-CM incorporates much greater clinical detail and specificity than ICD-9-CM. Terminology and disease classification have been updated to be consistent with current clinical practice. The modern classification system will provide much better data needed for:

➤ Measuring the quality, safety, and efficacy of care;

➤ Reducing the need for attachments to explain the patient's condition;

➤ Designing payment systems and processing claims for reimbursement;

➤ Conducting research, epidemiological studies, and clinical trials;

➤ Setting health policy;

➤ Operational and strategic planning;

➤ Designing health care delivery systems;

➤ Monitoring resource utilization;

➤ Improving clinical, financial, and administrative performance;

➤ Preventing and detecting health care fraud and abuse; and

➤ Tracking public health and risks.

Non-specific codes still exist for use when the medical record documentation does not support a more specific code.

SIMILARITIES AND DIFFERENCES BETWEEN THE TWO CODING SYSTEMS

ICD-10-CM uses 3–7 alpha and numeric digits and full code titles, but the format is very much the same as ICD-9-CM (e.g., ICD-10-CM has the same hierarchical structure as ICD-9-CM).

The 7th character in ICD-10-CM is used in several chapters (e.g., the Obstetrics, Injury, Musculoskeletal, and External Cause chapters). It has a different meaning depending on the section where it is being used (e.g., in the Injury and External Cause sections, the 7th character classifies an initial encounter, subsequent encounter, or sequelae (late effect)).

Primarily, changes in ICD-10-CM are in its organization and structure, code composition, and level of detail.

ICD-9-CM DIAGNOSES CODES:

➤ 3–5 digits;

➤ First digit is alpha (E or V) or numeric (alpha characters are not case sensitive);

➤ Digits 2–5 are numeric; and

➤ Decimal is used after third character.

Examples:

■ 496 – Chronic airway obstruction, not elsewhere classified (NEC);

■ 511.9 – Unspecified pleural effusion; and

■ V02.61 – Hepatitis B carrier.

ICD-10-CM DIAGNOSIS CODES:

➤ 3–7 digits;

➤ Digit 1 is alpha; Digit 2 is numeric;

➤ Digits 3–7 are alpha or numeric (alpha characters are not case sensitive); and

➤ Decimal is used after third character.

Examples:

■ A78 – Q fever;

■ A69.21 – Meningitis due to Lyme disease; and

■ S52.131A – Displaced fracture of neck of right radius, initial encounter for closed fracture.

NEW FEATURES FOUND IN ICD-10-CM

The following new features can be found in ICD-10-CM:

1) Laterality (left, right, bilateral)

Examples:

■ C50.511 – Malignant neoplasm of lower-outer quadrant of right female breast;

■ H16.013 – Central corneal ulcer, bilateral; and

■ L89.012 – Pressure ulcer of right elbow, stage II.   **1**

2) Combination codes for certain conditions and common associated symptoms and manifestations

Examples:

- K57.21 – Diverticulitis of large intestine with perforation and abscess with bleeding;
- E11.341 – Type 2 diabetes mellitus with severe nonproliferative diabetic retinopathy with macular edema; and
- I25.110 – Atherosclerotic heart disease of native coronary artery with unstable angina pectoris.

3) Combination codes for poisonings and their associated external cause

Example:

- T42.3x2S – Poisoning by barbiturates, intentional self-harm, sequela.

4) Obstetric codes identify trimester instead of episode of care

Example:

- O26.02 – Excessive weight gain in pregnancy, second trimester.

5) Character "x" is used as a 5th character placeholder in certain 6 character codes to allow for future expansion and to fill in other empty characters (e.g., character 5 and/or 6) when a code that is less than 6 characters in length requires a 7th character

Examples:

- T46.1x5A – Adverse effect of calcium-channel blockers, initial encounter; and
- T15.02xD – Foreign body in cornea, left eye, subsequent encounter.

6) Two types of Excludes notes

- ➤ Excludes 1 – Indicates that the code excluded should never be used with the code where the note is located (do not report both codes).

  Example:

  - **Q03** – Congenital hydrocephalus
    Excludes 1: Acquired hydrocephalus (**G91.-**)

- ➤ Excludes 2 – Indicates that the condition excluded is not part of the condition represented by the code but a patient may have both conditions at the same time, in which case both codes may be assigned together (both codes can be reported to capture both conditions).

  Example:

  - L27.2 – Dermatitis due to ingested food.
    Excludes 2: Dermatitis due to food in contact with skin (L23.6, L24.6, L25.4).

7) Inclusion of clinical concepts that do not exist in ICD-9-CM (e.g., underdosing, blood type, blood alcohol level)

Examples:

- T45.526D – Underdosing of antithrombotic drugs, subsequent encounter;
- Z67.40 – Type 0 blood, Rh positive; and
- Y90.6 – Blood alcohol level of 120–199 mg/100 ml.

8) A number of codes have been significantly expanded (e.g., injuries, diabetes, substance abuse, postoperative complications)

Examples:

- E10.610 – Type 1 diabetes mellitus with diabetic neuropathic arthropathy;
- F10.182 – Alcohol abuse with alcohol-induced sleep disorder; and
- T82.02xA – Displacement of heart valve prosthesis, initial encounter.

9) Codes for postoperative complications have been expanded and a distinction made between intraoperative complications and postprocedural disorders

Examples:

- D78.01 – Intraoperative hemorrhage and hematoma of spleen complicating a procedure on the spleen; and
- D78.21 – Postprocedural hemorrhage and hematoma of spleen following a procedure on the spleen.

ADDITIONAL CHANGES FOUND IN ICD-10-CM

The additional changes that can be found in ICD-10-CM are:

- ➤ Injuries are grouped by anatomical site rather than by type of injury;
- ➤ Category restructuring and code reorganization have occurred in a number of ICD-10-CM chapters, resulting in the classification of certain diseases and disorders that are different from ICD-9-CM;
- ➤ Certain diseases have been reclassified to different chapters or sections in order to reflect current medical knowledge;
- ➤ New code definitions (e.g., definition of acute myocardial infarction is now 4 weeks rather than 8 weeks); and
- ➤ The codes corresponding to ICD-9-CM V codes (Factors Influencing Health Status and Contact with Health Services) and E codes (External Causes of Injury and Poisoning) are incorporated into the main classification rather than separated into supplementary classifications as they were in ICD-9-CM.

To find additional information about ICD-10-CM/PCS, visit http://www.cms.hhs.gov/ICD10 on the Centers for Medicare & Medicaid Services (CMS) website.

Appendix C: Institutional Claim 4010A to 5010

INSTITUTIONAL CLAIM

4010A1

837-I 4010A1

Element Identifier	Description	ID	Min. Max.	Usage Reg.	Loop	Loop Repeat	Values
ISA	INTERCHANGE CONTROL HEADER		1	R	___	1	
ISA01	Authorization Information Qualifier	ID	2-2	R			00, 03
ISA02	Authorization Information	AN	10-10	R			
ISA03	Security Information Qualifier	ID	2-2	R			00, 01
ISA04	Security Information	AN	10-10	R			
ISA05	Interchange ID Qualifier	ID	2-2	R			01, 14, 20, 27, 28, 29, 30, 33, ZZ
ISA06	Interchange Sender ID	AN	15-15	R			
ISA07	Interchange ID Qualifier	ID	2-2	R			01, 14, 20, 27, 28, 29, 30, 33, ZZ
ISA08	Interchange Receiver ID	AN	15-15	R			
ISA09	Interchange Date	DT	6-6	R			YYMMDD
ISA10	Interchange Time	TM	4-4	R			HHMM
ISA11	Interchange Control Standards ID		1-1	R			
ISA12	Interchange Control Version Number	ID	5-5	R			
ISA13	Interchange Control Number	N0	9-9	R			
ISA14	Acknowledgement Requested	ID	1-1	R			0, 1
ISA15	Usage Indicator	ID	1-1	R			P, T
ISA16	Component Element Separator	AN	1-1	R			
GS	FUNCTIONAL GROUP HEADER		1	R	___	1	
GS01	Functional Identifier Code	ID	2-2	R			
GS02	Application Sender Code	AN	2-15	R			
GS03	Application Receiver Code	AN	2-15	R			
GS04	Date	DT	8-8	R			CCYYMMDD
GS05	Time	TM	4-8	R			HHMM, HHMMSS, HHMMSSD, HHMMSSDD
GS06	Group Control Number	N0	1-9	R			
GS07	Responsible Agency Code	ID	1-2	R			X
GS08	Version Identifier Code	AN	1-12	R			004010X096A1

5010

837-I 5010

Element Identifier	Description	ID	Min. Max.	Usage Reg.	Loop	Loop Repeat	Values	
ISA	INTERCHANGE CONTROL HEADER		1	R	___	1		
ISA01	Authorization Information Qualifier	ID	2-2	R			00, 03	
ISA02	Authorization Information	AN	10-10	R				
ISA03	Security Information Qualifier	ID	2-2	R			00, 01	
ISA04	Security Information	AN	10-10	R				
ISA05	Interchange ID Qualifier	ID	2-2	R			01, 14, 20, 27, 28, 29, 30, 33, ZZ	
ISA06	Interchange Sender ID	AN	15-15	R				
ISA07	Interchange ID Qualifier	ID	2-2	R			01, 14, 20, 27, 28, 29, 30, 33, ZZ	
ISA08	Interchange Receiver ID	AN	15-15	R				
ISA09	Interchange Date	DT	6-6	R			YYMMDD	
ISA10	Interchange Time	TM	4-4	R			HHMM	
ISA11	Interchange Control Standards ID		1-1	R				
ISA12	Interchange Control Version Number	ID	5-5	R			00501	
ISA13	Interchange Control Number	N0	9-9	R				
ISA14	Acknowledgement Requested	ID	1-1	R			0, 1	
ISA15	Usage Indicator	ID	1-1	R			P, T	
ISA16	Component Element Separator	AN	1-1	R				
GS	FUNCTIONAL GROUP HEADER		1	R	___	1		
GS01	Functional Identifier Code	ID	2-2	R				
GS02	Application Sender Code	AN	2-15	R				
GS03	Application Receiver Code	AN	2-15	R				
GS04	Date	DT	8-8	R			CCYYMMDD	
GS05	Time	TM	4-8	R			HHMM, HHMMSS, HHMMSSD, HHMMSSDD	
GS06	Group Control Number	N0	1-9	R				
GS07	Responsible Agency Code	ID	1-2	R			X	
GS08	Version Identifier Code	AN	1-12	R			005010X223	Code Change

Page 1 of 93

INSTITUTIONAL CLAIM

4010A1

837-I 4010A1

Element Identifier	Description	ID	Min. Max.	Usage Reg.	Loop	Loop Repeat	Values
ST	TRANSACTION SET HEADER		1	R	___	>1	
ST01	Transaction Set Identifier Code	ID	3-3	R			837
ST02	Transaction Set Control Number	AN	4-9	R			
BHT	BEGINNING OF HIERARCHICAL TRANSACTION		1	R	___	1	
BHT01	Hierarchical Structure Code	ID	4-4	R			0019
BHT02	Transaction Set Purpose Code	ID	2-2	R			00, 18
BHT03	Originator Application Transaction ID	AN	1-30	R			
BHT04	Transaction Set Creation Date	DT	8-8	R			CCYYMMDD
BHT05	Transaction Set Creation Time	TM	4-8	R			HHMM, HHMMSS, HHMMSSD, HHMMSSDD
BHT06	Claim or Encounter ID	ID	2-2	R.			CH, RP
REF	TRANSMISSION TYPE IDENTIFICATION		1	S			
REF01	Reference Identification Qualifier	ID	2-3	R			87
REF02	Reference Identification	AN	1-30	R			
REF03	Description	AN	1-80	N/U			
REF04	Reference Identifier			N/U			
NM1	SUBMITTER NAME		1	R	1000A	1	
NM101	Entity Identifier Code	ID	2-3	R			41
NM102	Entity Type Qualifier	ID	1-1	R			1, 2
NM103	Submitter Last or Organization Name	AN	1-35	R			
NM104	Submitter First Name	AN	1-25	S			
NM105	Submitter Middle Name	AN	1-25	S			
NM106	Name Prefix	AN	1-10	N/U			
NM107	Name Suffix	AN	1-10	N/U			
NM108	Identification Code Qualifier	ID	1-2	R			46
NM109	Submitter Identifier	AN	2-80	R			
NM110	Entity Relationship Code	ID	2-2	N/U			
NM111	Entity Identifier Code	ID	2-3	N/U			

5010

837-I 5010

Element Identifier	Description	ID	Min. Max.	Usage Reg.	Loop	Loop Repeat	Values	
ST	TRANSACTION SET HEADER		1	R	___	>1		
ST01	Transaction Set Identifier Code	ID	3-3	R			837	
ST02	Transaction Set Control Number	AN	4-9	R				
ST03	Implementation Convention Reference	AN	1-35	R				New Element
BHT	BEGINNING OF HIERARCHICAL TRANSACTION		1	R	___	1		
BHT01	Hierarchical Structure Code	ID	4-4	R			0019	
BHT02	Transaction Set Purpose Code	ID	2-2	R			00, 18	
BHT03	Originator Application Transaction ID	AN	1-50	R				Increase from 30 - 50
BHT04	Transaction Set Creation Date	DT	8-8	R			CCYYMMDD	
BHT05	Transaction Set Creation Time	TM	4-8	R			HHMM, HHMMSS, HHMMSSD, HHMMSSDD	
BHT06	Claim or Encounter ID	ID	2-2	R			31, CH, RP	Code Added
								Segment Deleted
NM1	SUBMITTER NAME		1	R	1000A	1		
NM101	Entity Identifier Code	ID	2-3	R			41	
NM102	Entity Type Qualifier	ID	1-1	R			1, 2	
NM103	Submitter Last or Organization Name	AN	1-60	R				Increase from 35 - 60
NM104	Submitter First Name	AN	1-35	S				Increase from 25 - 35
NM105	Submitter Middle Name	AN	1-25	S				
NM106	Name Prefix	AN	1-10	N/U				
NM107	Name Suffix	AN	1-10	N/U				
NM108	Identification Code Qualifier	ID	1-2	R			46	
NM109	Submitter Identifier	AN	2-80	R				
NM110	Entity Relationship Code	ID	2-2	N/U				
NM111	Entity Identifier Code	ID	2-3	N/U				
NM112	Name Last or Organization Name	AN	1-60	N/U				New Element

Page 2 of 93

INSTITUTIONAL CLAIM

Element Identifier	Description	ID	Min. Max.	Usage Req.	Loop	Loop Repeat	Values
	4010A1						
	837-I 4010A1						
PER	**SUBMITTER EDI CONTACT INFORMATION**		2	R	1000A		
PER01	Contact Function Code	ID	2-2	R			IC
PER02	Submitter Contact Name	AN	1-60	R			
PER03	Communication Number Qualifier	ID	2-2	R			ED, EM, FX. TE
PER04	Communication Number	AN	1-80	R			
PER05	Communication Number Qualifier	ID	2-2	S			ED, EM, EX, FX, TE
PER06	Communication Number	AN	1-80	S			
PER07	Communication Number Qualifier	ID	2-2	S			ED, EM, EX, FX, TE
PER08	Communication Number	AN	1-80	S			
PER09	Contact Inquiry Reference	AN	1-20	N/U			
NM1	**RECEIVER NAME**		1	R	1000B	1	
NM101	Entity Identifier Code	ID	2-3	R			40
NM102	Entity Type Qualifier	ID	1-1	R			2
NM103	Receiver Name	AN	1-35	R			
NM104	Name First	AN	1-25	N/U			
NM105	Name Middle	AN	1-25	N/U			
NM106	Name Prefix	AN	1-10	N/U			
NM107	Name Suffix	AN	1-10	N/U			
NM108	Identification Code Qualifier	ID	1-2	R			46
NM109	Receiver Primary Identifier	AN	2-80	R			
NM110	Entity Relationship Code	ID	2-2	N/U			
NM111	Entity Identifier Code	ID	2-3	N/U			
HL	**BILLING/PAY-TO PROVIDER HIERARCHICAL LEVEL**		1	R	2000A	>1	
HL01	Hierarchical ID Number	AN	1-12	R			
HL02	Hierarchical Parent ID Number	AN	1-12	N/U			
HL03	Hierarchical Level Code	ID	1-2	R			20
HL04	Hierarchical Child Code	ID	1-1	R			1
PRV	**BILLING/PAY-TO PROVIDER SPECIALTY INFORMATION**		1	S	2000A		
PRV01	Provider Code	ID	1-3	R			BI, PT
PRV02	Reference Identification Qualifier	ID	2-3	R			ZZ
PRV03	Provider Taxonomy Code	AN	1-30	R			
PRV04	State or Province Code	ID	2-2	N/U			

Element Identifier	Description	ID	Min. Max.	Usage Req.	Loop	Loop Repeat	Values	
	5010							
	837-I 5010							
PER	**SUBMITTER EDI CONTACT INFORMATION**		2	R	1000A			
PER01	Contact Function Code	ID	2-2	R			IC	
PER02	Submitter Contact Name	AN	1-60	S				Usage change to Situational
PER03	Communication Number Qualifier	ID	2-2	R			EM, FX. TE	Code deleted
PER04	Communication Number	AN	1-256	R				Increase from 80 - 256
PER05	Communication Number Qualifier	ID	2-2	S			EM, EX, FX, TE	Code deleted
PER06	Communication Number	AN	1-256	S				Increase from 80 - 256
PER07	Communication Number Qualifier	ID	2-2	S			EM, FX, TE	Code deleted
PER08	Communication Number	AN	1-256	S				Increase from 80 - 256
PER09	Contact Inquiry Reference	AN	1-20	N/U				
NM1	**RECEIVER NAME**		1	R	1000B	1		
NM101	Entity Identifier Code	ID	2-3	R			40	
NM102	Entity Type Qualifier	ID	1-1	R			2	
NM103	Receiver Name	AN	1-60	R				Increase from 35 - 60
NM104	Name First	AN	1-35	N/U				Increase from 25 - 35
NM105	Name Middle	AN	1-25	N/U				
NM106	Name Prefix	AN	1-10	N/U				
NM107	Name Suffix	AN	1-10	N/U				
NM108	Identification Code Qualifier	ID	1-2	R			46	
NM109	Receiver Primary Identifier	AN	2-80	R				
NM110	Entity Relationship Code	ID	2-2	N/U				
NM111	Entity Identifier Code	ID	2-3	N/U				
NM112	Name Last or Organization Name	AN	1-60	N/U				New Element
HL	**BILLING PROVIDER HIERARCHICAL LEVEL**		1	R	2000A	>1		Name Change
HL01	Hierarchical ID Number	AN	1-12	R				
HL02	Hierarchical Parent ID Number	AN	1-12	N/U				
HL03	Hierarchical Level Code	ID	1-2	R			20	
HL04	Hierarchical Child Code	ID	1-1	R			1	
PRV	**BILLING PROVIDER SPECIALTY INFORMATION**		1	S	2000A			Name Change
PRV01	Provider Code	ID	1-3	R			BI	Code Deleted
PRV02	Reference Identification Qualifier	ID	2-3	R			PXC	Code Change
PRV03	Provider Taxonomy Code	AN	1-50	R				Increase from 30 - 50
PRV04	State or Province Code	ID	2-2	N/U				

Page 3 of 93

INSTITUTIONAL CLAIM

4010A1							
Element Identifier	Description	ID	Min. Max.	Usage Reg.	Loop	Loop Repeat	Values
837-I 4010A1							
PRV05	PROVIDER SPECIALTY INFORMATION			N/U			
PRV06	Provider Organization Code	ID	3-3	N/U			
CUR	**FOREIGN CURRENCY INFORMATION**		1	S	2000A		
CUR01	Entity Identifier Code	ID	2-3	R			85
CUR02	Currency Code	ID	3-3	R			
CUR03	Exchange Rate	R	4-10	N/U			
CUR04	Entity Identifier Code	ID	2-3	N/U			
CUR05	Currency Code	ID	3-3	N/U			
CUR06	Currency Market/Exchange Code	ID	3-3	N/U			
CUR07	Date/Time Qualifier	ID	3-3	N/U			
CUR08	Date	DT	8-8	N/U			
CUR09	Time	TM	4-8	N/U			
CUR10	Date/Time Qualifier	ID	3-3	N/U			
CUR11	Date	DT	8-8	N/U			
CUR12	Time	TM	4-8	N/U			
CUR13	Date/Time Qualifier	ID	3-3	N/U			
CUR14	Date	DT	8-8	N/U			
CUR15	Time	TM	4-8	N/U			
CUR16	Date/Time Qualifier	ID	3-3	N/U			
CUR17	Date	DT	8-8	N/U			
CUR18	Time	TM	4-8	N/U			
CUR19	Date/Time Qualifier	ID	3-3	N/U			
CUR20	Date	DT	8-8	N/U			
CUR21	Time	TM	4-8	N/U			
NM1	**Billing Provider Name**		1	R	2010AA	1	
NM101	Entity Identifier Code	ID	2-3	R			85
NM102	Entity Type Qualifier	ID	1-1	R			2
NM103	Billing Provider Last or Organizational Name	AN	1-35	R			
NM104	Name First	AN	1-25	N/U			
NM105	Name Middle	AN	1-25	N/U			
NM106	Name Prefix	AN	1-10	N/U			
NM107	Name Suffix	AN	1-10	N/U			
NM108	Identification Code Qualifier	ID	1-2	R			24, 34, XX
NM109	Billing Provider Identifier	AN	2-80	S			
NM110	Entity Relationship Code	ID	2-2	N/U			
NM111	Entity Identifier Code	ID	2-3	N/U			

5010								
Element Identifier	Description	ID	Min. Max.	Usage Reg.	Loop	Loop Repeat	Values	
837-I 5010								
PRV05	PROVIDER SPECIALTY INFORMATION			N/U				
PRV06	Provider Organization Code	ID	3-3	N/U				
CUR	**FOREIGN CURRENCY INFORMATION**		1	S	2000A			
CUR01	Entity Identifier Code	ID	2-3	R			85	
CUR02	Currency Code	ID	3-3	R				
CUR03	Exchange Rate	R	4-10	N/U				
CUR04	Entity Identifier Code	ID	2-3	N/U				
CUR05	Currency Code	ID	3-3	N/U				
CUR06	Currency Market/Exchange Code	ID	3-3	N/U				
CUR07	Date/Time Qualifier	ID	3-3	N/U				
CUR08	Date	DT	8-8	N/U				
CUR09	Time	TM	4-8	N/U				
CUR10	Date/Time Qualifier	ID	3-3	N/U				
CUR11	Date	DT	8-8	N/U				
CUR12	Time	TM	4-8	N/U				
CUR13	Date/Time Qualifier	ID	3-3	N/U				
CUR14	Date	DT	8-8	N/U				
CUR15	Time	TM	4-8	N/U				
CUR16	Date/Time Qualifier	ID	3-3	N/U				
CUR17	Date	DT	8-8	N/U				
CUR18	Time	TM	4-8	N/U				
CUR19	Date/Time Qualifier	ID	3-3	N/U				
CUR20	Date	DT	8-8	N/U				
CUR21	Time	TM	4-8	N/U				
NM1	**Billing Provider Name**		1	R	2010AA	1		
NM101	Entity Identifier Code	ID	2-3	R			85	
NM102	Entity Type Qualifier	ID	1-1	R			2	
NM103	Billing Provider Last or Organizational Name	AN	1-60	R				Increase from 35 - 60
NM104	Billing Provider First Name	AN	1-35	N/U				Increase from 25 - 35
NM105	Billing Provider Middle Name	AN	1-25	N/U				
NM106	Name Prefix	AN	1-10	N/U				
NM107	Billing Provider Name Suffix	AN	1-10	N/U				
NM108	Identification Code Qualifier	ID	1-2	S			XX	Code Deleted Usage change to Situational
NM109	Billing Provider Identifier	AN	2-80	S				
NM110	Entity Relationship Code	ID	2-2	N/U				
NM111	Entity Identifier Code	ID	2-3	N/U				
NM112	Name Last or Organization Name	AN	1-60	N/U				New Element

Page 4 of 93

INSTITUTIONAL CLAIM

4010A1						
Element Identifier	Description	ID	Min. Max.	Usage Reg.	Loop	Loop Repeat	Values

837-I 4010A1

Element Identifier	Description	ID	Min. Max.	Usage Reg.	Loop	Loop Repeat	Values
N3	BILLING PROVIDER ADDRESS		1	R	2010AA		
N301	Billing Provider Address Line	AN	1-55	R			
N302	Billing Provider Address Line	AN	1-55	S			
N4	BILLING PROVIDER CITY/STATE/ZIP CODE		1	R	2010AA		
N401	Billing Provider City Name	AN	2-30	R			
N402	Billing Provider State or Province Code	ID	2-2	R			
N403	Billing Provider Postal Zone or ZIP Code	ID	3-15	R			
N404	Country Code	ID	2-3	S			
N405	Location Qualifier	ID	1-2	N/U			
N406	Location Identifier	AN	1-30	N/U			
REF	BILLING PROVIDER TAX IDENTIFICATION		8	R	2010AA		
REF01	Reference Identification Qualifier	ID	2-3	R			0B, 1A, 1B, 1C, 1D, 1G, 1H, 1J, B3, BQ, EI, FH, G2, G5, LU, SY, X5
REF02	Billing Provider Additional Identifier	AN	1-30	R			
REF03	Description	AN	1-80	N/U			
REF04	REFERENCE IDENTIFIER			N/U			
REF	CREDIT/DEBIT CARD BILLING INFORMATION		8	S	2010AA		
REF01	Reference Identification Qualifier	ID	2-3	R			06, 8U, EM, IJ, LU, RB, ST, TT
REF02	Billing Provider Additional Identifier	AN	1-30	R			
REF03	Description	AN	1-80	N/U			
REF04	REFERENCE IDENTIFIER			N/U			
PER	BILLING PROVIDER CONTACT INFORMATION		2	S	2010AA		
PER01	Contact Function Code	ID	2-2	R			IC
PER02	Billing Provider Contact Name	AN	1-60	R			
PER03	Communication Number Qualifier	ID	2-2	R			EM, FX, TE
PER04	Communication Number	AN	1-80	R			
PER05	Communication Number Qualifier	ID	2-2	S			EM, EX, FX, TE

5010						
Element Identifier	Description	ID	Min. Max.	Usage Reg.	Loop	Loop Repeat	Values

837-I 5010

Element Identifier	Description	ID	Min. Max.	Usage Reg.	Loop	Loop Repeat	Values	(notes)
N3	BILLING PROVIDER ADDRESS		1	R	2010AA			
N301	Billing Provider Address Line	AN	1-55	R				
N302	Billing Provider Address Line	AN	1-55	S				
N4	BILLING PROVIDER CITY/STATE/ZIP CODE		1	R	2010AA			
N401	Billing Provider City Name	AN	2-30	R				
N402	Billing Provider State or Province Code	ID	2-2	S				Usage change to Situational
N403	Billing Provider Postal Zone or ZIP Code	ID	3-15	S				Usage change to Situational
N404	Country Code	ID	2-3	S				
N405	Location Qualifier	ID	1-2	N/U				
N406	Location Identifier	AN	1-30	N/U				
N407	Country Subdivision Code	ID	1-3	S				New Element
REF	BILLING PROVIDER TAX IDENTIFICATION		1	R	2010AA			# Repeats change to 1
REF01	Reference Identification Qualifier	ID	2-3	R			EI	Code Deleted
REF02	Billing Provider Additional Identifier	AN	1-50	R				Increase from 30 - 50
REF03	Description	AN	1-80	N/U				
REF04	REFERENCE IDENTIFIER			N/U				
								Segment Deleted
PER	BILLING PROVIDER CONTACT INFORMATION		2	S	2010AA			
PER01	Contact Function Code	ID	2-2	R			IC	
PER02	Billing Provider Contact Name	AN	1-60	S				Usage change to Situational
PER03	Communication Number Qualifier	ID	2-2	R			EM, FX, TE	
PER04	Communication Number	AN	1-256	R				Increase from 80 - 256
PER05	Communication Number Qualifier	ID	2-2	S			EM, EX, FX, TE	

Page 5 of 93

INSTITUTIONAL CLAIM

4010A1

837-I 4010A1

Element Identifier	Description	ID	Min. Max.	Usage Reg.	Loop	Loop Repeat	Values
PER06	Communication Number	AN	1-80	S			
PER07	Communication Number Qualifier	ID	2-2	S			EM, EX, FX, TE
PER08	Communication Number	AN	1-80	S			
PER09	Contact Inquiry Reference	AN	1-20	N/U			
NM1	PAY-TO PROVIDER NAME		1	S	2010AB	1	
NM101	Entity Identifier Code	ID	2-3	R			87
NM102	Entity Type Qualifier	ID	1-1	R			2
NM103	Pay-to Provider Last or Organization Name	AN	1-35	N/U			
NM104	Name First	AN	1-25	N/U			
NM105	Name Middle	AN	1-25	N/U			
NM106	Name Prefix	AN	1-10	N/U			
NM107	Name Suffix	AN	1-10	N/U			
NM108	Identification Code Qualifier	ID	1-2	N/U			24, 34, XX
NM109	Pay-to Provider Identifier	AN	2-80	N/U			
NM110	Entity Relationship Code	ID	2-2	N/U			
NM111	Entity Identifier Code	ID	2-3	N/U			
N3	PAY-TO PROVIDER ADDRESS		1	R	2010AB		
N301	Pay-to Provider Address Line	AN	1-55	R			
N302	Pay-to Provider Address Line	AN	1-55	S			
N4	PAY-TO PROVIDER CITY/STATE/ZIP CODE		1	R	2010AB		
N401	Pay-to Provider City Name	AN	2-30	R			
N402	Pay-to Provider State Code	ID	2-2	R			
N403	Pay-to Provider Postal Zone or ZIP Code	ID	3-15	R			
N404	Pay-to Provider Country Code	ID	2-3	S			
N405	Location Qualifier	ID	1-2	N/U			
N406	Location Identifier	AN	1-30	N/U			
REF	PAY-TO PROVIDER SECONDARY IDENTIFICATION		5	S	2010AB		0B, 1A, 1B, 1C, 1D, 1G, 1H, 1J, B3, BQ, EI, FH, G2, G5, LU, SY, X5

5010

837-I 5010

Element Identifier	Description	ID	Min. Max.	Usage Reg.	Loop	Loop Repeat	Values	Notes
PER06	Communication Number	AN	1-256	S				Increase from 80 - 256
PER07	Communication Number Qualifier	ID	2-2	S			EM, EX, FX, TE	
PER08	Communication Number	AN	1-256	S				Increase from 80 - 256
PER09	Contact Inquiry Reference	AN	1-20	N/U				
NM1	PAY-TO ADDRESS NAME		1	S	2010AB	1		Name Change
NM101	Entity Identifier Code	ID	2-3	R			87	
NM102	Entity Type Qualifier	ID	1-1	R			2	
NM103	Pay-to Provider Last or Organization Name	AN	1-60	N/U				Increase from 35 - 60
NM104	Pay-to Provider First Name	AN	1-35	N/U				Increase from 25 - 35 / Name Change
NM105	Pay-to Provider Middle Name	AN	1-25	N/U				Name Change
NM106	Name Prefix	AN	1-10	N/U				
NM107	Pay-to Provider Name Suffix	AN	1-10	N/U				Name Change
NM108	Identification Code Qualifier	ID	1-2	N/U				Code Deleted
NM109	Pay-to Provider Identifier	AN	2-80	N/U				
NM110	Entity Relationship Code	ID	2-2	N/U				
NM111	Entity Identifier Code	ID	2-3	N/U				
NM112	Name Last or Organization Name	AN	1-60	N/U				New Element
N3	PAY-TO PROVIDER ADDRESS		1	R	2010AB			
N301	Pay-to Provider Address Line	AN	1-55	R				
N302	Pay-to Provider Address Line	AN	1-55	S				
N4	PAY-TO PROVIDER CITY/STATE/ZIP CODE		1	R	2010AB			
N401	Pay-to Provider City Name	AN	2-30	R				
N402	Pay-to Provider State Code	ID	2-2	S				Usage change to
N403	Pay-to Provider Postal Zone or ZIP Code	ID	3-15	S				Usage change to Situational
N404	Pay-to Provider Country Code	ID	2-3	S				
N405	Location Qualifier	ID	1-2	N/U				
N406	Location Identifier	AN	1-30	N/U				
N407	Country Subdivision Code	ID	1-3	S				New Element
								Segment Deleted

INSTITUTIONAL CLAIM

<table>
<thead>
<tr><th colspan="7">4010A1</th></tr>
<tr><th>Element Identifier</th><th>Description</th><th>ID</th><th>Min. Max.</th><th>Usage Reg.</th><th>Loop</th><th>Loop Repeat</th><th>Values</th></tr>
</thead>
<tbody>
<tr><td colspan="8">837-I 4010A1</td></tr>
<tr><td>REF01</td><td>Reference Identification Qualifier</td><td>ID</td><td>2-3</td><td>R</td><td></td><td></td><td></td></tr>
<tr><td>REF02</td><td>Billing Provider Additional Identifier</td><td>AN</td><td>1-30</td><td>R</td><td></td><td></td><td></td></tr>
<tr><td>REF03</td><td>Description</td><td>AN</td><td>1-80</td><td>N/U</td><td></td><td></td><td></td></tr>
<tr><td>REF04</td><td>REFERENCE IDENTIFIER</td><td></td><td></td><td>N/U</td><td></td><td></td><td></td></tr>
</tbody>
</table>

<table>
<thead>
<tr><th colspan="8">5010</th></tr>
<tr><th>Element Identifier</th><th>Description</th><th>ID</th><th>Min. Max.</th><th>Usage Reg.</th><th>Loop</th><th>Loop Repeat</th><th>Values</th></tr>
</thead>
<tbody>
<tr><td colspan="8">837-I 5010</td></tr>
<tr><td>NM1</td><td>PAY TO PLAN NAME</td><td></td><td>1</td><td>S</td><td>2010AC</td><td>1</td><td></td><td>New Segment</td></tr>
<tr><td>NM101</td><td>Entity Identifier Code</td><td>ID</td><td>2-3</td><td>R</td><td></td><td></td><td>PE</td></tr>
<tr><td>NM102</td><td>Entity Type Qualifier</td><td>ID</td><td>1-1</td><td>R</td><td></td><td></td><td>2</td></tr>
<tr><td>NM103</td><td>Pay to Plan Organizational Name</td><td>AN</td><td>1-60</td><td>R</td><td></td><td></td><td></td></tr>
<tr><td>NM104</td><td>Name First</td><td>AN</td><td>1-35</td><td>N/U</td><td></td><td></td><td></td></tr>
<tr><td>NM105</td><td>Name Middle</td><td>AN</td><td>1-25</td><td>N/U</td><td></td><td></td><td></td></tr>
<tr><td>NM106</td><td>Name Prefix</td><td>AN</td><td>1-10</td><td>N/U</td><td></td><td></td><td></td></tr>
<tr><td>NM107</td><td>Name Suffix</td><td>AN</td><td>1-10</td><td>N/U</td><td></td><td></td><td></td></tr>
<tr><td>NM108</td><td>Identification Code Qualifier</td><td>ID</td><td>1-2</td><td>R</td><td></td><td></td><td>PI, XV</td></tr>
<tr><td>NM109</td><td>Identification Code</td><td>AN</td><td>2-80</td><td>R</td><td></td><td></td><td></td></tr>
<tr><td>NM110</td><td>Entity Relationship Code</td><td>ID</td><td>2-2</td><td>N/U</td><td></td><td></td><td></td></tr>
<tr><td>NM111</td><td>Entity Identifier Code</td><td>ID</td><td>2-3</td><td>N/U</td><td></td><td></td><td></td></tr>
<tr><td>NM112</td><td>Name Last or Organization Name</td><td>AN</td><td>1-60</td><td>N/U</td><td></td><td></td><td></td></tr>
<tr><td>N3</td><td>PAY-TO PLAN ADDRESS</td><td></td><td>1</td><td>R</td><td>2010AC</td><td></td><td></td><td>New Segment</td></tr>
<tr><td>N301</td><td>Pay-to Plan Address Line</td><td>AN</td><td>1-55</td><td>R</td><td></td><td></td><td></td></tr>
<tr><td>N302</td><td>Pay-to Plan Address Line</td><td>AN</td><td>1-55</td><td>S</td><td></td><td></td><td></td></tr>
<tr><td>N4</td><td>PAY-TO PLAN CITY/STATE/ZIP CODE</td><td></td><td>1</td><td>R</td><td>2010AC</td><td></td><td></td><td>New Segment</td></tr>
<tr><td>N401</td><td>Pay-to Plan City Name</td><td>AN</td><td>2-30</td><td>R</td><td></td><td></td><td></td></tr>
<tr><td>N402</td><td>Pay-to Plan State Code</td><td>ID</td><td>2-2</td><td>S</td><td></td><td></td><td></td></tr>
<tr><td>N403</td><td>Pay-to Plan Postal Zone or ZIP Code</td><td>ID</td><td>3-15</td><td>S</td><td></td><td></td><td></td></tr>
<tr><td>N404</td><td>Pay-to Plan Country Code</td><td>ID</td><td>2-3</td><td>S</td><td></td><td></td><td></td></tr>
<tr><td>N405</td><td>Location Qualifier</td><td>ID</td><td>1-2</td><td>N/U</td><td></td><td></td><td></td></tr>
<tr><td>N406</td><td>Location Identifier</td><td>AN</td><td>1-30</td><td>N/U</td><td></td><td></td><td></td></tr>
<tr><td>N407</td><td>Country Subdivision Code</td><td>ID</td><td>1-3</td><td>S</td><td></td><td></td><td></td></tr>
<tr><td>REF</td><td>SECONDARY IDENTIFICATION</td><td></td><td>1</td><td>S</td><td>2010AC</td><td></td><td></td><td>New Segment</td></tr>
<tr><td>REF01</td><td>Reference Identification Qualifier</td><td>ID</td><td>2-3</td><td>R</td><td></td><td></td><td>2U, FY, NF</td></tr>
<tr><td>REF02</td><td>Reference Identification</td><td>AN</td><td>1-50</td><td>R</td><td></td><td></td><td></td></tr>
<tr><td>REF03</td><td>Description</td><td>AN</td><td>1-80</td><td>N/U</td><td></td><td></td><td></td></tr>
<tr><td>REF04</td><td>REFERENCE IDENTIFIER</td><td></td><td></td><td>N/U</td><td></td><td></td><td></td></tr>
<tr><td>REF</td><td>PAY-TO PLAN TAX IDENTIFICATION</td><td></td><td>1</td><td>R</td><td>2010AC</td><td></td><td></td><td>New Segment</td></tr>
</tbody>
</table>

Page 7 of 93

INSTITUTIONAL CLAIM

4010A1

837-I 4010A1

Element Identifier	Description	ID	Min. Max.	Usage Reg.	Loop	Loop Repeat	Values
HL	**SUBSCRIBER HIERARCHICAL LEVEL**		1	R	2000B	>1	
HL01	Hierarchical ID Number	AN	1-12	R			
HL02	Hierarchical Parent ID Number	AN	1-12	R			
HL03	Hierarchical Level Code	ID	1-2	R			22
HL04	Hierarchical Child Code	ID	1-1	R			0, 1
SBR	**SUBSCRIBER INFORMATION**		1	R	2000B		
SBR01	Payer Responsibility Sequence Number Code	ID	1-1	R			P, S, T
SBR02	Individual Relationship Code	ID	2-2	S			18
SBR03	Insured Group or Policy Number	AN	1-30	S			
SBR04	Insured Group Name	AN	1-60	S			
SBR05	Insurance Type Code	ID	1-3	N/U			
SBR06	Coordination of Benefits Code	ID	1-1	N/U			
SBR07	Yes/No Condition or Response Code	ID	1-1	N/U			
SBR08	Employment Status Code	ID	2-2	N/U			
SBR09	Claim Filing Indicator Code	ID	1-2	S			09, 10, 11, 12, 13, 14, 15, 16, AM, BL, CH, CI, DS, HM, LI, LM, MA, MB, MC, OF, TV, VA, WC, ZZ
NM1	**SUBSCRIBER NAME**		1	R	2010BA	1	
NM101	Entity Identifier Code	ID	2-3	R			IL
NM102	Entity Type Qualifier	ID	1-1	R			1, 2
NM103	Subscriber Last Name	AN	1-35	R			
NM104	Subscriber First Name	AN	1-25	S			
NM105	Subscriber Middle Name	AN	1-25	S			
NM106	Name Prefix	AN	1-10	N/U			
NM107	Subscriber Name Suffix	AN	1-10	S			
NM108	Identification Code Qualifier	ID	1-2	S			MI, ZZ
NM109	Subscriber Primary Identifier	AN	2-80	S			
NM110	Entity Relationship Code	ID	2-2	N/U			

5010

837-I 5010

Element Identifier	Description	ID	Min. Max.	Usage Reg.	Loop	Loop Repeat	Values	Notes
REF01	Reference Identification Qualifier	ID	2-3	R			EI	
REF02	Reference Identification	AN	1-50	R				
REF03	Description	AN	1-80	N/U				
REF04	REFERENCE IDENTIFIER			N/U				
HL	**SUBSCRIBER HIERARCHICAL LEVEL**		1	R	2000B	>1		
HL01	Hierarchical ID Number	AN	1-12	R				
HL02	Hierarchical Parent ID Number	AN	1-12	R				
HL03	Hierarchical Level Code	ID	1-2	R			22	
HL04	Hierarchical Child Code	ID	1-1	R			0, 1	
SBR	**SUBSCRIBER INFORMATION**		1	R	2000B			
SBR01	Payer Responsibility Sequence Number Code	ID	1-1	R			A, B, C, D, E, F, G, H, P, S, T, U	Code Added
SBR02	Individual Relationship Code	ID	2-2	S			18	
SBR03	Insured Group or Policy Number	AN	1-50	S				Increase from 30 - 50
SBR04	Insured Group Name	AN	1-60	S				
SBR05	Insurance Type Code	ID	1-3	N/U				
SBR06	Coordination of Benefits Code	ID	1-1	N/U				
SBR07	Yes/No Condition or Response Code	ID	1-1	N/U				
SBR08	Employment Status Code	ID	2-2	N/U				
SBR09	Claim Filing Indicator Code	ID	1-2	S			11, 12, 13, 14, 15, 16, 17, AM, BL, CH, CI, DS, FI, HM, LM, MA, MB, MC, OF, TV, VA, WC, ZZ	Code Change
NM1	**SUBSCRIBER NAME**		1	R	2010BA	1		
NM101	Entity Identifier Code	ID	2-3	R			IL	
NM102	Entity Type Qualifier	ID	1-1	R			1, 2	
NM103	Subscriber Last Name	AN	1-60	R				Increase from 35 - 60
NM104	Subscriber First Name	AN	1-35	S				Increase from 25 - 35
NM105	Subscriber Middle Name	AN	1-25	S				
NM106	Name Prefix	AN	1-10	N/U				
NM107	Subscriber Name Suffix	AN	1-10	S				
NM108	Identification Code Qualifier	ID	1-2	R			II, MI	Code Change Usage change to Required
NM109	Subscriber Primary Identifier	AN	2-80	R				Usage change to Required
NM110	Entity Relationship Code	ID	2-2	N/U				

INSTITUTIONAL CLAIM

4010A1

Element Identifier	Description	ID	Min. Max.	Usage Reg.	Loop	Loop Repeat	Values
	837-I 4010A1						
NM111	Entity Identifier Code	ID	2-3	N/U			
N3	**SUBSCRIBER ADDRESS**		1	S	2010BA		
N301	Subscriber Address Line	AN	1-55	R			
N302	Subscriber Address Line	AN	1-55	S			
N4	**SUBSCRIBER CITY/STATE/ZIP CODE**		1	S	2010BA		
N401	Subscriber City Name	AN	2-30	R			
N402	Subscriber State Code	ID	2-2	R			
N403	Subscriber Postal Zone or ZIP Code	ID	3-15	R			
N404	Subscriber Country Code	ID	2-3	S			
N405	Location Qualifier	ID	1-2	N/U			
N406	Location Identifier	AN	1-30	N/U			
DMG	**SUBSCRIBER DEMOGRAPHIC INFORMATION**		1	S	2010BA		
DMG01	Date Time Period Format Qualifier	ID	2-3	R			D8
DMG02	Subscriber Birth Date	AN	1-35	R			CCYYMMDD
DMG03	Subscriber Gender Code	ID	1-1	R			F, M, U
DMG04	Marital Status Code	ID	1-1	N/U			
DMG05	Race or Ethnicity Code	ID	1-1	N/U			
DMG06	Citizenship Status Code	ID	1-2	N/U			
DMG07	Country Code	ID	2-3	N/U			
DMG08	Basis of Verification Code	ID	1-2	N/U			
DMG09	Quantity	R	1-15	N/U			
REF	**SUBSCRIBER SECONDARY IDENTIFICATION**		4	S	2010BA		
REF01	Reference Identification Qualifier	ID	2-3	R			1W, 23, IG, SY
REF02	Subscriber Supplemental Identifier	AN	1-30	R			
REF03	Description	AN	1-80	N/U			
REF04	REFERENCE IDENTIFIER			N/U			
REF	**CASUALTY CLAIM NUMBER**		1	S	2010BA		
REF01	Reference Identification Qualifier	ID	2-3	R			Y4

5010

Element Identifier	Description	ID	Min. Max.	Usage Reg.	Loop	Loop Repeat	Values	
	837-I 5010							
NM111	Entity Identifier Code	ID	2-3	N/U				
NM112	Name Last or Organization Name	AN	1-60	N/U				New Element
N3	**SUBSCRIBER ADDRESS**		1	S	2010BA			
N301	Subscriber Address Line	AN	1-55	R				
N302	Subscriber Address Line	AN	1-55	S				
N4	**SUBSCRIBER CITY/STATE/ZIP CODE**		1	S	2010BA			
N401	Subscriber City Name	AN	2-30	R				
N402	Subscriber State Code	ID	2-2	S				Usage change to Situational
N403	Subscriber Postal Zone or ZIP Code	ID	3-15	S				Usage change to Situational
N404	Subscriber Country Code	ID	2-3	S				
N405	Location Qualifier	ID	1-2	N/U				
N406	Location Identifier	AN	1-30	N/U				
N407	Country Subdivision Code	ID	1-3	S				New Element
DMG	**SUBSCRIBER DEMOGRAPHIC INFORMATION**		1	S	2010BA			
DMG01	Date Time Period Format Qualifier	ID	2-3	R			D8	
DMG02	Subscriber Birth Date	AN	1-35	R			CCYYMMDD	
DMG03	Subscriber Gender Code	ID	1-1	R			F, M, U	
DMG04	Marital Status Code	ID	1-1	N/U				
DMG05	Race or Ethnicity Code	ID	1-1	N/U				
DMG06	Citizenship Status Code	ID	1-2	N/U				
DMG07	Country Code	ID	2-3	N/U				
DMG08	Basis of Verification Code	ID	1-2	N/U				
DMG09	Quantity	R	1-15	N/U				
DMG10	Code List Qualifier Code	ID	1-3	N/U				New Element
DMG11	Industry Code	AN	1-30	N/U				New Element
REF	**SUBSCRIBER SECONDARY IDENTIFICATION**		1	S	2010BA			
REF01	Reference Identification Qualifier	ID	2-3	R			SY	Code Deleted
REF02	Subscriber Supplemental Identifier	AN	1-50	R				Increase rom 30 - 50
REF03	Description	AN	1-80	N/U				
REF04	REFERENCE IDENTIFIER			N/U				
REF	**CASUALTY CLAIM NUMBER**		1	S	2010BA			
REF01	Reference Identification Qualifier	ID	2-3	R			Y4	

Page 9 of 93

INSTITUTIONAL CLAIM

4010A1

Element Identifier	Description	ID	Min. Max.	Usage Reg.	Loop	Loop Repeat	Values
	837-I 4010A1						
REF02	Property Casualty Claim Number	AN	1-30	R			
REF03	Description	AN	1-80	N/U			
REF04	REFERENCE IDENTIFIER			N/U			
NM1	**CREDIT/DEBIT CARD ACCOUNT HOLDER NAME**		1	S	2010BB	1	
NM101	Entity Identifier Code	ID	2-3	R			AO
NM102	Entity Type Qualifier	ID	1-1	R			1, 2
NM103	Credit or Debt Card Holder Last or Organization Name	AN	1-35	R			
NM104	Credit or Debt Card Holder First Name	AN	1-25	S			
NM105	Credit or Debt Card Holder Middle Name	AN	1-25	S			
NM106	Name Prefix	AN	1-10	N/U			
NM107	Credit or Debt Card Holder Name Suffix	AN	1-10	S			
NM108	Identification Code Qualifier	ID	1-2	R			MI
NM109	Payer Identifier	AN	2-80	R			
NM110	Entity Relationship Code	ID	2-2	N/U			
NM111	Entity Identifier Code	ID	2-3	N/U			
REF	**CREDIT/DEBT CARD INFORMATION**		2	S	2010BB		
REF01	Reference Identification Qualifier	ID	2-3	R			AB, BB
REF02	Credit or Debt Card Authorization Number	AN	1-30	R			
REF03	Description	AN	1-80	N/U			
REF04	REFERENCE IDENTIFIER			N/U			
NM1	**PAYER NAME**		1	R	2010BC	1	
NM101	Entity Identifier Code	ID	2-3	R			PR
NM102	Entity Type Qualifier	ID	1-1	R			2
NM103	Payer Name	AN	1-35	R			
NM104	Name First	AN	1-25	N/U			
NM105	Name Middle	AN	1-25	N/U			
NM106	Name Prefix	AN	1-10	N/U			
NM107	Name Suffix	AN	1-10	N/U			
NM108	Identification Code Qualifier	ID	1-2	R			PI, XV
NM109	Payer Identifier	AN	2-80	R			
NM110	Entity Relationship Code	ID	2-2	N/U			
NM111	Entity Identifier Code	ID	2-3	N/U			
N3	**PAYER ADDRESS**		1	S	2010BC		

5010

Element Identifier	Description	ID	Min. Max.	Usage Reg.	Loop	Loop Repeat	Values	
	837-I 5010							
REF02	Property Casualty Claim Number	AN	1-50	R				Increase rom 30 - 50
REF03	Description	AN	1-80	N/U				
REF04	REFERENCE IDENTIFIER	.		N/U				
								Segment Deleted
								Segment Deleted
NM1	**PAYER NAME**		1	R	2010BB	1		Loop Change
NM101	Entity Identifier Code	ID	2-3	R			PR	
NM102	Entity Type Qualifier	ID	1-1	R			2	
NM103	Payer Name	AN	1-60	R				Increase from 35 - 60
NM104	Name First	AN	1-35	N/U				Increase from 25 - 35
NM105	Name Middle	AN	1-25	N/U				
NM106	Name Prefix	AN	1-10	N/U				
NM107	Name Suffix	AN	1-10	N/U				
NM108	Identification Code Qualifier	ID	1-2	R			PI, XV	
NM109	Payer Identifier	AN	2-80	R				
NM110	Entity Relationship Code	ID	2-2	N/U				
NM111	Entity Identifier Code	ID	2-3	N/U				
NM112	Name Last or Organization Name	AN	1-60	N/U				New Element
N3	**PAYER ADDRESS**		1	S	2010BB			Loop Change

Page 10 of 93

INSTITUTIONAL CLAIM

4010A1

Element Identifier	Description	ID	Min. Max.	Usage Reg.	Loop	Loop Repeat	Values
				837-I 4010A1			
N301	Payer Address Line	AN	1-55	R			
N302	Payer Address Line	AN	1-55	S			
N4	**PAYER CITY/STATE/ZIP CODE**		**1**	**R**	**2010BC**		
N401	Payer City Name	AN	2-30	R			
N402	Payer State Code	ID	2-2	R			
N403	Payer Postal Zone or ZIP Code	ID	3-15	R			
N404	Payer Country Code	ID	2-3	S			
N405	Location Qualifier	ID	1-2	N/U			
N406	Location Identifier	AN	1-30	N/U			
REF	**PAYER SECONDARY IDENTIFICATION**		**3**	**S**	**2010BC**		
REF01	Reference Identification Qualifier	ID	2-3	R			2U, FY, NF, TJ
REF02	Payer Additional Identifier	AN	1-30	R			
REF03	Description	AN	1-80	N/U			
REF04	REFERENCE IDENTIFIER			N/U			
NM1	**RESPONSIBLE PARTY NAME**		**1**	**S**	**2010BD**	**1**	
NM101	Entity Identifier Code	ID	2-3	R			QD
NM102	Entity Type Qualifier	ID	1-1	R			
NM103	Payer Name	AN	1-35	R			
NM104	Name First	AN	1-25	S			
NM105	Name Middle	AN	1-25	S			
NM106	Name Prefix	AN	1-10	N/U			
NM107	Name Suffix	AN	1-10	S			
NM108	Identification Code Qualifier	ID	1-2	N/U			
NM109	Identification Code	AN	2-80	N/U			
NM110	Entity Relationship Code	ID	2-2	N/U			
NM111	Entity Identifier Code	ID	2-3	N/U			
N3	**RESPONSIBLE PARTY ADDRESS**		**1**	**S**	**2010BC**		

5010

Element Identifier	Description	ID	Min. Max.	Usage Reg.	Loop	Loop Repeat	Values	
				837-I 5010				
N301	Payer Address Line	AN	1-55	R				
N302	Payer Address Line	AN	1-55	S				
N4	**PAYER CITY/STATE/ZIP CODE**		**1**	**R**	**2010BB**			Loop Change
N401	Payer City Name	AN	2-30	R				
N402	Payer State Code	ID	2-2	S				Usage change to Situational
N403	Payer Postal Zone or ZIP Code	ID	3-15	S				Usage change to Situational
N404	Payer Country Code	ID	2-3	S				
N405	Location Qualifier	ID	1-2	N/U				
N406	Location Identifier	AN	1-30	N/U				
N407	Country Subdivision Code	ID	1-3	S				New Element
REF	**PAYER SECONDARY IDENTIFICATION**		**3**	**S**	**2010BB**			Loop Change
REF01	Reference Identification Qualifier	ID	2-3	R			2U, EI, FY, NF	Code Change
REF02	Payer Additional Identifier	AN	1-50	R				Increase from 30 - 50
REF03	Description	AN	1-80	N/U				
REF04	REFERENCE IDENTIFIER			N/U				
REF	**BILLING PROVIDER SECONDARY IDENTIFICATION**		**1**	**S**	**2010BB**			Segment Added
REF01	Reference Identification Qualifier	ID	2-3	R			G2, LU	
REF02	Payer Additional Identifier	AN	1-50	R				
REF03	Description	AN	1-80	N/U				
REF04	REFERENCE IDENTIFIER			N/U				
								Segment Deleted
								Segment Deleted

Page 11 of 93

INSTITUTIONAL CLAIM

Element Identifier	Description	ID	Min. Max.	Usage Reg.	Loop	Loop Repeat	Values
	4010A1						
	837-I 4010A1						
N301	Responsible Party Address Line	AN	1-55	R			
·N302	Responsible Party Address Line	AN	1-55	S			
N4	**RESPONSIBLE PARTY CITY/STATE/ZIP CODE**		1	R	2010BC		
N401	Responsible Party City Name	AN	2-30	R			
N402	Responsible Party State Code	ID	2-2	R			
N403	Responsible Party ZIP Code	ID	3-15	R			
N404	Responsible Party Country Code	ID	2-3	S			
N405	Location Qualifier	ID	1-2	N/U			
N406	Location Identifier	AN	1-30	N/U			
HL	**PATIENT HIERARCHICAL LEVEL**		1	S	2000C	>1	
HL01	Hierarchical ID Number	AN	1-12	R			
HL02	Hierarchical Parent ID Number	AN	1-12	R			
HL03	Hierarchical Level Code	ID	1-2	R			23
HL04	Hierarchical Child Code	ID	1-1	R			0
PAT	**PATIENT INFORMATION**		1	R	2000C		
PAT01	Individual Relationship Code	ID	2-2	R			01, 04, 05, 07, 10, 15, 17, 19, 20, 21, 22, 23, 24, 29, 32, 33, 36, 39, 40, 41, 43, 53, G8
PAT02	Patient Location Code	ID	1-1	N/U			
PAT03	Employment Status Code	ID	2-2	N/U			
PAT04	Student Status Code	ID	1-1	N/U			
PAT05	Date Time Period Format Qualifier	ID	2-3	N/U			
PAT06	Patient Death Date	AN	1-35	N/U			
PAT07	Measurement Code	ID	2-2	N/U			
PAT08	Patient Weight	R	1-10	N/U			
PAT09	Pregnancy Indicator	ID	1-1	N/U			
NM1	**PATIENT NAME**		1	R	2010CA	1	
NM101	Entity Identifier Code	ID	2-3	R			QC
NM102	Entity Type Qualifier	ID	1-1	R			1
NM103	Patient Last Name	AN	1-35	R			

Element Identifier	Description	ID	Min. Max.	Usage Reg.	Loop	Loop Repeat	Values	
	5010							
	837-I 5010							
								Segment Deleted
HL	**PATIENT HIERARCHICAL LEVEL**		1	S	2000C	>1		
HL01	Hierarchical ID Number	AN	1-12	R				
HL02	Hierarchical Parent ID Number	AN	1-12	R				
HL03	Hierarchical Level Code	ID	1-2	R			23	
HL04	Hierarchical Child Code	ID	1-1	R			0	
PAT	**PATIENT INFORMATION**		1	R	2000C			Code Deleted
PAT01	Individual Relationship Code	ID	2-2	R			01, 19, 20, 21, 39, 40, 53, G8	
PAT02	Patient Location Code	ID	1-1	N/U				
PAT03	Employment Status Code	ID	2-2	N/U				
PAT04	Student Status Code	ID	1-1	N/U				
PAT05	Date Time Period Format Qualifier	ID	2-3	N/U				
PAT06	Patient Death Date	AN	1-35	N/U				
PAT07	Measurement Code	ID	2-2	N/U				
PAT08	Patient Weight	R	1-10	N/U				
PAT09	Pregnancy Indicator	ID	1-1	N/U				
NM1	**PATIENT NAME**		1	R	2010CA	1		
NM101	Entity Identifier Code	ID	2-3	R			QC	
NM102	Entity Type Qualifier	ID	1-1	R			1	
NM103	Patient Last Name	AN	1-60	R				Increase from 35 - 60

Page 12 of 93

INSTITUTIONAL CLAIM

4010A1								5010							
Element Identifier	Description	ID	Min. Max.	Usage Reg.	Loop	Loop Repeat	Values	Element Identifier	Description	ID	Min. Max.	Usage Reg.	Loop	Loop Repeat	Values
	837-I 4010A1								837-I 5010						
NM104	Patient First Name	AN	1-25	R				NM104	Patient First Name	AN	1-35	S			
NM105	Patient Middle Name	AN	1-25	S				NM105	Patient Middle Name	AN	1-25	S			
NM106	Name Prefix	AN	1-10	N/U				NM106	Name Prefix	AN	1-10	N/U			
NM107	Patient Name Suffix	AN	1-10	S				NM107	Patient Name Suffix	AN	1-10	S			
NM108	Identification Code Qualifier	ID	1-2	S			MI, ZZ	NM108	Identification Code Qualifier	ID	1-2	N/U			
NM109	Patient Primary Identifier	AN	2-80	S				NM109	Patient Primary Identifier	AN	2-80	N/U			
NM110	Entity Relationship Code	ID	2-2	N/U				NM110	Entity Relationship Code	ID	2-2	N/U			
NM111	Entity Identifier Code	ID	2-3	N/U				NM111	Entity Identifier Code	ID	2-3	N/U			
								NM112	Name Last or Organization Name	AN	1-60	N/U			
N3	PATIENT ADDRESS		1	R	2010CA			N3	PATIENT ADDRESS		1	R	2010CA		
N301	Patient Address Line	AN	1-55	R				N301	Patient Address Line	AN	1-55	R			
N302	Patient Address Line	AN	1-55	S				N302	Patient Address Line	AN	1-55	S			
N4	PATIENT CITY/STATE/ZIP CODE		1	R	2010CA			N4	PATIENT CITY/STATE/ZIP CODE		1	R	2010CA		
N401	Patient City Name	AN	2-30	R				N401	Patient City Name	AN	2-30	R			
N402	Patient State Code	ID	2-2	R				N402	Patient State Code	ID	2-2	S			
N403	Patient Postal Zone or ZIP Code	ID	3-15	R				N403	Patient Postal Zone or ZIP Code	ID	3-15	S			
N404	Patient Country Code	ID	2-3	S				N404	Patient Country Code	ID	2-3	S			
N405	Location Qualifier	ID	1-2	N/U				N405	Location Qualifier	ID	1-2	N/U			
N406	Location Identifier	AN	1-30	N/U				N406	Location Identifier	AN	1-30	N/U			
								N407	Country Subdivision Code	ID	1-3	S			
DMG	PATIENT DEMOGRAPHIC INFORMATION		1	R	2010CA			DMG	PATIENT DEMOGRAPHIC INFORMATION		1	R	2010CA		
DMG01	Date Time Period Format Qualifier	ID	2-3	R			D8	DMG01	Date Time Period Format Qualifier	ID	2-3	R			D8
DMG02	Patient Birth Date	AN	1-35	R			CCYYMMDD	DMG02	Patient Birth Date	AN	1-35	R			CCYYMMDD
DMG03	Patient Gender Code	ID	1-1	R			F, M, U	DMG03	Patient Gender Code	ID	1-1	R			F, M, U
DMG04	Marital Status Code	ID	1-1	N/U				DMG04	Marital Status Code	ID	1-1	N/U			
DMG05	Race or Ethnicity Code	ID	1-1	N/U				DMG05	Race or Ethnicity Code	ID	1-1	N/U			
DMG06	Citizenship Status Code	ID	1-2	N/U				DMG06	Citizenship Status Code	ID	1-2	N/U			
DMG07	Country Code	ID	2-3	N/U				DMG07	Country Code	ID	2-3	N/U			
DMG08	Basis of Verification Code	ID	1-2	N/U				DMG08	Basis of Verification Code	ID	1-2	N/U			
DMG09	Quantity	R	1-15	N/U				DMG09	Quantity	R	1-15	N/U			
								DMG10	Code List Qualifier Code	ID	1-3	N/U			
								DMG11	Industry Code	AN	1-30	N/U			
REF	PATIENT SECONDARY IDENTIFICATION NUMBER		5	S	2010CA										

Notes (right margin):
- Increase from 25 - 35, Usage change to Situational (NM104)
- Code Deleted, Usage change to Not Used (NM108)
- Usage change to Not Used (NM109)
- New Element (NM112)
- Usage change to Situational (N402)
- Usage change to Situational (N403)
- New Element (N407)
- New Element (DMG10)
- New Element (DMG11)
- Segment Deleted (REF)

INSTITUTIONAL CLAIM

Element Identifier	Description	ID	Min. Max.	Usage Reg.	Loop	Loop Repeat	Values
		4010A1					
		837-I 4010A1					
REF01	Reference Identification Qualifier	ID	2-3	R			1W, 23, IG, SY
REF02	Patient Secondary Identifier	AN	1-30	R			
REF03	Description	AN	1-80	N/U			
REF04	REFERENCE IDENTIFIER			N/U			
REF	PROPERTY AND CASUALTY CLAIM NUMBER		1	S	2010CA		
REF01	Reference Identification Qualifier	ID	2-3	R			Y4
REF02	Property Casualty Claim Number	AN	1-30	R			
REF03	Description	AN	1-80	N/U			
REF04	REFERENCE IDENTIFIER			N/U			
CLM	CLAIM INFORMATION		1	R	2300	100	
CLM01	Patient Account Number	AN	1-38	R			
CLM02	Total Claim Charge Amount	R	1-18	R			
CLM03	Claim Filing Indicator Code	ID	1-2	N/U			
CLM04	Non-Institutional Claim Type Code	ID	1-2	N/U			
CLM05	HEALTH CARE SERVICE LOCATION INFORMATION			R			
CLM05-1	Facility Type Code	AN	1-2	R			
CLM05-2	Facility Code Qualifier	ID	1-2	R			A
CLM05-3	Claim Frequency Code	ID	1-1	R			
CLM06	Provider or Supplier Signature Indicator	ID	1-1	N/U			N, Y
CLM07	Medicare Assignment Code	ID	1-1	R			A, C
CLM08	Benefits Assignment Certification Indicator	ID	1-1	R			N
CLM09	Release of Information Code	ID	1-1	R			A, I, M, N, O, Y
CLM10	Patient Signature Source Code	ID	1-1	N/U			
CLM11	RELATED CAUSES INFORMATION			N/U			
CLM12	Special Program Indicator	ID	2-3	N/U			
CLM13	Yes/No Condition or Response Code	ID	1-1	N/U			
CLM14	Level of Service Code	ID	1-3	N/U			
CLM15	Yes/No Condition or Response Code	ID	1-1	N/U			

Element Identifier	Description	ID	Min. Max.	Usage Reg.	Loop	Loop Repeat	Values	
		5010						
		837-I 5010						
REF	PROPERTY AND CASUALTY CLAIM NUMBER		1	S	2010CA			
REF01	Reference Identification Qualifier	ID	2-3	R			Y4	
REF02	Property Casualty Claim Number	AN	1-50	R				Increase from 30 - 50
REF03	Description	AN	1-80	N/U				
REF04	REFERENCE IDENTIFIER			N/U				
CLM	CLAIM INFORMATION		1	R	2300	100		
CLM01	Patient Account Number	AN	1-38	R				
CLM02	Total Claim Charge Amount	R	1-18	R				
CLM03	Claim Filing Indicator Code	ID	1-2	N/U				
CLM04	Non-Institutional Claim Type Code	ID	1-2	N/U				
CLM05	HEALTH CARE SERVICE LOCATION INFORMATION			R				
CLM05-1	Facility Type Code	AN	1-2	R				
CLM05-2	Facility Code Qualifier	ID	1-2	R			A	
CLM05-3	Claim Frequency Code	ID	1-1	R				
CLM06	Provider or Supplier Signature Indicator	ID	1-1	N/U			N, Y	
CLM07	Medicare Assignment Code	ID	1-1	R			A, B, C	Code Added
CLM08	Benefits Assignment Certification Indicator	ID	1-1	R			N, W, Y	Code Added
CLM09	Release of Information Code	ID	1-1	R			I, Y	Code Deleted
CLM10	Patient Signature Source Code	ID	1-1	S			P	Usage change to Situational Code Added
CLM11	RELATED CAUSES INFORMATION			N/U				
CLM12	Special Program Indicator	ID	2-3	S			02, 03, 05, 09	Usage change to Situational Code Added
CLM13	Yes/No Condition or Response Code	ID	1-1	N/U				
CLM14	Level of Service Code	ID	1-3	N/U				
CLM15	Yes/No Condition or Response Code	ID	1-1	N/U				

INSTITUTIONAL CLAIM

4010A1							
Element Identifier	Description	ID	Min. Max.	Usage Reg.	Loop	Loop Repeat	Values
837-I 4010A1							
CLM16	Participation Agreement	ID	1-1	N/U			
CLM17	Claim Status Code	ID	1-2	N/U			
CLM18	Yes/No Condition or Response Code	ID	1-1	R			N, Y
CLM19	Claim Submission Reason Code	ID	2-2	N/U			
CLM20	Delay Reason Code	ID	1-2	S			1, 2, 3, 4, 5, 6, 7, 8, 9, 10, 11
DTP	**DATE - DISCHARGE HOUR**		1	S	2300		
DTP01	Date Time Qualifier	ID	3-3	R			96
DTP02	Date Time Period Format Qualifier	ID	2-3	R			TM
DTP03	Discharge Hour	AN	1-35	R			HHMM
DTP	**DATE - STATEMENT DATES**		1	R	2300		
DTP01	Date Time Qualifier	ID	3-3	R			434
DTP02	Date Time Period Format Qualifier	ID	2-3	R			D8, RD8
DTP03	Statement From or To Date	AN	1-35	R			CCYYMMDDCCYYMMDD
DTP	**DATE - ADMISSION DATE/HOUR**		1	S	2300		
DTP01	Date Time Qualifier	ID	3-3	R			435
DTP02	Date Time Period Format Qualifier	ID	2-3	R			DT
DTP03	Admission Date and Hour	AN	1-35	R			CCYYMMDDHHMM
CL1	**INSTITUTIONAL CLAIM CODE**		1	S	2300		
CL101	Admission Type Code	ID	1-1	S			
CL102	Admission Source Code	ID	1-1	S			
CL103	Patient Status Code	ID	1-2	S			
CL104	Nursing Home Code	ID	1-1	NU			
PWK	**CLAIM SUPPLEMENTAL INFORMATION**		10	S	2300		

5010								
Element Identifier	Description	ID	Min. Max.	Usage Reg.	Loop	Loop Repeat	Values	
837-I 5010								
CLM16	Participation Agreement	ID	1-1	N/U				
CLM17	Claim Status Code	ID	1-2	N/U				
CLM18	Yes/No Condition or Response Code	ID	1-1	N/U				Usage change to Not Used
CLM19	Claim Submission Reason Code	ID	2-2	N/U				
CLM20	Delay Reason Code	ID	1-2	S			1, 2, 3, 4, 5, 6, 7, 8, 9, 10, 11, 15	Code Added
DTP	**DATE - DISCHARGE HOUR**		1	S	2300			
DTP01	Date Time Qualifier	ID	3-3	R			96	
DTP02	Date Time Period Format Qualifier	ID	2-3	R			TM	
DTP03	Discharge Time	AN	1-35	R			HHMM	Name Change
DTP	**DATE - STATEMENT DATES**		1	S	2300			Usage change to Situational
DTP01	Date Time Qualifier	ID	3-3	R			434	
DTP02	Date Time Period Format Qualifier	ID	2-3	R			RD8	Code Deleted
DTP03	Statement From and To Date	AN	1-35	R			CCYYMMDDCCYYMMDD	Name Change
DTP	**DATE - ADMISSION DATE/HOUR**		1	S	2300			
DTP01	Date Time Qualifier	ID	3-3	R			435	
DTP02	Date Time Period Format Qualifier	ID	2-3	R			D8, DT	Code Added
DTP03	Admission Date and Hour	AN	1-35	R			CCYYMMDD, CCYYMMDDHHMM	Code Added
DTP	**DATE - REPRICER RECEIVED DATE**		1	S	2300			New Segment
DTP01	Date Time Qualifier	ID	3-3	R			050	
DTP02	Date Time Period Format Qualifier	ID	2-3	R			D8	
DTP03	Order Date	AN	1-35	R			CCYYMMDD	
CL1	**INSTITUTIONAL CLAIM CODE**		1	S	2300			
CL101	Admission Type Code	ID	1-1	S				
CL102	Admission Source Code	ID	1-1	S				
CL103	Patient Status Code	ID	1-2	R				Usage change to Required
CL104	Nursing Home Code	ID	1-1	NU				
PWK	**CLAIM SUPPLEMENTAL INFORMATION**		10	S	2300			

Page 15 of 93

INSTITUTIONAL CLAIM

4010A1

837-I 4010A1

Element Identifier	Description	ID	Min. Max.	Usage Reg.	Loop	Loop Repeat	Values
PWK01	Attachment Report Type Code	ID	2-2	R			AS, B2, B3, B4, CT, DA, DG, DS, EB, MT, NN, OB, OZ, PN, PO, PZ, RB, RR, RT
PWK02	Attachment Transmission Code	ID	1-2	R			AA, BM, EL, EM, FX
PWK03	Report Copies Needed	N0	1-2	N/U			
PWK04	Entity Identifier Code	ID	2-3	N/U			
PWK05	Identification Code Qualifier	ID	1-2	S			AC
PWK06	Attachment Control Number	AN	2-80	S			
PWK07	Description	AN	1-80	S			
PWK08	ACTIONS INDICATED			N/U			
PWK09	Request Category Code	ID	1-2	N/U			
CN1	CONTRACT INFORMATION		1	S	2300		
CN101	Contract Type Code	ID	2-2	R			01, 02, 03, 04, 05, 06, 09
CN102	Contract Amount	R	1-18	S			
CN103	Contract Percentage	R	1-6	S			
CN104	Contract Code	AN	1-30	S			
CN105	Terms Discount Percent	R	1-6	S			
CN106	Contract Version Identifier	AN	1-30	S			
AMT	PAYER ESTIMATED AMOUNT DUE		1	S	2300		
AMT01	Amount Qualifier Code	ID	1-3	R			C5
AMT02	Patient Responsibility Amount	R	1-18	R			
AMT03	Credit/Debit Flag Code	ID	1-1	N/U			
AMT	PATIENT ESTIMATED AMOUNT DUE		1	S	2300		
AMT01	Amount Qualifier Code	ID	1-3	R			F3

5010

837-I 5010

Element Identifier	Description	ID	Min. Max.	Usage Reg.	Loop	Loop Repeat	Values	Notes
PWK01	Attachment Report Type Code	ID	2-2	R			03, 04, 05, 06, 07, 08, 09, 10, 11, 13, 15, 21, A3, A4, AM, AS, B2, B3, B4, BR, BS, BT, CB, CK, CT, D2, DA, DB, DG, DJ, DS, EB, HC, HR, I5, IR, LA, M1, MT, NN, OB, OC, OD, OE, OX, OZ, P4, P5, PE, PN, PO, PQ, PY, PZ, RB, RR, RT, RX, SG, V5, XP	Code Added
PWK02	Attachment Transmission Code	ID	1-2	R			AA, BM, EL, EM, FT, FX	Code Added
PWK03	Report Copies Needed	N0	1-2	N/U				
PWK04	Entity Identifier Code	ID	2-3	N/U				
PWK05	Identification Code Qualifier	ID	1-2	S			AC	
PWK06	Attachment Control Number	AN	2-80	S				
PWK07	Description	AN	1-80	N/U				Usage change to Not Used
PWK08	ACTIONS INDICATED			N/U				
PWK09	Request Category Code	ID	1-2	N/U				
CN1	CONTRACT INFORMATION		1	S	2300			
CN101	Contract Type Code	ID	2-2	R			01, 02, 03, 04, 05, 06, 09	
CN102	Contract Amount	R	1-18	S				
CN103	Contract Percentage	R	1-6	S				
CN104	Contract Code	AN	1-50	S				Increase from 30 - 50
CN105	Terms Discount Percent	R	1-6	S				
CN106	Contract Version Identifier	AN	1-30	S				Segment Deleted
AMT	PATIENT ESTIMATED AMOUNT DUE		1	S	2300			
AMT01	Amount Qualifier Code	ID	1-3	R			F3	

Page 16 of 93

INSTITUTIONAL CLAIM

Element Identifier	Description	ID	Min. Max.	Usage Reg.	Loop	Loop Repeat	Values
			4010A1				
	837-I 4010A1						
AMT02	Patient Responsibility Amount	R	1-18	R			
AMT03	Credit/Debit Flag Code	ID	1-1	N/U			
AMT	**PATIENT PAID AMOUNT**		1	S	2300		
AMT01	Amount Qualifier Code	ID	1-3	R			F5
AMT02	Patient Paid Amount	R	1-18	R			
AMT03	Credit/Debit Flag Code	ID	1-1	N/U			
AMT	**CREDIT/DEBIT CARD MAXIMUM AMOUNT**		1	S	2300		
AMT01	Amount Qualifier Code	ID	1-3	R			MA
AMT02	Credit or Debit Card Maximum Amount	R	1-18	R			
AMT03	Credit/Debit Flag Code	ID	1-1	N/U			
REF	**SERVICE AUTHORIZATION EXCEPTION CODE**		1	S	2300		
REF01	Reference Identification Qualifier	ID	2-3	R			4N
REF02	Service Authorization Exception Code	AN	1-30	R			1, 2, 3, 4, 5, 6, 7
REF03	Description	AN	1-80	N/U			
REF04	REFERENCE IDENTIFIER			N/U			
REF	**PRIOR AUTHORIZATION**		2	S	2300		
REF01	Reference Identification Qualifier	ID	2-3	R			9F, G1
REF02	Prior Authorization Number	AN	1-30	R			
REF03	Description	AN	1-80	N/U			
REF04	REFERENCE IDENTIFIER			N/U			
REF	**ORIGINAL REFERENCE NUMBER (ICN/DCN)**		1	S	2300		
REF01	Reference Identification Qualifier	ID	2-3	R			F8
REF02	Claim Original Reference Number	AN	1-30	R			
REF03	Description	AN	1-80	N/U			

Element Identifier	Description	ID	Min. Max.	Usage Reg.	Loop	Loop Repeat	Values	
			5010					
	837-I 5010							
AMT02	Patient Responsibility Amount	R	1-18	R				
AMT03	Credit/Debit Flag Code	ID	1-1	N/U				
								Segment Deleted
								Segment Deleted
REF	**SERVICE AUTHORIZATION EXCEPTION CODE**		1	S	2300			
REF01	Reference Identification Qualifier	ID	2-3	R			4N	
REF02	Service Authorization Exception Code	AN	1-50	R			1, 2, 3, 4, 5, 6, 7	Increase from 30 - 50
REF03	Description	AN	1-80	N/U				
REF04	REFERENCE IDENTIFIER			N/U				
REF	**REFERRAL NUMBER**		1	S	2300			New Segment
REF01	Reference Identification Qualifier	ID	2-3	R			9F	
REF02	Prior Authorization or Referral Number	AN	1-50	R				
REF03	Description	AN	1-80	N/U				
REF04	REFERENCE IDENTIFIER			N/U				
REF	**PRIOR AUTHORIZATION**		1	S	2300			# Repeats change to 1 / Code Deleted
REF01	Reference Identification Qualifier	ID	2-3	R			G1	
REF02	Prior Authorization or Referral Number	AN	1-50	R				Increase from 30 - 50 / Name Change
REF03	Description	AN	1-80	N/U				
REF04	REFERENCE IDENTIFIER			N/U				
REF	**PAYER CLAIM CONTROL NUMBER**		1	S	2300			Name Change
REF01	Reference Identification Qualifier	ID	2-3	R			F8	
REF02	Claim Original Reference Number	AN	1-50	R				Increase from 30 - 50
REF03	Description	AN	1-80	N/U				

Page 17 of 93

INSTITUTIONAL CLAIM

4010A1

Element Identifier	Description	ID	Min. Max.	Usage Reg.	Loop	Loop Repeat	Values
	837-I 4010A1						
REF04	REFERENCE IDENTIFIER			N/U			
REF	**REPRICED CLAIM NUMBER**		1	S	2300		
REF01	Reference Identification Qualifier	ID	2-3	R			9A
REF02	Repriced Claim Reference Number	AN	1-30	R			
REF03	Description	AN	1-80	N/U			
REF04	REFERENCE IDENTIFIER			N/U			
REF	**ADJUSTED REPRICED CLAIM NUMBER**		1	S	2300		
REF01	Reference Identification Qualifier	ID	2-3	R			9C
REF02	Adjusted Repriced Claim Reference Number	AN	1-30	R			
REF03	Description	AN	1-80	N/U			
REF04	REFERENCE IDENTIFIER			N/U			
REF	**INVESTIGATIONAL DEVICE EXEMPTION NUMBER**		1	S	2300		
REF01	Reference Identification Qualifier	ID	2-3	R			LX
REF02	Investigational Device Exemption Number	AN	1-30	R			
REF03	Description	AN	1-80	N/U			
REF04	REFERENCE IDENTIFIER			N/U			
REF	**CLAIM IDENTIFIER FOR TRANSMISSION INTERMEDIARIES**		1	S	2300		
REF01	Reference Identification Qualifier	ID	2-3	R			D9
REF02	Value Added Network Trace Number	AN	1-30	R			
REF03	Description	AN	1-80	N/U			
REF04	REFERENCE IDENTIFIER			N/U			
REF	**DOCUMENT IDENTIFICATION CODE**		2	S	2300		
REF01	Reference Identification Qualifier	ID	2-3	R			DD
REF02	Document ControlIdentifier	AN	1-30	R			
REF03	Description	AN	1-80	N/U			
REF04	REFERENCE IDENTIFIER			N/U			

5010

Element Identifier	Description	ID	Min. Max.	Usage Reg.	Loop	Loop Repeat	Values	
	837-I 5010							
REF04	REFERENCE IDENTIFIER			N/U				
REF	**REPRICED CLAIM NUMBER**		1	S	2300			
REF01	Reference Identification Qualifier	ID	2-3	R			9A	
REF02	Repriced Claim Reference Number	AN	1-50	R				Increase from 30 - 50
REF03	Description	AN	1-80	N/U				
REF04	REFERENCE IDENTIFIER			N/U				
REF	**ADJUSTED REPRICED CLAIM NUMBER**		1	S	2300			
REF01	Reference Identification Qualifier	ID	2-3	R			9C	
REF02	Adjusted Repriced Claim Reference Number	AN	1-50	R				Increase from 30 - 50
REF03	Description	AN	1-80	N/U				
REF04	REFERENCE IDENTIFIER			N/U				
REF	**INVESTIGATIONAL DEVICE EXEMPTION NUMBER**		5	S	2300			
REF01	Reference Identification Qualifier	ID	2-3	R			LX	
REF02	Investigational Device Exemption Number	AN	1-50	R				Increase from 30 - 50
REF03	Description	AN	1-80	N/U				
REF04	REFERENCE IDENTIFIER			N/U				
REF	**CLAIM IDENTIFIER FOR TRANSMISSION INTERMEDIARIES**		1	S	2300			
REF01	Reference Identification Qualifier	ID	2-3	R			D9	
REF02	Clearinghouse Trace Number	AN	1-50	R				Increase from 30 - 50 Name Change
REF03	Description	AN	1-80	N/U				
REF04	REFERENCE IDENTIFIER			N/U				
								Segment Deleted
REF	**AUTO ACCIDENT STATE**		1	S	2300			New Segment

Page 18 of 93

INSTITUTIONAL CLAIM

Element Identifier	Description	ID	Min. Max.	Usage Reg.	Loop	Loop Repeat	Values
	4010A1						
	837-I 4010A1						
REF	**MEDICAL RECORD NUMBER**		1	S	2300		
REF01	Reference Identification Qualifier	ID	2-3	R			EA
REF02	Medical Record Number	AN	1-30	R			
REF03	Description	AN	1-80	N/U			
REF04	REFERENCE IDENTIFIER			N/U			
REF	**DEMONSTRATION PROJECT IDENTIFIER**		1	S	2300		
REF01	Reference Identification Qualifier	ID	2-3	R			P4
REF02	Demonstration Project Identifier	AN	1-30	R			
REF03	Description	AN	1-80	N/U			
REF04	REFERENCE IDENTIFIER			N/U			
REF	**PEER REVIEW ORGANIZARION (PRO) APPROVAL NUMBER**		1	S	2300		
REF01	Reference Identification Qualifier	ID	2-3	R			G4
REF02	PRO Number	AN	1-30	R			
REF03	Description	AN	1-80	N/U			
REF04	REFERENCE IDENTIFIER			N/U			
K3	**FILE INFORMATION**		10	S	2300		
K301	Fixed Format Information	AN	1-80	R			
K302	Record Format Code	ID	1-2	N/U			
K303	COMPOSITE UNIT OF MEASURE			N/U			
NTE	**CLAIM NOTE**		10	S	2300		
NTE01	Note Reference Code	ID	3-3	R			ALG, DCP, DGN, DME, MED, NTR, ODT, RHB, RLH, RNH, SET, SFM, SPT, UPI
NTE02	Claim Note Text	AN	1-80	R			
NTE	**BILLING NOTE**		1	S	2300		
NTE01	Note Reference Code	ID	3-3	R			ADD

Element Identifier	Description	ID	Min. Max.	Usage Reg.	Loop	Loop Repeat	Values	
	5010							
	837-I 5010							
REF01	Reference Identification Qualifier	ID	2-3	R			LU	
REF02	Auto Accident State or Province	AN	1-50	R				
REF03	Description	AN	1-80	N/U				
REF04	REFERENCE IDENTIFIER			N/U				
REF	**MEDICAL RECORD NUMBER**		1	S	2300			
REF01	Reference Identification Qualifier	ID	2-3	R			EA	
REF02	Medical Record Number	AN	1-50	R				Increase from 30 - 50
REF03	Description	AN	1-80	N/U				
REF04	REFERENCE IDENTIFIER			N/U				
REF	**DEMONSTRATION PROJECT IDENTIFIER**		1	S	2300			
REF01	Reference Identification Qualifier	ID	2-3	R			P4	
REF02	Demonstration Project Identifier	AN	1-50	R				Increase from 30 - 50
REF03	Description	AN	1-80	N/U				
REF04	REFERENCE IDENTIFIER			N/U				
REF	**PEER REVIEW ORGANIZARION (PRO) APPROVAL NUMBER**		1	S	2300			
REF01	Reference Identification Qualifier	ID	2-3	R			G4	
REF02	PRO Number	AN	1-50	R				Increase from 30 - 50
REF03	Description	AN	1-80	N/U				
REF04	REFERENCE IDENTIFIER			N/U				
K3	**FILE INFORMATION**		10	S	2300			
K301	Fixed Format Information	AN	1-80	R				
K302	Record Format Code	ID	1-2	N/U				
K303	COMPOSITE UNIT OF MEASURE			N/U				
NTE	**CLAIM NOTE**		10	S	2300			
NTE01	Note Reference Code	ID	3-3	R			ALG, DCP, DGN, DME, MED, NTR, ODT, RHB, RLH, RNH, SET, SFM, SPT, UPI	
NTE02	Claim Note Text	AN	1-80	R				
NTE	**BILLING NOTE**		1	S	2300			
NTE01	Note Reference Code	ID	3-3	R			ADD	

Page 19 of 93

INSTITUTIONAL CLAIM

Element Identifier	Description	ID	Min. Max.	Usage Reg.	Loop	Loop Repeat	Values
				4010A1			
				837-I 4010A1			
NTE02	Billing Note Text	AN	1-80	R			
CR6	HOME HEALTH CARE INFORMATION		1	S	2300		
CR601	Prognosis Indicator	ID	1-1	R			1, 2, 3, 4, 5, 6, 7, 8
CR602	Service From Date	DT	8-8	R			CCYYMMDD
CR603	Date Time Period Format Qualifier	ID	2-3	S			RD8
CR604	Home Health Certification Period	AN	1-35	S			
CR605	Diagnosis Date	DT	8-8	R			CCYYMMDD
CR606	Skilled Nursing Facility Indicator	ID	1-1	R			N, U, Y
CR607	Medicare Coverage Indicator	ID	1-1	R			N, Y
CR608	Certification Type Indicator	ID	1-1	R			I, R, S
CR609	Surgery Date	DT	8-8				CCYYMMDD
CR610	Product or Service ID Qualifier	ID	2-2	S			HC, ID
CR611	Surgical Procedure Code	AN	1-15	S			
CR612	Physician Order Date	DT	8-8	S			CCYYMMDD
CR613	Last Visit Date	DT	8-8	S			CCYYMMDD
CR614	Physician Contact Date	DT	8-8	S			CCYYMMDD
CR615	Date Time Period Format Qualifier	ID	2-3	S			RD8
CR616	Last Admission Period	AN	1-35	S			
CR617	Patient Discharge Facility Type Code	ID	1-1	R			A, B, C, D, E, F, G, H, L, M, O, R, S, T
CR618	Diagnosis Date	DT	8-8	S			CCYYMMDD
CR619	Diagnosis Date	DT	8-8	S			CCYYMMDD
CR620	Diagnosis Date	DT	8-8	S			CCYYMMDD
CR621	Diagnosis Date	DT	8-8	S			CCYYMMDD
CRC	HOME HEALTH FUNCTIONAL LIMITATIONS		3	S	2300		
CRC01	Code Category	ID	2-2	R			75
CRC02	Certification Condition Indicator	ID	1-1	R			N, Y
CRC03	Functional Limitations Code	ID	2-2	R			AA, AL, BL, CO, DY, EL, HL, LB, OL, PA, SL
CRC04	Functional Limitations Code	ID	2-2	S			
CRC05	Functional Limitations Code	ID	2-2	S			
CRC06	Functional Limitations Code	ID	2-2	S			
CRC07	Functional Limitations Code	ID	2-2	S			

Element Identifier	Description	ID	Min. Max.	Usage Reg.	Loop	Loop Repeat	Values
				5010			
				837-I 5010			
NTE02	Billing Note Text	AN	1-80	R			

Segment Deleted

Segment Deleted

Page 20 of 93

INSTITUTIONAL CLAIM

4010A1

837-I 4010A1

Element Identifier	Description	ID	Min. Max.	Usage Reg.	Loop	Loop Repeat	Values
CRC	HOME HEALTH FUNCTIONAL LIMITATIONS		3	S	2300		
CRC01	Code Category	ID	2-2	R			76
CRC02	Functional Limitations Code	ID	1-1	R			N, Y
CRC03	Activities Permitted Code	ID	2-2	R			BR, CA, CB, CR, EP, IH, NR, PW, TR, UT, WA, WR
CRC04	Activities Permitted Code	ID	2-2	S			
CRC05	Activities Permitted Code	ID	2-2	S			
CRC06	Activities Permitted Code	ID	2-2	S			
CRC07	Activities Permitted Code	ID	2-2	S			
CRC	HOME HEALTH MENTAL STATUS		2	S	2300		
CRC01	Certification Condition Indicator	ID	2-2	R			77
CRC02	Functional Limitations Code	ID	1-1	R			N, Y
CRC03	Mental Status Code	ID	2-2	R			AG, CM, DI, DP, FO, LE, MC, OT
CRC04	Mental Status Code	ID	2-2	S			
CRC05	Mental Status Code	ID	2-2	S			
CRC06	Mental Status Code	ID	2-2	S			
CRC07	Mental Status Code	ID	2-2	S			
HI	PRINCIPAL DIAGNOSIS		1	S	2300		
HI01	HEALTH CARE CODE INFORMATION			R			
HI01-1	Code List Qualifier Code	ID	1-3	R			BK
HI01-2	Industry Code	AN	1-30	R			
HI01-3	Date Time Period Format Qualifier	ID	2-3	N/U			
HI01-4	Date Time Period	AN	1-35	N/U			
HI01-5	Monetary Amount	R	1-18	N/U			
HI01-6	Quantity	R	1-15	N/U			
HI01-7	Version Identifier	AN	1-30	N/U			

5010

837-I 5010

Element Identifier	Description	ID	Min. Max.	Usage Reg.	Loop	Loop Repeat	Values	
								Segment Deleted
								Segment Deleted
CRC	EPSDT REFERRAL		1	S	2300			New Segment
CRC01	Code Category	ID	2-2	R			ZZ	
CRC02	Certification Condition Indicator	ID	1-1	R			N, Y	
CRC03	Condition Code	ID	2-3	R			AV, NU, S2, ST	
CRC04	Condition Code	ID	2-3	S			AV, NU, S2, ST	
CRC05	Condition Code	ID	2-3	S			AV, NU, S2, ST	
CRC06	Condition Indicator	ID	2-3	N/U				
CRC07	Condition Indicator	ID	2-3	N/U				
HI	PRINCIPAL DIAGNOSIS		1	R	2300			Usage change to Required
HI01	HEALTH CARE CODE INFORMATION			R				
HI01-1	Diagnosis Type Code	ID	1-3	R			ABK, BK	Name Change
HI01-2	Principal Diagnosis Code	AN	1-30	R				Name Change
HI01-3	Date Time Period Format Qualifier	ID	2-3	N/U				
HI01-4	Date Time Period	AN	1-35	N/U				
HI01-5	Monetary Amount	R	1-18	N/U				
HI01-6	Quantity	R	1-15	N/U				
HI01-7	Version Identifier	AN	1-30	N/U				

Page 21 of 93

INSTITUTIONAL CLAIM

4010A1							
Element Identifier	Description	ID	Min. Max.	Usage Reg.	Loop	Loop Repeat	Values
	837-I 4010A1						
HI02	HEALTH CARE CODE INFORMATION			S			
HI02-1	Code List Qualifier Code	ID	1-3	R			BJ, ZZ
HI02-2	Industry Code	AN	1-30	R			
HI02-3	Date Time Period Format Qualifier	ID	2-3	N/U			
HI02-4	Date Time Period	AN	1-35	N/U			
HI02-5	Monetary Amount	R	1-18	N/U			
HI02-6	Quantity	R	1-15	N/U			
HI02-7	Version Identifier	AN	1-30	N/U			
HI03	HEALTH CARE CODE INFORMATION			S			
HI03-1	Code List Qualifier Code	ID	1-3	R			BN
HI03-2	Industry Code	AN	1-30	R			
HI03-3	Date Time Period Format Qualifier	ID	2-3	N/U			
HI03-4	Date Time Period	AN	1-35	N/U			
HI03-5	Monetary Amount	R	1-18	N/U			
HI03-6	Quantity	R	1-15	N/U			
HI03-7	Version Identifier	AN	1-30	N/U			
HI04	HEALTH CARE CODE INFORMATION			N/U			

5010								
Element Identifier	Description	ID	Min. Max.	Usage Reg.	Loop	Loop Repeat	Values	
	837-I 5010							
HI01-8	Industry code	AN	1-30	N/U				New Element
HI01-9	Present on Admission indicator	ID	1-1	S			N, U, W, Y	New Element
HI02	HEALTH CARE CODE INFORMATION			N/U				Usage change to Not Used
HI02-1	Diagnosis Type Code	ID	1-3	N/U				Usage change to Not Used Name Change
HI02-2	Principal Diagnosis Code	AN	1-30	N/U				Usage change to Not Used Name Change
HI02-3	Date Time Period Format Qualifier	ID	2-3	N/U				
HI02-4	Date Time Period	AN	1-35	N/U				
HI02-5	Monetary Amount	R	1-18	N/U				
HI02-6	Quantity	R	1-15	N/U				
HI02-7	Version Identifier	AN	1-30	N/U				
HI02-8	Industry code	AN	1-30	N/U				New Element
HI02-9	Present on Admission indicator	ID	1-1	N/U				New Element
HI03	HEALTH CARE CODE INFORMATION			N/U				Usage change to Not Used
HI03-1	Diagnosis Type Code	ID	1-3	N/U				Usage change to Not Used Name Change
HI03-2	Principal Diagnosis Code	AN	1-30	N/U				Usage change to Not Used Name Change
HI03-3	Date Time Period Format Qualifier	ID	2-3	N/U				
HI03-4	Date Time Period	AN	1-35	N/U				
HI03-5	Monetary Amount	R	1-18	N/U				
HI03-6	Quantity	R	1-15	N/U				
HI03-7	Version Identifier	AN	1-30	N/U				
HI03-8	Industry code	AN	1-30	N/U				New Element
HI03-9	Present on Admission indicator	ID	1-1	N/U				New Element
HI04	HEALTH CARE CODE INFORMATION			N/U				
HI04-1	Diagnosis Type Code	ID	1-3	N/U				New Element
HI04-2	Principal Diagnosis Code	AN	1-30	N/U				New Element
HI04-3	Date Time Period Format Qualifier	ID	2-3	N/U				New Element
HI04-4	Date Time Period	AN	1-35	N/U				New Element
HI04-5	Monetary Amount	R	1-18	N/U				New Element
HI04-6	Quantity	R	1-15	N/U				New Element
HI04-7	Version Identifier	AN	1-30	N/U				New Element
HI04-8	Industry code	AN	1-30	N/U				New Element
HI04-9	Present on Admission indicator	ID	1-1	N/U				New Element

Page 22 of 93

INSTITUTIONAL CLAIM

4010A1

Element Identifier	Description	ID	Min. Max.	Usage Reg.	Loop	Loop Repeat	Values
	837-I 4010A1						
HI05	HEALTH CARE CODE INFORMATION			N/U			
HI06	HEALTH CARE CODE INFORMATION			N/U			
HI07	HEALTH CARE CODE INFORMATION			N/U			
HI08	HEALTH CARE CODE INFORMATION			N/U			

5010

Element Identifier	Description	ID	Min. Max.	Usage Reg.	Loop	Loop Repeat	Values	
	837-I 5010							
HI05	HEALTH CARE CODE INFORMATION			N/U				
HI05-1	Diagnosis Type Code	ID	1-3	N/U				New Element
HI05-2	Principal Diagnosis Code	AN	1-30	N/U				New Element
HI05-3	Date Time Period Format Qualifier	ID	2-3	N/U				New Element
HI05-4	Date Time Period	AN	1-35	N/U				New Element
HI05-5	Monetary Amount	R	1-18	N/U				New Element
HI05-6	Quantity	R	1-15	N/U				New Element
HI05-7	Version Identifier	AN	1-30	N/U				New Element
HI05-8	Industry code	AN	1-30	N/U				New Element
HI05-9	Present on Admission indicator	ID	1-1	N/U				New Element
HI06	HEALTH CARE CODE INFORMATION			N/U				
HI06-1	Diagnosis Type Code	ID	1-3	N/U				New Element
HI06-2	Principal Diagnosis Code	AN	1-30	N/U				New Element
HI06-3	Date Time Period Format Qualifier	ID	2-3	N/U				New Element
HI06-4	Date Time Period	AN	1-35	N/U				New Element
HI06-5	Monetary Amount	R	1-18	N/U				New Element
HI06-6	Quantity	R	1-15	N/U				New Element
HI06-7	Version Identifier	AN	1-30	N/U				New Element
HI06-8	Industry code	AN	1-30	N/U				New Element
HI06-9	Present on Admission indicator	ID	1-1	N/U				New Element
HI07	HEALTH CARE CODE INFORMATION			N/U				
HI07-1	Diagnosis Type Code	ID	1-3	N/U				New Element
HI07-2	Principal Diagnosis Code	AN	1-30	N/U				New Element
HI07-3	Date Time Period Format Qualifier	ID	2-3	N/U				New Element
HI07-4	Date Time Period	AN	1-35	N/U				New Element
HI07-5	Monetary Amount	R	1-18	N/U				New Element
HI07-6	Quantity	R	1-15	N/U				New Element
HI07-7	Version Identifier	AN	1-30	N/U				New Element
HI07-8	Industry code	AN	1-30	N/U				New Element
HI07-9	Present on Admission indicator	ID	1-1	N/U				New Element
HI08	HEALTH CARE CODE INFORMATION			N/U				
HI08-1	Diagnosis Type Code	ID	1-3	N/U				New Element
HI08-2	Principal Diagnosis Code	AN	1-30	N/U				New Element
HI08-3	Date Time Period Format Qualifier	ID	2-3	N/U				New Element
HI08-4	Date Time Period	AN	1-35	N/U				New Element
HI08-5	Monetary Amount	R	1-18	N/U				New Element
HI08-6	Quantity	R	1-15	N/U				New Element
HI08-7	Version Identifier	AN	1-30	N/U				New Element

Page 23 of 93

INSTITUTIONAL CLAIM

4010A1								
Element Identifier	Description	ID	Min. Max.	Usage Reg.	Loop	Loop Repeat	Values	
				837-I 4010A1				
HI09	HEALTH CARE CODE INFORMATION			N/U				
HI10	HEALTH CARE CODE INFORMATION			N/U				
HI11	HEALTH CARE CODE INFORMATION			N/U				
HI12	HEALTH CARE CODE INFORMATION			N/U				

5010								
Element Identifier	Description	ID	Min. Max.	Usage Reg.	Loop	Loop Repeat	Values	
				837-I 5010				
HI08-8	Industry code	AN	1-30	N/U				New Element
HI08-9	Present on Admission indicator	ID	1-1	N/U				New Element
HI09	HEALTH CARE CODE INFORMATION			N/U				
HI09-1	Diagnosis Type Code	ID	1-3	N/U				New Element
HI09-2	Principal Diagnosis Code	AN	1-30	N/U				New Element
HI09-3	Date Time Period Format Qualifier	ID	2-3	N/U				New Element
HI09-4	Date Time Period	AN	1-35	N/U				New Element
HI09-5	Monetary Amount	R	1-18	N/U				New Element
HI09-6	Quantity	R	1-15	N/U				New Element
HI09-7	Version Identifier	AN	1-30	N/U				New Element
HI09-8	Industry code	AN	1-30	N/U				New Element
HI09-9	Present on Admission indicator	ID	1-1	N/U				New Element
HI10	HEALTH CARE CODE INFORMATION			N/U				
HI10-1	Diagnosis Type Code	ID	1-3	N/U				New Element
HI10-2	Principal Diagnosis Code	AN	1-30	N/U				New Element
HI10-3	Date Time Period Format Qualifier	ID	2-3	N/U				New Element
HI10-4	Date Time Period	AN	1-35	N/U				New Element
HI10-5	Monetary Amount	R	1-18	N/U				New Element
HI10-6	Quantity	R	1-15	N/U				New Element
HI10-7	Version Identifier	AN	1-30	N/U				New Element
HI10-8	Industry code	AN	1-30	N/U				New Element
HI10-9	Present on Admission indicator	ID	1-1	N/U				New Element
HI11	HEALTH CARE CODE INFORMATION			N/U				
HI11-1	Diagnosis Type Code	ID	1-3	N/U				New Element
HI11-2	Principal Diagnosis Code	AN	1-30	N/U				New Element
HI11-3	Date Time Period Format Qualifier	ID	2-3	N/U				New Element
HI11-4	Date Time Period	AN	1-35	N/U				New Element
HI11-5	Monetary Amount	R	1-18	N/U				New Element
HI11-6	Quantity	R	1-15	N/U				New Element
HI11-7	Version Identifier	AN	1-30	N/U				New Element
HI11-8	Industry code	AN	1-30	N/U				New Element
HI11-9	Present on Admission indicator	ID	1-1	N/U				New Element
HI12	HEALTH CARE CODE INFORMATION			N/U				
HI12-1	Diagnosis Type Code	ID	1-3	N/U				New Element
HI12-2	Principal Diagnosis Code	AN	1-30	N/U				New Element
HI12-3	Date Time Period Format Qualifier	ID	2-3	N/U				New Element
HI12-4	Date Time Period	AN	1-35	N/U				New Element
HI12-5	Monetary Amount	R	1-18	N/U				New Element

Page 24 of 93

INSTITUTIONAL CLAIM

4010A1							
Element Identifier	Description	ID	Min. Max.	Usage Reg.	Loop	Loop Repeat	Values
				837-I 4010A1			

5010								
Element Identifier	Description	ID	Min. Max.	Usage Reg.	Loop	Loop Repeat	Values	
				837-I 5010				
HI12-6	Quantity	R	1-15	N/U				New Element
HI12-7	Version Identifier	AN	1-30	N/U				New Element
HI12-8	Industry code	AN	1-30	N/U				New Element
HI12-9	Present on Admission indicator	ID	1-1	N/U				New Element
HI	**ADMITTING DISGNOSIS**		1	R	2300			New Segment
HI01	HEALTH CARE CODE INFORMATION			R				
HI01-1	Diagnosis Type Code	ID	1-3	R			ABJ, BJ	
HI01-2	Admitting Diagnosis Code	AN	1-30	R				
HI01-3	Date Time Period Format Qualifier	ID	2-3	N/U				
HI01-4	Date Time Period	AN	1-35	N/U				
HI01-5	Monetary Amount	R	1-18	N/U				
HI01-6	Quantity	R	1-15	N/U				
HI01-7	Version Identifier	AN	1-30	N/U				
HI01-8	Industry code	AN	1-30	N/U				
HI01-9	Yes/No Condition or response Code	ID	1-1	N/U				
HI02	HEALTH CARE CODE INFORMATION			N/U				
HI02-1	Diagnosis Type Code	ID	1-3	N/U				
HI02-2	Principal Diagnosis Code	AN	1-30	N/U				
HI02-3	Date Time Period Format Qualifier	ID	2-3	N/U				
HI02-4	Date Time Period	AN	1-35	N/U				
HI02-5	Monetary Amount	R	1-18	N/U				
HI02-6	Quantity	R	1-15	N/U				
HI02-7	Version Identifier	AN	1-30	N/U				
HI02-8	Industry code	AN	1-30	N/U				
HI02-9	Present on Admission indicator	ID	1-1	N/U				
HI03	HEALTH CARE CODE INFORMATION			N/U				
HI03-1	Diagnosis Type Code	ID	1-3	N/U				
HI03-2	Principal Diagnosis Code	AN	1-30	N/U				
HI03-3	Date Time Period Format Qualifier	ID	2-3	N/U				
HI03-4	Date Time Period	AN	1-35	N/U				
HI03-5	Monetary Amount	R	1-18	N/U				
HI03-6	Quantity	R	1-15	N/U				
HI03-7	Version Identifier	AN	1-30	N/U				
HI03-8	Industry code	AN	1-30	N/U				
HI03-9	Present on Admission indicator	ID	1-1	N/U				
HI04	HEALTH CARE CODE INFORMATION			N/U				
HI04-1	Diagnosis Type Code	ID	1-3	N/U				
HI04-2	Principal Diagnosis Code	AN	1-30	N/U				

INSTITUTIONAL CLAIM

4010A1							
Element Identifier	Description	ID	Min. Max.	Usage Reg.	Loop	Loop Repeat	Values
837-I 4010A1							

5010							
Element Identifier	Description	ID	Min. Max.	Usage Reg.	Loop	Loop Repeat	Values
837-I 5010							
HI04-3	Date Time Period Format Qualifier	ID	2-3	N/U			
HI04-4	Date Time Period	AN	1-35	N/U			
HI04-5	Monetary Amount	R	1-18	N/U			
HI04-6	Quantity	R	1-15	N/U			
HI04-7	Version Identifier	AN	1-30	N/U			
HI04-8	Industry code	AN	1-30	N/U			
HI04-9	Present on Admission indicator	ID	1-1	N/U			
HI05	HEALTH CARE CODE INFORMATION			N/U			
HI05-1	Diagnosis Type Code	ID	1-3	N/U			
HI05-2	Principal Diagnosis Code	AN	1-30	N/U			
HI05-3	Date Time Period Format Qualifier	ID	2-3	N/U			
HI05-4	Date Time Period	AN	1-35	N/U			
HI05-5	Monetary Amount	R	1-18	N/U			
HI05-6	Quantity	R	1-15	N/U			
HI05-7	Version Identifier	AN	1-30	N/U			
HI05-8	Industry code	AN	1-30	N/U			
HI05-9	Present on Admission indicator	ID	1-1	N/U			
HI06	HEALTH CARE CODE INFORMATION			N/U			
HI06-1	Diagnosis Type Code	ID	1-3	N/U			
HI06-2	Principal Diagnosis Code	AN	1-30	N/U			
HI06-3	Date Time Period Format Qualifier	ID	2-3	N/U			
HI06-4	Date Time Period	AN	1-35	N/U			
HI06-5	Monetary Amount	R	1-18	N/U			
HI06-6	Quantity	R	1-15	N/U			
HI06-7	Version Identifier	AN	1-30	N/U			
HI06-8	Industry code	AN	1-30	N/U			
HI06-9	Present on Admission indicator	ID	1-1	N/U			
HI07	HEALTH CARE CODE INFORMATION			N/U			
HI07-1	Diagnosis Type Code	ID	1-3	N/U			
HI07-2	Principal Diagnosis Code	AN	1-30	N/U			
HI07-3	Date Time Period Format Qualifier	ID	2-3	N/U			
HI07-4	Date Time Period	AN	1-35	N/U			
HI07-5	Monetary Amount	R	1-18	N/U			
HI07-6	Quantity	R	1-15	N/U			
HI07-7	Version Identifier	AN	1-30	N/U			
HI07-8	Industry code	AN	1-30	N/U			
HI07-9	Present on Admission indicator	ID	1-1	N/U			
HI08	HEALTH CARE CODE INFORMATION			N/U			

Page 26 of 93

INSTITUTIONAL CLAIM

4010A1

Element Identifier	Description	ID	Min. Max.	Usage Req.	Loop	Loop Repeat	Values
				837-I 4010A1			

5010

Element Identifier	Description	ID	Min. Max.	Usage Req.	Loop	Loop Repeat	Values
				837-I 5010			
HI08-1	Diagnosis Type Code	ID	1-3	N/U			
HI08-2	Principal Diagnosis Code	AN	1-30	N/U			
HI08-3	Date Time Period Format Qualifier	ID	2-3	N/U			
HI08-4	Date Time Period	AN	1-35	N/U			
HI08-5	Monetary Amount	R	1-18	N/U			
HI08-6	Quantity	R	1-15	N/U			
HI08-7	Version Identifier	AN	1-30	N/U			
HI08-8	Industry code	AN	1-30	N/U			
HI08-9	Present on Admission indicator	ID	1-1	N/U			
HI09	HEALTH CARE CODE INFORMATION			N/U			
HI09-1	Diagnosis Type Code	ID	1-3	N/U			
HI09-2	Principal Diagnosis Code	AN	1-30	N/U			
HI09-3	Date Time Period Format Qualifier	ID	2-3	N/U			
HI09-4	Date Time Period	AN	1-35	N/U			
HI09-5	Monetary Amount	R	1-18	N/U			
HI09-6	Quantity	R	1-15	N/U			
HI09-7	Version Identifier	AN	1-30	N/U			
HI09-8	Industry code	AN	1-30	N/U			
HI09-9	Present on Admission indicator	ID	1-1	N/U			
HI10	HEALTH CARE CODE INFORMATION			N/U			
HI10-1	Diagnosis Type Code	ID	1-3	N/U			
HI10-2	Principal Diagnosis Code	AN	1-30	N/U			
HI10-3	Date Time Period Format Qualifier	ID	2-3	N/U			
HI10-4	Date Time Period	AN	1-35	N/U			
HI10-5	Monetary Amount	R	1-18	N/U			
HI10-6	Quantity	R	1-15	N/U			
HI10-7	Version Identifier	AN	1-30	N/U			
HI10-8	Industry code	AN	1-30	N/U			
HI10-9	Present on Admission indicator	ID	1-1	N/U			
HI11	HEALTH CARE CODE INFORMATION			N/U			
HI11-1	Diagnosis Type Code	ID	1-3	N/U			
HI11-2	Principal Diagnosis Code	AN	1-30	N/U			
HI11-3	Date Time Period Format Qualifier	ID	2-3	N/U			
HI11-4	Date Time Period	AN	1-35	N/U			
HI11-5	Monetary Amount	R	1-18	N/U			
HI11-6	Quantity	R	1-15	N/U			
HI11-7	Version Identifier	AN	1-30	N/U			
HI11-8	Industry code	AN	1-30	N/U			
HI11-9	Present on Admission indicator	ID	1-1	N/U			

Page 27 of 93

INSTITUTIONAL CLAIM

Element Identifier	Description	ID	Min. Max.	Usage Req.	Loop	Loop Repeat	Values
4010A1							
		837-I 4010A1					

Element Identifier	Description	ID	Min. Max.	Usage Req.	Loop	Loop Repeat	Values
5010							
		837-I 5010					
HI12	HEALTH CARE CODE INFORMATION			N/U			
HI12-1	Diagnosis Type Code	ID	1-3	N/U			
HI12-2	Principal Diagnosis Code	AN	1-30	N/U			
HI12-3	Date Time Period Format Qualifier	ID	2-3	N/U			
HI12-4	Date Time Period	AN	1-35	N/U			
HI12-5	Monetary Amount	R	1-18	N/U			
HI12-6	Quantity	R	1-15	N/U			
HI12-7	Version Identifier	AN	1-30	N/U			
HI12-8	Industry code	AN	1-30	N/U			
HI12-9	Present on Admission indicator	ID	1-1	N/U			
HI	**PATIENT REASON FOR VISIT**		1	R	2300		New Segment
HI01	HEALTH CARE CODE INFORMATION			R			
HI01-1	Diagnosis Type Code	ID	1-3	R			APR, PR
HI01-2	Patient Reason For Visit	AN	1-30	R			
HI01-3	Date Time Period Format Qualifier	ID	2-3	N/U			
HI01-4	Date Time Period	AN	1-35	N/U			
HI01-5	Monetary Amount	R	1-18	N/U			
HI01-6	Quantity	R	1-15	N/U			
HI01-7	Version Identifier	AN	1-30	N/U			
HI01-8	Industry code	AN	1-30	N/U			
HI01-9	Yes/No Condition or response Code	ID	1-1	N/U			
HI02	HEALTH CARE CODE INFORMATION			S			
HI02-1	Diagnosis Type Code	ID	1-3	R			APR, PR
HI02-2	Patient Reason For Visit	AN	1-30	R			
HI02-3	Date Time Period Format Qualifier	ID	2-3	N/U			
HI02-4	Date Time Period	AN	1-35	N/U			
HI02-5	Monetary Amount	R	1-18	N/U			
HI02-6	Quantity	R	1-15	N/U			
HI02-7	Version Identifier	AN	1-30	N/U			
HI02-8	Industry code	AN	1-30	N/U			
HI02-9	Yes/No Condition or response Code	ID	1-1	N/U			
HI03	HEALTH CARE CODE INFORMATION			S			
HI03-1	Diagnosis Type Code	ID	1-3	R			APR, PR
HI03-2	Patient Reason For Visit	AN	1-30	R			
HI03-3	Date Time Period Format Qualifier	ID	2-3	N/U			
HI03-4	Date Time Period	AN	1-35	N/U			
HI03-5	Monetary Amount	R	1-18	N/U			

INSTITUTIONAL CLAIM

	4010A1						
Element Identifier	Description	ID	Min. Max.	Usage Reg.	Loop	Loop Repeat	Values
	837-I 4010A1						

	5010						
Element Identifier	Description	ID	Min. Max.	Usage Reg.	Loop	Loop Repeat	Values
	837-I 5010						
HI03-6	Quantity	R	1-15	N/U			
HI03-7	Version Identifier	AN	1-30	N/U			
HI03-8	Industry code	AN	1-30	N/U			
HI03-9	Yes/No Condition or response Code	ID	1-1	N/U			
HI04	HEALTH CARE CODE INFORMATION			N/U			
HI04-1	Diagnosis Type Code	ID	1-3	N/U			
HI04-2	Principal Diagnosis Code	AN	1-30	N/U			
HI04-3	Date Time Period Format Qualifier	ID	2-3	N/U			
HI04-4	Date Time Period	AN	1-35	N/U			
HI04-5	Monetary Amount	R	1-18	N/U			
HI04-6	Quantity	R	1-15	N/U			
HI04-7	Version Identifier	AN	1-30	N/U			
HI04-8	Industry code	AN	1-30	N/U			
HI04-9	Present on Admission indicator	ID	1-1	N/U			
HI05	HEALTH CARE CODE INFORMATION			N/U			
HI05-1	Diagnosis Type Code	ID	1-3	N/U			
HI05-2	Principal Diagnosis Code	AN	1-30	N/U			
HI05-3	Date Time Period Format Qualifier	ID	2-3	N/U			
HI05-4	Date Time Period	AN	1-35	N/U			
HI05-5	Monetary Amount	R	1-18	N/U			
HI05-6	Quantity	R	1-15	N/U			
HI05-7	Version Identifier	AN	1-30	N/U			
HI05-8	Industry code	AN	1-30	N/U			
HI05-9	Present on Admission indicator	ID	1-1	N/U			
HI06	HEALTH CARE CODE INFORMATION			N/U			
HI06-1	Diagnosis Type Code	ID	1-3	N/U			
HI06-2	Principal Diagnosis Code	AN	1-30	N/U			
HI06-3	Date Time Period Format Qualifier	ID	2-3	N/U			
HI06-4	Date Time Period	AN	1-35	N/U			
HI06-5	Monetary Amount	R	1-18	N/U			
HI06-6	Quantity	R	1-15	N/U			
HI06-7	Version Identifier	AN	1-30	N/U			
HI06-8	Industry code	AN	1-30	N/U			
HI06-9	Present on Admission indicator	ID	1-1	N/U			
HI07	HEALTH CARE CODE INFORMATION			N/U			
HI07-1	Diagnosis Type Code	ID	1-3	N/U			
HI07-2	Principal Diagnosis Code	AN	1-30	N/U			
HI07-3	Date Time Period Format Qualifier	ID	2-3	N/U			

Page 29 of 93

INSTITUTIONAL CLAIM

4010A1							
Element Identifier	Description	ID	Min. Max.	Usage Reg.	Loop	Loop Repeat	Values
				837-I 4010A1			

5010							
Element Identifier	Description	ID	Min. Max.	Usage Reg.	Loop	Loop Repeat	Values
				837-I 5010			
HI07-4	Date Time Period	AN	1-35	N/U			
HI07-5	Monetary Amount	R	1-18	N/U			
HI07-6	Quantity	R	1-15	N/U			
HI07-7	Version Identifier	AN	1-30	N/U			
HI07-8	Industry code	AN	1-30	N/U			
HI07-9	Present on Admission indicator	ID	1-1	N/U			
HI08	HEALTH CARE CODE INFORMATION			N/U			
HI08-1	Diagnosis Type Code	ID	1-3	N/U			
HI08-2	Principal Diagnosis Code	AN	1-30	N/U			
HI08-3	Date Time Period Format Qualifier	ID	2-3	N/U			
HI08-4	Date Time Period	AN	1-35	N/U			
HI08-5	Monetary Amount	R	1-18	N/U			
HI08-6	Quantity	R	1-15	N/U			
HI08-7	Version Identifier	AN	1-30	N/U			
HI08-8	Industry code	AN	1-30	N/U			
HI08-9	Present on Admission indicator	ID	1-1	N/U			
HI09	HEALTH CARE CODE INFORMATION			N/U			
HI09-1	Diagnosis Type Code	ID	1-3	N/U			
HI09-2	Principal Diagnosis Code	AN	1-30	N/U			
HI09-3	Date Time Period Format Qualifier	ID	2-3	N/U			
HI09-4	Date Time Period	AN	1-35	N/U			
HI09-5	Monetary Amount	R	1-18	N/U			
HI09-6	Quantity	R	1-15	N/U			
HI09-7	Version Identifier	AN	1-30	N/U			
HI09-8	Industry code	AN	1-30	N/U			
HI09-9	Present on Admission indicator	ID	1-1	N/U			
HI10	HEALTH CARE CODE INFORMATION			N/U			
HI10-1	Diagnosis Type Code	ID	1-3	N/U			
HI10-2	Principal Diagnosis Code	AN	1-30	N/U			
HI10-3	Date Time Period Format Qualifier	ID	2-3	N/U			
HI10-4	Date Time Period	AN	1-35	N/U			
HI10-5	Monetary Amount	R	1-18	N/U			
HI10-6	Quantity	R	1-15	N/U			
HI10-7	Version Identifier	AN	1-30	N/U			
HI10-8	Industry code	AN	1-30	N/U			
HI10-9	Present on Admission indicator	ID	1-1	N/U			
HI11	HEALTH CARE CODE INFORMATION			N/U			
HI11-1	Diagnosis Type Code	ID	1-3	N/U			
HI11-2	Principal Diagnosis Code	AN	1-30	N/U			

Page 30 of 93

INSTITUTIONAL CLAIM

4010A1

Element Identifier	Description	ID	Min. Max.	Usage Reg.	Loop	Loop Repeat	Values
	837-I 4010A1						

5010

Element Identifier	Description	ID	Min. Max.	Usage Reg.	Loop	Loop Repeat	Values
	837-I 5010						
HI11-3	Date Time Period Format Qualifier	ID	2-3	N/U			
HI11-4	Date Time Period	AN	1-35	N/U			
HI11-5	Monetary Amount	R	1-18	N/U			
HI11-6	Quantity	R	1-15	N/U			
HI11-7	Version Identifier	AN	1-30	N/U			
HI11-8	Industry code	AN	1-30	N/U			
HI11-9	Present on Admission indicator	ID	1-1	N/U			
HI12	HEALTH CARE CODE INFORMATION			N/U			
HI12-1	Diagnosis Type Code	ID	1-3	N/U			
HI12-2	Principal Diagnosis Code	AN	1-30	N/U			
HI12-3	Date Time Period Format Qualifier	ID	2-3	N/U			
HI12-4	Date Time Period	AN	1-35	N/U			
HI12-5	Monetary Amount	R	1-18	N/U			
HI12-6	Quantity	R	1-15	N/U			
HI12-7	Version Identifier	AN	1-30	N/U			
HI12-8	Industry code	AN	1-30	N/U			
HI12-9	Present on Admission indicator	ID	1-1	N/U			
HI	EXTERNAL CAUSE OF INJURY		1	R	2300		New Segment
HI01	HEALTH CARE CODE INFORMATION			R			
HI01-1	Diagnosis Type Code	ID	1-3	R			ABN, BN
HI01-2	External Cause of Injury Code	AN	1-30	R			
HI01-3	Date Time Period Format Qualifier	ID	2-3	N/U			
HI01-4	Date Time Period	AN	1-35	N/U			
HI01-5	Monetary Amount	R	1-18	N/U			
HI01-6	Quantity	R	1-15	N/U			
HI01-7	Version Identifier	AN	1-30	N/U			
HI01-8	Industry code	AN	1-30	N/U			
HI01-9	Present on Admission indicator	ID	1-1	S			N, U, W, Y
HI02	HEALTH CARE CODE INFORMATION			S			
HI02-1	Diagnosis Type Code	ID	1-3	R			ABN, BN
HI02-2	External Cause of Injury Code	AN	1-30	R			
HI02-3	Date Time Period Format Qualifier	ID	2-3	N/U			
HI02-4	Date Time Period	AN	1-35	N/U			
HI02-5	Monetary Amount	R	1-18	N/U			
HI02-6	Quantity	R	1-15	N/U			
HI02-7	Version Identifier	AN	1-30	N/U			

Page 31 of 93

INSTITUTIONAL CLAIM

Element Identifier	Description	ID	Min. Max.	Usage Reg.	Loop	Loop Repeat	Values
	4010A1						
	837-I 4010A1						

Element Identifier	Description	ID	Min. Max.	Usage Reg.	Loop	Loop Repeat	Values
	5010						
	837-I 5010						
HI02-8	Industry code	AN	1-30	N/U			
HI02-9	Present on Admission indicator	ID	1-1	S			N, U, W, Y
HI03	HEALTH CARE CODE INFORMATION			S			
HI03-1	Diagnosis Type Code	ID	1-3	R			ABN, BN
HI03-2	External Cause of Injury Code	AN	1-30	R			
HI03-3	Date Time Period Format Qualifier	ID	2-3	N/U			
HI03-4	Date Time Period	AN	1-35	N/U			
HI03-5	Monetary Amount	R	1-18	N/U			
HI03-6	Quantity	R	1-15	N/U			
HI03-7	Version Identifier	AN	1-30	N/U			
HI03-8	Industry code	AN	1-30	N/U			
HI03-9	Present on Admission indicator	ID	1-1	S			N, U, W, Y
HI04	HEALTH CARE CODE INFORMATION			S			
HI04-1	Diagnosis Type Code	ID	1-3	R			ABN, BN
HI04-2	External Cause of Injury Code	AN	1-30	R			
HI04-3	Date Time Period Format Qualifier	ID	2-3	N/U			
HI04-4	Date Time Period	AN	1-35	N/U			
HI04-5	Monetary Amount	R	1-18	N/U			
HI04-6	Quantity	R	1-15	N/U			
HI04-7	Version Identifier	AN	1-30	N/U			
HI04-8	Industry code	AN	1-30	N/U			
HI04-9	Present on Admission indicator	ID	1-1	N/U			N, U, W, Y
HI05	HEALTH CARE CODE INFORMATION			S			
HI05-1	Diagnosis Type Code	ID	1-3	R			ABN, BN
HI05-2	Diagnosis Code	AN	1-30	R			
HI05-3	Date Time Period Format Qualifier	ID	2-3	N/U			
HI05-4	Date Time Period	AN	1-35	N/U			
HI05-5	Monetary Amount	R	1-18	N/U			
HI05-6	Quantity	R	1-15	N/U			
HI05-7	Version Identifier	AN	1-30	N/U			
HI05-8	Industry code	AN	1-30	N/U			
HI05-9	Present on Admission indicator	ID	1-1	S			N, U, W, Y
HI06	HEALTH CARE CODE INFORMATION			S			
HI06-1	Diagnosis Type Code	ID	1-3	R			ABN, BN
HI06-2	External Cause of Injury Code	AN	1-30	R			

Page 32 of 93

INSTITUTIONAL CLAIM

4010A1

Element Identifier	Description	ID	Min. Max.	Usage Reg.	Loop	Loop Repeat	Values
				837-I 4010A1			

5010

Element Identifier	Description	ID	Min. Max.	Usage Reg.	Loop	Loop Repeat	Values
				837-I 5010			
HI06-3	Date Time Period Format Qualifier	ID	2-3	N/U			
HI06-4	Date Time Period	AN	1-35	N/U			
HI06-5	Monetary Amount	R	1-18	N/U			
HI06-6	Quantity	R	1-15	N/U			
HI06-7	Version Identifier	AN	1-30	N/U			
HI06-8	Industry code	AN	1-30	N/U			
HI06-9	Present on Admission indicator	ID	1-1	S			N, U, W, Y
HI07	HEALTH CARE CODE INFORMATION			S			
HI07-1	Diagnosis Type Code	ID	1-3	R			ABN, BN
HI07-2	External Cause of Injury Code	AN	1-30	R			
HI07-3	Date Time Period Format Qualifier	ID	2-3	N/U			
HI07-4	Date Time Period	AN	1-35	N/U			
HI07-5	Monetary Amount	R	1-18	N/U			
HI07-6	Quantity	R	1-15	N/U			
HI07-7	Version Identifier	AN	1-30	N/U			
HI07-8	Industry code	AN	1-30	N/U			
HI07-9	Present on Admission indicator	ID	1-1	S			N, U, W, Y
HI08	HEALTH CARE CODE INFORMATION			S			
HI08-1	Diagnosis Type Code	ID	1-3	R			ABN, BN
HI08-2	External Cause of Injury Code	AN	1-30	R			
HI08-3	Date Time Period Format Qualifier	ID	2-3	N/U			
HI08-4	Date Time Period	AN	1-35	N/U			
HI08-5	Monetary Amount	R	1-18	N/U			
HI08-6	Quantity	R	1-15	N/U			
HI08-7	Version Identifier	AN	1-30	N/U			
HI08-8	Industry code	AN	1-30	N/U			
HI08-9	Present on Admission indicator	ID	1-1	S			N, U, W, Y
HI09	HEALTH CARE CODE INFORMATION			S			
HI09-1	Diagnosis Type Code	ID	1-3	R			ABN, BN
HI09-2	External Cause of Injury Code	AN	1-30	R			
HI09-3	Date Time Period Format Qualifier	ID	2-3	N/U			
HI09-4	Date Time Period	AN	1-35	N/U			
HI09-5	Monetary Amount	R	1-18	N/U			
HI09-6	Quantity	R	1-15	N/U			
HI09-7	Version Identifier	AN	1-30	N/U			
HI09-8	Industry code	AN	1-30	N/U			

INSTITUTIONAL CLAIM

4010A1

Element Identifier	Description	ID	Min. Max.	Usage Reg.	Loop	Loop Repeat	Values
	837-I 4010A1						
HI	DIAGNOSIS RELATED GROUP (DRG) INFORMATION		1	R	2300		

5010

Element Identifier	Description	ID	Min. Max.	Usage Reg.	Loop	Loop Repeat	Values
	837-I 5010						
HI09-9	Present on Admission indicator	ID	1-1	S			N, U, W, Y
HI10	HEALTH CARE CODE INFORMATION			S			
HI10-1	Diagnosis Type Code	ID	1-3	R			ABN, BN
HI10-2	External Cause of Injury Code	AN	1-30	R			
HI10-3	Date Time Period Format Qualifier	ID	2-3	N/U			
HI10-4	Date Time Period	AN	1-35	N/U			
HI10-5	Monetary Amount	R	1-18	N/U			
HI10-6	Quantity	R	1-15	N/U			
HI10-7	Version Identifier	AN	1-30	N/U			
HI10-8	Industry code	AN	1-30	N/U			
HI10-9	Present on Admission indicator	ID	1-1	S			N, U, W, Y
HI11	HEALTH CARE CODE INFORMATION			S			
HI11-1	Diagnosis Type Code	ID	1-3	R			ABN, BN
HI11-2	External Cause of Injury Code	AN	1-30	R			
HI11-3	Date Time Period Format Qualifier	ID	2-3	N/U			
HI11-4	Date Time Period	AN	1-35	N/U			
HI11-5	Monetary Amount	R	1-18	N/U			
HI11-6	Quantity	R	1-15	N/U			
HI11-7	Version Identifier	AN	1-30	N/U			
HI11-8	Industry code	AN	1-30	N/U			
HI11-9	Present on Admission indicator	ID	1-1	S			N, U, W, Y
HI12	HEALTH CARE CODE INFORMATION			S			
HI12-1	Diagnosis Type Code	ID	1-3	R			ABN, BN
HI12-2	External Cause of Injury Code	AN	1-30	R			
HI12-3	Date Time Period Format Qualifier	ID	2-3	N/U			
HI12-4	Date Time Period	AN	1-35	N/U			
HI12-5	Monetary Amount	R	1-18	N/U			
HI12-6	Quantity	R	1-15	N/U			
HI12-7	Version Identifier	AN	1-30	N/U			
HI12-8	Industry code	AN	1-30	N/U			
HI12-9	Present on Admission indicator	ID	1-1	S			N, U, W, Y
HI	DIAGNOSIS RELATED GROUP (DRG) INFORMATION		1	R	2300		

Page 34 of 93

INSTITUTIONAL CLAIM

4010A1

837-I 4010A1

Element Identifier	Description	ID	Min. Max.	Usage Reg.	Loop	Loop Repeat	Values
HI01	HEALTH CARE CODE INFORMATION			R			
HI01-1	Code List Qualifier Code	ID	1-3	R			DR
HI01-2	DRG Code	AN	1-30	R			
HI01-3	Date Time Period Format Qualifier	ID	2-3	N/U			
HI01-4	Date Time Period	AN	1-35	N/U			
HI01-5	Monetary Amount	R	1-18	N/U			
HI01-6	Quantity	R	1-15	N/U			
HI01-7	Version Identifier	AN	1-30	N/U			
HI02	HEALTH CARE CODE INFORMATION			S			
HI03	HEALTH CARE CODE INFORMATION			N/U			
HI04	HEALTH CARE CODE INFORMATION			N/U			

5010

837-I 5010

Element Identifier	Description	ID	Min. Max.	Usage Reg.	Loop	Loop Repeat	Values	
HI01	HEALTH CARE CODE INFORMATION			R				
HI01-1	Qualifier	ID	1-3	R			DR	Name Change
HI01-2	DRG Code	AN	1-30	R				
HI01-3	Date Time Period Format Qualifier	ID	2-3	N/U				
HI01-4	Date Time Period	AN	1-35	N/U				
HI01-5	Monetary Amount	R	1-18	N/U				
HI01-6	Quantity	R	1-15	N/U				
HI01-7	Version Identifier	AN	1-30	N/U				
HI01-8	Industry code	AN	1-30	N/U				New Element
HI01-9	Yes/No Condition or response Code	ID	1-1	N/U				New Element
HI02	HEALTH CARE CODE INFORMATION			S				
HI02-1	Diagnosis Type Code	ID	1-3	N/U				New Element
HI02-2	Principal Diagnosis Code	AN	1-30	N/U				New Element
HI02-3	Date Time Period Format Qualifier	ID	2-3	N/U				New Element
HI02-4	Date Time Period	AN	1-35	N/U				New Element
HI02-5	Monetary Amount	R	1-18	N/U				New Element
HI02-6	Quantity	R	1-15	N/U				New Element
HI02-7	Version Identifier	AN	1-30	N/U				New Element
HI02-8	Industry code	AN	1-30	N/U				New Element
HI02-9	Present on Admission indicator	ID	1-1	N/U				New Element
HI03	HEALTH CARE CODE INFORMATION			N/U				
HI03-1	Diagnosis Type Code	ID	1-3	N/U				New Element
HI03-2	Principal Diagnosis Code	AN	1-30	N/U				New Element
HI03-3	Date Time Period Format Qualifier	ID	2-3	N/U				New Element
HI03-4	Date Time Period	AN	1-35	N/U				New Element
HI03-5	Monetary Amount	R	1-18	N/U				New Element
HI03-6	Quantity	R	1-15	N/U				New Element
HI03-7	Version Identifier	AN	1-30	N/U				New Element
HI03-8	Industry code	AN	1-30	N/U				New Element
HI03-9	Present on Admission indicator	ID	1-1	N/U				New Element
HI04	HEALTH CARE CODE INFORMATION			N/U				
HI04-1	Diagnosis Type Code	ID	1-3	N/U				New Element
HI04-2	Principal Diagnosis Code	AN	1-30	N/U				New Element
HI04-3	Date Time Period Format Qualifier	ID	2-3	N/U				New Element
HI04-4	Date Time Period	AN	1-35	N/U				New Element
HI04-5	Monetary Amount	R	1-18	N/U				New Element
HI04-6	Quantity	R	1-15	N/U				New Element
HI04-7	Version Identifier	AN	1-30	N/U				New Element
HI04-8	Industry code	AN	1-30	N/U				New Element

INSTITUTIONAL CLAIM

4010A1							
Element Identifier	Description	ID	Min. Max.	Usage Req.	Loop	Loop Repeat	Values
		837-I 4010A1					
HI05	HEALTH CARE CODE INFORMATION			N/U			
HI06	HEALTH CARE CODE INFORMATION			N/U			
HI07	HEALTH CARE CODE INFORMATION			N/U			
HI08	HEALTH CARE CODE INFORMATION			N/U			

5010							
Element Identifier	Description	ID	Min. Max.	Usage Req.	Loop	Loop Repeat	Values
		837-I 5010					
HI04-9	Present on Admission indicator	ID	1-1	N/U			New Element
HI05	HEALTH CARE CODE INFORMATION			N/U			
HI05-1	Diagnosis Type Code	ID	1-3	N/U			New Element
HI05-2	Principal Diagnosis Code	AN	1-30	N/U			New Element
HI05-3	Date Time Period Format Qualifier	ID	2-3	N/U			New Element
HI05-4	Date Time Period	AN	1-35	N/U			New Element
HI05-5	Monetary Amount	R	1-18	N/U			New Element
HI05-6	Quantity	R	1-15	N/U			New Element
HI05-7	Version Identifier	AN	1-30	N/U			New Element
HI05-8	Industry code	AN	1-30	N/U			New Element
HI05-9	Present on Admission indicator	ID	1-1	N/U			New Element
HI06	HEALTH CARE CODE INFORMATION			N/U			
HI06-1	Diagnosis Type Code	ID	1-3	N/U			New Element
HI06-2	Principal Diagnosis Code	AN	1-30	N/U			New Element
HI06-3	Date Time Period Format Qualifier	ID	2-3	N/U			New Element
HI06-4	Date Time Period	AN	1-35	N/U			New Element
HI06-5	Monetary Amount	R	1-18	N/U			New Element
HI06-6	Quantity	R	1-15	N/U			New Element
HI06-7	Version Identifier	AN	1-30	N/U			New Element
HI06-8	Industry code	AN	1-30	N/U			New Element
HI06-9	Present on Admission indicator	ID	1-1	N/U			New Element
HI07	HEALTH CARE CODE INFORMATION			N/U			
HI07-1	Diagnosis Type Code	ID	1-3	N/U			New Element
HI07-2	Principal Diagnosis Code	AN	1-30	N/U			New Element
HI07-3	Date Time Period Format Qualifier	ID	2-3	N/U			New Element
HI07-4	Date Time Period	AN	1-35	N/U			New Element
HI07-5	Monetary Amount	R	1-18	N/U			New Element
HI07-6	Quantity	R	1-15	N/U			New Element
HI07-7	Version Identifier	AN	1-30	N/U			New Element
HI07-8	Industry code	AN	1-30	N/U			New Element
HI07-9	Present on Admission indicator	ID	1-1	N/U			New Element
HI08	HEALTH CARE CODE INFORMATION			N/U			
HI08-1	Diagnosis Type Code	ID	1-3	N/U			New Element
HI08-2	Principal Diagnosis Code	AN	1-30	N/U			New Element
HI08-3	Date Time Period Format Qualifier	ID	2-3	N/U			New Element
HI08-4	Date Time Period	AN	1-35	N/U			New Element
HI08-5	Monetary Amount	R	1-18	N/U			New Element
HI08-6	Quantity	R	1-15	N/U			New Element

Page 36 of 93

INSTITUTIONAL CLAIM

\	\	\	\	\

4010A1

Element Identifier	Description	ID	Min. Max.	Usage Req.	Loop	Loop Repeat	Values
		837-I 4010A1					
HI09	HEALTH CARE CODE INFORMATION			N/U			
HI10	HEALTH CARE CODE INFORMATION			N/U			
HI11	HEALTH CARE CODE INFORMATION			N/U			
HI12	HEALTH CARE CODE INFORMATION			N/U			

5010

Element Identifier	Description	ID	Min. Max.	Usage Req.	Loop	Loop Repeat	Values	
		837-I 5010						
HI08-7	Version Identifier	AN	1-30	N/U				New Element
HI08-8	Industry code	AN	1-30	N/U				New Element
HI08-9	Present on Admission indicator	ID	1-1	N/U				New Element
HI09	HEALTH CARE CODE INFORMATION			N/U				
HI09-1	Diagnosis Type Code	ID	1-3	N/U				New Element
HI09-2	Principal Diagnosis Code	AN	1-30	N/U				New Element
HI09-3	Date Time Period Format Qualifier	ID	2-3	N/U				New Element
HI09-4	Date Time Period	AN	1-35	N/U				New Element
HI09-5	Monetary Amount	R	1-18	N/U				New Element
HI09-6	Quantity	R	1-15	N/U				New Element
HI09-7	Version Identifier	AN	1-30	N/U				New Element
HI09-8	Industry code	AN	1-30	N/U				New Element
HI09-9	Present on Admission indicator	ID	1-1	N/U				New Element
HI10	HEALTH CARE CODE INFORMATION			N/U				
HI10-1	Diagnosis Type Code	ID	1-3	N/U				New Element
HI10-2	Principal Diagnosis Code	AN	1-30	N/U				New Element
HI10-3	Date Time Period Format Qualifier	ID	2-3	N/U				New Element
HI10-4	Date Time Period	AN	1-35	N/U				New Element
HI10-5	Monetary Amount	R	1-18	N/U				New Element
HI10-6	Quantity	R	1-15	N/U				New Element
HI10-7	Version Identifier	AN	1-30	N/U				New Element
HI10-8	Industry code	AN	1-30	N/U				New Element
HI10-9	Present on Admission indicator	ID	1-1	N/U				New Element
HI11	HEALTH CARE CODE INFORMATION			N/U				
HI11-1	Diagnosis Type Code	ID	1-3	N/U				New Element
HI11-2	Principal Diagnosis Code	AN	1-30	N/U				New Element
HI11-3	Date Time Period Format Qualifier	ID	2-3	N/U				New Element
HI11-4	Date Time Period	AN	1-35	N/U				New Element
HI11-5	Monetary Amount	R	1-18	N/U				New Element
HI11-6	Quantity	R	1-15	N/U				New Element
HI11-7	Version Identifier	AN	1-30	N/U				New Element
HI11-8	Industry code	AN	1-30	N/U				New Element
HI11-9	Present on Admission indicator	ID	1-1	N/U				New Element
HI12	HEALTH CARE CODE INFORMATION			N/U				
HI12-1	Diagnosis Type Code	ID	1-3	N/U				New Element
HI12-2	Principal Diagnosis Code	AN	1-30	N/U				New Element
HI12-3	Date Time Period Format Qualifier	ID	2-3	N/U				New Element
HI12-4	Date Time Period	AN	1-35	N/U				New Element

Page 37 of 93

INSTITUTIONAL CLAIM

4010A1

Element Identifier	Description	ID	Min. Max.	Usage Reg.	Loop	Loop Repeat	Values
837-I 4010A1							
HI	OTHER DIAGNOSIS INFORMATION		2	R	2300		
HI01	HEALTH CARE CODE INFORMATION			R			
HI01-1	Code List Qualifier Code	ID	1-3	R			BF
HI01-2	Other Diagnosis	AN	1-30	R			
HI01-3	Date Time Period Format Qualifier	ID	2-3	N/U			
HI01-4	Date Time Period	AN	1-35	N/U			
HI01-5	Monetary Amount	R	1-18	N/U			
HI01-6	Quantity	R	1-15	N/U			
HI01-7	Version Identifier	AN	1-30	N/U			
HI02	HEALTH CARE CODE INFORMATION			S			
HI02-1	Code List Qualifier Code	ID	1-3	R			BF
HI02-2	Other Diagnosis	AN	1-30	R			
HI02-3	Date Time Period Format Qualifier	ID	2-3	N/U			
HI02-4	Date Time Period	AN	1-35	N/U			
HI02-5	Monetary Amount	R	1-18	N/U			
HI02-6	Quantity	R	1-15	N/U			
HI02-7	Version Identifier	AN	1-30	N/U			
HI03	HEALTH CARE CODE INFORMATION			S			
HI03-1	Code List Qualifier Code	ID	1-3	R			BF
HI03-2	Other Diagnosis	AN	1-30	R			
HI03-3	Date Time Period Format Qualifier	ID	2-3	N/U			
HI03-4	Date Time Period	AN	1-35	N/U			
HI03-5	Monetary Amount	R	1-18	N/U			
HI03-6	Quantity	R	1-15	N/U			
HI03-7	Version Identifier	AN	1-30	N/U			

5010

Element Identifier	Description	ID	Min. Max.	Usage Reg.	Loop	Loop Repeat	Values	
837-I 5010								
HI12-5	Monetary Amount	R	1-18	N/U				New Element
HI12-6	Quantity	R	1-15	N/U				New Element
HI12-7	Version Identifier	AN	1-30	N/U				New Element
HI12-8	Industry code	AN	1-30	N/U				New Element
HI12-9	Present on Admission indicator	ID	1-1	N/U				New Element
HI	OTHER DIAGNOSIS INFORMATION		2	R	2300			
HI01	HEALTH CARE CODE INFORMATION			R				
HI01-1	Diagnosis Type Code	ID	1-3	R			ABF, BF	Name Change Code Added
HI01-2	Other Diagnosis	AN	1-30	R				
HI01-3	Date Time Period Format Qualifier	ID	2-3	N/U				
HI01-4	Date Time Period	AN	1-35	N/U				
HI01-5	Monetary Amount	R	1-18	N/U				
HI01-6	Quantity	R	1-15	N/U				
HI01-7	Version Identifier	AN	1-30	N/U				
HI01-8	Industry code	AN	1-30	N/U				New Element
HI01-9	Present on Admission indicator	ID	1-1	S			N, U, W, Y	New Element
HI02	HEALTH CARE CODE INFORMATION			S				
HI02-1	Diagnosis Type Code	ID	1-3	R			ABF, BF	Name Change Code Added
HI02-2	Other Diagnosis	AN	1-30	R				
HI02-3	Date Time Period Format Qualifier	ID	2-3	N/U				
HI02-4	Date Time Period	AN	1-35	N/U				
HI02-5	Monetary Amount	R	1-18	N/U				
HI02-6	Quantity	R	1-15	N/U				
HI02-7	Version Identifier	AN	1-30	N/U				
HI02-8	Industry code	AN	1-30	N/U				New Element
HI02-9	Present on Admission indicator	ID	1-1	N/U			N, U, W, Y	New Element
HI03	HEALTH CARE CODE INFORMATION			S				
HI03-1	Diagnosis Type Code	ID	1-3	R			ABF, BF	Name Change Code Added
HI03-2	Other Diagnosis	AN	1-30	R				
HI03-3	Date Time Period Format Qualifier	ID	2-3	N/U				
HI03-4	Date Time Period	AN	1-35	N/U				
HI03-5	Monetary Amount	R	1-18	N/U				
HI03-6	Quantity	R	1-15	N/U				
HI03-7	Version Identifier	AN	1-30	N/U				
HI03-8	Industry code	AN	1-30	N/U				New Element

Page 38 of 93

INSTITUTIONAL CLAIM

4010A1

Element Identifier	Description	ID	Min. Max.	Usage Reg.	Loop	Loop Repeat	Values
			837-I 4010A1				
HI04	HEALTH CARE CODE INFORMATION			S			
HI04-1	Code List Qualifier Code	ID	1-3	R			BF
HI04-2	Other Diagnosis	AN	1-30	R			
HI04-3	Date Time Period Format Qualifier	ID	2-3	N/U			
HI04-4	Date Time Period	AN	1-35	N/U			
HI04-5	Monetary Amount	R	1-18	N/U			
HI04-6	Quantity	R	1-15	N/U			
HI04-7	Version Identifier	AN	1-30	N/U			
HI05	HEALTH CARE CODE INFORMATION			S			
HI05-1	Code List Qualifier Code	ID	1-3	R			BF
HI05-2	Other Diagnosis	AN	1-30	R			
HI05-3	Date Time Period Format Qualifier	ID	2-3	N/U			
HI05-4	Date Time Period	AN	1-35	N/U			
HI05-5	Monetary Amount	R	1-18	N/U			
HI05-6	Quantity	R	1-15	N/U			
HI05-7	Version Identifier	AN	1-30	N/U			
HI06	HEALTH CARE CODE INFORMATION			S			
HI06-1	Code List Qualifier Code	ID	1-3	R			BF
HI06-2	Other Diagnosis	AN	1-30	R			
HI06-3	Date Time Period Format Qualifier	ID	2-3	N/U			
HI06-4	Date Time Period	AN	1-35	N/U			
HI06-5	Monetary Amount	R	1-18	N/U			
HI06-6	Quantity	R	1-15	N/U			
HI06-7	Version Identifier	AN	1-30	N/U			
HI07	HEALTH CARE CODE INFORMATION			S			
HI07-1	Code List Qualifier Code	ID	1-3	R			BF
HI07-2	Other Diagnosis	AN	1-30	R			

5010

Element Identifier	Description	ID	Min. Max.	Usage Reg.	Loop	Loop Repeat	Values	
			837-I 5010					
HI03-9	Present on Admission indicator	ID	1-1	N/U			N, U, W, Y	New Element
HI04	HEALTH CARE CODE INFORMATION			S				
HI04-1	Diagnosis Type Code	ID	1-3	R			ABF, BF	Name Change Code Added
HI04-2	Other Diagnosis	AN	1-30	R				
HI04-3	Date Time Period Format Qualifier	ID	2-3	N/U				
HI04-4	Date Time Period	AN	1-35	N/U				
HI04-5	Monetary Amount	R	1-18	N/U				
HI04-6	Quantity	R	1-15	N/U				
HI04-7	Version Identifier	AN	1-30	N/U				
HI04-8	Industry code	AN	1-30	N/U				New Element
HI04-9	Present on Admission indicator	ID	1-1	N/U			N, U, W, Y	New Element
HI05	HEALTH CARE CODE INFORMATION			S				
HI05-1	Diagnosis Type Code	ID	1-3	R			ABF, BF	Name Change Code Added
HI05-2	Other Diagnosis	AN	1-30	R				
HI05-3	Date Time Period Format Qualifier	ID	2-3	N/U				
HI05-4	Date Time Period	AN	1-35	N/U				
HI05-5	Monetary Amount	R	1-18	N/U				
HI05-6	Quantity	R	1-15	N/U				
HI05-7	Version Identifier	AN	1-30	N/U				
HI05-8	Industry code	AN	1-30	N/U				New Element
HI05-9	Present on Admission indicator	ID	1-1	N/U			N, U, W, Y	New Element
HI06	HEALTH CARE CODE INFORMATION			S				
HI06-1	Diagnosis Type Code	ID	1-3	R			ABF, BF	Name Change Code Added
HI06-2	Other Diagnosis	AN	1-30	R				
HI06-3	Date Time Period Format Qualifier	ID	2-3	N/U				
HI06-4	Date Time Period	AN	1-35	N/U				
HI06-5	Monetary Amount	R	1-18	N/U				
HI06-6	Quantity	R	1-15	N/U				
HI06-7	Version Identifier	AN	1-30	N/U				
HI06-8	Industry code	AN	1-30	N/U				New Element
HI06-9	Present on Admission indicator	ID	1-1	N/U			N, U, W, Y	New Element
HI07	HEALTH CARE CODE INFORMATION			S				
HI07-1	Diagnosis Type Code	ID	1-3	R			ABF, BF	Name Change Code Added
HI07-2	Other Diagnosis	AN	1-30	R				

INSTITUTIONAL CLAIM

4010A1

837-I 4010A1

Element Identifier	Description	ID	Min. Max.	Usage Reg.	Loop	Loop Repeat	Values
HI07-3	Date Time Period Format Qualifier	ID	2-3	N/U			
HI07-4	Date Time Period	AN	1-35	N/U			
HI07-5	Monetary Amount	R	1-18	N/U			
HI07-6	Quantity	R	1-15	N/U			
HI07-7	Version Identifier	AN	1-30	N/U			
HI08	HEALTH CARE CODE INFORMATION			S			
HI08-1	Code List Qualifier Code	ID	1-3	R			BF
HI08-2	Other Diagnosis	AN	1-30	R			
HI08-3	Date Time Period Format Qualifier	ID	2-3	N/U			
HI08-4	Date Time Period	AN	1-35	N/U			
HI08-5	Monetary Amount	R	1-18	N/U			
HI08-6	Quantity	R	1-15	N/U			
HI08-7	Version Identifier	AN	1-30	N/U			
HI09	HEALTH CARE CODE INFORMATION			S			
HI09-1	Code List Qualifier Code	ID	1-3	R			BF
HI09-2	Other Diagnosis	AN	1-30	R			
HI09-3	Date Time Period Format Qualifier	ID	2-3	N/U			
HI09-4	Date Time Period	AN	1-35	N/U			
HI09-5	Monetary Amount	R	1-18	N/U			
HI09-6	Quantity	R	1-15	N/U			
HI09-7	Version Identifier	AN	1-30	N/U			
HI10	HEALTH CARE CODE INFORMATION			S			
HI10-1	Code List Qualifier Code	ID	1-3	R			BF
HI10-2	Other Diagnosis	AN	1-30	R			
HI10-3	Date Time Period Format Qualifier	ID	2-3	N/U			
HI10-4	Date Time Period	AN	1-35	N/U			
HI10-5	Monetary Amount	R	1-18	N/U			
HI10-6	Quantity	R	1-15	N/U			
HI10-7	Version Identifier	AN	1-30	N/U			

5010

837-I 5010

Element Identifier	Description	ID	Min. Max.	Usage Reg.	Loop	Loop Repeat	Values	
HI07-3	Date Time Period Format Qualifier	ID	2-3	N/U				
HI07-4	Date Time Period	AN	1-35	N/U				
HI07-5	Monetary Amount	R	1-18	N/U				
HI07-6	Quantity	R	1-15	N/U				
HI07-7	Version Identifier	AN	1-30	N/U				
HI07-8	Industry code	AN	1-30	N/U				New Element
HI07-9	Present on Admission indicator	ID	1-1	N/U			N, U, W, Y	New Element
HI08	HEALTH CARE CODE INFORMATION			S				
HI08-1	Diagnosis Type Code	ID	1-3	R			ABF, BF	Name Change Code Added
HI08-2	Other Diagnosis	AN	1-30	R				
HI08-3	Date Time Period Format Qualifier	ID	2-3	N/U				
HI08-4	Date Time Period	AN	1-35	N/U				
HI08-5	Monetary Amount	R	1-18	N/U				
HI08-6	Quantity	R	1-15	N/U				
HI08-7	Version Identifier	AN	1-30	N/U				
HI08-8	Industry code	AN	1-30	N/U				New Element
HI08-9	Present on Admission indicator	ID	1-1	N/U			N, U, W, Y	New Element
HI09	HEALTH CARE CODE INFORMATION			S				
HI09-1	Diagnosis Type Code	ID	1-3	R			ABF, BF	Name Change Code Added
HI09-2	Other Diagnosis	AN	1-30	R				
HI09-3	Date Time Period Format Qualifier	ID	2-3	N/U				
HI09-4	Date Time Period	AN	1-35	N/U				
HI09-5	Monetary Amount	R	1-18	N/U				
HI09-6	Quantity	R	1-15	N/U				
HI09-7	Version Identifier	AN	1-30	N/U				
HI09-8	Industry code	AN	1-30	N/U				New Element
HI09-9	Present on Admission indicator	ID	1-1	N/U			N, U, W, Y	New Element
HI10	HEALTH CARE CODE INFORMATION			S				
HI10-1	Diagnosis Type Code	ID	1-3	R			ABF, BF	Name Change Code Added
HI10-2	Other Diagnosis	AN	1-30	R				
HI10-3	Date Time Period Format Qualifier	ID	2-3	N/U				
HI10-4	Date Time Period	AN	1-35	N/U				
HI10-5	Monetary Amount	R	1-18	N/U				
HI10-6	Quantity	R	1-15	N/U				
HI10-7	Version Identifier	AN	1-30	N/U				
HI10-8	Industry code	AN	1-30	N/U				New Element

Page 40 of 93

INSTITUTIONAL CLAIM

4010A1

837-I 4010A1

Element Identifier	Description	ID	Min. Max.	Usage Reg.	Loop	Loop Repeat	Values
HI11	HEALTH CARE CODE INFORMATION			S			
HI11-1	Code List Qualifier Code	ID	1-3	R			BF
HI11-2	Other Diagnosis	AN	1-30	R			
HI11-3	Date Time Period Format Qualifier	ID	2-3	N/U			
HI11-4	Date Time Period	AN	1-35	N/U			
HI11-5	Monetary Amount	R	1-18	N/U			
HI11-6	Quantity	R	1-15	N/U			
HI11-7	Version Identifier	AN	1-30	N/U			
HI12	HEALTH CARE CODE INFORMATION			S			
HI12-1	Code List Qualifier Code	ID	1-3	R			BF
HI12-2	Other Diagnosis	AN	1-30	R			
HI12-3	Date Time Period Format Qualifier	ID	2-3	N/U			
HI12-4	Date Time Period	AN	1-35	N/U			
HI12-5	Monetary Amount	R	1-18	N/U			
HI12-6	Quantity	R	1-15	N/U			
HI12-7	Version Identifier	AN	1-30	N/U			
HI	PRINCIPAL PROCEDURE INFORMATION		1	R	2300		
HI01	HEALTH CARE CODE INFORMATION			R			
HI01-1	Code List Qualifier Code	ID	1-3	R			BP
HI01-2	Principal Procedure Code	AN	1-30	R			
HI01-3	Date Time Period Format Qualifier	ID	2-3	S			D8
HI01-4	Date Time Period	AN	1-35	S			
HI01-5	Monetary Amount	R	1-18	N/U			
HI01-6	Quantity	R	1-15	N/U			
HI01-7	Version Identifier	AN	1-30	N/U			
HI02	HEALTH CARE CODE INFORMATION			N/U			

5010

837-I 5010

Element Identifier	Description	ID	Min. Max.	Usage Reg.	Loop	Loop Repeat	Values	
HI10-9	Present on Admission indicator	ID	1-1	N/U			N, U, W, Y	New Element
HI11	HEALTH CARE CODE INFORMATION			S				
HI11-1	Diagnosis Type Code	ID	1-3	R			ABF, BF	Name Change Code Added
HI11-2	Other Diagnosis	AN	1-30	R				
HI11-3	Date Time Period Format Qualifier	ID	2-3	N/U				
HI11-4	Date Time Period	AN	1-35	N/U				
HI11-5	Monetary Amount	R	1-18	N/U				
HI11-6	Quantity	R	1-15	N/U				
HI11-7	Version Identifier	AN	1-30	N/U				
HI11-8	Industry code	AN	1-30	N/U				New Element
HI11-9	Present on Admission indicator	ID	1-1	N/U			N, U, W, Y	New Element
HI12	HEALTH CARE CODE INFORMATION			S				
HI12-1	Diagnosis Type Code	ID	1-3	R			ABF, BF	Name Change Code Added
HI12-2	Other Diagnosis	AN	1-30	R				
HI12-3	Date Time Period Format Qualifier	ID	2-3	N/U				
HI12-4	Date Time Period	AN	1-35	N/U				
HI12-5	Monetary Amount	R	1-18	N/U				
HI12-6	Quantity	R	1-15	N/U				
HI12-7	Version Identifier	AN	1-30	N/U				
HI12-8	Industry code	AN	1-30	N/U				New Element
HI12-9	Present on Admission indicator	ID	1-1	N/U			N, U, W, Y	New Element
HI	PRINCIPAL PROCEDURE INFORMATION		1	R	2300			
HI01	HEALTH CARE CODE INFORMATION			R				
HI01-1	Qualifier	ID	1-3	R			BBR, BR	Name Change Code Change
HI01-2	Principal Procedure Code	AN	1-30	R				
HI01-3	Date Time Period Format Qualifier	ID	2-3	N/U				Usage change to Not Used
HI01-4	Date Time Period	AN	1-35	N/U				Usage change to Not Used
HI01-5	Monetary Amount	R	1-18	N/U				
HI01-6	Quantity	R	1-15	N/U				
HI01-7	Version Identifier	AN	1-30	N/U				
HI01-8	Industry code	AN	1-30	N/U				New Element
HI01-9	Present on Admission indicator	ID	1-1	N/U				New Element
HI02	HEALTH CARE CODE INFORMATION			N/U				

INSTITUTIONAL CLAIM

4010A1

Element Identifier	Description	ID	Min. Max.	Usage Reg.	Loop	Loop Repeat	Values
				837-I 4010A1			
HI03	HEALTH CARE CODE INFORMATION			N/U			
HI04	HEALTH CARE CODE INFORMATION			N/U			
HI05	HEALTH CARE CODE INFORMATION			N/U			

5010

Element Identifier	Description	ID	Min. Max.	Usage Reg.	Loop	Loop Repeat	Values	
				837-I 5010				
HI02-1	Diagnosis Type Code	ID	1-3	N/U				New Element
HI02-2	Principal Diagnosis Code	AN	1-30	N/U				New Element
HI02-3	Date Time Period Format Qualifier	ID	2-3	N/U				New Element
HI02-4	Date Time Period	AN	1-35	N/U				New Element
HI02-5	Monetary Amount	R	1-18	N/U				New Element
HI02-6	Quantity	R	1-15	N/U				New Element
HI02-7	Version Identifier	AN	1-30	N/U				New Element
HI02-8	Industry code	AN	1-30	N/U				New Element
HI02-9	Present on Admission indicator	ID	1-1	N/U				New Element
HI03	HEALTH CARE CODE INFORMATION			N/U				
HI03-1	Diagnosis Type Code	ID	1-3	N/U				New Element
HI03-2	Principal Diagnosis Code	AN	1-30	N/U				New Element
HI03-3	Date Time Period Format Qualifier	ID	2-3	N/U				New Element
HI03-4	Date Time Period	AN	1-35	N/U				New Element
HI03-5	Monetary Amount	R	1-18	N/U				New Element
HI03-6	Quantity	R	1-15	N/U				New Element
HI03-7	Version Identifier	AN	1-30	N/U				New Element
HI03-8	Industry code	AN	1-30	N/U				New Element
HI03-9	Present on Admission indicator	ID	1-1	N/U				New Element
HI04	HEALTH CARE CODE INFORMATION			N/U				
HI04-1	Diagnosis Type Code	ID	1-3	N/U				New Element
HI04-2	Principal Diagnosis Code	AN	1-30	N/U				New Element
HI04-3	Date Time Period Format Qualifier	ID	2-3	N/U				New Element
HI04-4	Date Time Period	AN	1-35	N/U				New Element
HI04-5	Monetary Amount	R	1-18	N/U				New Element
HI04-6	Quantity	R	1-15	N/U				New Element
HI04-7	Version Identifier	AN	1-30	N/U				New Element
HI04-8	Industry code	AN	1-30	N/U				New Element
HI04-9	Present on Admission indicator	ID	1-1	N/U				New Element
HI05	HEALTH CARE CODE INFORMATION			N/U				
HI05-1	Diagnosis Type Code	ID	1-3	N/U				New Element
HI05-2	Principal Diagnosis Code	AN	1-30	N/U				New Element
HI05-3	Date Time Period Format Qualifier	ID	2-3	N/U				New Element
HI05-4	Date Time Period	AN	1-35	N/U				New Element
HI05-5	Monetary Amount	R	1-18	N/U				New Element
HI05-6	Quantity	R	1-15	N/U				New Element
HI05-7	Version Identifier	AN	1-30	N/U				New Element
HI05-8	Industry code	AN	1-30	N/U				New Element
HI05-9	Present on Admission indicator	ID	1-1	N/U				New Element

Page 42 of 93

INSTITUTIONAL CLAIM

4010A1							
Element Identifier	Description	ID	Min. Max.	Usage Reg.	Loop	Loop Repeat	Values
	837-I 4010A1						
HI06	HEALTH CARE CODE INFORMATION			N/U			
HI07	HEALTH CARE CODE INFORMATION			N/U			
HI08	HEALTH CARE CODE INFORMATION			N/U			
HI09	HEALTH CARE CODE INFORMATION			N/U			

5010								
Element Identifier	Description	ID	Min. Max.	Usage Reg.	Loop	Loop Repeat	Values	
	837-I 5010							
HI06	HEALTH CARE CODE INFORMATION			N/U				
HI06-1	Diagnosis Type Code	ID	1-3	N/U				New Element
HI06-2	Principal Diagnosis Code	AN	1-30	N/U				New Element
HI06-3	Date Time Period Format Qualifier	ID	2-3	N/U				New Element
HI06-4	Date Time Period	AN	1-35	N/U				New Element
HI06-5	Monetary Amount	R	1-18	N/U				New Element
HI06-6	Quantity	R	1-15	N/U				New Element
HI06-7	Version Identifier	AN	1-30	N/U				New Element
HI06-8	Industry code	AN	1-30	N/U				New Element
HI06-9	Present on Admission indicator	ID	1-1	N/U				New Element
HI07	HEALTH CARE CODE INFORMATION			N/U				
HI07-1	Diagnosis Type Code	ID	1-3	N/U				New Element
HI07-2	Principal Diagnosis Code	AN	1-30	N/U				New Element
HI07-3	Date Time Period Format Qualifier	ID	2-3	N/U				New Element
HI07-4	Date Time Period	AN	1-35	N/U				New Element
HI07-5	Monetary Amount	R	1-18	N/U				New Element
HI07-6	Quantity	R	1-15	N/U				New Element
HI07-7	Version Identifier	AN	1-30	N/U				New Element
HI07-8	Industry code	AN	1-30	N/U				New Element
HI07-9	Present on Admission indicator	ID	1-1	N/U				New Element
HI08	HEALTH CARE CODE INFORMATION			N/U				
HI08-1	Diagnosis Type Code	ID	1-3	N/U				New Element
HI08-2	Principal Diagnosis Code	AN	1-30	N/U				New Element
HI08-3	Date Time Period Format Qualifier	ID	2-3	N/U				New Element
HI08-4	Date Time Period	AN	1-35	N/U				New Element
HI08-5	Monetary Amount	R	1-18	N/U				New Element
HI08-6	Quantity	R	1-15	N/U				New Element
HI08-7	Version Identifier	AN	1-30	N/U				New Element
HI08-8	Industry code	AN	1-30	N/U				New Element
HI08-9	Present on Admission indicator	ID	1-1	N/U				New Element
HI09	HEALTH CARE CODE INFORMATION			N/U				
HI09-1	Diagnosis Type Code	ID	1-3	N/U				New Element
HI09-2	Principal Diagnosis Code	AN	1-30	N/U				New Element
HI09-3	Date Time Period Format Qualifier	ID	2-3	N/U				New Element
HI09-4	Date Time Period	AN	1-35	N/U				New Element
HI09-5	Monetary Amount	R	1-18	N/U				New Element
HI09-6	Quantity	R	1-15	N/U				New Element
HI09-7	Version Identifier	AN	1-30	N/U				New Element
HI09-8	Industry code	AN	1-30	N/U				New Element

Page 43 of 93

INSTITUTIONAL CLAIM

Element Identifier	Description	ID	Min. Max.	Usage Reg.	Loop	Loop Repeat	Values
	4010A1						
	837-I 4010A1						
HI10	HEALTH CARE CODE INFORMATION			N/U			
HI11	HEALTH CARE CODE INFORMATION			N/U			
HI12	HEALTH CARE CODE INFORMATION			N/U			
HI	OTHER PROCEDURE INFORMATION		2	R	2300		
HI01	HEALTH CARE CODE INFORMATION			R			
HI01-1	Code List Qualifier Code	ID	1-3	R			BO, BQ
HI01-2	Procedure Code	AN	1-30	R			

Element Identifier	Description	ID	Min. Max.	Usage Reg.	Loop	Loop Repeat	Values	
	5010							
	837-I 5010							
HI09-9	Present on Admission indicator	ID	1-1	N/U				New Element
HI10	HEALTH CARE CODE INFORMATION			N/U				
HI10-1	Diagnosis Type Code	ID	1-3	N/U				New Element
HI10-2	Principal Diagnosis Code	AN	1-30	N/U				New Element
HI10-3	Date Time Period Format Qualifier	ID	2-3	N/U				New Element
HI10-4	Date Time Period	AN	1-35	N/U				New Element
HI10-5	Monetary Amount	R	1-18	N/U				New Element
HI10-6	Quantity	R	1-15	N/U				New Element
HI10-7	Version Identifier	AN	1-30	N/U				New Element
HI10-8	Industry code	AN	1-30	N/U				New Element
HI10-9	Present on Admission indicator	ID	1-1	N/U				New Element
HI11	HEALTH CARE CODE INFORMATION			N/U				
HI11-1	Diagnosis Type Code	ID	1-3	N/U				New Element
HI11-2	Principal Diagnosis Code	AN	1-30	N/U				New Element
HI11-3	Date Time Period Format Qualifier	ID	2-3	N/U				New Element
HI11-4	Date Time Period	AN	1-35	N/U				New Element
HI11-5	Monetary Amount	R	1-18	N/U				New Element
HI11-6	Quantity	R	1-15	N/U				New Element
HI11-7	Version Identifier	AN	1-30	N/U				New Element
HI11-8	Industry code	AN	1-30	N/U				New Element
HI11-9	Present on Admission indicator	ID	1-1	N/U				New Element
HI12	HEALTH CARE CODE INFORMATION			N/U				
HI12-1	Diagnosis Type Code	ID	1-3	N/U				New Element
HI12-2	Principal Diagnosis Code	AN	1-30	N/U				New Elemont
HI12-3	Date Time Period Format Qualifier	ID	2-3	N/U				New Element
HI12-4	Date Time Period	AN	1-35	N/U				New Element
HI12-5	Monetary Amount	R	1-18	N/U				New Element
HI12-6	Quantity	R	1-15	N/U				New Element
HI12-7	Version Identifier	AN	1-30	N/U				New Element
HI12-8	Industry code	AN	1-30	N/U				New Element
HI12-9	Present on Admission indicator	ID	1-1	N/U				New Element
HI	OTHER PROCEDURE INFORMATION		2	R	2300			
HI01	HEALTH CARE CODE INFORMATION			R				
HI01-1	Qualifier Code	ID	1-3	R			BBQ, BQ	Name Change Code Change
HI01-2	Procedure Code	AN	1-30	R				

Page 44 of 93

INSTITUTIONAL CLAIM

4010A1

Element Identifier	Description	ID	Min. Max.	Usage Reg.	Loop	Loop Repeat	Values
	837-I 4010A1						
HI01-3	Date Time Period Format Qualifier	ID	2-3	S			D8
HI01-4	Date Time Period	AN	1-35	S			CCYYMMDD
HI01-5	Monetary Amount	R	1-18	N/U			
HI01-6	Quantity	R	1-15	N/U			
HI01-7	Version Identifier	AN	1-30	N/U			
HI02	HEALTH CARE CODE INFORMATION			S			
HI02-1	Code List Qualifier Code	ID	1-3	R			BO, BQ
HI02-2	Procedure Code	AN	1-30	R			
HI02-3	Date Time Period Format Qualifier	ID	2-3	S			D8
HI02-4	Date Time Period	AN	1-35	S			CCYYMMDD
HI02-5	Monetary Amount	R	1-18	N/U			
HI02-6	Quantity	R	1-15	N/U			
HI02-7	Version Identifier	AN	1-30	N/U			
HI03	HEALTH CARE CODE INFORMATION			S			
HI03-1	Code List Qualifier Code	ID	1-3	R			BO, BQ
HI03-2	Procedure Code	AN	1-30	R			
HI03-3	Date Time Period Format Qualifier	ID	2-3	S			D8
HI03-4	Date Time Period	AN	1-35	S			CCYYMMDD
HI03-5	Monetary Amount	R	1-18	N/U			
HI03-6	Quantity	R	1-15	N/U			
HI03-7	Version Identifier	AN	1-30	N/U			
HI04	HEALTH CARE CODE INFORMATION			S			
HI04-1	Code List Qualifier Code	ID	1-3	R			BO, BQ
HI04-2	Procedure Code	AN	1-30	R			
HI04-3	Date Time Period Format Qualifier	ID	2-3	S			D8
HI04-4	Date Time Period	AN	1-35	S			CCYYMMDD
HI04-5	Monetary Amount	R	1-18	N/U			

5010

Element Identifier	Description	ID	Min. Max.	Usage Reg.	Loop	Loop Repeat	Values	
	837-I 5010							
HI01-3	Date Time Period Format Qualifier	ID	2-3	R			D8	Usage change to Required
HI01-4	Date Time Period	AN	1-35	R			CCYYMMDD	Usage change to Required
HI01-5	Monetary Amount	R	1-18	N/U				
HI01-6	Quantity	R	1-15	N/U				
HI01-7	Version Identifier	AN	1-30	N/U				
HI01-8	Industry code	AN	1-30	N/U				New Element
HI01-9	Yes/No Condition or response Code	ID	1-1	N/U				New Element
HI02	HEALTH CARE CODE INFORMATION			S				
HI02-1	Qualifier Code	ID	1-3	R			BBQ, BQ	Name Change Code Change
HI02-2	Procedure Code	AN	1-30	R				
HI02-3	Date Time Period Format Qualifier	ID	2-3	R			D8	Usage change to Required
HI02-4	Date Time Period	AN	1-35	R			CCYYMMDD	Usage change to Required
HI02-5	Monetary Amount	R	1-18	N/U				
HI02-6	Quantity	R	1-15	N/U				
HI02-7	Version Identifier	AN	1-30	N/U				
HI02-8	Industry code	AN	1-30	N/U				New Element
HI02-9	Yes/No Condition or response Code	ID	1-1	N/U				New Element
HI03	HEALTH CARE CODE INFORMATION			S				
HI03-1	Qualifier Code	ID	1-3	R			BBQ, BQ	Name Change Code Change
HI03-2	Procedure Code	AN	1-30	R				
HI03-3	Date Time Period Format Qualifier	ID	2-3	R			D8	Usage change to Required
HI03-4	Date Time Period	AN	1-35	R			CCYYMMDD	Usage change to Required
HI03-5	Monetary Amount	R	1-18	N/U				
HI03-6	Quantity	R	1-15	N/U				
HI03-7	Version Identifier	AN	1-30	N/U				
HI03-8	Industry code	AN	1-30	N/U				New Element
HI03-9	Yes/No Condition or response Code	ID	1-1	N/U				New Element
HI04	HEALTH CARE CODE INFORMATION			S				
HI04-1	Qualifier Code	ID	1-3	R			BBQ, BQ	Name Change Code Change
HI04-2	Procedure Code	AN	1-30	R				
HI04-3	Date Time Period Format Qualifier	ID	2-3	R			D8	Usage change to Required
HI04-4	Date Time Period	AN	1-35	R			CCYYMMDD	Usage change to Required
HI04-5	Monetary Amount	R	1-18	N/U				

INSTITUTIONAL CLAIM

4010A1

Element Identifier	Description	ID	Min. Max.	Usage Req.	Loop	Loop Repeat	Values
				837-I 4010A1			
HI04-6	Quantity	R	1-15	N/U			
HI04-7	Version Identifier	AN	1-30	N/U			
HI05	HEALTH CARE CODE INFORMATION			S			
HI05-1	Code List Qualifier Code	ID	1-3	R			BO, BQ
HI05-2	Procedure Code	AN	1-30	R			
HI05-3	Date Time Period Format Qualifier	ID	2-3	S			D8
HI05-4	Date Time Period	AN	1-35	S			CCYYMMDD
HI05-5	Monetary Amount	R	1-18	N/U			
HI05-6	Quantity	R	1-15	N/U			
HI05-7	Version Identifier	AN	1-30	N/U			
HI06	HEALTH CARE CODE INFORMATION			S			
HI06-1	Code List Qualifier Code	ID	1-3	R			BO, BQ
HI06-2	Procedure Code	AN	1-30	R			
HI06-3	Date Time Period Format Qualifier	ID	2-3	S			D8
HI06-4	Date Time Period	AN	1-35	S			CCYYMMDD
HI06-5	Monetary Amount	R	1-18	N/U			
HI06-6	Quantity	R	1-15	N/U			
HI06-7	Version Identifier	AN	1-30	N/U			
HI07	HEALTH CARE CODE INFORMATION			S			
HI07-1	Code List Qualifier Code	ID	1-3	R			BO, BQ
HI07-2	Procedure Code	AN	1-30	R			
HI07-3	Date Time Period Format Qualifier	ID	2-3	S			D8
HI07-4	Date Time Period	AN	1-35	S			CCYYMMDD
HI07-5	Monetary Amount	R	1-18	N/U			
HI07-6	Quantity	R	1-15	N/U			
HI07-7	Version Identifier	AN	1-30	N/U			

5010

Element Identifier	Description	ID	Min. Max.	Usage Req.	Loop	Loop Repeat	Values	
				837-I 5010				
HI04-6	Quantity	R	1-15	N/U				
HI04-7	Version Identifier	AN	1-30	N/U				
HI04-8	Industry code	AN	1-30	N/U				New Element
HI04-9	Yes/No Condition or response Code	ID	1-1	N/U				New Element
HI05	HEALTH CARE CODE INFORMATION			S				
HI05-1	Qualifier Code	ID	1-3	R			BBQ, BQ	Name Change / Code Change
HI05-2	Procedure Code	AN	1-30	R				
HI05-3	Date Time Period Format Qualifier	ID	2-3	R			D8	Usage change to Required
HI05-4	Date Time Period	AN	1-35	R			CCYYMMDD	Usage change to Required
HI05-5	Monetary Amount	R	1-18	N/U				
HI05-6	Quantity	R	1-15	N/U				
HI05-7	Version Identifier	AN	1-30	N/U				
HI05-8	Industry code	AN	1-30	N/U				New Element
HI05-9	Yes/No Condition or response Code	ID	1-1	N/U				New Element
HI06	HEALTH CARE CODE INFORMATION			S				
HI06-1	Qualifier Code	ID	1-3	R			BBQ, BQ	Name Change / Code Change
HI06-2	Procedure Code	AN	1-30	R				
HI06-3	Date Time Period Format Qualifier	ID	2-3	R			D8	Usage change to Required
HI06-4	Date Time Period	AN	1-35	R			CCYYMMDD	Usage change to Required
HI06-5	Monetary Amount	R	1-18	N/U				
HI06-6	Quantity	R	1-15	N/U				
HI06-7	Version Identifier	AN	1-30	N/U				
HI06-8	Industry code	AN	1-30	N/U				New Element
HI06-9	Yes/No Condition or response Code	ID	1-1	N/U				New Element
HI07	HEALTH CARE CODE INFORMATION			S				
HI07-1	Qualifier Code	ID	1-3	R			BBQ, BQ	Name Change / Code Change
HI07-2	Procedure Code	AN	1-30	R				
HI07-3	Date Time Period Format Qualifier	ID	2-3	R			D8	Usage change to Required
HI07-4	Date Time Period	AN	1-35	R			CCYYMMDD	Usage change to Required
HI07-5	Monetary Amount	R	1-18	N/U				
HI07-6	Quantity	R	1-15	N/U				
HI07-7	Version Identifier	AN	1-30	N/U				
HI07-8	Industry code	AN	1-30	N/U				New Element
HI07-9	Yes/No Condition or response Code	ID	1-1	N/U				New Element

Page 46 of 93

INSTITUTIONAL CLAIM

4010A1

837-I 4010A1

Element Identifier	Description	ID	Min. Max.	Usage Reg.	Loop	Loop Repeat	Values
HI08	HEALTH CARE CODE INFORMATION			S			
HI08-1	Code List Qualifier Code	ID	1-3	R			BO, BQ
HI08-2	Procedure Code	AN	1-30	R			
HI08-3	Date Time Period Format Qualifier	ID	2-3	S			D8
HI08-4	Date Time Period	AN	1-35	S			CCYYMMDD
HI08-5	Monetary Amount	R	1-18	N/U			
HI08-6	Quantity	R	1-15	N/U			
HI08-7	Version Identifier	AN	1-30	N/U			
HI09	HEALTH CARE CODE INFORMATION			S			
HI09-1	Code List Qualifier Code	ID	1-3	R			BO, BQ
HI09-2	Procedure Code	AN	1-30	R			
HI09-3	Date Time Period Format Qualifier	ID	2-3	S			D8
HI09-4	Date Time Period	AN	1-35	S			CCYYMMDD
HI09-5	Monetary Amount	R	1-18	N/U			
HI09-6	Quantity	R	1-15	N/U			
HI09-7	Version Identifier	AN	1-30	N/U			
HI10	HEALTH CARE CODE INFORMATION			S			
HI10-1	Code List Qualifier Code	ID	1-3	R			BO, BQ
HI10-2	Procedure Code	AN	1-30	R			
HI10-3	Date Time Period Format Qualifier	ID	2-3	S			D8
HI10-4	Date Time Period	AN	1-35	S			CCYYMMDD
HI10-5	Monetary Amount	R	1-18	N/U			
HI10-6	Quantity	R	1-15	N/U			
HI10-7	Version Identifier	AN	1-30	N/U			
HI11	HEALTH CARE CODE INFORMATION			S			
HI11-1	Code List Qualifier Code	ID	1-3	R			BO, BQ
HI11-2	Procedure Code	AN	1-30	R			

5010

837-I 5010

Element Identifier	Description	ID	Min. Max.	Usage Reg.	Loop	Loop Repeat	Values	Notes
HI08	HEALTH CARE CODE INFORMATION			S				
HI08-1	Qualifier Code	ID	1-3	R			BBQ, BQ	Name Change / Code Change
HI08-2	Procedure Code	AN	1-30	R				
HI08-3	Date Time Period Format Qualifier	ID	2-3	R			D8	Usage change to Required
HI08-4	Date Time Period	AN	1-35	R			CCYYMMDD	Usage change to Required
HI08-5	Monetary Amount	R	1-18	N/U				
HI08-6	Quantity	R	1-15	N/U				
HI08-7	Version Identifier	AN	1-30	N/U				
HI08-8	Industry code	AN	1-30	N/U				New Element
HI08-9	Yes/No Condition or response Code	ID	1-1	N/U				New Element
HI09	HEALTH CARE CODE INFORMATION			S				
HI09-1	Qualifier Code	ID	1-3	R			BBQ, BQ	Name Change / Code Change
HI09-2	Procedure Code	AN	1-30	R				
HI09-3	Date Time Period Format Qualifier	ID	2-3	R			D8	Usage change to Required
HI09-4	Date Time Period	AN	1-35	R			CCYYMMDD	Usage change to Required
HI09-5	Monetary Amount	R	1-18	N/U				
HI09-6	Quantity	R	1-15	N/U				
HI09-7	Version Identifier	AN	1-30	N/U				
HI09-8	Industry code	AN	1-30	N/U				New Element
HI09-9	Yes/No Condition or response Code	ID	1-1	N/U				New Element
HI10	HEALTH CARE CODE INFORMATION			S				
HI10-1	Qualifier Code	ID	1-3	R			BBQ, BQ	Name Change / Code Change
HI10-2	Procedure Code	AN	1-30	R				
HI10-3	Date Time Period Format Qualifier	ID	2-3	R			D8	Usage change to Required
HI10-4	Date Time Period	AN	1-35	R			CCYYMMDD	Usage change to Required
HI10-5	Monetary Amount	R	1-18	N/U				
HI10-6	Quantity	R	1-15	N/U				
HI10-7	Version Identifier	AN	1-30	N/U				
HI10-8	Industry code	AN	1-30	N/U				New Element
HI10-9	Yes/No Condition or response Code	ID	1-1	N/U				New Element
HI11	HEALTH CARE CODE INFORMATION			S				
HI11-1	Qualifier Code	ID	1-3	R			BBQ, BQ	Name Change / Code Change
HI11-2	Procedure Code	AN	1-30	R				

Page 47 of 93

INSTITUTIONAL CLAIM

4010A1

837-I 4010A1

Element Identifier	Description	ID	Min. Max.	Usage Reg.	Loop	Loop Repeat	Values
HI11-3	Date Time Period Format Qualifier	ID	2-3	S			D8
HI11-4	Date Time Period	AN	1-35	S			CCYYMMDD
HI11-5	Monetary Amount	R	1-18	N/U			
HI11-6	Quantity	R	1-15	N/U			
HI11-7	Version Identifier	AN	1-30	N/U			
HI12	HEALTH CARE CODE INFORMATION			S			
HI12-1	Code List Qualifier Code	ID	1-3	R			BO, BQ
HI12-2	Procedure Code	AN	1-30	R			
HI12-3	Date Time Period Format Qualifier	ID	2-3	S			D8
HI12-4	Date Time Period	AN	1-35	S			CCYYMMDD
HI12-5	Monetary Amount	R	1-18	N/U			
HI12-6	Quantity	R	1-15	N/U			
HI12-7	Version Identifier	AN	1-30	N/U			
HI	OCCURRENCE SPAN INFORMATION		2	S	2300		
HI01	HEALTH CARE CODE INFORMATION			R			
HI01-1	Code List Qualifier Code	ID	1-3	R			BI
HI01-2	Occurrence Span Code	AN	1-30	R			
HI01-3	Date Time Period Format Qualifier	ID	2-3	R			RD8
HI01-4	Date Time Period	AN	1-35	R			CCYYMMDD CCYYMMDD
HI01-5	Monetary Amount	R	1-18	N/U			
HI01-6	Quantity	R	1-15	N/U			
HI01-7	Version Identifier	AN	1-30	N/U			
HI02	HEALTH CARE CODE INFORMATION			S			
HI02-1	Code List Qualifier Code	ID	1-3	R			BI
HI02-2	Occurrence Span Code	AN	1-30	R			
HI02-3	Date Time Period Format Qualifier	ID	2-3	R			RD8
HI02-4	Date Time Period	AN	1-35	R			CCYYMMDD-CCYYMMDD

5010

837-I 5010

Element Identifier	Description	ID	Min. Max.	Usage Reg.	Loop	Loop Repeat	Values	Notes
HI11-3	Date Time Period Format Qualifier	ID	2-3	R			D8	Usage change to Required
HI11-4	Date Time Period	AN	1-35	R			CCYYMMDD	Usage change to Required
HI11-5	Monetary Amount	R	1-18	N/U				
HI11-6	Quantity	R	1-15	N/U				
HI11-7	Version Identifier	AN	1-30	N/U				
HI11-8	Industry code	AN	1-30	N/U				New Element
HI11-9	Yes/No Condition or response Code	ID	1-1	N/U				New Element
HI12	HEALTH CARE CODE INFORMATION			S				
HI12-1	Qualifier Code	ID	1-3	R			BBQ, BQ	Name Change / Code Change
HI12-2	Procedure Code	AN	1-30	R				
HI12-3	Date Time Period Format Qualifier	ID	2-3	R			D8	Usage change to Required
HI12-4	Date Time Period	AN	1-35	R			CCYYMMDD	Usage change to Required
HI12-5	Monetary Amount	R	1-18	N/U				
HI12-6	Quantity	R	1-15	N/U				
HI12-7	Version Identifier	AN	1-30	N/U				
HI12-8	Industry code	AN	1-30	N/U				New Element
HI12-9	Yes/No Condition or response Code	ID	1-1	N/U				New Element
HI	OCCURRENCE SPAN INFORMATION		2	R	2300			Usage change to Required
HI01	HEALTH CARE CODE INFORMATION			R				
HI01-1	Qualifier	ID	1-3	R			BI	Name Change
HI01-2	Occurrence Span Code	AN	1-30	R				
HI01-3	Date Time Period Format Qualifier	ID	2-3	R			RD8	
HI01-4	Date Time Period	AN	1-35	R			CCYYMMDD-CCYYMMDD	
HI01-5	Monetary Amount	R	1-18	N/U				
HI01-6	Quantity	R	1-15	N/U				
HI01-7	Version Identifier	AN	1-30	N/U				
HI01-8	Industry code	AN	1-30	N/U				New Element
HI01-9	Yes/No Condition or response Code	ID	1-1	N/U				New Element
HI02	HEALTH CARE CODE INFORMATION			S				
HI02-1	Qualifier	ID	1-3	R			BI	Name Change
HI02-2	Occurrence Span Code	AN	1-30	R				
HI02-3	Date Time Period Format Qualifier	ID	2-3	R			RD8	
HI02-4	Date Time Period	AN	1-35	R			CCYYMMDD-CCYYMMDD	

INSTITUTIONAL CLAIM

4010A1

Element Identifier	Description	ID	Min. Max.	Usage Reg.	Loop	Loop Repeat	Values
	837-I 4010A1						
HI02-5	Monetary Amount	R	1-18	N/U			
HI02-6	Quantity	R	1-15	N/U			
HI02-7	Version Identifier	AN	1-30	N/U			
HI03	HEALTH CARE CODE INFORMATION			S			
HI03-1	Code List Qualifier Code	ID	1-3	R			BI
HI03-2	Occurrence Span Code	AN	1-30	R			
HI03-3	Date Time Period Format Qualifier	ID	2-3	R			RD8
HI03-4	Date Time Period	AN	1-35	R			CCYYMMDD-CCYYMMDD
HI03-5	Monetary Amount	R	1-18	N/U			
HI03-6	Quantity	R	1-15	N/U			
HI03-7	Version Identifier	AN	1-30	N/U			
HI03-8	Industry code	AN	1-30	N/U			
HI03-9	Yes/No Condition or response Code	ID	1-1	N/U			
HI04	HEALTH CARE CODE INFORMATION			S			
HI04-1	Code List Qualifier Code	ID	1-3	R			BI
HI04-2	Occurrence Span Code	AN	1-30	R			
HI04-3	Date Time Period Format Qualifier	ID	2-3	R			RD8
HI04-4	Date Time Period	AN	1-35	R			CCYYMMDD-CCYYMMDD
HI04-5	Monetary Amount	R	1-18	N/U			
HI04-6	Quantity	R	1-15	N/U			
HI04-7	Version Identifier	AN	1-30	N/U			
HI05	HEALTH CARE CODE INFORMATION			S			
HI05-1	Code List Qualifier Code	ID	1-3	R			BI
HI05-2	Occurrence Span Code	AN	1-30	R			
HI05-3	Date Time Period Format Qualifier	ID	2-3	R			RD8
HI05-4	Date Time Period	AN	1-35	R			CCYYMMDD-CCYYMMDD
HI05-5	Monetary Amount	R	1-18	N/U			
HI05-6	Quantity	R	1-15	N/U			
HI05-7	Version Identifier	AN	1-30	N/U			
HI06	HEALTH CARE CODE INFORMATION			S			

5010

Element Identifier	Description	ID	Min. Max.	Usage Reg.	Loop	Loop Repeat	Values	
	837-I 5010							
HI02-5	Monetary Amount	R	1-18	N/U				
HI02-6	Quantity	R	1-15	N/U				
HI02-7	Version Identifier	AN	1-30	N/U				
HI02-8	Industry code	AN	1-30	N/U				New Element
HI02-9	Yes/No Condition or response Code	ID	1-1	N/U				New Element
HI03	HEALTH CARE CODE INFORMATION			S				
HI03-1	Qualifier	ID	1-3	R			BI	Name Change
HI03-2	Occurrence Span Code	AN	1-30	R				
HI03-3	Date Time Period Format Qualifier	ID	2-3	R			RD8	
HI03-4	Date Time Period	AN	1-35	R			CCYYMMDD-CCYYMMDD	
HI03-5	Monetary Amount	R	1-18	N/U				
HI03-6	Quantity	R	1-15	N/U				
HI03-7	Version Identifier	AN	1-30	N/U				
HI03-8	Industry code	AN	1-30	N/U				New Element
HI03-9	Yes/No Condition or response Code	ID	1-1	N/U				New Element
HI04	HEALTH CARE CODE INFORMATION			S				
HI04-1	Qualifier	ID	1-3	R			BI	Name Change
HI04-2	Occurrence Span Code	AN	1-30	R				
HI04-3	Date Time Period Format Qualifier	ID	2-3	R			RD8	
HI04-4	Date Time Period	AN	1-35	R			CCYYMMDDCCYYMMDD	
HI04-5	Monetary Amount	R	1-18	N/U				
HI04-6	Quantity	R	1-15	N/U				
HI04-7	Version Identifier	AN	1-30	N/U				
HI04-8	Industry code	AN	1-30	N/U				New Element
HI04-9	Yes/No Condition or response Code	ID	1-1	N/U				New Element
HI05	HEALTH CARE CODE INFORMATION			S				
HI05-1	Qualifier	ID	1-3	R			BI	Name Change
HI05-2	Occurrence Span Code	AN	1-30	R				
HI05-3	Date Time Period Format Qualifier	ID	2-3	R			RD8	
HI05-4	Date Time Period	AN	1-35	R			CCYYMMDD-CCYYMMDD	
HI05-5	Monetary Amount	R	1-18	N/U				
HI05-6	Quantity	R	1-15	N/U				
HI05-7	Version Identifier	AN	1-30	N/U				
HI05-8	Industry code	AN	1-30	N/U				New Element
HI05-9	Yes/No Condition or response Code	ID	1-1	N/U				New Element
HI06	HEALTH CARE CODE INFORMATION			S				

Page 49 of 93

INSTITUTIONAL CLAIM

Element Identifier	Description	ID	Min. Max.	Usage Reg.	Loop	Loop Repeat	Values
			4010A1				
			837-I 4010A1				
HI06-1	Code List Qualifier Code	ID	1-3	R			BI
HI06-2	Occurrence Span Code	AN	1-30	R			
HI06-3	Date Time Period Format Qualifier	ID	2-3	R			RD8
HI06-4	Date Time Period	AN	1-35	R			CCYYMMDD-CCYYMMDD
HI06-5	Monetary Amount	R	1-18	N/U			
HI06-6	Quantity	R	1-15	N/U			
HI06-7	Version Identifier	AN	1-30	N/U			
HI07	HEALTH CARE CODE INFORMATION			S			
HI07-1	Code List Qualifier Code	ID	1-3	R			BI
HI07-2	Occurrence Span Code	AN	1-30	R			
HI07-3	Date Time Period Format Qualifier	ID	2-3	R			RD8
HI07-4	Date Time Period	AN	1-35	R			CCYYMMDD-CCYYMMDD
HI07-5	Monetary Amount	R	1-18	N/U			
HI07-6	Quantity	R	1-15	N/U			
HI07-7	Version Identifier	AN	1-30	N/U			
HI08	HEALTH CARE CODE INFORMATION			S			
HI08-1	Code List Qualifier Code	ID	1-3	R			BI
HI08-2	Occurrence Span Code	AN	1-30	R			
HI08-3	Date Time Period Format Qualifier	ID	2-3	R			RD8
HI08-4	Date Time Period	AN	1-35	R			CCYYMMDD-CCYYMMDD
HI08-5	Monetary Amount	R	1-18	N/U			
HI08-6	Quantity	R	1-15	N/U			
HI08-7	Version Identifier	AN	1-30	N/U			
HI09	HEALTH CARE CODE INFORMATION			S			
HI09-1	Code List Qualifier Code	ID	1-3	R			BI
HI09-2	Occurrence Span Code	AN	1-30	R			
HI09-3	Date Time Period Format Qualifier	ID	2-3	R			RD8
HI09-4	Date Time Period	AN	1-35	R			CCYYMMDD-CCYYMMDD
HI09-5	Monetary Amount	R	1-18	N/U			
HI09-6	Quantity	R	1-15	N/U			

Element Identifier	Description	ID	Min. Max.	Usage Reg.	Loop	Loop Repeat	Values	
			5010					
			837-I 5010					
HI06-1	Qualifier	ID	1-3	R			BI	Name Change
HI06-2	Occurrence Span Code	AN	1-30	R				
HI06-3	Date Time Period Format Qualifier	ID	2-3	R			RD8	
HI06-4	Date Time Period	AN	1-35	R			CCYYMMDD-CCYYMMDD	
HI06-5	Monetary Amount	R	1-18	N/U				
HI06-6	Quantity	R	1-15	N/U				
HI06-7	Version Identifier	AN	1-30	N/U				
HI06-8	Industry code	AN	1-30	N/U				New Element
HI06-9	Yes/No Condition or response Code	ID	1-1	N/U				New Element
HI07	HEALTH CARE CODE INFORMATION			S				
HI07-1	Qualifier	ID	1-3	R			BI	Name Change
HI07-2	Occurrence Span Code	AN	1-30	R				
HI07-3	Date Time Period Format Qualifier	ID	2-3	R			RD8	
HI07-4	Date Time Period	AN	1-35	R			CCYYMMDD-CCYYMMDD	
HI07-5	Monetary Amount	R	1-18	N/U				
HI07-6	Quantity	R	1-15	N/U				
HI07-7	Version Identifier	AN	1-30	N/U				
HI07-8	Industry code	AN	1-30	N/U				New Element
HI07-9	Yes/No Condition or response Code	ID	1-1	N/U				New Element
HI08	HEALTH CARE CODE INFORMATION			S				
HI08-1	Qualifier	ID	1-3	R			BI	Name Change
HI08-2	Occurrence Span Code	AN	1-30	R				
HI08-3	Date Time Period Format Qualifier	ID	2-3	R			RD8	
HI08-4	Date Time Period	AN	1-35	R			CCYYMMDD-CCYYMMDD	
HI08-5	Monetary Amount	R	1-18	N/U				
HI08-6	Quantity	R	1-15	N/U				
HI08-7	Version Identifier	AN	1-30	N/U				
HI08-8	Industry code	AN	1-30	N/U				New Element
HI08-9	Yes/No Condition or response Code	ID	1-1	N/U				New Element
HI09	HEALTH CARE CODE INFORMATION			S				
HI09-1	Qualifier	ID	1-3	R			BI	Name Change
HI09-2	Occurrence Span Code	AN	1-30	R				
HI09-3	Date Time Period Format Qualifier	ID	2-3	R			RD8	
HI09-4	Date Time Period	AN	1-35	R			CCYYMMDD-CCYYMMDD	
HI09-5	Monetary Amount	R	1-18	N/U				
HI09-6	Quantity	R	1-15	N/U				

Page 50 of 93

INSTITUTIONAL CLAIM

4010A1

837-I 4010A1

Element Identifier	Description	ID	Min. Max.	Usage Reg.	Loop	Loop Repeat	Values
HI09-7	Version Identifier	AN	1-30	N/U			
HI10	HEALTH CARE CODE INFORMATION			S			
HI10-1	Code List Qualifier Code	ID	1-3	R			BI
HI10-2	Occurrence Span Code	AN	1-30	R			
HI10-3	Date Time Period Format Qualifier	ID	2-3	R			RD8
HI10-4	Date Time Period	AN	1-35	R			CCYYMMDD-CCYYMMDD
HI10-5	Monetary Amount	R	1-18	N/U			
HI10-6	Quantity	R	1-15	N/U			
HI10-7	Version Identifier	AN	1-30	N/U			
HI11	HEALTH CARE CODE INFORMATION			S			
HI11-1	Code List Qualifier Code	ID	1-3	R			BI
HI11-2	Occurrence Span Code	AN	1-30	R			
HI11-3	Date Time Period Format Qualifier	ID	2-3	R			RD8
HI11-4	Date Time Period	AN	1-35	R			CCYYMMDD-CCYYMMDD
HI11-5	Monetary Amount	R	1-18	N/U			
HI11-6	Quantity	R	1-15	N/U			
HI11-7	Version Identifier	AN	1-30	N/U			
HI12	HEALTH CARE CODE INFORMATION			S			
HI12-1	Code List Qualifier Code	ID	1-3	R			BI
HI12-2	Occurrence Span Code	AN	1-30	R			
HI12-3	Date Time Period Format Qualifier	ID	2-3	R			RD8
HI12-4	Date Time Period	AN	1-35	R			CCYYMMDD-CCYYMMDD
HI12-5	Monetary Amount	R	1-18	N/U			
HI12-6	Quantity	R	1-15	N/U			
HI12-7	Version Identifier	AN	1-30	N/U			
HI	OCCURRENCE INFORMATION		2	R	2300		

5010

837-I 5010

Element Identifier	Description	ID	Min. Max.	Usage Reg.	Loop	Loop Repeat	Values	
HI09-7	Version Identifier	AN	1-30	N/U				
HI09-8	Industry code	AN	1-30	N/U				New Element
HI09-9	Yes/No Condition or response Code	ID	1-1	N/U				New Element
HI10	HEALTH CARE CODE INFORMATION			S				
HI10-1	Qualifier	ID	1-3	R			BI	Name Change
HI10-2	Occurrence Span Code	AN	1-30	R				
HI10-3	Date Time Period Format Qualifier	ID	2-3	R			RD8	
HI10-4	Date Time Period	AN	1-35	R			CCYYMMDD-CCYYMMDD	
HI10-5	Monetary Amount	R	1-18	N/U				
HI10-6	Quantity	R	1-15	N/U				
HI10-7	Version Identifier	AN	1-30	N/U				
HI10-8	Industry code	AN	1-30	N/U				New Element
HI10-9	Yes/No Condition or response Code	ID	1-1	N/U				New Element
HI11	HEALTH CARE CODE INFORMATION			S				
HI11-1	Qualifier	ID	1-3	R			BI	Name Change
HI11-2	Occurrence Span Code	AN	1-30	R				
HI11-3	Date Time Period Format Qualifier	ID	2-3	R			RD8	
HI11-4	Date Time Period	AN	1-35	R			CCYYMMDD-CCYYMMDD	
HI11-5	Monetary Amount	R	1-18	N/U				
HI11-6	Quantity	R	1-15	N/U				
HI11-7	Version Identifier	AN	1-30	N/U				
HI11-8	Industry code	AN	1-30	N/U				New Element
HI11-9	Yes/No Condition or response Code	ID	1-1	N/U				New Element
HI12	HEALTH CARE CODE INFORMATION			S				
HI12-1	Qualifier	ID	1-3	R			BI	Name Change
HI12-2	Occurrence Span Code	AN	1-30	R				
HI12-3	Date Time Period Format Qualifier	ID	2-3	R			RD8	
HI12-4	Date Time Period	AN	1-35	R			CCYYMMDD-CCYYMMDD	
HI12-5	Monetary Amount	R	1-18	N/U				
HI12-6	Quantity	R	1-15	N/U				
HI12-7	Version Identifier	AN	1-30	N/U				
HI12-8	Industry code	AN	1-30	N/U				New Element
HI12-9	Yes/No Condition or response Code	ID	1-1	N/U				New Element
HI	OCCURRENCE INFORMATION		2	R	2300			

Page 51 of 93

INSTITUTIONAL CLAIM

4010A1

837-I 4010A1

Element Identifier	Description	ID	Min. Max.	Usage Reg.	Loop	Loop Repeat	Values
HI01	HEALTH CARE CODE INFORMATION			R			
HI01-1	Code List Qualifier Code	ID	1-3	R			BH
HI01-2	Occurrence Code	AN	1-30	R			
HI01-3	Date Time Period Format Qualifier	ID	2-3	R			D8
HI01-4	Date Time Period	AN	1-35	R			CCYYMMDD
HI01-5	Monetary Amount	R	1-18	N/U			
HI01-6	Quantity	R	1-15	N/U			
HI01-7	Version Identifier	AN	1-30	N/U			
HI02	HEALTH CARE CODE INFORMATION			S			
HI02-1	Code List Qualifier Code	ID	1-3	R			BH
HI02-2	Occurrence Code	AN	1-30	R			
HI02-3	Date Time Period Format Qualifier	ID	2-3	R			D8
HI02-4	Date Time Period	AN	1-35	R			CCYYMMDD
HI02-5	Monetary Amount	R	1-18	N/U			
HI02-6	Quantity	R	1-15	N/U			
HI02-7	Version Identifier	AN	1-30	N/U			
HI03	HEALTH CARE CODE INFORMATION			S			
HI03-1	Code List Qualifier Code	ID	1-3	R			BH
HI03-2	Occurrence Code	AN	1-30	R			
HI03-3	Date Time Period Format Qualifier	ID	2-3	R			D8
HI03-4	Date Time Period	AN	1-35	R			CCYYMMDD
HI03-5	Monetary Amount	R	1-18	N/U			
HI03-6	Quantity	R	1-15	N/U			
HI03-7	Version Identifier	AN	1-30	N/U			
HI04	HEALTH CARE CODE INFORMATION			S			
HI04-1	Code List Qualifier Code	ID	1-3	R			BH
HI04-2	Occurrence Code	AN	1-30	R			
HI04-3	Date Time Period Format Qualifier	ID	2-3	R			D8
HI04-4	Date Time Period	AN	1-35	R			CCYYMMDD
HI04-5	Monetary Amount	R	1-18	N/U			
HI04-6	Quantity	R	1-15	N/U			
HI04-7	Version Identifier	AN	1-30	N/U			

5010

837-I 5010

Element Identifier	Description	ID	Min. Max.	Usage Reg.	Loop	Loop Repeat	Values	
HI01	HEALTH CARE CODE INFORMATION			R				
HI01-1	Qualifier	ID	1-3	R			BH	Name Change
HI01-2	Occurrence Code	AN	1-30	R				
HI01-3	Date Time Period Format Qualifier	ID	2-3	R			D8	
HI01-4	Date Time Period	AN	1-35	R			CCYYMMDD	
HI01-5	Monetary Amount	R	1-18	N/U				
HI01-6	Quantity	R	1-15	N/U				
HI01-7	Version Identifier	AN	1-30	N/U				
HI01-8	Industry code	AN	1-30	N/U				New Element
HI01-9	Yes/No Condition or response Code	ID	1-1	N/U				New Element
HI02	HEALTH CARE CODE INFORMATION			S				
HI02-1	Qualifier	ID	1-3	R			BH	Name Change
HI02-2	Occurrence Code	AN	1-30	R				
HI02-3	Date Time Period Format Qualifier	ID	2-3	R			D8	
HI02-4	Date Time Period	AN	1-35	R			CCYYMMDD	
HI02-5	Monetary Amount	R	1-18	N/U				
HI02-6	Quantity	R	1-15	N/U				
HI02-7	Version Identifier	AN	1-30	N/U				
HI02-8	Industry code	AN	1-30	N/U				New Element
HI02-9	Yes/No Condition or response Code	ID	1-1	N/U				New Element
HI03	HEALTH CARE CODE INFORMATION			S				
HI03-1	Qualifier	ID	1-3	R			BH	Name Change
HI03-2	Occurrence Code	AN	1-30	R				
HI03-3	Date Time Period Format Qualifier	ID	2-3	R			D8	
HI03-4	Date Time Period	AN	1-35	R			CCYYMMDD	
HI03-5	Monetary Amount	R	1-18	N/U				
HI03-6	Quantity	R	1-15	N/U				
HI03-7	Version Identifier	AN	1-30	N/U				
HI03-8	Industry code	AN	1-30	N/U				New Element
HI03-9	Yes/No Condition or response Code	ID	1-1	N/U				New Element
HI04	HEALTH CARE CODE INFORMATION			S				
HI04-1	Qualifier	ID	1-3	R			BH	Name Change
HI04-2	Occurrence Code	AN	1-30	R				
HI04-3	Date Time Period Format Qualifier	ID	2-3	R			D8	
HI04-4	Date Time Period	AN	1-35	R			CCYYMMDD	
HI04-5	Monetary Amount	R	1-18	N/U				
HI04-6	Quantity	R	1-15	N/U				
HI04-7	Version Identifier	AN	1-30	N/U				
HI04-8	Industry code	AN	1-30	N/U				New Element

Page 52 of 93

INSTITUTIONAL CLAIM

4010A1

Element Identifier	Description	ID	Min. Max.	Usage Reg.	Loop	Loop Repeat	Values
	837-I 4010A1						
HI05	HEALTH CARE CODE INFORMATION			S			
HI05-1	Code List Qualifier Code	ID	1-3	R			BH
HI05-2	Occurrence Code	AN	1-30	R			
HI05-3	Date Time Period Format Qualifier	ID	2-3	R			D8
HI05-4	Date Time Period	AN	1-35	R			CCYYMMDD
HI05-5	Monetary Amount	R	1-18	N/U			
HI05-6	Quantity	R	1-15	N/U			
HI05-7	Version Identifier	AN	1-30	N/U			
HI06	HEALTH CARE CODE INFORMATION			S			
HI06-1	Code List Qualifier Code	ID	1-3	R			BH
HI06-2	Occurrence Code	AN	1-30	R			
HI06-3	Date Time Period Format Qualifier	ID	2-3	R			D8
HI06-4	Date Time Period	AN	1-35	R			CCYYMMDD
HI06-5	Monetary Amount	R	1-18	N/U			
HI06-6	Quantity	R	1-15	N/U			
HI06-7	Version Identifier	AN	1-30	N/U			
HI07	HEALTH CARE CODE INFORMATION			S			
HI07-1	Code List Qualifier Code	ID	1-3	R			BH
HI07-2	Occurrence Code	AN	1-30	R			
HI07-3	Date Time Period Format Qualifier	ID	2-3	R			D8
HI07-4	Date Time Period	AN	1-35	R			CCYYMMDD
HI07-5	Monetary Amount	R	1-18	N/U			
HI07-6	Quantity	R	1-15	N/U			
HI07-7	Version Identifier	AN	1-30	N/U			
HI08	HEALTH CARE CODE INFORMATION			S			
HI08-1	Code List Qualifier Code	ID	1-3	R			BH
HI08-2	Occurrence Code	AN	1-30	R			
HI08-3	Date Time Period Format Qualifier	ID	2-3	R			D8
HI08-4	Date Time Period	AN	1-35	R			CCYYMMDD
HI08-5	Monetary Amount	R	1-18	N/U			
HI08-6	Quantity	R	1-15	N/U			

5010

Element Identifier	Description	ID	Min. Max.	Usage Reg.	Loop	Loop Repeat	Values	
	837-I 5010							
HI04-9	Yes/No Condition or response Code	ID	1-1	N/U				New Element
HI05	HEALTH CARE CODE INFORMATION			S				
HI05-1	Qualifier	ID	1-3	R			BH	Name Change
HI05-2	Occurrence Code	AN	1-30	R				
HI05-3	Date Time Period Format Qualifier	ID	2-3	R			D8	
HI05-4	Date Time Period	AN	1-35	R			CCYYMMDD	
HI05-5	Monetary Amount	R	1-18	N/U				
HI05-6	Quantity	R	1-15	N/U				
HI05-7	Version Identifier	AN	1-30	N/U				
HI05-8	Industry code	AN	1-30	N/U				New Element
HI05-9	Yes/No Condition or response Code	ID	1-1	N/U				New Element
HI06	HEALTH CARE CODE INFORMATION			S				
HI06-1	Qualifier	ID	1-3	R			BH	Name Change
HI06-2	Occurrence Code	AN	1-30	R				
HI06-3	Date Time Period Format Qualifier	ID	2-3	R			D8	
HI06-4	Date Time Period	AN	1-35	R			CCYYMMDD	
HI06-5	Monetary Amount	R	1-18	N/U				
HI06-6	Quantity	R	1-15	N/U				
HI06-7	Version Identifier	AN	1-30	N/U				
HI06-8	Industry code	AN	1-30	N/U				New Element
HI06-9	Yes/No Condition or response Code	ID	1-1	N/U				New Element
HI07	HEALTH CARE CODE INFORMATION			S				
HI07-1	Qualifier	ID	1-3	R			BH	Name Change
HI07-2	Occurrence Code	AN	1-30	R				
HI07-3	Date Time Period Format Qualifier	ID	2-3	R			D8	
HI07-4	Date Time Period	AN	1-35	R			CCYYMMDD	
HI07-5	Monetary Amount	R	1-18	N/U				
HI07-6	Quantity	R	1-15	N/U				
HI07-7	Version Identifier	AN	1-30	N/U				
HI07-8	Industry code	AN	1-30	N/U				New Element
HI07-9	Yes/No Condition or response Code	ID	1-1	N/U				New Element
HI08	HEALTH CARE CODE INFORMATION			S				
HI08-1	Qualifier	ID	1-3	R			BH	Name Change
HI08-2	Occurrence Code	AN	1-30	R				
HI08-3	Date Time Period Format Qualifier	ID	2-3	R			D8	
HI08-4	Date Time Period	AN	1-35	R			CCYYMMDD	
HI08-5	Monetary Amount	R	1-18	N/U				
HI08-6	Quantity	R	1-15	N/U				

Page 53 of 93

INSTITUTIONAL CLAIM

Element Identifier	Description	ID	Min. Max.	Usage Reg.	Loop	Loop Repeat	Values
		4010A1					
		837-I 4010A1					
HI08-7	Version Identifier	AN	1-30	N/U			
HI09	HEALTH CARE CODE INFORMATION			S			
HI09-1	Code List Qualifier Code	ID	1-3	R			BH
HI09-2	Occurrence Code	AN	1-30	R			
HI09-3	Date Time Period Format Qualifier	ID	2-3	R			D8
HI09-4	Date Time Period	AN	1-35	R			CCYYMMDD
HI09-5	Monetary Amount	R	1-18	N/U			
HI09-6	Quantity	R	1-15	N/U			
HI09-7	Version Identifier	AN	1-30	N/U			
HI10	HEALTH CARE CODE INFORMATION			S			
HI10-1	Code List Qualifier Code	ID	1-3	R			BH
HI10-2	Occurrence Code	AN	1-30	R			
HI10-3	Date Time Period Format Qualifier	ID	2-3	R			D8
HI10-4	Date Time Period	AN	1-35	R			CCYYMMDD
HI10-5	Monetary Amount	R	1-18	N/U			
HI10-6	Quantity	R	1-15	N/U			
HI10-7	Version Identifier	AN	1-30	N/U			
HI11	HEALTH CARE CODE INFORMATION			S			
HI11-1	Code List Qualifier Code	ID	1-3	R			BH
HI11-2	Occurrence Code	AN	1-30	R			
HI11-3	Date Time Period Format Qualifier	ID	2-3	R			D8
HI11-4	Date Time Period	AN	1-35	R			CCYYMMDD
HI11-5	Monetary Amount	R	1-18	N/U			
HI11-6	Quantity	R	1-15	N/U			
HI11-7	Version Identifier	AN	1-30	N/U			
HI12	HEALTH CARE CODE INFORMATION			S			
HI12-1	Code List Qualifier Code	ID	1-3	R			BH
HI12-2	Occurrence Code	AN	1-30	R			
HI12-3	Date Time Period Format Qualifier	ID	2-3	R			D8
HI12-4	Date Time Period	AN	1-35	R			CCYYMMDD

Element Identifier	Description	ID	Min. Max.	Usage Reg.	Loop	Loop Repeat	Values	
		5010						
		837-I 5010						
HI08-7	Version Identifier	AN	1-30	N/U				
HI08-8	Industry code	AN	1-30	N/U				New Element
HI08-9	Yes/No Condition or response Code	ID	1-1	N/U				New Element
HI09	HEALTH CARE CODE INFORMATION			S				
HI09-1	Qualifier	ID	1-3	R			BH	Name Change
HI09-2	Occurrence Code	AN	1-30	R				
HI09-3	Date Time Period Format Qualifier	ID	2-3	R			D8	
HI09-4	Date Time Period	AN	1-35	R			CCYYMMDD	
HI09-5	Monetary Amount	R	1-18	N/U				
HI09-6	Quantity	R	1-15	N/U				
HI09-7	Version Identifier	AN	1-30	N/U				
HI09-8	Industry code	AN	1-30	N/U				New Element
HI09-9	Yes/No Condition or response Code	ID	1-1	N/U				New Element
HI10	HEALTH CARE CODE INFORMATION			S				
HI10-1	Qualifier	ID	1-3	R			BH	Name Change
HI10-2	Occurrence Code	AN	1-30	R				
HI10-3	Date Time Period Format Qualifier	ID	2-3	R			D8	
HI10-4	Date Time Period	AN	1-35	R			CCYYMMDD	
HI10-5	Monetary Amount	R	1-18	N/U				
HI10-6	Quantity	R	1-15	N/U				
HI10-7	Version Identifier	AN	1-30	N/U				
HI10-8	Industry code	AN	1-30	N/U				New Element
HI10-9	Yes/No Condition or response Code	ID	1-1	N/U				New Element
HI11	HEALTH CARE CODE INFORMATION			S				
HI11-1	Qualifier	ID	1-3	R			BH	Name Change
HI11-2	Occurrence Code	AN	1-30	R				
HI11-3	Date Time Period Format Qualifier	ID	2-3	R			D8	
HI11-4	Date Time Period	AN	1-35	R			CCYYMMDD	
HI11-5	Monetary Amount	R	1-18	N/U				
HI11-6	Quantity	R	1-15	N/U				
HI11-7	Version Identifier	AN	1-30	N/U				
HI11-8	Industry code	AN	1-30	N/U				New Element
HI11-9	Yes/No Condition or response Code	ID	1-1	N/U				New Element
HI12	HEALTH CARE CODE INFORMATION			S				
HI12-1	Qualifier	ID	1-3	R			BH	Name Change
HI12-2	Occurrence Code	AN	1-30	R				
HI12-3	Date Time Period Format Qualifier	ID	2-3	R			D8	
HI12-4	Date Time Period	AN	1-35	R			CCYYMMDD	

Page 54 of 93

INSTITUTIONAL CLAIM

4010A1

Element Identifier	Description	ID	Min. Max.	Usage Reg.	Loop	Loop Repeat	Values
	837-I 4010A1						
HI12-5	Monetary Amount	R	1-18	N/U			
HI12-6	Quantity	R	1-15	N/U			
HI12-7	Version Identifier	AN	1-30	N/U			
HI	**VALUE INFORMATION**		2	R	2300		
HI01	HEALTH CARE CODE INFORMATION			R			
HI01-1	Code List Qualifier Code	ID	1-3	R			BE
HI01-2	Value Code	AN	1-30	R			
HI01-3	Date Time Period Format Qualifier	ID	2-3	N/U			
HI01-4	Date Time Period	AN	1-35	N/U			
HI01-5	Value Code Associated Amount	R	1-18	R			
HI01-6	Quantity	R	1-15	N/U			
HI01-7	Version Identifier	AN	1-30	N/U			
HI02	HEALTH CARE CODE INFORMATION			S			
HI02-1	Code List Qualifier Code	ID	1-3	R			BE
HI02-2	Value Code	AN	1-30	R			
HI02-3	Date Time Period Format Qualifier	ID	2-3	N/U			
HI02-4	Date Time Period	AN	1-35	N/U			
HI02-5	Value Code Associated Amount	R	1-18	R			
HI02-6	Quantity	R	1-15	N/U			
HI02-7	Version Identifier	AN	1-30	N/U			
HI03	HEALTH CARE CODE INFORMATION			S			
HI03-1	Code List Qualifier Code	ID	1-3	R			BE
HI03-2	Value Code	AN	1-30	R			
HI03-3	Date Time Period Format Qualifier	ID	2-3	N/U			
HI03-4	Date Time Period	AN	1-35	N/U			
HI03-5	Value Code Associated Amount	R	1-18	R			
HI03-6	Quantity	R	1-15	N/U			
HI03-7	Version Identifier	AN	1-30	N/U			

5010

Element Identifier	Description	ID	Min. Max.	Usage Reg.	Loop	Loop Repeat	Values	
	837-I 5010							
HI12-5	Monetary Amount	R	1-18	N/U				
HI12-6	Quantity	R	1-15	N/U				
HI12-7	Version Identifier	AN	1-30	N/U				
HI12-8	Industry code	AN	1-30	N/U				New Element
HI12-9	Yes/No Condition or response Code	ID	1-1	N/U				New Element
HI	**VALUE INFORMATION**		2	R	2300			
HI01	HEALTH CARE CODE INFORMATION			R				
HI01-1	Qualifier	ID	1-3	R			BE	Name Change
HI01-2	Value Code	AN	1-30	R				
HI01-3	Date Time Period Format Qualifier	ID	2-3	N/U				
HI01-4	Date Time Period	AN	1-35	N/U				
HI01-5	Value Code Amount	R	1-18	R				Name Change
HI01-6	Quantity	R	1-15	N/U				
HI01-7	Version Identifier	AN	1-30	N/U				
HI01-8	Industry code	AN	1-30	N/U				New Element
HI01-9	Yes/No Condition or response Code	ID	1-1	N/U				New Element
HI02	HEALTH CARE CODE INFORMATION			S				
HI02-1	Qualifier	ID	1-3	R			BE	Name Change
HI02-2	Value Code	AN	1-30	R				
HI02-3	Date Time Period Format Qualifier	ID	2-3	N/U				
HI02-4	Date Time Period	AN	1-35	N/U				
HI02-5	Value Code Amount	R	1-18	R				Name Change
HI02-6	Quantity	R	1-15	N/U				
HI02-7	Version Identifier	AN	1-30	N/U				
HI02-8	Industry code	AN	1-30	N/U				New Element
HI02-9	Yes/No Condition or response Code	ID	1-1	N/U				New Element
HI03	HEALTH CARE CODE INFORMATION			S				
HI03-1	Qualifier	ID	1-3	R			BE	Name Change
HI03-2	Value Code	AN	1-30	R				
HI03-3	Date Time Period Format Qualifier	ID	2-3	N/U				
HI03-4	Date Time Period	AN	1-35	N/U				
HI03-5	Value Code Amount	R	1-18	R				Name Change
HI03-6	Quantity	R	1-15	N/U				
HI03-7	Version Identifier	AN	1-30	N/U				
HI03-8	Industry code	AN	1-30	N/U				New Element
HI03-9	Yes/No Condition or response Code	ID	1-1	N/U				New Element

Page 55 of 93

INSTITUTIONAL CLAIM

4010A1									5010								
Element Identifier	Description	ID	Min. Max.	Usage Reg.	Loop	Loop Repeat	Values		Element Identifier	Description	ID	Min. Max.	Usage Reg.	Loop	Loop Repeat	Values	
	837-I 4010A1									837-I 5010							
HI04	HEALTH CARE CODE INFORMATION			S					HI04	HEALTH CARE CODE INFORMATION			S				
HI04-1	Code List Qualifier Code	ID	1-3	R			BE		HI04-1	Qualifier	ID	1-3	R			BE	Name Change
HI04-2	Value Code	AN	1-30	R					HI04-2	Value Code	AN	1-30	R				
HI04-3	Date Time Period Format Qualifier	ID	2-3	N/U					HI04-3	Date Time Period Format Qualifier	ID	2-3	N/U				
HI04-4	Date Time Period	AN	1-35	N/U					HI04-4	Date Time Period	AN	1-35	N/U				
HI04-5	Value Code Associated Amount	R	1-18	R					HI04-5	Value Code Amount	R	1 18	R				Name Change
HI04-6	Quantity	R	1-15	N/U					HI04-6	Quantity	R	1-15	N/U				
HI04-7	Version Identifier	AN	1-30	N/U					HI04-7	Version Identifier	AN	1-30	N/U				
									HI04-8	Industry code	AN	1-30	N/U				New Element
									HI04-9	Yes/No Condition or response Code	ID	1-1	N/U				New Element
HI05	HEALTH CARE CODE INFORMATION			S					HI05	HEALTH CARE CODE INFORMATION			S				
HI05-1	Code List Qualifier Code	ID	1-3	R			BE		HI05-1	Qualifier	ID	1-3	R			BE	Name Change
HI05-2	Value Code	AN	1-30	R					HI05-2	Value Code	AN	1-30	R				
HI05-3	Date Time Period Format Qualifier	ID	2-3	N/U					HI05-3	Date Time Period Format Qualifier	ID	2-3	N/U				
HI05-4	Date Time Period	AN	1-35	N/U					HI05-4	Date Time Period	AN	1-35	N/U				
HI05-5	Value Code Associated Amount	R	1-18	R					HI05-5	Value Code Amount	R	1-18	R				Name Change
HI05-6	Quantity	R	1-15	N/U					HI05-6	Quantity	R	1-15	N/U				
HI05-7	Version Identifier	AN	1-30	N/U					HI05-7	Version Identifier	AN	1-30	N/U				
									HI05-8	Industry code	AN	1-30	N/U				New Element
									HI05-9	Yes/No Condition or response Code	ID	1-1	N/U				New Element
HI06	HEALTH CARE CODE INFORMATION			S					HI06	HEALTH CARE CODE INFORMATION			S				
HI06-1	Code List Qualifier Code	ID	1-3	R			BE		HI06-1	Qualifier	ID	1-3	R			BE	Name Change
HI06-2	Value Code	AN	1-30	R					HI06-2	Value Code	AN	1-30	·R				
HI06-3	Date Time Period Format Qualifier	ID	2-3	N/U					HI06-3	Date Time Period Format Qualifier	ID	2-3	N/U				
HI06-4	Date Time Period	AN	1-35	N/U					HI06-4	Date Time Period	AN	1-35	N/U				
HI06-5	Value Code Associated Amount	R	1-18	R					HI06-5	Value Code Amount	R	1-18	R				Name Change
HI06-6	Quantity	R	1-15	N/U					HI06-6	Quantity	R	1-15	N/U				
HI06-7	Version Identifier	AN	1-30	N/U					HI06-7	Version Identifier	AN	1-30	N/U				
									HI06-8	Industry code	AN	1-30	N/U				New Element
									HI06-9	Yes/No Condition or response Code	ID	1-1	N/U				New Element
HI07	HEALTH CARE CODE INFORMATION			S					HI07	HEALTH CARE CODE INFORMATION			S				
HI07-1	Code List Qualifier Code	ID	1-3	R			BE		HI07-1	Qualifier	ID	1-3	R			BE	Name Change
HI07-2	Value Code	AN	1-30	R					HI07-2	Value Code	AN	1-30	R				
HI07-3	Date Time Period Format Qualifier	ID	2-3	N/U					HI07-3	Date Time Period Format Qualifier	ID	2-3	N/U				
HI07-4	Date Time Period	AN	1-35	N/U					HI07-4	Date Time Period	AN	1-35	N/U				

INSTITUTIONAL CLAIM

4010A1

Element Identifier	Description	ID	Min. Max.	Usage Reg.	Loop	Loop Repeat	Values
	837-I 4010A1						
HI07-5	Value Code Associated Amount	R	1-18	R			
HI07-6	Quantity	R	1-15	N/U			
HI07-7	Version Identifier	AN	1-30	N/U			
HI08	HEALTH CARE CODE INFORMATION			S			
HI08-1	Code List Qualifier Code	ID	1-3	R			BE
HI08-2	Value Code	AN	1-30	R			
HI08-3	Date Time Period Format Qualifier	ID	2-3	N/U			
HI08-4	Date Time Period	AN	1-35	N/U			
HI08-5	Value Code Associated Amount	R	1-18	R			
HI08-6	Quantity	R	1-15	N/U			
HI08-7	Version Identifier	AN	1-30	N/U			
HI09	HEALTH CARE CODE INFORMATION			S			
HI09-1	Code List Qualifier Code	ID	1-3	R			BE
HI09-2	Value Code	AN	1-30	R			
HI09-3	Date Time Period Format Qualifier	ID	2-3	N/U			
HI09-4	Date Time Period	AN	1-35	N/U			
HI09-5	Value Code Associated Amount	R	1-18	R			
HI09-6	Quantity	R	1-15	N/U			
HI09-7	Version Identifier	AN	1-30	N/U			
HI10	HEALTH CARE CODE INFORMATION			S			
HI10-1	Code List Qualifier Code	ID	1-3	R			BE
HI10-2	Value Code	AN	1-30	R			
HI10-3	Date Time Period Format Qualifier	ID	2-3	N/U			
HI10-4	Date Time Period	AN	1-35	N/U			
HI10-5	Value Code Associated Amount	R	1-18	R			
HI10-6	Quantity	R	1-15	N/U			
HI10-7	Version Identifier	AN	1-30	N/U			

5010

Element Identifier	Description	ID	Min. Max.	Usage Reg.	Loop	Loop Repeat	Values	
	837-I 5010							
HI07-5	Value Code Amount	R	1-18	R				Name Change
HI07-6	Quantity	R	1-15	N/U				
HI07-7	Version Identifier	AN	1-30	N/U				
HI07-8	Industry code	AN	1-30	N/U				New Element
HI07-9	Yes/No Condition or response Code	ID	1-1	N/U				New Element
HI08	HEALTH CARE CODE INFORMATION			S				
HI08-1	Qualifier	ID	1-3	R			BE	Name Change
HI08-2	Value Code	AN	1-30	R				
HI08-3	Date Time Period Format Qualifier	ID	2-3	N/U				
HI08-4	Date Time Period	AN	1-35	N/U				
HI08-5	Value Code Amount	R	1-18	R				Name Change
HI08-6	Quantity	R	1-15	N/U				
HI08-7	Version Identifier	AN	1-30	N/U				
HI08-8	Industry code	AN	1-30	N/U				New Element
HI08-9	Yes/No Condition or response Code	ID	1-1	N/U				New Element
HI09	HEALTH CARE CODE INFORMATION			S				
HI09-1	Qualifier	ID	1-3	R			BE	Name Change
HI09-2	Value Code	AN	1-30	R				
HI09-3	Date Time Period Format Qualifier	ID	2-3	N/U				
HI09-4	Date Time Period	AN	1-35	N/U				
HI09-5	Value Code Amount	R	1-18	R				Name Change
HI09-6	Quantity	R	1-15	N/U				
HI09-7	Version Identifier	AN	1-30	N/U				
HI09-8	Industry code	AN	1-30	N/U				New Element
HI09-9	Yes/No Condition or response Code	ID	1-1	N/U				New Element
HI10	HEALTH CARE CODE INFORMATION			S				
HI10-1	Qualifier	ID	1-3	R			BE	Name Change
HI10-2	Value Code	AN	1-30	R				
HI10-3	Date Time Period Format Qualifier	ID	2-3	N/U				
HI10-4	Date Time Period	AN	1-35	N/U				
HI10-5	Value Code Amount	R	1-18	R				Name Change
HI10-6	Quantity	R	1-15	N/U				
HI10-7	Version Identifier	AN	1-30	N/U				
HI10-8	Industry code	AN	1-30	N/U				New Element
HI10-9	Yes/No Condition or response Code	ID	1-1	N/U				New Element

INSTITUTIONAL CLAIM

4010A1

837-I 4010A1

Element Identifier	Description	ID	Min. Max.	Usage Reg.	Loop	Loop Repeat	Values
HI11	HEALTH CARE CODE INFORMATION			S			
HI11-1	Code List Qualifier Code	ID	1-3	R			BE
HI11-2	Value Code	AN	1-30	R			
HI11-3	Date Time Period Format Qualifier	ID	2-3	N/U			
HI11-4	Date Time Period	AN	1-35	N/U			
HI11-5	Value Code Associated Amount	R	1-18	R			
HI11-6	Quantity	R	1-15	N/U			
HI11-7	Version Identifier	AN	1-30	N/U			
HI12	HEALTH CARE CODE INFORMATION			S			
HI12-1	Code List Qualifier Code	ID	1-3	R			BE
HI12-2	Value Code	AN	1-30	R			
HI12-3	Date Time Period Format Qualifier	ID	2-3	N/U			
HI12-4	Date Time Period	AN	1-35	N/U			
HI12-5	Value Code Associated Amount	R	1-18	R			
HI12-6	Quantity	R	1-15	N/U			
HI12-7	Version Identifier	AN	1-30	N/U			
HI	CONDITION INFORMATION		2	R	2300		
HI01	HEALTH CARE CODE INFORMATION			R			
HI01-1	Code List Qualifier Code	ID	1-3	R			BG
HI01-2	Condition Code	AN	1-30	R			
HI01-3	Date Time Period Format Qualifier	ID	2-3	N/U			
HI01-4	Date Time Period	AN	1-35	N/U			
HI01-5	Monetary Amount	R	1-18	N/U			
HI01-6	Quantity	R	1-15	N/U			
HI01-7	Version Identifier	AN	1-30	N/U			
HI02	HEALTH CARE CODE INFORMATION			S			
HI02-1	Code List Qualifier Code	ID	1-3	R			BG
HI02-2	Condition Code	AN	1-30	R			
HI02-3	Date Time Period Format Qualifier	ID	2-3	N/U			

5010

837-I 5010

Element Identifier	Description	ID	Min. Max.	Usage Reg.	Loop	Loop Repeat	Values	
HI11	HEALTH CARE CODE INFORMATION			S				
HI11-1	Qualifier	ID	1-3	R			BE	Name Change
HI11-2	Value Code	AN	1-30	R				
HI11-3	Date Time Period Format Qualifier	ID	2-3	N/U				
HI11-4	Date Time Period	AN	1-35	N/U				
HI11-5	Value Code Amount	R	1-18	R				Name Change
HI11-6	Quantity	R	1-15	N/U				
HI11-7	Version Identifier	AN	1-30	N/U				
HI11-8	Industry code	AN	1-30	N/U				New Element
HI11-9	Yes/No Condition or response Code	ID	1-1	N/U				New Element
HI12	HEALTH CARE CODE INFORMATION			S				
HI12-1	Qualifier	ID	1-3	R			BE	Name Change
HI12-2	Value Code	AN	1-30	R				
HI12-3	Date Time Period Format Qualifier	ID	2-3	N/U				
HI12-4	Date Time Period	AN	1-35	N/U				
HI12-5	Value Code Amount	R	1-18	R				Name Change
HI12-6	Quantity	R	1-15	N/U				
HI12-7	Version Identifier	AN	1-30	N/U				
HI12-8	Industry code	AN	1-30	N/U				New Element
HI12-9	Yes/No Condition or response Code	ID	1-1	N/U				New Element
HI	CONDITION INFORMATION		2	R	2300			
HI01	HEALTH CARE CODE INFORMATION			R				
HI01-1	Qualifier	ID	1-3	R			BG	Name Change
HI01-2	Condition Code	AN	1-30	R				
HI01-3	Date Time Period Format Qualifier	ID	2-3	N/U				
HI01-4	Date Time Period	AN	1-35	N/U				
HI01-5	Monetary Amount	R	1-18	N/U				
HI01-6	Quantity	R	1-15	N/U				
HI01-7	Version Identifier	AN	1-30	N/U				
HI01-8	Industry code	AN	1-30	N/U				New Element
HI01-9	Yes/No Condition or response Code	ID	1-1	N/U				New Element
HI02	HEALTH CARE CODE INFORMATION			S				
HI02-1	Qualifier	ID	1-3	R			BG	Name Change
HI02-2	Condition Code	AN	1-30	R				
HI02-3	Date Time Period Format Qualifier	ID	2-3	N/U				

INSTITUTIONAL CLAIM

4010A1							
Element Identifier	Description	ID	Min. Max.	Usage Reg.	Loop	Loop Repeat	Values
837-I 4010A1							
HI02-4	Date Time Period	AN	1-35	N/U			
HI02-5	Monetary Amount	R	1-18	N/U			
HI02-6	Quantity	R	1-15	N/U			
HI02-7	Version Identifier	AN	1-30	N/U			
HI03	HEALTH CARE CODE INFORMATION			S			
HI03-1	Code List Qualifier Code	ID	1-3	R			BG
HI03-2	Condition Code	AN	1-30	R			
HI03-3	Date Time Period Format Qualifier	ID	2-3	N/U			
HI03-4	Date Time Period	AN	1-35	N/U			
HI03-5	Monetary Amount	R	1-18	N/U			
HI03-6	Quantity	R	1-15	N/U			
HI03-7	Version Identifier	AN	1-30	N/U			
HI04	HEALTH CARE CODE INFORMATION			S			
HI04-1	Code List Qualifier Code	ID	1-3	R			BG
HI04-2	Condition Code	AN	1-30	R			
HI04-3	Date Time Period Format Qualifier	ID	2-3	N/U			
HI04-4	Date Time Period	AN	1-35	N/U			
HI04-5	Monetary Amount	R	1-18	N/U			
HI04-6	Quantity	R	1-15	N/U			
HI04-7	Version Identifier	AN	1-30	N/U			
HI05	HEALTH CARE CODE INFORMATION			S			
HI05-1	Code List Qualifier Code	ID	1-3	R			BG
HI05-2	Condition Code	AN	1-30	R			
HI05-3	Date Time Period Format Qualifier	ID	2-3	N/U			
HI05-4	Date Time Period	AN	1-35	N/U			
HI05-5	Monetary Amount	R	1-18	N/U			
HI05-6	Quantity	R	1-15	N/U			
HI05-7	Version Identifier	AN	1-30	N/U			
HI06	HEALTH CARE CODE INFORMATION			S			
HI06-1	Code List Qualifier Code	ID	1-3	R			BG
HI06-2	Condition Code	AN	1-30	R			

5010								
Element Identifier	Description	ID	Min. Max.	Usage Reg.	Loop	Loop Repeat	Values	
837-I 5010								
HI02-4	Date Time Period	AN	1-35	N/U				
HI02-5	Monetary Amount	R	1-18	N/U				
HI02-6	Quantity	R	1-15	N/U				
HI02-7	Version Identifier	AN	1-30	N/U				
HI02-8	Industry code	AN	1-30	N/U				New Element
HI02-9	Yes/No Condition or response Code	ID	1-1	N/U				New Element
HI03	HEALTH CARE CODE INFORMATION			S				
HI03-1	Qualifier	ID	1-3	R			BG	Name Change
HI03-2	Condition Code	AN	1-30	R				
HI03-3	Date Time Period Format Qualifier	ID	2-3	N/U				
HI03-4	Date Time Period	AN	1-35	N/U				
HI03-5	Monetary Amount	R	1-18	N/U				
HI03-6	Quantity	R	1-15	N/U				
HI03-7	Version Identifier	AN	1-30	N/U				
HI03-8	Industry code	AN	1-30	N/U				New Element
HI03-9	Yes/No Condition or response Code	ID	1-1	N/U				New Element
HI04	HEALTH CARE CODE INFORMATION			S				
HI04-1	Qualifier	ID	1-3	R			BG	Name Change
HI04-2	Condition Code	AN	1-30	R				
HI04-3	Date Time Period Format Qualifier	ID	2-3	N/U				
HI04-4	Date Time Period	AN	1-35	N/U				
HI04-5	Monetary Amount	R	1-18	N/U				
HI04-6	Quantity	R	1-15	N/U				
HI04-7	Version Identifier	AN	1-30	N/U				
HI04-8	Industry code	AN	1-30	N/U				New Element
HI04-9	Yes/No Condition or response Code	ID	1-1	N/U				New Element
HI05	HEALTH CARE CODE INFORMATION			S				
HI05-1	Qualifier	ID	1-3	R			BG	Name Change
HI05-2	Condition Code	AN	1-30	R				
HI05-3	Date Time Period Format Qualifier	ID	2-3	N/U				
HI05-4	Date Time Period	AN	1-35	N/U				
HI05-5	Monetary Amount	R	1-18	N/U				
HI05-6	Quantity	R	1-15	N/U				
HI05-7	Version Identifier	AN	1-30	N/U				
HI05-8	Industry code	AN	1-30	N/U				New Element
HI05-9	Yes/No Condition or response Code	ID	1-1	N/U				New Element
HI06	HEALTH CARE CODE INFORMATION			S				
HI06-1	Qualifier	ID	1-3	R			BG	Name Change
HI06-2	Condition Code	AN	1-30	R				

Page 59 of 93

INSTITUTIONAL CLAIM

4010A1

Element Identifier	Description	ID	Min. Max.	Usage Reg.	Loop	Loop Repeat	Values
	837-I 4010A1						
HI06-3	Date Time Period Format Qualifier	ID	2-3	N/U			
HI06-4	Date Time Period	AN	1-35	N/U			
HI06-5	Monetary Amount	R	1-18	N/U			
HI06-6	Quantity	R	1-15	N/U			
HI06-7	Version Identifier	AN	1-30	N/U			
HI07	HEALTH CARE CODE INFORMATION			S			
HI07-1	Code List Qualifier Code	ID	1-3	R			BG
HI07-2	Condition Code	AN	1-30	R			
HI07-3	Date Time Period Format Qualifier	ID	2-3	N/U			
HI07-4	Date Time Period	AN	1-35	N/U			
HI07-5	Monetary Amount	R	1-18	N/U			
HI07-6	Quantity	R	1-15	N/U			
HI07-7	Version Identifier	AN	1-30	N/U			
HI08	HEALTH CARE CODE INFORMATION			S			
HI08-1	Code List Qualifier Code	ID	1-3	R			BG
HI08-2	Condition Code	AN	1-30	R			
HI08-3	Date Time Period Format Qualifier	ID	2-3	N/U			
HI08-4	Date Time Period	AN	1-35	N/U			
HI08-5	Monetary Amount	R	1-18	N/U			
HI08-6	Quantity	R	1-15	N/U			
HI08-7	Version Identifier	AN	1-30	N/U			
HI09	HEALTH CARE CODE INFORMATION			S			
HI09-1	Code List Qualifier Code	ID	1-3	R			BG
HI09-2	Condition Code	AN	1-30	R			
HI09-3	Date Time Period Format Qualifier	ID	2-3	N/U			
HI09-4	Date Time Period	AN	1-35	N/U			
HI09-5	Monetary Amount	R	1-18	N/U			
HI09-6	Quantity	R	1-15	N/U			
HI09-7	Version Identifier	AN	1-30	N/U			
HI10	HEALTH CARE CODE INFORMATION			S			

5010

Element Identifier	Description	ID	Min. Max.	Usage Reg.	Loop	Loop Repeat	Values	
	837-I 5010							
HI06-3	Date Time Period Format Qualifier	ID	2-3	N/U				
HI06-4	Date Time Period	AN	1-35	N/U				
HI06-5	Monetary Amount	R	1-18	N/U				
HI06-6	Quantity	R	1-15	N/U				
HI06-7	Version Identifier	AN	1-30	N/U				
HI06-8	Industry code	AN	1-30	N/U				New Element
HI06-9	Yes/No Condition or response Code	ID	1-1	N/U				New Element
HI07	HEALTH CARE CODE INFORMATION			S				
HI07-1	Qualifier	ID	1-3	R			BG	Name Change
HI07-2	Condition Code	AN	1-30	R				
HI07-3	Date Time Period Format Qualifier	ID	2-3	N/U				
HI07-4	Date Time Period	AN	1-35	N/U				
HI07-5	Monetary Amount	R	1-18	N/U				
HI07-6	Quantity	R	1-15	N/U				
HI07-7	Version Identifier	AN	1-30	N/U				
HI07-8	Industry code	AN	1-30	N/U				New Element
HI07-9	Yes/No Condition or response Code	ID	1-1	N/U				New Element
HI08	HEALTH CARE CODE INFORMATION			S				
HI08-1	Qualifier	ID	1-3	R			BG	Name Change
HI08-2	Condition Code	AN	1-30	R				
HI08-3	Date Time Period Format Qualifier	ID	2-3	N/U				
HI08-4	Date Time Period	AN	1-35	N/U				
HI08-5	Monetary Amount	R	1-18	N/U				
HI08-6	Quantity	R	1-15	N/U				
HI08-7	Version Identifier	AN	1-30	N/U				
HI08-8	Industry code	AN	1-30	N/U				New Element
HI08-9	Yes/No Condition or response Code	ID	1-1	N/U				New Element
HI09	HEALTH CARE CODE INFORMATION			S				
HI09-1	Qualifier	ID	1-3	R			BG	Name Change
HI09-2	Condition Code	AN	1-30	R				
HI09-3	Date Time Period Format Qualifier	ID	2-3	N/U				
HI09-4	Date Time Period	AN	1-35	N/U				
HI09-5	Monetary Amount	R	1-18	N/U				
HI09-6	Quantity	R	1-15	N/U				
HI09-7	Version Identifier	AN	1-30	N/U				
HI09-8	Industry code	AN	1-30	N/U				New Element
HI09-9	Yes/No Condition or response Code	ID	1-1	N/U				New Element
HI10	HEALTH CARE CODE INFORMATION			S				

INSTITUTIONAL CLAIM

	4010A1						
Element Identifier	Description	ID	Min. Max.	Usage Reg.	Loop	Loop Repeat	Values
	837-I 4010A1						
HI10-1	Code List Qualifier Code	ID	1-3	R			BG
HI10-2	Condition Code	AN	1-30	R			
HI10-3	Date Time Period Format Qualifier	ID	2-3	N/U			
HI10-4	Date Time Period	AN	1-35	N/U			
HI10-5	Monetary Amount	R	1-18	N/U			
HI10-6	Quantity	R	1-15	N/U			
HI10-7	Version Identifier	AN	1-30	N/U			
HI11	HEALTH CARE CODE INFORMATION			S			
HI11-1	Code List Qualifier Code	ID	1-3	R			BG
HI11-2	Condition Code	AN	1-30	R			
HI11-3	Date Time Period Format Qualifier	ID	2-3	N/U			
HI11-4	Date Time Period	AN	1-35	N/U			
HI11-5	Monetary Amount	R	1-18	N/U			
HI11-6	Quantity	R	1-15	N/U			
HI11-7	Version Identifier	AN	1-30	N/U			
HI12	HEALTH CARE CODE INFORMATION			S			
HI12-1	Code List Qualifier Code	ID	1-3	R			BG
HI12-2	Condition Code	AN	1-30	R			
HI12-3	Date Time Period Format Qualifier	ID	2-3	N/U			
HI12-4	Date Time Period	AN	1-35	N/U			
HI12-5	Monetary Amount	R	1-18	N/U			
HI12-6	Quantity	R	1-15	N/U			
HI12-7	Version Identifier	AN	1-30	N/U			
HI	TREATMENT CODE INFORMATION		2	R	2300		
HI01	HEALTH CARE CODE INFORMATION			R			
HI01-1	Code List Qualifier Code	ID	1-3	R			TC
HI01-2	Treatment Code	AN	1-30	R			
HI01-3	Date Time Period Format Qualifier	ID	2-3	N/U			
HI01-4	Date Time Period	AN	1-35	N/U			
HI01-5	Monetary Amount	R	1-18	N/U			
HI01-6	Quantity	R	1-15	N/U			
HI01-7	Version Identifier	AN	1-30	N/U			

	5010							
Element Identifier	Description	ID	Min. Max.	Usage Reg.	Loop	Loop Repeat	Values	
	837-I 5010							
HI10-1	Qualifier	ID	1-3	R			BG	Name Change
HI10-2	Condition Code	AN	1-30	R				
HI10-3	Date Time Period Format Qualifier	ID	2-3	N/U				
HI10-4	Date Time Period	AN	1-35	N/U				
HI10-5	Monetary Amount	R	1-18	N/U				
HI10-6	Quantity	R	1-15	N/U				
HI10-7	Version Identifier	AN	1-30	N/U				
HI10-8	Industry code	AN	1-30	N/U				New Element
HI10-9	Yes/No Condition or response Code	ID	1-1	N/U				New Element
HI11	HEALTH CARE CODE INFORMATION			S				
HI11-1	Qualifier	ID	1-3	R			BG	Name Change
HI11-2	Condition Code	AN	1-30	R				
HI11-3	Date Time Period Format Qualifier	ID	2-3	N/U				
HI11-4	Date Time Period	AN	1-35	N/U				
HI11-5	Monetary Amount	R	1-18	N/U				
HI11-6	Quantity	R	1-15	N/U				
HI11-7	Version Identifier	AN	1-30	N/U				
HI11-8	Industry code	AN	1-30	N/U				New Element
HI11-9	Yes/No Condition or response Code	ID	1-1	N/U				New Element
HI12	HEALTH CARE CODE INFORMATION			S				
HI12-1	Qualifier	ID	1-3	R			BG	Name Change
HI12-2	Condition Code	AN	1-30	R				
HI12-3	Date Time Period Format Qualifier	ID	2-3	N/U				
HI12-4	Date Time Period	AN	1-35	N/U				
HI12-5	Monetary Amount	R	1-18	N/U				
HI12-6	Quantity	R	1-15	N/U				
HI12-7	Version Identifier	AN	1-30	N/U				
HI12-8	Industry code	AN	1-30	N/U				New Element
HI12-9	Yes/No Condition or response Code	ID	1-1	N/U				New Element
HI	TREATMENT CODE INFORMATION		2	R	2300			
HI01	HEALTH CARE CODE INFORMATION			R				
HI01-1	Qualifier	ID	1-3	R			TC	Name Change
HI01-2	Treatment Code	AN	1-30	R				
HI01-3	Date Time Period Format Qualifier	ID	2-3	N/U				
HI01-4	Date Time Period	AN	1-35	N/U				
HI01-5	Monetary Amount	R	1-18	N/U				
HI01-6	Quantity	R	1-15	N/U				
HI01-7	Version Identifier	AN	1-30	N/U				

Page 61 of 93

INSTITUTIONAL CLAIM

4010A1

837-I 4010A1

Element Identifier	Description	ID	Min. Max.	Usage Reg.	Loop	Loop Repeat	Values
HI02	HEALTH CARE CODE INFORMATION			S			
HI02-1	Code List Qualifier Code	ID	1-3	R			TC
HI02-2	Treatment Code	AN	1-30	R			
HI02-3	Date Time Period Format Qualifier	ID	2-3	N/U			
HI02-4	Date Time Period	AN	1-35	N/U			
HI02-5	Monetary Amount	R	1-18	N/U			
HI02-6	Quantity	R	1-15	N/U			
HI02-7	Version Identifier	AN	1-30	N/U			
HI03	HEALTH CARE CODE INFORMATION			S			
HI03-1	Code List Qualifier Code	ID	1-3	R			TC
HI03-2	Treatment Code	AN	1-30	R			
HI03-3	Date Time Period Format Qualifier	ID	2-3	N/U			
HI03-4	Date Time Period	AN	1-35	N/U			
HI03-5	Monetary Amount	R	1-18	N/U			
HI03-6	Quantity	R	1-15	N/U			
HI03-7	Version Identifier	AN	1-30	N/U			
HI04	HEALTH CARE CODE INFORMATION			S			
HI04-1	Code List Qualifier Code	ID	1-3	R			TC
HI04-2	Treatment Code	AN	1-30	R			
HI04-3	Date Time Period Format Qualifier	ID	2-3	N/U			
HI04-4	Date Time Period	AN	1-35	N/U			
HI04-5	Monetary Amount	R	1-18	N/U			
HI04-6	Quantity	R	1-15	N/U			
HI04-7	Version Identifier	AN	1-30	N/U			
HI05	HEALTH CARE CODE INFORMATION			S			
HI05-1	Code List Qualifier Code	ID	1-3	R			TC
HI05-2	Treatment Code	AN	1-30	R			
HI05-3	Date Time Period Format Qualifier	ID	2-3	N/U			
HI05-4	Date Time Period	AN	1-35	N/U			
HI05-5	Monetary Amount	R	1-18	N/U			

5010

837-I 5010

Element Identifier	Description	ID	Min. Max.	Usage Reg.	Loop	Loop Repeat	Values	
HI01-8	Industry code	AN	1-30	N/U				New Element
HI01-9	Yes/No Condition or response Code	ID	1-1	N/U				New Element
HI02	HEALTH CARE CODE INFORMATION			S				
HI02-1	Qualifier	ID	1-3	R			TC	Name Change
HI02-2	Treatment Code	AN	1-30	R				
HI02-3	Date Time Period Format Qualifier	ID	2-3	N/U				
HI02-4	Date Time Period	AN	1-35	N/U				
HI02-5	Monetary Amount	R	1-18	N/U				
HI02-6	Quantity	R	1-15	N/U				
HI02-7	Version Identifier	AN	1-30	N/U				
HI02-8	Industry code	AN	1-30	N/U				New Element
HI02-9	Yes/No Condition or response Code	ID	1-1	N/U				New Element
HI03	HEALTH CARE CODE INFORMATION			S				
HI03-1	Qualifier	ID	1-3	R			TC	Name Change
HI03-2	Treatment Code	AN	1-30	R				
HI03-3	Date Time Period Format Qualifier	ID	2-3	N/U				
HI03-4	Date Time Period	AN	1-35	N/U				
HI03-5	Monetary Amount	R	1-18	N/U				
HI03-6	Quantity	R	1-15	N/U				
HI03-7	Version Identifier	AN	1-30	N/U				
HI03-8	Industry code	AN	1-30	N/U				New Element
HI03-9	Yes/No Condition or response Code	ID	1-1	N/U				New Element
HI04	HEALTH CARE CODE INFORMATION			S				
HI04-1	Qualifier	ID	1-3	R			TC	Name Change
HI04-2	Treatment Code	AN	1-30	R				
HI04-3	Date Time Period Format Qualifier	ID	2-3	N/U				
HI04-4	Date Time Period	AN	1-35	N/U				
HI04-5	Monetary Amount	R	1-18	N/U				
HI04-6	Quantity	R	1-15	N/U				
HI04-7	Version Identifier	AN	1-30	N/U				
HI04-8	Industry code	AN	1-30	N/U				New Element
HI04-9	Yes/No Condition or response Code	ID	1-1	N/U				New Element
HI05	HEALTH CARE CODE INFORMATION			S				
HI05-1	Qualifier	ID	1-3	R			TC	Name Change
HI05-2	Treatment Code	AN	1-30	R				
HI05-3	Date Time Period Format Qualifier	ID	2-3	N/U				
HI05-4	Date Time Period	AN	1-35	N/U				
HI05-5	Monetary Amount	R	1-18	N/U				

Page 62 of 93

INSTITUTIONAL CLAIM

4010A1

Element Identifier	Description	ID	Min. Max.	Usage Reg.	Loop	Loop Repeat	Values
	837-I 4010A1						
HI05-6	Quantity	R	1-15	N/U			
HI05-7	Version Identifier	AN	1-30	N/U			
HI06	HEALTH CARE CODE INFORMATION			S			
HI06-1	Code List Qualifier Code	ID	1-3	R			TC
HI06-2	Treatment Code	AN	1-30	R			
HI06-3	Date Time Period Format Qualifier	ID	2-3	N/U			
HI06-4	Date Time Period	AN	1-35	N/U			
HI06-5	Monetary Amount	R	1-18	N/U			
HI06-6	Quantity	R	1-15	N/U			
HI06-7	Version Identifier	AN	1-30	N/U			
HI07	HEALTH CARE CODE INFORMATION			S			
HI07-1	Code List Qualifier Code	ID	1-3	R			TC
HI07-2	Treatment Code	AN	1-30	R			
HI07-3	Date Time Period Format Qualifier	ID	2-3	N/U			
HI07-4	Date Time Period	AN	1-35	N/U			
HI07-5	Monetary Amount	R	1-18	N/U			
HI07-6	Quantity	R	1-15	N/U			
HI07-7	Version Identifier	AN	1-30	N/U			
HI08	HEALTH CARE CODE INFORMATION			S			
HI08-1	Code List Qualifier Code	ID	1-3	R			TC
HI08-2	Treatment Code	AN	1-30	R			
HI08-3	Date Time Period Format Qualifier	ID	2-3	N/U			
HI08-4	Date Time Period	AN	1-35	N/U			
HI08-5	Monetary Amount	R	1-18	N/U			
HI08-6	Quantity	R	1-15	N/U			
HI08-7	Version Identifier	AN	1-30	N/U			
HI09	HEALTH CARE CODE INFORMATION			S			
HI09-1	Code List Qualifier Code	ID	1-3	R			TC
HI09-2	Treatment Code	AN	1-30	R			
HI09-3	Date Time Period Format Qualifier	ID	2-3	N/U			

5010

Element Identifier	Description	ID	Min. Max.	Usage Reg.	Loop	Loop Repeat	Values	
	837-I 5010							
HI05-6	Quantity	R	1-15	N/U				
HI05-7	Version Identifier	AN	1-30	N/U				
HI05-8	Industry code	AN	1-30	N/U				New Element
HI05-9	Yes/No Condition or response Code	ID	1-1	N/U				New Element
HI06	HEALTH CARE CODE INFORMATION			S				
HI06-1	Qualifier	ID	1-3	R			TC	Name Change
HI06-2	Treatment Code	AN	1-30	R				
HI06-3	Date Time Period Format Qualifier	ID	2-3	N/U				
HI06-4	Date Time Period	AN	1-35	N/U				
HI06-5	Monetary Amount	R	1-18	N/U				
HI06-6	Quantity	R	1-15	N/U				
HI06-7	Version Identifier	AN	1-30	N/U				
HI06-8	Industry code	AN	1-30	N/U				New Element
HI06-9	Yes/No Condition or response Code	ID	1-1	N/U				New Element
HI07	HEALTH CARE CODE INFORMATION			S				
HI07-1	Qualifier	ID	1-3	R			TC	Name Change
HI07-2	Treatment Code	AN	1-30	R				
HI07-3	Date Time Period Format Qualifier	ID	2-3	N/U				
HI07-4	Date Time Period	AN	1-35	N/U				
HI07-5	Monetary Amount	R	1-18	N/U				
HI07-6	Quantity	R	1-15	N/U				
HI07-7	Version Identifier	AN	1-30	N/U				
HI07-8	Industry code	AN	1-30	N/U				New Element
HI07-9	Yes/No Condition or response Code	ID	1-1	N/U				New Element
HI08	HEALTH CARE CODE INFORMATION			S				
HI08-1	Qualifier	ID	1-3	R			TC	Name Change
HI08-2	Treatment Code	AN	1-30	R				
HI08-3	Date Time Period Format Qualifier	ID	2-3	N/U				
HI08-4	Date Time Period	AN	1-35	N/U				
HI08-5	Monetary Amount	R	1-18	N/U				
HI08-6	Quantity	R	1-15	N/U				
HI08-7	Version Identifier	AN	1-30	N/U				
HI08-8	Industry code	AN	1-30	N/U				New Element
HI08-9	Yes/No Condition or response Code	ID	1-1	N/U				New Element
HI09	HEALTH CARE CODE INFORMATION			S				
HI09-1	Qualifier	ID	1-3	R			TC	Name Change
HI09-2	Treatment Code	AN	1-30	R				
HI09-3	Date Time Period Format Qualifier	ID	2-3	N/U				

Page 63 of 93

INSTITUTIONAL CLAIM

4010A1

Element Identifier	Description	ID	Min. Max.	Usage Reg.	Loop	Loop Repeat	Values
	837-I 4010A1						
HI09-4	Date Time Period	AN	1-35	N/U			
HI09-5	Monetary Amount	R	1-18	N/U			
HI09-6	Quantity	R	1-15	N/U			
HI09-7	Version Identifier	AN	1-30	N/U			
HI10	HEALTH CARE CODE INFORMATION			S			
HI10-1	Code List Qualifier Code	ID	1-3	R			TC
HI10-2	Treatment Code	AN	1-30	R			
HI10-3	Date Time Period Format Qualifier	ID	2-3	N/U			
HI10-4	Date Time Period	AN	1-35	N/U			
HI10-5	Monetary Amount	R	1-18	N/U			
HI10-6	Quantity	R	1-15	N/U			
HI10-7	Version Identifier	AN	1-30	N/U			
HI11	HEALTH CARE CODE INFORMATION			S			
HI11-1	Code List Qualifier Code	ID	1-3	R			TC
HI11-2	Treatment Code	AN	1-30	R			
HI11-3	Date Time Period Format Qualifier	ID	2-3	N/U			
HI11-4	Date Time Period	AN	1-35	N/U			
HI11-5	Monetary Amount	R	1-18	N/U			
HI11-6	Quantity	R	1-15	N/U			
HI11-7	Version Identifier	AN	1-30	N/U			
HI12	HEALTH CARE CODE INFORMATION			S			
HI12-1	Code List Qualifier Code	ID	1-3	R			TC
HI12-2	Treatment Code	AN	1-30	R			
HI12-3	Date Time Period Format Qualifier	ID	2-3	N/U			
HI12-4	Date Time Period	AN	1-35	N/U			
HI12-5	Monetary Amount	R	1-18	N/U			
HI12-6	Quantity	R	1-15	N/U			
HI12-7	Version Identifier	AN	1-30	N/U			
QTY	CLAIM QUANTITY		4	S	2300		
QTY01	Quantity Qualifier	ID	2-2	R			CA, CD, LA, NA
QTY02	Claim Days Count	R	1-15	R			

5010

Element Identifier	Description	ID	Min. Max.	Usage Reg.	Loop	Loop Repeat	Values	
	837-I 5010							
HI09-4	Date Time Period	AN	1-35	N/U				
HI09-5	Monetary Amount	R	1-18	N/U				
HI09-6	Quantity	R	1-15	N/U				
HI09-7	Version Identifier	AN	1-30	N/U				
HI09-8	Industry code	AN	1-30	N/U				New Element
HI09-9	Yes/No Condition or response Code	ID	1-1	N/U				New Element
HI10	HEALTH CARE CODE INFORMATION			S				
HI10-1	Qualifier	ID	1-3	R			TC	Name Change
HI10-2	Treatment Code	AN	1-30	R				
HI10-3	Date Time Period Format Qualifier	ID	2-3	N/U				
HI10-4	Date Time Period	AN	1-35	N/U				
HI10-5	Monetary Amount	R	1-18	N/U				
HI10-6	Quantity	R	1-15	N/U				
HI10-7	Version Identifier	AN	1-30	N/U				
HI10-8	Industry code	AN	1-30	N/U				New Element
HI10-9	Yes/No Condition or response Code	ID	1-1	N/U				New Element
HI11	HEALTH CARE CODE INFORMATION			S				
HI11-1	Qualifier	ID	1-3	R			TC	Name Change
HI11-2	Treatment Code	AN	1-30	R				
HI11-3	Date Time Period Format Qualifier	ID	2-3	N/U				
HI11-4	Date Time Period	AN	1-35	N/U				
HI11-5	Monetary Amount	R	1-18	N/U				
HI11-6	Quantity	R	1-15	N/U				
HI11-7	Version Identifier	AN	1-30	N/U				
HI11-8	Industry code	AN	1-30	N/U				New Element
HI11-9	Yes/No Condition or response Code	ID	1-1	N/U				New Element
HI12	HEALTH CARE CODE INFORMATION			S				
HI12-1	Qualifier	ID	1-3	R			TC	Name Change
HI12-2	Treatment Code	AN	1-30	R				
HI12-3	Date Time Period Format Qualifier	ID	2-3	N/U				
HI12-4	Date Time Period	AN	1-35	N/U				
HI12-5	Monetary Amount	R	1-18	N/U				
HI12-6	Quantity	R	1-15	N/U				
HI12-7	Version Identifier	AN	1-30	N/U				
HI12-8	Industry code	AN	1-30	N/U				New Element
HI12-9	Yes/No Condition or response Code	ID	1-1	N/U				New Element
								Segment Deleted

Page 64 of 93

INSTITUTIONAL CLAIM

4010A1

Element Identifier	Description	ID	Min. Max.	Usage Reg.	Loop	Loop Repeat	Values
	837-I 4010A1						
QTY03	COMPOSITE UNIT OF MEASURE			R			
QTY03-1	Unit or Basis for Measurement Code	ID	2-2	R			DA
QTY03-2	Exponent	R	1-15	N/U			
QTY03-3	Multiplier	R	1-10	N/U			
QTY03-4	Unit or Basis for Measurement Code	ID	2-2	N/U			
QTY03-5	Exponent	R	1-15	N/U			
QTY03-6	Multiplier	R	1-10	N/U			
QTY03-7	Unit or Basis for Measurement Code	ID	2-2	N/U			
QTY03-8	Exponent	R	1-15	N/U			
QTY03-9	Multiplier	R	1-10	N/U			
QTY03-10	Unit or Basis for Measurement Code	ID	2-2	N/U			
QTY03-11	Exponent	R	1-15	N/U			
QTY03-12	Multiplier	R	1-10	N/U			
QTY03-13	Unit or Basis for Measurement Code	ID	2-2	N/U			
QTY03-14	Exponent	R	1-15	N/U			
QTY03-15	Multiplier	R	1-10	N/U			
QTY04	Free-Form Message	AN	1-30	N/U			
HCP	**CLAIM PRICING/REPRICING INFORMATION**		1	S	2300		
HCP01	Pricing Methodology	ID	2-2	R			00, 01, 02, 03, 04, 05, 06, 07, 08, 09, 10 ,11, 12, 13, 14
HCP02	Repriced Allowed Amount	R	1-18	R			
HCP03	Repriced Saving Amount	R	1-18	S			
HCP04	Repricing Organization Identifier	AN	1-30	S			
HCP05	Repricing Per Diem or Flat Rate Amount	R	1-9	S			
HCP06	Repriced Approved DRG Code	AN	1-30	S			
HCP07	Repriced Approved Amount	R	1-18	S			
HCP08	Product/Service ID	AN	1-48	S			
HCP09	Product/Service ID Qualifier	ID	2-2	S			HC
HCP10	Product/Service ID	AN	1-48	S			
HCP11	Unit or Basis for Measurement Code	ID	2-2	S			DA, UN
HCP12	Quantity	R	1-15	S			

5010

Element Identifier	Description	ID	Min. Max.	Usage Reg.	Loop	Loop Repeat	Values	
	837-I 5010							
HCP	**CLAIM PRICING/REPRICING INFORMATION**		1	S	2300			
HCP01	Pricing Methodology	ID	2-2	R			00, 01, 02, 03, 04, 05, 06, 07, 08, 09, 10 ,11, 12, 13, 14	
HCP02	Repriced Allowed Amount	R	1-18	R				
HCP03	Repriced Saving Amount	R	1-18	S				
HCP04	Repricing Organization Identifier	AN	1-50	S				Increase from 30 - 50
HCP05	Repricing Per Diem or Flat Rate Amount	R	1-9	S				
HCP06	Ambulatory Patient Group Code	AN	1-50	S				Increase from 30 - 50 Name Change
HCP07	Ambulatory Patient Group Amount	R	1-18	S		'		Name Change
HCP08	Product/Service ID	AN	1-48	S				
HCP09	Product/Service ID Qualifier	ID	2-2	N/U				Usage change to Not Used
HCP10	Product/Service ID	AN	1-48	N/U				Usage change to Not Used
HCP11	Unit or Basis for Measurement Code	ID	2-2	S			DA, UN	
HCP12	Quantity	R	1-15	S				

Page 65 of 93

INSTITUTIONAL CLAIM

4010A1

Element Identifier	Description	ID	Min. Max.	Usage Reg.	Loop	Loop Repeat	Values
	837-I 4010A1						
HCP13	Reject Reason Code	ID	2-2	S			T1, T2, T3, T4, T5, T6
HCP14	Policy Compliance Code	ID	1-2	S			1, 2, 3, 4, 5
HCP15	Exception Code	ID	1-2	S			1, 2, 3, 4, 5, 6
CR7	**HOME HEALTH CARE PLAN INFORMATION**		1	S	2305	6	
CR701	Disipline Type Code	ID	2-2	R			AI, MS, OT, PT, SN, ST
CR702	Vsits Prior to Recertification Date Count	NO	1-9	R			
CR703	Total Visits Projected This Certification Count	NO	1-9	R			
HSD	**HOME CARE SERVICES DELIVERY**		12	S	2305		
HSD01	Visits	ID	2-2	S			
HSD02	Number of Visits	R	1-15	S			
HSD03	Frequency Period	ID	2-2	S			DA, MO, Q1, WK
HSD04	Frequency Count	R	1-6	S			
HSD05	Duration of Visits Units	ID	1-2	S			7, 35
HSD06	Duration of Visits, Number of Units	NO	1-3	S			
HSD07	Ship, Delivery or Caledar Pattern Code	ID	1-2	S			1, 2, 3, 4, 5, 6, 7, 8, 9, A, B, C, D, E, F, G, J, K, L, N, O, S, SA, SB, SC, SD, SG, SL, SP, SX, SY, SZ, W,
HSD08	Delivery Pattern Time Code	ID	1-1	S			D, E, F
NM1	**ATTENDING PHYSICIAN NAME**		1	S	2310A	1	
NM101	Entity Identifier Code	ID	2-3	R			71
NM102	Entity Type Qualifier	ID	1-1	R			1, 2
NM103	Name Last	AN	1-35	R			
NM104	NameFirst	AN	1-25	S			
NM105	Name Middle	AN	1-25	S			
NM106	Name Prefix	AN	1-10	N/U			
NM107	Name Suffix	AN	1-10	S			
NM108	Identification Code Qualifier	ID	1-2	R			24, 34, XX
NM109	Provider Identifier	AN	2-80	R			
NM110	Entity Relationship Code	ID	2-2	N/U			
NM111	Entity Identifier Code	ID	2-3	N/U			

5010

Element Identifier	Description	ID	Min. Max.	Usage Reg.	Loop	Loop Repeat	Values	
	837-I 5010							
HCP13	Reject Reason Code	ID	2-2	S			T1, T2, T3, T4, T5, T6	
HCP14	Policy Compliance Code	ID	1-2	S			1, 2, 3, 4, 5	
HCP15	Exception Code	ID	1-2	S			1, 2, 3, 4, 5, 6	
								Segment Deleted
								Segment Deleted
NM1	**ATTENDING PROVIDER NAME**		1	S	2310A	1		Name Change
NM101	Entity Identifier Code	ID	2-3	R			71	
NM102	Entity Type Qualifier	ID	1-1	R			1	Code Deleted
NM103	Last Name	AN	1-60	R				Name Change Increase from 35 - 60
NM104	First Name	AN	1-35	S				Name Change Increase 25 - 35
NM105	Middle Name	AN	1-25	S				Name Change
NM106	Name Prefix	AN	1-10	N/U				
NM107	Name Suffix	AN	1-10	S				
NM108	Identification Code Qualifier	ID	1-2	S			XX	Code Deleted Usage change to Situational
NM109	Provider Identifier	AN	2-80	S				Usage change to Situational
NM110	Entity Relationship Code	ID	2-2	N/U				
NM111	Entity Identifier Code	ID	2-3	N/U				

INSTITUTIONAL CLAIM

Element Identifier	Description	ID	Min. Max.	Usage Reg.	Loop	Loop Repeat	Values		Element Identifier	Description	ID	Min. Max.	Usage Reg.	Loop	Loop Repeat	Values	
	4010A1									**5010**							
	837-I 4010A1									**837-I 5010**							
									NM112	Name Last or Organization Name	AN	1-60	N/U				New Element
PRV	**ATTENDING PHYSICIAN SPECIALTY INFORMATION**		1	S	2310A				**PRV**	**ATTENDING PROVIDER SPECIALTY INFORMATION**		1	S	2310A			Name Change
PRV01	Provider Code	ID	1-3	R			AT, SU		PRV01	Provider Code	ID	1-3	R			AT	Code Deleted
PRV02	Reference Identification Qualifier	ID	2-3	R			ZZ		PRV02	Reference Identification Qualifier	ID	2-3	R			PXC	Code Change
PRV03	Provider Taxonomy Code	AN	1-30	R					PRV03	Provider Taxonomy Code	AN	1-50	R				Increase from 30 - 50
PRV04	State or Province Code	ID	2-2	N/U					PRV04	State or Province Code	ID	2-2	N/U				
PRV05	PROVIDER SPECIALTY INFORMATION			N/U					PRV05	PROVIDER SPECIALTY INFORMATION			N/U				
PRV06	Provider Organization Code	ID	3-3	N/U					PRV06	Provider Organization Code	ID	3-3	N/U				
REF	**ATTENDING PHYSICIAN SECONDARY IDENTIFICATION**		5	S	2310A				**REF**	**ATTENDING PROVIDER SECONDARY IDENTIFICATION**		4	S	2310A			Name Change # Repeats change to 4
REF01	Reference Identification Qualifier	ID	2-3	R			0B, 1A, 1B, 1C, 1D, 1G, 1H, EI, G2, LU, N5, SY, X5		REF01	Reference Identification Qualifier	ID	2-3	R			0B, 1G, G2, LU	Code Deleted
REF02	Attending Physician Secondary Identifier	AN	1-30	R					REF02	Secondary Identifier	AN	1-50	R				Increase from 30 - 50 Name Change
REF03	Description	AN	1-80	N/U					REF03	Description	AN	1-80	N/U				
REF04	REFERENCE IDENTIFIER			N/U					REF04	REFERENCE IDENTIFIER			N/U				
NM1	**OPERATING PHYSICIAN NAME**		1	S	2310B	1			**NM1**	**OPERATING PHYSICIAN NAME**		1	S	2310B	1		
NM101	Entity Identifier Code	ID	2-3	R			72		NM101	Entity Identifier Code	ID	2-3	R			72	
NM102	Entity Type Qualifier	ID	1-1	R			1		NM102	Entity Type Qualifier	ID	1-1	R			1	
NM103	Last or Organization Name	AN	1-35	R					NM103	Last or Organization Name	AN	1-60	R				Increase from 35 - 60
NM104	Name First	AN	1-25	R					NM104	First Name	AN	1-35	S				Increase from 25 - 35 Usage change to Situational
NM105	Middle Name	AN	1-25	S					NM105	Middle Name	AN	1-25	S				
NM106	Name Prefix	AN	1-10	N/U					NM106	Name Prefix	AN	1-10	N/U				
NM107	Name Suffix	AN	1-10	S					NM107	Name Suffix	AN	1-10	S				
NM108	Identification Code Qualifier	ID	1-2	R			24, 34, XX		NM108	Identification Code Qualifier	ID	1-2	S			XX	Code Deleted Usage change to Situational
NM109	Identifier	AN	2-80	R					NM109	Identifier	AN	2-80	S				Usage change to Situational
NM110	Entity Relationship Code	ID	2-2	N/U					NM110	Entity Relationship Code	ID	2-2	N/U				
NM111	Entity Identifier Code	ID	2-3	N/U					NM111	Entity Identifier Code	ID	2-3	N/U				
									NM112	Name Last or Organization Name	AN	1-60	N/U				New Element

Page 67 of 93

INSTITUTIONAL CLAIM

4010A1

837-I 4010A1

Element Identifier	Description	ID	Min. Max.	Usage Req.	Loop	Loop Repeat	Values
REF	OPERATING PHYSICIAN SECONDARY IDENTIFICATION		5	S	2310B		
REF01	Reference Identification Qualifier	ID	2-3	R			0B, 1A, 1B, 1C, 1D, 1G, 1H, EI, G2, LU, N5, SY, X5
REF02	Secondary Identifier	AN	1-30	R			
REF03	Description	AN	1-80	N/U			
REF04	REFERENCE IDENTIFIER			N/U			
NM1	OTHER PROVIDER NAME		1	S	2310C	1	
NM101	Entity Identifier Code	ID	2-3	R			73
NM102	Entity Type Qualifier	ID	1-1	R			1, 2
NM103	Last or Organization Name	AN	1-35	R			
NM104	First Name	AN	1-25	R			
NM105	Middle Name	AN	1-25	S			
NM106	Name Prefix	AN	1-10	N/U			
NM107	Name Suffix	AN	1-10	S			
NM108	Identification Code Qualifier	ID	1-2	R			24, 34, XX
NM109	Identifier	AN	2-80	S			
NM110	Entity Relationship Code	ID	2-2	N/U			
NM111	Entity Identifier Code	ID	2-3	N/U			
REF	OTHER PROVIDER SECONDARY IDENTIFICATION		5	S	2310C		
REF01	Reference Identification Qualifier	ID	2-3	R			0B, 1A, 1B, 1C, 1D, 1G, 1H, EI, G2, LU, N5, SY, X5
REF02	Rendering Provider Secondary Identifier	AN	1-30	R			
REF03	Description	AN	1-80	N/U			
REF04	REFERENCE IDENTIFIER			N/U			

5010

837-I 5010

Element Identifier	Description	ID	Min. Max.	Usage Req.	Loop	Loop Repeat	Values	
REF	OPERATING PHYSICIAN SECONDARY IDENTIFICATION		4	S	2310B			# Repeats change to 4
REF01	Qualifier	ID	2-3	R			0B, 1G, G2, LU	Code Deleted
REF02	Secondary Identifier	AN	1-50	R				Increase from 30 - 50
REF03	Description	AN	1-80	N/U				
REF04	REFERENCE IDENTIFIER			N/U				
NM1	OTHER OPERATING PHYSICIAN NAME		1	S	2310C	1		Name Change
NM101	Entity Identifier Code	ID	2-3	R			ZZ	Code Change
NM102	Entity Type Qualifier	ID	1-1	R			1	Code Deleted
NM103	Last or Organization Name	AN	1-60	R				Increase from 35 - 60
NM104	First Name	AN	1-35	S				Increase from 25 - 35 Usage change to Situational
NM105	Middle Name	AN	1-25	S				
NM106	Name Prefix	AN	1-10	N/U				
NM107	Name Suffix	AN	1-10	S				
NM108	Identification Code Qualifier	ID	1-2	S			XX	Code Deleted Usage change to Situational
NM109	Identifier	AN	2-80	S				
NM110	Entity Relationship Code	ID	2-2	N/U				
NM111	Entity Identifier Code	ID	2-3	N/U				
NM112	Name Last or Organization Name	AN	1-60	N/U				New Element
REF	OPERATING PHYSICIAN SECONDARY IDENTIFICATION		4	S	2310C			Name Chnge # of Repeats change to 4
REF01	Reference Identification Qualifier	ID	2-3	R			0B, 1G, G2, LU	Code Deleted
REF02	Rendering Provider Secondary Identifier	AN	1-50	R				Increase from 30 - 50
REF03	Description	AN	1-80	N/U				
REF04	REFERENCE IDENTIFIER			N/U				
NM1	RENDERING PHYSICIAN NAME		1	S	2310D	1		New Segment
NM101	Entity Identifier Code	ID	2-3	R			82	
NM102	Entity Type Qualifier	ID	1-1	R			1	
NM103	Rendering Provider Last or Organization Name	AN	1-60	R				

INSTITUTIONAL CLAIM

Element Identifier	Description	ID	Min. Max.	Usage Reg.	Loop	Loop Repeat	Values
				4010A1			
	837-I 4010A1						
NM1	**SERVICE FACILITY NAME**		1	S	2310E	1	
NM101	Entity Identifier Code	ID	2-3	R			FA
NM102	Entity Type Qualifier	ID	1-1	R			2
NM103	Laboratory or Facility Name	AN	1-35	R			
NM104	Name First	AN	1-25	N/U			
NM105	Name Middle	AN	1-25	N/U			
NM106	Name Prefix	AN	1-10	N/U			
NM107	Name Suffix	AN	1-10	N/U			
NM108	Identification Code Qualifier	ID	1-2	S			24, 34, XX
NM109	Laboratory or Facility Primary Identifier	AN	2-80	S			
NM110	Entity Relationship Code	ID	2-2	N/U			
NM111	Entity Identifier Code	ID	2-3	N/U			
N3	**SERVICE FACILITY ADDRESS**		1	R	2310E		
N301	Laboratory or Facility Address Line	AN	1-55	R			

Element Identifier	Description	ID	Min. Max.	Usage Reg.	Loop	Loop Repeat	Values	
				5010				
	837-I 5010							
NM104	Rendering Provider First Name	AN	1-35	S				
NM105	Rendering Provider Middle Name	AN	1-25	S				
NM106	Name Prefix	AN	1-10	N/U				
NM107	Rendering Provider Name Suffix	AN	1-10	S				
NM108	Identification Code Qualifier	ID	1-2	S			XX	
NM109	Rendering Provider Identifier	AN	2-80	S				
NM110	Entity Relationship Code	ID	2-2	N/U				
NM111	Entity Identifier Code	ID	2-3	N/U				
NM112	Name Last or Organization Name	AN	1-60	N/U				
REF	**RENDERING PHYSICIAN SECONDARY IDENTIFICATION**		4	S	2310D			New Segment
REF01	Reference Identification Qualifier	ID	2-3	R			0B, 1G, G2, LU	
REF02	Rendering Provider Secondary Identifier	AN	1-50	R				
REF03	Description	AN	1-80	N/U				
REF04	REFERENCE IDENTIFIER			N/U				
NM1	**SERVICE FACILITY LOCATION**		1	S	2310E	1		Name Change
NM101	Entity Identifier Code	ID	2-3	R			77	Code Change
NM102	Entity Type Qualifier	ID	1-1	R			2	
NM103	Laboratory or Facility Name	AN	1-60	R				Increase from 35 - 60
NM104	Name First	AN	1-35	N/U				Increase from 25 - 35
NM105	Name Middle	AN	1-25	N/U				
NM106	Name Prefix	AN	1-10	N/U				
NM107	Name Suffix	AN	1-10	N/U				
NM108	Identification Code Qualifier	ID	1-2	S			XX	Code Deleted
NM109	Laboratory or Facility Primary Identifier	AN	2-80	S				
NM110	Entity Relationship Code	ID	2-2	N/U				
NM111	Entity Identifier Code	ID	2-3	N/U				
NM112	Name Last or Organization Name	AN	1-60	N/U				New Element
N3	**SERVICE FACILITY LOCATION ADDRESS**		1	R	2310E			Name Change
N301	Laboratory or Facility Address Line	AN	1-55	R				

Page 69 of 93

INSTITUTIONAL CLAIM

	4010A1						
Element Identifier	Description	ID	Min. Max.	Usage Reg.	Loop	Loop Repeat	Values
	837-I 4010A1						
N302	Laboratory or Facility Address Line	AN	1-55	S			
N4	**SERVICE FACILITY CITY/STATE/ZIP CODE**		1	R	2310E		
N401	Laboratory or Facility City Name	AN	2-30	R			
N402	Laboratory or Facility State or Province Code	ID	2-2	R			
N403	Laboratory or Facility Postal Zone or ZIP Code	ID	3-15	R			
N404	Laboratory/Facility Country Code	ID	2-3	S			
N405	Location Qualifier	ID	1-2	N/U			
N406	Location Identifier	AN	1-30	N/U			
REF	**SERVICE FACILITY SECONDARY IDENTIFICATION**		5	S	2310E		
REF01	Reference Identification Qualifier	ID	2-3	R			0B, 1A, 1B, 1C, 1D, 1G, 1H, EI, G2, LU, N5, SY, X5
REF02	Laboratory or Facility Secondary Identifier	AN	1-30	R			
REF03	Description	AN	1-80	N/U			
REF04	REFERENCE IDENTIFIER			N/U			

	5010							
Element Identifier	Description	ID	Min. Max.	Usage Reg.	Loop	Loop Repeat	Values	
	837-I 5010							
N302	Laboratory or Facility Address Line	AN	1-55	S				
N4	**SERVICE FACILITY LOCATION CITY/STATE/ZIP**		1	R	2310E			Name Change
N401	Laboratory or Facility City Name	AN	2-30	R				
N402	Laboratory or Facility State or Province Code	ID	2-2	S				Usage change to Situational
N403	Laboratory or Facility Postal Zone ZIP Code	ID	3-15	S				Usage change to Situational
N404	Laboratory/Facility Country Code	ID	2-3	S				
N405	Location Qualifier	ID	1-2	N/U				
N406	Location Identifier	AN	1-30	N/U				
N407	Country Subdivision Code	ID	1-3	S				New Element
REF	**SERVICE FACILITY LOCATION SECONDARY IDENTIFICATION**		3	S	2310E			Name Change # of Repeats change to 3
REF01	Reference Identification Qualifier	ID	2-3	R			0B, G2, LU	Code Deleted
REF02	Laboratory or Facility Secondary Identifier	AN	1-50	R				Increase from 30 - 50
REF03	Description	AN	1-80	N/U				
REF04	REFERENCE IDENTIFIER			N/U				
NM1	**REFERRING PROVIDER NAME**		1	S	2310F	1		New Segment
NM101	Entity Identifier Code	ID	2-3	R			DN	
NM102	Entity Type Qualifier	ID	1-1	R			1	
NM103	Referring Provider Last Name	AN	1-60	R				
NM104	Referring Provider First Name	AN	1-35	S				
NM105	Referring Provider Middle Name	AN	1-25	S				
NM106	Name Prefix	AN	1-10	N/U				
NM107	Referring Provider Name Suffix	AN	1-10	S				
NM108	Identification Code Qualifier	ID	1-2	S			XX	
NM109	Referring Provider Identifier	AN	2-80	S				
NM110	Entity Relationship Code	ID	2-2	N/U				
NM111	Entity Identifier Code	ID	2-3	N/U				
NM112	Name Last or Organization Name	AN	1-60	N/U				

INSTITUTIONAL CLAIM

4010A1

Element Identifier	Description	ID	Min. Max.	Usage Reg.	Loop	Loop Repeat	Values
	837-I 4010A1						
SBR	**OTHER SUBSCRIBER INFORMATION**		1	S	2320	10	
SBR01	Payer Responsibility Sequence Number Code	ID	1-1	R			P, S, T
SBR02	Individual Relationship Code	ID	2-2	R			01, 04, 05, 07, 10, 15, 17, 18, 19, 20, 21, 22, 23, 24, 29, 32, 33, 36, 39, 40, 41, 43, 53, G8
SBR03	Insured Group or Policy Number	AN	1-30	S			
SBR04	Other Insured Group Name	AN	1-60	S			
SBR05	Insurance Type Code	ID	1-3	N/U			
SBR06	Coordination of Benefits Code	ID	1-1	N/U			
SBR07	Yes/No Condition or Response Code	ID	1-1	N/U			
SBR08	Employment Status Code	ID	2-2	N/U			
SBR09	Claim Filing Indicator Code	ID	1-2	S			09, 10, 11, 12, 13, 14, 15, 16, AM, BL, CH, CI, DS, HM, LI, LM, MA, MB, MC, OF, TV, VA, WC, ZZ
CAS	**CLAIM LEVEL ADJUSTMENTS**		5	S	2320		
CAS01	Claim Adjustment Group Code	ID	1-2	R			CO, CR, OA, PI, PR
CAS02	Adjustment Reason Code	ID	1-5	R			
CAS03	Adjustment Amount	R	1-18	R			
CAS04	Adjustment Quantity	R	1-15	S			
CAS05	Adjustment Reason Code	ID	1-5	S			
CAS06	Adjustment Amount	R	1-18	S			
CAS07	Adjustment Quantity	R	1-15	S			
CAS08	Adjustment Reason Code	ID	1-5	S			
CAS09	Adjustment Amount	R	1-18	S			

5010

Element Identifier	Description	ID	Min. Max.	Usage Reg.	Loop	Loop Repeat	Values	
	837-I 5010							
REF	**REFERRING PROVIDER SECONDARY IDENTIFICATION**		3	S	2310F			New Segment
REF01	Reference Identification Qualifier	ID	2-3	R			0B, 1G, G2	
REF02	Referring Provider Secondary Identifier	AN	1-50	R				
REF03	Description	AN	1-80	N/U				
REF04	REFERENCE IDENTIFIER			N/U				
SBR	**OTHER SUBSCRIBER INFORMATION**		1	S	2320	10		
SBR01	Payer Responsibility Sequence Number Code	ID	1-1	R			A, B, C, D, E, F, G, H, P, S, T, U	Code Added
								Code Deleted
SBR02	Individual Relationship Code	ID	2-2	R			01, 18, 19, 20, 21, 39, 40, 53, G8	
SBR03	Insured Group or Policy Number	AN	1-50	S				Increase from 30 - 50
SBR04	Other Insured Group Name	AN	1-60	S				
SBR05	Insurance Type Code	ID	1-3	N/U				
SBR06	Coordination of Benefits Code	ID	1-1	N/U				
SBR07	Yes/No Condition or Response Code	ID	1-1	N/U				
SBR08	Employment Status Code	ID	2-2	N/U				
SBR09	Claim Filing Indicator Code	ID	1-2	S			11, 12, 13, 14, 15, 16, 17, AM, BL, CH, CI, DS, FI, HM, LM, MA, MB, MC, OF, TV, VA, WC, ZZ	Code Change
CAS	**CLAIM LEVEL ADJUSTMENTS**		5	S	2320			
CAS01	Claim Adjustment Group Code	ID	1-2	R			CO, CR, OA, PI, PR	
CAS02	Adjustment Reason Code	ID	1-5	R				
CAS03	Adjustment Amount	R	1-18	R				
CAS04	Adjustment Quantity	R	1-15	S				
CAS05	Adjustment Reason Code	ID	1-5	S				
CAS06	Adjustment Amount	R	1-18	S				
CAS07	Adjustment Quantity	R	1-15	S				
CAS08	Adjustment Reason Code	ID	1-5	S				
CAS09	Adjustment Amount	R	1-18	S				

Page 71 of 93

INSTITUTIONAL CLAIM

4010A1							
Element Identifier	Description	ID	Min. Max.	Usage Reg.	Loop	Loop Repeat	Values
837-I 4010A1							
CAS10	Adjustment Quantity	R	1-15	S			
CAS11	Adjustment Reason Code	ID	1-5	S			
CAS12	Adjustment Amount	R	1-18	S			
CAS13	Adjustment Quantity	R	1-15	S			
CAS14	Adjustment Reason Code	ID	1-5	S			
CAS15	Adjustment Amount	R	1-18	S			
CAS16	Adjustment Quantity	R	1-15	S			
CAS17	Adjustment Reason Code	ID	1-5	S			
CAS18	Adjustment Amount	R	1-18	S			
CAS19	Adjustment Quantity	R	1-15	S			
AMT	**PAYER PRIOR PAYMENT**		1	S	2320		
AMT01	Amount Qualifier Code	ID	1-3	R			C4
AMT02	Other Payer Patient Paid Amount	R	1-18	R			
AMT03	Credit/Debit Flag Code	ID	1-1	N/U			
AMT	**COORDINATION OF BENEFITS (COB) TOTAL ALLOWED AMOUNT**		1	S	2320		
AMT01	Amount Qualifier Code	ID	1-3	R			B6
AMT02	Allowed Amount	R	1-18	R			
AMT03	Credit/Debit Flag Code	ID	1-1	N/U			
AMT	**COORDINATION OF BENEFITS (COB) TOTAL SUBMITED CHARGES**		1	S	2320		
AMT01	Amount Qualifier Code	ID	1-3	R			T3
AMT02	Coordination of Benefits Total Submitted Charge Amount	R	1-18	R			
AMT03	Credit/Debit Flag Code	ID	1-1	N/U			
AMT	**DIAGNOSTIC RELATED GROUP (DRG) OUTLIER AMOUNT**		1	S	2320		
AMT01	Amount Qualifier Code	ID	1-3	R			ZZ
AMT02	Claim DRG Outlier Amount	R	1-18	R			
AMT03	Credit/Debit Flag Code	ID	1-1	N/U			
AMT	**COORDINATION OF BENEFITS (COB) TOTAL MEDICARE PAID AMOUNT**		1	S	2320		
AMT01	Amount Qualifier Code	ID	1-3	R			N1
AMT02	Total Medicare Paid Amout	R	1-18	R			
AMT03	Credit/Debit Flag Code	ID	1-1	N/U			
AMT	**MEDICARE PAID AMOUNT - 100%**		1	S	2320		

5010								
Element Identifier	Description	ID	Min. Max.	Usage Reg.	Loop	Loop Repeat	Values	
837-I 5010								
CAS10	Adjustment Quantity	R	1-15	S				
CAS11	Adjustment Reason Code	ID	1-5	S				
CAS12	Adjustment Amount	R	1-18	S				
CAS13	Adjustment Quantity	R	1-15	S				
CAS14	Adjustment Reason Code	ID	1-5	S				
CAS15	Adjustment Amount	R	1-18	S				
CAS16	Adjustment Quantity	R	1-15	S				
CAS17	Adjustment Reason Code	ID	1-5	S				
CAS18	Adjustment Amount	R	1-18	S				
CAS19	Adjustment Quantity	R	1-15	S				
AMT	**COB PAYER PAID AMOUNT**		1	S	2320			Name Change
AMT01	Amount Qualifier Code	ID	1-3	R			D	Code Change
AMT02	Payer Paid Amount	R	1-18	R				Name Change
AMT03	Credit/Debit Flag Code	ID	1-1	N/U				
								Segment Deleted
								Segment Deleted
								Segment Deleted
								Segment Deleted
								Segment Deleted

INSTITUTIONAL CLAIM

4010A1						
Element Identifier	Description	ID	Min. Max.	Usage Reg.	Loop	Loop Repeat	Values

Element Identifier	Description	ID	Min. Max.	Usage Reg.	Loop	Loop Repeat	Values
	837-I 4010A1						
AMT01	Amount Qualifier Code	ID	1-3	R			KF
AMT02	Medicare Paid at 100% Amount	R	1-18	R			
AMT03	Credit/Debit Flag Code	ID	1-1	N/U			
AMT	**MEDICARE PAID AMOUNT - 80%**		1	S	2320		
AMT01	Amount Qualifier Code	ID	1-3	R			PG
AMT02	Medicare Paid at 80% Amount	R	1-18	R			
AMT03	Credit/Debit Flag Code	ID	1-1	N/U			
AMT	**COORDINATION OF BENEFITS (COB) MEDICARE A TRUST FUND PAID AMOUNT**		1	S	2320		
AMT01	Amount Qualifier Code	ID	1-3	R			AA
AMT02	Paid From Part A Medicare Trust Fund Amount	R	1-18	R			
AMT03	Credit/Debit Flag Code	ID	1-1	N/U			
AMT	**COORDINATION OF BENEFITS (COB) MEDICARE B TRUST FUND PAID AMOUNT**		1	S	2320		
AMT01	Amount Qualifier Code	ID	1-3	R			B1
AMT02	Paid From Part B Medicare Trust Fund Amount	R	1-18	R			
AMT03	Credit/Debit Flag Code	ID	1-1	N/U			
AMT	**COORDINATION OF BENEFITS (COB) TOTAL NON-COVERED AMOUNT**		1	S	2320		
AMT01	Amount Qualifier Code	ID	1-3	R			A8
AMT02	Non-Covered Charge Amount	R	1-18	R			
AMT03	Credit/Debit Flag Code	ID	1-1	N/U			
AMT	**COORDINATION OF BENEFITS (COB) TOTAL DENIED AMOUNT**		1	S	2320		
AMT01	Amount Qualifier Code	ID	1-3	R			YT
AMT02	Claim Total Denied Charge Amount	R	1-18	R			
AMT03	Credit/Debit Flag Code	ID	1-1	N/U			

5010						
Element Identifier	Description	ID	Min. Max.	Usage Reg.	Loop	Loop Repeat	Values

Element Identifier	Description	ID	Min. Max.	Usage Reg.	Loop	Loop Repeat	Values	
	837-I 5010							
								Segment Deleted
								Segment Deleted
								Segment Deleted
								Segment Deleted
								Segment Deleted
								Segment Deleted
AMT	**REMAINING PATIENT LIABILITY**		1	S	2320			New Segment
AMT01	Amount Qualifier Code	ID	1-3	R			EAF	

INSTITUTIONAL CLAIM

Element Identifier	Description	ID	Min. Max.	Usage Reg.	Loop	Loop Repeat	Values
	4010A1						
	837-I 4010A1						
DMG	**OTHER SUBSCRIBER DEMOGRAPHIC INFORMATION**		1	S	2320		
DMG01	Date Time Period Format Qualifier	ID	2-3	R			D8
DMG02	Other Insured Birth Date	AN	1-35	R			
DMG03	Gender Code	ID	1-1	R			F, M, U
DMG04	Marital Status Code	ID	1-1	N/U			
DMG05	Race or Ethnicity Code	ID	1-1	N/U			
DMG06	Citizenship Status Code	ID	1-2	N/U			
DMG07	Country Code	ID	2-3	N/U			
DMG08	Basis of Veification Code	ID	1-2	N/U			
DMG09	Quantity	R	1-15	N/U			
OI	**OTHER INSURANCE COVERAGE INFORMATION**		1	R	2320		
OI01	Claim Filing Indicator Code	ID	1-2	N/U			
OI02	Claim Submission Reason Code	ID	2-2	N/U			
OI03	Benefits Assignment Certification Indicator	ID	1-1	R			N, Y
OI04	Patient Signature Source Code	ID	1-1	N/U			
OI05	Provider Agroemont Code	ID	1 1	N/U			
OI06	Release of Information Code	ID	1-1	R			A, I, M, N, O, Y
MIA	**MEDICARE INPATIENT ADJUDICATION INFORMATION**		1	S	2320		
MIA01	Covered Days or Visits Count	R	1-15	R			
MIA02	Lifetime Reserve Days Count	R	1-15	S			
MIA03	Lifetime Psychiatric Days	R	1-15	S			
MIA04	Claim DRG Amount	R	1-18	S			

Element Identifier	Description	ID	Min. Max.	Usage Reg.	Loop	Loop Repeat	Values	
	5010							
	837-I 5010							
AMT02	Remaining Patient Liability Amount	R	1-18	R				
AMT03	Credit/Debit Flag Code	ID	1-1	N/U				
AMT	**COB TOTAL NON-COVERED AMOUNT**		1	S	2320			New Segment
AMT01	Amount Qualifier Code	ID	1-3	R			A8	
AMT02	Non-Covered Amount	R	1-18	R				
AMT03	Credit/Debit Flag Code	ID	1-1	N/U				
								Segment Deleted
OI	**OTHER INSURANCE COVERAGE INFORMATION**		1	R	2320			
OI01	Claim Filing Indicator Code	ID	1-2	N/U				
OI02	Claim Submission Reason Code	ID	2-2	N/U				
OI03	Benefits Assignment Certification Indicator	ID	1-1	R			N, W, Y	Code Added
OI04	Patient Signature Source Code	ID	1-1	N/U				
OI05	Provider Agreement Code	ID	1-1	N/U				
OI06	Release of Information Code	ID	1-1	R			I, Y	Code Deleted
MIA	**INPATIENT ADJUDICATION INFORMATION**		1	S	2320			
MIA01	Covered Days or Visits Count	R	1-15	S				Usage change to Situational
MIA02	Amount	R	1-18	N/U				Usage change to Not Used Increase from 15 - 18 Name Change
MIA03	Lifetime Psychiatric Days	R	1-15	S				
MIA04	Remaining Patient Liability Amount	R	1-18	S				Name Change

Page 74 of 93

INSTITUTIONAL CLAIM

4010A1							
Element Identifier	Description	ID	Min. Max.	Usage Reg.	Loop	Loop Repeat	Values
837-I 4010A1							
MIA05	Remark Code	AN	1-30	S			
MIA06	Claim Disproportionate Share Amount	R	1-18	S			
MIA07	Claim MSP Pass-through Amount	R	1-18	S			
MIA08	Claim PPS Capital Amount	R	1-18	S			
MIA09	PPS-Capital FSP DRG Amount	R	1-18	S			
MIA10	PPS-Capital HSP DRG Amount	R	1-18	S			
MIA11	PPS-Capital DSH DRG Amount	R	1-18	S			
MIA12	Old Capital Amount	R	1-18	S			
MIA13	PPS-Capital IME Amount	R	1-18	S			
MIA14	PPS-Operating Hospital Specific DRG Amount	R	1-18	S			
MIA15	Cost Report Day Count	R	1-15	S			
MIA16	PPS-Operating Federal Specific DRG Amount	R	1-18	S			
MIA17	Claim PPS Capital Outlier Amount	R	1-18	S			
MIA18	Claim Indirect Teaching Amount	R	1-18	S			
MIA19	Non-Payable Professional Component Amount	R	1-18	S			
MIA20	Remark Code	AN	1-30	S			
MIA21	Remark Code	AN	1-30	S			
MIA22	Remark Code	AN	1-30	S			
MIA23	Remark Code	AN	1-30	S			
MIA24	PPS-Capital Exception Amount	R	1-18	S			
MOA	MEDICARE OUTPATIENT ADJUDICATION INFORMATION		1	S	2320		
MOA01	Reimbursement Rate	R	1-10	S			
MOA02	Claim HCPCS Payable Amount	R	1-18	S			
MOA03	Remark Code	AN	1-30	S			
MOA04	Remark Code	AN	1-30	S			
MOA05	Remark Code	AN	1-30	S			
MOA06	Remark Code	AN	1-30	S			
MOA07	Remark Code	AN	1-30	S			

5010								
Element Identifier	Description	ID	Min. Max.	Usage Reg.	Loop	Loop Repeat	Values	
837-I 5010								
MIA05	Claim Payment Remark Code	AN	1-50	S				Increase from 30 - 50 Name Change
MIA06	Claim Disproportionate Share Amount	R	1-18	S				
MIA07	Claim MSP Pass-through Amount	R	1-18	S				
MIA08	Claim PPS Capital Amount	R	1-18	S				
MIA09	PPS-Capital FSP DRG Amount	R	1-18	S				
MIA10	PPS-Capital HSP DRG Amount	R	1-18	S				
MIA11	PPS-Capital DSH DRG Amount	R	1-18	S				
MIA12	Old Capital Amount	R	1-18	S				
MIA13	PPS-Capital IME Amount	R	1-18	S				
MIA14	PPS-Operating Hospital Specific DRG Amount	R	1-18	S				
MIA15	Cost Report Day Count	R	1-15	S				
MIA16	PPS-Operating Federal Specific DRG Amount	R	1-18	S				
MIA17	Claim PPS Capital Outlier Amount	R	1-18	S				
MIA18	Claim Indirect Teaching Amount	R	1-18	S				
MIA19	Non-Payable Professional Component Billed Amount	R	1-18	S				Name Change
MIA20	Claim Payment Remark Code	AN	1-50	S				Increase from 30 - 50 Name Change
MIA21	Claim Payment Remark Code	AN	1-50	S				Increase from 30 - 50 Name Change
MIA22	Claim Payment Remark Code	AN	1-50	S				Increase from 30 - 50 Name Change
MIA23	Claim Payment Remark Code	AN	1-50	S				Increase from 30 - 50 Name Change
MIA24	PPS-Capital Exception Amount	R	1-18	S				
MOA	MEDICARE OUTPATIENT ADJUDICATION INFORMATION		1	S	2320			
MOA01	Reimbursement Rate	R	1-10	S				
MOA02	HCPCS Payable Amount	R	1-18	S				Name Change
MOA03	Remark Code	AN	1-50	S				Increase from 30 - 50
MOA04	Remark Code	AN	1-50	S				Increase from 30 - 50
MOA05	Remark Code	AN	1-50	S				Increase from 30 - 50
MOA06	Remark Code	AN	1-50	S				Increase from 30 - 50
MOA07	Remark Code	AN	1-50	S				Increase from 30 - 50

INSTITUTIONAL CLAIM

Element Identifier	Description	ID	Min. Max.	Usage Reg.	Loop	Loop Repeat	Values
	4010A1						
	837-I 4010A1						
MOA08	Claim ESRD Payment Amount	R	1-18	S			
MOA09	Non-Payable Professional Component Amount	R	1-18	S			
NM1	**OTHER SUBSCRIBER NAME**		1	R	2330A	1	
NM101	Entity Identifier Code	ID	2-3	R			IL
NM102	Entity Type Qualifier	ID	1-1	R			1, 2
NM103	Other Insured Last Name	AN	1-35	R			
NM104	Other Insured First Name	AN	1-25	S			
NM105	Other Insured Middle Name	AN	1-25	S			
NM106	Name Prefix	AN	1-10	N/U			
NM107	Other Insured Name Suffix	AN	1-10	S			
NM108	Identification Code Qualifier	ID	1-2	R			MI, ZZ
NM109	Other Insured Identifier	AN	2-80	R			
NM110	Entity Relationship Code	ID	2-2	N/U			
NM111	Entity Identifier Code	ID	2-3	N/U			
N3	**OTHER SUBSCRIBER ADDRESS**		1	S	2330A		
N301	Other Insured Address Line	AN	1-55	R			
N302	Other Insured Address Line	AN	1-55	S			
N4	**OTHER SUBSCRIBER CITY/STATE/ZIP CODE**		1	S	2330A		
N401	Other Insured City Name	AN	2-30	R			
N402	Other Insured State Code	ID	2-2	R			
N403	Other Insured Postal Zone or ZIP Code	ID	3-15	R			
N404	Subscriber Country Code	ID	2-3	S			
N405	Location Qualifier	ID	1-2	N/U			
N406	Location Identifier	AN	1-30	N/U			
REF	**OTHER SUBSCRIBER SECONDARY IDENTIFICATION**		3	S	2330A		
REF01	Reference Identification Qualifier	ID	2-3	R			1W, 23, !G, SY
REF02	Other Insured Additional Identifier	AN	1-30	R			
REF03	Description	AN	1-80	N/U			
REF04	REFERENCE IDENTIFIER			N/U			

Element Identifier	Description	ID	Min. Max.	Usage Reg.	Loop	Loop Repeat	Values	
	5010							
	837-I 5010							
MOA08	End Stage Renal Disease Payment Amount	R	1-18	S				Name Change
MOA09	Non-Payable Professional Component Billed Amount	R	1-18	S				Name Change
NM1	**OTHER SUBSCRIBER NAME**		1	R	2330A	1		
NM101	Entity Identifier Code	ID	2-3	R			IL	
NM102	Entity Type Qualifier	ID	1-1	R			1, 2	
NM103	Other Insured Last Name	AN	1-60	R				Increase from 35 - 60
NM104	Other Insured First Name	AN	1-35	S				Increase from 25 - 35
NM105	Other Insured Middle Name	AN	1-25	S				
NM106	Name Prefix	AN	1-10	N/U				
NM107	Other Insured Name Suffix	AN	1-10	S				
NM108	Identification Code Qualifier	ID	1-2	R			II, MI	Code Change
NM109	Other Insured Identifier	AN	2-80	R				
NM110	Entity Relationship Code	ID	2-2	N/U				
NM111	Entity Identifier Code	ID	2-3	N/U				
NM112	Name Last or Organization Name	AN	1-60	N/U				New Element
N3	**OTHER SUBSCRIBER ADDRESS**		1	S	2330A			
N301	Other Insured Address Line	AN	1-55	R				
N302	Other Insured Address Line	AN	1-55	S				
N4	**OTHER SUBSCRIBER CITY/STATE/ZIP CODE**		1	R	2330A			
N401	Other Insured City Name	AN	2-30	R				
N402	Other Insured State Code	ID	2-2	S				Usage change to Situational
N403	Other Insured Postal Zone or ZIP Code	ID	3-15	S				Usage change to Situational
N404	Subscriber Country Code	ID	2-3	S				
N405	Location Qualifier	ID	1-2	N/U				
N406	Location Identifier	AN	1-30	N/U				
N407	Country Subdivision Code	ID	1-3	S				New Element
REF	**OTHER SUBSCRIBER SECONDARY IDENTIFICATION**		2	S	2330A			# of Repeat change to 2
REF01	Reference Identification Qualifier	ID	2-3	R			SY	Code Deleted
REF02	Other Insured Additional Identifier	AN	1-50	R				Increase from 30 - 50
REF03	Description	AN	1-80	N/U				
REF04	REFERENCE IDENTIFIER			N/U				

Page 76 of 93

INSTITUTIONAL CLAIM

4010A1							
Element Identifier	Description	ID	Min. Max.	Usage Reg.	Loop	Loop Repeat	Values
	837-I 4010A1						
NM1	**OTHER PAYER NAME**		1	R	2330B	1	
NM101	Entity Identifier Code	ID	2-3	R			PR
NM102	Entity Type Qualifier	ID	1-1	R			2
NM103	Other Payer Last or Organization Name	AN	1-35	R			
NM104	Name First	AN	1-25	N/U			
NM105	Name Middle	AN	1-25	N/U			
NM106	Name Prefix	AN	1-10	N/U			
NM107	Name Suffix	AN	1-10	N/U			
NM108	Identification Code Qualifier	ID	1-2	R			PI, XV
NM109	Other Payer Primary Identifier	AN	2-80	R			
NM110	Entity Relationship Code	ID	2-2	N/U			
NM111	Entity Identifier Code	ID	2-3	N/U			
N3	**OTHER PAYER ADDRESS**		1	S	2330B		
N301	Other Payer Address Line	AN	1-55	R			
N302	Other Payer Address Line	AN	1-55	S			
N4	**OTHER PAYER CITY/STATE/ZIP CODE**		1	S	2330B		
N401	Other Payer City Name	AN	2-30	R			
N402	Other Payer State Code	ID	2-2	R			
N403	Other Payer Postal Zone or ZIP Code	ID	3-15	R			
N404	Payer Country Code	ID	2-3	S			
N405	Location Qualifier	ID	1-2	N/U			
N406	Location Identifier	AN	1-30	N/U			
DTP	**CLAIM ADJUDICATION DATE**		1	S	2330B		
DTP01	Date Time Qualifier	ID	3-3	R			573
DTP02	Date Time Period Format Qualifier	ID	2-3	R			D8
DTP03	Adjudication or Payment Date	AN	1-35	R			CCYYMMDD
REF	**OTHER PAYER SECONDARY IDENTIFICATION AND REFERENCE NUMBER**		2	S	2330B		
REF01	Reference Identification Qualifier	ID	2-3	R			2U, F8, FY, NF, TJ
REF02	Other Payer Secondary Identifier	AN	1-30	R			
REF03	Description	AN	1-80	N/U			

5010								
Element Identifier	Description	ID	Min. Max.	Usage Reg.	Loop	Loop Repeat	Values	
	837-I 5010							
NM1	**OTHER PAYER NAME**		1	R	2330B	1		
NM101	Entity Identifier Code	ID	2-3	R			PR	
NM102	Entity Type Qualifier	ID	1-1	R			2	
NM103	Other Payer Last or Organization Name	AN	1-60	R				Increase from 35 - 60
NM104	Name First	AN	1-35	N/U				Increase from 25 - 35
NM105	Name Middle	AN	1-25	N/U				
NM106	Name Prefix	AN	1-10	N/U				
NM107	Name Suffix	AN	1-10	N/U				
NM108	Identification Code Qualifier	ID	1-2	R			PI, XV	
NM109	Other Payer Primary Identifier	AN	2-80	R				
NM110	Entity Relationship Code	ID	2-2	N/U				
NM111	Entity Identifier Code	ID	2-3	N/U				
NM112	Name Last or Organization Name	AN	1-60	N/U				New Element
N3	**OTHER PAYER ADDRESS**		1	S	2330B			
N301	Other Payer Address Line	AN	1-55	R				
N302	Other Payer Address Line	AN	1-55	S				
N4	**OTHER PAYER CITY/STATE/ZIP CODE**		1	R	2330B			Usage change to Required
N401	Other Payer City Name	AN	2-30	R				
N402	Other Payer State Code	ID	2-2	S				Usage change to Situational
N403	Other Payer Postal Zone or ZIP Code	ID	3-15	S				Usage change to Situational
N404	Other Payer Country Code	ID	2-3	S				Name Change
N405	Location Qualifier	ID	1-2	N/U				
N406	Location Identifier	AN	1-30	N/U				
N407	Country Subdivision Code	ID	1-3	S				New Element
DTP	**DATE - CLAIM CHECK OR REMITTANCE DATE**		1	S	2330B			Name Change
DTP01	Date Time Qualifier	ID	3-3	R			573	
DTP02	Date Time Period Format Qualifier	ID	2-3	R			D8	
DTP03	Adjudication or Payment Date	AN	1-35	R			CCYYMMDD	
REF	**OTHER PAYER SECONDARY IDENTIFICATION**		2	S	2330B			Name Change
REF01	Reference Identification Qualifier	ID	2-3	R			2U, EI, FY, NF	Code Change
REF02	Other Payer Secondary Identifier	AN	1-50	R				Increase from 30 - 50
REF03	Description	AN	1-80	N/U				

INSTITUTIONAL CLAIM

4010A1

Element Identifier	Description	ID	Min. Max.	Usage Reg.	Loop	Loop Repeat	Values
	837-I 4010A1						
REF04	REFERENCE IDENTIFIER			N/U			
REF	**OTHER PAYER PRIOR AUTHORIZATION OR REFERRAL NUMBER**		1	S	2330B		
REF01	Reference Identification Qualifier	ID	2-3	R			9F, G1
REF02	Authorization or Referral Number	AN	1-30	R			
REF03	Description	AN	1-80	N/U			
REF04	REFERENCE IDENTIFIER			N/U			
NM1	**OTHER PAYER PATIENT INFORMATION**		1	S	2330C	1	
NM101	Entity Identifier Code	ID	2-3	R			QC
NM102	Entity Type Qualifier	ID	1-1	R			1
NM103	Name Last or Organization Name	AN	1-35	N/U			
NM104	Name First	AN	1-25	N/U			
NM105	Name Middle	AN	1-25	N/U			
NM106	Name Prefix	AN	1-10	N/U			
NM107	Name Suffix	AN	1-10	N/U			

5010

Element Identifier	Description	ID	Min. Max.	Usage Reg.	Loop	Loop Repeat	Values	
	837-I 5010							
REF04	REFERENCE IDENTIFIER			N/U				
REF	**OTHER PAYER PRIOR AUTHORIZATION NUMBER**		1	S	2330B			
REF01	Reference Identification Qualifier	ID	2-3	R			G1	Code Change
REF02	Other Payer Prior Authorization Number	AN	1-50	R				Increase from 30 - 50
REF03	Description	AN	1-80	N/U				
REF04	REFERENCE IDENTIFIER			N/U				
REF	**OTHER PAYER REFERRAL NUMBER**		1	S	2330B			New Segment
REF01	Reference Identification Qualifier	ID	2-3	R			9F	
REF02	Other Payer Referral Number	AN	1-50	R				
REF03	Description	AN	1-80	N/U				
REF04	REFERENCE IDENTIFIER			N/U				
REF	**OTHER PAYER CLAIM ADJUSTMENT INDICATOR**		1	S	2330B			New Segment
REF01	Reference Identification Qualifier	ID	2-3	R			T4	
REF02	Other Payer Claim Adjustment Indicator	AN	1-50	R				
REF03	Description	AN	1-80	N/U				
REF04	REFERENCE IDENTIFIER			N/U				
REF	**OTHER PAYER CLAIM CONTROL NUMBER**		1	S	2330B			New Segment
REF01	Reference Identification Qualifier	ID	2-3	R			F8	
REF02	Other Payer Claim Control Number	AN	1-50	R				
REF03	Description	AN	1-80	N/U				
REF04	REFERENCE IDENTIFIER			N/U				Segment Deleted

Page 78 of 93

INSTITUTIONAL CLAIM

4010A1							
Element Identifier	Description	ID	Min. Max.	Usage Reg.	Loop	Loop Repeat	Values
837-I 4010A1							
NM108	Identification Code Qualifier	ID	1-2	R			EI, MI
NM109	Other Payer Patient Primary Identifier	AN	2-80	R			
NM110	Entity Relationship Code	ID	2-2	N/U			
NM111	Entity Identifier Code	ID	2-3	N/U			
REF	**OTHER PAYER PATIENT IDENTIFICATION NUMBER**		3	S	2330C		
REF01	Reference Identification Qualifier	ID	2-3	R			1W, IG, SY
REF02	Other Payer Patient Secondary Identifier	AN	1-30	R			
REF03	Description	AN	1-80	N/U			
REF04	REFERENCE IDENTIFIER			N/U			
NM1	**OTHER PAYER ATTENDING PROVIDER**		1	S	2330D	1	
NM101	Entity Identifier Code	ID	2-3	R			71
NM102	Entity Type Qualifier	ID	1-1	R			1, 2
NM103	Name Last or Organization Name	AN	1-35	N/U			
NM104	Name First	AN	1-25	N/U			
NM105	Name Middle	AN	1-25	N/U			
NM106	Name Prefix	AN	1-10	N/U			
NM107	Name Suffix	AN	1-10	N/U			
NM108	Identification Code Qualifier	ID	1-2	N/U			
NM109	Identification Code	AN	2-80	N/U			
NM110	Entity Relationship Code	ID	2-2	N/U			
NM111	Entity Identifier Code	ID	2-3	N/U			
REF	**OTHER PAYER ATTENDING PROVIDER SECONDARY IDENTIFICATION**		3	R	2330D		
REF01	Reference Identification Qualifier	ID	2-3	R			1A, 1B, 1C, 1D, 1G, 1H, EI, G2, LU, N5
REF02	Secondary Identifier	AN	1-30	R			
REF03	Description	AN	1-80	N/U			
REF04	REFERENCE IDENTIFIER			N/U			
NM1	**OTHER PAYER OPERATING PROVIDER**		1	S	2330E	1	
NM101	Entity Identifier Code	ID	2-3	R			72
NM102	Entity Type Qualifier	ID	1-1	R			1
NM103	Name Last or Organization Name	AN	1-35	N/U			

5010								
Element Identifier	Description	ID	Min. Max.	Usage Reg.	Loop	Loop Repeat	Values	
837-I 5010								
								Segment Deleted
NM1	**OTHER PAYER ATTENDING PROVIDER**		1	S	2330C	1		Loop Change
NM101	Entity Identifier Code	ID	2-3	R			71	
NM102	Entity Type Qualifier	ID	1-1	R			1	Code Deleted
NM103	Name Last or Organization Name	AN	1-60	N/U				Increase from 35 - 60
NM104	Name First	AN	1-35	N/U				Increase from 25 - 35
NM105	Name Middle	AN	1-25	N/U				
NM106	Name Prefix	AN	1-10	N/U				
NM107	Name Suffix	AN	1-10	N/U				
NM108	Identification Code Qualifier	ID	1-2	N/U				
NM109	Other Payer Primary Identifier	AN	2-80	N/U				Name Change
NM110	Entity Relationship Code	ID	2-2	N/U				
NM111	Entity Identifier Code	ID	2-3	N/U				
NM112	Name Last or Organization Name	AN	1-60	N/U				New Element
REF	**OTHER PAYER ATTENDING PROVIDER SECONDARY IDENTIFICATION**		4	R	2330C			Loop Change # Repeats change to 4
REF01	Reference Identification Qualifier	ID	2-3	R			0B, 1G, G2, LU	Code Change
REF02	Secondary Identifier	AN	1-50	R				Increase from 30 - 50
REF03	Description	AN	1-80	N/U				
REF04	REFERENCE IDENTIFIER			N/U				
NM1	**OTHER PAYER OPERATING PROVIDER**		1	S	2330D	1		Loop Change
NM101	Entity Identifier Code	ID	2-3	R			72	
NM102	Entity Type Qualifier	ID	1-1	R			1	
NM103	Name Last or Organization Name	AN	1-60	N/U				Increase from 35 - 60

INSTITUTIONAL CLAIM

4010A1							
Element Identifier	Description	ID	Min. Max.	Usage Reg.	Loop	Loop Repeat	Values
		837-I 4010A1					
NM104	Name First	AN	1-25	N/U			
NM105	Name Middle	AN	1-25	N/U			
NM106	Name Prefix	AN	1-10	N/U			
NM107	Name Suffix	AN	1-10	N/U			
NM108	Identification Code Qualifier	ID	1-2	N/U			
NM109	Other Payer Primary Identifier	AN	2-80	N/U			
NM110	Entity Relationship Code	ID	2-2	N/U			
NM111	Entity Identifier Code	ID	2-3	N/U			
REF	OTHER PAYER OPERATING PROVIDER IDENTIFICATION		3	R	2330E		
REF01	Reference Identification Qualifier	ID	2-3	R			1A, 1B, 1C, 1D, 1G, 1H, EI, G2, LU, N5
REF02	Secondary Identifier	AN	1-30	R			
REF03	Description	AN	1-80	N/U			
REF04	REFERENCE IDENTIFIER			N/U			
NM1	OTHER PAYER OTHER PROVIDER		1	S	2330F	1	
NM101	Entity Identifier Code	ID	2-3	R			73
NM102	Entity Type Qualifier	ID	1-1	R			1, 2
NM103	Name Last or Organization Name	AN	1-35	N/U			
NM104	Name First	AN	1-25	N/U			
NM105	Name Middle	AN	1-25	N/U			
NM106	Name Prefix	AN	1-10	N/U			
NM107	Name Suffix	AN	1-10	N/U			
NM108	Identification Code Qualifier	ID	1-2	N/U			
NM109	Other Payer Primary Identifier	AN	2-80	N/U			
NM110	Entity Relationship Code	ID	2-2	N/U			
NM111	Entity Identifier Code	ID	2-3	N/U			
REF	OTHER PAYER OTHER PROVIDER IDENTIFICATION		3	R	2330F		
REF01	Reference Identification Qualifier	ID	2-3	R			1A, 1B, 1C, 1D, 1G, 1H, EI, G2, LU, N5, SY
REF02	Secondary Identifier	AN	1-30	R			

5010								
Element Identifier	Description	ID	Min. Max.	Usage Reg.	Loop	Loop Repeat	Values	
		837-I 5010						
NM104	Name First	AN	1-35	N/U				Increase from 25 - 35
NM105	Name Middle	AN	1-25	N/U				
NM106	Name Prefix	AN	1-10	N/U				
NM107	Name Suffix	AN	1-10	N/U				
NM108	Identification Code Qualifier	ID	1-2	N/U				
NM109	Other Payer Primary Identifier	AN	2-80	N/U				
NM110	Entity Relationship Code	ID	2-2	N/U				
NM111	Entity Identifier Code	ID	2-3	N/U				
NM112	Name Last or Organization Name	AN	1-60	N/U				
REF	OTHER PAYER OPERATING PROVIDER SECONDARY IDENTIFICATION		4	R	2330D			Loop Change Name Change # Repeats change to 4
REF01	Reference Identification Qualifier	ID	2-3	R			0B, 1G, G2, LU	Code Change
REF02	Secondary Identifier	AN	1-50	R				Increase from 30 - 50
REF03	Description	AN	1-80	N/U				
REF04	REFERENCE IDENTIFIER			N/U				
NM1	OTHER PAYER OTHER PROVIDER		1	S	2330E	1		Loop Change Name Change
NM101	Entity Identifier Code	ID	2-3	R			ZZ	Code Change
NM102	Entity Type Qualifier	ID	1-1	R			1	Code Deleted
NM103	Name Last or Organization Name	AN	1-60	N/U				Increase from 35 - 60
NM104	Name First	AN	1-35	N/U				Increase from 25 - 35
NM105	Name Middle	AN	1-25	N/U				
NM106	Name Prefix	AN	1-10	N/U				
NM107	Name Suffix	AN	1-10	N/U				
NM108	Identification Code Qualifier	ID	1-2	N/U				
NM109	Other Payer Primary Identifier	AN	2-80	N/U				
NM110	Entity Relationship Code	ID	2-2	N/U				
NM111	Entity Identifier Code	ID	2-3	N/U				
NM112	Name Last or Organization Name	AN	1-60	N/U				New Element
REF	OTHER PAYER OTHER OPERATING PROVIDER SECONDARY IDENTIFICATION		4	R	2330E			Loop Change Name Change # Repeats change to 4
REF01	Reference Identification Qualifier	ID	2-3	R			0B, 1G, G2, LU	Code Change
REF02	Secondary Identifier	AN	1-50	R				Increase from 30 - 50

Page 80 of 93

INSTITUTIONAL CLAIM

4010A1

Element Identifier	Description	ID	Min. Max.	Usage Reg.	Loop	Loop Repeat	Values
	837-I 4010A1						
REF03	Description	AN	1-80	N/U			
REF04	REFERENCE IDENTIFIER			N/U			
NM1	**OTHER PAYER SERVICE FACILITY PROVIDER**		1	S	2330H	1	
NM101	Entity Identifier Code	ID	2-3	R			FA
NM102	Entity Type Qualifier	ID	1-1	R			2
NM103	Name Last or Organization Name	AN	1-35	N/U			
NM104	Name First	AN	1-25	N/U			
NM105	Name Middle	AN	1-25	N/U			
NM106	Name Prefix	AN	1-10	N/U			
NM107	Name Suffix	AN	1-10	N/U			
NM108	Identification Code Qualifier	ID	1-2	N/U			
NM109	Other Payer Primary Identifier	AN	2-80	N/U			
NM110	Entity Relationship Code	ID	2-2	N/U			
NM111	Entity Identifier Code	ID	2-3	N/U			
NM112	Name Last or Organization Name	AN	1-60	N/U			
REF	**OTHER PAYER SERVICE FACILITY PROVIDER IDENTIFICATION**		3	R	2330H		
REF01	Reference Identification Qualifier	ID	2-3	R			1B, 1C, 1D, EI, G2, LU, N5
REF02	Other Payer Service Facility Location Secondary Identifier	AN	1-30	R			
REF03	Description	AN	1-80	N/U			
REF04	REFERENCE IDENTIFIER			N/U			

5010

Element Identifier	Description	ID	Min. Max.	Usage Reg.	Loop	Loop Repeat	Values	
	837-I 5010							
REF03	Description	AN	1-80	N/U				
REF04	REFERENCE IDENTIFIER			N/U				
NM1	**OTHER PAYER SERVICE FACILITY LOCATION**		1	S	2330F	1		Loop Change Name Change
NM101	Entity Identifier Code	ID	2-3	R			77	Code Change
NM102	Entity Type Qualifier	ID	1-1	R			2	
NM103	Name Last or Organization Name	AN	1-60	N/U				Increase from 35 - 60
NM104	Name First	AN	1-35	N/U				Increase from 25 - 35
NM105	Name Middle	AN	1-25	N/U				
NM106	Name Prefix	AN	1-10	N/U				
NM107	Name Suffix	AN	1-10	N/U				
NM108	Identification Code Qualifier	ID	1-2	N/U				
NM109	Other Payer Primary Identifier	AN	2-80	N/U				
NM110	Entity Relationship Code	ID	2-2	N/U				
NM111	Entity Identifier Code	ID	2-3	N/U				
NM112	Name Last or Organization Name	AN	1-60	N/U				
REF	**OTHER PAYER SERVICE FACILITY LOCATION SECONDARY IDENTIFIER**		3	R	2330F			Loop Change Name Change
REF01	Reference Identification Qualifier	ID	2-3	R			0B, G2, LU	Code Change
REF02	Other Payer Service Facility Location Secondary Identifier	AN	1-50	R				Increase from 30 - 50
REF03	Description	AN	1-80	N/U				
REF04	REFERENCE IDENTIFIER			N/U				
NM1	**OTHER PAYER RENDERING PROVIDER**		1	S	2330G	1		New Segment
NM101	Entity Identifier Code	ID	2-3	R			82	
NM102	Entity Type Qualifier	ID	1-1	R			1	
NM103	Name Last or Organization Name	AN	1-60	N/U				
NM104	Name First	AN	1-35	N/U				
NM105	Name Middle	AN	1-25	N/U				
NM106	Name Prefix	AN	1-10	N/U				
NM107	Name Suffix	AN	1-10	N/U				
NM108	Identification Code Qualifier	ID	1-2	N/U				
NM109	Other Payer Primary Identifier	AN	2-80	N/U				
NM110	Entity Relationship Code	ID	2-2	N/U				
NM111	Entity Identifier Code	ID	2-3	N/U				
NM112	Name Last or Organization Name	AN	1-60	N/U				

Page 81 of 93

INSTITUTIONAL CLAIM

Element Identifier	Description	ID	Min. Max.	Usage Reg.	Loop	Loop Repeat	Values
4010A1							
837-I 4010A1							

Element Identifier	Description	ID	Min. Max.	Usage Reg.	Loop	Loop Repeat	Values	
5010								
837-I 5010								
REF	OTHER PAYER RENDERING PROVIDER SECONDARY IDENTIFIER		4	R	2330G			New Segment
REF01	Reference Identification Qualifier	ID	2-3	R			0B, 1G, G2, LU	
REF02	Other Payer Rendering Provider Secondary Identifier	AN	1-50	R				
REF03	Description	AN	1-80	N/U				
REF04	REFERENCE IDENTIFIER			N/U				
NM1	OTHER PAYER REFERRING PROVIDER		1	S	2330H	1		New Segment
NM101	Entity Identifier Code	ID	2-3	R			DN	
NM102	Entity Type Qualifier	ID	1-1	R			1	
NM103	Name Last or Organization Name	AN	1-60	N/U				
NM104	Name First	AN	1-35	N/U				
NM105	Name Middle	AN	1-25	N/U				
NM106	Name Prefix	AN	1-10	N/U				
NM107	Name Suffix	AN	1-10	N/U				
NM108	Identification Code Qualifier	ID	1-2	N/U				
NM109	Other Payer Primary Identifier	AN	2-80	N/U				
NM110	Entity Relationship Code	ID	2-2	N/U				
NM111	Entity Identifier Code	ID	2-3	N/U				
NM112	Name Last or Organization Name	AN	1-60	N/U				
REF	OTHER PAYER REFERRING PROVIDER SECONDARY IDENTIFIER		3	R	2330H			New Segment
REF01	Reference Identification Qualifier	ID	2-3	R			0B, 1G, G2	
REF02	Other Payer Referring Provider Secondary Identifier	AN	1-50	R				
REF03	Description	AN	1-80	N/U				
REF04	REFERENCE IDENTIFIER			N/U				
NM1	OTHER PAYER BILLING PROVIDER		1	S	2330I	1		New Segment
NM101	Entity Identifier Code	ID	2-3	R			85	
NM102	Entity Type Qualifier	ID	1-1	R			2	
NM103	Name Last or Organization Name	AN	1-60	N/U				
NM104	Name First	AN	1-35	N/U				
NM105	Name Middle	AN	1-25	N/U				
NM106	Name Prefix	AN	1-10	N/U				
NM107	Name Suffix	AN	1-10	N/U				

Page 82 of 93

INSTITUTIONAL CLAIM

4010A1								
Element Identifier	Description	ID	Min. Max.	Usage Reg.	Loop	Loop Repeat	Values	
				837-I 4010A1				
LX	**SERVICE LINE NUMBER**		1	R	2400	999		
LX01	Assigned Number	N0	1-6	R				
SV2	**INSTITUTIONAL SERVICE LINE**		1	R	2400			
SV201	Revenue Code	AN	1-48	R				
SV202	COMPOSITE			S				
SV202-1	Product or Service ID Qualifier	ID	2-2	R			HC, IV, ZZ	
SV202-2	Procedure Code	AN	1-48	R				
SV202-3	Procedure Modifier	AN	2-2	S				
SV202-4	Procedure Modifier	AN	2-2	S				
SV202-5	Procedure Modifier	AN	2-2	S				
SV202-6	Procedure Modifier	AN	2-2	S				
SV202-7	Description	AN	1-80	N/U				
SV203	Line Item Charge Amount	R	1-18	R				
SV204	Unit or Basis for Measurement Code	ID	2-2	R			DA, F2, UN	
SV205	Service Unit Count	R	1-15	R				
SV206	Unit Rate	ID	1-10	S				
SV207	Monetary Amount	R	1-18	S				
SV208	Y/N	ID	1-1	N/U				
SV209	NHRSC	ID	1-1	N/U				
SV210	Level of Care Code	ID	1-1	N/U				
PWK	**LINE SUPPLEMENTAL INFORMATION**		5	S	2400			

5010								
Element Identifier	Description	ID	Min. Max.	Usage Reg.	Loop	Loop Repeat	Values	
				837-I 5010				
NM108	Identification Code Qualifier	ID	1-2	N/U				
NM109	Other Payer Primary Identifier	AN	2-80	N/U				
NM110	Entity Relationship Code	ID	2-2	N/U				
NM111	Entity Identifier Code	ID	2-3	N/U				
NM112	Name Last or Organization Name	AN	1-60	N/U				
REF	**OTHER PAYER BILLING PROVIDER SECONDARY IDENTIFICATION**		2	R	2330I			New Segment
REF01	Reference Identification Qualifier	ID	2-3	R			G2, LU	
REF02	Other Payer Billing Provider Secondary Identification	AN	1-50	R				
REF03	Description	AN	1-80	N/U				
REF04	REFERENCE IDENTIFIER			N/U				
LX	**SERVICE LINE**		1	R	2400	999		Name Change
LX01	Assigned Number	N0	1-6	R				
SV2	**INSTITUTIONAL SERVICE LINE**		1	R	2400			
SV201	Revenue Code	AN	1-48	R				
SV202	COMPOSITE			R				Usage change to Required
SV202-1	Product or Service ID Qualifier	ID	2-2	R			ER, HC, HP, IV, WK	Code Change
SV202-2	Procedure Code	AN	1-48	R				
SV202-3	Procedure Modifier	AN	2-2	S				
SV202-4	Procedure Modifier	AN	2-2	S				
SV202-5	Procedure Modifier	AN	2-2	S				
SV202-6	Procedure Modifier	AN	2-2	S				
SV202-7	Description	AN	1-80	S				Usage change to Situational
SV202-8	Product/Service ID	AN	1-48	N/U				New Element
SV203	Line Item Charge Amount	R	1-18	R				
SV204	Unit or Basis for Measurement Code	ID	2-2	R			DA, UN	Code Deleted
SV205	Service Units/Days	R	1-15	R				Name Change
SV206	Unit Rate	ID	1-10	N/U				Usage change to Not Used
SV207	Monetary Amount	R	1-18	S				
SV208	Y/N	ID	1-1	N/U				
SV209	NHRSC	ID	1-1	N/U				
SV210	Level of Care Code	ID	1-1	N/U				
PWK	**LINE SUPPLEMENTAL INFORMATION**		10	S	2400			# Repeats change to 10

Page 83 of 93

INSTITUTIONAL CLAIM

Element Identifier	Description	ID	Min. Max.	Usage Req.	Loop	Loop Repeat	Values
4010A1							
837-I 4010A1							
PWK01	Attachment Report Type Code	ID	2-2	R			AS, B2, B3, B4, CT, D2, DA, DG, DS, EB, MT, NN, OB, OZ, PN, PO, PZ, RB, RR, RT
PWK02	Attachment Transmission Code	ID	1-2	R			AA, AB, AD, AF, AG, BM, EL, EM, FX
PWK03	Report Copies Needed	N0	1-2	N/U			
PWK04	Entity Identifier Code	ID	2-3	N/U			
PWK05	Identification Code Qualifier	ID	1-2	S			AC
PWK06	Identification Code	AN	2-80	S			
PWK07	Description	AN	1-80	N/U			
PWK08	ACTIONS INDICATED			N/U			
PWK09	Request Category Code	ID	1-2	N/U			
DTP	**SERVICE LINE DATE**		1	R	2400		
DTP01	Date Time Qualifier	ID	3-3	R			472
DTP02	Date Time Period Format Qualifier	ID	2-3	R			D8, RD8
DTP03	Service Date	AN	1-35	R			CYYMMDD, CCYYMMDD-CCYYMMDD
DTP	**ASSESSMENT DATE**		1	S	2400		
DTP01	Date Time Qualifier	ID	3-3	R			866
DTP02	Date Time Period Format Qualifier	ID	2-3	R			D8
DTP03	Assessment Date	AN	1-35	R			CCYYMMDD

Element Identifier	Description	ID	Min. Max.	Usage Req.	Loop	Loop Repeat	Values	
5010								
837-I 5010								Code Added
PWK01	Attachment Report Type Code	ID	2-2	R			03, 04, 05, 06, 07, 08, 09, 10, 11, 13, 15, 21, A3, A4, AM, AS, B2, B3, B4, BR, BS, BT, CB, CK, CT, D2, DA, DB, DG, DJ, DS, EB, HC, HR, I5, IR, LA, M1, MT, NN, OB, OC, OD, OE, OX, OZ, P4, P5, PE, PN, PO, PQ, PY, PZ, RB, RR, RT, RX, SG, V5, XP	
PWK02	Attachment Transmission Code	ID	1-2	R			AA, BM, EL, EM, FT, FX	Code Change
PWK03	Report Copies Needed	N0	1-2	N/U				
PWK04	Entity Identifier Code	ID	2-3	N/U				
PWK05	Identification Code Qualifier	ID	1-2	S			AC	
PWK06	Identification Code	AN	2-80	S				
PWK07	Description	AN	1-80	N/U				
PWK08	ACTIONS INDICATED			N/U				
PWK09	Request Category Code	ID	1-2	N/U				
DTP	**DATE - SERVICE DATE**		1	R	2400			Name Change / Usage change to Required
DTP01	Date Time Qualifier	ID	3-3	R			472	
DTP02	Date Time Period Format Qualifier	ID	2-3	R			D8, RD8	
DTP03	Service Date	AN	1-35	R			CYYMMDD, CCYYMMDD-CCYYMMDD	
								Segment Deleted
REF	**LINE ITEM CONTROL NUMBER**		1	S	2400			New Segment
REF01	Reference Identification Qualifier	ID	2-3	R			6R	
REF02	Line Item Control Number	AN	1-50	R				

INSTITUTIONAL CLAIM

4010A1

837-I 4010A1

Element Identifier	Description	ID	Min. Max.	Usage Reg.	Loop	Loop Repeat	Values
AMT	**SERVICE TAX AMOUNT**		1	S	2400		
AMT01	Amount Qualifier Code	ID	1-3	R			GT
AMT02	Service Tax Amount	R	1-18	R			
AMT03	Credit/Debit Flag Code	ID	1-1	N/U			
AMT	**FACILITY TAX AMOUNT**		1	S	2400		
AMT01	Amount Qualifier Code	ID	1-3	R			N8
AMT02	Facility Tax Amount	R	1-18	R			
AMT03	Credit/Debit Flag Code	ID	1-1	N/U			
HCP	**LINE PRICING/REPRICING INFORMATION**		1	S	2400		
HCP01	Pricing Methodology	ID	2-2	R			00, 01, 02, 03, 04, 05, 06, 07, 08, 09, 10, 11, 12, 13, 14
HCP02	Repriced Allowed Amount	R	1-18	R			
HCP03	Repriced Saving Amount	R	1-18	S			
HCP04	Repricing Organization Identifier	AN	1-30	S			
HCP05	Repricing Per Diem or Flat Rate Amount	R	1-9	S			

5010

837-I 5010

Element Identifier	Description	ID	Min. Max.	Usage Reg.	Loop	Loop Repeat	Values	Notes
REF03	Description	AN	1-80	N/U				
REF04	REFERENCE IDENTIFIER			N/U				
REF	**REPRICED LINE ITEM REFERENCE NUMBER**		1	S	2400			New Segment
REF01	Reference Identification Qualifier	ID	2-3	R			9B	
REF02	Repriced Line Item Reference Number	AN	1-50	R				
REF03	Description	AN	1-80	N/U				
REF04	REFERENCE IDENTIFIER			N/U				
REF	**ITEM REFERENCE NUMBER**		1	S	2400			New Segment
REF01	Reference Identification Qualifier	ID	2-3	R			9D	
REF02	Adjusted Repriced Line Item Reference Number	AN	1-50	R				
REF03	Description	AN	1-80	N/U				
REF04	REFERENCE IDENTIFIER			N/U				
AMT	**SERVICE TAX AMOUNT**		1	S	2400			
AMT01	Amount Qualifier Code	ID	1-3	R			GT	
AMT02	Tax Amount	R	1-18	R				Name Change
AMT03	Credit/Debit Flag Code	ID	1-1	N/U				
AMT	**FACILITY TAX AMOUNT**		1	S	2400			
AMT01	Amount Qualifier Code	ID	1-3	R			N8	
AMT02	Facility Tax Amount	R	1-18	R				
AMT03	Credit/Debit Flag Code	ID	1-1	N/U				
NTE	**THIRD PARTY ORGANIZATION NOTES**		1	S	2400			Segment Added
NTE01	Note Reference Code	ID	3-3	R			TPO	
NTE02	Claim Note Text	AN	1-80	R				
HCP	**LINE PRICING/REPRICING INFORMATION**		1	S	2400			
HCP01	Pricing Methodology	ID	2-2	R			00, 01, 02, 03, 04, 05, 06, 07, 08, 09, 10, 11, 12, 13, 14	
HCP02	Repriced Allowed Amount	R	1-18	R				
HCP03	Repriced Saving Amount	R	1-18	S				
HCP04	Repricing Organization Identifier	AN	1-50	S				Increase from 30 - 50
HCP05	Repricing Per Diem or Flat Rate Amount	R	1-9	S				

INSTITUTIONAL CLAIM

4010A1

837-I 4010A1

Element Identifier	Description	ID	Min. Max.	Usage Reg.	Loop	Loop Repeat	Values
HCP06	Ambulatory Patient Group Code	AN	1-30	S			
HCP07	Ambulatory Patient Group Amount	R	1-18	S			
HCP08	Product/Service ID	AN	1-48	S			
HCP09	Product or Service ID Qualifier	ID	2-2	S			HC
HCP10	Procedure Code	AN	1-48	S			
HCP11	Measurement Code	ID	2-2	S			DA, UN
HCP12	Repriced Approved Service Unit Count "DA" "UN"	R	1-15	S			
HCP13	Reject Reason Code	ID	2-2	S			T1, T2, T3, T4, T5, T6
HCP14	Policy Compliance Code	ID	1-2	S			1, 2, 3, 4, 5
HCP15	Exception Code	ID	1-2	S			1, 2, 3, 4, 5, 6
LIN	DRUG IDENTIFICATION		1	S	2410	25	
LIN01	Assigned Identification	AN	1-20	N/U			
LIN02	Product or Service ID Qualifier	ID	2-2	R			N4
LIN03	National Drug Code	AN	1-48	R			
LIN04	Product/Service ID Qualifier	ID	2-2	N/U			
LIN05	Product/Service ID	AN	1-48	N/U			
LIN06	Product/Service ID Qualifier	ID	2-2	N/U			
LIN07	Product/Service ID	AN	1-48	N/U			
LIN08	Product/Service ID Qualifier	ID	2-2	N/U			
LIN09	Product/Service ID	AN	1-48	N/U			
LIN10	Product/Service ID Qualifier	ID	2-2	N/U			
LIN11	Product/Service ID	AN	1-48	N/U			
LIN12	Product/Service ID Qualifier	ID	2-2	N/U			
LIN13	Product/Service ID	AN	1-48	N/U			
LIN14	Product/Service ID Qualifier	ID	2-2	N/U			
LIN15	Product/Service ID	AN	1-48	N/U			
LIN16	Product/Service ID Qualifier	ID	2-2	N/U			
LIN17	Product/Service ID	AN	1-48	N/U			
LIN18	Product/Service ID Qualifier	ID	2-2	N/U			
LIN19	Product/Service ID	AN	1-48	N/U			
LIN20	Product/Service ID Qualifier	ID	2-2	N/U			
LIN21	Product/Service ID	AN	1-48	N/U			
LIN22	Product/Service ID Qualifier	ID	2-2	N/U			
LIN23	Product/Service ID	AN	1-48	N/U			
LIN24	Product/Service ID Qualifier	ID	2-2	N/U			
LIN25	Product/Service ID	AN	1-48	N/U			
LIN26	Product/Service ID Qualifier	ID	2-2	N/U			
LIN27	Product/Service ID	AN	1-48	N/U			
LIN28	Product/Service ID Qualifier	ID	2-2	N/U			
LIN29	Product/Service ID	AN	1-48	N/U			
LIN30	Product/Service ID Qualifier	ID	2-2	N/U			

5010

837-I 5010

Element Identifier	Description	ID	Min. Max.	Usage Reg.	Loop	Loop Repeat	Values	Notes
HCP06	Ambulatory Patient Group Code	AN	1-50	S				Increase from 30 - 50
HCP07	Ambulatory Patient Group Amount	R	1-18	S				
HCP08	Product/Service ID	AN	1-48	N/U				Usage change to Not Used
HCP09	Product or Service ID Qualifier	ID	2-2	S			ER, HC, HP, IV, WK	Code Added
HCP10	Procedure Code	AN	1-48	S				
HCP11	Measurement Code	ID	2-2	S			DA, UN	
HCP12	Repriced Approved Service Unit Count "DA" "UN"	R	1-15	S				
HCP13	Reject Reason Code	ID	2-2	S			T1, T2, T3, T4, T5, T6	
HCP14	Policy Compliance Code	ID	1-2	S			1, 2, 3, 4, 5	
HCP15	Exception Code	ID	1-2	S			1, 2, 3, 4, 5, 6	
LIN	DRUG IDENTIFICATION		1	S	2410	1		# Loop Repeats change to 1
LIN01	Assigned Identification	AN	1-20	N/U				
LIN02	Product or Service ID Qualifier	ID	2-2	R			N4	
LIN03	National Drug Code	AN	1-48	R				
LIN04	Product/Service ID Qualifier	ID	2-2	N/U				
LIN05	Product/Service ID	AN	1-48	N/U				
LIN06	Product/Service ID Qualifier	ID	2-2	N/U				
LIN07	Product/Service ID	AN	1-48	N/U				
LIN08	Product/Service ID Qualifier	ID	2-2	N/U				
LIN09	Product/Service ID	AN	1-48	N/U				
LIN10	Product/Service ID Qualifier	ID	2-2	N/U				
LIN11	Product/Service ID	AN	1-48	N/U				
LIN12	Product/Service ID Qualifier	ID	2-2	N/U				
LIN13	Product/Service ID	AN	1-48	N/U				
LIN14	Product/Service ID Qualifier	ID	2-2	N/U				
LIN15	Product/Service ID	AN	1-48	N/U				
LIN16	Product/Service ID Qualifier	ID	2-2	N/U				
LIN17	Product/Service ID	AN	1-48	N/U				
LIN18	Product/Service ID Qualifier	ID	2-2	N/U				
LIN19	Product/Service ID	AN	1-48	N/U				
LIN20	Product/Service ID Qualifier	ID	2-2	N/U				
LIN21	Product/Service ID	AN	1-48	N/U				
LIN22	Product/Service ID Qualifier	ID	2-2	N/U				
LIN23	Product/Service ID	AN	1-48	N/U				
LIN24	Product/Service ID Qualifier	ID	2-2	N/U				
LIN25	Product/Service ID	AN	1-48	N/U				
LIN26	Product/Service ID Qualifier	ID	2-2	N/U				
LIN27	Product/Service ID	AN	1-48	N/U				
LIN28	Product/Service ID Qualifier	ID	2-2	N/U				
LIN29	Product/Service ID	AN	1-48	N/U				
LIN30	Product/Service ID Qualifier	ID	2-2	N/U				

Page 86 of 93

INSTITUTIONAL CLAIM

4010A1

Element Identifier	Description	ID	Min. Max.	Usage Reg.	Loop	Loop Repeat	Values
	837-I 4010A1						
LIN31	Product/Service ID	AN	1-48	N/U			
CTP	**DRUG QUANTITY**		1	S	2410		
CTP01	Class of Trade Code	ID	2-2	N/U			
CTP02	Price Identifier Code	ID	3-3	N/U			
CTP03	Unit Price	R	1-17	R			
CTP04	National Drug Unit Count	R	1-15	R			
CTP05	COMPOSITE UNIT OF MEASURE			R			
CTP05-1	Unit or Basis For Measurement Code	ID	2-2	R			F2, GR, ML, UN
CTP05-2	Exponent	R	1-15	N/U			
CTP05-3	Multiplier	R	1-10	N/U			
CTP05-4	Unit or Basis For Measurement Code	ID	2-2	N/U			
CTP05-5	Exponent	R	1-15	N/U			
CTP05-6	Multiplier	R	1-10	N/U			
CTP05-7	Unit or Basis For Measurement Code	ID	2-2	N/U			
CTP05-8	Exponent	R	1-15	N/U			
CTP05-9	Multiplier	R	1-10	N/U			
CTP05-10	Unit or Basis For Measurement Code	ID	2-2	N/U			
CTP05-11	Exponent	R	1-15	N/U			
CTP05-12	Multiplier	R	1-10	N/U			
CTP05-13	Unit or Basis For Measurement Code	ID	2-2	N/U			
CTP05-14	Exponent	R	1-15	N/U			
CTP05-15	Multiplier	R	1-10	N/U			
CTP06	Price Multiplier Qualifier	ID	3-3	N/U			
CTP07	Multiplier	R	1-10	N/U			
CTP08	Monetary Amount	R	1-18	N/U			
CTP09	Basis of Unit Price Code	ID	2-2	N/U			
CTP10	Condition Value	AN	1-10	N/U			
CTP11	Multiple Price Quantity	N0	1-2	N/U			
REF	**PRESCRIPTION NUMBER**		1	S	2410		
REF01	Reference Identification Qualifier	ID	2-3	R			XZ
REF02	Prescription Number	AN	1-30	R			
REF03	Desciption	AN	1-80	N/U			
REF04	REFERENCE IDENTIFIER			N/U			
NM1	**ATTENDING PHYSICIAN NAME**		1	S	2420A	1	

5010

Element Identifier	Description	ID	Min. Max.	Usage Reg.	Loop	Loop Repeat	Values	
	837-I 5010							
LIN31	Product/Service ID	AN	1-48	N/U				
CTP	**DRUG QUANTITY**		1	R	2410			Usage Change to Required
CTP01	Class of Trade Code	ID	2-2	N/U				
CTP02	Price Identifier Code	ID	3-3	N/U				
CTP03	Unit Price	R	1-17	N/U				Usage change to Not Used
CTP04	National Drug Unit Count	R	1-15	R				
CTP05	COMPOSITE UNIT OF MEASURE			R				
CTP05-1	Unit or Basis For Measurement Code	ID	2-2	R			F2, GR, ME, ML, UN	Code Added
CTP05-2	Exponent	R	1-15	N/U				
CTP05-3	Multiplier	R	1-10	N/U				
CTP05-4	Unit or Basis For Measurement Code	ID	2-2	N/U				
CTP05-5	Exponent	R	1-15	N/U				
CTP05-6	Multiplier	R	1-10	N/U				
CTP05-7	Unit or Basis For Measurement Code	ID	2-2	N/U				
CTP05-8	Exponent	R	1-15	N/U				
CTP05-9	Multiplier	R	1-10	N/U				
CTP05-10	Unit or Basis For Measurement Code	ID	2-2	N/U				
CTP05-11	Exponent	R	1-15	N/U				
CTP05-12	Multiplier	R	1-10	N/U				
CTP05-13	Unit or Basis For Measurement Code	ID	2-2	N/U				
CTP05-14	Exponent	R	1-15	N/U				
CTP05-15	Multiplier	R	1-10	N/U				
CTP06	Price Multiplier Qualifier	ID	3-3	N/U				
CTP07	Multiplier	R	1-10	N/U				
CTP08	Monetary Amount	R	1-18	N/U				
CTP09	Basis of Unit Price Code	ID	2-2	N/U				
CTP10	Condition Value	AN	1-10	N/U				
CTP11	Multiple Price Quantity	N0	1-2	N/U				
REF	**PRESCRIPTION OR COMPOUND DRUG ASSOCIATION NUMBER**		1	S	2410			Name Change
REF01	Reference Identification Qualifier	ID	2-3	R			VY, XZ	Code Added
REF02	Prescription Number	AN	1-50	R				Increase from 30 - 50
REF03	Desciption	AN	1-80	N/U				
REF04	REFERENCE IDENTIFIER			N/U				
								Segment Deleted

INSTITUTIONAL CLAIM

4010A1

Element Identifier	Description	ID	Min. Max.	Usage Reg.	Loop	Loop Repeat	Values
	837-I 4010A1						
NM101	Entity Identifier Code	ID	2-3	R			71
NM102	Entity Type Qualifier	ID	1-1	R			1, 2
NM103	Last Name	AN	1-35	R			
NM104	First Name	AN	1-25	S			
NM105	Middle Name	AN	1-25	S			
NM106	Name Prefix	AN	1-10	N/U			
NM107	Name Suffix	AN	1-10	S			
NM108	Identification Code Qualifier	ID	1-2	S			24, 34, XX
NM109	Identifier	AN	2-80	S			
NM110	Entity Relationship Code	ID	2-2	N/U			
NM111	Entity Identifier Code	ID	2-3	N/U			
REF	**ATTENDING PHYSICIAN SECONDARY IDENTIFICATION**		1	S	2420A		
REF01	Reference Identification Qualifier	ID	2-3	R			OB, 1A, 1B, 1C, 1D, 1G, 1H, EI, G2, LU, N5, SY, X5
REF02	Secondary Identifier	AN	1-30	R			
REF03	Description	AN	1-80	N/U			
REF04	REFERENCE IDENTIFIER			S			
NM1	**OPERATING PHYSICIAN NAME**		1	S	2420B	1	
NM101	Entity Identifier Code	ID	2-3	R			72
NM102	Entity Type Qualifier	ID	1-1	R			1
NM103	Last Name	AN	1-35	R			
NM104	First Name	AN	1-25	S			
NM105	Middle Name	AN	1-25	S			
NM106	Name Prefix	AN	1-10	N/U			
NM107	Name Suffix	AN	1-10	S			
NM108	Identification Code Qualifier	ID	1-2	S			24, 34, XX
NM109	Identifier	AN	2-80	S			
NM110	Entity Relationship Code	ID	2-2	N/U			
NM111	Entity Identifier Code	ID	2-3	N/U			
REF	**OPERATING PHYSICIAN SECONDARY IDENTIFICATION**		1	S	2420B		
REF01	Reference Identification Qualifier	ID	2-3	R			OB, 1A, 1B, 1C, 1D, 1G, 1H, EI, G2, LU, N5, SY, X5
REF02	Secondary Identifier	AN	1-30	R			
REF03	Description	AN	1-80	N/U			
REF04	REFERENCE IDENTIFIER			N/U			

5010

Element Identifier	Description	ID	Min. Max.	Usage Reg.	Loop	Loop Repeat	Values	Comments
	837-I 5010							
								Segment Deleted
NM1	**OPERATING PHYSICIAN NAME**		1	S	2420A	1		
NM101	Entity Identifier Code	ID	2-3	R			72	
NM102	Entity Type Qualifier	ID	1-1	R			1	
NM103	Last Name	AN	1-60	R				Increase from 35 - 60
NM104	First Name	AN	1-35	S				Increase from 25 - 35
NM105	Middle Name	AN	1-25	S				
NM106	Name Prefix	AN	1-10	N/U				
NM107	Name Suffix	AN	1-10	S				
NM108	Identification Code Qualifier	ID	1-2	S			XX	Code Deleted
NM109	Identifier	AN	2-80	S				
NM110	Entity Relationship Code	ID	2-2	N/U				
NM111	Entity Identifier Code	ID	2-3	N/U				
NM112	Name Last or Organization Name	AN	1-60	N/U				New Element
REF	**OPERATING PHYSICIAN SECONDARY IDENTIFICATION**		20	S	2420A			# Reeats change to 20
REF01	Reference Identification Qualifier	ID	2-3	R			OB, 1G, G2, LU	Code Change
REF02	Secondary Identifier	AN	1-50	R				Increase from 30 - 50
REF03	Description	AN	1-80	N/U				
REF04	REFERENCE IDENTIFIER			S				Usage change to Siuational

Page 88 of 93

INSTITUTIONAL CLAIM

4010A1

837-I 4010A1

Element Identifier	Description	ID	Min. Max.	Usage Reg.	Loop	Loop Repeat	Values
NM1	OTHER PROVIDER NAME		1	S	2420C	1	
NM101	Entity Identifier Code	ID	2-3	R			73
NM102	Entity Type Qualifier	ID	1-1	R			1, 2
NM103	Other Physician Last Name	AN	1-35	R			
NM104	Other Physician First Name	AN	1-25	S			

5010

837-I 5010

Element Identifier	Description	ID	Min. Max.	Usage Reg.	Loop	Loop Repeat	Values	
REF04-1	Reference Identifier Qualifier	ID	2-3	R			2U	New Element
REF04-2	Idenitifer	AN	1-50	R				New Element
REF04-3	Reference Identification Qualifier	ID	2-3	N/U				New Element
REF04-4	Reference Identification	AN	1-50	N/U				New Element
REF04-5	Reference Identification Qualifier	ID	2-3	N/U				New Element
REF04-6	Reference Identification	AN	1-50	N/U				New Element
NM1	OTHER OPERATING PHYSICIAN NAME		1	S	2420B	1		New Segment
NM101	Entity Identifier Code	ID	2-3	R			ZZ	
NM102	Entity Type Qualifier	ID	1-1	R			1	
NM103	Last Name	AN	1-60	R				
NM104	First Name	AN	1-35	S				
NM105	Middle Name	AN	1-25	S				
NM106	Name Prefix	AN	1-10	N/U				
NM107	Name Suffix	AN	1-10	S				
NM108	Identification Code Qualifier	ID	1-2	S			XX	
NM109	Identifier	AN	2-80	S				
NM110	Entity Relationship Code	ID	2-2	N/U				
NM111	Entity Identifier Code	ID	2-3	N/U				
NM112	Name Last or Organization Name	AN	1-60	N/U				
REF	OTHER OPERATING PHYSICIAN SECONDARY IDENTIFICATION		20	S	2420B			New Segment
REF01	Reference Identification Qualifier	ID	2-3	R			OB, 1G, G2, LU	
REF02	Secondary Identifier	AN	1-50	R				
REF03	Description	AN	1-80	N/U				
REF04	REFERENCE IDENTIFIER			S				
REF04-1	Reference Identifier Qualifier	ID	2-3	R			2U	
REF04-2	Idenitifer	AN	1-50	R				
REF04-3	Reference Identification Qualifier	ID	2-3	N/U				
REF04-4	Reference Identification	AN	1-50	N/U				
REF04-5	Reference Identification Qualifier	ID	2-3	N/U				
REF04-6	Reference Identification	AN	1-50	N/U				
								Segment Deleted

Page 89 of 93

INSTITUTIONAL CLAIM

4010A1

Element Identifier	Description	ID	Min. Max.	Usage Reg.	Loop	Loop Repeat	Values
	837-I 4010A1						
NM105	Middle Name	AN	1-25	S			
NM106	Name Prefix	AN	1-10	N/U			
NM107	Name Suffix	AN	1-10	S			
NM108	Identification Code Qualifier	ID	1-2	R			24, 34, XX
NM109	Identifier	AN	2-80	R			
NM110	Entity Relationship Code	ID	2-2	N/U			
NM111	Entity Identifier Code	ID	2-3	N/U			
REF	**OTHER PROVIDER SECONDARY IDENTIFICATION**		1	S	2420B		
REF01	Reference Identification Qualifier	ID	2-3	R			OB, 1A, 1B, 1C, 1D, 1G, 1H, EI, G2, LU, N5, SY, X5
REF02	Secondary Identifier	AN	1-30	R			
REF03	Description	AN	1-80	N/U			
REF04	REFERENCE IDENTIFIER			S			

5010

Element Identifier	Description	ID	Min. Max.	Usage Reg.	Loop	Loop Repeat	Values	
	837-I 5010							Segment Deleted
NM1	**RENDERING PROVIDER NAME**		1	S	2420C	1		New Segment
NM101	Entity Identifier Code	ID	2-3	R			82	
NM102	Entity Type Qualifier	ID	1-1	R			1	
NM103	Rendering Provider Last or Organization Name	AN	1-60	R				
NM104	Rendering Provider First Name	AN	1-35	S				
NM105	Rendering Provider Middle Name	AN	1-25	S				
NM106	Name Prefix	AN	1-10	N/U				
NM107	Rendering Provider Name Suffix	AN	1-10	S				
NM108	Identification Code Qualifier	ID	1-2	S			XX	
NM109	Rendering Provider Identifier	AN	2-80	S				
NM110	Entity Relationship Code	ID	2-2	N/U				
NM111	Entity Identifier Code	ID	2-3	N/U				
NM112	Name Last or Organization Name	AN	1-60	N/U				
REF	**RENDERING PROVIDER SECONDARY IDENTIFICATION**		20	S	2420C			New Segment
REF01	Reference Identification Qualifier	ID	2-3	R			OB, 1G, G2, LU	
REF02	Rendering Provider Secondary Identifier	AN	1-50	R				
REF03	Description	AN	1-80	N/U				
REF04	REFERENCE IDENTIFIER			S				

Page 90 of 93

INSTITUTIONAL CLAIM

4010A1							
Element Identifier	Description	ID	Min. Max.	Usage Reg.	Loop	Loop Repeat	Values
837-I 4010A1							

5010								
Element Identifier	Description	ID	Min. Max.	Usage Reg.	Loop	Loop Repeat	Values	
837-I 5010								
REF04-1	Reference Identifier Qualifier	ID	2-3	R			2U	
REF04-2	Other Payer Primary Idenitifer	AN	1-50	R				
REF04-3	Reference Identification Qualifier	ID	2-3	N/U				
REF04-4	Reference Identification	AN	1-50	N/U				
REF04-5	Reference Identification Qualifier	ID	2-3	N/U				
REF04-6	Reference Identification	AN	1-50	N/U				
NM1	**REFERRING PROVIDER NAME**		1	S	2420D	1		New Segment
NM101	Entity Identifier Code	ID	2-3	R			DN	
NM102	Entity Type Qualifier	ID	1-1	R			1	
NM103	Referring Provider Last Name	AN	1-60	R				
NM104	Referring Provider First Name	AN	1-35	S				
NM105	Referring Provider Middle Name or Initial	AN	1-25	S				
NM106	Name Prefix	AN	1-10	N/U				
NM107	Referring Provider Name Suffix	AN	1-10	S				
NM108	Identification Code Qualifier	ID	1-2	S			XX	
NM109	Other Payer Primary Identifier	AN	2-80	S				
NM110	Entity Relationship Code	ID	2-2	N/U				
NM111	Entity Identifier Code	ID	2-3	N/U				
NM112	Name Last or Organization Name	AN	1-60	N/U				
REF	**REFERRING PROVIDER SECONDARY IDENTIFICATION**		20	S	2420D			New Segment
REF01	Reference Identification Qualifier	ID	2-3	R			OB, 1G, G2	
REF02	Referring Provider Secondary Identifier	AN	1-50	R				
REF03	Description	AN	1-80	N/U				
REF04	REFERENCE IDENTIFIER			S				
REF04-1	Reference Identifier Qualifier	ID	2-3	R			2U	
REF04-2	Other Payer Primary Idenitifer	AN	1-50	R				
REF04-3	Reference Identification Qualifier	ID	2-3	N/U				
REF04-4	Reference Identification	AN	1-50	N/U				
REF04-5	Reference Identification Qualifier	ID	2-3	N/U				

Page 91 of 93

INSTITUTIONAL CLAIM

4010A1

Element Identifier	Description	ID	Min. Max.	Usage Req.	Loop	Loop Repeat	Values
	837-I 4010A1						
SVD	**LINE ADJUDICATION INFORMATION**		1	S	2430	25	
SVD01	Payer Identifier	AN	2-80	R			
SVD02	Service Line Paid Amount	R	1-18	R			
SVD03	COMPOSITE MEDICAL PROCEDURE IDENTIFIER			R			
SVD03-1	Product or Service ID Qualifier	ID	2-2	R			HC, IV, ZZ
SVD03-2	Procedure Code	AN	1-48	R			
SVD03-3	Procedure Modifier	AN	2-2	S			
SVD03-4	Procedure Modifier	AN	2-2	S			
SVD03-5	Procedure Modifier	AN	2-2	S			
SVD03-6	Procedure Modifier	AN	2-2	S			
SVD03-7	Procedure Code Description	AN	1-80	S			
SVD04	Product or Service ID	AN	1-48	R			
SVD05	Paid Service Unit Count	R	1-15	R			
SVD06	Bundled or Unbundled Line Number	N0	1-6	S			
CAS	**LINE ADJUSTMENT**		99	S	2430		
CAS01	Claim Adjustment Group Code	ID	1-2	R			CO, CR, OA, PI, PR
CAS02	Adjustment Reason Code	ID	1-5	R			
CAS03	Adjustment Amount	R	1-18	R			
CAS04	Adjustment Quantity	R	1-15	S			
CAS05	Adjustment Reason Code	ID	1-5	S			
CAS06	Adjustment Amount	R	1-18	S			
CAS07	Adjustment Quantity	R	1-15	S			
CAS08	Adjustment Reason Code	ID	1-5	S			
CAS09	Adjustment Amount	R	1-18	S			
CAS10	Adjustment Quantity	R	1-15	S			
CAS11	Adjustment Reason Code	ID	1-5	S			
CAS12	Adjustment Amount	R	1-18	S			
CAS13	Adjustment Quantity	R	1-15	S			
CAS14	Adjustment Reason Code	ID	1-5	S			
CAS15	Adjustment Amount	R	1-18	S			
CAS16	Adjustment Quantity	R	1-15	S			
CAS17	Adjustment Reason Code	ID	1-5	S			
CAS18	Adjustment Amount	R	1-18	S			
CAS19	Adjustment Quantity	R	1-15	S			
DTP	**SERVICE ADJUDICATION DATE**		1	S	2430		

5010

Element Identifier	Description	ID	Min. Max.	Usage Req.	Loop	Loop Repeat	Values	
	837-I 5010							
REF04-6	Reference Identification	AN	1-50	N/U				
SVD	**LINE ADJUDICATION INFORMATION**		1	S	2430	15		
SVD01	Other Payer Primary Identifier	AN	2-80	R				Name Change
SVD02	Service Line Paid Amount	R	1-18	R				
SVD03	COMPOSITE MEDICAL PROCEDURE IDENTIFIER			R				
SVD03-1	Product or Service ID Qualifier	ID	2-2	R			ER, HC, HP, IV, WK	Code Change
SVD03-2	Procedure Code	AN	1-48	R				
SVD03-3	Procedure Modifier	AN	2-2	S				
SVD03-4	Procedure Modifier	AN	2-2	S				
SVD03-5	Procedure Modifier	AN	2-2	S				
SVD03-6	Procedure Modifier	AN	2-2	S				
SVD03-7	Procedure Code Description	AN	1-80	S				
SVD03-8	Product/Service ID	AN	1-48	N/U				New Element Usage change to Not Used
SVD04	Product or Service ID	AN	1-48	N/U				
SVD05	Paid Service Unit Count	R	1-15	R				
SVD06	Bundled or Unbundled Line Number	N0	1-6	S				
CAS	**LINE ADJUSTMENT**		5	S	2430			
CAS01	Claim Adjustment Group Code	ID	1-2	R			CO, CR, OA, PI, PR	
CAS02	Adjustment Reason Code	ID	1-5	R				
CAS03	Adjustment Amount	R	1-18	R				
CAS04	Adjustment Quantity	R	1-15	S				
CAS05	Adjustment Reason Code	ID	1-5	S				
CAS06	Adjustment Amount	R	1-18	S				
CAS07	Adjustment Quantity	R	1-15	S				
CAS08	Adjustment Reason Code	ID	1-5	S				
CAS09	Adjustment Amount	R	1-18	S				
CAS10	Adjustment Quantity	R	1-15	S				
CAS11	Adjustment Reason Code	ID	1-5	S				
CAS12	Adjustment Amount	R	1-18	S				
CAS13	Adjustment Quantity	R	1-15	S				
CAS14	Adjustment Reason Code	ID	1-5	S				
CAS15	Adjustment Amount	R	1-18	S				
CAS16	Adjustment Quantity	R	1-15	S				
CAS17	Adjustment Reason Code	ID	1-5	S				
CAS18	Adjustment Amount	R	1-18	S				
CAS19	Adjustment Quantity	R	1-15	S				
								Name Change Usage change to Required
DTP	**LINE CHECK OR REMITTANCE DATE**		1	R	2430			

Page 92 of 93

INSTITUTIONAL CLAIM

4010A1

837-I 4010A1

Element Identifier	Description	ID	Min. Max.	Usage Reg.	Loop	Loop Repeat	Values
DTP01	Date Time Qualifier	ID	3-3	R			573
DTP02	Date Time Period Format Qualifier	ID	2-3	R			D8
DTP03	Adjudication or Payment Date	AN	1-35	R			CCYYMMDD
SE	**TRANSACTION SET TRAILER**		1	R	___	>1	
SE01	Transaction Segment Count	N0	1-10	R			
SE02	Transaction Set Control Number	AN	4-9	R			
GE	**FUNCTION GROUP TRAILER**		1	R	___	1	
GE01	Number of Transaction Sets Included	N0	1-6	R			
GE02	Group Control Number	N0	1-9	R			
IEA	**INTERCHANGE CONTROL TRAILER**		1	R	___	1	
IEA01	Number of Included Functional Groups	N0	1-5	R			
IEA02	Interchange Control Number	N0	9-9	R			

5010

837-I 5010

Element Identifier	Description	ID	Min. Max.	Usage Reg.	Loop	Loop Repeat	Values	
DTP01	Date Time Qualifier	ID	3-3	R			573	
DTP02	Date Time Period Format Qualifier	ID	2-3	R			D8	
DTP03	Adjudication or Payment Date	AN	1-35	R			CCYYMMDD	
AMT	**REMAINING PATIENT LIABILITY**		1	S	2430			New Segment
AMT01	Amount Qualifier Code	ID	1-3	R			EAF	
AMT02	Remaining Patient Liability Amount	R	1-18	R				
AMT03	Credit/Debit Flag Code	ID	1-1	N/U				
SE	**TRANSACTION SET TRAILER**		1	R	___	>1		
SE01	Transaction Segment Count	N0	1-10	R				
SE02	Transaction Set Control Number	AN	4-9	R				
GE	**FUNCTION GROUP TRAILER**		1	R	___	1		
GE01	Number of Transaction Sets Included	N0	1-6	R				
GE02	Group Control Number	N0	1-9	R				
IEA	**INTERCHANGE CONTROL TRAILER**		1	R	___	1		
IEA01	Number of Included Functional Groups	N0	1-5	R				
IEA02	Interchange Control Number	N0	9-9	R				

Appendix D: Professional Claim 4010A to 5010

PROFESSIONAL CLAIM

4010A1

837-P 4010A1

Element Identifier	Description	ID	Min. Max.	Usage Req.	Loop	Loop Repeat	Values
ISA	**INTERCHANGE CONTROL HEADER**		1	R	___	1	
ISA01	Authorization Information Qualifier	ID	2-2	R			00, 03
ISA02	Authorization Information	AN	10-10	R			
ISA03	Security Information Qualifier	ID	2-2	R			00, 01
ISA04	Security Information	AN	10-10	R			
ISA05	Interchange ID Qualifier	ID	2-2	R			01, 14, 20, 27, 28, 29, 30, 33, ZZ
ISA06	Interchange Sender ID	AN	15-15	R			
ISA07	Interchange ID Qualifier	ID	2-2	R			01, 14, 20, 27, 28, 29, 30, 33, ZZ
ISA08	Interchange Receiver ID	AN	15-15	R			
ISA09	Interchange Date	DT	6-6	R			YYMMDD
ISA10	Interchange Time	TM	4-4	R			HHMM
ISA11	Interchange Control Standards ID	ID	1-1	R			U
ISA12	Interchange Control Version Number	ID	5-5	R			00401
ISA13	Interchange Control Number	N0	9-9	R			
ISA14	Acknowledgement Requested	ID	1-1	R			0, 1
ISA15	Usage Indicator	ID	1-1	R			P, T
ISA16	Component Element Separator	AN	1-1	R			
GS	**FUNCTIONAL GROUP HEADER**		1	R	___	>1	
GS01	Functional Identifier Code	ID	2-2	R			HC
GS02	Application Sender Code	AN	2-15	R			
GS03	Application Receiver Code	AN	2-15	R			
GS04	Date	DT	8-8	R			CCYYMMDD
GS05	Time	TM	4-8	R			HHMMSSDD
GS06	Group Control Number	N0	1-9	R			
GS07	Responsible Agency Code	ID	1-2	R			X
GS08	Version Identifier Code	AN	1-12	R			004010X098A1

5010

837-P 5010

Element Identifier	Description	ID	Min. Max.	Usage Req.	Loop	Loop Repeat	Values	
ISA	**INTERCHANGE CONTROL HEADER**		1	R	___	1		
ISA01	Authorization Information Qualifier	ID	2-2	R			00, 03	
ISA02	Authorization Information	AN	10-10	R				
ISA03	Security Information Qualifier	ID	2-2	R			00, 01	
ISA04	Security Information	AN	10-10	R				
ISA05	Interchange ID Qualifier	ID	2-2	R			01, 14, 20, 27, 28, 29, 30, 33, ZZ	
ISA06	Interchange Sender ID	AN	15-15	R				
ISA07	Interchange ID Qualifier	ID	2-2	R			01, 14, 20, 27, 28, 29, 30, 33, ZZ	
ISA08	Interchange Receiver ID	AN	15-15	R				
ISA09	Interchange Date	DT	6-6	R			YYMMDD	
ISA10	Interchange Time	TM	4-4	R			HHMM	
ISA11	Interchange Control Standards ID		1-1	R				
ISA12	Interchange Control Version Number	ID	5-5	R			00501	
ISA13	Interchange Control Number	N0	9-9	R				
ISA14	Acknowledgement Requested	ID	1-1	R			0, 1	
ISA15	Usage Indicator	ID	1-1	R			P, T	
ISA16	Component Element Separator	AN	1-1	R				
GS	**FUNCTIONAL GROUP HEADER**		1	R	___	1		
GS01	Functional Identifier Code	ID	2-2	R				
GS02	Application Sender Code	AN	2-15	R				
GS03	Application Receiver Code	AN	2-15	R				
GS04	Date	DT	8-8	R			CCYYMMDD	
GS05	Time	TM	4-8	R			HHMM	
GS06	Group Control Number	N0	1-9	R				
GS07	Responsible Agency Code	ID	1-2	R			X	
GS08	Version Identifier Code	AN	1-12	R			005010X222	Code Change

Page 1 of 93

PROFESSIONAL CLAIM

<table>
<tr><td colspan="7" align="center">**4010A1**</td><td colspan="7" align="center">**5010**</td><td></td></tr>
<tr>
<td>Element Identifier</td><td>Description</td><td>ID</td><td>Min. Max.</td><td>Usage Req.</td><td>Loop</td><td>Loop Repeat</td><td>Values</td>
<td>Element Identifier</td><td>Description</td><td>ID</td><td>Min. Max.</td><td>Usage Req.</td><td>Loop</td><td>Loop Repeat</td><td>Values</td>
<td></td>
</tr>
<tr><td colspan="8" align="center">837-P 4010A1</td><td colspan="8" align="center">837-P 5010</td><td></td></tr>
<tr>
<td>ST</td><td>TRANSACTION SET HEADER</td><td></td><td>1</td><td>R</td><td>___</td><td>>1</td><td></td>
<td>ST</td><td>TRANSACTION SET HEADER</td><td></td><td>1</td><td>R</td><td>___</td><td>>1</td><td></td>
<td></td>
</tr>
<tr>
<td>ST01</td><td>Transaction Set Identifier Code</td><td>ID</td><td>3-3</td><td>R</td><td></td><td></td><td>837</td>
<td>ST01</td><td>Transaction Set Identifier Code</td><td>ID</td><td>3-3</td><td>R</td><td></td><td></td><td>837</td>
<td></td>
</tr>
<tr>
<td>ST02</td><td>Transaction Set Control Number</td><td>AN</td><td>4-9</td><td>R</td><td></td><td></td><td></td>
<td>ST02</td><td>Transaction Set Control Number</td><td>AN</td><td>4-9</td><td>R</td><td></td><td></td><td></td>
<td></td>
</tr>
<tr>
<td></td><td></td><td></td><td></td><td></td><td></td><td></td><td></td>
<td>ST03</td><td>Implementation Convention Reference</td><td>AN</td><td>1-35</td><td>R</td><td></td><td></td><td></td>
<td>New Element</td>
</tr>
<tr>
<td>BHT</td><td>BEGINNING OF HIERARCHICAL TRANSACTION</td><td></td><td>1</td><td>R</td><td>___</td><td>1</td><td></td>
<td>BHT</td><td>BEGINNING OF HIERARCHICAL TRANSACTION</td><td></td><td>1</td><td>R</td><td>___</td><td>1</td><td></td>
<td></td>
</tr>
<tr>
<td>BHT01</td><td>Hierarchical Structure Code</td><td>ID</td><td>4-4</td><td>R</td><td></td><td></td><td>0019</td>
<td>BHT01</td><td>Hierarchical Structure Code</td><td>ID</td><td>4-4</td><td>R</td><td></td><td></td><td>0019</td>
<td></td>
</tr>
<tr>
<td>BHT02</td><td>Transaction Set Purpose Code</td><td>ID</td><td>2-2</td><td>R</td><td></td><td></td><td>00, 18</td>
<td>BHT02</td><td>Transaction Set Purpose Code</td><td>ID</td><td>2-2</td><td>R</td><td></td><td></td><td>00, 18</td>
<td></td>
</tr>
<tr>
<td>BHT03</td><td>Originator Application Transaction ID</td><td>AN</td><td>1-30</td><td>R</td><td></td><td></td><td></td>
<td>BHT03</td><td>Originator Application Transaction ID</td><td>AN</td><td>1-50</td><td>R</td><td></td><td></td><td></td>
<td></td>
</tr>
<tr>
<td>BHT04</td><td>Transaction Set Creation Date</td><td>DT</td><td>8-8</td><td>R</td><td></td><td></td><td>CCYYMMDD</td>
<td>BHT04</td><td>Transaction Set Creation Date</td><td>DT</td><td>8-8</td><td>R</td><td></td><td></td><td>CCYYMMDD</td>
<td></td>
</tr>
<tr>
<td>BHT05</td><td>Transaction Set Creation Time</td><td>TM</td><td>4-8</td><td>R</td><td></td><td></td><td>HHMM, HHMMSS, HHMMSSD, HHMMSSDD</td>
<td>BHT05</td><td>Transaction Set Creation Time</td><td>TM</td><td>4-8</td><td>R</td><td></td><td></td><td>HHMM, HHMMSS, HHMMSSD, HHMMSSDD</td>
<td></td>
</tr>
<tr>
<td>BHT06</td><td>Claim or Encounter ID</td><td>ID</td><td>2-2</td><td>R</td><td></td><td></td><td>CH, RP</td>
<td>BHT06</td><td>Claim or Encounter ID</td><td>ID</td><td>2-2</td><td>R</td><td></td><td></td><td>31, CH, RP</td>
<td></td>
</tr>
<tr>
<td>REF</td><td>TRANSMISSION TYPE IDENTIFICATION</td><td></td><td>1</td><td>R</td><td>___</td><td>1</td><td></td>
<td></td><td></td><td></td><td></td><td></td><td></td><td></td><td></td>
<td>Segment Deleted</td>
</tr>
<tr>
<td>REF01</td><td>Reference Identification Qualifier</td><td>ID</td><td>2-3</td><td>R</td><td></td><td></td><td>87</td>
<td></td><td></td><td></td><td></td><td></td><td></td><td></td><td></td>
<td></td>
</tr>
<tr>
<td>REF02</td><td>Transmission Type Code</td><td>AN</td><td>1-30</td><td>R</td><td></td><td></td><td>004010X098A1, 004010X098DA1</td>
<td></td><td></td><td></td><td></td><td></td><td></td><td></td><td></td>
<td></td>
</tr>
<tr>
<td>REF03</td><td>Description</td><td>AN</td><td>1-80</td><td>N/U</td><td></td><td></td><td></td>
<td></td><td></td><td></td><td></td><td></td><td></td><td></td><td></td>
<td></td>
</tr>
<tr>
<td>REF04</td><td>REFERENCE IDENTIFIER</td><td></td><td></td><td>N/U</td><td></td><td></td><td></td>
<td></td><td></td><td></td><td></td><td></td><td></td><td></td><td></td>
<td></td>
</tr>
<tr>
<td>NM1</td><td>SUBMITTER NAME</td><td></td><td>1</td><td>R</td><td>1000A</td><td>1</td><td></td>
<td>NM1</td><td>SUBMITTER NAME</td><td></td><td>1</td><td>R</td><td>1000A</td><td>1</td><td></td>
<td></td>
</tr>
<tr>
<td>NM101</td><td>Entity Identifier Code</td><td>ID</td><td>2-3</td><td>R</td><td></td><td></td><td>41</td>
<td>NM101</td><td>Entity Identifier Code</td><td>ID</td><td>2-3</td><td>R</td><td></td><td></td><td>41</td>
<td></td>
</tr>
<tr>
<td>NM102</td><td>Entity Type Qualifier</td><td>ID</td><td>1-1</td><td>R</td><td></td><td></td><td>1, 2</td>
<td>NM102</td><td>Entity Type Qualifier</td><td>ID</td><td>1-1</td><td>R</td><td></td><td></td><td>1, 2</td>
<td></td>
</tr>
<tr>
<td>NM103</td><td>Submitter Last or Organization Name</td><td>AN</td><td>1-35</td><td>R</td><td></td><td></td><td></td>
<td>NM103</td><td>Submitter Last or Organization Name</td><td>AN</td><td>1-60</td><td>R</td><td></td><td></td><td></td>
<td>Increase from 35 - 60</td>
</tr>
<tr>
<td>NM104</td><td>Submitter First Name</td><td>AN</td><td>1-25</td><td>S</td><td></td><td></td><td></td>
<td>NM104</td><td>Submitter First Name</td><td>AN</td><td>1-35</td><td>S</td><td></td><td></td><td></td>
<td>Increase from 25 - 35</td>
</tr>
<tr>
<td>NM105</td><td>Submitter Middle Name</td><td>AN</td><td>1-25</td><td>S</td><td></td><td></td><td></td>
<td>NM105</td><td>Submitter Middle Name</td><td>AN</td><td>1-25</td><td>S</td><td></td><td></td><td></td>
<td></td>
</tr>
<tr>
<td>NM106</td><td>Name Prefix</td><td>AN</td><td>1-10</td><td>N/U</td><td></td><td></td><td></td>
<td>NM106</td><td>Name Prefix</td><td>AN</td><td>1-10</td><td>N/U</td><td></td><td></td><td></td>
<td></td>
</tr>
<tr>
<td>NM107</td><td>Name Suffix</td><td>AN</td><td>1-10</td><td></td><td></td><td></td><td></td>
<td>NM107</td><td>Name Suffix</td><td>AN</td><td>1-10</td><td>N/U</td><td></td><td></td><td></td>
<td></td>
</tr>
<tr>
<td>NM108</td><td>Identification Code Qualifier</td><td>ID</td><td>1-2</td><td>R</td><td></td><td></td><td>46</td>
<td>NM108</td><td>Identification Code Qualifier</td><td>ID</td><td>1-2</td><td>R</td><td></td><td></td><td>46</td>
<td></td>
</tr>
<tr>
<td>NM109</td><td>Submitter Identifier</td><td>AN</td><td>2-80</td><td>R</td><td></td><td></td><td></td>
<td>NM109</td><td>Submitter Identifier</td><td>AN</td><td>2-80</td><td>R</td><td></td><td></td><td></td>
<td></td>
</tr>
<tr>
<td>NM110</td><td>Entity Relationship Code</td><td>ID</td><td>2-2</td><td>N/U</td><td></td><td></td><td></td>
<td>NM110</td><td>Entity Relationship Code</td><td>ID</td><td>2-2</td><td>N/U</td><td></td><td></td><td></td>
<td></td>
</tr>
<tr>
<td>NM111</td><td>Entity Identifier Code</td><td>ID</td><td>2-3</td><td>N/U</td><td></td><td></td><td></td>
<td>NM111</td><td>Entity Identifier Code</td><td>ID</td><td>2-3</td><td>N/U</td><td></td><td></td><td></td>
<td></td>
</tr>
</table>

Page 2 of 93

PROFESSIONAL CLAIM

4010A1

Element Identifier	Description	ID	Min. Max.	Usage Reg.	Loop	Loop Repeat	Values
837-P 4010A1							
PER	**SUBMITTER EDI CONTACT INFORMATION**		**2**	**R**	1000A		
PER01	Contact Function Code	ID	2-2	R			IC
PER02	Submitter Contact Name	AN	1-60	R			
PER03	Communication Number Qualifier	ID	2-2	R			ED, EM, FX. TE
PER04	Communication Number	AN	1-80	R			
PER05	Communication Number Qualifier	ID	2-2	S			ED, EM, EX, FX, TE
PER06	Communication Number	AN	1-80	S			
PER07	Communication Number Qualifier	ID	2-2	S			ED, EM, EX, FX, TE
PER08	Communication Number	AN	1-80	S			
PER09	Contact Inquiry Reference	AN	1-20	N/U			
NM1	**RECEIVER NAME**		**1**	**R**	1000B	1	
NM101	Entity Identifier Code	ID	2-3	R			40
NM102	Entity Type Qualifier	ID	1-1	R			2
NM103	Receiver Name	AN	1-35	R			
NM104	Name First	AN	1-25	N/U			
NM105	Name Middle	AN	1-25	N/U			
NM106	Name Prefix	AN	1-10	N/U			
NM107	Name Suffix	AN	1-10	N/U			
NM108	Identification Code Qualifier	ID	1-2	R			46
NM109	Receiver Primary Identifier	AN	2-80	R			
NM110	Entity Relationship Code	ID	2-2	N/U			
NM111	Entity Identifier Code	ID	2-3	N/U			
HL	**BILLING/PAY-TO PROVIDER HIERARCHICAL LEVEL**		**1**	**R**	2000A	>1	
HL01	Hierarchical ID Number	AN	1-12	R			
HL02	Hierarchical Parent ID Number	AN	1-12	N/U			
HL03	Hierarchical Level Code	ID	1-2	R			20
HL04	Hierarchical Child Code	ID	1-1	R			1
PRV	**BILLING/PAY-TO PROVIDER SPECIALTY INFORMATION**		**1**	**S**	2000A		
PRV01	Provider Code	ID	1-3	R			BI, PT
PRV02	Reference Identification Qualifier	ID	2-3	R			ZZ

5010

Element Identifier	Description	ID	Min. Max.	Usage Reg.	Loop	Loop Repeat	Values	Notes
NM112	Name Last or Organization Name	AN	1-60	N/U				NewElement
837-P 5010								
PER	**SUBMITTER EDI CONTACT INFORMATION**		**2**	**R**	1000A			
PER01	Contact Function Code	ID	2-2	R			IC	
PER02	Submitter Contact Name	AN	1-60	S				
PER03	Communication Number Qualifier	ID	2-2	R			EM, FX. TE	Code Deleted
PER04	Communication Number	AN	1-256	R				Increase from 80 - 256
PER05	Communication Number Qualifier	ID	2-2	S			EM, EX, FX, TE	Code Deleted
PER06	Communication Number	AN	1-256	S				Increase from 80 - 256
PER07	Communication Number Qualifier	ID	2-2	S			EM, EX, FX, TE	Code Deleted
PER08	Communication Number	AN	1-256	S				Increase from 80 - 256
PER09	Contact Inquiry Reference	AN	1-20	N/U				
NM1	**RECEIVER NAME**		**1**	**R**	1000B	1		
NM101	Entity Identifier Code	ID	2-3	R			40	
NM102	Entity Type Qualifier	ID	1-1	R			2	
NM103	Receiver Name	AN	1-60	R				Increase from 35 - 60
NM104	Name First	AN	1-35	N/U				Increase from 25 - 35
NM105	Name Middle	AN	1-25	N/U				
NM106	Name Prefix	AN	1-10	N/U				
NM107	Name Suffix	AN	1-10	N/U				
NM108	Identification Code Qualifier	ID	1-2	R			46	
NM109	Receiver Primary Identifier	AN	2-80	R				
NM110	Entity Relationship Code	ID	2-2	N/U				
NM111	Entity Identifier Code	ID	2-3	N/U				
NM112	Name Last or Organization Name	AN	1-60	N/U				New Element
HL	**BILLING PROVIDER HIERARCHICAL LEVEL**		**1**	**R**	2000A	>1		Name Change
HL01	Hierarchical ID Number	AN	1-12	R				
HL02	Hierarchical Parent ID Number	AN	1-12	N/U				
HL03	Hierarchical Level Code	ID	1-2	R			20	
HL04	Hierarchical Child Code	ID	1-1	R			1	
PRV	**BILLING PROVIDER SPECIALTY INFORMATION**		**1**	**S**	2000A			Name Change
PRV01	Provider Code	ID	1-3	R			BI	
PRV02	Reference Identification Qualifier	ID	2-3	R			PXC	

Page 3 of 93

PROFESSIONAL CLAIM

4010A1

837-P 4010A1

Element Identifier	Description	ID	Min. Max.	Usage Reg.	Loop	Loop Repeat	Values
PRV03	Provider Taxonomy Code	AN	1-30	R			
PRV04	State or Province Code	ID	2-2	N/U			
PRV05	PROVIDER SPECIALTY INFORMATION			N/U			
PRV06	Provider Organization Code	ID	3-3	N/U			
CUR	FOREIGN CURRENCY INFORMATION		1	S	2000A		
CUR01	Entity Identifier Code	ID	2-3	R			85
CUR02	Currency Code	ID	3-3	R			
CUR03	Exchange Rate	R	4-10	N/U			
CUR04	Entity Identifier Code	ID	2-3	N/U			
CUR05	Currency Code	ID	3-3	N/U			
CUR06	Currency Market/Exchange Code	ID	3-3	N/U			
CUR07	Date/Time Qualifier	ID	3-3	N/U			
CUR08	Date	DT	8-8	N/U			
CUR09	Time	TM	4-8	N/U			
CUR10	Date/Time Qualifier	ID	3-3	N/U			
CUR11	Date	DT	8-8	N/U			
CUR12	Time	TM	4-8	N/U			
CUR13	Date/Time Qualifier	ID	3-3	N/U			
CUR14	Date	DT	8-8	N/U			
CUR15	Time	TM	4-8	N/U			
CUR16	Date/Time Qualifier	ID	3-3	N/U			
CUR17	Date	DT	8-8	N/U			
CUR18	Time	TM	4-8	N/U			
CUR19	Date/Time Qualifier	ID	3-3	N/U			
CUR20	Date	DT	8-8	N/U			
CUR21	Time	TM	4-8	N/U			
NM1	Billing Provider Name Suffix		1	R	2010AA	1	
NM101	Entity Identifier Code	ID	2-3	R			85
NM102	Entity Type Qualifier	ID	1-1	R			1, 2
NM103	Billing Provider Last or Organizational Name	AN	1-35	R			
NM104	Billing Provider First Name	AN	1-25	S			
NM105	Billing Provider Middle Name	AN	1-25	S			
NM106	Name Prefix	AN	1-10	N/U			
NM107	Billing Provider Name Suffix	AN	1-10	S			
NM108	Identification Code Qualifier	ID	1-2	R			24, 34, XX
NM109	Billing Provider Identifier	AN	2-80	R			
NM110	Entity Relationship Code	ID	2-2	N/U			

5010

837-P 5010

Element Identifier	Description	ID	Min. Max.	Usage Reg.	Loop	Loop Repeat	Values	Notes
PRV03	Provider Taxonomy Code	AN	1-50	R				Increase 30 - 50
PRV04	State or Province Code	ID	2-2	N/U				
PRV05	PROVIDER SPECIALTY INFORMATION			N/U				
PRV06	Provider Organization Code	ID	3-3	N/U				
CUR	FOREIGN CURRENCY INFORMATION		1	S	2000A			
CUR01	Entity Identifier Code	ID	2-3	R			85	
CUR02	Currency Code	ID	3-3	R				
CUR03	Exchange Rate	R	4-10	N/U				
CUR04	Entity Identifier Code	ID	2-3	N/U				
CUR05	Currency Code	ID	3-3	N/U				
CUR06	Currency Market/Exchange Code	ID	3-3	N/U				
CUR07	Date/Time Qualifier	ID	3-3	N/U				
CUR08	Date	DT	8-8	N/U				
CUR09	Time	TM	4-8	N/U				
CUR10	Date/Time Qualifier	ID	3-3	N/U				
CUR11	Date	DT	8-8	N/U				
CUR12	Time	TM	4-8	N/U				
CUR13	Date/Time Qualifier	ID	3-3	N/U				
CUR14	Date	DT	8-8	N/U				
CUR15	Time	TM	4-8	N/U				
CUR16	Date/Time Qualifier	ID	3-3	N/U				
CUR17	Date	DT	8-8	N/U				
CUR18	Time	TM	4-8	N/U				
CUR19	Date/Time Qualifier	ID	3-3	N/U				
CUR20	Date	DT	8-8	N/U				
CUR21	Time	TM	4-8	N/U				
NM1	Billing Provider Name		1	R	2010AA	1		Name Change
NM101	Entity Identifier Code	ID	2-3	R			85	
NM102	Entity Type Qualifier	ID	1-1	R			1, 2	
NM103	Billing Provider Last or Organizational Name	AN	1-60	R				Increase from 35 - 60
NM104	Billing Provider First Name	AN	1-35	S				Increase from 25 - 35
NM105	Billing Provider Middle Name	AN	1-25	S				
NM106	Name Prefix	AN	1-10	N/U				
NM107	Billing Provider Name Suffix	AN	1-10	S				Usage changed to Situational
NM108	Identification Code Qualifier	ID	1-2	S			XX	Code Deleted Usage changed to Situational
NM109	Billing Provider Identifier	AN	2-80	S				Usage changed to Situational
NM110	Entity Relationship Code	ID	2-2	N/U				

PROFESSIONAL CLAIM

	4010A1						
Element Identifier	Description	ID	Min. Max.	Usage Reg.	Loop	Loop Repeat	Values
	837-P 4010A1						
NM111	Entity Identifier Code	ID	2-3	N/U			
N3	**BILLING PROVIDER ADDRESS**		1	R	2010AA		
N301	Billing Provider Address Line	AN	1-55	R			
N302	Billing Provider Address Line	AN	1-55	S			
N4	**BILLING PROVIDER CITY/STATE/ZIP CODE**		1	R	2010AA		
N401	Billing Provider City Name	AN	2-30	R			
N402	Billing Provider State or Province Code	ID	2-2	R			
N403	Billing Provider Postal Zone or ZIP Code	ID	3-15	R			
N404	Country Code	ID	2-3	S			
N405	Location Qualifier	ID	1-2	N/U			
N406	Location Identifier	AN	1-30	N/U			
REF	**BILLING PROVIDER SECONDARY IDENTIFICATION**		8	S	2010AA		
REF01	Reference Identification Qualifier	ID	2-3	R			0B, 1A, 1B, 1C, 1D, 1G, 1H, 1J, B3, BQ, EI, FH, G2, G5, LU, SY, U3, X5
REF02	Billing Provider Additional Identifier	AN	1-30	R			
REF03	Description	AN	1-80	N/U			
REF04	REFERENCE IDENTIFIER			N/U			
REF	**CREDIT/DEBIT CARD BILLING INFORMATION**		8	S	2010AA		

	5010							
Element Identifier	Description	ID	Min. Max.	Usage Reg.	Loop	Loop Repeat	Values	
	837-P 5010							
NM111	Entity Identifier Code	ID	2-3	N/U				
NM112	Name Last or Organization Name	AN	1-60	N/U				New Element
N3	**BILLING PROVIDER ADDRESS**		1	R	2010AA			
N301	Billing Provider Address Line	AN	1-55	R				
N302	Billing Provider Address Line	AN	1-55	S				
N4	**BILLING PROVIDER CITY/STATE/ZIP CODE**		1	R	2010AA			
N401	Billing Provider City Name	AN	2-30	R				
N402	Billing Provider State or Province Code	ID	2-2	S				Usage changed to Situational
N403	Billing Provider Postal Zone or ZIP Code	ID	3-15	S				Usage changed to Situational
N404	Country Code	ID	2-3	S				
N405	Location Qualifier	ID	1-2	N/U				
N406	Location Identifier	AN	1-30	N/U				
N407	Country Subdivision Code	ID	1-3	S				New Element
REF	**BILLING PROVIDER TAX IDENTIFICATION**		1	R	2010AA			Name Change Usage changed to Required
REF01	Reference Identification Qualifier	ID	2-3	R			EI, SY	Code Deleted
REF02	Billing Provider Additional Identifier	AN	1-50	R				Increase from 30 - 50
REF03	Description	AN	1-80	N/U				
REF04	REFERENCE IDENTIFIER			N/U				
REF04-1	Reference Identifier Qualifier	ID	2-3	N/U				New Element
REF04-2	Other Payer Primary Idenitifer	AN	1-50	N/U				New Element
REF04-3	Reference Identification Qualifier	ID	2-3	N/U				New Element
REF04-4	Reference Identification	AN	1-50	N/U				New Element
REF04-5	Reference Identification Qualifier	ID	2-3	N/U				New Element
REF04-6	Reference Identification	AN	1-50	N/U				New Element
REF	**BILLING PROVIDER UPIN/LICENSE INFORMATION**		2	S	2010AA			Name Change

PROFESSIONAL CLAIM

Element Identifier	Description	ID	Min. Max.	Usage Req.	Loop	Loop Repeat	Values
	4010A1						
	837-P 4010A1						
REF01	Reference Identification Qualifier	ID	2-3	R			06, 8U, EM, IJ, LU, RB, ST, TT
REF02	Billing Provider Credit Card Identifier	AN	1-30	R			
REF03	Description	AN	1-80	N/U			
REF04	REFERENCE IDENTIFIER			N/U			
PER	**BILLING PROVIDER CONTACT INFORMATION**		2	S	2010AA		
PER01	Contact Function Code	ID	2-2	R			IC
PER02	Billing Provider Contact Name	AN	1-60	R			
PER03	Communication Number Qualifier	ID	2-2	R			EM, FX, TE
PER04	Communication Number	AN	1-80	R			
PER05	Communication Number Qualifier	ID	2-2	S			EM, EX, FX, TE
PER06	Communication Number	AN	1-80	S			
PER07	Communication Number Qualifier	ID	2-2	S			EM, EX, FX, TE
PER08	Communication Number	AN	1-80	S			
PER09	Contact Inquiry Reference	AN	1-20	N/U			
NM1	**PAY-TO PROVIDER NAME**		1	S	2010AB	1	
NM101	Entity Identifier Code	ID	2-3	R			87
NM102	Entity Type Qualifier	ID	1-1	R			1, 2
NM103	Pay-to Provider Last or Organization Name	AN	1-35	R			
NM104	Pay-to Provider First Name	AN	1-25	S			
NM105	Pay-to Provider Middle Name	AN	1-25	S			
NM106	Name Prefix	AN	1-10	N/U			
NM107	Pay-to Provider Name Suffix	AN	1-10	S			

Element Identifier	Description	ID	Min. Max.	Usage Req.	Loop	Loop Repeat	Values	
	5010							
	837-P 5010							
REF01	Reference Identification Qualifier	ID	2-3	R			0B, 1G	Code Deleted
REF02	Billing Provider Additional Identifier	AN	1-50	R				Increase from 30 - 50
REF03	Description	AN	1-80	N/U				
REF04	REFERENCE IDENTIFIER			N/U				New Element
REF04-1	Reference Identifier Qualifier	ID	2-3	N/U				New Element
REF04-2	Other Payer Primary Idenitifer	AN	1-50	N/U				New Element
REF04-3	Reference Identification Qualifier	ID	2-3	N/U				New Element
REF04-4	Reference Identification	AN	1-50	N/U				New Element
REF04-5	Reference Identification Qualifier	ID	2-3	N/U				New Element
REF04-6	Reference Identification	AN	1-50	N/U				New Element
PER	**BILLING PROVIDER CONTACT INFORMATION**		2	S	2010AA			
PER01	Contact Function Code	ID	2-2	R			IC	
PER02	Billing Provider Contact Name	AN	1-60	S				Usage changed to Situational
PER03	Communication Number Qualifier	ID	2-2	R			EM, FX, TE	
PER04	Communication Number	AN	1-256	R				Increase from 80 - 256
PER05	Communication Number Qualifier	ID	2-2	S			EM, EX, FX, TE	
PER06	Communication Number	AN	1-256	S				Increase from 80 - 256
PER07	Communication Number Qualifier	ID	2-2	S			EM, EX, FX, TE	
PER08	Communication Number	AN	1-256	S				Increase from 80 - 256
PER09	Contact Inquiry Reference	AN	1-20	N/U				
NM1	**PAY-TO ADDRESS NAME**		1	S	2010AB	1		Name Change
NM101	Entity Identifier Code	ID	2-3	R			87	
NM102	Entity Type Qualifier	ID	1-1	R			1, 2	
NM103	Pay-to Provider Last or Organization Name	AN	1-60	N/U				Increase from 35 - 60 Usage changed to Not Used
NM104	Pay-to Provider First Name	AN	1-35	N/U				Increase from 25 - 35 Usage changed to Not Used
NM105	Pay-to Provider Middle Name	AN	1-25	N/U				Usage changed to Not Used
NM106	Name Prefix	AN	1-10	N/U				Usage changed to Not Used
NM107	Pay-to Provider Name Suffix	AN	1-10	N/U				Usage changed to Not Used

Page 6 of 93

PROFESSIONAL CLAIM

Element Identifier	Description	ID	Min. Max.	Usage Req.	Loop	Loop Repeat	Values
		4010A1					
		837-P 4010A1					
NM108	Identification Code Qualifier	ID	1-2	R			24, 34, XX
NM109	Pay-to Provider Identifier	AN	2-80	R			
NM110	Entity Relationship Code	ID	2-2	N/U			
NM111	Entity Identifier Code	ID	2-3	N/U			
N3	**PAY-TO PROVIDER ADDRESS**		1	R	2010AB		
N301	Pay-to Provider Address Line	AN	1-55	R			
N302	Pay-to Provider Address Line	AN	1-55	S			
N4	**PAY-TO PROVIDER CITY/STATE/ZIP CODE**		1	R	2010AB		
N401	Pay-to Provider City Name	AN	2-30	R			
N402	Pay-to Provider State Code	ID	2-2	R			
N403	Pay-to Provider Postal Zone or ZIP Code	ID	3-15	R			
N404	Pay-to Provider Country Code	ID	2-3	S			
N405	Location Qualifier	ID	1-2	N/U			
N406	Location Identifier	AN	1-30	N/U			
REF	**PAY-TO PROVIDER SECONDARY IDENTIFICATION**		5	S	2010AB		
REF01	Reference Identification Qualifier	ID	2-3	R			0B, 1A, 1B, 1C, 1D, 1G, 1H, 1J, B3, BQ, EI, FH, G2, G5, LU, SY, U3, X5
REF02	Pay-to Provider Identifier	AN	1-30	R			
REF03	Description	AN	1-80	N/U			
REF04	REFERENCE IDENTIFIER			N/U			

Element Identifier	Description	ID	Min. Max.	Usage Req.	Loop	Loop Repeat	Values	
		5010						
		837-P 5010						
NM108	Identification Code Qualifier	ID	1-2	N/U				Code Deleted Usage changed to Not Used
NM109	Pay-to Provider Identifier	AN	2-80	N/U				Usage changed to Not Used
NM110	Entity Relationship Code	ID	2-2	N/U				Usage changed to Not Used
NM111	Entity Identifier Code	ID	2-3	N/U				Usage changed to Not Used
NM112	Name Last or Organization Name	AN	1-60	N/U				New Element
N3	**PAY-TO PROVIDER ADDRESS**		1	R	2010AB			
N301	Pay-to Provider Address Line	AN	1-55	R				
N302	Pay-to Provider Address Line	AN	1-55	S				
N4	**PAY-TO PROVIDER CITY/STATE/ZIP CODE**		1	R	2010AB			
N401	Pay-to Provider City Name	AN	2-30	R				
N402	Pay-to Provider State Code	ID	2-2	S				Usage changed to Situational
N403	Pay-to Provider Postal Zone or ZIP Code	ID	3-15	S				Usage changed to Situational
N404	Pay-to Provider Country Code	ID	2-3	S				
N405	Location Qualifier	ID	1-2	N/U				
N406	Location Identifier	AN	1-30	N/U				
N407	Country Subdivision Code	ID	1-3	S				New Element
								Segment Deleted
NM1	**PAY TO PLAN NAME**		1	S	2010AC	1		New Segment
NM101	Entity Identifier Code	ID	2-3	R			PE	
NM102	Entity Type Qualifier	ID	1-1	R			2	
NM103	Pay to Plan Organizational Name	AN	1-60	R				
NM104	Name First	AN	1-35	N/U				

Page 7 of 93

PROFESSIONAL CLAIM

4010A1							
Element Identifier	Description	ID	Min. Max.	Usage Reg.	Loop	Loop Repeat	Values
837-P 4010A1							

5010							
Element Identifier	Description	ID	Min. Max.	Usage Reg.	Loop	Loop Repeat	Values
837-P 5010							
NM105	Name Middle	AN	1-25	N/U			
NM106	Name Prefix	AN	1-10	N/U			
NM107	Name Suffix	AN	1-10	N/U			
NM108	Identification Code Qualifier	ID	1-2	R			PI, XV
NM109	Identification Code	AN	2-80	R			
NM110	Entity Relationship Code	ID	2-2	N/U			
NM111	Entity Identifier Code	ID	2-3	N/U			
NM112	Name Last or Organization Name	AN	1-60	N/U			
N3	**PAY-TO PLAN ADDRESS**		1	R	2010AC		New Segment
N301	Pay-to Plan Address Line	AN	1-55	R			
N302	Pay-to Plan Address Line	AN	1-55	S			
N4	**PAY-TO PLAN CITY/STATE/ZIP CODE**		1	R	2010AC		New Segment
N401	Pay-to Plan City Name	AN	2-30	R			
N402	Pay-to Plan State Code	ID	2-2	S			
N403	Pay-to Plan Postal Zone or ZIP Code	ID	3-15	S			
N404	Pay-to Plan Country Code	ID	2-3	S			
N405	Location Qualifier	ID	1-2	N/U			
N406	Location Identifier	AN	1-30	N/U			
N407	Country Subdivision Code	ID	1-3	S			
REF	**PAY-TO PLAN SECONDARY IDENTIFICATION**		1	S	2010AC		New Segment
REF01	Reference Identification Qualifier	ID	2-3	R			2U, FY, NF
REF02	Reference Identification	AN	1-50	R			
REF03	Description	AN	1-80	N/U			
REF04	REFERENCE IDENTIFIER			N/U			
REF04-1	Reference Identifier Qualifier	ID	2-3	N/U			
REF04-2	Other Payer Primary Idenitifer	AN	1-50	N/U			
REF04-3	Reference Identification Qualifier	ID	2-3	N/U			
REF04-4	Reference Identification	AN	1-50	N/U			
REF04-5	Reference Identification Qualifier	ID	2-3	N/U			
REF04-6	Reference Identification	AN	1-50	N/U			
REF	**PAY-TO PLAN TAX IDENTIFICATION**		1	R	2010AC		New Segment
REF01	Reference Identification Qualifier	ID	2-3	R			EI
REF02	Reference Identification	AN	1-50	R			

Page 8 of 93

PROFESSIONAL CLAIM

4010A1

Element Identifier	Description	ID	Min./Max.	Usage Reg.	Loop	Loop Repeat	Values
				837-P 4010A1			
HL	**SUBSCRIBER HIERARCHICAL LEVEL**		1	R	2000B	>1	
HL01	Hierarchical ID Number	AN	1-12	R			
HL02	Hierarchical Parent ID Number	AN	1-12	R			
HL03	Hierarchical Level Code	ID	1-2	R			22
HL04	Hierarchical Child Code	ID	1-1	R			0, 1
SBR	**SUBSCRIBER INFORMATION**		1	R	2000B		
SBR01	Payer Responsibility Sequence Number Code	ID	1-1	R			P, S, T
SBR02	Individual Relationship Code	ID	2-2	S			18
SBR03	Insured Group or Policy Number	AN	1-30	S			
SBR04	Insured Group Name	AN	1-60	S			
SBR05	Insurance Type Code	ID	1-3	S			12, 13, 14, 15, 16, 41, 42, 43, 47
SBR06	Coordination of Benefits Code	ID	1-1	N/U			
SBR07	Yes/No Condition or Response Code	ID	1-1	N/U			
SBR08	Employment Status Code	ID	2-2	N/U			
SBR09	Claim Filing Indicator Code	ID	1-2	S			09, 10, 11, 12, 13, 14, 15, 16, AM, BL, CH, CI, DS, HM, LI, LM, MB, MC, OF, TV, VA, WC, ZZ
PAT	**PATIENT INFORMATION**		1	S	2000B		
PAT01	Individual Relationship Code	ID	2-2	N/U			
PAT02	Patient Location Code	ID	1-1	N/U			
PAT03	Employment Status Code	ID	2-2	N/U			

5010

Element Identifier	Description	ID	Min./Max.	Usage Reg.	Loop	Loop Repeat	Values	
				837-P 5010				
REF03	Description	AN	1-80	N/U				
REF04	REFERENCE IDENTIFIER			N/U				
REF04-1	Reference Identifier Qualifier	ID	2-3	N/U				
REF04-2	Other Payer Primary Idenitifer	AN	1-50	N/U				
REF04-3	Reference Identification Qualifier	ID	2-3	N/U				
REF04-4	Reference Identification	AN	1-50	N/U				
REF04-5	Reference Identification Qualifier	ID	2-3	N/U				
REF04-6	Reference Identification	AN	1-50	N/U				
HL	**SUBSCRIBER HIERARCHICAL LEVEL**		1	R	2000B	>1		
HL01	Hierarchical ID Number	AN	1-12	R				
HL02	Hierarchical Parent ID Number	AN	1-12	R				
HL03	Hierarchical Level Code	ID	1-2	R			22	
HL04	Hierarchical Child Code	ID	1-1	R			0, 1	
SBR	**SUBSCRIBER INFORMATION**		1	R	2000B			
SBR01	Payer Responsibility Sequence Number Code	ID	1-1	R			A, B, C, D, E, F, G, H, P, S, T, U	Code Deleted
SBR02	Individual Relationship Code	ID	2-2	S			18	
SBR03	Insured Group or Policy Number	AN	1-50	S				Increase from 30 - 50
SBR04	Insured Group Name	AN	1-60	S				
SBR05	Insurance Type Code	ID	1-3	S			12, 13, 14, 15, 16, 41, 42, 43, 47	
SBR06	Coordination of Benefits Code	ID	1-1	N/U				
SBR07	Yes/No Condition or Response Code	ID	1-1	N/U				
SBR08	Employment Status Code	ID	2-2	N/U				
SBR09	Claim Filing Indicator Code	ID	1-2	S			11, 12, 13, 14, 15, 16, 17, AM, BL, CH, CI, DS, FI, HM, LM, MA, MB, MC, OF, TV, VA, WC, ZZ	Code Change
PAT	**PATIENT INFORMATION**		1	S	2000B			
PAT01	Individual Relationship Code	ID	2-2	N/U				
PAT02	Patient Location Code	ID	1-1	N/U				
PAT03	Employment Status Code	ID	2-2	N/U				

PROFESSIONAL CLAIM

4010A1 — 837-P 4010A1

Element Identifier	Description	ID	Min. Max.	Usage Reg.	Loop	Loop Repeat	Values
PAT04	Student Status Code	ID	1-1	N/U			
PAT05	Date Time Period Format Qualifier	ID	2-3	S			D8
PAT06	Insured Individual Death Date	AN	1-35	S			CCYYMMDD
PAT07	Unit or Basis for Measurement Code	ID	2-2	S			01
PAT08	Patient Weight 9(6)V99	R	1-10	S			
PAT09	Pregnancy Indicator	ID	1-1	S			Y
NM1	SUBSCRIBER NAME		1	R	2010BA	1	
NM101	Entity Identifier Code	ID	2-3	R			IL
NM102	Entity Type Qualifier	ID	1-1	R			1, 2
NM103	Subscriber Last Name	AN	1-35	R			
NM104	Subscriber First Name	AN	1-25	S			
NM105	Subscriber Middle Name	AN	1-25	S			
NM106	Name Prefix	AN	1-10	N/U			
NM107	Subscriber Name Suffix	AN	1-10	S			
NM108	Identification Code Qualifier	ID	1-2	S			MI, ZZ
NM109	Subscriber Primary Identifier	AN	2-80	S			
NM110	Entity Relationship Code	ID	2-2	N/U			
NM111	Entity Identifier Code	ID	2-3	N/U			
N3	SUBSCRIBER ADDRESS		1	S	2010BA		
N301	Subscriber Address Line	AN	1-55	R			
N302	Subscriber Address Line	AN	1-55	S			
N4	SUBSCRIBER CITY/STATE/ZIP CODE		1	S	2010BA		
N401	Subscriber City Name	AN	2-30	R			
N402	Subscriber State Code	ID	2-2	R			
N403	Subscriber Postal Zone or ZIP Code	ID	3-15	R			
N404	Subscriber Country Code	ID	2-3	S			
N405	Location Qualifier	ID	1-2	N/U			
N406	Location Identifier	AN	1-30	N/U			
DMG	SUBSCRIBER DEMOGRAPHIC INFORMATION		1	S	2010BA		
DMG01	Date Time Period Format Qualifier	ID	2-3	R			D8
DMG02	Subscriber Birth Date	AN	1-35	R			CCYYMMDD

5010 — 837-P 5010

Element Identifier	Description	ID	Min. Max.	Usage Reg.	Loop	Loop Repeat	Values	Notes
PAT04	Student Status Code	ID	1-1	N/U				
PAT05	Date Time Period Format Qualifier	ID	2-3	S			D8	
PAT06	Insured Individual Death Date	AN	1-35	S			CCYYMMDD	
PAT07	Unit or Basis for Measurement Code	ID	2-2	S			01	
PAT08	Patient Weight 9(6)V99	R	1-10	S				
PAT09	Pregnancy Indicator	ID	1-1	S			Y	
NM1	SUBSCRIBER NAME		1	R	2010BA	1		
NM101	Entity Identifier Code	ID	2-3	R			IL	
NM102	Entity Type Qualifier	ID	1-1	R			1, 2	
NM103	Subscriber Last Name	AN	1-60	R				Increase from 35 - 60
NM104	Subscriber First Name	AN	1-35	S				Increase from 25 - 35
NM105	Subscriber Middle Name	AN	1-25	S				
NM106	Name Prefix	AN	1-10	N/U				
NM107	Subscriber Name Suffix	AN	1-10	S				
NM108	Identification Code Qualifier	ID	1-2	R			II, MI	Code Change / Usage changed to Reqired
NM109	Subscriber Primary Identifier	AN	2-80	R				Usage changed to Required
NM110	Entity Relationship Code	ID	2-2	N/U				
NM111	Entity Identifier Code	ID	2-3	N/U				
NM112	Name Last or Organization Name	AN	1-60	N/U				New Element
N3	SUBSCRIBER ADDRESS		1	S	2010BA			
N301	Subscriber Address Line	AN	1-55	R				
N302	Subscriber Address Line	AN	1-55	S				
N4	SUBSCRIBER CITY/STATE/ZIP CODE		1	S	2010BA			
N401	Subscriber City Name	AN	2-30	R				
N402	Subscriber State Code	ID	2-2	S				Usage changed to Situational
N403	Subscriber Postal Zone or ZIP Code	ID	3-15	S				Usage changed to Situational
N404	Subscriber Country Code	ID	2-3	S				
N405	Location Qualifier	ID	1-2	N/U				
N406	Location Identifier	AN	1-30	N/U				
N407	Country Subdivision Code	ID	1-3	S				New Element
DMG	SUBSCRIBER DEMOGRAPHIC INFORMATION		1	S	2010BA			
DMG01	Date Time Period Format Qualifier	ID	2-3	R			D8	
DMG02	Subscriber Birth Date	AN	1-35	R			CCYYMMDD	

PROFESSIONAL CLAIM

4010A1

Element Identifier	Description	ID	Min. Max.	Usage Reg.	Loop	Loop Repeat	Values
	837-P 4010A1						
DMG03	Subscriber Gender Code	ID	1-1	R			F, M, U
DMG04	Marital Status Code	ID	1-1	N/U			
DMG05	Race or Ethnicity Code	ID	1-1	N/U			
DMG06	Citizenship Status Code	ID	1-2	N/U			
DMG07	Country Code	ID	2-3	N/U			
DMG08	Basis of Verification Code	ID	1-2	N/U			
DMG09	Quantity	R	1-15	N/U			
REF	**SUBSCRIBER SECONDARY IDENTIFICATION**		4	S	2010BA		
REF01	Reference Identification Qualifier	ID	2-3	R			1W, 23, IG, SY
REF02	Subscriber Supplemental Identifier	AN	1-30	R			
REF03	Description	AN	1-80	N/U			
REF04	REFERENCE IDENTIFIER			N/U			
REF	**PROPERTY AND CASUALTY CLAIM NUMBER**		1	S	2010BA		
REF01	Reference Identification Qualifier	ID	2-3	R			Y4
REF02	Property Casualty Claim Number	AN	1-30	R			
REF03	Description	AN	1-80	N/U			
REF04	REFERENCE IDENTIFIER			N/U			

5010

Element Identifier	Description	ID	Min. Max.	Usage Reg.	Loop	Loop Repeat	Values	
	837-P 5010							
DMG03	Subscriber Gender Code	ID	1-1	R			F, M, U	
DMG04	Marital Status Code	ID	1-1	N/U				
DMG05	Race or Ethnicity Code	ID	1-1	N/U				
DMG06	Citizenship Status Code	ID	1-2	N/U				
DMG07	Country Code	ID	2-3	N/U				
DMG08	Basis of Verification Code	ID	1-2	N/U				
DMG09	Quantity	R	1-15	N/U				
DMG10	Code List Qualifier Code	ID	1-3	N/U				New Element
DMG11	Industry Code	AN	1-30	N/U				New Element
REF	**SUBSCRIBER SECONDARY IDENTIFICATION**		1	S	2010BA			Code Removed
REF01	Reference Identification Qualifier	ID	2-3	R			SY	
REF02	Subscriber Supplemental Identifier	AN	1-50	R				Increase from 30 - 50
REF03	Description	AN	1-80	N/U				
REF04	REFERENCE IDENTIFIER			N/U				
REF04-1	Reference Identifier Qualifier	ID	2-3	N/U				New Element
REF04-2	Other Payer Primary Idenitifer	AN	1-50	N/U				New Element
REF04-3	Reference Identification Qualifier	ID	2-3	N/U				New Element
REF04-4	Reference Identification	AN	1-50	N/U				New Element
REF04-5	Reference Identification Qualifier	ID	2-3	N/U				New Element
REF04-6	Reference Identification	AN	1-50	N/U				New Element
REF	**PROPERTY AND CASUALTY CLAIM NUMBER**		1	S	2010BA			
REF01	Reference Identification Qualifier	ID	2-3	R			Y4	
REF02	Property Casualty Claim Number	AN	1-50	R				Increase from 30 - 50
REF03	Description	AN	1-80	N/U				
REF04	REFERENCE IDENTIFIER			N/U				
REF04-1	Reference Identifier Qualifier	ID	2-3	N/U				New Element
REF04-2	Other Payer Primary Idenitifer	AN	1-50	N/U				New Element
REF04-3	Reference Identification Qualifier	ID	2-3	N/U				New Element
REF04-4	Reference Identification	AN	1-50	N/U				New Element
REF04-5	Reference Identification Qualifier	ID	2-3	N/U				New Element
REF04-6	Reference Identification	AN	1-50	N/U				New Element

Page 11 of 93

PROFESSIONAL CLAIM

4010A1

837-P 4010A1

Element Identifier	Description	ID	Min. Max.	Usage Reg.	Loop	Loop Repeat	Values
NM1	**PAYER NAME**		1	R	2010BB	1	
NM101	Entity Identifier Code	ID	2-3	R			PR
NM102	Entity Type Qualifier	ID	1-1	R			2
NM103	Payer Name	AN	1-35	R			
NM104	Name First	AN	1-25	N/U			
NM105	Name Middle	AN	1-25	N/U			
NM106	Name Prefix	AN	1-10	N/U			
NM107	Name Suffix	AN	1-10	N/U			
NM108	Identification Code Qualifier	ID	1-2	R			PI, XV
NM109	Payer Identifier	AN	2-80	R			
NM110	Entity Relationship Code	ID	2-2	N/U			
NM111	Entity Identifier Code	ID	2-3	N/U			
N3	**PAYER ADDRESS**		1	S	2010BB		
N301	Payer Address Line	AN	1-55	R			
N302	Payer Address Line	AN	1-55	S			
N4	**PAYER CITY/STATE/ZIP CODE**		1	S	2010BB		
N401	Payer City Name	AN	2-30	R			
N402	Payer State Code	ID	2-2	R			
N403	Payer Postal Zone or ZIP Code	ID	3-15	R			
N404	Payer Country Code	ID	2-3	S			
N405	Location Qualifier	ID	1-2	N/U			
N406	Location Identifier	AN	1-30	N/U			

5010

837-P 5010

Element Identifier	Description	ID	Min. Max.	Usage Reg.	Loop	Loop Repeat	Values	Notes
PER	**PROPERTY AND CASUALTY SUBSCRIBER CONTACT INFORMATION**		1	S	2010BA			New Segment
PER01	Contact Function Code	ID	2-2	R			IC	
PER02	Billing Provider Contact Name	AN	1-60	S				
PER03	Communication Number Qualifier	ID	2-2	R			TE	
PER04	Communication Number	AN	1-256	R				
PER05	Communication Number Qualifier	ID	2-2	S			EX	
PER06	Communication Number	AN	1-256	S				
PER07	Communication Number Qualifier	ID	2-2	N/U				
PER08	Communication Number	AN	1-256	N/U				
PER09	Contact Inquiry Reference	AN	1-20	N/U				
NM1	**PAYER NAME**		1	R	2010BB	1		
NM101	Entity Identifier Code	ID	2-3	R			PR	
NM102	Entity Type Qualifier	ID	1-1	R			2	
NM103	Payer Name	AN	1-60	R				Increase from 35 - 60
NM104	Name First	AN	1-35	N/U				Increase from 25 - 35
NM105	Name Middle	AN	1-25	N/U				
NM106	Name Prefix	AN	1-10	N/U				
NM107	Name Suffix	AN	1-10	N/U				
NM108	Identification Code Qualifier	ID	1-2	R			PI, XV	
NM109	Payer Identifier	AN	2-80	R				
NM110	Entity Relationship Code	ID	2-2	N/U				
NM111	Entity Identifier Code	ID	2-3	N/U				
NM112	Name Last or Organization Name	AN	1-60	N/U				New Element
N3	**PAYER ADDRESS**		1	S	2010BB			
N301	Payer Address Line	AN	1-55	R				
N302	Payer Address Line	AN	1-55	S				
N4	**PAYER CITY/STATE/ZIP CODE**		1	R	2010BB			Usage changed to Required
N401	Payer City Name	AN	2-30	R				
N402	Payer State Code	ID	2-2	S				Usage changed to Situational
N403	Payer Postal Zone or ZIP Code	ID	3-15	S				Usage changed to Situational
N404	Payer Country Code	ID	2-3	S				
N405	Location Qualifier	ID	1-2	N/U				
N406	Location Identifier	AN	1-30	N/U				
N407	Country Subdivision Code	ID	1-3	S				New Element

Page 12 of 93

PROFESSIONAL CLAIM

4010A1

Element Identifier	Description	ID	Min. Max.	Usage Req.	Loop	Loop Repeat	Values
	837-P 4010A1						
REF	**PAYER SECONDARY IDENTIFICATION**		3	S	2010BB		
REF01	Reference Identification Qualifier	ID	2-3	R			2U, FY, NF, TJ
REF02	Payer Additional Identifier	AN	1-30	R			
REF03	Description	AN	1-80	N/U			
REF04	REFERENCE IDENTIFIER			N/U			
NM1	**RESPONSIBLE PARTY NAME**		1	S	2010BC	1	
NM101	Entity Identifier Code	ID	2-3	R			QD
NM102	Entity Type Qualifier	ID	1-1	R			1, 2
NM103	Responsible Party Last or Organization Name	AN	1-35	R			
NM104	Responsible Party First Name	AN	1-25	S			
NM105	Responsible Party Middle Name	AN	1-25	S			
NM106	Name Prefix	AN	1-10	N/U			
NM107	Responsible Party Suffix Name	AN	1-10	S			

5010

Element Identifier	Description	ID	Min. Max.	Usage Req.	Loop	Loop Repeat	Values	Notes
	837-P 5010							
REF	**PAYER SECONDARY IDENTIFICATION**		3	S	2010BB			
REF01	Reference Identification Qualifier	ID	2-3	R			2U, EI, FY, NF	Code Change
REF02	Payer Additional Identifier	AN	1-50	R				Increase from 30 - 50
REF03	Description	AN	1-80	N/U				
REF04	REFERENCE IDENTIFIER			N/U				New Element
REF04-1	Reference Identifier Qualifier	ID	2-3	N/U				New Element
REF04-2	Other Payer Primary Idenitfer	AN	1-50	N/U				New Element
REF04-3	Reference Identification Qualifier	ID	2-3	N/U				New Element
REF04-4	Reference Identification	AN	1-50	N/U				New Element
REF04-5	Reference Identification Qualifier	ID	2-3	N/U				New Element
REF04-6	Reference Identification	AN	1-50	N/U				New Segment
REF	**BILLING PROVIDER SECONDARY IDENTIFICATION**		2	S	2010BB			
REF01	Reference Identification Qualifier	ID	2-3	R			G2, LU	
REF02	Payer Additional Identifier	AN	1-50	R				
REF03	Description	AN	1-80	N/U				
REF04	REFERENCE IDENTIFIER			N/U				
REF04-1	Reference Identifier Qualifier	ID	2-3	N/U				
REF04-2	Other Payer Primary Idenitfer	AN	1-50	N/U				
REF04-3	Reference Identification Qualifier	ID	2-3	N/U				
REF04-4	Reference Identification	AN	1-50	N/U				
REF04-5	Reference Identification Qualifier	ID	2-3	N/U				
REF04-6	Reference Identification	AN	1-50	N/U				Segment Deleted

Page 13 of 93

PROFESSIONAL CLAIM

Element Identifier	Description	ID	Min. Max.	Usage Reg.	Loop	Loop Repeat	Values
	4010A1						
	837-P 4010A1						
NM108	Identification Code Qualifier	ID	1-2	N/U			
NM109	Identification Code	AN	2-80	N/U			
NM110	Entity Relationship Code	ID	2-2	N/U			
NM111	Entity Identifier Code	ID	2-3	N/U			
N3	**RESPONSIBLE PARTY ADDRESS**		1	R	2010BC		
N301	Responsible Party Address Line	AN	1-55	R			
N302	Responsible Party Address Line	AN	1-55	S			
N4	**RESPONSIBLE PARTY CITY/STATE/ZIP CODE**		1	R	2010BC		
N401	Responsible Party City Name	AN	2-30	R			
N402	Responsible Party State Code	ID	2-2	R			
N403	Responsible Party Postal Zone or ZIP Code	ID	3-15	R			
N404	Responsible Party Country Code	ID	2-3	S			
N405	Location Qualifier	ID	1-2	N/U			
N406	Location Identifier	AN	1-30	N/U			
NM1	**CREDIT/DEBIT CARD HOLDER NAME**		1	S	2010BD	1	
NM101	Entity Identifier Code	ID	2-3	R			AO
NM102	Entity Type Qualifier	ID	1-1	R			1,2
NM103	Credit or Debit Card Holder Last or Organizational Name	AN	1-35	R			
NM104	Credit or Debit Card Holder First Name	AN	1-25	S			
NM105	Credit or Debit Card Holder Middle Name	AN	1-25	S			
NM106	Name Prefix	AN	1-10	N/U			
NM107	Credit or Debit Card Holder Name Suffix	AN	1-10	S			
NM108	Identification Code Qualifier	ID	1-2	R			MI
NM109	Credit or Debit Card Number	AN	2-80	R			
NM110	Entity Relationship Code	ID	2-2	N/U			
NM111	Entity Identifier Code	ID	2-3	N/U			
REF	**CREDIT/DEBIT CARD INFORMATION**		2	S	2010BD		

Element Identifier	Description	ID	Min. Max.	Usage Reg.	Loop	Loop Repeat	Values
	5010						
	837-P 5010						
							Segment Deleted
							Segment Deleted
							Segment Deleted
							Segment Deleted

Page 14 of 93

PROFESSIONAL CLAIM

	4010A1								**5010**						
Element Identifier	Description	ID	Min. Max.	Usage Reg.	Loop	Loop Repeat	Values	Element Identifier	Description	ID	Min. Max.	Usage Reg.	Loop	Loop Repeat	Values
	837-P 4010A1								**837-P 5010**						
REF01	Reference Identification Qualifier	ID	2-3	R			AB, BB								
REF02	Credit or Debit Card Authorization Number	AN	1-30	R											
REF03	Description	AN	1-80	N/U											
REF04	REFERENCE IDENTIFIER			N/U											
HL	**PATIENT HIERARCHICAL LEVEL**		1	S	2000C	>1		**HL**	**PATIENT HIERARCHICAL LEVEL**		1	S	2000C	>1	
HL01	Hierarchical ID Number	AN	1-12	R				HL01	Hierarchical ID Number	AN	1-12	R			
HL02	Hierarchical Parent ID Number	AN	1-12	R				HL02	Hierarchical Parent ID Number	AN	1-12	R			
HL03	Hierarchical Level Code	ID	1-2	R			23	HL03	Hierarchical Level Code	ID	1-2	R			23
HL04	Hierarchical Child Code	ID	1-1	R			0	HL04	Hierarchical Child Code	ID	1-1	R			0
PAT	**PATIENT INFORMATION**		1	R	2000C			**PAT**	**PATIENT INFORMATION**		1	R	2000C		
PAT01	Individual Relationship Code	ID	2-2	R			01, 04, 05, 07, 09, 10, 15, 17, 19, 20, 21, 22, 23, 24, 29, 32, 33, 34, 36, 39, 40, 41, 43, 53, G8	PAT01	Individual Relationship Code	ID	2-2	R			01, 19, 20, 21, 39, 40, 53, G8
PAT02	Patient Location Code	ID	1-1	N/U				PAT02	Patient Location Code	ID	1-1	N/U			
PAT03	Employment Status Code	ID	2-2	N/U				PAT03	Employment Status Code	ID	2-2	N/U			
PAT04	Student Status Code	ID	1-1	N/U				PAT04	Student Status Code	ID	1-1	N/U			
PAT05	Date Time Period Format Qualifier	ID	2-3	S			D8	PAT05	Date Time Period Format Qualifier	ID	2-3	S			D8
PAT06	Patient Death Date	AN	1-35	S			CCYYMMDD	PAT06	Patient Death Date	AN	1-35	S			CCYYMMDD
PAT07	Unit or Basis for Measurement Code	ID	2-2	S			01	PAT07	Unit or Basis for Measurement Code	ID	2-2	S			01
PAT08	Patient Weight 9(6)V99	R	1-10	S				PAT08	Patient Weight 9(6)V99	R	1-10	S			
PAT09	Pregnancy Indicator	ID	1-1	S			Y	PAT09	Pregnancy Indicator	ID	1-1	S			Y
NM1	**PATIENT NAME**		1	R	2010CA	1		**NM1**	**PATIENT NAME**		1	R	2010CA	1	
NM101	Entity Identifier Code	ID	2-3	R			QC	NM101	Entity Identifier Code	ID	2-3	R			QC
NM102	Entity Type Qualifier	ID	1-1	R			1	NM102	Entity Type Qualifier	ID	1-1	R			1
NM103	Patient Last Name	AN	1-35	R				NM103	Patient Last Name	AN	1-60	R			
NM104	Patient First Name	AN	1-25	R				NM104	Patient First Name	AN	1-35	S			
NM105	Patient Middle Name	AN	1-25	S				NM105	Patient Middle Name	AN	1-25	S			
NM106	Name Prefix	AN	1-10	N/U				NM106	Name Prefix	AN	1-10	N/U			
NM107	Patient Name Suffix	AN	1-10	S				NM107	Patient Name Suffix	AN	1-10	S			
NM108	Identification Code Qualifier	ID	1-2	S			MI, ZZ	NM108	Identification Code Qualifier	ID	1-2	N/U			
NM109	Patient Primary Identifier	AN	2-80	S				NM109	Patient Primary Identifier	AN	2-80	N/U			
NM110	Entity Relationship Code	ID	2-2	N/U				NM110	Entity Relationship Code	ID	2-2	N/U			

Notes on 5010 column (right margin):
- PAT: Code Deleted
- NM103: Increase from 35 - 60
- NM104: Increase from 25 - 35 / Usage changed to Situational
- NM108: Code Deleted / Usage changed to Not Used
- NM109: Usage changed to Not Used

Page 15 of 93

PROFESSIONAL CLAIM

4010A1

837-P 4010A1

Element Identifier	Description	ID	Min. Max.	Usage Reg.	Loop	Loop Repeat	Values
NM111	Entity Identifier Code	ID	2-3	N/U			
N3	PATIENT ADDRESS		1	R	2010CA		
N301	Patient Address Line	AN	1-55	R			
N302	Patient Address Line	AN	1-55	S			
N4	PATIENT CITY/STATE/ZIP CODE		1	R	2010CA		
N401	Patient City Name	AN	2-30	R			
N402	Patient State Code	ID	2-2	R			
N403	Patient Postal Zone or ZIP Code	ID	3-15	R			
N404	Patient Country Code	ID	2-3	S			
N405	Location Qualifier	ID	1-2	N/U			
N406	Location Identifier	AN	1-30	N/U			
DMG	PATIENT DEMOGRAPHIC INFORMATION		1	R	2010CA		
DMG01	Date Time Period Format Qualifier	ID	2-3	R			D8
DMG02	Patient Birth Date	AN	1-35	R			CCYYMMDD
DMG03	Patient Gender Code	ID	1-1	R			F, M, U
DMG04	Marital Status Code	ID	1-1	N/U			
DMG05	Race or Ethnicity Code	ID	1-1	N/U			
DMG06	Citizenship Status Code	ID	1-2	N/U			
DMG07	Country Code	ID	2-3	N/U			
DMG08	Basis of Verification Code	ID	1-2	N/U			
DMG09	Quantity	R	1-15	N/U			
REF	PATIENT SECONDARY IDENTIFICATION		5	S	2010CA		
REF01	Reference Identification Qualifier	ID	2-3	R			1W, 23, IG, SY
REF02	Patient Secondary Identifier	AN	1-30	R			
REF03	Description	AN	1-80	N/U			
REF04	REFERENCE IDENTIFIER			N/U			
REF	PROPERTY AND CASUALTY CLAIM NUMBER		1	S	2010CA		
REF01	Reference Identification Qualifier	ID	2-3	R			Y4

5010

837-P 5010

Element Identifier	Description	ID	Min. Max.	Usage Reg.	Loop	Loop Repeat	Values	Notes
NM111	Entity Identifier Code	ID	2-3	N/U				
NM112	Name Last or Organization Name	AN	1-60	N/U				New Element
N3	PATIENT ADDRESS		1	R	2010CA			
N301	Patient Address Line	AN	1-55	R				
N302	Patient Address Line	AN	1-55	S				
N4	PATIENT CITY/STATE/ZIP CODE		1	R	2010CA			
N401	Patient City Name	AN	2-30	R				
N402	Patient State Code	ID	2-2	S				Usage changed to Situational
N403	Patient Postal Zone or ZIP Code	ID	3-15	S				Usage changed to Situational
N404	Patient Country Code	ID	2-3	S				
N405	Location Qualifier	ID	1-2	N/U				
N406	Location Identifier	AN	1-30	N/U				
N407	Country Subdivision Code	ID	1-3	S				New Element
DMG	PATIENT DEMOGRAPHIC INFORMATION		1	R	2010CA			
DMG01	Date Time Period Format Qualifier	ID	2-3	R			D8	
DMG02	Patient Birth Date	AN	1-35	R			CCYYMMDD	
DMG03	Patient Gender Code	ID	1-1	R			F, M, U	
DMG04	Marital Status Code	ID	1-1	N/U				
DMG05	Race or Ethnicity Code	ID	1-1	N/U				
DMG06	Citizenship Status Code	ID	1-2	N/U				
DMG07	Country Code	ID	2-3	N/U				
DMG08	Basis of Verification Code	ID	1-2	N/U				
DMG09	Quantity	R	1-15	N/U				
DMG10	Code List Qualifier Code	ID	1-3	N/U				New Element
DMG11	Industry Code	AN	1-30	N/U				New Element
								Segment Deleted
REF	PROPERTY AND CASUALTY CLAIM NUMBER		1	S	2010CA			
REF01	Reference Identification Qualifier	ID	2-3	R			Y4	

Page 16 of 93

PROFESSIONAL CLAIM

Element Identifier	Description	ID	Min. Max.	Usage Reg.	Loop	Loop Repeat	Values
4010A1							
837-P 4010A1							
REF02	Property Casualty Claim Number	AN	1-30	R			
REF03	Description	AN	1-80	N/U			
REF04	REFERENCE IDENTIFIER			N/U			
CLM	CLAIM INFORMATION		1	R	2300	100	
CLM01	Patient Account Number	AN	1-38	R			
CLM02	Total Claim Charge Amount S9(7)V99	R	1-18	R			
CLM03	Claim Filing Indicator Code	ID	1-2	N/U			
CLM04	Non-Institutional Claim Type Code	ID	1-2	N/U			
CLM05	HEALTH CARE SERVICE LOCATION INFORMATION			R			
CLM05-1	Facility Type Code	AN	1-2	R			11, 12, 21, 22, 23, 24, 25, 26, 31, 32, 33, 34, 41, 42, 51, 52, 53, 54, 55, 56, 50, 60, 61, 62, 65, 71, 72, 81, 99

Element Identifier	Description	ID	Min. Max.	Usage Reg.	Loop	Loop Repeat	Values	
5010								
837-P 5010								
REF02	Property Casualty Claim Number	AN	1-50	R				Increase from 30 - 50
REF03	Description	AN	1-80	N/U				
REF04	REFERENCE IDENTIFIER			N/U				
REF04-1	Reference Identifier Qualifier	ID	2-3	N/U				New Element
REF04-2	Other Payer Primary Idenitifer	AN	1-50	N/U				New Element
REF04-3	Reference Identification Qualifier	ID	2-3	N/U				New Element
REF04-4	Reference Identification	AN	1-50	N/U				New Element
REF04-5	Reference Identification Qualifier	ID	2-3	N/U				New Element
REF04-6	Reference Identification	AN	1-50	N/U				New Element
PER	PROPERTY AND CASUALTY PATIENT CONTACT INFORMATION		1	S	2010CA			New Segment
PER01	Contact Function Code	ID	2-2	R			IC	
PER02	Billing Provider Contact Name	AN	1-60	S				
PER03	Communication Number Qualifier	ID	2-2	R			TE	
PER04	Communication Number	AN	1-256	R				
PER05	Communication Number Qualifier	ID	2-2	S			EX	
PER06	Communication Number	AN	1-256	S				
PER07	Communication Number Qualifier	ID	2-2	N/U				
PER08	Communication Number	AN	1-256	N/U				
PER09	Contact Inquiry Reference	AN	1-20	N/U				
CLM	CLAIM INFORMATION		1	R	2300	100		
CLM01	Patient Account Number	AN	1-38	R				
CLM02	Total Claim Charge Amount S9(7)V99	R	1-18	R				
CLM03	Claim Filing Indicator Code	ID	1-2	N/U				
CLM04	Non-Institutional Claim Type Code	ID	1-2	N/U				
CLM05	HEALTH CARE SERVICE LOCATION INFORMATION			R				Code Deleted
CLM05-1	Facility Type Code	AN	1-2	R				

Page 17 of 93

PROFESSIONAL CLAIM

Element Identifier	Description	ID	Min. Max.	Usage Reg.	Loop	Loop Repeat	Values		Element Identifier	Description	ID	Min. Max.	Usage Reg.	Loop	Loop Repeat	Values	
4010A1									**5010**								
837-P 4010A1									837-P 5010								
																	Usage changed to Required
CLM05-2	Facility Code Qualifier	ID	1-2	N/U					CLM05-2	Facility Code Qualifier	ID	1-2	R			B	
																	Code Deleted
CLM05-3	Claim Frequency Code	ID	1-1	R			Refer to Code Source 235		CLM05-3	Claim Frequency Code	ID	1-1	R				
CLM06	Provider or Supplier Signature Indicator .	ID	1-1	R			N, Y		CLM06	Provider or Supplier Signature Indicator	ID	1-1	R			N, Y	
																	Code Deleted
CLM07	Medicare Assignment Code	ID	1-1	R			A, B, C, P		CLM07	Medicare Assignment Code	ID	1-1	R			A, B, C	
																	Code Added
CLM08	Benefits Assignment Certification Indicator	ID	1-1	R			N, Y		CLM08	Benefits Assignment Certification Indicator	ID	1-1	R			N, W, Y	
																	Code Deleted
CLM09	Release of Information Code	ID	1-1	R			A, I, M, N, O, Y		CLM09	Release of Information Code	ID	1-1	R			I, Y	
																	Code Deleted
CLM10	Patient Signature Source Code	ID	1-1	S			B, C, M, P, S		CLM10	Patient Signature Source Code	ID	1-1	S			P	
CLM11	RELATED CAUSES INFORMATION			S					CLM11	RELATED CAUSES INFORMATION			S				
CLM11-1	Related Causes Code	ID	2-3	R			AA, AP, EM, OA		CLM11-1	Related Causes Code	ID	2-3	R			AA, EM, OA	Code Deleted
CLM11-2	Related Causes Code	ID	2-3	S			AA, AP, EM, OA		CLM11--2	Related Causes Code	ID	2-3	S			AA, EM, OA	Code Deleted
																	Code Deleted Usage changed to Not Used
CLM11-3	Related Causes Code	ID	2-3	S			AA, AP, EM, OA		CLM11-3	Related Causes Code	ID	2-3	N/U				
CLM11-4	Auto Accident State or Province Code	ID	2-2	S					CLM11-4	Auto Accident State or Province Code	ID	2-2	S				
CLM11-5	Country Code	ID	2-3	S					CLM11-5	Country Code	ID	2-3	S				
																	Code Deleted
CLM12	Special Program Indicator	ID	2-3	S			01, 02, 03, 05, 07, 08, 09		CLM12	Special Program Indicator	ID	2-3	S			02, 03, 05, 09	
CLM13	Yes/No Condition or Response Code	ID	1-1	N/U					CLM13	Yes/No Condition or Response Code	ID	1-1	N/U				
CLM14	Level of Service Code	ID	1-3	N/U					CLM14	Level of Service Code	ID	1-3	N/U				
CLM15	Yes/No Condition or Response Code	ID	1-1	N/U					CLM15	Yes/No Condition or Response Code	ID	1-1	N/U				
CLM16	Participation Agreement	ID	1-1	S			P		CLM16	Participation Agreement	ID	1-1	N/U				Coe Deleted
CLM17	Claim Status Code	ID	1-2	N/U					CLM17	Claim Status Code	ID	1-2	N/U				
CLM18	Yes/No Condition or Response Code	ID	1-1	N/U					CLM18	Yes/No Condition or Response Code	ID	1-1	N/U				
CLM19	Claim Submission Reason Code	ID	2-2	N/U					CLM19	Claim Submission Reason Code	ID	2-2	N/U				
																	Code Added
CLM20	Delay Reason Code	ID	1-2	S			1, 2, 3, 4, 5, 6, 7, 8, 9, 10, 11		CLM20	Delay Reason Code	ID	1-2	S			1, 2, 3, 4, 5, 6, 7, 8, 9, 10, 11, 15	
																	New Segment
									DTP	DATE - ONSET OF CURRENT ILLNESS/SYMPTOM		1	S	2300			
									DTP01	Date Time Qualifier	ID	3-3	R			431	
									DTP02	Date Time Period Format Qualifier	ID	2-3	R			D8	
									DTP03	Onset of Current Illness or Injury Date	AN	1-35	R			CCYYMMDD	

Page 18 of 93

PROFESSIONAL CLAIM

Element Identifier	Description	ID	Min. Max.	Usage Reg.	Loop	Loop Repeat	Values
4010A1							
837-P 4010A1							
DTP	**DATE - INITIAL TREATMENT**		1	S	2300		
DTP01	Date Time Qualifier	ID	3-3	R			454
DTP02	Date Time Period Format Qualifier	ID	2-3	R			D8
DTP03	Initial Treatment Date	AN	1-35	R			CCYYMMDD
DTP	**DATE - DATE LAST SEEN**		1	S	2300		
DTP01	Date Time Qualifier	ID	3-3	R			304
DTP02	Date Time Period Format Qualifier	ID	2-3	R			D8
DTP03	Last Seen Date	AN	1-35	R			CCYYMMDD
DTP	**DATE - ONSET OF CURRENT ILLNESS/SYMPTOM**		1	S	2300		
DTP01	Date Time Qualifier	ID	3-3	R			431
DTP02	Date Time Period Format Qualifier	ID	2-3	R			D8
DTP03	Onset of Current Illness or Injury Date	AN	1-35	R			CCYYMMDD
DTP	**DATE - ACUTE MANIFESTATION**		5	S	2300		
DTP01	Date Time Qualifier	ID	3-3	R			453
DTP02	Date Time Period Format Qualifier	ID	2-3	R			D8
DTP03	Acute Manifestation Date	AN	1-35	R			CCYYMMDD
DTP	**DATE - SIMILAR ILLNESS/SYMPTOM ONSET**		10	S	2300		
DTP01	Date Time Qualifier	ID	3-3	R			438
DTP02	Date Time Period Format Qualifier	ID	2-3	R			D8
DTP03	Similar Illness or Symptom Date	AN	1-35	R			CCYYMMDD
DTP	**DATE - ACCIDENT**		10	S	2300		
DTP01	Date Time Qualifier	ID	3-3	R			439
DTP02	Date Time Period Format Qualifier	ID	2-3	R			D8, DT
DTP03	Accident Date	AN	1-35	R			CCYYMMDD, CCYYMMDDHHMM
DTP	**DATE - LAST MENSTRUAL PERIOD**		1	S	2300		
DTP01	Date Time Qualifier	ID	3-3	R			484

Element Identifier	Description	ID	Min. Max.	Usage Reg.	Loop	Loop Repeat	Values
5010							
837-P 5010							
DTP	**DATE - INITIAL TREATMENT**		1	S	2300		
DTP01	Date Time Qualifier	ID	3-3	R			454
DTP02	Date Time Period Format Qualifier	ID	2-3	R			D8
DTP03	Initial Treatment Date	AN	1-35	R			CCYYMMDD
DTP	**DATE - DATE LAST SEEN**		1	S	2300		
DTP01	Date Time Qualifier	ID	3-3	R			304
DTP02	Date Time Period Format Qualifier	ID	2-3	R			D8
DTP03	Last Seen Date	AN	1-35	R			CCYYMMDD
							Segment Deleted
DTP	**DATE - ACUTE MANIFESTATION**		1	S	2300		
DTP01	Date Time Qualifier	ID	3-3	R			453
DTP02	Date Time Period Format Qualifier	ID	2-3	R			D8
DTP03	Acute Manifestation Date	AN	1-35	R			CCYYMMDD
							Segment Deleted
DTP	**DATE - ACCIDENT**		1	S	2300		
DTP01	Date Time Qualifier	ID	3-3	R			439
DTP02	Date Time Period Format Qualifier	ID	2-3	R			D8,
DTP03	Accident Date	AN	1-35	R			CCYYMMDD
							Code Deleted
DTP	**DATE - LAST MENSTRUAL PERIOD**		1	S	2300		
DTP01	Date Time Qualifier	ID	3-3	R			484

PROFESSIONAL CLAIM

Element Identifier	Description	ID	Min. Max.	Usage Reg.	Loop	Loop Repeat	Values
	4010A1						
	837-P 4010A1						
DTP02	Date Time Period Format Qualifier	ID	2-3	R			D8
DTP03	Last Menstrual Period Date	AN	1-35	R			CCYYMMDD
DTP	**DATE - LAST X-RAY**		1	S	2300		
DTP01	Date Time Qualifier	ID	3-3	R			455
DTP02	Date Time Period Format Qualifier	ID	2-3	R			D8
DTP03	Last X-Ray Date	AN	1-35	R			CCYYMMDD
DTP	**DATE - HEARING AND VISION PRESCRIPTION DATE**		1	S	2300		
DTP01	Date Time Qualifier	ID	3-3	R			471
DTP02	Date Time Period Format Qualifier	ID	2-3	R			D8
DTP03	Prescription Date	AN	1-35	R			CCYYMMDD
DTP	**DATE - DISABILITY BEGIN**		5	S	2300		
DTP01	Date Time Qualifier	ID	3-3	R			360
DTP02	Date Time Period Format Qualifier	ID	2-3	R			D8
DTP03	Disability From Date	AN	1-35	R			CCYYMMDD
DTP	**DATE - DISABILITY END**		5	S	2300		
DTP01	Date Time Qualifier	ID	3-3	R			361
DTP02	Date Time Period Format Qualifier	ID	2-3	R			D8
DTP03	Disability To Date	AN	1-35	R			CCYYMMDD
DTP	**DATE - LAST WORKED**		1	S	2300		
DTP01	Date Time Qualifier	ID	3-3	R			297
DTP02	Date Time Period Format Qualifier	ID	2-3	R			D8
DTP03	Last Worked Date	AN	1-35	R			CCYYMMDD
DTP	**DATE - AUTHORIZED RETURN TO WORK**		1	S	2300		
DTP01	Date Time Qualifier	ID	3-3	R			296
DTP02	Date Time Period Format Qualifier	ID	2-3	R			D8
DTP03	Work Return Date	AN	1-35	R			CCYYMMDD

Element Identifier	Description	ID	Min. Max.	Usage Reg.	Loop	Loop Repeat	Values	
	5010							
	837-P 5010							
DTP02	Date Time Period Format Qualifier	ID	2-3	R			D8	
DTP03	Last Menstrual Period Date	AN	1-35	R			CCYYMMDD	
DTP	**DATE - LAST X-RAY**		1	S	2300			
DTP01	Date Time Qualifier	ID	3-3	R			455	
DTP02	Date Time Period Format Qualifier	ID	2-3	R			D8	
DTP03	Last X-Ray Date	AN	1-35	R			CCYYMMDD	
DTP	**DATE - HEARING AND VISION PRESCRIPTION DATE**		1	S	2300			
DTP01	Date Time Qualifier	ID	3-3	R			471	
DTP02	Date Time Period Format Qualifier	ID	2-3	R			D8	
DTP03	Prescription Date	AN	1-35	R			CCYYMMDD	
								Segment Deleted
								New Segment
DTP	**DATE - DISABILITY DATES**		1	S	2300			
DTP01	Date Time Qualifier	ID	3-3	R			314, 360, 361	
DTP02	Date Time Period Format Qualifier	ID	2-3	R			D8, RD8	
DTP03	Disability From Date	AN	1-35	R			CCYYMMDD	
								Segment Deleted
DTP	**DATE - LAST WORKED**		1	S	2300			
DTP01	Date Time Qualifier	ID	3-3	R			297	
DTP02	Date Time Period Format Qualifier	ID	2-3	R			D8	
DTP03	Last Worked Date	AN	1-35	R			CCYYMMDD	
DTP	**DATE - AUTHORIZED RETURN TO WORK**		1	S	2300			
DTP01	Date Time Qualifier	ID	3-3	R			296	
DTP02	Date Time Period Format Qualifier	ID	2-3	R			D8	
DTP03	Work Return Date	AN	1-35	R			CCYYMMDD	

PROFESSIONAL CLAIM

	4010A1							**5010**						
Element Identifier	Description	ID	Min. Max.	Usage Req.	Loop	Loop Repeat	Values	Element Identifier	Description	ID	Min. Max.	Usage Req.	Loop	Loop Repeat	Values
	837-P 4010A1								**837-P 5010**						
DTP	**DATE - ADMISSION**		1	S	2300			DTP	**DATE - ADMISSION**		1	S	2300		
DTP01	Date Time Qualifier	ID	3-3	R			435	DTP01	Date Time Qualifier	ID	3-3	R			435
DTP02	Date Time Period Format Qualifier	ID	2-3	R			D8	DTP02	Date Time Period Format Qualifier	ID	2-3	R			D8
DTP03	Related Hospitalization Admission Date	AN	1-35	R			CCYYMMDD	DTP03	Related Hospitalization Admission Date	AN	1-35	R			CCYYMMDD
DTP	**DATE - DISCHARGE**		1	S	2300			DTP	**DATE - DISCHARGE**		1	S	2300		
DTP01	Date Time Qualifier	ID	3-3	R			096	DTP01	Date Time Qualifier	ID	3-3	R			096
DTP02	Date Time Period Format Qualifier	ID	2-3	R			D8	DTP02	Date Time Period Format Qualifier	ID	2-3	R			D8
DTP03	Related Hospitalization Discharge Date	AN	1-35	R			CCYYMMDD	DTP03	Related Hospitalization Discharge Date	AN	1-35	R			CCYYMMDD
DTP	**DATE - ASSUMED AND RELINQUISHED CARE DATES**		2	S	2300			DTP	**DATE - ASSUMED AND RELINQUISHED CARE DATES**		2	S	2300		
DTP01	Date Time Qualifier	ID	3-3	R			090, 091	DTP01	Date Time Qualifier	ID	3-3	R			090, 091
DTP02	Date Time Period Format Qualifier	ID	2-3	R			D8	DTP02	Date Time Period Format Qualifier	ID	2-3	R			D8
DTP03	Assumed or Relinquished Care Date	AN	1-35	R			CCYYMMDD	DTP03	Assumed or Relinquished Care Date	AN	1-35	R			CCYYMMDD
								DTP	**DATE - PROPERTY AND CASUALTY DATE OF FIRST CONTACT**		1	S	2300			New Segment
								DTP01	Date Time Qualifier	ID	3-3	R			444
								DTP02	Date Time Period Format Qualifier	ID	2-3	R			D8
								DTP03	Order Date	AN	1-35	R			CCYYMMDD
								DTP	**DATE - REPRICER RECEIVED DATE**		1	S	2300			New Segment
								DTP01	Date Time Qualifier	ID	3-3	R			050
								DTP02	Date Time Period Format Qualifier	ID	2-3	R			D8
								DTP03	Order Date	AN	1-35	R			CCYYMMDD
PWK	**CLAIM SUPPLEMENTAL INFORMATION**		10	S	2300			PWK	**CLAIM SUPPLEMENTAL INFORMATION**		10	S	2300		

Page 21 of 93

PROFESSIONAL CLAIM

4010A1

Element Identifier	Description	ID	Min. Max.	Usage Reg.	Loop	Loop Repeat	Values
				837-P 4010A1			
PWK01	Attachment Report Type Code	ID	2-2	R			77, AS, B2, B3, B4, CT, DA, DG, DS, EB, MT, NN, OB, OZ, PN, PO, PZ, RB, RR, RT
PWK02	Attachment Transmission Code	ID	1-2	R			AA, BM, EL, EM, FX
PWK03	Report Copies Needed	N0	1-2	N/U			
PWK04	Entity Identifier Code	ID	2-3	N/U			
PWK05	Identification Code Qualifier	ID	1-2	S			AC
PWK06	Attachment Control Number	AN	2-80	S			
PWK07	Description	AN	1-80	N/U			
PWK08	ACTIONS INDICATED			N/U			
PWK09	Request Category Code	ID	1-2	N/U			
CN1	CONTRACT INFORMATION		1	S	2300		
CN101	Contract Type Code	ID	2-2	R			02, 03, 04, 05, 06, 09
CN102	Contract Amount S9(7)V99	R	1-18	S			
CN103	Contract Percentage 9(2)V99	R	1-6	S			
CN104	Contract Code	AN	1-30	S			
CN105	Terms Discount Percent 9(2)V99	R	1-6	S			
CN106	Contract Version Identifier	AN	1-30	S			
AMT	CREDIT/DEBIT CARD MAXIMUM AMOUNT		1	S	2300		
AMT01	Amount Qualifier Code	ID	1-3	R			
AMT02	Credit or Debit Card Maximum Amount S9(7)V99	R	1-18	R			
AMT03	Credit/Debit Flag Code	ID	1-1	N/U			
AMT	PATIENT AMOUNT PAID		1	S	2300		

5010

Element Identifier	Description	ID	Min. Max.	Usage Reg.	Loop	Loop Repeat	Values	
				837-P 5010				Code Added
PWK01	Attachment Report Type Code	ID	2-2	R			03, 04, 05, 06, 07, 08, 09, 10, 11, 13, 15, 21, A3, A4, AM, AS, B2, B3, B4, BR, BS, BT, CB, CK, CT, D2, DA, DB, DG, DJ, DS, EB, HC, HR, I5, IR, LA, M1, MT, NN, OB, OC, OD, OE, OX, OZ, P4, P5, PE, PN, PO, PQ, PY, PZ, RB, RR, RT, RX, SG, V5, XP	
PWK02	Attachment Transmission Code	ID	1-2	R			AA, BM, EL, EM, FT, FX	Code Deleted
PWK03	Report Copies Needed	N0	1-2	N/U				
PWK04	Entity Identifier Code	ID	2-3	N/U				
PWK05	Identification Code Qualifier	ID	1-2	S			AC	
PWK06	Attachment Control Number	AN	2-80	S				
PWK07	Description	AN	1-80	N/U				
PWK08	ACTIONS INDICATED			N/U				
PWK09	Request Category Code	ID	1-2	N/U				
CN1	CONTRACT INFORMATION		1	S	2300			
CN101	Contract Type Code	ID	2-2	R			01, 02, 03, 04, 05, 06, 09	Code Deleted
CN102	Contract Amount S9(7)V99	R	1-18	S				
CN103	Contract Percentage 9(2)V99	R	1-6	S				
CN104	Contract Code	AN	1-50	S				Increase from 30 - 50
CN105	Terms Discount Percent 9(2)V99	R	1-6	S				
CN106	Contract Version Identifier	AN	1-30	S				
								Segment Deleted
AMT	PATIENT AMOUNT PAID		1	S	2300			

Page 22 of 93

PROFESSIONAL CLAIM

4010A1

Element Identifier	Description	ID	Min. Max.	Usage Req.	Loop	Loop Repeat	Values
	837-P 4010A1						
AMT01	Amount Qualifier Code	ID	1-3	R			F5
AMT02	Patient Amount Paid S9(7)V99	R	1-18	R			
AMT03	Credit/Debit Flag Code	ID	1-1	N/U			
AMT	**TOTAL PURCHASED SERVICE AMOUNT**		1	S	2300		
AMT01	Amount Qualifier Code	ID	1-3	R			NE
AMT02	Total Purchased Service Amount S9(7)V99	R	1-18	R			
AMT03	Credit/Debit Flag Code	ID	1-1	N/U			
REF	**SERVICE AUTHORIZATION EXCEPTION CODE**		1	S	2300		
REF01	Reference Identification Qualifier	ID	2-3	R			4N
REF02	Service Authorization Exception Code	AN	1-30	R			1, 2, 3, 4, 5, 6, 7
REF03	Description	AN	1-80	N/U			
REF04	REFERENCE IDENTIFIER			N/U			
REF	**MANDATORY MEDICARE (SECTION 4081) CROSSOVER INDICATOR**		1	S	2300		
REF01	Reference Identification Qualifier	ID	2-3	R			F5
REF02	Medicare Section 4081 Indicator	AN	1-30	R			Y,N
REF03	Description	AN	1-80	N/U			
REF04	REFERENCE IDENTIFIER			N/U			

5010

Element Identifier	Description	ID	Min. Max.	Usage Req.	Loop	Loop Repeat	Values	
	837-P 5010							
AMT01	Amount Qualifier Code	ID	1-3	R			F5	
AMT02	Patient Amount Paid S9(7)V99	R	1-18	R				
AMT03	Credit/Debit Flag Code	ID	1-1	N/U				
								Segment Deleted
REF	**SERVICE AUTHORIZATION EXCEPTION CODE**		1	S	2300			
REF01	Reference Identification Qualifier	ID	2-3	R			4N	
REF02	Service Authorization Exception Code	AN	1-50	R			1, 2, 3, 4, 5, 6, 7	Increase from 30 - 50
REF03	Description	AN	1-80	N/U				
REF04	REFERENCE IDENTIFIER			N/U				
REF04-1	Reference Identifier Qualifier	ID	2-3	N/U				New Element
REF04-2	Other Payer Primary Idenitifer	AN	1-50	N/U				New Element
REF04-3	Reference Identification Qualifier	ID	2-3	N/U				New Element
REF04-4	Reference Identification	AN	1-50	N/U				New Element
REF04-5	Reference Identification Qualifier	ID	2-3	N/U				New Element
REF04-6	Reference Identification	AN	1-50	N/U				New Element
REF	**MANDATORY MEDICARE (SECTION 4081) CROSSOVER INDICATOR**		1	S	2300			
REF01	Reference Identification Qualifier	ID	2-3	R			F5	
REF02	Medicare Section 4081 Indicator	AN	1-50	R			Y,N	Increase from 30 - 50
REF03	Description	AN	1-80	N/U				
REF04	REFERENCE IDENTIFIER			N/U				
REF04-1	Reference Identifier Qualifier	ID	2-3	N/U				New Element
REF04-2	Other Payer Primary Idenitifer	AN	1-50	N/U				New Element
REF04-3	Reference Identification Qualifier	ID	2-3	N/U				New Element
REF04-4	Reference Identification	AN	1-50	N/U				New Element
REF04-5	Reference Identification Qualifier	ID	2-3	N/U				New Element

PROFESSIONAL CLAIM

4010A1

837-P 4010A1

Element Identifier	Description	ID	Min. Max.	Usage Reg.	Loop	Loop Repeat	Values
REF	**MAMMOGRAPHY CERTIFICATION NUMBER**		1	S	2300		
REF01	Mammography Certification Number	ID	2-3	R			EW
REF02	Mammography Certification Number	AN	1-30	R			
REF03	Description	AN	1-80	N/U			
REF04	REFERENCE IDENTIFIER			N/U			
REF	**PRIOR AUTHORIZATION OR REFERRAL NUMBER**		2	S	2300		
REF01	Reference Identification Qualifier	ID	2-3	R			9F, G1
REF02	Prior Authorization or Referral Number	AN	1-30	R			
REF03	Description	AN	1-80	N/U			
REF04	REFERENCE IDENTIFIER			N/U			
REF	**ORIGINAL REFERENCE NUMBER (ICN/DCN)**		1	S	2300		
REF01	Reference Identification Qualifier	ID	2-3	R			F8
REF02	Claim Original Reference Number	AN	1-30	R			
REF03	Description	AN	1-80	N/U			
REF04	REFERENCE IDENTIFIER			N/U			

5010

837-P 5010

Element Identifier	Description	ID	Min. Max.	Usage Reg.	Loop	Loop Repeat	Values	
REF04-6	Reference Identification	AN	1-50	N/U				New Element
REF	**MAMMOGRAPHY CERTIFICATION NUMBER**		1	S	2300			
REF01	Mammography Certification Number	ID	2-3	R			EW	
REF02	Mammography Certification Number	AN	1-50	R				Increase from 30 - 50
REF03	Description	AN	1-80	N/U				
REF04	REFERENCE IDENTIFIER			N/U				New Element
REF04-1	Reference Identifier Qualifier	ID	2-3	N/U				New Element
REF04-2	Other Payer Primary Idenitifer	AN	1-50	N/U				New Element
REF04-3	Reference Identification Qualifier	ID	2-3	N/U				New Element
REF04-4	Reference Identification	AN	1-50	N/U				New Element
REF04-5	Reference Identification Qualifier	ID	2-3	N/U				New Element
REF04-6	Reference Identification	AN	1-50	N/U				Segment Deleted
								Segment Deleted
REF	**REFERRAL NUMBER**		1	S	2300			New Segment
REF01	Reference Identification Qualifier	ID	2-3	R			9F	
REF02	Prior Authorization or Referral Number	AN	1-50	R				
REF03	Description	AN	1-80	N/U				
REF04	REFERENCE IDENTIFIER			N/U				
REF04-1	Reference Identifier Qualifier	ID	2-3	N/U				
REF04-2	Other Payer Primary Idenitifer	AN	1-50	N/U				

PROFESSIONAL CLAIM

	4010A1						
Element Identifier	Description	ID	Min. Max.	Usage Reg.	Loop	Loop Repeat	Values
	837-P 4010A1						
REF	**CLINICAL LABORATORY IMPROVEMENT AMENDMENT (CLIA) NUMBER**		3	S	2300		
REF01	Reference Identification Qualifier	ID	2-3	R			X4

	5010							
Element Identifier	Description	ID	Min. Max.	Usage Reg.	Loop	Loop Repeat	Values	
	837-P 5010							
REF04-3	Reference Identification Qualifier	ID	2-3	N/U				
REF04-4	Reference Identification	AN	1-50	N/U				
REF04-5	Reference Identification Qualifier	ID	2-3	N/U				
REF04-6	Reference Identification	AN	1-50	N/U				
REF	**PRIOR AUTHORIZATION**		**1**	**S**	**2300**			New Segment
REF01	Reference Identification Qualifier	ID	2-3	R			G1	
REF02	Prior Authorization or Referral Number	AN	1-50	R				
REF03	Description	AN	1-80	N/U				
REF04	REFERENCE IDENTIFIER			N/U				
REF04-1	Reference Identifier Qualifier	ID	2-3	N/U				
REF04-2	Other Payer Primary Idenitifer	AN	1-50	N/U				
REF04-3	Reference Identification Qualifier	ID	2-3	N/U				
REF04-4	Reference Identification	AN	1-50	N/U				
REF04-5	Reference Identification Qualifier	ID	2-3	N/U				
REF04-6	Reference Identification	AN	1-50	N/U				
REF	**PAYER CLAIM CONTROL NUMBER**		**1**	**S**	**2300**			New Segment
REF01	Reference Identification Qualifier	ID	2-3	R			F8	
REF02	Claim Original Reference Number	AN	1-50	R				
REF03	Description	AN	1-80	N/U				
REF04	REFERENCE IDENTIFIER			N/U				
REF04-1	Reference Identifier Qualifier	ID	2-3	N/U				
REF04-2	Other Payer Primary Idenitifer	AN	1-50	N/U				
REF04-3	Reference Identification Qualifier	ID	2-3	N/U				
REF04-4	Reference Identification	AN	1-50	N/U				
REF04-5	Reference Identification Qualifier	ID	2-3	N/U				
REF04-6	Reference Identification	AN	1-50	N/U				
REF	**CLINICAL LABORATORY IMPROVEMENT AMENDMENT (CLIA) NUMBER**		**1**	**S**	**2300**			
REF01	Reference Identification Qualifier	ID	2-3	R			X4	

Page 25 of 93

PROFESSIONAL CLAIM

4010A1

837-P 4010A1

Element Identifier	Description	ID	Min. Max.	Usage Reg.	Loop	Loop Repeat	Values
REF02	Clinical Laboratory Improvement Amendment Number	AN	1-30	R			
REF03	Description	AN	1-80	N/U			
REF04	REFERENCE IDENTIFIER			N/U			
REF	**REPRICED CLAIM NUMBER**		1	S	2300		
REF01	Reference Identification Qualifier	ID	2-3	R			9A
REF02	Repriced Claim Reference Number	AN	1-30	R			
REF03	Description	AN	1-80	N/U			
REF04	REFERENCE IDENTIFIER			N/U			
REF	**ADJUSTED REPRICED CLAIM NUMBER**		1	S	2300		
REF01	Reference Identification Qualifier	ID	2-3	R			9C
REF02	Adjusted Repriced Claim Reference Number	AN	1-30	R			
REF03	Description	AN	1-80	N/U			
REF04	REFERENCE IDENTIFIER			N/U			

5010

837-P 5010

Element Identifier	Description	ID	Min. Max.	Usage Reg.	Loop	Loop Repeat	Values	Notes
REF02	Clinical Laboratory Improvement Amendment Number	AN	1-50	R				Increase from 30 - 50
REF03	Description	AN	1-80	N/U				
REF04	REFERENCE IDENTIFIER			N/U				
REF04-1	Reference Identifier Qualifier	ID	2-3	N/U				New Element
REF04-2	Other Payer Primary Idenitifer	AN	1-50	N/U				New Element
REF04-3	Reference Identification Qualifier	ID	2-3	N/U				New Element
REF04-4	Reference Identification	AN	1-50	N/U				New Element
REF04-5	Reference Identification Qualifier	ID	2-3	N/U				New Element
REF04-6	Reference Identification	AN	1-50	N/U				New Element
REF	**REPRICED CLAIM NUMBER**		1	S	2300			
REF01	Reference Identification Qualifier	ID	2-3	R			9A	
REF02	Repriced Claim Reference Number	AN	1-50	R				Increase from 30 - 50
REF03	Description	AN	1-80	N/U				
REF04	REFERENCE IDENTIFIER			N/U				
REF04-1	Reference Identifier Qualifier	ID	2-3	N/U				New Element
REF04-2	Other Payer Primary Idenitifer	AN	1-50	N/U				New Element
REF04-3	Reference Identification Qualifier	ID	2-3	N/U				New Element
REF04-4	Reference Identification	AN	1-50	N/U				New Element
REF04-5	Reference Identification Qualifier	ID	2-3	N/U				New Element
REF04-6	Reference Identification	AN	1-50	N/U				New Element
REF	**ADJUSTED REPRICED CLAIM NUMBER**		1	S	2300			
REF01	Reference Identification Qualifier	ID	2-3	R			9C	
REF02	Adjusted Repriced Claim Reference Number	AN	1-50	R				Increase from 30 - 50
REF03	Description	AN	1-80	N/U				
REF04	REFERENCE IDENTIFIER			N/U				
REF04-1	Reference Identifier Qualifier	ID	2-3	N/U				New Element
REF04-2	Other Payer Primary Idenitifer	AN	1-50	N/U				New Element
REF04-3	Reference Identification Qualifier	ID	2-3	N/U				New Element
REF04-4	Reference Identification	AN	1-50	N/U				New Element

PROFESSIONAL CLAIM

Element Identifier	Description	ID	Min. Max.	Usage Reg.	Loop	Loop Repeat	Values
	4010A1						
	837-P 4010A1						
REF	**INVESTIGATIONAL DEVICE EXEMPTION NUMBER**		1	S	2300		
REF01	Reference Identification Qualifier	ID	2-3	R			LX
REF02	Investigational Device Exemption Number	AN	1-30	R			
REF03	Description	AN	1-80	N/U			
REF04	REFERENCE IDENTIFIER			N/U			
REF	**CLAIM IDENTIFICATION NUMBER FOR CLEARING HOUSES AND OTHER TRANSMISSION INTERMEDIARIES**		1	S	2300		
REF01	Reference Identification Qualifier	ID	2-3	R			D9
REF02	Clearinghouse Trace Number	AN	1-30	R			
REF03	Description	AN	1-80	N/U			
REF04	REFERENCE IDENTIFIER			N/U			
REF	**AMBULATORY PATIENT GROUP (APG)**		4	S	2300		
REF01	Reference Identification Qualifier	ID	2-3	R			1S

Element Identifier	Description	ID	Min. Max.	Usage Reg.	Loop	Loop Repeat	Values	
	5010							
	837-P 5010							
REF04-5	Reference Identification Qualifier	ID	2-3	N/U				New Element
REF04-6	Reference Identification	AN	1-50	N/U				New Element
REF	**INVESTIGATIONAL DEVICE EXEMPTION NUMBER**		1	S	2300			
REF01	Reference Identification Qualifier	ID	2-3	R			LX	
REF02	Investigational Device Exemption Number	AN	1-50	R				Increase from 30 - 50
REF03	Description	AN	1-80	N/U				
REF04	REFERENCE IDENTIFIER			N/U				
REF04-1	Reference Identifier Qualifier	ID	2-3	N/U				New Element
REF04-2	Other Payer Primary Idenitifer	AN	1-50	N/U				New Element
REF04-3	Reference Identification Qualifier	ID	2-3	N/U				New Element
REF04-4	Reference Identification	AN	1-50	N/U				New Element
REF04-5	Reference Identification Qualifier	ID	2-3	N/U				New Element
REF04-6	Reference Identification	AN	1-50	N/U				New Element
REF	**CLAIM IDENTIFIER FOR TRANSMISSION INTERMEDIARIES**		1	S	2300			Name Change
REF01	Reference Identification Qualifier	ID	2-3	R			D9	
REF02	Clearinghouse Trace Number	AN	1-50	R				Increase from 30 - 50
REF03	Description	AN	1-80	N/U				
REF04	REFERENCE IDENTIFIER			N/U				
REF04-1	Reference Identifier Qualifier	ID	2-3	N/U				New Element
REF04-2	Other Payer Primary Idenitifer	AN	1-50	N/U				New Element
REF04-3	Reference Identification Qualifier	ID	2-3	N/U				New Element
REF04-4	Reference Identification	AN	1-50	N/U				New Element
REF04-5	Reference Identification Qualifier	ID	2-3	N/U				New Element
REF04-6	Reference Identification	AN	1-50	N/U				New Element
								Segment Deleted

PROFESSIONAL CLAIM

4010A1

837-P 4010A1

Element Identifier	Description	ID	Min. Max.	Usage Reg.	Loop	Loop Repeat	Values
REF02	Ambulatory Patient Group Number	AN	1-30	R			
REF03	Description	AN	1-80	N/U			
REF04	REFERENCE IDENTIFIER			N/U			
REF	MEDICAL RECORD NUMBER		1	S	2300		
REF01	Reference Identification Qualifier	ID	2-3	R			EA
REF02	Medical Record Number	AN	1-30	R			
REF03	Description	AN	1-80	N/U			
REF04	REFERENCE IDENTIFIER			N/U			
REF	DEMONSTRATION PROJECT IDENTIFIER		1	S	2300		
REF01	Reference Identification Qualifier	ID	2-3	R			P4
REF02	Demonstration Project Identifier	AN	1-30	R			
REF03	Description	AN	1-80	N/U			
REF04	REFERENCE IDENTIFIER			N/U			

5010

837-P 5010

Element Identifier	Description	ID	Min. Max.	Usage Reg.	Loop	Loop Repeat	Values	Notes
REF	MEDICAL RECORD NUMBER		1	S	2300			
REF01	Reference Identification Qualifier	ID	2-3	R			EA	
REF02	Medical Record Number	AN	1-50	R				Increase from 30 - 50
REF03	Description	AN	1-80	N/U				
REF04	REFERENCE IDENTIFIER			N/U				New Element
REF04-1	Reference Identifier Qualifier	ID	2-3	N/U				New Element
REF04-2	Other Payer Primary Idenitifer	AN	1-50	N/U				New Element
REF04-3	Reference Identification Qualifier	ID	2-3	N/U				New Element
REF04-4	Reference Identification	AN	1-50	N/U				New Element
REF04-5	Reference Identification Qualifier	ID	2-3	N/U				New Element
REF04-6	Reference Identification	AN	1-50	N/U				New Element
REF	DEMONSTRATION PROJECT IDENTIFIER		1	S	2300			
REF01	Reference Identification Qualifier	ID	2-3	R			P4	
REF02	Demonstration Project Identifier	AN	1-50	R				Increase from 30 - 50
REF03	Description	AN	1-80	N/U				
REF04	REFERENCE IDENTIFIER			N/U				New Element
REF04-1	Reference Identifier Qualifier	ID	2-3	N/U				Now Element
REF04-2	Other Payer Primary Idenitifer	AN	1-50	N/U				New Element
REF04-3	Reference Identification Qualifier	ID	2-3	N/U				New Element
REF04-4	Reference Identification	AN	1-50	N/U				New Element
REF04-5	Reference Identification Qualifier	ID	2-3	N/U				New Element
REF04-6	Reference Identification	AN	1-50	N/U				New Element
REF	CARE PLAN OVERSIGHT		1	S	2300			New Segment
REF01	Reference Identification Qualifier	ID	2-3	R			1J	
REF02	Care Plan Oversight Number	AN	1-50	R				
REF03	Description	AN	1-80	N/U				
REF04	REFERENCE IDENTIFIER			N/U				

Page 28 of 93

PROFESSIONAL CLAIM

Element Identifier	Description	ID	Min. Max.	Usage Reg.	Loop	Loop Repeat	Values
			4010A1				
			837-P 4010A1				
K3	**FILE INFORMATION**		10	S	2300		
K301	Fixed Format Information	AN	1-80	R			
K302	Record Format Code	ID	1-2	N/U			
K303	COMPOSITE UNIT OF MEASURE			N/U			
NTE	**CLAIM NOTE**		1	S	2300		
NTE01	Note Reference Code	ID	3-3	R			ADD, CER, DCP,DGN,PMT,TPO
NTE02	Claim Note Text	AN	1-80	R			
CR1	**AMBULANCE TRANSPORT INFORMATION**		1	S	2300		
CR101	Unit or Basis for Measurement Code	ID	2-2	S			LB
CR102	Patient Weight 9(3)	R	1-10	S			
CR103	Ambulance Transport Code	ID	1-1	R			I, R, T, X
CR104	Ambulance Transport Reason Code	ID	1-1	R			A, B, C, D, E
CR105	Unit or Basis for Measurement Code	ID	2-2	R			DH
CR106	Transport Distance 9(4)	R	1-15	R			
CR107	Address Information	AN	1-55	N/U			
CR108	Address Information	AN	1-55	N/U			
CR109	Round Trip Purpose Description	AN	1-80	S			
CR110	Stretcher Purpose Description	AN	1-80	S			
CR2	**SPINAL MANIPULATION SERVICE INFORMATION**		1	S	2300		
CR201	Treatment Series Number 9(3)	N0	1-9	N/U			
CR202	Treatment Count 9(3)	R	1-15	N/U			

Element Identifier	Description	ID	Min. Max.	Usage Reg.	Loop	Loop Repeat	Values	
			5010					
			837-P 5010					
REF04-1	Reference Identifier Qualifier	ID	2-3	N/U				
REF04-2	Other Payer Primary Idenitifer	AN	1-50	N/U				
REF04-3	Reference Identification Qualifier	ID	2-3	N/U				
REF04-4	Reference Identification	AN	1-50	N/U				
REF04-5	Reference Identification Qualifier	ID	2-3	N/U				
REF04-6	Reference Identification	AN	1-50	N/U				
K3	**FILE INFORMATION**		10	S	2300			
K301	Fixed Format Information	AN	1-80	R				
K302	Record Format Code	ID	1-2	N/U				
K303	COMPOSITE UNIT OF MEASURE			N/U				
NTE	**CLAIM NOTE**		1	S	2300			Code Deleted
NTE01	Note Reference Code	ID	3-3	R			ADD, CER, DCP, DGN, TPO	
NTE02	Claim Note Text	AN	1-80	R				
CR1	**AMBULANCE TRANSPORT INFORMATION**		1	S	2300			
CR101	Unit or Basis for Measurement Code	ID	2-2	S			LB	
CR102	Patient Weight 9(3)	R	1-10	S				
CR103	Ambulance Transport Code	ID	1-1	N/U				Code Deleted Usage changed to Not Used
CR104	Ambulance Transport Reason Code	ID	1-1	R			A, B, C, D, E	
CR105	Unit or Basis for Measurement Code	ID	2-2	R			DH	
CR106	Transport Distance 9(4)	R	1-15	R				
CR107	Address Information	AN	1-55	N/U				
CR108	Address Information	AN	1-55	N/U				
CR109	Round Trip Purpose Description	AN	1-80	S				
CR110	Stretcher Purpose Description	AN	1-80	S				
CR2	**SPINAL MANIPULATION SERVICE INFORMATION**		1	S	2300			
CR201	Treatment Series Number 9(3)	N0	1-9	N/U				
CR202	Treatment Count 9(3)	R	1-15	N/U				

Page 29 of 93

PROFESSIONAL CLAIM

4010A1							
Element Identifier	Description	ID	Min. Max.	Usage Reg.	Loop	Loop Repeat	Values
837-P 4010A1							
CR203	Subluxation Level Code	ID	2-3	N/U			C1, C2, C3, C4, C5, C6, C7, CO, IL, L1, L2, L3, L4, L5, OC, SA, T1, T10, T11, T12, T2, T3, T4, T5, T6, T7, T8, T9
CR204	Subluxation Level Code	ID	2-3	N/U			C1, C2, C3, C4, C5, C6, C7, CO, IL, L1, L2, L3, L4, L5, OC, SA, T1, T10, T11, T12, T2, T3, T4, T5, T6, T7, T8, T9
CR205	Unit or Basis for Measurement Code	ID	2-2	N/U			DA, MO, WK, YR
CR206	Treatment Period Count 9(3)	R	1-15	N/U			
CR207	Monthly Treatment Count 9(2)	R	1-15	N/U			
CR208	Patient Condition Code	ID	1-1	R			A, C, D, E, F, G, M
CR209	Complication Indicator	ID	1-1	N/U			N, Y
CR210	Patient Condition Description	AN	1-80	S			
CR211	Patient Condition Description	AN	1-80	S			
CR212	X-ray Availability Indicator	ID	1-1	S			N, Y
CRC	AMBULANCE CERTIFICATION		3	S	2300		
CRC01	Code Category	ID	2-2	R			07
CRC02	Certification Condition Indicator	ID	1-1	R			N, Y
CRC03	Condition Code	ID	2-2	R			01, 02, 03, 04, 05, 06, 07, 08, 09, 60
CRC04	Condition Code	ID	2-2	S			01, 02, 03, 04, 05, 06, 07, 08, 09, 60
CRC05	Condition Code	ID	2-2	S			01, 02, 03, 04, 05, 06, 07, 08, 09, 60
CRC06	Condition Code	ID	2-2	S			01, 02, 03, 04, 05, 06, 07, 08, 09, 60

5010								
Element Identifier	Description	ID	Min. Max.	Usage Reg.	Loop	Loop Repeat	Values	
837-P 5010								
CR203	Subluxation Level Code	ID	2-3	N/U				Code Deleted
CR204	Subluxation Level Code	ID	2-3	N/U				Code Deleted
CR205	Unit or Basis for Measurement Code	ID	2-2	N/U				Code Deleted
CR206	Treatment Period Count 9(3)	R	1-15	N/U				
CR207	Monthly Treatment Count 9(2)	R	1-15	N/U				
CR208	Patient Condition Code	ID	1-1	R			A, C, D, E, F, G, M	
CR209	Complication Indicator	ID	1-1	N/U				Code Deleted
CR210	Patient Condition Description	AN	1-80	S				
CR211	Patient Condition Description	AN	1-80	S				
CR212	Yes/No Condition or Response Code	ID	1-1	N/U				Code Deleted Usage changed to Not Used
CRC	AMBULANCE CERTIFICATION		3	S	2300			
CRC01	Code Category	ID	2-2	R			07	
CRC02	Certification Condition Indicator	ID	1-1	R			N, Y	
CRC03	Condition Code	ID	2-3	R			01, 04, 05, 06, 07, 08, 09, 12	Code Deleted Increase from 2 - 3
CRC04	Condition Code	ID	2-3	S			01, 04, 05, 06, 07, 08, 09, 12	Code Deleted Increase from 2 - 3
CRC05	Condition Code	ID	2-3	S			01, 04, 05, 06, 07, 08, 09, 12	Code Deleted Increase from 2 - 3
CRC06	Condition Code	ID	2-3	S			01, 04, 05, 06, 07, 08, 09, 12	Code Deleted Increase from 2 - 3

Page 30 of 93

PROFESSIONAL CLAIM

4010A1								5010							
Element Identifier	Description	ID	Min. Max.	Usage Reg.	Loop	Loop Repeat	Values	Element Identifier	Description	ID	Min. Max.	Usage Reg.	Loop	Loop Repeat	Values	
837-P 4010A1								**837-P 5010**								
CRC07	Condition Code	ID	2-2	S			01, 02, 03, 04, 05, 06, 07, 08, 09, 60	CRC07	Condition Code	ID	2-3	S			01, 04, 05, 06, 07, 08, 09, 12	Code Deleted Increase from 2 - 3
CRC	**PATIENT CONDITION INFORMATION: VISION**		3	S	2300			**CRC**	**PATIENT CONDITION INFORMATION: VISION**		3	S	2300			
CRC01	Code Category	ID	2-2	R			E1, E2, E3	CRC01	Code Category	ID	2-2	R			E1, E2, E3	
CRC02	Certification Condition Indicator	ID	1-1	R			N, Y	CRC02	Certification Condition Indicator	ID	1-1	R			N, Y	
CRC03	Condition Code	ID	2-2	R			L1, L2, L3, L4, L5	CRC03	Condition Code	ID	2-3	R			L1, L2, L3, L4, L5	Increase from 2 - 3
CRC04	Condition Code	ID	2-2	S			L1, L2, L3, L4, L5	CRC04	Condition Code	ID	2-3	S			L1, L2, L3, L4, L5	Increase from 2 - 3
CRC05	Condition Code	ID	2-2	S			L1, L2, L3, L4, L5	CRC05	Condition Code	ID	2-3	S			L1, L2, L3, L4, L5	Increase from 2 - 3
CRC06	Condition Code	ID	2-2	S			L1, L2, L3, L4, L5	CRC06	Condition Code	ID	2-3	S			L1, L2, L3, L4, L5	Increase from 2 - 3
CRC07	Condition Code	ID	2-2	S			L1, L2, L3, L4, L5	CRC07	Condition Code	ID	2-3	S			L1, L2, L3, L4, L5	Increase from 2 - 3
CRC	**HOMEBOUND INDICATOR**		1	S	2300			**CRC**	**HOMEBOUND INDICATOR**		1	S	2300			
CRC01	Code Category	ID	2-2	R			75	CRC01	Code Category	ID	2-2	R			75	
CRC02	Certification Condition Indicator	ID	1-1	R			Y	CRC02	Certification Condition Indicator	ID	1-1	R			Y	
CRC03	Homebound Indicator	ID	2-2	R			IH	CRC03	Homebound Indicator	ID	2-3	R			IH	Increase from 2 - 3
CRC04	Condition Indicator	ID	2-2	N/U				CRC04	Condition Indicator	ID	2-3	N/U				Increase from 2 - 3
CRC05	Condition Indicator	ID	2-2	N/U				CRC05	Condition Indicator	ID	2-3	N/U				Increase from 2 - 3
CRC06	Condition Indicator	ID	2-2	N/U				CRC06	Condition Indicator	ID	2-3	N/U				Increase from 2 - 3
CRC07	Condition Indicator	ID	2-2	N/U				CRC07	Condition Indicator	ID	2-3	N/U				Increase from 2 - 3
CRC	**EPSDT REFERRAL**		1	S	2300			**CRC**	**EPSDT REFERRAL**		1	S	2300			
CRC01	Code Category	ID	2-2	R			ZZ	CRC01	Code Category	ID	2-2	R			ZZ	
CRC02	Certification Condition Indicator	ID	1-1	R			N, Y	CRC02	Certification Condition Indicator	ID	1-1	R			N, Y	
CRC03	Condition Code	ID	2-2	R			AV, NU, S2, ST	CRC03	Condition Code	ID	2-3	R			AV, NU, S2, ST	Increase from 2 - 3
CRC04	Condition Code	ID	2-2	S			AV, NU, S2, ST	CRC04	Condition Code	ID	2-3	S			AV, NU, S2, ST	Increase from 2 - 3
CRC05	Condition Code	ID	2-2	S			AV, NU, S2, ST	CRC05	Condition Code	ID	2-3	S			AV, NU, S2, ST	Increase from 2 - 3
CRC06	Condition Indicator	ID	2-2	N/U				CRC06	Condition Indicator	ID	2-3	N/U				Increase from 2 - 3
CRC07	Condition Indicator	ID	2-2	N/U				CRC07	Condition Indicator	ID	2-3	N/U				Increase from 2 - 3
HI	**HEALTH CARE DIAGNOSIS CODE**		1	S	2300			**HI**	**HEALTH CARE DIAGNOSIS CODE**		1	R	2300			Usage changed to Required
HI01	HEALTH CARE CODE INFORMATION			R				HI01	HEALTH CARE CODE INFORMATION			R				
HI01-1	Diagnosis Type Code	ID	1-3	R			BK	HI01-1	Diagnosis Type Code	ID	1-3	R			ABK, BK	Code Added
HI01-2	Diagnosis Code	AN	1-30	R				HI01-2	Diagnosis Code	AN	1-30	R				
HI01-3	Date Time Period Format Qualifier	ID	2-3	N/U				HI01-3	Date Time Period Format Qualifier	ID	2-3	N/U				
HI01-4	Date Time Period	AN	1-35	N/U				HI01-4	Date Time Period	AN	1-35	N/U				
HI01-5	Monetary Amount	R	1-18	N/U				HI01-5	Monetary Amount	R	1-18	N/U				

Page 31 of 93

PROFESSIONAL CLAIM

4010A1

Element Identifier	Description	ID	Min. Max.	Usage Reg.	Loop	Loop Repeat	Values
	837-P 4010A1						
HI01-6	Quantity	R	1-15	N/U			
HI01-7	Version Identifier	AN	1-30	N/U			
HI02	HEALTH CARE CODE INFORMATION			S			
HI02-1	Diagnosis Type Code	ID	1-3	R			BF
HI02-2	Diagnosis Code	AN	1-30	R			
HI02-3	Date Time Period Format Qualifier	ID	2-3	N/U			
HI02-4	Date Time Period	AN	1-35	N/U			
HI02-5	Monetary Amount	R	1-18	N/U			
HI02-6	Quantity	R	1-15	N/U			
HI02-7	Version Identifier	AN	1-30	N/U			
HI03	HEALTH CARE CODE INFORMATION			S			
HI03-1	Diagnosis Type Code	ID	1-3	R			BF
HI03-2	Diagnosis Code	AN	1-30	R			
HI03-3	Date Time Period Format Qualifier	ID	2-3	N/U			
HI03-4	Date Time Period	AN	1-35	N/U			
HI03-5	Monetary Amount	R	1-18	N/U			
HI03-6	Quantity	R	1-15	N/U			
HI03-7	Version Identifier	AN	1-30	N/U			
HI04	HEALTH CARE CODE INFORMATION			S			
HI04-1	Diagnosis Type Code	ID	1-3	R			BF
HI04-2	Diagnosis Code	AN	1-30	R			
HI04-3	Date Time Period Format Qualifier	ID	2-3	N/U			
HI04-4	Date Time Period	AN	1-35	N/U			
HI04-5	Monetary Amount	R	1-18	N/U			
HI04-6	Quantity	R	1-15	N/U			
HI04-7	Version Identifier	AN	1-30	N/U			
HI05	HEALTH CARE CODE INFORMATION			S			
HI05-1	Diagnosis Type Code	ID	1-3	R			BF
HI05-2	Diagnosis Code	AN	1-30	R			
HI05-3	Date Time Period Format Qualifier	ID	2-3	N/U			

5010

Element Identifier	Description	ID	Min. Max.	Usage Reg.	Loop	Loop Repeat	Values	
	837-P 5010							
HI01-6	Quantity	R	1-15	N/U				
HI01-7	Version Identifier	AN	1-30	N/U				
HI01-8	Industry code	AN	1-30	N/U				New Element
HI01-9	Yes/No Condition or response Code	ID	1-1	N/U				New Element
HI02	HEALTH CARE CODE INFORMATION			S				
HI02-1	Diagnosis Type Code	ID	1-3	R			ABF, BF	Code Added
HI02-2	Diagnosis Code	AN	1-30	R				
HI02-3	Date Time Period Format Qualifier	ID	2-3	N/U				
HI02-4	Date Time Period	AN	1-35	N/U				
HI02-5	Monetary Amount	R	1-18	N/U				
HI02-6	Quantity	R	1-15	N/U				
HI02-7	Version Identifier	AN	1-30	N/U				
HI02-8	Industry code	AN	1-30	N/U				New Element
HI02-9	Yes/No Condition or response Code	ID	1-1	N/U				New Element
HI03	HEALTH CARE CODE INFORMATION			S				
HI03-1	Diagnosis Type Code	ID	1-3	R			ABF, BF	Code Added
HI03-2	Diagnosis Code	AN	1-30	R				
HI03-3	Date Time Period Format Qualifier	ID	2-3	N/U				
HI03-4	Date Time Period	AN	1-35	N/U				
HI03-5	Monetary Amount	R	1-18	N/U				
HI03-6	Quantity	R	1-15	N/U				
HI03-7	Version Identifier	AN	1-30	N/U				
HI03-8	Industry code	AN	1-30	N/U				New Element
HI03-9	Yes/No Condition or response Code	ID	1-1	N/U				New Element
HI04	HEALTH CARE CODE INFORMATION			S				
HI04-1	Diagnosis Type Code	ID	1-3	R			ABF, BF	Code Added
HI04-2	Diagnosis Code	AN	1-30	R				
HI04-3	Date Time Period Format Qualifier	ID	2-3	N/U				
HI04-4	Date Time Period	AN	1-35	N/U				
HI04-5	Monetary Amount	R	1-18	N/U				
HI04-6	Quantity	R	1-15	N/U				
HI04-7	Version Identifier	AN	1-30	N/U				
HI04-8	Industry code	AN	1-30	N/U				New Element
HI04-9	Yes/No Condition or response Code	ID	1-1	N/U				New Element
HI05	HEALTH CARE CODE INFORMATION			S				
HI05-1	Diagnosis Type Code	ID	1-3	R			ABF, BF	Code Added
HI05-2	Diagnosis Code	AN	1-30	R				
HI05-3	Date Time Period Format Qualifier	ID	2-3	N/U				

PROFESSIONAL CLAIM

4010A1

837-P 4010A1

Element Identifier	Description	ID	Min. Max.	Usage Reg.	Loop	Loop Repeat	Values
HI05-4	Date Time Period	AN	1-35	N/U			
HI05-5	Monetary Amount	R	1-18	N/U			
HI05-6	Quantity	R	1-15	N/U			
HI05-7	Version Identifier	AN	1-30	N/U			
HI06	HEALTH CARE CODE INFORMATION			S			
HI06-1	Diagnosis Type Code	ID	1-3	R			BF
HI06-2	Diagnosis Code	AN	1-30	R			
HI06-3	Date Time Period Format Qualifier	ID	2-3	N/U			
HI06-4	Date Time Period	AN	1-35	N/U			
HI06-5	Monetary Amount	R	1-18	N/U			
HI06-6	Quantity	R	1-15	N/U			
HI06-7	Version Identifier	AN	1-30	N/U			
HI07	HEALTH CARE CODE INFORMATION			S			
HI07-1	Diagnosis Type Code	ID	1-3	R			BF
HI07-2	Diagnosis Code	AN	1-30	R			
HI07-3	Date Time Period Format Qualifier	ID	2-3	N/U			
HI07-4	Date Time Period	AN	1-35	N/U			
HI07-5	Monetary Amount	R	1-18	N/U			
HI07-6	Quantity	R	1-15	N/U			
HI07-7	Version Identifier	AN	1-30	N/U			
HI08	HEALTH CARE CODE INFORMATION			S			
HI08-1	Diagnosis Type Code	ID	1-3	R			BF
HI08-2	Diagnosis Code	AN	1-30	R			
HI08-3	Date Time Period Format Qualifier	ID	2-3	N/U			
HI08-4	Date Time Period	AN	1-35	N/U			
HI08-5	Monetary Amount	R	1-18	N/U			
HI08-6	Quantity	R	1-15	N/U			
HI08-7	Version Identifier	AN	1-30	N/U			
HI09	HEALTH CARE CODE INFORMATION			N/U			

5010

837-P 5010

Element Identifier	Description	ID	Min. Max.	Usage Reg.	Loop	Loop Repeat	Values	Notes
HI05-4	Date Time Period	AN	1-35	N/U				
HI05-5	Monetary Amount	R	1-18	N/U				
HI05-6	Quantity	R	1-15	N/U				
HI05-7	Version Identifier	AN	1-30	N/U				
HI05-8	Industry code	AN	1-30	N/U				New Element
HI05-9	Yes/No Condition or response Code	ID	1-1	N/U				New Element
HI06	HEALTH CARE CODE INFORMATION			S				
HI06-1	Diagnosis Type Code	ID	1-3	R			ABF, BF	Code Added
HI06-2	Diagnosis Code	AN	1-30	R				
HI06-3	Date Time Period Format Qualifier	ID	2-3	N/U				
HI06-4	Date Time Period	AN	1-35	N/U				
HI06-5	Monetary Amount	R	1-18	N/U				
HI06-6	Quantity	R	1-15	N/U				
HI06-7	Version Identifier	AN	1-30	N/U				
HI06-8	Industry code	AN	1-30	N/U				New Element
HI06-9	Yes/No Condition or response Code	ID	1-1	N/U				New Element
HI07	HEALTH CARE CODE INFORMATION			S				
HI07-1	Diagnosis Type Code	ID	1-3	R			ABF, BF	Code Added
HI07-2	Diagnosis Code	AN	1-30	R				
HI07-3	Date Time Period Format Qualifier	ID	2-3	N/U				
HI07-4	Date Time Period	AN	1-35	N/U				
HI07-5	Monetary Amount	R	1-18	N/U				
HI07-6	Quantity	R	1-15	N/U				
HI07-7	Version Identifier	AN	1-30	N/U				
HI07-8	Industry code	AN	1-30	N/U				New Element
HI07-9	Yes/No Condition or response Code	ID	1-1	N/U				New Element
HI08	HEALTH CARE CODE INFORMATION			S				
HI08-1	Diagnosis Type Code	ID	1-3	R			ABF, BF	Code Added
HI08-2	Diagnosis Code	AN	1-30	R				
HI08-3	Date Time Period Format Qualifier	ID	2-3	N/U				
HI08-4	Date Time Period	AN	1-35	N/U				
HI08-5	Monetary Amount	R	1-18	N/U				
HI08-6	Quantity	R	1-15	N/U				
HI08-7	Version Identifier	AN	1-30	N/U				
HI08-8	Industry code	AN	1-30	N/U				New Element
HI08-9	Yes/No Condition or response Code	ID	1-1	N/U				New Element
HI09	HEALTH CARE CODE INFORMATION			S				Usage changed to Situational
HI09-1	Diagnosis Type Code	ID	1-3	R			ABF, BF	New Element
HI09-2	Diagnosis Code	AN	1-30	R				New Element

Page 33 of 93

PROFESSIONAL CLAIM

Element Identifier	Description	ID	Min. Max.	Usage Req.	Loop	Loop Repeat	Values
	4010A1						
	837-P 4010A1						
HI10	HEALTH CARE CODE INFORMATION			N/U			
HI11	HEALTH CARE CODE INFORMATION			N/U			
HI12	HEALTH CARE CODE INFORMATION			N/U			

Element Identifier	Description	ID	Min. Max.	Usage Req.	Loop	Loop Repeat	Values	
	5010							
	837-P 5010							
HI09-3	Date Time Period Format Qualifier	ID	2-3	N/U				New Element
HI09-4	Date Time Period	AN	1-35	N/U				New Element
HI09-5	Monetary Amount	R	1-18	N/U				New Element
HI09-6	Quantity	R	1-15	N/U				New Element
HI09-7	Version Identifier	AN	1-30	N/U				New Element
HI09-8	Industry code	AN	1-30	N/U				New Element
HI09-9	Yes/No Condition or response Code	ID	1-1	N/U				New Element
HI10	HEALTH CARE CODE INFORMATION			S				Usage changed to Situational
HI10-1	Diagnosis Type Code	ID	1-3	R			ABF, BF	New Element
HI10-2	Diagnosis Code	AN	1-30	R				New Element
HI10-3	Date Time Period Format Qualifier	ID	2-3	N/U				New Element
HI10-4	Date Time Period	AN	1-35	N/U				New Element
HI10-5	Monetary Amount	R	1-18	N/U				New Element
HI10-6	Quantity	R	1-15	N/U				New Element
HI10-7	Version Identifier	AN	1-30	N/U				New Element
HI10-8	Industry code	AN	1-30	N/U				New Element
HI10-9	Yes/No Condition or response Code	ID	1-1	N/U				New Element
HI11	HEALTH CARE CODE INFORMATION			S				Usage changed to Situational
HI11-1	Diagnosis Type Code	ID	1-3	R			ABF, BF	New Element
HI11-2	Diagnosis Code	AN	1-30	R				New Element
HI11-3	Date Time Period Format Qualifier	ID	2-3	N/U				New Element
HI11-4	Date Time Period	AN	1-35	N/U				New Element
HI11-5	Monetary Amount	R	1-18	N/U				New Element
HI11-6	Quantity	R	1-15	N/U				New Element
HI11-7	Version Identifier	AN	1-30	N/U				New Element
HI11-8	Industry code	AN	1-30	N/U				New Element
HI11-9	Yes/No Condition or response Code	ID	1-1	N/U				New Elomont
HI12	HEALTH CARE CODE INFORMATION			S				Usage changed to Situational
HI12-1	Diagnosis Type Code	ID	1-3	R			ABF, BF	New Element
HI12-2	Diagnosis Code	AN	1-30	R				New Element
HI12-3	Date Time Period Format Qualifier	ID	2-3	N/U				New Element
HI12-4	Date Time Period	AN	1-35	N/U				New Element
HI12-5	Monetary Amount	R	1-18	N/U				New Element
HI12-6	Quantity	R	1-15	N/U				New Element
HI12-7	Version Identifier	AN	1-30	N/U				New Element
HI12-8	Industry code	AN	1-30	N/U				New Element
HI12-9	Yes/No Condition or response Code	ID	1-1	N/U				New Element

PROFESSIONAL CLAIM

4010A1							
Element Identifier	Description	ID	Min. Max.	Usage Req.	Loop	Loop Repeat	Values
837-P 4010A1							

5010								
Element Identifier	Description	ID	Min. Max.	Usage Req.	Loop	Loop Repeat	Values	
837-P 5010								
HI	ANESTHESIA RELATED PROCEDURE		1	S	2300			New Segment
HI01	HEALTH CARE CODE INFORMATION			R				
HI01-1	Code List Qualifier	ID	1-3	R			BP	
HI01-2	Anesthesia Related Surgical Procedure	AN	1-30	R				
HI01-3	Date Time Period Format Qualifier	ID	2-3	N/U				
HI01-4	Date Time Period	AN	1-35	N/U				
HI01-5	Monetary Amount	R	1-18	N/U				
HI01-6	Quantity	R	1-15	N/U				
HI01-7	Version Identifier	AN	1-30	N/U				
HI01-8	Industry code	AN	1-30	N/U				
HI01-9	Yes/No Condition or response Code	ID	1-1	N/U				
HI02	HEALTH CARE CODE INFORMATION			S				
HI02-1	Code List Qualifier	ID	1-3	R			BO	
HI02-2	Anesthesia Related Surgical Procedure	AN	1-30	R				
HI02-3	Date Time Period Format Qualifier	ID	2-3	N/U				
HI02-4	Date Time Period	AN	1-35	N/U				
HI02-5	Monetary Amount	R	1-18	N/U				
HI02-6	Quantity	R	1-15	N/U				
HI02-7	Version Identifier	AN	1-30	N/U				
HI02-8	Industry code	AN	1-30	N/U				
HI02-9	Yes/No Condition or response Code	ID	1-1	N/U				
HI03	HEALTH CARE CODE INFORMATION			N/U				
HI03-1	Code List Qualifier	ID	1-3	N/U				
HI03-2	Anesthesia Related Surgical Procedure	AN	1-30	N/U				
HI03-3	Date Time Period Format Qualifier	ID	2-3	N/U				
HI03-4	Date Time Period	AN	1-35	N/U				
HI03-5	Monetary Amount	R	1-18	N/U				
HI03-6	Quantity	R	1-15	N/U				
HI03-7	Version Identifier	AN	1-30	N/U				
HI03-8	Industry code	AN	1-30	N/U				
HI03-9	Yes/No Condition or response Code	ID	1-1	N/U				
HI04	HEALTH CARE CODE INFORMATION			N/U				
HI04-1	Code List Qualifier	ID	1-3	N/U				
HI04-2	Anesthesia Related Surgical Procedure	AN	1-30	N/U				

Page 35 of 93

PROFESSIONAL CLAIM

	4010A1						
Element Identifier	Description	ID	Min. Max.	Usage Req.	Loop	Loop Repeat	Values
	837-P 4010A1						

	5010						
Element Identifier	Description	ID	Min. Max.	Usage Req.	Loop	Loop Repeat	Values
	837-P 5010						
HI04-3	Date Time Period Format Qualifier	ID	2-3	N/U			
HI04-4	Date Time Period	AN	1-35	N/U			
HI04-5	Monetary Amount	R	1-18	N/U			
HI04-6	Quantity	R	1-15	N/U			
HI04-7	Version Identifier	AN	1-30	N/U			
HI04-8	Industry code	AN	1-30	N/U			
HI04-9	Yes/No Condition or response Code	ID	1-1	N/U			
HI05	HEALTH CARE CODE INFORMATION			N/U			
HI05-1	Code List Qualifier	ID	1-3	N/U			
HI05-2	Anesthesia Related Surgical Procedure	AN	1-30	N/U			
HI05-3	Date Time Period Format Qualifier	ID	2-3	N/U			
HI05-4	Date Time Period	AN	1-35	N/U			
HI05-5	Monetary Amount	R	1-18	N/U			
HI05-6	Quantity	R	1-15	N/U			
HI05-7	Version Identifier	AN	1-30	N/U			
HI05-8	Industry code	AN	1-30	N/U			
HI05-9	Yes/No Condition or response Code	ID	1-1	N/U			
HI06	HEALTH CARE CODE INFORMATION			N/U			
HI06-1	Code List Qualifier	ID	1-3	N/U			
HI06-2	Anesthesia Related Surgical Procedure	AN	1-30	N/U			
HI06-3	Date Time Period Format Qualifier	ID	2-3	N/U			
HI06-4	Date Time Period	AN	1-35	N/U			
HI06-5	Monetary Amount	R	1-18	N/U			
HI06-6	Quantity	R	1-15	N/U			
HI06-7	Version Identifier	AN	1-30	N/U			
HI06-8	Industry code	AN	1-30	N/U			
HI06-9	Yes/No Condition or response Code	ID	1-1	N/U			
HI07	HEALTH CARE CODE INFORMATION			N/U			
HI07-1	Code List Qualifier	ID	1-3	N/U			
HI07-2	Anesthesia Related Surgical Procedure	AN	1-30	N/U			
HI07-3	Date Time Period Format Qualifier	ID	2-3	N/U			
HI07-4	Date Time Period	AN	1-35	N/U			
HI07-5	Monetary Amount	R	1-18	N/U			
HI07-6	Quantity	R	1-15	N/U			
HI07-7	Version Identifier	AN	1-30	N/U			
HI07-8	Industry code	AN	1-30	N/U			

PROFESSIONAL CLAIM

4010A1							
Element Identifier	Description	ID	Min. Max.	Usage Req.	Loop	Loop Repeat	Values
837-P 4010A1							

5010							
Element Identifier	Description	ID	Min. Max.	Usage Req.	Loop	Loop Repeat	Values
837-P 5010							
HI07-9	Yes/No Condition or response Code	ID	1-1	N/U			
HI08	HEALTH CARE CODE INFORMATION			N/U			
HI08-1	Code List Qualifier	ID	1-3	N/U			
HI08-2	Anesthesia Related Surgical Procedure	AN	1-30	N/U			
HI08-3	Date Time Period Format Qualifier	ID	2-3	N/U			
HI08-4	Date Time Period	AN	1-35	N/U			
HI08-5	Monetary Amount	R	1-18	N/U			
HI08-6	Quantity	R	1-15	N/U			
HI08-7	Version Identifier	AN	1-30	N/U			
HI08-8	Industry code	AN	1-30	N/U			
HI08-9	Yes/No Condition or response Code	ID	1-1	N/U			
HI09	HEALTH CARE CODE INFORMATION			N/U			
HI09-1	Code List Qualifier	ID	1-3	N/U			
HI09-2	Anesthesia Related Surgical Procedure	AN	1-30	N/U			
HI09-3	Date Time Period Format Qualifier	ID	2-3	N/U			
HI09-4	Date Time Period	AN	1-35	N/U			
HI09-5	Monetary Amount	R	1-18	N/U			
HI09-6	Quantity	R	1-15	N/U			
HI09-7	Version Identifier	AN	1-30	N/U			
HI09-8	Industry code	AN	1-30	N/U			
HI09-9	Yes/No Condition or response Code	ID	1-1	N/U			
HI10	HEALTH CARE CODE INFORMATION			N/U			
HI10-1	Code List Qualifier	ID	1-3	N/U			
HI10-2	Anesthesia Related Surgical Procedure	AN	1-30	N/U			
HI10-3	Date Time Period Format Qualifier	ID	2-3	N/U			
HI10-4	Date Time Period	AN	1-35	N/U			
HI10-5	Monetary Amount	R	1-18	N/U			
HI10-6	Quantity	R	1-15	N/U			
HI10-7	Version Identifier	AN	1-30	N/U			
HI10-8	Industry code	AN	1-30	N/U			
HI10-9	Yes/No Condition or response Code	ID	1-1	N/U			
HI11	HEALTH CARE CODE INFORMATION			N/U			
HI11-1	Code List Qualifier	ID	1-3	N/U			
HI11-2	Anesthesia Related Surgical Procedure	AN	1-30	N/U			

Page 37 of 93

PROFESSIONAL CLAIM

4010A1							
Element Identifier	Description	ID	Min. Max.	Usage Req.	Loop	Loop Repeat	Values
837-P 4010A1							

5010							
Element Identifier	Description	ID	Min. Max.	Usage Req.	Loop	Loop Repeat	Values
837-P 5010							
HI11-3	Date Time Period Format Qualifier	ID	2-3	N/U			
HI11-4	Date Time Period	AN	1-35	N/U			
HI11-5	Monetary Amount	R	1-18	N/U			
HI11-6	Quantity	R	1-15	N/U			
HI11-7	Version Identifier	AN	1-30	N/U			
HI11-8	Industry code	AN	1-30	N/U			
HI11-9	Yes/No Condition or response Code	ID	1-1	N/U			
HI12	HEALTH CARE CODE INFORMATION			N/U			
HI12-1	Code List Qualifier	ID	1-3	N/U			
HI12-2	Anesthesia Related Surgical Procedure	AN	1-30	N/U			
HI12-3	Date Time Period Format Qualifier	ID	2-3	N/U			
HI12-4	Date Time Period	AN	1-35	N/U			
HI12-5	Monetary Amount	R	1-18	N/U			
HI12-6	Quantity	R	1-15	N/U			
HI12-7	Version Identifier	AN	1-30	N/U			
HI12-8	Industry code	AN	1-30	N/U			
HI12-9	Yes/No Condition or response Code	ID	1-1	N/U			
HI	CONDITION INFORMATION		2	S	2300		New Segment
HI01	HEALTH CARE CODE INFORMATION			R			
HI01-1	Code List Qualifier	ID	1-3	R			BG
HI01-2	Condition Code	AN	1-30	R			
HI01-3	Date Time Period Format Qualifier	ID	2-3	N/U			
HI01-4	Date Time Period	AN	1-35	N/U			
HI01-5	Monetary Amount	R	1-18	N/U			
HI01-6	Quantity	R	1-15	N/U			
HI01-7	Version Identifier	AN	1-30	N/U			
HI01-8	Industry code	AN	1-30	N/U			
HI01-9	Yes/No Condition or response Code	ID	1-1	N/U			
HI02	HEALTH CARE CODE INFORMATION			S			
HI02-1	Code List Qualifier	ID	1-3	R			BG
HI02-2	Condition Code	AN	1-30	R			
HI02-3	Date Time Period Format Qualifier	ID	2-3	N/U			
HI02-4	Date Time Period	AN	1-35	N/U			
HI02-5	Monetary Amount	R	1-18	N/U			
HI02-6	Quantity	R	1-15	N/U			
HI02-7	Version Identifier	AN	1-30	N/U			
HI02-8	Industry code	AN	1-30	N/U			

Page 38 of 93

PROFESSIONAL CLAIM

4010A1								**5010**						
Element Identifier	Description	ID	Min. Max.	Usage Req.	Loop	Loop Repeat	Values	Element Identifier	Description	ID	Min. Max.	Usage Req.	Loop	Loop Repeat	Values
837-P 4010A1								**837-P 5010**						
								HI02-9	Yes/No Condition or response Code	ID	1-1	N/U			
								HI03	HEALTH CARE CODE INFORMATION			S			
								HI03-1	Code List Qualifier	ID	1-3	R			BG
								HI03-2	Condition Code	AN	1-30	R			
								HI03-3	Date Time Period Format Qualifier	ID	2-3	N/U			
								HI03-4	Date Time Period	AN	1-35	N/U			
								HI03-5	Monetary Amount	R	1-18	N/U			
								HI03-6	Quantity	R	1-15	N/U			
								HI03-7	Version Identifier	AN	1-30	N/U			
								HI03-8	Industry code	AN	1-30	N/U			
								HI03-9	Yes/No Condition or response Code	ID	1-1	N/U			
								HI04	HEALTH CARE CODE INFORMATION			S			
								HI04-1	Code List Qualifier	ID	1-3	R			BG
								HI04-2	Condition Code	AN	1-30	R			
								HI04-3	Date Time Period Format Qualifier	ID	2-3	N/U			
								HI04-4	Date Time Period	AN	1-35	N/U			
								HI04-5	Monetary Amount	R	1-18	N/U			
								HI04-6	Quantity	R	1-15	N/U			
								HI04-7	Version Identifier	AN	1-30	N/U			
								HI04-8	Industry code	AN	1-30	N/U			
								HI04-9	Yes/No Condition or response Code	ID	1-1	N/U			
								HI05	HEALTH CARE CODE INFORMATION			S			
								HI05-1	Code List Qualifier	ID	1-3	R			BG
								HI05-2	Condition Code	AN	1-30	R			
								HI05-3	Date Time Period Format Qualifier	ID	2-3	N/U			
								HI05-4	Date Time Period	AN	1-35	N/U			
								HI05-5	Monetary Amount	R	1-18	N/U			
								HI05-6	Quantity	R	1-15	N/U			
								HI05-7	Version Identifier	AN	1-30	N/U			
								HI05-8	Industry code	AN	1-30	N/U			
								HI05-9	Yes/No Condition or response Code	ID	1-1	N/U			
								HI06	HEALTH CARE CODE INFORMATION			S			
								HI06-1	Code List Qualifier	ID	1-3	R			BG
								HI06-2	Condition Code	AN	1-30	R			
								HI06-3	Date Time Period Format Qualifier	ID	2-3	N/U			
								HI06-4	Date Time Period	AN	1-35	N/U			
								HI06-5	Monetary Amount	R	1-18	N/U			
								HI06-6	Quantity	R	1-15	N/U			

Page 39 of 93

PROFESSIONAL CLAIM

Element Identifier	Description	ID	Min. Max.	Usage Reg.	Loop	Loop Repeat	Values
	4010A1						
	837-P 4010A1						

Element Identifier	Description	ID	Min. Max.	Usage Reg.	Loop	Loop Repeat	Values
	5010						
	837-P 5010						
HI06-7	Version Identifier	AN	1-30	N/U			
HI06-8	Industry code	AN	1-30	N/U			
HI06-9	Yes/No Condition or response Code	ID	1-1	N/U			
HI07	HEALTH CARE CODE INFORMATION			S			
HI07-1	Code List Qualifier	ID	1-3	R			BG
HI07-2	Condition Code	AN	1-30	R			
HI07-3	Date Time Period Format Qualifier	ID	2-3	N/U			
HI07-4	Date Time Period	AN	1-35	N/U			
HI07-5	Monetary Amount	R	1-18	N/U			
HI07-6	Quantity	R	1-15	N/U			
HI07-7	Version Identifier	AN	1-30	N/U			
HI07-8	Industry code	AN	1-30	N/U			
HI07-9	Yes/No Condition or response Code	ID	1-1	N/U			
HI08	HEALTH CARE CODE INFORMATION			S			
HI08-1	Code List Qualifier	ID	1-3	R			BG
HI08-2	Condition Code	AN	1-30	R			
HI08-3	Date Time Period Format Qualifier	ID	2-3	N/U			
HI08-4	Date Time Period	AN	1-35	N/U			
HI08-5	Monetary Amount	R	1-18	N/U			
HI08-6	Quantity	R	1-15	N/U			
HI08-7	Version Identifier	AN	1-30	N/U			
HI08-8	Industry code	AN	1-30	N/U			
HI08-9	Yes/No Condition or response Code	ID	1-1	N/U			
HI09	HEALTH CARE CODE INFORMATION			S			
HI09-1	Code List Qualifier	ID	1-3	R			BG
HI09-2	Condition Code	AN	1-30	R			
HI09-3	Date Time Period Format Qualifier	ID	2-3	N/U			
HI09-4	Date Time Period	AN	1-35	N/U			
HI09-5	Monetary Amount	R	1-18	N/U			
HI09-6	Quantity	R	1-15	N/U			
HI09-7	Version Identifier	AN	1-30	N/U			
HI09-8	Industry code	AN	1-30	N/U			
HI09-9	Yes/No Condition or response Code	ID	1-1	N/U			
HI10	HEALTH CARE CODE INFORMATION			S			
HI10-1	Code List Qualifier	ID	1-3	R			BG
HI10-2	Condition Code	AN	1-30	R			
HI10-3	Date Time Period Format Qualifier	ID	2-3	N/U			
HI10-4	Date Time Period	AN	1-35	N/U			

Page 40 of 93

PROFESSIONAL CLAIM

4010A1

837-P 4010A1

Element Identifier	Description	ID	Min./Max.	Usage Reg.	Loop	Loop Repeat	Values
HCP	CLAIM PRICING/REPRICING INFORMATION		1	S	2300		
HCP01	Pricing Methodology	ID	2-2	R			00, 01, 02, 03, 04, 05, 07, 08, 09, 10 ,11, 12, 13, 14
HCP02	Repriced Allowed Amount S9(7)V99	R	1-18	R			
HCP03	Repriced Saving Amount S9(7)V99	R	1-18	S			
HCP04	Repricing Organization Identifier	AN	1-30	S			
HCP05	Repricing Per Diem or Flat Rate Amount S9(5)V99	R	1-9	S			

5010

837-P 5010

Element Identifier	Description	ID	Min./Max.	Usage Reg.	Loop	Loop Repeat	Values
HI10-5	Monetary Amount	R	1-18	N/U			
HI10-6	Quantity	R	1-15	N/U			
HI10-7	Version Identifier	AN	1-30	N/U			
HI10-8	Industry code	AN	1-30	N/U			
HI10-9	Yes/No Condition or response Code	ID	1-1	N/U			
HI11	HEALTH CARE CODE INFORMATION			S			
HI11-1	Code List Qualifier	ID	1-3	R			BG
HI11-2	Condition Code	AN	1-30	R			
HI11-3	Date Time Period Format Qualifier	ID	2-3	N/U			
HI11-4	Date Time Period	AN	1-35	N/U			
HI11-5	Monetary Amount	R	1-18	N/U			
HI11-6	Quantity	R	1-15	N/U			
HI11-7	Version Identifier	AN	1-30	N/U			
HI11-8	Industry code	AN	1-30	N/U			
HI11-9	Yes/No Condition or response Code	ID	1-1	N/U			
HI12	HEALTH CARE CODE INFORMATION			S			
HI12-1	Code List Qualifier	ID	1-3	R			BG
HI12-2	Condition Code	AN	1-30	R			
HI12-3	Date Time Period Format Qualifier	ID	2-3	N/U			
HI12-4	Date Time Period	AN	1-35	N/U			
HI12-5	Monetary Amount	R	1-18	N/U			
HI12-6	Quantity	R	1-15	N/U			
HI12-7	Version Identifier	AN	1-30	N/U			
HI12-8	Industry code	AN	1-30	N/U			
HI12-9	Yes/No Condition or response Code	ID	1-1	N/U			
HCP	CLAIM PRICING/REPRICING INFORMATION		1	S	2300		
HCP01	Pricing Methodology	ID	2-2	R			00, 01, 02, 03, 04, 05, 07, 08, 09, 10 ,11, 12, 13, 14
HCP02	Repriced Allowed Amount S9(7)V99	R	1-18	R			
HCP03	Repriced Saving Amount S9(7)V99	R	1-18	S			
HCP04	Repricing Organization Identifier	AN	1-50	S			
HCP05	Repricing Per Diem or Flat Rate Amount S9(5)V99	R	1-9	S			

Increase from 30 - 50

Page 41 of 93

PROFESSIONAL CLAIM

4010A1								5010							
Element Identifier	Description	ID	Min. Max.	Usage Reg.	Loop	Loop Repeat	Values	Element Identifier	Description	ID	Min. Max.	Usage Reg.	Loop	Loop Repeat	Values
	837-P 4010A1								837-P 5010						
HCP06	Repriced Approved Ambulatory Patient Group Code	AN	1-30	S				HCP06	Repriced Approved Ambulatory Patient Group Code	AN	1-50	S			Increase from 30 - 50
HCP07	Repriced Approved Ambulatory Patient Group Amount S9(7)V99	R	1-18	S				HCP07	Repriced Approved Ambulatory Patient Group Amount S9(7)V99	R	1-18	S			
HCP08	Product/Service ID	AN	1-48	N/U				HCP08	Product/Service ID	AN	1-48	N/U			
HCP09	Product/Service ID Qualifier	ID	2-2	N/U				HCP09	Product/Service ID Qualifier	ID	2-2	N/U			
HCP10	Product/Service ID	AN	1-48	N/U				HCP10	Product/Service ID	AN	1-48	N/U			
HCP11	Unit or Basis for Measurement Code	ID	2-2	N/U				HCP11	Unit or Basis for Measurement Code	ID	2-2	N/U			
HCP12	Quantity 9(3)V9	R	1-15	N/U				HCP12	Quantity 9(3)V9	R	1-15	N/U			
HCP13	Reject Reason Code	ID	2-2	S			T1, T2, T3, T4, T5, T6	HCP13	Reject Reason Code	ID	2-2	S			T1, T2, T3, T4, T5, T6
HCP14	Policy Compliance Code	ID	1-2	S			1, 2, 3, 4, 5	HCP14	Policy Compliance Code	ID	1-2	S			1, 2, 3, 4, 5
HCP15	Exception Code	ID	1-2	S			1, 2, 3, 4, 5, 6	HCP15	Exception Code	ID	1-2	S			1, 2, 3, 4, 5, 6
CR7	HOME HEALTH CARE PLAN INFORMATION		1	S	2305	6									Segment Deleted
CR701	Discipline Type Code	ID	2-2	R			AI, MS, OT, PT, SN, ST								
CR702	Total Visits Rendered Count	N0	1-9	R											
CR703	Certification Period Projected Visit Count	N0	1-9	R											
HSD	HEALTH CARE SERVICES DELIVERY		3	S	2305										Segment Deleted
HSD01	Visits	ID	2-2	S			VS								
HSD02	Number of Visits 9(3)	R	1-15	S											
HSD03	Frequency Period	ID	2-2	S			DA, MO, Q1, WK								
HSD04	Frequency Count 9(2)V9	R	1-6	S											
HSD05	Duration of Visits Units	ID	1-2	S			7, 35								
HSD06	Duration of Visits, Number of Units	N0	1-3	S											
HSD07	Ship, Delivery or Calendar Pattern Code	ID	1-2	S			1-7, A-H, J-L, N, O, S, SA, SB, SC, SD, SG, SL, SP, SX, SY, SZ, W								
HSD08	Delivery Pattern Time Code	ID	1-1	S			D, E, F								
NM1	REFERRING PROVIDER NAME		1	S	2310A	2		NM1	REFERRING PROVIDER NAME		1	S	2310A	2	
NM101	Entity Identifier Code	ID	2-3	R			DN, P3	NM101	Entity Identifier Code	ID	2-3	R			DN, P3
NM102	Entity Type Qualifier	ID	1-1	R			1, 2	NM102	Entity Type Qualifier	ID	1-1	R			1	Code Deleted
NM103	Referring Provider Last Name	AN	1-35	R				NM103	Referring Provider Last Name	AN	1-60	R			Increase from 35 - 60

PROFESSIONAL CLAIM

4010A1							
Element Identifier	Description	ID	Min. Max.	Usage Reg.	Loop	Loop Repeat	Values
837-P 4010A1							
NM104	Referring Provider First Name	AN	1-25	S			
NM105	Referring Provider Middle Name	AN	1-25	S			
NM106	Name Prefix	AN	1-10	N/U			
NM107	Referring Provider Name Suffix	AN	1-10	S			
NM108	Identification Code Qualifier	ID	1-2	S			24, 34, XX
NM109	Referring Provider Identifier	AN	2-80	S			
NM110	Entity Relationship Code	ID	2-2	N/U			
NM111	Entity Identifier Code	ID	2-3	N/U			
PRV	**REFERRING PROVIDER SPECIALTY INFORMATION**		1	S	2310A		
PRV01	Provider Code	ID	1-3	R			RF
PRV02	Reference Identification Qualifier	ID	2-3	R			ZZ
PRV03	Provider Taxonomy Code	AN	1-30	R			
PRV04	State or Province Code	ID	2-2	N/U			
PRV05	PROVIDER SPECIALTY INFORMATION			N/U			
PRV06	Provider Organization Code	ID	3-3	N/U			
REF	**REFERRING PROVIDER SECONDARY IDENTIFICATION**		5	S	2310A		
REF01	Reference Identification Qualifier	ID	2-3	R			0B, 1B, 1C, 1D, 1G, 1H, EI, G2, LU, N5, SY, X5
REF02	Referring Provider Secondary Identifier	AN	1-30	R			
REF03	Description	AN	1-80	N/U			
REF04	REFERENCE IDENTIFIER			N/U			

5010								
Element Identifier	Description	ID	Min. Max.	Usage Reg.	Loop	Loop Repeat	Values	
837-P 5010								
NM104	Referring Provider First Name	AN	1-35	S				Increase from 25 - 35
NM105	Referring Provider Middle Name	AN	1-25	S				
NM106	Name Prefix	AN	1-10	N/U				
NM107	Referring Provider Name Suffix	AN	1-10	S				
NM108	Identification Code Qualifier	ID	1-2	S			XX	Code Deleted
NM109	Referring Provider Identifier	AN	2-80	S				
NM110	Entity Relationship Code	ID	2-2	N/U				
NM111	Entity Identifier Code	ID	2-3	N/U				
NM112	Name Last or Organization Name	AN	1-60	N/U				New Element
								Segment Deleted
REF	**REFERRING PROVIDER SECONDARY IDENTIFICATION**		3	S	2310A			
REF01	Reference Identification Qualifier	ID	2-3	R			0B, 1G, G2	Code Deleted
REF02	Referring Provider Secondary Identifier	AN	1-50	R				Increase from 30 - 50
REF03	Description	AN	1-80	N/U				
REF04	REFERENCE IDENTIFIER			N/U				
REF04-1	Reference Identifier Qualifier	ID	2-3	N/U				New Element
REF04-2	Other Payer Primary Idenitifer	AN	1-50	N/U				New Element
REF04-3	Reference Identification Qualifier	ID	2-3	N/U				New Element
REF04-4	Reference Identification	AN	1-50	N/U				New Element
REF04-5	Reference Identification Qualifier	ID	2-3	N/U				New Element
REF04-6	Reference Identification	AN	1-50	N/U				New Element

Page 43 of 93

PROFESSIONAL CLAIM

4010A1

Element Identifier	Description	ID	Min. Max.	Usage Reg.	Loop	Loop Repeat	Values
	837-P 4010A1						
NM1	**RENDERING PROVIDER NAME**		1	S	2310B	1	
NM101	Entity Identifier Code	ID	2-3	R			82
NM102	Entity Type Qualifier	ID	1-1	R			1, 2
NM103	Rendering Provider Last or Organization Name	AN	1-35	R			
NM104	Rendering Provider First Name	AN	1-25	S			
NM105	Rendering Provider Middle Name	AN	1-25	S			
NM106	Name Prefix	AN	1-10	N/U			
NM107	Rendering Provider Name Suffix	AN	1-10	S			
NM108	Identification Code Qualifier	ID	1-2	R			24, 34, XX
NM109	Rendering Provider Identifier	AN	2-80	R			
NM110	Entity Relationship Code	ID	2-2	N/U			
NM111	Entity Identifier Code	ID	2-3	N/U			
PRV	**RENDERING PROVIDER SPECIALTY INFORMATION**		1	S	2310B		
PRV01	Provider Code	ID	1-3	R			PE
PRV02	Reference Identification Qualifier	ID	2-3	R			ZZ
PRV03	Provider Taxonomy Code	AN	1-30	R			
PRV04	State or Province Code	ID	2-2	N/U			
PRV05	PROVIDER SPECIALTY INFORMATION			N/U			
PRV06	Provider Organization Code	ID	3-3	N/U			
REF	**RENDERING PROVIDER SECONDARY IDENTIFICATION**		5	S	2310B		
REF01	Reference Identification Qualifier	ID	2-3	R			0B, 1B, 1C, 1D, 1G, 1H, EI, G2, LU, N5, SY, X5
REF02	Rendering Provider Secondary Identifier	AN	1-30	R			
REF03	Description	AN	1-80	N/U			
REF04	REFERENCE IDENTIFIER			N/U			

5010

Element Identifier	Description	ID	Min. Max.	Usage Reg.	Loop	Loop Repeat	Values	
	837-P 5010							
NM1	**RENDERING PROVIDER NAME**		1	S	2310B	1		
NM101	Entity Identifier Code	ID	2-3	R			82	
NM102	Entity Type Qualifier	ID	1-1	R			1, 2	
NM103	Rendering Provider Last or Organization Name	AN	1-60	R				Increase from 35 - 60
NM104	Rendering Provider First Name	AN	1-35	S				Increase from 25 - 35
NM105	Rendering Provider Middle Name	AN	1-25	S				
NM106	Name Prefix	AN	1-10	N/U				
NM107	Rendering Provider Name Suffix	AN	1-10	S				
NM108	Identification Code Qualifier	ID	1-2	S			XX	Code Deleted Usage Changed to Situational
NM109	Rendering Provider Identifier	AN	2-80	S				Usage Canged to Situational
NM110	Entity Relationship Code	ID	2-2	N/U				
NM111	Entity Identifier Code	ID	2-3	N/U				
NM112	Name Last or Organization Name	AN	1-60	N/U				New Element
PRV	**RENDERING PROVIDER SPECIALTY INFORMATION**		1	S	2310B			
PRV01	Provider Code	ID	1-3	R			PE	
PRV02	Reference Identification Qualifier	ID	2-3	R			PXC	Code Change
PRV03	Provider Taxonomy Code	AN	1-50	R				Increase from 30 - 50
PRV04	State or Province Code	ID	2-2	N/U				
PRV05	PROVIDER SPECIALTY INFORMATION			N/U				
PRV06	Provider Organization Code	ID	3-3	N/U				
REF	**RENDERING PROVIDER SECONDARY IDENTIFICATION**		4	S	2310B			
REF01	Reference Identification Qualifier	ID	2-3	R			0B, 1G, G2, LU	
REF02	Rendering Provider Secondary Identifier	AN	1-50	R				Increase from 30 - 50
REF03	Description	AN	1-80	N/U				
REF04	REFERENCE IDENTIFIER			N/U				
REF04-1	Reference Identifier Qualifier	ID	2-3	N/U				New Element
REF04-2	Other Payer Primary Idenitifer	AN	1-50	N/U				New Element

Page 44 of 93

PROFESSIONAL CLAIM

Element Identifier	Description	ID	Min. Max.	Usage Reg.	Loop	Loop Repeat	Values
	4010A1						
	837-P 4010A1						
NM1	**PURCHASED SERVICE PROVIDER NAME**		1	S	2310C	1	
NM101	Entity Identifier Code	ID	2-3	R			QB
NM102	Entity Type Qualifier	ID	1-1	R			1 , 2
NM103	Name Last or Organization Name	AN	1-35	R			
NM104	Name First	AN	1-25	S			
NM105	Name Middle	AN	1-25	S			
NM106	Name Prefix	AN	1-10	N/U			
NM107	Name Suffix	AN	1-10	N/U			
NM108	Identification Code Qualifier	ID	1-2	S			24, 34, XX
NM109	Purchased Service Provider Identifier	AN	2-80	S			
NM110	Entity Relationship Code	ID	2-2	N/U			
NM111	Entity Identifier Code	ID	2-3	N/U			
REF	**PURCHASED SERVICE PROVIDER SECONDARY IDENTIFICATION**		5	S	2310C		
REF01	Reference Identification Qualifier	ID	2-3	R			0B,1A,1B,1C,1D,1G,1H,EI,G2,LU,N5,SY,U3,X5
REF02	Purchased Service Provider Secondary Identifier	AN	1-30	R			
REF03	Description	AN	1-80	N/U			
REF04	REFERENCE IDENTIFIER			N/U			
NM1	**SERVICE FACILITY LOCATION**		1	S	2310D	1	
NM101	Entity Identifier Code	ID	2-3	R			77, FA, LI, TL
NM102	Entity Type Qualifier	ID	1-1	R			2
NM103	Laboratory or Facility Name	AN	1-35	S			
NM104	Name First	AN	1-25	N/U			
NM105	Name Middle	AN	1-25	N/U			
NM106	Name Prefix	AN	1-10	N/U			
NM107	Name Suffix	AN	1-10	N/U			
NM108	Identification Code Qualifier	ID	1-2	S			24, 34, XX

Element Identifier	Description	ID	Min. Max.	Usage Reg.	Loop	Loop Repeat	Values	
	5010							
	837-P 5010							
REF04-3	Reference Identification Qualifier	ID	2-3	N/U				New Element
REF04-4	Reference Identification	AN	1-50	N/U				New Element
REF04-5	Reference Identification Qualifier	ID	2-3	N/U				New Element
REF04-6	Reference Identification	AN	1-50	N/U				New Element
								Segment Deleted
								Segment Deleted
NM1	**SERVICE FACILITY LOCATION**		1	S	2310C	1		Loop Change
NM101	Entity Identifier Code	ID	2-3	R			77	Code Deleted
NM102	Entity Type Qualifier	ID	1-1	R			2	
NM103	Laboratory or Facility Name	AN	1-60	R				Increase from 35 - 60 / Usage changed to required
NM104	Name First	AN	1-35	N/U				Increase from 25 - 35
NM105	Name Middle	AN	1-25	N/U				
NM106	Name Prefix	AN	1-10	N/U				
NM107	Name Suffix	AN	1-10	N/U				
NM108	Identification Code Qualifier	ID	1-2	S			XX	Code Deleted

Page 45 of 93

PROFESSIONAL CLAIM

4010A1

837-P 4010A1

Element Identifier	Description	ID	Min. Max.	Usage Reg.	Loop	Loop Repeat	Values
NM109	Laboratory or Facility Primary Identifier	AN	2-80	S			
NM110	Entity Relationship Code	ID	2-2	N/U			
NM111	Entity Identifier Code	ID	2-3	N/U			
N3	**SERVICE FACILITY LOCATION ADDRESS**		1	R	2310D		
N301	Laboratory or Facility Address Line	AN	1-55	R			
N302	Laboratory or Facility Address Line	AN	1-55	S			
N4	**SERVICE FACILITY LOCATION CITY/STATE/ZIP**		1	R	2310D		
N401	Laboratory or Facility City Name	AN	2-30	R			
N402	Laboratory or Facility State or Province Code	ID	2-2	R			
N403	Laboratory or Facility Postal Zone ZIP Code	ID	3-15	R			
N404	Laboratory/Facility Country Code	ID	2-3	S			
N405	Location Qualifier	ID	1-2	N/U			
N406	Location Identifier	AN	1-30	N/U			
REF	**SERVICE FACILITY LOCATION SECONDARY IDENTIFICATION**		5	S	2310D		
REF01	Reference Identification Qualifier	ID	2-3	R			0B,1A,1B,1C,1D,1G,1H,G2,LU,N5,TJ,X4,X5
REF02	Laboratory or Facility Secondary Identifier	AN	1-30	R			
REF03	Description	AN	1-80	N/U			
REF04	REFERENCE IDENTIFIER			N/U			

5010

837-P 5010

Element Identifier	Description	ID	Min. Max.	Usage Reg.	Loop	Loop Repeat	Values	
NM109	Laboratory or Facility Primary Identifier	AN	2-80	S				
NM110	Entity Relationship Code	ID	2-2	N/U				
NM111	Entity Identifier Code	ID	2-3	N/U				
NM112	Name Last or Organization Name	AN	1-60	N/U				New Element
N3	**SERVICE FACILITY LOCATION ADDRESS**		1	R	2310C			Loop Change
N301	Laboratory or Facility Address Line	AN	1-55	R				
N302	Laboratory or Facility Address Line	AN	1-55	S				
N4	**SERVICE FACILITY LOCATION CITY/STATE/ZIP**		1	R	2310C			Loop Change
N401	Laboratory or Facility City Name	AN	2-30	R				
N402	Laboratory or Facility State or Province Code	ID	2-2	S				Usage changed to Situational
N403	Laboratory or Facility Postal Zone ZIP Code	ID	3-15	S				Usage changed to Situational
N404	Laboratory/Facility Country Code	ID	2-3	S				
N405	Location Qualifier	ID	1-2	N/U				
N406	Location Identifier	AN	1-30	N/U				
N407	Country Subdivision Code	ID	1-3	S				New Element
REF	**SERVICE FACILITY LOCATION SECONDARY IDENTIFICATION**		3	S	2310C			Loop Change
REF01	Reference Identification Qualifier	ID	2-3	R			0B, G2, LU	Code Deleted
REF02	Laboratory or Facility Secondary Identifier	AN	1-50	R				Increase from 30 - 50
REF03	Description	AN	1-80	N/U				
REF04	REFERENCE IDENTIFIER			N/U				
REF04-1	Reference Identifier Qualifier	ID	2-3	N/U				New Element
REF04-2	Other Payer Primary Idenitifer	AN	1-50	N/U				New Element
REF04-3	Reference Identification Qualifier	ID	2-3	N/U				New Element
REF04-4	Reference Identification	AN	1-50	N/U				New Element
REF04-5	Reference Identification Qualifier	ID	2-3	N/U				New Element
REF04-6	Reference Identification	AN	1-50	N/U				New Element

Page 46 of 93

PROFESSIONAL CLAIM

4010A1

837-P 4010A1

Element Identifier	Description	ID	Min. Max.	Usage Reg.	Loop	Loop Repeat	Values
NM1	**SUPERVISING PROVIDER NAME**		1	S	2310E	1	
NM101	Entity Identifier Code	ID	2-3	R			DQ
NM102	Entity Type Qualifier	ID	1-1	R			1
NM103	Supervising Provider Last Name	AN	1-35	R			
NM104	Supervising Provider First Name	AN	1-25	R			
NM105	Supervising Provider Middle Name	AN	1-25	S			
NM106	Name Prefix	AN	1-10	N/U			
NM107	Supervising Provider Name Suffix	AN	1-10	S			
NM108	Identification Code Qualifier	ID	1-2	S			24, 34, XX
NM109	Supervising Provider Identifier	AN	2-80	S			
NM110	Entity Relationship Code	ID	2-2	N/U			
NM111	Entity Identifier Code	ID	2-3	N/U			
REF	**SUPERVISING PROVIDER SECONDARY IDENTIFIER**		5	S	2310E		
REF01	Reference Identification Qualifier	ID	2-3	R			0B, 1B, 1C, 1D, 1G, 1H, EI, G2, LU, N5, SY, X5
REF02	Supervising Provider Secondary Identifier	AN	1-30	R			
REF03	Description	AN	1-80	N/U			
REF04	REFERENCE IDENTIFIER			N/U			

5010

837-P 5010

Element Identifier	Description	ID	Min. Max.	Usage Reg.	Loop	Loop Repeat	Values	
PER	**SERVICE FACILITY CONTACT INFORMATION**		1	R	2310C			New Segment
PER01	Contact Function Code	ID	2-2	R			IC	
PER02	Submitter Contact Name	AN	1-60	S				
PER03	Communication Number Qualifier	ID	2-2	R			TE	
PER04	Communication Number	AN	1-256	R				
PER05	Communication Number Qualifier	ID	2-2	S			EX	
PER06	Communication Number	AN	1-256	S				
PER07	Communication Number Qualifier	ID	2-2	N/U				
PER08	Communication Number	AN	1-256	N/U				
PER09	Contact Inquiry Reference	AN	1-20	N/U				
NM1	**SUPERVISING PROVIDER NAME**		1	S	2310D	1		Loop Change
NM101	Entity Identifier Code	ID	2-3	R			DQ	
NM102	Entity Type Qualifier	ID	1-1	R			1	
NM103	Supervising Provider Last Name	AN	1-60	R				Increase from 35 - 60
NM104	Supervising Provider First Name	AN	1-35	S				Increase from 25 - 35 Usage changed to Situational
NM105	Supervising Provider Middle Name	AN	1-25	S				
NM106	Name Prefix	AN	1-10	N/U				
NM107	Supervising Provider Name Suffix	AN	1-10	S				
NM108	Identification Code Qualifier	ID	1-2	S			XX	Code Deleted
NM109	Supervising Provider Identifier	AN	2-80	S				
NM110	Entity Relationship Code	ID	2-2	N/U				
NM111	Entity Identifier Code	ID	2-3	N/U				
NM112	Name Last or Organization Name	AN	1-60	N/U				New Element
REF	**SUPERVISING PROVIDER SECONDARY IDENTIFIER**		4	S	2310D			Loop Change Code Deleted
REF01	Reference Identification Qualifier	ID	2-3	R			0B, 1G, G2, LU	
REF02	Supervising Provider Secondary Identifier	AN	1-50	R				Increase from 30 - 50
REF03	Description	AN	1-80	N/U				
REF04	REFERENCE IDENTIFIER			N/U				New Element
REF04-1	Reference Identifier Qualifier	ID	2-3	N/U				

Page 47 of 93

PROFESSIONAL CLAIM

Element Identifier	Description	ID	Min. Max.	Usage Reg.	Loop	Loop Repeat	Values
	4010A1						
	837-P 4010A1						

Element Identifier	Description	ID	Min. Max.	Usage Reg.	Loop	Loop Repeat	Values	
	5010							
	837-P 5010							
REF04-2	Other Payer Primary Idenitifer	AN	1-50	N/U				New Element
REF04-3	Reference Identification Qualifier	ID	2-3	N/U				New Element
REF04-4	Reference Identification	AN	1-50	N/U				New Element
REF04-5	Reference Identification Qualifier	ID	2-3	N/U				New Element
REF04-6	Reference Identification	AN	1-50	N/U				New Element
NM1	**AMBULANCE PICK UP LOCATION**		1	S	2310E	1		New Segment
NM101	Entity Identifier Code	ID	2-3	R			PW	
NM102	Entity Type Qualifier	ID	1-1	R			2	
NM103	Name Last or Organization Name	AN	1-60	N/U				
NM104	Name First	AN	1-35	N/U				
NM105	Name Middle	AN	1-25	N/U				
NM106	Name Prefix	AN	1-10	N/U				
NM107	Name Suffix	AN	1-10	N/U				
NM108	Identification Code Qualifier	ID	1-2	N/U				
NM109	Identification Code	AN	2-80	N/U				
NM110	Entity Relationship Code	ID	2-2	N/U				
NM111	Entity Identifier Code	ID	2-3	N/U				
NM112	Name Last or Organization Name	AN	1-60	N/U				
N3	**AMBULANCE PICK UP LOCATION ADDRESS**		1	R	2310E			New Segment
N301	Ambulance Pick Up Address Line	AN	1-55	R				
N302	Ambulance Pick Up Address Line	AN	1-55	S				
N4	**AMBULANCE PICK UP LOCATION CITY/STATE/ZIP**		1	R	2310E			New Segment
N401	Ambulance Pick Up City Name	AN	2-30	R				
N402	Ambulance Pick Up State or Province Code	ID	2-2	S				
N403	Ambulance Pick Up Postal Zone ZIP Code	ID	3-15	S				
N404	Ambulance Pick Up Country Code	ID	2-3	S				
N405	Location Qualifier	ID	1-2	N/U				
N406	Location Identifier	AN	1-30	N/U				
N407	Country Subdivision Code	ID	1-3	S				

Page 48 of 93

PROFESSIONAL CLAIM

Element Identifier	Description	ID	Min. Max.	Usage Reg.	Loop	Loop Repeat	Values
			4010A1				
			837-P 4010A1				
SBR	OTHER SUBSCRIBER INFORMATION		1	S	2320	10	
SBR01	Payer Responsibility Sequence Number Code	ID	1-1	R			P, S, T
SBR02	Individual Relationship Code	ID	2-2	R			01, 04, 05, 07, 10, 15, 17, 18, 19, 20, 21, 22, 23, 24, 29, 32, 33, 36, 39, 40, 41, 43, 53, G8

Element Identifier	Description	ID	Min. Max.	Usage Reg.	Loop	Loop Repeat	Values	
			5010					
			837-P 5010					
NM1	AMBULANCE DROP OFF LOCATION		1	S	2310F	1		New Segment
NM101	Entity Identifier Code	ID	2-3	R			45	
NM102	Entity Type Qualifier	ID	1-1	R			2	
NM103	Ambulance Drop Off Location	AN	1-60	S				
NM104	Name First	AN	1-35	N/U				
NM105	Name Middle	AN	1-25	N/U				
NM106	Name Prefix	AN	1-10	N/U				
NM107	Name Suffix	AN	1-10	N/U				
NM108	Identification Code Qualifier	ID	1-2	N/U				
NM109	Identification Code	AN	2-80	N/U				
NM110	Entity Relationship Code	ID	2-2	N/U				
NM111	Entity Identifier Code	ID	2-3	N/U				
NM112	Name Last or Organization Name	AN	1-60	N/U				
N3	AMBULANCE DROP OFF LOCATION ADDRESS		1	R	2310F			New Segment
N301	Ambulance Drop Off Address Line	AN	1-55	R				
N302	Ambulance Drop Off Address Line	AN	1-55	S				
N4	AMBULANCE DROP OFF LOCATION CITY/STATE/ZIP		1	R	2310F			New Segment
N401	Ambulance Drop Off City Name	AN	2-30	R				
N402	Ambulance Drop Off State or Province Code	ID	2-2	S				
N403	Ambulance Drop Off Postal Zone ZIP Code	ID	3-15	S				
N404	Ambulance Drop Off Country Code	ID	2-3	S				
N405	Location Qualifier	ID	1-2	N/U				
N406	Location Identifier	AN	1-30	N/U				
N407	Country Subdivision Code	ID	1-3	S				
SBR	OTHER SUBSCRIBER INFORMATION		1	S	2320	10		
SBR01	Payer Responsibility Sequence Number Code	ID	1-1	R			A, B, C, D, E, F, G, H, P, S, T, U	Code Added / Code Deleted
SBR02	Individual Relationship Code	ID	2-2	R			01, 18, 19, 20, 21, 39, 40, 53, G8	

Page 49 of 93

PROFESSIONAL CLAIM

4010A1

837-P 4010A1

Element Identifier	Description	ID	Min. Max.	Usage Reg.	Loop	Loop Repeat	Values
SBR03	Insured Group or Policy Number	AN	1-30	S			
SBR04	Other Insured Group Name	AN	1-60	S			
SBR05	Insurance Type Code	ID	1-3	R			AP, C1, CP, GP, HM, IP, LD, LT, MB, MC, MI, MP, OT, PP, SP
SBR06	Coordination of Benefits Code	ID	1-1	N/U			
SBR07	Yes/No Condition or Response Code	ID	1-1	N/U			
SBR08	Employment Status Code	ID	2-2	N/U			
SBR09	Claim Filing Indicator Code	ID	1-2	S			09, 10, 11, 12, 13, 14, 15, 16, AM, BL, CH, CI, DS, HM, LI, LM, MB, MC, OF, TV, VA, WC, ZZ
CAS	CLAIM LEVEL ADJUSTMENTS		5	S	2320		
CAS01	Claim Adjustment Group Code	ID	1-2	R			CO, CR, OA, PI, PR
CAS02	Adjustment Reason Code	ID	1-5	R			
CAS03	Adjustment Amount S9(7)V99	R	1-18	R			
CAS04	Adjustment Quantity 9(7)	R	1-15	S			
CAS05	Adjustment Reason Code	ID	1-5	S			
CAS06	Adjustment Amount S9(7)V99	R	1-18	S			
CAS07	Adjustment Quantity 9(7)	R	1-15	S			
CAS08	Adjustment Reason Code	ID	1-5	S			
CAS09	Adjustment Amount S9(7)V99	R	1-18	S			
CAS10	Adjustment Quantity 9(7)	R	1-15	S			
CAS11	Adjustment Reason Code	ID	1-5	S			
CAS12	Adjustment Amount S9(7)V99	R	1-18	S			
CAS13	Adjustment Quantity 9(7)	R	1-15	S			
CAS14	Adjustment Reason Code	ID	1-5	S			
CAS15	Adjustment Amount S9(7)V99	R	1-18	S			
CAS16	Adjustment Quantity 9(7)	R	1-15	S			
CAS17	Adjustment Reason Code	ID	1-5	S			
CAS18	Adjustment Amount S9(7)V99	R	1-18	S			
CAS19	Adjustment Quantity 9(7)	R	1-15	S			
AMT	COB PAYER PAID AMOUNT		1	S	2320		

5010

837-P 5010

Element Identifier	Description	ID	Min. Max.	Usage Reg.	Loop	Loop Repeat	Values	
SBR03	Insured Group or Policy Number	AN	1-50	S				Increase from 30 - 50
SBR04	Other Insured Group Name	AN	1-60	S				
SBR05	Insurance Type Code	ID	1-3	S			12, 13, 14, 15, 16, 41, 42, 43, 47	Code Change Usage changed to Situational
SBR06	Coordination of Benefits Code	ID	1-1	N/U				
SBR07	Yes/No Condition or Response Code	ID	1-1	N/U				
SBR08	Employment Status Code	ID	2-2	N/U				
SBR09	Claim Filing Indicator Code	ID	1-2	S			11, 12, 13, 14, 15, 16, 17, AM, BL, CH, CI, DS, FI, HM, LM, MA, MB, MC, OF, TV, VA, WC, ZZ	Code Change
CAS	CLAIM LEVEL ADJUSTMENTS		5	S	2320			
CAS01	Claim Adjustment Group Code	ID	1-2	R			CO, CR, OA, PI, PR	
CAS02	Adjustment Reason Code	ID	1-5	R				
CAS03	Adjustment Amount S9(7)V99	R	1-18	R				
CAS04	Adjustment Quantity 9(7)	R	1-15	S				
CAS05	Adjustment Reason Code	ID	1-5	S				
CAS06	Adjustment Amount S9(7)V99	R	1-18	S				
CAS07	Adjustment Quantity 9(7)	R	1-15	S				
CAS08	Adjustment Reason Code	ID	1-5	S				
CAS09	Adjustment Amount S9(7)V99	R	1-18	S				
CAS10	Adjustment Quantity 9(7)	R	1-15	S				
CAS11	Adjustment Reason Code	ID	1-5	S				
CAS12	Adjustment Amount S9(7)V99	R	1-18	S				
CAS13	Adjustment Quantity 9(7)	R	1-15	S				
CAS14	Adjustment Reason Code	ID	1-5	S				
CAS15	Adjustment Amount S9(7)V99	R	1-18	S				
CAS16	Adjustment Quantity 9(7)	R	1-15	S				
CAS17	Adjustment Reason Code	ID	1-5	S				
CAS18	Adjustment Amount S9(7)V99	R	1-18	S				
CAS19	Adjustment Quantity 9(7)	R	1-15	S				
AMT	COB PAYER PAID AMOUNT		1	S	2320			

Page 50 of 93

PROFESSIONAL CLAIM

	4010A1						
Element Identifier	Description	ID	Min. Max.	Usage Reg.	Loop	Loop Repeat	Values
	837-P 4010A1						
AMT01	Amount Qualifier Code	ID	1-3	R			D
AMT02	Payer Paid Amount S9(7)V99	R	1-18	R			
AMT03	Credit/Debit Flag Code	ID	1-1	N/U			
AMT	**COB APPROVED AMOUNT**		1	S	2320		
AMT01	Amount Qualifier Code	ID	1-3	R			AAE
AMT02	Approved Amount S9(7)V99	R	1-18	R			
AMT03	Credit/Debit Flag Code	ID	1-1	N/U			
AMT	**COB ALLOWED AMOUNT**		1	S	2320		
AMT01	Amount Qualifier Code	ID	1-3	R			B6
AMT02	Allowed Amount S9(7)V99	R	1-18	R			
AMT03	Credit/Debit Flag Code	ID	1-1	N/U			
AMT	**COB PATIENT RESPONSIBILITY AMOUNT**		1	S	2320		
AMT01	Amount Qualifier Code	ID	1-3	R			F2
AMT02	Other Payer Patient Responsibility Amount S9(7)V99	R	1-18	R			
AMT03	Credit/Debit Flag Code	ID	1-1	N/U			
AMT	**COB COVERED AMOUNT**		1	S	2320		
AMT01	Amount Qualifier Code	ID	1-3	R			AU
AMT02	Other Payer Covered Amount S9(7)V99	R	1-18	R			
AMT03	Credit/Debit Flag Code	ID	1-1	N/U			
AMT	**COB DISCOUNT AMOUNT**		1	S	2320		
AMT01	Amount Qualifier Code	ID	1-3	R			D8

	5010							
Element Identifier	Description	ID	Min. Max.	Usage Reg.	Loop	Loop Repeat	Values	
	837-P 5010							
AMT01	Amount Qualifier Code	ID	1-3	R			D	
AMT02	Payer Paid Amount S9(7)V99	R	1-18	R				
AMT03	Credit/Debit Flag Code	ID	1-1	N/U				
								Segment Deleted
AMT	**COB TOTAL NON-COVERED AMOUNT**		1	S	2320			New Segment
AMT01	Amount Qualifier Code	ID	1-3	R			A8	
AMT02	Non-Covered Amount S9(7)V99	R	1-18	R				
AMT03	Credit/Debit Flag Code	ID	1-1	N/U				
								Segment Deleted
AMT	**REMAINING PATIENT LIABILITY**		1	S	2320			New Segment
AMT01	Amount Qualifier Code	ID	1-3	R			EAF	
AMT02	Remaining Patient Liability Amount S9(7)V99	R	1-18	R				
AMT03	Credit/Debit Flag Code	ID	1-1	N/U				
								Segment Deleted
								Segment Deleted
								Segment Deleted

Page 51 of 93

PROFESSIONAL CLAIM

4010A1							
Element Identifier	Description	ID	Min. Max.	Usage Reg.	Loop	Loop Repeat	Values
	837-P 4010A1						
AMT02	Other Payer Discount Amount S9(7)V99	R	1-18	R			
AMT03	Credit/Debit Flag Code	ID	1-1	N/U			
AMT	**COB PER DAY LIMIT AMOUNT**		1	S	2320		
AMT01	Amount Qualifier Code	ID	1-3	R			DY
AMT02	Other Payer Per Day Limit Amount S9(7)V99	R	1-18	R			
AMT03	Credit/Debit Flag Code	ID	1-1	N/U			
AMT	**COB PATIENT PAID AMOUNT**		1	S	2320		
AMT01	Amount Qualifier Code	ID	1-3	R			F5
AMT02	Other Payer Patient Paid Amount S9(7)V99	R	1-18	R			
AMT03	Credit/Debit Flag Code	ID	1-1	N/U			
AMT	**COB TAX AMOUNT**		1	S	2320		
AMT01	Amount Qualifier Code	ID	1-3	R			T
AMT02	Other Payer Tax Amount S9(7)V99	R	1-18	R			
AMT03	Credit/Debit Flag Code	ID	1-1	N/U			
AMT	**COB TOTAL CLAIM BEFORE TAXES AMOUNT**		1	S	2320		
AMT01	Amount Qualifier Code	ID	1-3	R			T2
AMT02	Other Payer Pre-Tax Claim Total Amount S9(7)V99	R	1-18	R			
AMT03	Credit/Debit Flag Code	ID	1-1	N/U			
DMG	**SUBSCRIBER DEMOGRAPHIC INFORMATION**		1	S	2320		
DMG01	Date Time Period Format Qualifier	ID	2-3	R			D8
DMG02	Other Insured Birth Date	AN	1-35	R			CCYYMMDD
DMG03	Other Insured Gender Code	ID	1-1	R			F, M, U
DMG04	Marital Status Code	ID	1-1	N/U			
DMG05	Race or Ethnicity Code	ID	1-1	N/U			
DMG06	Citizenship Status Code	ID	1-2	N/U			
DMG07	Country Code	ID	2-3	N/U			
DMG08	Basis of Verification Code	ID	1-2	N/U			
DMG09	Quantity	R	1-15	N/U			
OI	**OTHER INSURANCE COVERAGE INFORMATION**		1	R	2320		
OI01	Claim Filing Indicator Code	ID	1-2	N/U			

5010							
Element Identifier	Description	ID	Min. Max.	Usage Reg.	Loop	Loop Repeat	Values
	837-P 5010						
							Segment Deleted
							Segment Deleted
							Segment Deleted
							Segment Deleted
							Segment Deleted
OI	**OTHER INSURANCE COVERAGE INFORMATION**		1	R	2320		
OI01	Claim Filing Indicator Code	ID	1-2	N/U			

Page 52 of 93

PROFESSIONAL CLAIM

4010A1

Element Identifier	Description	ID	Min. Max.	Usage Reg.	Loop	Loop Repeat	Values
	837-P 4010A1						
OI02	Claim Submission Reason Code	ID	2-2	N/U			
OI03	Benefits Assignment Certification Indicator	ID	1-1	R			N, Y
OI04	Patient Signature Source Code	ID	1-1	S			B, C, M, P, S
OI05	Provider Agreement Code	ID	1-1	N/U			
OI06	Release of Information Code	ID	1-1	R			A, I, M, N, O, Y
MOA	**MEDICARE OUTPATIENT ADJUDICATION INFORMATION**		**1**	**S**	**2320**		
MOA01	Reimbursement Rate 9(3)V99	R	1-10	S			
MOA02	HCPCS Payable Amount S9(7)V99	R	1-18	S			
MOA03	Remark Code	AN	1-30	S			
MOA04	Remark Code	AN	1-30	S			
MOA05	Remark Code	AN	1-30	S			
MOA06	Remark Code	AN	1-30	S			
MOA07	Remark Code	AN	1-30	S			
MOA08	End Stage Renal Disease Payment Amount S9(7)V99	R	1-18	S			
MOA09	Non-Payable Professional Component Billed Amount S9(7)V99	R	1-18	S			
NM1	**OTHER SUBSCRIBER NAME**		**1**	**R**	**2330A**	**1**	
NM101	Entity Identifier Code	ID	2-3	R			IL
NM102	Entity Type Qualifier	ID	1-1	R			1, 2
NM103	Other Insured Last Name	AN	1-35	R			
NM104	Other Insured First Name	AN	1-25	S			
NM105	Other Insured Middle Name	AN	1-25	S			
NM106	Name Prefix	AN	1-10	N/U			
NM107	Other Insured Name Suffix	AN	1-10	S			
NM108	Identification Code Qualifier	ID	1-2	R			MI, ZZ
NM109	Other Insured Identifier	AN	2-80	R			
NM110	Entity Relationship Code	ID	2-2	N/U			
NM111	Entity Identifier Code	ID	2-3	N/U			
N3	**OTHER SUBSCRIBER ADDRESS**		**1**	**S**	**2330A**		
N301	Other Insured Address Line	AN	1-55	R			

5010

Element Identifier	Description	ID	Min. Max.	Usage Reg.	Loop	Loop Repeat	Values	
	837-P 5010							
OI02	Claim Submission Reason Code	ID	2-2	N/U				
OI03	Benefits Assignment Certification Indicator	ID	1-1	R			N, W, Y	Code Added
OI04	Patient Signature Source Code	ID	1-1	S			P	Code Deleted
OI05	Provider Agreement Code	ID	1-1	N/U				
OI06	Release of Information Code	ID	1-1	R			I, Y	Code Deleted
MOA	**MEDICARE OUTPATIENT ADJUDICATION INFORMATION**		**1**	**S**	**2320**			
MOA01	Reimbursement Rate 9(3)V99	R	1-10	S				
MOA02	HCPCS Payable Amount S9(7)V99	R	1-18	S				
MOA03	Remark Code	AN	1-50	S				Increase from 30 - 50
MOA04	Remark Code	AN	1-50	S				Increase from 30 - 50
MOA05	Remark Code	AN	1-50	S				Increase from 30 - 50
MOA06	Remark Code	AN	1-50	S				Increase from 30 - 50
MOA07	Remark Code	AN	1-50	S				Increase from 30 - 50
MOA08	End Stage Renal Disease Payment Amount S9(7)V99	R	1-18	S				
MOA09	Non-Payable Professional Component Billed Amount S9(7)V99	R	1-18	S				
NM1	**OTHER SUBSCRIBER NAME**		**1**	**R**	**2330A**	**1**		
NM101	Entity Identifier Code	ID	2-3	R			IL	
NM102	Entity Type Qualifier	ID	1-1	R			1, 2	
NM103	Other Insured Last Name	AN	1-60	R				Increase from 35 - 60
NM104	Other Insured First Name	AN	1-35	S				Increase from 25 - 35
NM105	Other Insured Middle Name	AN	1-25	S				
NM106	Name Prefix	AN	1-10	N/U				
NM107	Other Insured Name Suffix	AN	1-10	S				
NM108	Identification Code Qualifier	ID	1-2	R			II, MI	Code Change
NM109	Other Insured Identifier	AN	2-80	R				
NM110	Entity Relationship Code	ID	2-2	N/U				
NM111	Entity Identifier Code	ID	2-3	N/U				
NM112	Name Last or Organization Name	AN	1-60	N/U				New Element
N3	**OTHER SUBSCRIBER ADDRESS**		**1**	**S**	**2330A**			
N301	Other Insured Address Line	AN	1-55	R				

Page 53 of 93

PROFESSIONAL CLAIM

4010A1

837-P 4010A1

Element Identifier	Description	ID	Min. Max.	Usage Reg.	Loop	Loop Repeat	Values
N302	Other Insured Address Line	AN	1-55	S			
N4	**OTHER SUBSCRIBER CITY/STATE/ZIP CODE**		1	S	2330A		
N401	Other Insured City Name	AN	2-30	S			
N402	Other Insured State Code	ID	2-2	S			
N403	Other Insured Postal Zone or ZIP Code	ID	3-15	S			
N404	Subscriber Country Code	ID	2-3	S			
N405	Location Qualifier	ID	1-2	N/U			
N406	Location Identifier	AN	1-30	N/U			
REF	**OTHER SUBSCRIBER SECONDARY IDENTIFICATION**		3	S	2330A		
REF01	Reference Identification Qualifier	ID	2-3	R			1W, 23, IG, SY
REF02	Other Insured Additional Identifier	AN	1-30	R			
REF03	Description	AN	1-80	N/U			
REF04	REFERENCE IDENTIFIER			N/U			
NM1	**OTHER PAYER NAME**		1	R	2330B	1	
NM101	Entity Identifier Code	ID	2-3	R			PR
NM102	Entity Type Qualifier	ID	1-1	R			2
NM103	Other Payer Last or Organization Name	AN	1-35	R			
NM104	Name First	AN	1-25	N/U			
NM105	Name Middle	AN	1-25	N/U			
NM106	Name Prefix	AN	1-10	N/U			
NM107	Name Suffix	AN	1-10	N/U			
NM108	Identification Code Qualifier	ID	1-2	R			PI, XV
NM109	Other Payer Primary Identifier	AN	2-80	R			
NM110	Entity Relationship Code	ID	2-2	N/U			
NM111	Entity Identifier Code	ID	2-3	N/U			

5010

837-P 5010

Element Identifier	Description	ID	Min. Max.	Usage Reg.	Loop	Loop Repeat	Values	Notes
N302	Other Insured Address Line	AN	1-55	S				
N4	**OTHER SUBSCRIBER CITY/STATE/ZIP CODE**		1	R	2330A			Usage changed to Required
N401	Other Insured City Name	AN	2-30	R				Usage changed to Required
N402	Other Insured State Code	ID	2-2	S				
N403	Other Insured Postal Zone or ZIP Code	ID	3-15	S				
N404	Subscriber Country Code	ID	2-3	S				
N405	Location Qualifier	ID	1-2	N/U				
N406	Location Identifier	AN	1-30	N/U				
N407	Country Subdivision Code	ID	1-3	S				New Element
REF	**OTHER SUBSCRIBER SECONDARY IDENTIFICATION**		1	S	2330A			
REF01	Reference Identification Qualifier	ID	2-3	R			SY	Code Deleted
REF02	Other Insured Additional Identifier	AN	1-50	R				Increase from 30 - 50
REF03	Description	AN	1-80	N/U				
REF04	REFERENCE IDENTIFIER			N/U				
REF04-1	Reference Identifier Qualifier	ID	2-3	N/U				New Element
REF04-2	Other Payer Primary Idenitifer	AN	1-50	N/U				New Element
REF04-3	Reference Identification Qualifier	ID	2-3	N/U				New Element
REF04-4	Reference Identification	AN	1-50	N/U				New Element
REF04-5	Reference Identification Qualifier	ID	2-3	N/U				New Element
REF04-6	Reference Identification	AN	1-50	N/U				New Element
NM1	**OTHER PAYER NAME**		1	R	2330B	1		
NM101	Entity Identifier Code	ID	2-3	R			PR	
NM102	Entity Type Qualifier	ID	1-1	R			2	
NM103	Other Payer Last or Organization Name	AN	1-60	R				Increase from 35 - 60
NM104	Name First	AN	1-35	N/U				Increase from 25 - 35
NM105	Name Middle	AN	1-25	N/U				
NM106	Name Prefix	AN	1-10	N/U				
NM107	Name Suffix	AN	1-10	N/U				
NM108	Identification Code Qualifier	ID	1-2	R			PI, XV	
NM109	Other Payer Primary Identifier	AN	2-80	R				
NM110	Entity Relationship Code	ID	2-2	N/U				
NM111	Entity Identifier Code	ID	2-3	N/U				

Page 54 of 93

PROFESSIONAL CLAIM

4010A1

Element Identifier	Description	ID	Min. Max.	Usage Reg.	Loop	Loop Repeat	Values
	837-P 4010A1						
PER	**OTHER PAYER CONTACT INFORMATION**		2	S	2330B		
PER01	Contact Function Code	ID	2-2	R			IC
PER02	Other Payer Contact Name	AN	1-60	R			
PER03	Communication Number Qualifier	ID	2-2	R			ED, EM, FX, TE
PER04	Communication Number	AN	1-80	R			
PER05	Communication Number Qualifier	ID	2-2	S			ED, EM, EX, FX, TE
PER06	Communication Number	AN	1-80	S			
PER07	Communication Number Qualifier	ID	2-2	S			ED, EM, EX, FX, TE
PER08	Communication Number	AN	1-80	S			
PER09	Contact Inquiry Reference	AN	1-20	N/U			
DTP	**CLAIM ADJUDICATION DATE**		1	S	2330B		
DTP01	Date Time Qualifier	ID	3-3	R			573
DTP02	Date Time Period Format Qualifier	ID	2-3	R			D8
DTP03	Adjudication or Payment Date	AN	1-35	R			CCYYMMDD

5010

Element Identifier	Description	ID	Min. Max.	Usage Reg.	Loop	Loop Repeat	Values	
	837-P 5010							
NM112	Name Last or Organization Name	AN	1-60	N/U				New Element
N3	**OTHER PAYER ADDRESS**		1	S	2330B			New Segment
N301	Other Payer Address Line	AN	1-55	R				
N302	Other Payer Address Line	AN	1-55	S				
N4	**OTHER PAYER CITY/STATE/ZIP CODE**		1	R	2330B			New Segment
N401	Other Payer City Name	AN	2-30	R				
N402	Other Payer State Code	ID	2-2	S				
N403	Other Payer Postal Zone or ZIP Code	ID	3-15	S				
N404	Other Payer Country Code	ID	2-3	S				
N405	Location Qualifier	ID	1-2	N/U				
N406	Location Identifier	AN	1-30	N/U				
N407	Country Subdivision Code	ID	1-3	S				
								Segment Deleted
								Segment Deleed
DTP	**DATE - CLAIM CHECK OR REMITTANCE DATE**		1	S	2330B			New Segment
DTP01	Date Time Qualifier	ID	3-3	R			573	
DTP02	Date Time Period Format Qualifier	ID	2-3	R			D8	
DTP03	Adjudication or Payment Date	AN	1-35	R			CCYYMMDD	

Page 55 of 93

PROFESSIONAL CLAIM

	4010A1						
Element Identifier	Description	ID	Min. Max.	Usage Reg.	Loop	Loop Repeat	Values
	837-P 4010A1						
REF	**OTHER PAYER SECONDARY IDENTIFIER**		2	S	2330B		
REF01	Reference Identification Qualifier	ID	2-3	R			2U, F8, FY, NF, TJ
REF02	Other Payer Secondary Identifier	AN	1-30	R			
REF03	Description	AN	1-80	N/U			
REF04	REFERENCE IDENTIFIER			N/U			
REF	**OTHER PAYER PRIOR AUTHORIZATION OR REFERRAL NUMBER**		2	S	2330B		
REF01	Reference Identification Qualifier	ID	2-3	R			9F, G1
REF02	Other Payer Prior Authorization or Referral Number	AN	1-30	R			
REF03	Description	AN	1-80	N/U			
REF04	REFERENCE IDENTIFIER			N/U			

	5010							
Element Identifier	Description	ID	Min. Max.	Usage Reg.	Loop	Loop Repeat	Values	
	837-P 5010							
REF	**OTHER PAYER SECONDARY IDENTIFICATION**		2	S	2330B			Name Change
REF01	Reference Identification Qualifier	ID	2-3	R			2U, EI, FY, NF	Code Deleted
REF02	Other Payer Secondary Identifier	AN	1-50	R				Increase from 30 - 50
REF03	Description	AN	1-80	N/U				
REF04	REFERENCE IDENTIFIER			N/U				
REF04-1	Reference Identifier Qualifier	ID	2-3	N/U				New Element
REF04-2	Other Payer Primary Idenitifer	AN	1-50	N/U				New Element
REF04-3	Reference Identification Qualifier	ID	2-3	N/U				New Element
REF04-4	Reference Identification	AN	1-50	N/U				New Element
REF04-5	Reference Identification Qualifier	ID	2-3	N/U				New Element
REF04-6	Reference Identification	AN	1-50	N/U				New Element
REF	**OTHER PAYER PRIOR AUTHORIZATION NUMBER**		1	S	2330B			Name Change
REF01	Reference Identification Qualifier	ID	2-3	R			G1	Code Deleted
REF02	Other Payer Prior Authorization Number	AN	1-50	R				Increase from 30 - 50
REF03	Description	AN	1-80	N/U				
REF04	REFERENCE IDENTIFIER			N/U				
REF04-1	Reference Identifier Qualifier	ID	2-3	N/U				New Element
REF04-2	Other Payer Primary Idenitifer	AN	1-50	N/U				New Element
REF04-3	Reference Identification Qualifier	ID	2-3	N/U				New Element
REF04-4	Reference Identification	AN	1-50	N/U				New Element
REF04-5	Reference Identification Qualifier	ID	2-3	N/U				New Element
REF04-6	Reference Identification	AN	1-50	N/U				New Element
REF	**OTHER PAYER REFERRAL NUMBER**		1	S	2330B			New Segment
REF01	Reference Identification Qualifier	ID	2-3	R			9F	
REF02	Other Payer Referral Number	AN	1-50	R				
REF03	Description	AN	1-80	N/U				
REF04	REFERENCE IDENTIFIER			N/U				

Page 56 of 93

PROFESSIONAL CLAIM

4010A1

Element Identifier	Description	ID	Min. Max.	Usage Reg.	Loop	Loop Repeat	Values
	837-P 4010A1						
REF	**OTHER PAYER CLAIM ADJUSTMENT INDICATOR**		2	S	2330B		
REF01	Reference Identification Qualifier	ID	2-3	R			T4
REF02	Other Payer Claim Adjustment Indicator	AN	1-30	R			Y
REF03	Description	AN	1-80	N/U			
REF04	REFERENCE IDENTIFIER			N/U			
NM1	**OTHER PAYER PATIENT INFORMATION**		1	S	2330C	1	
NM101	Entity Identifier Code	ID	2-3	R			QC
NM102	Entity Type Qualifier	ID	1-1	R			1
NM103	Patient Last Name	AN	1-35	N/U			
NM104	Name First	AN	1-25	N/U			
NM105	Name Middle	AN	1-25	N/U			
NM106	Name Prefix	AN	1-10	N/U			
NM107	Name Suffix	AN	1-10	N/U			
NM108	Identification Code Qualifier	ID	1-2	R			MI
NM109	Other Payer Patient Primary Identifier	AN	2-80	R			
NM110	Entity Relationship Code	ID	2-2	N/U			
NM111	Entity Identifier Code	ID	2-3	N/U			

5010

Element Identifier	Description	ID	Min. Max.	Usage Reg.	Loop	Loop Repeat	Values	
	837-P 5010							
REF04-1	Reference Identifier Qualifier	ID	2-3	N/U				
REF04-2	Other Payer Primary Idenitifer	AN	1-50	N/U				
REF04-3	Reference Identification Qualifier	ID	2-3	N/U				
REF04-4	Reference Identification	AN	1-50	N/U				
REF04-5	Reference Identification Qualifier	ID	2-3	N/U				
REF04-6	Reference Identification	AN	1-50	N/U				
REF	**OTHER PAYER CLAIM ADJUSTMENT INDICATOR**		1	S	2330B			
REF01	Reference Identification Qualifier	ID	2-3	R			T4	
REF02	Other Payer Claim Adjustment Indicator	AN	1-50	R				Code Deleted Increase from 30 - 50
REF03	Description	AN	1-80	N/U				
REF04	REFERENCE IDENTIFIER			N/U				New Element
REF04-1	Reference Identifier Qualifier	ID	2-3	N/U				New Element
REF04-2	Other Payer Primary Idenitifer	AN	1-50	N/U				New Element
REF04-3	Reference Identification Qualifier	ID	2-3	N/U				New Element
REF04-4	Reference Identification	AN	1-50	N/U				New Element
REF04-5	Reference Identification Qualifier	ID	2-3	N/U				New Element
REF04-6	Reference Identification	AN	1-50	N/U				Segment Deleted
REF	**OTHER PAYER CLAIM CONTROL NUMBER**		1	S	2330B			New Segment

Page 57 of 93

PROFESSIONAL CLAIM

	4010A1						
Element Identifier	Description	ID	Min. Max.	Usage Reg.	Loop	Loop Repeat	Values
	837-P 4010A1						
REF	OTHER PAYER PATIENT IDENTIFICATION		3	S	2330C		
REF01	Reference Identification Qualifier	ID	2-3	R			1W, 23, IG, SY
REF02	Other Payer Patient Secondary Identifier	AN	1-30	R			
REF03	Description	AN	1-80	N/U			
REF04	REFERENCE IDENTIFIER			N/U			
NM1	OTHER PAYER REFERRING PROVIDER		1	S	2330D	2	
NM101	Entity Identifier Code	ID	2-3	R			DN, P3
NM102	Entity Type Qualifier	ID	1-1	R			1, 2
NM103	Referring Provider Last Name	AN	1-35	N/U			
NM104	Name First	AN	1-25	N/U			
NM105	Name Middle	AN	1-25	N/U			
NM106	Name Prefix	AN	1-10	N/U			
NM107	Name Suffix	AN	1-10	N/U			
NM108	Identification Code Qualifier	ID	1-2	N/U			
NM109	Identification Code	AN	2-80	N/U			
NM110	Entity Relationship Code	ID	2-2	N/U			
NM111	Entity Identifier Code	ID	2-3	N/U			
REF	OTHER PAYER REFERRING PROVIDER IDENTIFICATION		3	R	2330D		
REF01	Reference Identification Qualifier	ID	2-3	R			1B, 1C, 1D, EI, G2, LU, N5

	5010							
Element Identifier	Description	ID	Min. Max.	Usage Reg.	Loop	Loop Repeat	Values	
	837-P 5010							
REF01	Reference Identification Qualifier	ID	2-3	R			F8	
REF02	Other Payer Claim Control Number	AN	1-50	R				
REF03	Description	AN	1-80	N/U				
REF04	REFERENCE IDENTIFIER			N/U				
REF04-1	Reference Identifier Qualifier	ID	2-3	N/U				
REF04-2	Other Payer Primary Identifier	AN	1-50	N/U				
REF04-3	Reference Identification Qualifier	ID	2-3	N/U				
REF04-4	Reference Identification	AN	1-50	N/U				
REF04-5	Reference Identification Qualifier	ID	2-3	N/U				
REF04-6	Reference Identification	AN	1-50	N/U				Segment Deleted
NM1	OTHER PAYER REFERRING PROVIDER		1	S	2330C	2		Loop Change
NM101	Entity Identifier Code	ID	2-3	R			DN, P3	
NM102	Entity Type Qualifier	ID	1-1	R			1	Code Deleted
NM103	Name Last or Organization Name	AN	1-60	N/U				Increase from 35 - 60
NM104	Name First	AN	1-35	N/U				Increase from 25 - 35
NM105	Name Middle	AN	1-25	N/U				
NM106	Name Prefix	AN	1-10	N/U				
NM107	Name Suffix	AN	1-10	N/U				
NM108	Identification Code Qualifier	ID	1-2	N/U				
NM109	Other Payer Primary Identifier	AN	2-80	N/U				
NM110	Entity Relationship Code	ID	2-2	N/U				
NM111	Entity Identifier Code	ID	2-3	N/U				
NM112	Name Last or Organization Name	AN	1-60	N/U				New Element
REF	OTHER PAYER REFERRING PROVIDER SECONDARY IDENTIFIER		3	R	2330C			Loop Change
REF01	Reference Identification Qualifier	ID	2-3	R			0B, 1G, G2	Code Change

Page 58 of 93

PROFESSIONAL CLAIM

4010A1

837-P 4010A1

Element Identifier	Description	ID	Min. Max.	Usage Reg.	Loop	Loop Repeat	Values
REF02	Other Payer Referring Provider Identification	AN	1-30	R			
REF03	Description	AN	1-80	N/U			
REF04	REFERENCE IDENTIFIER			N/U			
NM1	OTHER PAYER RENDERING PROVIDER		1	S	2330E	1	
NM101	Entity Identifier Code	ID	2-3	R			82
NM102	Entity Type Qualifier	ID	1-1	R			1, 2
NM103	Rendering Provider Last or Organization Name	AN	1-35	N/U			
NM104	Name First	AN	1-25	N/U			
NM105	Name Middle	AN	1-25	N/U			
NM106	Name Prefix	AN	1-10	N/U			
NM107	Name Suffix	AN	1-10	N/U			
NM108	Identification Code Qualifier	ID	1-2	N/U			
NM109	Identification Code	AN	2-80	N/U			
NM110	Entity Relationship Code	ID	2-2	N/U			
NM111	Entity Identifier Code	ID	2-3	N/U			
REF	OTHER PAYER RENDERING PROVIDER SECONDARY IDENTIFICATION		3	R	2330E		
REF01	Reference Identification Qualifier	ID	2-3	R			1B, 1C, 1D, EI, G2, LU, N5
REF02	Other Payer Rendering Provider Secondary Identifier	AN	1-30	R			
REF03	Description	AN	1-80	N/U			
REF04	REFERENCE IDENTIFIER			N/U			

5010

837-P 5010

Element Identifier	Description	ID	Min. Max.	Usage Reg.	Loop	Loop Repeat	Values	Changes
REF02	Other Payer Referring Provider Secondary Identifier	AN	1-50	R				Increase from 30 - 50
REF03	Description	AN	1-80	N/U				
REF04	REFERENCE IDENTIFIER			N/U				
REF04-1	Reference Identifier Qualifier	ID	2-3	N/U				New Element
REF04-2	Other Payer Primary Idenitifer	AN	1-50	N/U				New Element
REF04-3	Reference Identification Qualifier	ID	2-3	N/U				New Element
REF04-4	Reference Identification	AN	1-50	N/U				New Element
REF04-5	Reference Identification Qualifier	ID	2-3	N/U				New Element
REF04-6	Reference Identification	AN	1-50	N/U				New Element
NM1	OTHER PAYER RENDERING PROVIDER		1	S	2330D	1		Loop Change
NM101	Entity Identifier Code	ID	2-3	R			82	
NM102	Entity Type Qualifier	ID	1-1	R			1, 2	
NM103	Name Last or Organization Name	AN	1-60	N/U				Increase from 35 - 60
NM104	Name First	AN	1-35	N/U				Increase from 25 - 35
NM105	Name Middle	AN	1-25	N/U				
NM106	Name Prefix	AN	1-10	N/U				
NM107	Name Suffix	AN	1-10	N/U				
NM108	Identification Code Qualifier	ID	1-2	N/U				
NM109	Other Payer Primary Identifier	AN	2-80	N/U				
NM110	Entity Relationship Code	ID	2-2	N/U				
NM111	Entity Identifier Code	ID	2-3	N/U				
NM112	Name Last or Organization Name	AN	1-60	N/U				New Element
REF	OTHER PAYER RENDERING PROVIDER SECONDARY IDENTIFIER		3	R	2330D			Loop Change Name Change
REF01	Reference Identification Qualifier	ID	2-3	R			0B, 1G, G2, LU	Code Change
REF02	Other Payer Rendering Provider Secondary Identifier	AN	1-50	R				Increase from 30 - 50
REF03	Description	AN	1-80	N/U				
REF04	REFERENCE IDENTIFIER			N/U				
REF04-1	Reference Identifier Qualifier	ID	2-3	N/U				New Element
REF04-2	Other Payer Primary Idenitifer	AN	1-50	N/U				New Element

Page 59 of 93

PROFESSIONAL CLAIM

Element Identifier	Description	ID	Min. Max.	Usage Reg.	Loop	Loop Repeat	Values
	837-P 4010A1						
NM1	OTHER PAYER PURCHASED SERVICE PROVIDER		1	S	2330F	1	

Element Identifier	Description	ID	Min. Max.	Usage Reg.	Loop	Loop Repeat	Values	
	837-P 5010							
REF04-3	Reference Identification Qualifier	ID	2-3	N/U				New Element
REF04-4	Reference Identification	AN	1-50	N/U				New Element
								New Element
REF04-5	Reference Identification Qualifier	ID	2-3	N/U				
REF04-6	Reference Identification	AN	1-50	N/U				New Element
NM1	OTHER PAYER SERVICE FACILITY LOCATION		1	S	2330E	1		New Segment
NM101	Entity Identifier Code	ID	2-3	R			77	
NM102	Entity Type Qualifier	ID	1-1	R			2	
NM103	Name Last or Organization Name	AN	1-60	N/U				
NM104	Name First	AN	1-35	N/U				
NM105	Name Middle	AN	1-25	N/U				
NM106	Name Prefix	AN	1-10	N/U				
NM107	Name Suffix	AN	1-10	N/U				
NM108	Identification Code Qualifier	ID	1-2	N/U				
NM109	Other Payer Primary Identifier	AN	2-80	N/U				
NM110	Entity Relationship Code	ID	2-2	N/U				
NM111	Entity Identifier Code	ID	2-3	N/U				
NM112	Name Last or Organization Name	AN	1-60	N/U				
REF	OTHER PAYER SERVICE FACILITY LOCATION SECONDARY IDENTIFIER		3	R	2330E			New Segment
REF01	Reference Identification Qualifier	ID	2-3	R			0B, G2, LU	
REF02	Other Payer Service Facility Location Secondary Identifier	AN	1-50	R				
REF03	Description	AN	1-80	N/U				
REF04	REFERENCE IDENTIFIER			N/U				
REF04-1	Reference Identifier Qualifier	ID	2-3	N/U				
REF04-2	Other Payer Primary Idenitifer	AN	1-50	N/U				
REF04-3	Reference Identification Qualifier	ID	2-3	N/U				
REF04-4	Reference Identification	AN	1-50	N/U				
REF04-5	Reference Identification Qualifier	ID	2-3	N/U				
REF04-6	Reference Identification	AN	1-50	N/U				
								Segment Deleted

Page 60 of 93

PROFESSIONAL CLAIM

4010A1

837-P 4010A1

Element Identifier	Description	ID	Min. Max.	Usage Reg.	Loop	Loop Repeat	Values
NM101	Entity Identifier Code	ID	2-3	R			QB
NM102	Entity Type Qualifier	ID	1-1	R			1, 2
NM103	Purchased Service Provider Name	AN	1-35	N/U			
NM104	Name First	AN	1-25	N/U			
NM105	Name Middle	AN	1-25	N/U			
NM106	Name Prefix	AN	1-10	N/U			
NM107	Name Suffix	AN	1-10	N/U			
NM108	Identification Code Qualifier	ID	1-2	N/U			
NM109	Identification Code	AN	2-80	N/U			
NM110	Entity Relationship Code	ID	2-2	N/U			
NM111	Entity Identifier Code	ID	2-3	N/U			
REF	**OTHER PAYER PURCHASED SERVICE PROVIDER IDENTIFICATION**		3	R	2330F		
REF01	Reference Identification Qualifier	ID	2-3	R			1A, 1B, 1C, 1D, EI, G2, LU, N5
REF02	Other Payer Purchased Service Provider Identifier	AN	1-30	R			
REF03	Description	AN	1-80	N/U			
REF04	REFERENCE IDENTIFIER			N/U			

5010

837-P 5010

Element Identifier	Description	ID	Min. Max.	Usage Reg.	Loop	Loop Repeat	Values	
								Segment Deleted
NM1	**OTHER PAYER SUPERVISING PROVIDER**		1	S	2330F	1		New Segment
NM101	Entity Identifier Code	ID	2-3	R			DQ	
NM102	Entity Type Qualifier	ID	1-1	R			1	
NM103	Name Last or Organization Name	AN	1-60	N/U				
NM104	Name First	AN	1-35	N/U				
NM105	Name Middle	AN	1-25	N/U				
NM106	Name Prefix	AN	1-10	N/U				
NM107	Name Suffix	AN	1-10	N/U				
NM108	Identification Code Qualifier	ID	1-2	N/U				
NM109	Other Payer Primary Identifier	AN	2-80	N/U				
NM110	Entity Relationship Code	ID	2-2	N/U				
NM111	Entity Identifier Code	ID	2-3	N/U				
NM112	Name Last or Organization Name	AN	1-60	N/U				
REF	**OTHER PAYER SUPERVISING PROVIDER SECONDARY IDENTIFICATION**		3	R	2330F			New Segment
REF01	Reference Identification Qualifier	ID	2-3	R			0B, 1G, G2, LU	

Page 61 of 93

PROFESSIONAL CLAIM

4010A1

Element Identifier	Description	ID	Min. Max.	Usage Reg.	Loop	Loop Repeat	Values
	837-P 4010A1						
NM1	**OTHER PAYER SERVICE FACILITY LOCATION**		1	S	2330G	1	
NM101	Entity Identifier Code	ID	2-3	R			77, FA, LI, TL
NM102	Entity Type Qualifier	ID	1-1	R			2
NM103	Service Facility Name	AN	1-35	N/U			
NM104	Name First	AN	1-25	N/U			
NM105	Name Middle	AN	1-25	N/U			
NM106	Name Prefix	AN	1-10	N/U			
NM107	Name Suffix	AN	1-10	N/U			
NM108	Identification Code Qualifier	ID	1-2	N/U			
NM109	Identification Code	AN	2-80	N/U			
NM110	Entity Relationship Code	ID	2-2	N/U			
NM111	Entity Identifier Code	ID	2-3	N/U			
REF	**OTHER PAYER SERVICE FACILITY LOCATION IDENTIFICATION**		3	R	2330G		
REF01	Reference Identification Qualifier	ID	2-3	R			1A, 1B, 1C, 1D,G2, LU, N5
REF02	Other Payer Service Facility Location Identifier	AN	1-30	R			
REF03	Description	AN	1-80	N/U			
REF04	REFERENCE IDENTIFIER			N/U			

5010

Element Identifier	Description	ID	Min. Max.	Usage Reg.	Loop	Loop Repeat	Values	
	837-P 5010							
REF02	Other Payer Supervising Provider Secondary Identifier	AN	1-50	R				
REF03	Description	AN	1-80	N/U				
REF04	REFERENCE IDENTIFIER			N/U				
REF04-1	Reference Identifier Qualifier	ID	2-3	N/U				
REF04-2	Other Payer Primary Idenitifer	AN	1-50	N/U				
REF04-3	Reference Identification Qualifier	ID	2-3	N/U				
REF04-4	Reference Identification	AN	1-50	N/U				
REF04-5	Reference Identification Qualifier	ID	2-3	N/U				
REF04-6	Reference Identification	AN	1-50	N/U				
								Segment Deleted
								Segment Deleted
NM1	**OTHER PAYER BILLING PROVIDER**		1	S	2330G	1		New Segment
NM101	Entity Identifier Code	ID	2-3	R			85	
NM102	Entity Type Qualifier	ID	1-1	R			1, 2	
NM103	Name Last or Organization Name	AN	1-60	N/U				
NM104	Name First	AN	1-35	N/U				
NM105	Name Middle	AN	1-25	N/U				
NM106	Name Prefix	AN	1-10	N/U				

Page 62 of 93

PROFESSIONAL CLAIM

4010A1

837-P 4010A1

Element Identifier	Description	ID	Min. Max.	Usage Reg.	Loop	Loop Repeat	Values
NM1	OTHER PAYER SUPERVISING PROVIDER		1	S	2330H	1	
NM101	Entity Identifier Code	ID	2-3	R			DQ
NM102	Entity Type Qualifier	ID	1-1	R			1
NM103	Supervising Provider Last Name	AN	1-35	N/U			
NM104	Name First	AN	1-25	N/U			
NM105	Name Middle	AN	1-25	N/U			
NM106	Name Prefix	AN	1-10	N/U			
NM107	Name Suffix	AN	1-10	N/U			
NM108	Identification Code Qualifier	ID	1-2	N/U			
NM109	Identification Code	AN	2-80	N/U			
NM110	Entity Relationship Code	ID	2-2	N/U			
NM111	Entity Identifier Code	ID	2-3	N/U			
REF	OTHER PAYER SUPERVISING PROVIDER IDENTIFICATION		3	R	2330H		

5010

837-P 5010

Element Identifier	Description	ID	Min. Max.	Usage Reg.	Loop	Loop Repeat	Values	
NM107	Name Suffix	AN	1-10	N/U				
NM108	Identification Code Qualifier	ID	1-2	N/U				
NM109	Other Payer Primary Identifier	AN	2-80	N/U				
NM110	Entity Relationship Code	ID	2-2	N/U				
NM111	Entity Identifier Code	ID	2-3	N/U				
NM112	Name Last or Organization Name	AN	1-60	N/U				
REF	OTHER PAYER BILLING PROVIDER SECONDARY IDENTIFICATION		2	R	2330G			New Segment
REF01	Reference Identification Qualifier	ID	2-3	R			G2, LU	
REF02	Other Payer Billing Provider Secondary Identification	AN	1-50	R				
REF03	Description	AN	1-80	N/U				
REF04	REFERENCE IDENTIFIER			N/U				
REF04-1	Reference Identifier Qualifier	ID	2-3	N/U				
REF04-2	Other Payer Primary Idenitifer	AN	1-50	N/U				
REF04-3	Reference Identification Qualifier	ID	2-3	N/U				
REF04-4	Reference Identification	AN	1-50	N/U				
REF04-5	Reference Identification Qualifier	ID	2-3	N/U				
REF04-6	Reference Identification	AN	1-50	N/U				
								Segment Deleted
								Segment Deleted

Page 63 of 93

PROFESSIONAL CLAIM

4010A1

Element Identifier	Description	ID	Min. Max.	Usage Reg.	Loop	Loop Repeat	Values
	837-P 4010A1						
REF01	Reference Identification Qualifier	ID	2-3	R			1B, 1C, 1D,EI, G2, N5
REF02	Other Payer Supervising Provider Identifier	AN	1-30	R			
REF03	Description	AN	1-80	N/U			
REF04	REFERENCE IDENTIFIER			N/U			
LX	**SERVICE LINE**		1	R	2400	50	
LX01	Assigned Number	N0	1-6	R			
SV1	**PROFESSIONAL SERVICE**		1	R	2400		
SV101	COMPOSITE MEDICAL PROCEDURE IDENTIFIER			R			
SV101-1	Product or Service ID Qualifier	ID	2-2	R			HC, IV, ZZ
SV101-2	Procedure Code	AN	1-48	R			
SV101-3	Procedure Modifier	AN	2-2	S			
SV101-4	Procedure Modifier	AN	2-2	S			
SV101-5	Procedure Modifier	AN	2-2	S			
SV101-6	Procedure Modifier	AN	2-2	S			
SV101-7	Description	AN	1-80	N/U			
SV102	Line Item Charge Amount S9(7)V99	R	1-18	R			
SV103	Unit or Basis for Measurement Code	ID	2-2	R			F2,MJ,UN
SV104	Service Unit Count "F2" = 9(7)V999 "MJ" = 9(4) "UN" = 9(3)V9	R	1-15	R			
SV105	Place of Service Code	AN	1-2	S			11, 12, 21, 22, 23, 24, 25, 26, 31, 32, 33, 34, 41, 42, 50, 51, 52, 53, 54, 55, 56, 60, 61, 62, 65, 71, 72, 81, 99
SV106	Service Type Code	ID	1-2	N/U			
SV107	COMPOSITE DIAGNOSIS CODE POINTER			S			
SV107-1	Diagnosis Code Pointer	N0	1-2	R			
SV107-2	Diagnosis Code Pointer	N0	1-2	S			
SV107-3	Diagnosis Code Pointer	N0	1-2	S			
SV107-4	Diagnosis Code Pointer	N0	1-2	S			
SV108	Monetary Amount	R	1-18	N/U			
SV109	Emergency Indicator	ID	1-1	S			Y
SV110	Multiple Procedure Code	ID	1-2	N/U			
SV111	EPSDT Indicator	ID	1-1	S			Y
SV112	Family Planning Indicator	ID	1-1	S			Y
SV113	Review Code	ID	1-2	N/U			

5010

Element Identifier	Description	ID	Min. Max.	Usage Reg.	Loop	Loop Repeat	Values	
	837-P 5010							
LX	**SERVICE LINE**		1	R	2400	50		
LX01	Assigned Number	N0	1-6	R				
SV1	**PROFESSIONAL SERVICE**		1	R	2400			
SV101	COMPOSITE MEDICAL PROCEDURE IDENTIFIER			R				
SV101-1	Product or Service ID Qualifier	ID	2-2	R			ER, HC, IV, WK	Coe Change
SV101-2	Procedure Code	AN	1-48	R				
SV101-3	Procedure Modifier	AN	2-2	S				
SV101-4	Procedure Modifier	AN	2-2	S				
SV101-5	Procedure Modifier	AN	2-2	S				
SV101-6	Procedure Modifier	AN	2-2	S				
SV101-7	Description	AN	1-80	S				
SV101-8	Product/Service ID	AN	1-48	N/U				New Element
SV102	Line Item Charge Amount S9(7)V99	R	1-18	R				
SV103	Unit or Basis for Measurement Code	ID	2-2	R			MJ, UN	
SV104	Service Unit Count "MJ" = 9(4) "UN" = 9(3)V9	R	1-15	R				
SV105	Place of Service Code	AN	1-2	S				
SV106	Service Type Code	ID	1 2	N/U				
SV107	COMPOSITE DIAGNOSIS CODE POINTER			R				Usage changed to Required
SV107-1	Diagnosis Code Pointer	N0	1-2	R				
SV107-2	Diagnosis Code Pointer	N0	1-2	S				
SV107-3	Diagnosis Code Pointer	N0	1-2	S				
SV107-4	Diagnosis Code Pointer	N0	1-2	S				
SV108	Monetary Amount	R	1-18	N/U				
SV109	Emergency Indicator	ID	1-1	S			Y	
SV110	Multiple Procedure Code	ID	1-2	N/U				
SV111	EPSDT Indicator	ID	1-1	S			Y	
SV112	Family Planning Indicator	ID	1-1	S			Y	
SV113	Review Code	ID	1-2	N/U				

PROFESSIONAL CLAIM

4010A1

837-P 4010A1

Element Identifier	Description	ID	Min. Max.	Usage Reg.	Loop	Loop Repeat	Values
SV114	National or Local Assigned Review Value	AN	1-2	N/U			
SV115	Co-Pay Status Code	ID	1-1	S			0
SV116	Health Care Professional Shortage Area Code	ID	1-1	N/U			
SV117	Reference Identification	AN	1-30	N/U			
SV118	Postal Code	ID	3-15	N/U			
SV119	Monetary Amount	R	1-18	N/U			
SV120	Level of Care Code	ID	1-1	N/U			
SV121	Provider Agreement Code	ID	1-1	N/U			
SV5	**DURABLE MEDICAL EQUIPMENT SERVICE**		1	S	2400		
SV501	COMPOSITE MEDICAL PROCEDURE			R			
SV501-1	Procedure Identifier	ID	2-2	R			HC
SV501-2	Procedure Code	AN	1-48	R			
SV501-3	Procedure Modifier	AN	2-2	N/U			
SV501-4	Procedure Modifier	AN	2-2	N/U			
SV501-5	Procedure Modifier	AN	2-2	N/U			
SV501-6	Procedure Modifier	AN	2-2	N/U			
SV501-7	Desription	AN	1-80	N/U			
SV502	Unit or Basis for Measurement Code	ID	2-2	R			DA
SV503	Length of Medical Necessity 9(3)	R	1-15	R			
SV504	DME Rental Price S9(7)V99	R	1-18	S			
SV505	DME Purchase Price S9(7)V99	R	1-18	S			
SV506	Rental Unit Price Indicator	ID	1-1	S			1, 4, 6
SV507	Prognosis Code	ID	1-1	N/U			

5010

837-P 5010

Element Identifier	Description	ID	Min. Max.	Usage Reg.	Loop	Loop Repeat	Values	
SV114	National or Local Assigned Review Value	AN	1-2	N/U				
SV115	Co-Pay Status Code	ID	1-1	S			0	
SV116	Health Care Professional Shortage Area Code	ID	1-1	N/U				
SV117	Reference Identification	AN	1-30	N/U				
SV118	Postal Code	ID	3-15	N/U				
SV119	Monetary Amount	R	1-18	N/U				
SV120	Level of Care Code	ID	1-1	N/U				
SV121	Provider Agreement Code	ID	1-1	N/U				
SV5	**DURABLE MEDICAL EQUIPMENT SERVICE**		1	S	2400			
SV501	COMPOSITE MEDICAL PROCEDURE			R				
SV501-1	Procedure Identifier	ID	2-2	R			HC	
SV501-2	Procedure Code	AN	1-48	R				
SV501-3	Procedure Modifier	AN	2-2	N/U				
SV501-4	Procedure Modifier	AN	2-2	N/U				
SV501-5	Procedure Modifier	AN	2-2	N/U				
SV501-6	Procedure Modifier	AN	2-2	N/U				
SV501-7	Desription	AN	1-80	N/U				
SV501-8	Product/Service ID	AN	1-48	N/U				New Element
SV502	Unit or Basis for Measurement Code	ID	2-2	R			DA	
SV503	Length of Medical Necessity 9(3)	R	1-15	R				
SV504	DME Rental Price S9(7)V99	R	1-18	R				Usage changed to Required
SV505	DME Purchase Price S9(7)V99	R	1-18	R				Usage changed to Required
SV506	Rental Unit Price Indicator	ID	1-1	R			1, 4, 6	Usage changed to Required
SV507	Prognosis Code	ID	1-1	N/U				
PWK	**LINE SUPPLEMENTAL INFORMATION**		10	S	2400			New Segment

Page 65 of 93

PROFESSIONAL CLAIM

Element Identifier	Description	ID	Min. Max.	Usage Reg.	Loop	Loop Repeat	Values
				4010A1			
	837-P 4010A1						
PWK	**DMERC CMN INDICATOR**		1	S	2400		
PWK01	Attachment Report Type Code	ID	2-2	R			CT
PWK02	Attachment Transmission Code	ID	1-2	R			AB, AD, AF, AG, NS
PWK03	Report Copies Needed	N0	1-2	N/U			
PWK04	Entity Identifier Code	ID	2-3	N/U			
PWK05	Identification Code Qualifier	ID	1-2	N/U			
PWK06	Identification Code	AN	2-80	N/U			
PWK07	Description	AN	1-80	N/U			
PWK08	ACTIONS INDICATED			N/U			
PWK09	Request Category Code	ID	1-2	N/U			
CR1	**AMBULANCE TRANSPORT INFORMATION**		1	S	2400		
CR101	Unit or Basis for Measurement Code	ID	2-2	S			LB

Element Identifier	Description	ID	Min. Max.	Usage Reg.	Loop	Loop Repeat	Values
				5010			
	837-P 5010						
PWK01	Attachment Report Type Code	ID	2-2	R			03, 04, 05, 06, 07, 08, 09, 10, 11, 13, 15, 21, A3, A4, AM, AS, B2, B3, B4, BR, BS, BT, CB, CK, CT, D2, DA, DB, DG, DJ, DS, EB, HC, HR, I5, IR, LA, M1, MT, NN, OB, OC, OD, OE, OX, OZ, P4, P5, PE, PN, PO, PQ, PY, PZ, RB, RR, RT, RX, SG, V5, XP
PWK02	Attachment Transmission Code	ID	1-2	R			AA, BM, EL, EM, FT, FX
PWK03	Report Copies Needed	N0	1-2	N/U			
PWK04	Entity Identifier Code	ID	2-3	N/U			
PWK05	Identification Code Qualifier	ID	1-2	S			AC
PWK06	Identification Code	AN	2-80	S			
PWK07	Description	AN	1-80	N/U			
PWK08	ACTIONS INDICATED			N/U			
PWK09	Request Category Code	ID	1-2	N/U			
PWK	**DURABLE MEDICAL EQUIPMENT CERTIFICATE OF MEDICAL NECESSITY INDICATOR**		1	S	2400		
PWK01	Attachment Report Type Code	ID	2-2	R			CT
PWK02	Attachment Transmission Code	ID	1-2	R			AB, AD, AF, AG, NS
PWK03	Report Copies Needed	N0	1-2	N/U			
PWK04	Entity Identifier Code	ID	2-3	N/U			
PWK05	Identification Code Qualifier	ID	1-2	N/U			
PWK06	Identification Code	AN	2-80	N/U			
PWK07	Description	AN	1-80	N/U			
PWK08	ACTIONS INDICATED			N/U			
PWK09	Request Category Code	ID	1-2	N/U			
CR1	**AMBULANCE TRANSPORT INFORMATION**		1	S	2400		
CR101	Unit or Basis for Measurement Code	ID	2-2	S			LB

Name Change

Page 66 of 93

PROFESSIONAL CLAIM

Element Identifier	Description	ID	Min. Max.	Usage Reg.	Loop	Loop Repeat	Values
				4010A1			
				837-P 4010A1			
CR102	Patient Weight 9(3)	R	1-10	S			
CR103	Ambulance Transport Code	ID	1-1	R			I, R, T, X
CR104	Ambulance Transport Reason Code	ID	1-1	R			A, B, C, D, E
CR105	Unit or Basis for Measurement Code	ID	2-2	R			DH
CR106	Transport Distance 9(4)	R	1-15	R			
CR107	Address Information	AN	1-55	N/U			
CR108	Address Information	AN	1-55	N/U			
CR109	Round Trip Purpose Description	AN	1-80	S			
CR110	Stretcher Purpose Description	AN	1-80	S			
CR2	**SPINAL MANIPULATION SERVICE INFORMATION**		5	S	2400		
CR201	Treatment Series Number 9(3)	N0	1-9	N/U			
CR202	Treatment Count 9(3)	R	1-15	N/U			
CR203	Subluxation Level Code	ID	2-3	N/U			C1, C2, C3, C4, C5, C6, C7, CO, IL, L1, L2, L3, L4, L5, OC, SA, T1, T10, T11, T12, T2, T3, T4, T5, T6, T7, T8, T9
CR204	Subluxation Level Code	ID	2-3	N/U			C1, C2, C3, C4, C5, C6, C7, CO, IL, L1, L2, L3, L4, L5, OC, SA, T1, T10, T11, T12, T2, T3, T4, T5, T6, T7, T8, T9
CR205	Unit or Basis for Measurement Code	ID	2-2	N/U			DA, MO, WK, YR
CR206	Treatment Period Count 9(3)	R	1-15	N/U			
CR207	Monthly Treatment Count 9(2)	R	1-15	N/U			
CR208	Patient Condition Code	ID	1-1	R			A, C, D, E, F, G, M
CR209	Complication Indicator	ID	1-1	N/U			N, Y
CR210	Patient Condition Description	AN	1-80	S			
CR211	Patient Condition Description	AN	1-80	S			
CR212	X-ray Availability Indicator	ID	1-1	S			N, Y

Element Identifier	Description	ID	Min. Max.	Usage Reg.	Loop	Loop Repeat	Values	
				5010				
				837-P 5010				
CR102	Patient Weight 9(3)	R	1-10	S				
CR103	Ambulance Transport Code	ID	1-1	N/U				Code Deleted Usage changed to Not Used
CR104	Ambulance Transport Reason Code	ID	1-1	R			A, B, C, D, E	
CR105	Unit or Basis for Measurement Code	ID	2-2	R			DH	
CR106	Transport Distance 9(4)	R	1-15	R				
CR107	Address Information	AN	1-55	N/U				
CR108	Address Information	AN	1-55	N/U				
CR109	Round Trip Purpose Description	AN	1-80	S				
CR110	Stretcher Purpose Description	AN	1-80	S				Segment Deleted

PROFESSIONAL CLAIM

4010A1

Element Identifier	Description	ID	Min. Max.	Usage Reg.	Loop	Loop Repeat	Values
	837-P 4010A1						
CR3	**DURABLE MEDICAL EQUIPMENT CERTIFICATION**		1	S	2400		
CR301	Certification Type Code	ID	1-1	R			I,R,S
CR302	Unit or Basis for Measurement Code	ID	2-2	R			MO
CR303	Durable Medical Equipment Duration 9(2)	R	1-15	R			
CR304	Insulin Dependent Code	ID	1-1	N/U			
CR305	Description	AN	1-80	N/U			
CR5	**HOME OXYGEN THERAPY INFORMATION**		1	S	2400		
CR501	Certification Type Code	ID	1-1	R			I,R,S
CR502	Treatment Period Count 9(2)	R	1-15	R			
CR503	Oxygen Equipment Type Code	ID	1-1	N/U			
CR504	Oxygen Equipment Type Code	ID	1-1	N/U			
CR505	Description	AN	1-80	N/U			
CR506	Quantity	R	1-15	N/U			
CR507	Quantity	R	1-15	N/U			
CR508	Quantity	R	1-15	N/U			
CR509	Description	AN	1-80	N/U			
CR510	Arterial Blood Gas Quantity 9(2)V9	R	1-15	S			
CR511	Oxygen Saturation Quantity 9(2)V9	R	1-15	S			
CR512	Oxygen Test Condition Code	ID	1-1	R			E,R,S
CR513	Oxygen Test Findings Code	ID	1-1	S			1
CR514	Oxygen Test Findings Code	ID	1-1	S			2
CR515	Oxygen Test Findings Code	ID	1-1	S			3
CR516	Quantity	R	1-15	N/U			
CR517	Oxygen Delivery System code	ID	1-1	N/U			
CR518	Oxygen Equipment Type Code	ID	1-1	N/U			
CRC	**AMBULANCE CERTIFICATION**		3	S	2400		
CRC01	Code Category	ID	2-2	R			07
CRC02	Certification Condition Indicator	ID	1-1	R			N, Y

5010

Element Identifier	Description	ID	Min. Max.	Usage Reg.	Loop	Loop Repeat	Values
	837-P 5010						
CR3	**DURABLE MEDICAL EQUIPMENT CERTIFICATION**		1	S	2400		
CR301	Certification Type Code	ID	1-1	R			I,R,S
CR302	Unit or Basis for Measurement Code	ID	2-2	R			MO
CR303	Durable Medical Equipment Duration 9(2)	R	1-15	R			
CR304	Insulin Dependent Code	ID	1-1	N/U			
CR305	Description	AN	1-80	N/U			
CRC	**AMBULANCE CERTIFICATION**		3	S	2400		
CRC01	Code Category	ID	2-2	R			07
CRC02	Certification Condition Indicator	ID	1-1	R			N, Y

Segment Deleted

Page 68 of 93

PROFESSIONAL CLAIM

Element Identifier	Description	ID	Min. Max.	Usage Reg.	Loop	Loop Repeat	Values	Element Identifier	Description	ID	Min. Max.	Usage Reg.	Loop	Loop Repeat	Values	
			4010A1								**5010**					
			837-P 4010A1								837-P 5010					
CRC03	Condition Code	ID	2-2	R			01, 02, 03, 04, 05, 06, 07, 08, 09, 60	CRC03	Condition Code	ID	2-3	R			01, 04, 05, 06, 07, 08, 09, 12	Code Deleted
CRC04	Condition Code	ID	2-2	S			01, 02, 03, 04, 05, 06, 07, 08, 09, 60	CRC04	Condition Code	ID	2-3	S			01, 04, 05, 06, 07, 08, 09, 12	Code Deleted
CRC05	Condition Code	ID	2-2	S			01, 02, 03, 04, 05, 06, 07, 08, 09, 60	CRC05	Condition Code	ID	2-3	S			01, 04, 05, 06, 07, 08, 09, 12	Code Deleted
CRC06	Condition Code	ID	2-2	S			01, 02, 03, 04, 05, 06, 07, 08, 09, 60	CRC06	Condition Code	ID	2-3	S			01, 04, 05, 06, 07, 08, 09, 12	Code Deleted
CRC07	Condition Code	ID	2-2	S			01, 02, 03, 04, 05, 06, 07, 08, 09, 60	CRC07	Condition Code	ID	2-3	S			01, 04, 05, 06, 07, 08, 09, 12	Code Deleted
CRC	**HOSPICE EMPLOYEE INDICATOR**		1	S	2400			**CRC**	**HOSPICE EMPLOYEE INDICATOR**		1	S	2400			
CRC01	Code Category	ID	2-2	R			70	CRC01	Code Category	ID	2-2	R			70	
CRC02	Hospice Employed Provider Indicator	ID	1-1	R			N, Y	CRC02	Hospice Employed Provider Indicator	ID	1-1	R			N, Y	
CRC03	Condition Indicator	ID	2-2	R			65	CRC03	Condition Indicator	ID	2-3	R			65	Increase from 2 - 3
CRC04	Condition Indicator	ID	2-2	N/U				CRC04	Condition Indicator	ID	2-3	N/U				Increase from 2 - 3
CRC05	Condition Indicator	ID	2-2	N/U				CRC05	Condition Indicator	ID	2-3	N/U				Increase from 2 - 3
CRC06	Condition Indicator	ID	2-2	N/U				CRC06	Condition Indicator	ID	2-3	N/U				Increase from 2 - 3
CRC07	Condition Indicator	ID	2-2	N/U				CRC07	Condition Indicator	ID	2-3	N/U				Increase from 2 - 3
CRC	**DMERC CONDITION INDICATOR**		2	S	2400			**CRC**	**CONDITION INDICATOR DURABLE MEDICAL EQUIPMENT**		1	S	2400			
CRC01	Code Category	ID	2-2	R			09,11	CRC01	Code Category	ID	2-2	R			09	Code Deleted
CRC02	Certification Condition Indicator	ID	1-1	R			N, Y	CRC02	Certification Condition Indicator	ID	1-1	R			N, Y	
CRC03	Condition Indicator	ID	2-2	R			37,38,AL,P1, ZV	CRC03	Condition Indicator	ID	2-3	R			38, ZV	Code Deleted Increase from 2 - 3
CRC04	Condition Indicator	ID	2-2	S			37,38,AL,P1, ZV	CRC04	Condition Indicator	ID	2-3	S			38, ZV	Code Deleted Increase from 2 - 3
CRC05	Condition Indicator	ID	2-2	S			37,38,AL,P1, ZV	CRC05	Condition Indicator	ID	2-3	N/U				Usage changed to Not Used
CRC06	Condition Indicator	ID	2-2	S			37,38,AL,P1, ZV	CRC06	Condition Indicator	ID	2-3	N/U				Usage changed to Not Used
CRC07	Condition Indicator	ID	2-2	S			37,38,AL,P1, ZV	CRC07	Condition Indicator	ID	2-3	N/U				Usage changed to Not Used
DTP	**DATE - SERVICE DATE**		1	R	2400			**DTP**	**DATE - SERVICE DATE**		1	R	2400			
DTP01	Date Time Qualifier	ID	3-3	R			472	DTP01	Date Time Qualifier	ID	3-3	R			472	
DTP02	Date Time Period Format Qualifier	ID	2-3	R			D8, RD8	DTP02	Date Time Period Format Qualifier	ID	2-3	R			D8, RD8	

Page 69 of 93

PROFESSIONAL CLAIM

4010A1

837-P 4010A1

Element Identifier	Description	ID	Min. Max.	Usage Reg.	Loop	Loop Repeat	Values
DTP03	Service Date	AN	1-35	R			CYYMMDD, CCYYMMDDCCYYMMDD
DTP	DATE - CERTIFICATION REVISION DATE		1	S	2400		
DTP01	Date Time Qualifier	ID	3-3	R			607
DTP02	Date Time Period Format Qualifier	ID	2-3	R			D8
DTP03	Certification Revision Date	AN	1-35	R			CCYYMMDD
DTP	DATE - BEGIN THERAPY DATE		1	S	2400		
DTP01	Date Time Qualifier	ID	3-3	R			463
DTP02	Date Time Period Format Qualifier	ID	2-3	R			D8
DTP03	Begin Therapy Date	AN	1-35	R			CCYYMMDD
DTP	DATE - LAST CERTIFICATION DATE		1	S	2400		
DTP01	Date Time Qualifier	ID	3-3	R			461
DTP02	Date Time Period Format Qualifier	ID	2-3	R			D8
DTP03	Last Certification Date	AN	1-35	R			CCYYMMDD
DTP	DATE - DATE LAST SEEN		1	S	2400		
DTP01	Date Time Qualifier	ID	3-3	R			304
DTP02	Date Time Period Format Qualifier	ID	2-3	R			D8
DTP03	Last Seen Date	AN	1-35	R			CCYYMMDD
DTP	DATE - TEST		2	S	2400		
DTP01	Date Time Qualifier	ID	3-3	R			738, 739
DTP02	Date Time Period Format Qualifier	ID	2-3	R			D8
DTP03	Test Performed Date	AN	1-35	R			CCYYMMDD

5010

837-P 5010

Element Identifier	Description	ID	Min. Max.	Usage Reg.	Loop	Loop Repeat	Values	
DTP03	Service Date	AN	1-35	R			CYYMMDD, CCYYMMDDCCYYMMDD	
DTP	DATE - PRESCRIPTION DATE		1	S	2400			New Segment
DTP01	Date Time Qualifier	ID	3-3	R			471	
DTP02	Date Time Period Format Qualifier	ID	2-3	R			D8	
DTP03	Prescription Date	AN	1-35	R			CCYYMMDD	
DTP	DATE - CERTIFICATION REVISION/RECERTIFICATION DATE		1	S	2400			
DTP01	Date Time Qualifier	ID	3-3	R			607	
DTP02	Date Time Period Format Qualifier	ID	2-3	R			D8	
DTP03	Certification Revision Recertification Date	AN	1-35	R			CCYYMMDD	
DTP	DATE - BEGIN THERAPY DATE		1	S	2400			
DTP01	Date Time Qualifier	ID	3-3	R			463	
DTP02	Date Time Period Format Qualifier	ID	2-3	R			D8	
DTP03	Begin Therapy Date	AN	1-35	R			CCYYMMDD	
DTP	DATE - LAST CERTIFICATION DATE		1	S	2400			
DTP01	Date Time Qualifier	ID	3-3	R			461	
DTP02	Date Time Period Format Qualifier	ID	2-3	R			D8	
DTP03	Last Certification Date	AN	1-35	R			CCYYMMDD	
DTP	DATE - DATE LAST SEEN		1	S	2400			
DTP01	Date Time Qualifier	ID	3-3	R			304	
DTP02	Date Time Period Format Qualifier	ID	2-3	R			D8	
DTP03	Last Seen Date	AN	1-35	R			CCYYMMDD	
DTP	DATE - TEST		2	S	2400			
DTP01	Date Time Qualifier	ID	3-3	R			738, 739	
DTP02	Date Time Period Format Qualifier	ID	2-3	R			D8	
DTP03	Test Performed Date	AN	1-35	R			CCYYMMDD	

Page 70 of 93

PROFESSIONAL CLAIM

4010A1							
Element Identifier	Description	ID	Min. Max.	Usage Req.	Loop	Loop Repeat	Values
837-P 4010A1							
DTP	**DATE - OXYGEN SATURATION/ARTERIAL BLOOD GAS TEST**		3	S	2400		
DTP01	Date Time Qualifier	ID	3-3	R			119, 480, 481
DTP02	Date Time Period Format Qualifier	ID	2-3	R			D8
DTP03	Oxygen Saturation Test Date	AN	1-35	R			CCYYMMDD
DTP	**DATE - SHIPPED**		1	S	2400		
DTP01	Date Time Qualifier	ID	3-3	R			011
DTP02	Date Time Period Format Qualifier	ID	2-3	R			D8
DTP03	Shipped Date	AN	1-35	R			CCYYMMDD
DTP	**DATE - ONSET OF CURRENT SYMPTOM/ILLNESS**		1	S	2400		
DTP01	Date Time Qualifier	ID	3-3	R			431
DTP02	Date Time Period Format Qualifier	ID	2-3	R			D8
DTP03	Onset Date	AN	1-35	R			CCYYMMDD
DTP	**DATE - LAST X-RAY**		1	S	2400		
DTP01	Date Time Qualifier	ID	3-3	R			455
DTP02	Date Time Period Format Qualifier	ID	2-3	R			D8
DTP03	Last X-Ray Date	AN	1-35	R			CCYYMMDD
DTP	**DATE - ACUTE MANIFESTATION**		1	S	2400		
DTP01	Date Time Qualifier	ID	3-3	R			453
DTP02	Date Time Period Format Qualifier	ID	2-3	R			D8
DTP03	Acute Manifestation Date	AN	1-35	R			CCYYMMDD
DTP	**DATE - INITIAL TREATMENT**		1	S	2400		
DTP01	Date Time Qualifier	ID	3-3	R			454
DTP02	Date Time Period Format Qualifier	ID	2-3	R			D8
DTP03	Initial Treatment Date	AN	1-35	R			CCYYMMDD
DTP	**DATE - SIMILAR ILLNESS/SYMPTOM ONSET**		1	S	2400		
DTP01	Date Time Qualifier	ID	3-3	R			438

5010								
Element Identifier	Description	ID	Min. Max.	Usage Req.	Loop	Loop Repeat	Values	
837-P 5010								
								Segment Deleted
DTP	**DATE - SHIPPED**		1	S	2400			
DTP01	Date Time Qualifier	ID	3-3	R			011	
DTP02	Date Time Period Format Qualifier	ID	2-3	R			D8	
DTP03	Shipped Date	AN	1-35	R			CCYYMMDD	
								Segment Deleted
DTP	**DATE - LAST X-RAY**		1	S	2400			
DTP01	Date Time Qualifier	ID	3-3	R			455	
DTP02	Date Time Period Format Qualifier	ID	2-3	R			D8	
DTP03	Last X-Ray Date	AN	1-35	R			CCYYMMDD	
								Segment Deleted
DTP	**DATE - INITIAL TREATMENT**		1	S	2400			
DTP01	Date Time Qualifier	ID	3-3	R			454	
DTP02	Date Time Period Format Qualifier	ID	2-3	R			D8	
DTP03	Initial Treatment Date	AN	1-35	R			CCYYMMDD	
								Segment Deleted

Page 71 of 93

PROFESSIONAL CLAIM

4010A1							
Element Identifier	Description	ID	Min. Max.	Usage Reg.	Loop	Loop Repeat	Values
	837-P 4010A1						
DTP02	Date Time Period Format Qualifier	ID	2-3	R			D8
DTP03	Similar Illness or Symptom Date	AN	1-35	R			CCYYMMDD
MEA	**TEST RESULTS**		20	S	2400		
MEA01	Measurement Reference Identification Code	ID	2-2	R			OG, TR
MEA02	Measurement Qualifier	ID	1-3	R			GRA, HT, R1, R2, R3, R4, ZO
MEA03	Test Result 9(3) "GRA", "R1", "R2", "R4", & "ZO" = 9(2)V9	R	1-20	R			
MEA04	COMPOSITE UNIT OF MEASURE			N/U			
MEA05	Range Minimum	R	1-20	N/U			
MEA06	Range Maximum	R	1-20	N/U			
MEA07	Measurement Significance Code	ID	2-2	N/U			
MEA08	Measurement Attribute Code	ID	2-2	N/U			
MEA09	Surface/Layer/Position Code	ID	2-2	N/U			
MEA10	Measurement Method or Device	ID	2-4	N/U			
CN1	**CONTRACT INFORMATION**		1	S	2400		

5010								
Element Identifier	Description	ID	Min. Max.	Usage Reg.	Loop	Loop Repeat	Values	
	837-P 5010							
QTY	**AMBULANCE PATIENT COUNT**		1	S	2400			Segment Added
QTY01	Quantity Qualifier	ID	2-2	R			PT	
QTY02	Ambulance Patient Count 9(2)	R	1-15	R				
QTY03	COMPOSITE UNIT OF MEASURE			N/U				
QTY04	Fee-Form Message	AN	1-30	N/U				
QTY	**OBSTETRIC ANESTHESIA ADDITIONAL UNITS**		1	S	2400			Segment Added
QTY01	Quantity Qualifier	ID	2-2	R			FL	
QTY02	Obstetric Additional Units 9(2)	R	1-15	R				
QTY03	COMPOSITE UNIT OF MEASURE			N/U				
QTY04	Fee-Form Message	AN	1-30	N/U				
MEA	**TEST RESULTS**		5	S	2400			
MEA01	Measurement Reference Identification Code	ID	2-2	R			OG, TR	
MEA02	Measurement Qualifier	ID	1-3	R			HT, R1, R2, R3, R4	Code Deleted
MEA03	Test Result "HT" 9(2), "R1", "R2", "R3", "R4" = 9(2)V9	R	1-20	R				
MEA04	COMPOSITE UNIT OF MEASURE			N/U				
MEA05	Range Minimum	R	1-20	N/U				
MEA06	Range Maximum	R	1-20	N/U				
MEA07	Measurement Significance Code	ID	2-2	N/U				
MEA08	Measurement Attribute Code	ID	2-2	N/U				
MEA09	Surface/Layer/Position Code	ID	2-2	N/U				
MEA10	Measurement Method or Device	ID	2-4	N/U				
MEA11	Code List Qualifier Code	ID	1-3	N/U				New Element
MEA12	Industry Code	AN	1-30	N/U				New Element
CN1	**CONTRACT INFORMATION**		1	S	2400			

PROFESSIONAL CLAIM

4010A1

Element Identifier	Description	ID	Min. Max.	Usage Reg.	Loop	Loop Repeat	Values
	837-P 4010A1						
CN101	Contract Type Code	ID	2-2	R			01, 02, 03, 04, 05, 06, 09
CN102	Contract Amount S9(7)V99	R	1-18	S			
CN103	Contract Percentage 9(2)V99	R	1-6	S			
CN104	Contract Code	AN	1-30	S			
CN105	Terms Discount Percent 9(2)V99	R	1-6	S			
CN106	Contract Version Identifier	AN	1-30	S			
REF	**REPRICED LINE ITEM REFERENCE NUMBER**		1	S	2400		
REF01	Reference Identification Qualifier	ID	2-3	R			9B
REF02	Repriced Line Item Reference Number	AN	1-30	R			
REF03	Description	AN	1-80	N/U			
REF04	REFERENCE IDENTIFIER			N/U			
REF	**ADJUSTED REPRICED LINE ITEM REFERENCE NUMBER**		1	S	2400		
REF01	Reference Identification Qualifier	ID	2-3	R			9D
REF02	Adjusted Repriced Line Item Reference Number	AN	1-30	R			
REF03	Description	AN	1-80	N/U			
REF04	REFERENCE IDENTIFIER			N/U			

5010

Element Identifier	Description	ID	Min. Max.	Usage Reg.	Loop	Loop Repeat	Values	
	837-P 5010							
CN101	Contract Type Code	ID	2-2	R			01, 02, 03, 04, 05, 06, 09	
CN102	Contract Amount S9(7)V99	R	1-18	S				
CN103	Contract Percentage 9(2)V99	R	1-6	S				
CN104	Contract Code	AN	1-50	S				Increase from 30 - 50
CN105	Terms Discount Percent 9(2)V99	R	1-6	S				
CN106	Contract Version Identifier	AN	1-30	S				
REF	**REPRICED LINE ITEM REFERENCE NUMBER**		1	S	2400			
REF01	Reference Identification Qualifier	ID	2-3	R			9B	
REF02	Repriced Line Item Reference Number	AN	1 50	R				Increase from 30 - 50
REF03	Description	AN	1-80	N/U				
REF04	REFERENCE IDENTIFIER			N/U				
REF04-1	Reference Identifier Qualifier	ID	2-3	N/U				New Element
REF04-2	Other Payer Primary Identifer	AN	1-50	N/U				New Element
REF04-3	Reference Identification Qualifier	ID	2-3	N/U				New Element
REF04-4	Reference Identification	AN	1-50	N/U				New Element
REF04-5	Reference Identification Qualifier	ID	2-3	N/U				New Element
REF04-6	Reference Identification	AN	1-50	N/U				New Element
REF	**ADJUSTED REPRICED LINE ITEM REFERENCE NUMBER**		1	S	2400			
REF01	Reference Identification Qualifier	ID	2-3	R			9D	
REF02	Adjusted Repriced Line Item Reference Number	AN	1-50	R				Increase from 30 - 50
REF03	Description	AN	1-80	N/U				
REF04	REFERENCE IDENTIFIER			N/U				
REF04-1	Reference Identifier Qualifier	ID	2-3	N/U				New Element
REF04-2	Other Payer Primary Idenitifer	AN	1-50	N/U				New Element
REF04-3	Reference Identification Qualifier	ID	2-3	N/U				New Element
REF04-4	Reference Identification	AN	1-50	N/U				New Element
REF04-5	Reference Identification Qualifier	ID	2-3	N/U				New Element
REF04-6	Reference Identification	AN	1-50	N/U				New Element

PROFESSIONAL CLAIM

4010A1

837-P 4010A1

Element Identifier	Description	ID	Min. Max.	Usage Reg.	Loop	Loop Repeat	Values
REF	PRIOR AUTHORIZATION OR REFERRAL NUMBER		2	S	2400		
REF01	Reference Identification Qualifier	ID	2-3	R			9F, G1
REF02	Prior Authorization or Referral Number	AN	1-30	R			
REF03	Description	AN	1-80	N/U			
REF04	REFERENCE IDENTIFIER			N/U			
REF	LINE ITEM CONTROL NUMBER		1	S	2400		
REF01	Reference Identification Qualifier	ID	2-3	R			6R
REF02	Line Item Control Number	AN	1-30	R			
REF03	Description	AN	1-80	N/U			
REF04	REFERENCE IDENTIFIER			N/U			
REF	MAMMOGRAPHY CERTIFICATION NUMBER		1	S	2400		
REF01	Reference identification Qualifier	ID	2-3	R			EW
REF02	Mammography Certification Number	AN	1-30	R			
REF03	Description	AN	1-80	N/U			
REF04	REFERENCE IDENTIFIER			N/U			

5010

837-P 5010

Element Identifier	Description	ID	Min. Max.	Usage Reg.	Loop	Loop Repeat	Values	
REF	PRIOR AUTHORIZATION		5	S	2400			
REF01	Reference Identification Qualifier	ID	2-3	R			G1	Code Deleted
REF02	Prior Authorization or Referral Number	AN	1-50	R				Increase from 30 - 50
REF03	Description	AN	1-80	N/U				
REF04	REFERENCE IDENTIFIER							New Element
REF04-1	Reference Identifier Qualifier	ID	2-3	R			2U	New Element
REF04-2	Other Payer Primary Idenitifer	AN	1-50	R				New Element
REF04-3	Reference Identification Qualifier	ID	2-3	N/U				New Element
REF04-4	Reference Identification	AN	1-50	N/U				New Element
REF04-5	Reference Identification Qualifier	ID	2-3	N/U				New Element
REF04-6	Reference Identification	AN	1-50	N/U				New Element
REF	LINE ITEM CONTROL NUMBER		1	S	2400			
REF01	Reference Identification Qualifier	ID	2-3	R			6R	
REF02	Line Item Control Number	AN	1-50	R				Increase from 30 - 50
REF03	Description	AN	1-80	N/U				
REF04	REFERENCE IDENTIFIER			N/U				New Element
REF04-1	Reference Identifier Qualifier	ID	2-3	N/U				New Element
REF04-2	Other Payer Primary Idenitifer	AN	1-50	N/U				New Element
RFF04-3	Reference Identification Qualifier	ID	2-3	N/U				New Element
REF04-4	Reference Identification	AN	1-50	N/U				New Element
REF04-5	Reference Identification Qualifier	ID	2-3	N/U				New Element
REF04-6	Reference Identification	AN	1-50	N/U				New Element
REF	MAMMOGRAPHY CERTIFICATION NUMBER		1	S	2400			
REF01	Reference identification Qualifier	ID	2-3	R			EW	
REF02	Mammography Certification Number	AN	1-50	R				Increase from 30 - 50
REF03	Description	AN	1-80	N/U				
REF04	REFERENCE IDENTIFIER			N/U				New Element
REF04-1	Reference Identifier Qualifier	ID	2-3	N/U				

PROFESSIONAL CLAIM

Element Identifier	Description	ID	Min. Max.	Usage Reg.	Loop	Loop Repeat	Values
	4010A1						
	837-P 4010A1						
REF	**CLINICAL LABORATORY IMPROVEMENT AMENDMENT (CLIA) IDENTIFICATION**		1	S	2400		
REF01	Reference Identification Qualifier	ID	2-3	R			X4
REF02	Clinical Laboratory Improvement Amendment Number	AN	1-30	R			
REF03	Description	AN	1-80	N/U			
REF04	REFERENCE IDENTIFIER			N/U			
REF	**REFERRING CLINICAL LABORATORY IMPROVEMENT AMENDMENT (CLIA) FACILITY IDENTIFICATION**		1	S	2400		
REF01	Reference Identification Qualifier	ID	2-3	R			F4
REF02	Referring CLIA Number	AN	1-30	R			
REF03	Description	AN	1-80	N/U			
REF04	REFERENCE IDENTIFIER			N/U			

Element Identifier	Description	ID	Min. Max.	Usage Reg.	Loop	Loop Repeat	Values	
	5010							
	837-P 5010							
REF04-2	Other Payer Primary Idenitifer	AN	1-50	N/U				New Element
REF04-3	Reference Identification Qualifier	ID	2-3	N/U				New Element
REF04-4	Reference Identification	AN	1-50	N/U				New Element
REF04-5	Reference Identification Qualifier	ID	2-3	N/U				New Element
REF04-6	Reference Identification	AN	1-50	N/U				New Element
REF	**CLINICAL LABORATORY IMPROVEMENT AMENDMENT (CLIA) IDENTIFICATION**		1	S	2400			
REF01	Reference Identification Qualifier	ID	2-3	R			X4	
REF02	Clinical Laboratory Improvement Amendment Number	AN	1-50	R				Increase from 30 - 50
REF03	Description	AN	1-80	N/U				
REF04	REFERENCE IDENTIFIER			N/U				
REF04-1	Reference Identifier Qualifier	ID	2-3	N/U				New Element
REF04-2	Other Payer Primary Idenitifer	AN	1-50	N/U				New Element
REF04-3	Reference Identification Qualifier	ID	2-3	N/U				New Element
REF04-4	Reference Identification	AN	1-50	N/U				New Element
REF04-5	Reference Identification Qualifier	ID	2-3	N/U				New Element
REF04-6	Reference Identification	AN	1-50	N/U				New Element
REF	**REFERRING CLINICAL LABORATORY IMPROVEMENT AMENDMENT (CLIA) FACILITY IDENTIFICATION**		1	S	2400			
REF01	Reference Identification Qualifier	ID	2-3	R			F4	
REF02	Referring CLIA Number	AN	1-50	R				Increase from 30 - 50
REF03	Description	AN	1-80	N/U				
REF04	REFERENCE IDENTIFIER			N/U				
REF04-1	Reference Identifier Qualifier	ID	2-3	N/U				New Element
REF04-2	Other Payer Primary Idenitifer	AN	1-50	N/U				New Element
REF04-3	Reference Identification Qualifier	ID	2-3	N/U				New Element
REF04-4	Reference Identification	AN	1-50	N/U				New Element

Page 75 of 93

PROFESSIONAL CLAIM

4010A1

Element Identifier	Description	ID	Min. Max.	Usage Req.	Loop	Loop Repeat	Values
	837-P 4010A1						
REF	**IMMUNIZATION BATCH NUMBER**		1	S	2400		
REF01	Reference Identification Qualifier	ID	2-3	R			BT
REF02	Immunization Batch Number	AN	1-30	R			
REF03	Description	AN	1-80	N/U			
REF04	REFERENCE IDENTIFIER			N/U			
REF	**AMBULATORY PATIENT GROUP (APG)**		4	S	2400		
REF01	Reference Identification Qualifier	ID	2-3	R			1S
REF02	Ambulatory Patient Group Number	AN	1-30	R			
REF03	Description	AN	1-80	N/U			
REF04	REFERENCE IDENTIFIER			N/U			
REF	**OXYGEN FLOW RATE**		1	S	2400		
REF01	Reference Identification Qualifier	ID	2-3	R			TP
REF02	Oxygen Flow Rate	AN	1-30	R			
REF03	Description	AN	1-80	N/U			
REF04	REFERENCE IDENTIFIER			N/U			
REF	**UNIVERSAL PRODUCT NUMBER (UPN)**		1	S	2400		
REF01	Reference Identification Qualifier	ID	2-3	R			OZ, VP
REF02	Universal Product Number	AN	1-30	R			
REF03	Description	AN	1-80	N/U			
REF04	REFERENCE IDENTIFIER			N/U			

5010

Element Identifier	Description	ID	Min. Max.	Usage Req.	Loop	Loop Repeat	Values	
	837-P 5010							
REF04-5	Reference Identification Qualifier	ID	2-3	N/U				New Element
REF04-6	Reference Identification	AN	1-50	N/U				New Element
REF	**IMMUNIZATION BATCH NUMBER**		1	S	2400			
REF01	Reference Identification Qualifier	ID	2-3	R			BT	
REF02	Immunization Batch Number	AN	1-50	R				Increase from 30 - 50
REF03	Description	AN	1-80	N/U				
REF04	REFERENCE IDENTIFIER			N/U				
REF04-1	Reference Identifier Qualifier	ID	2-3	N/U				New Element
REF04-2	Other Payer Primary Idenitifer	AN	1-50	N/U				New Element
REF04-3	Reference Identification Qualifier	ID	2-3	N/U				New Element
REF04-4	Reference Identification	AN	1-50	N/U				New Element
REF04-5	Reference Identification Qualifier	ID	2-3	N/U				New Element
REF04-6	Reference Identification	AN	1-50	N/U				New Element
								Segment Deleted
								Segment Deleted
								Segment Deleted
REF	**REFERRAL NUMBER**		5	S	2400			New Segment

Page 76 of 93

PROFESSIONAL CLAIM

4010A1							
Element Identifier	Description	ID	Min. Max.	Usage Req.	Loop	Loop Repeat	Values
837-P 4010A1							
AMT	**SALES TAX AMOUNT**		1	S	2400		
AMT01	Amount Qualifier Code	ID	1-3	R			T
AMT02	Sales Tax Amount S9(7)V99	R	1-18	R			
AMT03	Credit/Debit Flag Code	ID	1-1	N/U			
AMT	**APPROVED AMOUNT**		1	S	2400		
AMT01	Amount Qualifier Code	ID	1-3	R			AAE
AMT02	Approved Amount S9(7)V99	R	1-18	R			
AMT03	Credit/Debit Flag Code	ID	1-1	N/U			
AMT	**POSTAGE CLAIMED AMOUNT**		1	S	2400		
AMT01	Amount Qualifier Code	ID	1-3	R			F4
AMT02	Postage Claimed Amount S9(7)V99	R	1-18	R			
AMT03	Credit/Debit Flag Code	ID	1-1	N/U			
K3	**FILE INFORMATION**		10	S	2400		
K301	Fixed Format Information	AN	1-80	R			
K302	Record Format Code	ID	1-2	N/U			
K303	COMPOSITE UNIT OF MEASURE			N/U			
NTE	**LINE NOTE**		1	S	2400		
NTE01	Note Reference Code	ID	3-3	R			ADD, DCP, PMT, TPO
NTE02	Line Note Text	AN	1-80	R			

5010								
Element Identifier	Description	ID	Min. Max.	Usage Req.	Loop	Loop Repeat	Values	
837-P 5010								
REF01	Reference Identification Qualifier	ID	2-3	R			9F	
REF02	Referral Number	AN	1-50	R				
REF03	Description	AN	1-80	N/U				
REF04	REFERENCE IDENTIFIER							
REF04-1	Reference Identifier Qualifier	ID	2-3	R			2U	
REF04-2	Other Payer Primary Idenitifer	AN	1-50	R				
REF04-3	Reference Identification Qualifier	ID	2-3	N/U				
REF04-4	Reference Identification	AN	1-50	N/U				
REF04-5	Reference Identification Qualifier	ID	2-3	N/U				
REF04-6	Reference Identification	AN	1-50	N/U				
AMT	**SALES TAX AMOUNT**		1	S	2400			
AMT01	Amount Qualifier Code	ID	1-3	R			T	
AMT02	Sales Tax Amount S9(7)V99	R	1-18	R				
AMT03	Credit/Debit Flag Code	ID	1-1	N/U				
								Segment Deleted
AMT	**POSTAGE CLAIMED AMOUNT**		1	S	2400			
AMT01	Amount Qualifier Code	ID	1-3	R			F4	
AMT02	Sales Tax Amount S9(7)V99	R	1-18	R				
AMT03	Credit/Debit Flag Code	ID	1-1	N/U				
K3	**FILE INFORMATION**		10	S	2400			
K301	Fixed Format Information	AN	1-80	R				
K302	Record Format Code	ID	1-2	N/U				
K303	COMPOSITE UNIT OF MEASURE			N/U				
NTE	**LINE NOTE**		1	S	2400			
NTE01	Note Reference Code	ID	3-3	R			ADD, DCP	Code Deleted
NTE02	Line Note Text	AN	1-80	R				

PROFESSIONAL CLAIM

4010A1

Element Identifier	Description	ID	Min. Max.	Usage Reg.	Loop	Loop Repeat	Values
	837-P 4010A1						
PS1	**PURCHASED SERVICE INFORMATION**		1	S	2400		
PS101	Purchased Service Provider Identifier	AN	1-30	R			
PS102	Purchased Service Charge Amount S9(7)V99	R	1-18	R			
PS103	State or Province Code	ID	2-2	N/U			
HSD	**HEALTH CARE SERVICES DELIVERY**		1	S	2400		
HSD01	Visits	ID	2-2	S			VS
HSD02	Number of Visits 9(3)	R	1-15	S			
HSD03	Frequency Period	ID	2-2	S			DA, MO, Q1, WK
HSD04	Frequency Count 9(2)V9	R	1-6	S			
HSD05	Duration of Visits Units	ID	1-2	S			7, 34, 35
HSD06	Duration of Visits, Number of Units	N0	1-3	S			
HSD07	Ship, Delivery or Calendar Pattern Code	ID	1-2	S			1, 2, 3, 4, 5, 6, 7, A, B, C, D, E, F, G, H, J, K, L, N, O, SA, SB, SC, SD, SG, SL, SP, SX, SY, SZ, W
HSD08	Delivery Pattern Time Code	ID	1-1	S			D, E, F
HCP	**LINE PRICING/REPRICING INFORMATION**		1	S	2400		
HCP01	Pricing Methodology	ID	2-2	R			00, 01, 02, 03, 04, 05, 06, 07, 08, 09, 10, 11, 12, 13, 14
HCP02	Repriced Allowed Amount S9(7)V99	R	1-18	R			
HCP03	Repriced Saving Amount S9(7)V99	R	1-18	S			
HCP04	Repricing Organization Identifier	AN	1-30	S			
HCP05	Repricing Per Diem or Flat Rate Amount S9(5)V99	R	1-9	S			
HCP06	Repriced Approved Ambulatory Patient Group Code	AN	1-30	S			

5010

Element Identifier	Description	ID	Min. Max.	Usage Reg.	Loop	Loop Repeat	Values	
	837-P 5010							
NTE	**THIRD PARTY ORGANIZATION NOTE**		1	S	2400			New Segment
NTE01	Third Party Organization Notes	ID	3-3	R			TPO	
NTE02	Line Note Text	AN	1-80	R				
PS1	**PURCHASED SERVICE INFORMATION**		1	S	2400			
PS101	Purchased Service Provider Identifier	AN	1-50	R				Increase from 30 - 50
PS102	Purchased Service Charge Amount S9(7)V99	R	1-18	R				
PS103	State or Province Code	ID	2-2	N/U				
								Segment Deleted
HCP	**LINE PRICING/REPRICING INFORMATION**		1	S	2400			
HCP01	Pricing Methodology	ID	2-2	R			00, 01, 02, 03, 04, 05, 06, 07, 08, 09, 10, 11, 12, 13, 14	
HCP02	Repriced Allowed Amount S9(7)V99	R	1-18	R				
HCP03	Repriced Saving Amount S9(7)V99	R	1-18	S				
HCP04	Repricing Organization Identifier	AN	1-50	S				Increase from 30 - 50
HCP05	Repricing Per Diem or Flat Rate Amount S9(5)V99	R	1-9	S				
HCP06	Repriced Approved Ambulatory Patient Group Code	AN	1-50	S				Increase from 30 - 50

PROFESSIONAL CLAIM

	4010A1						
Element Identifier	Description	ID	Min. Max.	Usage Reg.	Loop	Loop Repeat	Values
	837-P 4010A1						
HCP07	Repriced Approved Ambulatory Patient Group Amount S9(7)V99	R	1-18	S			
HCP08	Product/Service ID	AN	1-48	N/U			
HCP09	Product or Service ID Qualifier	ID	2-2	S			HC, IV, ZZ
HCP10	Procedure Code	AN	1-48	S			
HCP11	Unit or Basis for Measurement Code	ID	2-2	S			DA, UN
HCP12	Repriced Approved Service Unit Count "DA" = 9(3) "UN" = 9(3)V9	R	1-15	S			
HCP13	Reject Reason Code	ID	2-2	S			T1, T2, T3, T4, T5, T6
HCP14	Policy Compliance Code	ID	1-2	S			1, 2, 3, 4, 5
HCP15	Exception Code	ID	1-2	S			1, 2, 3, 4, 5, 6
LIN	**DRUG IDENTIFICATION**		1	S	2410	25	
LIN01	Assigned Identification	AN	1-20	N/U			
LIN02	Product or Service ID Qualifier	ID	2-2	R			N4
LIN03	National Drug Code	AN	1-48	R			
LIN04	Product/Service ID Qualifier	ID	2-2	N/U			
LIN05	Product/Service ID	AN	1-48	N/U			
LIN06	Product/Service ID Qualifier	ID	2-2	N/U			
LIN07	Product/Service ID	AN	1-48	N/U			
LIN08	Product/Service ID Qualifier	ID	2-2	N/U			
LIN09	Product/Service ID	AN	1-48	N/U			
LIN10	Product/Service ID Qualifier	ID	2-2	N/U			
LIN11	Product/Service ID	AN	1-48	N/U			
LIN12	Product/Service ID Qualifier	ID	2-2	N/U			
LIN13	Product/Service ID	AN	1-48	N/U			
LIN14	Product/Service ID Qualifier	ID	2-2	N/U			
LIN15	Product/Service ID	AN	1-48	N/U			
LIN16	Product/Service ID Qualifier	ID	2-2	N/U			
LIN17	Product/Service ID	AN	1-48	N/U			
LIN18	Product/Service ID Qualifier	ID	2-2	N/U			
LIN19	Product/Service ID	AN	1-48	N/U			
LIN20	Product/Service ID Qualifier	ID	2-2	N/U			

	5010							
Element Identifier	Description	ID	Min. Max.	Usage Reg.	Loop	Loop Repeat	Values	
	837-P 5010							
HCP07	Repriced Approved Ambulatory Patient Group Amount S9(7)V99	R	1-18	S				
HCP08	Product/Service ID	AN	1-48	N/U				
HCP09	Product or Service ID Qualifier	ID	2-2	S			ER, HC, IV, WK	Code Deleted
HCP10	Procedure Code	AN	1-48	S				
HCP11	Unit or Basis for Measurement Code	ID	2-2	S			MJ, UN	Code Change
HCP12	Repriced Approved Service Unit Count "MJ" = 9(4) "UN" = 9(3)V9	R	1-15	S				
HCP13	Reject Reason Code	ID	2-2	S			T1, T2, T3, T4, T5, T6	
HCP14	Policy Compliance Code	ID	1-2	S			1, 2, 3, 4, 5	
HCP15	Exception Code	ID	1-2	S			1, 2, 3, 4, 5, 6	
LIN	**DRUG IDENTIFICATION**		1	S	2410	1		
LIN01	Assigned Identification	AN	1-20	N/U				
LIN02	Product or Service ID Qualifier	ID	2-2	R			N4	
LIN03	National Drug Code	AN	1-48	R				
LIN04	Product/Service ID Qualifier	ID	2-2	N/U				
LIN05	Product/Service ID	AN	1-48	N/U				
LIN06	Product/Service ID Qualifier	ID	2-2	N/U				
LIN07	Product/Service ID	AN	1-48	N/U				
LIN08	Product/Service ID Qualifier	ID	2-2	N/U				
LIN09	Product/Service ID	AN	1-48	N/U				
LIN10	Product/Service ID Qualifier	ID	2-2	N/U				
LIN11	Product/Service ID	AN	1-48	N/U				
LIN12	Product/Service ID Qualifier	ID	2-2	N/U				
LIN13	Product/Service ID	AN	1-48	N/U				
LIN14	Product/Service ID Qualifier	ID	2-2	N/U				
LIN15	Product/Service ID	AN	1-48	N/U				
LIN16	Product/Service ID Qualifier	ID	2-2	N/U				
LIN17	Product/Service ID	AN	1-48	N/U				
LIN18	Product/Service ID Qualifier	ID	2-2	N/U				
LIN19	Product/Service ID	AN	1-48	N/U				
LIN20	Product/Service ID Qualifier	ID	2-2	N/U				

Page 79 of 93

PROFESSIONAL CLAIM

4010A1								**5010**							
Element Identifier	Description	ID	Min. Max.	Usage Reg.	Loop	Loop Repeat	Values	Element Identifier	Description	ID	Min. Max.	Usage Reg.	Loop	Loop Repeat	Values
837-P 4010A1								**837-P 5010**							
LIN21	Product/Service ID	AN	1-48	N/U				LIN21	Product/Service ID	AN	1-48	N/U			
LIN22	Product/Service ID Qualifier	ID	2-2	N/U				LIN22	Product/Service ID Qualifier	ID	2-2	N/U			
LIN23	Product/Service ID	AN	1-48	N/U				LIN23	Product/Service ID	AN	1-48	N/U			
LIN24	Product/Service ID Qualifier	ID	2-2	N/U				LIN24	Product/Service ID Qualifier	ID	2-2	N/U			
LIN25	Product/Service ID	AN	1-48	N/U				LIN25	Product/Service ID	AN	1-48	N/U			
LIN26	Product/Service ID Qualifier	ID	2-2	N/U				LIN26	Product/Service ID Qualifier	ID	2-2	N/U			
LIN27	Product/Service ID	AN	1-48	N/U				LIN27	Product/Service ID	AN	1-48	N/U			
LIN28	Product/Service ID Qualifier	ID	2-2	N/U				LIN28	Product/Service ID Qualifier	ID	2-2	N/U			
LIN29	Product/Service ID	AN	1-48	N/U				LIN29	Product/Service ID	AN	1-48	N/U			
LIN30	Product/Service ID Qualifier	ID	2-2	N/U				LIN30	Product/Service ID Qualifier	ID	2-2	N/U			
LIN31	Product/Service ID	AN	1-48	N/U				LIN31	Product/Service ID	AN	1-48	N/U			
CTP	**DRUG PRICING**		1	S	2410			**CTP**	**DRUG PRICING**		1	R	2410		
CTP01	Class of Trade Code	ID	2-2	N/U				CTP01	Class of Trade Code	ID	2-2	N/U			
CTP02	Price Identifier Code	ID	3-3	N/U				CTP02	Price Identifier Code	ID	3-3	N/U			
CTP03	Drug Unit Price S9(7)V99	R	1-17	R				CTP03	Unit Price	R	1-17	N/U			
CTP04	National Drug Unit Count - when CTP05 = "UN" 9(3)V9, CTP05 = "F2" 9(7)V999, CTP05 = "ML" or "GR" 9(2)V99	R	1-15	R				CTP04	National Drug Unit Count - when CTP05-1 = "UN" 9(3)V9, "F2" 9(7)V999, "ML" or "GR" 9(2)V99, ME 9(5)V999	R	1-15	R			
CTP05	COMPOSITE UNIT OF MEASURE							CTP05	COMPOSITE UNIT OF MEASURE			R			
CTP05-1	Unit or Basis For Measurement Code	ID	2-2	R			F2, GR, ML, UN	CTP05-1	Unit or Basis For Measurement Code	ID	2-2	R			F2, GR, ME, ML, UN
CTP05-2	Exponent	R	1-15	N/U				CTP05-2	Exponent	R	1-15	N/U			
CTP05-3	Multiplier	R	1-10	N/U				CTP05-3	Multiplier	R	1-10	N/U			
CTP05-4	Unit or Basis For Measurement Code	ID	2-2	N/U				CTP05-4	Unit or Basis For Measurement Code	ID	2-2	N/U			
CTP05-5	Exponent	R	1-15	N/U				CTP05-5	Exponent	R	1-15	N/U			
CTP05-6	Multiplier	R	1-10	N/U				CTP05-6	Multiplier	R	1-10	N/U			
CTP05-7	Unit or Basis For Measurement Code	ID	2-2	N/U				CTP05-7	Unit or Basis For Measurement Code	ID	2-2	N/U			
CTP05-8	Exponent	R	1-15	N/U				CTP05-8	Exponent	R	1-15	N/U			
CTP05-9	Multiplier	R	1-10	N/U				CTP05-9	Multiplier	R	1-10	N/U			
CTP05-10	Unit or Basis For Measurement Code	ID	2-2	N/U				CTP05-10	Unit or Basis For Measurement Code	ID	2-2	N/U			
CTP05-11	Exponent	R	1-15	N/U				CTP05-11	Exponent	R	1-15	N/U			
CTP05-12	Multiplier	R	1-10	N/U				CTP05-12	Multiplier	R	1-10	N/U			
CTP05-13	Unit or Basis For Measurement Code	ID	2-2	N/U				CTP05-13	Unit or Basis For Measurement Code	ID	2-2	N/U			
CTP05-14	Exponent	R	1-15	N/U				CTP05-14	Exponent	R	1-15	N/U			

Notes in right margin:
- Usage changed to Not Used (CTP03)
- Usage changed to Required (CTP05)
- Code Added (CTP05-1)

Page 80 of 93

PROFESSIONAL CLAIM

4010A1							
Element Identifier	Description	ID	Min. Max.	Usage Reg.	Loop	Loop Repeat	Values
	837-P 4010A1						
CTP05-15	Multiplier	R	1-10	N/U			
CTP06	Price Multiplier Qualifier	ID	3-3	N/U			
CTP07	Multiplier	R	1-10	N/U			
CTP08	Monetary Amount	R	1-18	N/U			
CTP09	Basis of Unit Price Code	ID	2-2	N/U			
CTP10	Condition Value	AN	1-10	N/U			
CTP11	Multiple Price Quantity	N0	1-2	N/U			
REF	**PRESCRIPTION NUBER**		1	S	2410		
REF01	Reference Identification Qualifier	ID	2-3	R			XZ
REF02	Prescription Number	AN	1-30	R			
REF03	Desciption	AN	1-80	N/U			
REF04	REFERENCE IDENTIFIER			N/U			
NM1	**RENDERING PROVIDER NAME**		1	S	2420A	1	
NM101	Entity Identifier Code	ID	2-3	R			82
NM102	Entity Type Qualifier	ID	1-1	R			1,2
NM103	Rendering Provider Last or Organization Name	AN	1-35	R			
NM104	Rendering Provider First Name	AN	1-25	S			
NM105	Rendering Provider Middle Name	AN	1-25	S			
NM106	Name Prefix	AN	1-10	N/U			
NM107	Rendering Provider Name Suffix	AN	1-10	S			
NM108	Identification Code Qualifier	ID	1-2	R			24, 34, XX
NM109	Rendering Provider Identifier	AN	2-80	R			
NM110	Entity Relationship Code	ID	2-2	N/U			
NM111	Entity Identifier Code	ID	2-3	N/U			

5010								
Element Identifier	Description	ID	Min. Max.	Usage Reg.	Loop	Loop Repeat	Values	
	837-P 5010							
CTP05-15	Multiplier	R	1-10	N/U				
CTP06	Price Multiplier Qualifier	ID	3-3	N/U				
CTP07	Multiplier	R	1-10	N/U				
CTP08	Monetary Amount	R	1-18	N/U				
CTP09	Basis of Unit Price Code	ID	2-2	N/U				
CTP10	Condition Value	AN	1-10	N/U				
CTP11	Multiple Price Quantity	N0	1-2	N/U				
REF	**PRESCRIPTION OR COMPOUND DRUG ASSOCIATION NUMBER**		1	S	2410			Name change
REF01	Reference Identification Qualifier	ID	2-3	R			VY, XZ	Code Added
REF02	Prescription Number	AN	1-50	R				Increase from 30 - 50
REF03	Desciption	AN	1-80	N/U				
REF04	REFERENCE IDENTIFIER			N/U				
REF04-1	Reference Identifier Qualifier	ID	2-3	N/U				New Element
REF04-2	Other Payer Primary Idenitifer	AN	1-50	N/U				New Element
REF04-3	Reference Identification Qualifier	ID	2-3	N/U				New Element
REF04-4	Reference Identification	AN	1-50	N/U				New Element
REF04-5	Reference Identification Qualifier	ID	2-3	N/U				New Element
REF04-6	Reference Identification	AN	1-50	N/U				New Element
NM1	**RENDERING PROVIDER NAME**		1	S	2420A	1		
NM101	Entity Identifier Code	ID	2-3	R			82	
NM102	Entity Type Qualifier	ID	1-1	R			1,2	
NM103	Rendering Provider Last or Organization Name	AN	1-60	R				
NM104	Rendering Provider First Name	AN	1-35	S				
NM105	Rendering Provider Middle Name	AN	1-25	S				
NM106	Name Prefix	AN	1-10	N/U				
NM107	Rendering Provider Name Suffix	AN	1-10	S				
NM108	Identification Code Qualifier	ID	1-2	S			XX	Code Deleted
NM109	Rendering Provider Identifier	AN	2-80	S				
NM110	Entity Relationship Code	ID	2-2	N/U				
NM111	Entity Identifier Code	ID	2-3	N/U				
NM112	Name Last or Organization Name	AN	1-60	N/U				New Element

Page 81 of 93

PROFESSIONAL CLAIM

	4010A1							
Element Identifier	Description	ID	Min. Max.	Usage Reg.	Loop	Loop Repeat	Values	
	837-P 4010A1							
PRV	**RENDERING PROVIDER SPECIALTY INFORMATION**		1	S	2420A			
PRV01	Provider Code	ID	1-3	R			PE	
PRV02	Reference Identification Qualifier	ID	2-3	R			ZZ	
PRV03	Provider Taxonomy Code	AN	1-30	R				
PRV04	State or Province Code	ID	2-2	N/U				
PRV05	PROVIDER SPECIALTY INFORMATION			N/U				
PRV06	Provider Organization Code	ID	3-3	N/U				
REF	**RENDERING PROVIDER SECONDARY IDENTIFICATION**		5	S	2420A			
REF01	Reference Identification Qualifier	ID	2-3	R			0B, 1B, 1C, 1D, 1G, 1H, EI, G2, LU, N5, SY, X5	
REF02	Rendering Provider Secondary Identifier	AN	1-30	R				
REF03	Description	AN	1-80	N/U				
REF04	REFERENCE IDENTIFIER			N/U				
NM1	**PURCHASED SERVICE PROVIDER NAME**		1	S	2420B	1		
NM101	Entity Identifier Code	ID	2-3	R			QB	
NM102	Entity Type Qualifier	ID	1-1	R			1, 2	
NM103	Name Last or Organization Name	AN	1-35	N/U				
NM104	Name First	AN	1-25	N/U				
NM105	Name Middle	AN	1-25	N/U				
NM106	Name Prefix	AN	1-10	N/U				
NM107	Name Suffix	AN	1-10	N/U				
NM108	Identification Code Qualifier	ID	1-2	S			24, 34, XX	

	5010							
Element Identifier	Description	ID	Min. Max.	Usage Reg.	Loop	Loop Repeat	Values	
	837-P 5010							
PRV	**RENDERING PROVIDER SPECIALTY INFORMATION**		1	S	2420A			
PRV01	Provider Code	ID	1-3	R			PE	
PRV02	Reference Identification Qualifier	ID	2-3	R			PXC	Code change
PRV03	Provider Taxonomy Code	AN	1-50	R				Increase from 30 - 50
PRV04	State or Province Code	ID	2-2	N/U				
PRV05	PROVIDER SPECIALTY INFORMATION			N/U				
PRV06	Provider Organization Code	ID	3-3	N/U				
REF	**RENDERING PROVIDER SECONDARY IDENTIFICATION**		20	S	2420A			
REF01	Reference Identification Qualifier	ID	2-3	R			OB, 1G, G2, LU	Code Deleted
REF02	Rendering Provider Secondary Identifier	AN	1-50	R				Increase from 30 - 50
REF03	Description	AN	1-80	N/U				
REF04	REFERENCE IDENTIFIER			S				New Element
REF04-1	Reference Identifier Qualifier	ID	2-3	R			2U	New Element
REF04-2	Other Payer Primary Idenitifer	AN	1-50	R				New Element
REF04-3	Reference Identification Qualifier	ID	2-3	N/U				New Element
REF04-4	Reference Identification	AN	1-50	N/U				New Element
REF04-5	Reference Identification Qualifier	ID	2-3	N/U				New Element
REF04-6	Reference Identification	AN	1-50	N/U				
NM1	**PURCHASED SERVICE PROVIDER NAME**		1	S	2420B	1		
NM101	Entity Identifier Code	ID	2-3	R			QB	
NM102	Entity Type Qualifier	ID	1-1	R			1, 2	
NM103	Name Last or Organization Name	AN	1-60	N/U				Increase from 35 - 60
NM104	Name First	AN	1-35	N/U				Increase from 25 - 35
NM105	Name Middle	AN	1-25	N/U				
NM106	Name Prefix	AN	1-10	N/U				
NM107	Name Suffix	AN	1-10	N/U				
NM108	Identification Code Qualifier	ID	1-2	S			XX	Code Deleted

Page 82 of 93

PROFESSIONAL CLAIM

4010A1

837-P 4010A1

Element Identifier	Description	ID	Min. Max.	Usage Reg.	Loop	Loop Repeat	Values
NM109	Purchased Service Provider Identifier	AN	2-80	S			
NM110	Entity Relationship Code	ID	2-2	N/U			
NM111	Entity Identifier Code	ID	2-3	N/U			
REF	PURCHASED SERVICE PROVIDER SECONDARY IDENTIFICATION		5	S	2420B		
REF01	Reference Identification Qualifier	ID	2-3	R			0B, 1A, 1B, 1C, 1D, 1G, 1H, EI, G2, LU, N5, SY, U3, X5
REF02	Purchased Service Provider Secondary Identifier	AN	1-30	R			
REF03	Description	AN	1-80	N/U			
REF04	REFERENCE IDENTIFIER			N/U			
NM1	SERVICE FACILITY LOCATION		1	S	2420C	1	
NM101	Entity Identifier Code	ID	2-3	R			77, FA, LI, TL
NM102	Entity Type Qualifier	ID	1-1	R			2
NM103	Laboratory or Facility Name	AN	1-35	S			
NM104	Name First	AN	1-25	N/U			
NM105	Name Middle	AN	1-25	N/U			
NM106	Name Prefix	AN	1-10	N/U			
NM107	Name Suffix	AN	1-10	N/U			
NM108	Identification Code Qualifier	ID	1-2	S			24, 34, XX
NM109	Laboratory or Facility Primary Identifier	AN	2-80	S			
NM110	Entity Relationship Code	ID	2-2	N/U			
NM111	Entity Identifier Code	ID	2-3	N/U			

5010

837-P 5010

Element Identifier	Description	ID	Min. Max.	Usage Reg.	Loop	Loop Repeat	Values	
NM109	Other Payer Primary Identifier	AN	2-80	S				
NM110	Entity Relationship Code	ID	2-2	N/U				
NM111	Entity Identifier Code	ID	2-3	N/U				
NM112	Name Last or Organization Name	AN	1-60	N/U				New Element
REF	PURCHASED SERVICE PROVIDER SECONDARY IDENTIFICATION		20	S	2420B			
REF01	Reference Identification Qualifier	ID	2-3	R			0B, 1G, G2	Code Deleted
REF02	Purchased Service Provider Secondary Identifier	AN	1-50	R				Increase from 30 - 50
REF03	Description	AN	1-80	N/U				
REF04	REFERENCE IDENTIFIER			S				
REF04-1	Reference Identifier Qualifier	ID	2-3	R			2U	New Element
REF04-2	Other Payer Primary Idenitifer	AN	1-50	R				New Element
REF04-3	Reference Identification Qualifier	ID	2-3	N/U				New Element
REF04-4	Reference Identification	AN	1-50	N/U				New Element
REF04-5	Reference Identification Qualifier	ID	2-3	N/U				New Element
REF04-6	Reference Identification	AN	1-50	N/U				New Element
NM1	SERVICE FACILITY LOCATION NAME		1	S	2420C	1		
NM101	Entity Identifier Code	ID	2-3	R			77	
NM102	Entity Type Qualifier	ID	1-1	R			2	
NM103	Name Last or Organization Name	AN	1-60	R				Increase from 35 - 60
NM104	Name First	AN	1-35	N/U				Increase from 25 - 35
NM105	Name Middle	AN	1-25	N/U				
NM106	Name Prefix	AN	1-10	N/U				
NM107	Name Suffix	AN	1-10	N/U				
NM108	Identification Code Qualifier	ID	1-2	S			XX	Code Deleted
NM109	Other Payer Primary Identifier	AN	2-80	S				
NM110	Entity Relationship Code	ID	2-2	N/U				
NM111	Entity Identifier Code	ID	2-3	N/U				
NM112	Name Last or Organization Name	AN	1-60	N/U				New Element

Page 83 of 93

PROFESSIONAL CLAIM

4010A1

837-P 4010A1

Element Identifier	Description	ID	Min. Max.	Usage Reg.	Loop	Loop Repeat	Values
N3	SERVICE FACILITY LOCATION ADDRESS		1	R	2420C		
N301	Laboratory or Facility Address Line	AN	1-55	R			
N302	Laboratory or Facility Address Line	AN	1-55	S			
N4	SERVICE FACILITY LOCATION CITY/STATE/ZIP		1	R	2420C		
N401	Laboratory or Facility City Name	AN	2-30	R			
N402	Laboratory or Facility State or Province Code	ID	2-2	R			
N403	Laboratory or Facility Postal Zone or ZIP Code	ID	3-15	R			
N404	Country Code	ID	2-3	S			
N405	Location Qualifier	ID	1-2	N/U			
N406	Location Identifier	ID	1-30	N/U			
REF	SERVICE FACILITY LOCATION SECONDARY IDENTIFICATION		5	S	2420C		
REF01	Reference Identification Qualifier	ID	2-3	R			0B, 1A, 1B, 1C, 1D, 1G,1H, G2, LU, N5, TJ, X4, X5
REF02	Service Facility Location Secondary Identifier	AN	1-30	R			
REF03	Description	AN	1-80	N/U			
REF04	REFERENCE IDENTIFIER			N/U			
NM1	SUPERVISING PROVIDER NAME		1	S	2420D	1	
NM101	Entity Identifier Code	ID	2-3	R			DQ

5010

837-P 5010

Element Identifier	Description	ID	Min. Max.	Usage Reg.	Loop	Loop Repeat	Values	
N3	SERVICE FACILITY LOCATION ADDRESS		1	R	2420C			
N301	Laboratory or Facility Address Line	AN	1-55	R				
N302	Laboratory or Facility Address Line	AN	1-55	S				
N4	SERVICE FACILITY LOCATION CITY/STATE/ZIP		1	R	2420C			
N401	Laboratory or Facility City Name	AN	2-30	R				
N402	Laboratory or Facility State or Province Code	ID	2-2	S				Usage changed to Situational
N403	Laboratory or Facility Postal Zone ZIP Code	ID	3-15	S				Usage changed to Situational
N404	Laboratory or Facility Country Code	ID	2-3	S				
N405	Location Qualifier	ID	1-2	N/U				
N406	Location Identifier	AN	1-30	N/U				
N407	Country Subdivision Code	ID	1-3	S				New Element
REF	SERVICE FACILITY LOCATION SECONDARY IDENTIFICATION		3	S	2420C			Code Deleted
REF01	Reference Identification Qualifier	ID	2-3	R			G2, LU	
REF02	Service Facility Location Secondary Identifier	AN	1-50	R				Increase from 30 - 50
REF03	Description	AN	1-80	N/U				
REF04	REFERENCE IDENTIFIER			S				Usage changed to Situational
REF04-1	Reference Identifier Qualifier	ID	2-3	R			2U	New Element
REF04-2	Other Payer Primary Idenitifer	AN	1-50	R				New Element
REF04-3	Reference Identification Qualifier	ID	2-3	N/U				New Element
REF04-4	Reference Identification	AN	1-50	N/U				New Element
REF04-5	Reference Identification Qualifier	ID	2-3	N/U				New Element
REF04-6	Reference Identification	AN	1-50	N/U				New Element
NM1	SUPERVISING PROVIDER NAME		1	S	2420D	1		
NM101	Entity Identifier Code	ID	2-3	R			DQ	

Page 84 of 93

PROFESSIONAL CLAIM

4010A1								5010							
Element Identifier	Description	ID	Min. Max.	Usage Reg.	Loop	Loop Repeat	Values	Element Identifier	Description	ID	Min. Max.	Usage Reg.	Loop	Loop Repeat	Values	
837-P 4010A1								**837-P 5010**								
NM102	Entity Type Qualifier	ID	1-1	R			1	NM102	Entity Type Qualifier	ID	1-1	R			1	
NM103	Supervising Provider Last Name	AN	1-35	R				NM103	Supervising Provider Last Name	AN	1-60	R				Increase from 35 - 60
NM104	Supervising Provider First Name	AN	1-25	R				NM104	Name First	AN	1-35	S				Increase from 25 - 35 Usage changed to Situational
NM105	Supervising Provider Middle Name	AN	1-25	S				NM105	Name Middle	AN	1-25	S				
NM106	Name Prefix	AN	1-10	N/U				NM106	Name Prefix	AN	1-10	N/U				
NM107	Supervising Provider Name Suffix	AN	1-10	S				NM107	Name Suffix	AN	1-10	S				
NM108	Identification Code Qualifier	ID	1-2	S			24, 34, XX	NM108	Identification Code Qualifier	ID	1-2	S			XX	Code Deleted
NM109	Supervising Provider Identifier	AN	2-80	S				NM109	Other Payer Primary Identifier	AN	2-80	S				
NM110	Entity Relationship Code	ID	2-2	N/U				NM110	Entity Relationship Code	ID	2-2	N/U				
NM111	Entity Identifier Code	ID	2-3	N/U				NM111	Entity Identifier Code	ID	2-3	N/U				
								NM112	Name Last or Organization Name	AN	1-60	N/U				New Element
REF	SUPERVISING PROVIDER SECONDARY IDENTIFICATION		5	S	2420D			REF	SUPERVISING PROVIDER SECONDARY IDENTIFICATION		20	S	2420D			
REF01	Reference Identification Qualifier	ID	2-3	R			0B, 1B, 1C, 1D, 1G, 1H, EI, G2, LU, N5, SY, X5	REF01	Reference Identification Qualifier	ID	2-3	R			0B, 1G, G2, LU	Code Deleted
REF02	Supervising Provider Secondary Identifier	AN	1-30	R				REF02	Supervising Provider Secondary Identifier	AN	1-50	R				Increase from 30 - 50
REF03	Description	AN	1-80	N/U				REF03	Description	AN	1-80	N/U				
REF04	REFERENCE IDENTIFIER			N/U				REF04	REFERENCE IDENTIFIER			S				Usage changed to Situational
								REF04-1	Reference Identifier Qualifier	ID	2-3	R			2U	New Element
								REF04-2	Other Payer Primary Idenitifer	AN	1-50	R				New Element
								REF04-3	Reference Identification Qualifier	ID	2-3	N/U				New Element
								REF04-4	Reference Identification	AN	1-50	N/U				New Element
								REF04-5	Reference Identification Qualifier	ID	2-3	N/U				New Element
								REF04-6	Reference Identification	AN	1-50	N/U				New Element
NM1	ORDERING PROVIDER NAME		1	S	2420E	1		NM1	ORDERING PROVIDER NAME		1	S	2420E	1		
NM101	Entity Identifier Code	ID	2-3	R			DK	NM101	Entity Identifier Code	ID	2-3	R			DK	
NM102	Entity Type Qualifier	ID	1-1	R			1	NM102	Entity Type Qualifier	ID	1-1	R			1	
NM103	Ordering Provider Last Name	AN	1-35	R				NM103	Ordering Provider Last Name	AN	1-60	R				Increase from 35 - 60

Page 85 of 93

PROFESSIONAL CLAIM

4010A1

837-P 4010A1

Element Identifier	Description	ID	Min. Max.	Usage Reg.	Loop	Loop Repeat	Values
NM104	Ordering Provider First Name	AN	1-25	R			
NM105	Ordering Provider Middle Name	AN	1-25	S			
NM106	Name Prefix	AN	1-10	N/U			
NM107	Ordering Provider Name Suffix	AN	1-10	S			
NM108	Identification Code Qualifier	ID	1-2	S			24, 34, XX
NM109	Ordering Provider Identifier	AN	2-80	S			
NM110	Entity Relationship Code	ID	2-2	N/U			
NM111	Entity Identifier Code	ID	2-3	N/U			
N3	ORDERING PROVIDER ADDRESS		1	S	2420E		
N301	Ordering Provider Address Line	AN	1-55	R			
N302	Ordering Provider Address Line	AN	1-55	S			
N4	ORDERING PROVIDER CITY/STATE/ZIP CODE		1	S	2420E		
N401	Ordering Provider City Name	AN	2-30	R			
N402	Ordering Provider State Code	ID	2-2	R			
N403	Ordering Provider Postal Zone or ZIP Code	ID	3-15	R			
N404	Country Code	ID	2-3	S			
N405	Location Qualifier	ID	1-2	N/U			
N406	Location Identifier	AN	1-30	N/U			
REF	ORDERING PROVIDER SECONDARY IDENTIFICATION		5	S	2420E		
REF01	Reference Identification Qualifier	ID	2-3	R			0B, 1B, 1C, 1D, 1G, 1H, EI, G2, LU, N5, SY, X5
REF02	Ordering Provider Secondary Identifier	AN	1-30	R			
REF03	Description	AN	1-80	N/U			
REF04	REFERENCE IDENTIFIER			N/U			

5010

837-P 5010

Element Identifier	Description	ID	Min. Max.	Usage Reg.	Loop	Loop Repeat	Values	Notes
NM104	Ordering Provider First Name	AN	1-35	S				Increase from 25 - 35 Usage changed to Situational
NM105	Ordering Provider Middle Name or Initial	AN	1-25	S				
NM106	Name Prefix	AN	1-10	N/U				
NM107	Ordering Provider Name Suffix	AN	1-10	S				
NM108	Identification Code Qualifier	ID	1-2	S			XX	Code Deleted
NM109	Other Payer Primary Identifier	AN	2-80	S				
NM110	Entity Relationship Code	ID	2-2	N/U				
NM111	Entity Identifier Code	ID	2-3	N/U				
NM112	Name Last or Organization Name	AN	1-60	N/U				New Element
N3	ORDERING PROVIDER ADDRESS		1	S	2420E			
N301	Ordering Provider Address Line	AN	1-55	R				
N302	Ordering Provider Address Line	AN	1-55	S				
N4	ORDERING PROVIDER CITY/STATE/ZIP CODE		1	R	2420E			Usage changed to Required
N401	Ordering Provider City Name	AN	2-30	R				
N402	Ordering Provider State or Province Code	ID	2-2	S				Usage changed to Situational
N403	Ordering Provider Postal Zone ZIP Code	ID	3-15	S				Usage changed to Situational
N404	Ordering Provider Country Code	ID	2-3	S				
N405	Location Qualifier	ID	1-2	N/U				
N406	Location Identifier	AN	1-30	N/U				
N407	Country Subdivision Code	ID	1-3	S				New Element
REF	ORDERING PROVIDER SECONDARY IDENTIFICATION		20	S	2420E			
REF01	Reference Identification Qualifier	ID	2-3	R			OB, 1G, G2	Code Deleted
REF02	Ordering Provider Secondary Identifier	AN	1-50	R				Increase from 30 - 50
REF03	Description	AN	1-80	N/U				
REF04	REFERENCE IDENTIFIER			S				Usage changed to Situational

PROFESSIONAL CLAIM

4010A1

837-P 4010A1

Element Identifier	Description	ID	Min. Max.	Usage Reg.	Loop	Loop Repeat	Values
PER	**ORDERING PROVIDER CONTACT INFORMATION**		1	S	2420E		
PER01	Contact Function Code	ID	2-2	R			1C
PER02	Ordering Provider Contact Name	AN	1-60	R			
PER03	Communication Number Qualifier	ID	2-2	R			EM, FX, TE
PER04	Communication Number	AN	1-80	R			
PER05	Communication Number Qualifier	ID	2-2	S			EM, EX, FX, TE
PER06	Communication Number	AN	1-80	S			
PER07	Communication Number Qualifier	ID	2-2	S			EM, EX, FX, TE
PER08	Communication Number	AN	1-80	S			
PER09	Contact Inquiry Reference	AN	1-20	N/U			
NM1	**REFERRING PROVIDER NAME**		1	S	2420F	2	
NM101	Entity Identifier Code	ID	2-3	R			DN, P3
NM102	Entity Type Qualifier	ID	1-1	R			1
NM103	Referring Provider Last Name	AN	1-35	R			
NM104	Referring Provider First Name	AN	1-25	R			
NM105	Referring Provider Middle Name	AN	1-25	S			
NM106	Name Prefix	AN	1-10	N/U			
NM107	Referring Provider Name Suffix	AN	1-10	S			
NM108	Identification Code Qualifier	ID	1-2	S			24, 34, XX
NM109	Referring Provider Identifier	AN	2-80	S			
NM110	Entity Relationship Code	ID	2-2	N/U			
NM111	Entity Identifier Code	ID	2-3	N/U			

5010

837-P 5010

Element Identifier	Description	ID	Min. Max.	Usage Reg.	Loop	Loop Repeat	Values	
REF04-1	Reference Identifier Qualifier	ID	2-3	R			2U	New Element
REF04-2	Other Payer Primary Idenitifer	AN	1-50	R				New Element
REF04-3	Reference Identification Qualifier	ID	2-3	N/U				New Element
REF04-4	Reference Identification	AN	1-50	N/U				New Element
REF04-5	Reference Identification Qualifier	ID	2-3	N/U				New Element
REF04-6	Reference Identification	AN	1-50	N/U				New Element
PER	**ORDERING PROVIDER CONTACT INFORMATION**		1	S	2420E			
PER01	Contact Function Code	ID	2-2	R			1C	
PER02	Ordering Provider Contact Name	AN	1-60	S				Usage changed to Situational
PER03	Communication Number Qualifier	ID	2-2	R			EM, FX, TE	
PER04	Communication Number	AN	1-256	R				
PER05	Communication Number Qualifier	ID	2-2	S			EM, EX, FX, TE	
PER06	Communication Number	AN	1-256	S				
PER07	Communication Number Qualifier	ID	2-2	S			EM, EX, FX, TE	
PER08	Communication Number	AN	1-256	S				
PER09	Contact Inquiry Reference	AN	1-20	N/U				
NM1	**REFERRING PROVIDER NAME**		1	S	2420F	2		
NM101	Entity Identifier Code	ID	2-3	R			DN, P3	
NM102	Entity Type Qualifier	ID	1-1	R			1	
NM103	Referring Provider Last Name	AN	1-60	R				Increase from 35 - 60
NM104	Referring Provider First Name	AN	1-35	S				Increase from 25 - 35
NM105	Referring Provider Middle Name or Initial	AN	1-25	S				
NM106	Name Prefix	AN	1-10	N/U				
NM107	Referring Provider Name Suffix	AN	1-10	S				
NM108	Identification Code Qualifier	ID	1-2	S			XX	Code Deleted
NM109	Other Payer Primary Identifier	AN	2-80	S				
NM110	Entity Relationship Code	ID	2-2	N/U				
NM111	Entity Identifier Code	ID	2-3	N/U				

Page 87 of 93

PROFESSIONAL CLAIM

4010A1

Element Identifier	Description	ID	Min. Max.	Usage Reg.	Loop	Loop Repeat	Values
	837-P 4010A1						
PRV	**REFERRING PROVIDER SPECIALTY INFORMATION**		1	S	2420F		
PRV01	Provider Code	ID	1-3	R			RF
PRV02	Reference Identification Code	ID	2-3	R			ZZ
PRV03	Provider Taxonomy Code	AN	1-30	R			
PRV04	State or Province Code	ID	2-2	N/U			
PRV05	PROVIDER SPECIALTY INFORMATION			N/U			
PRV06	Provider Organization Code	ID	3-3	N/U			
REF	**REFERRING PROVIDER SECONDARY IDENTIFICATION**		5	S	2420F		
REF01	Reference Identification Qualifier	ID	2-3	R			0B, 1B, 1C, 1D, 1G, 1H, EI, G2, LU, N5, SY, X5
REF02	Referring Provider Secondary Identifier	AN	1-30	R			
REF03	Description	AN	1-80	N/U			
REF04	REFERENCE IDENTIFIER			N/U			
NM1	**OTHER PAYER PRIOR AUTHORIZATION OR REFERRAL NUMBER**		1	S	2420G	4	
NM101	Entity Identifier Code	ID	2-3	R			PR
NM102	Entity Type Qualifier	ID	1-1	R			2
NM103	Payer Name	AN	1-35	R			
NM104	Name First	AN	1-25	N/U			
NM105	Name Middle	AN	1-25	N/U			
NM106	Name Prefix	AN	1-10	N/U			
NM107	Name Suffix	AN	1-10	N/U			

5010

Element Identifier	Description	ID	Min. Max.	Usage Reg.	Loop	Loop Repeat	Values	
	837-P 5010							
NM112	Name Last or Organization Name	AN	1-60	N/U				New Element
								Segment Deleted
REF	**REFERRING PROVIDER SECONDARY IDENTIFICATION**		20	S	2420F			
REF01	Reference Identification Qualifier	ID	2-3	R			0B, 1G, G2	Code Deleted
REF02	Referring Provider Secondary Identifier	AN	1-50	R				Increase from 30 - 50
REF03	Description	AN	1-80	N/U				
REF04	REFERENCE IDENTIFIER			S				Usage changed to Situational
REF04-1	Reference Identifier Qualifier	ID	2-3	R			2U	New Element
REF04-2	Other Payer Primary Identifier	AN	1-50	R				New Element
REF04-3	Reference Identification Qualifier	ID	2-3	N/U				New Element
REF04-4	Reference Identification	AN	1-50	N/U				New Element
REF04-5	Reference Identification Qualifier	ID	2-3	N/U				New Element
REF04-6	Reference Identification	AN	1-50	N/U				New Element
								Segment Deleted

Page 88 of 93

PROFESSIONAL CLAIM

4010A1						
Element Identifier	Description	ID	Min. Max.	Usage Reg.	Loop	Loop Repeat	Values

837-P 4010A1

Element Identifier	Description	ID	Min. Max.	Usage Reg.	Loop	Loop Repeat	Values
NM108	Identification Code Qualifier	ID	1-2	R			PI, XV
NM109	Other Payer Identification Number	AN	2-80	R			
NM110	Entity Relationship Code	ID	2-2	N/U			
NM111	Entity Identifier Code	ID	2-3	N/U			
REF	**OTHER PAYER PRIOR AUTHORIZATION OR REFERRAL NUMBER**		2	R	2420G		
REF01	Reference Identification Qualifier	ID	2-3	R			9F, G1
REF02	Other Payer Prior Authorization or Referral Number	AN	1-30	R			
REF03	Description	AN	1-80	N/U			
REF04	REFERENCE IDENTIFIER			N/U			

5010						
Element Identifier	Description	ID	Min. Max.	Usage Reg.	Loop	Loop Repeat	Values

837-P 5010

Element Identifier	Description	ID	Min. Max.	Usage Reg.	Loop	Loop Repeat	Values	
								Segment Deleted
NM1	**AMBULANCE PICK UP LOCATION**		1	S	2420G	1		New Segment
NM101	Entity Identifier Code	ID	2-3	R			PW	
NM102	Entity Type Qualifier	ID	1-1	R			2	
NM103	Name Last or Organization Name	AN	1-60	N/U				
NM104	Name First	AN	1-35	N/U				
NM105	Name Middle	AN	1-25	N/U				
NM106	Name Prefix	AN	1-10	N/U				
NM107	Name Suffix	AN	1-10	N/U				
NM108	Identification Code Qualifier	ID	1-2	N/U				
NM109	Identification Code	AN	2-80	N/U				
NM110	Entity Relationship Code	ID	2-2	N/U				
NM111	Entity Identifier Code	ID	2-3	N/U				
NM112	Name Last or Organization Name	AN	1-60	N/U				
N3	**AMBULANCE PICK UP LOCATION ADDRESS**		1	R	2420G			New Segment
N301	Ambulance Pick Up Address Line	AN	1-55	R				
N302	Ambulance Pick Up Address Line	AN	1-55	S				
N4	**AMBULANCE PICK UP LOCATION CITY/STATE/ZIP**		1	R	2420G			New Segment
N401	Ambulance Pick Up City Name	AN	2-30	R				

Page 89 of 93

PROFESSIONAL CLAIM

	4010A1						
Element Identifier	Description	ID	Min. Max.	Usage Req.	Loop	Loop Repeat	Values
	837-P 4010A1						

	5010							
Element Identifier	Description	ID	Min. Max.	Usage Req.	Loop	Loop Repeat	Values	
	837-P 5010							
N402	Ambulance Pick Up State or Province Code	ID	2-2	S				
N403	Ambulance Pick Up Postal Zone ZIP Code	ID	3-15	S				
N404	Ambulance Pick Up Country Code	ID	2-3	S				
N405	Location Qualifier	ID	1-2	N/U				
N406	Location Identifier	AN	1-30	N/U				
N407	Country Subdivision Code	ID	1-3	S				
NM1	**AMBULANCE DROP OFF LOCATION**		1	S	2420H	1		New Segment
NM101	Entity Identifier Code	ID	2-3	R			45	
NM102	Entity Type Qualifier	ID	1-1	R			2	
NM103	Ambulance Drop Off Location	AN	1-60	S				
NM104	Name First	AN	1-35	N/U				
NM105	Name Middle	AN	1-25	N/U				
NM106	Name Prefix	AN	1-10	N/U				
NM107	Name Suffix	AN	1-10	N/U				
NM108	Identification Code Qualifier	ID	1-2	N/U				
NM109	Identification Code	AN	2-80	N/U				
NM110	Entity Relationship Code	ID	2-2	N/U				
NM111	Entity Identifier Code	ID	2-3	N/U				
NM112	Name Last or Organization Name	AN	1-60	N/U				
N3	**AMBULANCE DROP OFF LOCATION ADDRESS**		1	R	2420H			New Segment
N301	Ambulance Drop Off Address Line	AN	1-55	R				
N302	Ambulance Drop Off Address Line	AN	1-55	S				
N4	**AMBULANCE DROP OFF LOCATION CITY/STATE/ZIP**		1	R	2420H			New Segment
N401	Ambulance Drop Off City Name	AN	2-30	R				
N402	Ambulance Drop Off State or Province Code	ID	2-2	S				
N403	Ambulance Drop Off Postal Zone ZIP Code	ID	3-15	S				
N404	Ambulance Drop Off Country Code	ID	2-3	S				
N405	Location Qualifier	ID	1-2	N/U				
N406	Location Identifier	AN	1-30	N/U				

Page 90 of 93

PROFESSIONAL CLAIM

4010A1

Element Identifier	Description	ID	Min. Max.	Usage Req.	Loop	Loop Repeat	Values
				837-P 4010A1			
SVD	LINE ADJUDICATION INFORMATION		1	S	2430	25	
SVD01	Other Payer Primary Identifier	AN	2-80	R			
SVD02	Service Line Paid Amount S9(7)V99	R	1-18	R			
SVD03	COMPOSITE MEDICAL PROCEDURE IDENTIFIER			R			
SVD03-1	Product or Service ID Qualifier	ID	2-2	R			HC, IV, ZZ
SVD03-2	Procedure Code	AN	1-48	R			
SVD03-3	Procedure Modifier	AN	2-2	S			
SVD03-4	Procedure Modifier	AN	2-2	S			
SVD03-5	Procedure Modifier	AN	2-2	S			
SVD03-6	Procedure Modifier	AN	2-2	S			
SVD03-7	Procedure Code Description	AN	1-80	S			
SVD04	Product or Service ID	AN	1-48	N/U			
SVD05	Paid Service Unit Count 9(7)V999	R	1-15	R			
SVD06	Bundled Line Number	N0	1-6	S			
CAS	LINE ADJUSTMENT		99	S	2430		
CAS01	Claim Adjustment Group Code	ID	1-2	R			CO, CR, OA, PI, PR
CAS02	Adjustment Reason Code	ID	1-5	R			
CAS03	Adjustment Amount S9(7)V99	R	1-18	R			
CAS04	Adjustment Quantity 9(7)	R	1-15	S			
CAS05	Adjustment Reason Code	ID	1-5	S			
CAS06	Adjustment Amount S9(7)V99	R	1-18	S			
CAS07	Adjustment Quantity 9(7)	R	1-15	S			
CAS08	Adjustment Reason Code	ID	1-5	S			
CAS09	Adjustment Amount S9(7)V99	R	1-18	S			
CAS10	Adjustment Quantity 9(7)	R	1-15	S			
CAS11	Adjustment Reason Code	ID	1-5	S			
CAS12	Adjustment Amount S9(7)V99	R	1-18	S			
CAS13	Adjustment Quantity 9(7)	R	1-15	S			
CAS14	Adjustment Reason Code	ID	1-5	S			
CAS15	Adjustment Amount S9(7)V99	R	1-18	S			

5010

Element Identifier	Description	ID	Min. Max.	Usage Req.	Loop	Loop Repeat	Values	
				837-P 5010				
N407	Country Subdivision Code	ID	1-3	S				
SVD	LINE ADJUDICATION INFORMATION		1	S	2430	15		
SVD01	Other Payer Primary Identifier	AN	2-80	R				
SVD02	Service Line Paid Amount S9(7)V99	R	1-18	R				
SVD03	COMPOSITE MEDICAL PROCEDURE IDENTIFIER			R				
SVD03-1	Product or Service ID Qualifier	ID	2-2	R			ER, HC, IV, WK	Code Change
SVD03-2	Procedure Code	AN	1-48	R				
SVD03-3	Procedure Modifier	AN	2-2	S				
SVD03-4	Procedure Modifier	AN	2-2	S				
SVD03-5	Procedure Modifier	AN	2-2	S				
SVD03-6	Procedure Modifier	AN	2-2	S				
SVD03-7	Procedure Code Description	AN	1-80	S				
SVD03-8	Product/Service ID	AN	1-48	N/U				New Element
SVD04	Product or Service ID	AN	1-48	N/U				
SVD05	Paid Service Unit Count 9(7)V999	R	1-15	R				
SVD06	Bundled or Unbundled Line Number	N0	1-6	S				Name Change
CAS	LINE ADJUSTMENT		5	S	2430			
CAS01	Claim Adjustment Group Code	ID	1-2	R			CO, CR, OA, PI, PR	
CAS02	Adjustment Reason Code	ID	1-5	R				
CAS03	Adjustment Amount S9(7)V99	R	1-18	R				
CAS04	Adjustment Quantity 9(7)	R	1-15	S				
CAS05	Adjustment Reason Code	ID	1-5	S				
CAS06	Adjustment Amount S9(7)V99	R	1-18	S				
CAS07	Adjustment Quantity 9(7)	R	1-15	S				
CAS08	Adjustment Reason Code	ID	1-5	S				
CAS09	Adjustment Amount S9(7)V99	R	1-18	S				
CAS10	Adjustment Quantity 9(7)	R	1-15	S				
CAS11	Adjustment Reason Code	ID	1-5	S				
CAS12	Adjustment Amount S9(7)V99	R	1-18	S				
CAS13	Adjustment Quantity 9(7)	R	1-15	S				
CAS14	Adjustment Reason Code	ID	1-5	S				
CAS15	Adjustment Amount S9(7)V99	R	1-18	S				

Page 91 of 93

PROFESSIONAL CLAIM

4010A1							
Element Identifier	Description	ID	Min. Max.	Usage Reg.	Loop	Loop Repeat	Values
837-P 4010A1							
CAS16	Adjustment Quantity 9(7)	R	1-15	S			
CAS17	Adjustment Reason Code	ID	1-5	S			
CAS18	Adjustment Amount S9(7)V99	R	1-18	S			
CAS19	Adjustment Quantity 9(7)	R	1-15	S			
DTP	LINE ADJUDICATION DATE		1	R	2430		
DTP01	Date Time Qualifier	ID	3-3	R			573
DTP02	Date Time Period Format Qualifier	ID	2-3	R			D8
DTP03	Adjudication or Payment Date	AN	1-35	R			CCYYMMDD
LQ	FORM IDENTIFICATION CODE		1	S	2440	5	
LQ01	Code List Qualifier Code	ID	1-3	R			AS, UT
LQ02	Form Identifier	AN	1-30	R			
FRM	SUPPORTING DOCUMENTATION		99	S	2440		
FRM01	Question Number/Letter	AN	1-20	R			
FRM02	Question Response	ID	1-1	S			N, W, Y
FRM03	Question Response	AN	1-30	S			
FRM04	Question Response	DT	8-8	S			CCYYMMDD
FRM05	Question Response 9(3)V9	R	1-6	S			
SE	TRANSACTION SET TRAILER		1	R	_____	>1	
SE01	Transaction Segment Count	N0	1-10	R			
SE02	Transaction Set Control Number	AN	4-9	R			
GE	FUNCTION GROUP TRAILER		1	R	_____	>1	
GE01	Number of Transaction Sets Included	N0	1-6	R			
GE02	Group Control Number	N0	1-9	R			

5010								
Element Identifier	Description	ID	Min. Max.	Usage Reg.	Loop	Loop Repeat	Values	
837-P 5010								
CAS16	Adjustment Quantity 9(7)	R	1-15	S				
CAS17	Adjustment Reason Code	ID	1-5	S				
CAS18	Adjustment Amount S9(7)V99	R	1-18	S				
CAS19	Adjustment Quantity 9(7)	R	1-15	S				
DTP	LINE CHECK OR REMITTANCE DATE		1	R	2430			
DTP01	Date Time Qualifier	ID	3-3	R			573	
DTP02	Date Time Period Format Qualifier	ID	2-3	R			D8	
DTP03	Adjudication or Payment Date	AN	1-35	R			CCYYMMDD	
AMT	REMAINING PATIENT LIABILITY		1	S	2430			New Segment
AMT01	Amount Qualifier Code	ID	1-3	R			EAF	
AMT02	Remaining Patient Liability Amount S9(7)V99	R	1-18	R				
AMT03	Credit/Debit Flag Code	ID	1-1	N/U				
LQ	FORM IDENTIFICATION CODE		1	S	2440	>1		
LQ01	Code List Qualifier Code	ID	1-3	R			AS, UT	
LQ02	Form Identifier	AN	1-30	R				
FRM	SUPPORTING DOCUMENTATION		99	S	2440			
FRM01	Question Number/Letter	AN	1-20	R				
FRM02	Question Response	ID	1-1	S			N, W, Y	
FRM03	Question Response	AN	1-50	S				Increase from 30 - 50
FRM04	Question Response	DT	8-8	S			CCYYMMDD	
FRM05	Question Response 9(3)V9	R	1-6	S				
SE	TRANSACTION SET TRAILER		1	R	_____	>1		
SE01	Transaction Segment Count	N0	1-10	R				
SE02	Transaction Set Control Number	AN	4-9	R				
GE	FUNCTION GROUP TRAILER		1	R	_____	1		
GE01	Number of Transaction Sets Included	N0	1-6	R				
GE02	Group Control Number	N0	1-9	R				

Page 92 of 93

PROFESSIONAL CLAIM

Element Identifier	Description	ID	Min. Max.	Usage Req.	Loop	Loop Repeat	Values
4010A1							
837-P 4010A1							
IEA	**INTERCHANGE CONTROL TRAILER**		1	R	___	1	
IEA01	Number of Included Functional Groups	N0	1-5	R			
IEA02	Interchange Control Number	N0	9-9	R			

Element Identifier	Description	ID	Min. Max.	Usage Req.	Loop	Loop Repeat	Values
5010							
837-P 5010							
IEA	**INTERCHANGE CONTROL TRAILER**		1	R	___	1	
IEA01	Number of Included Functional Groups	N0	1-5	R			
IEA02	Interchange Control Number	N0	9-9	R			

Page 93 of 93

Appendix E: GEM Fact Sheet

Official CMS Industry Resources for the ICD-10 Transition
www.cms.gov/ICD10

The General Equivalence Mappings

Use the GEMs When...

- You are translating lists of codes, code tables, or other coded data

- You are converting a system or application containing ICD-9-CM codes

- You are creating a "one-to-one" applied mapping (aka crosswalk) between code sets that will be used in an ongoing way to translate records or other coded data

- You want to study the differences in meaning between the ICD-9-CM classification systems and the ICD-10-CM/PCS classification systems by looking at the GEMs entries for a given code or area of classification

Use the ICD-10-CM/PCS and ICD-9-CM Code Books When...

- You have a short list of ICD-9-CM codes with their code descriptions

- You have access to the medical record

- You have access to other forms of clinical information, such as text descriptions or clinical terms from surveys, research, or clinical software applications

Note: A medical record that will be processed and stored as ICD-10 data should always be coded directly in ICD-10-CM/PCS, using the code books or an encoder.

Compliance Timeline

JANUARY 1, 2010

- Payers and providers should begin internal testing of Version 5010 standards for electronic claims

DECEMBER 31, 2010

- Internal testing of Version 5010 must be complete to achieve Level I Version 5010 compliance

JANUARY 1, 2011

- Payers and providers should begin external testing of Version 5010 for electronic claims

- CMS begins accepting Version 5010 claims

- Version 4010 claims continue to be accepted

DECEMBER 31, 2011

- External testing of Version 5010 for electronic claims must be complete to achieve Level II Version 5010 compliance

JANUARY 1, 2012

- All electronic claims must use Version 5010

- Version 4010 claims are no longer accepted

OCTOBER 1, 2013

- Claims for services provided on or after this date must use ICD-10 codes for medical diagnosis and inpatient procedures

- CPT codes will continue to be used for outpatient services

Visit *www.cms.gov/ICD10* for ICD-10 and Version 5010 resources from CMS.

IO62 Rheumatic aortic stenosis with insufficiency
IO68 Other rheumatic aortic valve diseases
IO69 Rheumatic aortic valve disease, unspecified
IO70 Rheumatic tricuspid stenosis
IO71 Rheumatic tricuspid insufficiency

GEMs Files at a Glance

ICD-10-CM (diagnosis) GEM	ICD-9-CM Diagnosis GEM	ICD-10-PCS (procedure) GEM	ICD-9-CM Procedure GEM
[year]_I10gem.txt	[year]_I9gem.txt	gem_pcsi9.txt	gem_i9pcs.txt
ICD-10-CM is the code to be translated (source system)	ICD-9-CM is the code to be translated (source system)	ICD-10-PCS is the code to be translated (source system)	ICD-9-CM is the code to be translated (source system)
Contains all ICD-10-CM codes *Note:* Each GEM file contains all of the source system codes for that GEM, but not all of the target system codes	Contains all ICD-9-CM diagnosis codes *Note:* Each GEM file contains all of the source system codes for that GEM, but not all of the target system codes	Contains all ICD-10-PCS codes *Note:* Each GEM file contains all of the source system codes for that GEM, but not all of the target system codes	Contains all ICD-9-CM procedure codes *Note:* Each GEM file contains all of the source system codes for that GEM, but not all of the target system codes
Translation determined by ICD-10-CM meaning and specificity *Note:* The GEM translation is determined by the meaning and specificity of the source system code	Translation determined by ICD-9-CM meaning and specificity *Note:* The GEM translation is determined by the meaning and specificity of the source system code	Translation determined by ICD-10-PCS meaning and specificity *Note:* The GEM translation is determined by the meaning and specificity of the source system code	Translation determined by ICD-9-CM meaning and specificity *Note:* The GEM translation is determined by the meaning and specificity of the source system code
Contains ICD-9-CM clusters	Contains ICD-10-CM clusters	Contains ICD-9-CM clusters	Contains ICD-10-PCS clusters
Contains entries with no target system translation (No Map Flag is 1)	Contains entries with no target system translation (No Map Flag is 1)	All source system entries have a target system translation (No Map Flag is 0)	Contains entries with no target system translation (No Map Flag is 1)
Recommended use – Convert an existing application that uses ICD-9-CM codes to ICD-10-CM – Create a backward mapping from ICD-10-CM to ICD-9-CM – Research the translation differences between the two diagnosis code sets	*Recommended use* – Convert stored data containing ICD-9-CM codes to ICD-10-CM – Research the translation differences between the two diagnosis code sets	*Recommended use* – Convert an existing application that uses ICD-9-CM codes to ICD-10-PCS – Create a backward mapping from ICD-10-PCS to ICD-9-CM – Research the translation discontinuities between the two procedure code sets	*Recommended use* – Convert stored data containing ICD-9-CM codes to ICD-10-PCS – Research the translation discontinuities between the two procedure code sets

MAY 2010

Official CMS Industry Resources for the ICD-10 Transition
www.cms.gov/ICD10

I062 Rheumatic aortic stenosis with insufficiency
I068 Other rheumatic aortic valve diseases
I069 Rheumatic aortic valve disease, unspecified
I070 Rheumatic tricuspid stenosis
I071 Rheumatic tricuspid insufficiency

Using GEMs File(s) for Specific Projects

Mapping Project	GEMs File to Use	How to Use the GEMs File
Convert an existing system or application that uses ICD-9-CM codes to an ICD-10-CM/PCS based system	ICD-10-CM (diagnosis) GEM [year]_I10gem.txt ICD-10-PCS (procedure) GEM gem_pcsi9.txt	– **Re-sort** the file so that you can look up the relevant GEMs entry based on the ICD-9-CM code (aka reverse lookup) – **Find** all translation alternatives for the ICD-9-CM code(s) in your applications list or table – **Replace** the ICD-9-CM code(s) with the ICD-10-CM/PCS translation alternatives – **Review** the translated ICD-10-CM/PCS list for relevance of the code detail to the specific use for the list and application
Convert an existing data warehouse or other stored data containing ICD-9-CM codes to ICD-10-CM/PCS (create a forward mapping)	ICD-9-CM diagnosis GEM [year]_I9gem.txt ICD-9-CM procedure GEM gem_i9pcs.txt	– **Find** all GEMs entries for every ICD-9-CM code that contains multiple ICD-10-CM/PCS translation alternatives – Based on a consistent set of rules or reference data, **choose one** ICD-10-CM/PCS mapping for each ICD-9-CM code that translates to multiple ICD-10-CM/PCS alternatives *Note:* Because of translation differences between the two systems, "one" ICD-9-CM code may map to "one" ICD-10-CM/PCS cluster
Create a "one to one" backward mapping from ICD-10-CM/PCS to ICD-9-CM for a specific purpose	ICD-10-CM (diagnosis) GEM [year]_I10gem.txt ICD-10-PCS (procedure) GEM gem_pcsi9.txt	– **Find** all GEMs entries for every ICD-10-CM/PCS code that contains multiple ICD-9-CM translation alternatives – Based on a consistent set of rules or reference data (rules that pick the correct code for a service area or the most frequently recorded ICD-9-CM code), **choose one** ICD-9-CM mapping for each ICD-10-CM/PCS code that translates to multiple ICD-9-CM alternatives *Note:* Because of translation differences between the two systems, "one" ICD-10-CM/PCS code may map to "one" ICD-9-CM cluster

ICD-10

Official CMS Industry Resources for the ICD-10 Transition
www.cms.gov/ICD10

MAY 2010

I062 Rheumatic aortic stenosis with insufficiency
I068 Other rheumatic aortic valve diseases
I069 Rheumatic aortic valve disease, unspecified
I070 Rheumatic tricuspid stenosis
I071 Rheumatic tricuspid insufficiency

Mapping Project	GEMs File to Use	How to Use the GEMs File
Research the translation differences between the two diagnosis code sets, for your own understanding or for planning future changes to a system or application	ICD-10-CM (diagnosis) GEM [year]_I10gem.txt ICD-9-CM diagnosis GEM [year]_I9gem.txt	– **Find** the code of interest in both GEM files – **Compare** the translation alternatives for the code of interest, when it is the source system code (the code being translated) and when it is the target system code (a translation alternative of a code in the other code set) *Note:* The code of interest may not be listed as a target system alternative; this in itself is useful information, to learn that the code is not considered a plausible translation based on the meaning and specificity of the source system code
Research the translation discontinuities between the two procedure code sets, for your own understanding or for planning future changes to a system or application	ICD-10-PCS (procedure) GEM gem_pcsi9.txt ICD-9-CM procedure GEM gem_i9pcs.txt	– **Find** the code of interest in both GEM files – **Compare** the translation alternatives for the code of interest, when it is the source system code (the code being translated) and when it is the target system code (a translation alternative of a code in the other code set) *Note:* The code of interest may not be listed as a target system alternative; this in itself is useful information, to learn that the code is not considered a plausible translation based on the meaning and specificity of the source system code

Glossary

Applied mapping: distillation of a reference mapping to conform to the needs of a particular application (e.g., data quality, research)

Backward mapping: mapping that proceeds from a newer code set to an older code set

Cluster: in a combination entry, one instance where a code is chosen from each of the choice lists in the target system entry, that when combined satisfies the equivalent meaning of the corresponding code in the source system

Forward mapping: mapping that proceeds from an older code set to a newer code set

General Equivalence Map (GEM): reference mapping that attempts to include all valid relationships between the codes in the ICD-9-CM diagnosis classification and the ICD-10-CM diagnosis classification

ICD-9-CM: International Classification of Diseases 9th Revision Clinical Modification

ICD-10-CM: International Classification of Diseases 10th Revision Clinical Modification

No map flag: attribute in a GEM that when turned on indicates that a code in the source system is not linked to any code in the target system

Reverse lookup: using a GEM by looking up a target system code to see all the codes in the source system that translate to it

Source system: code set of origin in the mapping; the set being mapped 'from'

Target system: destination code set in the mapping; the set being mapped 'to'

Official CMS Industry Resources for the ICD-10 Transition
www.cms.gov/ICD10

MAY 2010

Appendix F: GEM Guidelines

Diagnosis Code Set General Equivalence Mappings
ICD-10-CM to ICD-9-CM and ICD-9-CM to ICD-10-CM
2012 Version
Documentation and User's Guide

Preface

Purpose and Audience
This document accompanies the 2012 release of the National Center for Health Statistics (NCHS) public domain diagnosis code reference mappings of the International Classification of Diseases 10th Revision Clinical Modification (ICD-10-CM) and the International Classification of Diseases 9th Revision (ICD-9-CM) Volumes 1 & 2. The purpose of this document is to give readers the information they need to understand the structure and relationships contained in the mappings so they can use the information correctly. The intended audience includes but is not limited to professionals working in health information, medical research and informatics. General interest readers may find section 1 useful. Those who may benefit from the material in both sections 1 and 2 include clinical and health information professionals who plan to directly use the mappings in their work. Software engineers and IT professionals interested in the details of the file format will find this information in Appendix A.

Document Overview
For readability, ICD-9-CM is abbreviated "I-9," and ICD-10-CM is abbreviated "I-10." The network of relationships between the two code sets described herein is named the General Equivalence Mappings (GEMs).

- **Section 1** is a general interest discussion of mapping as it pertains to the GEMs. It includes a discussion of the difficulties inherent in translating between two coding systems. The specific conventions and terms employed in the GEMs are discussed in more detail.

- **Section 2** contains detailed information on how to use the GEM files for users who will be working directly with applied mappings now or in the future—as coding experts, researchers, claims processing personnel, software developers, etc.

- The **Glossary** provides a reference list of the terms and conventions used—some unique to this document—with their accompanying definitions.

- **Appendix A** contains tables describing the technical details of the file formats, one for each of the two GEM files:
    1) ICD-9-CM to ICD-10-CM (I-9 to I-10)
    2) ICD-10-CM to ICD-9-CM (I-10 to I-9)

1

<u>Section 1—Mapping and the GEMs</u>

Translating Between the ICD-9 and ICD-10 Diagnosis Code Sets

Mappings between I-9 and I-10 attempt to find corresponding diagnosis codes between the two code sets, insofar as this is possible. In some areas of the classification the correlation between codes is fairly close, and since the two code sets share the conventions of organization and formatting common to both revisions of the International Classification of Diseases, translating between them is straightforward. Many infectious disease, neoplasm, eye, and ear codes are examples of fairly straightforward correspondence between the two code sets. In other areas—obstetrics, for example— whole chapters are organized along a different axis of classification. In such cases, translating between them the majority of the time can offer only a series of possible compromises rather than the mirror image of one code in the other code set.

I-10 Description	Correlation	I-9 Description	Unequal Axis of classification
A02.21 Salmonella meningitis	=	003.21 Salmonella meningitis	None
C92.01 Acute myeloid leukemia, in remission	=	205.01 Myeloid leukemia, acute, in remission	None

I-10 Description	Correlation	I-9 Description	Unequal Axis of classification
O26.851 Spotting complicating pregnancy, first trimester O26.852 Spotting complicating pregnancy, second trimester O26.853 Spotting complicating pregnancy, third trimester O26.859 Spotting complicating pregnancy, unspecified trimester	≠	649.50 Spotting complicating pregnancy, unspecified episode of care 649.51 Spotting complicating pregnancy, delivered 649.53 Spotting complicating pregnancy, antepartum	Stage of pregnancy (I-10) vs. Episode of care (I-9)

2

A sentence translated from English to Chinese may not be able to capture the full meaning of the original because of fundamental differences in the structure of the language. Likewise, a code set may not be able to seamlessly link the codes in one set to identical counterparts in the other code set. For these two diagnosis code sets, it is often difficult to find two corresponding descriptions that are identical in level of specificity and terminology used. This is understandable. Indeed, there would be little point in changing from the old system to the new system if the differences between the two, and the benefits available in the new system, were not significant.

There is no simple "crosswalk from I-9 to I-10" in the GEM files. A mapping that forces a simple correspondence—each I-9 code mapped only once—from the smaller, less detailed I-9 to the larger, more detailed I-10 defeats the purpose of upgrading to I-10. It obscures the differences between the two code sets and eliminates any possibility of benefiting from the improvement in data quality that I-10 offers. Instead of a simple crosswalk, the GEM files attempt to organize those differences in a meaningful way, by linking a code to all valid alternatives in the other code set from which choices can be made depending on the use to which the code is put.

It is important to understand the kinds of differences that need to be reconciled in linking coded data. The method used to reconcile those differences may vary, depending on whether the data is used for research, claims adjudication, or analyzing coding patterns between the two code sets; whether the desired outcome is to present an all-embracing look at the possibilities (one-to-many mapping) or to offer the one "best" compromise for the application (one-to-one mapping); whether the desired outcome is to translate existing coded data to their counterparts in the new code set ("forward mapping") or to track newly coded data back to what they may have been in the previous code set ("backward mapping"), or any number of other factors. The scope of the differences varies, is complex, and cannot be overlooked if quality mapping and useful coded data are the desired outcomes. Several common types of differences between the code sets will be examined here in detail to give the reader a sense of the scope.

Diagnosis Codes and Differences in Classification

ICD-10-CM has been updated to reflect the current clinical understanding and technological advancements of medicine, and the code descriptions are designed to provide a more consistent level of detail. It contains a more extensive vocabulary of clinical concepts, body part specificity, patient encounter information, and other components from which codes are built.

For example, an I-9 code description containing the words "complicated open wound" does not have a simple one-to-one correspondent in I-10. The I-9 description identifies the clinical concept "complicated," but according to the note at the beginning of the section, that one concept includes any of the following: delayed healing, delayed treatment, foreign body or infection. I-10 does not classify open wound codes based on the general concept "complicated." It categorizes open wounds by wound type— laceration or puncture wound, for example—and then further classifies each type of open

3

wound according to whether a foreign body is present. I-10 open wound codes do not mention delayed healing or delayed treatment, and instructional notes advise the coder to code any associated infection separately. Therefore, depending on the documentation in the record, the correct correspondence between and I-9 and I-10 code could be one of several.

Diagnosis Codes and Levels of Specificity

I-9 and I-10 Code Sets Compared:
Code Length and Set Size

Comparison	ICD-9-CM	ICD-10-CM
# of Characters	3-5 Numeric (+V and E codes)	3-7 Alphanumeric
# of Codes	~14,500	~70,000

As shown in the table above, I-10 codes may be longer, and there are about five times as many of them. Consequently, in an unabridged I-9 to I-10 mapping, each I-9 code is typically linked to more than one I-10 code, because each I-10 code is more specific.

I-10 is much more specific than I-9, and, just as important for purposes of mapping, the level of precision in an I-10 code is more consistent within clinically pertinent ranges of codes. In I-9, on the other hand, the level of detail among code categories varies greatly. For example, category 733, Other disorders of bone and cartilage, contains the codes:

> 733.93 Stress fracture of tibia or fibula
> 733.94 Stress fracture of the metatarsals
> 733.95 Stress fracture of other bone
> 733.96 Stress fracture of femoral neck
> 733.97 Stress fracture of shaft of femur
> 733.98 Stress fracture of pelvis

Five of the six codes specify the site of the fracture. The third code is an "umbrella" code for all other bones in the body. In practical terms this means that the general I-9 code 733.95 must represent a whole host of disparate fracture sites. Diagnoses that are identified by umbrella codes lose their uniqueness as coded data. When only the coded I-9 data is available, it is impossible to tell which bone was fractured. On the other hand, in many instances I-10 provides specific codes for all likely sites of a stress fracture, including more specificity for the bones of the extremities, the pelvis and the vertebra. Stress fracture data coded in I-10 possesses a consistent level of specificity.

One might expect an I-10 to I-9 mapping never to contain one-to-many mappings, since I-10 is so much larger and more specific. However, there are cases where I-9 contains more detail than I-10, especially where a clinical concept or axis of classification is no longer deemed essential information. Aspects of some individual I-9 code descriptions, such as information about how a diagnosis was confirmed, were intentionally not included in I-10. This means a single I-10 code could be linked to more than one I-9 code

4

option, depending on the purpose of the mapping and the specific documentation in the medical record.

Below are two examples where a distinction made in I-9 is not made in I-10. The result is that the I-10 code could be linked to more than one I-9 code, because a particular area of the I-9 classification contains detail purposely left out of I-10.

Specificity in I-9 and not in I-10:
Method of Detection

I-9 contains	I-10 contains
010.90 Primary tuberculous infection, unspecified examination 010.91 Primary tuberculous infection, bacteriological/histological exam not done 010.92 Primary tuberculous infection, bacteriological/histological exam unknown (at present) 010.93 Primary tuberculous infection, tubercle bacilli found by microscopy 010.94 Primary tuberculous infection, tubercle bacilli found by bacterial culture 010.95 Primary tuberculous infection, tubercle bacilli confirmed histologically 010.96 Primary tuberculous infection, tubercle bacilli confirmed by other methods	A15.7 Primary respiratory tuberculosis

Specificity in I-9 and not in I-10:
Legal Status and completeness of procedure

I-9 contains	I-10 contains
635.50 Legally induced abortion, complicated by shock, unspecified 635.51 Legally induced abortion, complicated by shock, incomplete 635.52 Legally induced abortion, complicated by shock, complete 636.50 Illegal abortion, complicated by shock, unspecified 636.51 Illegal abortion, complicated by shock, incomplete 636.52 Illegal abortion, complicated by shock, complete	O04.81 Shock following (induced) termination of pregnancy

Diagnosis Codes in Combination

One I-9 or I-10 code can contain more than one diagnosis. For purposes of mapping, these are called combination codes. A combination code consists of more than one diagnosis. For example, a combination code can consist of a chronic condition with a current acute manifestation, as in I-9 code *250.21 Diabetes with hyperosmolarity, type I (juvenile type), not stated as uncontrolled.* Or a combination code can consist of two acute conditions found together, as in I-10 code *R65.21 Severe sepsis with septic shock.* Or a combination code can consist of an acute condition and its external cause, as in I-10 code *T58.01 Toxic effect of carbon monoxide from motor vehicle exhaust, accidental (unintentional).*

If a combination code in one code set has a corresponding combination code in the other code set, then the two entries are linked in the usual way. It is only when a combination

5

code in one set is broken into discrete diagnosis codes in the other set that another method of mapping is needed.

Mapping in cases where a combination code in one set corresponds to two or more discrete diagnosis codes in the other set requires that the combination code be linked as a unit to two or more codes in the other code set. Each discrete diagnosis code is a partial expression of the information contained in the combination code and must be linked together as one GEM entry to fully describe the same conditions specified in the combination code. Entries of this type are linked using a special mapping flag that indicates the allowable A+B+C choices.

I-9 to I-10 mapping, combination entry:
Histoplasma duboisii meningitis

ICD-9-CM Source	to	ICD-10-CM Target
115.11 Histoplasma duboisii meningitis	≈	B39.5 Histoplasmosis duboisii **AND** G02 Meningitis in other infectious and parasitic diseases classified elsewhere

I-10 to I-9 mapping, combination entry:
Atherosclerosis of autologous vein coronary artery bypass graft(s) with unstable angina pectoris

ICD-10-CM Source	to	ICD-9-CM Target
I25.710 Atherosclerosis of autologous vein coronary artery bypass graft(s) with unstable angina pectoris	≈	414.02 Coronary atherosclerosis of autologous vein bypass graft **AND** 411.1 Intermediate coronary syndrome

Introduction to the GEMs

The I-10 and I-9 GEMs are used to facilitate linking between the procedure codes in I-9 volume 3 and the new I-10 code set. The GEMs are the raw material from which providers, health information vendors and payers can derive specific applied mappings to meet their needs. This is covered in more detail in section 2.

The I-9 to I-10 GEM contains an entry for every I-9 code. Not all I-10 codes are contained in the I-9 to I-10 GEM; the I-9 to I-10 GEM contains only those I-10 codes which are plausible translations of the I-9 codes. As with a bi-directional translation dictionary, the translations given are based on the code looked up, called the source system code.

The I-9 to I-10 GEM can be used to migrate I-9 historical data to a I-10 based representation for comparable longitudinal analysis between I-9 coded data and I-10 coded data. It can be used to create I-10 based test records from a repository of I-9 based test records. The I-9 to PCS GEM can also be used for general reference.

The I-10 to I-9 GEM contains an entry for every I-10 code. Not all I-10 codes are contained in the I-10 to I-9 GEM; the I-10 to I-9 GEM contains only those I-9 codes which are plausible translations of the I-10 codes. The translations given are based on the I-10 code looked up, the source system code in the I-10 to I-9 GEM.

The I-10 to I-9 GEM can be used to convert I-9 based systems or applications to I-10 based applications, or create one-to-one backwards mappings (also known as a crosswalk) from incoming I-10 based records to I-9 based legacy systems. This is accomplished by using the I-10 to I-9 GEM, but looking up the *target system* code (I-9) to see all the *source system* possibilities (I-10). This is called reverse lookup. For more information on converting I-9 based systems and applications to I-10, see the MS-DRG conversion project report at:
http://www.cms.gov/ICD10/17_ICD10_MS_DRG_Conversion_Project.asp

The word "crosswalk" is often used to refer to mappings between annual code updates of I-9. Crosswalk carries with it a comfortable image: clean white lines mark the boundary on either side; the way across the street is the same in either direction; a traffic signal, or perhaps even a crossing guard, aids you from one side to the other. Please be advised: *GEMs are not crosswalks.* They are reference mappings, to help the user navigate the complexity of translating meaning from one code set to the other. They are tools to help the user understand, analyze, and make distinctions that manage the complexity, and to derive their own applied mappings if that is the goal. The GEMs are more complex than a simple one-to-one crosswalk, but ultimately more useful. They reflect the relative complexity of the code sets clearly so that it can be managed effectively, rather than masking it in an oversimplified way.

One entry in a GEM identifies relationships between one code in the source system and its possible equivalents in the target system. If a mapping is described as having a direction, the source is the code one is mapping from, and the target is the code being mapped to.

Source		Target		a.k.a.
From	ICD-9-CM	**To**	ICD-10-CM	"forward mapping"
From	ICD-10-CM	**To**	ICD-9-CM	"backward mapping"

The correspondence between codes in the source and target systems is approximate in most cases. As with translating between languages, translating between coding systems does not necessarily yield an exact match. Context is everything, and the specific purpose of an applied mapping must be identified before the most appropriate option can be selected.

The GEMs together provide a general (many to many) reference mapping that can be refined to fit the requirements of an applied mapping. For a particular code entry, a GEM may contain several possible translations, each on a separate row. The code in the source system is listed on a new row as many times as there are alternatives in the target system. Each correspondence is formatted as a code pair. The user must choose from among the alternatives a single code in the target system if a one-to-one mapping is desired.

The word "entry," as used to describe the format of a GEM, refers to all rows in a GEM file having the same first listed code, the code in the source system. The word "row" refers to a single line in the file, containing a code pair—one code from the source system and one code from the target system—along with its associated attributes. An entry typically encompasses multiple rows.

There are two basic types of entries in the GEM. They are "single entry" and "combination entry." In special cases, a code in the source system may be mapped using both types of entries.

- *Single entry*—an entry in a GEM for which a code in the source system linked to one code option in the target system is a valid entry

An entry of the single type is characterized by a single correspondence: code A in the source system corresponds to code A **or** code B **or** code C in the target system. Each row in the entry can be one of several valid correspondences, and each is an option for a "one to one" applied mapping. An entry may consist of one row, if there is a close correspondence between the two codes in the code pair.

An entry of the single type is not the same as a one-to-one mapping. A code in the source system may be used multiple times in a GEM, each time linked to a different code in the target system. This is because a GEM contains alternatives from which the appropriate applied mapping can be selected. Taken together, all rows containing the same source system code linked to single code alternatives are considered one entry of the single type.

Here is an entry of the single type, consisting of two rows. The rows can be thought of as rows A **or** B. Each row of the entry is considered a valid applied mapping option if a one-to-one mapping is desired.

I-9 to I-10 GEM:
Single type entry for ICD-9-CM code 599.72

ICD-9-CM Source	to	ICD-10-CM Target
599.72 Microscopic hematuria	≈	R31.1 Benign essential microscopic hematuria
599.72 Microscopic hematuria	≈	R31.2 Other microscopic hematuria

Because I-10 codes are for the most part more specific than I-9 codes, an entry of the single type in the I-9 to I-10 GEM is typically linked to multiple I-10 codes. The user must know, or must model, the level of detail contained in the original medical record to be able to choose one of the I-10 codes. The I-9 code itself cannot contain the answer; it

8

cannot be made to describe detail it does not have. The same is occasionally true for the I-10 to I-9 GEM as well. An I-10 code may be linked to more than one I-9 code because detail in I-9 was purposely left out of I-10, as discussed earlier.

Both I-9 and I-10 contain what we refer to as "combination codes." These are codes that contain more than one diagnosis in the code description. An example is I-10 code *R65.21 Severe sepsis with septic shock.* In this case, I-9 does not have an equivalent combination code, so in order to link the I-10 code to its I-9 equivalent, a combination entry must be used in the GEM.

- *Combination entry*—an entry in a GEM for which a code in the source system must be linked to more than one code option in the target system to be a valid entry

An entry of the combination type is characterized by a compound correspondence: code A in the source system must be linked as a unit to code A **and** code B **and** code C in the target system to be a valid correspondence. Attributes in a GEM file clearly signal these special cases.

Stated another way, it takes more than one code in the target system to satisfy all of the meaning contained in one code in the source system. As discussed in this section, the situation occurs both when I-9 is the source system and when I-10 is the source system.

Here is an entry of the combination type, consisting of two rows in the format of a GEM file. The rows can be thought of as rows A **and** B. The rows of the entry combined are considered one complete translation.

I-10 to I-9 GEM:
Combination type entry for ICD-10-CM code R65.21

ICD-10-CM Source	to	ICD-9-CM Target
R65.21 Severe sepsis with septic shock	≈	995.92 Severe sepsis **AND** 785.52 Septic shock

Linking a code in the source system to a combination of codes in the target system is accomplished by using conventions in the GEMs called *scenarios* and *choice lists.*

- *Scenario*—in a combination entry, a collection of codes from the target system containing the necessary codes that combined as directed will satisfy the equivalent meaning of a code in the source system

- *Choice list*—in a combination entry, a list of one or more codes in the target system from which one code must be chosen to satisfy the equivalent meaning of a code in the source system

9

Here is the combination type entry for *R65.21,*
Severe sepsis with septic shock as it is depicted
in the "flat text" GEM format, and repeated below
in table format with the code descriptions and attributes labeled.

```
R6521   99592 101 1 1
R6521   78552 101 1 2
```

There are two rows in the I-10 to I-9 GEM for combination code R65.21. The entry is of
the combination type, meaning that each row—code R65.21 linked to both of the two I-9
codes—is considered a valid entry. The combination flag is the third attribute in a GEM
file. The scenario number is 1, because there is only one variation of the diagnoses
specified in the combination code. There are two choice lists in this entry, and only one
code in each choice list.

I-10 Code	I-10 Description	I-9 Code	I-9 Description	Approximate [FLAG]	No Map [FLAG]	Combination [FLAG]	Scenario	Choice list
R65.21	Severe sepsis with septic shock	995.92	Severe sepsis	1	0	1	1	1
R65.21	Severe sepsis with septic shock	785.52	Septic shock	1	0	1	1	2

It is important to make the distinction between a single row in a combination entry and an
entry of the single type. An entry of the single type is one code in the source system
linked to multiple one-code alternatives in the target system. It presents the option of
linking one code in the source system to code A **or** B **or** C in the target system. Each
code correspondence is considered a viable option. Each row of the source system code
entry linked with target code A **or** B **or** C is one valid entry in an applied map.

An entry of the combination type is one code in the source system linked to a multiple-
code alternative in the target system. If the source system is I-10, for example, the user
must include I-9 codes A **and** B **and** C in order to cover all the diagnoses identified in
the I-10 code. Further, there may be more than one multiple-code alternative. If a GEM
contains a range of I-9 code alternatives for each partial expression of the I-10 code, then
the number of solutions increases. Each instance of the I-10 combination code paired
with one code of the allowed range A and one code of the allowed range B and one code
of the allowed range C is sometimes referred to as a "cluster," and is considered a valid
entry. The combination flag in a GEM will clearly signal an entry of the combination
type.

10

The two entry types and their main features are summarized in the table below.

Entry Type	Summary Description	Approximate [FLAG]	No Map [FLAG]	Combination [FLAG]	Scenario	Choice list
Single	Source system code has one or more single target code alternatives	On or Off	N/A	Off	0	0
Combination	Source system code has one or more multiple target code alternatives	On	N/A	On	1-9	1-9

11

<u>Section 2—How to Use GEM Files</u>

For ease of use, we recommend loading the GEM files into a database along with the code descriptions for both code sets. With roughly 85,000 codes and their descriptions in both code sets, a desktop database like MS Access is adequate.

ICD-10-CM code descriptions can be found on the NCHS website with this documentation at: http://www.cdc.gov/nchs/icd/icd10cm.htm

ICD-9-CM code descriptions can be found at: http://www.cdc.gov/nchs/icd/icd9cm.htm

A general process for using the GEMs consists of three basic steps. In most cases it is expected these steps will be performed by software designed to integrate the GEMs content and translate codes or lists of codes from I-9 to I-10 or vice versa. In that case that a small number of records need to be translated, and the user has access to the original medical record, it is more efficient and accurate to look the codes up directly in the respective ICD-9-CM or ICD-10-CM book.

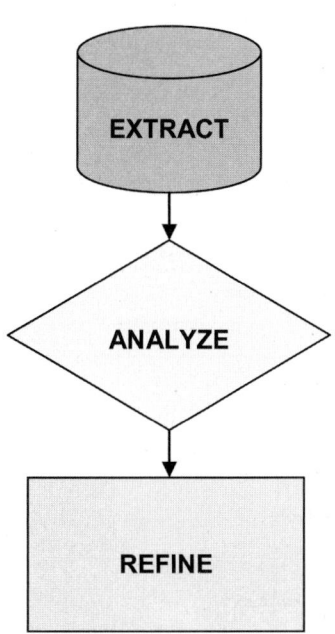

Step 1: EXTRACT
Select all rows containing the code in the source system.

Step 2: ANALYZE
Note any flags applied to the code and understand what they convey about the entry.

Step 3: REFINE
Select the row(s) of an entry that meet the requirements of the applied mapping.

Step 1: EXTRACT

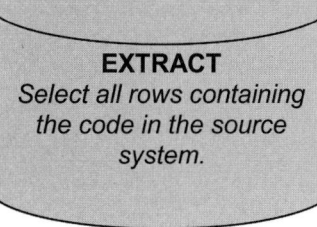

EXTRACT
Select all rows containing the code in the source system.

- *Have all rows that contain the same code from the source system been selected?*

- *Does the entry include multiple rows?*

- *Is the entry of the single type or combination type, or both?*

12

The code we will use for purposes of demonstration is I-9 code *599.72, Microscopic hematuria.*

I-9 to I-10 GEM:
599.72 Microscopic hematuria

```
59972 R311   10000
59972 R312   10000
59981 N3641  00000
59982 N3642  00000
59983 N368   10000
59984 N368   00000
59989 N398   00000
5999  N369   10000
5999  N399   10000
```

The illustrations at left and below display the I-9 code 599.72 as it appears in the I-9 to I-10 GEM. At left is the entry in text file format with its adjacent GEM entries, and below is the same information as it would appear in a desktop database. Note that the codes do not contain decimals in the GEMs.

The code in the source system is listed first, followed by the code in the target system. Here the source system is the I-9 code and the target system is the I-10 code. The final group of digits is used to indicate additional attributes for entries in the map. The first three digits are called flags. The last two digits are used in combination entries, and will be discussed later. The GEM entry contains a flag characterizing the degree of correspondence between codes in one row ("approximate" flag), a flag for codes with no correspondence in the target system ("no map" flag) and a flag indicating the row is part of a combination entry ("combination" flag). If the digit is 1, the flag applies (is "turned on") to that entry in the GEM. If the digit is 0, the flag does not apply (is "turned off") to that entry in the GEM. In other words, 1 means "yes," the flag applies to the entry in a GEM and 0 means, "no," the flag does not apply. There are two rows in the I-9 to I-10 GEM for code 599.72. The entry is of the single type, meaning that each row—code 599.72 linked to one of two I-10 code alternatives—is considered a valid entry.

I-9 Code	I-9 Description	I-10 Code	I-10 Description	Approximate [FLAG]	No Map [FLAG]	Combination [FLAG]
599.72	Microscopic hematuria	R31.1	Benign essential microscopic hematuria	1	0	0
599.72	Microscopic hematuria	R31.2	Other microscopic hematuria	1	0	0

13

Step 2: ANALYZE

```
          ANALYZE
  Note any flags applied
     to the code and
  understand what they
 convey about the entry.
```

Is the "approximate" flag turned on?
* If yes, the correspondence is not a precise equivalent.

Is the "no map" flag turned on?
* If yes, there is no corresponding code in the target system.

Is the "combination" flag turned on?
* If yes, more than one code is the target system is required to satisfy the meaning of the code in the source system.

In the GEMs, there are three flags:

Approximate   *indicates that the entry is not considered equivalent*

No Map   *indicates that a code in the source system is not linked to any code in the target system*

Combination   *indicates that more than one code in the target system is required to satisfy the full equivalent meaning of a code in the source system*

The Approximate Flag

I-9 Code	I-9 Description	I-10 Code	I-10 Description	Approximate [FLAG]	No Map [FLAG]	Combination [FLAG]
599.72	Microscopic hematuria	R31.1	Benign essential microscopic hematuria	1	0	0
599.72	Microscopic hematuria	R31.2	Other microscopic hematuria	1	0	0

The approximate flag is turned on when no one code in the target system or linked combination of codes in the target system expresses the same essential meaning as the code in the source system. The difference between the two systems is typically in level of detail between the codes, and in nearly all cases the I-10 code is more detailed than the I-9 code.

The approximate flag is on for both rows in the source system GEM entry for I-9 code 599.72. The level of detail differs here—the type of hematuria is specified in I-10 and not

14

in I-9. Although *599.72 Microscopic hematuria* in I-9 and *R31.2 Other microscopic hematuria* in I-10 could be said to be equal, in fact they are not, because the I-9 code represents all varieties of microscopic hematuria and the I-10 code represents only microscopic hematuria not classified in the other code. The approximate flag is turned on to indicate no single code in I-10 expresses the same meaning as 599.72.

The approximate flag is on for the majority of entries in the GEMs. This may include code pairs that have the same description in both code sets. In such cases, neighboring codes in a subcategory are more specific in one code set than another, and so the number of clinical conditions included in a code is different—hence it does not express the same essential meaning. Codes containing the word "other" in their description are a common example.

I-10 Code	I-10 Description	I-9 Code	I-9 Description	Approximate [FLAG]	No Map [FLAG]	Combination [FLAG]
B37.41	Candidal cystitis and urethritis	112.2	Candidiasis of other urogenital sites	1	0	0
B37.42	Candidal balanitis	112.2	Candidiasis of other urogenital sites	1	0	0
B37.49	Other urogenital candidiasis	112.2	Candidiasis of other urogenital sites	1	0	0

In this example, the body sites included in the "other candidiasis" code differs between code sets, so the approximate flag is on for all entries in this subcategory. I-10 has specific codes for cystitis/urethritis and balanitis. I-9 does not. In I-9, balanitis is listed as an "includes" note under the code *112.2 Candidiasis of other urogenital sites,* and cystitis or urethritis have no specific entry in tabular.

The No Map Flag

I-9 Code	I-9 Description	I-10 Code	I-10 Description	Approximate [FLAG]	No Map [FLAG]	Combination [FLAG]
V64.41	Laparoscopic surgical procedure converted to open procedure	NoDx	No Description	0	1	0
V64.42	Thoracoscopic surgical procedure converted to open procedure	NoDx	No Description	0	1	0
V64.43	Arthroscopic surgical procedure converted to open procedure	NoDx	No Description	0	1	0

In the I-9 to I-10 GEM, the "no map" flag is on for a subset of I-9 codes. In this example, the I-9 codes do not identify a diagnosis, but instead further specify the reason why a procedure was performed differently than planned. The recommendation was made that I-10 diagnosis codes do not contain information regarding procedures, so I-10 does not contain an equivalent group of codes. Therefore, the I-9 codes cannot be linked to I-10 at all. In the I-9 to I-10 GEM they are listed without a corresponding I-10 entry, and with the "no map" flag on.

The Combination Flag

The combination flag is turned on when a code in the source system must be linked to more than one code in the target system to be a valid entry. When the combination flag is on, the *scenario* and *choice list* fields in a GEM file contain a number. They appear last in a GEM file, after the flags. These numbers allow the user to collate the combination entries in the GEM.

```
T422X1A 9662   10111
T422X1A E8558 10112
T422X1A 9660   10121
T422X1A E8558 10122
T422X1D V5889 10000
T422X1S 9090   10111
T422X1S E9292 10112
T422X2A 9662   10111
T422X2A E9504 10112
T422X2A 9660   10121
T422X2A E9504 10122
T422X2D V5889 10000
T422X2S 9090   10111
T422X2S E959   10112
```

I-10 to I-9 GEM:

T42.2X1A Poisoning by succinimides and oxazolidinediones, accidental (unintentional),initial encounter

The illustrations at left and below display the I-10 to I-9 GEM entry for I-10 diagnosis code *T42.2X1A Poisoning by succinimides and oxazolidinediones, accidental (unintentional), initial encounter*. At left is the entry in text file format, and below is the same information as it would appear in a desktop database. The I-10 combination code T42.2X1A specifies both the diagnosis and the external cause, so it requires a combination entry in the GEM. A combination entry is subdivided hierarchically on two levels: 1) By *scenario*, the number of variations of diagnosis combinations included in the source system code, and 2) By *choice list*, the possible target system codes that combined are one valid expression of a scenario.

Each of the two types of drug listed in the I-10 code T42.2X1A is a unique I-9 code, so there are two scenarios from which to choose an applied mapping: one that specifies poisoning by succinimides and one that specifies poisoning by oxazolidinediones. Because each drug type listed in the I-10 combination code requires its own diagnosis code in I-9, each variation of the diagnosis is assigned a separate *scenario* number in the GEM entry.

A scenario designates one variation of the meaning of the source system diagnosis as specified in a combination code. In other words, it identifies one roughly equivalent expression of the source system code. In this example, scenario 1 contains the I-9 codes needed to satisfy the equivalent meaning of "Poisoning by succinimides, accidental

16

(unintentional), initial encounter" Scenario 2 contains all the I-9 codes needed to specify "Poisoning by oxazolidinediones, accidental (unintentional), initial encounter."

A scenario is subdivided into two or more choice lists of codes in the target system. These are the codes that must be linked together as a unit in an applied mapping to satisfy the equivalent meaning of the combination code in the source system. A choice list contains one or more codes in the target system that express a portion of the meaning of the code in the source system. A code must be included from each choice list in a scenario to satisfy the equivalent meaning of the code in the source system.

Scenario 1

I-10 Code	I-10 Description	I-9 Code	I-9 Description	Approximate [FLAG]	Combination [FLAG]	Scenario	Choice list
T42.2X1A	Poisoning by succinimides and oxazolidinediones, accidental (unintentional), initial encounter	966.2	Poisoning by succinimides	1	1	1	1
T42.2X1A	Poisoning by succinimides and oxazolidinediones, accidental (unintentional), initial encounter	E855.8	Other specified drugs acting on central and autonomic nervous systems	1	1	1	2

Scenario 2

I-10 Code	I-10 Description	I-9 Code	I-9 Description	Approximate [FLAG]	Combination [FLAG]	Scenario	Choice list
T42.2X1A	Poisoning by succinimides and oxazolidinediones, accidental (unintentional), initial encounter	966.0	Poisoning by oxazolidine derivatives	1	1	2	1
T42.2X1A	Poisoning by succinimides and oxazolidinediones, accidental (unintentional), initial encounter	E855.8	Other specified drugs acting on central and autonomic nervous systems	1	1	2	2

17

In this example there are two I-9 choice lists in scenario 1 and two I-9 choice lists in scenario 2, with one I-9 code in each list.

This is a comparatively simple example of a combination entry because each choice list contains only one code. The user does not need to choose among alternatives beyond the scenario.

The result is that for this I-10 combination entry, there are only two applied mapping alternatives:

Scenario 1

ICD-10-CM Source	to	ICD-9-CM Target
T42.2X1A Poisoning by succinimides and oxazolidinediones, accidental (unintentional), initial encounter	≈	966.2 Poisoning by succinimides **AND** E855.8 Other specified drugs acting on central and autonomic nervous systems

OR

Scenario 2

ICD-10-CM Source	to	ICD-9-CM Target
T42.2X1A Poisoning by succinimides and oxazolidinediones, accidental (unintentional), initial encounter	≈	966.0 Poisoning by oxazolidine derivatives **AND** E855.8 Other specified drugs acting on central and autonomic nervous systems

18

Step 3: REFINE

REFINE
Select the row(s) of an entry that meet the requirements of the applied mapping.

- *What is the purpose of the applied mapping?*

- *Does the applied mapping require that the code in the source system be mapped to only one "best" alternative in the target system?*

- *Will the correct applied mapping vary depending on the documentation in the record?*

Once the user has analyzed all rows for an entry in a GEM, it is possible to select the row or rows most appropriate to an applied mapping. We will use two different sample entries—one combination entry from the I-9 to I-10 GEM and one single entry from the I-10 to I-9 GEM—in order to discuss the process of refining an entry and deriving an applied mapping.

Sample Entry 1—I-9 to I-10 GEM

896.2 Traumatic amputation of foot (complete) (partial), bilateral, without mention of complication

I-9 Code	I-9 Description	I-10 Code	I-10 Description	Approximate [FLAG]	No Map [FLAG]	Combination [FLAG]	Scenario	Choice list
896.2	Traumatic amputation of foot (complete) (partial), bilateral, without mention of complication	S98.011A	Complete traumatic amputation of right foot at ankle level, initial encounter	1	0	1	1	1
896.2	Traumatic amputation of foot (complete) (partial), bilateral, without mention of complication	S98.012A	Partial traumatic amputation of left foot at ankle level, initial encounter	1	0	1	1	2
896.2	Traumatic amputation of foot (complete) (partial), bilateral, without mention of complication	S98.021A	Complete traumatic amputation of right foot at ankle level, initial encounter	1	0	1	1	1
896.2	Traumatic amputation of foot (complete) (partial), bilateral, without mention of complication	S98.022A	Partial traumatic amputation of left foot at ankle level, initial encounter	1	0	1	1	2

In this instance the I-9 code specifies that the traumatic amputation is bilateral but does not specify whether it is partial or complete. Since both types of information—left or right foot, and whether the amputation is partial or complete—are specified in separate codes in I-10, the entry in the I-9 to I-10 GEM is a combination entry. There are two choice lists in this entry, because two codes in I-10 are required to satisfy the equivalent meaning in the I-9 combination code. And because the injury can be partial on one side and complete on the other, both sides partial, or both sides complete, there are two choices in each choice list.

19

After collating the combination entries into their respective choice lists (there is only one scenario), the four valid clusters are:

ICD-9-CM Source	to	ICD-10-CM Target
896.2 Traumatic amputation of foot (complete) (partial), bilateral, without mention of complication	≈	S98.011A Complete traumatic amputation of right foot at ankle level **AND** S98.012A Complete traumatic amputation of left foot at ankle level
		OR
	≈	S98.011A Complete traumatic amputation of right foot at ankle level **AND** S98.022A Partial traumatic amputation of left foot at ankle level
		OR S98.021A Partial traumatic amputation of right foot at ankle level **AND**
	≈	S98.012A Complete traumatic amputation of left foot at ankle level
		OR S98.021A Partial traumatic amputation of right foot at ankle level **AND**
	≈	S98.022A Partial traumatic amputation of left foot at ankle level

To refine this entry, first the user must decide whether or not it is possible to choose a single cluster—the correct combination of left and right, partial and complete—and if possible, whether or not it is necessary. This decision of course depends on the use of the mapping.

A health information professional or health statistics researcher who is converting a limited number of old I-9 records to I-10, and has access to the individual medical record, can make use of the increased specificity in I-10 codes to re-code the record directly in I-10. The user can simply refer to the original record to see the specific nature of the bilateral traumatic amputation and assign the correct pair of I-10 codes to the record.

However, a health statistics analyst or data modeler who is translating aggregate I-9 data forward to I-10, and has no access to individual medical records, cannot make use of the fine distinctions in I-10 since they are not present in the old data. In this case, choosing a single cluster that is the closest equivalent cannot be the goal. The user must choose an I-10 code or pair of codes to represent all the I-10 alternatives, and could choose to fashion a rule by which to map similar cases. Rules specific to the applied mapping would

20

promote consistency and document the decisions made. For example, here the applied mapping could use only the partial traumatic amputation codes.

Sample Entry 2—I-10 to I-9 GEM:
G92 Toxic encephalopathy

I-10 Code	I-10 Description	I-9 Code	I-9 Description	Approximate [FLAG]	No Map [FLAG]	Combination [FLAG]
G92	Toxic encephalopathy	323.71	Toxic encephalitis and encephalomyelitis	1	0	0
G92	Toxic encephalopathy	323.72	Toxic myelitis	1	0	0
G92	Toxic encephalopathy	349.82	Toxic encephalopathy	1	0	0

This same method could be used to translate a record coded in I-10 back to I-9, and could then be processed by a legacy payment system for reimbursement. The approximate flag is on, indicating that the relationship between the code in the source system and the code in the target system is an approximate equivalent. The approximate flag is on for all three target system I-9 code translations of I-10 code G92, because the complete meaning of *G92 Toxic encephalopathy*— as encompassed by the tabular instruction and index entries that refer to G92—includes the clinical concepts toxic encephalitis and encephalomyelitis, toxic myelitis, and toxic encephalopathy specified in three separate I-9 diagnosis codes.

To choose among the alternatives in I-9 is not possible based on the meaning of the codes themselves. Because the applied mapping is intended to establish general rules for translation rather than deciding on a case-by-case basis, then a consistent method must be derived and documented for resolving the disparity in classification between the two systems. Depending on the applied mapping, the user may choose the closest matching code description or the most frequently recorded of the I-9 code alternatives based on I-9 data.

For example, for mapping research data on toxic encephalitis during a period that overlaps the use of both I-10 and I-9, a valid one-to-one mapping from G92 to 323.72 could be derived. But for patient records coded in I-10 and mapped internally to an I-9 based medical necessity edit system during the transition period, it would depend on the classification of the I-9 code alternatives in the edit system. If all three I-9 codes were included in the same edit grouping, a valid one-to-one applied mapping to any of the three I-9 mapping choices could be derived.

21

Glossary

Approximate flag—attribute in a GEM that when turned on indicates that the entry is not considered equivalent

Applied mapping—distillation of a reference mapping to conform to the needs of a particular application (e.g., data quality, research)

Backward mapping—mapping that proceeds from a newer code set to an older code set

Cluster—in a combination entry, one instance where a code is chosen from each of the choice lists in the target system entry, that when combined satisfies the equivalent meaning of the corresponding code in the source system

Choice list—in a combination entry, a list of one or more codes in the target system from which one code must be chosen to satisfy the equivalent meaning of a code in the source system

Combination flag—attribute in a GEM that when turned on indicates that more than one code in the target system is required to satisfy the full equivalent meaning of a code in the source system

Combination entry—an entry in a GEM for which a code in the source system must be linked to more than one code option in the target system to be a valid entry

Complete meaning [of a code]— all correctly coded conditions or procedures that would be classified to a code based on the code title, all associated tabular instructional notes, and all index references that refer to a code

Forward mapping—mapping that proceeds from an older code set to a newer code set

General Equivalence Map (GEM)—reference mapping that attempts to include all valid relationships between the codes in the ICD-9-CM diagnosis classification and the ICD-10-CM diagnosis classification

ICD-9-CM—International Classification of Diseases 9th Revision Clinical Modification (I-9)

ICD-10-CM—International Classification of Diseases 10th Revision Clinical Modification (I-10)

No map flag—attribute in a GEM that when turned on indicates that a code in the source system is not linked to any code in the target system

Reference mapping—mapping that includes all possible valid relationships between a source system and a target system

Reverse lookup—using a GEM by looking up a target system code to see all the codes in the source system that translate to it

Scenario—in a combination entry, a collection of codes from the target system containing the necessary codes that when combined as directed will satisfy the equivalent meaning of a code in the source system

Single entry—an entry in a GEM for which a code in the source system linked to one code option in the target system is a valid entry

Source system—code set of origin in the mapping; the set being mapped 'from'

Target system—destination code set in the mapping; the set being mapped 'to'

Diagnosis Code Set
General Equivalence Mappings
2012 Version Documentation

Appendix A—File and Format Detail

ICD-9-CM to ICD-10-CM
General Equivalence Mapping (GEM)

FILE NAME: 2012_l9gem.txt

FILE FORMAT

FIELD	POSITION	LENGTH	VALUE
ICD-9-CM Code [source]	1 – 5	5	Left justified, blank filled No decimal
Filler	6	1	*Blank*
ICD-10-CM Code [target]	7 – 13	7	All seven characters used, no decimal
Filler	14	1	*Blank*
Approximate [FLAG]	15	1	1 = Yes/On 0 = No/Off
No Map [FLAG]	16	1	1 = Yes/On 0 = No/Off
Combination [FLAG]	17	1	1 = Yes/On 0 = No/Off
Scenario	18	1	0 – 9
Choice list	19	1	0 – 9

24

ICD-10-CM to ICD-9-CM
General Equivalence Mapping (GEM)

FILE NAME: 2012_I10gem.txt

FILE FORMAT

FIELD	POSITION	LENGTH	VALUE
ICD-10-CM Code [source]	1 – 7	7	Left justified, blank filled No decimal
Filler	8	1	*Blank*
ICD-9-CM Code [target]	9 – 13	5	All seven characters used, no decimal
Filler	14	1	*Blank*
Approximate [FLAG]	15	1	1 = Yes/On 0 = No/Off
No Map [FLAG]	16	1	1 = Yes/On 0 = No/Off
Combination [FLAG]	17	1	1 = Yes/On 0 = No/Off
Scenario	18	1	0 – 9
Choice list	19	1	0 – 9

25

Appendix G: GEM 2012 Updates

ICD-10-CM/PCS to ICD-9-CM Reimbursement Mappings
2012 Version
Documentation and User's Guide

Preface

Purpose and Audience

This document accompanies the 2012 update of the Centers for Medicare and Medicaid Studies (CMS) public domain one-to-one applied reimbursement mappings of the ICD-10-CM (diagnosis) and ICD-10-PCS (procedure) code systems to the ICD-9-CM Volume 1 (diagnosis) and ICD-9-CM Volume 3 (procedure) code systems respectively. The Reimbursement Mappings can be found on the CMS ICD-10 website at http://www.cms.gov/ICD10. The purpose of this document is to give readers the information they need to understand the intent and structure of the mappings so they can use the information correctly. The intended audience includes but is not limited to professionals working with health services reimbursement systems. General readers may find section 1 useful. Software engineers and IT professionals interested in the details of the file formats will find this information in Appendix A.

Document Overview

For readability, when no distinction is necessary between diagnosis codes and procedure codes, ICD-10-CM or ICD-10-PCS is abbreviated "ICD-10", and ICD-9-CM Volumes 1 or 3 is abbreviated "ICD-9".

- **Section 1** is a general interest discussion of mapping between ICD-10 and ICD-9 and the rationale for the development of the Reimbursement Mappings. The meaning of "one-to-one" in the context of an applied mapping is discussed.

- **Section 2** contains detailed information on how to use the Reimbursement Mappings, for users who will be working directly with mapping between applications.

- **Appendix A** describes the technical details of the file formats. One mapping file is provided for diagnosis codes and one for procedures, both in the same format.

- **Appendix B** contains the frequency rule set applied to make the mapping choices for the Reimbursement Mappings. Also included are codes whose frequencies are so low that they did not fall within the parameters of any rule in the frequency rule set. In such cases, the coding and clinical members of the team chose the code deemed the closest match.

Section 1 – Reimbursement Mapping Rationale

Converting ICD-10 Data for ICD-9 Systems

After the ICD-10 implementation date as specified in the Final Rule, health care claims for services on or after October 1, 2013 will be submitted to payers with diagnoses coded in ICD-10-CM for all provider types, and procedures coded in ICD-10-PCS for hospital inpatient services only. The Reimbursement Mappings were created to provide a temporary but reliable mechanism for mapping records containing ICD-10 diagnosis and procedure codes to "reimbursement equivalent" ICD-9 diagnosis and procedure codes, so that while systems are being converted to process ICD-10 claims directly, the claims may be processed by the legacy systems.

The ICD-10 diagnosis codes submitted on the claim are mapped via the Diagnosis Reimbursement Mapping into ICD-9 diagnosis codes that can then be processed by the ICD-9-based reimbursement system. Similarly the ICD-10 procedure codes submitted on the claim are mapped via the Procedure Reimbursement Mapping into ICD-9 procedure codes that can then be processed by the ICD-9-based reimbursement system. The claim may then be priced using the rules written for ICD-9 codes.

Derivation from General Equivalence Mappings (GEMs)

CMS annually publishes updates of the General Equivalence Mappings (GEMs). The GEMs are mappings between ICD-10-CM and PCS and ICD-9-CM codes. These annual updates can be found on the CMS ICD-10 website at http://www.cms.gov/ICD10 .

The reader is advised to see the User's Guides provided with the GEM files. Each contains a general discussion of the challenges inherent in translating between code sets, and the strategies that may be adopted to develop mappings from the GEMs for specific applications. Those discussions are not repeated here. The GEM User's Guides also provide a comprehensive glossary, which may be of use to readers unfamiliar with the terminology of code set translation.

The Reimbursement Mappings were derived from the GEMs using the techniques discussed below.

One-to-one and one-to-many mappings

The ICD-10 to ICD-9 General Equivalence Mappings are one-to-many mappings in two different senses:

Alternatives. More than one ICD-9 code may be a valid translation of a given ICD-10 code. Which one of those ICD-9 codes is the most correct translation cannot be determined based on the meaning of the codes themselves. For example, ICD-10 procedure 0LQ70ZZ, *Repair Right Hand Tendon, Open Approach*, translates to ICD-9 procedure 83.61, *Suture of tendon sheath*, or to procedure 83.64, *Other suture of tendon*. Both are valid translations of the ICD-10 procedure code.

Clusters. At times it requires multiple ICD-9 codes combined to reproduce the complete meaning of one ICD-10 code. This is the case with ICD-9 principal procedure codes such as coronary angioplasty that require the use of "adjunct"

Reimbursement Mapping User's Guide   2   2012 Version

ICD-9 codes to provide additional detail. For example, ICD-10 procedure code 02733ZZ, *Dilation of Coronary Artery, Four or More Sites, Percutaneous Approach*, requires two ICD-9 codes to be fully represented in ICD-9: 00.66, *PTCA or coronary atherectomy*, and 00.43, *Procedure on four or more vessels*. Reimbursement systems may depend for correct pricing on the additional meaning provided by adjunct ICD-9 codes. A reimbursement system which pays more for a procedure performed on four or more vessels would pay incorrectly if the 02733ZZ were translated into 00.66 only.

The Reimbursement Mappings are one-to-one mappings only in the sense that they choose one ICD-9 translation for each ICD-10 code. The translation may be one ICD-9 code or one ICD-9 cluster. For ICD-10 codes that translate to multiple single ICD-9 codes in the GEMs, one ICD-9 code was selected for reimbursement purposes. For ICD-10 codes that translate to multiple ICD-9 clusters in the GEMs, one ICD-9 cluster was selected for reimbursement purposes. The mapping of one ICD-10 may require as many as six ICD-9 codes to reproduce the meaning of the ICD-10 code. In such cases, where an ICD-10 code maps to an ICD-9 cluster in the Reimbursement Mappings, the ICD-9 codes comprising the cluster are *not* to be treated as alternatives. All of them must be included in the translated ICD-9 claim sent to the ICD-9 legacy reimbursement system in order to reproduce the information in the submitted ICD-10 claim.

Frequency data used to derive ICD-9 mapping

The Reimbursement Mappings are an applied mapping of the ICD-10 to ICD-9 GEMs. More than 66,000 of the 70,000 ICD-10 diagnosis codes (95%) in the ICD-10 to ICD-9 diagnosis GEM translate to a single ICD-9 code. Similarly, more than 66,000 of the 72,000 ICD-10 procedure codes (93%) in the ICD-10 to ICD-9 procedure GEM translate to a single ICD-9 code. Approximately 3,500 ICD-10 diagnosis codes and 5,000 ICD-10 procedure codes required rules for choosing among ICD-9 code alternatives.

Translation Alternatives in ICD-10 to ICD-9 GEMs

Code set	ICD-10 Codes with only 1 ICD-9 alternative	ICD-10 Codes with >1 ICD-9 alternative	ICD-10 Codes with no ICD-9 alternative	Total ICD-10 codes
ICD-10-CM (diagnosis)	66,032	3,801 (5%)	669	69,833
ICD-10-PCS (procedure)	66,538	5,580 (7%)	0	71,918

The rules for choosing among ICD-9 code alternatives operated on frequency data from ICD-9 based records. Selection of a single ICD-9 code for both diagnosis and procedure codes made use of two *reference data sources*:

> <u>Medicare</u> Approximately 35 million MedPAR records, from 10/1/2006 to 9/30/2009

All-payer Approximately 12 million inpatient hospital records available from the California Office of Statewide Health Planning and Development (OSHPD) from 10/1/2005 to 9/30/2008

Because both data sets come from hospital inpatient data, the resultant mapping reflects frequencies characteristic of inpatient rather than outpatient data when the two differ. A clear example of this can be found in the obstetrics codes specifying complications of pregnancy. Because ICD-10 does not specify encounter information, i.e., whether the patient delivered during the encounter, the reimbursement mapping must choose between two ICD-9 alternatives, one that specifies antepartum encounter, the other a delivery. For inpatient hospital data, the ICD-9 codes specifying delivery are far more frequent, while in outpatient and physician data, one would expect the ICD-9 codes specifying antepartum encounter to dominate.

When the ICD-10 to ICD-9 GEM offered more than one translation for an ICD-10 code, these reference data sources were queried to find the most frequently coded of the alternative ICD-9 codes. For all but about 300 diagnosis codes and 60 procedure codes, one of the ICD-9 alternatives was clearly dominant—often more than twice as frequent as any of the other alternatives.

Reimbursement Mapping of dominant ICD-9 code alternative

ICD-10 code	ICD-9 code alternatives in the ICD-10 to ICD-9 GEM	MedPAR records	MedPAR %	Calif. Records	Calif. %	Reimbursement Mapping
J45.22 Mild intermittent asthma with status asthmaticus	493.01 Extrinsic asthma with status asthmaticus	657	86%	5,416	99%	X
	493.11 Intrinsic asthma with status asthmaticus	94	14%	55	1%	

The dominant ICD-9 alternative was chosen as the ICD-9 code for the Reimbursement Mapping. Where an ICD-10 code translated to multiple ICD-9 clusters, the first ICD-9 code in the cluster as determined by the GEM "choice list" order was used to determine the dominant alternative.

When the Medicare reference data set and the all-payer reference data set disagreed, the code with the highest Medicare frequency was chosen for non-obstetric and non-newborn diagnosis codes, and for non-obstetric procedure codes. For obstetric and newborn diagnosis codes, and obstetric procedure codes, the all-payer data set was given precedence. When there were too few records (defined as <30 records) in either reference data set alone, the two were combined to achieve a higher frequency. Finally, coding expertise was used to select the mapping deemed the "closest match in meaning between the codes," for approximately 300 diagnosis and 60 procedure codes which were so rarely recorded (fewer than 30 records in the combined reference data sets) that the reference data sets were unable to identify a dominant alternative.

Reimbursement Mapping of ICD-9 "closest match" code alternative

ICD-10 code	ICD-9 code alternatives in the GEM	MedPAR records	MedPAR %	Calif. Records	Calif. %	Reimbursement Mapping
3E0B7KZ Introduction of Other Diagnostic Substance into Ear, Via Natural or Artificial Opening	**20.72** Injection into inner ear	3	27%	1	20%	X
	20.94 Injection of tympanum	11	88%	4	80%	

This process resulted in the Reimbursement Mapping files documented in Appendix A. Each mapping file has one and only one entry for each valid ICD-10 code. An entry contains one ICD-10 code and from one to six ICD-9 codes. An ICD-9 cluster (more than one ICD-9 code combined to represent one ICD-10 code) is used to ensure that potentially reimbursable components of the meaning of the ICD-10 code are reproduced in the ICD-9 translation. The distribution of mappings from one ICD-10 code to one ICD-9 code, and from one ICD-10 code to one ICD-9 cluster, are shown in the following table.

ICD-10 Reimbursement Mapping
Distribution of mappings to single ICD-9 codes and ICD-9 code clusters

Code set	Mapped to single ICD-9 code	Mapped to two-code cluster	Mapped to three-code cluster	Mapped to four-code cluster	Mapped to five-code cluster	Mapped to six-code cluster	Total ICD-10 codes
ICD-10-CM (diagnosis)	66,104	3,692	31	6	0	0	69,833
ICD-10-PCS (procedure)	69,962	1,110	340	458	36	12	71,918

Section 2 – Using the Reimbursement Mapping

Accommodating system requirements

The two text files accompanying this document—one for diagnosis codes, one for procedure codes—are listed in ICD-10 code order. Users are advised to download the files and load them into a database or table structure that allows efficient lookup based on the ICD-10 code at the beginning of each mapping entry.

Certain ICD-10-CM diagnosis codes specify conditions or external causes which are not represented in ICD-9-CM. For those codes, the mapping entry contains the text "NODX" in the ICD-9 code field. ICD-10 codes that have no equivalent in ICD-9 can safely be ignored by an ICD-9 based pricing system, since they represent conditions or external causes which could never have been coded with ICD-9-CM, and which an ICD-9 based pricing system would therefore not have used.

A health care claim will typically contain a list of ICD-10 diagnosis codes, one of which is designated as principal diagnosis. The Reimbursement Mapping can be adapted to a claims system using the following:

- Reserve space in the system for the maximum number of ICD-9 codes possible in a mapping entry. Since one ICD-10 code may map to a cluster of multiple ICD-9 codes, the mapped output ICD-9 entry may be longer than the input ICD-10 entry. Though the use of clusters in the mapping is uncommon, as shown in the table above, the way to ensure that there is enough space for the mapped ICD-9 output is to reserve space for four ICD-9 diagnosis codes and six ICD-9 procedure codes.

- Map the ICD-10 principal diagnosis first, by looking up the ICD-10 designated principal diagnosis code in the mapping. If the ICD-10 code maps to one ICD-9 code, then this becomes the ICD-9 principal diagnosis. If the ICD-10 code maps to an ICD-9 code cluster, then take the first ICD-9 diagnosis code in the cluster as the principal diagnosis, and use the remaining diagnosis codes in the cluster as ICD-9 secondary diagnosis codes on the translated record. All of the ICD-9-CM diagnosis code clusters are arranged so that the first listed ICD-9 code in a cluster is the recommended principal diagnosis when the combination ICD-10 code it translates from is the principal diagnosis.

- For each additional diagnosis, look up the ICD-10 code in the mapping. If the ICD-9 mapping is "NODX" then do not place anything in the ICD-9 code list for this input ICD-10 code and move on to the next ICD-10 input code. Because a mapping entry may contain more than one ICD-9 code, the placement of the secondary codes in the output ICD-9 space must be tracked independently from the input ICD-10 codes if a correlation between input and output codes is desired.

- For procedures, the process for translating ICD-10 codes on the record is straightforward. Map the codes in the order in which they were received. If the mapping supplies an ICD-9 code cluster, all of the codes in the cluster must be included in the mapping to equal the detail contained in the ICD-10 procedure code.

Testing the mapping

The Reimbursement Mapping contains an entry for every ICD-10 code. However, not every ICD-9 code is used in the mapping. Because the mapping was developed using hospital inpatient frequency data to choose among ICD-9 mapping alternatives in the GEMs, the resultant mapping reflects the coding patterns characteristic of inpatient rather than outpatient records when the two differ. An ICD-10 code is mapped to the clearly dominant ICD-9 code in the recorded data, or mapped according to additional frequency rules in Appendix B, or mapped to the "closest match" ICD-9 code, in the process outlined in Section 1. Naturally, a process that chooses a single ICD-9 code among alternatives must leave the other ICD-9 alternatives unused.

Users of the Reimbursement Mapping may want to sort the mapping entries by ICD-9 code to determine if any particular ICD-9 codes used by their legacy systems (for example, those qualifying for carve-outs or other special treatment) are not mapped. Such codes would not be used when ICD-10 codes are mapped to their legacy systems via the Reimbursement Mapping.

If ICD-9 codes not used by the Reimbursement Mapping are essential to a legacy system then the Reimbursement Mapping can be modified for that system's needs by doing the following:

- Consult the relevant ICD-9 to ICD-10 GEM, or one of the commercial tools built from it. This will enumerate the valid ICD-10 translations of the unused ICD-9 code.

- Find the valid ICD-10 codes enumerated above in the first column of the Reimbursement Mapping.

- Substitute the unused ICD-9 code into the Reimbursement Mapping entry or entries found, and document the change as appropriate.

Appendix A – Format of the Reimbursement Mapping Files

reimb_map_dx_2012.txt contains the Reimbursement Mapping from ICD-10-CM
diagnosis codes to ICD-9-CM diagnosis codes or diagnosis clusters.

reimb_map_pr_2012.txt contains the Reimbursement Mapping from ICD-10-PCS
procedure codes to ICD-9-CM (Volume 3) procedure codes or procedure clusters.

Both files are formatted the same way. "Code" below means either "diagnosis code" or
"procedure code" depending on which file is being used. Decimal points have all been
removed. F10.151, for example, is F10151 in the file. Codes may contain both alphabetic
and numeric characters. All alphabetic characters are upper case.

There is one entry in the file for each valid ICD-10 code. Each entry is from 16 to 40
characters long. The files may be made fixed length by padding each record less than 40
characters out to 40 characters with blanks.

Each Reimbursement Mapping record is formatted as follows:

Position	Length	Contents
1	8	ICD-10 code (3 to 7 characters) left justified in 8-character field. Last character in field is blank.
9	1	Number of ICD-9 codes this ICD-10 code maps to. Values 1 through 6.
10	6	First ICD-9 code (2 to 5 characters) left justified in a 6-character field. Last character in field is blank.
16	6	Second ICD-9 code (2 to 5 characters) left justified in a 6-character field if ICD-10 code mapped to two or more ICD-9 codes. Last character in field is blank.
22	6	Third ICD-9 code (2 to 5 characters) left justified in a 6-character field if ICD-10 code mapped to three or more ICD-9 codes. Last character in field is blank.
28	6	Fourth ICD-9 code (2 to 5 characters) left justified in a 6-character field if ICD-10 code mapped to four or more ICD-9 codes. Last character in field is blank.
34	6	Fifth ICD-9 code (2 to 5 characters) left justified in a 6-character field if ICD-10 code mapped to five ICD-9 codes. Last character in field is blank.
40	6	Sixth ICD-9 code (2 to 5 characters) left justified in a 6-character field if ICD-10 code mapped to six ICD-9 codes. Last character in field is blank.

Appendix B – Reimbursement Mapping Rule Set

The following table presents a detailed breakdown of the frequency based rules used to choose among ICD-9-CM code alternatives, where more than one translation alternative was given in the 10 to 9 GEM. The first two columns give the number and percentage of ICD-10 codes mapped using a given rule. The third column contains the name of the rule and the last column describes the specific components of the rule, i.e., the specific conditions that are met when a map choice is made using the rule.

ICD-10 Diagnosis codes mapped	ICD-10 Procedure codes mapped	Mapping Rule	Rule Detail
66,032 (95%)	66,538 (93%)	None	There is only one ICD-9 translation alternative for the ICD-10 code, and therefore no mapping rule is necessary.
1,566 (2%)	4,244 (6%)	Not OB/NB, Medpar >= 30, pct >= 60, Calif agree	The ICD-10 code is not an obstetric diagnosis, a newborn diagnosis, or an obstetric procedure.
			There are at least 30 records in the MedPAR data for the ICD-9 code alternative with the highest frequency.
			The ICD-9 code alternative with the highest frequency represents at least 60% of the total number of records of all ICD-9 alternatives.
			The ICD-9 code alternative with the highest MedPAR frequency also has the highest frequency in the OSHPD data.
203 (0.3%)	437 (0.6%)	Not OB/NB, Medpar >= 30, pct > 50, Calif agree, All same DRG	The ICD-10 code is not an obstetric diagnosis, a newborn diagnosis, or an obstetric procedure.
			There are at least 30 records in the MedPAR data for the ICD-9 code alternative with the highest frequency.
			The ICD-9 code alternative with the highest frequency represents more than 50% of the total number of records of all ICD-9 alternatives.
			The ICD-9 code alternative with the highest MedPAR frequency also has the highest frequency in the OSHPD data.
			All of the ICD-9 code alternatives available reside in the same list in the DRG logic. (This is only meant as a general indicator that though the highest frequency ICD-9 code is not overwhelmingly dominant, the other available choices are not strikingly different.)

ICD-10 Diagnosis codes mapped	ICD-10 Procedure codes mapped	Mapping Rule	Rule Detail
1,251 (2%)	81 (0.1%)	OB/NB, Calif >= 30, pct >= 60	The ICD-10 code is an obstetric diagnosis, a newborn diagnosis, or an obstetric procedure. There are at least 30 records in the OSHPD data for the ICD-9 code alternative with the highest frequency. The ICD-9 code alternative with the highest frequency represents at least 60% of the total number of records of all ICD-9 alternatives.
91 (0.1%)	2 (0%)	OB/NB, Calif >= 30, pct > 50, All same DRG	The ICD-10 code is an obstetric diagnosis, a newborn diagnosis, or an obstetric procedure. There are at least 30 records in the OSHPD data containing the ICD-9 code alternative with the highest frequency. The ICD-9 code alternative with the highest frequency represents more than 50% of the total number of records of all ICD-9 alternatives. All of the ICD-9 code alternatives available reside in the same list in the DRG logic. (This is only meant as a general indicator that though the highest frequency ICD-9 code is not overwhelmingly dominant, the other available choices are not strikingly different.)
325 (0.4%)	62 (0.1%)	Combined < 30, Closest match	The MedPAR and OSHPD frequency data combined equal less than 30 records for the ICD-9 code alternative with the highest frequency. Coding expertise was used to determine the closest matching ICD-9 code alternative for the ICD-9 code.
365 (0.5%)	554 (0.7%)	Combined >=30, Combined pct > 50, All same DRG	The MedPAR and OSHPD frequency data combined equal at least 30 records for the ICD-9 code alternative with the highest frequency. The ICD-9 code alternative with the highest frequency represents more than 50% of the total number of records of all ICD-9 alternatives. All of the ICD-9 code alternatives available reside in the same list in the DRG logic. (This is only meant as a general indicator that though the highest frequency ICD-9 code is not overwhelmingly dominant, the other available choices are not strikingly different.)
69,833	**71,918**	N/A	N/A

Index

Note: Page numbers followed by a 't' or 'f' indicate that the entry is included in a table or figure.

A

Abdominohysterectomy, 141–142, 143f
Ablation therapy, 138
Abortifacient, 232
Abortion, 232–233
Access location, 192
Accredited Standards Committee (ASC) X12, 30, 38, 41–42
    version 5010 standards, 43–53
Activities of daily living (ADL) assessment, 400f
Acuity, 287
Acupuncture, 330t
Adhesiolysis procedures, 154
Administration section (302–3E1), 258, 259
    root operations in, 270–281
        approaches used in, 273–276
        introduction, 270, 271f, 272, 276–277
        irrigation, 270, 271f, 277–278
        transfusion, 270, 273f, 278–281
Administrative Simplification, HIPAA Title II, 25, 26, 27–28
Administrative Simplification Compliance Act (ASCA), of 2001, 41
Allogenic, 204
Alphabetic Index, 9, 104–106
Alteration (0), root operation, 177
American Health Information Management Association (AHIMA), 3
American Hospital Association (AHA), 3, 4
American National Standards Institute (ANSI), 38, 40–41
American Public Health Association (APHA), 3
American Recovery and Reinvestment Act (ARRA)/ Health Information Technology for Economic and Clinical Health (HITECH), 33–36
Amniocentesis, 148
Antabuse, 409
Anterior cruciate ligament (ACL), 191
Antiarrhythmic drug, 275
Antineoplastic, 273
Aphasia, 389
Appendices, in ICD-10-PCS, 122–123, 124f
Applied mapping, 69
Approach/technique, 14, 114–115
Arthrocentesis, 149
Articulatory-raising approach used in osteopathic treatment, 324t
Assessments, in physical rehabilitation, 385, 386–387, 386t
Assistance, 303–308

Atmospheric control, 314
Attributes, 70
Audiometer, 397
Audiometry, 393
Audiovisual hearing disorders counseling, coding procedure, 400–401
Augmentative or alternative communication (AAC), 393
Autologous, 279
Autotransplant, 161

B

Backward mapping, 69
Balanced tension technique, 324t
Balloon pump, 304
Banding, 163
Beam radiation. *See* External radiation therapy
Bekesy audiometer, 393
Bertillon Classification of Causes of Death, 3
Bertillon, Jacques, 3
Bilateral body part values, 191
Binaural, 393
Bioactive intraluminal device, 163
Biofeedback, 403t
Biopsies followed by more definitive procedures, 135
Body part (character 4) values, 15, 16
    in imaging section, 335, 336–341t, 342f, 343f
    in medical and surgical section, 187–189
        guidelines, 189–192
    in nuclear medicine section, 357–361
    in obstetrics section, 234–236
Body regions
    in osteopathic section, 323
    in Other Procedures, 327, 328–329f
Body system (character 2) values, 14
    of ICD-10-PCS code, 109–110
    in imaging section, 333–334
    in medical and surgical section, 186–187
    in nuclear medicine, 355, 356t
    in radiation oncology section, 367, 368t
Body system and region, character 4
    physical rehabilitation and diagnostic audiology, 387, 388–389t
    placement section, anatomical regions, 259, 261, 265t
Body system specific coding guidelines, 187t

Bone morphogenetic proteins (BMPs), 276
Bone scan, 357
Brachytherapy, 367, 368, 372
Breech, 246
Bupropion, 409
Business associate (BA), 29
    identifying, 29f
Bypass
    of the jejunum, 120f
    root operation, 165–168

C

C-section, 247
Cardiac resynchronization therapy (CRT), 205
Cardiopulmonary bypass device, 308f
Cardioversion, 313
Caregiver training, 385, 386t
Carpal tunnel release procedure, 154
Centers for Medicare and Medicaid Services (CMS), 3, 4, 13, 30, 41
    CMS-1500 provider paper insurance claim form, 43f
Central arteries, 272
Certain infectious and parasitic diseases (A00-B99) (ICD-10-CM: Chapter 1), 11f
Certification and Authorization of Referrals, 277 transaction, 38t, 39
Cesarean sections, 247
Change, root operation, 176, 268f, 269
Character, 93, 94
Character assignment, ICD-10-PCS, 14f
    definitions, 15t
    examples, 15f
Charge ticket. *See* Encounter form
Chiropractic section (9WB), 324
    coding chiropractic root operation manipulation in ICD-10-PCS, 325–326
Cholecystectomy, 142–143, 150–151
Classical cesarean section, 247
Clonidine, 409
Cluster (codes), 62
Cochlear implant, 398
    prosthesis, 386, 387f
Code 0JH63M7, character values for, 94t
Code sets, 4
    ASC x12, version 5010 standards and transactions, 52–53
    HIPAA, 51–52
Code structure, ICD-10-PCS (Procedural Coding System), 14

Code value, 91

Coding. *See also* Medical/surgical section coding
  assistance root operations, in
    ICD-10-PCS, 306, 308
  chiropractic root operation manipulation,
    in ICD-10-PCS, 325–326
  Extracorporeal Therapies, in
    ICD-10-PCS, 316–317
  imaging section procedures using ICD-10-PCS,
    344–349
  mental health, in ICD-10-PCS, 405–406
  monitoring root operations,
    294–295
  nuclear medicine procedures, 361–366
  osteopathic root operation treatment,
    in ICD-10-PCS, 324
  Other Procedures in ICD-10-PCS, 332
  performance root operations,
    in ICD-10-PCS, 312–313
  physical rehabilitation and diagnostic
    audiology, in ICD-10-PCS, 398–402
  radiation oncology procedures, 375–377
  substance abuse procedures,
    in ICD-10-PCS, 409–410

Coding Clinics, 62

Coding manual, ICD-10-PCS
  (Procedural Coding System), 15

Cognitive integration skills,
  393–394

Collection method, 330t, 331

Combination codes, 65

Complete breech, 246

Completeness, 13, 94

Compression, 259

Computer assisted procedures, 330

Conductivity, 287

Continuous positive airway
  pressure (CPAP), 306

Contractility, 287

Contrast (character 5) values
  in imaging section, 335,
    342, 344f, 344t

Contrast agents, 335

Contrast, defined, 335

Control, root operation,
  168–169

Conversion, 69

Cooperating parties, 3

Counseling, 403t

Covered entities (CE), 28

Creation (4), root operation, 177

Crisis intervention, 403t

Current Dental Terminology (CDT)
  procedure codes, 51

Current Procedural Terminology
  (CPT), 4, 14
  procedure codes, 51

Cutting/separation
  division procedure, 154
    using index to search for root operation
      division, 154–156
  release procedure, 154
    using index to search for root operation
      release, 156–157

D

Decompression, 314

Deep Inferior Epigastric Artery Perforator (DIEP)
  Flap, 205

Delivery, 233

Delivery forceps, types of, 234f

Densitometry, 343

Dental Content Committee of the American Dental
  Association (DeCC), 30

Department of Health and Human Services (HHS/
  DHHS), 29–30

Designated record set, 32, 33

Designated Standard Maintenance Organizations
  (DSMO), 30

Destruction (5), 138
  root operation, 218f
  using index to search root operation,
    144–146

Detachment (6), 138
  coding, root operation, 208–209
  using index to search root operation,
    143–144

Device, 14, 262–265, 266t

Device (character 6) values, in medical and surgical
  section, 194–198

Diagnosis-Related Groups
  (DRGs), 78–79

Diagnostic myocardial imaging (3D), contrast
  Tc-99m, 363

Dialysate, 275

Dialysis filtration system, 311f

Dichotic, 394

Dilation, root operation, 164–165, 209

Discharge summary, 98, 101f

Discontinued procedures, 135

Division procedure, 154
  using index to search for root operation,
    154–156

Dix-Hallpike test, 394

Documentation, root operations and, 136

Drainage (9), 148
  using index to search for root operation,
    149, 150f

Dressing, 261f, 267, 268f

Ductus arteriosus, 200
  qualifier, 209

Duration, defined, 302

Duration values, 303
  in assistance root operation,
    304t, 310t
  in performance root operations, 309–310

Dynamic orthosis, 398

E

Ectopic pregnancy, 248

Electrocardiogram (EKG), 288

Electroconvulsive therapy (ECT),
  403, 403t

Electroencephalogram, 288–289

Electromagnetic therapy, 315

Electron beam, 372

Electronic data interchange (EDI), 4, 25

Electronic Fetal Monitoring (EFM), 242

Electronic Health Record (EHR),
  33, 34–35

Electronic Protected Health Information (EPHI), 32

Electrophysiologic somatosensory, 394

Encounter form, 96, 97f, 98

Enrollment or Disenrollment in a Health Plan, 834
  transaction, 38t, 40

Enterprise Integration. *See* Health Information
  Exchange (HIE)

Equipment, character 6
  physical rehabilitation and diagnostic
    audiology, 394–398

Excision, 215, 216f

Excision (B) and resection (T), 136–138
  using index to search root operation,
    139–143

Expandability, 94

Explanation of Benefits (EOB), 40

External approach, 183

External radiation therapy, 367, 368

Extirpation (C), 149
  using index to search for root operation,
    150–151, 152f

Extracorporeal membrane oxygenation
  (ECMO), 306

Extracorporeal sections, 300
  Extracorporeal Assistance and Performance
    5A0–5A2, 302
    root operations, 303–313
  Extracorporeal Therapies
    6A0–6A9, 314
    body system, duration, and qualifier
      values for, 316
    coding, in root operations in
      ICD-10-PCS, 316–317
    root operations, 314–316

Extracorporeal shock wave lithotripsy (ESWL),
  149, 151

Extraction (D), 138–139
  using index to search root operation,
    146–147

Extraperitoneal cesarean section, 248

F

Family psychotherapy, 403t

Farr, William, 3

Fascia, 215, 216f

Fascial and myofascial release approach used in
  osteopathic treatment, 324t

Fee slip. *See* Encounter form

Female reproductive system,
  229, 230f

Filtered speech, 394

Filtration, 310

Fittings, 160, 385, 386t

Fixation, 160

Flags, 70

Fluoroscopy, 335

Footling breech, 246

Forceps delivery, 246

Forward mapping, 69

Fractionated radiation therapy, 368

Fragmentation (F), 149
using index to search for root operation, 151–152, 153f
Frank breech, 246
Free TRAM Flap, 205
Function, 125
Fusion (G), root operation, 177

G

Gallbladder, 143, 144f
Gamma beam, 372
Gamma rays, 372
General Equivalency Mappings (GEMs), 61
10 steps for using, 75–76, 77f
diagnosis codes, 67–68
in combination, 65–66
and levels of specificity, 62–66
fact sheet, 620–624
guidelines, 625–650
ICD-9-CM to ICD-10-CM, 69–86
for ICD-10-PCS coding, 76–78
migration choices for systems and applications, 69
needs, 62
reading, 72t
and reimbursement mapping, 84–85
v26 Medicare Severity-Diagnosis Related Groups (MS-DRGs), 78–79
and reimbursement conversion, 79–84
updates (2011), 651–661
General mobilization approach used in osteopathic treatment, 324t
Graunt, John, 3
Group psychotherapy, 403t

H

Halo orthosis, 398
Health and Human Services (HHS), 28, 29–30, 34
Health care, 32
Health Care Claim
Dental, 837-D transaction, 38t, 40
Institutional, 837-I transaction, 38t, 40
Professional, 837-P transaction, 38t, 40
Health Care Claim Payment/Remittance Advice, 835 transaction, 38t, 40
Health Care Claim Status Request, 276 transaction, 38t, 39, 44
Health Care Claim Status Response, 277 transaction, 38t, 39
Health Care Claims Attachment, 275 transaction, 38t, 40
Health care clearinghouses, 28–29, 47–48, 51
Health Care Common Procedural Coding System (HCPCS), 14
level II, 51–52
Health care operations, 32
Health care providers, 28
Health care systems, types of, 26t
Health Information Exchange (HIE), 33, 34, 35
Health information technology (HIT), 34
Health Information Technology for Economic and Clinical Health (HITECH)

American Recovery and Reinvestment Act (ARRA), 33–36
Health Insurance Portability and Accountability Act (HIPAA), 4, 25
Accredited Standards Committee (ASC) X12, 38, 41–42
American National Standards Institute (ANSI), 38, 40–41
ARRA Title XIII/ HITECH, 33–36
business associate (BA), 29
identifying, 29f
code sets, 51–52
compliance deadlines, 28
covered entities (CE), 28
designated record set, 33
and Electronic Health Record (EHR), 33
government organizations involving in
Centers for Medicare and Medicaid Services (CMS), 30
Office of Civil Rights (OCR), 30
U.S. Department of Health and Human Services (HHS), 29–30
health care, 32
clearinghouses, 28–29, 47–48, 51
high-level overview, 25f
organizations involving in, 28–29
Protected Health Information (PHI), 31
definition, 31f
identifiers, 32t
standards organizations, 30–31
Title II: Administrative Simplification, 27–28
Titles, 27t
transaction standards, 37–40, 38t
treatment, payment and health care operations (TPO), 32–33
Health Level Seven (HL7), 30, 40
Health plan, 28
Health Plan Eligibility Inquiry, transaction 270, 38–39, 38t
Health Plan Eligibility Response, 271 transaction, 38t, 39
Health Plan Premium Payments, 820 transaction, 38t, 39
Healthcare Common Procedural Coding System (HCPCS), 4
Hearing treatment, 401–402
High velocity low amplitude (HVLA) approach used in osteopathic treatment, 324t
Hip arthroplasty total, 219, 220f
History and Physical Exam (H&P, HPE), 98, 99–100f
Holter® Monitor, 295
Hyperbaric oxygenation, 305
Hyperthermia, 315, 375, 376f
Hypnosis, 403t
Hypothermia, 315

I

ICD. See International Classification of Diseases (ICD)
ICD-9. See International Classification of Diseases, Ninth Revision (ICD-9)

ICD-9-CM. See International Classification of Diseases, Ninth Revision, Clinical Modification (ICD-9-CM)
ICD-10. See International Classification of Diseases, 10th Edition (ICD-10)
ICD-10-CM. See International Classification of Diseases, 10th Edition, Clinical Modification (ICD-10-CM)
ICD-10-PCS. See International Classification of Diseases, 10th Edition, Procedural Coding System (ICD-10-PCS)
Identifiers, 31–32
Protected Health Information (PHI), 32t
Imaging section
body part (character 4) values in, 335, 336–341t, 342f, 343f
body system (character 2) values in, 333–334
coding, procedures using ICD-10-PCS, 344–349
contrast (character 5) values in, 335, 342, 344t, 344f
qualifier (characters 6 and 7) values used in, 342–343, 345f, 346f
root type (character 3) values in, 334–335
Immobilization, 259
Implant therapy. See Internal radiation therapy
Implantable cardiac defibrillator (ICD), 205
Incision and drainage (I&D), 148
Incomplete abortion, 233
Index, 104–106
Indirect approach, used in osteopathic treatment, 324t
Individual psychotherapy, 403t
Induced abortion, 233
Indwelling catheter, body system, 326, 327f
Injection, percutaneous, 270
Insertion (H), root operation, 173, 174f
Inspection
with another procedure, 171
of body part, 171
guidelines for root operation, 171–172
of multiple body parts, 171
Institutional claim, 4010A to 5010, 432–525
Instrumentation, 193
Intensity Modulated Radiation Therapy (IMRT), 368
Interleukin-2, 276
Intermittent pressure device, 263–264
Internal radiation therapy (IRT), 367, 368
International Classification of Diseases (ICD)
diagnostic and procedural codes, 2–3
history of, 3–4
reasons for changing, 4
International Classification of Diseases, 9th Edition, volumes 1, 2, and 3 (ICD-9) procedure and diagnosis codes, 51
International Classification of Diseases, Ninth Revision (ICD-9), 3
and ICD-10 diagnostic and procedure codes, comparison of, 5f

International Classification of Diseases, Ninth Revision, Clinical Modification (ICD-9-CM), 3
excerpt from code 041.12 in, 73f
and ICD-10-CM
comparison, 8t, 63f
General Equivalency Mappings (GEMs), 69–86
terminology differences, 64–65, 64t
ICD-10-PCS, terminology differences, 77–78t
International Classification of Diseases, 10th Edition (ICD-10), 2–6
and ICD-9 diagnostic and procedure codes, comparison of, 5f
implementation, guidelines for, 4
quick reference, 429–431
v5010 and, 53f
International Classification of Diseases, 10th Edition, Clinical Modification (ICD-10-CM), 3, 4, 7, 51
Alphabetic Index, 9
for orthopnea, 11f
codes, 4
coding manual, 9
example, 9t
excerpt from code B95.6 in, 74f
features of, 8
guidelines (2011)
and ICD-9-CM
comparison, 8t, 63f
terminology differences, 64–65, 64t
implementation, 7
layout of, 8–9
for MRSA, 74f
stress fracture codes in, 63f
structure of, 9
Tabular Index, for MRSA, 74f
Tabular List, 9, 11f
for category R06, 12f
International Classification of Diseases, 10th Edition, Procedural Coding System (ICD-10-PCS), 3, 51
alphabetic index and tables, 16–17
appendices in, 122–123, 124f
benefits of, 94
biopsies followed by more definitive procedures, 135
character assignment, 14f, 15f, 15t
values, 95t
character assignment and definitions, 107–118, 123, 125
approach, 114–115
body part, 112–114
body system, 109–110
character values for table sections, 107t
device, 115–116, 117t
not elsewhere classified (NEC), 110
qualifier, 117–118
root operation, 110, 111t
character numbers and names, 95f
code, 92
structure, 14, 93–95

codebook layout, 95–96
coding guidelines, 118–119
coding manual, 15
coding mental health in, 405–406
coding physical rehabilitation and diagnostic audiology in, 398–402
coding substance abuse procedures in, 409–410
development, 13–14
discontinued procedures, 135
General Equivalency Mappings for, 76–78
guidelines (2011), 414–428
and ICD-9-CM, terminology differences, 77–78t
legislation, 93
medical documentation, 96–107
alphabetic index, 104–106
Discharge Summary, 98, 101f
encounter form, 96, 97f, 98
History and Physical Exam (H&P, HPE), 98, 99–100f
main and modifying terms, 103–104
operative report, 98, 102f
tables, 106–107
treatment notes, 98
multiple procedures, 133–135
overlapping body parts, 135–136
root operations in, guidelines, 132–136
steps in, 119–121
International Classification System of Causes of Death, 3
International List of Causes of Death, 3
Intradermal, 270
Intramuscular, 270
Intraoperative electron beam radiation to abdomen procedure, 376, 377f
Intraoperative radiation therapy (IORT), 373, 376–377
Intravenous, 270
Introduction, 270
root operation, 270, 271f, 272
Iodine-131, 357
Irrigation, 270
root operation, 270, 271f
Isotope, 367
administration, 375, 376f
Isotopes (character 6) values, in radiation oncology section, 373–374

K

Kassebaum, Nancy, 27
Kennedy, Edward, 27
Kennedy-Kassebaum bill. *See* Health Insurance Portability and Accountability Act (HIPAA)

L

Laminaria, 232
Latissimus Dorsi (LD) Flap breast reconstruction, 205
Left hip joint value, 222
Levo-alpha-acetyl-methadol (LAAM), 409

Light therapy, 403t
Lithotripsy, 149, 151
London Bills of Mortality, 3
Lymphatic drainage massage, 324t
Lymphatic pump approach used in osteopathic treatment, 324t
Lysis procedures, 154

M

Magnetic resonance imaging (MRI), 335
Major Diagnostic Category (MDC), 78
Male reproductive system, 229, 230f
Manipulation, defined, 325
Manual chest compressions, 312
Mapping, root operation, 172
Measurement, 283
approaches, 284–285
function/devices, 285–287
and physiological devices, 289–290
and physiological systems, 290–296
qualifiers, 287–289
Measurement and Monitoring section (4A0–4B0), 258, 281
root operations, 282–289
physiological devices, 289–290
with physiological system body system values, 283–289
physiological systems, 290–296
Mechanical means, 233
Mechanical traction, 261
Medicaid, 30, 34
Medical/surgical section coding, 182
approach (character 5) values in, 192
guidelines for, 193–194
body part (character 4) values in, 187
guidelines, 189–192
body system (character 2) values in, 186
guidelines, 187
coding by detachment root operation, 208–209, 210f
coding device procedures, 209, 211
coding steps review, 207
device (character 6) values in, 194–198
match procedural statements, assigning code character values to, 207
coding extraction root operation, 207–208
multiple procedures, 212, 214–219
from operative report, 219–222
qualifiers (character 7) values in, 199
with applicable root operations and body system values, 201–202t
insertion for body system ear, nose, and sinus, 204
insertion for body system subcutaneous tissue and fascia, 204–205
qualifier ductus arteriosus, 200
qualifiers with root operation detachment, 203–204
replacement for body system lower joints, 204

Medical/surgical section coding (*Continued*)
   skin and breast body system, 205–206
   transplantation, 204
  Table 00D, 208
Medicare, 30, 34
Medicare Severity-Diagnosis Related Groups (MS-DRGs), v26, 78–79
  and reimbursement conversion
    using General Equivalency Mappings for, 79–84
Medication abortion, 233
Medication management, 403t
Mental health (GZ1-GZJ), 402
  coding, in ICD-10-PCS, 405–406
  root type, character 3, 403
  type qualifiers, character 4, 403, 404–405
Metabolism, 287
Methadone, 408, 409
Methotrexate, 248
Millions of electron volts (MeV), 374
Miscarriage, 233
Missed abortion, 233
Modality qualifier (character 5), 367
  other radiation (root type Y) modalities, 372–373
  in radiation oncology section, 372, 373t
  stereotactic radiosurgery (root type 2) modalities, 372
Monitoring, 281
Monoaural, 394
Monoclonal antibody, 276
Motility, 287
Multiplanar, defined, 335
Multiple procedures
  ICD-10-PCS root operations guideline, 133–135
Muscle energy (isometric, isotonic)
  approach used in osteopathic treatment, 324t
Myocardial Perfusion Imaging (MPI) procedures, 361

N

Naltrexone, 409
Narcosynthesis, 403, 403t
National Center for Health Statistics (NCHS), 3, 13, 61
National Committee on Vital and Health Statistics (NCVHS), 31, 33
National Council for Prescription Drug Programs (NCPDP), 30
  NCPDP 3.0, 41
National Uniform Billing Committee (NUBC), 31
National Uniform Claim Committee (NUCC), 31
Natriuretic, 276
Near-infrared spectroscopy, 330
Neurophysiologic intraoperative, 394
Nonautologous, 279
Nonimaging nuclear medicine assay, 356t, 365f
Nonimaging nuclear medicine probe, 356t, 357, 365f

Nonimaging nuclear medicine uptake, 356, 356t, 364f
Not elsewhere classified (NEC), 110, 170
Nuclear medicine (C01–CW7)
  body part (character 4) values in, 357–361
  body system (character 2) values in, 355, 356t
  coding nuclear medicine procedures, 361–366
  radionuclides (character 5) values in, 361, 362t
  root type (character 3) values in, 355–357
Nylen-Barany test. *See* Dix-Hallpike test

O

Obama, Barack, 33, 41
Obstetrics, 228, 229
  approach (character 5) values in, 236–242
  body parts, 234
  device (character 6) values in, 242
    Electronic Fetal Monitoring (EFM), 242
    telemetry, 243
  guidelines specific to, 232
  qualifier (character 7) values in, 243
    ectopic pregnancy, 248
    used with extraction root operation, 245–248
    used with repair and transplantation root operation, 248–249
  root operations
    abortion, 232–233
    delivery, 233
Occlusion root operation, 163–164, 209, 211f
Office of Civil Rights (OCR), 30
Office of E-Health Standards & Services (OESS), 41
One-to-many mapping, 62
One-to-one mapping, 62
Open approach, 193
Open central nervous system monitoring procedure, 290
Open endoscopic approach, 193
Operative Report, 98, 102f
Oral peripheral mechanism, 394
Orthopnea, ICD-10-CM Alphabetic Index for, 11f
Orthosis, 397
  dynamic orthosis, 398
  static orthosis, 398
Osmolarity, 335
Osmole, 335
Osteopathic Manipulation Technique (OMT), 323
Osteopathic section, 322
  body regions in, 323
  coding, root operation treatment in ICD-10-PCS, 324
  treatment approaches, 323–324
Other Procedures section (8E0)
  approach (character 5) values used with, 327, 329
  body regions used in, 327, 328–329f
  coding, in ICD-10-PCS, 332
  indwelling catheter, body system, 326, 327f

  method (character 6) values used with, 330–331
  physiological systems and anatomical regions body system, 326–327
  qualifiers (character 7) values used with, 331
Otoacoustic emission (OAE), 398
Output, 304
Overlapping body parts, 135–136
Oxazolidinones, 276
Oxygenation, 304
  hyperbaric, 305
  supersaturated, 305

P

Pacemaker, 204
Pacing function, 310
Packing, 259
  root operation, 268f, 269
Paracentesis, 148
Particle Beam Radiation therapy/Particulate Radiation, 372
Particle beams, 372
Particulate, 372
Patent ductus arteriosus (PDA), 200, 209
Payment, 32
Percutaneous approach, 193
Percutaneous endoscopic, 211
Percutaneous injection, 270
Percutaneous peripheral venous flow test, 284
Percutaneous transluminal angioplasty (PTA), 164
Percutaneous transluminal coronary angioplasty (PTCA), 164
Percutaneous venous flow monitoring procedure, 293
Performance, 308–313
Peripheral artery, 270, 272
Phacoemulsification, 139
Pheresis, 315, 316
Phonetically balanced speech discrimination, 394
Phosphorus-32, 357
Photon, 372
Phototherapy, 315
Physical rehabilitation and diagnostic audiology (F00-F15), 384
  body system and region, character 4, 387, 388–389t
  coding, in ICD-10-PCS, 398–402
  equipment, character 6, 394–398
  root types, character 3, 385–387
  type qualifier, character 5, 389, 390–393t, 390f
    definitions, 389, 393–394
Physiological device measurements, 289–290
Physiological systems, monitoring, 290–296
  approaches in, 292–294
  coding monitoring, 294–296
Placement section, 258
  anatomical orifices (2Y0–2Y5), 267–269
  anatomical regions (2W0–2W6), 258
    approach, 262
    body system/region, 259, 261, 265t

device, 262–265, 266t

ICD-10-PCS code book, 267

qualifiers, 265–266

root operations, 258–259, 260f, 261f, 262f, 263f, 264f

Plain radiography, 335

Planar imaging, 356, 356t

Planar nuclear medicine imaging, 354, 355f, 363f

Plaque therapy, 372

Pneumatic tourniquet system, 304, 306f

Port, 368

Positron Emission Tomography (PET) scan, 356, 356t, 364f

Procedural Coding System. See International Classification of Diseases, 10th Edition, Procedural Coding System (ICD-10-PCS)

Products of conception, 229

Professional claim, 4010A to 5010, 526–619

837 Professional transaction format, 44, 45f

version 5010, 837 Institutional (837-I) claim electronic transaction, 44, 47, 49–50f

Progress notes. See Treatment notes

Prospective Payment Systems (PPS), 4

Prosthesis, 397

Protected Health Information (PHI), 31

and Electronic Protected Health Information (EPHI), 32

HIPAA definition of, 31f

identifiers, 32t

Proton beam therapy, 372–373

Provider, 3–4, 14

Psychological tests, 403t

Public Law 104-191 [H.R. 3103]. See Health Insurance Portability and Accountability Act (HIPAA)

Pulsatile compression device, 304, 306f

Q

Qualifier (character 7) values, 14–15, 117–118, 165

for extracorporeal therapies, 316

in imaging section, 342–343, 345f, 346f

in medical and surgical section, 199–206

with applicable root operations and body system values, 201–202t

insertion for body system ear, nose, and sinus, 204

insertion for body system subcutaneous tissue and fascia, 204–205

qualifier ductus arteriosus, 200

qualifiers with root operation detachment, 203–204

replacement for body system lower joints, 204

skin and breast body system, 205–206

transplantation, 204

in placement section, 265–266

in radiation oncology section, 375

used with Other Procedures, 331

used with root operation assistance, 304–306

used with root operation performance, 310–311

R

Radiation oncology

body systems (character 2) values in, 367, 368t

coding radiation oncology procedures, 375–377

isotope (character 6) values in, 373–374

modality qualifier (character 5) in, 372, 373t

Other Radiation (root type Y) modalities, 372–373

Stereotactic Radiosurgery (root type 2) modalities, 372

qualifier (character 7) values in radiation oncology section, 375

root types (character 3) values in, 368

treatment site (character 4) in, 368–371

Radioactive isotope, 373

Radiocontrast agents. See Contrast agents

Radioisotopes, 373

Radionuclides (character 5) values, in nuclear medicine section, 361, 362t

Range of motion integrity, 394

Ray, 203–204

Reattachment (M), root operation, 159

Recombinant Bone Morphogenetic Protein, 276

Recombinant Human-activated Protein C, 276

Reduction, 161

Regional Health Information Organization (RHIO), 35

Release procedure, 154

using index to search for root operation, 156–157

Remittance Advice (RA), 40

Removal, root operation, 138, 176, 268f, 269

Repair, root operation, 169–170

Replacement

hip, 221f

root operation, 173–174, 175f

Reposition, root operation, 160–162

Reproductive system, 229, 230f

Resection (T) and excision (B), 136–138

using index to search root operation, 139–143

Respiratory system, 307f

Restoration, 313

Restriction, root operation, 163, 209

Reverse mapping. See Backward mapping

Revision (W), root operation, 177

Robotic-assisted procedures, 330

Root operations, 14, 110, 111t, 303–313

in administration section (302–3E1), 270–281

alter diameter or route of a body part, 162

bypass (1), 165–168

dilation (7), 164–165

occlusion (L), 163–164

restriction (V), 163

Appendix E, 123f

assistance, 303–308

definitions, 122f

and examples, 314–316

and documentation, 136

examination only

inspection, 171–172

mapping, 172

in ICD-10-PCS, guidelines, 132–136

biopsies followed by more definitive procedures, 135

discontinued procedures, 135

multiple procedures, 133–135

overlapping body parts, 135–136

involving cutting/separation

division procedure, 154

release procedure, 154

using index to search for division, 154–156

using index to search for release, 156–157

involving device

change (2), 176

insertion (H), 173, 174f

removal (P), 176

replacement (R), 173–174, 175f

revision (W), 177

supplement (U), 175–176

Measurement and Monitoring section, 282–289

physiological devices, 289–290

physiological systems, 290–296

in medical and surgical section, 122f, 130–177

other objectives

alteration (0), 177

creation (4), 177

fusion (G), 177

other repairs

control, 168–169

repair, 169–170

performance, 308–313

in placement section, 258–259, 260f, 261f, 262f, 263f, 264f

put in/put back, or move some or all of a body part

reattachment (M), 159

reposition (S), 160–162

transfer (X), 159–160

transplantation (Y), 157–159

restoration, 313

take out a solid, fluid, or gas from a body part

drainage (9), 148

extirpation (C), 149

fragmentation (F), 149

using index for root objectives, 149–153

take out some or all of a body part

destruction (5), 138, 144–146

detachment (6), 138, 143–144

excision (B) and resection (T), 136–138, 139–143

Root operations (*Continued*)

    extraction (D), 138–139, 146–147

    using index for root objectives, 139–147

Root type (character 3) values

    in imaging section, 334–335

    in mental health, 403

    in nuclear medicine, 355–357

    physical rehabilitation and diagnostic audiology, 385–387

    in radiation oncology section, 368

    substance abuse, 407–408

S

Salpingostomy, 248

Saturation, 287

Scan, 361, 362f

Scintigraphy, 357

Section, 14

    qualifier, 385

Separation/cutting, 154

Shock wave therapy, 316

Sigmoid colon, 215, 217f

Single photon emission computed tomography (SPECT), 357

Skin and breast body system, replacement of, 205–206

Source codes, 69

Speech Discrimination (SD) test, 394

Speech Reception Threshold (SRT) test, 394

SPET. *See* Single photon emission computed tomography (SPECT)

Sphygmomanometers, 263–264

Spinal cord cordotomy, 154

Spondee (words), 394

Spontaneous abortions, 233

Stable isotopes, 373

Staggered spondaic words, 394

Standardized terminology, 94

State Children's Health Insurance Program (SCHIP), 30

Static orthosis, 398

Stereotactic apparatus, 263, 267f

Stereotactic radiosurgery, 367, 368

    (root type 2) modalities, 372

Stress fracture codes, in ICD-10-CM, 63f

Subcutaneous tissue, 215, 216f

Substance abuse (HZ2–HZ9)

    coding, in ICD-10-PCS, 409–410

    root types and type qualifiers, characters 3 and 4, 407–408

Suffix, 161

Superbill. *See* Encounter form

Supplement (U), root operation, 175–176

Syngeneic, 204

Systemic nuclear medicine therapy, 356t, 357, 365f

Systemic thyroid therapy, I-131, 363–364

T

Tables, 106–107

Tabular List, 9

    ICD-10-CM (2011), 11f

        for category R06, 12f

    ICD-10-PCS, 16–17

Target code, 69

Tattoos, 368

Technetium-99m, 361

Technique/approach, 14, 114–115

Telemetry, 243

Thallium-201 chloride, 361

Therapeutic massage, 330t

Third Party Administrator (TPA), 51

Thoracentesis (pleural tap), 148

Three-dimensional (3-D) conformal radiation therapy (3DCRT), 372

Title XIII of American Recovery and Reinvestment Act (ARRA), 33–36

Titles, HIPAA, 27t. *See also* Health Insurance Portability and Accountability Act (HIPAA)

Tomographic (tomo) imaging, 356, 356t

Tomography Nuclear Medicine Imaging, 364f

Tracers. *See* Radionuclides

Traction, 261, 264f

TRAM Flap procedure, 205

Transaction and code sets (TCS), 4

Transaction standards, 37–40

Transactions, 4, 33

    ASC x12, version 5010 standards and code sets, 52–53

    defined, 37

    HIPAA, 38t

Transfer, root operation, 159–160

Transfusion root operation, 270, 273f, 278–279

    ICD-10-PCS code book for, 280–281

Transplantation (Y), root operation, 157–159

Transurethral resection of the prostate (TURP), 137–138

Transverse rectus abdomini myocutaneous (TRAM)

    muscle flap reconstruction, 174

    replacement, 174

Treatment, 32, 385, 386t, 387

    Osteopathic section

        approaches in, 323–324

        root operation for, 322

    payment and health care operations (TPO), 32

Treatment notes, 98

Treatment site (character 4), in radiation oncology section, 367, 368–371

Tympanometry, 397

Type of Instrumentation, 193

Type qualifiers

    definitions, 389, 393–394

    in mental health, 403, 404–405

    physical rehabilitation and diagnostic audiology, 389, 390–393t, 390f

    substance abuse, 407–408

U

UB-04 Institutional paper insurance claim form, 44, 48f

Ultrasonography, 335

Ultrasound therapy, 316

Ultraviolet light therapy, 316

Unstable/radioactive isotopes, 373

U.S. Department of Health and Human Services (HHS), 28, 29–30

U.S. Government Accounting Office (GAO), 37

U.S. Public Health Service, 3

Uterine curettes, types of, 233f

V

Vacuum-assisted birth, 246

Vaginal birth after cesarean (VBAC), 247

Vasopressor, 275

Ventilation, 304

Version 5010 standards

    837 professional transaction format, 44, 45f

    Accredited Standards Committee (ASC) X12, 43–53

    transactions, and code sets, 52–53

    UB-04 institutional paper insurance claim form, 44, 48f

    v4010A1 to v5010 837 professional conversion, 44, 46–47f

    v5010, 837 institutional claim electronic transaction, 44, 47, 49–50f

Version technique, 246

Vertex presentation, 246

Via natural or artificial opening approach, 193

Via natural or artificial opening approach endoscopic, 193

W

Washington Publishing Company (WPC), 31

Word recognition test. *See* Speech Discrimination (SD) test

Workgroup for Electronic Data Interchange (WEDI), 31

World Health Organization (WHO), 3

X

X-rays, 372

Z

Zooplastic tissue, 20